ACTA CONVENTUS
NEO-LATINI CANTABRIGIENSIS

Medieval and Renaissance
Texts and Studies

Volume 259

ACTA CONVENTUS NEO-LATINI CANTABRIGIENSIS

Proceedings of the Eleventh International Congress of Neo-Latin Studies

Cambridge 30 July–5 August 2000

GENERAL EDITOR

RHODA SCHNUR

EDITED BY

JEAN LOUIS CHARLET, LUCIA GUALDA ROSA,
HEINZ HOFMANN, BRENDA HOSINGTON,
ELENA RODRÍGUEZ PEREGRINA,
and RONALD TRUMAN

Arizona Center for Medieval and Renaissance Studies
Tempe, Arizona
2003

A generous grant from Pegasus Limited for the Promotion
of Neo-Latin Studies has helped meet publication costs of this book.

© Copyright 2003
Arizona Board of Regents for Arizona State University

Library of Congress Cataloging-in-Publication Data
International Congress of Neo-Latin Studies (11th : 2000 : Cambridge, England)
    Acta Conventus Neo-Latini Cantabrigiensis : proceedings of the eleventh International Congress of Neo-Latin Studies, Cambridge, 30 July–5 August 2000 / general editor Rhoda Schnur ; edited by Jean Louis Charlet . . . [et al.]
       p. cm. — (Medieval and Renaissance Texts and Studies ; v. 259)
    Includes bibliographical references and index.
    ISBN 0–86698–302–3 (acid-free paper)
    1. Latin literature, Medieval and modern — History and criticism — Congresses. 2. Latin philology, Medieval and modern — Congresses. I. Schnur, Rhoda. II. Charlet, Jean Louis. III. Title. IV. Medieval & Renaissance Texts & Studies (Series) ; v. 259.

PA8002.I57 2003
477–dc21   2003052335

This book is made to last.
It is set in Bembo, smythe-sewn
and printed on acid-free paper
to library specifications.

Printed in the United States of America

International Association for Neo-Latin Studies

Eleventh International Congress

Cambridge, 30 July – 5 August 2000

PROGRAMME

**Res Publica Litterarum:
Unity and Diversity**

Sponsors

The British Academy
Cambridge University Press
Clare College, Cambridge
Classics Faculty, University of Cambridge
French Department, University of Cambridge
French Embassy, London
Girton College, Cambridge
Jesus College, Cambridge
Pembroke College, Cambridge
Pegasus Ltd.
The Scandinavian Studies Fund, University of Cambridge
The Tiarks Fund, Department of German, Cambridge
Trinity College, Cambridge
Trinity Hall, Cambridge

Executive Committee

President: Prof. Gilbert Tournoy, Katholieke Universiteit Leuven
Past President: Prof. Brenda M. Hosington, Université de Montréal
First Vice President: Prof. Stella Revard, St. Louis, MO
Second Vice President: Dr. Philip Ford, University of Cambridge
Treasurer: Prof. Chris Heesakkers, Universiteit Leiden
Secretary: Dr. Karl-August Neuhausen, Universität Bonn
Chair of Publications: Mrs. Rhoda Schnur, St. Gallen

Advisory Board

for the Eleventh International IANLS Congress
Chair: Professor Stella Revard, USA
Professor Charles Béné, France
Professor Judith Rice Henderson, Canada
Professor Jean-Claude Margolin, France
Professor Outi Merisalo, Finland
Professor Colette Nativel, France
Professor Fred Nichols, USA
Professor Fiammetta Palladini, Italy/Germany
Professor Jerzy Starnawski, Poland

Sunday, 30 July

18.30 Reception in Clare College

Monday, 31 July

08.30 Registration

09.15 Official Opening
Philip Ford (Chair of Organising Committee)
Anne Lonsdale (Pro-Vice Chancellor, University of Cambridge)
Gilbert Tournoy (President, IANLS)

09.45 Plenary Session I
JULIA GAISSER, Allegorizing Apuleius: Fulgentius, Boccaccio, Beroaldo, and the Chain of Receptions

10.45 Coffee

11.15–12.45 Papers I

Session 1
FRANZ RÖMER, *Connubio stabili*: ein Extremfall habsburgischer Heiratspolitik in poetischer Darstellung
UELI DILL, Gilbertus Cognatus als Herausgeber und Kommentator von Janus Secundus' *Regina Pecuniae*
FIDEL RÄDLE, L. Geizkofler: *De miseriis studiosorum declamatio* (1576)

Session 2
JÖRG ROBERT, *Exulis haec uox est*: Ovidische Selbstentwürfe in der neulateinischen Dichtung (Velius, Celtis, Lotichius, Du Bellay)
ANGELA FRITSEN, The Renaissance Search for Roman Roots: The Venetian *gens Cornelia* and Ovid's *Fasti*
KATHRYN McKINLEY, Raphael Regius: The Editor as Reader of Ovid's *Metamorphoses*

Session 3
MONIQUE MUND-DOPCHIE, Traductions et commentaires latins des *Voyages des frères Zeno en Septentrion* (1558) aux XVIe et XVIIe siècles: tradition ou trahison?
MARC LAUREYS, The Unity of Christendom and the Diversity of Europe in Uberto Foglietta's Treatise on the Greatness of the Turkish Empire
ROBERT W. CARRUBBA, The Preface of the *Amoenitates exoticae*

Session 4
STELLA REVARD, Milton and Cambridge
MARIO A. DiCESARE, George Herbert's Latin Poetry and the Quest for a Liturgical Poetics: Introductory Notes
FIAMMETTA PALLADINI, Pufendorf on Milton and Divorce

Session 5
RICHARD I. FRANK, Budé: Humanists and the Republic of Letters
INGRID DE SMET, The Fourth Man? J.-A. de Thou and the Republic of Letters
JOHN CONSIDINE, Philology and Autobiography in Isaac Casaubon, *Animadversionum in Athenaei Deipnosophistas Libri XV* (1600)

13.00 Lunch

14.00–15.30 Papers II

Session 1

ARNOLD L. KERSON, Fray Alonso de la Veracruz's Views on the Legitimacy of the Spanish Conquest of America as Revealed in his *De dominio infidelium et iusto bello* (1553-54)

YASMIN HASKELL, Chocolate and Other Unsavoury Subjects: Jesuit Latin Georgic Poetry about the New World

AVELINA CARRERA, ¿Por qué se prohibieron las *Adnotationes* de Philipp Melanchthon a la obra de Salustio en México a finales del siglo XVI?

Session 2

ANNE L. SAUNDERS, Reflections on Marriage in Early Modern Europe: Giovanni Nevizzano's *Sylva nuptialis*

JOLANTA MALINOWSKA, The *Epithalamium Sigismundi Secundi Augusti et Elisabes Ferdinandi filiae* as a Good Specimen of Petrus Royzius' Epic Poetry

Session 3

ALBERT R. BACA, Apuleius' *Tale of Cupid and Psyche* in Art and Myth

JUDITH DEITCH, Prefacing *Axiochus:* The Renaissance Plato and the *Res publica litterarum*

GEORGE HUGO TUCKER, Versions of a 'Picture': Giovanni Battista Pio di Bologna's *Tabula Cebetis* of 1496 and Two Other Latin Versions of the *Tabula* Also Produced either in the Circle of Filippo Beroaldo or for Isabella d'Este in 1495–97

Session 4

ZLATA BOJOVIC, Humanism in Boka Kotorska

JAN OKÓN, Erasmo da Rotterdam e il primo rinascimento in Polonia

15.30 Tea

16.00–17.30 Papers III

Session 1

JOSÉ MANUEL RODRÍGUEZ PEREGRINA, El diálogo en el renacimiento portugués: el *Duarum virginum colloquium* de Luisa Sigea

JUAN JESÚS VALVERDE ABRIL, El testamento literario de Juan Ginés de Sepúlveda: sus *Epistolarum libri VII*, Salamanca, 1557

JOAQUÍN J. SÁNCHEZ GÁZQUEZ, Erasmus' *De libero arbitrio* in the Reading of Sepúlveda and his Italian Contemporaries

Session 2

ALISON FRAZIER, Advertising Virtue in the *res publica litterarum*: Renaissance Experiments with *vitae sanctorum*

OLGA PUGLIESE, The Role of Latin in the Composition of Castiglione's *Il libro del Cortegiano*

MARYANNE CLINE HOROWITZ, *Semina virtutum* in Early Education for Aeneas Sylvius Piccolomini and Desiderius Erasmus

Session 3

ADRIE VAN DER LAAN, Rudolph Agricola and the Construction of Self-Image in his Letters

JEANINE DE LANDTSHEER, In Praise of the Holy Trinity, Justus Lipsius and German Beer: Forty-four Parodies on Horace, *Odes* IV.3

JAN WASZINK, Lipsius and Cicero

Session 4
MINNA SKAFTE JENSEN, Nationalism and Internationalism in Danish Latin Poetry of the Sixteenth and Seventeenth Centuries
VIBEKE ROGGEN, Entertainment and Learning in Neo-Latin Rebuses by the Seventeenth-Century Norwegian Nils Thomasson

19.00 Dinner

20.15 Concert
Emmanuel United Reformed Church, Trumpington Street
Latin Sacred Songs and Elegies of the Seventeenth and Eighteenth Centuries
Invocation: Julia Gooding and Ana-Maria Rincón, sopranos
Timothy Roberts, organ and harpsichord

Tuesday, 1 August

09.15–11.15 Papers IV
Session 1
THOMAS LINDNER, Leonardo Datis *Trophaeum Anglaricum*
ELISABETH KLECKER, Die Rezeption von Vergils Heldenschau in der neulateinischen Habsburg-Epik
LÁSZLÓ SZÖRÉNYI, La poesia epica di Elias Berger

Session 2
EVRARD DELBEY, Pontano élégiaque: l'énonciation de la subjectivité dans la République des lettres
ABBAS MIROUZE, Giovanni Pontano et le modèle aristotélicien
BÉATRICE CHARLET-MESDJIAN, Tito Vespasiano Strozzi et Janus Pannonius: un commerce poétique au sein de la *Res publica litterarum*

Session 3
LUIS PARRA GARCÍA, Las fuentes sobre la concepción histórica de Alfonso de Cartagena en el discurso *Propositio super altercatione praeminentiae sedium inter oratores regum Castellae et Angliae in concilio Basilensi*
FERRAN GRAU CODINA, *Orationes* concerning Letters in the University of Valencia in the Sixteenth Century
DANIEL LÓPEZ CAÑETE, La obra latina de Manuel Sousa Coutinho

Session 4
JAN BLOEMENDAL, Senecan Drama: Unity and Diversity
HOWARD NORLAND, Gager's *Meleager*: An Inventive Adaptation of Senecan Form
VICENTE PICON GARCIA and ANGEL SIERRA DE COZAR, Nuevos textos del teatro jesuitico en España
JAMES A. PARENTE, Historical Tragedy and the End of Christian Humanism: Nicolaus Vernulaeus (1583–1649)

11.15 Coffee

11.45–12.45 Plenary Session II
LUCIA GUALDO ROSA, L'Accademia Pontaniana e la sua ideologia in alcuni componimenti giovanili del Sannazaro

13.00 Lunch

14.00–15.30 Papers V

Session 1
CLARE M. MURPHY, Thomas More's *De tristitia Christi* as Theo-Drama
ELIZABETH N. McCUTCHEON, Laughter and Humanism: Unity and Diversity in Thomas More's *Epigrammata*
THOMAS FINAN, Sir Thomas More's Translations and Use of Lucian

Session 2
SEBASTIANO VALERIO, Paolo Palladino, militare e letterato alla corte di Federico d'Aragona
ANTONIO IURILLI, *Auctor in re publica litteraria*: Antonio Galateo e i suoi lettori
CARLO SANTINI, La versione latina dell'*Iliade* di Giuseppe Pasquali Marinelli

Session 3
MARIANO MADRID CASTRO, Sources for the Commentaries of Jodocus Badius Ascensius
MARIANNE PADE, Style and Intention in the Latin Translations of Lapo da Castiglionchio the Younger
GINETTE VAGENHEIM, Marquard Gude (1635–1689), citoyen méconnu de la *res publica litterarum* du XVIIe siècle en Europe

Session 4
PETER FISHER, What is a Hippopotamus? A Problem in Renaissance Taxonomy and Description
FABIO STOK, L'umanesimo scandinavo di Olaus Magnus
HANS HELANDER, Latin as a Vehicle of Pro-Swedish Propaganda during the Thirty Years' War

15.30 Tea

16.00–17.30 Papers VI

Session 1
DAVIDE CANFORA, L'anonimo carme pastorale intitolato *Cinthias*
JOHN B. DILLON, Pontano, the Aqueduct, and the Neapolitan Graces of 1495 and 1496: Towards an Occasion for *Eridanus*, 2.23
STEPHEN MURPHY, The Capilupi, Masters of the Cento

Session 2
JOSÉ GONZÁLEZ-VÁSQUEZ and MANUEL LÓPEZ-MUÑOZ, El papel de la *actio* en los tratados neolatinos españoles de retórica
JOAQUÍN PASCUAL, Particularidades y coincidencias en la obra latina y castellana de Rodrigo Caro

Session 3
MAIA WELLINGTON GAHTAN, A Renaissance Treatise on Time: Lilio Gregorio Giraldi's *De annis et mensibus* ...
PHILLIPS SALMAN, Johannes Kepler on Geometry as Language
MARIA BERGGREN, New Words for New Findings

Session 4
PETER L. SCHMIDT, Huttens Loetze-Elegien: ein humanistisches Gesellenstück

WALTHER LUDWIG, Der Ritter und der Tyrann: die humanistischen Invektiven des Ulrich von Hutten gegen Herzog Ulrich von Württemberg

ECKHARD BERNSTEIN, Bartholomaeus Latomus' *Factio memorabilis ab Siccingen* and its Historical Background

18.00 Reception
Cambridge University Press

19.30 Dinner

Wednesday, 2 August

09.15–11.15 Papers VII

Special Session
Autobiographical Self-Representation in the *Res Publica Litterarum*

SIEGMAR WALTER DÖPP, Ioannes Fabricius Montanus: The Two Autobiographies

JAN PAPY, Lipsius's Correspondence: From Draft Letter to Literary Monument, from Philologist to Philosopher

TOON VAN HOUDT, Writing Letters, Rewriting the Self: Psychotherapeutic Dimensions of Lipsius' Correspondence

Session 2
ZWEDER VON MARTELS, Influences of Late Antiquity on the Work of Aeneas Silvius Piccolomini

MARJORIE C. WOODS, Medieval Latin Rhetoric in a Neo-Latin Context

ROBERT GINSBERG, Philosophy and Pedagogy in the Rhetoric of Giambattista Vico's *De nostri temporis studiorum ratione* (1709)

JOHN R. C. MARTYN, Memory Training in Renaissance Education

Session 3
LEE PIEPHO, Paul Melissus Schede's Poem to Sir Philip Sidney: A German Humanist at the Court of Elizabeth

STEPHEN RYLE, A Romano-British Epic: The *Reliquiae Eboracenses* (1743) of Heneage Dering

JOHN BARRY, The Latinity of Richard Stanihurst

AUGUST A. IMHOLTZ, Neo-Latin Nonsense: From Carroll's *Alice* to Nabokov's *Lolita*

Session 4
GERHARD HOLK, Petrus Martyr de Angleria (Pietro Martire d'Anghiera): A Remarkable Italian Humanist and Historian of the New World

GEOFFREY EATOUGH, Mission to Egypt: What Peter Martyr Saw with his Own Eyes

DAG NIKOLAUS HASSE, Die humanistische Polemik gegen arabische Autoritäten

11.15 Coffee

11.45–12.45 Plenary Session III
ELENA RODRÍGUEZ PEREGRINA, Lutero y su influencia en la España de Carlos V

13.00 Lunch

14.00 Excursion to Hatfield House

19.30 Dinner

Thursday, 3 August

09.15–10.45 Papers VIII

Session 1
BENJAMÍN GARCÍA HERNÁNDEZ, Los reflejos plautinos en el latín de Descartes (*Meditationes* I–III)
CORINNA VERMEULEN, A Latin Translation of Descartes
PIET STEENBAKKERS, Philosophy in the Republic of Letters: Jean Le Clerc

Session 2
PAUL GERHARD SCHMIDT, Erasmus von Rotterdam, *Ratio seu methodus verae theologiae*
CARL SPRINGER, Arms and the Theologian: Martin Luther's *Adversus armatum virum Cocleum*
JENNIFER MORRISH-TUNBERG, Samuel Gott's *Nova Solyma* and the Tradition of the Neo-Latin *Utopia*

Session 3
AGNIESZKA DZIUBA, The Renaissance Portrait of the Polish King: Sigismundus I in Bernard Wapowski's *Chronica Polonorum*
PIOTR URBAŃSKI, Jan Dantyszek (Joannes Dantiscus) and Italian Neo-Latin Poetry
JERZY STARNAWSKI, Zamość: die letzte Redoute der Renaissance in Polen

10.45 Coffee

11.15 Business Meeting

13.00 Lunch

14.00–15.00 Plenary Session IV
JEAN-LOUIS CHARLET, Une querelle au sein de la *Res publica litterarum*: la question de Pline l'Ancien de 1469 au milieu du XVIe siècle

15.00 Tea

15.30–17.30 Papers IX

Special Session
Neo-Latin Literature in Cambridge

HILAIRE and CRAIG KALLENDORF, Exorcism and the Interstices of Language: Ruggle's *Ignoramus* and the Demonization of Renaissance English Neo-Latin
JOHN HALE, George Herbert's Oration before King James, Cambridge 1623
DAVID MONEY, Quantity or Quality? A Quick Look at 2000 Cambridge Latin Poets
JAMES BINNS, Victorian Latin at Cambridge

Session 2
JOHANN RAMMINGER, Hermolao Barbaros *Corollarium* zu Dioskurides und die humanistische Kommentarliteratur am Ende des Quattrocento
MICHAEL VERWEIJ, The Cranevelt Letters and Rome
NIKOLAUS THURN, Die *Disputationes Camaldulenses* von Cristoforo Landino

Session 3
MARIA AURELIA MASTRONARDI, *Imago urbis* e sistema delle arti: il *Libellus de magnificis ornamentis regie civitatis Padue*
ELLEN S. GINSBERG, Theory and Practice of Genre(s) in the French Renaissance
COLETTE NATIVEL, L'Apport de la République des lettres à la République des arts: le *Gallus Romae hospes* de Montjosieu

Session 4
JUDITH RICE HENDERSON, Renaissance Epistolary Rhetoric: The Political Phase
DIRK VAN MIERT, The Letters of Hadrianus Junius on the Anglican Church
HENK J. M. NELLEN, Hugo Grotius' Correspondence with his Brother Willem de Groot

Session 5
JOSÉ C. MIRALLES MALDONADO, *Traductio* and *imitatio* in Faerno's Neo-Latin Fables
PERRINE GALAND-HALLYN, Jean Salmon Macrin: l'ode latine comme support d'un lyrisme familial dans les recueils de 1537
DIRK SACRÉ, Some Technical Aspects of Neo-Latin Echo Poetry

19.00 Dinner

20.15 Performance
George Ruggle's *Ignoramus*

Friday, 4 August

09.15–10.45 Papers X
Session 1
DONALD GILMAN, Petrarch's Poetics: A Definition and Defense of Creativity in the *Familiares* and *Seniles*
JOHN N. GRANT, Domizio Calderini and his Commentary on Suetonius' *Vitae Caesarum*
HANS-ERIK JOHANNESSON, Poetics and Ideology in Neo-Latin Poetry

Session 2
RAPHAEL FALCO, Rupture and Remythicization in Boccaccio's *Genealogia deorum gentilium*
PHILIP FORD, Syncretism in the Teaching of Jean Dorat
FRANÇOIS ROUGET, *Illustris Blondelli comparatio Pindari et Horatii*: les commentaires sur les oeuvres d'Horace et de Pindare en France à la fin du XVIIe siècle

Session 3
ELIA BORZA, Étude de quelques traductions latines de Sophocle au XVIe siècle
JEAN-FRÉDÉRIC CHEVALIER, La 'victime tragique' depuis les premières tragédies néo-latines jusqu'à *Jephthes* de Buchanan
HEIDRUN FÜHRER, Jacob Balde's *Jephtias*: A Christian Drama on a Classical Background

Session 4
TERENCE TUNBERG, On the Italian Pronunciation of Latin
KLÁRA PAJORIN, Funzione e importanza dei nomi antichizzanti degli umanisti
MARÍA PILAR GARCÍA RUIZ, Posible influencia de las lenguas vernáculas en el uso de diminutivos en textos humanísticos

Session 5
BRENDA HOSINGTON, On the Glory of Women: English and French Translations of Agrippa's *Declamatio de nobilitate et praecellentia foeminei sexus* (1530–1726)
PIETA VAN BEEK, 'Ius fasque esse in Rempublicam litterariam foeminas adscribi': Anna Maria van Schurman (1607–1678) and her European Women's Republic of Letters
JOSÉ MANUEL RUIZ VILA, Personajes femeninos en el *De viris illustribus* (1779) de Charles François Lhomond

10.45 Coffee

11.15–12.15 Plenary Session V
HEINZ HOFMANN, Die neuen Leiden des jungen Aristaeus: Mythologische Kreativität in neulateinischer Lehrdichtung

13.00 Lunch

14.00–16.00 Papers XI

Session 1
CARMEN PERAITA, Furió's *Bononia*: On Translating the Bible and the Art of *Relegere*
NIELS W. BRUUN, Søren Kierkegaard and his Latin Translation of the New Testament

Session 2
SYLVIA BROWN, In Praise of the *filia docta*: Elizabeth Weston and the Female Line
DONALD CHENEY, Elizabeth Jane Weston as Cultural Icon
JANE STEVENSON, Martha Marchina as Baroque Poet and Model of Style
ELISABET GÖRANSSON, The Making of a Poetess

Session 3
MICHAEL J. HEATH, Confession and Concession: The Texts of Erasmus's *Exomologesis*
TINEKE L. TER MEER, *De pueris instituendis* and the *Apophthegmata*: Two Writings of Erasmus Dedicated to William of Cleves
ARI WESSELING, The Rhetoric of Adages and Vernacular Proverbs in Erasmus

Session 4
JUAN MARIA NUÑEZ, De Gasparini Barzizii *De compositione* opusculo quaestiunculae
KARL AUGUST NEUHAUSEN, Lusus quidam Westmonasterienses ab oblivione nunc vindicandi
ISTVÁN DÁVID LÁZAR, De fontibus historiaque operis Antonii Bonfinii: *De architectura*

16.00 Tea

16.15 Meeting of the Amici Thomae Mori

19.30 Banquet

Saturday, 5 August

9.00 Excursion
Eton College and Windsor Castle

§§§

Organizing Committee
Chair: Prof. Philip Ford
Prof. Philip Hardie
Prof. Yasmin Haskell
Prof. David Money

Executive Committee
President: Prof. Gilbert Tournoy, Katholieke Universiteit Leuven
Past President: Prof. Brenda M. Hosington, Université de Montréal
First Vice President: Prof. Stella Revard, St. Louis, MO
Second Vice President: Dr. Philip Ford, University of Cambridge
Treasurer: Prof. Chris Heesakkers, Universiteit Leiden
Secretary: Dr. Karl-August Neuhausen, Universität Bonn
Chair of Publications: Mrs. Rhoda Schnur, St. Gallen

ACTA CONVENTUS
NEO-LATINI CANTABRIGIENSIS

GILBERT TOURNOY, Presidential Address   1

PLENARY PAPERS

JEAN-LOUIS CHARLET, Une querelle au sein de la Res publica litterarum: la question de Pline l'Ancien de 1469 au milieu du XVIème siècle   7

JULIA HAIG GAISSER, Allegorizing Apuleius: Fulgentius, Boccaccio, Beroaldo, and the Chain of Receptions   23

HEINZ HOFMANN, Die neuen Leiden des jungen Aristaeus: Mythologische Kreativität in neulateinischer Lehrdichtung   43

LUCIA GUALDO ROSA, L'Accademia Pontaniana e la sua ideologia in alcuni componimenti giovanili del Sannazaro   61

ELENA RODRÍGUEZ PEREGRINA, Lutero y su influencia en la España de Carlos V   83

COMMUNICATIONS

SYLVIA BROWN, In Praise of the *Filia Docta*: Elizabeth Weston and the Female Line   105

DAVIDE CANFORA, L'anonimo carme pastorale iutitolato *Cinthias*   115

AVELINA CARRERA DE LA RED, ¿Por qué se prohibieron las *Adnotationes* de Philipp Melanchthon a la obra de Salustio en México a finales del siglo XVI?   121

ROBERT W. CARRUBBA, The *Preface* to the *Amoenitates Exoticae*   131

DONALD CHENEY, Elizabeth Jane Weston as Cultural Icon   139

JEAN-FRÉDÉRIC CHEVALIER, La victime tragique depuis les premières tragédies néo-latines jusqu'à *Jephthes* de G. Buchanan   145

JOHN CONSIDINE, Philology and Autobiography in Isaac Casaubon, *Animadversionum in Athenaei Deipnosophistas libri XV* (1600)   155

JUDITH DEITCH, Prefacing *Axiochus*: The Renaissance Plato and the *res publica litterarum*   163

E. DELBEY, Pontano élégiaque : l'énonciation de la subjectivité élégiaque dans la République des Lettres   171

SIEGMAR DÖPP, Ioannes Fabricius Montanus: The Two Autobiographies 181
AGNIESZKA DZIUBA, The Renaissance Portrait of the Polish King
  Sigismund I in Bernard Wapowski's *Chronica Polonorum* 187
PETER FISHER, What is a Hippopotamus? A Problem in Renaissance
  Taxonomy and Description 193
RICHARD I. FRANK, Budé and the Republic of Letters 201
MAIA WELLINGTON GAHTAN, A Renaissance Treatise on Time:
  Lilio Gregorio Giraldi's *De annis et mensibus* 207
BENJAMIN GARCÍA HERNÁNDEZ, Los reflejos plautinos en el latín de
  Descartes (*Med.* 1–3) 217
DONALD GILMAN, Petrarch's Poetics: A Definition and Defense of
  Creativity in the *Familiares* and *Seniles* 229
ROBERT GINSBERG, Philosophy and Pedagogy in the Rhetoric of
  Giambattista Vico's *De nostri temporis studiorum ratione* (1709) 239
FERRAN GRAU CODINA, *Orationes* concerning Letters at the University
  of Valencia in the Sixteenth Century 247
JOHN K. HALE, George Herbert's Oration before King James,
  Cambridge 1623 253
MICHAEL J. HEATH, Confession and Concession: The Texts of
  Erasmus's *Exomologesis* 263
GERHARD HOLK, Petrus Martyr de Angleria (Pietro Martire d'Anghiera):
  A Remarkable Italian Humanist and Historian of the New World 271
BRENDA M. HOSINGTON, On the Glory of Women: English and French
  Translations of Agrippa's *Declamatio de nobilitate et praecellentia foeminei
  sexus* (1542–1726) 279
AUGUST A. IMHOLTZ, Neo-Latin Nonsense in Nabokov 287
HANS-ERIK JOHANNESSON, Poetics and Ideology in Neo-Latin Poetry 297
HILAIRE KALLENDORF, Exorcism and the Interstices of Language: Ruggle's
  Ignoramus and the Demonization of Renaissance English Neo-Latin 303
ARNOLD L. KERSON, Fray Alonso de la Veracruz's Views on the
  Legitimacy of the Spanish Conquest of America as Revealed in His
  De dominio infidelium et iusto bello (1553–1554) 311
THOMAS LINDNER, Bemerkungen zum *Trophaeum Anglaricum* von
  Leonardo Dati 321
DANIEL LÓPEZ-CAÑETE QUILES, Un Soneto de Quevedo y un Epigrama
  de Falcó 329
MARIANO MADRID CASTRO, Fuentes para los Comentarios de Jodocus
  Badius Ascensius 337
JOHN R. C. MARTYN, Memory Training in Renaissance Education 345
ELIZABETH N. MCCUTCHEON, Laughter and Humanism: Unity and Diversity
  in Thomas More's *Epigrammata* 351
DAVID MONEY, The Politics of Poetry: A Quick Look at Robert Walpole,
  and Two Thousand Other Cambridge Latin Poets 361
CLARE M. MURPHY, Thomas More's *De tristitia Christi* as Theo-Drama 371
STEPHEN MURPHY, The Metamorphoses of *De vita monachorum* 377

H. J. M. NELLEN, Hugo Grotius's Correspondence with His Brother
  Willem de Groot   385
KARL AUGUST NEUHAUSEN, *Lusus* quidam *Westmonasterienses* ab oblivione
  nunc vindicandi: Appendix sive Contemporaneas res bina per saecula
  (1704–1905) orbe toto terrarum feliciter gestas quam lepide nonnulli
  poetae Londinienses Latinis versibus singulas usque depinxerint   395
HOWARD B. NORLAND, Gager's *Meleager:* An Inventive Adaptation of
  Senecan Form   409
JUAN Mª NÚÑEZ GONZÁLEZ, In Gasparini Barzizzii *De compositione*
  opusculum quaestiunculae   419
KLÁRA PAJORIN, La funzione e l'importanza dei nomi umanistici   427
JOAQUÍN PASCUAL BAREA, Coincidences and Differences between the Latin
  and the Spanish Poems, Treatises, and Epistles of Rudericus Carus
  (Rodrigo Caro)   435
VICENTE PICON GARCIA, Nuevos textos del teatro jesuítico en España, II:
  Las comedias *Techmitius* y *Triunfo de la fe*   443
OLGA ZORZI PUGLIESE, The Role of Latin in the Composition of
  Castiglione's *Il libro del cortegiano*   449
STELLA P. REVARD, Milton and Cambridge   455
VIBEKE ROGGEN, Entertainment and Learning in the Neo-Latin Rebuses by
  the Seventeenth-Century Norwegian Nils Thomassøn   463
FRANÇOIS ROUGET, *Illustris Blondelli Comparatio Pindari et Horatii*:
  Les commentaires sur les œuvres de Pindare et d'Horace à la fin du
  XVIIe siècle   473
JOSÉ MANUEL RUIZ VILA, Personajes femeninos en el *De viris illustribus
  Urbis Romae a Romulo ad Augustum* (1779) de Charles François Lhomond   483
CARLO SANTINI, La versione latina dell'*Iliade* di Giuseppe Pasquali
  Marinelli   493
PAUL GERHARD SCHMIDT, Erasmus von Rotterdam, "Ratio seu methodus verae
  theologiae"   503
ANGEL SIERRA DE COZAR, Nuevos textos del teatro jesuítico en España, I:
  Parenesia y *Demophilus*   509
JERZY STARNAWSKI, Zamość: Das letzte Bollwerk der Renaissance in Polen   517
FABIO STOK, L'Umanesimo scandinavo di Olaus Magnus   525
LÁSZLÓ SZÖRÉNYI, L'epopea di Elia Berger sulla Santa Croce e la
  storia ungherese   535
NIKOLAUS THURN, Die Aeneis-Allegorese in Cristoforo Landinos
  Disputationes Camaldulenses   545
PIOTR URBAŃSKI, Joannes Dantiscus and Italian Neo-Latin Poetry   555
SEBASTIANO VALERIO, Paolo Paladino: militare e umanista alla corte di
  Federico d'Aragona   565
JUAN JESÚS VALVERDE ABRIL, Juan Ginés de Sepúlveda, *Epistolarum
  libri Septem*, Salamanca, 1557: Testamento Literario de un Humanista   573
DIRK VAN MIERT, The Religious Beliefs of Hadrianus Junius (1511–1575)   583
MICHIEL VERWEIJ, The Cranevelt Letters and Rome   595

ZWEDER VON MARTELS, The Central Position of the Authors of Late
   Antiquity in Humanist Thought: The Case of Aeneas Silvius Piccolomini   603

INDEX   611

ACTA CONVENTUS
NEO-LATINI CANTABRIGIENSIS

Presidential Address at the Opening Ceremony of the Eleventh International Congress for Neo-Latin Studies

GILBERT TOURNOY

Ladies and gentlemen, dear friends and colleagues,
The theme chosen for this conference is "*Res Publica Litterarum*: Unity and Diversity." We are all familiar with the term "Res Publica Litterarum" or "Res Publica Litteraria," which, by common agreement, signifies a community of scholars where communication is free and unbiased, exactly as was envisaged by Pierre Bayle in the *Préface* to the first issue of his famous *Nouvelles de la République des Lettres*, published at Amsterdam in March 1684:[1]

> Car nous déclarons premiérement, que nous ne prétendons pas établir aucun préjugé ou pour, ou contre les Auteurs ... Si nous approuvons, ou si nous réfutons quelque chose, ce sera sans consequence, nous n'aurons pour but que de fournir aux Sçavans de nouvelles occasions de perfectionner l'instruction publique. Nous déclarons en second lieu, que nous soûmettons, ou plûtôt que nous abandonnons nos sentimens à la censure de tout le monde. ...

> Il ne s'agit point ici de Religion: il s'agit de Science: on doit donc mettre bas tous les termes qui divisent les hommes en differentes factions, et considerer seulement le point dans lequel ils se réunissent, qui est la qualité d'Homme illustre dans la République des Lettres. En ce sens-là tous les Sçavans se doivent regarder comme freres, ou comme d'aussi bonne maison les uns que les autres. Ils doivent dire,
>
>> Nous sommes tous égaux / Nous sommes tous parens /
>> Comme enfans d'Apollon.

---

[1] *Nouvelles de la République des Lettres. Mois de Mars 1684,* seconde édition revuë et corrigée par l'Auteur (Amsterdam, 1684), fols. A4r and A6r.

Looking for the origin of this term, which is attested neither in Classical Antiquity nor in the Middle Ages, Fritz Schalk argued nearly a quarter of a century ago that it first made its appearance in the *Antibarbarorum liber* by Erasmus.[2] According to Marc Fumaroli,[3] however,

> cette expression ... apparaît pour la première fois en 1417, dans une lettre latine adressée par le jeune humaniste Francesco Barbaro à Poggio Bracciolini, pour le féliciter des découvertes de manuscrits qu'il lui a annoncées, et entre autres de l'*Institutio Oratoria* de Quintilien. A plusieurs reprises dans cette même lettre, comme dans d'autres occurrences ultérieures de la correspondance de F. Barbaro, l'idée d'une communauté savante transcendante aux frontières et aux générations, qui a contracté une dette de reconnaissance envers le Pogge et qui se doit de lui rendre honneur, se fait jour par d'autres formules: *eruditi homines, doctissimi homines ubicumque*, unis entre eux par la *necessitudo literarum* (le lien des Lettres), en rendant hommage par la plume de F. Barbaro aux *pro communi utilitate labores* (les travaux utiles au bien commun) du Pogge. Voici trois générations que de Pétrarque à Boccace, de Boccace à Salutati, selon un réseau qui inclut Milan et Padoue, Florence et Rome, la *renovatio literarum* a créé entre savants qui l'ont adoptée pour leur idéal des liens de solidarité et de collaboration: soudain celles-ci prennent un nom: *Respublica litteraria*.

The unity and diversity of this *Res Publica* have to do essentially with the possession of a single language on the one hand, Latin being for many centuries the main vehicle for communication and education within this community, and on the other hand with the multitude of disciplines pursued (art, history, literature, music, philosophy, theology, science, and so on), the nearly infinite choice of topics for discussion, and the different ways of treating them. In the case of our Association, specifically, these topics are reflected in the great variety of themes dealt with during our successive conferences, all aiming, however, at the common goal set out in our Statutes, namely, to promote by various means interest, research, and teaching in the field of

---

[2] Fritz Schalk, "Von Erasmus' *Respublica literaria* zur Gelehrtenrepublik der Aufklärung," in idem, *Studien zur Französischen Aufklärung* (Frankfurt am Main, 1977), 143–163.

[3] Marc Fumaroli, "La République des Lettres," *Diogenes* 143 (1988): 131–150 (here 137–138). More recent studies in this field include Hans Bots, *Republiek der Letteren: Ideaal en Werkelijkheid* (Amsterdam, 1977); S. Neumeister and C. Wiedemann, eds., *Res Publica Litteraria* (Wiesbaden, 1987); Daniel Roche, *Les Républicains des Lettres. Gens de culture et Lumières au XVIIIe siècle* (Paris, 1988); Françoise Waquet, "Qu'est-ce que la République des Lettres? Essai de sémantique historique," *Bibliothèque de l'Ecole des Chartes* 147 (1989): 473–502; Hans Bots and François Waquet, eds., *Commercium litterarium. La communication dans la République des Lettres ... 1600–1750* (Amsterdam–Maarssen, 1994); D. Goodman, *The Republic of Letters. A Cultural History of the French Enlightenment* (Ithaca–London, 1994); Herbert Jaumann, "Gibt es eine katholische Respublica litteraria? Zum problematischen Konzept der Gelehrtenrepublik in der frühen Neuzeit," in idem, ed., *Kaspar Schoppe (1576–1649), Philologe im Dienste der Gegenreformation. Beiträge zur Gelehrtenkultur des europäischen Späthumanismus* (Frankfurt am Main, 1998), 361–379.

Neo-Latin. Since the time of its foundation, now more than twenty-five years ago, our Association has developed out of a small *granum sinapis* into a great tree, populated by an abundance of birds of multicoloured plumage and varied song and melody, and one can justifiably state that our Association has by now grown to maturity.

Browsing through the list of papers proposed for this conference, it also caught my eye that the number of scholars who participated in the First Conference make up only a small group among those taking part this time, the vast majority being relatively new members who have joined our Association during the last decade. American scholars continue to be the largest group, but it is heartwarming to see that Spain, a country only recently described by the late Jozef IJsewijn[4] as "Hispania, quae terra Renatarum Litterarum Latinarum admodum inops habebatur," has acquired for itself in such a short span of time an important position in the field of Neo-Latin studies. Equally promising is the fact that contributions from countries such as Poland, Sweden, and Hungary are rapidly increasing. We should seriously consider the possibility of organizing one of our next congresses in one of these countries, not only in order to further this blossoming interest for Neo-Latin, but to underline also the geographical unity and diversity of this republic of letters.

In any case, still more than this geographical expansion, the founding of several local Neo-Latin societies, the organisation of conferences, and the publishing of new journals and series entirely or almost entirely devoted to Neo-Latin studies are most promising signs of a bright future. Let me mention, in addition to the *American Association of Neo-Latin Studies*, the *Cambridge Neo-Latin Association, Orbis Neolatinus*, and the *Nederlands Neolatinistenverband*, only the recently established societies in France and Germany, namely, *La Société française d'études néo-latines*, founded in April 1996 and presided over first by Pierre Laurens and now by Jean-Louis Charlet, and the *Deutsche Neulateinische Gesellschaft*, founded in the autumn of 1998 and presided over by Wilhelm Kühlmann. The possibilities for publishing Neo-Latin texts have been greatly improved by the appearance of no fewer than three new journals last year and this, namely the *Neulateinisches Jahrbuch*, the first issue of which appeared in 1999, *Les Cahiers de l'humanisme*, and the Spanish journal *Calamus Renascens*, both of these publishing their first volume in 2000. Moreover, the editors of these journals have all made it clear that larger Neo-Latin texts can find a place in the new series they are planning. Together with the American *Library of Renaissance Humanism*, the *Bibliotheca Neolatina*, the Italian *Parthenias: collezione di poesia neolatina*, and the *Bibliotheca Latinitatis Novae*, they will help to place at our disposal many first-class studies and especially many much-needed critical editions of Neo-Latin authors.

At this point it is only just and equitable to look back for a moment and remember the persons who are no longer with us but who devoted all their knowledge, their abilities and energy, to the promotion of our discipline. I want to mention here in the first place Paul Oskar Kristeller († 7 June 1999) and Giuseppe Billanovich († 2 February 2000), who were, each in his own way, shining examples for an entire

---

[4] In the *Praefatio* to J. M. Maestre Maestre, *El Humanismo alcañizano del siglo XVI. Textos y estudios de latín renacentista* (Cádiz, 1990), xi.

postwar generation; and, beyond them, the Erasmus specialists Aloïs Gerlo († 3 September 1998), Léon-E. Halkin († 29 December 1998), and Cornelis Reedijk († 7 May 2000). More closely associated with our Association were our lifelong members Jacques Chomarat († 9 June 1998), Philip Dust († 3 May 1998), James Mehl († 16 November 1998), and Virginia Woods Callahan († 7 December 1999). But above all, we lament the passing of the man who was for nearly all of us the figurehead of Neo-Latin Studies, Jozef IJsewijn († 27 November 1998), founder, first president, and honorary member of our Association. His name will be written in gold in our hearts and in our memory. Let us observe a minute's silence in his honour and in honour of our other deceased colleagues.

At the end of this opening ceremony I am most happy to be able, on my own behalf and on behalf of our entire Association, to express our sincere thanks to the University of Cambridge, represented here by its Pro-Vice-Chancellor, Mrs. Anne Lonsdale, for the hospitality we have been offered. Needless to say, a special word of thanks must go to our Vice-President, Dr. Philip Ford, who over the last few years has shown himself to be a paragon of British competence and efficiency. We cannot thank them better, I believe, than to do our utmost to make this Conference a major success. It is in this expectation that I declare the Eleventh Conference for Neo-Latin Studies open.

Seminarium Philologiae Humanisticae, Leuven

Plenary Papers

Une querelle au sein de la Res publica litterarum: la question de Pline l'Ancien de 1469 au milieu du XVIème siècle

JEAN-LOUIS CHARLET

La réception de Pline l'Ancien à l'époque humaniste a fait l'objet de nombreuses études. Depuis 1980, c'est-à-dire depuis le gros chapitre écrit par Ch. G. Nauert pour le quatrième volume du *Catalogus Translationum et Commentariorum*, on relève les études de P. Casciano ("Il ms. Angelicano 1097"), H. Walter ("Studien zur Handschriftengeschichte," "An Illustrated Incunable," "La vicenda del *Regius antiquus*," "Codice parigino latino 6808," "Incunabolo N614"), J. Monfasani ("The First Call for Press Censorship"), M. Davies ("Making Sense of Pliny"), V. Fera ("Un laboratorio filologico," "Poliziano, Ermolao Barbaro e Plinio"), P. De Capua ("Fortune esegetiche"), M. E. Boutroue ("Pline ou le trésor du monde," "Giovanni Andrea Bussi," "Les *Annotationes in Plinium*,"), M. T. Scaramuzza ("Le note filologiche," "Un nuovo autografo") et pour ma part, après deux articles ("La lettre de N. Perotti," "Philippe Strozzi le Jeune"), j'achève une édition critique commentée qui replace dans la perspective de la querelle sur Pline la *Lettre à Guarnieri* de N. Perotti et la *Lettre à Partenio di Salò* de C. Vitelli, réplique à la lettre de Perotti. Ici je voudrais, en passant très rapidement sur ce qui est déjà connu, faire le point sur cette querelle qui constitue, selon la belle expression de V. Fera, "un laboratorio filologico" et ouvrir de nouvelles perspectives.

L'intérêt des humanistes pour le texte de Pline l'Ancien remonte à Pétrarque, au génois Lodovico de' Guasti et à Guarino de Vérone. Mais c'est avec l'apparition de l'imprimerie que va commencer la querelle proprement dite. Nous verrons même, et ce point n'a pas jusqu'ici été mis suffisamment en valeur, que le document qui lance cette querelle est étroitement lié à l'impression des textes classiques à Rome.

Mais ce n'est pas à Rome qu'apparaît la première édition imprimée de l'*Historia naturalis*, c'est à Venise, chez Jean de Spire, en 1469. Nous ignorons le nom de celui qui a préparé cette édition (le *curatore*). Mais une étude d'H. Walter, publiée en 1983 ("Studien zur Handschriftengeschichte"), a jeté quelque lumière sur le travail préparatoire de cette édition. J'insiste sur l'importance de cette contribution parce que presque tous ceux qui ont travaillé depuis sur la réception de Pline semblent l'ignorer. Or H. Walter a retrouvé le manuscrit qui a servi de base à cette édition à partir du livre 2.[1] Comme ce manuscrit, qui porte des marques du travail de l'imprimeur et des indications à l'intention de ce dernier, a été écrit par plusieurs mains, H. Walter conclut à l'existence d'une équipe éditoriale pour la préparation de cette *editio princeps*. Les humanistes semblent n'avoir jamais cité explicitement cette édition, mais certains d'entre eux l'ont utilisée sans le dire.

C'est avec la deuxième édition que va commencer la querelle. Imprimée à Rome par Sweynheym et Pannartz avant la fin du mois d'août 1470, et très probablement entre le mois d'avril et le début du mois de juillet, elle est due à G. A. Bussi, l'*Aleriense*, avec l'aide de quelques collaborateurs au premier rang desquels on remarque Teodoro Gaza. Les études de A. Marucchi ("Note sul manoscritto [Vat. Lat. 5991]"), P. Casciano ("Il ms. Angelicano 1097"), M. Davies ("Making Sense of Pliny"), et M. E. Boutroue ("Pline ou le trésor du monde") ont permis de reconstituer les phases préparatoires de cette édition. M. E. Boutroue, en particulier, a montré que, dans la phase ultime du travail, Bussi a utilisé, à côté de sources manuscrites, un exemplaire de l'*editio princeps*.

Selon son habitude, Bussi avait travaillé à la hâte et son édition subit au moins trois attaques. La première, chronologiquement, est celle de N. Perotti. Depuis G. Mercati (*Per la cronologia della vita e degli scritti di Niccolò Perotti*), plusieurs critiques ont attiré l'attention sur la lettre adressée par l'archevêque de Siponto à Fr. Guarnieri, secrétaire du cardinal vénitien Marco Barbo, lui-même neveu du pape Paul II, en montrant qu'elle propose un contrôle, voire une censure, philologique sur l'édition des textes classiques à Rome et S. Prete, lors du troisième congrès de notre association à Tours, en 1976 ("La lettera di Niccolò Perotti"), avait insisté sur les principes de critique textuelle qu'elle contient. J. Monfasani ("The First Call for Press Censorship") a ouvert de nouvelles perspectives en précisant le concept de censure philologique et surtout en corrigeant la datation de cette lettre, qu'il ne faut pas placer au début de 1473, comme le pensait G. Mercati, mais en 1470. On peut préciser la fourchette chronologique compte-tenu de ce que l'on sait du travail de Bussi: entre mai et début juillet 1470. Perotti voulait obtenir du pape un contrôle philologique sur toutes les éditions romaines des classiques. Or, en 1470, Rome est encore le centre d'impression le plus important des textes antiques, et l'entreprise de Sweynheym et Pannartz joue en ce domaine un rôle prépondérant. Perotti n'obtint pas satisfaction. Mais son intervention polémique contribua à déstabiliser une entreprise déjà chancelante dont il prendra le contrôle scientifique à l'automne 1472. Nous y reviendrons.

Pour montrer la mauvaise qualité de l'édition Bussi, Perotti a annexé à sa lettre un commentaire ecdotique et philologique de la *Praefatio* de Pline qui fait ressortir vingt-deux prétendues erreurs de Bussi. Pour Perotti, si l'on dénombre autant d'erreurs dans

---

[1] Par. lat. 6805.

un texte aussi court et aussi facile (dit-il!), le reste du texte doit être pire encore. Ce premier commentaire humaniste à la *Praefatio* de Pline ouvre plusieurs points de controverse, en particulier sur le nom du dédicataire de l'œuvre et sur la patrie de Pline l'Ancien. Perotti reproche à Bussi d'avoir corrompu le texte des manuscrits en remplaçant *Vespasiano* par *Domitiano* dans la dédicace de cette lettre-préface. Pour Perotti, le dédicataire de l'œuvre est Titus, souvent appelé *Vespasianus* tout court, et non son frère Domitien. Sur ce point, la philologie donnera raison à Perotti, mais la leçon erronée de Bussi vient très probablement... de l'*editio princeps* vénitienne! Sur le deuxième point, Perotti croit trouver dans le texte du premier paragraphe de la *Praefatio* la preuve que Pline l'Ancien est originaire de Vérone et non de Côme (*Guarn.* 16). Ici, Perotti se trompe, mais son intervention déclenchera toute une série de prises de position en faveur soit de Vérone, soit de Côme. Nous reviendrons sur certaines d'entre elles.

Le texte envoyé par Perotti à Guarnieri va circuler dans les milieux humanistes vénitiens. Le manuscrit de Pérouse[2] est, avec une curieuse *editio princeps* dont nous parlerons plus loin, le seul témoin direct conservé de ce premier état du texte; mais les témoignages de C. Vitelli et de R. Regio, sur lesquels nous reviendrons, en sont des témoins indirects. Perotti apportera ensuite quelques corrections à son texte et en fera un manifeste philologique sous le titre plus général: *Epistola aduersus eos qui temere corrigunt errores ueterum librorum cum expositione prohoemii Plyniani*, en le faisant circuler dans l'entourage de Bessarion, lié, comme l'a montré M. D. Feld, à l'entreprise Sweynheym-Pannartz. Les deux manuscrits jumeaux qui donnent ce deuxième état du texte l'associent à des œuvres de Bessarion.[3] Un dernier manuscrit, provenant de la bibliothèque d'Urbino,[4] dont j'ai pu établir qu'il est la copie probablement directe, mais non exempte d'erreurs, de l'exemplaire de l'auteur, c'est-à-dire du texte conservé et corrigé par Perotti, représente le troisième et dernier état. Mais seuls Perotti, Federico d'Urbino, et éventuellement certains de leurs proches ont pu y avoir accès, et il dort, d'un sommeil presque complet (comme aussi le deuxième état), depuis plus de cinq siècles. Touchante ironie de l'histoire, c'est par l'imprimerie, au cœur du débat, que la *Lettre à Guarnieri* connaîtra une grande diffusion et un rayonnement dans toute l'Europe, mais plus tard, après la mort de Niccolò et dans des conditions étonnantes auxquelles Perotti n'avait sûrement pas songé.

Pour le moment, restons en 1470–1471 pour assister à la seconde attaque contre l'édition de Bussi. Elle est l'œuvre d'un élève de Filelfo, Giorgio Merula. Sur ce point, je passe vite, en renvoyant à la belle étude de V. Fera ("Poliziano, Ermolao Barbaro e Plinio"). V. Fera a retrouvé la première version manuscrite de cette attaque: il s'agit d'une lettre datée du 28 février 1471 et adressée à Bussi lui-même ("o nostri temporis Aristarche"), après l'achat de son édition à Venise le 5 décembre 1470. Vers 1474, Merula fera imprimer ce texte sous une forme modifiée et en l'adressant à Antonio Vinciguerra, secrétaire de l'ambassadeur vénitien à Rome: il le

---

[2] Perugia, Badia di S. Pietro, CM 53.
[3] Berlin, St. Pr. Kult., lat. 4–566; Mantova, biblioteca comunale, H I 35.
[4] Cité du Vatican, Urb. lat. 297.

charge de transmettre sa lettre au *corrector* de l'édition, c'est-à-dire Bussi. Merula ne fait pas la moindre allusion à la lettre de Perotti, mais il ne me semble pas l'ignorer: à mon avis, son silence est volontaire, il écarte à dessein la *Praefatio* pour éviter d'avoir à se situer par rapport à Perotti. C'est que son point de vue est différent: Perotti attaquait Bussi en s'efforçant d'épargner Gaza, son collègue de l'Académie de Bessarion. Merula, au contraire, ménage quelque peu Bussi pour attaquer *Graeculus aliquis* qui ne saurait être que Gaza. Les critiques de Merula portent surtout sur l'ignorance des *realia* (en particulier les noms géographiques) . . . et du grec, ce qui est un comble pour un *Graeculus*! Une allusion désenchantée dans la dédicace de l'édition des *Lettres* de Cicéron (antérieure au 29 août 1470) montre que Bussi a été atteint par les critiques de Perotti. Mais nous n'avons pas trace d'une réponse de l'*Aleriense* ni à Perotti ni à Merula.

En revanche, la lettre de Perotti à Guarnieri suscita une réplique de C. Vitelli dans une courte lettre adressée à son ami Partenio di Salò. Vitelli y explique que Partenio lui avait donné une copie de la lettre de Perotti, mais que des empêchements ont retardé sa réponse. J'ai pu établir que Vitelli se réfère non à l'édition romaine de Bussi, mais à sa réédition avec quelques modifications par Nicolas Jenson à Venise en 1472. Comme par ailleurs Vitelli ne parle pas de l'édition romaine de Perotti, datée du 7 mai 1473, sa lettre a été écrite en 1472 ou au début de 1473. Vitelli reconnaît le soin avec lequel Perotti a corrigé certaines fautes de Bussi, mais il estime que, dans sa rage contre l'*Aleriense*, Perotti s'est laissé emporter jusqu'à l'aveuglement et qu'il a lui-même commis des fautes de jugement ou d'interprétation. Vitelli les relève, dit-il, non par esprit de dénigrement ou pour se faire valoir, mais pour montrer sa bonne foi. En réalité, il cherche à se mettre en valeur pour obtenir un poste universitaire à Padoue ou à Venise. La *res publica litterarum* était déjà agitée par des préoccupations de carrière universitaire. Il est difficile de dire quelle fut en 1472 ou 1473 la diffusion de la lettre de Vitelli. Mais on notera qu'à la fin de cette lettre Vitelli institue juge de cette querelle, à côté de Partenio, un certain Raffaele de Bergame qui n'est autre que Raffaele Regio qui interviendra activement dans une phase ultérieure de la querelle et qui donc, dès 1472 ou 1473, lisait en manuscrit les deux lettres de Perotti et Vitelli. Mais on ne sait dans quelle mesure le texte de Vitelli a circulé alors en dehors de l'ambiance vénitienne. Le seul manuscrit qui le conserve, lié au milieu culturel vénitien et non, comme le pensait J. Monfasani ("The First Call for Press Censorship"), à la présence de Perotti à Pérouse, l'associe au premier état du texte de Perotti,[5] et nous verrons que sa première édition imprimée, liée elle aussi au premier état du texte de Perotti, sera issue de Venise, et nettement postérieure. Nous avons un témoin de la querelle entre Perotti et Vitelli, un poème de trente-quatre vers composé par l'évêque de Gaète Francesco Patrizi, qui semble vouloir réconcilier les deux adversaires: des savants devraient se respecter et éviter de se battre inutilement pour le texte de Pline. Mais nous ne pouvons dater ce poème. Toutefois, si l'on prend Patrizi au pied de la lettre, les deux protagonistes s'attaquent *mutuellement*, ce qui laisse supposer une réplique (perdue) de Perotti.

---

[5] Perugia, Badia di S. Pietro, CM 53.

À la fin de 1472, Perotti semble avoir réussi, au moins en partie, son offensive contre Bussi, puisqu'il prend auprès de Sweynheym et Pannartz la place de *curatore* scientifique laissée vacante par Bussi appelé à d'autres fonctions auprès de Sixte IV. Perotti mettra en application ses principes et ses convictions en supprimant les longues préfaces dans lesquelles le *curatore* (Bussi) se mettait en avant (dans la *Lettre à Guarnieri*, il disait qu'il les arrachait ou les biffait!) et en adoptant une ligne éditoriale de philologie pure et dure: l'éditeur doit s'effacer devant le texte qu'il publie (ses éditions de Martial et Pline ne portent même pas son nom!), puisque sa seule tâche est de restaurer les chefs-d'œuvre de l'antiquité dans leur pureté originelle. Pour lui, l'édition des textes classiques ne répond pas à un programme idéologique, comme cela avait été le cas pour Bussi qui cherchait, grâce au livre imprimé, à faire partager par une communauté de lecteurs humanistes le souci d'unir la culture païenne et le christianisme comme l'avaient fait dans l'antiquité chrétienne les Pères de l'Église. Pour le philologue Perotti, le livre n'est pas un moyen (il ne se préoccupe pas du lecteur, d'où l'absence de préface), mais une fin en soi: il s'agit de restaurer les livres antiques (= les Belles Lettres) dans leur texte authentique purifié des corruptions médiévales. C'est sa notion de *liber integer*.[6] Ce désintérêt du lecteur et des conditions du marché ne fera qu'accroître les difficultés financières de l'entreprise, et, comme les éditions préparées par Perotti lui-même (son Martial du 30 avril 1473 et son Pline du 7 mai 1473) feront l'objet d'une attaque philologique en règle de la part de son ancien ami Domizio Calderini, on comprend la fragilité de l'entreprise, et on ne s'étonne pas de la séparation de Sweynheym et Pannartz précisément après la publication du Pline de Perotti, destiné à remplacer celui de Bussi.

La querelle Calderini-Perotti a déjà été étudiée (Dunston, "Studies in Domizio Calderini"; Ramminger, "Brotheus e Timon"), même s'il subsiste à mon avis encore quelques zones d'ombre. Elle éclate à propos de Martial. Un certain Matteo Rufo, disciple de Perotti qui interviendra plus tard dans la querelle sur Pline, informe son maître que, dans son cours sur Martial au *Studio* de Rome, Calderini ne se prive pas de critiquer ses interventions sur ce texte. Ce qui nous intéresse ici, c'est que, dans sa *Defensio aduersus Brotheum grammaticum* (imprimée en 1475), Calderini fait intervenir Pline dans la controverse. Il déclare être en train de terminer une œuvre polémique en quatre livres, dont deux démontreraient que Perotti a corrompu le texte de Pline en 275 passages. Pour le moment (et il en restera là), il se contente de réfuter neuf corrections intempestives de Perotti à Pline, en sus de quelques erreurs concernant Martial et Juvénal. Il considère que Perotti est incompétent, notamment en géographie, et commet les fautes qu'il reproche aux autres (ajouts, suppressions, ou déplacements arbitraires). Le chiffre de 275 "corruptions" surprend par sa précision. Mais Calderini affirme avoir en main le *codex* remis par Perotti aux imprimeurs, avec en marge ses propres interventions. Avec G. Mercati (*Cronologia*) et M. Davies ("Making Sense of Pliny"), je crois que ce *codex* n'est autre qu'un exemplaire de l'édition Bussi corrigé (et même insuffisamment corrigé pour la *Praefatio* puisque l'édition Perotti

---

[6] *Guarn.* 6 et 7. Voir J.-L. Charlet, *Deux pièces de la controverse humaniste sur Pline* (Paris, 2003). Voir aussi A. Grafton, "Printers' Corrections," 149–150.

conserve des erreurs évidentes de Bussi dénoncées dans la *Lettre à Guarnieri*!) à l'intention des typographes. Ce *codex* a très probablement été donné à Calderini par Sweynheym, et Calderini a pu très facilement compter le nombre de retouches apportées par Perotti au texte de Bussi. Calderini conclut que les quatre cents exemplaires de cette édition doivent être *brûlés* à défaut de pouvoir être corrigés. Mais l'un d'entre eux connaîtra un destin particulier.

La polémique sur Pline rebondit en 1476 avec une troisième attaque contre l'édition de Bussi, pourtant mort en février 1475. En annexe à son édition de l'*Historia naturalis* (maintes fois rééditée), Beroaldo publie un petit commentaire en forme de lettre qui critique Bussi et justifie les changements apportés dans son édition. Il édicte aussi quelques conseils pour la correction du texte qui ne sont pas sans rapport avec ceux donnés par Perotti dans la *Lettre à Guarnieri*. En ce qui concerne la *Praefatio*, Beroaldo reprend un certain nombre de leçons propres à Perotti. Par ailleurs, grâce à la *recollecta* de son étudiant allemand Richard Graman,[7] on sait qu'il fit un cours sur la *Praefatio* en 1480. Il s'y attache plus au sens des mots qu'à l'établissement du texte, mais ses gloses sont parfois si proches de celles de Perotti qu'on peut conclure à une utilisation de la *Lettre à Guarnieri*, même si le nom de Perotti n'apparaît pas.

Cette année 1480 marque une nouvelle étape dans l'étude de Pline et les controverses sur son texte. D'une part, grâce à un exemplaire de l'édition Perotti conservé à Oxford,[8] nous savons que Politien a fait une première lecture critique la plume à la main du texte de Pline durant l'été 1480, avant de commencer son enseignement au *Studio* de Florence. D'autre part, c'est au début des années 1480 que la querelle proprement dite va reprendre. Merula avait attaqué en 1478 les commentaires de Calderini à Martial et à Juvénal. Vitelli remonta au créneau et dédia à E. Barbaro (ami de Merula!) son *In defensionem Plinii et Domitii Calderini contra Georgium Merulam*. Cet ouvrage fut publié à Venise entre la fin de l'été 1481 (allusion à la mort de Filelfo) et l'automne 1482, puisque Vitelli fut à son tour attaqué par un partisan de Merula, Paolo Romuleio (*Pro Georgio Merula . . . aduersus quendam Cornelium Vitellium apologia* [Venise, 14 novembre 1482]). Vitelli accuse Calderini d'avoir corrompu le texte de Pline.

Est-ce un hasard si, au même moment, sont publiées ensemble à Venise, fort discrètement, sans date ni nom de typographe (. . . comme pour le libelle de Vitelli!), les lettres de Perotti et de Vitelli? Je ne le pense pas. Perotti est mort en décembre 1480. On peut supposer que Vitelli, en pleine polémique avec Merula et ses partisans, a jugé utile pour lui de faire imprimer sa première intervention publique sur le texte de Pline avec la lettre de Perotti sans laquelle sa réponse n'était pas compréhensible. Mais ce n'est pas cette petite plaquette de dix feuillets, de faible diffusion, qui assurera le succès de la *Lettre à Guarnieri*, d'autant que Vitelli semble, après cette publication, avoir quitté Venise pour d'autres cieux plus ou moins favorables (Louvain, Paris, et surtout Oxford où il jouera un rôle important dans le développement des études humanistes, en particulier dans le domaine grec).

---

[7] Trèves, bibl. munic. 1110/2037, fols. 245r–246r.
[8] Bodl. Auct. Q. 1.2.

En 1488, le travail philologique de Beroaldo se concrétise par les fameuses *Annotationes centum*, consacrées en grande partie à Pline l'Ancien, qui imposent dans la *res publica litterarum* un genre philologique proposé par Calderini avec ses *Obseruationes* inachevées: celui des notes critiques ponctuelles et discontinues, qui sera porté à la perfection par Politien, l'année suivante, avec la première centurie de ses *Miscellanea*.

Cette même année 1489 avait vu l'édition posthume, toujours à Venise, du grand œuvre de Perotti, le *Cornu copiae*. E. Barbaro, chef de file de l'école philologique vénitienne depuis le départ de Merula, s'empressa de l'attaquer dans une lettre du 25 décembre 1489 adressée à Iacopo Antiquario. Ce texte fut remanié et adressé (au printemps 1490 d'après V. Branca) à Giorgio Valla, puis imprimé avec le *Cornu copiae* dans l'édition préparée par Brugnolo (Venise, 1508). On l'appelle généralement *Animaduersiones in Perotti Cornucopiam*. La *Corne d'abondance* de Perotti se prétend un commentaire à Martial, mais Pline l'Ancien y occupe une place très importante dans la mesure où ce commentaire tourne à l'encyclopédie, et les critiques de Barbaro portent souvent sur Pline. Mais dans ses *Castigationes*, écrites à Rome un peu plus tard, Barbaro atténuera ses critiques en disant que Perotti n'a pas eu le temps de polir son œuvre.

À partir de la fin 1489, l'*Historia naturalis* est au centre des débats et des études humanistes, non plus seulement d'un point de vue philologique, mais en tant qu'œuvre scientifique qui donne accès au savoir des anciens et dont il faut rétablir le texte corrompu durant la moyen âge avant d'en vérifier l'exactitude scientifique. À Florence, à la demande d'étudiants anglais et portugais, Politien fait, d'octobre 1489 à avril 1490, un cours privé sur Pline dont nous avons quelques éléments dans une *recollecta* conservée dans un *zibaldone*.[9] Ce cours lui donne l'occasion d'une nouvelle lecture critique de l'édition Perotti déjà mentionnée, avec une collation systématique de plusieurs manuscrits. Le travail de Politien sur cet exemplaire continua après ce cours: il y collationna les *Castigationes* de Barbaro. Et Pline occupe une place importante dans la seconde centurie des *Miscellanea*.

À Rome, où il était venu en ambassadeur, Barbaro rédigea ses *Primae* et *Secundae castigationes* (dédicaces respectives du 25 août 1492 et du 13 janvier 1493). Il y porte à un point jamais atteint la méthode exégétique fondée sur l'examen des sources et sur une solide documentation littéraire, historique et scientifique: il s'agit de reconstituer la science antique, et c'est l'image d'un *Plinius triumphans* qui émerge d'une fameuse lettre à Pic de la Mirandole datée de la fin de l'été 1491.[10] L'édition de Perotti représente pour Barbaro un point de référence.

Au moment même où Barbaro rédige ses *Castigationes*, Marcantonio Coccio dit Sabellico, élève de Calderini et Pomponio Leto, travaille à ses *Emendationes seu annotationes in Plinium* qui ne seront imprimées qu'en 1497, probablement à cause du succès des *Castigationes* (dédicace antérieure au 20 septembre 1493 qui présente l'ouvrage comme résultant d'un cours donné trois ans auparavant). On notera que dans cette

---

[9] Munich, Clm 754.

[10] Lettre de la fin de l'été 1491: *Ermolao Barbaro: Epistolare, orationes et carmina*, éd. V. Branca, 2 vols. (Firenze, 1943 [1942]), 2: 92.

dédicace Sabellico dit avoir été poussé à achever son travail par un certain Antonio Moreto dont nous allons très bientôt reparler.

Toujours en 1490 surgit une nouvelle controverse sur Pline. Raffaele Regio, celui que Vitelli avait choisi comme juge en 1472–1473 et qui avait enseigné à Padoue de 1482 à 1486, publie à Venise ses *Epistolae Plynii qua libri Naturalis historiae Tito Vespasiano dedicantur enarrationes* (23 mai 1490). Ce commentaire de la *Praefatio* a pour but déclaré d'approuver ce qui a été écrit de juste et de réfuter les erreurs de ses prédécesseurs. Il s'agit donc d'une exégèse sélective et normative, assez souvent polémique. En réalité, Regio cherche surtout à critiquer, en sus de Perotti et Vitelli, l'enseignement de celui qui lui a soufflé en 1486 la chaire de rhétorique de Padoue, Giovanni Calfurnio.

C'est probablement aussi au milieu de 1490 qu'a commencé le premier travail philologique sur Pline de Francesco Pucci, élève de Politien arrivé à Naples comme professeur en 1483. Le manuscrit de Naples V. F. 2 conserve un travail critique sur Pline que V. Fera ("Un laboratorio filologico") estime écrit de la main de Pucci. Par ailleurs, Pucci a aussi collationné le fameux *Regius* sur un exemplaire mutilé de l'édition Palmarius (1497 = 1498).[11]

Cette effervescence autour de Pline à partir de 1490 explique à mes yeux l'initiative d'Antonio Moreto qui, chargé par Battista de Tortis de préparer la troisième édition vénitienne du *Cornu copiae* (achevée le 19 octobre 1490) ajoute en appendice la *Lettre à Guarnieri* qui n'avait plus été imprimée depuis la *princeps* confidentielle. Cette publication est précédée d'une lettre où Sabellico félicite Moreto (retour d'ascenseur!) et déclare que dans l'entreprise de "Latinam linguam reparare," il ne trouve personne "qui Sypontino antistiti in omni scribendi genere praeferri possit," et il enchaîne un éloge appuyé de Perotti. Mais Moreto se rend coupable d'une falsification dont il est coutumier: il change le nom du destinataire de la lettre de Perotti pour se l'adresser à lui-même, en modifiant çà et là le texte afin de l'harmoniser avec cette supercherie. Nous avons noté plus haut, à propos de Sabellico, l'intérêt de Moreto pour le texte de Pline, et c'est encore Moreto qui poussera Palmarius à faire une nouvelle édition de Pline, la première à intégrer massivement le travail de Barbaro. On comprend que Moreto ait voulu faire d'une pierre deux coups: diffuser le premier commentaire humaniste à la *Praefatio* et s'assurer une gloire personnelle en se présentant comme le destinataire de ce travail. Par cette falsification, Moreto oblittère le contexte particulier de 1470 et déactualise la *Lettre à Guarnieri*, mais en même temps il lui donne la portée méthodologique générale . . . que Perotti avait souhaité lui donner en diffusant une version corrigée de cette lettre! La lettre acquiert une valeur générale dans le contexte d'autres polémiques: elle devient un manuel à l'usage de ceux qui éditent les classiques et un commentaire à la *Praefatio*. Bien entendu, Moreto ne reprend pas la réplique critique de Vitelli. C'est à cette supercherie que la lettre de Perotti doit sa grande diffusion, puisqu'elle sera désormais associée au succès de librairie qu'est le *Cornu copiae*. Quand Alde Manuce s'apercevra, en 1499, de la falsification, il rétablira

---

[11] Possédé successivement par Salutati, Bruni, Beccadelli, et le roi de Naples (d'où son nom), ce manuscrit est actuellement démembré entre l'Oxf. Bodl. Auct. T. 1. 27 et le Par. lat. 6798.

le nom du destinataire véritable et, à partir d'un exemplaire de l'*editio princeps* (il n'est pas surprenant qu'il ait trouvé cette édition vénitienne à Venise), corrigera en partie le texte falsifié par Moreto (en quelques cas, il conservera la leçon de Moreto contre celle de la *princeps*). Par ailleurs, Alde Manuce reprendra aussi la réplique de Vitelli, écartée par Moreto, et lui assurera ainsi une large diffusion. L'aldine sera suivie par toutes les éditions italiennes du *Cornu copiae*, mais, en Europe du nord, le texte rétabli ne s'imposera, à Bâle, qu'à partir de 1521 (jusqu'en 1536), et à Paris, qu'à partir de 1528, si bien que la falsification de Moreto sera encore imprimée huit fois avec le *Cornu copiae*, sans compter une édition particulière sur laquelle nous reviendrons. Je rappelle que le texte imprimé dont nous parlons correspond au premier état de la lettre de Perotti et qu'il faudra attendre un article de J. Monfasani ("The First Call for Press Censorship") pour qu'on prenne conscience des corrections apportées par Perotti à son texte (deux états pour Monfasani, qui a négligé un manuscrit; trois pour moi).

À l'époque où Barbaro publie ses *Castigationes*, la controverse entre Niccolò Leoniceno, professeur de médecine à Ferrare (*De Plinii ... erroribus*, 1492), et le juriste Pandolfo Collenuccio (*Pliniana defensio ...* [1493?]) concerne les erreurs de Pline, en particulier des confusions fâcheuses dans l'identification des plantes par mauvaise compréhension des sources grecques, notamment Dioscoride, et montre le souci nouveau de confronter les affirmations de Pline avec les réalités de l'expérience: cette attitude novatrice annonce le développement des sciences expérimentales.

Dans la nouvelle édition de Pline par les frères Angelo et Iacopo Britannici (Brescia, 1496), on lit une lettre de Matteo Rufo à l'évêque de Vérone Giusto sur la patrie de Pline l'Ancien. Une lettre liminaire de Giovanni, frère d'Angelo et Iacopo, nous apprend que ces éditeurs sont tombés sur ce texte au moment où ils avaient déjà imprimé une bonne partie de leurs exemplaires. Une troisième lettre, du médecin de Vérone Alessandro Benedetti qui donnera lui-même une édition de Pline en 1507, adressée à Matteo Rufo, le félicite pour sa mise au point. La lettre de Rufo, disciple de Perotti comme nous l'avons vu plus haut, se rattache directement à la *Lettre à Guarnieri*. Rufo y fait un éloge appuyé de son maître et entreprend, par reconnaissance pour lui, de réfuter ceux qui ont voulu contredire Perotti, en particulier sur l'identification de la patrie de Pline avec Vérone: il repousse comme falsifiés les témoignages de Suétone, Jérôme, et Macrobe en faveur de Côme et invoque l'autorité de Pétrarque, Biondo, Pie II, Valla, Politien (l'allusion aux *Miscellanea* prouve que la lettre est postérieure à 1489), et Landino, ainsi que des témoignages épigraphiques. Rufo sera suivi par A. Benedetti dans l'édition de 1507 que je viens de mentionner. Mais d'autres découvertes épigraphiques par Benedetto Giovio,[12] suivi par Alciato, ruineront les prétentions des Véronais.

Comme je l'avais annoncé, la polémique entre Regio et un élève dalmate de Calfurnio, Marino Becichemo, reprend au début du XVIe siècle. Dès 1500, Becichemo et Regio sont en concurrence à Venise où ils enseignent tous deux. Appelé au Studio

---

[12] Notamment dans l'*Enarratio Praefationis Historiae Naturalis C. Plinii Secundi*, conservée dans deux manuscrits: Cité du Vatican, Vat. lat. 5896 et Milan, Ambr. J 47 inf.

de Brescia en 1503, après avoir été chassé de sa chaire de rhétorique à Padoue par Regio (!), Becichemo récite alors, peut-être les 25 et 27 août, si l'on se fie aux dates de dédicace de l'une et l'autre œuvre, une *In C. Plinium Secundum praelectio*, puis des *In primum Naturalis historiae librum obseruationum collectanea*, dont la composition remonte à 1501 et qui constituent un commentaire à la *Praefatio*. Ces deux ouvrages seront publiés ensemble à Brescia vers 1504–1505, par Angelo et/ou Iacopo Britannici. Dans la dédicace, Becichemo déclare que certains de ses élèves, à son insu, ont publié la *Praelectio*, qu'il n'a pas pu la corriger comme il l'aurait voulu et qu'il doit se défendre contre les calomnies d'un *Homeromastix* (qualifié plus loin de *Calpurniomastix* = Regio!) qui s'attaque aux savants et a corrompu Quintilien et surtout Pline, garant de la science romaine.

La *Praelectio* a une portée générale et concerne le genre et le titre de l'œuvre. Il y est question du dédicataire de Pline et de la patrie de ce dernier. Mais dix-neuf feuillets sont consacrés à la polémique avec Regio, calomniateur de tous les savants, et à sa propre apologie. Becichemo se flatte d'avoir fait chasser ce "fanaticus senex," ce calomniateur impénitent, "ex celeberrimo Italiæ gymnasio." Il s'est opposé à lui à Venise, à Padoue, et maintenant à Brescia, qui a expulsé Regio pour l'engager lui, Becichemo, avec un traitement supérieur (*maiore salario*). Aussi a-t-il conçu ses *Collectanea*, annoncés dans la *Praelectio*, comme une réfutation des *errores pueriles* de Regio.[13] Becichemo affirme avoir eu le temps de corriger les *Collectanea*, dont il souligne l'originalité par rapport à quatre précurseurs qu'il loue dans l'ordre (Politien, Barbaro, Sabellico, et Beroaldo): son commentaire à lui n'est pas sélectif. Pour l'heure, il a déclaré la guerre (*bellum indixi*) à l'ennemi de la vérité, des hommes de bien, et des savants (= Regio!). Les *Collectanea* se présentent donc comme une réfutation des positions de Regio. Mais, du point de vue méthodologique, Becichemo se rapproche de la manière de Perotti dans le *Cornu copiae*: à partir d'un mot du texte, il explique le sens, les *realia*, et le contexte historique; mais il en profite aussi pour explorer le champ sémantique en l'illustrant de nombreuses citations.

Regio répliquera en publiant à Venise le 2 octobre 1508 une *Apologia* adressée à Giovanni Badoer. Il faut dire qu'en 1508 Regio et Becichemo se retrouvent une nouvelle fois en concurrence, pour lors à Venise, où ils enseignent tous deux! Regio défend son propre travail éditorial et exégétique sur la *Praefatio*, en revenant notamment sur certains points de la controverse entre Perotti et Vitelli, et accuse Becichemo de s'être approprié les travaux de son maître Calfurnio.

Jusqu'ici, nous sommes restés en Italie, mais au XVIe siècle la question de Pline devient européenne et il est impossible d'en suivre tous les développements dans le cadre d'une simple relation. Aussi me contenterai-je d'évoquer quatre figures qui nous mèneront en France, puis en Espagne, puis à nouveau en Italie, mais pour introduire finalement un grand représentant de la philologie germanique.

En France, Nicolas Bérault donne en 1516 une édition de Pline dont le texte, peu original, a été étudié par M. M. de la Garanderie ("Travaux italiens et français").

---

[13] Par une inversion de la topique traditionnelle, Becichemo présente Regio comme un *senex puer*.

Mais, ce qui à mes yeux est beaucoup plus original et peut-être nouveau dans son projet éditorial recommandé par une lettre d'Érasme, c'est que ce *curatore* de Pline prend la peine d'éditer trois ans après sa propre édition (1519) un recueil des quatre commentaires à ses yeux les plus importants de la *Praefatio* de Pline: les deux travaux de Becichemo et les lettres de Perotti (dans la version falsifiée, mais "normalisée", de Moreto) et Vitelli. On peut s'étonner de certaines absences: Bérault avait déjà repris dans la préface de son édition le premier commentaire de Beroaldo et, se rangeant du côté de Becichemo, il a écarté Regio. Quant à Barbaro, auquel il voue une grande admiration,[14] ses interventions sur la *Praefatio* avaient été fort limitées en volume. Ce livre composite est, en dehors de la *princeps*, la seule édition des lettres de Perotti et Vitelli indépendantes du *Cornu copiae*. Par ailleurs, pour la commodité du lecteur, Bérault donne aussi le texte de la *Praefatio* de Pline. Or ce texte n'est pas celui qu'il a lui-même édité en 1516, mais revient assez souvent à celui défendu par Perotti dans la *Lettre à Guarnieri*, ce qui signifie que Bérault a lu attentivement les textes qu'il faisait publier et qu'il en a tenu compte pour l'établissement du texte de Pline.

C'est encore beaucoup plus ouvertement que Francesco Lopez de Villalobos, médecin de Charles Quint, rend justice au mérite de Perotti, premier commentateur de la *Praefatio* de Pline, dans l'avertissement au lecteur de son propre commentaire (*Glossa litteralis*) à la Préface et au livre 2 de l'*Histoire naturelle* (Alcalà de Henares, 1524). Il cite ensuite C. Vitelli, mais de façon dépréciative: "Deinde Cornelius Vitellius quasdam expositionis Sipontini partes aliquantulum iracunde corrigere professus est." De fait, l'utilisation de la *Lettre à Guarnieri* dans son commentaire de la *Praefatio* est massive et tourne souvent au plagiat, même si elle n'est que rarement avouée dans le détail des emprunts. Ce qui est plus étrange, c'est que Villalobos ne cite dans son avertissement aucun autre humaniste que Perotti et Vitelli, alors qu'après 1500 le point de référence privilégié des philologues pour Pline est Ermolao Barbaro. Manifestement, Villalobos disposait, comme la plupart des hommes cultivés de son époque, d'une édition du *Cornu copiae*, et il s'est contenté des deux pièces annexées à cette édition depuis Alde Manuce.

Nous revenons un instant en Italie pour nous attacher à un commentateur de Pline qui ne figure pas, du moins sous son vrai nom, dans l'étude de Nauert. On doit en effet à H. Walter ("La vicenda del *Regius antiquus*," "Codice parigino latino 6808") la restitution à Filippo Strozzi le Jeune, le banquier qui à la fin de sa vie deviendra le chef des républicains florentins et fournira à Musset l'une des grandes figures de *Lorenzaccio*, d'un commentaire de Pline jusque là attribué à Guillaume Pellicier et connu seulement par deux manuscrits autographes, l'un conservé à Paris et l'autre à Budapest, mais provenant de Paris,[15] jusqu'à la découverte à Florence en 1998 dans les *Carte Strozziane* par M. T. Scaramuzza ("Le note filologiche," "Un nuovo autografo"), sur les conseils d'H. Walter, d'un troisième manuscrit en partie autographe

---

[14] Bérault achètera en 1534 un exemplaire des *Castigationes Plinianae* que j'ai identifié à la Bibliothèque Universitaire de la Sorbonne (rés. XVI,896 in-4°).

[15] Par. lat. 6808 (*Praefatio* et livres 2 et 10); Bibl. Sechényi, cod. fol. lat. 201,I (*Praefatio* et livres 3 à 9).

donnant trois états antérieurs du commentaire à la *Praefatio* et au livre II,[16] dont j'ai proposé un classement chronologique dans l'ordre inverse des feuillets (Charlet, "Philippe Strozzi le Jeune"). Le manuscrit de Budapest est une sorte de collation critique du commentaire de Beatus Rhenanus (1526) avec lequel j'achèverai mon exposé; il est donc postérieur à 1526, alors que les trois états du manuscrit de Florence, qui ne font aucune référence à l'humaniste rhénan, sont antérieurs à cette date. Quant au manuscrit de Paris, il apparaît, à M. T. Scaramuzza comme à moi, comme la rédaction ultime, du moins en l'état actuel de nos connaissances, du commentaire de F. Strozzi. Globalement, pour le commentaire à la *Praefatio*, Perotti est, après Barbaro, l'humaniste le plus cité. Strozzi ne l'approuve pas toujours, mais il le loue explicitement au moins une fois et le considère comme le représentant d'une sorte de vulgate dont il part pour la critiquer au nom du respect dû aux manuscrits. Strozzi est dans la ligne de Politien et se concentre sur les problèmes ecdotiques, alors que Perotti, même dans la *Lettre à Guarnieri* dont l'objet est l'édition du texte de la *Praefatio*, accorde une place plus importante aux *realia* et au commentaire linguistique ou littéraire.

Mais l'examen du manuscrit de Budapest pour le commentaire à la *Praefatio* m'amène à terminer ce panorama des querelles, mais aussi des échanges, autour de Pline dans la *res publica litterarum* un peu plus au nord, dans le monde rhénan et germanique de Beatus Rhenanus, dont nous avons déjà cité le commentaire publié à Bâle en 1526. Rhenanus me semble connaître les travaux de Perotti, mais ne le nomme jamais et paraît le considérer comme une sorte de vulgate insatisfaisante qu'il s'agit de corriger. J'ai retrouvé aussi dans son commentaire deux lignes de Vitelli, caché derrière un pluriel anonyme (*inquiunt*).[17] Mais le plus intéressant, c'est peut-être ses rapports avec F. Strozzi. Que Strozzi ait collationné son commentaire et en ait tiré profit est prouvé, comme nous l'avons vu, par les manuscrits de Budapest et de Paris. Mais deux faits troublants observés quand je préparais une séance du colloque de Sassoferrato consacrée à F. Strozzi (Charlet, "Philippe Strozzi le Jeune") m'amènent à formuler l'hypothèse que des rapports ont peut-être existé entre le banquier florentin et l'humaniste rhénan *avant* la publication à Bâle du commentaire sur Pline (1526). À propos du paragraphe 30 de la *Praefatio*, là où les manuscrits donnent *attineo, atteneo* ou *attento*, Strozzi propose, dans les deux premiers états du manuscrit de Florence (fols. 95r et 54r) antérieurs au commentaire de Rhenanus, de lire *"ait in eo" ex uetustis*. Le manuscrit de Budapest, qui mentionne que cette conjecture apparaît aussi chez Rhenanus (où les éditeurs modernes sont allés chercher cette correction), et le manuscrit de Paris, qui lui, en revanche, ne dit mot sur ce point de Rhenanus, précisent que cette leçon s'appuie sur le *Mediceus*, manuscrit florentin auquel avait accès Strozzi, qui donne *attineo*. Ici, on peut invoquer une simple coïncidence: deux grands esprits peuvent, indépendamment l'un de l'autre, faire la même

---

[16] Archivio di Stato di Firenze, Carte Strozziane, Va serie, 1221, vol. 3.

[17] Commentaire à Plin. *praef.* 22: '*Iuratissimos*', inquiunt, *uocat Plinius 'litteratos et quasi iureiurando doctissimos affirmatos. Proximos autem* [*uero* Vitelli] *qui propter doctrinam propius sunt famae.*' À part *autem*, il s'agit d'une citation exacte de Vitelli 12 (mon édition).

conjecture presque au même moment. Mais il y a plus troublant. À propos du paragraphe 9 de cette même *Praefatio* (*ineptis* codd.), Rhenanus conjecture *meritis*, mais rapporte anonymement une autre conjecture, *inemptis*, retenue par les éditeurs modernes en référence à cet anonyme. Or la leçon *inemptis* est proposée par Strozzi dans le manuscrit de Florence (fol. 27r) avant que ce même Strozzi ait pris connaissance du travail de Rhenanus et, sur le manuscrit de Budapest (fol. 213v), après avoir nommément cité la conjecture de Rhenanus (*meritis*), il reprend explicitement comme sienne, mais sans la moindre polémique avec Rhenanus, la leçon *inemptis*. Cette leçon reparaît deux fois dans le Parisinus (fol. 12r) et, la seconde fois, est explicitement revendiquée comme personnelle (*nos*), toujours sans polémique. Strozzi donne l'impression d'identifier l'anonyme cité par Rhenanus (ou de s'identifier avec lui). Je ne puis rien affirmer dans la mesure où nous n'avons aucune trace d'échange épistolaire avec F. Strozzi dans la correspondance conservée de Rhenanus. Mais Strozzi, par ses relations bancaires, pouvait nouer de nombreux contacts, et on ne peut exclure l'hypothèse qu'il ait pu entretenir des relations philologiques avec un membre éminent de la *Res publica litterarum* intéressé comme lui au texte de Pline l'Ancien.

Sur cette hypothèse, je m'arrête pour conclure. La querelle sur Pline, véritable "laboratorio filologico", pour reprendre la belle expression de V. Fera déjà citée, a mis en évidence les grandeurs et les misères de la *Res publica litterarum*: grandeur dans la quête impossible du texte originel, dans la volonté presque démiurgique de ressusciter un *Plinius triumphans* pour reconstituer la science antique. Misères aussi dans les petitesses, les mesquineries, les chamailleries d'universitaires jaloux de la chaire occupée par le "collègue". Mais, en tout état de cause, la culture occidentale est héritière des efforts de cette *Res publica litterarum*. Et à nous, néo-latinistes, cette *Res publica litterarum* offre un champ d'investigation privilégié pour ce que je me plais à appeler une "philologie biologique" qui s'inscrit dans l'évolution des sciences. Le XIXe siècle a été le siècle des mathématiques et la physique est devenue la science dominante à partir du début du XXe siècle. Mais, depuis quelques dizaines d'années, et cette évolution est en train de s'accélérer, c'est la biologie qui devient le fer de lance de la conquête du savoir. Le néo-latin est particulièrement propice à la mise en œuvre d'une philologie biologique, c'est-à-dire une philologie attachée à comprendre et à reconstituer à la fois les processus vitaux de l'élaboration d'un texte par son auteur (l'existence de manuscrits d'auteur ou corrigés par l'auteur et des états successifs d'un texte — données qui font presque toujours défaut pour les auteurs antiques — permet souvent de reconstituer à la fois le mouvement qui a porté un texte à la vie)[18] et la vie, parfois même la mutation, de ce texte dans les différentes phases de sa réception: dans certains cas privilégiés, ici la *Lettre à Guarnieri* de N. Perotti, nous pouvons reconstruire la vie d'un texte dans les décennies qui ont suivi son élaboration.

Université de Provence (Aix-Marseille I)

---

[18] Sur ce point, comme l'a rappelé L. Gualdo Rosa dans la relation plénière en italien, P. O. Kristeller, G. Billanovich et quelques autres nous ont montré la voie.

Bibliographie

Boutroue, Marie-Elisabeth. "Pline ou le trésor du monde. Recherches sur quelques aspects de la transmission et de la fortune de l'*Histoire naturelle* de Pline l'Ancien (XVe–XVIe siècles)." Thèse de l'Université de Paris, 1998.

———. "Giovanni Andrea Bussi et la deuxième édition de l'*Histoire naturelle* de Pline l'Ancien." À paraître dans les *Actes du séminaire sur Pline*. (Paris, 2001).

———. "Les *Annotationes in Plinium* de Rhenanus et la tradition textuelle de l'*Histoire Naturelle* à la Renaissance." In *Beatus Rhenanus (1485–1547), lecteur et éditeur des textes anciens*, éd. James Hirstein, 327–375. Turnhout, 2000 [2001].

Casciano, Paola. "Il ms. Angelicano 1097, fase preparatoria per l'edizione del Plinio di Sweynheym e Pannartz." In *Scrittura, biblioteche e stampa a Roma nel Quattrocento*, ed. C. Bianca, M. Miglio et al., 383–394. Roma, 1980.

Charlet, Jean-Louis. "La lettre de N. Perotti à Francesco Guarnieri: un commentaire à la *Préface* de Pline qui annonce le *Cornu copiae*." *Studi Umanistici Piceni* 19 (1999): 38–46.

———. "Philippe Strozzi le Jeune lecteur de Perotti dans son commentaire à la *Praefatio* de Pline." *Studi Umanistici Piceni* 20 (2000): 86–107.

———. *Deux pièces de la controverse humaniste sur Pline: N. Perotti, Lettre à Guarnieri, C. Vitelli, Lettre à Partenio di Salò. Édition critique et commentaire.* Paris, 2003.

Davies, Martin. "Making Sense of Pliny in the Quattrocento." *Renaissance Studies* 9 (1995): 240–257.

De Capua, Paola. "Fortune esegetiche della *Praefatio* alla *Naturalis historia* tra Quattro- e Cinquecento." In *Filologia umanistica. Per Gianvito Resta*, ed. Vincenzo Fera e Giacomo Ferraú, 1:495–526. Padova, 1997.

Dunston, John. "Studies in Domizio Calderini." *Italia Medievale e Umanistica* 11 (1968): 71–150.

Feld, M. D. "Sweynheym and Pannartz, Cardinal Bessarion, Neoplatonism: Renaissance Humanism and Two Early Printers' Choice of Texts." *Harvard Library Bulletin* 30 (1982): 282–335.

———. "The Sybils of Subiaco, Sweynheym and Pannartz and the 'Editio Princeps' of Lactantius." In *Renaissance Studies in Honor of Craig Hugh Smyth*, ed. A. Morrogh, 301–315. Firenze, 1985.

———. "A Theory of the Early Italian Printing Firm. Part I: Variants of Humanism." *Harvard Library Bulletin* 33 (1985): 282–335; "... Part II: The Political Economy of Patronage." *Harvard Library Bulletin* 34 (1986): 294–332.

——— "The First Roman Printers and the Idioms of Humanism. An Introduction." *Harvard Library Bulletin* 36 (1988): 9–91.

Fera, Vincenzo. "Un laboratorio filologico di fine Quattrocento: la *Naturalis historia*." In *Formative Stages of Classical Traditions: Latin Texts from Antiquity to the Renaissance*, ed. O. Pecere and M. D. Reeve, 435–466. Spoleto, 1995.

———. "Poliziano, Ermolao Barbaro e Plinio." In *Una famiglia veneziana nella storia: i Barbaro*, ed. Michela Marangoni e Manlio Pastore Stocchi, 193–234. Venezia, 1996.

de la Garanderie, Marie Madeleine. "Travaux italiens et français sur Pline l'Ancien: l'édition parisienne de Nicolas Bérault (1516)." In *L'aube de la Renaissance*, éd. D.

Cecchetti, L. Sozzi et L. Terreaux, 209–224. Genève, 1991.

Grafton, Antony. "Printers' Correctors and the Publication of Classical Texts." In idem, *Bring Out Your Dead: The Past as Revelation*, 141–155. Cambridge, MA, 2001.

Marucchi, Adriana. "Note sul manoscritto (Vat. Lat. 5991) di cui si è servito Giovanni Andrea Bussi per l'edizione di Plinio del 1470." *Bulletin d'information de l'Institut de Recherche et d'Histoire des Textes* 15 (1967–1968): 175–182.

Mercati, Giovanni. *Per la cronologia della vita e degli scritti di Niccolò Perotti arcivescovo di Siponto*. Studi e testi 44. Roma, 1925.

Monfasani, John. "The First Call for Press Censorship: Niccolò Perotti, Giovanni Andrea Bussi, Antonio Moreto, and the Editing of Pliny's *Natural History*." *Renaissance Quarterly* 41 (1988): 1–31.

Nauert, Charles G. Jr. "Plinius." In *Catalogus Translationum et Commentariorum*, ed. E. F. Cranz and P. O. Kristeller, 4:297–422. Medieval and Renaissance Latin Translations and Commentaries 4. Washington, 1980.

Prete, Sesto. "La lettera di Niccolò Perotti a Francesco Guarnieri." *Studi Piceni* 43 (1976): 115–126.

―――. "Problems of Textual Criticism: Niccolò Perotti's Letter to Francesco Guarnieri." In *Acta conventus neo-latini Turonensis (1976)*, éd. Jean-Claude Margolin, 15–26. Paris, 1980.

Ramminger, Johann. "Die *animadversiones in Perotti Cornucopiam* von Ermolao Barbaro dem Jüngeren." *Studi Umanistici Piceni* 16 (1996): 87–99.

―――. "Die 'Irrtümer Perottis' von Ermolao Barbaro d. J. Ausgabe und Kommentar von Brief 135." *Wiener Studien* 114 (2001): 677–700.

―――. "Brotheus e Timon: il vocabulario della polemica tra Domizio Calderini e N. Perotti." *Studi Umanistici Piceni* 21 (2001): 147–155.

Scaramuzza, Maria Teresa. "Le note filologiche di Filippo Strozzi a Plinio il Vecchio." Tesi di laurea, Università di Ferrara, 1998.

―――. "Un nuovo autografo del commentario alla *Storia Naturale* pliniana di Filippo Strozzi il Giovane (Archivio di Stato di Firenze, Carte Strozziane V, 1221, vol. 3)." *Studi Umanistici Piceni* 20 (2000): 117–135.

Walter, Hermann. "Studien zur Handschriftengeschichte der Naturalis Historia des Älteren Plinius. Ein Erfahrungsbericht." In *Forschungsbericht Universität Mannheim 1978–1982*, 227–239. Mannheim, 1983.

―――. "An Illustrated Incunable of Pliny's *Natural History* in the Biblioteca Palatina, Parma." *Journal of the Warburg and Courtauld Institutes* 53 (1990): 208–216.

―――. "La vicenda del *Regius antiquus* di Angelo Poliziano (Bodl. auct. T. 1. 27/Par. lat. 6798) e un presunto commentario di Guillaume Pellicier alla *Storia Naturale* di Plinio il Vecchio (Par. lat. 6808)." In *Poliziano nel suo tempo*, ed. Luisa Secchi Tarugi, 387–409. Firenze, 1996.

―――. "Il commentario pliniano di Guillaume Pellicier, vescovo di Montpellier, e il codice parigino latino 6808." *Studi Umanistici Piceni* 17 (1997): 179–194.

―――. "Il commentario pliniano di Guillaume Pellicier, vescovo di Montpellier, e l'incunabolo N 614 della Biblioteca Palatina di Parma." *Studi Umanistici Piceni* 18 (1998): 187–196.

Allegorizing Apuleius:
Fulgentius, Boccaccio, Beroaldo,
and the Chain of Receptions

JULIA HAIG GAISSER

Apuleius was a very lucky man. He cultivated the arts of all the nine Muses, married a rich widow, defended himself brilliantly against a charge of practicing magic, and, by his own account at least, achieved fame and fortune as a sophist and Platonic philosopher.[1] His works enjoyed similar good fortune. Most came through the ravages of the Middle Ages unscathed. His novel, the *Metamorphoses* or *Golden Ass*, received an allegorical interpretation by Fulgentius in late antiquity and then went on to slumber peacefully through the centuries in a single manuscript in the great library of Monte Cassino. At the dawn of the Renaissance, Apuleius had the good luck to fall into the hands of one of the greatest — and most Apuleian — figures in Italian literature, Giovanni Boccaccio. At the end of the fifteenth century Fortune smiled on him again, when he was taken up by another kindred spirit, the Bolognese humanist Filippo Beroaldo. Both encounters were decisive. Boccaccio did not "discover" the manuscript at Monte Cassino, as scholars often maintain, but he transcribed Apuleius's works, imitated two of his stories in the *Decameron*, and produced an allegorical reading of the story of Cupid and Psyche. Beroaldo, one of the most influential teachers in Italy, lectured on the *Golden Ass* at the University of Bologna and interpreted it in a major literary and philological commentary. Boccaccio brought Apuleius to the attention of Florentine humanists and artists in the fourteenth and fifteenth centuries. Beroaldo made him famous all over Europe.

My topic is reception — of the *Golden Ass*, to be sure — but also of *interpretations* of the *Golden Ass*, particularly allegorical interpretations of its two most important stories: the transformation of its hero Lucius into an ass, and the tale of Cupid and Psyche. I will be talking about a chain of receptions (a term I have borrowed from

---

[1] Most of what we know about the life of Apuleius (c. A.D. 125–c. 169) comes from autobiographical remarks in his *Apology* and *Florida*.

Charles Martindale) that stretches from late antiquity through the sixteenth century.[2] The major links of the chain were forged by Fulgentius, Boccaccio, and Beroaldo, but it also has some more obscure links, as well as offshoots leading into vernacular translations and the realm of art. As we will see, the chain is neither tidy nor unbroken. It has dead ends and new beginnings and a few loose strands along the way. It begins as a single chain of interpretations of Psyche, but doubles in the fourteenth century, when allegorical readers turn their attention also to the transformations of Lucius.

Our story begins in the late fifth century, with two allegorical readers of the story of Cupid and Psyche, Martianus Capella and Fulgentius the mythographer.[3] We know very little about either — except that both, like Apuleius, were north Africans and that Martianus was a pagan and Fulgentius a Christian. Martianus gives Psyche a cameo role in his strange allegorical work, *The Marriage of Mercury and Philology*, but her story is not the one told by Apuleius. The main difference for our purposes is that in Apuleius her parents are the unnamed "king and queen" of fairy tale, while Martianus calls them Apollo and Endelichia (*De Nuptiis* 1.7). This is an important point, and we shall return to it presently.

Fulgentius, on the other hand, does follow Apuleius, even to the point of imitating his language and turns of phrase.[4] Yet he tells — and allegorizes — a story that is essentially different from that in Apuleius. We must look at his treatment in some detail, both because it is artistic in its own right (a claim that may require some demonstration) and because it is the first link in our chain of allegories.

Fulgentius tells the story of Psyche in three parts or sections, each related in a different style, yet please note that her name never appears in his account. Part 1 is straight narrative and goes like this. The king and queen of a certain city had three daughters. The two older ones were pretty enough, but the youngest was so beautiful that she was believed to be an earthly Venus. The older daughters married, but no one dared to court the youngest. Instead, she was worshipped like a goddess with prayers and sacrifices. Venus was outraged and commanded Cupid to punish the girl, but he fell in love with her instead. Apollo commanded that she be placed alone on a mountain peak and escorted as in a funeral procession to her marriage to a winged serpent. Zephyr wafted her down into a beautiful golden house, where she was waited on by invisible servants whom she perceived only as voices. Her husband

---

[2] For "chain of receptions" see Charles Martindale, *Redeeming the Text. Latin Poetry and the Hermeneutics of Reception* (Cambridge, 1993), 7 and 28.

[3] For Martianus see especially Danuta Shanzer, *A Philosophical and Literary Commentary on Martianus Capella's De Nuptiis Philologiae et Mercurii Book I* (Berkeley, 1986). Shanzer dates the work to the 470s or 480s: see *Commentary*, 8–17. For Fulgentius see Bradford Gregory Hays, "Fulgentius the Mythographer" (Ph.D. diss., Cornell University, 1996). Hays (1–24) dates the *Mitologiae* after the 480s, probably during the reign of Thrasamund (496–523), placing it in the cultural world of Vandal Africa.

[4] *Mitologiae* 3.6. I cite the Latin text from *Fabii Planciadis Fulgentii V. C. Opera*, ed. R. Helm, rev. J. Preaux (Leipzig, 1898; repr. Stuttgart, 1970). The translations are my own.

came to her at night, made love to her in the darkness, and departed at dawn unseen. The section ends with a neat little summary in very Apuleian style:

> Habuit ergo vocale servitium, ventosum dominium, nocturnum commercium, ignotum coniugium. (*Mit.* 3.6.115)
>
> [In short, she had voices for servants, an insubstantial domain, nocturnal intercourse, and an unknown husband.]

Part 2 continues the narration but adds moralizing comments. The two sisters climbed the mountain and loudly lamented her death. Her husband forbade her to see them, but, as Fulgentius says, "the unbreakable ardor of kindred affection overshadowed her husband's command."[5] Zephyr wafted the sisters down and she agreed to their poisonous advice to find out what her husband looked like. Fulgentius says: "she seized curiosity, a stepmother of her safety, and she seized easy credulity, which is always the mother of deception, neglecting the voice of caution."[6] Her sisters told her that she was married to a serpent. Believing them, she planned to kill him and hid a dagger under the pillow and a lighted lamp under a bushel. When her husband was asleep, she armed herself with the weapon and uncovered her lamp. She recognized Cupid — it is important to remember here that *Cupido*, "Cupid," also means "erotic desire" — and while "she was on fire with the licentious passion of love,"[7] she burned her husband with a drop of oil from her lamp. Cupid fled, chastising her curiosity, and left her homeless and a refugee. In the end, after she had been greatly persecuted by Venus, he accepted her in marriage at the urging of Jupiter. The section ends with a rush, omitting much of the story, and differing from Apuleius's account, in which it is Cupid who desires the marriage, and Jupiter who agrees to allow it.

Part 3 summarizes the girl's trials in an elegant *praeteritio*: "I could tell the whole story — how she fetched water from the Styx and stole fleece from the flocks of the Sun and sorted the seeds and nearly died when she took a bit of Proserpina's beauty for herself."[8] Having just mentioned these matters, Fulgentius declines to relate them in detail, explaining that they have already been told at length by both Apuleius and an otherwise unknown author called Aristophontes the Athenian.

Fulgentius's narrative is often taken as a mere summary of Apuleius's "Cupid and Psyche," but it is not, for he has omitted every detail connected with Psyche's

---

[5] "tamen consanguineae caritatis invincibilis ardor maritale obumbravit imperium": *Mit.* 3.6.115.

[6] "curiositam, suae salutis novercam, arripuit et facillimam credulitatem, quae semper deceptionum mater est, postposito cautelae suffragio arripit": *Mit.* 3.6.115.

[7] "dum inmodesto amoris torretur affectu": *Mit.* 3.6.115.

[8] "Poteram quidem totius fabulae ordinem hoc libello percurrere, qualiter et ad infernum descenderit et ex Stigiis aquis urnulam delibaverit et Solis armenta vellere spoliaverit et seminum germina confusa discreverit et de Proserpinae pulchritudine particulam moritura praesumpserit": *Mit.* 3.6.116.

redemption and final happiness: her pregnancy, Cupid's assistance in completing the tasks set by Venus, his plea to Jupiter to allow the marriage, Psyche's divinity and wedding, and the birth of her child, Voluptas (Pleasure), the emblem of her joyous and everlasting union with Cupid. Instead, all we have is a shotgun wedding: "At last," says Fulgentius, "at Jupiter's urging, he took her in marriage."[9]

The result of Fulgentius's omissions is a darker and more pessimistic story than that in Apuleius, one that is focused far more on the girl's error than on her subsequent sufferings and final redemption. It is this story, subtly but surely different from Apuleius's "Cupid and Psyche," that he explains in his allegory. We might allegorize Apuleius's tale as the story of the union of the Soul with Love. Fulgentius's allegory is about the sins of the flesh and the evils of sexual desire. Here it is:

The city of the girl's birth represents the world, and her parents, the king and queen, are god and matter. The three daughters are *caro* (Flesh), *ultronietas* (a very rare word that Fulgentius defines as Free Will), and *anima* or Psice (Soul).[10] Soul is younger because the body is already made when the soul is placed in it. She is more beautiful because Soul is both superior to Free Will and nobler than Flesh. She is envied by Venus, that is, Lust, who sends *Cupiditas* or Desire to destroy her. Desire, which can be of either good or evil, esteems Soul and joins with her as if in a marriage and persuades her not to see his face — that is, says Fulgentius, not to learn the delights of desire. He expands this explanation with one of the most fascinating and revealing comments in the allegory:

Whence also Adam, although he sees, does not see that he is naked, until he eats from the tree of concupiscence.[11]

Fulgentius does not explain the connection, but leaves it to us to infer that seeing the face of Desire is equivalent to eating the apple: each is a fall from innocence into carnal awareness and lust; each is a sin.[12]

The allegory continues. Desire urges Soul not to be persuaded by her sisters to satisfy her curiosity about his appearance. But terrified by their urging, she takes the lamp from beneath the bushel — "that is," says Fulgentius, "she reveals the flame of longing hidden in her heart, sees that it is sweet, and falls in love with it."[13] His

---

[9] "postea Iove petente in coniugio accepit": *Mit.* 3.6.116.

[10] The name Psice appears only twice in *Mit* 3.6: in the title and in the explanation of the name at 3.6.117.

[11] "unde et Adam quamvis videat nudum se non videt, donec de concupiscentiae arbore comedat": *Mit.* 3.6.118.

[12] The parallel between Adam and Psyche is often noted, but usually attributed — with only partial accuracy — to their sharing in "the sin of disobedient curiosity." See Luisa Vertova, "Cupid and Psyche in Renaissance Painting before Raphael," *Journal of the Warburg and Courtauld Institutes* 42 (1979): 104–121, here 104–105.

[13] "id est desiderii flammam in pectore absconsam depalat visamque taliter dulcem amat ac diligit": *Mit.* 3.6.118. Fulgentius uses the image of Psyche's lamp quite differently in the prologue of Book 1: *Mit.* prol. 1.4 and 1.20.

heroine sees what has been there all along — her own sexual longing, its light unfortunately no longer hidden under a bushel. I suspect that some of you are shaking your heads by now, remembering the New Testament and its repeated injunction *not* to keep one's light hidden under a bushel. Thus, in the Sermon on the Mount, Jesus says:

> Neither do men light a candle, and put it under a bushel, but on a candlestick: and it giveth light unto all that are in the house. Let your light so shine before men, that they may see your good works, and glorify your father which is in heaven. (Matthew 5:15–16)[14]

Fulgentius wants us to remember this good light, which *should* be revealed, and to contrast it with the sinful flame of carnal desire, which should remain hidden from us. The flame does double duty in his allegory: it is Soul's desire, but it also enflames Soul's desire. We might say that the flame burns and damages itself. Here is the way Fulgentius puts it: "[Soul] is said to kindle the flame with the spurting of the lamp because every Desire burns as much as it is loved and fixes the stain of sin on its own flesh."[15] He continues: "Therefore, as if made naked by Desire, she is deprived of her mighty fortune and tossed by dangers and driven from her royal palace."[16] Here the allegory ends — with Fulgentius implicitly keeping the example of Adam before us. Soul, like Adam, has succumbed to temptation and gained forbidden knowledge; and like Adam, she is driven from her Eden.

The next links in our chain of allegories appear over eight hundred years later, around the middle of the fourteenth century. The story of Apuleius's reception in this period is yet to be understood: we know only that someone, at some point, removed or copied the manuscript from Monte Cassino, and the cat (or perhaps we should say, the *Golden Ass*) was out of the bag. Among the twenty-three fourteenth-century manuscripts of the novel are three illuminated codices in the Vatican Library: Vat. lat. 2193 (c. 1330–1340), Vat. lat. 2194 (1345), and Vat. lat. 2195 (1358).[17] Vat. lat. 2195 gives no hint of how its scribe or illuminator interpreted the novel: its sole illumination is a cheerful-looking ass on the first folio. The other two are more interesting.

---

[14] "neque accendunt lucernam et ponunt eam sub modio, sed super candelabrum ut luceat omnibus qui in domo sunt: sic luceat lux vestra coram hominibus, ut videant vestra bona opera et glorificent Patrem vestrum qui in caelis est." See also Mark 4:21 and Luke 11:33.

[15] "Quam ideo lucernae ebullitione dicitur incendisse, quia omnis cupiditas quantum diligitur tantum ardescit et peccatricem suae carni configit maculam": *Mit.* 3.6.118.

[16] "Ergo quasi cupiditate nudata et potenti fortuna privatur et periculis iactatur et regia domo expellitur": *Mit.* 3.6.118. The phrase I have translated as "made naked by Desire" might also mean "denuded of Desire".

[17] Twenty-two are listed by D. S. Robertson, "The Manuscripts of the *Metamorphoses* of Apuleius," *Classical Quarterly* 18 (1924): 27–42, 85–99. The twenty-third is University of Illinois MS. 7.

Vat. lat. 2193 was owned by Petrarch, who annotated it in the 1340s.[18] Four of the Apuleian works in the manuscript have illuminated initials: each depicts Apuleius in an appropriate character. At the beginning of *De deo Socratis* he is shown as a bearded philosopher, in the *Florida* as a busy writer, and in the *Apology* as a magician.[19] In the illumination for the *Golden Ass* he is shown as Lucius, the asinine hero of the novel.[20] The illumination shows Apuleius/Lucius above the bar of the initial A, his alter ego the ass below. (The arrangement perhaps indicates his dual nature as man and beast — human above the waist and animal below.) The artist is clearly interpreting the novel as autobiographical. The scribe has the same view, for in the title he awards Apuleius the *praenomen* of his hero: "Lucii Apulegii Platonici Madaurensis Methamorphoseos liber primus incipit."

Apuleius's actual *praenomen* is unknown, and no *praenomen* appears in the oldest manuscripts.[21] The awarding of the name Lucius, which became general in the Renaissance and is still frequent today, may date from this manuscript, for this is the earliest occurrence of it that I have been able to find. The scribe and illuminator perhaps remembered that Augustine had considered the *Golden Ass* autobiography (whether real or fictitious),[22] or perhaps they arrived at the idea independently, when they saw that the story is told in the first person. In any case, Petrarch himself evidently accepted this identification, for in *Ep. fam.* 1.4.4 he refers to the hero of the novel as Apuleius.

In Vat. lat. 2194 we find hints of an almost mystical interpretation of Lucius's adventures, for the artist shows him protected by divine or angelic forces.[23] At the beginning of book 2 we see Lucius waking up on his first morning in Thessaly.[24]

---

[18] See Elisabeth Pellegrin, *Les manuscrits classiques latins de la Bibliothèque Vaticane* 3.1 (Paris, 1991), 514–517, with earlier bibliography. For the annotations see Caterina Tristano, "Le postille del Petrarca nel Vaticano Lat. 2193 (Apuleio, Frontino, Vegezio, Palladio)," *Italia Medioevale e Umanistica* 17 (1974): 365–468. See also A. Petrucci, *La scrittura di Francesco Petrarca*, Studi e Testi 248 (Vatican City, 1967), 117–118 and plates IX and X. For the illuminations see Pierre de Nolhac, "Manuscrits à miniatures de la bibliothèque de Pétrarque," *Gazette archéologique* 14 (1889): 25–32; and Marco Buonocore, ed., *Vedere i classici: L'illustrazione libraria dei testi antichi dall' età romana al tardo medioevo* ([Rome], 1996), 268–274, with earlier bibliography.

[19] Philosopher: Vat. lat. 2193, fol. 1; writer: fol. 19v; magician: fol 27r. Fol. 19v is shown in de Nolhac, "Manuscrits," plate 8a.

[20] Vat. lat. 2193, fol. 43; illustrated in Buonocore, *Vedere i classici*, 269 fig. 192.

[21] In Florence, MS. Bibl. Laur. 68.2, the oldest manuscript of the *Apology*, *Metamorphoses*, and *Florida*, he is called Apuleius Platonicus Madaurensis (fols. 125v–126r). In Brussels, MS. Bibliothèque royale 10054–56, the best manuscript of *De Deo Socratis*, *Asclepius*, *De Platone*, and *De Mundo*, he is called Apuleius Platonicus Madaurensis (fol. 2r), Apuleius Platonicus philosophus Madaurensis (fol. 16v), and Apuleius Madaurensis (fol. 60v).

[22] See Augustine, *De Civitate Dei* 18.18: "... sicut Apuleius in libris, quos 'asini aurei' titulo inscripsit, sibi ipsi accidisse, ut accepto veneno humano animo permanente asinus fieret, aut indicavit aut finxit."

[23] For a description see Pellegrin, *Les manuscrits classiques latins*, 517–518, with earlier bibliography. For the illuminations see Buonocore, *Vedere i classici*, 267–268, with earlier bibliography.

[24] Vat. lat. 2194, fol. 5v; shown in Buonocore, *Vedere i classici*, 267, fig. 189.

Two birds (of ill omen?) perch in the trees, and an angelic figure reaches out from heaven — perhaps in warning. The illumination from book 9 shows the ass at a dangerous moment: his present owners, thinking he may be suffering from hydrophobia (literally "fear of water"), are about to put him to the test. If he shuns the water, they will conclude that he is rabid and put him to death.[25] We see the pail of water, a nervous keeper peering through the door, and an angelic figure complete with halo reaching down protectively to the ass. The last illumination shows a shadowy Lucius on the shore in Book 11; here he is human in form, perhaps in anticipation of his imminent redemption.[26]

We can only guess at the interpretation behind the illuminations in Vat. lat. 2194, since no explanatory text accompanies them. But we are on surer ground with two other fourteenth-century works that are independent of both the illuminations and each other: Boccaccio's allegory of Psyche and an anonymous allegory of the story of Lucius.[27] The existence of the two textual interpretations and the manuscript illuminations we have just been considering, all so different from each other, and all arising in central and northern Italy within a few decades, suggests something of the interpretative ferment that resulted when the early humanists first encountered — and tried to understand — Apuleius's novel.

Boccaccio's allegory of Psyche appears in his *Genealogy of the Pagan Gods*, a massive encyclopedia of classical mythology that he began around 1350, at about the same time that he was writing the *Decameron* and transcribing his own manuscript of Apuleius.[28] He continued to work on the *Genealogy* for many years and was still revising it in the early 1370s, just a few years before his death. The work exists in two slightly different versions, which scholars have dubbed the "autograph" and the "vulgate." Neither is fully authoritative, but in the case of Psyche it has been established that the vulgate supersedes the autograph.[29] In both versions Boccaccio makes major corrections to Fulgentius; in the vulgate he makes small but important alterations to his

---

[25] Vat. lat. 2194, fol. 48v; shown in Buonocore, *Vedere i classici*, 268, fig. 191.

[26] Vat. lat. 2194, fol. 65v; shown in Alessandro Conti, *La Miniatura Bolognese. Scuole e botteghe 1270–1340* (Bologna, 1981), fig. 293.

[27] *Psyche*: Boccaccio, *Genealogia deorum gentilium* 5.22: "De Psyce XV^a Apollinis filia." *Lucius*: Florence, Biblioteca Nazionale, MS. II.V.2, fols. 2r–15r.

[28] For the chronology see Vincenzo Romano, ed., *Boccaccio: Genealogia deorum gentilium* (Bari, 1951), 843–857; Pier Giorgio Ricci, "Contributi per un' edizione critica della 'Genealogia deorum gentilium'," *Rinascimento* 2 (1951): 195–208, here 205–207. Giuseppe Billanovich demonstrated that Boccaccio embarked on his final revisions in 1372: "Pietro Piccolo da Monteforte tra il Petrarca e il Boccaccio," in *Medioevo e Rinascimento. Studi in onore di Bruno Nardi*, 2 vols. (Florence, 1955), 1:15, 39–40.

[29] See Guido Martellotti, "Le due redazioni delle *Genealogie* del Boccaccio," repr. in idem, *Dante e Boccaccio e altri scrittori dall' umanesimo al romanticismo* (Florence, 1983), 137–163. I follow the vulgate, in which Boccaccio condensed the narration of the autograph and changed his account of Psyche and her sisters to bring it into conformity with contemporary doctrine on the soul (see notes 41 and 42 below). For further discussion of the two redactions, see Romano, ed., *Genealogia*, 789–864 (but note that he favors the autograph); Ricci, "Contributi." See also Billanovich, "Pietro Piccolo."

own earlier treatment in the autograph. To put it another way, we might say that Boccaccio's allegory constitutes a *double* link in our chain of receptions.

First Fulgentius. Since Boccaccio repeatedly cites and criticizes him elsewhere in the *Genealogy*, we may assume that he was well aware of Fulgentius's allegory, and that his own radically different treatment, which avoids all mention of Fulgentius and almost all echoes of his language and style, was intended to refute or correct it.[30] He departs from Fulgentius at the outset. On the authority of Martianus Capella, he tells us that Psyche's parents are Apollo and Endelichia (in Fulgentius, one recalls, they were God and Matter).[31] Apollo, according to Boccaccio, is the sun — "the god which is the true light of the world, since it is for no other power except god to create a rational soul."[32] He identifies Endelichia as "the fullness of time," who brings to fulfillment the rational soul that we have from "the Father of lights" (James 1:17) even in the womb.[33] Boccaccio's Psyche is not merely "soul" as in Fulgentius, but the rational faculty of the soul.[34] Her sisters are the vegetative and feeling faculties of the soul.

In Boccaccio Psyche's marriage is not with Desire as in Fulgentius. Rather, it is a divine union with God himself. He forbids her to want to see him:

that is, she must not wish to see concerning his eternity, or the first causes of things, or his omnipotence, for the good reason that these things are known to

---

[30] B. L. Hijmans, Jr. suggests that Boccaccio in his allegory "opposes" Fulgentius ("Boccaccio's *Amor and Psyche*," in B. L. Hijmans, Jr. and V. Schmidt, eds., *Symposium Apuleianum Groninganum* [Groningen, 1981], 30–45, esp. 33 and 40, n. 8). In the *Genealogia* Boccaccio invokes Fulgentius many times (see Romano's index s.n. Fulgentius) and occasionally criticises his interpretations as far-fetched (e.g., at *Genealogia* 2.52, 4.24, 4.30, 10.10, and 11.7). But he does not avoid all echoes of him: like Fulgentius, but unlike Apuleius, he has Psyche hide her lamp under a "bushel" (*modio*, the biblical word). Boccaccio says: "novaculam paravit, et lucernam abscondit sub modio": *Genealogia*, ed. Romano, 5.22 (257); cf. Fulgentius: "novaculam sub pulvinal abscondit lucernamque modio contegit" (*Mit.* 3.6.115). (The phrasing is very similar in the *First Vatican Mythographer*, which is based on Fulgentius: "novaculam sub pulvinari abscondit lucernamque modio contegit": *Mythographus primus vaticanus* 3.29.9.) In Apuleius Psyche's sisters tell her to put the lamp under "aliquo claudentis aululae tegmine" (*Met.* 5.20.2).

[31] "Psyches, ut dicit Martianus Capella in libro, quem De nuptiis Mercurii et phylologie scripsit, filia fuit Apollinis et Endilichie": *Genealogia*, ed. Romano, 5.22 (254). Cf. Mart. Cap., *Nupt.* 1.7; Fulg., *Mit.* 3.6.

[32] "... qui mundi vera lux est deus, cum nullius alterius potentie sit rationalem creare animam, nisi dei": *Genealogia*, ed. Romano, 5.22 (259).

[33] "Endelichia autem, ut dicit Calcidius super Tymeo Platonis, perfecta etas interpretatur; cuius ideo rationalis anima dicitur filia, qui et si in utero matris illam a patre luminum suscipiamus, non tamen eius apparent opera, nisi in etate perfecta": *Genealogia*, ed. Romano, 5.22 (259). Boccaccio is confusing Martianus's Endelichia ("continuous motion") with Aristotelian Entelechia (entelechy), a confusion that goes back at least to the tenth century. See Shanzer, *Commentary*, 68, and Peter Dronke, *Fabula: Explorations into the Uses of Myth in Medieval Platonism* (Leiden and Cologne, 1974), 109–110; both with earlier bibliography.

[34] See notes 41 and 42 below.

him alone. For whenever we mortals examine such matters, we destroy him, or rather we destroy ourselves, by straying from the right path.[35]

But the sisters try to persuade her to see her husband, "to see what she loves by means of natural reason, and not to know it through faith."[36] When she gives in to their urgings, she sees "a beautiful likeness of a man," that is, the external works of God, but not his true form or divinity, "since no one has ever seen God."[37] Through the harmful spark of her lamp, which Boccaccio explains as "haughty desire,"[38] she loses the good of contemplation and is thus separated from her divine marriage. At last, however, all is well. Psyche is penitent and destroys her sisters, thereby overpowering the vegetative and feeling faculties that brought her into disaster. Here is how the allegory ends:

> When she is purged through suffering of her haughty presumption and disobedience she regains the good of divine love and contemplation and is joined to it for ever, since leaving behind transitory things she is carried to everlasting glory and there gives birth to Pleasure, or eternal joy and happiness, the child of love.[39]

Fulgentius had suppressed Psyche's happy ending. Boccaccio restores it — and that makes all the difference. Boccaccio, like Apuleius, tells of Redemption, while Fulgentius presents only the Fall. Boccaccio's changes to the identity of Psyche and her family, moreover, produce a more religious and and more overtly Christian reading than that in Fulgentius. Boccaccio's revisions in the vulgate to his earlier treatment in the autograph work to the same end, refining and clarifying the Christian vision of his allegory. Since Boccaccio's "Christianizing" changes to Fulgentius and the autograph are similar in kind and effect, I will consider them together.

By changing Psyche's parents to Apollo and Endelichia from Fulgentius's God and Matter, Boccaccio achieved two results. The change allowed him to fit Psyche into

---

[35] "hoc est nolit de eternitate sua, de principiis rerum, de omnipotentia videre per causas, que soli sibi nota sunt; nam quotiens talia mortales perquirimus, illum, imo nosmet ipsos deviando perdimus": *Genealogia*, ed. Romano, 5.22 (260).

[36] "ut virum videat, id est velut naturali ratione videre quod amat, et non per fidem cognoscere": *Genealogia*, ed. Romano, 5.22 (260).

[37] "videt effigiem viri pulcherrimam, id est extrinseca Dei opera, formam, id est divinitatem, videre non potest, quia Deum nemo vidit unquam": *Genealogia*, ed. Romano, 5.22 (260).

[38] "et cum favillula ledit et vulnerat, id est superbo desiderio, per quod inobediens facta, et sensualitati credula, bonum contemplationis amittit, et sic a divino separatur coniugio": *Genealogia*, ed. Romano, 5.22 (260).

[39] "et erumnis et miseriis purgata presumptuosa superbia atque inobedientia, bonum divine dilectionis atque contemplationis iterum reassumit, eique se iniungit perpetuo, dum perituris dimissis rebus in eternam defertur gloriam, et ibi ex amore parturit Voluptatem, id est delectationem et letitiam sempiternam": *Genealogia*, ed. Romano, 5.22 (260–261).

the genealogical scheme of his work, in which she appears as the "fifteenth daughter of Apollo." More important, however, the change brought her birth into line with contemporary teaching on the soul.[40] This doctrine, which maintained that God created each soul *ex nihilo*, made it impossible for Psyche to be the daughter of Matter. Boccaccio makes similar changes in Psyche and her sisters. In the autograph they are no longer Fulgentius's Soul, Flesh, and Free Will, entities somehow separate from one another and different in kind, but rather three souls: Psyche is the rational soul, her sisters the vegetative and feeling souls.[41] In the vulgate, however, Boccaccio changes his conception. The essential singleness of the soul had become an important point in fourteenth-century theology. Boccaccio's revision conforms to the orthodox view: the three sisters, he now explains, are not three souls, but three *faculties* of the soul.[42]

In the vulgate Boccaccio also revises his *narrative*. He drastically condenses the story, but also changes and suppresses some important details.[43] In the autograph, as in Apuleius, Psyche is pregnant when she spies on the sleeping Cupid. After completing her tasks for Venus, she is escorted to Heaven by Mercury, made immortal, and officially married to Cupid.[44] Afterwards she gives birth to Voluptas. In the vulgate Boccaccio makes no mention of her pregnancy, her "official" marriage, or her being made immortal. He ends the revised narrative in these words:

> At last through [her husband's] prayers to Jupiter it was brought to pass that she came into favor with Venus, was received into heaven, and enjoyed her eternal marriage with Cupid, to whom she bore Voluptas.[45]

---

[40] As Hijmans suggested, "Boccaccio's *Amor and Psyche*," 40 n. 8.

[41] "Sunt huic due sorores maiores natu, quarum una est anima vegetativa, altera vero sensitiva, sed Psyces pulchritudine illas excedit, et hoc ideo quia vegetativa anima communicamus cum plantis, sensitiva autem cum brutis, rationali quidem cum angelis et Deo, quo nil pulchrius": *Genealogia*, ed. Romano, 5.22 (259–260).

[42] "Sunt huic due sorores maiores natu, non quia primo natae sint, sed quoniam primo potentia utuntur sua, quarum una vegetativa dicitur, altero vero sensitiva, quae non animae sunt, ut quidam voluerunt, sed huius animae sunt potentiae, quarum ideo Psyche dicitur iunior, quia longe ante eam vegetativa potentia conceditur foetui, et inde tractu temporis sensitiva. Postremo autem huic Psyche conceditur ratio": *Genealogia*, ed. Romano, 5.22 (855 n. 2). For contemporary doctrine on the soul, see Martellotti (note 29 above) 146. Both Martellotti, "Le due redazioni," 145–146, and Ricci, "Contributi," 210–211 use the fact that Boccaccio gives a similar account of the three faculties of the soul in his commentary on Dante (*Inferno* 13) to demonstrate that his account in the vulgate corrects that in the autograph.

[43] Boccaccio's condensed narrative leaves out some details important for the sense, particularly the fact that Psyche's sisters claim that her lover is a snake. See Martellotti, "Le due redazioni," 143–144.

[44] "Quam [i.e., Psycen] Mercurius Iovis iussu devexit in celum et ibidem, immortalis effecta, nuptie celebrate sunt": *Genealogia*, ed. Romano, 5.22 (259).

[45] "cuius postremo ad Iovem precibus actum est, ut in Veneris deveniret gratiam, et in caelis assumpta Cupidinis perpetuo frueretur coniugio, cui peperit Voluptatem": *Genealogia*, ed. Romano, 5.22 (855 n. 2).

The second ending is abstract and metaphysical, where the first had been concrete and matter of fact; but it is also more overtly Christian, especially in its omission of the awarding of immortality to Psyche, since in Christian doctrine the soul is immortal by definition and is naturally "received into heaven."

Boccaccio's treatment had an interesting reception in fifteenth-century Florence. There, artists under Medici patronage painted his version of Psyche's story both on marriage chests (*cassoni*) and on panels (which presumably hung on the walls of bridal chambers).[46] The use of Boccaccio on the *cassoni* was demonstrated over a hundred years ago by Richard Foerster, who noted that they follow Boccaccio in presenting Psyche's parents as Apollo and Endelichia.[47] There is more than that to be said, however, for the *cassoni* follow Boccaccio not only at the beginning of the story, but at the end as well — although with an interesting "correction," as we shall see.[48]

There are several sets of these paintings, all similar in iconography.[49] Most interesting for our purposes is the earliest, a pair of *cassone* frontals now in Berlin that were made by an anonymous master for the marriage in 1444 of Piero de' Medici and Lucrezia Tornabuoni, the parents of Lorenzo the Magnificent.[50] The painter tells Psyche's story in two parts: the first panel takes us from Psyche's conception to Cupid's flight; the second shows her wanderings and the happy ending.[51]

The first frontal is full of detail, but contains three primary scenes: the marriage chamber of Psyche's parents on the left, the marriage chamber of Cupid and Psyche on the right, and in the center the mountain from which Psyche will be carried to her bridegroom. The chamber on the left shows a woman in bed, and a golden spherical object just above her. These are the parents of Psyche in Boccaccio's

---

[46] See Vertova, "Cupid and Psyche," with earlier bibliography. The definitive study of *cassoni* is Paul Schubring, *Cassoni. Truhen und Truhenbilder der italienischen Frührenaissance*, 2 vols. (Leipzig, 1923). See also Graham Hughes, *Renaissance Cassoni* (London, 1997); Cristelle L. Baskins, *Cassone Painting, Humanism, and Gender in Early Modern Italy* (Cambridge, 1998); P. Schubring, "Zwei Cassonetafeln mit Apuleius' Märchen von Amor und Psyche," *Zeitschrift für bildende Kunst* 51 (1916): 315–320.

[47] R. Foerster, "Amor und Psyche vor Raffael," *Jahrbuch der königlichen preussischen Kunstsammlungen* 16 (1893): 221. Foerster discusses only the panel by Jacopo Sellaio now in the Fitzwilliam Museum in Cambridge.

[48] *Pace* Vertova, "Cupid and Psyche," 112: "the painted narrative draws on the Christian mythographers and on Boccaccio's *De genealogiis* (*edita vulgata*) only at the beginning of the story."

[49] For a list see Ellen Callman, "Subjects from Boccaccio in Italian Painting, 1375–1525," *Studi sul Boccaccio* 23 (1995): 57–60.

[50] The panels are discussed and illustrated by Schubring, *Cassoni*, 422–423, plates CXCIII–CXCV; Vertova, "Cupid and Psyche," plates 30, a–b, 33a. For fine color illustrations, see Hughes, *Renaissance Cassoni*, 134–135. For their association with the marriage of Piero de' Medici, see Wilhelm Bode, "Zwei Cassone-Tafeln aus dem Besitz des Piero de' Medici in der Sammlung Eduard Simon zu Berlin," *Mitteilungen des kunsthistorischen Institutes in Florenz* 2 (1971): 150–151. Vertova, "Cupid and Psyche," 112, dates the marriage to 1444.

[51] But Vertova argues that these *cassoni* also had side panels with additional scenes and believes that she has identified one showing Psyche's journey to Hades "in a small painting formerly in the Lanckoronski collection in Vienna": Vertova, "Cupid and Psyche," 110–112 and plate 31a.

allegory: her mother, Endelichia, and her father, Apollo, the sun. In the chamber on the right Psyche stands over the sleeping Cupid; then he flies out the window as she holds on to his ankle.

The second Medici frontal, which shows chapter two of Psyche's story, focuses on Psyche's encounters with the gods. On the left side she is scolded by Cupid from his cypress tree, rejected by Ceres and Juno, and scourged by a minion of Venus. On the right, the action is shown in two registers corresponding to heaven and earth. In the upper right a kneeling Cupid pleads with Jupiter for Psyche's hand. The marriage takes place below, but still in heaven, as the clouds underfoot are meant to indicate.[52] (I will return to this point presently.) Jupiter performs the ceremony, which looks for all the world like a nice Christian wedding — except for the wings and nudity of the bridegroom.

The story of Psyche is obviously an appropriate subject for wedding chests and panels in marriage chambers — and certainly much more cheerful than many from the standpoint of the bride. (The Sabine women, Lucretia, and Dido, for example, appear on *cassoni* with depressing regularity.)[53] But the painter of the Medici *cassoni* and his patron had something more in mind than just a love story with a happy ending. As we have seen, their adherence to Boccaccio (and for that matter Martianus Capella) is shown in the depiction of Psyche's parents as Endelichia and Apollo, the sun — "the god which is the true light of the world," as Boccaccio says. But their adherence to Boccaccio is also shown by omission, for the panel picturing Psyche's happy ending does not show her either being escorted to heaven or drinking the cup of immortality, as in Apuleius. And for good reason: in Boccaccio's Christian allegory, Psyche, the soul, does not need to be made immortal. She already is.

But the artist also *corrects* or revises Boccaccio. Boccaccio omits the "official" marriage of Cupid and Psyche; the artist includes it — and for an obvious reason: he is painting the story on a wedding chest. Boccaccio, as we have seen, treats the marriage of Psyche as the union of the soul with God. The *cassone* presents this allegory as a model or symbol for human marriage — specifically, in this case, for the marriage of Piero de' Medici and Lucrezia Tornabuoni. To put it another way, the marriage of Piero and Lucrezia is an earthly or a mortal reflection of the everlasting oneness of the soul with God. The fusion or conflation of the divine and human unions is reflected in the placement of Psyche's wedding on the *cassone*: the members of the wedding party are standing on the ground, but with clouds under their feet, so that the wedding seems to take place in heaven and earth at the same time.

After the Florentine *cassoni* Boccaccio's allegory seems to have no further descendants. Instead, interest returns to Fulgentius, whose interpretation remains the dominant strand in the chain of allegories. Fulgentius's allegory was cited as authoritative in the *editio princeps*, and, as we shall see presently, was discussed in Beroaldo's

---

[52] Vertova, "Cupid and Psyche," 112, suggests that the wedding is placed on earth because the painter lacked room for it in the upper register.

[53] For a sophisticated discussion of Dido and Lucretia (and other female subjects on *cassoni*), see Baskins, *Cassone Painting*.

commentary on the *Golden Ass*. It was taught in schools.[54] It even made its way into later vernacular poetry. In the middle of the seventeenth century, for example, Shakerly Marmion prefaced his English version, "A Morall Poem Intituled the Legend of Cupid and Psyche," with Fulgentius — adding details, and making an interesting change.[55] Fulgentius assimilated Psyche to Adam. Marmion likens her to *Eve*: "Like Eve," he tells us, "being made naked through desire, she is cast out of all happinesse, exhil'd from her house, and tost with many dangers."[56]

But we are getting too far afield. We still have not thought about that fourteenth-century allegory of Lucius that I mentioned above. Like the mysterious illuminations in Vat. lat. 2194, the allegory is tantalizing evidence of very early discussions and interpretations of Apuleius's novel that are otherwise unknown to us. The allegory appears in the margin of a fourteenth-century manuscript of the Third Vatican Mythographer now in Florence.[57] It is written in a fourteenth-century hand, and although it could have been composed much earlier, I am inclined to place it in the fourteenth century for two reasons: first, because that is when Apuleius bursts on the scene in central and northern Italy; and second, because the author knows Apuleius's philosophical treatise *De deo Socratis*, which seems to have been joined with the literary works first in the fourteenth century. Both manuscript and allegory, however, require much more attention than we can give them in the present discussion.

For now I want to make only two observations. First, the author reads Apuleius's *Apology* and *Metamorphoses* together, as virtually a single work, and takes the novel as Apuleius's personal testimony of the dangers of magic, written in order to deter others from his mistakes. This means, of course, that he sees the novel as autobiographical and equates its hero with Apuleius himself. Second, like many allegorical readers, he is able to entertain several meanings at the same time. He tells us first that Lucius is transformed into an ass because he tried to learn about magic and that he at last regained his freedom by the grace of heaven.[58] A few lines later he says that Lucius's asinine imprisonment symbolises the misery of human existence, from the vileness of conception to the frightening and lamentable finality of death.[59] On the next page he asserts that it signifies the enslavement of the inner man to anxious passions

---

[54] On the title page of a German school edition published in Erfurt around 1515 Psyche's sisters are identified as *Caro* and *Libertas*, more or less the names awarded them by Fulgentius. See Raymond Klibansky and Frank Regen, *Die Handschriften der philosophischen Werken des Apuleius: Ein Beitrag zur Überlieferungsgeschichte*. Abhandlungen der Akademie der Wissenschaften in Göttingen, Philologisch-historische Klasse 3.204 (Göttingen, 1993), Tafel VIII.

[55] Shakerly Marmion, *Cupid and Psyche, or an Epick Poem of Cupid, and his Mistress* (London, 1637).

[56] Marmion, *Cupid and Psyche*, ed. Alice Jones Nearing (Philadelphia, 1944), 105.

[57] Florence, Biblioteca Nazionale ms. II. VI. 2, fols. 2r–16r. The work was first noticed by Eugenio Garin, "Noterelle sulla filosofia del rinascimento," *Rinascimento* 2 (1951): 319–336, here 320. It was edited by Gian Carlo Garfagnini, "Un accessus ad Apuleio e un nuovo codice del Terzo Mitografo vaticano," *Studi Medioevali* 17 (1976): 306–362.

[58] Garfagnini, "Un accessus ad Apuleio," lines 25–30.

[59] Garfagnini, "Un accessus ad Apuleio," lines 42–51.

of the mind, or "bestial anxieties," and that the man regains his human shape when he has recovered his lost grace.[60] His favorite idea, however, seems to be that Lucius's transformation is caused by lust, symbolized by the kiss of his mistress, Photis: "The kiss of Photis is the idle delight of this world, which gives human souls into the hands of demons and twists them into the appearance of beasts."[61] In all these interpretations, however, Lucius's sufferings as an ass are a necessary penance: it is hardly going too far to call them a kind of purgatory. The author says: "condemned for his mistakes, he cannot eat the fresh roses [which will return him to his human shape] until he endures much trouble and distress."[62] After he has completed his "time of correction," he receives the rose remedy, which the author defines as "the sedation of lascivious passion and the restoration of his human nature so that he may no longer live like an animal, but preserve himself in religion and chastity."[63]

This fourteenth-century allegory seems unrelated to other interpretations — a loose strand, so to speak, in the chain of receptions. Isolated though it appears, however, it does have some similarities with the readings of Beroaldo and his successors, as we shall see presently. Perhaps these are merely accidental: it would not be surprising if different readers looking at Lucius's transformation from a Christian perspective arrived at similar ideas independently. But perhaps — and I confess that I find this thought more attractive — we can imagine an *underground* chain of reception: fourteenth- and fifteenth-century discussions and conversations on the novel now lost to us, some of whose ideas became part of the written record only in a later period.

Three principal fifteenth-century discussions of Apuleius have come down to us. First, Poggio's brief preface to his 1450 translation of Lucian's (or I should say, pseudo-Lucian's) *Onos* (*The Ass*), in which he concludes both that Apuleius did not invent the story of *The Metamorphoses* and that it was fiction, not autobiography. Second, Giovanni Andrea Bussi's preface to the first edition of Apuleius, which was printed in 1469.[64] The overworked and impoverished Bussi had been persecuted all his life by Duke Francesco Sforza, who maliciously blocked all his ecclesiastical appointments and income. Not surprisingly, he seems to have interpreted Lucius's story in the light of of his own experience, not seeing the adventures in religious or even moral terms, but rather as examples of the depravity of human nature. "In this whole

---

[60] Garfagnini, "Un accessus ad Apuleio," lines 79–85.

[61] "Osculum istud Photis est otiosa deliciositas huius mundi, que in manus demonum et in facies brutorum animas pervertit humanas": Garfagnini, "Un accessus ad Apuleio," lines 243–245. Her kiss is also the kiss of Judas (lines 241–243).

[62] "[Est igitur in predam latronum ductus, honeribus sarcinatus et multis anxietatibus et erumnis oppressus,] nec potest rosas recentes comedere donec plures patiatur damnatus errorum": Garfagnini, "Un accessus ad Apuleio," lines 246–248.

[63] "correctionis spatium": Garfagnini, "Un accessus ad Apuleio," line 264. "impetravit habere rosarum medelas, scilicet sedationem ardoris lascivi et reformationem nature humane ne amplius bestialiter vivat sed religiose casteque se servet": lines 267–269.

[64] See M. Miglio, "Giovanni Andrea Bussi," *Dizionario Biografico degli Italiani* 15 (1972): 565–572.

story," Bussi says, "the attentive reader will clearly see human nature depicted and revealed, and he will learn the unexpected cunning of deceit, by which even cautious men are often taken in."[65] He goes on to say that Lucius regained his human form after surviving and surmounting many labors, which has a nice moral ring to it, and "after passing through the manifold tricks and trials of treacherous men," which seems much less edifying.[66] For Bussi, Lucius's happy ending is a matter not of redemption, but of simple survival, of living through the worst that human beings can plot either against each other or against unfortunate asses. His interpretation had no Renaissance antecedents or descendants that I know of, but it has plenty of relatives in our own time.

The third fifteenth-century discussion is the final major link in our chain of allegories: the massive and influential commentary of Filippo Beroaldo, which was printed in Bologna in 1500.[67] Beroaldo was an important scholar and critic, to be sure, but above all he was a teacher, one of the most famous and influential in Italy. His commentary, written to be promoted and sold to his students, brings us into his classroom to hear his voice and instruction.

At once we find ourselves in a different world from that of previous interpreters. Fulgentius, Boccaccio, and the anonymous fourteenth-century allegorist all seem to be writing in a historical vacuum, quite unconcerned with the realities of Apuleius's time, and saying very little about their own. Beroaldo, however, is historical in both senses. He is passionately interested in the details of Apuleius's world, and even more interested in those of late fifteenth-century Bologna. His commentary is full of information on both, and he constantly uses the one to elucidate the other, linking the world of everyday experience in the *Golden Ass* to the life and customs of his own time. Laundry methods, time-keeping, medical problems, dowries, baldness — all draw his attention and provide the occasion for lively comparisons.[68] These digressions undoubtedly brought the novel to life for Beroaldo's students, but they create

---

[65] "Quo in toto sermone, si quis recte intendat, mores humanos effictos liquido perspiciet explicari et impraemeditatas fallaciarum argutias discet, quibus etiam cauti saepissime capiantur": Giovanni Andrea de'Bussi, *Prefazioni alle edizioni di Sweynheym e Pannartz prototipografi romani*, ed. Massimo Miglio (Rome, 1978), 13.

[66] "Tandem exanclatis multis aerumnosisque laboribus, ut ipse ait, id est cum summa animi anxietate et corporis molestia superatis ac victis, transcursisque multiplicibus vitae huius fallacium hominum machinamentis atque excitiis": Bussi, *Prefazioni*, ed. Miglio, 14.

[67] For Beroaldo see M. Gilmore, "Filippo Beroaldo, senior," *Dizionario Biografico degli Italiani* 9 (1967): 382–384; Ezio Raimondi, *Codro e l'umanesimo a Bologna* (Bologna, 1950), 90–107; Eugenio Garin, "Note sull'insegnamento di Filippo Beroaldo il vecchio," *Studi e memorie per la Storia dell'Università di Bologna* n.s. 1 (1956): 357–376; idem, "Note in margine all'opera di Filippo Beroaldo il vecchio," in *Tra latino e volgare. Per Carlo Dionisotti*, ed. G. B. Trezzini et al., 2 vols. (Padua, 1974), 2:437–456. For Beroaldo as a commentator, see Maria Teresa Casella, "Il metodo dei commentatori umanistici esemplato sul Beroaldo," *Studi medievali* 16 (1975): 627–701. For his Apuleius commentary the fundamental work is Konrad Krautter, *Philologische Methode und humanistische Existenz. Filippo Beroaldo und sein Kommentar zum Goldenen Esel des Apuleius* (Munich, 1971).

[68] See Krautter, *Philologische Methode*, passim. Casella, "Il metodo," 685–701 lists Beroaldo's digressions.

an even more interesting effect for the modern reader, who is given a glimpse into Apuleius's world and Beroaldo's at the same time.

Beroaldo's down-to-earth contemporary vision is evident in his interpretations of Cupid and Psyche and the transformations of Lucius. At the beginning of the story of Psyche he quotes Fulgentius and explains the fourfold system of allegory, using the familiar medieval example of Jerusalem: on the historical level Jerusalem is the city of Judaea, on the allegorical or tropological level the church, on the moral level the soul, on the spiritual level "the heavenly city to which the prayers of all aspire and desire to be made its inhabitants."[69] For Beroaldo himself, however, the historical level is quite sufficient. He says: "But I will not pursue allegories in the explanation of this story so much as the historical sense, and I will explain the meaning of words and obscure matters, lest I appear a bad philosopher instead of a commentator."[70]

True to his word, Beroaldo does explain the tale on "the historical level" of language and plot. But he does much more, for he punctuates his account with two long digressions relating the story to his own life in present-day Bologna. In each case he gets into the digression in the same way — by using a significant word from Apuleius as the jumping-off point for a little riff or arpeggio on his own world. The words he plays on are "soul" (or "Psyche") and "pleasure" (the child of Cupid and Psyche). Here we have time to consider only the second digression, which appears in Book 6, at the end of the story. Here Beroaldo adds to "soul" and "pleasure" a major new theme: marriage. Apuleius's story of Cupid and Psyche ends with these words: "So Psyche was duly married to Cupid, and in the fullness of time a daughter was born to them, whom we call Pleasure."[71] Beroaldo notes:

> Both wisely and cleverly they say that Pleasure was born of the marriage of Cupid and Psyche, since pleasure — by which the most notable philosophers measure the highest good — comes into being from the desire and love of the soul.[72]

He continues:

---

[69] "et ut res exemplo magis colliquescat, Hierusalem historice significat civitatem Iudaeae metropolim. allegorice. ecclesiam, moraliter animam. spiritaliter celestem civitatem, ad quam cunctorum vota suspirant, et illius coloni effici concupiscunt": Filippo Beroaldo, *Commentarii . . . conditi in Asinum Aureum Lucii Apuleii* (Bologna, 1500), fol. 95v.

[70] "Sed nos non tam allegorias in explicatione huiusce fabulae sectabimur, quam historicum sensum, et rerum reconditarum verborumque interpretationem explicabimus, ne philosophaster magis videar quam commentator": Beroaldo, *Commentarii*, fol. 95v.

[71] "Sic rite Psyche convenit in manum Cupidinis et nascitur illis maturo partu filia, quam Voluptatem nominamus": Apuleius, *Met.* 6.24.4.

[72] "Conducenter et scite voluptatem ex connubio cupidinis et psyches natam esse finxerunt, cum ex cupiditate animae et dilectione voluptas progignatur, qua summum bonum clarissimi philosophorum metiuntur": Beroaldo, *Commentarii*, fol. 134.

> While I was writing these things and commenting on this marriage of Psyche and Cupid, it so happened ... that I took a wife — it was fated by the stars, I believe. ... May the gods make this marriage fertile and happy and fortunate for us, so that from it pleasure may be born. ... May the offspring born of us be pleasure-bringing, like that born of Psyche and Cupid.[73]

A page later he proudly announces that his young wife is pregnant and concludes his digression: "I hope and predict that in this memorable jubilee year [1500] a son will be born, to be the pleasure and ornament of his parents."[74]

In this digression Beroaldo's marriage both re-enacts the union of Cupid and Psyche and explains it — rather movingly, I think — in terms of real human feelings and experiences. We could say that he gives meaning to Apuleius's fairy tale. But he does not interpret it. There are no allegories, no other-worldly or metaphysical explanations, no attempts to tell us what it is really about. There *is* something familiar about his discussion, though. Like the *cassoni* paintings made for the marriage of Piero de' Medici and Lucrezia Tornabuoni fifty years earlier, it links a contemporary human marriage to the mythological union of Cupid and Psyche. The important difference is that Beroaldo makes a direct connection, not using an allegorical interface to bring together his own experience and the world of myth.

Beroaldo does not reject allegory altogether, however — just metaphysics.[75] He quite willingly uses allegory to interpret the transformations of Lucius, which he sees in down-to-earth moral and ethical terms applicable to ordinary human life, and especially — one suspects — to the life of his young students. Like the fourteenth-century allegorist, he lists several interpretations without reconciling them. In each, however, Lucius's experience is an allegory of the human condition. Beroaldo begins with his most fully developed idea, and the one that ultimately emerges as dominant.

> We turn into asses when we have sunk into bestial pleasures and are so brutish in our asinine stupidity that we lack any spark of reason and virtue. ... The reformation from an ass to a man signifies that reason is coming back to its senses, having trampled pleasures underfoot and thrown off bodily delights, and that the inner man, who is the real man, has come back from that dung-filled prison to a shining habitation with the guidance of virtue and religion.[76]

---

[73] "Condentibus haec nobis et has psyches ac cupidinis nuptias commentantibus siderali opinor decreto factum est, ut ego ... uxorem duceremV. ... Dii faxint, ut hoc connubium sit nobis foelix faustum ac fortunatum, utque ex eo voluptas gignatur": Beroaldo, *Commentarii*, fol. 134r–v.

[74] "spero et ominor filium anno hoc Iubilei memorando nasciturum, qui parentibus sit voluptati futurus et ornamento": Beroaldo, *Commentarii*, fol. 135r.

[75] On this point, see Krautter, *Philologische Methode*, 29–30, 149–151.

[76] "[Verum sub hoc transmutationis involucro, naturam mortalium et mores humanos quasi transeunter designare voluisse], ut admoneremur ex hominibus Asinos fieri, quando voluptatibus belluinis immersi Asinali stoliditate brutescimus, nec ulla rationis virtutisque scintilla in nobis elucescit. ... Rursus ex Asino in hominem reformatio significat calcatis voluptatibus, exutisque corporalibus deliciis rationem resipiscere, et hominem interiorem, qui verus est homo ex ergastulo illo

Young men, he continues — no doubt for the benefit of his students — are particularly prone to sink into pleasures and turn into asses, but as they mature they tend to resume their humanity.[77] The rose cure is wisdom.[78] Having taken it, one can throw off the bestiality that deforms the inner man and serve God free of sin, just like Lucius.[79]

In the next breath he moves on to another idea: that in life many men are wolves or pigs or other beasts, since the world is Circe's way-station and her transforming drugs are forgetfulness, error, and ignorance; the rose cure is knowledge, which restores human shape, that is, rational intelligence. But it can also be, he says, that the metamorphosis is caused by the manifold toils and changes of human life, by which man is transformed almost every day, or, more probably, that Apuleius as a good Platonist and Pythagorean is using the story to set out the doctrine of metempsychosis and transmigration of souls.

As I suggested a moment ago, Beroaldo's ideas have some similarities with those of the fourteenth-century allegorist. The most obvious are that both relate the transformation to the vicissitudes of human life, imagine an "inner man" trapped in an alien body, and think of Lucius's asinine shape as a prison. But Beroaldo is unlike his predecessor in remaining almost entirely on the moral, human level (the only exception is his brief reference to metempsychosis, which makes no further appearance in his discussion). For Beroaldo, Lucius's transformation is not a necessary purgatory from which he can be rescued only by divine grace, but a consequence of foolish human conduct that can be remedied by human effort, that is, by the acquisition of wisdom.

The success of Beroaldo's commentary was instant and long-lasting. The initial print run was twelve hundred copies, and it was reprinted ten times in the sixteenth century.[80] In the sixteenth century Apuleius traveled all over Europe, principally by way of Beroaldo, whose commentary was so ubiquitous and so influential that it overshadowed the work of all his predecessors. Boccaccio's treatment of Psyche was available in the many printed editions of the *Genealogy of the Pagan Gods*, but Beroaldo had ignored it, and later readers did as well. The interpretation of the fourteenth–century allegorist was long forgotten. Only Fulgentius remained — largely, I believe, because his allegory had been incorporated in Beroaldo's commentary, which had become the easiest and most convenient place to find it. We might say that he had been co–opted or subsumed by Beroaldo.

---

cenoso, ad lucidum habitaculum, virtute et religione ducibus remigrasse": Beroaldo, *Commentarii*, fol. 2v.

[77] Beroaldo, *Commentarii*, fol. 2v.

[78] "ut mystice intelligas coronam rosaceam esse sapientiam": Beroaldo, *Commentarii*, fol. 266r.

[79] "Qua vita [i.e., serving God with a pure heart] nihil beatius esse potest, ad quam utinam nos quoque pervenire possimus sicut Apuleius noster, post exudatos labores multiiugos post exutas terrenas sordes aliquando felicissime pervenit": Beroaldo, *Commentarii*, fol. 266r.

[80] See the bibliography in Krautter, *Philologische Methode*, 193–194. The last edition mentioned by Krautter was printed in 1823.

So Beroaldo held the field, not only for his text and commentary, but also for the interpretation of the novel. Readers looked to him for the allegory of Psyche as well as for that of Lucius, often conveniently forgetting that although he had quoted Fulgentius's interpretation, he had not promoted or subscribed to it. The first French, Spanish, German, and English translators all either cited or plagiarized his ideas.[81] Interpreters used and regarded Beroaldo as their source, even when they altered or misunderstood his views — reading Apuleius through him, and both writers through the lenses of their own time and place. In short, Beroaldo had become the starting point for a new chain of receptions, but that is a subject for another time.

Bryn Mawr College

---

[81] French: Guillaume Michel, *Lucius Apuleius de Lasne dore* (Paris, 1518); Spanish: Diego López de Cortegana, *Lucio Apuleyo del Asno de oro* [Seville, c. 1525]; German: Johann Sieder, *Ain schön lieblich auch kurtzweylig gedichte Lucii Apuleii von ainem gulden Esel* (Augsburg, 1538); English: William Adlington, *The xi Bookes of the Golden Asse* (London, 1566).

Die neuen Leiden des jungen Aristaeus: Mythologische Kreativität in neulateinischer Lehrdichtung[1]

HEINZ HOFMANN

Während das lateinische Lehrgedicht im Mittelalter durch die 1997 erschienene Darstellung von Thomas Haye eine erste umfassende Behandlung erfuhr,[2] hat das neulateinische Lehrgedicht bisher noch nicht die Aufmerksamkeit in der Forschung auf sich gezogen, die es eigentlich verdiente. Sicher, wir haben an neueren Studien die 1975 erschienene Monographie von Georg Roellenbleck über *Das epische Lehrgedicht Italiens im fünfzehnten und sechzehnten Jahrhundert*[3] und mehrere wichtige Aufsätze, die in den letzten 25 Jahren veröffentlicht wurden, darunter W. Ludwigs Beitrag über "Neulateinische Lehrgedichte und Vergils *Georgica*" von 1982[4] und die 1988 in den *Acta Conventus Neo-Latini Guelpherbytani* erschienenen Vorträge von Bernd Effe, Fokke Akkerman, Georg Roellenbleck und Mario Di Cesare, die im Rahmen eines Seminars 1985 in Wolfenbüttel gehalten wurden.[5] Dazu kommen

---

[1] Der vorliegende Beitrag gibt den Text meines Plenarvortrags in Cambridge vom 4. August 2000 wieder, lediglich um einige Nachweise in den Anmerkungen ergänzt. Eine ausführlichere Fassung dieser Untersuchung wird in der Zeitschrift *Humanistica Lovaniensia* 52 (2003) erscheinen.

[2] T. Haye, *Das lateinische Lehrgedicht im Mittelalter. Analyse einer Gattung*, Mittellateinische Studien und Texte 22 (Leiden, 1997).

[3] G. Roellenbleck, *Das epische Lehrgedicht Italiens im fünfzehnten und sechzehnten Jahrhundert. Ein Beitrag zur Literaturgeschichte des Humanismus und der Renaissance*, Münchner Romanistische Arbeiten 43 (München, 1975).

[4] W. Ludwig, "Neulateinische Lehrgedichte und Vergils *Georgica*," in *From Wolfram and Petrarch to Goethe and Grass. Studies in Literature in Honour of Leonard Forster*, ed. D. H. Green, L. P. Johnson, and D. Wuttke (Baden-Baden, 1982), 151–180; Ndr. in W. Ludwig, *Litterae Neolatinae. Schriften zur neulateinischen Literatur*, ed. L. Braun, W.-W. Ehlers, P. G. Schmidt und B. Seidensticker, Humanistische Bibliothek 35 (München, 1989), 100–127 (im folgenden hiernach zitiert).

[5] H. Hofmann, "Seminar: Das neulateinische Lehrgedicht," mit Beiträgen von B. Effe, F. Akkerman, G. Roellenbleck und M. Di Cesare, in *Acta Conventus Neo-Latini Guelpherbytani*. Pro-

einige neuere Aufsätze von Yasmin Haskell[6] sowie der von ihr und Philip Hardie 1999 herausgegebene Band *Poets and Teachers*.[7]

Daneben sind auch neuere Ausgaben und Kommentare zu verzeichnen: Mario Di Cesares Edition sämtlicher Fassungen von Vidas *Scacchia Ludus* (1975)[8] und die seiner Poetik von Ralph G. Williams (1976) und R. Girardi (1982),[9] die von Pontanos *Meteorum liber* von Mauro de Nichilo (1975),[10] die kommentierten Ausgaben von Fracastoros *Syphilis* von Geoffrey Eatough (1984)[11] und Aonius Palearius' *De animorum immortalitate* von Dirk Sacré (1986),[12] dazu seine kritische Edition mit englischer Einleitung von 1992,[13] die zweisprachigen Ausgaben der *Rhetoricorum libri IV* von Benedictus Arias Montanus durch M. V. Pérez Custodio (1994),[14] des *Zodiacus Vitae* von Palingenius Stellatus durch Jacques Chomarat (1996)[15] und von Bernardo Zamagnas *Navis Aëria* von Diane Bitzel (1997)[16] sowie die 1999 erschienene erste

---

ceedings of the Sixth International Congress of Neo-Latin Studies, Wolfenbüttel, 12 to 16 August 1985, ed. S. P. Revard, F. Rädle, and M. A. Di Cesare, Medieval & Renaissance Texts & Studies 53 (Binghamton, NY: MRTS, 1988), 401–436.

[6] Y. Haskell, "Round and Round We Go: The Alchemical *Opus Circulatorium* of Giovanni Aurelio Augurello," *Bibliothèque d'Humanisme et Renaissance* 59 (1997): 583–606; eadem, "Renaissance Latin Didactic Poetry on the Stars: Wonder, Myth, and Science," *Renaissance Studies* 12 (1998): 495–522; eadem, "Work or Play? Latin 'Recreational' Georgic Poetry of the Italian Renaissance," *Humanistica Lovaniensia* 48 (1999): 132–159.

[7] Y. Haskell and P. Hardie, eds., *Poets and Teachers: Latin Didactic Poetry and the Didactic Authority of the Latin Poet from the Renaissance to the Present. Proceedings of the Fifth Annual Symposium of the Cambridge Society for Neo-Latin Studies, Clare College, Cambridge, 9–11 September 1996*, Kleos 4 (Bari, 1999).

[8] M. A. Di Cesare, ed., *The Game of Chess: Marco Girolamo Vida's "Scacchia Ludus". With English Verse Translation and the Text of the Three Earlier Versions* (Nieuwkoop, 1975).

[9] R. G. Williams, ed., *The "De arte poetica" of Marco Girolamo Vida, Translated with Commentary and with the Text of c. 1517* (New York, 1976); R. Girardi, ed., *Marco Girolamo Vida, "L'arte poetica". Introduzione, testo, traduzione e note*, Biblioteca di critica e letteratura 20 (Bari, 1982).

[10] M. de Nichilo, ed., *I poemi astrologici di Giovanni Pontano. Storia del testo. Con un saggio di edizione critica del "Meteorum liber"*, Contributi alla storia della cultura umanistica 1 (Bari, 1975).

[11] G. Eatough, ed., *Fracastoro's "Syphilis". Introduction, Text, Translation and Notes*, ARCA 12 (Liverpool, 1984).

[12] D. Sacré, "*Aonii Palearii Verulani 'De animorum immortalitate libri III'*. Kritische editie met een Nederlandse vertaling en toelichtingen, voorafgegaan door een biobibliografie van de auteur," 2 vols. (Ph.D. diss., Katholieke Universiteit Leuven, 1986).

[13] D. Sacré, ed., *Aonii Palearii Verulani "De animorum immortalitate libri III". Introduction and Text*, Verhandelingen van de Koninklijke Academie voor Wetenschappen, Letteren en Schone Kunsten van België, Klasse der Letteren, Jaargang 54, Nr. 144 (Brussel, 1992).

[14] M. V. Pérez Custodio, ed., *Los "Rhetoricorum libri quattuor" de Benito Arias Montano. Introducción, edición crítica, traducción y notas* (Badajoz, 1994).

[15] J. Chomarat, *Palingène (Pier Angelo Manzolli, dit Marzello Palingenio Stellato), Le Zodiaque de la vie ("Zodiacus Vitae"). XII livres. Texte latin établi, traduit et annoté*, Travaux d'Humanisme et Renaissance 307 (Genève, 1996).

[16] D. Bitzel, *Bernardo Zamagna "Navis Aëria". Eine Metamorphose des Lehrgedichts im Zeichen des technischen Fortschritts*, Studien zur Klassischen Philologie 109 (Frankfurt, 1997).

kritische Ausgabe der beiden Lehrgedichte von Lorenzo Bonincontri (*De rebus naturalibus et divinis*) durch Stephan Heilen.[17]

Dennoch bedarf es dringend weiterer Editionen, Kommentare und Studien, um gerade diese Gattung noch mehr zu erschließen, ihre politischen und gesellschaftlichen Funktionen besser verstehen und ihren Platz im literarischen Diskurs ihrer jeweiligen Zeit präziser beschreiben zu können. Ein wichtiges Kriterium zur Bestimmung ihres innovativen Charakters ist dabei von jeder ihr Verhältnis zu den antiken Vorbildern, die sie teils rezipierend weitergeführt, teils transzendiert und sowohl formal als auch thematisch hinter sich gelassen hat. So haben die neulateinischen Lehrdichter sich mit Vorliebe jenen Themen zugewandt, die von den Alten noch nicht oder nicht hinreichend behandelt worden waren, oder solchen, die erst durch die wissenschaftlichen, technischen und gesellschaftlichen Entwicklungen der Neuzeit möglich wurden: der Medizin und Pharmakologie etwa, insbesondere der Diätetik, also Fragen der Ernährung, Gesundheit und allgemeinen Lebensführung, des Badewesens, der Anatomie und einzelnen Krankheiten, ferner der Vogelbeize, der Seidenraupenzucht und der neuzeitlichen Genußpflanzen, der Teichwirtschaft, aber auch der Entdeckungen und der Neuen Welt, der Mineralogie und Alchemie, der Zoologie und Elektrizität, der Musik und der Bildenden Künste, der Handwerke und technischen Erfindungen, der Politik und Pädagogik, des Schachspiels und des Baus von Luftschiffen.

Neben Fragen von Inhalt, Aufbau und Struktur hat Walter Ludwig in seinem vorhin genannten Aufsatz auch einen kurzen Überblick über die Mythen in jenen Lehrgedichten gegeben, ohne diese Thematik, die ja nicht sein Hauptanliegen war, erschöpfend zu behandeln. Eine erschöpfende Behandlung ist auch nicht mein Ziel, kann es hier und heute auch gar nicht sein; dennoch möchte ich im folgenden versuchen, die verschiedenen Formen der Einbindung von Mythen in neulateinischer Lehrdichtung voneinander abzugrenzen und Ihnen einen kleinen Eindruck von der mythenbildenden Kreativität neulateinischer Lehrdichter zu vermitteln. Beginnen wir aber, wie es sich gehört, in der Antike und mit Vergil!

Vergil hat am Ende seiner *Georgica* zum erstenmal im Lehrgedicht eine umfangreiche mythologische Erzählung hinzugefügt und folgte damit dem Vorbild Lukrezens, der sein Lehrgedicht ebenfalls mit einem Epyllion beschlossen hat: freilich nicht einer mythologischen, sondern einer historischen Erzählung vom Wüten der Pest in Athen, die als Exempel deutende Funktion für das Phänomen der Krankheit im Kontext der falschen Haltung gegenüber dem Tod hat und als Epyllion alexandrinische Traditionen aufnimmt, sie aber gleichzeitig kennzeichnend umformt. Vergil behandelt die Bienenzucht, und auch er spricht dabei über Krankheiten der Bienen und Maßnahmen, die der Imker dagegen ergreifen soll. Für den Fall, daß ein ganzes Bienenvolk zugrundegeht, empfiehlt er das von einem Meister aus Arkadien (*Arcadii ... magistri, Georg.* 4.283) erfundene Verfahren der Gewinnung neuer Bienen aus den

---

[17] S. Heilen, ed., *Laurentius Bonincontrius Miniatensis, "De rebus naturalibus et divinis". Zwei Lehrgedichte an Lorenzo de' Medici und Ferdinand von Aragon. Einleitung und kritische Edition*, Beiträge zur Altertumskunde 129 (Stuttgart und Leipzig, 1999).

faulenden Kadavern von Stieren (*Georg.* 4.281 ff.), das unter dem Begriff der Bugonie seit hellenistischer Zeit von Dichtern mehrfach erwähnt wird,[18] wenn freilich die Imker es in der Praxis niemals ernstlich als Mittel zur Wiedergewinnung neuer Bienen erprobt haben dürften.

Die nun folgende mythologische Erzählung (4.317 ff.) berichtet in kunstvoll verschlungener Weise, wie Aristaeus seine Bienen verlor und seiner Mutter, der Nymphe Cyrene, den Verlust klagte. Sie rät ihm, sich zum Seher Proteus zu begeben, der ihm weiteren Aufschluß über den Grund des Bienensterbens geben könne. Proteus verkündet ihm, er habe durch große Schuld göttlichen Zorn auf sich geladen: Orpheus habe ihn so gestraft und zürne ihm wegen des Verlusts seiner Gattin. Dann erzählt er ihm ausführlich die Geschichte von Orpheus und Eurydike (4.457–527), entzieht sich danach jedoch durch einen Sprung ins Meer weiteren Erklärungen. Damit hinterließ er nicht nur Aristaeus, sondern ganze Generationen von Philologen ratlos, was diese Erzählung von Orpheus und Eurydike nun im Zusammenhang mit dem Tod der Bienen bedeuten solle. Doch Cyrene, die alles mitgehört hatte, weiß die Lösung (jedenfalls für Aristaeus): Er trage durch sein Werben um Eurydike Schuld an ihrem Tod; denn als sie sich seinen Zudringlichkeiten entziehen wollte, sei sie auf der Flucht auf eine Giftschlange getreten und an ihrem Biß gestorben. Daher hätten Orpheus und die Nymphen zur Strafe seine Bienen getötet; nun müsse er sie durch ein Opfer versöhnen, für das sie ihm genaue Vorschriften gibt. Aristaeus befolgt alles, und als er nach neun Tagen zurückkommt, entdeckt er, daß sich in den verwesenden Eingeweiden der getöteten Stiere ein neues Bienenvolk gebildet hat, das ausschwärmt und in einer dicken Traube vom Baum hängt.

Dieser kunstvolle aitiologische Mythos am Ende eines Lehrgedichts, auf dessen viele Probleme ich hier nicht eingehen kann, wurde bereits in der Antike mißtrauisch beäugt und als Ergebnis einer späteren erzwungenen Umarbeitung der ominösen *Laudes Galli* gedeutet, mit denen Vergil angeblich zunächst die *Georgica* beschlossen haben soll.[19] Für die Geschichte der Gattung blieb er folgenlos; denn das lateinische Lehrgedicht kam nach Vergil die ganze Spätantike und das Mittelalter hindurch ohne mythologische Erzählungen in diesem großen Stile aus: Das Aristaeus-Epyllion hatte kein Nachleben. Dies änderte sich auch nicht, als Mitte des 15. Jahrhunderts italienische Humanisten mit der Gattung des Lehrgedichts experimentierten und ver-

---

[18] Philitas *fr.* 22 Powell und Kallimachos *fr.* 383.4 Pfeiffer nennen die Biene βουγενής, Theokrit (*Syrinx* 3) nennt sie ταυροπάτωρ, die ägyptischen Dichter Archelaos (bei Varro *R.R.* 3.16.4; vgl. 2.5.5;) und Nikander (*Ther.* 741, *Alex.* 446 f.) erwähnen kurz die Entstehung von Bienen aus Rindern und Wespen aus Pferden; vgl. Mynors im Kommentar zu *Georg.* 4.282 (S. 294 f.). W. Richter im Kommentar zu *Georg.* 4.284 ff. behauptet, daß bereits Empedokles die Angabe kenne, "daß aus dem Leichnam eines Rindes Bienen entstehen könnten" (S. 370); allerdings ist es fraglich, ob mit den βουγενή ἀνδρόπρωρα von 31 B 61, 2 D.-K. (aus Aelian, *Nat. anim.* 16.29) ("Kuhsprößlinge mit Menschenvorderteil" übersetzen D.-K.) dasselbe gemeint ist wie mit der Bugonie der Bienen bei Vergil.

[19] Vgl. zur Forschungsgeschichte J. Hermes, "C. Cornelius Gallus und Vergil. Das Problem der Umarbeitung des vierten Georgica-Buches" (Ph.D. diss., Universität Münster, 1977).

suchten, die durch Lukrez, Vergil und Manilius repräsentierte antike Tradition[20] fortzusetzen und jene Wissensgebiete zu behandeln, welche den Alten noch unbekannt waren oder von ihnen nicht als Gegenstand für ein Lehrgedicht gewählt wurden. Erst mit den drei Lehrgedichten des Giovanni Pontano vom Ende des 15. Jahrhunderts finden Erzählungen antiker Mythen Eingang ins neulateinische Lehrgedicht.

Im Gedicht *De hortis Hesperidum*, das vom Anbau der Zitrusfrüchte handelt, sind mehrere Mythen eingestreut, bei denen von den antiken Vorbildern nur die aitiologische Funktion übernommen ist. Dabei stützt sich Pontano — wie viele andere Lehrdichter nach ihm — in erster Linie auf Ovids *Metamorphosen*. Aus ihnen übernimmt er einzelne Mythen, aber er dichtet auch neue Mythen nach ihrem Vorbild und weist auch mit diesem Verfahren seinen Nachfolgern den Weg. Bekanntestes Beispiel ist seine Version der Sage von Venus und Adonis (1.67 ff.): Im Unterschied zu Ovids *Metamorphosen* (10.708–739) wird der von einem Eber tödlich verwundete Adonis von seiner Geliebten Venus in einen Orangenbaum (*citris*)[21] verwandelt, der im Garten der Hesperiden wächst und dessen goldene Äpfel Venus geweiht waren. Diese waren es, die Herakles auf seiner letzten Arbeit raubte und auf diese Weise die Orangenbaumkultur in Italien einführte. Damit geriet Pontano jedoch in Konflikt mit Vergil: denn dieser hätte die Orangen dann ja erwähnen müssen. Doch Pontanos List der poetischen Vernunft versteht es, den historischen Sachverhalt — daß nämlich der Orangenbaum erst im Mittelalter durch die Araber in Europa bekannt wurde — mit seiner Deutung zu harmonisieren (1.168–177): Aus Zorn über ein ihr vorenthaltenes Erstlingsopfer habe Juno die Orangenkulturen völlig vernichtet. Erst Venus habe viele Jahrhunderte später den ihr teuren Baum, der ja der verwandelte Adonis war, erneut aus Persien nach Italien eingeführt. So kann Pontano das Fehlen des Orangenbaums bei Vergil erklären und gleichzeitig für sich den Anspruch erheben, als erster dieses Thema im Lehrgedicht behandelt zu haben. Trotz dieser "Überbietung" Vergils knüpft aber Pontano für die Kenner ganz bewußt bei Vergil an, der im zweiten Buch der *Georgica* (2.126–135) bereits eine andere aus Persien importierte Zitrusfrucht, nämlich die Zitrone (*citrus medica*), genannt hatte.

Pontano sucht also die *aemulatio* mit Ovid in der Erfindung neuer Metamorphosen und die spielerische Überbietung Vergils in der Formulierung des neoterischen Erstheitsanspruchs. Diese Technik von Anlehnung und Abgrenzung wendet Pontano bereits in seinem gegen 1496 abgeschlossen Lehrgedicht *Urania* an. Im erstem Buch erzählt er bei den Planeten und ihren Göttern gelegentlich die dazugehörigen Mythen teils knapp, teils ausführlicher, darunter auch die Sage von Venus und Adonis (1.474–506), aber noch ohne die spätere Metamorphose des Adonis in den Orangenbaum,

---

[20] Daneben waren natürlich auch die anderen lateinischen Lehrdichtungen bekannt, insbesondere die *Aratea* des Germanicus, die seit dem 9. Jahrhundert reich überliefert sind, später häufig zusammen mit Ciceros und Avienus' *Aratea*, welch letztere freilich nur in 2 Hss. (s. IX/X und XV²) auf uns gekommen sind und nach der ed. pr. (Venedig 1488, dann 1499 von Aldus Manutius in den *Astronomici veteres*) bis ins 19. Jahrhundert in Vergessenheit gerieten; daneben wurde auch Horazens *Ars poetica* als Lehrgedicht gelesen und häufig nachgeahmt.

[21] Zur Identifikation der Zitrusfrüchte vgl. Ludwig, "Lateinische Lehrgedichte," 107 mit Anm. 24.

und die Flucht des Saturn nach Latium und sein kulturstiftendes Wirken unter der noch unzivilisierten Bevölkerung (1.711–726), von der bereits Euander dem Aeneas berichtet hatte (Verg. *Aen.* 8.319 ff.). Ausführliche mythologische Erzählungen ebenfalls überwiegend aitiologischer Art und mehrfach durch einen Musenanruf besonders hervorgehoben, finden sich auch in den folgenden Büchern, etwa im zweiten anläßlich der Tierkreisbilder von Krebs (2.578 ff.), Jungfrau (2.805 ff.), Skorpion (2.1070 ff.) und Schütze (2.1184 ff.); dieser war in der antiken Vorstellung der Kentaur Chiron, der Sohn des Saturn und der Nymphe Philyra; denn Saturn hatte sich bekanntlich in einen Hengst verwandelt, um nicht von seiner Gemahlin Rhea beim Seitensprung erwischt zu werden.[22] Vergil spielt darauf in einem berühmten Vergleich in den *Georgica* (3.92–94) an:

> talis et ipse iubam cervice effundit equina
> coniugis adventu pernix Saturnus et altum
> Pelion hinnitu fugiens implevit acuto.

Pontano arbeitet diese Anspielung zu einem langen aitiologischen Mythos aus, den Chiron dem Lehrdichter selbst erzählt (2.1190–1324).[23] Zu den berühmtesten Mythen Pontanos gehört der von Andromeda, ihrer Rettung durch Perseus und ihrer Verstirnung (4.181–344), der seine bekannteste Ausprägung in Ovids *Metamorphosen* (4.665–5.235) erfahren hatte, der aber auch bei Pontanos Vorbild Manilius ausführlich erzählt ist (5.538–618) und von späteren Dichtern in Latein und den Volkssprachen bis ins 18. Jahrhundert vielfältig umgestaltet wurde.

Pontano beschließt die *Urania* mit einer Klage über den Tod seiner Tochter Lucia (5.819–911): Diese Klage geht in eine Traumvision ihres Katasterismos über und endet mit dem Preis seines eigenen Ruhms durch die Nachwelt, in den im Stil der antiken Sphragis eine Bio-Bibliographie eingefügt ist. Der Wille zu einem Schluß wie bei Vergil ist deutlich erkennbar, doch hat Pontano noch nicht den Weg des Aristaeus-Epyllions eingeschlagen, sondern nur die Sphragis der *Georgica* als Vorbild gewählt, sie freilich zu einem großen persönlichen Finale von 125 Versen geweitet.

Mit seiner überreichen Verwendung von Mythen hat Pontano den späteren Lehrdichtern einen Weg gewiesen, den allzu viele allzu freudig eingeschlagen haben, darunter auch Girolamo Fracastoro, der das zweite und dritte Buch der *Syphilis* mit zwei aitiologischen Mythen krönte, die er jedoch — im Gegensatz zu Pontano, der

---

[22] Diese Geschichte wird nicht von Ovid in den *Metamorphosen* erzählt, nur in den Benennungen des Kentauren Chiron als *Philyreius heros* (2.676) und des Pelion als *Philyreia tecta* (7.352) spielt er kurz darauf an. Ausführlicher erzählt sie Apollonios von Rhodos als Aition für die Insel Philyra (2.1231–1241), auf welche Stelle sich Vergil offensichtlich bezieht.

[23] Später wird dieser Mythos, wohl wegen seines Vorkommens in den *Georgica*, ein beliebtes Sujet in der Lehrdichtung u.a. bei Vida, *Bombyces* 1.397 ff. und Claude Quillet, *Callipaedia seu de pulchrae prolis habendae ratione* (Leiden 1655, ²1656); vgl. dazu P. Ford, "Claude Quillet's *Callipaedia* (1655): Eugenics Treatise or Pregnancy Manual?," in Haskell and idem, eds., *Poets and Teachers*, 125–139, hier 133 ff.

sich im wesentlichen an die tradierten Vorgaben der Antike hielt — unter Verwendung antiker Elemente völlig neu dichtete.

Am Ende des zweiten Buches erzählt er die Entdeckung der Quecksilbertherapie durch den Jäger Ilceus, der von jener neuen Krankheit befallen ist und sein Leid der Quellnymphe Callirhoe klagt (2.281 ff.). Sie erklärt ihm in einem Traum die Krankheit als Strafe Dianas für den Abschuß eines ihr geweihten Hirsches. Heilung dafür müsse er *unter* der Erde suchen; daher gibt sie ihm genaue Anweisungen für den Abstieg in die unterirdische Welt (2.310 ff.). Wie Aristaeus und Orpheus im Lied des Proteus, so steigt auch Ilceus in die Tiefe, wo die Nymphe Lipare ihm bei einem Rundgang durch die Unterwelt die Gewinnung des Quecksilbers zeigt und ihn über dessen Heilkraft belehrt (2.361 ff.). Schließlich taucht sie ihn dreimal in den Quecksilberfluß, wodurch er von Krankheit und Aussatz geheilt wird (2.409 ff.), und entläßt ihn mit Vorschriften für ein Opfer an die Oberwelt, das er nach seiner Rückkehr ans Tageslicht ausführt.

Damit ist Fracastoro der erste neulateinische Lehrdichter, der den Schluß der *Georgica* als Modell für den Schluß eines Lehrgedichts wählt. Wenn auch die Struktur des Ilceus-Mythos einfacher ist, so hat Fracastoro doch die tragenden Elemente des Aristaeus-Epyllions verwendet: das Unglück des Helden, Klage und Zuflucht bei einer Nymphe, Instruktion über den einzuschlagenden Weg, Belehrung über die Ursache des Übels — eine gekränkte Gottheit — durch eine wissende Person, Abstieg in die Unterwelt (bei Vergil zweifach [Aristaeus und Orpheus], bei Fracastoro nur einmal), Eröffnung des Wegs zur Heilung, und abschließende Opfer zur Reinigung von der Schuld und zur Versöhnung der erzürnten Gottheit.

Eine ähnliche Struktur zeigt das dritte Buch der *Syphilis*. Entgegen dem Rat von Pietro Bembo, die mythologische Kopflastigkeit der ursprünglichen Fassung in zwei Büchern zu reduzieren, gestaltete Fracastoro es als selbständiges Epyllion, das die Ursachen für die Entstehung jener Krankheit im Kontext der ersten Entdeckungsfahrt von Christoph Columbus erzählt (3.30–404). Fracastoro hat in diesen von ihm konstruierten aitiologischen Mythos noch zwei weitere Mythentraditionen eingeflochten:[24] die Odysseus-Abenteuer der Bücher 9–12 der *Odyssee*, die von Vergil bereits in Buch III der *Aeneis* integriert wurden, und die Geschichte von Niobe aus dem sechsten Buch der *Metamorphosen* Ovids. Das Raffinierte an Fracastoros Mythos ist nun, daß die zentralen Motive sowohl der Columbus-Handlung als auch der Syphilus-Geschichte verdoppelt sind: Sowohl Columbus und die Spanier als auch Syphilus und seine Landsleute in jener fernen Vergangenheit, in der die Geschichte spielt, müssen dieselben Stationen durchlaufen wie der vergilische Aristaeus; denn beide haben Schuld auf sich geladen, ohne sich dessen bewußt zu sein, beide werden dafür gestraft, beide müssen bei Nymphen um Aufklärung und Hilfe bitten, und beide müssen Opfer und Riten vollziehen, um sich von dieser Schuld zu befreien und die erzürnte Gottheit zu versöhnen. Doch während von Aristaeus der Bann genommen

---

[24] Walter Ludwig hat das Wichtigste dazu gesagt, so daß ich mich hier kurz fassen kann: vgl. W. Ludwig, "Julius Caesar Scaligers Kanon der neulateinischen Dichter," *Antike und Abendland* 25 (1979): 20–40; Ndr. in idem, *Litterae Neolatinae* (o. Anm. 4), 220–241; hier: 236f.

wird und er neue Bienen erhält, bleibt bei den Spaniern und den Ureinwohnern des zerstörten Atlantis die Strafe für ihr Fehlverhalten über den Versöhnungsakt hinaus (und erreicht dadurch fast die Dimensionen der alttestamentlichen Erbschuld): Sie und ihre Nachfahren werden *immer* an dieser Krankheit leiden und können höchstens *Linderung*, nie aber *Heilung* davon erfahren (3.174 ff., 343 ff.).

Mit Pontanos und Fracastoros mythologischen Kreationen sind zwei Möglichkeiten vorgezeichnet, wie die vergilische Vorgabe jeweils variiert, modifiziert und aktualisiert werden kann. Im folgenden will ich die Variationsbreite dieses vorgegebenen Grundschemas an einigen bekannten und weniger bekannten Beispielen vorführen.

Ich beginne mit Marco Girolamo Vidas Lehrgedicht über Seidenraupenzucht (*Bombycum libri II*). Vida entwickelt darin eine spezielle "Fortsetzungstechnik", d.h. ein Mythos wird nicht auf einmal erzählt, sondern in verschiedene Erzählsequenzen unterteilt, die über das ganze Werk hin verstreut werden und durch Vorausdeutungen und Rückverweise aufeinander bezogen sind. Dadurch werden verschiedene Mythen thematisch miteinander verflochten und schaffen eine narrative "Superstruktur", die in ihren Verweisfunktionen die Einheit des Gedichts verstärkt.

In den Proömien der beiden Bücher wird durch die Anrufung der *Seriades*, der Seidennymphen, bereits auf den Schlußmythos vorausgewiesen, der seinerseits zwei andere mythologische Erzählungen aus Buch I und II aufnimmt und sie in das abschließende Aition integriert. Gegen Ende von Buch I erzählt Vida den Mythos von der Liebe des Saturn zur Nymphe Philyra, den sich schon Pontano in der *Urania* vom Kentauren Chiron hatte erzählen lassen. Bei Vida ist die Erzählung in den Kontext einer "Kulturentstehungslehre" eingebettet (1.385 ff.), mit der Vida an eine Tradition anknüpft, die über Ovid, Vergil und Lukrez auf Arat und Hesiod zurückgeht:[25] Minerva lehrt die Menschen, die sich bis dahin nur mit Fellen und Blättern gegen die Kälte geschützt hatten, das Weben und Spinnen, so daß sie sich Kleider aus Wolle und Leinen machen können, und gibt auch allen Göttinnen solche Kleider bis auf Venus, die ihr wegen ihrer Schönheit verhaßt ist. Venus und ihre Kinder, die Eroten, müssen daher weiter nackt bleiben und verbergen sich aus Scham in den tiefen Wäldern. Dort hatte Venus einst Saturn bei seinem Liebesabenteuer mit Philyra geholfen; denn sie war es gewesen, die ihm geraten hatte, sich in ein Roß zu verwandeln. Dafür schenkte er ihr zarte Samen und lehrte sie die Kunst, daraus die feinsten Gewebe zu wirken, ohne auf Minervas Wolle und Linnen angewiesen zu sein.

Mit diesem Geschenk läßt Saturn Venus und Vida den Leser allein, bis im zweiten Buch aus den Samen Seidenraupen ausgeschlüpft sind, mit denen die Eroten spielen, aber zu unvorsichtig damit umgehen und ihren Tod verursachen (2.223 ff.). Nun ist Vida glücklich beim Ausgangspunkt des Aristaeus-Epyllions angelangt — dem Verlust von Nutztieren — und konstruiert seinen Mythos in analoger, wenn auch vereinfachender Weise: Venus ist nun Aristaeus und Orpheus zugleich und zieht wie diese in die Unterwelt, wo sie von Pluto erreicht, daß die Raupen, deren Seelen in

---

[25] Ov. *Ars* 2.467 ff.; *Met.* 1.5 ff., 89 ff.; *Fasti* 4.395 ff.; Verg. *Georg.* 1.121 ff.; Lucr. 5.925 ff., 1011 ff.; Arat. *Phaen.* 96 ff.; Hes. *Op.* 109 ff.

der Unterwelt sind, wieder lebendig werden. Pluto gibt ihnen zusätzlich Flügel, bindet sie aber an das Gesetz, zweimal jährlich sterben und in die Unterwelt gehen zu müssen.[26] Auf dieser Weise deutet Vida den Vorgang der halbjährlichen Verpuppung der Raupen als Tod und das Ausschlüpfen der geflügelten Raupen, d.h. der Schmetterlinge, die auf Griechisch *psychai* "Seelen" heißen, als Auferstehung. Vida gelingt es sogar, die Bugonie selbst in sein Gedicht einzubauen, und schildert ebenfalls kurz das Entstehen neuer Raupen aus den Kadavern von Stieren (2.332–343), doch ist diese "Bombycogonie" losgelöst vom eigentlichen Mythos.[27]

Dieser wird am Ende des zweiten Buches nochmals aufgenommen und erhält eine neue aitiologische Wendung. Da Vergil in den *Georgica* (2.121) die Seide als Produkt der Serer, d.h. der Chinesen bezeichnet hatte,[28] läßt Vida im dritten Teil seines Mythos die Seide von einem chinesischen Prinzen nach Europa einführen (3.387 ff.). Nachdem dieser gehört hatte, daß Phaëthusa, eine der Schwestern Phaëthons, Tag und Nacht am Ufer des Po ihren Bruder beweine — Vida läßt uns im unklaren, ob durch Lektüre Ovids (vielleicht sogar in chinesischer Übersetzung!) oder auf andere Weise —, entbrannte er in heißer Liebe zu ihr, verließ sein Reich und begab sich nach Oberitalien. Doch als er dort ankam, war sie bereits in eine hohe Pappel verwandelt. All sein Jammern, seine Umarmungen des Stammes fruchteten nichts, und so verbrachte er ein ganzes Jahr unter Klagen und Weinen, bis sein Körper ganz in Tränen zerfloß, sich in Wasser auflöste und zum Fluß wurde.[29] Dieser Fluß mündete in die Adda, die ihrerseits kurz vor Cremona, der Heimat Vidas, in den Po fließt (so verband Vida etymologisch kühn den in den Bergamasker Alpen entspringenden Fluß *Serio* mit dem *Serius*, dem Prinzen aus China). Dort konnte er die Wurzeln des Baums benetzen, und endlich gelang es ihm, die Liebe der Baumnymphe zu gewinnen und sich mit ihr in richtiger Ehe (*licitisque hymenaeis*, 2.426) zu vereinen. Als Hochzeitsgeschenk brachte er ihr kostbare Seidenkleider und -stoffe und auch Eier der Seidenraupe und zeigte ihr, wie man daraus Seide gewinnt. Phaëthusa lehrte später ihre Töchter, die *Seriades Nymphae*, die Seidengewinnung, und diese verbrei-

---

[26] Hier spielt die ovidische Erzählung von Ceres und Proserpina aus dem fünften Buch der *Metamorphosen* mit herein, insbesondere die von Jupiter verfügte Verweildauer Proserpinas von je einem halben Jahr auf der Ober- und in der Unterwelt (*Met.* 5.564 ff.).

[27] Bereits vor Vida hatten Giustolo in seinem Seidenraupengedicht *De sere seu de saetivomis animalibus opusculum* (gedruckt in seinen *Opera*, Rom 1510) und Nicolò Perotti in der *Cornucopia* (Lib. I, Epigr. 2.487; ed. J.-L. Charlet [Sassoferrato, 1991], 2:181.16ff) die Bugonie in eine Bombycogonie verwandelt: vgl. Ludwig, "Neulateinische Lehrgedichte" (o. Anm. 4), 112.

[28] Das chinesische Wort *si* "Seide" erscheint im Griechischen als σηρικόν, im Lateinischen als *sericum* ('Seidenstoff').

[29] Ähnliche Verwandlungen berichtet Ovid mehrfach in den *Metamorphosen*: Cyane zerfließt in ein *stagnum* aus Trauer über die Verletzung ihrer *iura fontis* durch Pluto (5.409 ff.), Byblis löst sich in Tränen in eine Quelle auf, weil ihr Bruder Caunus ihre Liebe verschmäht (9.663 f.), und Egeria wird aus Schmerz über den Tod ihres Gatten Numa Pompilius zu der gleichnamigen Quelle (15.547 ff.); vgl. W. Ludwig, *Marcus Hieronymus Vida, Schachspiel der Götter. "Scacchia Ludus"*. Eingeleitet und mit der Übersetzung von Joh. Jos. Ign. Hoffmann hg. von W. Ludwig (Zürich und München, 1979), 6 ff.

teten in ganz Italien die Seidenraupenzucht und den Maulbeerbaum, aus dessen grünen Zweigen sich der Dichter ob seiner Verdienste von den Mädchen, die er mit seinem Gedicht in dieser Kunst unterwiesen hat, einen Kranz wünscht (2.435 ff.).

In seinem Kunstmythos hat Vida die Hauptstrukturen des vergilischen Aristaeus-Epyllions geschickt mit dem mythologischen Schatz von Ovids *Metamorphosen* angereichert, nicht ohne auf andere Reminiszenzen aus den *Georgica* zu verzichten. Das Ganze verband er mit einer Reverenz vor seiner Geburtsstadt Cremona, kulminierend im Wunsch nach dem Dichterkranz, womit er auf eine antike Tradition anspielt, die durch Petrarcas Dichterkrönung am Ostersonntag des Jahres 1341 wiederaufgenommen wurde und seitdem ein wesentliches Element humanistischer Dichterehrung bildete.

Innerhalb dieses von Pontano, Fracastoro und Vida vorgezeichneten Rahmens bewegen sich die meisten neulateinischen Lehrdichter, die einerseits für ihre aitiologischen Mythen Erzählungen, die sie bei Ovid vorgefunden haben, adaptieren oder im Stile der *Metamorphosen* neu erfinden und andrerseits versuchen, die Grundstruktur des Aristaeus-Epyllions beizubehalten, es aber an Erfindungsreichtum und Originalität zu übertreffen.

René Rapin hat die vier Bücher seines Lehrgedichts über Gartenbau und Parkanlagen[30] mit zahlreichen ovidianisierenden Mythen über die Entstehung von Pflanzen angereichert: Die Mythen von Narcissus (1.230–233), Hyacinthus (1.263–272) und Cyparissus (2.394–418) hat er mit wörtlichen Anklängen, wenn auch erheblich gekürzt, aus Ovid übernommen,[31] die der Entstehung des Veilchens (1.234–262) und der Tulpe (1.289–333) sind neu erfundene Metamorphosen nach dem Modell von Apollo und Daphne bzw. Pomona und Vertumnus: Die Nymphe Ianthis war Begleiterin der Diana und konnte dem erotischen Drängen Apollos nur dadurch entgehen, daß sie von Diana in eine Blume (Viola) verwandelt wurde. Tulipa war die Tochter der Nymphe der Timavusquelle und des Proteus; sie floh vor den Nachstellungen des Vertumnus und wurde in die Tulpe verwandelt. Mit dieser Erzählung hat Rapin auch insofern die Alten übertroffen, als die Tulpe erst ein Jahrhundert vorher aus der Türkei in Europa eingeführt wurde und daher noch auf ihre Metamorphose aus der Feder eines neuen Ovid warten mußte.[32]

Weitere originelle Neuschöpfungen Rapins sind die Aitia von der Entstehung des Wasserfalls und des Springbrunnens. Die Anlage von künstlichen Wasserfällen in den großen Parks von Versailles und anderen Schlössern und Villenanlagen ist ein wichtiger Lehrgegenstand im dritten Buch, das den Fontänen und Wasserläufen gewidmet ist; die Enstehung der Kaskaden wird auf Apollo zurückgeführt, der die unglückliche

---

[30] *Hortorum libri IV*, Paris 1665; abgedruckt bei F. Oudin, ed., *Poemata Didascalica*, vol. 2 (Paris, 1813), 225–340. Letzte Ausgabe von Irving T. McDonald mit der alten englischen Versübersetzung von James Gardiner (†1732) (Worcester, MA, 1932).

[31] Narcissus-Narzisse: Ov. *Met.* 3.339–510; Hyacinthus-Hyazinthe: Ov. *Met.* 10.162–219; Cyparissus-Zypresse: Ov. *Met.* 10.106–142 (vgl. *Hort.* 2.394b = *Met.* 10.120b).

[32] Vgl. *Augerius Gislenius Busbequius, Vier brieven over het gezantschap naar Turkije.* "Legationis Turcicae Epistolae Quattuor", ed. Z. von Martels, vertaling door M. Goldstein, inleiding en aantekeningen door Z. von Martels (Hilversum, 1994).

Sappho, als sie sich aus Liebeskummer um ihren untreuen Phaon von der Höhe des Leukadischen Felsens ins Meer stürzen wollte, noch rechtzeitig in einen Wasserfall verwandelte (3.510–524). Das Aition von der Entstehung des Springbrunnens (3.293–339) verbindet Rapin in geistreicher Weise mit der Sage von Herakles und Hylas, die schon Pontano in der *Urania* erzählt hatte, die aber in der Antike nie mit einer Metamorphose verbunden war, so daß Rapin die Alten gleich zweifach übertreffen kann: In den schönen Knaben Hylas verliebte sich die Nymphe Isis. Als er an ihrem Teich Wasser schöpfte, zog sie ihn zu sich herab und wollte ihn für immer als Geliebten behalten; doch Hylas weigerte sich, die Liebe der Isis zu erwidern, und versuchte sich aus ihrer Umarmung zu befreien.[33] Die verschmähte Isis verleiht Hylas *excelsum ingenium moresque superbos* (3.328) und verwandelt ihn in eine Fontäne, die hoch emporsteigend aus ihrem Teich entkommen will, aber dennoch immer wieder dorthin zurückfällt, und verewigt in diesem vergeblichen Versuch symbolisch den hoch aufschießenden und dennoch wieder zum Nachgeben gezwungenen Sinn des Hylas.

Diese und alle anderen der knapp vierzig Mythen in Rapins Lehrgedicht sind alte und neue Metamorphosen, die zwar aus der falschen Gattungstradition stammen, aber seinem strengen Klassizismus entsprachen und die antike Wunderwelt des Mythos auch im Frankreich Ludwigs XIV. heimisch machen sollten. Der letzte Mythos des Lehrgedichts im vierten, dem Obstbau gewidmeten Buch basiert dagegen auf dem Aristaeus-Epyllion und behandelt die Erfindung des Spalierobstbaus durch den aus der *Odyssee* bekannten Phäakenkönig Alcinous (4.606–682). Auch dieser Mythos nimmt seinen Ausgang von einer Naturkatastrophe, nämlich der Vernichtung der Gärten des Alcinous durch einen Sturm. Sowohl Alcinous, der hier die Rolle des Aristaeus übernimmt, als auch die meisten der herbeigerufenen Seher sind sich, wie das bei Sehern häufig so ist, über die Ursache im unklaren, bis der Phoebuspriester Eurymedon erkennt, daß sie, die Phäaken selbst, schuld sind und der Sturm eine Strafe der *dei agrestes* für den Hochmut des Königs und die Vernachlässigung ihres Kultes war. Wie Aristaeus seine Mutter Cyrene, Ilceus die Nymphe Lipare und Syphilus die Nymphe Ammerice, so fragt Alcinous die Nymphe Hesperis um Rat. Diese empfiehlt, Jupiter und Phoebus durch ein Opfer zu versöhnen. Der König befolgt diesen Rat und auch den weiteren, eine Schutzmauer gegen den Nordwind zu errichten und die neuen Bäume gegen diese Mauer anzupflanzen, so daß sie gegen Stürme geschützt sind und gleichzeitig durch die Reflektion der warmen Sonnenstrahlen ihre Früchte besser reifen. Freilich enden die *Hortorum libri* nicht mit dem Alcinous-Epyllion, sondern mit einer an *Georgica* 4.559–566 orientierten Sphragis (820–825) mit dem Preis Ludwigs XIV., der nach einer schlimmen Zeit kriegerischer Unruhen mit seinem Regierungsantritt 1661[34] ein neues Goldenes Zeitalter heraufgeführt

---

[33] Hier übernimmt Rapin Motive aus Ovids Erzählung von Salmacis und Hermaphroditus in *Met.* 4.285 ff.

[34] Ludwig, am 5.9.1638 geboren, wurde nach dem frühen Tod seines Vaters Ludwig XIII. im Jahre 1643 König von Frankreich; solange er unmündig war, führten seine Mutter Anna von Österreich und Kardinal Mazarin (1602–1661) für ihn die Regierungsgeschäfte. Er selbst trat die Herrschaft erst im Jahre 1661 im Alter von 23 Jahren an. Auf diesen Zeitpunkt bezieht sich das Finale der *Hortorum libri*.

habe. Rapins Herrscherlob deckt sich mit der offiziellen Propaganda des Königshofs, wonach Ludwigs Herrschaft eine Erneuerung des Prinzipats von Augustus sei und in Frankreich und Paris der politische und kulturelle Glanz des alten Rom neu erstehe.

Nach dem Vorbild des Aristaeus-Epyllions ist auch der Schlußmythos im achten Buch des Lehrgedichts über Schiffsbau und Seefahrt (*Nautica*) des neapolitanischen Jesuiten Nicolò Partenio Giannettasio vom Ende des 17. Jahrhunderts strukturiert, über den ich mich kurz fassen kann, da ich bereits an anderer Stelle ausführlicher darüber gehandelt habe.[35] Hier ist es der junge Columbus, der von seiner Mutter, der Nymphe Urania, ungeduldig die Einlösung ihres Versprechens fordert, daß sie ihn neue Länder und Völker jenseits des Ozeans entdecken lassen werde. Urania besteigt mit ihm den höchsten Berg Teneriffas und zeigt ihm den Kontinent, der westlich des Ozeans sichtbar wird. Sie erklärt ihm den Bau und die Gesetze des Kosmos und weist ihm die Orte in der neuen Welt an, die er auf seiner Reise entdecken wird, und prophezeit ihm dafür bleibenden Ruhm bei der Nachwelt; ferner gibt sie ihm praktische Hinweise über die Technik der Navigation und den Zeitpunkt der Fahrt und instruiert ihn, mit welchen Opfern er vorher die Götter des Meeres und des neuen Kontinents zu versöhnen habe. Schließlich warnt sie ihn vor den Strapazen und Gefahren, die er erdulden muß, und versichert ihm, daß sie ihm jederzeit beistehen werde. Hier hat freilich nicht nur das Aristaeus-Epyllion als Vorlage gedient, sondern Giannettasio hat auch zentrale Teile des *Somnium Scipionis* eingearbeitet und auf diese Weise zwei zentrale Texte der antiken Literatur zu einer neuen kunstvollen Einheit verbunden.[36]

Weit häufiger dagegen als solche kunstvollen Gebilde finden sich in den Lehrgedichten vor allem des 17. und 18. Jahrhunderts einfachere aitiologische Mythen, mit denen sich die Dichter nicht nur bemühten, den neuen, den Entdeckungen und Erkenntnissen ihrer eigenen Zeit entnommenen Themen einen antikisierenden Goldrand zu verleihen, sondern auch den Lehrgegenstand selbst in mythologisch-antikisierender Form zu verschlüsseln.

Das längste und einflußreichste dieser Werke ist das zwischen 1683 und 1746 entstandene, in seiner definitiven Form 16 Bücher umfassende landwirtschaftliche Lehrgedicht *Praedium rusticum* des Jesuiten Jacques Vanière (1664–1759). Es enthält zahlreiche solcher Mythen: neben mehr traditionellen wie dem Mythos der Königin Pristera von Zypern (Buch XIII), die den Verfolgungen eines Räubers dadurch entkommt, daß die Götter sie in eine Taube (griech. *peristerá*) verwandeln, während ihr Verfolger in einen Raubvogel verwandelt wird,[37] hat Vanière als Neuerung gegenüber der Antike einige Fisch-Metamorphosen eingebaut, die das der Teichwirtschaft gewidmete 15. Buch auflockern, darunter die der schönen Jungfrau Truta in eine Fo-

---

[35] H. Hofmann, "Variations on an Ending: Scipio, Aristaeus, and the Dream of Columbus," *Res Publica Litterarum* 16 (1993): 227–238; vgl. jetzt auch Bitzel, *Bernardo Zamagna "Navis Aëria*," 187 ff., und vor allem Claudia Schindler, "Nicolò Partenio Giannettasios *Nauticorum libri VIII*. Ein neulateinisches Lehrgedicht des 17. Jahrhunderts," *Neulateinisches Jahrbuch* 3 (2001): 145–176.

[36] Ähnlich verfuhr siebzig Jahre vor ihm Giovanni Pietro d'Alessandro in seinem Epos *Hierosolymae eversae* (1613), worüber Elisabeth Klecker in Cambridge sprach.

[37] Vorbilder sind u.a. Ovids Sagen von Apollo und Daphne, Io, Arethusa und Tereus-Progne.

relle, die des alten Fischers Barbus in die Barbe oder die des Carpus in den Karpfen, den man, wie die französische Anmerkung zu dieser Stelle besagt, vor allem im Gardasee finde: denn als Saturn auf seiner Flucht vor Jupiter nach Oberitalien kam und den Gardasee auf dem Boot des Fährmanns Carpus überqueren wollte, versuchte dieser, ihn zu überwältigen und sich in den Besitz seines Goldes zu bringen. Doch Saturn, der ihm seinen niederträchtigen Plan aus dem Gesicht ablas (*mentem ex vultu praesensit iniquam*), warf ihn und seine Schiffer ins Wasser, wo sie zu *carpiones* (Karpfen) wurden, die noch heute die Schiffe im Gardasee verfolgen *aurique cupidine flagrant / seque adeo humana testantur origine cretos*.[38] Das *tertium comparationis* für dieses Aition ist der zu Beginn erwähnte Umstand, daß auch dieser Fisch von Ausoniens Gewässern stammt, *ramentis fulvi qui vescitur auri / atque alio priscos in corpore servat amores*; doch diese *priscos amores* sind nicht, wie der Leser zunächst geneigt sein könnte zu glauben, ein schönes Mädchen am Gardasee, sondern in Vanières moralisierender Interpretation die durch den Mythos begründete *auri sacra fames*.

Ebenfalls mit einer alten Liebe erklärt der Jesuit Thomas Fellon (1672–1759) in seinem 1696 in Lyon erschienenen Lehrgedicht *Magnes* die Entstehung des Magnetismus.[39] Bereits nach dem Proömium kündigt er an, er wolle die von vielen vergebens gesuchten Ursachen dafür, daß die Magnetnadel im Kompaß immer nach Norden zeige, darlegen und deutet an, daß das Eisen im Norden eine verlorene Liebe suche (*amissos scrutatur amores*, 95). Darauf folgt bereits *vor* der wissenschaftlichen Darlegung das mythologische Aition mit der Geschichte der Zwillinge Siderites und Siderus, Söhnen der Ceres und Brüder der Proserpina, die sich in gegenseitiger Liebe zugetan waren (97–184): Als Proserpina von Pluto geraubt wurde, jagten sie im Wagen ihrer Mutter Ceres Plutos Gespann hinterher und verfolgten es bis ans äußerste Ende der Welt, wo der Nordwind zuhause ist. Sie hatten Pluto beinahe erreicht, als er mit seinem Stab eine Öffnung in die Erde schlug, in der er mit Wagen und Proserpina verschwand und die sich hinter ihm sofort wieder schloß. Also war beiden Brüdern der Weg zur Rettung ihrer Schwester abgeschnitten. Ohnmächtig vor Wut rief Siderus die Götter an und schalt sie, daß sie hart wie Eisen seien, weil

---

[38] Dieses Aition scheint eine Erfindung Girolamo Fracastoros zu sein, der es um 1535 in einer poetischen Epistel an den Bischof von Verona, Giovanni Matteo Giberti, erzählt: *Hieronymi Fracastorii Veronensis [. . .] Carminum Editio II* (Padova, 1739), 1:117–120, Carmen V: *Ad Joannem Matthaeum Gibertum episcopum Veronensem*; später wird es mit Verweis auf Fracastoros Behandlung nochmals ausführlicher von Georgius Iodocus Berganus (d.h. Georg Jodocus aus Bergen in Brabant, der als Benediktinermönch in S. Zeno in Verona lebte) in Buch IV (77 ff.) seines Lobgedichts auf den Gardasee (*Benacus*, Veronae apud Antonium Puteolum, 1546, fols. 54r ff.) erzählt. Ein völlig anderes Aition bietet Pierius Valerianus (Giampietro Valeriano Bolzani [1477–1558] aus Belluno) in einer Elegie seiner *Amorum libri V* (Venetiis 1549, 93–100). Vgl. G.B. Pighi, *Benacensia. La leggenda del Carpione di Girolamo Fracastoro* (Verona, 1966), 10–20; A. Valerini, *Le bellezze di Verona* (Verona, 1586; Ndr. Verona, 1974), 27–44; W.Th. Elwert, "Il Lago di Garda nella poesia latina del Cinquecento," in idem, *Aufsätze zur provenzalischen, französischen und neulateinischen Dichtung*, Studien zu den Romanischen Sprachen und Literaturen 4 (Wiesbaden, 1971), 164–206 (Siegmar Döpp [Göttingen] danke ich herzlich für diese Hinweise und eine Kopie von Georgius Iodocus Berganus' *Benacus*).

[39] Abgedruckt bei Oudin, *Poemata Didascalica*, 1:174–202.

sie sich seiner nicht erbarmten. Da erstarrte seine Zunge, und er wandelte sich in eine *frigida massa*, eine starre Masse von Eisen. Während Siderites noch das Los seines Bruders Siderus beklagte, wurde er selbst zu einem harten Felsen (*durum saxum*); doch beide Brüder bewahrten auch nach der Verwandlung in Stein und Eisen ihre frühere Liebe und ziehen sich gegenseitig an. Daher neigt sich der Magnetstein (*Siderites*) noch immer nach Norden zu seinem zu Eisen gewordenen Bruder (*Siderus*), und das Eisen will noch immer in die Tiefe der Erde dringen und Proserpina von Pluto zurückfordern.

In der Antike gibt es keine mythologische Erklärung des Magnetismus,[40] nur eine bei Plinius (*Nat. hist.* 36.128 ff.) angedeutete und von ihm auf Nikander zurückgeführte Anekdote von der Entdeckung des Magnetsteins durch einen Hirten Magnes, der, als er auf dem Berge Ida seine Herde weidete, mit den Nägeln seiner Sandalen und seines Speeres Spitze an diesem Stein hängen blieb. Bei Plinius hatte unser Lehrdichter jedenfalls das Wort *sideritis* bzw. *siderites* für den Magnetstein gefunden, den er als Eigennamen auf den Bruder übertrug, der in diesen Stein verwandelt wurde, während der andere, Siderus, einfach "der Eiserne" ist. Eine Bemerkung des Plinius mag ihn auch zu seinem Mythos der *amissos amores*, der verlorenen Liebe, angeregt haben: "Das Eisen," so schreibt Plinius (36.127), "wird vom Magnetstein angezogen, und jenes alles beherrschende Material (*domitrix illa rerum omnium materia*) läuft auf ein unerklärliches Leeres zu (*ad inane nescio quid currit*), springt, sobald es ihm näher kommt, heran, wird festgehalten und hängt in der Umarmung fest (*tenetur amplexuque haeret*)": eine poetische Formulierung, die der Sprache der Liebesdichtung entlehnt ist und gleichsam das Grundmotiv formte, aus dem Fellon seinen Mythos entfaltete. Die Bewahrung der Liebe zueinander auch nach der Verwandlung ist schließlich ein Motiv, das Fellon verschiedenen ovidischen Metamorphosen entnehmen konnte, vor allem jener von Ceyx und Alcyone, von denen es am Schluß ebenfalls heißt: *fatis obnoxius isdem / tunc quoque mansit amor* (Ov. *Met.* 11.742 f.).

In ähnlicher Weise verwenden viele andere Lehrdichter des 17. und 18. Jahrhunderts zur Auflockerung und antikisierenden Gestaltung ihres Lehrvortrags aitiologische Mythen, die auch ohne Rekurs auf das Aristaeus-Epyllion zu einem festen Bestandteil neulateinischer Lehrdichtung geworden sind. Der Jesuit François Tarillon (1666–1735) schließt sein 1692 in Paris erschienenes Lehrgedicht über das Schießpulver (*Pulvis Pyrius*)[41] mit einem kurzen Schlußmythos, den er mit einer ähnlichen Frage einleitet wie Vergil das Aristaeus-Epyllion und mit einer sich an die *Georgica* anlehnenden Sphragis abrundet (303–333). Im Mythos stellt er der Goldenen Zeit *ante Iovem* die Verschlechterung *sub Iove* entgegen, die begann, als Vulkan von Juno aus dem Himmel gestoßen wurde. Aus Zorn hierüber habe Vulkan die Kyklopen unter dem Ätna erstmals in der Kunst unterwiesen, *fulmineos imitari sulphure motus* (312); dadurch wurde der Krater in den Ätna gesprengt und wurden das Schießpulver und die dadurch ermöglichten *saevae artes* in der Welt bekannt.

---

[40] Zum Thema vgl. A. Radl, *Der Magnetstein in der Antike. Quellen und Zusammenhänge*, Boethius 19 (Stuttgart, 1988). Zu Plinius: Radl, *Magnetstein*, 48 ff.

[41] Gedruckt bei Oudin, *Poemata Didascalica*, 1:117–128.

Louis Clairambault eröffnet sein 1737 gedrucktes Lehrgedicht über die Zucht von Kanarienvögeln (*Acanthides Canariae sive Spini*)[42] mit dem Mythos von der Nymphe Acanthis und dem Jüngling Spinus (26–83). Beide waren sangeskundig und einander in treuer Liebe ergeben, doch weigerten sich beide, an den ekstatischen Riten der Venus, die inzwischen auch die *Fortunatae Insulae* erreicht hatten, teilzunehmen und obszöne Lieder zu Ehren der Göttin anzustimmen. Aus Wut über diese Mißachtung befahl Venus, Amor solle die beiden mit seinen Pfeilen zur Liebesraserei treiben, doch wurden sie auf der Flucht vor dem *saevus amor* von den Göttern in Kanarienvögel verwandelt.

Der Jesuit Charles Noceti (1694–1759) erzählt in seinem Lehrgedicht über den Regenbogen (*Iris*)[43] den Mythos vom Troianer Xanthus (388–443), dem Geliebten der Venus, der sich in die Göttin Iris verliebte und, da er von ihr trotz seines Werbens nicht erhört wurde, sich aus Verzweiflung in jenen Fluß stürzte, der seitdem nach ihm benannt ist. Von Venus aber wurde die vermeintliche Nebenbuhlerin Iris im Zorn zu ewiger Jungfräulichkeit verurteilt. Seitdem zerfließt sie immerdar in Tränen über ihr Schicksal und weint vergebens und zu spät über die nicht erwiderte Liebe des Xanthus.

Indes fand auch Vidas Experiment mit seinem Schachgedicht zumindest einen Nachfolger. Im *Scacchia Ludus* hat Vida bekanntlich das Lehrgedicht in ein mythologisches Epyllion verwandelt und die Gattung fiktionalisiert, indem er die Regeln anläßlich der ersten Schachpartie erläuterte, die nach der Hochzeit von Herakles und Hebe im Olymp von Apollo und Merkur gespielt wurde. In ähnlicher Weise hat der Jesuit François-Antoine Le Febvre (ca. 1670–1737) in seinem Lehrgedicht über die Musik (*Musica*)[44] die Entstehung der Musik, der wichtigsten Instrumente und Tonarten gänzlich in einer fiktionalen antiken Welt lokalisiert, so daß das Gedicht eher ein mythologisches Epyllion ist als ein Lehrgedicht.

Zusammenfassend können wir also festhalten, daß das Aristaeus-Epyllion erst spät als Modell für einen aitiologischen Schlußmythos im Lehrgedicht übernommen wurde, nämlich erstmals 1530 in Fracastoros *Syphilis*. Spätere Mythen, die nach diesem Vorbild konstruiert wurden, etwa bei Vida, Rapin und Giannettasio, reduzieren die Komplexität des vergilischen Schlußmythos auf einfache Sequenzen und stellen selbst dort, wo es sich wie in Vidas Seidenraupengedicht angeboten hätte, keinen Bezug zur Bugonie her, die bei Vergil bekanntlich der thematische Ausgangspunkt für das Aristaeus-Epyllion war. Keiner dieser Lehrdichter hat zudem eine Erzählung innerhalb seiner Version des Aristaeus-Epyllions, die der von Proteus erzählten Geschichte von Orpheus und Eurydice entspricht und erst durch eine andere Person in ihrem Bezug zum Anliegen des Geschädigten gedeutet werden muß. Offensichtlich hatten jene Lehrdichter die Komplexität der vergilischen Orpheus-Erzählung nicht erkannt — darin vielen Philologen bis in unser Jahrhundert nicht unähnlich — und

---

[42] Gedruckt bei Oudin, *Poemata Didascalica*, 2:155–166.

[43] Erstmals gedruckt Venedig 1729, zweite Auflage Rom 1747; wieder abgedruckt bei Oudin, *Poemata Didascalica*, 2:71–88.

[44] Erstausgabe Paris 1704, wieder abgedruckt bei Oudin, *Poemata Didascalica*, 1:230–243.

daher von vornherein ihr Epyllion linearer und daher meist auch kürzer angelegt.

Neben diesen an Vergil orientierten Versuchen in mythologischer Kreativität haben es die meisten Lehrdichter vorgezogen, aitiologische Mythen nach dem Vorbild Ovids einzufügen, die sie den *Metamorphosen* entnahmen oder nach der Struktur der dort erzählten Verwandlungssagen neu dichteten. Insbesondere haben sie sich dabei, wie wir gesehen haben, bemüht, neue Metamorphosen zu ersinnen, die es in der Antike noch nicht gab, und zwar sowohl von den Personen her, die verwandelt wurden, als auch von den Lebewesen und Objekten, in die sie verwandelt wurden (z.B. Tulpe, Veilchen, Taube, Wasserfall, Fontäne etc.). Neu sind dabei insbesondere die Fischmetamorphosen, für die es in der Antike kaum Vorbilder gibt und die durch ähnliche Bestrebungen, die Alten zu übertreffen, angeregt worden sein dürften wie die Ausweitung der Eklogendichtung von den Hirten auf andere Lebensbereiche (ich verweise nur auf die *Eclogae Piscatoriae* von Lorenzo Gambara di Brescia und die *Eclogae Nauticae* des Nicolò Partenio Giannettasio).

Der erklärende, begründende oder illustrierende Mythos im neulateinischen Lehrgedicht konnte allerdings schon seit dem Ende des 16. Jahrhunderts durch andere narrative Einlagen ersetzt werden: Scévole de Sainte-Marthe (Scaevola Sammarthanus, 1536–1623) schließt das erste Buch seines 1584 in Paris gedruckten Lehrgedichts über Kindererziehung (*Paedotrophiae sive de puerorum educatione libri III*)[45] mit einer epischen Paraphrase der biblischen Erzählung vom Sündenfall (1.396–510), womit der Umstand, daß die Geburt eines Kindes unter Schmerzen verläuft, wie in der Genesis (3:16) als Strafe für die Frauen wegen Evas Verfehlung im Paradies gedeutet wird. Im zweiten Buch bringt Sammarthanus als Exemplum für eine falsche Temperatur im Kinderschlafzimmer — nämlich zuviel Wärme — eine historische Erzählung vom Tode des einzigen Sohnes des Herzogs der Bretagne (2.156–212). Seine Beweinung wird in ein mythisches Ambiente verlegt, in dem Oceanus und die Nymphen der Bretagne um das Kind trauern; eine dieser Nymphen jedoch tröstet die Trauernden mit einer Prophezeiung über die spätere Hochzeit Annas, der Tochter des Herzogspaares, mit dem französischen König Karl VIII. (1483–1498): dadurch würden die *fata* diesen schweren Verlust wieder kompensieren und werde das Haus Valois ruhmreiche Nachkommenschaft haben (2.181 ff.). Erst das dritte Buch, in dem die Kinderkrankheiten besprochen werden, endet mit einem aitiologischen Mythos, der den Ursprung der Epilepsie erklären will, von der gerade die hervorragendsten Männer befallen werden. Als mythologisches Beispiel — für das er sich am Schluß mit der Bemerkung entschuldigt, auch die großen Dichter hätten Ernstes mit Fiktivem gemischt (*ficto variarunt seria ludo / saepe sacri vates*) und die Camenen liebten solche *figmenta* (3.596–598) — erzählt Sammartin, wie Herakles einst nach der Bezwingung des Nemeischen Löwen von einem Epilepsieanfall heimgesucht und von Paeonis, der Tochter des berühmten Arztes Paieon, geheilt wurde, die auf seine Fragen ihm (und damit auch dem interessierten Leser) erklärte, wie man bei solch einem Anfall vorgehen müsse. Herakles, immer schnell für schöne Frauen entflammt, verliebte sich sofort in das Mädchen und verwandelte sie nach vielen Jahren, als sie alt und er schon

---

[45] Gedruckt bei Oudin, *Poemata Didascalica*, 2:167–224.

längst unter die Götter des Olymps aufgenommen war, in die Päonie, die berühmteste Heilpflanze des Altertums, die wegen ihrer Breitbandwirkung auch in der Medizin der Folgezeit vor allem als magisches Mittel gegen "dämonische" Krankheiten wie Epilepsie und Lähmungen hoch geschätzt wurde (3.466–595).

Eine historische Erzählung von der Erfindung des Barometers durch Galilei und seinen Schüler Torricelli setzte auch der Jesuit Loup Thomas in seinem 1749 in Paris erschienenen Lehrgedicht über das Barometer (*Barometrum*)[46] an die Stelle des aitiologischen Mythos (257–399). Eine Anekdote aus den Perserkriegen des 5. Jahrhunderts v. Chr. verwendete der Jesuit Louis Doissin (1727–1753) im ersten Buch seiner *Sculpturae libri III*[47] als historisches Aition für die "Erfindung" von Karyatiden und ihrer Verwendung anstelle von Säulen (1.296–352). In seinem Gedicht über die Orangenbäume (*Mala Aurea*)[48] von 1692 wählt der Jesuit Guillaume Veschambez das Mittel der Ekphrasis statt des Mythos: Die Töpfe, in die man die Orangenbäume im Park von Versailles gepflanzt hat, sind mit Darstellungen der Heldentaten König Ludwigs XIV. verziert, die der Lehrdichter dem Leser ausführlich vorstellt (214–268). Und der Proteus aus dem Aristaeus-Epyllion, der den Ausgangspunkt meiner Betrachtungen bildete, wird von dem Jesuiten Jean Lucas (1638–1716) in seinem Lehrgedicht über Gestik und Vortrag des Redners und Schauspielers (*Actio oratoris seu De gestu et voce libri II*)[49] geradezu entmythologisiert: denn dieser Proteus bei Vergil, so behauptet Lucas, war kein Gott, wie die *credula posteritas* gemeint hat, sondern ein Schauspieler, der durch seine glänzende theatralische Ausbildung den Mythos von Orpheus und Eurydice so wirkungsvoll vortrug und mit Hilfe der Bühnentechnik sich in all die genannten Gestalten — Wildschwein, Tigerin, Schlange, Löwin, Feuer, Wasser — mühelos verwandeln konnte (1.165–197): eine für das theaterbegeisterte Barockzeitalter durchaus angemessene Interpretation!

So sind wir am Ende wieder bei Proteus angelangt, der also nur ein Schauspieler gewesen sein soll: Der Übernahme von Mythen im Lehrgedicht, ihrer Adaption und Konstruktion nach antikem Vorbild folgt ihre Ersetzung durch Anekdoten, historische Erzählungen, biblische Geschichten, Bildbeschreibungen und schließlich ihre Destruktion durch den Rationalismus des ausgehenden 17. Jahrhunderts, das — wie später auch die Aufklärung — das Lehrgedicht liebte und pflegte,[50] wenn freilich mehr in den modernen Sprachen als in Latein, dessen Vormachtstellung als *lingua franca* der Gelehrsamkeit und Schönen Literatur schon damals weit zurückgedrängt war. Auf diesem Weg hat uns unser Streifzug eine Fülle von Gestaltungsmöglichkeiten für den Mythos im Lehrgedicht vorgeführt, der zwar stets in enger Verbindung zum Lehrgegenstand blieb, dessen Bereich die Lehrdichter jedoch über alle vier

---

[46] Wieder abgedruckt bei Oudin, *Poemata Didascalica*, 2:341–356.
[47] Paris 1752, wieder abgedruckt bei Oudin, *Poemata Didascalica*, 3:28–109.
[48] Wieder abgedruckt bei Oudin, *Poemata Didascalica*, 2:33–51.
[49] Paris 1675, wieder abgedruckt bei Oudin, *Poemata Didascalica*, 1:66–116.
[50] Vgl. L.L. Albertsen, *Das Lehrgedicht. Eine Geschichte der antikisierenden Sachepik in der neueren deutschen Literatur, mit einem unbekannten Gedicht Albrecht von Hallers* (Aarhus, 1967), 108 ff., 132 ff.; C. Siegrist, *Das Lehrgedicht der Aufklärung*, Germanistische Abhandlungen 43 (Stuttgart, 1974).

Kontinente ausdehnten: von China im Osten bis Amerika im Westen, vom magnetischen Pol im Norden bis nach Afrika und zu den Inseln der Seligen im Süden. Vergils Vorbild hat die Phantasie der Lehrdichter angeregt und sie doch immer wieder auf Ovids Geschichten von Liebesfreud und Liebesleid und die neuen Leiden des jungen Aristaeus zurückgeführt.

Universität Tübingen

L'*Accademia Pontaniana* e la sua ideologia in alcuni componimenti giovanili del Sannazaro

LUCIA GUALDO ROSA

Quando, nel lontano 1973,[1] io parlai nel congresso di Amsterdam degli epigrammi latini del Sannazaro, potevo contare su pochi sussidi bibliografici. In particolare, per il testo delle *Elegie* e degli *Epigrammi* latini, ben poco era stato aggiunto all'edizione olandese del 1728 e allo *Spicilegium Romanum* di Angelo Mai;[2] per la tradizione manoscritta delle poesie latine, esisteva solo lo studio dell'Altamura,[3] mentre un esame critico complessivo dell'opera sannazariana, sul doppio versante latino e volgare, era stato abbozzato solo, in forma assai raffinata ma tuttora incompleta, dal Tateo e dal Dionisotti.[4]

Oggi, a quasi trent'anni di distanza, la situazione è nettamente migliorata. Abbiamo innanzitutto il pilastro dell'edizione critica del *De partu Virginis*, che rappresenta un buon punto di partenza anche per la storia delle prime raccolte dei carmi latini, pubblicate, tra il 1528 e il 1533, in appendice al poema maggiore.[5] Una promettente anticipazione di quell'edizione critica dei carmi latini che tutti continuiamo ad auspicare è inoltre la tesi di dottorato di Anita Di Stefano, presentata all'università di Messina, relatore Vincenzo Fera) nel 1994 e consultabile, come tutte le tesi di dottorato,

---

[1] L. Gualdo Rosa, "A proposito degli epigrammi latini del Sannazaro," in *Acta Conventus Neo-Latini Amstelodamensis, Amsterdam 19–24 August 1973*, ed. P. Tuynmann, G.-C. Kuiper, and E. Kessler (München, 1978), 453–476.

[2] *Actii Sinceri Sannazarii Opera latine scripta, ex secundis curis Jani Broukhusii. Accedunt . . . Vitae Sannazarianae et Notae Petri Vlamingii* (Amstelaedami, 1728), e A. Mai, "Actii Synceri Sannazarii Carmina inedita," in *Spicilegium Romanum* 8 (1842): 508–511.

[3] A. Altamura, *La tradizione manoscritta dei "Carmina" del Sannazaro* (Napoli, 1957).

[4] F. Tateo, "La crisi culturale di Jacopo Sannazaro," in Id., *Tradizione e realtà nell'Umanesimo italiano* (Bari, 1967), 9–109, e C. Dionisotti, "Appunti sulle rime di Iacopo Sannazaro," *Giornale Storico della Letteratura Italiana* 140 (1963): 61–111.

[5] Iacopo Sannazaro, *De partu Virginis*, ed. C. Fantazzi e A. Perosa (Firenze, 1988).

nelle biblioteche nazionali di Firenze e di Roma.[6] Molto importanti per la storia del metodo di lavoro del Sannazaro, ma anche per quella della tradizione manoscritta di elegie ed epigrammi, gli studi condotti da Carlo Vecce sui manoscritti del Sannazaro e di altri poeti della sua cerchia che — grazie alla mediazione dell'umanista ungherese Giovanni Sambuco — si conservano nella Biblioteca Palatina di Vienna.[7] In questi stessi anni, un giovane allievo di Alain Michel, Marc Deramaix, ha pubblicato molti significativi contributi tesi ad illustrare da un lato i precedenti del *De partu Virginis*, dall'altro il significato estetico e religioso del poema e i suoi rapporti col classicismo romano del primo '500.[8]

Questa ripresa di studi sul Sannazaro (ma anche su Michele Marullo e su altri rappresentanti dell'Accademia pontaniana) si inserisce nel quadro più ampio di una complessiva rivalutazione del classicismo in generale, e in particolare del ruolo che in questo movimento culturale europeo ebbero i più importanti maestri della "sodalitas" pontaniana.[9] Sull'importanza di questo cenacolo culturale per l'elaborazione di una poetica dell'*excellentia* e dell'imitazione dei modelli più perfetti di ciascun genere letterario, mi basterà ricordare — accanto ai più recenti saggi del Deramaix e del Vecce — lo studio del Ferraù sul Pontano critico e quelli di De Caprio sui cenacoli umanistici del '400 e sulla Roma del primo '500.[10]

L'interesse attuale per l'opera del Marullo, ampiamente dimostrato dalle tre edizioni dei suoi *Hymni Naturales* apparse quasi contemporaneamente in Francia, in Austria e in Italia,[11] non è estraneo al nostro discorso; perché il Marullo fece — come è noto — il suo apprendistato poetico a Napoli, alla scuola dell'Accademia pontaniana, e a quegli ideali poetici e teorici rimase fedele durante tutta la sua breve esistenza, anche quando fu costretto ad allontanarsi da Napoli per andare prima a

---

[6] A. Di Stefano, "Per l'edizione delle 'Elegie' e degli 'Epigrammi' di Jacopo Sannazaro," tesi di dottorato, VI ciclo, Università degli Studi di Messina, 1994.

[7] C. Vecce, *Iacopo Sannazaro in Francia. Scoperte di codici all'inizio del XVI secolo* (Padova, 1988); Id. *Gli zibaldoni di Iacopo Sannazaro* (Messina, 1998); Id., " 'In Actii Sinceri bibliotheca.' Appunti sui libri di Sannazaro," in *Studi vari di lingua e letteratura italiana in onore di Giuseppe Velli*, Quaderni di Acme 41 (2000), 301–310.

[8] M. Deramaix, "La genèse du 'De partu Virginis' de J. Sannazare et trois églogues inédites de Gilles de Viterbe," *Mélanges de l'École française de Rome. Moyen Âge-Temps modernes* 99 (1987): 171–212; Id., " 'Christias 1513'. La 'forma antiquior' du 'De partu Virginis' de Sannazar et l'Académie Romaine de Léon X, dans un manuscrit inédit de Séville," *Cahiers de l'Humanisme* 1 (2000): 151–172.

[9] Per la rivalutazione del classicismo cattolico e controriformistico, cf. M. Fumaroli, *L'âge de l'éloquence. Rhétorique et 'res literaria' de la Renaissance au seuil de l'époque classique* (Genève, 1980), e A. Michel, *La parole et la beauté. Rhétorique et esthétique dans la tradition occidentale* (Paris, 1982).

[10] G. Ferraù, *Pontano critico* (Messina, 1983), e V. De Caprio, "I cenacoli umanistici," in A. Asor Rosa, ed., *Letteratura italiana*, vol. 1, *Il letterato e le istituzioni* (Torino, 1982), 799–822; e Id., "Roma," in *Storia e geografia*, vol. 2, *L'età moderna,* 1 (Torino, 1988), 360–453.

[11] Chr. Harrauer, *Kosmos und Mythos. Die Weltgotthymnen und die mythologische Hymnen des Michel Marullus*, Text, Übersetzung und Kommentar (Wien, 1994); Michel Marulle, *Hymnes naturels*, éd, J. Chomarat (Genève, 1995); Michele Marullo Tarcaniota, *Inni naturali*, ed. D. Coppini (Firenze, 1995); vedi anche la recensione di P. Laurens, *Cahiers de l'Humanisme* 1 (2000): 271–274.

Roma e poi a Firenze.¹² Ed è proprio dal rapporto di stretta solidarietà ed affinità poetica che intercorse tra Sannazaro e Marullo che intendiamo prendere le mosse, partendo dall'analisi delle liriche latine del Sannazaro e dimostrando come la presenza del Marullo in quei componimenti sia assai più significativa se, accanto alle testimonianze rimaste dell'edizione definitiva, si aggiungono quelle espunte, nel corso degli anni, nella scelta e nella redazione finale dei componimenti accolti nell'*editio princeps*.

Questa edizione apparve, come è noto, cinque anni dopo la morte del poeta, a Venezia, nel 1535.¹³ Si tratta dunque di un'edizione postuma, fortemente voluta dal cardinale Girolamo Seripando e da Scipione Capece e curata non tanto e non solo da Antonio Diaz Garlon, conte d'Alife, cui la dedica Paolo Manuzio,¹⁴ quanto dal poeta neolatino Onorato Fascitelli da Isernia.¹⁵

Chiunque sia stato il responsabile dell'*editio princeps* aldina, egli dovette servirsi di un manoscritto — perduto — che dava elegie ed epigrammi in un testo e in una disposizione assai diversi anche rispetto al ben noto Vat. lat. 3361, che è la maggiore testimonianza dell'instancabile *labor limae* esercitato dal Sannazaro sulle sue liriche latine.¹⁶ Il codice è interamente autografo, ad eccezione dei due indici degli epigrammi, che si leggono uno al fol. 63 e l'altro al fol. 83a; gli studi della Di Stefano ci consentono ora di attribuire il primo indice alla mano di Antonio Seripando ed il se-

---

¹² Cf. C. Minieri Riccio, *Biografie degli accademici alfonsini, detti poi pontaniani dal 1442 al 1543* (Napoli, 1881; repr. Bologna, 1969), 128–133. Cf. anche L. Gualdo Rosa, "L'"Académie Pontanienne' et l'élaboration d'une poétique du classicisme," *Cahiers de l'Humanisme* 1 (2000): 209–215.

¹³ Iacobi Sannazarii *Opera omnia latine scripta* . . . (Venetiis: in aedibus Aldi Manutii et Andreae Asulani soceri, mense septembri, MDXXXV).

¹⁴ L'Aldina è dedicata ad Antonio Diaz Garlon, conte d'Alife, che fu uno dei curatori testamentari del Sannazaro: cf. E. Percopo, *Vita di Jacobo Sannazaro*, ed. G. Brognoligo (Napoli, 1931), 194. Ma per questa edizione e per i problemi relativi alla sua attribuzione, cf. Gualdo Rosa, "A proposito degli epigrammi," 456 e note.

¹⁵ Per l'importanza del Fascitelli (e di Girolamo Seripando e Scipione Capece) come curatori dell'edizione delle poesie latine del Sannazaro (e non solo), cf. il fol. 2 delle note aggiunte dall'erudito napoletano Gian Vincenzo Meola (1744–1814) in calce all'esemplare della sua edizione che si conserva alla Biblioteca Nazionale di Napoli (ms. XIII B 66 bis = *Honorati Fascitelli Aeserniensis Opera*, Neapoli, 1776): "Annis vero MDXXXIV et MDXXXV, iure dedignatis quas Aldus Pater fecerat carminum editiones nostri Sannazarii, et acceptis per litteras quae purgatiora essent tanti Poete ab Hieronymo Seripando et Scipione Capycio, fere eius a prima aetate fautoribus cum esset Neapoli, in meliorem ordinem et lectionem expurgatissimam digessit, typisque Manutianis prodire fecit, cum hoc titulo: *Sonetti et Canzoni del Sannazaro*, primum, deinde, *Sannazarii Opera latine nuper edita* . . ."; cf. inoltre Vecce, *Iacopo Sannazaro in Francia*, 161–165, e note. Per un buon profilo biografico del Fascitelli, cf. F. Calitti, *Dizionario Biografico degli Italiani* (d'ora in poi *DBI*), 45 (Roma, 1995), 228–231.

¹⁶ Questo manoscritto — come ha rilevato il Vecce (*Iacopo Sannazaro in Francia*, 161, n. 10) — fu donato con altri due autografi sannazariani da Giambattista Crispo a Fulvio Orsini. Per questo codice, oltre a quanto detto dal Vecce, cf. Gualdo Rosa, "A proposito degli epigrammi," 458–459.

condo a quella di Angelo Colocci.[17] Accanto a questo importantissimo codice (d'ora in poi V), in cui alcuni componimenti sono scritti più volte in redazioni diverse, la fase redazionale più antica di molti epigrammi ed elegie sembra in molti casi essere rappresentata dal Vindob. Lat. 9477 (d'ora in poi W), lo zibaldone raccolto dal Sambuco ed attentamente studiato dal Vecce, dove ai fols. 114–141 si leggono molti componimenti lirici del nostro, in parte autografi.[18] Anche qui, come e ancor più che nel codice V, i testi autografi sono irti di correzioni e di riscritture, tanto da risultare in alcuni casi assai poco leggibili; i più leggibili di questi componimenti, rimasti inediti, furono pubblicati nel 1842 da Angelo Mai, che si basava tuttavia non sul codice viennese, ma su un suo tardo apografo vaticano.[19]

Ma torniamo al Marullo ed alla sua presenza nell'opera poetica del Sannazaro. Di lui il Sannazaro parla con affetto nelle due elegie, comprese nell'*editio princeps*, in cui presenta i suoi compagni dell'Accademia pontaniana e ne celebra le virtù morali e poetiche; di queste la più antica è la 1.11, *In maledicos detractores*,[20] su cui ritorneremo, e dove al Marullo sono dedicati i vv. 31–32, in cui si allude solo alle sue poesie liriche sull'esilio:

> Tu quoque, quid cessas doctis deflere querelis
>   Excidium patriae, culte Marulle, tuae?

Più tarda — ma comunque non anteriore al 1501, data della morte di Marullo — deve essere l'elegia 2.2,[21] in cui, in occasione del suo genetliaco, egli torna a celebrare la dotta brigata dei suoi sodali. Qui i versi dedicati al Marullo sono quattro, 25–28:

> Nec gemat exilium Spartani Musa Marulli,
>   Ventura ad nostras ingeniosa dapes.
> Verba sed antiqui reddat numerosque Lucreti,
>   Dum magnis divos laudibus accumulat,

---

[17] Cf. Di Stefano, "Per l'edizione," 27–28 e soprattutto 95–125. Ma sul rapporto Sannazaro-Colocci dovremo ritornare.

[18] Per il codice W, cf. soprattutto Vecce, *Gli zibaldoni*, 9–60, e Di Stefano, "Per l'edizione," 37 e 70–94.

[19] Cf. Mai, "Actii Synceri Sannazarii Carmina," 508–511. L'edizione del Mai si fonda sul codice settecentesco Ottobon. lat. 3172, per il quale cf. Altamura, *La tradizione manoscritta*, 48, e Di Stefano, "Per l'edizione," 32.

[20] Già l' Altamura (*Iacopo Sannazaro, con appendice di documenti e testi inediti* [Napoli, 1951], 172–175) tentava di dare una data ad ogni singola elegia o epigramma, basandosi su elementi interni; per questa elegia egli giustamente proponeva una data anteriore al 1493, anno della morte di Giuniano Maio, che qui compare come ben vivo. Cf. per il Maio, P. Garbini, in Asor Rosa, ed., *Letteratura italiana. Gli autori*, vol. 2 (Torino, 1991), 1110.

[21] L'el. 2.2 è edita, con traduzione italiana e commento, in *Poeti latini del Quattrocento*, ed. F. Arnaldi, L. Gualdo Rosa, e L. Monti Sabia (Milano–Napoli, 1964), 1134–1137. Il *terminus ante quem* per questa elegia è proprio la data di morte del Marullo, e cioè il 1501.

dove si ricordano anche le cure filologiche dedicate dal Marullo al testo di Lucrezio e i suoi *Hymni naturales*, composti negli ultimi anni di vita del poeta e da lui pubblicati nel 1497. Ma accanto a questi ricordi affettuosi, pur abbastanza significativi, il Marullo era presente, come dedicatario, in una redazione antica dell'elegia 1.10, che nell'Aldina e nelle edizioni che ne derivano è dedicata *Ad Ioannem Sangrium, patricium Neapolitanum*, mentre in tutte le redazioni precedenti manca di titolo.

L'elegia 1.10 è una squisita *rêverie* malinconica, sul tema, tipicamente petrarchesco e sannazariano, della propria morte, e morte d'amore; composta sicuramente in età giovanile, sembrerebbe addirittura — se si prende alla lettera il primo distico — risalire ad epoca anteriore alla morte della madre del poeta, Masella Santomango:

> Si me saevus Amor patriis pateretur in oris
> Vivere, vel saltem *matre vidente* mori.[22]

Il componimento è così bello, e riflette così perfettamente la sensibilità del Sannazaro, che in tutte le fasi redazionali è rimasto sostanzialmente immutato; l'unica variante significativa è quella del dedicatario, immaginato come esecutore testamentario delle ultime volontà del poeta, il che ha comportato la successiva riscrittura del v. 17.

W = Vind. Lat. 9447, fol. 115 r–v	V¹ = Vat. Lat. 3361, fol. 11r–v	V² = Vat. lat. 3361, foll. 54v–55	Ald. 1535 Ad Ioannem Sangrium, patricium Neapolitanum, de suo immaturo obitu.
Senza titolo	Senza titolo	Senza titolo	
17 At tu, quandoquidem iubet hoc fortuna, Rabiri	At tu, quandoquidem iubet hoc fortuna, Marulle,	Lepyri *corr. ex* Marulle	At tu, quandoquidem Nemesis iubet, optime Sangri,

Come si può vedere dallo schema, sia nel codice W — dove il testo non è autografo — come nelle due stesure autografe del codice V, l'elegia non ha titolo. Il titolo con dedica si legge solo nell'Aldina, e nelle innumerevoli edizioni che ne derivano.

Il primo dedicatario, Rabirio, sembra essere il nome accademico di un amico degli anni giovanili: un amico non ancora identificato, al quale tuttavia furono dedicate, nella loro primitiva stesura, ben due elegie: l'elegia 1.4, e l'elegia 2.10: la prima nell'edizione definitiva ha il titolo: "Ad Lucinam, parturiente Cornelia Piccolominea,

---

[22] Anche per l'el. 1.10, cf. *Poeti latini*, 1132–1135. La madre del Sannazaro, pianta come morta nell'*Arcadia*, col nome di Massilia, sarebbe morta tra il 1474 e il 1478; cf. F. Tateo, "L'umanesimo meridionale," in C. Muscetta, ed., *Letteratura italiana Laterza,* vol. 16 (Bari, 1972), 190–191.

Antonii Garlonii Allifarum domini coniuge";[23] la seconda, nell'edizione finale non ha dedicatario, mentre nel codice W ha questo titolo: "Mala punica, ad Rabirium egrotantem."[24]

Ma qui è opportuno aprire una parentesi. Il carattere postumo dell'*editio princeps* rende essenziale la ricostruzione delle precedenti fasi redazionali di tutte le liriche latine. Questa indagine è ancora più importante per quei pochi componimenti che — sull'onda del successo della doppia edizione del *De partu Virginis* nel 1526[25] — furono inseriti, in appendice al poema sacro, nelle sette edizioni stampate a Venezia tra il 1527 e il 1533. Per il testo delle elegie, non interessa l'Aldina del 1527, dove si leggono solo quattro epigrammi. Ma nelle successive sei edizioni, è importante studiare la disposizione e la fase redazionale della silloge di cinque elegie (diventate sei a partire dall'edizione dei fratelli Nicolini da Sabbio del 1530), che vi troviamo costantemente, insieme ad un manipolo sempre più cospicuo di epigrammi.[26] Ma sulle redazioni precanoniche delle elegie e sulla loro circolazione, più o meno tacitamente autorizzata dall'autore, ritorneremo. Qui ci premeva sottolineare come la presenza del *sodalis* Rabirio nella prima fase redazionale dell'elegia 1.10 non sia, nella complessa stratificazione dell'opera sannazariana, un fatto isolato.

Mentre nell'elegia 1.4 — che in queste edizioni è sempre al primo posto — Rabirio rimane presente in tutte le numerose redazioni sia manoscritte che a stampa che precedono la *princeps*, nell'elegia 1.10 egli è presto sostituito dal ben più illustre Marullo. Dopo la morte del poeta, il Sannazaro pensò di dedicare l'elegia ad un altro personaggio dai contorni per noi evanescenti; infatti, nella seconda stesura dell'elegia, che si legge in V (V²), al fol. 54v, troviamo nell'interlinea, di mano del Sannazaro, la variante "Lepyri", al posto del "Marulle", cancellato, ma perfettamente leggibile nel testo. Ma chi è questo "Lepirio"? Nel ms. XIII AA 63 della Biblioteca Nazionale di

---

[23] Il titolo della redazione più antica dell'el. 1.4 si legge nella forma più ampia nel ms. Vat. Lat. 2847, fol. 4v: "Ad Lucinam ut puellae Rabirii sodalis parturienti subveniat, precatio." Per questo codice — su cui dovremo ritornare — cf. P. O. Kristeller, *Iter Italicum*, 2 (London–Leiden, 1967), 23b–24a; cf. anche qui, n. 43.

[24] L'elegia fu pubblicata per la prima volta nel 1529, insieme alle Odi latine, ad alcuni epigrammi del Sannazaro e ai carmi latini di Giovanni Cotta e di Marco Antonio Flaminio in un'edizione veneziana anonima, ma che si può senz'altro attribuire ai fratelli Nicolini da Sabbio, col titolo *De malo punico*. Per questa edizione, cf. Di Stefano, "Per l'edizione."

[25] Nel 1526 il *De partu Virginis* fu pubblicato prima a Napoli, nel mese di maggio, "per Antonium Fretiam," e poi a Roma, nel mese di dicembre, "in aedibus P. Minitii Calvi." Cf. Sannazaro, *De partu*, xlv–li.

[26] Le sei edizioni — accuratamente elencate da Perosa-Fantazzi (Sannazaro, *De partu*, xcviii–c) — tutte veneziane, sono le seguenti: 1528, Aldina; 1528, anonima, ma probabilmente dei fratelli Nicolini da Sabbio; 1530, fratelli Nicolini da Sabbio; 1530, Francesco Bindoni e Maffeo Pasini; 1531, Bernardino Stagnino; 1533, Melchiorre Sessa; 1533, Aldina. A partire dalla prima edizione del 1530, alle cinque elegie, che hanno un testo identico e identico ordinamento, se ne aggiunge una sesta, l'el. 2.10, *De malo Punico,* pubblicata per la prima volta nell'ed. del 1529 (cf. qui n. 24). Le cinque elegie si leggono nell'ordine seguente: 1.4 (*Affer opem*); 1.11 (*Quid ruis?*); 1.1 (*Te foecunda*); 1.3 (*Nulla meos*); 1.2 (*Parde, decus*).

Napoli,[27] al fol. 22, si legge un componimento poetico in endecasillabi faleci, indirizzato ad Antonio Seripando e firmato "tuus Hadr.<ianus> Lepyrius." Il Fuiano, che ha pubblicato il componimento, insieme con altri testi che si leggono in questa interessante raccolta, pensa che anche in questo caso si tratti di un nome accademico; tuttavia l'identificazione da lui proposta in via ipotetica non è affatto convincente.[28]

L'ultimo dedicatario, Giovanni di Sangro, è sicuramente da identificare con il "Sangriolus", caro a Decio Apranio e ad Antonio Seripando, e molto presente nelle lettere e nei componimenti poetici dello zibaldone dei Seripando;[29] egli è ricordato affettuosamente, insieme all'Apranio, anche da Girolamo Carbone in una importante elegia da lui indirizzata ad Agostino Nifo, in cui si dà un quadro dettagliato di quella "seconda Accademia Pontaniana" che nei primi decenni del '500 tentava, tra Roma e Napoli, di mantenere in vita gli ideali estetico-cortigiani dell'antica "sodalitas".[30] Così l'elegia 1.10, che è come un testamento spirituale del Sannazaro, cambia successivamente il suo destinatario, passando da Rabirio a Marullo, e da questi al fantomatico Lepirio, per approdare infine a quel Giovanni di Sangro che fu tra gli esecutori testamentari del poeta napoletano:[31] questo mutamento di nomi, nelle diverse fasi redazionali, scandisce le diverse tappe di un complesso percorso esistenziale.

Tra le poesie escluse dall'edizione definitiva, c'è un epigramma in trimetri giambici scazonti, che si legge solo, autografo, e ricco di correzioni e cancellature, nel codice W.[32] E' un delizioso componimento, di schietta impronta catulliana: decisamente catulliano è il verso iniziale, che ricorda l'apertura del carme 22, come catulliano è il

---

[27] Si tratta di un codice composito, che raccoglie lettere e poesie autografe, di mani e formato diversi, indirizzate ai fratelli Antonio e Girolamo Seripando o da loro composte. Da questo manoscritto Gian Vincenzo Meola trascrisse, ai fols. 33–55 del ms. V E 53 della Biblioteca Nazionale di Napoli, una raccolta di poesie latine dal titolo: "Clarissimorum aevi Caroli Caesaris V poetarum carmina, ex schedis Seripandi Cardinalis, in Bibliotheca S. Io. ad Carbonariam, quae nunc in Regiam Bibliothecam deductae sunt." Per il Meola, cf. A. Nunziana, "Interrogativi su Gian Vincenzo Meola: uno spregiudicato falsario o un erudito perseguitato dalla sfortuna?" *Quaderni dell'Istituto Nazionale di studi per il Rinascimento meridionale* 11 (1996): 43–75. Per il codice, che contiene anche un fascicolo di mano di Antonio Serassi, cf. anche C. Vecce, "Esercizi di traduzione nella Napoli del Rinascimento. I. Sannazaro e Pindaro," *Annali dell'Istituto Universitario Orientale, Sezione romanza* 31 (1989): 324, n. 16.

[28] Cf. M. Fuiano, *Insegnamento e cultura a Napoli nel Rinascimento* (Napoli, 1973), 166–167.

[29] Cf. Fuiano, *Insegnamento e cultura*, 165–166, dove si legge un componimento poetico a lui dedicato, probabilmente da Antonio Seripando.

[30] Cf. P. de Montera, *L'humaniste napolitain Girolamo Carbone et ses poésies inédites* (Napoli, 1936), el. 30, vv. 61–62: "Nam quis Aprani, qui te, placidissime Sangri, / Ignoret curas demere saepe meas?" Per Giovanni, figlio di Lucido di Sangro e di Lucrezia Spinelli ed esattamente identificato dal Montera, cf. F. Campanile, *L'historia dell'illustrissima famiglia di Sangro* (Napoli, 1615), 67–68. Il nome di Giovanni di Sangro non figura nell'edizione ufficiale di Minieri Riccio, *Biografie degli accademici alfonsini*, ma si legge nei ritagli del giornale *Italia reale* del 1880, che si conservano alla BN di Napoli, S.Q. XXXIII.C 40, 37.

[31] Cf. Percopo, *Vita*, 194.

[32] Ms. W, fol. 137 r–v, trascritto nel ms. Ottobon. Lat. 3172, fol. 171 r–v ed edito in Mai, "Actii Sannazarii Carmina," 510–511. Qualche correzione all'ed. del Mai in Altamura, *Jacopo Sannazaro*, 170–171. Cf. anche Altamura, *La tradizione*, 48.

cinediorem del v. 30.³³ E soprattutto catulliana è la presentazione che in questo epigramma, sicuramente giovanile, egli fa — ai vv. 15–19 — del piccolo gruppo dei suoi *sodales*: come i *poetae novi* cari a Catullo, anche il membri della *sodalitas* napoletana sono presentati qui come dei giovani spensierati e pronti allo scherzo, ma al tempo stesso ben consapevoli della loro superiore dignità di poeti, prediletti di Apollo e delle Muse. La stessa scelta del modello catulliano è un significativo omaggio al Marullo, che nel primo libro degli *Epigrammi* si rifaceva esplicitamente al poeta veronese.³⁴ Ma accanto a Catullo, non mancano citazioni preziose di altre fonti. Così al v. 11 i rari attributi *pexatus* e *coccinatus* sono due sapienti riferimenti a due epigrammi di Marziale³⁵ mentre al v. 17 il *virens Aon*, identificato con l'Elicona caro alle Muse, è un chiaro richiamo alla *Lyra* del Pontano.³⁶

Non mi è stato per ora possibile identificare questo *Priscus*, sciocco e borioso, che, venuto a Napoli da Roma, si era circondato di schiamazzanti filosofi e che, pur avendo incontrato il *parvulus coetus* dei pontaniani, dichiarava che a Napoli non aveva visto né poeti, né oratori. Abbiamo tuttavia un *terminus post quem* per la composizione di questo epigramma; infatti i due epiteti marzialiani che si leggono qui al v. 11 furono trascritti dal Sannazaro nel suo *Repertorium* edito dal Vecce e sono stati sicuramente tratti dall'edizione veneziana del 1482 degli epigrammi di Marziale, col commento di Domizio Calderini, il cui esemplare, utilizzato dal Sannazaro e da lui annotato, si conserva alla Biblioteca Nazionale di Napoli.³⁷ Il *terminus ante quem* potrebbe essere la data della partenza di Marullo da Napoli, e cioè al più tardi il 1486.

Pochi anni dopo la composizione dell'elegia 1.10 (1476c) e dell'epigramma *De Prisco* (1482–1486), si colloca la prima redazione dell'elegia 1.11, che nell'edizione Aldina ha il titolo, molto generico, *In maledicos detractores*.³⁸ Si tratta, come abbiamo già detto, di una delle due elegie in cui il Sannazaro ci dà un dettagliato elenco dei suoi compagni di Accademia, e tra le due è senz'altro la più antica. Come ha sottolineato il De Caprio, per tutto il secolo XV quelle che si sogliono definire accademie

---

³³ Catullo, 22.1:0 "Suffenus iste, Vare, quem probe nosti" e, per il v. 30, Catullo, 10.24: "Hic illa, ut decuit *cinaediorem*."

³⁴ Basterà a questo proposito citare gli epigrammi 30 e 31, che il Poliziano, non ancora ostile a Marullo, compose in suo onore, dedicandoli al suo protettore fiorentino, Lorenzo di Pierfrancesco de' Medici; cf. *Poeti latini*, 1008–1009.

³⁵ Per *pexatus*, cf. Marziale, 2.58, v. 1; per *coccinatus*, Marziale, 3.2, v. 11. Entrambe le parole sono annotate e commentate dal Sannazaro nel *Repertorium rerum antiquarum*, che il Vecce ha pubblicato, traendolo dal ms. Vindobon. Lat. 9477 (W). Cf. Vecce, *Gli zibaldoni*, 167, linn. 118–119 (*pexatus*) e 169, linn. 202–203 (*coccinatus*).

³⁶ Per *Aon*, considerato sinonimo di Elicona, cf. Pontano, *Lyra*, 3.14 e 12.6, in L. Monti Sabia, "La *Lyra* di Giovanni Pontano, edita secondo l'autografo codice Reginense latino 1527," *Rendiconti dell'Accademia di Archeologia, Lettere e Belle Arti di Napoli* 47 (1972): 39, 56.

³⁷ Si tratta di un esemplare dell'edizione di Marziale, col commento di Domizio Calderini (Venezia, 1482), che si conserva alla Biblioteca Nazionale di Napoli (S.Q. X.D.26). Cf. Vecce, *Gli zibaldoni*, 41, n. 2.

³⁸ Pubblico l'elegia in Appendice, 2, seguendo il testo dell'edizione olandese del 1728 (cf. Sannazarii *Opera*, 116–117). Per questa importante edizione, curata dal filologo belga Peter Vlaming, che ha ristampato le note di Johann Broekhuizen, cf. Sannazaro, *De partu*, cxix–cxx.

non avevano il carattere formalizzato ed organizzato che assumeranno a partire dalla seconda metà del '500. E' certo tuttavia che i vari cenacoli umanistici si andavano definendo non solo in base ad una precisa identità in positivo, ma anche, se non soprattutto, in funzione polemica nei confronti di altri gruppi rivali. In questo senso, dunque, un'elegia come la 1.11, che è una vera e propria invettiva, ha un significato tutto speciale, per caratterizzare gli ideali estetici e morali della *sodalitas* pontaniana. Tanto più che proprio questa elegia, così poco elegiaca, è stata inserita al secondo posto della piccola silloge, pubblicata, in redazione precanonica, in appendice al *De partu Virginis*: lo studio della sua tradizione manoscritta ci può aprire uno spiraglio sulla formazione di questa raccolta, e sulla sua circolazione, in ambienti legati agli ideali politici ed estetici dell'Accademia pontaniana.

La più antica redazione dell'elegia 1.11 non si legge nel codice W; come si può osservare dall'apparato, il codice del Sambuco ci dà solo i vv. 1–35, che si leggono, autografi, ma con qualche lacuna, al fol. 130r–v; essi ci conservano la redazione finale del testo, accolta nella *princeps*; lo dimostra la lezione *Ioviani* del v. 15 e soprattutto la presenza dei vv. 25–26, che in V si leggono solo a margine, con la variante *Concelebretque suae*, al fol. 7v. Evidentemente il materiale sannazariano che il Sambuco si procurò a Napoli nel suo soggiorno del 1562–1563, conteneva, accanto a molti abbozzi giovanili e a testi rimasti inediti, anche alcuni *specimina* di quella redazione definitiva che fu utilizzata dai curatori dell'Aldina del 1535.[39]

Uno dei tramiti tra i pontaniani rimasti a Napoli e i circoli culturali romani fu indubbiamente l'umanista Angelo Colocci, che fu membro dell'Accademia pontaniana, raccoglitore appassionato di epigrammi neolatini e presente — come abbiamo visto — anche nel codice V.[40] E dalla biblioteca del Colocci provengono i due più autorevoli manoscritti vaticani che ci conservano in redazione precanonica l'elegia 1.11: il Vat. Lat. 2836 (A)[41] e il Vat. Lat. 2847 (B); un terzo codice, il Vat. Lat. 6250 (C), è decisamente più tardo e probabilmente *descriptus* non da qualcuna delle edizioni precanoniche — come erroneamente ipotizza la Di Stefano — ma dallo stesso codice B.[42]

---

[39] Per Giovanni Sambuco (János Zsámboky, 1531–1584) e per il suo fruttuoso soggiorno napoletano, cf. Vecce, *Gli zibaldoni*, 11–22.

[40] Per Angelo Colocci (Jesi, 1474–Roma, 1549), cf. S. Lattès, "Recherches sur la bibliothèque d'Angelo Colocci," *École Française de Rome, Mélanges d'Archéologie et d'Histoire* 48 (1931): 308–344; A. Campana, "Angelo Colocci conservatore ed editore di letteratura neolatina," in *Atti del convegno di studi su Angelo Colocci. Jesi, 13–14 settembre 1969* (Jesi, 1972), 257–272; cf. infine, voce redazionale in *DBI*, 27 (Roma, 1982), 105–111. Fu senz'altro membro dell'Accademia pontaniana; il suo nome non figura nella pubblicazione più nota del Minieri Riccio, ma come "Colucci <sic> Basso Angelo," nei ritagli dell'*Italia reale* (n. 30), fol. 40.

[41] Per il Vat. Lat. 2836, cf. Kristeller, *Iter*, 2, 353a; Altamura, *La tradizione*, 46–47; e Di Stefano, "Per l'edizione," 24. Del Sannazaro il codice contiene solo, ai foll. 123–124r, le elegie 1.2 e 1.11, oltre ad una ventina di epigrammi, divisi tra loro in base al contenuto.

[42] Per il Vat. Lat. 6250, cf. Kristeller, *Iter*, 2, 339a; M. Vattasso, "I codici molziani della Biblioteca Vaticana, con un'appendice di carmi inediti o rari," in *Miscellanea A. M. Ceriani* (Milano, 1910), 540–541.

All'interno di questa tradizione precanonica, il codice B è comunque il più antico ed autorevole. Come molti altri zibaldoni colocciani, anche B è un codice composito, frutto dell'assemblaggio di fascicoli di mani ed epoche diverse.[43] Nel primo fascicolo, i fols. 1–9v sono scritti in una bella corsiva calligrafica, che è sicuramente da attribuire ad un copista di buona e solida formazione: i titoli e qualche nota marginale sono scritti dalla stessa mano in un inchiostro rosso assai scolorito. La raccolta si apre (foll. 1r–2v) con otto epigrammi.[44] Seguono le cinque elegie della raccolta precanonica, in una disposizione diversa e con titoli più ampi e dettagliati di quelli delle redazioni successive: foll. 2r–3r: "Acci Sinceri Nazarij Neapolitani ad puellam de foederibus inter se et illam iunctis, elegia prima" (= El. 1.3); foll. 3r–4r: "Eiusdem Accij ad Io. Pardum philosophum ac poetam clarissimum de animi sui voto ad vitam rusticam" (= El. 1.2); fol. 4r–v "Ioannis Pardi Hispani philosophi doctissimi ad Accium Sincerum responsio"; foll. 4v–5r: "Acci Sinceri ad Lucinam ut puellae Rabirii sodalis parturienti subveniat precatio, Elegia tertia" (= El. 1.4); foll. 5r–6v: "Acci Sinceri ad Lucium Crassum Neapolitanum, amicum suavissimum, de mora eius ad Petrinum oppidum" (= El. 1.1); foll. 7r–8v: "Eiusdem Accii in livides detractores, Scucchae grammatici alumnos, homicidas furesque nocturnos" (= El. 1.11). La silloge si chiude

---

[43] La sezione sannazariana del codice si chiude col fol. 11v (bianco); i foll. 12–163 contengono varie raccolte (di mani ed epoche diverse) di poemetti, elegie, ed epigrammi dell'umanista ungherese Janus Pannonius; foll. 164–172: Petri Gravinae Canonici Neapolitani *Poema ad illustrissimi Consalvi Ferdinandi Magni invictique ducis gloriam et immortalitatem*; foll. 173r–174v: epigrammi di vari autori, di mano del Colocci; fol. 175r–v: lettera di Blosius Palladius, dat. "Romae, die XVI octobris 1516"; foll. 176–177: Io. Fr. Picus Petro Bembo, lettera, dat. "Romae, tertio decimo Kal. Octobris MDXII"; foll. 180–189: acquarelli simbolici, che illustrano la storia dell'utilizzazione, presso diversi popoli antichi, della quercia come albero sacro; fol. 190: splendida raffigurazione di un rinoceronte; foll. 191–199: commento storico alle illustrazioni precedenti (tese evidentemente alla celebrazione dello stemma dei Della Rovere), con ampie citazioni di fonti classiche; foll. 201–228: Galli Epidii Romani *De Viridario Augustini Chisii Patritii Senensis Vera libellus* . . . Impressum Romae per Stephanum Guillereti et Herculem Nani consocium, Anno Domini MDXI; foll. 229–240v: scrittura semigotica, s. XIV ex./XVin.: Magistri Christiani de Camerino *Super contiones partium guelfe et gibelline et ipsarum obiurgatione*, poemetto in esametri (inc.: "Impia terribili nunc tempestate furentum"). Per questo importante manoscritto, oltre al Kristeller (*Iter*, 2, 23b–24a), cf. L. Juhász, *Commentatio critica ad edendas Jani Pannonii Elegias* (Szeged, 1929), 16–17; idem, *Quaestiones criticae de epigrammatibus Iani Pannonii* (Roma, 1929), 23–24; G. Santangelo, "La polemica fra Pietro Bembo e Gian Francesco Pico intorno al principio dell'imitazione," *Rinascimento* n.s. 1 (1950): 332–334; M. Dewar, "Encomium of Agostino Chigi and Pope Julius II in the *Suburbanum Augustini Chigi* of Blosius Palladius," *Res publica litterarum* 14 (1991): 61–68.

[44] Ecco, nell'ordine, gli epigrammi, con i rispettivi titoli: *De Alphonso, Calabrum duce, exercitum ducente per Apennini iugum in Xistum quartum Pontificem Maximum* (1.37); *De Diana, Iove et Amore* (2.23); *De Luna, Pane et Endimione* (1.18); *De Iove et Cupidine* (2.50); *De Pane, Luna et Syringe* (2.1); *De Venere et Priapo* (2.13); *De Cyparisso et Apolline* (1.49); *De Venere et Pallade* (1.17). Nell'ed. Aldina 1527, si leggono solo tre di questi epigrammi (2.13, 1.17 e 1.49) + l'ep. 1.36 (*De mirabili urbe Venetiis*); in quella del 1528 (fols. 3–4), gli epigrammi che coincidono sono sette: 2.13, 1.17, 1.49, 2.56, 2.23, 1.18, 2.7 + l'ep. 1.36 e gli epp. 2.10 (*De Summontii pietate*) e 3.9 (*Ad patriam, antequam iret in exilium*). Manca solo l'ep. 1.37, che compare a partire dall'ed. Venetiis 1530, col titolo banalizzato: *De Alphonso, duce Calabriae.*

con una lettera di Gabriele Altilio al Chariteo, che è un vero e proprio commento dell'elegia 1.11:[45] di questa lettera — pubblicata più volte — B è il solo testimone manoscritto. Nell'inviare all'amico una copia dell'elegia sannazariana, l'Altilio la presenta come la risposta — straordinariamente pacata ed elegante — del Sannazaro alle invettive lanciate contro i pontaniani da anonimi κακολόγοι. La lettera non ci fornisce purtroppo elementi per identificare gli infami detrattori, paragonati dall'Altilio a ragni velenosi o a topi infetti, e nemmeno per una datazione precisa. Altrettanto deludente a questo scopo è la lettura della canzone che lo stesso Chariteo, sollecitato evidentemente dalla lettera dell'Altilio, scrisse in volgare, parafrasando, anche nel titolo (*Risposta del Chariteo contra li malivoli*), l'elegia del Sannazaro:[46] secondo il Percopo, che pubblica e commenta la canzone del Chariteo, il testo anonimo che aveva suscitato le ire dei pontaniani sarebbe una composizione poetica dal titolo "Triumphi", in stile petrarchesco. Non è questo il luogo per un'analisi dettagliata di queste due composizioni, che abbiamo ricordato perché esse servono a sottolineare l'importanza dell'elegia 1.11, che ai contemporanei apparve come un vero e proprio manifesto programmatico della poetica pontaniana.

Il *terminus ante quem* per datare questa elegia è — come aveva già osservato l'Altamura — il 20 aprile 1493, data in cui Giuniano Maio era sicuramente morto, come si ricava da un documento pubblicato dal Percopo.[47] Nell'elegia il venerato maestro è presentato al centro della dotta brigata (vv. 33–36); prima sono ricordati il Pontano (vv. 15–16), Gabriele Altilio (vv. 17–18), Pietro Golino, detto il Compare (vv. 19–20), Elisio Calenzio, soprannominato Galluccio (vv. 21–22), Andrea Matteo Acquaviva, duca di Atri (vv. 23–24), Leonardo Corvino (vv. 27–28), Giovanni Albino (vv. 29–30), e Michele Marullo (vv. 31–32).[48] Seguono, con elegante parallelismo,

---

[45] La lettera (foll. 8v–9v) ha l'*inscriptio*, in rosso: "Gabriel Altilius, Episcopus Polycastrensis ac ill. Principis Campani ab Epistolis, Chariteo amico charissimo." L'Altilio — per il quale cf. F. Nicolini, *DBI*, 2 (Roma, 1960), 505–506 — divenne vescovo di Policastro l'8 gennaio 1493; tuttavia non è affatto escluso che la lettera sia precedente alla nomina e che il titolo sia stato aggiunto dal copista. La lettera fu pubblicata per la prima volta, insieme con la risposta poetica di Giovanni Pardo all' 1.2 del Sannazaro, nell'edizione del *De partu Virginis* del 1531 (Venetiis, 1531); poi in Sannazarii *Opera*, 595–596, fra le note di Petrus Vlamingius; cf. inoltre Benedetto Gareth, detto il Chariteo, *Rime*, ed. E. Percopo (Napoli, 1892), app. XI, 192–193; e Gabriele Altilio, *Poesie*, ed. G. Lamattina (Salerno, 1978), 145–147.

[46] Per la canzone, cf. Benedetto Gareth, *Rime*, 355–367.

[47] Cf. E. Percopo, "Nuovi documenti su gli scrittori e gli artisti dei tempi aragonesi, con un profilo dell'autore," ed. M. Del Treppo, *Archivio Storico delle province Napoletane* 19 (1894): 756 (rist. Napoli, 1997), 127, doc. LIX. Per Giuniano Maio, oltre al prezioso saggio del Percopo, cf. P. Garbini, in Asor Rosa, ed., *Letteratura italiana. Gli autori*, vol. 2, 1110.

[48] Per Pietro Golino, detto "il Compare" (*Petrus Compater*), cf. A. Altamura, *L'umanesimo nel Mezzogiorno d'Italia. Storia, bibliografia e testi inediti* (Firenze, 1941), 56–57; per Elisio Calenzio, detto Galluccio con una curiosa inversione, certificata dal suo testamento, cf. S. Foà, "Gallucci Luigi (Elisio Calenzio)," *DBI*, 51 (Roma, 1998), 743–745; per Andrea Matteo Acquaviva, duca di Atri (1458–1529), cf. M. Perugini, in Asor Rosa, ed., *Letteratura italiana. Gli autori*, vol. 1 (Torino: Einaudi, 1990), 23. Leonardo Cermini da Cerbara, detto Corvino, "clericus Barchinonensis," fu vescovo di Montepeloso dal 1491 e poi di Trivento dal 21 febbraio 1498, fino

Benedetto Gareth, detto il Chariteo (vv. 37–38), Francesco Pucci, che nella redazione finale sarà sostituito da Francesco Elio Marchese, zio di Cassandra (vv. 39–40), Francesco Scala (vv. 41–42), Rutilio Zenone (vv. 43–44), Giovanni Pardo (vv. 47–48), e alla fine lo stesso Sannazaro, cui sono consacrati i vv. 51–54.[49] Abbiamo volutamente escluso dall'elenco Troiano Cabanilla, o Cavaniglia (vv. 25–26) e Girolamo Carbone (vv. 45–46), i cui nomi furono aggiunti — come si nota dall'apparato — in un secondo più tardo rifacimento.[50]

La centralità del vecchio maestro, che regge la sua verga professorale come uno scettro regale, non ha solo una funzione architettonica. Se leggiamo infatti il titolo più ampio, che si legge solo in B, vediamo che i "malevoli detrattori" sono definiti "Scucchae grammatici alumnos, homicidas furesque nocturnos." Si tratta dunque, ancora una volta, di un componimento indirizzato contro i grammatici, da accostare ai due famosi epigrammi 1.66 e 1.67, che il Sannazaro compose contro il Poliziano, e su cui ci siamo fermati in altra sede.[51] Il *terminus post quem* per la datazione di questa elegia è dunque, senza alcun dubbio, il settembre del 1489, data di pubblicazione della prima centuria dei *Miscellanea* del Poliziano. Qui tuttavia la posizione preminente assegnata al Maio e la presenza del Pucci (poi sostituito da un altro poeta-filologo, Francesco Elio Marchese) ci fa capire che l'invettiva non è genericamente indirizzata contro i grammatici troppo pedanti, ma che si tratta di una precisa e netta contrapposizione tra due modi diversi di concepire la grammatica e la filologia.[52]

Ma chi è il grammatico che Sannazaro chiama *Scuccha* e chi sono i suoi discepoli, definiti "assassini e ladri notturni"? Se si leggono i ruoli dei professori di discipline umanistiche che insegnarono a Napoli in quegli anni, si nota che l'unico nome pos-

---

al 16 marzo 1502, quando fu sostituito "per obitum" da Tommaso Caracciolo. La sua origine catalana, sostenuta dal Dionisotti ("Miscellanea umanistica transalpina," *Giornale Storico della Letteratura Italiana* 110 [1937]: 262–267) è confermata, senza ombra di dubbio, dalla canzone del Chariteo, vv. 224–226 (cf. Benedetto Gareth, *Rime*, 367): "Et tu Corvino mio, per ch'io ti mostro / Che di sangue et d'amor son teco giunto, / Parla di me con penna et con inchiostro"; infine per Giovanni Albino (1456–1520c.), cf. *DBI*, 2 (Roma, 1960), 85–86.

[49] Per Benedetto Gareth, detto il Chariteo (1450c.–1514), oltre alla preziosa edizione curata dal Percopo, cf. F. Tateo, *L'umanesimo meridionale*, 121–133, e M. Moschella, in Asor Rosa, ed., *Letteratura italiana. Gli autori*, vol. 1, 537–538; per Francesco Pucci (Firenze, 1463–Roma, 1512), cf. Percopo, "Nuovi documenti," 59–78; per Francesco Elio Marchese (1430c.–1517), cf. P. Rocchi, in Asor Rosa, ed., *Letteratura italiana. Gli autori*, vol. 2, 1137. Per Francesco Scala o Scales (m. prima del 1497), cf. Minieri Riccio, *Biografie*, 27–33; per Rutilio Zenone, cf. Percopo, "Nuovi documenti," 98–101; per Giovanni Pardo, cf. Percopo, "Nuovi documenti," 173–182, e Altamura, *L'umanesimo meridionale*, 58–59.

[50] Per Troiano Cabanilla (Cavaniglia), conte di Troia e Montella, dedicatario dei *Salices*, cf. *Poeti latini*, 1137; cfr. inoltre Minieri Riccio, in *Italia reale*, fol. 27r–v. Per Girolamo Carbone (1465c.–1528), oltre alla bella monografia del Montera, cf. R. Pastore, *DBI*, 19 (Roma, 1976), 695–696.

[51] Cf. Gualdo Rosa, "L'Académie Pontanienne," 212–215.

[52] Cf. V. Fera, "Il dibattito umanistico sui *Miscellanea*," in *Agnolo Poliziano poeta, scrittore e filologo. Atti del Convegno Internazionale di Studi, Montepulciano, 3–6 novembre 1994*, ed. V. Fera e M. Martelli (Firenze, 1998), 334–362.

sibile, al di fuori di Giuniano Maio e di Francesco Pucci, perfettamente integrati nel cenacolo pontaniano, è quello del milanese Aurelio Bienato.⁵³ Dopo aver insegnato grammatica e retorica allo Studio di Napoli dal 1470 al 1480, il Bienato ottenne diversi privilegi ecclesiastici, fino a diventare, nel 1485, vescovo di Martirano (Catanzaro). Il favore di cui godette a corte, anche dopo la condanna a morte del suo protettore Antonello Petrucci (1486), è testimoniato dal fatto che egli fu, fino al 1490, precettore di don Pietro d'Aragona, secondogenito del duca di Calabria Alfonso e di Isabella Maria Sforza. Compose un'epitome dei sei libri delle *Elegantiae* del Valla, più volte ristampata, ed un commento alle *Institutiones* di Quintiliano, di cui si conserva una parte in un codice napoletano.⁵⁴ Il Bienato fu coinvolto, nella notte del 20 febbraio del 1490, in un grave fatto di sangue. Come ci racconta il Leostello, il duca Alfonso "ebbe nova che lo mastro dell'Illustre Signoria Don Pietro, suo figlio, che era episcopo et chiamavasi per nome M. Aurelio, poeta excellentissimo et docto, avea ferito malamente uno suo preite con una sua spada in li fianchi, et, per sospecto di non venire in mano della Corte, se ferio se medesmo in la gola con un rasoro." Il duca fece portare i due feriti a Castel Nuovo e li fece curare dal suo medico personale.⁵⁵ Non sappiamo cosa sia successo al prete. Certo il Bienato guarì e riconquistò i favori della corte, tanto che il 25 aprile del 1492 ebbe l'incarico di leggere in Santa Maria la Nova, alla presenza dei sovrani, l'elogio funebre di Lorenzo de' Medici.⁵⁶ L'orazione, edita dal Capialbi, è un caldo elogio non solo di Lorenzo, ma anche di Firenze, considerata come la vera e sola madre della rinascita degli studi letterari ed artistici.

E' ovvio che un grammatico, seguace e ammiratore del Valla, esaltatore dell'umanesimo fiorentino e per di più commentatore di Quintiliano, non poteva essere gradito ai nostri pontaniani, impegnati, proprio nel 1490, in un'aspra polemica contro il Poliziano, che del Valla era considerato il più autorevole seguace. L'ostilità era senz'altro reciproca; basta leggere l'introduzione all'*Epitoma* del Bienato indirizzata al discepolo Sebastiano degli Agostini: accanto all'esaltazione del Valla, vi troviamo tutto il disprezzo per coloro che non condividono le sue teorie. Particolare interesse ha il passaggio in cui si polemizza contro coloro che studiano le parole rare ed arcaiche: "Quod si aliqua preter illius (*scil.* del Valla) preceptionem in autoribus antiquis legeris, nihil te moveant; illa adeo rara sunt, ut potius licentiose cuidam autoritati ascribenda,

---

⁵³ Cf. V. Capialbi, *Memorie di Rutilio Zeno e Aurelio Bienato* (Napoli, 1848); Percopo, "Nuovi documenti," 102–109; M. Miglio, *DBI*, 10 (Roma, 1968), 369–370.

⁵⁴ Cf. Aurelii Bienati *Elegantiarum epithomata in sex libros Laurentii Vallae disertissimi*. L'opera ebbe tre edizioni napoletane nel '400; la prima, da attribuire a Francesco di Dino, è del 1479/1480; la seconda, di Francesco del Tuppo, del 1488; e la terza, di Christian Preller, del 1491. Cf. M. Santoro, *La stampa a Napoli nel Quattrocento* (Napoli, 1984), 102–103. Il codice, dove si legge il commento parziale del Bienato alle *Institutiones oratoriae* di Quintiliano, datato 1475/1476, è il ms. della Biblioteca Nazionale di Napoli V D 30, foll. 34–216, per il quale cf. Kristeller, *Iter Italicum* 1 (London–Leiden, 1963), 415b.

⁵⁵ Cf. J. P. Leostello, "Effemeridi delle cose fatte per il Duca di Calabria," in G. Filangieri, *Documenti per la storia, le arti e le industrie delle province napoletane* 1 (Napoli, 1883), 307.

⁵⁶ Cf. Capialbi, *Memorie*, 71–86.

quam ratione usquam comprobanda videantur. Quem igitur — si placet — de posteris cum hoc (*scil.* col Valla) conferes? An Servium, an Priscianum, ab eo merito toties castigatos? An Papiam, an Marcellum, quibus satius fuisset tacere?"[57] Sicché quando a Napoli cominciò a circolare una composizione poetica anonima, piena di malevole critiche contro i pontaniani, questi risalirano facilmente al Bienato (definito dal Leostello "poeta ecellentissimo") e ai suoi discepoli. E poiché il Bienato era stato coinvolto in un brutto fatto di cronaca, l'occasione fu colta al volo dal Sannazaro per definire globalmente lui e i suoi discepoli "homicidae furesque nocturni." Accanto agli insulti indirizzati contro i discepoli dello Scucca-Bienato, creature delle tenebre, immersi nella paludi dello Stige, allevati dalle Erinni, contrapposti all'eletta schiera dei pontaniani, luminosi seguaci di Apollo e delle Muse, altri elementi interni mi sembrano alludere alla rissa sanguinosa in cui era stato coinvolto il Bienato.

Ai vv. 7–8, si legge:

> An monet hoc Stygiis immersus Scucca lacunis
> Dum flens Eumenidum verbera torta timet?

Il Bienato era rinchiuso a Castel dell'Ovo, affidato alle cure del medico di corte; ma non è improbabile che — come del resto dice esplicitamente lo stesso Leostello — egli potesse temere una qualche severa punizione per il suo gesto sconsiderato. Più avanti, ai vv. 59–60, nel descrivere le male arti introdotte dai seguaci dello Scucca nella pacifica Partenope, il Sannazaro aggiunge:

> Nocturnisque dolis agitate et caedibus urbem
> Perque fora infestam reddite, perque vias.

Anche qui l'allusione alla cronaca mi sembra molto precisa.

Il codice B è utile anche perché sui suoi margini si leggono, in un inchiostro rosso molto scolorito, i nomi completi dei pontaniani ricordati nel testo. Così possiamo identificare con sicurezza in Francesco Scala, lo Scala ricordato ai vv. 41–42, che ancora il Broekhuizen (Janus Broukhusius), nel suo commento seicentesco, pubblicato da Peter Vlaming nel 1728, identificava erroneamente con il fiorentino Bartolomeo Scala.[58] Si tratta dello stesso Scala o Scales, cui il Marullo dedica l'ep. I 9 ("Scala, delicium tui Marulli"), autorevole funzionario al servizio dei sovrani aragonesi, e membro dell'Accademia pontaniana.[59]

---

[57] Aurelii Bienati *Elegantiarum Epithomata* (Napoli, 1479–1480), fol. ii. L'esemplare che ho visto a Napoli (BN, S.Q. VII B 30), ha i fogli non numerati. Oggetto delle critiche del Bienato sembra essere proprio Giuniano Maio, che nel 1475 pubblicò a Napoli il *De priscorum proprietate verborum*, in cui si attingeva abbondantemente proprio ai grammatici qui così aspramente scherniti.

[58] Cf. Sannazarii *Opera*, 124–125. Per una corretta identificazione, cf. Michaelis Marulli *Carmina*, ed. A. Perosa (Turici, 1951), 257.

[59] L'identificazione esatta è già in Capialbi, *Memorie*, 19–22. Un più preciso riferimento al codice W ai molti pontaniani amici dello Scala nell'introduzione del Percopo a Benedetto Gareth, *Rime*, ccxi.

Questa identificazione ci serve anche per correggere l'*inscriptio* di una bella elegia ("Dic mihi tam grato quid volvis, Scala, recessu?"), ingiustamente esclusa dall'edizione canonica, elegia che nel codice W è dedicata ad un Fulvio Scala non meglio identificato, mentre nell'autografo V, manca come al solito di intestazione. Basandosi sul codice viennese, il Mai la pubblicò con l'*inscriptio* misteriosa. Molto opportunamente il Percopo suggeriva di correggere il Fulvio in Francesco; ma l'Altamura, nel commentare l'elegia nella sua monografia sul Sannazaro, difendeva l'intestazione del codice, fondandosi sulla sua presunta autografia.[60] Purtroppo per l'Altamura e fortunatamente per noi, la famosa *inscriptio* "Ad Fulvium Scalam" che si legge al fol. 120v di W non è affatto autografa, per cui il *Fulvium* può e deve essere corretto in *Franciscum,* sulla base anche della nota marginale di B, oltre che della logica storica e dell'analisi del testo.

Abbiamo visto quanto importante e autorevole sia il codice B. A questo punto non mi sembra azzardato avanzare l'ipotesi che la raccolta, che si legge ai foll. 1r–9v, sia stata amorosamente preparata e fatta trascrivere da un esperto copista, proprio per il Chariteo (cui è indirizzata la lettera dell'Altilio, che si conserva solo in B), un poeta che — anche per le sue origini catalane — rimase fedele per tutta la vita agli ideali poetici dell'Accademia e al ricordo nostalgico della dinastia aragonese; e che proprio il Chariteo l'abbia portata con sé, quando nel 1501, dopo la caduta definitiva dei sovrani aragonesi, egli si trasferì a Roma, entrando a far parte del circolo del Colocci.[61]

Ma il fascicolo sannazariano del codice B non si conclude con la lettera dell'Altilio. I foll. 10r–11r (il fol. 11v è bianco) contengono infatti, scritti da una mano diversa, in una scrittura corsiva e personale e senza titoli rubricati, alcuni componimenti sannazariani più tardi. Il primo, al fol. 10r–v è la *Fabula de salicibus Sarno amni imminentibus*: si tratta dell'epillio *Salices*, dedicato a Troiano Cabanilla, e stampato, a partire dall'*editio princeps* del *De partu Virginis,* dopo la quinta ecloga.[62] Seguono, al fol. 11r, due epigrammi, databili entrambi agli anni 1502/1503. Il primo è l'ep. 1.14 che qui ha il titolo *De tauro et ursis*, mentre nell'edizione definitiva avrà quello, assai più banale, *De Borgia, Alexandri pontificis filio*. Come si ricava dal contenuto, l'epigramma fu scritto quando Cesare Borgia, dopo la morte del padre, nell'autunno del 1503, si era rifugiato in Castel S. Angelo, dove era assediato da quegli stessi Orsini, che poco

---

[60] Cf. Altamura, *Jacopo Sannazaro,* 170–171 e n. 1.

[61] Il Chariteo, dopo la cacciata definitiva dei Francesi (maggio 1503), tornò a Napoli, dove rimase fino alla morte (1514). Per le vicende biografiche del Chariteo in quegli anni, cf. Percopo, in Benedetto Gareth, *Rime,* xxxviii–xxxix. Che egli sia l'autore o il destinatario della raccolta di componimenti sannazariani che si leggono in B, lo dimostra anche la presenza, in una silloge così selettiva, dell'elegia 1.2, indirizzata allo spagnolo Giovanni Pardo e della risposta poetica dello stesso Pardo (cf. B, fols. 3r–4v). La poesia del Pardo e la lettera dell'Altilio non furono stampate nelle edizioni precanoniche, con l'unica eccezione — su cui bisognerà riflettere — dell'edizione del 1531 (cf. qui, n. 45).

[62] L'epillio fu pubblicato, con la *Lamentatio de morte Christi* e con le *Eclogae piscatoriae* insieme al *De partu Virginis,* fin dalle due prime edizioni del 1526. Cf. Sannazaro, *De partu Virginis,* xlv–lii.

tempo prima egli aveva perseguitato.[63] Si tratta, con ogni probabilità, dell'epigramma di cui parla Iacopo d'Atri, ambasciatore del marchese di Mantova presso il re di Francia, in una lettera inviata da Lione a Isabella d'Este Gonzaga, e datata 24 dicembre 1503: "Sannazaro me ha promesso uno epigramma facto per il duca Valentinois."[64] L'altro è l'ep. 2.60, composto dal Sannazaro per celebrare la bellezza della poetessa Camilla Scarampa, da lui incontrata a Pavia nell'agosto del 1502; anche questo epigramma fu inviato da Iacopo d'Atri a Isabella Gonzaga, avidissima di conoscere per prima la produzione poetica del poeta napoletano.[65] Orbene, nel codice B questo epigramma ha il titolo *In laudem Camillae Scarampae Ticinensis*, che è con tutta evidenza il solo titolo corretto, visto che a partire dalla *princeps*, lo leggiamo in questa forma: *De Camilla Scalampa Mediolanensi*.[66]

E' evidente che i testi raccolti ai foll. 10r–11r sono stati composti in un momento diverso ed hanno una provenienza diversa, rispetto alla silloge, calligraficamente trascritta nei fogli precedenti. Tra l'altro i due epigrammi non sono accolti nelle edizioni precanoniche. E tuttavia la redazione dei testi che vi si leggono ha un'identica autorità e sembra risalire, se non direttamente al Sannazaro, certo ad ambienti a lui molto vicini. Sappiamo che il codice B è uno zibaldone appartenuto ad Angelo Colocci; dai testi che vi si leggono possiamo arguire che esso fu messo insieme durante il pontificato di Giulio II.[67] In quel periodo, i contatti tra i pontaniani rimasti a Napoli, e i circoli umanistici romani, non erano tuttavia assicurati dal solo Colocci. Un ruolo importante lo dovette svolgere anche quel Francesco Pucci che — come ci insegna il Percopo — a partire dal 1504 fu segretario del cardinale Luigi d'Aragona, si stabilì con lui a Roma almeno dal 1506 e lì morì il 24 agosto del 1512. Sappiamo che il Sannazaro mantenne col cardinale una costante corrispondenza, proprio per il tramite del Pucci[68] e che, proprio nel 1512, correva voce che Giulio II intendeva "far re di Napoli il cardinal di Ragona."[69] Con quanta commozione, negli ambienti vicini al cardinale, si dovevano leggere i componimenti del Sannazaro ed in particolare quell'elegia 1.11 che è una vera e propria glorificazione dell'Accademia pontaniana e insieme una sapiente esaltazione di quell'ideale puristico e classicistico che fu il manifesto culturale del pontificato "imperiale" del papa Della Rovere !

Poche sono le certezze che abbiamo ricavato dalla nostra analisi, molti sono i dubbi ancora da chiarire. E tuttavia, come ci hanno insegnato i grandi maestri della scuola storica del tardo '800 (e per Sannazaro e i pontaniani, soprattutto il Percopo), e come ci è stato più di recente insegnato dal Kristeller, dal Billanovich e, per il

---

[63] Cf. L. v. Pastor, *Storia dei papi dalla fine del Medioevo*, trad. A. Mercati, 3 (Roma, 1959), 657.

[64] A. Luzio e R. Renier, "La coltura e le relazioni letterarie di Isabella D'Este Gonzaga," *Giornale Storico della letteratura Italiana* 40 (1901): 307.

[65] Cf. Luzio e Renier, "La coltura," 306–307.

[66] Cf. *Sannazarii Opera omnia*, fol. 57v. Cf. anche Vecce, *Iacopo Sannazaro in Francia*, 51, 182.

[67] Cf. qui, n. 43.

[68] Cf. Iacobo Sannazaro, *Opere volgari*, ed. A. Mauro (Bari, 1961), 311, lettera 3 ad Antonio Seripando, del 27 giugno 1517.

[69] Cf. F. Stefani, G. Berchet e N. Barone, edd., *I Diarii di Marino Sanuto*, vol. 15 (Venezia, 1887), col. 10.

Sannazaro e il Marullo, soprattutto dal Perosa, se pure il Sannazaro, da buon petrarchista, tendeva ad eliminare nei suoi autografi i riferimenti precisi (in V mancano tutti i titoli!); se pure i curatori dell'edizione postuma hanno ordinato elegie ed epigrammi con un criterio che non tiene alcun conto né della storia né della cronologia, lo studio dei documenti di archivio, affiancato da quello dei manoscritti e delle edizioni — e della loro storia — sono i soli strumenti che ci possono aiutare a comprendere il vero significato dei suoi componimenti latini, inquadrandoli in un contesto in cui non solo la storia, ma persino la cronaca contribuiscono ad illuminare l'evoluzione di uno stile e di una poetica assolutamente esemplari.

Università di Roma, "La Sapienza"

Appendici

1. De Prisco

1   Priscus, Marulle, Priscus ille quem nosti:
    Sectarum ocellus, dogmatum omnium cultor,
    Antiqua solus dicta qui senum septem
    Omnesque callet Atticae sales linguae,
5   Et quicquid alto cum silentio dixit
    Osor fabarum ille Samius lupinique;
    Zenonis haeres Socratisque successor,
    Aristotelis idem et Platonis auditor,
    Cuius per orbem fama iam volat totum;
10 Romam perosus, cum Neapolim nuper
    Pexatus atque coccinatus intraret,
    Et disputantum vocibus sophistarum
    Hinc inde septus per theatra, per thermas
    Iret supinus et scholas poëtarum,
15 Occurrit illi parvulus quidem coetus,
    Sed nec Minervae poenitendus aut Musis,
    Qualem biceps Parnasus et virens Aon,
    Vix ante natum annis fuisse sexcentis
    Credunt, et hoc verissimum esse contendunt.
20 Hic, post salutes obviosque congressus
    Cum iam putaret Pittacum aut Solonem ipsum
    Venisse, miro prosecutus adfectu,
    Per templa duxit, per vireta, per fontes;
    Nec ullum omisit offici genus. At ille
25 Utpote malignus, insolens, inurbanus,
    Negavit ullum rhetorem poëtamve
    Vidisse se Neapoli. Sed hi porro
    Deos per omneis caelitumque supremum

W = Vindob. Lat. 9477, fol. 137r–v; O = Ottob. Lat. 3172, fol. 171r–v; ed.= Mai, *Spicilegium Romanum*, 8:510–511.

6.   Osor] *corr. ex* Hostis W ille Samius] *corr. ex* Pythagoras W
8.   Idem et] *corr. ex* hospes W auditor] *corr. ex* adfinis W
18. Vix ... sexcentis] *add. sin.m.*] Hic (*corr. ex* Vix) ante natum annos fuisse sexcentos *d.m. add. et exc.* W
19. Credunt] *corr. ex* Dicunt W
22. Vidisse] *corr. ex* Videre W

Iovem parentem, deierare non cessant
30 Cinediorem huc usque philosophum sese
Nec hic nec alibi praenotasse terrarum.

2. El. 1.11
In maledicos detractores
(da Actii Sinceri Sannazarii *Opera latine scripta*, 116–127)

1   Quid ruis in sacros, temeraria turba, poetas
   Saevaque mordaci praelia dente moves?
Desine sacrilega convicia fundere lingua,
   Desine: pro populo stat Deus ipse suo.
5   Quis novus in furias armat dolor? Ite, profani!
   Ite, nec immeritas conscelerate Deas.
An monet hoc Stygiis immersus Scuccha lacunis,
   Dum flens Eumenidum verbera torta timet?
Illum olim tinctae iuverunt felle sagittae,
10   Nunc miserum facti paenitet usque sui.
Parcite tam cari manes violare parentis:
   Per stupra et talos, per cyathosque rogo!
Ars sua quenque iuvet: non vos Helicona subire,
   Non fas virginei polluere amnis aquam.

---

25.   inurbanus] *corr. ex* inhumanus W
27.   porro] *corr. ex* prorsus W
30–31. .] *sin. m. add.* W
30.   Cinediorem] *omm.* O ed. huc usque ... sese] *corr. ex* se philosophum nunquam quenquam W.

A = Vat. Lat. 2836, foll. 124–125v; B = Vat. Lat. 2847, foll. 7–8v; W = Vindob. Lat. 9477, fol. 130r–v: vv. 1–36; V¹ = Vat. Lat. 3361, foll. 7–9; V² = Vat. Lat. 3361, foll. 51–53; V = *consensus* V¹ et V²; e¹ = Venetiis, apud haeredes Aldi 1528; e² = Venetiis, B. Stagnini, 1531; e³ = Venetiis, ap. haerr. Aldi 1533; e = *consensus harum edd.*; Ald. = Venetiis ap. haerr. Aldi 1535.

Titulus: omm. AWV; Eiusdem Accii in lividos detractores Scucchae grammatici alumnos homicidas furesque nocturnos B; Actii Sinceri in lividos detractores Scucchae grammatici alumnos C; Eiusdem dirae in detractores quosdam Scucchae grammatici alumnos *e*

2.   dente] mente A
6.   immeritas] innumeras *e*
7.   monet] movet *e*
12. et] per *e*
13. Iuvet] Iuvat A*e*

15 Scilicet hanc sumpto Ioviani Musa cothurno
        Hauriat, et magno digna Marone sonet;
    Cui comes, intactae lustrans sacraria sylvae
        Altilius, docto pectore carmen hiet.
    Nec minus et Musae repetens monimenta iocosae,
20   Compater argutos ingerat ore sales.
    Elisiusque, hedera comptus florente capillos,
        Rara, sed Aoniis concinat apta choris.
    Extendatque armis titulos Aquivivus avitos
        Et doceat nostras cernere castra Deas.
25 Ipse suae referat Cabanilius ardua Troiae
        Moenia et antiquos, Appula regna, lares.
    Quique velut tenera surgit novus arbore ramus,
        Corvinus quavis aure probanda canat.
    Et qui Pieriis resonat non ultimus antris
30   Albinus referat principis acta sui.
    Tu quoque, quid cessas doctis deflere querelis
        Excidium patriae, culte Marulle, tuae?
    Quique tot egregias animas, tot clara virorum
        Ingenia enixu format alitque suo,
35 Nectat honorata Maius sua dicta corona,
        Tamque pias ferulas regia sceptra vocet.
    Quin et rite suos genio Chariteus honores
        Praebeat et festas concinat ante dapes.
    Aelius et blandae fretus dulcedine linguae
40   Facunda totos conterat arte dies.
    Nec te iam pudeat venturo ostendere saeclo

---

15. hanc] hinc e³ Ioviani] Pontani ABV*e*
19. Monumenta V*e* monumenta iocosae *om*. W (*add. Sambucus*)
24. cernere] quaerere AB*e*
25–26. *omm*. AB *e* Con<ce>lebretque suae Cabanilius ardua Troiae / Moenia et antiquos, Appula regna, lares *laevo marg. add.* V¹
28. *om*. W (*add. Sambucus*)
29. Pieriis] *corr.* Musarum V²
30. *om*. W (*add. Sambucus*) principis] consulis *e*
34. format] firmat A
35. honorata] odorata *e*
37–84. *om*. W
37. Quin et rite suos] Ipse suo sacros ABV*e*
39. Aelius et] Puccius et AB*e* fretus] flendus B
40. arte] ante C

Eloquii vires, Scala diserte, tui.
Certent Socraticis Zenonis scripta libellis,
   Cuius apis vernos intulit ore favos.
45 At tu, Castaliis non inficiande choreis
   Castalidos, Carbo, concine regna tuae.
Te quoque, quem gemina mulcet sapientia lingua,
   Parde, iuvet studiis invigilare tuis.
Atque alii, quorum doctas it fama per aures,
50   Extremo properent vincere fata die.
Nos quoque, si magnus non aversatur Apollo,
   Cantemus Nymphas capripedesque Deos.
Nam bene Thespiacas, livor licet audiat, undas
   Novimus et dextro pressimus antra pede.
55 At vos incautis sociis aconita parate,
   Et furtis miseras extimulate domos;
Oedipodisque modo, thalamos foedate paternos,
   Si modo dat certum vulgus habere patrem.
Nocturnisque dolis agitate et caedibus urbem,
60   Perque fora infestam reddite, perque vias.
Haec studia, has artes primis didicistis ab annis,
   Non Aganippaeae tangere fila lyrae.
Nam neque Calliope vobis, nec dexter Apollo
   Permessi sanctos exhibuere lacus;
65 Dira sed Alecto, gemina comitata sorore,
   Pocula coenoso de Phlegethonte tulit.
Nimirum hinc nigro mores et carmina tabo
   Pallent et foedo livor in ore sedet.
Fallor, an hos nobis misit gravis Aetna Cyclopas,
70   Mitis et hanc sentis tu quoque, terra, luem?
Heu, mea Parthenope, quae te contagia laedunt?

---

42.   Eloquii] Ingenii *e*
45.   At] Et V
45–46. *omm.* AB*e post* v. 38 *dextro vel laevo marg. add.* V¹ *et* V² Carbo concine regna tuae] *corr.*
       ex dulces dic mihi, Carbo, iocos V²
46.   concine] nunc cane V'
47.   Te quoque] Et te ABV*e*
49.   aures] urbes *e*
50.   Extremo] Extrema *e*
51.   aversatur] adversatur *e*
53.   Thespiacas] Castalios V¹ Castalias *corr.* Pierias V² Castalias AB*e*
58.   patrem] patrum *e*¹*e*²
64.   sanctos] liquidos *e*

>   Talia tu nunquam gignere monstra soles.
>   Dii patrii, quorum monitis huc advena classis
>   Appulit, Euboicas constituitque domos,
> 75 Littoribus talem nostris avertite pestem,
>   Moenia felici si posuistis ave.
>   Vosque, umbrae insontes, quas iam lethale venenum,
>   Ante diem Stygias ire coëgit aquas,
>   Ultrices huc ferte faces, fumoque sequaci,
> 80   Authores vestrae sollicitate necis.
>   Et vos, o vatum certissima numina Musae,
>   Numina, carminibus non violanda meis,
>   Parcite, si vestras nunc primum laesimus aures:
>   Iusta lacessita sumpsimus arma manu.

---

74. constituitque] deseruitque AB*e* V
80. Authores] Auctores ABV¹*e*

Lutero y su influencia en la España de Carlos V

ELENA RODRÍGUEZ PEREGRINA

Soy plenamente consciente de la multiplicidad y diversidad de enfoques que admite un tema como el que da título a esta ponencia. No obstante, en razón del tiempo del que dispongo, y de mi procedencia del campo de la filología latina, he decidido centrar mi exposición fundamentalmente en dos aspectos. Primero analizaré cómo reflejó la historiografía latina escrita en España lo que estaba sucediendo en Alemania. Y después, cómo se reaccionó desde el seno de la ortodoxia católica contra los libros de corte reformista escritos en el extranjero con la aparición de una serie de obras, entre las que destaca el *De fato et libero arbitrio adversus Lutherum* de Juan Ginés de Sepúlveda.

1.
Lutero y el movimiento luterano en la historiografía española de la época de Carlos V escrita en latín

Las dos fuentes históricas españolas en lengua latina de que me voy a servir en este estudio son el *Opus Epistolarum* de Pedro Mártir de Anglería, que llega hasta el año 1525, y el *De rebus gestis Caroli V* de Juan Ginés de Sepúlveda, que abarca desde el nacimiento del Emperador en el año 1500 hasta su muerte en 1558. Otras historias contemporáneas, como la de Pedro Mejía, que se extiende hasta el año 1530, la de Alonso de Santa Cruz, que lo hace hasta 1549, o la completa, pero ya escrita en el s. XVII, de Fray Prudencio de Sandoval las desestimaré por estar escritas en castellano.

Las figuras de Pedro Mártir y de Juan Ginés de Sepúlveda son tan conocidas que cualquier presentación resulta de todo punto innecesaria. Llama si acaso la atención el hecho de que uno, Pedro Mártir, sea un italiano afincado en España; el otro, Juan Ginés de Sepúlveda, un español con largos años de formación y permanencia en Italia. Del *Opus Epistolarum* de Pedro Mártir existen dos ediciones: la primera fue realizada en 1530 en Alcalá de Henares por Miguel de Eguía;[1] la segunda en 1670 en

---

[1] Petri Martyris Anglerii *Opus Epistolarum* (Compluti: in aedibus Michaelis de Eguia, 1530).

Amsterdam por Daniel Elsevier.[2] El *De rebus gestis Caroli V*, por razones que ahora no hace al caso explicar, permaneció inédito hasta que en 1780 la Real Academia de la Historia procedió a su edición junto con otras obras del autor.[3] Actualmente el Excmo. Ayuntamiento de Pozoblanco (Córdoba) está financiando una edición nueva de las obras de Sepúlveda, entre otras, de esta Historia de Carlos V, de la que ya han aparecido dos volúmenes.[4]

Pues bien, para empezar por el principio, Lutero colgaba sus 95 Tesis sobre las Indulgencias en la puerta de la iglesia del castillo de Wittenberg el 31 de octubre de 1517; daba comienzo con ello a una revolución religiosa que iba a sacudir no sólo a Alemania, sino también a toda la cristiandad.[5] En España, puede que para 1519 el comercio editorial alemán hubiese logrado introducir algunas partidas de los escritos latinos de Lutero. Eso, al menos, sostiene L. Pfandl, que extrae la noticia de una carta que el editor de Basilea, Frobenius, escribe a Lutero. En ella se dice lo siguiente:

> Dono dedit mihi Blasius Salmonius, bibliopola Lipsensis, in proximis nundinis Francofordensibus libellos varios a te elucubratos, quos ... typis meis statim excudi. Sexcentos in Galliam misimus et in Hispaniam.[6]

De otro lado, es más que probable que los ecos de las tesis de Lutero contra las indulgencias, de la negativa de éste a retractarse en Augsburgo en 1518, y de la disputa mantenida en Leipzig en 1519 con Eck atravesaran los Pirineos tanto por vía oral como escrita. Precisamente hacia finales de ese año, el cardenal Adriano de Utrecht, el que luego sería Adriano VI, que por entonces desempeñaba el cargo de Inquisidor General de España, se adhería a la condena que sus antiguos colegas de la Universidad de Lovaina realizaban de la recopilación de escritos de Lutero llevada a cabo por Frobenius. Su postura antiluterana queda reflejada en la carta-prólogo que se publicó en febrero de 1520 junto a la censura de Lovaina y la de Colonia.[7] Está claro, pues, que si algún consejo dio ya entonces al joven Carlos sería de índole represiva. En cambio, el embajador de Carlos en Roma, D. Juan Manuel, analizaba la cuestión en términos diplomáticos y veía que se podía sacar partido del movimiento anti-papista

---

[2] Petri Martyris Anglerii *Opus Epistolarum* (Amstelodami: typis Elzevirianis, 1670).

[3] Io. Genesii Sepulvedae *Opera Omnia cum edita tum inedita*, 4 vols. (Matriti: ex typographia regia de la Gazeta, 1780), vols. 1–2 os *Epistolarum libri* en el vol. 3.

[4] Juan Ginés de Sepúlveda, *Historia de Carlos V. Libros I–V*, ed. y trad. E. Rodríguez Peregrina; estudio histórico B. Cuart Moner (Pozoblanco, 1995). Idem, *Historia de Carlos V. Libros VI–X*, ed. y trad. E. Rodríguez Peregrina; estudio histórico B. Cuart Moner (Pozoblanco, 1996).

[5] Dos importantes estudios sobre los orígenes del luteranismo español son: J. Longhurst, "Luther in Spain (1520–1540)," *Proceedings of the American Philosophical Society* 103 (1959): 63–93. A. Redondo, "Luther et l'Espagne de 1520 à 1536," *Mélanges de la casa de Velázquez* 1 (1965): 109–165.

[6] Cf. L. Pfandl, "Das spanische Lutherbild des 16. Jahrhunderts," *Historisches Jahrbuch* 50 (1930): 464–497, 464.

[7] Cf. E. de Moreau, "Luther et l'Université de Louvain," *Nouvelle Revue Théologique* 54 (1927): 401–435, 405 ss.

en Alemania obligando a León X a abandonar su alianza con Francia y a aproximarse al rey de España. Así se lo comunica por carta a éste cuando en mayo de 1520 se disponía a marchar desde la Coruña a los Países Bajos; desconocemos la respuesta que se dio a esta carta.

En los Países Bajos la corte debió entrar en contacto con las ideas luteranas, pues, por una parte, la regente Margarita de Austria, tía de Carlos, había dejado desarrollarse la propaganda reformista, y, por otra, en el periodo 1518–1520 los nombres de Lutero y Erasmo no dejaban de aparecer ligados. La bula *Exsurge Domine*, publicada en Roma en junio de 1520, aunque era conocida, no se publica en los Países Bajos hasta el mes de septiembre. El 8 de octubre, tras la quema de libros de Lutero en Lovaina, la corte se dirige a Aquisgrán, donde Carlos sería coronado el 23 de octubre, y de allí se dirige a Worms adonde llega a final de año, el 11 de diciembre de 1520. Ni la condena de la bula —corría el rumor de que era falsa— ni la declaración de apoyo a la Santa Sede efectuada por Carlos V habían disminuido la simpatía que numerosos cortesanos —entre ellos, bastantes españoles— sentían por Lutero. Que por la corte circulaban ampliamente los escritos de Lutero lo ponen de manifiesto las palabras de Alfonso de Valdés, futuro secretario de Carlos V, a Pedro Mártir de Anglería en carta fechada en Worms a 13 de mayo de 1521:

> después de salir a la luz los libros de Lutero se venden sin cesar impunemente por calles y plazas.[8]

Y cuando se supo en la corte que Lutero había quemado públicamente en Wittenberg, el 10 de diciembre de 1520, la bula del Papa, muchos españoles aplaudieron este hecho, poniendo el énfasis no tanto en la bula, cuanto en los otros libros que la habían acompañado. Dice Juan de Vergara en su proceso:

> bien hizo Lutero en quemar los libros de canones y decretos pues no se usa dellos.[9]

Lo que vino después, el decreto de destierro para Lutero y sus partidarios y la bula de excomunión, *Decet Romanum Pontificem*, de fecha 3 de enero de 1521, hizo que los españoles que habían leído sus obras, sin el pretexto ya de que Lutero no había sido aún condenado, decidieran echar marcha atrás y permanecer en la ortodoxia. Así lo confirma el nuncio Aleandro en una carta probablemente de fecha 14 de enero de 1521 en que se felicita de la ortodoxia del duque de Alba, que, según él, es común a todos los españoles, exceptuados los marranos o judíos conversos.

---

[8] Hay traducción castellana del *Opus Epistolarum* de Pedro Mártir, realizada por J. López de Toro en *Documentos Inéditos para la Historia de España* IX–XII (Madrid, 1953–1955). A ella remitimos en adelante.

[9] Cf. Redondo, "Luther et l'Espagne," 117 n. 4.

Los protectores de Lutero lograron, sin embargo, que a éste se le diera oportunidad de comparecer y explicarse ante la Dieta reunida en Worms, a cuyo objeto se le remitió un salvaconducto con fecha 26 de marzo. Ese mismo día se publicaba en Alemania un edicto que condenaba al fuego los escritos del monje, y dos días después el papa León X confirmaba la excomunión con la bula *Tu coena Domini*. A pesar de lo revuelto del ambiente, el viaje y entrada de Lutero en Worms el 16 de abril de 1521 fue triunfal y muchos los cortesanos que acudieron a verle durante su estancia allí, "especialmente los españoles," a decir de Vergara.[10]

De entre las diversas fuentes que transmiten lo allí ocurrido hay que destacar dos de procedencia española: un informe anónimo, en castellano, — atribuido por algunos a Galíndez de Carvajal — titulado *Relación de lo que pasó al Emperador en Bormes con Luthero en 1521*, y una carta en latín de Alfonso de Valdés dirigida a Pedro Mártir de Anglería. En cuanto al primer informe, es evidente que no ha sido redactado por ningún partidario de Lutero; así lo delatan el tono y posicionamiento del mismo.[11] Respecto al autor del segundo, Alfonso de Valdés, que no puede ser adscrito sin más a las filas luteranas, por más que algunos lo intenten, podemos tener una idea de su posicionamiento inicial al respecto y de su primera visión de los hechos acudiendo a dos tempranos testimonios, ambos en forma de carta, en los que informa al humanista Pedro Mártir, y a través de él a sus compatriotas españoles, de lo que está sucediendo en tierras alemanas. Los dos testimonios aparecen recogidos en las ediciones mencionadas del *Opus Epistolarum* de Pedro Mártir, donde figuran con los números 689 y 722. A pesar de haber sido publicados en su momento, estos testimonios pasaron desapercibidos hasta que un par de siglos después Lessing los puso de relieve: a decir de éste, no había sido Johannes Cochlaeus, como era opinión generalizada, sino Alfonso de Valdés el primero que había hablado de que la Reforma había surgido en Alemania de los recelos y disputas entre dos órdenes religiosas.[12]

Hay que decir inmediatamente que los datos cronológicos con que ambas cartas se presentan en el *Opus Epistolarum* carecen de relevancia. Y es que el hecho de que la obra se publicara cuatro años después de muerto su autor sin que éste tuviera ocasión de participar en la edición de la misma ha acarreado, en general, múltiples problemas de datación de cartas. En el caso concreto de las que aquí nos ocupan — las de Alfonso de Valdés — la problemática es aún más compleja. El contenido de sus dos cartas concernientes al movimiento luterano es de índole tal, que o bien hay que concluir que las redactó largo tiempo después de la fecha con que figuran en la edición — entonces habría que atribuir la culpa de la datación errónea a los editores — o bien las escribió efectivamente en la fecha con que aparecen datadas y después las reelaboró con vistas a una publicación de las mismas. Ambas hipótesis resultan de difícil confirmación, dado que no contamos con manuscrito alguno de esta obra de Pedro Mártir. Hay quien va más allá en la crítica, como J. Bernays, que las considera sin más una ficción introducida *a posteriori* por Valdés con motivo de la edición póstuma del

---

[10] Cf. Redondo, "Luther et l'Espagne," 118 n. 2.
[11] Cf. Pfandl, "Das spanische Lutherbild," 472–479.
[12] Cf. Pfandl, "Das spanische Lutherbild," 482.

Opus Epistolarum, si bien no aporta pruebas concluyentes en apoyo de su hipótesis.[13] En cualquier caso, lo cierto es que las cartas tal y como hoy las leemos pudieron ser escritas en una fecha más tardía de la que aparece consignada en ellas.

La primera, la número 689, está fechada en Bruselas a 31 de agosto de 1520. En ella Alfonso de Valdés informa a su amigo acerca de las noticias que a él le han llegado a través de personas fidedignas sobre el origen, los progresos, y el estado actual de la nueva secta de los luteranos, nacida en Alemania. En el informe se pasa revista a los acontecimientos más destacados desde que se decidió sufragar mediante indulgencias los gastos de San Pedro hasta la quema de los libros canónicos y de la bula de excomunión en Wittenberg en 1520. Valdés considera como primera causa de los sucesos las disputas entre el fraile dominico y el agustino por el asunto de las indulgencias. La segunda la atribuye a la envidia que Federico, duque de Sajonia, siente por el también elector Alberto, cardenal y arzobispo de Maguncia, al que había oído contar que sacaba gran utilidad de tales indulgencias, según lo convenido entre él y el Pontífice Romano. Éste último separa al duque de la comunión de los fieles y Lutero se granjea su favor afirmando que la sentencia del Papa, toda vez que era injusta, no obligaba en conciencia. A partir de ahí — dice Valdés — empezó a sacar a la luz muchas y muy graves obras impresas contra el Pontífice y la curia romana. Una situación que vino a agravar el propio León X con su negativa a celebrar un concilio general, como se le solicitaba desde diferentes instancias. Valdés aprovecha la ocasión para dejar constancia de su opinión al respecto:

> ojalá así se hubiera hecho; pero mientras el Pontífice defiende tenazmente su derecho; mientras teme la reunión de los cristianos; mientras que (hablando con libertad) tiene en más su propia utilidad, que tal vez saldría un tanto menoscabada en el Sínodo general, que la salud del pueblo cristiano; mientras desea condenar sin discusión los escritos de Lutero, manda un legado *a latere* al César Maximiliano para que procure que con la autoridad del César y de todo el imperio romano se imponga silencio a Lutero.
>
> (Pedro Mártir de Anglería, *Epistolario*, carta nº 689)

Así pues, en lugar del concilio se celebraron comicios imperiales en Augsburgo, adonde se hizo venir a Lutero para defender sus escritos frente a Cayetano, legado del Papa, que se retiró sin haber conseguido nada. Lutero, despedido con mayores muestras de alegría que las que se le dispensaron en su recibimiento, y confiado en la protección del duque de Sajonia, dio a luz otros nuevos dogmas contra las instituciones apostólicas. Entonces el Pontífice envió contra él y sus secuaces una enérgica bula. De esta manera un tanto ingenua y simplista explica Valdés a Pedro Mártir de Anglería los comienzos de la división religiosa en Alemania. Todavía se le desliza a Valdés un error cronológico al final de su informe. Cree que el escrito polémico de Lutero que lleva por título *De la cautividad babilónica de la Iglesia* era la airada respuesta de éste a

---

[13] Cf. J. Bernays, *Petrus Martyr Anglerius und sein Opus Epistolarum* (Strassburg, 1891).

la bula de excomunión, cuando en realidad fue consecuencia de la primera bula en que se le amenazaba con ella. Y concluye:

> Y no satisfecho aún con esto, quemó públicamente cuantos libros de derecho pontificio encontró en Wittenberg, diciendo que éstos habían pervertido y corrompido la piedad cristiana.
> (Pedro Mártir de Anglería, *Epistolario*, carta nº 689)

De la bula de excomunión no dice nada Valdés, quizás es que en este último punto su fuente de información era Melanchthon, con el que mantenía contacto.

Si nos detenemos en la problemática de la datación de esta carta, aunque en ella reza el 31 de agosto de 1520, hay puntos en el propio texto que la contradicen: en primer lugar, la carta se cierra con la quema de libros por parte de Lutero en Wittenberg, algo que sucedió el 20 de diciembre de 1520; en segundo lugar, se habla de la exigencia por parte de los alemanes de celebrar un concilio, cosa que ciertamente pudo haber ocurrido a finales de 1520, si bien Bernays la pospone hasta 1523 o 1524;[14] en tercer lugar, Valdés confunde al nuncio Aleandro con el cardenal Cayetano y traslada la experiencia negativa de Aleandro en los preparativos para la Dieta de Worms a la actuación de Cayetano en Augsburgo. De todo lo dicho se infiere que en absoluto puede ser exacta la fecha que aparece en la carta; más bien tiene que fecharse entre finales de 1520 y principios de 1521. La posible objeción de que Carlos V estaba en Worms desde el 18 de noviembre de 1520 y con él debería estar también Valdés, con lo que la carta no podría haberse datado en Bruselas, como efectivamente lo está, no resulta tal objeción, pues Valdés no fue nombrado secretario general hasta 1526, con lo que su presencia en Worms no habría sido imprescindible y habría podido permanecer en Bruselas. Eso explicaría, según Pfandl, los errores y confusiones de la carta, que de haber estado Valdés en Worms resultarían menos explicables. No es necesario ir tan lejos como Bernays y postular una intromisión posterior de Valdés en el *Opus Epistolarum*.[15]

El segundo informe de Valdés, el referido propiamente a la Dieta de Worms, lleva como fecha el 13 de mayo de 1521, aunque esta vez tampoco haya por qué tomar el dato al pie de la letra. Más oportuno parece fecharlo tras el último acontecimiento que en él se narra, en torno, pues, al 30 de mayo. Que Valdés estaba en Worms cuando redactó la carta se infiere de la propia datación de ésta en Worms y de las palabras del comienzo en que se dice textualmente:

> El César, convocados en esta ciudad de Worms los electores y demás órdenes del imperio romano, dispuso ante todo tratar de la causa de Lutero.
> (Pedro Mártir de Anglería, *Epistolario*, carta nº 722)

Que estuviera presente o no en los interrogatorios a Lutero ya es más cuestionable,

---

[14] Cf. Bernays, *Petrus Martyr Anglerius*, 138–139.
[15] Cf. Pfandl, "Das spanische Lutherbild," 487.

puede incluso que llegara allí cuando ya Lutero se había marchado. Sin embargo, su informe resulta tan fiable y tan exacto que no puede proceder sino de un testigo presencial de los hechos. A decir de Pfandl, a este informe se le puede caracterizar con tres palabras: conciso, claro, veraz.[16] Aunque en forma sucinta, todo lo esencial está dicho en él, y lo que se dice coincide con la realidad histórica. Abarca desde los preparativos de la Dieta hasta la promulgación del edicto del Emperador proscribiendo a Lutero, esto es, desde más o menos comienzos de abril hasta el 8 de mayo de 1521. En él se distinguen claramente cinco partes: 1. Preparativos de la Dieta, con la concesión a Lutero de un salvoconducto. 2. Transcurso de las dos sesiones: en la primera, a la pregunta de si los libros que continuamente circulaban bajo su nombre eran suyos y si quería o no revocar lo que en ellos había escrito, respondió:

> que todos los libros cuyos títulos se leyeron a su petición eran suyos, lo que no quería negar ni lo negaría jamás. En cuanto a la segunda parte de la pregunta que se le había hecho, a saber, si quería revocar lo que había escrito, pidió que el César le diese tiempo para deliberar, lo cual le fue concedido por el César hasta el día siguiente. En ese mismo día ... Martín Lutero ... después de un largo y prolijo discurso que pronunció ya en latín, ya en alemán, dijo que él no podía revocar cosa alguna de lo contenido en sus escritos, si no se le probaba por la doctrina evangélica y por los testimonios del Antiguo Testamento que había errado y escrito impíamente ... Y ... que no podía atenerse tampoco a los decretos de los concilios, toda vez que los mismos concilios alguna vez habían sido contrarios entre sí.
> (Pedro Mártir de Anglería, *Epistolario*, carta nº 722)

3. Orden del César de que Lutero se marche y disolución por aquel día de la Junta. Nuevos y vanos intentos de los electores y otros órdenes del Imperio por llegar a un acuerdo con Lutero. 4. Notificación a Lutero de la orden de proscripción y edicto del Emperador ordenando quemar los libros del hereje. 5. Valdés, muy sagazmente, llega a la conclusión de que aquello no era, como algunos querían ver, el final de la tragedia, sino tan sólo su comienzo. De nuevo insiste en que todo aquello podría haberse evitado si el Papa hubiese atendido más al bien de la cristiandad que al suyo propio y hubiese convocado un sínodo general. No hay nada en este informe de anecdótico, nada se dice sobre el aspecto de Lutero o el comportamiento de partidarios y detractores. Todo eso, en cambio, aparece descrito con todo lujo de detalles en la *Relación anónima de lo que pasó al emperador en Bormes*, a que antes nos referíamos, de suerte que la una, contando aspectos externos, y la otra, haciendo un fino análisis de la situación, vienen a complementarse mutuamente. De esta forma, los españoles pudieron hacerse una idea de un momento importante sin duda en la vida de Lutero, el que representó la Dieta de Worms. En cambio, sobre los comienzos del movimiento luterano y las razones internas del surgimiento del mismo los españoles tuvieron más bien escasa, por no decir nula información.

---

[16] Pfandl, "Das spanische Lutherbild," 488.

Más sorprendente aún resulta constatar cómo en una obra de una extensión considerable —treinta libros— y dedicada a relatar la Historia de Carlos V, el *De rebus gestis Caroli V* de Juan Ginés de Sepúlveda, ni siquiera se menciona la Dieta de Worms.[17] Hay que esperar al libro X para que de forma bastante superflua y con motivo del viaje de Carlos a Alemania después de su coronación en Bolonia se trate de la Dieta de Augsburgo de 1530. Nada se nos ha dicho del Coloquio de Marburgo en 1529, en el que Lutero y Zwinglio trataron sin éxito de solucionar sus diferencias. La Confesión de Augsburgo no satisfizo ni a católicos ni a protestantes. La división de estos últimos hizo creer a Carlos V que podría con ellos, pero no fue así. Después de la elección y coronación de Fernando como rey de Romanos, los príncipes protestantes respondieron fundando la Liga de Esmalcalda en 1531, dato que Sepúlveda desconoce, pues la sitúa en 1534. Tampoco se hace alusión a la paz de Nuremberg de 1532.

En el libro XIV se hace referencia a las gestiones de Carlos —a su llegada triunfante a Italia tras la guerra de Túnez en 1535— ante el papa Paulo III para que convocase un concilio general, llegando éste incluso a promulgar una bula convocatoria el 2 de junio de 1536.

A pesar de lo ampliamente que Iohannes Sleidanus —la fuente principal de Sepúlveda en los asuntos alemanes— trata de las conversaciones de Hagenau y Worms en 1540, presididas por Granvela y que condujeron a la Dieta de Ratisbona, que se celebró de abril a julio de 1541, Sepúlveda las despacha sumariamente en los capítulos finales del libro XIX.[18] No parece que le haya servido de mucho haber enviado a uno de sus servidores a Alemania para que le mantuviera informado al respecto, según afirma en carta dirigida a Contarini y fechada el 12 de junio de 1541.[19] En el capítulo 34 de este libro XIX se describe la postura decididamente católica de Sepúlveda en el tema de la controversia religiosa. Después de lo cual, y muy en línea con su concepción de la historiografía, no tiene inconveniente en dedicar hasta cinco capítulos a relatar con todo lujo de detalles el asesinato de Juan Díaz a manos de su hermano Alfonso por discrepancias religiosas. Un hecho que dice haberle contado el propio Alfonso, pero que Sepúlveda sitúa mal, pues no ocurrió en ésta, sino en la Dieta de Ratisbona de 1546.[20] Sleidanus también recoge el suceso y parece fuera de toda duda que tomó la noticia de la *Historia vera de morte sancti viri Iohannis Diazii Hispani* de su amigo Francisco de Enzinas, un protestante burgalés, amigo íntimo a su vez de Juan Díaz;[21] en muchos *Acta martyrum* protestantes aparece extractada esta historia.

---

[17] Sobre J. Ginés de Sepúlveda son fundamentales dos obras: O. A. von Looz-Corswarem, *Juan Ginés de Sepúlveda* (Göttingen, 1931) y Á. Losada, *Juan Ginés de Sepúlveda a través de su "Epistolario" y nuevos documentos* (Madrid, 1949; repr. 1973).

[18] Sepúlveda desvela cuáles son sus fuentes de información en la carta a Diego de Neila, con la que los editores de la Academia tuvieron a bien encabezar la *Historia de Carlos V*.

[19] Es la carta 2. 16.

[20] Cf. I. J. García Pinilla, "Un ejemplo del uso de las fuentes en J. Ginés de Sepúlveda: La historia de Juan Díaz," in *Actas del Congreso Internacional sobre el V Centenario del nacimiento del Dr. J. Ginés de Sepúlveda* (Córdoba, 1993), 99–106.

[21] Aunque Senarclaeus se declara autor de la obra, hoy día parece probado que el autor de la

Juan Díaz se transformó así en tópico literario.[22] También sirvió como elemento de propaganda antiespañola y con tal finalidad es reseñada esta anécdota por el Thuanus en la *Historia sui temporis*.[23]

Bien, en el libro XXII se cuenta que bajo la influencia de Bucero se llegó a redactar un texto común sobre la justificación por la fe y que nunca el acuerdo había parecido más próximo. Pero Contarini fue desautorizado por Paulo III y Bucero por Lutero. Después de este intento de reconciliación el luteranismo hizo nuevos progresos. Sólo en 1542 el duque de Clèves y el arzobispo de Colonia se inscribieron en sus filas; el duque Enrique de Brunswick, pilar del catolicismo en el norte de Alemania, fue depuesto por Felipe de Hesse y el elector Juan Federico de Sajonia. Tras el conflicto entre el Emperador y el duque de Clèves a propósito de Güeldres, en que el duque no fue apoyado por la Liga de Esmalcalda, éste tuvo que someterse y volver al catolicismo en 1543.

Carlos, que necesitaba del apoyo financiero de los príncipes para luchar contra Francisco I y contra los turcos, prometió en la Dieta de Spira de 1544 trabajar para la reunión de un concilio nacional. Paulo III manifestó su reprobación y convocó de nuevo a concilio general. En 1545 propuso al Emperador, mediante el cardenal Farnesio, una acción militar común contra los protestantes. Finalmente, el concilio se abrió el 13 de diciembre de 1545 en Trento y estuvo presidido por del Monte, Cervino y Pole. Sepúlveda, bien informado como estaba acerca de los asuntos españoles, nos ofrece una lista completa de los prelados y teólogos que asistieron al Concilio. Todo ello en el libro XXIII de la crónica.

En lo referente a la Dieta de Ratisbona de 1546 y a la descripción de la Liga de Esmalcalda, que se hace en el libro XXIV, la fuente utilizada ha sido Sleidanus. Por si esto parece extraño, aclaro que Sepúlveda, al referirse a las fuentes utilizadas en la crónica, dice que ha leído a Sleidanus antes de haber sido censurado por la Iglesia católica, y aunque su estilo desaliñado, dice en otra carta, le provoca risa, su escrupulosidad le resulta casi excesiva. Sorprendentemente, y en contradicción con Sleidanus, Sepúlveda sitúa la formación de la Liga en 1534. Es también de resaltar cómo Sepúlveda considera la guerra de Esmalcalda una guerra de religión. Por lo general, como ya observó Voigt,[24] la narración de la guerra de Esmalcalda se ciñe estrechamente a los comentarios de Luis de Ávila y Zúñiga, esto es, a *El primer comentario de la guerra de Alemania*, cuya edición príncipe está realizada en 1550 en Amberes.[25] Se observa, sin embargo, que Sepúlveda extracta sensiblemente la obra de que se sirve,

---

misma fue F. de Enzinas, también conocido como Dryander. Cf. Francisco de Enzinas, *Memorias*, trad. F. Socas (Madrid, 1992), 39.

[22] Cf. I. J. García Pinilla, "Juan Díaz, conquense: humanista, mártir y tópico literario," in J. M. Maestre, J. Pascual y L. Charlo, eds. *Humanismo y pervivencia del mundo clásico. Homenaje al Profesor Luis Gil* (Cádiz, 1997), 3:1495–1505.

[23] Iac. Augusti Thuani *Historiarum sui temporis libri CXXV* (Lutetiae: apud Hieronymum Drouart, 1609–1614).

[24] Cf. G. Voigt, *Die Geschichtsschreibung über den Schmalkaldischen Krieg* (Leipzig, 1874), 45–47.

[25] D. Luis de Ávila y Zúñiga, *Comentario de la guerra de Alemania*, in C. Rosell (dir.), *Biblioteca de autores españoles. Historiadores de sucesos particulares* (Madrid, 1852), 1:409–449.

publicando sólo lo esencial y omitiendo muchas marchas y escaramuzas de menor importancia, con lo que a menudo se pierden detalles que hubieran dado más vivacidad y color a la narración. Un dato se permite Sepúlveda corregir en el cap. 45 donde da la fecha correcta de un 22 de noviembre, en lugar de un 27, que aparece en Ávila. Que Sepúlveda manejó estos comentarios lo sabemos por una carta fechada hacia 1548, en la que responde a una que había recibido de Pedro de Ávila, dándole las gracias por haberle enviado junto a la carta la historia de la guerra contra la Liga de Esmalcalda de su hermano Luis, un libro que —dice— le ha sido de enorme utilidad en su trabajo.[26]

El libro XXV está dedicado a las campañas de Bohemia y Sajonia. La fuente principal sigue siendo Ávila. El 24 de abril de 1547 tenía lugar la victoria de Mühlberg. Son interesantes las observaciones que hace el cronista en el cap. 15, relativas a la captura de Juan Federico, duque de Sajonia. Al parecer, el Emperador estaba decidido a condenarlo a muerte, pero los consejos del juez Muñatones le hicieron desistir del empeño. Asimismo, en el cap. 39 se narra cómo el Emperador hizo oídos sordos al consejo que muchos le daban de que debía envenenar a Felipe de Hesse. La Liga de Esmalcalda parecía aplastada. Mauricio de Sajonia recibió en recompensa una parte de los territorios de Juan Federico junto con la dignidad electoral. Carlos V se creyó lo suficientemente fuerte como para arreglar la cuestión religiosa en Alemania. Hizo que una Dieta reunida en Augsburgo en mayo de 1548 adoptara el *Interim*, por el que se restablecía en todas partes el catolicismo y además se concedía a los luteranos la comunión bajo las dos especies y el matrimonio de los sacerdotes. La Santa Sede lo desautorizó. Del lado protestante varios príncipes aceptaron; pero Magdeburgo rehusó hacerlo, convirtiéndose así en el bastión del luteranismo. La victoria fue incompleta, pero durante unos pocos años Carlos V pareció ser el dueño de Alemania.

En el libro XXVI cuenta Sepúlveda los esfuerzos de Paulo III por trasladar el concilio de Trento a Bolonia, así como la muerte de éste, que es sucedido por Julio III. Como consecuencia de una reunión familiar en Augsburgo con Fernando, María de Hungría y el príncipe Felipe se decidió en marzo de 1551 que Fernando, cuando fuese Emperador, haría elegir a Felipe rey de Romanos, y que éste a su vez haría lo mismo con su primo Maximiliano, una combinación singular que fue aceptada de mala gana por la rama austriaca. Carlos V pensó que era necesario reunir todas las fuerzas de la familia para mantener a raya a los protestantes. El año 1551 destacó por la continuación de los trabajos del concilio de Trento, gracias al nuevo Papa. Como anteriormente, se discutieron las cuestiones dogmáticas, y el decreto del 11 de octubre sobre la transubstanciación convirtió en ilusorio todo acercamiento con los protestantes.

En el libro XXVII Sepúlveda sigue a Sleidanus en lo que se conoce como la *Fürstenrevolution* hasta el sitio de Metz, y únicamente pone de su cosecha ciertos detalles referentes a obispos españoles asistentes al concilio y caballeros de la misma nacionalidad que acompañaban al Emperador. El protagonista fue Mauricio de Sajonia, que se pasó bruscamente al bando opuesto. A la cabeza de un ejército se lanzó hacia el sur. El concilio de Trento debió suspender sus sesiones una vez más. Carlos, que se

---

[26] Es la carta 3. 8.

encontraba en Innsbruck sin dinero y sin tropas, sólo tuvo tiempo de escapar y refugiarse en Villach. Comprendió que la partida en Alemania estaba perdida y dejó a Fernando que entablase negociaciones con los protestantes en Passau. Ayudado por A. Fugger pudo reunir tropas para atacar Metz. Fracasó y se retiró a los Países Bajos, donde prosiguió las hostilidades contra Enrique II, dejando de lado los asuntos de Alemania. Mauricio de Sajonia murió en 1553 en combate contra Alberto Alcibíades de Brandenburgo. En Fernando recayó la carga de preparar la paz definitiva, la cual se firmó en Augsburgo el 25 de septiembre de 1555. Una paz que estaba basada en el principio *cuius regio, eius religio*, esto es, los súbditos debían adoptar la religión de su príncipe; en el reconocimiento de las secularizaciones efectuadas hasta 1552, sin que pudiesen llevarse a cabo otras nuevas; y en la admisión únicamente del catolicismo y el luteranismo. Tales fueron las características de la paz que sancionó el fracaso de la política religiosa del Emperador.

Los últimos capítulos del libro XXX están dedicados a narrar el final del reinado de Carlos V, su retirada a Yuste y el traspaso del Imperio a Fernando. Estando en su retiro de Yuste le llegan noticias sobre movimientos heréticos en España, concretamente, en Valladolid y Sevilla, unos movimientos que decide reprimir a toda costa. Sepúlveda describe este episodio sin relación con ninguna obra anterior. Finalmente y de forma rápida da cuenta del fallecimiento del Emperador el 21 de septiembre de 1558, sin mencionar siquiera que fue asistido en sus últimos momentos por el arzobispo Bartolomé de Carranza, que se vería después envuelto en un proceso por heterodoxia.[27]

De todo lo expuesto se deduce que Sepúlveda en esta *Historia de Carlos V* selecciona el material de que dispone y sólo publica una parte del mismo. Así, por ejemplo, desde la coronación de Carlos en Aquisgrán en 1520 hasta la Dieta de Augsburgo en 1530 no se hace mención alguna a lo que está ocurriendo en Alemania, y eso que el autor conocía perfectamente la importancia del movimiento luterano —como se desprende de su obra contra Lutero—, y sus fuentes —Sleidanus principalmente— le brindaban abundante material. Y es que intencionadamente no se ocupa de Alemania ni de los países del norte más que durante los periodos en que el Emperador permanece en ellos, y aun así de forma deficiente muy a menudo. El verdadero marco de su historia, por tanto, lo componen los países mediterráneos: España, Italia y el norte de África, como zona de influencia española. Añádase a ello su extraordinario cuidado por la forma, en claro contraste con otras historias de su tiempo, como la de Alonso de Santa Cruz, en la que encontramos todas las noticias que echamos en falta en Sepúlveda, pero en descuidado amontonamiento. Una característica que no pasó desapercibida a Leopold von Ranke, quien a este respecto afirma:

Die Darstellung übergeht vieles; aber was sie berichtet, erzählt sie genau ... Was bei historischen Werken so selten möglich ist, man kann das Buch zu geistiger Erfrischung in die Hand nehmen.[28]

Hasta aquí el primer punto.

---

[27] Cf. J. I. Tellechea Idígoras, *Tiempos recios. Inquisición y heterodoxias* (Salamanca, 1977).
[28] Cf. L. von Ranke, *Zur Kritik neuerer Geschichtsschreiber* (Leipzig, 1884), 109.

2.
La reacción española ante el movimiento luterano. El *De fato et libero arbitrio* de J. Ginés de Sepúlveda

Las ideas de la Reforma habían ido infiltrándose poco a poco en España. En esa difusión había jugado un papel importante la imprenta, siempre bajo el punto de mira de la Inquisición. Este tribunal, que había sido creado para vigilar a musulmanes y judíos conversos, ejerce pronto su vigilancia tanto sobre los antiguos cristianos como sobre los nuevos. Las normas que impone son cada vez más estrechas, hasta el punto de que libros que habían obtenido anteriormente el beneplácito de la censura se ven de nuevo sometidos a examen. Hay ediciones que desaparecen por completo o si sobreviven es en reducidísimos ejemplares. Resulta, pues, complicado intentar medir el impacto de la Reforma a partir del análisis de los libros supervivientes, ya que a menudo sólo se encuentran huellas de esos libros en las actas notariales o inquisitoriales, y a menudo esas huellas son bastante vagas y fruto del azar; con mucha frecuencia ha desaparecido incluso la propia huella de esos libros. Y es que el primer *Índice* español, aparecido a la vez en Valladolid, Sevilla, Valencia, y Toledo, no data sino de 1551, si bien con el paso del tiempo experimentó varias actualizaciones y reediciones.

Tan gran celo desplegó este tribunal en la represión de las ideas reformadoras que, a decir de A. G. Kinder, la que imposibilitó la introducción de las ideas de la Reforma protestante en España fue precisamente esta institución, no, como defienden algunos, el hecho de que a finales del s. XV y principios del XVI ya se hubiesen adoptado diferentes medidas para reformar la Iglesia española.[29] Un caso especial de persecución por parte de la Inquisición lo constituye el movimiento de los alumbrados, un movimiento que, según sus más fervientes seguidores, habría surgido antes de 1517, con lo que habría precedido incluso al propio Lutero. Con el paso del tiempo los alumbrados tuvieron al menos conocimiento de las obras de Lutero, si bien no hay ninguna prueba de lectura directa de sus libros. Para el Santo Oficio los calificativos de "alumbrado, erasmiano y luterano" iban muy a menudo de la mano. Juan de Valdés, hermano del Alfonso de Valdés de que hablábamos antes, entra en contacto con uno de estos alumbrados, Pedro Ruiz de Alcaraz.[30] En 1529 publica en las prensas de Miguel de Eguía en Alcalá de Henares su *Dialogo de doctrina christiana*, un tratado de un protestantismo ciertamente muy velado, pero que obligó a comparecer ante el Santo Oficio al impresor y a cada uno de sus censores. La muerte en 1532 de Alfonso de Valdés, conocido erasmista, que había escrito dos obras realmente críticas para con la institución eclesiástica le evitaron un posible encontronazo con la Inquisición.[31] Ésta arremete contra el grupo de discípulos de Erasmo en Alcalá, entre ellos, Juan de Valdés, que se ve obligado a huir a Italia. Muchos teólogos formados en

---

[29] Cf. A. G. Kinder, "Le livre et les idées réformés en Espagne," in *La Réforme et le livre*, ed. G. F. Gilmont (Paris, 1990), 301–326, 305.

[30] Cf. C. Gilly, "Juan de Valdés: Übersetzer und Bearbeiter von Luthers Schriften in seinem *Dialogo de doctrina*," *Archiv für Reformationsgeschichte* 74 (1983): 257–306.

[31] El *Dialogo en que particularmente se tratan las cosas acaecidas en Roma el año de 1527* y el *Dialogo de Mercurio y Caron*.

Alcalá emigraron a su vez a Sevilla y allí constituyeron un movimiento evangélico, que se mantuvo en contacto con otro surgido en Valladolid; entre los integrantes del grupo sevillano destacan Juan Gil (el Doctor Egidio) y Constantino Ponce de la Fuente. Los escritos de este último fueron incluidos en el *Índice* y sus huesos y su efigie condenados a la hoguera; no obstante, el inventario de su biblioteca revela la posesión de muy pocas obras de carácter netamente protestante.

En cuanto a los libros de ideas protestantes que se introducen en España provenientes del extranjero, su infiltración comienza relativamente pronto; así lo pone de manifiesto el envío ya en 1521 de sendos Breves del papa León X al condestable y al almirante de Castilla, entonces gobernadores del reino, pidiéndoles que tomen medidas para prevenir la introducción en España de los escritos de Lutero y sus simpatizantes. Los años siguientes vienen jalonados por varios apresamientos y quema de libros por distintas ramas provinciales de la Inquisición. Es cierto, pues, que los libros producidos en el extranjero lograron un cierto grado de difusión en España. Resulta, en cambio, de difícil comprobación afirmar que libros de autores protestantes se publicaran en España en traducción española. Y, aunque está fuera de toda duda que las doctrinas verdaderamente protestantes arraigaron durante un corto espacio de tiempo en las ciudades de Sevilla y Valladolid, no está suficientemente probado que estos protestantes hayan publicado algo en España.

Por otra parte, en el bando de los defensores de la ortodoxia católica son de destacar, entre otros, los siguientes títulos: el inédito de Jaime de Olesa *Contra errores Martini Lutheri*; el *Monoctium, sive unius noctis opusculum* de Jerónimo Pérez, publicado en Nápoles en 1525; el mencionado en una carta de León X a su corresponsal, Diego de Muros, fechada en 1522, *Adversus Lutherum*, desaparecido posteriormente; el *De fato et libero arbitrio* de Juan Ginés de Sepúlveda, publicado en Roma en 1526. Los *Adversus omnes haereses libri XIII* de Alfonso de Castro, publicados en París en 1534, conocieron hasta doce ediciones, la mayoría fuera de España, salvo una edición aparecida en Salamanca en 1541. Asimismo, el traductor de Erasmo, Alonso de Virués, compone unas *Philippicae disputationes viginti adversus Lutherana dogmata per Philippum Melanchthonem defensa*, que se publican en Amberes en 1541. Andrés Vega concentra sus ataques sobre la justificación por la fe en sus *De justificatione doctrina universa libri XV*, que conocieron sucesivas ediciones: una en Venecia en 1546, otra en Alcalá en 1564 y otra en Colonia en 1572. Gaspar Cardillo de Villalpando escribe un tratado *De traditionibus Ecclesiae* y unas *Disputationes adversus protestationem trigintaquattuor haereticorum Augustanae confessionis*, que aparecieron en Venecia en 1564, en donde se refuta a Lutero y sus discípulos. Martín Pérez de Ayala se centra principalmente en el protestantismo en su *De divinis Apostolicis atque ecclesiasticis traditionibus*, publicada en Colonia en 1549.

Como hemos visto, una de las reacciones más tempranas a Lutero la constituye la obra del cordobés Juan Ginés de Sepúlveda *De fato et libero arbitrio libri III*.[32] En el año 1526, Juan Ginés de Sepúlveda, tras una estancia de ocho años en el Colegio San Clemente de Bolonia y un par de años en Carpi, se encuentra en Roma junto a

---

[32] Cf. F. Lauchert, *Die italienischen literarischen Gegner Luthers* (Freiburg, 1912), 306–311.

Alberto Pío y continúa al servicio de la corte pontificia como traductor oficial de Aristóteles. En el mes de junio publica la mencionada obra en un ambiente de abierta confrontación entre las tropas imperiales y las pontificias. Y es que en septiembre de ese mismo año, en unión de otros sacerdotes, contempla en Roma desde una ventana —según él mismo cuenta en la *Historia de Carlos V*—[33] el avance de los Colonna guibelinos capitaneados por Hugo de Moncada. Tras el *sacco di Roma* en 1527 se ve obligado a buscar refugio junto con la corte pontificia en las ciudades del sur de Italia, siendo testigo del sitio de la ciudad de Nápoles. Afortunadamente para él, el cardenal Cayetano, el célebre Tomás Vío, lo llama a Gaeta para que colabore con él en sus trabajos exegéticos.

La primera edición, pues, del *De fato et libero arbitrio adversus Lutherum* ve la luz en Roma el año 1526. La obra conocería aún otras tres ediciones, pero formando parte entonces de unas pretendidas obras completas del autor: así, en la de París de 1541 (ex officina Simonis Colinaei) aparece en primer lugar, ocupando los folios 2–56; en la de Colonia de 1602 (in officina Birkmannica, sumptibus Arnoldi Mylii) aparece en duodécimo lugar y ocupa de la página 536 a la 594; y en la de Madrid de 1780 (ex typographia regia de la Gazeta) aparece en el volumen IV entre las páginas 468 y 541. Al final del texto de la edición romana aparece una carta del autor, que omitieron las siguientes ediciones de París y Colonia y que los editores académicos insertaron en el *Epistolario*.[34] Va dirigida a Juan Ruiz, canónigo de Córdoba, y está fechada "el día siguiente de las nonas de junio." En ella nos dice que Ruiz le había encargado que, puesto que no podía hacerlo en persona, saludase por carta al obispo de Córdoba, Juan de Toledo, pues, según Ruiz le aseguraba, el obispo se alegraría mucho de mantener correspondencia epistolar con él, ya que era muy aficionado a los estudios literarios y tenía un elevado concepto del autor. Juan Ginés para satisfacer los deseos de su amigo, le envió esta obra para que se la entregase al obispo, a quien iba dedicada. Sabemos, por otra parte, que el autor entregó un ejemplar de esta edición romana a Hernando Colón, célebre bibliófilo, fundador de la Biblioteca Colombina de Sevilla, cuando éste asistía en 1530 en Bolonia al esperado encuentro entre Carlos V y el papa Clemente VII, si bien no aguarda allí hasta que el 24 de febrero se produzca la coronación del Emperador, sino que continúa su camino en dirección a Venecia.[35]

Y es que Erasmo, en vista de la gravedad de los acontecimientos de la Reforma y los continuos ataques de luteranismo de que era objeto, había publicado en 1524 su *De libero arbitrio*, al que había replicado Lutero en 1525 con su *De servo arbitrio*. A decir de Sepúlveda, Erasmo se había quedado corto en sus razonamientos, y es por eso por lo que él se siente en la obligación de llenar los huecos dejados por el de Rotterdam y acomete la redacción de su *De fato et libero arbitrio*. Dice Sepúlveda:

---

[33] *Historia de Carlos V*, 6. 40.
[34] El *Epistolario* en *Opera* 3: 1–389. Es la carta 7. 13.
[35] Cf. K. Wagner, "Hernando Colón: semblanza de un bibliófilo y de su biblioteca," in M. L. López-Vidriero y P. M. Cátedra, eds., *El libro antiguo español. Actas del segundo Coloquio Internacional* (Madrid, 1992), 475–492, 491.

cum hic [Erasmus] de libero arbitrio librum docte et eleganter ac perinde religiose conscripsisset, quo Lutheranum hunc errorem ac potius fraudem et malitiosam impietatem scienter ille quidem et peracute, sed iusto tamen modestius, ne dicam parcius et timidius, insectatur. Qui si totam causam fuisset complexus nec bonam partem intactam reliquisset, consuluisset vir eloquens et eruditus labori meo meque gravi hoc scribendi munere liberasset.[36]

La obra consta de tres libros. El plan de la misma, según palabras del propio Sepúlveda en el cap. 16 del libro I, es el siguiente:

> en esta cuestión confirmaremos primeramente nuestra tesis con argumentos filosóficos y teológicos. A continuación, en un segundo libro, expondremos las razones de los filósofos contrarios y las refutaremos desde el plano de la filosofía. Por último, en el libro tercero, una vez descubiertos los inconvenientes que siguen de ordinario a este error, rebatiremos por separado los sofismas de Martín, tal como exige la razón de la religión cristiana.[37]

Pero antes de abordar su objetivo, Sepúlveda considera oportuno aclarar cuál ha sido el origen del que se han derivado tan grandes males y pasar revista a las depravadas artes y costumbres de Lutero. Éste aparece no sólo como subvertidor de la religión, sino más aún como aniquilador de la dignidad humana. Resulta interesante a este respecto comprobar qué grado de deformación alcanza la figura de Lutero a la vista de un humanista en la Roma de ese momento. El Reformador es, en opinión de Sepúlveda, un desvergonzado y un subversivo, que se aprovecha del descontento existente en Alemania hacia el Papado para abandonar las estrecheces de una vida monástica en aras de otra más disipada. Él, en cambio, se reconoce a sí mismo como hijo fiel de la Iglesia católica. Lutero antes de exigir santidad de costumbres en Papas y cardenales debería intentar corregir la conducta de los hombres. No es sino un Catilina cualquiera, que se rodea de hombres de escandalosa conducta, intrigantes y atormentados por la conciencia de sus crímenes. Ahí está si no el caso de Ulrich von Hutten para confirmarlo, quien después de sumar a otros delitos un homicidio junto a las termas de Viterbo se vio obligado a salir de Italia y refugiarse en Alemania, sumándose activamente a los secuaces de Lutero, como si es que hubiera huido no para evitar el castigo de su crimen, sino por hastío de las costumbres de los sacerdotes romanos. A este retrato poco favorable de Lutero añade Sepúlveda la afirmación categórica de que ha sido la afición a la elocuencia y a la literatura lo que ha llevado a los alemanes a esta ruina fatal. Más les hubiera valido, dice,

---

[36] Io. Genesii Sepulvedae *De fato et libero arbitrio*, 1. 1.

[37] "Primum igitur in hac quaestione tum philosophorum, tum theologorum rationibus causam nostram confirmabimus. Deinde adversariorum philosophorum argumenta secundo libro proponemus, eademque ut philosophi refutabimus. Tum in tertio incommodis, quae eiusmodi errorem communiter consequuntur, explicatis, Martini captiones privatim, ut ratio poscit Christianae religionis, refellemus" (*De fato* 1. 16).

expresar las artes liberales al estilo de sus antepasados con un lenguaje sencillo y claro, que haber adquirido con tal perversión los recursos literarios de la totalidad de escritores griegos y latinos.[38]

Años después Sepúlveda suavizaría un tanto esta postura tan radical y en carta a Martín de Oliva, Inquisidor apostólico, de fecha 13 de diciembre de 1547 asegura que, si bien todos los jerifaltes de la herejía en Alemania han sido hombres de extraordinaria cultura en el campo de las letras griegas, sería un error imperdonable llegar a la conclusión de que hay que condenar la cultura helénica, pues lo que ha ocurrido sencillamente es que se ha hecho un mal uso de ella.[39] A él, en cambio, dedicado desde niño a su estudio, le ha servido para abrirse paso por el campo general de la filosofía y, particularmente, en el ámbito cristiano del Nuevo Testamento, ya que gracias a ello ha podido beber en las fuentes originales sin necesidad de recurrir a traducciones, como les ocurre a tantos otros.

Lutero ha enardecido también al pueblo en contra de los obispos y los monjes, las consecuencias de lo cual son bien conocidas por todos (se está refiriendo a la guerra de los campesinos). Con su libelo *De servo arbitrio* arremete contra toda la religión y sus prácticas; su intención era empezar atacando las prácticas para llegar poco a poco a lo fundamental. Así, después de proclamar que ambos sexos están liberados de la obligación de los votos y de concederles la facultad de contrar matrimonio, él mismo lo hizo con

> una muy bella joven sacada de entre las vírgenes consagradas, en el caso de que fuera virgen y no hubiera sido mancillada por él mismo hacía ya cuatro años, como he oído contar a algunos alemanes.[40]

Por todo ello Sepúlveda se ve obligado a rebatirlo, y lo hace apoyándose fundamentalmente en argumentos filosóficos. Se muestra seguidor al respecto de las tesis de Aristóteles y Alejandro de Afrodisias, su más importante comentarista. En un estilo típicamente humanista saca a la palestra en el libro II a los defensores y a los detractores del libre albedrío: de los antiguos filósofos griegos hasta los nuevos teólogos, pasando por los padres de la Iglesia. Lutero aparece alineado junto a los maniqueos y a Wyclif. Más adelante pasa a definir la ley natural como

> lo que creen comúnmente todos los hombres ... en todo tiempo, en todo lugar ... Y nada ha sido dictaminado con un consentimiento mayor del género

---

[38] "quibus [Germanis] longe optabilius commodiusque fuisset ingenuas artes more maiorum rudi ac simplici sermone tractare, quam sibi cum tanta pernicie omnia omnium Latinorum Graecorumque ornamenta orationis peperisse" (*De fato* 1. 5).

[39] Es la carta 5. 2.

[40] "ipse sibi pulcherrimam adolescentulam ex sacris virginibus, si tamen virgo erat et non ab ipso iam ante quattuor annos, ut quosdam Germanos dicere audio, polluta, sanctissimo connubio copulavit" (*De fato* 1. 12).

humano, como el que existen muchos actos en manos del hombre, para cuya acción u omisión goza de absoluta y plena libertad.[41]

De ese "consenso", pues, de los hombres hace derivar Sepúlveda el libre albedrío. Rechaza toda influencia de los astros en las acciones humanas, a pesar de lo cual en el cap. 18 del libro II alude al horóscopo de Lutero, un Capricornio,

> que si no está contrarrestado con la presencia de otros astros algo más favorables, suele imbuir la naturaleza de los recién nacidos de una falsa religión, y hace a los hombres embusteros, simuladores, inconstantes, charlatanes, desleales y lujuriosos. Además la oposición de Marte y Mercurio marca la vanidad y el carácter mentiroso de Martín.[42]

Por lo demás, no voy a extenderme en su exposición del punto de vista de Aristóteles y en la doctrina de los estoicos, contraria a éste. En opinión de Sepúlveda, el libre albedrío va aparejado al concepto persona. Su moral es aristotélica: las virtudes no nacen con nosotros, el alcanzarlas, en cambio, sí que depende de nosotros, motivo por el que con razón son alabados los buenos y justamente censurados los viciosos, son necesarias las exhortaciones y son convenientes las leyes, al objeto de poder disponer de ellas como normas para vivir racional y felizmente. Y aún más, las virtudes y los vicios dependen de nosotros, porque, una vez formados tales hábitos, aún depende de nosotros la posibilidad de rechazarlos o, mediante la conducta opuesta, cambiarlos en los contrarios. Las virtudes las alcanzamos, pues, mediante la dedicación y el esfuerzo.

El libro III se ocupa más de cuestiones teológicas —la mayoría de las veces desplegando una fina ironía contra Lutero— ; pasa revista a temas tales como qué es el pecado, cómo puede compaginarse el conocimiento que Dios tiene de todo con la libertad humana, etc.

A decir de los editores de la Academia, Sepúlveda se nos muestra en esta obra como un eximio teólogo y un acérrimo defensor de la religión, a la vez que profundo filósofo conocedor de las opiniones de todos cuantos habían tratado el tema con anterioridad a él. Todo ello hace exclamar a Miguel de Medina:

---

[41] "quidquid homines in omni aetate, in omni regione, in omni civitate, docti pariter et indocti communiter opinantur, id legem esse naturae ... Nihil est autem maiore consensu omnium mortalium iudicatum, quam esse multa in potestate hominum, quae ut agendi, sic omittendi liberam atque integram habeant facultatem" (*De fato* 1. 17).

[42] "Habuit enim horoscopum capricornum, qui, nisi aliorum astrorum benigniore aspectu temperetur, falsa religione solet nascentium animos imbuere et homines facit simulatores, mendaces, inconstantes, loquaces, infidos, libidinosos. Oppositio Martis et Mercurii vanitatem rursus et mendacitatem Martinis confirmat" (*De fato* 2. 18).

En esta obra encontramos la elocuencia de Cicerón, la filosofía de Aristóteles y, lo que es más importante todavía, la integridad de un corazón cristiano.[43]

El propio Erasmo, al pasar revista en su *Ciceroniano* a todos los escritores que imitaron a Cicerón, comenta en relación con esta obra de Sepúlveda las grandes esperanzas que se pueden depositar en el autor de la misma.[44] Una alabanza que, sin duda, satisfizo a Sepúlveda, pero que estimó insuficiente, pues —creía él— estaba hecha en unos términos más propios para estimular a un joven incipiente que para reconocer los méritos de un autor maduro —ya tenía 36 años— con una trayectoria de más de once años en Italia dedicado exclusivamente al estudio. Por este motivo decidió escribir una carta a Erasmo exponiéndole sus quejas. Los editores de la Academia dicen no encontrar esta carta entre las editadas por Sepúlveda. A pesar de no haberse entrevistado personalmente, los dos humanistas mantuvieron un intercambio epistolar entre los años 1532 y 1536.[45] Las relaciones entre ellos se pueden reducir a tres puntos :1. Enemistad de Erasmo con Alberto Pío, amigo íntimo de Sepúlveda, a quien defiende contra las acusaciones de aquél en su *Antapologia pro Alberto Pio principe Carpensi in Erasmum Roterodamum*.[46] 2. Intervención en las polémicas con Erasmo de otro amigo suyo, López de Stúñiga o Zúñiga. 3. Discusión sobre la exégesis de ciertos pasajes del Nuevo Testamento. A pesar de sus diferencias con el de Rotterdam, Sepúlveda dejó constancia de la muerte de Erasmo en julio de 1536 al final del libro XV de la *Historia de Carlos V* en estos términos:

> Este año ... murió Erasmo de Rotterdam ... varón esclarecido por su elocuencia y vasta erudición, de ingenio agudo, copioso y sutil, y festivo más de lo que puede creerse ... hubiera llegado a ser considerado como uno de los autores y sabios más beneméritos de las letras, no sólo profanas sino también sagradas, si hubiese tratado de los asuntos sagrados y sus ministros con mayor reverencia y compostura ... y se hubiese abstenido de sembrar peligrosas sospechas; males fueron estos que muchos varones graves eruditos y religiosos no dudaron en considerar como las semillas de las locuras luteranas ... mientras vivía los Sumos Pontífices transigían con él, no porque aprobasen sus escritos y doctrinas, sino para evitar que, exasperado por ellos, públicamente se apartase de la Iglesia Católica, se pasase al reducto luterano abiertamente y estorbase así los planes de la Iglesia ...[47]

---

[43] *De vita et scriptis Io. Genesii Sepulvedae Cordubensis*, 14 (un comentario redactado por los editores de la Academia como introducción a los *Opera*).

[44] Cf. M. Menéndez Pelayo, "Apuntes sobre el ciceronianismo en España," in *Bibliografía hispano-latina clásica*, ed. E. Sánchez Reyes, 10 vols. (Santander, 1950–1953), 3: 228–232.

[45] En *Opera* 3: 77–97.

[46] La primera edición de esta obra lleva por título: *Io. Genesii Sepulvedae Antapologia pro Alberto Pio Comite Carpensi in Erasmum Roterodamum* (Lutetiae: apud A. Augerellum, 1532).

[47] "Hoc anno ... Desiderius Erasmus Roterodamus ... decessit ... vir eloquentia et multarum rerum cognitione clarus, acri ingenio et copioso, arguto et supra quam credi potest festivo ... Quibus rebus id erat assecutus, ut de litteris non modo profanis, sed etiam sacris ac litterarum

Vemos, pues, que Sepúlveda, como tantos otros, es de la opinión de que Lutero no había hecho sino incubar los huevos que había puesto Erasmo. Pero esto ya es otro tema.[48]

Yo me propongo no alargar más mi exposición y finalizar aquí. Pero es que, como dice Sepúlveda a Juan de Toledo, obispo de Córdoba, al final del *De fato et libero arbitrio*:

> In qua quaestione disserenda, si tibi forte vel longior aliquanto, vel . . . concitatior visus fuero, illud tribues difficultati, quae cum maxima sit iudicio omnium . . . sermonis angustias non patitur.[49]

Universidad de Granada

---

studiosis optime meritus esse videretur, si de rebus sacris ac eorum ministris maiore adhibita reverentia temperatusque disseruisset . . . postremo, si periculosis suspicionibus serendis abstinuisset; quae mala multi viri graves, eruditi et religiosi non dubitaverunt seminaria Lutheranarum insaniarum fuisse confirmare . . . Nam viventi Pontifices Maximi parcebant, non quod eius mentem et scripta probarent, sed ne exagitatus ab ipsis palam desciceret ab ecclesia catholica et in castra Lutherana coniectus apertius ecclesiae rationibus officeret" (*De rebus gestis Caroli V*, 15. 31).

[48] Cf. Joaquín J. Sánchez Gázquez, "Juan Ginés de Sepúlveda, Un hispano a la altura del siglo XVI: Lutero y Erasmo", in *Acta Conventus Neo-Latini Abulensis*, ed. R. Schnur et al., MRTS 207 (Tempe, AZ, 2001), 575–583.

[49] Io. Genesii Sepulvedae *De fato* 3. 31.

Communications

In Praise of the Filia Docta: Elizabeth Weston and the Female Line[1]

SYLVIA BROWN

1612 marked the end of the reign of the Emperor Rudolph II. It was also the year in which a young Englishwoman, just thirty-one, died in exile in Bohemia. She had presented herself as coming from a noble English family, although even her near contemporaries were not sure exactly who that family was or where it had come from.[2] At some point, her widowed mother had married the notorious alchemist Edward Kelley, who had been at first favored, then imprisoned and ruined by Rudolph II. Edward Kelley himself died in a Bohemian prison in 1597.[3] Six years later, his

---

[1] I would like to thank Susan Bassnett, John Considine, and Paddy Considine for their generous assistance during the writing of this paper.

[2] John Fuller's *Worthies of England* (1662) placed her in Surrey (where there was a family of Westons) for want of a more certain origin. For this, and for a full version of the biographical details summarized in this paragraph, see Susan Bassnett, "Revising a Biography: A New Interpretation of the Life of Elizabeth Jane Weston (Westonia), Based on her Autobiographical Poem on the Occasion of the Death of her Mother," *Cahiers élisabéthains* 37 (1990): 1–8, here 2; also eadem, "Absent Presences: Edward Kelley's Family in the Writings of John Dee," [forthcoming] in *John Dee: Interdisciplinary Studies in English Renaissance Thought*, ed. S. Clucas (Dordrecht, 2000). (I am grateful to Professor Bassnett for providing me with an advance copy of this paper.)

[3] Bassnett proposes ("Revising a Biography") that Kelley married a Jane Weston (née Cooper) in England, and that the couple then moved across Europe with John Dee's ménage (although, problematically, there is no mention of Weston's children, Elizabeth and her brother, in Dee's diaries for this period). Louise Schleiner proposed a different identity for Westonia's mother in "Elizabeth Weston, Alchemist's Step-Daughter and Published Poet," *Cauda Pavonis: The Hermetic Text Society Newsletter* 11 (1992): 8–16. Schleiner proposed that Jane Cooper married and left Kelley *before* he was married a second time to Elizabeth Weston's mother, who was already resident in Bohemia when Kelley arrived there. In her later book, *Tudor and Stuart Women Writers* (Bloomington, 1994), Schleiner revised her account to agree with Bassnett's identification. She plausibly proposed that a Bohemian wedding between Kelley and a "Lady Weston," reported without documentation by Václav Kaplicky in his *Zivot Alchymistuv* [The Life of an Alchemist]

unfortunate stepdaughter seems to have found some stability in marriage, at the age of twenty-two, to a lawyer at the imperial court named Johannes Leo. But after nine years of a marriage which produced seven children (of whom only three daughters survived), this young wife and mother was herself dead.

The woman whose biography I have sketched was, of course, Elizabeth Jane Weston, known to her male contemporaries as "Westonia." On her death, the principal poets of Bohemia (all men) poured out funeral elegies which praised her as a learned goddess, *DEA docta*. Indeed, during her life she was celebrated by an impressive range of humanists and Neo-Latin poets, whose various discourses of praise have been surveyed and analyzed by Brenda Hosington.[4]

In my brief sketch of her life, I have deliberately left out all of the qualities that made Elizabeth Weston "Westonia": her impressive linguistic attainments (which included fluency in English, German, Italian, and Czech, as well as Latin); her ambitious poetry, wherein she associated herself with the best Latin poets, including another poet of exile, Ovid; and, finally, her publications, which comprised the two books of the *Poëmata* (published 1602) and the three books of the *Parthenicôn* (probably first published, according to Donald Cheney, in 1608).[5] The bare outlines of Weston's life — minus the prodigious learning so unusual for a woman of the period, minus the copious output of Neo-Latin verse — make her sound like a very unfortunate person, born into unpropitious circumstances and dogged by bad luck. All the more remarkable, then, we might say, that she was able to rise above circumstances and the constraints placed on her by reason of her sex and earn the esteem of her learned contemporaries.

It is my contention in this paper, however, that her male contemporaries' praise of her exceptional talents was perhaps *more* constraining, *more* of a hurdle to overcome than her straitened material circumstances, for after all, it was her family's misfortunes which prompted the majority of her verse epistles. It was not, however, the mere fact of praise which was a problem; rather, it was *how* Weston was praised. I shall therefore examine some of the terms in which she was praised, arguing that the laudatory comparisons to which she and her poetry were subjected worked not to

---

(Prague, 1980), might have been a *second* wedding necessary for the marriage to be recognized as Catholic. See Schleiner, *Tudor and Stuart Women Writers*, 96–97.

[4] Brenda M. Hosington, "Elizabeth Jane Weston and Men's Discourse of Praise," in *La femme lettrée à la Renaissance/De geleerde vrouw in de Renaissance: Actes du Colloque international, Bruxelles, 27–29 mars 1996*, ed. Michel Bastiaensen (Brussels, 1997), 107–118. Hosington quotes "DEA docta" from a poem by Weston's patron Georg Martinius von Baldhoven (116).

[5] Donald Cheney, "Virgo Angla: The Self-Fashioning of Westonia," in *La femme lettrée/De geleerde vrouw*, ed. Bastiaensen, here 120 n. 3. On Weston's linguistic and poetic learning, see Hosington, "Elizabeth Jane Weston," 110–111. For Weston's poem "In 2 Ovidij. Trist." (On Ovid's *Tristia*, II) see *Elizabeth Jane Weston: Collected Writings*, ed. and trans. Donald Cheney and Brenda M. Hosington (Toronto, 2000), 70–73. The first draft of this paper was written without the benefit of this invaluable edition. I am glad to have been able to consult and benefit from it since. It will subsequently be referred to as Cheney and Hosington, *Weston: Collected Writings*.

affirm her talent, but rather to limit possibilities for its development, and this not only for Weston herself, but, perhaps more seriously, for other early modern women who might seek to imitate her and establish a tradition of learned female poetry. (Here I am thinking about the *discursive* reasons why exceptional "learned ladies," like Lady Jane Grey or Olympia Morata or Westonia, did not seem to prepare the way for any sort of general "Renaissance" of female erudition.) In the second half of the paper, I shall turn to Weston's poetry, arguing that she herself had problems with the conventional language used to praise the learned woman and found it difficult to represent herself as a poet on those terms. I shall end by suggesting that, at the end of her poetic career, and perhaps especially with the death of her mother, Weston began to find an alternative, more helpful idiom in which to conceive of herself as a woman poet.

In her survey of the women with whom Weston is compared, Brenda Hosington concludes that the "Muses, of course, provide the first and foremost model for a female poet, with the Graces and Venus close behind."[6] The main problem with these analogues is that none of them is human: they deny the possibility of a poetic tradition composed of and available to *women*, rather than "learned goddesses." Hosington gives us Jan Dousa's superficially flattering, but ultimately unhelpful, judgement that Westonia produced "writing which it seems no mortal hand could have portrayed."[7]

Better then, perhaps, are the comparisons of Weston with mortals. Pavel Stránský's poem, *AD ELISABETHAM WESTHONIANAM nobilem Poëtriam*, provides a typical example. In it, Stránský commands Perilla as well as Sappho to cede their places to Weston: "Cede Perhilla inquam, Nasonis vivida versu, / Cumque tua Sappho Lesbia cede lyra."[8] The comparison with Sappho is conventional and I shall return to it. Perilla is a less familiar name, but she was a particularly apt historical poet for Stránský to invoke. She was Ovid's stepdaughter, and we know about her because she was addressed and indeed "lives" (*vivida*) in one of the elegies of the *Tristia*. From his exile, Ovid pictured Perilla enjoying the company of her mother, her books, and her muses ["aut illam invenies dulci cum matre sedentem, / aut inter libros Pieridasque suas"].[9] He recalled how he first recognized and cultivated his stepdaughter's poetic gifts, and hoped that his fate would not deter her from continuing to write verses. By putting Weston in Perilla's place, Stránský aptly locates *her* in the company of her books, muses, and mother. But his comparison also places Weston in a filial position and himself, as the one who addresses her, in the position of Ovid: he is an encouraging father-figure as well as a patron who grants her the reward of his praise.[10]

---

[6] Hosington, "Elizabeth Jane Weston," 114.

[7] "Litera, mortalis quam non manus ulla videri / Pinxê. . . .": quoted in Hosington, "Elizabeth Jane Weston," 110. The translation is hers.

[8] Cheney and Hosington, *Weston: Collected Writings*, 98–99 [*Parthenicôn* 1:51], lines 13–14. Cheney and Hosington describe Stránský (1583–1657) as a "Bohemian nationalist and defender of the Czech language, historian, political observer, and commentator on Rudolf's court." See also R. J. W. Evans, *Rudolf II and His World: A Study of Intellectual History, 1576–1612* (Oxford, 1973), 23 and passim.

[9] Ovid, *Tristia*, 3.7.1–2.

[10] Stránský is also patronizing in that his praise is rather grudging. In his poem he admits that

As for Sappho, she at least was cited for her own prodigious talent, not because she "lived" in another's verses. But she *was* a prodigy, and herein lies the crux of the problem of praise. Stránský sees Weston replacing Sappho: she is, again in a conventional early modern compliment, the Sappho of her age, with the implicit assumption that there can only be, at most, one Sappho at a time.[11] A prodigious and unusual talent appears only now and again. So each exceptionally learned woman is a freak, a *lusus naturae*, or, as the French Carmelite Louis Jacob said of another learned woman, Anna Maria van Schurman, *miraculum seu naturae monstrum*.[12]

In other words, all the praise Weston received assumed she was *exceptional*. Nice as it is to be considered exceptional, none of these compliments suggests that Weston's learned poetry could be imitated or reproduced by other women. On the contrary, her male praisers locate her at the *end* of a line of exceptional women, who do not so much comprise an inheritable female tradition as a line of unique exemplars whom Weston, phoenix-like, replaces and surpasses. In literary terms, she is barren. As the apogee of learned female poets, she will have no successor.[13] A strong illustration of this tendency of male praise is the catalogue of "learned maidens and women" which was appended to the *Parthenicôn*: Weston is the very last name.[14]

A final example from a poem by Václav Ripa serves to illustrate the problem of praise: the closing down, rather than the enabling, of a female tradition of learned

---

he at first hesitated to believe in the reports of Weston's talent. See Cheney and Hosington, *Weston: Collected Writings*, on lines 5–8.

[11] Paul Melissus also said of Weston that she was "equal in genius to Sappho, or wholly exceeds Sappho herself": quoted and translated by Hosington, "Elizabeth Jane Weston," 110. Westonia is also praised as a second Sappho (or as surpassing Sappho) in poems by Balthasar Caminaeus, Andreas Calagius, and Matthias Zuber (Cheney and Hosington, *Weston: Collected Writings*, 310–311, 388–389, 434–435). Other early modern women poets praised as equivalents to Sappho include Louise Labé (c. 1520–1566), Anne Bradstreet (c. 1612–1672), and Sor Juana Inés de la Cruz (1648–1695).

[12] Jacob, *Elogium* (1646), quoted in Mirjam de Baar and Brita Rang, "Anna Maria van Schurman: A Historical Survey of her Reception since the Seventeenth Century," in *Choosing the Better Part: Anna Maria van Schurman (1607–1678)*, ed. Mirjam de Baar et al. (Dordrecht, 1996), 5. Bernhard Praetorius addresses Weston as a "Miracle of nature and of your sex." Matthias Zuber enthuses, "You are an illustrious miracle of your sex" and also writes her a dubiously complimentary epigram: "What did Nature deny you, learned Westonia? / Nothing. Aside from your being born a woman." See Cheney and Hosington, *Weston: Collected Writings*, 416–417, lines 15–16, and 436–437. It is because he regarded her as a prodigy or curiosity that Justus Lipsius scorned to write in praise of Westonia. According to him, such female learning was superficial, just for show. See Cheney, "Virgo Angla," 121–122.

[13] Perhaps this accounts for the odd persistence of the categorization of Weston as *virgo*, even after she had married and borne children. The persistence of *virgo* is discussed by Cheney, "Virgo Angla," 125–127.

[14] Cheney and Hosington, *Weston: Collected Writings*, 282–307. Weston is the sixty-fifth, as well as the last, woman in the catalogue, which was probably put together by her editor Baldhoven. The first fifty-seven entries reproduce verbatim a list of learned women by Ravisius Textor (1552), which itself was based on an earlier list by Raffaele Maffei. See Cheney and Hosington, *Weston: Collected Writings*, 282.

poetry.¹⁵ Ripa compares Weston with the Roman poet Sulpicia. Sulpicia, whom Ripa admires as *docta virago*, did teach other Roman women to compose divine poetry to rival even that of the Greeks: "Prima hæc Romanas docuit contendere Graijs / Carmine divino, docta virago, nurus." She thus potentially begins an *inheritable* tradition of learned female poetry. Weston, as her counterpart, might similarly teach other women. Yet Ripa does not allow this productive comparison to stand. Instead of seeing Sulpicia as the founding mother of a female tradition and Weston as an inheriting daughter, Ripa decides, some lines into the poem, to undo the connection. Weston cannot after all be compared to Sulpicia, who was a vernacular poet. Vernacular poets avoid imitating the ancient bards because they are lazy: "Hæc aliter sentit WESTONIA virgo, Poëtas / Illos dùm superat carmine docta suo" [The maiden Weston feels quite differently, when she learnedly surpasses those poets in her song].¹⁶ Ripa means to compliment Weston. She is different from vernacular poets; indeed she outdoes, even vanquishes, them [*superat*] because she writes in a language other than her own. But in ultimately denying the connection to Sulpicia, Ripa denies Weston what one might call "a tradition of her own."

What was Elizabeth Weston's response to all of this double-edged praise? One place to look for an answer to this question is the poetry of the *Poëmata* and the *Parthenicôn*. The poems by Weston in these collections are, for the most part, dialogic: they respond to other poems by her friends and admirers.¹⁷ We thus have a great deal of evidence for Weston's response to praise. Even when the praiser's poem has not been printed, careful attention to the language of Weston's response enables us not only to reconstruct, at least in part, the original exchange, but also to gauge Weston's reaction to the recurrent patterns of male praise which would isolate her as a female prodigy. One response which repays this kind of attention is a poem addressed by Weston to George Carolides, the premier poet of the Rudolfine court. When Carolides sent Weston verses congratulating her on her poems on the Nativity of Christ, Weston answered him with another poem.¹⁸ Weston's response to Carolides's praise is one of those self-referential poems in which the poet meditates aloud

---

¹⁵ Cheney and Hosington, *Weston: Collected Writings*, 98–99. Ripa (1579–1616) was himself a poet, a composer of elegies, and "a prominent figure in Prague, involved in church disputes in that city." See Cheney and Hosington, *Weston: Collected Writings*, 99 n.

¹⁶ The translation is from Cheney and Hosington, *Weston: Collected Writings*, 99, lines 15–16.

¹⁷ About a third of the *Parthenicôn* (especially Book III) consists of poems by Weston's admirers, most of which have no printed response by Weston. Conversely, most of Weston's responses are to poems *not* printed in her collection.

¹⁸ The religious poems which Carolides praised were likely those later reprinted at the beginning of Book II of the *Parthenicôn*. See Cheney and Hosington, *Weston: Collected Writings*, particularly 100–107. For Carolides, see Evans, *Rudolf II and His World*, 150. I have been unable to locate his poem praising Weston's Nativity poems. I would like to know whether it is extant and, if so, whether it explicitly refers to Weston as "Lesbia." Weston's response is in Cheney and Hosington, *Weston: Collected Writings*, 62–66 [*Parthenicôn* 1:34]. Her poem addresses Carolides deferentially as *Clarissimo Viro, Dno GEORGIO CAROLIDÆ á Carlsberga, Civi Pragensi, artium liberalium Magistro, & Poëtæ Cæsareo*.

on her art and ambitions. In doing so, Weston complicates and rewrites the vocabulary of praise which I have been tracing in her male admirers. Subtly but firmly, she refuses the conventional terms with which the imperial poet has praised her. Her refusal is partly disguised as the ritual dance of modesty, performed in the republic of letters whenever compliments were exchanged. But beneath the gesture of self-deprecation is a more distinctive, less pliable voice, telling Carolides that his praise does not quite "fit" Weston's sense of her self or her future as a poet.

Weston begins her poem to Carolides with disarming self-deprecation, declaring her nativity poems to be the "uncertain issue of a female brain."[19] She is nonetheless not at all surprised that Carolides found them agreeable ("At minùs admiror consonuisse tibi"). Still, the reasons she finds for Carolides's approval have little to do with her personal poetic talent or ambitions: anything put into "numbers" or verse sounds musically to the ear; moreover, her subject matter is the worthiest that could be.[20]

While the first half of her poem declares a modest, almost self-effacing, wish to please God with her poetry ("Vnde placere DEO valeam"), the second half focuses more directly on her sense of herself as a poet. Here Weston thinks very precisely about her poetic reputation and the terms on which she wishes to be praised. Specifically, she considers the suitability of the identification of herself with Sappho — here *Lesbia*, the Lesbian woman. She introduces Sappho into her poem (which has heretofore been more concerned with how her verses may praise Christ and please God) by considering how she, Weston, ought to be placed in relation to the ancient pagan poets or bards, the *vates*. She declares that she hardly wishes to be placed before the ancient poets: "Vatibus haud cupiam dici prælata vetustis." Note here that she is conscious of what is *said* about her: she would hardly wish to be said [*dici*] to be before [them]. That she is thinking primarily about ancient *female* poets is clear in subsequent lines. She is content that the reputations of all women writers who worship the Muses of Helicon (including Sappho) should flourish from the first to the last age: "Floreat à primo postremum Lesbia in ævum, / Ac Heliconiades quæ coluêre DEAS." While executing the modesty topos, Weston is also paying tribute to an enduring female literary tradition, as well as implying that she does not wish to replace that tradition by being known as a singular prodigy. She sees herself, in time, joining the ancient line of female poets. She asks Carolides to pray to the highest power in order that she might be what Sappho was: not a pagan of course (that would nullify the devout intentions of the first part of the poem), but a poet with an enduring and deserved reputation, like Sappho's ("Deprecor à summo deposcas Numine tandem, / Vt sim, qualis erat Lesbia: sorte puto"). And if Weston is fated to achieve an immortality like Sappho's: "Tunc tibi carminibus gratabor, Culte Georgi; / Altera tunc pro me Lesbia, vota feram" [Then, and only then, cultivated George Carolides —

---

[19] "Fæmineo cernis titubare profecta cerebrô": Cheney and Hosington, *Weston: Collected Writings*, 62–63, line 3. My translations and paraphrases of this poem are informed by those of Cheney and Hosington. Any translation of theirs quoted verbatim is enclosed in quotation marks.

[20] Cheney and Hosington, *Weston: Collected Writings*, 62–65, lines 5–16.

(note the repetition of *tunc* for emphasis) — shall I thank you in poems]. In other words, he must wait for his thanks until Weston does become *altera Lesbia*, another Sappho. Weston sees herself still learning and developing as a poet. She also implies that she is capable of future work of enduring fame.

In this last line, I find significant the interpolation of the solid *pro me* in the midst of the significantly split *Altera . . . Lesbia*. Perhaps one day she will offer prayers for George Carolides, just as he is offering to pray for her future as the other Sappho now. But, even if one day she is another Sappho, she will still offer those prayers *on her own behalf, pro me*. I believe this speaks of the stubborn survival of Elizabeth Weston, a real woman, even as she concedes a hypothetical future as a mythic Sapphic poet.[21]

The response to Carolides is one of the few poems by Weston which mention Sappho. This alone suggests that Weston found figures like her problematic.[22] One other poem — a reply to Eric Lymburch, who Weston claims had excessively praised her — also mentions Sappho, as well as the Greek poet Praxilla and the "learned Corinna," but only, again, in order to refuse the title of Sappho's conqueror.[23]

I think Weston came to find the recurring clichés of praise exasperating. Such praise does not seem, after all, to have helped her in her material misfortunes. In a manuscript addition to the *Parthenicôn*, she commented with explicit displeasure at

---

[21] This is a markedly different ending from the one printed in an earlier version of the poem in Carolides's *Parentalia* (1601). There the prayers are offered *pro te*, on behalf of Carolides. Also, there is no mention of Lesbia in the final lines. See Cheney and Hosington, *Weston: Collected Writings*, 66. Although Weston complained of her editor Baldhoven's tampering with her verses, the revision is arguably Weston's: it suggests an increasing self-consciousness about the trajectory of her poetic reputation.

[22] In her essay, "Female Authority and Authorization Strategies in Early Modern Europe," in *This Double Voice: Gendered Writing in Early Modern England*, ed. Danielle Clarke and Elizabeth Clarke (Basingstoke, 2000), 16–40, Jane Stevenson has noted that, while early modern men may have been fond of characterizing women poets as "the Tenth Muse," women themselves avoided this identification. Stevenson writes, "the Tenth Muse is a difficult figure, from a woman's point of view: the main problem is that she is singular. It is notable that, while a number of poems survive written by one woman Latinist to congratulate another, they do *not* use this trope." In her essay she discusses the unsatisfactory models of female authorship available to women (for instance, jumping from Sappho to "the second Sappho"), and argues that women authors themselves rejected these models, invoking instead "a tradition of *auctrices* . . . a succession of women writers across time." My thanks to Professor Stevenson for her helpful comments after the delivery of this paper at the IANLS Congress and for supplying me with an advance copy of her essay.

[23] In the same poem, Weston also mentions more recent learned women, deferring to the learned "Fulvia" (Olympia Morata) and hoping only to equal the famous Morel sisters. See Cheney and Hosington, *Weston: Collected Writings*, 58–61 [*Parthenicôn* 1:30]. (The preceding poem [*Parthenicôn* 1:29] questions Lymburch's excessive praises.) Stevenson ("Female Authority") discusses *Parthenicôn* 1:30 to show that learned Renaissance women knew the work of both their ancient predecessors and their near contemporaries. By contrast, poems praising Westonia conventionally deny her connection with her learned female contemporaries, declaring that she "vanquishes" them or that they must "yield" to her. See, for example, Janus Dousa to Baldhoven, in Cheney and Hosington, *Weston: Collected Writings*, 243–245, especially lines 11–14.

how the verses of others were mixed up with hers in publication: "It would be better to form these brief praises into a separate book."[24] Although we might appreciate the glimpse of the social milieu which the mixed, dialogic collections of Weston's verse give, she herself clearly longed for a much more independent expression of herself as an author.

This manuscript note is dated Prague, 16 August 1610, two years before Weston's death. Sometime in the last half-decade of her life, Weston also published a poem commemorating the death of her mother: *In Obitum NOBILIS ET GENEROSÆ FÆMINÆ Dæ Ioannæ*.[25] I shall conclude by suggesting that this autobiographical poem, although founded upon grief and loss, nonetheless offered Weston the possibility of bypassing the problem of the female poet as I have been setting it out in this paper. There are no Muses or Graces, no Sappho, in this funeral poem. The only mythic female is Atropos, who exercises her fury again and again against Weston's diminishing family. The pain in this poem is very disturbing. But it enables her to write, much more vividly and sincerely than she is able to do in many of her verse supplications. Weston laments the loss of an intimate relationship of trust and help, not of the formal and always compromising relations of patron and client. She regrets the loss of her mother's blessing and touch, making the sign of the cross on her forehead and breast; she regrets the loss of maternal advice and maternal words.

> Non plus maternis me vocibus illa monebit,
> Nec mihi cui dicam, consule mater, erit.
> Non ea plus soboli benedicens prona mihiq[ue],
> Signa dabit fronti, pectoribusq[ue] crucis.

"Non plus maternis me vocibus illa monebit": "No more will she counsel me with a mother's words, nor will there be one to whom I can say 'Advise me, mother!'" I think it not a frivolous question to wonder *in what language* Joanna Weston

---

[24] The translation is by Connie McQuillen. Parts of the manuscript addition, with McQuillen's translation, are reproduced in Schleiner, "Elizabeth Weston," 14, n. 5. The complete manuscript verses (which are found in copies of the *Parthenicôn* in the British Library and the National Museum Library of Prague) are reproduced in Cheney and Hosington, *Weston: Collected Writings*, 304–307. In them Weston also expresses dissatisfaction with her inclusion in the catalogue of learned women, finding some items (e.g., the entry for Sappho?) less welcome than others. In other manuscript additions (Cheney and Hosington, *Weston: Collected Writings*, 307), she demands that George Carolides remove his verses from her book (a series of his epigrams were printed in Book I of *Parthenicôn*) — a considerably less polite attitude than in her response to Carolides discussed earlier!

[25] I am grateful to Professor Susan Bassnett for generously sending me a copy of her photocopy of this poem, which was published only in pamphlet form and together with two smaller epitaphs on Joanna Kelley by Nicolaus Maius and George Carolides. It is undated, but could not have appeared before 1606 since Elizabeth married in April 1603 and had had three children by the time her mother died, as she tells us in the poem. The original text was in the Strahov Library but disappeared in the early 1990s. Fortunately, the text is now preserved in Cheney and Hosington, *Weston: Collected Writings*, 335–343.

might have advised her daughter. According to the short epitaph by George Carolides, appended to *In Obitum*, Weston's mother was herself a learned lady: "Docta fuit vario, Latiæque idiomate lingvæ / Edere, quod memori finxerat ingenio" [she was learned in various languages and could give out, in the Latin tongue, what her ingenious memory had retained]. We do not really know where Elizabeth Weston learned her Latin. Susan Bassnett speculates that Edward Kelley supervised the education of both Elizabeth and her brother, and that perhaps the children also benefited from the tutors hired by Kelley's notorious associate, John Dee.[26] It would seem to me fitting if Elizabeth Weston learned at least her first Latin words at her mother's knee. For, after all, what she is doing in the poem on her mother's death is commemorating a real female line. *In Obitum* is very different from the historical catalogues of learned ladies of every age, in which Westonia herself was included. The difference is that Weston wrote from her *experience*,[27] of the pain of losing her mother, but also of the particular social and familial ties of her own time and place. As a necessarily mimetic Neo-Latin poet, she would draw upon this to enrich her poetry. As a female Neo-Latin poet, she would use it to create an accessibly domestic rather than a problematically mythic genealogy. This late poem for her mother leaves us to wonder what *more* Weston might have achieved, had she lived longer.

University of Alberta

---

[26] Bassnett, "Revising a Biography," 5–6, and "Absent Presences." In an essay about Edward Kelley published in the *London Review of Books*, Charles Nicholl quotes a manuscript by the Czech alchemist Simon Tadeas Budeck of Leslin which gave an account of Elizabeth Weston and her mother visiting Kelley on his deathbed at Most Castle. Budeck reported that Kelley "spoke English to his wife, and Flemish and Latin to his daughter." See "The Last Years of Edward Kelley, Alchemist to the Emperor," *LRB* 23, no. 8 (19 April 2001): 8. This adds weight to Bassnett's proposal that Weston learned Latin from her stepfather, but it does not preclude a pedagogical role as well for her mother, who was also praised as *docta*.

[27] In this poem she declares that she speaks "as one who has been wounded and is experienced" ("læsam / Vulnere, & expertam me facit ista loqui"). See Cheney and Hosington, *Weston: Collected Writings*, 336–337, lines 5–6.

L'anonimo carme pastorale iutitolato
Cinthias

DAVIDE CANFORA

La poesia bucolica è attestata nella storia letteraria italiana a partire dal principio del XIV secolo.[1] Ebbe luogo, a quel tempo, il noto scambio epistolare in forma di ecloghe latine tra Dante Alighieri e il maestro bolognese Giovanni del Virgilio. Anche Petrarca e Boccaccio nutrirono notevole interesse per il genere.

Si può affermare che la produzione pastorale trecentesca si richiamò apertamente al modello antico, latino e virgiliano in particolare (i personaggi di Titiro e Melibeo sono appunto i pastori protagonisti della prima ecloga dantesca, così come della prima ecloga di Virgilio). Di questo modello fu valorizzato in primo luogo l'aspetto allegorico, conformemente all'interpretazione più tipicamente medievale del genere bucolico.

La lezione dei tre grandi del Trecento non rimase naturalmente inascoltata. Il genere pastorale fu ampiamente frequentato in latino e, successivamente, anche in volgare. Tra la fine del Quattrocento e i primi anni del Cinquecento, dopo una ricca sperimentazione avviatasi all'incirca alla metà del secolo, si datano le poesie pastorali in volgare di Boiardo (autore, peraltro, anche di *Pastoralia* virgiliani in latino) e soprattutto l'*Arcadia* di Sannazaro, che deve considerarsi una tappa essenziale e rifondativa del genere. Quanto alla produzione bucolica latina, essa conobbe, dopo Petrarca

---

[1] Lo studio ancora oggi fondamentale, con riferimento al genere bucolico nella letteratura italiana, rimane E. Carrara, *La poesia pastorale* (Milano, 1909). Per quanto riguarda il *Bucolicum carmen* petrarchesco, il testo che certo esercitò maggiore influenza sul genere nel XIV secolo, mi limito qui a rinviare alla recente edizione diplomatica dell'autografo: D. De Venuto, *Il "Bucolicum carmen" di Petrarca. Edizione diplomatica dell'autografo Vat. lat. 3358* (Pisa, 1990). Del carme esiste anche un'utile concordanza: N. Mann, *A Concordance to Petrarch's "Bucolicum carmen"* (Pisa, 1984). Per una recente rilettura del poema, con particolare riferimento agli elementi di esso derivanti dalla cultura medievale, si veda M. Ariani, *Petrarca* (Roma, 1999), 203–213. Sulla riscoperta del genere bucolico nella letteratura del XIV secolo rinvio a G. Billanovich, F. Čįda, A. Campana, e P. O. Kristeller, "Scuola di retorica e poesia bucolica nel Trecento italiano," *Italia Medioevale e Umanistica* 4 (1961): 181–221; K. Krautter, *Die Renaissance des Bukolik in der lateinischen Literatur des XIV. Jahrhunderts: von Dante bis Petrarca* (München, 1983).

e Boccaccio, una fioritura notevole nel tardo Trecento e soprattutto nel secolo dell'Umanesimo, in particolare presso gli ambienti cortigiani, in cui più abitualmente si ricorse alla rappresentazione pastorale con intenti narrativi ed encomiastici. Ricordiamo le ecloghe composte in questo periodo in ambiente mantovano e ferrarese, nonché napoletano. Maestro del genere, nel secondo Quattrocento napoletano, fu Giovanni Gioviano Pontano.

A Napoli la lezione dei grandi autori del Trecento si era comunque affermata già prima del periodo pontaniano. Particolare influenza esercitò il magistero di Boccaccio, il quale aveva a lungo soggiornato nella città partenopea in giovane età e aveva fatto esplicitamente riferimento, nell'allegorico *Bucolicum Carmen*, al casato angioino, mettendone in scena i personaggi di maggiore rilievo sotto le spoglie di pastori. Di un'anonima ecloga latina napoletana, avente come protagonisti i pastori Dafni, Titiro e Mopso, in cui si narravano le vicende della guerra per la successione angioina (1435–1442), diede notizia Enrico Carrara nel già citato volume *La poesia pastorale*. Si tratta di una bucolica "forte imperfecta" — secondo la descrizione di Angelo Maria Bandini — trascritta su un codice conservato presso la Biblioteca Medicea Laurenziana.

Mi occuperò qui dell'anonimo *Pastorale carmen cuius titulus Cinthias*: un testo, non datato, che potrebbe essere, come vedremo, di alcuni anni più antico rispetto all'ecloga laurenziana. Di esso rimane, che io sappia, un'unica copia in un manoscritto, vergato nella seconda metà del Quattrocento, della Library of the Earl of Leicester, Holkham Hall.[2] Si tratta di una bucolica costituita da 295 esametri latini di contenuto storico-allegorico, della quale sto preparando l'edizione.

Il racconto ripercorre gli eventi del regno di Napoli e del casato angioino a partire dalla morte di Roberto di Angiò fino almeno agli ultimi anni del Trecento.[3] Ap-

---

[2] Holkham Hall, Library of the Earl of Leicester MS 483. Si tratta di un codice cartaceo databile al XV secolo (l'ultimo foglio reca la data 1486), di contenuto vario: oltre a testi molto circolanti nella tradizione umanistica (il *Tyrannus* di Senofonte nella traduzione di Leonardo Bruni, la *Historia de duobus amantibus* di Enea Silvio Piccolomini, Esopo tradotto da Valla), figurano nel manoscritto testi anonimi e vere e proprie pagine che sembrano esercitazioni di scuola, disordinate e di non agevole lettura. Il carme *Cinthias* è ai fol. 118r–124r. Per una descrizione, comunque parziale, del codice, rinvio a: S. De Ricci, *A Handlist of Manuscripts in the Library of the Earl of Leicester at Holkham Hall* (Oxford, 1932), 42; P. O. Kristeller, *Iter*, 4: 46. Una descrizione più dettagliata è nel catalogo manoscritto della Biblioteca: W. Roscoe e F. Madden, *Catalogue of Manuscripts in the Library of Holkham Hall* (8 ms. vols., 1815–1828).

[3] La bibliografia relativa al casato angioino è naturalmente vastissima e non si intende qui dare conto di essa in modo dettagliato. Mi limiterò a segnalare, da ultimo S. Tramontana, *Il Mezzogiorno medievale: Normanni, Svevi, Angioini, Aragonesi nei secoli XI–XV* (Roma, 2000). Con particolare riferimento ai rapporti tra gli angioini di Napoli e gli angioini di Ungheria, rinvio a *Colloquio italo-ungherese sul tema: gli Angioini di Napoli e di Ungheria*, organizzato d'intesa con l'Accademia delle Scienze di Ungheria, Roma, 23–24 maggio 1972 (Roma, 1974). Studi ancora validi sulla dinastia in generale sono A. Cutolo, *Gli Angioini* (Firenze, 1934); V. Epifanio, *Gli Angioini di Napoli e la Sicilia: dall'inizio del regno di Giovanna I alla pace di Catania* (Napoli, 1936). Si vedano altresì E. G. Léonard, *Gli Angioini di Napoli*, trad. R. Liguori (Milano, 1967); B. Ruggiero, *Potere, istituzioni, chiese locali: aspetti e motivi del Mezzogiorno medievale dai Longobardi agli Angioni* (Bologna, 1977).

paiono sulla scena in primo luogo due pastori, Arion e Eschinus, il secondo dei quali, in apertura, invoca la morte per sé e paventa immense sciagure a causa delle gravi condizioni di salute di Cinzia, figura femminile presentata come "noster amor", "silvarum regina", "astrorum decus", "spes unica ruris", "tranquilla quies et grata voluptas"; descritta inoltre nella sua grazia femminile secondo i canoni della poesia erotica latina ("Quid memorem auratos labi per colla capillos? [...] Quid roseas super ora notas tenerumque labellum?") e, al tempo stesso, definita "dea" e ninfa ("nimphas tantum hec supereminet omnes"); appellata infine "requies" e "spes gratissima nostra", di fronte alla quale avevano un tempo tremato, quando ancora godeva di buona salute, i "Calabri lupi", le fiere della Sicilia, il "Pelignus aper" e l' "ursus atrox".

Passato quel tempo, tuttavia, Cinzia — così si lamenta Eschinus — "mesta iacens macie vix egros substinet artus". Le sue gote sono sfiorite, il collo rimane immobile, le tenebre stigie hanno oscurato i suoi occhi e la casta fronte a stento conserva l'antico pudore; la sua pelle è secca e malata, le membra sono pallide, madide e consunte da un turpe veleno. "En virgo moritura iacet" — esclama ancora Eschinus con parole oraziane — "nec curat olive [...]: nec sum qualis eram, periit pars maxima nostri": e subito dopo il pastore invita le proprie caprette a rifugiarsi in luoghi riparati, a fronte di imminenti e terribili sventure. Da queste ultime immagini usate da Eschinus si ricava con chiarezza che Cinzia, oltre ad essere raffigurata come donna bella e potente ("dum stabula et montes, silvas et rura regebat") e come ninfa e dea, è altresì descritta come personaggio direttamente partecipe del mondo dei pastori ("nec curat olive").

Fin qui si estende la prima parte del carme pastorale, che rievoca in modo evidente l'ambientazione tipica delle bucoliche virgiliane: due pastori si incontrano e, attraverso immagini allegoriche, fanno riferimento a vicende storiche presenti, o comunque vicine nel tempo, in modo invero alquanto oscuro (chi si celi dietro l'immagine di Cinzia non risulta ancora chiaro al lettore, né emerge ancora in modo esplicito alcun riferimento agli angioini).

Con il v. 104 prende avvio la seconda parte del componimento. Qui l'ecloga si articola notevolmente. Eschinus — dopo essersi chiesto "sed que causa mali fuerit?" ed essersi anche dato una risposta ("discordia demens / et rebus non equa diu fortuna secundis") — si dilunga in un'ampia serie di allusioni a personaggi che furono a vario titolo protagonisti della storia del regno di Napoli tra Trecento e primo Quattrocento: Roberto di Angiò, re Andrea di Ungheria (marito di Giovanna I di Angiò), papa Urbano VI, Ladislao di Angiò-Durazzo, Luigi II di Angiò.

In questa seconda parte del carme non viene meno l'oscurità del testo allegorico e solo grazie ad alcune glosse apposte dal copista sui margini è possibile ricostruire in modo immediato quali figure storiche siano via via evocate nell'intervento di Eschinus. Appare in ogni caso chiaro che siamo di fronte ad una nostalgica rievocazione del tempo glorioso della monarchia angioina a Napoli e ad una dolorosa ricostruzione delle vicende che minarono alla base la solidità del regno nel corso dei decenni, a partire dalla morte di re Roberto.

Sempre utile potrà risultare la consultazione del III tomo ("in cui contiensi la politia del Regno sotto Angioini ed Aragonesi") della *Istoria civile del Regno di Napoli* di Pietro Giannone.

La scomparsa di quest'ultimo, avvenuta nel 1343, è descritta come "summa dies lugenda per urbem". Dopo quell'evento luttuoso, i fati diedero libero sfogo alle furie, che devastarono i pascoli dei pastori, fino a quel tempo fiorenti e felici, e trascinarono con sé nel regno delle ombre il duce dei Pannoni: l'allusione, come chiarisce il copista con una glossa sul margine, è ad Andrea di Ungheria. A quest'ultimo, secondogenito del re di Ungheria, re Roberto aveva promesso in sposa la sorella, Giovanna I di Angiò: le nozze si erano celebrate nel 1342; la corona di Napoli fu peraltro concessa ad Andrea solo nel 1345, a seguito delle pressioni esercitate su Giovanna da papa Clemente VI e dal re Luigi di Ungheria, padre di Andrea; nello stesso anno 1345 Andrea morì in una congiura, promossa forse dalla stessa regina.

Quest'ultimo episodio causò l'invasione del regno di Napoli da parte di Luigi di Ungheria. La guerra — che conobbe alterne vicende e vide il coinvolgimento anche di Carlo di Durazzo, conte di Gravina, il quale ambiva a prendere il posto di Giovanna, di cui aveva sposato la nipote ed erede Margherita — si concluse nel 1352, con il ritiro dall'Italia meridionale delle truppe ungheresi, dopo che Napoli era stata presa per ben due volte.

Anche l'attacco di Luigi viene allusivamente rievocato nell'egloga: "tunc quales sonuere unde qualesque procelle! / In miserum cecidere gregem, ruit asper ab oris / Argus Illiricis fraterna morte cruentus." Che Argo rappresenti qui Luigi di Ungheria è chiarito ancora una volta dal glossatore del manoscritto, che annota sul margine, in corrispondenza dei versi appena citati: "rex Ungarie". Ad Argo l'autore del carme aveva già fatto riferimento poco prima, osservando che, quando ancora Cinzia "silvas et rura regebat", "Argus iratus procul hinc pascebat onagros." Si noti qui incidentalmente che l'uso di "hinc" rappresenta un ragionevole indizio del fatto che chi scrisse il carme era, se non napoletano, comunque presente presso la corte angioina.

I versi in cui si rammenta la discesa in Italia di Luigi di Ungheria rappresentano un passaggio cruciale del carme, poiché in questa sede per la prima volta l'immagine di Cinzia viene associata a fatti concreti e non solo a raffigurazioni oscuramente allegoriche. L'autore scrive che, al tempo dell'invasione ungherese, "quantos illa tulit miseranda tunc labores Cinthia!". Cinzia fu dunque duramente provata dalla guerra scatenata da re Luigi a seguito della congiura contro il figlio Andrea. "Ex illo" — prosegue Eschinus—"adversis fluxerunt tempora fatis", in una interminabile successione di sventure. E ancora: "sed nunc flere libet [...]: gemino sponsata viro complexibus heret [scil.: Cinthia]." Cinzia è dunque "nunc" legata ad un "vir geminus", ai cui abbracci si abbandona lascivamente. Il che suggerisce all'autore del carme una breve e topica invettiva contro l'ambizione umana e l'avidità di gloria e di denaro.

Ora, la sdegnata allusione al "vir geminus" — alla luce della quale si spiega l'iniziale riferimento dell'autore alla castità perduta dalla sua adorata Cinzia — potrebbe essere motivata nel modo seguente: Giovanna I, dopo l'uccisione del marito Andrea, si era avvicinata a Roberto, principe di Taranto, legandosi successivamente al fratello di Roberto, Luigi di Taranto, con il quale si sposò ventunenne nel 1347. L'odio di Carlo di Durazzo nei confronti del casato tarantino era stato uno dei motivi da cui lo stesso Carlo aveva tratto il pretesto per inserirsi nel già ricordato conflitto tra la corona angioina e quella di Ungheria. Cinzia potrebbe dunque essere l'immagine allegorica dietro cui si cela la figura di Giovanna I di Angiò. Si ricordi, in proposito, anche quanto l'autore del carme aveva precedentemente scritto riguardo ai "labores" toccati a Cinzia, definita in quel caso "miseranda", a causa della discesa in Italia di Luigi di Ungheria: nessuno più di Giovanna, evidentemente, era stato danneggiato dall'invasione ungherese. Anche il riferimento al fatto che Cinzia non "curat olive" è in accordo con lo scenario fin qui delineato: il disinteresse per la pianta dell'olivo, notoriamente simbolo di pace già per gli antichi, si adatta bene, infatti, ad una regina il cui regno fu funestato da numerose guerre.

Attraverso un'ampia serie di altre immagini allegoriche il carme prosegue raccontando gli eventi relativi agli anni successivi alla guerra tra ungheresi e angioini. E' qui incidentalmente opportuno precisare che la narrazione presentata nel carme è diacronica: perciò il "nunc" pronunciato da Eschinus nella citata frase "nunc flere libet, gemino sponsata viro complexibus heret" non fa riferimento al tempo presente, non deve dunque intendersi nel senso di "oggi", bensì segnala una delle varie tappe della vicenda angioina via via raccontata.

Si coglie, in particolare, un'allusione alla persona di papa Urbano VI, uno dei responsabili del Grande Scisma di Occidente. Urbano VI fu uno dei sostenitori di Carlo III di Durazzo, il quale — rivendicando le stesse pretese che avevano animato l'azione del fratello Carlo di Durazzo — irruppe in Napoli nel 1382, conquistò il regno e fece decapitare l'ormai anziana Giovanna. Quest'ultima, prima della fine, fece peraltro in tempo a nominare erede al trono Luigi I di Angiò, fratello del re di Francia, Carlo V. Luigi I di Angiò morì a Bari di lì a due anni, nel 1384, prima di potersi scontrare sul campo di battaglia con il rivale Carlo III di Durazzo. Il titolo di erede al trono, attribuito da Giovanna a Luigi I, si trasmise a quel punto a Luigi II di Angiò, figlio di Luigi I.

Alla morte di Cinzia nel carme non si fa espressamente riferimento: si fa tuttavia riferimento, nel finale, alla fuga disperata dei "coloni" di fronte ad una nefasta invasione straniera ("sic miseros cecus subit furor undique, tandem / dispersi sine lege ruunt et tecta relinquunt / dulcia, nec cari possunt renovare penates") e si chiamano altresì in causa le figure di "Ladixlaus" (Ladislao di Angiò-Durazzo) e di "Lodovicus" (Luigi II di Angiò), il primo definito "generosus avis, Grayo cognomine Fedrus", il secondo "formosus Alexis". L'uso di associare i personaggi storici al mondo dei pastori — allo stesso modo in cui Giovanna, come si è visto, prendeva il nome di Cinzia — è ovviamente tipico del genere pastorale allegorico: si noti, in particolare, che in Boccaccio ricorrono molti dei nomi di pastori presenti anche nell'anonimo carme *Cinthias* (nel *Buccolicum Carmen* Argo era ad esempio Roberto di Angiò, Alessi era Andrea di Ungheria).

Si è detto che il "generosus avis" e "Alexis" rappresentano qui, rispettivamente, Ladislao di Angiò-Durazzo e Luigi II di Angiò, come ci viene chiarito dal glossatore del manoscritto. Ladislao e Luigi si contesero il regno di Napoli nell'ultimo decennio del Trecento, fino al 1414 (anno della morte di Ladislao). Ora, poiché questi due personaggi entrarono in scena dopo la morte di Giovanna I di Angiò, si ricava da ciò che il carme pastorale intitolato *Cinthias* fu verosimilmente scritto dopo la morte della regina.

Di Ladislao si dice che "errat periturus in undis" come un marinaio sorpreso dalla tempesta. Né il nome di Luigi II è associato ad immagini benauguranti: "quid terimus sermone diem?", si chiede al v. 228 Arion, interrompendo finalmente il lungo discorso di Eschinus, il quale aveva nominato Luigi II un attimo prima; e soggiunge: "sic astra minantur / et manifesta mali micuerunt signa futuri." A quali "signa" alluda Arion non è del tutto chiaro. Non è cioè dato di sapere fino a quale punto l'autore del carme ebbe modo di seguire personalmente la vicenda del lento e faticoso declino della corona angioina a Napoli. L'apparente assenza di riferimenti a Giovanna II di Angiò — sorella di Ladislao e ultima regina angioina di Napoli prima che Alfonso di Aragona, da lei stessa chiamato in aiuto già nel 1421, si impadronisse del regno nel 1442 — lascia intendere che il carme è precedente al 1414, anno della morte di Ladislao, e forse anche al 1411, anno in cui Ladislao prevalse definitivamente su Luigi II di Angiò e lo costrinse a riparare in Francia. La guerra tra Ladislao e Luigi II appare infatti, nel carme, ancora in corso ("non arma iuvant" si legge al v. 222). Ovvio termine *post quem* deve, per altro verso, considerarsi il 1389, l'anno in cui ebbe di fatto inizio la lotta tra Luigi II e Ladislao, all'epoca ancora fanciulli (Ladislao fu riconosciuto "maggiorenne" solo nel 1393).

Non è comunque da escludersi che il riferimento a Ladislao errante "periturus in undis" consenta una datazione più precisa. Potrebbe infatti trattarsi di un riferimento alla spedizione di Ladislao in Ungheria, svoltasi nel 1402–1403: il rivale di Luigi II, dopo avere sottratto a quest'ultimo Napoli nel 1399, si mise per mare e sbarcò a Zara con l'assenso dei Veneziani, proclamandosi re di Ungheria. Quanto alla pessimistica e drammatica espressione usata da Eschinus nel carme a proposito di Ladislao ("errat periturus in undis"), essa allude, forse, al fatto che l'impresa di Ungheria fallì quasi subito e Ladislao fu ben presto costretto a rientrare a Napoli per riprendere la lotta con Luigi II.

Università degli Studi di Bari

¿Por qué se prohibieron las Adnotationes de Philipp Melanchthon a la obra de Salustio en México a finales del siglo XVI?

AVELINA CARRERA DE LA RED

Son numerosas las prescripciones oficiales que tratan de neutralizar la llegada de las ideas protestantes a América; las que afectan a la producción literaria son las más tempranas, pues pronto se comprende la importante función del libro en la transmisión de las nuevas ideas. Disposiciones civiles y eclesiásticas representan la censura libresca oficial, que atiende las directrices del Concilio de Trento (1545–1563) en cuanto a la necesidad de limitar la circulación de libros "sospechosos o perniciosos." Fechas como 1554, 1558, 1569, y 1598, años de celebración de las Cortes de Toledo, La Coruña, Valladolid, y Madrid, marcan los hitos más destacados en el tema de la censura en la circulación de libros. Paralelamente, en España y América se regula toda una legislación relativa a la impresión e importación de libros en el Nuevo Mundo.[1]

Entre los primeros decretos sancionados por la autoridad real que regulan la importación de libros a América, se encuentra la *Cedula que manda que no consientan que se lleuen a las Indias libros de historias profanas*, cédula firmada el 29 de septiembre de 1543, en la que se prohíbe llevar a aquellas tierras libros de materia profana, fábulas y novelas, "de mentirosas historias," pues de ello "se siguen muchos inconvenientes: porque los Indios que supieren leer, dandose a ellos" —dice—, "dexaran los libros de sancta y buena doctrina, y leyendo los de mentirosas historias deprenderan en ellos malas costumbres y vicios. . . ."[2] La disposición de 9 de octubre de 1556 insiste en

---

[1] Véase la introducción de J. M. de Bujanda a *Index de l'Inquisition Espagnole: 1551, 1554, 1559* (Sherbrooke, 1984), 35–37, e *Index de l'Inquisition Espagnole: 1583, 1584* (Sherbrooke, 1993), 17–49. Numerosa documentación se encuentra también en Antonio Sierra Corella, *La censura de libros y papeles en España y los índices y catálogos españoles de los prohibidos y expurgados* (Madrid, 1947). Para el tema de la Inquisición en América, puede consultarse la obra de Juan Blázquez Miguel, *La inquisición en América (1569–1820)* ([s.n., s.l.], 1994).

[2] de Bujanda, *Index de l'Inquisition Espagnole: 1551*, 36.

que no se envíen a América libros prohibidos por la Inquisición, y solicita a las autoridades civiles y religiosas de Perú vigilar la llegada de navíos y ejercer un control para incautar los libros que ya estuviesen en aquellas tierras; y ello, "porque en tierra nueva donde se planta agora nuestra sancta fee catolica, conuiene y es necessario que se arraygue y siembre buena doctrina y no doctrina perjudicial, y escandalosa."[3] De tales libros se llenan los Índices o Catálogos de libros prohibidos publicados en la segunda mitad del siglo XVI. En 1551, impresos en Valladolid y en Toledo, aparecen en España los primeros. Pocos años más tarde, en 1554, se publica en Valladolid, por orden del Santo Oficio, una censura general contra los errores introducidos en las ediciones de la Sagrada Escritura. Nuevos Catálogos serán impresos en 1559, 1583, y 1584. En América la censura libresca oficial está regulada por estos *Indices Librorum Prohibitorum* y por el *Manuale Qualificatorum Sanctae Inquisitionis* en el que se enumeraban los libros sujetos a expurgación o bien aquellos que debían ser quemados.[4] En 1571, el inquisidor Moya de Contreras ordenó que cuantos poseyeran libros presentaran un catálogo de los mismos ante el Tribunal y mandó que sus funcionarios visitasen las librerías de la ciudad de México para retirar los prohibidos. Los comisarios tenían instrucciones especiales para que en los puertos vigilasen los navíos que pudiesen transportar tales libros prohibidos.

En una de estas revisiones, hacia 1573, a Juan Rodríguez se le requisan "el libro de Officiis de Cicerón, con las anotaciones de Philipo Melantón, y tiene las Epístolas del mismo Cicerón con los argumentos y Escholias de Crisóforo Engendorfino,[5] que son autores cuyas obras están prohibidas por el cathálogo." En el mismo requerimiento, a un tal Rodrigo Maldonado se le requisan como libros prohibidos "que se han de recoger," "las Epístolas de Cicerón, con Scholias de Xophar Engendorphino y Copia verborum con los Comentarios de Bethischio,[6] y Salustio, con las anotaciones de Philipo Melantón y Horas."[7]

Un recorrido por decretos y dictados de esta naturaleza parece suficiente para responder a la pregunta que encabeza este trabajo. Los libros de Melanchthon aparecen en todos los Índices (en algunos casos, sus *Opera omnia*) por ser fruto de uno de los *recentes haeretici* que han llenado la sagrada doctrina de errores, y como autor de obras llenas de "falsa, mala o sospechosa doctrina." Sin embargo, me parece interesante contrastar esta condena con la doctrina del propio Melanchthon, la que él quiso transmitir a todos aquellos jóvenes que como Rodrigo Maldonado leían sus anotaciones al tiempo que estudiaban a Salustio. Trato, pues, de presentar el espíritu de este trabajo historiográfico melanchtoniano, para poder así comprender mejor los recelos que en muchos momentos de la historia americana mostraron las autoridades frente a la enseñanza de la historia de la Antigüedad, sobre todo entre la población indígena.

---

[3] de Bujanda, *Index de l'Inquisition Espagnole: 1551*, 36–37.
[4] Cf. Francisco Fernández del Castillo, *Libros y libreros en el siglo XVI*, 2ª ed. (México, 1982), 12.
[5] Cristóbal Hegendorf, Leipzig 1500–Lüneburgo 1561.
[6] Juan Velcurio (Veltkirchius), m. 1534.
[7] Cf. Fernández del Castillo, *Libros y libreros en el siglo XVI*, 480 y 490.

La historiografía en América se desarrolla ante todo a partir de crónicas contemporáneas o recopilaciones generales de época antigua. A comienzos de siglo se traslada la historiografía clásica con la cultura renacentista. El hecho histórico de la conjuración de Catilina, por ejemplo, se conoce y tiene un gran arraigo en el espíritu revolucionario americano de algunas épocas. También Jugurta y la Guerra de Numidia se encuentran a menudo citados entre las fuentes utilizadas por los cronistas de Indias para la elaboración de sus obras. Y es que la presencia de Salustio en el mundo intelectual del Renacimiento es importante. En 1529, en La Haya, se imprimen unos breves comentarios de Melanchthon y Hulderichus Huttenus a las dos monografías de este autor, junto con algunos fragmentos de sus *Historiae*, las *Catilinarias* de Cicerón, y la pseudo-ciceroniana *Inuectiua in Sallustium*.[8] Años más tarde, en 1533, aparecerán en Lyon las *Adnotationes* de Melanchton a la obra de Salustio.[9] Además de algunas ediciones alemanas, como la de Mainz en 1544, la obra de Melanchthon conocerá en Lyon reediciones sucesivas localizadas sobre todo en la primera mitad del siglo XVI (1536, 1545, 1551, 1561). El interés de este autor por la obra de Salustio se inscribe en el interés general que el historiador clásico despierta en el Renacimiento. Toda una labor de crítica textual, traducción, y comentario se elabora en torno a su obra. Motivaciones ideológicas y vitales, además de estilísticas, explican que Salustio, su lengua y forma de construir y expresarse atraigan a los escritores renacentistas, quienes durante décadas lo van a considerar uno de los más destacados guías del arte y del pensamiento en historiografía. El nacimiento de las ciudades a la vida, sobre todo en territorio italiano, el sentimiento del patriotismo que aflora en tantos autores de la época, el "catilinarismo" que significa que algunos hombres políticos del Renacimiento desarrollen un espíritu de libertad y de gloria que a veces estalla en exaltación y a menudo roza el delito político (megalomanía, organización de conjuras, e incluso, inducción al tiranicidio),[10] encuentran en las monografías salustianas los mejores modelos de orientación de la filosofía y de la práctica políticas, además de una inmejorable fuente de información histórica sobre los acontecimientos que en ella se narran. Por otra parte, Salustio informa sus escritos de juicios morales. Persigue el descubrimiento de las causas de los acontecimientos. Estudia la psicología de los protagonistas de la historia. Incluye vivos discursos de los personajes que explican por sí mismos sus motivaciones en la acción. Condena a quienes han llenado la vida de Roma de corrupción, y defiende el patriotismo y la lealtad al Estado. Escribe con una prosa breve, vibrante, a veces coloquial, llena de novedad y variedad, que contrasta con la unifor-

---

[8] Ejemplar de la Bibliothèque Nationale de París: *C. Crispi Salustii . . . In Catilinam atque Jugurtham opuscula, per Hulderichum Huttenum atque Phil. Melanchthonem scholiis . . . illustrata . . . [M.T. Ciceronis Oratio contra Salustium. Ejusdem Orationes contra Catilinam. Portii Latronis Declamatio contra Catilinam. Orationes quaedam ex libris Historiarum C. Crispi Sallustii]* (Haganoe: per J. Secerium, 1529).

[9] *C. Crispi Sallustii de L. Sergii Catilinae coniuratione, et Bello Iugurthino historiae, cum reliquis orationibus . . . His accesserunt Philippi Melanchthonis . . . adnotationes. Praeterea flosculorum Sallustianorum ac rerum notarum dignarum indices duo* (Lugduni: apud Sebastianum Gryphium, 1533). Utilizo el ejemplar de la Bibliothèque de Lyon. El único ejemplar de esta obra que se encuentra en la Biblioteca Nacional de Madrid (la misma edición anterior) está censurado.

[10] Cf. Ezio Bolaffi, *Sallustio e la sua fortuna nei secoli* (Roma, 1949), 257ss.

midad de César y los simétricos períodos ciceronianos.¹¹ La enseñanza de Salustio durante el Renacimiento se asocia estrechamente a la formación en poética y retórica. No en vano, el primer comentarista del historiador clásico fue Lorenzo Valla, precisamente el pionero de la corriente retoricista en el género historiográfico; para él, escribir historia es una forma de literatura y, como tal, ha de ser valorada por los *praecepta de apte dicendo*.¹²

Hasta América se trasladan estos postulados retoricistas para la creación de obras históricas; allí se comprueba que los cronistas se inspiran, dentro de su originalidad, en el discurso que había inaugurado la historiografía del Humanismo italiano. "En la historiografía del Nuevo Mundo se desarrolló, espléndidamente, la pesquisa filológica y el anhelo por lograr un embellecimiento sobrio de la materia narrativa," dice Enrique Pupo-Walker.¹³

En este sentido se orientan las anotaciones de Philipp Melanchthon a las dos monografías de Salustio, *Catilina* y *Jugurta*. Melanchthon sitúa en los primeros niveles de los estudios la gramática, la dialéctica, la filosofía, y la moral. La enseñanza de la historia ha de estar rigurosamente garantizada, pues ella permite valorar en toda su dimensión la gloria universal de las Artes, enseña lo que está bien y lo que está mal, lo que es útil y lo que no lo es, no deja de lado ningún aspecto de la vida, pública o privada; es la regla (*ratio*) de las relaciones humanas. "Poetas e historiadores" — dice — "deben ser conocidos por los jóvenes desde el principio de su formación."¹⁴ En general, las *Adnotationes* son un excelente ejercicio de retórica. Es una visión técnica, pero no tecnificada, pues el objetivo último de su autor es estimular la conducta moral de los jóvenes adolescentes, principales destinatarios de su comentario, a través de la belleza literaria de una obra clásica.

Melanchthon abre sus notas al texto de Salustio con la que podría considerarse declaración de principios de todo historiador humanista. Ante el famoso pasaje del prólogo de *Catilina* en el que Salustio anuncia su decisión de narrar algunos de los capítulos esenciales de la historia del pueblo romano, una vez que había conseguido liberarse de la servidumbre que impone la política, Melanchthon señala: "Nam in historico potissimum loqueri solet fides, et M. Cicero lumen ueritatis appellat historiam," una afirmación en la que hay que subrayar la humanista unión de conceptos como *fides, ueritas e historia*.

Los ejes sobre los que se mueven las apreciaciones de Melanchthon al texto de Salustio son dos, retórica y moralismo; ambos conforman la retórica-moralizante o el moralismo-retoricista que sostiene el espíritu crítico del alemán en toda su obra. Las

---

[11] Cf. Avelina Carrera, "Comentarios humanistas del siglo XVI a la obra de Salustio," in F. Grau Codina et al., eds., *La Universitat de Valencia i l'Humanisme:* Studia Humanitatis *i renovació cultural a Europa i al Nou Món* (Valencia, 2003), 383–391.

[12] Cf. Linda Gardiner Janik, "Lorenzo Valla: The Primacy of Rhetoric and the De-moralization of History," *History and Theory* 12 (1973): 389–404.

[13] Enrique Pupo-Walker, *La vocación literaria del pensamiento histórico en América: Desarrollo de la prosa de ficción: Siglos XVI, XVII, XVIII y XIX* (Madrid, 1982), 80ss.

[14] *Encomion eloquentiae* 3:50, citado en Jean-François Boisset, *Mélanchthon. Éducateur de l'Allemagne* (Paris, 1967), 110.

referencias que dan forma a las anotaciones de Melanchthon confirman el texto de Salustio como fuente literaria bella, expresiva y de elegante estilo, en la línea del juicio que este historiador merece a muchos críticos del Renacimiento. Además esta fuente literaria es fuente histórica, transmisora de valores imperecederos.

En realidad, Melanchthon parece concebir *Catilina* y *Jugurta* como dos grandes discursos. De hecho, los famosos discursos pronunciados por los personajes de Salustio se analizan en todos sus componentes; véase, por ejemplo, el discurso de Adérbal ante la asamblea romana *(Iug. 14): Exordium ab officio (1); Propositio (2); Confirmatio a suae personae meritis (3); A meritis familiae (5); Ab ipso casu (6);* Πάθος *a beneficiis Micipsae erga Iugurtham a regni illius calamitatibus aliis (9); A facili (13); Amplificatio sceleris (14); A necessario cur confugiat ad Romanos (15); Amplificatio superioris argumenti (16); A necessario (17); Confutatio (20); A uoto (21);* Πάθος *per apostrophen (22); Id est, ostendo quam instabiles sint res humanae (23); Peroratio (24).* Pues bien, las partes narrativas del texto de Salustio tienen unas anotaciones muy similares. Las numerosas consideraciones retóricas que subraya en los márgenes del texto le sirven al alumno como guía para su interpretación. Allí se apuntan *schemata, captationes beneuolentiae, concessiones, confirmationes, decorum, loci communes, exempla, comparationes, aetiologiae, perorationes, epiphonemata, insinuationes, confutationes, apostrophes, amplificationes, excursus,* ὑποτιπόσεις, πάθος. Y cuando algún pasaje, sentencia, o afirmación le interesa especialmente, incita al alumno a que lo lea por medio de breves y pregnantes llamadas de atención, combinando retórica y moral; "collationes egregiae, nam raro plures diuitiae honeste parantur," apunta ante la presentación de las virtudes de los primeros romanos (*Cat.* 7.6); César elabora en su discurso un magnífico "schema quo eleuat autoritatem aliorum, qui contra coniuratos dixerant sententias liberiores" (*Cat.* 51.10); la batalla de Zama, por ejemplo, se describe en Salustio con una "egregia hypotiposis quae iterum atque iterum est legenda" (*Iug.* 60.3–4); la presentación que el clásico hace de Mario como candidato popular, íntegro y honesto hasta que la ambición lo llevó a la ruina, es un "locus ille iucundus et plenus eruditionis" (*Iug.* 63).

La fuerza expresiva se asocia a la fuerza del contenido. Retórica y oratoria se utilizan para persuadir, y aparece entonces el humanista atento al hombre, y sobre todo, al joven a quien se dirigen un sinfín de mensajes moralizantes, tratando de moldear sus permeables espíritus en las virtudes del valor, la honradez, la lealtad, el servicio a los demás, la amistad, la prudencia, el buen gobierno, o la libertad, opuestas a los vicios de la servidumbre, la ambición, o la envidia tan denostados en el autor de Amiterno: "Exemplum corruptae ciuitatis" (*Cat.* 10.6); "Ambitio" (*Cat.* 11.1); "Luxus" (*Cat.* 11.3); "His artibus inescabat adolescentes" (*Cat.* 14.5); "Seueritas in Catone" (*Cat.* 54.5); "Non est obnoxius mortalitati animus" (*Iug.* 2.3); "Reprehensio morum" (*Iug.* 4.7); "Docilitas" (*Iug.* 5.2); "Sine inuidia laudem inuenit, quae laus modesta est" (*Iug.* 6.1); "Munimenta regnorum sunt boni amici, inquit Cicero" (*Iug.* 10.5); "Magna ingenia aegre ferunt iniuriam" (*Iug.* 22.3); "Adhortatio ad recuperandam libertatem, et est a minori" (*Iug.* 31.11); "Vt discernatis bonos a malis" (*Iug.* 31.28); "Abusi sunt uictoria" (*Iug.* 42.2); "Vtrinque peccatum est, Gracchi nimis magno motu rem agebant, Senatus nimis crudeliter uindicabat" (*Iug.* 42.5); "Nomen romanum ubique male audiit propter auaritiam" (*Iug.* 43.5); "Neque nimium indulgebat militi, quod est ambitionis, neque defatigabat, quod est saeuitiae" (*Iug.* 46.1);

"Animus tyranni nunquam quietus aut securus esse potest, timetur enim ab omnibus, et contra ipse omnes timet" (*Iug.* 72.2); "Nouus homo qui inclarescit uirtute sua" (*Iug.* 73.6); "Crudelis uictoria. Excusat crudelitatem Romanam" (*Iug.* 91.6); "Parum sancte coluit matrimonium" (*Iug.* 95.3); "Exemplum boni principis" (*Iug.* 100.5); etc.

Se comprueban en las notas al texto de Salustio las características de la *exegesis methodica* de Philipp Melanchthon, magníficamente sintetizadas por Kees Meerhoff. El profesor, pedagogo y teólogo alemán, partiendo de su amplio dominio de la tradición clásica y de las directrices pedagógicas del Humanismo italiano, persigue la interpretación del texto a través de las reglas del discurso y de las normas que ofrece la retórica, como paso previo para la elaboración de un texto propio. Es éste un curioso sistema en el que el método de desarrollo lógico tiende a coincidir con el método de amplificación oratoria y en el que, incluso, los *loci communes* se revisten de emoción. Partiendo de sus convicciones religiosas y de su profundo humanismo, Melanchthon estudia el texto de Salustio, su lengua y su cultura, como transmisor de una doctrina sólida y un mensaje de los que él quiere persuadir al alumno utilizando un método claro, sencillo y pregnante.[15]

Es la nueva historiografía del Renacimiento; en ella, la nueva forma de ver a los clásicos trae consigo una nueva perspectiva histórica.[16] Autores como N. Maquiavelo subrayan que la historia debe ser útil moral y políticamente, al tiempo que amena en su relato, despertando con su ejemplo "un intenso deseo de seguir el ejemplo del bien," e incentivando la acción política en momentos históricos de tanta calamidad y falta de reglas morales, religiosas, civiles, o militares. Lorenzo Valla había puesto de manifiesto el potencial revolucionario que la historia lleva consigo. Antes que él, Leonardo Bruni mostraba cómo escribir historia política se relaciona con numerosos temas como la libertad y el engrandecimiento del Estado. Aeneas Silvius Piccolomini exhorta al joven heredero al trono de Bohemia y Hungría a que lea a los ilustres historiadores de la Antigüedad y no las crónicas medievales, llenas de barbarismos, mentiras, y fábulas. Battista Guarini empuja al estudio de los historiadores romanos para aprender costumbres, leyes, instituciones, y la variabilidad de la fortuna humana.[17]

Mal habían de parecerle estas amonestaciones, tan del gusto humanista, a un personaje como Jerónimo López, quien en 1545 en México denunciaba cómo los indios a través de la lengua latina y *por los libros que leen* han podido conocer nuestra historia, "de dónde procedemos e cómo fuimos sojuzgados de los romanos e convertidos a la fe de gentiles, e todo lo demás que se escribió en este caso, que les causa decir que también nosotros venimos de gentiles e fuimos sujetos e ganados e sojuzgados, e fuimos sujetos a los romanos e nos alzamos e rebelamos"; el peligro de sublevación

---

[15] Kees Meerhoff, "Philippe Melanchthon (1497–1560)," in *Centuriae Latinae. Cent une figures humanistes de la Renaissance aux Lumières offertes à Jacques Chomarat*, réunies par Colette Nativel (Genève, 1997), 537–549.

[16] Cf. Charles G. Nauert, Jr., *Humanism and the Culture of Renaissance Europe*, 3ª ed. (Cambridge, 1998), 19ss.

[17] Cf. Eric Cochrane, *Historians and Historiography in the Italian Renaissance* (Chicago–London, 1981), 266ss.

que este ejemplo podía provocar parecía claro para este mexicano.[18] Además, no faltan voces críticas que ponen en cuestión los supuestos valores morales y estéticos que proporciona la lectura de estos autores. Algunos consideran al historiador una especie de falaz embaucador que propone convencer a sus lectores, aunque su narración no responda del todo a la verdad. Se denuncia también la falta de una auténtica base epistemológica de esta disciplina, en la que se comprueba cómo se mezclan realidad y fantasía. Al hacer balance de la consideración que la historia merece entre los intelectuales en México a finales del siglo XVI, la relación de libros que, procedentes de la Península, arriban allí en este tiempo puede ser una fuente muy útil.

En cumplimiento de lo dispuesto por las autoridades civiles y eclesiásticas, los encargados de la revisión de los navíos trasladan las listas de libros que éstos transportan a los responsables de su supervisión. El repaso de estas listas es para nosotros, como señala Elías Trabulse, un adecuado índice para conocer tanto el estado de la cultura en la Nueva España como de las diversas características que adoptó la represión libresca a lo largo del siglo XVI.[19] Si nos detenemos a comprobar la posición de la historia antigua en este panorama, lo primero que llama la atención es el muy reducido número de libros de esta naturaleza que se mencionan en los envíos, comparándolo con los pertenecientes a otras materias. De 1573 a 1599, se limita prácticamente a éstos: *Chronica de Spana, Historia romana de los emperadores, Historia de Cristóbal Colón, cuando vino a descubrir la costa y la de Santo Domingo, Varones ilustres, Las Repúblicas de toda la cristiandad e Gentilidad, Las tierras de Jerusalem, Los Césares* de Pedro Mexía, *Lo de Cartago, La Conquista de Chile, La Araucana, Uno de Historia, Historia del Africa, La Conquista de la India de Portugal, La Conquista de esta tierra, Historia de Europa, Marco Aurelio, Un Sumario de las Guerras Civiles*, Primera parte de la *Historia* de Paulo Jovio en toscano, *La Descripción del Africa, La Rebelión de Flandes, Luciadas* de Camões, *Descubrimiento del Perú, Historia de los Girones y linajes de España, Guerra y entrada del Rey en Portugal, Historia Pontifical, Historia* de Guicciardino, *Viaje de la Tierra Sancta, Valerio Máximo, El descubrimiento de las Indias, Chrónica baldiana de España, Carlomagno, Historia de Malta,* y expresamente vedados como libros prohibidos, *Suma de corónicas de todo el mundo, Morales* de Plutarco en latín, *Josepho, De las antigüedades, Justino Historiador, Salustio con las anotaciones de Philipo Melantón, Vida de Julio César, Las guerras del Perú, Gesta Romanorum, Discursos de Nicolao Machiavello para la gobernación de la república y mantener los estados en paz,* y *Un pedazo de la Chrónica de los Reyes Cathólicos*.

La dimensión política de los textos históricos, temida y rechazada en algunos círculos de la intelectualidad americana por su carácter de educadora de conciencias, explica la prohibición de estas obras. Además, el carácter paganizante de los autores antiguos provocará a lo largo de todo el siglo XVI recelos de censores, religiosos y políticos en América y en toda Europa. Los autores de la Antigüedad comienzan a contemplarse en algunos casos como una amenaza para la sociedad cristiana. Juicios extremos se comprueban en México, como ocurre en 1575, durante la revisión de

---

[18] Citado en Lino Gómez, *La educación de los marginados durante la época colonial* (México, 1982), 186.

[19] Fernández del Castillo, *Libros y libreros en el siglo XVI*, 175.

"La Candelaria", una de las naves que llegaron al puerto de San Juan de Ulúa, donde se encontraron un *Amadís y dos o tres más de caballerías, Calvario, Flossantorum, Horas en latín y romance, La Vida de San Francisco y Vida de Julio César*, "que leía un estudiante llamado San Clemente, y porque le dijeron que por qué no leía mejor la vida de San Francisco que era cristiano y no la de Julio César que estaba en el infierno, por no estar bautizado, se suscitó una disputa y se levantó información contra el estudiante por sospechoso de la fe."[20]

Como recoge Jill Kraye, el siglo XVI presencia una reacción de escritores y maestros, protestantes y católicos, cuyo objetivo era expulsar del currículo escolar a las obras clásicas.[21] El propio Melanchthon, quien, al igual que Lutero y Calvino, insiste en la necesidad de mantener este *curriculum* en la educación protestante, se opone firmemente a las inclinaciones paganizantes del ciceronianismo, casi tanto como los propios representantes de la Contrarreforma. Y los recelos se convierten en oposición frontal en numerosos representantes de la Europa de la Cristiandad, cuando a lo largo del siglo XVI se conoce aquí la que probablemente haya sido su más intensa sacudida espiritual hasta época moderna, en un momento en que la tradicional unidad espiritual europea se resquebraja y la vida de la Iglesia se somete a juicio crítico.

Si los humanistas italianos se habían propuesto recuperar la Roma clásica en su príntina pureza, liberándola del lastre acumulado en épocas pasadas, el espíritu reformista de Lutero se propone restaurar la fe de la Roma pura y eterna, removiendo las capas de corrupción acumuladas en la Iglesia durante siglos.[22] Siendo el eje central de la confrontación entre protestantes y católicos la valoración de la tradición de la Iglesia, se comprende el valor que alcanza la historia como instrumento al servicio de los intereses de unos y otros. En el fondo, espíritu humanista y espíritu reformista se acercan. Autores y pedagogos como Philipp Melanchthon parecen aunar ambos espíritus a través de sus programas educativos, en los que la historia ocupa un lugar destacado, como fuente de conocimiento y base fundamental de cualquier reforma.

En sus *Adnotationes* a Salustio, Melanchthon aborda el texto original poniendo en juego sus principios religiosos, éticos, e intelectuales. La conjuración de Catilina o la guerra de Jugurta se convierten así en modelos de historia en los que, además de un estilo elegantemente adaptado al *usus latinus*, y la historia y geografía romanas que Salustio describe, el alumno puede aprender las consecuencias negativas que los vicios acarrean, el valor de la virtud y la recta conducta, qué cualidades ha de tener el buen príncipe y la inquietud de vida de un tirano, y, por encima de todo, el sentido de la libertad y la lucha por la dignidad personal y colectiva. Era la "creencia en el nuevo horizonte de la visión histórica, y el criticar la tradición eclesiástica," de los que habla Marcel Bataillon.[23] En el fondo, todos, humanistas dados al estudio de los poetas y

---

[20] Fernández del Castillo, *Libros y libreros en el siglo XVI*, 510–511.

[21] Jill Kraye, ed., *Introducción al humanismo renacentista*, ed. española Carlos Clavería, trad. Lluis Cabré (Cambridge, 1998), esp. 111–114.

[22] Cf. Ernst Breisach, *Historiography: Ancient, Medieval and Modern* (Chicago, 1983), 166ss.

[23] Marcel Bataillon, "Humanismo, Erasmismo y represión cultural en la España del siglo XVI," in *Erasmo y el Erasmismo*, trad. cast. Carlos Pujol, 2ª ed. (Barcelona, 1983), 163.

los historiadores de la Antigüedad greco-latina, y reformadores eclesiásticos pretendían "asomarse a problemas humanos permanentes de moral y de política."[24] Y, como señala Elías Trabulse, el seguimiento contrarreformista de libros prohibidos no consigue evitar que las obras censuradas circularan entre los doctos e intelectuales mexicanos, atraídos por estos valores. Quizá fueran todavía más nefastas para la ciencia las "revueltas entre clérigos y frailes" que tan a menudo son denunciadas por los mercaderes como causa de las malas ventas de libros.[25]

Universidad de Valladolid

---

[24] Bataillon, "Humanismo, Erasmismo," 162.
[25] Cf. Fernández del Castillo, *Libros y libreros en el siglo XVI*, 284.

The Preface *to the* Amoenitates Exoticae

ROBERT W. CARRUBBA

Engelbert Kaempfer (1651–1716), the German scholar, physician, and traveler, devoted more than ten years (1683–1693) to exotic investigations in history, culture, and science.[1] As secretary of the Swedish mission to the Persian court, Kaempfer traveled to Moscow, made a perilous crossing of the Caspian Sea, and journeyed through Persia to Isfahan. When the embassy completed its affairs, Kaempfer entered into the service of the Dutch East India Company (1684) as a physician. This position afforded him the opportunities to visit Arabia, India, Ceylon, Java, Siam, and Japan, where he resided for two years at Nagasaki (1691–1692) and twice visited Edo (Tokyo) to pay homage to the Shogun. His tour of duty completed, Kaempfer returned to Europe by way of Java and the Cape of Good Hope. Before settling in his native Germany, Kaempfer was awarded an M.D. by the National University of Leiden. His doctoral thesis, *A Decade of Exotic Observations*,[2] published in 1694, presented a rich sampling of Kaempfer's scientific research and discoveries: a discussion of the fabled plant-animal called the Scythian Lamb; an explanation of the extreme bitterness of the Caspian Sea; a description of the sources and medicinal properties of the substance of Persian mummy; a first description of the torpedo fish of the Persian Gulf in which Kaempfer likens the effect of the fish to that of lightning; a report of the tree which produces the resin called dragon's blood; a medical analysis of the guinea worm and the method of extracting it from a patient's body; accounts of two diseases endemic to Malabar, Andrum (hydrocele of the scrotum) and Perical (swelling of the foot); and lastly, accounts of the Oriental therapeutic techniques of acupuncture and moxibustion. Once established as a physician in Lemgo, Kaempfer in-

---

[1] For an account of Kaempfer's life based on the most recent scholarship, see Detlef Haberland, *Engelbert Kaempfer 1651–1716: A Biography*, trans. Peter Hogg (London, 1996).

[2] See John Z. Bowers and Robert W. Carrubba, "The Doctoral Thesis of Engelbert Kaempfer On the Tropical Diseases, Oriental Medicine, and Exotic Natural Phenomena," *Journal of the History of Medicine and Allied Sciences* 25 (1970): 270–310.

tended to edit for publication his extensive papers recorded in various languages in the course of his travels. The Preface to the *Amoenitates Exoticae* reveals how his plans were long frustrated by the burdens of his duties as physician to the Count of Lippe (from 1698). In addition, his marriage to Maria Sophia Wilstach in December of 1700 was filled with discord and their two daughters and one son all died of smallpox. On 2 November 1716 Kaempfer himself succumbed to colic. Before the end of a customary year of mourning, his widow had remarried. From the Preface to the *Amoenitates*[3] Sir Hans Sloane (1660–1753), an avid naturalist and collector, learned of the existence of Kaempfer's manuscripts, which he arranged to have purchased and which eventually became the possession of the British Library. Johannes Casparus Scheuchzer, Sir Hans's secretary, translated a portion of Kaempfer's original German papers into an English version entitled *The History of Japan,* which was published in London in 1727. Like Sir Hans Sloane, president of the Royal College of Physicians (1719–1735), we too can approach the Preface to the *Amoenitates Exoticae* for an understanding of Kaempfer's life and achievements. And in the tradition of Scheuchzer, his amanuensis, I have endeavored to make available from the Latin original a first translation of the *Praefatio* to the *Amoenitates Exoticae*.

The structure of Kaempfer's Preface is quite straightforward. First, he explains that domestic affairs and his duties as a physician to the Count of Lippe frustrated his intention to edit and organize his manuscripts for publication immediately upon his return eighteen years previously. Second, Kaempfer relates that recently he had been relieved of some of his duties and had more time available to ready the *Amoenitates Exoticae,* which represents only a small portion of his research. He intended also to publish a work entitled *Japan of Our Time* in German with about forty illustrations (this is the manuscript which Scheuchzer translated into English), a *Specimen of a Trans-Ganges Herbarium* in Latin with about five hundred illustrations, and a *Journey in Three Parts* with many illustrations and in Latin, German, or Dutch, containing Russo-Tartaric materials, items for Asia this side of the Ganges, and lastly topics from Asia beyond the Ganges. Third, Kaempfer reviews his travels of more than a decade, the initial phase of which was from Stockholm to Moscow, across the Caspian Sea, and on to Isfahan. Upon the dismissal of the Swedish embassy Kaempfer reports that he considered going to Egypt, accepting a position as court physician in the country of Georgia, or joining the Dutch fleet occupying the Bay of Hormuz. Thanks to the good counsel of a Capuchin and royal interpreter, Father du Mans, Kaempfer chose to join the Dutch East India Company, in whose employ he visited the Orient and eventually returned to Amsterdam. And Kaempfer reminds his reader that the *Amoenitates* contains only a few blossoms from his large garden of reports. Fourth, Kaempfer reveals that he chose the title *Pleasures* because of the "agreeable variety of subject matter which merits reading by the cultivator of any discipline." He also underscores the fact that his reports are not embroidered, but present his original research con-

---

[3] *Amoenitatum exoticarum politico-physico-medicarum, fasciculi V, quibus continentur variae relationes, observationes, & descriptiones rerum Persicarum & Ulterioris Asiae* (Lemgo, 1712). The pages [xi–xx] of the *Praefatio* are not numbered sequentially.

ducted with considerable risk to his safety and at the cost of much labor and expense. Fifth, Kaempfer apologizes to his reader for the occasional unevenness of the style, which resulted from the preoccupations of a traveler on land and sea, and for the poor quality of the copper engravings, for which he blames unskilled and peevish engravers. So vexed was Kaempfer with the engravings that he kept back a number of illustrations and completely omitted a sixth fascicle, entitled *Letters to Learned Gentlemen in Asia*. Nor did the printer escape Kaempfer's disapproval for improperly reproducing certain Chinese characters and for departing considerably from their native elegance and genius. Sixth, Kaempfer records his method of transcription of foreign words so that the reader may correctly pronounce them, and he clarifies the distances represented by the terms "paces" and "parasangs." Lastly, Kaempfer bids his reader a farewell, asks that his work may be favorably received, and records the place and date of authorship as "my small estate, called Steinhof, in the County of Lippe, in the Year of Christ, 1712."[4]

Before, however, presenting the Preface itself in translation and with notes, it may be useful to review briefly the fascinating contents of the five fascicles of the *Amoenitates*. Fascicle I treats the present state of the Persian court, including the person of the Shah, his coronation, the military, financial, religious, and spiritual leaders, the splendor of the palace, the royal harem, and a royal audience. Fascicle II presents historical and scientific reports on various things, including the mythical whirlpools of the Caspian Sea, the archaeological remains at Persepolis, the Christians of St. Thomas, the Oriental ordeals by fire and crocodile, and the wisdom of the closing of the Japanese empire. Fascicle III offers curious scientific and medical observations, elaborating upon the ten topics of Kaempfer's doctoral thesis and including additional observations on the harvesting of asafetida, snake charming with cobras, two reputed antidotes to snakebite (the Mungo root and snake stones), a lengthy treatise on Japanese tea and the implements for preparing and serving it, ambergris, Persian and Indian drugs, and sexual spells practiced by the Makassars.[5] Fascicle IV is devoted to botanical and historical reports concerning the date palm growing in Persia, along with accounts of visiting the palms and the utility of the tree. Fascicle V presents a description of various classes of Japanese plants, along with many illustrations. The entire volume of the *Amoenitates Exoticae,* including dedication, preface, fascicles, illustrations, index, and errata, fills more than nine hundred pages. All in all, Kaempfer's *Amoenitates Exoticae* offers a stunning and detailed array of scientific, historical, and cultural discoveries based on eyewitness observation and placed within a scholarly context.[6]

Fordham University

---

[4] Steinhof in Lieme bei Lemgo was acquired by Kaempfer's father. The house, located in a pleasant rural area, no longer exists.

[5] For a translation and commentary, see Robert W. Carrubba, *Engelbert Kaempfer, Exotic Pleasures: Fascicle III, Curious Scientific and Medical Observations* (Carbondale and Edwardsville, 1996).

[6] Haberland (*Engelbert Kaempfer*, 54) observes that in the *Amoenitates* Kaempfer refers to more than one hundred and fifty books by other authors.

Preface

Eighteen years have passed since I returned to my native land from the Indies. Unlike the usual returnee, I was laden not with the spoils of profit and trade, but rather with pages on which I had written exotic reports gathered through much labor, expense, and danger in various regions. I intended to publish these immediately in a number of volumes which were complete except for a few months of work on their organization and interrelationships. I also needed to add illustrations from copper engravings, since exotica are very difficult to comprehend without these clarifying aids. But in fact a host of duties and impediments confronted me and led me astray from my fervent plan. Scarcely had I landed when domestic cares, difficult in this area, ensnared me and against my will a most burdensome medical practice (which I had decided to forego for the future) overwhelmed me. I add that the most illustrious Lord and Count Regent of Lippe, my most kind master, generously appointed this humble person to the position of court physician at his most renowned seat. Although I consider the appointment a singular honor and I had hoped for it, nevertheless it claimed, as was appropriate, the greater and principal part of my life and leisure time. For this reason my spoils were set aside and stored in chests where they hitherto lay buried, much to my sorrow.

Recently, upon being relieved of a certain part of my duties, I regained some spare hours and with them the disposition and resolve to save from destruction my papers which were already eaten by roaches and worms, moldy, and in great part erased by sea water which earlier inundated them in shipwrecks. In keeping with this decision, I am pleased to offer, in this present little book, a kind of selection or sample of my writings through which the good reader may have a preview of the range of my observations. I will imitate our salesmen who, upon returning from markets, exhibit samples of their wares in order to explore the buyers' pleasures. In the *Cyclops* of Euripides, Ulysses asks in a polite manner before selling wine to Silenus: "Do you wish to taste what I bring first?" Silenus replies: "That is appropriate, for a taste invites a buyer."[1] If I find that the samples are appealing, I will immediately unfold the display itself and from it I will offer to publishers:

1. *Japan of Our Time*, to be published in quarto, as they say, and in German with about forty illustrations.[2]
2. *Specimen of a Trans-Ganges Herbarium*, in folio and in Latin with about five hundred illustrations. If the distinguished gentleman Rumpf publishes his *Hortus Amboinensis* first, may I not repeat his work and appear to be carrying wood to a forest.[3]

---

[1] Euripides' play *The Cyclops* is the only example extant of the humorous type of ancient play called a satyr drama. The subject is the escape of Ulysses (Odysseus) from the cave of the Cyclops as related in book nine of Homer's Odyssey.

[2] Englebert Kaempfer, *The History of Japan*, trans. J. G. Scheuchzer, 2 vols. (London, 1727).

[3] Georg Eberhard Rumpf (Rumphius, 1627–1706), *Herbarium Amboinense*, 6 vols. (Amsterdam, 1741-1750).

3. *Journey in Three Parts*,[4] in folio, with as many illustrations as the publisher's budget will support and giving him the choice of the language — Latin, German, or indeed Dutch. At present the work is complete, but unorganized, and is recorded at random in my diaries in several languages. The work will contain three parts: the first presents Russo-Tartaric materials; the second presents materials from Asia this side of the Ganges; and the third, materials from Asia beyond the Ganges. This sequence follows my exhausting itinerary.

I will here very briefly outline my travels for the good reader so that he may know what observations of things and places he can expect from me. In 1682 the Most Serene King of Sweden[5] created a secret embassy, as a member of which I left Stockholm and traveled through Finland, Livonia,[6] and Russia to the Court of Moscow. When negotiations were concluded there, I journeyed through the expanses of Kazan and Nagaja in Tartaria,[7] crossed the Caspian Sea and arrived in Media.[8] While the embassy refreshed itself during a three-month period of leisure in the capital city of Shemakha,[9] I undertook my own trips to other places. When summoned to the Persian court, we were led through Hyrcania and Parthia to the Royal Palace at Isfahan, within whose confines we passed two years during which time I was frequently free to make private excursions.

At length I separated from the embassy upon its dismissal. I considered going to Egypt, was invited to Georgia[10] as court physician, and was besieged with various offers of positions. The elderly Father du Mans, a Capuchin and royal interpreter, persuaded me to accept the invitation of the Dutch admiral whose fleet occupied the Bay of Hormuz. After the delivery of arms, I journeyed to Arabia, and from there to the lands of the Great Mogul, the realms of Malabar, Ceylon, and the region of the Bay of the Ganges. After traveling along the Coast of Sumatra to Java and proceeding from its capital to the more distant provinces and islands, at length I visited the Court of Siam. From there, I arrived in Japan, the farthest island of the Orient, after observing, in passing, Cambodia, southern China, and the adjacent regions. My visit to Japan lasted for two full, and by no means idle, years and my stay in Asia consumed

---

[4] Titles two and three (Specimen and Journey) were never published; original materials are in the British Library. See Karl Meier-Lemgo, *Die Reisetagebücher Englebert Kaempfers* (Wiesbaden, 1968).

[5] Charles XI, who ruled from 1660–1697, was among Sweden's greatest kings.

[6] Livonia included present-day Estonia and parts of Latvia.

[7] Tartaria, or the region of the Great Khan, extended in upper Asia from the area of the Caspian Sea to the Pacific Ocean. Kazan is located on the Volga; Nagaja is found to the east of the Volga and to the north of the Caspian Sea.

[8] On pages 134 and 135 of the *Amoenitates Exoticae*, Kaempfer explains that the whole of the Persian Empire is divided into five parts: (1) *Australis* (Fars) or Southern; (2) *Orientalis* (Chorasmia) or Eastern; (3) *Occidentalis* (Azerbaijan) or Western; (4) *Septentrionalis* (Hyrcania) or Northern; (5) *Media* (Parthia) or Central.

[9] The city is near to Baku and the Apsheron Peninsula.

[10] The country on the Black Sea.

ten years. I returned to Holland by a direct route over the ocean. I was at sea for one year, except for a few weeks during which I traveled the wilds of the African promontory.[11]

These, I say, are the expanses of the globe which I describe in the log of my journey from which I selected and compiled, in the greater part, the descriptions and observations of this initial work. This book does not, as a result, deplete the record of my journey nor is it the case that — as happens in smaller gardens — when a few blossoms have been plucked, only stems and leaves remain. If it were my desire to divide my complete travel log into separate reports of this type and to transcribe them here, this book would be expanded into very many fascicles. It is preferable, however, to display at a future time the finished artifice itself rather than its rough components.

I distinguish this introductory work with the title *Pleasures* because of the agreeable variety of subject matter which merits reading by the cultivator of any discipline. I have not reported anything in this book which is the creation of my imagination nor anything which suggests polish or the odor of midnight oil. Nor am I reheating a stew cooked by others (unless methodology or the need for logical sequence required it). Rather, matters reported by others have been omitted. Indeed, I have my hands full describing things which are new or which others have not reported in depth or thoroughly. To be sure, as I traveled, I had no other goal than to put together reports of things not at all or inadequately known to us. Consequently, I have never tired of traveling for many days to out-of-the-way places, even at the risk of my safety, provided that my labor obtained its reward of some knowledge discovered about something desirable, memorable, or disputed in the community of learned men. However insignificant these Asiatic spoils of mine may have been or may appear to be, they are assuredly the results of my considerable labors and expenses.

Kind reader, you have, however, two things in this book with whose awkwardness you may find fault: the style, to be sure, and certain illustrations. The style, I confess, is occasionally uneven, and less than appropriate for an historical report. The first deficiency was brought about by the circumstances of the journey, which did not permit the traveler to compose anything with a leisurely hand and tranquil spirit. Who, indeed, does not understand the tasks of voyagers? Now the baggage must from day to day be packed, unpacked, transported and guarded from thieves and robbers; now a crowd of people, gathering to see the European guests, disturbs them when they have scarcely entered their lodging; now the insane clamor of the soldiers on board, the storms in the sky, and the shaking motion of the ship itself impede the pen of the sea voyagers. And so let me pass over in silence the conditions which assail us and repeatedly interrupt the course of writing and even more entangle the thinkers' minds with concerns and difficulties. This variety of activity and disposition, I say, begot an unevenness of style for whose correction I now have neither the leisure nor, after long pauses in my studies, the inclination.

---

[11] Ships sailing to and from Asia would normally put in at the Cape of Good Hope for rest and provisions.

I blame the second deficiency on certain copper engravers whom I found to be unskilled and of a peevish disposition. They so distorted pictures, which with my own hand I had drawn carefully and in varying sizes, and which they needed to reduce or enlarge to the proper dimensions, that were these pictures not necessary for clarifying the subject matter, I would reject them as a disgrace to the book. And it is for this reason that I am completely omitting Fascicle Six, namely, my *Letters to Learned Gentlemen in Asia*. The Letters, indeed, treat matters which are not understandable without illustrations engraved with an accurate hand in my presence. Hence, I have even held back illustrations pertaining to Fascicle I: a plan of the city of Isfahan, painstakingly compiled by me during three months of study; a depiction of the Royal way, Tsjahaar baag, and the adjacent Gardens, especially the Hadsar dsjeriib, and the houses situated in them; illustrations of the quadrupeds to be seen in the city and in the royal wildlife preserves; and also many inscriptions and particular views of ancient Persepolis, which pertain to Fascicle II; and as well a new and accurate geographic table of Japan and many other illustrations appropriate to Fascicles III and IV, which I now retain in the hope of a better occasion. I make the same complaint concerning my printer as I did about the copper engravers. He has, indeed, negligently treated certain Chinese characters, with strokes curved, lengthened or shortened otherwise than suitable, and others improperly placed, and by this very action he has departed considerably from the native elegance and genius of the characters.

For the rest, it is necessary to inform the reader that with respect to my transcription of exotic vocabulary words I have adapted myself to Germanic pronunciation: thus, I wish a to be read as the Greek ου; g as the French gu; ch like the Greek χ, or the Polish ch without the guttural, or as the Italian g before a; s at times must be pronounced with a hiss, at other times more softly like the Polish z without accent. Here we do not have available a double letter, with which we might indicate such a difference, and so I have expressed in Persian words the letter ﺽ by ds and dsj, which, however, needed to be brought out a little more softly by the French g before e and i. By sj, in the Dutch manner, I express the Arabic and Persian ﺵ, which the French do with ch, the English with sh, and Germans with sch. The Japanese sounds seo, sio, meo, mio and the like ought to be pronounced as one syllable, with the inserted vowel heard slightly, and even a little more lightly than if written sjo and mjo. I have expressed the orthotone native to any people by accents and duplicate vowels, from which it is easy to comprehend the lengthening or shortening of the syllables; thus, aa must be read as Greek α, ii as ι, oo as ω, and so forth. I call attention to these matters so that exotic vocabulary words, when read by non-Germans and people of foreign tongues, may have an authentic sound and may not, as commonly happens, degenerate into entirely different words. In Persian words, the syllable ﻭ is quite the same, whether you pronounce it aan, oon, or ουν, since Persian dialects differ on it, as in ﮐﺮﻣﺎﻥ Kirmaan (Kerman), ﺁﺳﻤﻮﻥ aasmoon (sky), ﺟﻬﻮﻥ Dsjehuun (world), and countless other words. Concerning units of measure, which on various occasions I have used for distances, I very briefly advise: that by paces I do not mean the linear ones which consist of two footprints but my own simple common ones, with which a man of average height or a little taller than average walks, and which comprise at the minimum two linear feet. By parasangs also should be understood lengths or distances from place to place of such an extent that twenty-two and one-half of them equal one celestial degree or fifteen German miles.

I bid the reader thus advised to fare well and to favor my writings. I wrote from the study of my small estate, called Steinhoff, in the County of Lippe, in the Year of Christ, 1712.

Elizabeth Jane Weston
as Cultural Icon

DONALD CHENEY

The praise lavished on Elizabeth Jane Weston and her Latin verses during her lifetime both encourages and frustrates speculation as to just what she represented to those citizens of the republic of letters who exchanged compliments with her during her brief period of international fame in the first decade of the seventeenth century.[1] Indeed, it was only during the final decade of the twentieth century that Western scholars learned why this noble English maiden, *virgo angla nobilissima*, spent her lifetime in and around the court of Rudolph II: her mother had married the alchemist Edward Kelley and accompanied him to Bohemia shortly after the death of her first husband, a certain John Weston described only as "clerk" in his burial record of 1582.[2]

Thus, we now know what Czech scholars[3] had discovered in 1928 from a unique copy of her poem on her mother's death, namely that Weston apparently owed any claims of noble origin less to a presumed connection with aristocratic English Westons than to a title bestowed on her stepfather by the Emperor Rudolph, and to Kelley's own dubious prior claim to an Irish title. And the earlier assumption of biographers and biographical dictionaries, that she was the orphaned daughter of a recusant English Weston who had fled to Catholic Prague where he had bankrupted himself like a good English aristocrat, was a reasonable but mistaken deduction based on the evidence of her published writings, which avoided all mention of Kelley, whose

---

[1] *Elizabeth Jane Weston: Collected Writings*, ed. and trans. Donald Cheney and Brenda M. Hosington (Toronto, 2000).

[2] Susan Bassnett, "Elizabeth Jane Weston — the Hidden Roots of Poetry," in E. Fučiková, ed., *Prag um 1600* (Freren/Emsland, 1988), 9–15, and eadem, "Revising a Biography," *Cahiers élisabéthains* 37 (1990): 1–8; James Binns, *Intellectual Culture in Elizabethan and Jacobean England: The Latin Writings of the Age* (Leeds, 1990), 110–114, 759 (index).

[3] Karel Hrdina, "Dvě prácě z dějin českého humanismu," *Listy filologické* 55 (1928): 14–19; Bohumil Ryba, "Westonia," *Listy filologické* 56 (1929): 14–28.

death in prison and in debt around 1598 had made her an orphan for the second time and necessitated her literary career.

To summarize the story of Weston as it may be most plausibly and simply understood today, the parish records of Chipping Norton in Oxfordshire show that John Weston and Jane Cooper were married in 1579; a son, John Francis, was christened there in 1580, as was Elizabeth, apparently in 1581. John Weston, husband and father, was buried on 6 May 1582.[4] During the week prior to this burial, Edward Kelley, who had been serving as skryer or crystal-gazer to Doctor John Dee at his house outside London, twice reported that the Archangel Michael had told him that he must marry; and shortly afterward he reluctantly obeyed this injunction, marrying the widowed Jane Weston.[5] The following year, Dee and Kelley set off with their wives and the children of Dee on an extended voyage to Poland and later to Prague, where Kelley was to spend the rest of his life in service to Rudolph. The Weston children apparently stayed with their grandparents at first but joined their stepfather's household subsequently.

In her elegy for her mother, Weston states that Kelley cared for his new stepchildren "like another father,"[6] and this seems borne out by his having provided a superior education for them even as he fell further into debt and out of favor with the emperor. Elsewhere, Elizabeth gives thanks to a Latin master named John Hammond, who may be the man of that name whom Dr Dee had employed in Trebon in 1588.[7] Weston's brother was sent to the local Clementine College in Prague and later to the university of Ingolstadt, enrolling there in the summer term of 1598 as "Ioannis Westonius Oxoniensis Anglus nobilis," an early instance of the Weston children's tendency to elide their claims to nobility with their Oxfordshire origins.[8]

Kelley's fortunes declined after 1591, when he killed one of Rudolph's courtiers in a duel; and after a series of prison stays he died sometime around 1597, leaving his family destitute and their properties in the hands of creditors. John Francis Weston had been in poor health himself and died in late 1600. In an attempt to gain sympathy for her plight and that of her newly-widowed mother, Elizabeth turned to the writing of the Latin poetry that would shortly make her famous.

From our perspective today, a number of factors may have contributed to the extravagant praise Weston's elegiac laments immediately elicited. As a young maiden in distress, appealing to the protection of the learned and powerful men of her time, she could capitalize on the very simplicity and monotony of her material. Granted that she had a talent for writing directly and clearly in classical Latin, this was a talent that was more likely to be valued in a young woman than in a sophisticated man of the

---

[4] Chipping Norton parish register, typescript of September 1992 checked against an anonymous copy of ca. 1790.

[5] Meric Casaubon, *A True and Faithful Relation of What passed for many Years between Dr. John Dee . . . and Some Spirits . . .* (London, 1659), fol. 39v.

[6] *Weston: Collected Writings*, 336–341.

[7] *Weston: Collected Writings*, 313.

[8] *Annales Ingolstadiensis Academiae*, Part 2 (Ingolstadt, 1782), 152; Götz Freiherr von Pölnitz, *Die Matrikel der Ludwig-Maximilians-Universität* (Munich, 1937), 1:1374.

worlds of court or academe. And as recent feminist approaches to early modern literature have suggested, the position of an orphan can be positively liberating for a woman who is hoping to be heard, for she has neither father nor brother to speak for her and — we have been led to believe — to silence her in the process.[9] Although we may be somewhat skeptical of this latter principle, chiefly based as it is on a small and familiar collection of examples like that of Isotta Nogarola in Italy, there is a letter from one of Weston's own contemporaries, another learned Elizabeth who signs herself "Elizabeth Albert of Kameneck, Bohemian maiden," who laments that most Bohemians consider letters "not only useless for a virgin's concern but actually shameful," and says that it both "grieves and shames" her father to have taught his daughters to write in the classical tongues.[10] So we may have some basis for believing that Weston had reason to insist repeatedly in her poems and letters on the cloistered world of mother and daughter to which she was confined. This was a world to which the men of the greater world could address their compliments with confidence that their praise could not be taken amiss by some protective male in the virgin's circle.

In fact, however, Weston *did* have a male patron who played a crucial role in promoting her writings. George Martinius von Baldhoven, a Silesian nobleman a few years her senior, edited two collections of her writings and forwarded her poems and letters to the learned men of Europe, who responded in kind. It was Baldhoven who brought out the first collection, *Poëmata*, published in two books at Frankfurt am Oder in 1602, and who immediately afterward urged her to assemble a fuller, three-book edition, with letters to and from her, which was eventually to be published in Prague around 1608, as *Parthenica*.

We may wonder at the precise role played by Baldhoven in promoting his friend's career. He seems to have been responsible for persuading Paul Melissus of Heidelberg, the translator of Marot, to send her a laurel wreath, and thereby give her the laureate status enjoyed rather informally by the Latin poets of the day. And he seems to have attempted, often rather ineptly, to polish her verses. Born in 1578, Baldhoven was close enough in age to have entertained thoughts of marriage with Weston, or at least close enough for others to have imagined such a thing. When George Carolides praises Weston in 1601 as a virgin "worthy of marriage to a good poet,"[11] the line seems to point toward the laureated Baldhoven (who was certainly good, though not necessarily a good poet) rather than toward the lawyer, Johannes Leo, whom Weston did marry in 1603.

Weston's marriage in fact provoked an oddly awkward letter (*Parth.* III.30) to her editor, in which she formally informs Baldhoven of her marriage (three months after

---

[9] See Anthony Grafton and Lisa Jardine, *From Humanism to the Humanities* (Cambridge, MA, 1986), esp. chap. 2, "Woman Humanists: Education for What?", 29–57; and Louise Schleiner and Winfried Schleiner, "Elizabeth Weston: A Woman Poet among the Humanists," in *Form and Reform in Renaissance England: Essays in Honor of Barbara Kiefer Lewalski*, ed. Amy Boesky and Mary Thomas Crane (Newark and London, 1999), 185–219.

[10] *Weston: Collected Writings*, 402–403.

[11] *Weston: Collected Writings*, 390–393, "Virgo digna boni toro Poëtæ."

the event) "in case you are ignorant of my present state and condition," and expresses surprise that Baldhoven should have alluded to some sense of distress. Whether or not Baldhoven was a disappointed suitor, or Weston feared he might have been, it is also true that her marriage had put an end to that image of a *virgo angla* that he had been so carefully cultivating. Baldhoven may simply — or also — have felt that his grand editorial project was being undercut by his protégée's failing to keep to the script that had been so hugely successful thus far.

In the same letter, Weston affirms that she wishes to continue her friendship, and her publishing plans, as if nothing had happened; that she has been slow to send on additional materials only because of the press of other matters and a problem of locating some missing letters; that her husband would prefer that the collected volume be published in Prague or Leipzig rather than Leiden as Baldhoven wishes (since he is living there at present). There is a certain poignancy in the fact that the expanded collection was in fact published in Prague: Weston's new condition was one in which her husband was now making the decisions. At the same time, Baldhoven apparently was responsible for labeling the collection *Parthenica* or "maidenly writings" — even though Weston would protest in manuscript verses[12] that some of the works in the volume were those of a newlywed matron, and that others had been carelessly proofread to boot. Unquestionably, things had changed, even though we cannot put a single simple name to the change.

Indeed, Weston's marriage in April 1603 coincided as well with the death on 24 March of another English virgin named Elizabeth. We may wonder just how much the appeal of Elizabeth Jane Weston may have been affected by an implicit allusion to that grander figure at the margins of the Holy Roman Empire. Weston was adroit in evoking the pathos of her own literally helpless position, and in suggesting that a truly "august" emperor, a worthy successor to Caesar Augustus himself, would show his worth by accepting the prayers of this client and by bringing her thereby into the circle of his grace and favor. A poem like that to Johann Barvitius, Rudolph's counselor, praises the gardens of a man who resembles his master in retiring to a flourishing space where he can "hear the prayers of widows and take up the petitions of clients" (*Parth.* I.13).[13] Such widows and clients can bless and indeed authenticate the claims of an imperial court. Perhaps those learned scholars and courtiers who responded so enthusiastically to Weston's laments were recognizing that she was shrewdly articulating something of their own sense of dependency and helplessness in the greater world that threatened them increasingly with its religious and nationalist divisions. The republic of letters itself had an uneasy relationship with the Holy Roman Empire, as did the Empire with the increasingly fragmented world it still claimed as its own.

It may have seemed all the more apt, then, that Weston could lay claim to the names not only of orphan and virgin but also to those of Elisabetha and Angla; for by

---

[12] *Weston: Collected Writings*, 304–307.

[13] Donald Cheney, "Westonia on the Gardens of Barvitius," *American Notes and Queries* 5 (1992): 64–67.

doing so she could suggest a further dimension of her alienated condition, representing a Protestant and insular nation in an imperial court that was itself located on the eastern fringe of its own empire. The operative word in the preceding sentence is "suggest," however. What is peculiarly characteristic of Weston's poetry is a suggestiveness which always eludes explicit identification of just who she is and where she stands, what she represents. In writing on Ovid's *Tristia* (*Parth.* I.39), she compares her own exile with that of the poet who was similarly exiled to the savage east:

> You leave your fatherland, but the friends there are unharmed;
> Here for me both my father and his household are gone.
> You are troubled by repeated incursions of Sarmatian hordes;
> but from me a furious race steals what it does not give![14]

These lines skilfully conflate two kinds of isolation: she is far from her native English home and she is alienated from her emperor's grace; but she stops short of identifying Rudolph's court, or Bohemia in general, with the furious race that has confiscated her family's property. As a distressed damsel she does not need to specify the precise parameters of her exile; nor, in fact, could she do so, since the England of her origins is a world she scarcely knew and one to which she does not aspire to return.

It is remarkable that Weston's presentation of herself before her marriage as a *virgo angla* is silent on the matter of her lost English home and family, and that she makes no appeals to Queen Elizabeth or her courtiers. An obvious reason for this is that she is chiefly concerned to advance her mother's claims for restitution of family properties in Bohemia; she has every reason to avoid suggesting that a return fare to Chipping Norton might satisfy the family's needs. Once she is married, however, one of her first poetic acts is to compose an ode to James I (*Parth.* III.1) on his coronation, and to affirm her loyalties to her native land; subsequently, she is greatly distressed at a rumour that James or his courtiers may have been indifferent or contemptuous of this appeal (*Parth.* III.3). Beyond this ode, however, and a similarly enthusiastic one addressed to Rudolph's successor Matthias, we have little evidence of Weston's later writings that might shed light on the new directions of her literary career. Between her marriage in 1603 and her death nine years later, she bore seven children to Johannes Leo, a lawyer representing Anhalt interests at the imperial court; at some point during this time her widowed mother died, and presumably the claims on the Kelley estate were rendered moot or became less pressing for the new household. Weston and her husband continued to exchange complimentary verses with members of the inner circle around Prague, as well as some further afield; increasingly, these celebrated the arrival of new, infant muses on the scene; so we might conclude that the phenomenon of the *virgo angla* had come to a natural conclusion.

---

[14] Tu patriam, incolumes patriæ sed linquis amicos:
   Mi pater & patrij hic interiêre lares.
   Sauromatæ infestant crebris tibi cuncta rapinis:
   Et mihi, quæ non dat, gens furibunda rapit!

Indeed, it is possible to tell a coherent story about Weston without insisting on the possibility of larger speculative dimensions. Weston's silences are surely explicable in terms either of a seemly maidenly modesty or of the strategic demands of her position, appealing to Rudolph and his associates for a speedy resolution of her family's needs. If she, or her editor, omitted mentioning Kelley by name, that was only prudent; most people would know the identity of this respected "parent" anyway. She could show respect for him without insisting on redeeming his name — only his property. Yet nothing is completely simple in the Prague of Rudolph, and the "nobility" attributed to Weston is inextricable from the prestige associated with Edward Kelley and his grand alchemical projects. A later century's categorical scorn for alchemy in general, and for the controversial Kelley in particular, has almost certainly blinded us to the potency of the language associated with the grand dreams of the day, of which the transformation of base metals to gold was a part. Indeed, we can scarcely claim that our modern science has none of these magical, transcendent overtones.

The fact remains that there is evidence to suggest, but only suggest, that Weston may have been seen as figuring in the grander cultural dreams of her place and time, or at least trying to exploit them. For instance, the eagerness of the Paracelsan physcian Oswald Croll to have a poem of hers in the prefatory materials to his *Basilica Chymica* of 1609 most likely reflects a high regard for the learned world of the Kelley household, even though Kelley as usual goes unmentioned in the exchanges between Croll and Weston. Similarly, references to the grand projects of their "parent" in letters between Weston and her brother suggest — or may have been intended to suggest — ideas and plans that we can only guess at, and that may well have been equally obscure to many readers at the time. Nor have we any evidence of the degree to which the Anhalt interest in promoting Protestant causes might have led Joannes Leo to form a union with his English maiden. I can only conclude that there seems to be an unbroken continuum between the domestic biography of Weston that is developed in her collected works and a larger cultural story that her readers and admirers were likely to intuit. Perhaps it is only a coincidence that a few months after the death of Elizabeth Jane Weston, another *virgo angla*, the daughter of James I, similarly named Elizabeth, was to marry Frederick, the elector palatine, and after a few happy years in Heidelberg come to Bohemia for a tragically brief season of rule. Frances Yates has argued that Rosicrucianism emerged from the cultural ferment in Bohemia during this period, and that its rhetoric of chemical and moral transformation spoke to a dream of transformation and reconciliation of opposites that the modern world was denying with ever-increasing effect.[15] Edward Kelley brought his wife and stepchildren into a world that was fostering this dream; and I think that his stepdaughter's poetry owes much of its power, in its own day at least, to the vividness of the figure of a *virgo nobilissima* from a distant country who must be allowed to be a part of the transformative work if wholeness is to be achieved.

University of Massachusetts, Amherst

---

[15] Frances Yates, *The Rosicrucian Enlightenment* (London, 1972).

La victime tragique
depuis les premières tragédies néo-latines
jusqu'à Jephthes de G. Buchanan

JEAN-FRÉDÉRIC CHEVALIER

Les premières tragédies néo-latines (*Ecerinis* d'Albertino Mussato, *Achilles* d'Antonio Loschi, *Progne* de Gregorio Correr, et *Hiensal* de Leonardo Dati) sont caractérisées par un déchaînement de violence dû à la métamorphose d'un homme en monstre. Le *furor* est l'agent de cette transformation au terme de laquelle les héros furieux présentent leurs actes comme autant de défis à l'ordre divin. Leurs victimes sont assassinées dans des conditions qui rappellent le sacrifice rituel d'un animal. La victime humaine se substitue ainsi à la victime animale et assume le rôle de "bouc émissaire". Pourtant, même si les tragédies néo-latines, héritières du modèle sénéquien, présentent toutes la scène du sacrifice de la victime comme la perversion d'un rituel sacré, la place accordée à la victime dans les tragédies évolue très nettement entre les premières tragédies néo-latines et celles de Muret (*Iulius Caesar*) ou de G. Buchanan (*Jephthes*, *Baptistes*): l'héroïsation de la victime s'accroît à mesure de l'intériorisation du conflit tragique.

Les premières tragédies néo-latines (XIVe et XVe siècles)[1] présentent des scènes de massacre assimilables à des sacrifices. La victime est collective dans l'*Ecerinis* d'Albertino Mussato, où le chœur présente la soumission du peuple padouan comme analogue au sacrifice de jeunes taureaux:

---

[1] Albertino Mussato, *Ecerinide*, éd. L. Padrin (Bologna, 1900); ainsi que *Écérinide, Épîtres métriques sur la poésie, Songe*, éd. J.-F. Chevalier (Paris, 2000). Antonio Loschi, *Achilles*, éd. V. Zaccaria, *Il teatro umanistico veneto, la tragedia* (Ravenna, 1981), 9–96. Gregorio Correr, *Progne*, ed. J. R. Berrigan, G. Tournoy, "Gregorii Corrarii Veneti Tragoedia, cui titulus Progne," *Humanistica Lovaniensia* 29 (1980): 23–99; ainsi que éd. L. Casarsa, *Teatro umanistico veneto. La tragedia: "Achilles"–"Progne"* (Ravenna, 1981), 129–181; et éd. A. Onorato (Messina, 1994), 1:159–218. Leonardo Dati, *Hiensal*, éd. J. R. Berrigan, *Humanistica Lovaniensia* 25 (1976): 84–145; ainsi que *Hyempsal*, éd. A. Onorato (Messina, 2000).

> Plebe cum tota populus subegit
> Colla, deuoti ueluti iuuenci
> Victimis sacras ueniunt ad aras.² (v. 252–254)

Cette assimilation est confirmée par les propos du tyran, Ezzelino da Romano:

> fumus ad summos polos
> A me litatas uictimas tales ferat.³ (v. 336–337)

La rage du despote sanguinaire s'abat sur tous les citoyens à la fois (les nobles et le peuple). Comme leur mort est présentée telle une provocation envers Dieu, ce défi rapproche Ezzelino da Romano de son père, Satan. Les victimes sont en fait immolées à Satan puisque Ezzelino s'était voué à son père dès le début de la tragédie (v. 86–112).

La victime peut également être unique. La vengeance d'Hécube, dans l'*Achilles* d'Antonio Loschi, se concentre sur Achille, le meurtrier de ses fils, Hector et Troïlus. Quand Pâris accède à la prière de sa mère, il fait revêtir à Achille le statut d'une victime immolée en sacrifice:

> Si tantus dolor pectus inflammat, parens,
> Peribit hostis, uictima ut templis cadet.⁴ (v. 206–207)

Comme dans *Médée* ou *Thyeste* de Sénèque, un enfant paie le crime de son père dans *Progne* de Gregorio Correr. Itys est la victime innocente que sa mère immolera pour se venger de Térée. Au moment où Procné, accompagnée de ses compagnes célébrant le culte de Bacchus, délivre sa sœur, elle s'écrie:

> Eruite propere carceris duri minas
> Atque hos ministros regii iussus neci
> Mandate! Maior uictima his cadet manibus!
> Eruite propere: iam satis Baccho datum.
> Insaniendum est nunc mihi: instigat furor.⁵ (*Progne*, v. 555–559)

La victime annoncée est son fils. La célébration du culte de Bacchus pourrait permettre à Procné de justifier son geste sacrilège par l'exemple de Penthée déchiré par

---

² "Les citoyens et tout le menu peuple ont tendu le cou au joug, comme les jeunes taureaux consacrés s'approchent des autels des sacrifices."

³ "Que la fumée, jusqu'au sommet du ciel, porte ces victimes par moi immolées."

⁴ "Si une si profonde douleur, ma mère, enflamme ton cœur, l'ennemi périra; il tombera comme une victime dans le temple."

⁵ "Détruisez à la hâte les murs de cette cruelle prison et livrez à la mort ceux qui ont exécuté l'ordre du roi. Mes mains immoleront une victime plus grande. Nous avons désormais suffisamment donné à Bacchus. Il me faut maintenant perdre la raison. La fureur m'aiguillonne."

les mains de sa mère.⁶ Le rappel du corps déchiré de Penthée (Ovide, *Métamorphoses* 3) préfigure le corps mutilé d'Itys, qui sera, en outre, offert en banquet sacrificiel à son père. Gregorio Correr, en situant le crime tragique dans le cadre du culte mystique de Dionysos, s'inspirait peut-être du mythe orphique selon lequel Dionysos, fils de Zeus et de Perséphone, avait été tué, dépecé et mangé par les Titans. La longue comparaison au début de la tragédie entre Térée et Orphée invite à une pareille lecture.

La vengeance personnelle transforme également Jugurtha en meurtrier. La mort d'Hiempsal et de ses compagnons, dans la tragédie de Leonardo Dati, ressemble elle aussi à la célébration d'un sacrifice. Les victimes sont renversées à terre. L'emploi du verbe *mactare* accentue cette impression de rituel sacré au cours duquel Hiempsal est décapité:

> Nam res eo ducta est loci ut satellites
> Noctu Iugurtae in Hiensalis domum dolis
> Irruperint illicque diuersi ocius
> Regem frequentes quaeritant, internecant.
> Alii oscitantis dormientisque obuios
> Omnis et impetu et mucrone competunt,
> Mactant et inuersos tenus sternunt solo.
> Scrutari et alii abdita, alii diffringere
> Clausa loca non cessant, domusque omnis simul
> Cadentium gemitu et fragore et aspero
> Plagis tumultu exterrita intus uoluitur.
> Tandem repertum Hiensalem opprimunt, caput
> Ferro amputant. Res hunc igitur acta in modum est.⁷ (v. 667–679)

Dès la scène suivante la Pythonisse conseille aux femmes de Libye, en proie au *furor* des Bacchantes, d'offrir des sacrifices à Dis et aux Mânes, c'est-à-dire aux divinités de la mort:

> Io Libes, Libes, io parens, parens,
> Ditique Manibusque litandum tibi.⁸ (v. 696–697)

---

⁶ En dépit des dénégations du chœur (*Progne*, v. 520–522).

⁷ "La situation en est arrivée au point que les hommes de main de Jugurtha ont fait irruption de nuit et par ruse dans la demeure d'Hiempsal; et là, rapidement, ils recherchent de tous côtés le roi et tuent un grand nombre d'hommes. Les uns, en chargeant l'épée à la main, traquent tous ceux qui, sur leur route, somnolent ou dorment, les sacrifient et les renversent face contre terre. D'autres fouillent les recoins; d'autres, sans relâche, fracturent les portes fermées: toute la demeure, terrifiée à la fois par les gémissements des mourants, par le fracas et le violent tumulte provoqué par les coups, est sens dessus dessous. Ils trouvent enfin Hiempsal, se jettent sur lui et le décapitent. Voilà les faits."

⁸ "Io, Libyennes, Libyennes, Io, mère, mère, tu dois offrir un sacrifice à Dis et aux Mânes."

Dans chacune des tragédies néo-latines mentionnées, on assiste à la substitution d'une victime humaine à une victime animale. La personne sacrifiée est ainsi victime de la perversion de l'ordre sacré du monde. En bouleversant les lois de l'univers pour perpétrer son sacrilège, le héros en proie au *furor* revendique une liberté totale. Un seul homme fait assassiner des milliers de Padouans (*Ecerinis*); une vieille femme obtient la mort du plus brillant des héros grecs (*Achilles*); une mère assassine son fils (*Progne*); un jeune prince fait décapiter celui qui partage avec lui le pouvoir (*Hiensal*). Plus la victime est innocente, plus le héros *furiosus* apparaît tel un monstre. L'hypertrophie du "moi" du héros en mal accentue la revendication de l'instauration d'un monde nouveau, fondé sur les ruines de l'ancien. Ezzelino da Romano cherche à obtenir la ruine de la puissance du Dieu des chrétiens; Hécube cherche à abattre la puissance des Grecs; Procné renonce à la puissance des liens du sang; Jugurtha passe outre les dernières volontés de Micipsa. Chaque décision est un défi dicté par le ressentiment exacerbé du héros.

Mais, même s'il est vrai qu'Achille, Térée, et Hiempsal ne sont pas des victimes innocentes, leur châtiment est monstrueux parce qu'il est présenté comme la transgression d'un rituel sacré. Achille est assassiné dans un temple au cours du rituel du mariage. Persuadé d'épouser la princesse troyenne Polyxène, il se rend seul dans le temple d'Apollon. La parole donnée par les Troyens n'était que fourberie.

> Dubia dum martis labat
> sors, inquit: "Hec est prolis Assaraci fides?
> Hec iura thalami? Pacis hec false quies?"[9] (v. 672–674)

Le chœur des Grecs insiste ensuite sur le sacrilège du sang profanant l'autel d'Apollon:

> Pelides genitus dea
> olim qui timor Ylios
> sublimis stetit incliti,
> cesus templa rigat suo
> ferro sanguine Apollinis.[10] (v. 755–759)

Le participe *caesus*, déjà employé au vers 21 pour désigner Hector tué par Achille, associe les deux héros dans le même destin. Pâris avait d'ailleurs refusé d'assassiner Achille par traîtrise avant de céder au *furor* de sa mère. La haine des Troyens se focalise sur Achille. Considéré comme le responsable des malheurs de Troie, Achille devient la victime expiatoire. Véritable bouc émissaire, sur lui retombent tous les torts des Grecs.[11]

---

[9] "Tandis que le sort du combat hésite et reste incertain, il s'écrie: 'Telle est la loyauté de la descendance d'Assaracus? Telles sont les lois nuptiales? Tel est le repos procuré par une fausse paix?'"

[10] "Le fils de Pélée et d'une déesse, dont la grandeur depuis longtemps suscitait la crainte de l'illustre Ilion, baigne de son sang, frappé par le fer, le temple d'Apollon."

[11] Voir R. Girard, *La violence et le sacré* (Paris, 1972).

Le sacrilège le plus horrible est l'assassinat d'Itys par sa mère, puis le banquet sacrificiel perverti dans *Progne*. Gregorio Correr accentue, en effet, le sacrilège de la mort de l'enfant puisque Itys non seulement n'a commis aucune faute, mais qu'en plus son corps sert à l'accomplissement d'un rite sacrificiel perverti. Reprenant simultanément le rôle de Médée et d'Atrée, Procné tue son fils avant de servir son corps en repas à Térée. Le père devient le tombeau de son fils:

> Impiae matris
> Victima caesus dirique premis
> Viscera patris.[12] (*Progne*, v. 953–955)

On retrouve l'emploi de *caesus*, emprunté ici à un passage des *Troyennes* de Sénèque où il désigne Priam:

> Magnoque Ioui uictima caesus
> Sigea premis litora truncus.[13] (Sénèque, *Les Troyennes*, v. 140–141)

L'effort d'*imitatio* accentue le sacrilège puisque Priam avait été assassiné dans un temple. Procné assassine son fils comme une bête sauvage dévore sa proie:

> Sic fata, Furiis concita, infantem trahit
> de more uituli, quem aspra lactentem rapit
> Hyrcana tigris.[14] (v. 899–901)

Les circonstances dans lesquelles l'enfant est mis à mort s'écartent pourtant du rituel dionysiaque dont nous avons déjà parlé. L'enfant lacéré (*sparagmos*) n'est pas dévoré cru par les Bacchantes. L'ômophagie,[15] qui marque la régression à l'animalité, est ici remplacée par la perversion du rituel du sacrifice: le recours à la broche et au chaudron pour faire cuire non un animal, mais un être humain. Gregorio Correr suit fidèlement le modèle ovidien de la préparation du festin de Térée (*Métamorphoses* 6), tout en l'enrichissant de nombreuses expressions empruntées au *Thyeste* de Sénèque (v. 760–779). Une partie des membres de l'enfant bout dans un chaudron en bronze alors que l'autre partie est rôtie sur des broches:

---

[12] "Ta mère, impie, t'a immolé comme une victime et tu accables les viscères de ton funeste père." La formule *Tumulus est nati pater* apparaît au vers 1010.

[13] "Immolé comme une victime offerte au grand Jupiter, tu reposes sur le rivage de Sigée, toi qui n'es plus qu'un tronc." L'influence de Virgile (*Énéide*, 2.557–558) est vraisemblable; la description par Lucain du corps mutilé de Pompée a également pu servir de modèle (*Guerre Civile*, 1.685 et 8.698). L'atmosphère pathétique du poème de Lucain est une source importante de toutes les tragédies néo-latines.

[14] "À ces mots, excitée par les Furies, elle tire à part l'enfant comme s'il s'agissait d'un veau qu'une tigresse d'Hyrcanie arrache avec cruauté alors qu'il tète encore."

[15] Voir M. Detienne et J.-P. Vernant, *La cuisine du sacrifice en pays grec* (Paris, 1979); F. Dupont, *Les monstres de Sénèque* (Paris, 1995).

> Pars haec aheno uoluitur, aestu laticem
> miscente, at illa uerubus[16] affixa ingemit.
> Fumus penates obsidet totos niger.
> Disponit ipsa lancibus diras dapes,
> gnatum parenti. (v. 937-941)[17]

Le corps partagé en deux (*haec . . . illa*), les membres qui s'agitent dans l'eau contenue dans un chaudron d'airain, le gémissement émis par les morceaux du corps, la fumée noire envahissant les Pénates sont autant de motifs empruntés à Sénèque. Contrairement à Agavé (Euripide, *Les Bacchantes*) ou à Héraclès (*Hercule Furieux* de Sénèque) dont la prise de conscience est douloureuse, le sacrificateur criminel exulte à la vue de son crime. Médée et Atrée sont ici les modèles de cette mise en scène tragique d'un récit ovidien.

Il arrive que la célébration d'un sacrifice avec victimes animales annonce la mort prochaine d'un héros. Quand Hiempsal, dans la tragédie de Leonardo Dati, procède à un sacrifice, des prodiges effrayants épouvantent les esprits:

> Ruptisque uinclis taurus excepto fugax
> Ceruice ferro cessit ex ara petens
> Cruore sparsos regios iuuenes suo.
> Quin etiam Hiensal ipse prodiens domo
> Pollice sub illiso moleste limiti
> Faciem in suam pronus propere lapsus gemit.[18] (v. 583-590)

La chute d'Hiempsal et le sang versé préfigurent la scène où les compagnons d'Hiempsal sont immolés sur le sol, face contre terre, tandis que le jeune roi est décapité.

La mort de la victime tragique plonge le monde dans le chaos. Ezzelino da Romano fait régner la terreur dans Padoue et Fra Luca Belludi, compagnon de saint Antoine de Padoue, lui rappelle qu'il ne peut longtemps bouleverser les lois de l'univers. Dans chaque tragédie, les messagers sont frappés de terreur. Paralysés, ils ne peuvent dans un premier temps s'exprimer tant le spectacle du crime sacrilège obsède leur pensée. À l'imitation des pièces de Sénèque, les tragédies néo-latines centrent leur intrigue sur la violence des passions et la monstruosité des personnages rendus furieux.

---

[16] La forme *uerubus* employée par Gregorio Correr est peut-être l'indice de l'utilisation d'un manuscrit de Sénèque appartenant à la famille A alors que le manuscrit *Etruscus* présente la forme *ueribus*.

[17] "Une partie est remuée dans un chaudron où l'eau bout; l'autre partie, fixée à des broches, gémit. Une fumée noire investit totalement la demeure. Elle-même dispose sur des plats le funeste festin, le fils offert à son père."

[18] "Alors que le fer était suspendu à son cou, un taureau brisa ses chaînes, s'enfuit de l'autel et se dirigea vers les jeunes rois en les aspergeant de son sang. Bien plus Hiempsal lui-même, en sortant de chez lui, se blessa grièvement le pied en chemin, tomba en avant lourdement, la tête la première, et gémit."

Dans les quatre tragédies néo-latines évoquées, le héros furieux est toujours le personnage principal et la tragédie repose sur la mise en scène du ressentiment exacerbé qui se transforme en folie furieuse. La place accordée à la victime est ainsi toujours secondaire: le spectacle tragique offre un tel déchaînement de violence que la victime ne sert que de faire-valoir à la monstruosité du héros. Les Padouans ne s'expriment qu'à travers les chœurs de la tragédie dans l'*Ecerinis*. Si Achille hésite à épouser Polyxène parce qu'il craint la réaction des autres chefs grecs, à aucun moment la pièce n'offre une analyse profonde du cœur du héros dans l'*Achilles* d'Antonio Loschi. Le chœur assume cette fonction en se contentant de rappeler la puissance de l'amour qui règne même sur les dieux. Itys est réduit au rôle d'instrument de la vengeance de sa mère dans la tragédie de Gregorio Correr tandis que Procné elle-même n'est que fureur. Hiempsal et Jugurtha sont aveuglés par leurs ressentiments dans *Hiensal* de Leonardo Dati. La souffrance des victimes est, à chaque fois, réduite à sa plus simple expression. Il faut attendre le XVIe siècle pour que les tragédies latines offrent un spectacle plus intime en permettant aux victimes d'exprimer leur souffrance. Progressivement le tragique ne naît plus seulement de l'exacerbation d'un moi meurtrier, mais de l'intériorisation d'une souffrance inouïe.

Nous prendrons l'exemple le plus significatif: *Jephthes* de G. Buchanan.[19] Alors que le nom du héros guerrier a donné à la pièce son titre, Jephté n'entre en scène qu'au vers 433 alors que sa fille, Iphis, parle dès le vers 84 et que près de 130 vers lui reviennent dans toute la pièce. L'horreur provient, il est vrai, de la décision inexorable et cruelle de son père, mais la beauté tragique de la pièce revient intégralement à Iphis qui, héritière de la grandeur d'Iphigénie ou de Polyxène, offre sa vie. Sans l'insistance sur l'héroïsme de la jeune fille, la pièce n'aurait été que le développement de la monstruosité d'un père aveuglé. Dans les quatre premières tragédies néo-latines que nous avons évoquées, jamais la victime n'était à ce point au cœur de la tragédie. Les poètes tragiques du Trecento et du Quattrocento auraient pourtant pu puiser leur inspiration dans certaines tragédies de Sénèque où les victimes jouaient le rôle principal (*Les Troyennes* par exemple). La nouveauté du théâtre de Sénèque n'était pas pour eux l'intériorisation d'une souffrance assumée, mais le spectacle de la transformation d'un héros en monstre. G. Buchanan offre une inversion de la perspective tragique par rapport aux premières tragédies néo-latines. La douleur de la condamnée à mort est au centre de la pièce alors que l'héroïsme jusqu'à la pièce de Gregorio Correr était toujours un héroïsme assassin et monstrueux. Le héros était un tortionnaire qui rejoignait dans l'horreur les grands maudits de la religion ou de la mythologie. Dans la pièce de G. Buchanan, le héros tragique n'est peut-être pas le père, mais la fille. Le héros retrouve sa grandeur magnanime. Dans le théâtre de langue française, cette même voie est explorée. La première tragédie de Garnier s'intitule *Porcie*, une femme illustre, la fille de Caton.[20]

---

[19] George Buchanan, *Jephthes* . . . , ed. P. Sharrat et P. H. Walsh (Edinburgh, 1983). Voir Ph. Ford, "George Buchanan," dans *Centuriae Latinae: Cent une figures humanistes de la Renaissance aux Lumières offertes à Jacques Chomarat*, éd. C. Nativel (Genève, 1997), 213–220.
[20] Voir R. Garnier, *Porcie*, éd. J.-Cl. Ternaux (Paris, 1999).

Les raisons d'un tel changement de perspective sont multiples. Le martyrologe chrétien a certainement offert à G. Buchanan un modèle d'héroïsme. Le *Peristephanon* de Prudence a servi de modèle durant tout le Moyen Âge à la poésie hagiographique. Les premières traductions des tragédies grecques permettaient également d'enrichir la personnalité du héros tragique, victime d'une faute (*hamartia*) dont il n'est pas coupable. Le modèle d'*Hécube* et d'*Iphigénie à Aulis* d'Euripide est d'autant plus déterminant qu'Érasme avait proposé dès 1506 une traduction latine de ces deux pièces. La première traduction en français d'*Hécube*[21] date de 1544 alors que *Jephthes* de G. Buchanan a été composé vers 1540 avant d'être publié en 1554. Même s'il ne connaissait pas le *Traité du sublime*, G. Buchanan rejoint l'idéal de grandeur décrit dans cet ouvrage grâce à l'influence conjointe des modèles tragiques grecs et latins. La grandeur spirituelle de l'héroïne tragique consiste précisément dans l'alliance de la sobriété de l'acceptation et l'intensité de l'amour éprouvé. L'élévation sublime offre à la tragédie des perspectives qui n'avaient pas été explorées au Trecento et au Quattrocento. Il est significatif de remarquer que Polyxène ne s'exprime jamais dans les *Troyennes* de Sénèque alors qu'Iphis, dans la pièce de G. Buchanan, dépasse tout sentiment de révolte pour finalement plaindre son père: "Aeque atque nos aut amplius etiam miser" (v. 1262),[22] et prier Dieu pour le salut de ses parents et de son peuple. Ce sublime d'acceptation consiste dans l'élévation spirituelle de l'héroïne, qui parvient à la gloire et à l'immortalité par le renoncement et le sacrifice volontaire de sa vie.[23] La victime sacrifiée assure l'équilibre du monde tandis que le vœu de Jephté bouleversait les lois humaines et divines. Alors que la souffrance des victimes ne servait auparavant qu'à accentuer la cruauté de leurs bourreaux, le sacrifice d'Iphis permet de mettre un terme à la crise tragique en réalisant le vœu de son père. L'héroïsme d'Iphis correspond à la définition du sublime considéré comme "l'écho d'une grande âme" (*Traité du sublime*, 9.2).

Il n'est pas étonnant de retrouver cette héroïsation de la victime dans une tragédie néo-latine contemporaine de *Jephthes*: *Iulius Caesar* de Marc-Antoine de Muret[24] (composée sans doute vers 1545 et publiée dans les *Iuuenilia* en 1552). La scène de l'assassinat de Jules César est, elle aussi, décrite comme un sacrifice et Calpurnie réclame d'être assassinée par les mêmes bourreaux:

> Secunda uestras hostia exspecto manus.
> Cupide madentem coniugali sanguine,
> Iugulo mucronem, aut pectore excipiam meo.
> Nondum litasti, Brute, perficito sacrum. (v. 487–490)[25]

---

[21] Voir B. Garnier, *Pour une poétique de la traduction: L'Hécube d'Euripide en France de la traduction humaniste à la tragédie classique* (Paris, 1999).

[22] "Tu es aussi malheureux que nous, et même plus encore."

[23] Voir A. Michel, "Rhétorique et poétique: la théorie du sublime de Platon aux modernes," *Revue des Études Latines* 54 (1976): 278–279.

[24] Marc-Antoine de Muret, *Iulius Caesar*, éd. P. Blanchard (Thonon-les-Bains, 1995).

[25] "Et docile victime, / j'en appelle à vos coups. Car j'ai soif et j'ai faim / d'accueillir et mêler dans ma gorge ou mon sein / le poignard ruisselant du sang de mon époux. / Tu n'as pas bien

Et César apparaît pour révéler son apothéose dans une scène imitée de l'épilogue d'*Hercule sur l'Œta* de Sénèque: "Ego ad alta caeli tecta stellantis feror" (v. 545).[26]

La renaissance de la tragédie au début du Trecento est due à la découverte des manuscrits des *Tragédies* de Sénèque, mais les poètes humanistes ont toujours su conjuguer l'influence simultanée de l'épopée et de la tragédie. Leur esthétique tragique était empruntée à Sénèque, mais aussi à Virgile (notamment le livre 7 de l'*Énéide* décrivant le *furor* insufflé par Allecto), à Ovide (par exemple le livre 4 des *Métamorphoses* retraçant le *furor* d'Ino et d'Athamas), à Lucain, à Stace, à Claudien, et à Boèce. On retrouve dans les premières tragédies néo-latines le surgissement d'un *furor* qui s'acharne sur des victimes expiatoires, mais l'importance accordée à la victime ne sera grandissante qu'à partir de la traduction en latin, puis en langue vernaculaire, des tragédies grecques. *Iphigénie* et *Hécube* d'Euripide ont sans aucun doute marqué un tournant dans l'histoire de la tragédie à la Renaissance, histoire que la connaissance de la *Poétique* d'Aristote continuera d'enrichir dès la fin du XVIe siècle.

Université de Reims

---

encore immolé ta victime, / Brutus, accomplis jusqu'au bout ton sacrifice." Trad. P. Blanchard.
[26] "Me voici emporté vers les hautes demeures / du ciel étincelant." Trad. P. Blanchard.

Philology and Autobiography in *Isaac Casaubon,* Animadversionum in Athenaei Deipnosophistas libri XV *(1600)*

JOHN CONSIDINE

The citizens of ancient Athens very much liked eating fish. They knew a wide variety of edible species of fish, and a wide variety of recipes for cooking them. Their desire to eat fish was sometimes pursued at the expense of health; it could become something of a mania. The Athenian culture of fish-eating is described most fully by Athenaeus of Naucratis, in his *Deipnosophistae*, a very long dialogue on the pleasures of the table, which was written in the first century A.D., and of which the abridged version which has come down to the present day takes up seven volumes in the Loeb edition. Athenaeus is no longer much in demand by the non-specialist reader — there is, for instance, no paperback translation into English — although the attractiveness of his material is suggested by the recent success of James Davidson's book *Courtesans and Fishcakes*, which trawls, as it were, in Athenaean waters.[1]

The subject of this paper is an earlier reader of Athenaeus, the philologist Isaac Casaubon (1559–1614). He published an edition of the *Deipnosophistae* in 1597, accompanied by a reprint of the Latin translation of Jacques Daléchamps. The title page of this edition announced that the editor's notes formed a part of it; however, it was only in 1600 that Casaubon's *Animadversionum in Athenaei Deipnosophistas libri XV* appeared.[2] It may at first glance seem surprising that Casaubon of all people should

---

[1] James Davidson, *Courtesans and Fishcakes: The Consuming Passions of Classical Athens* (London, 1997).

[2] Athenaeus of Naucratis, *Deipnosophistarum libri XV. Isaacus Casaubonis recensuit, et ex antiquis membranis suppleuit, auxitque. Adiecti sunt eiusdem Casauboni in eundem scriptorem animaduersionum libri XV* (Heidelberg: apud Hieronymum Commelinum [printed Geneva: Paul Estienne], 1597); Isaac Casaubon, *Animadversionum in Athenaei Deipnosophistas libri XV* (Lyon: apud Antonium de Harsy, 1600).

have animadverted upon Athenaeus's text, or at least that he should have done so at great length — the *Animadversiones* run to 648 pages plus indexes, closely printed, in folio. After all, the image of Casaubon which haunts the imaginations of students of the history of scholarship has little in common with the happy, fish-loving Athenians of the *Deipnosophistae*. That image comes chiefly from Mark Pattison's splendid biography of 1875.³ There, Casaubon appears as a rather tragic figure, born into poverty and kept there by a wife who, with female inconsiderateness, never seemed to stop producing children; groaning under an excessively heavy teaching load; often isolated from other scholars; loathing the pagan authors on whom he worked and longing to turn his attention to holier writings; dying at last as a result of a deformity of the bladder which could be ascribed to his reluctance to interrupt his studies even to urinate, so that the poet Peter Levi has, with poetic licence, called him "a martyr to the lack of sanitary arrangements in the Bodleian Library."⁴ He is also called a martyr, a "martyr of learning," by Sir John Sandys, and Rudolf Pfeiffer, an admirer of Pattison's biography, describes Casaubon as "always in a state of despondency."⁵ Why, it is reasonable to ask, did Pattison's lonely and thwarted Casaubon, Sandys's martyred Casaubon, Pfeiffer's despondent Casaubon, spend so much time working on the *Deipnosophistae*, a big book about the pagan pleasures of the flesh?

Some answers to that question can be found in the *Animadversiones* itself. These answers not only illuminate Casaubon's interest in one work, but permit a general reassessment of his character and his relationship with his scholarship. This move from the specific to the general can be made because the commentary on Athenaeus is so representative of Casaubon's output. So, for instance, what Ulrich von Wilamowitz said of the whole oeuvre applies perfectly to Casaubon's work on the *Animadversiones*: "By nature an expositor, pre-eminently of subject-matter, he specialized in authors who required the widest learning for their elucidation, and whatever author he tackled the result was decisive." So does the point he made directly afterwards: "The learning is marvellous, but it is not displayed for its own sake."⁶ Casaubon's aim, working on Athenaeus or any other text, was to reconstruct the cultures of the ancient world as fully and carefully as he could from the textual sources. And that, indeed, suggests what Athenaeus offered him: a mine of cultural information. Erasmus's annotations in the margins of his copy of Athenaeus show that to him, the

---

³ Mark Pattison, *Isaac Casaubon 1559–1614* (Oxford, 1875; rev. ed. Oxford, 1892).

⁴ Peter Levi, *Eden Renewed: The Public and Private Life of John Milton* (London, 1996), 96, just after a reference to Pattison's biography.

⁵ John Edwin Sandys, *A History of Classical Scholarship* (Cambridge, 1908), 2:208; Rudolf Pfeiffer, *History of Classical Scholarship 1300–1850* (Oxford, 1976), 121, praising Pattison's work as "a detailed, well-documented, sympathetic modern biography such as hardly exists of any classical scholar" (120 n. 1).

⁶ Ulrich von Wilamowitz-Moellendorff, *History of Classical Scholarship,* trans. Alan Harris (London, 1982), 54.

Deipnosophistae was a source of proverbs, of historical anecdotes, or interesting lexical items.[7] To Casaubon, it was something quite different.

This passage, for instance, occurs very early in the *Animadversiones*:

> A most amusing story is told by Athenaeus from Clearchus, about Pithyllus the Gourmand, who, in order that he might devour his food as hot as possible without pain to his tongue, not only wrapped it [his tongue] up in a protective membrane, but went further than that, and put a casing or piece of armour over it.[8]

The discussion which follows deals with the philological evidence for the precise means by which the greedy Pithyllus did protect his tongue. Athenaeus, Casaubon observes, uses two words to describe those means. The first, the noun *periglōttis*, must mean "a covering for the tongue," but the second, the verb *proselutroun*, which is a *hapax legomenon*, is more tricky. Its first element indicates an action which adds to another, and its second element is certainly the rare verb *elutroō*. This must elsewhere be understood to mean, as Casaubon summarizes it, "cover with a coating, as is done with earthenware vases: the French call this *vernisser*." Could Pithyllus have varnished his tongue? In Greek, Casaubon continues, the proper word for glazing or varnishing is a derivative of *petalon* — and this leads him to a passage in St. John Chrysostom, which describes the King of Persia as decorating his beard with *petala* of gold.[9] The question in Casaubon's mind at present is clearly still the thickness of the protection which Pithyllus wore: how thick a covering is implied by *petalon*? In the case of the King of Persia, he argues, we are surely to imagine an application of gold leaf to his beard rather than a rigid golden casing. Elsewhere, in an early Graeco-Latin glossary, a derivative of *petalon* is translated by *stanno*, "I line or cover with tin." This leads to a discussion of the history of the practice of tinning copper vessels, especially to provide safely inert containers for medical use, which takes in Eustathius of Thessalonica's commentary on Homer; then Pliny's natural history; then Dioscorides; then the *Problemata* of Alexander of Aphrodisias; and finally the Byzantine anthology of agricultural writings called the *Geoponica*, before referring to a similar expression in Hebrew. After this great sweep of lexical erudition, Casaubon returns for a moment to the present day, remarking that there is no longer any need to make vessels of

---

[7] Erasmus's copy of the 1514 Aldine *editio princeps* of Athenaeus is now in the Bodleian Library, Oxford, pressmark Auct. I. R. inf. 1.1.

[8] Casaubon, *Animadversiones*, 12: "Lepidissima historia est quam refert ex Clearcho Athenæus, de Pithyllo Ligurritore: qui vt cibos quam feruentissimos posset vorare sine offensione linguæ, non solum membraneo tegmine eam inuoluebat: sed hoc amplius, crustam illi ceu loricam inducebat."

[9] Casaubon, *Animadversiones*, 12, quoting Chrysostom and commenting, "Videtur Persarum rex non veris laminis barbae pilos inuoluisse: verum bracteae aureae illitu aureum colorem barbae conciliasse."

tinned copper, since porcelain can be used instead.[10] His conclusion, that Pithyllus did indeed protect his tongue with a hard casing, is almost overwhelmed by the vigour and scope of his argument.

There is much to be said about this discussion; particularly striking is the lexicographical sophistication with which Casaubon maps his semantic field, working towards a unified comparative study of the different Greek words for kinds of thin casing or covering. But the autobiographical elements, both explicit and implicit, of the passage are even more fascinating than its philological elegance. Perhaps the foremost of these is Casaubon's pleasure in his material. Athenaeus himself speaks of Pithyllus in moralizing terms, calling him *trisathlios*, "thrice wretched," on account of his greed. Casaubon does not moralize: rather, he calls the story "most amusing," *lepidissima*. It is difficult to read Casaubon's *lepidissima* here as anything but a statement that he liked the story of Pithyllus's revolting greed for its own sake.[11]

A second respect in which the commentary illuminates Casaubon's character is its demonstration that he has no difficulty reading Athenaeus's report of the immoral behavior of a pagan side by side with the words of St. John Chrysostom, "sanctissimus pater" as the latter is. What can be seen in the *Animadversiones* is a readiness to use Christian and pagan authors together, an understanding that both can be read as part of the same philology. The legacy of Casaubon's work on Athenaeus can be seen in the eleven references to the *Deipnosophistae* in his last book, his response to the Catholic world-history of Cardinal Barono. Athenaeus gives him material for a commentary on all the possible senses of the word *epiphania*, for a discussion of what exactly St. John the Baptist ate (was it really locusts?), for an account of a spring which supposedly emulated the miracle at Cana by flowing spontaneously with wine, for a history of the practice of saying a prayer before eating, and much more.[12] Casaubon's philology merges seamlessly into his Protestantism: animadverting on Athenaeus could be a holy activity as well as an amusing one. At one point, indeed, Athenaeus leads Casaubon into a reflection on the politics of contemporary Protestantism which, although oblique, is courageous: citing uses of the Greek word *psephos*, "a vote," in Gregory of Nazianzen, he quotes from a sermon in which Gregory refers to those for whom grace is a matter of the reversal of votes, and explains that this may mean people "who readily change their faith itself. For such, in those days, was the state of

---

[10] Casaubon, *Animadversiones,* 13: "quo artificio hodie non est opus: cum incrustatione ea quae sit martiae coctae oblitu, fictilia porcellanas aemulentur, quibus nullum *arguroma,* si sapiam praetulerim."

[11] It is in fact the word *lepidissima* which opens the chapter of the *Animadversiones* given over to this discussion. Although my sense is that *lepidus* is quite often applied in humanistic Latin to texts with some moral dimension, I do not think that it ever comes simply to mean "morally attractive." After all, the connotative range of the word can hardly exclude its Catullan *locus classicus.*

[12] Isaac Casaubon, *De rebus sacris et ecclesiasticis exercitationes XVI ad Cardinalis Baronii Prolegomena in Annales, et primam eorum partem, de Domini Nostri Iesu Christi natiuitate, vita, passione, assumtione* (London: ex officina Nortoniana apud Ioan. Billium, 1614), 186, 247, 278, 590–591.

the Church of God."[13] Bearing in mind the pressure put on Casaubon to become a Catholic at just the time at which he was writing, and the notoriously opportunistic recent conversion of Henri IV, "in those days" is evidently pointed.

A third point is that Casaubon was fascinated by the daily lives of people around him. The discussion of glazed earthenware summarized above leads him to the modern French word *vernisser*, the discussion of tinning to the advantages of porcelain; but there is much more of this sort besides. For instance, he remarks that the practice of adding wine to water (rather than water to wine) to avoid the making of too strong a mixture, reported by Athenaeus, continues in Languedoc.[14] He emends the statement that wine encourages *philosophia* to say that it encourages *philia*, with the dry observation that wine does not make men more disposed to study.[15] A long list of similar examples was compiled by Mark Pattison from a number of Casaubon's philological works. It concludes as follows:

> The use of dogs to carry despatches through the enemy's lines; the checked plaids of the Swiss peasantry; the Spanish almonds he had seen at Lyon; the practice of fixing the antlers of the deer over the gates of the château — these are a few among many examples, which might be culled from his various notes, of his general remark that everyday life is constantly reproducing its old incident.[16]

What can be seen, then, in the *Animadversiones* and other commentaries of Casaubon's is a careful attention to contemporary material culture, and a readiness to apply it in philological work. "How," it has been asked, "can we profess an interest in the history of peasants when we hate our students?"[17] That readiness to scorn, when it occurs in the present, what is loved when it occurs in the past is a problem, but it was not Casaubon's.

This interest in the lives of ordinary people is matched by the record in the *Animadversiones* of Casaubon's place in an extensive network of friends and fellow-scholars. References to the work, and especially to the friendly cooperation, of others abound in his text, and one in particular stands out. In one of his notes, Casaubon had had occasion to edit the so-called Decree of Timotheus, a document which pur-

---

[13] Casaubon, *Animadversiones*, 635: "de iis qui temere eundem modo pro orthodoxo, modo pro haeretico haberent: aut qui facile ipsi fidem mutarent. Ea namque fuit Ecclesiae Dei illis temporibus conditio."

[14] Casaubon, *Animadversiones*, 495: "Durat hic mos hodieque in Narbonensi Gallia: vbi pueri a poculis aquam in scypho offerunt, deinde vinum ex oenophoro aut lagena infundunt."

[15] Casaubon, *Animadversiones*, 207: "Absurdum dictu est, vini potu fieri homines ad studia philosophi[a]e proniores."

[16] Pattison, *Isaac Casaubon*, 446; cf. the materials for this passage in Bodleian Library MS Pattison 79, fols. 47v–48r.

[17] I remember this as the formulation of Arthur Burns, in a conversation arising from the similar questions of Gerald Strauss, "The Dilemma of Popular History," *Past and Present* 132 (1991): 130–149.

ports to be the official order for the expulsion from Sparta of Timotheus of Miletus after he had invented a lyre which, being provided with extra strings, could play more subtle and less chaste music than the Spartans liked. If it were, as Casaubon and his contemporaries mistakenly supposed it to be, authentic, it would be a very ancient witness to the Laconian dialect of Greek. It had been transmitted in highly corrupt form, copied by scribes more familiar with Latin than Greek, in Boethius's treatise on music, and had caused great difficulty to other early modern scholars.[18] Casaubon had reason to be pleased with his emendations to it. While he was in Paris early in 1600, making some final notes to be published as addenda to the *Animadversiones*, he had a surprise. A parcel arrived from Joseph Scaliger in Leiden, containing a copy of Scaliger's third edition of the *Astronomicon* of Manilius — one of the notes to which included a beautifully emended text of the Decree of Timotheus.[19] Having his laborious and original work so narrowly anticipated by another scholar's publication might understandably have moved Casaubon to irritation, or at least have cast him into dignified silence. Instead, he wrote as follows in the addenda:

> After my material on the decree of Timotheus had been written, and after it had been set up in type by the printer, the new edition of the *Astronomicon* of Manilius was sent to me by the kindness of its editor, the incomparable Joseph Scaliger. I looked at once and eagerly through this splendid work, and found that this exceptionally learned and accurate scholar had published an emended text of this decree or proclamation of the Lacedemonians, which I had set out to edit, with a commentary. I rejoiced more than a little to find that the two of us, setting out at the same time on this byway for different reasons, he at Lugdunum Batavorum and I at Lugdunum Convenarum, should have made very much the same judgments, and should have written very much the same.[20]

What matters to Casaubon here is a sense of shared enterprise, and Scaliger's anticipation of his publication only reinforces that sense.

---

[18] See comments on the manuscripts, and collation, in Boethius, *De institutione arithmetica [et] De institutione musica,* ed. G. Friedlein (Leipzig, 1867), 175–176 and 182–184, and Glareanus's marginal collation in Boethius, *Opera* (Basle: ex officina Henricpetrina, 1570), 1372; for other sixteenth-century treatments, see Lilius Gregorius Gyraldus, *Operum quæ extant omnium tomus secundus* (Basle: per Thomam Guarinum, 1580), 347 and Paulus Leopardus, *Emendationum et miscellaneorum libri viginti,* tomus prior (Antwerp: ex officina Christophori Plantini, 1568), 213–216.

[19] Joseph Justus Scaliger, *Notae,* in Manilius, *Astronomicon* (Leiden: ex officina Plantiniana, apud Christophorum Raphelengium, Academiae Lugduno-Batauae Typographum, 1600), 425–427.

[20] Casaubon, *Animadversiones,* 644: "Postquam haec a nobis scripta essent, et iam chalcographi typis dudum expressa, perlata ad nos est Maniliani Astronomici noua editio, a praestantissimo viro Iosepho Scaligero eius auctore muneri missa. Quod opus aureum dum auide statim percurreremus, reperimus doctissimum, acuratissimumque virum hoc ipsum Lacedaemoniorum, siue *psephisma* siue *prosoulemna,* cuius emendationem eramus hic aggressi, correctum a se publicasse, atque illustrasse. Gauisi sumus nec mediocriter, eodem tempore ipsum quidem Lugduni Batauorum, nos vero Lugduni Conuenarum, idem, *odou parergon* occasione diuersa aggressos, idem propemodum sensisse, idem scripsisse."

This leads to a fifth point: the sociable, collaborative scholarly work which the *Animadversiones* record is matched by solitary work — but solitary work which is presented to his readers with great vividness. Flashes of inspiration glitter through the whole commentary. Casaubon is thinking with his pen in his hand. A solution to a problem "has just now occurred to me for the very first time"; a few pages later, another "now comes into my mind."[21] What is evident here is the manner of a great teacher, confident in his work and in the participation of his pupils, his readers, in a shared enterprise of analysis and discovery. Casaubon invites his readers to consider problems from different angles: "even if I had not at first remembered which tragedy these lines were taken from," he explains, it would still have been beyond doubt that it must be by Euripides.[22] He warns them that the sources are unreliable on a particular point: "Beware of agreeing with the highly learned men who identify Augustus himself as the originator of this disgraceful practice."[23] He invites them to join him in exasperation at the shortcomings of secondary sources: "O human credulity!" he exclaims of those who have accepted an impossible reading in Aristophanes. He remarks on the stupidity of the Byzantine encyclopedist whom he knows as Suidas, adding "why should I not call a spade a spade?"[24] He even shares his frustration at the points where analysis breaks down: "If only I could gloss over the difficulty of these words," he says at one particularly intractable passage, and a few lines later, with good-humoured irony, "I have to confess the slowness of my intelligence: I make no sense of this passage."[25]

All this suggests that the writing of the *Animadversiones* actually gave Casaubon a great deal of pleasure. How, it might even be asked, did Pattison turn this model of academic wit and panache — a man whose readers see him laughing over the thrice-wretched greed of Pithyllus, watching as the sparks of interpretation crackle between sacred and profane texts, turning an observant eye on his own world and on that of ancient Athens, enjoying an extensive correspondence, and teaching energetically — into the ill-starred Casaubon with whom scholars are now acquainted? Part of the answer is that he had been too deeply impressed by Casaubon's fascinating diaries, the so-called *Ephemerides*, which are preserved at Canterbury Cathedral, and had been

---

[21] Casaubon, *Animadversiones*, 8: "Gulielmus Canterus . . . emendabat, *alla pant'apix*. Puto verius quod venit nobis nunc primulum in mentem"; 25: "Sed non dubitamus verum esse quod iam nobis venit in mentem."

[22] Casaubon, *Animadversiones*, 8: "Etsi non memineram initio ex qua tragedia esset hic versus, Euripidis tamen esse non dubitabam."

[23] Casaubon, *Animadversiones*, 31: "Caue assentiaris eruditissimis viris qui infamis huius inuenti auctorem produnt Augustum ipsum."

[24] Casaubon, *Animadversiones*, 10: "Fidem hominum! quis fando audiuit aut legit vsquam *vinacea plebiscitorum*?"; 14: "Pari stupore, (cur enim non dicam ligonem ligonem?) *skolia* alibi legit et probauit pro *askolia*."

[25] Casaubon, *Animadversiones*, 20: "Vtinam liceret mihi difficultatem horum verborum dissimulare"; again, "Tarditatem ingenij mei necesse est confitear: nihil enim hic intelligo."

published in 1850 in an edition which was reviewed by Pattison.[26] They constitute a true journal, written day by day, and when Casaubon was feeling tired and despondent at the end of the day, he tended to express himself gloomily, and in particular to question the value of his work. We all do that. But to say, as Pfeiffer does after reading Pattison, that the *Animadversiones* "were written with groaning and sighing, day and night, through more than three years" is to exaggerate, and to say, as Pattison himself does, that to Casaubon "the labour [of writing the *Animadversiones*] and its result were equally repulsive and disappointing" is to exaggerate quite gravely.[27]

The true story is, indeed, vividly apparent elsewhere in Casaubon's diaries. Late in 1597, to his devastating grief, his beloved daughter Elizabeth died. He read the Bible on the day of her death; and, on that day, at the end of a deeply moving journal entry, resolved, "with my soul cast down by the death of my little girl," to turn back to Athenaeus. Just as work on Polybius would help him cope with the death of his daughter Philippa in 1608, so now work on Athenaeus gave him strength; and in the coming days, he refers repeatedly to hard labor on the *Animadversiones*, and asks God repeatedly to help him in his labors.[28] This is not the behavior of a man carrying the repulsive burden which Pattison claims the work on Athenaeus was; it is that of one turning to a vital personal resource.

Pattison's unforgettable evocation of Casaubon's gloom, and virtual dismissal of his happiness, is characteristic — for Pattison was himself a deeply unhappy man. He was seeing himself in the mirror of Casaubon; he was, in tremendously powerful and memorable prose, putting his own autobiography into his philological work. But Casaubon's autobiography is worth the reading as well as Pattison's, and it is to be found not only in his *Ephemerides* and in his letters, but also in his philological works. In the *Animadversiones* on the *Deipnosophistae*, among the convivial Athenians who are eating their fish and drinking their wine and talking so copiously about both, Casaubon is to be seen, a cheerful stranger, bright-eyed and observant, trying to understand the conversation, taking notes at every turn, and, from time to time, unexpectedly, laughing.

University of Alberta

---

[26] Isaac Casaubon, *Ephemerides*, ed. John Russell (Oxford, 1850), reviewed by Pattison in the *Quarterly Review* 93 (1853): 462–500. It was this review which suggested the name of Edward Casaubon to George Eliot as she wrote her novel *Middlemarch*.

[27] Pfeiffer, *History of Classical Scholarship 1300–1850*, 121; Pattison, *Isaac Casaubon*.

[28] Casaubon, *Ephemerides*, 37: "jacente animo ex obitu filiolae, hodie tamen solennia studiorum repetiimus; ac mane totum studiis *enkukliois*, praesertim Athenaeo impendimus"; cf. 38: "tuo, mi Deus, beneficio Athenaei censurae impendimus, et gratiae immortales, O Deus salutis meae, quod eo die secundum librum recensere absolvimus," et seqq. For Polybius and the death of Philippa, see Pattison, *Isaac Casaubon*, 244.

Prefacing Axiochus:
The Renaissance Plato and the
res publica litterarum

JUDITH DEITCH

The purpose of this paper is to raise the profile of the dialogue entitled *Axiochus*. Although it is now known to have been composed around the first century B.C., this short *consolatio* on how to die well, which exhibits Stoic and Epicurean doctrines, was quite simply the most popular work by Plato in the Renaissance. "Popular" means having the widest-ranging appeal, and this is evident from the bibliographic data. Throughout Europe printers printed and readers bought up successive editions of the Latin version of the dialogue, alone and in collations with other Platonic texts. According to a tabulation derived from James Hankins's "Census of Printed Editions," *Axiochus* was printed sixty-one times between 1474 and 1600, nearly double the number of the nearest Platonic contenders (*Charmides, Epistles,* and *Amatores* at thirty-three printings), and two-and-a-half times as often as some of the dialogues we now consider representative of the essential Plato, such as the *Symposium*.[1] It was certainly used as a school text; for example, the title page of a Greek-Latin edition of 1577 declares the work to contain the "doctrine for living and dying well, in order to fashion the morals of an adult dutifully and honestly, especially profiting for youth in the exercising of both languages."[2]

---

[1] James Hankins, Appendix B, "Census of Printed Editions," in *Plato in the Italian Renaissance* (Leiden, 1990), 738–796. My tabulation yields the following numbers of printings for the period: *Timaeus*: 31; *Phaedo, Hipparchus, Meno, Theages*: 28; *Republic, Alcibiades 1 and 2*: 27; *Crito, Euthyphro, Apology, Theaetetus*: 26; *Symposium, Sophist, Minos, Laws, Epinomis*: 25; the Complete Works, often including the *spuria*: 24.

[2] "Doctrina recte vivendi ac moriendi ad mores pie ac honeste conformandos etiam adultis, ad linguae utriusque exercitia iuuenibus potissimum conducens." (Hankins, "Census," #122.) All translations are mine unless otherwise stated. A 1543 edition, published as a pendant to Aristotle's *Topica* (Hankins, "Census," #57), refers to the zealous student comparing both languages. Padelford reports seeing a copy which "shows the Greek heavily larded with cribs and one of the mar-

Besides schoolboys and layfolk interested in this brief *praeparatio ad mortem*, a steady stream of Renaissance humanist scholars enjoyed popular success by translating it into Latin. This started in the fifteenth century with Cencio de'Rustici, Rinuccio Aretino, and Antonio Cassarino, whose translations were already widely disseminated when the text started coming out in print.[3] As Jacques Chevalier remarked in his 1915 monograph on the work:

> The Renaissance read, translated, and commented on the *Axiochus* with passion. It is through this apocryphal dialogue that the humanists discovered Plato: they studied and admired it as much as, and more often than, the great authentic works. And their enthusiasm was sincere.[4]

This statement has found little resonance in Renaissance studies over the past eighty-five years. Not only is current awareness of the dialogue low, but it is often readily dismissed by scholars — as if once it has been said that it is not authentic there is nothing left to say, except perhaps to smile at the Hellenistic doctrines issuing from the mouth of Socrates. The question most frequently asked by modern scholars, "Didn't they know it wasn't by Plato?," reveals more about our notions of authorship than about how Plato was perceived in the Renaissance. (My answer to that question is that they "knew" it was!) It is thus fascinating and revealing to ponder how and why this particular dialogue came to represent "the Renaissance Plato."

Of all Renaissance readers, two of the highest-ranking humanists of the age showed great interest in this pseudo-Platonic work, approaching it with forethought and respect for its content. Ficino and Agricola not only translated the *Axiochus* into Latin but also published it with other serious works. Although Ficino attributed the work to Plato's disciple Xenocrates (on evidence construed from Diogenes Laertius, who listed the dialogue among the *spuria*), it is important to note that he still incorporated the *Axiochus* within the legitimate canon of the Platonic Academy: he did not see it as a forgery or clumsy imitation. It was printed during Ficino's lifetime in the 1497 volume of Neoplatonic works headed by Iamblichus, and in a 1498 edition

---

gins ... decorated with that type of aimless drawing which a tired schoolboy employs to relieve the ennui of a weary task": Frederick Padelford, "Introduction," in *The Axiochus of Plato Translated by Edmund Spenser* (Baltimore, 1934), 17.

[3] See Hankins, *Plato*, 95–97. Cencio de'Rustici's translation was printed in the sixteenth century and is extant in thirty-eight MSS; sixteenth-century vernacular translations were executed by Etienne Dolet and Philippe de Mornay in French, Vincentio Belprato in Italian, and Edmund Spenser in English.

[4] "La Renaissance lut, traduisit et commenta l'*Axiochos* avec passion. C'est à travers ce dialogue apocryphe que les humanistes découvrirent Platon: ils l'étudient et l'admirent autant, et souvent plus, que les grandes oeuvres authentiques. Et leur enthousiasme fut sincère": Jacques Chevalier, *Etudes critiques du dialogue pseudo-platonicien l'Axiochos sur la mort et sur l'immortalité de l'âme* (Paris, 1915), 117.

with Athenagoras's *De resurrectione*; in 1507, eight years after Ficino's death, it appeared with his *De religione christiana*.[5]

But it is Agricola's translation which appeared most frequently, and, almost always from 1518 onward, as an addition to Ficino's *Platonis Opera*.[6] Agricola's *Axiochus* was also consistently printed with collections of his own works, notably in the *Opuscula* of 1511 edited by Peter Gilles, and the *Lucubrationes* of 1539, in a companion volume to the first complete text of the *De inventione dialectica* edited by Alardus of Amsterdam.[7] Many of the works by Agricola which appeared in the 1511 *Opuscula* — including letters, poems, and translations — had already been printed in one of the earliest editions of the *Axiochus*, published in 1483 at Leuven.[8] In yet another edition, a school text produced at Deventer, the dialogue was printed amidst a new humanist selection of works by Jerome, Cicero, Basil, and Horace.[9] Thus one great appeal of the *Axiochus* was that it was Janus-faced, looking both forward and back: in addition to demonstrating compatibility with the new humanist context, it seemed to accomplish the feat of making Plato conform to the medieval *ars moriendi*. There is codicological evidence for the latter contention in a volume at Deventer in which the Platonic dialogue was bound with traditional literature of purgatorial visions and apparitions.[10]

Not only was the *Axiochus* printed with important texts, but both Ficino and Agricola chose to preface this work with mythologization both of self and of the *res publica litterarum*. I will examine how the dialogue was presented in three prefaces: Ficino's dedication to Piero de'Medici, Agricola's letter to Rodolphus Langius, and Jacob Canter's letter to Johann Rinck which appeared as a second preface to Agricola's translation in the 1495, 1500, and 1506 editions.[11]

The great adaptability of the text is apparent in the different ways it has been prefaced. Four topics help reveal the respective constructions of the *res publica litterarum*: power, genealogy, knowledge transfer, and geopolitical boundaries. These aspects are handled quite differently by Ficino and the Dutch humanists. First, in terms of power, Ficino's dedication emphasizes a patronage relationship with a prince who exemplifies the Platonic philosopher-king. Agricola and Canter, on the other hand, construct a relationship of Aristotelian primary friendship or Ciceronian *amicitia* where power derives from personal bonds between equals. Second, in terms of genealogy,

---

[5] Hankins, "Census," #10, #11, and #18 respectively. Ficino translated only one other spurious work, the *Definitiones*.

[6] See G. Tournoy, "Marsile Ficin, Agricola et leurs traductions de l'*Axiochos*," in *Rodolphus Agricola Phrisius 1444–1485*, ed. F. Akkerman and A. J. Vanderjagt (Leiden, 1988), 211–228.

[7] Hankins, "Census," #22 and #53.

[8] Hankins, "Census," #4. One curious reversal of the practice with the *Opera Omnia* occurred in 1508, when Jacobus de Breda published a collection of works by Agricola without the pseudo-Platonic text, and published Ficino's translation of *Axiochus* as a separate item.

[9] Hankins, "Census," #17.

[10] Deventer Stads- of Athenaeumbibliotheek (SAB) verzamelband 103, originally from the Heer Florenshuis.

[11] Hankins, "Census," #9 and #17; the Deventer edition of 1500 is missing.

Ficino establishes a hereditary succession of three generations of Medici rulers. Canter, however, following Agricola, uses intellectual succession in order to provide Northern humanist legitimation of the kind carried on by Erasmus. Third, the transfer of knowledge in Ficino's state is limited to an elite, but Agricola revels in *universitas*, making Plato accessible to all. Lastly, Ficino sets boundaries for his republic of letters within the confines of "patria," one country or homeland; however, because of their shifting places of residence around Europe, the conceptual community of scholars Agricola and Canter invoke transcends geopolitical boundaries.

Ficino's short preface to the *Axiochus* is most widely known for its narration of Cosimo de'Medici's last days. Significantly, Cosimo is seen ordering translations of Aristotle and Plato, and on his deathbed Ficino reads him the *Axiochus*:

> When he had discoursed acutely and at length on many things concerning the contempt for this life — he was then aspiring to the life of heavenly bliss — and when he had made an end of his speaking, I said to him, "Cosimo, Xenocrates, a just man and beloved disciple of our Plato, has treated this same subject in his book on death." Then he said, "Marsilio, recount in Latin what Xenocrates discoursed in Greek." I recounted it; he approved. He ordered it to be translated; I translated it.[12]

The scene of reading is programmatic because here in the preface the dying Cosimo already anticipates and pre-empts doctrines of *contemptus mundi* and "death as a gain" which Socrates endorses in the dialogue.

This dedication is a species of that genre familiar to the modern academic: the application for funding. In hopes of securing Cosimo's son Piero as a patron for his scholarly projects, Ficino emphasizes the need to join wisdom and power. But, as Hankins notes, this in itself is Platonic:

> The need for joining wisdom to power ... Ficino regarded as a peculiarly Platonic teaching; the *sententia aurea* of *Republic* VII — that states would be blessed when philosophers ruled or rulers philosophized — was the most famous of all Plato's dicta.[13]

In the preface this conjunction is handled in two ways. First, wisdom must be derived from learned men; as Ficino wrote in the argument to one of the Platonic letters: "Princes should honor the wise; the wise should willingly consult the interest of

---

[12] "Ubi per multa et acute et copiose de huius vitae contemptu disseruit: utpote qui iam ad supernam beatitudinem adspiraret. Cum ille finem dicendi fecisset: Haec eadem, Cosme, inquam, Xenocrates vir sanctus atque dilectus Platonis nostri discipulus in libro de morte tractavit. Tum ille: referas, inquit, latine Marsili quae grece Xenocrates disputat. Retuli; probavit. Transferri iussit: transtuli. ...": Ficino, "Preface," *Xenocrates De Morte* (Augsburg: Sylvan Othmar, 1515 [Hankins, "Census," #26]) a.ii.r. I have repunctuated and normalized spelling. The text of this and some of the other prefaces are conveniently reproduced by Chevalier, *Axiochos*.

[13] Hankins, *Plato*, 304.

princes."[14] Thus in complying with Cosimo's order to translate ten books of Plato,[15] Ficino takes up his own position in the dynamic of power relations which constitute patronage. Wisdom and power are also united in the person of Cosimo de'Medici himself who exemplifies the Platonic philosopher-king. As the text of the preface says, he was "wise in both humane learning and things divine," and throughout his life kept "the fellowship of the Muses even when on the highest business."[16] In old age "when he had given himself wholly to the study of philosophy and sacred letters," he called for translations of Plato, Aristotle, and Mercury [i.e., "Hermes Trismegistus", the Hermetic Corpus] "in order to be initiated into the sacred service of philosophy."[17] Cosimo's grasp of learning is considerable: he is said to have read these translations "carefully and comprehended them perfectly."[18]

Second, with regard to genealogy, Ficino involves three generations in the hereditary descent of Medici patrons: for, although he is not mentioned here, in a later letter Ficino reminds Lorenzo, Cosimo's grandson, that he was present at the deathbed.[19] In the preface, although Ficino laments that Cosimo must die, both "patria et academia" are blessed in still having Piero, who is "parenti quam simillimus" (most like his father). Thus a dynasty of philosopher-kings will herald a golden age.[20] The other way genealogy is construed in the preface is in the historical descent of philosophers mentioned. In a broad sweep, the syncretic continuum stretches from Egyptian hermetic wisdom ("Mercury"), through the Platonists to the Renaissance — or from Plato to his disciples Xenocrates and Aristotle, and eventually to Ficino himself. Xenocrates, and thus his dialogue the *Axiochus*, fits perfectly into this direct line of philosophical succession.

The third aspect of this republic of letters, knowledge transfer, is restricted to an elite class: the members of Ficino's Platonic academy, for example. Platonic wisdom is here referred to as "archana," something to be kept from the vulgar eye and revealed only to the initiated. The sacred mysteries are opened to Cosimo as being an

---

[14] Quoted by Hankins, *Plato*, 304.

[15] According to Allen, eight of these were spurious; only two were authentic, the *Parmenides* and the *Philebus*: M. J. B. Allen, "Ficino's Theory of the Five Substances and the Neoplatonists' *Parmenides*," in idem, *Plato's Third Eye: Studies in Marsilio Ficino's Metaphysics and its Sources* (Aldershot, 1995), 22.

[16] "non modo rerum humanarum prudentia, verumetiam sapientia divinarum . . . in summis negociis absque consortio Musarum."

[17] "in senectute praecipue philosophiae studiis sacrisque literis totum se tradidit. Utque in primis philosophiae sacris iniciaretur, nonnullos Aristotelis libros converti ab Iohanne Argyrophylo viro doctissimo voluit: . . . Deinde . . . divi Platonis libros decem et unum Mercurii e greca lingua in latinam a nobis transferri iussit."

[18] "Haec omnia Cosmus et accurate legit et absolute comprehendit." As Hankins wryly notes, he was much in advance of modern scholarship (*Plato*, 268 n. 3).

[19] Hankins, *Plato*, 268, n. 4.

[20] See Hankins on the Medici family as patrons "acting as local agents for Divine Providence" (*Plato*, 304).

example of the kind of initiate who correctly regards Plato's philosophy as veiled truth.[21]

Lastly, geopolitical boundaries are inscribed in the word "patria," which here indicates an actual nation within real identifiable borders. It is the nation and homeland that is said to bewail Cosimo's death but affirms its hope in his son as successor. This *res publica* is equivalent to a self-standing and locatable political entity, to the Italy mentioned at the very opening of the preface.[22]

For the Dutch humanists the cohesive power of their *res publica litterarum* runs along friendship ties. Agricola dedicates his translation to Rodolphus Langius, a school friend from his university days; both "Rudolphs" studied at Erfurt and matriculated in the same year, 1456. Langen was part of the circle of friends which included Alexander Hegius, Wessel Gansfort, and Antonius Liber.[23] Agricola's prefatory letter to the *Axiochus* is in the genre of *epistulae ad familiares*, although the somewhat playful tone is less like that of Cicero to Atticus than it is like the poetic envoy of Catullus 1:

> I have translated into Latin the little book of Plato entitled Axiochus. You might object, to whom would I dedicate this piece? But I was hoping that I would easily be able to impose on your kindness, in order that, should you accept [the book], you would afford it not the haughtiness of a critic, but the protection of a friend.[24]

As opposed to an exchange of intellectual prestige for financial backing, Agricola invokes a relationship which grants his friend the status of ideal reader. Agricola hopes that Langius will be a friend to his work, rather than a critic. This attitude of ideal reader is further evident in the invocation of *benevolentia*, as well as in the fiction of the "sole reader": "Therefore I have dedicated it to you and to you alone".[25] He ends the short preface emphatically on this note: "I consider that you alone abundantly make up the great audience for my efforts."[26] His object will be achieved if

---

[21] "Quibus omnia vitae praecepta, omnia naturae principia, omnia divinarum rerum mysteria sancta panduntur."

[22] Cosimo is "Italiae decus," the glory of Italy, the tag being taken from Vergil, *Aeneid*, 2.508.

[23] For basic information on the circle see individual entries in *The Contemporaries of Erasmus*, ed. P. G. Bietenholz and Th. B. Deutscher, 3 vols. (Toronto, 1985–1987).

[24] "Libellum Platonis qui Axiochus inscribitur latinum feci. Tuque potissimum cui eum dicarem occurrebas? Quod facillime sperabam posse me tuae benevolentiae imponere, ut, cum acciperes eum, amici sinum illi non iudicis supercilium offeres": Agricola, *Axiochus Platonis de contemnenda morte*, ed. Jacob Canter Phyrsius (Mainz: Peter von Friedberg, 1495 [Hankins, "Census," #9]), A.iii.r. I have repunctuated and normalized spelling. Agricola's preface appeared in all four incunables and frequently afterwards. Compare Catullus: "To whom shall I dedicate my charming new book? . . . / Cornelius, to you." ("Cui dono lepidum novum libellum . . . ? / Corneli tibi." [*Carmina*, 1.1–3])

[25] "Tibi igitur — atque adeo uni tibi — illum dicavi."

[26] "quem solum ego meorum studiorum abunde magnum theatrum puto."

Langen approves the work, "because I delight greatly in your love for me," but it will be a failure if he is displeased.[27] It is his friend's opinion and critical judgment ("tuis ... auribus tuoque iudicio"), not reward or political status, which will determine the success or failure of the work *as a literary project*.

The intimacy between the two friends forms the basis for a community of scholars which is, paradoxically, open to all. For each reader is invited to identify himself with these friends by means of the very specificity of the dedication. Each reader can be both ideal reader, like Langen, and producer of texts for friendship exchange, like Agricola.

This rhetorical community is also important for the concept of genealogy, inscribed in the additional or second preface, Jacob Canter's letter-dedication to Johann Rinck. Written in the same intimate tone of *amicitia*, Canter explicitly states that the dialogue's importance partially rests on the fact that it was translated by Agricola: "the worthiest man of all my compatriots. ..."[28] Thus in 1495, somewhat predating Erasmus's efforts,[29] we already have Agricola as the man whose intellectual reputation is a standard for Northern humanism. This intellectual succession presents an unrestricted form of genealogy open to any Dutch or German humanist who wishes to claim descent from the eloquent Frisian.

With genealogy and power governed by the construction of a rhetorical community, the boundaries of this republic of letters are necessarily conceptual rather than actual, fluid rather than fixed. In another way, such fluidity is explicitly inscribed by Canter in the second preface by reference to his traveling. For example, he opens by referring to the dialogue as a gift from Rinck which has been traveling with him for a long time.[30] But Agricola, Langius, and other Northern humanists too, occupied many different places of residence around Europe, either for purposes of their own education (as students), or for the education of others (as teachers). The nation of the itinerant is conceptual, exceeding geopolitical borders.

This connects directly with the topic of knowledge transfer. Agricola, Langen, Canter, and Rinck were all concerned with reforming public education, with opening new schools and incorporating new learning in the classroom. In concert with this, Agricola sees his translation as transferring knowledge of Plato's philosophy to the general public; he dares to publish such a stream in order that the flood be made

---

[27] "Tu itaque si probabis hunc meum laborem, erit (quod gaudeam magis pro tuo in me amore) quem ego in causa putabo, qui ut ingenio meo blandiar. Sin displicebit haec tibi opera mea perierit."

[28] "Rodolpho Agricola conterraneo me viro nestorea, mehercule, vita dignissimo": Jacob Canter Phrysius, "Letter to Rinck," in Agricola, *Axiochus* (Mainz, 1495), A.i.v–A.ii.r. I have re-punctuated and normalized spelling.

[29] Erasmus's first reference to Agricola as intellectual predecessor appears in the "Quid canis in balneo" entry of the *Adages* of 1508.

[30] "Axiochum, quem mihi ante annos aliquot dono dedisti, Joannes suavissime, eo sane tempore (si satis memini) quo in latinum profectus sum, iam mecum diu terra marique peregrinantem."

known to the general public.³¹ Instead of veiled truths or sacred mysteries, the popular reader is invited to be instructed by this consolation of philosophy.

Furthermore, such a conception of knowledge transfer fits Agricola's overall view of Socrates, and the representation of Socrates in a dialogue by his disciple Plato. As A. J. Vanderjagt has observed, Agricola viewed Socrates as a practical philosopher, most concerned with ethics. As he says, Socrates is the philosopher *par excellence* because he brings philosophy down from the heavens for everyday use by human beings. Agricola believes that in his work he is reiterating the philosophical attitude of this Socrates who taught men to reflect upon themselves and their way of doing things.³² Not only by making Plato accessible, but also by choosing a Socrates who speaks those most practical philosophies — Stoicism and Epicureanism — is Agricola, in his translation of *Axiochus*, purveying a trenchant representation of the Renaissance Plato. A Stoic Plato who provides practical advice on dying a good death makes perfect sense, as much sense, in fact, as a Neoplatonist Plato who conceals truths about the soul's ascent.³³

In this paper I have attempted to detail how the *Axiochus* was placed in a privileged position as an important text in the period. The large differences in application bespeak the remarkable adaptability of the *Axiochus*. Both Ficino and Agricola esteemed it sufficiently to attach to it foundational statements which frame the dialogue within a *res publica litterarum*. Those who inherited the work propagated it widely. Surely it is worthy of our serious attention, whether Renaissance readers — from the most learned scholar to the most sluggish schoolboy — "knew it wasn't by Plato" or not. "The Renaissance Plato" is necessarily a much larger conceptual field than the Modern Plato; and the Postmodern Plato may be something yet again. As Derrida cautions, "What we have in the history of philosophy is ... a series of different accounts that have some common elements, but that all also leave something out. We should beware of taking any version of the story [as] simply authoritative."³⁴

York University, Canada

---

[31] "ut audeam immensum illud divinumque Platonis dicendi flumen populo meis verbis cognoscendum proponere."

[32] A. J. Vanderjagt, "Rudolph Agricola on Ancient and Medieval Philosophy," in *Rodolphus Agricola Phrisius 1444–1485*, 225.

[33] And the Hellenistic philosophers, just as the Neoplatonists, claimed descent from Socrates.

[34] Quoted by Catherine H. Zuckert, *Postmodern Platos: Nietzsche, Heidegger, Gadamer, Strauss, Derrida* (Chicago, 1996), 6.

Pontano élégiaque : l'énonciation de la subjectivité élégiaque dans la République des Lettres

E. DELBEY

Nous avons choisi de poser la question d'une possible esthétique de la subjectivité, à la fois intériorité et individualité, par l'analyse d'exemples empruntés à la poésie élégiaque de Pontano: énonce-t-elle une prise en considération du moi par le je de l'écriture? Comment parler de la personnalité littéraire de Pontano? Le problème est d'autant plus important que, par tradition littéraire, l'élégie peut paraître, dans ses artifices mêmes d'expression, impersonnelle; P. Veyne, au cours de son ouvrage *L'élégie érotique romaine* daté de 1983, s'était attaché à vouloir démontrer que l'aspect proprement littéraire d'une expression savante de la mythologie interdisait au sentiment amoureux toute réalité et faisait de la passion l'objet d'un discours représentant l'esthétique alexandrine et callimachéenne dont le code amoureux n'est précisément qu'un code. Properce et Ovide seraient les meilleurs poètes de cette littérature des "topoi". Pontano, poète élégiaque, entre donc au sein d'une République des Lettres où le style élégiaque paraît être l'objet d'une esthétique de l'imitation-émulation plutôt que de l'énonciation subjective. Rivaliser avec Properce, Ovide, ou Tibulle reviendrait en effet à s'écarter toujours plus d'une écriture personnelle dès lors que, par cette pratique de l'*imitatio*, le poète néo-latin n'engage de lui-même que son art; abordant la matière élégiaque, il la traite sans se laisser arrêter par les réalisations d'illustres prédécesseurs qui n'ont pas accaparé tout ce que l'on pouvait dire, mais ont ouvert une voie. Nous retrouvons alors un art de l'invention dont Sénèque avait dit le plus grand bien dans la lettre 9.79.6 à Lucilius: "La différence est grande entre une matière usée et une matière déjà travaillée par d'autres: celle-ci s'enrichit de jour en jour et les inventions anciennes ne sont pas une gêne à qui est fait pour inventer. D'autre part, le mieux avantagé, c'est le dernier venu. Il trouve tout prêt un fonds d'expressions qui, différemment agencées, offrent une physionomie nouvelle."

Toutefois la poésie élégiaque de l'époque classique peut continuer d'être lue aussi, encore, comme célébration du désir et des plaisirs en relation étroite avec l'idéal hédoniste de la liberté amoureuse; art de l'érôs léger et ludique, les textes qui le composent, apparaissent traversés par les corps "de manière réelle et concrète, jusque dans les plus précieux détails" ainsi que l'écrit M. Onfray à la page 118 de sa *Théorie du corps amoureux* parue en 2000; Catulle, Tibulle, Properce, Ovide sont des individus vivants qui, chacun à sa manière, enseignent à aimer la vie. Charnelle, l'élégie romaine serait donc à comprendre selon sa seule dimension d'apparition à la conscience subjective par une poétique des sentiments fondée sur une théorie des possibilités du corps qu'illustre l'*Art d'aimer*. Dès lors le souci de soi n'est plus à exclure des poèmes élégiaques; le tout est de savoir où situer ce moi.

Nous nous proposons d'étudier l'énonciation de la subjectivité chez Pontano élégiaque en privilégiant l'étude de l'acte d'écriture comme faculté mimétique et mise en forme d'une conscience de soi. Déictiques, première personne de l'indicatif présent sont des marqueurs importants du subjectif comme registre d'expression dans l'élégie classique, chez Properce par exemple, ainsi que nous pensons l'avoir démontré dans notre thèse sur les poétiques élégiaques (Paris IV-Sorbonne, 1995). Comment Pontano donc se pose-t-il en héritier sans renoncer à être lui-même?

Répondre à cette question, c'est d'abord noter que l'éventualité d'une possible contradiction entre la technique d'écriture et l'inspiration comme élément subjectif n'est pas envisagée par Pontano qui fait preuve du plus grand soin dans l'imitation des modèles sans pour autant se rendre identique à eux. A la différence de Politien, qui s'efforce de formuler l'idée d'un style personnel, préparant ainsi une esthétique nouvelle, Pontano ne s'engage pas dans un mouvement d'affirmation de la stylistique subjective; alors que Politien s'attache à une esthétique du caractère (*indoles* / èthos), sensible aux effets de présence subjective qui sont les marques de l'improvisation, Pontano, tout en ne contestant pas la spécificité de l'*ingenium* — que renforce d'ailleurs la thématique astrale — , situe la faculté mimétique — représenter en imitant — au centre de la conscience de soi comme poète.

L'élégie 1.18 des *Libri Parthenopei siue Amorum* met en scène précisément cette force de l'héritage dans la poésie élégiaque telle que la conçoit l'auteur néo-latin; l'appel de l'épopée homérique — écrire une nouvelle *Iliade* — et l'imitation de Virgile (v. 1–12) ne prévalent pas, même si le souci de la gloire littéraire fondée sur le prestige de la grande composition épique demeure; nous indiquerons en caractères gras les mots qui mettent en valeur la personnalité littéraire, il en sera de même pour les autres citations.

> Scilicet in magnis quaerenda est gloria rebus,
>   hinc ueniant **capiti** laurea serta **meo**;
> quod si forte **animis** respondent carmina **nostris**,
>   uel Croesi fuerint uilia regna **mihi** (1.18.13–16).

A cet endroit du texte, Pontano accumule les références à sa propre personne de poète — jusqu'alors, pour désigner ses poèmes élégiaques, il avait simplement utilisé l'expression *nostra scripta* au vers 2 — ; mais l'idée de postérité littéraire s'inscrit selon la perspective élégiaque de l'héritage propertien (v. 21–24): l'Ombrie pourra s'enorgueillir de compter parmi ses enfants illustres Pontano lui-même, si seulement la renommée survit à la mort du poète. Ornement de sa terre natale, Pontano fait alors l'éloge de cette patrie de Properce qui perpétue la tradition de l'élégie:

> Umbria Pieridum cultrix, patria alta Properti
> quae **me** non humili candida monte tulit... (v. 25–26).

Il est à remarquer l'emploi de l'adjectif *candida* qui qualifie la beauté éclatante; il est possible de le rapporter au style *humilis* des élégiaques. Chez Pontano et Sannazar, en effet, les biographes notent le *candor*, vertu principale des élégiaques classiques, expression de leur caractère; à l'écart du sublime de l'épopée, cette clarté éthique est celle de la simplicité et de la transparence. Ainsi la grâce du style entre en harmonie avec les qualités d'un caractère serein: le jugement esthétique porte sur des tempéraments — ceux de Properce et de Pontano — exempts de toute humeur mélancolique.

Le moi de l'individu se confond alors avec le je de l'écrivain. S'ensuit dans le même poème la représentation d'une scène idyllique illustrant le moi personnel en personnage littéraire; le décor en est l'Ombrie transformée en "topos" du *locus amoenus*:

> **Hic** ubi **me** uiridi **puerum** sub ualle **canentem**
> audiit irrigui coerula nympha loci
> atque ait: "Antra, **puer**, muscosi fontis et ista
> tecta petas, en haec quae **tibi** serta paro;
> si mecum hoc uiridi libeat considere prato,
> **tu** mea cura, **puer**, **tu** meus ardor eris;
> hanc **tibi** nos dabimus, ne sis modo durus amanti,
> quam dederat nobis Delius ante lyram" (v. 29–36).

Cette campagne idéale, éloignée du tumulte et des vices qui caractérisent les cités, n'est pas celle d'un univers révolu, puisqu'elle permet cette mise en images du je littéraire. Le genre pastoral facilite la représentation thématique de l'Erôs élégiaque (v. 33–34). Le jeu des références tient à l'expression de la sensualité dans un lieu commun où Properce observait encore les principes esthétiques d'une convenance quelque peu figée par la présence de l'Arcadisme apollinien et des Muses du Parnasse. Les guirlandes tressées de fleurs que la nymphe aux yeux bleus confectionne pour le futur poète sont le signe d'une inspiration érotique à prendre, dont la lyre se fera l'instrument (v. 35–36). C'est donc par une variation sur des poèmes de Properce signifiant le choix de l'inspiration élégiaque — *Elégies*, 2.30; 3.1 et 3 — que se met à exister Pontano poète/individu. Afin de faciliter la comparaison avec Properce nous citerons d'abord l'élégie 2.30, où le poète augustéen déclare, comme il le fera en 3.1, la toute-puissance de l'*Amor*. Nous marquerons encore par des caractères gras les mots indiquant des effets de mise en scène à propos de la personnalité littéraire.

> Una contentum pudeat **me** uiuere amica?
> Hoc si crimen erit, crimen Amoris erit:

> **mi** nemo obiciat. Libeat **tibi, Cynthia, mecum**
>   rorida muscosis antra tenere iugis.
> Illic aspicies scopulis haerere Sorores
>   et canere antiqui dulcia furta Iouis,
> ut Semela est combustus, ut est deperditus Io,
>   denique ut ad Troiae tecta uolarit auis.
> Quod si nemo exstat qui uicerit Alitis arma,
>   communis culpae cur reus unus agor?
> Nec **tu** Virginibus reuerentia moueris ora:
>   hic quoque non nescit quid sit amare chorus,
> si tamen Oeagri quaedam compressa figura
>   Bistoniis olim rupibus accubuit.
> **Hic** ubi **me** prima statuent in parte choreae
>   et medius docta cuspide Bacchus erit,
> tum capiti sacros patiar pendere corymbos.
>   Nam sine **te nostrum** non ualet **ingenium**
>   (Properce, 2.30.23–40);

> Callimachi Manes et Coi sacra Philetae,
>   in uestrum, quaeso, **me** sinite ire nemus.
> Primus **ego** ingredior puro de fonte sacerdos
>   Itala per Graios orgia ferre choros.
> Dicite, quo pariter carmen tenuastis in antro?
>   quoue pede ingressi? quamue bibistis aquam?
> . . . .
> Multi, Roma, tuas laudes annalibus addent,
>   qui finem imperii Bactra futura canent.
> Sed, quod pace legas, opus hoc de monte Sororum
>   detulit intacta **pagina nostra** uia.
> Mollia, Pegasides, date uestro serta poetae:
>   non faciet **capiti** dura corona **meo**
>   (Properce, 3.1.1–6, 15–20);

l'élégie 3.3, quant à elle, représente le *Somnium Propertii* dont nous mentionnons les éléments caractéristiques:

> Visus eram molli recubans Heliconis in umbra,
>   Bellerophontei qua fluit umor equi,
> reges, Alba, tuos et regnum facta tuorum,
>   tantum operis, **neruis** hiscere posse **meis**;
> paruaque tam magnis admoram fontibus ora
>   unde pater sitiens Ennius ante bibit
> . . . .
> cum **me** Castalia speculans ex arbore Phoebus
>   sic ait, aurata nixus ad antra lyra:

"Quid **tibi** cum tali, demens, est flumine? quis **te**
 carminis heroi tangere iussit opus?
Non hinc ulla **tibi** speranda est fama, **Properti**:
 mollia sunt paruis prata terenda rotis,
ut **tuus** in scamno iactetur saepe **libellus**
 quem legat exspectans sola puella uirum"
. . . .
Dixerat, et plectro sedem **mihi** monstrat eburno,
 qua noua muscoso semita facta solo est.
Hic erat affixis uiridis spelunca lapillis
 pendebantque cauis tympana pumicibus,
orgia Musarum et Sileni patris imago
 fictilis et calami, Pan Tegeaee, tui;
et Veneris dominae uolucres, **mea turba**, columbae
 tingunt Gorgoneo punica rostra lacu;
diuersaeque nouem sortita rura Puellae
 exercent teneras in sua dona manus:
haec hederas legit in thyrsos, haec carmina neruis
 aptat, at illa manu texit utraque rosam.
                    (Properce, 3.3.1–6, 13–20, 25–36)

Pontano reprend le motif du paysage merveilleux, lieu d'une révélation; mais il met en évidence, parmi ses réminiscences littéraires, les éléments d'un symbolisme essentiellement érotique. Properce, plutôt que de représenter un rêve amoureux où significativement c'est la *coerula nympha* qui apostrophe le *puer* Pontano (v. 31–32, 34–35), avait choisi un point de vue autre: celui qui consistait à interpeller lui-même Cynthie (2.30, 25–26, 33, 40). D'où la dimension didactique de la représentation de l'*ingenium*: le territoire des Muses est l'objet d'une description (v. 27) suivie de l'énumération de quelques histoires d'amour dont Jupiter est le protagoniste (v. 29–30). Lieu mental pour le poète et surtout lieu de mémoire collective, le *locus amoenus* se donne de l'extérieur comme paysage idéal à admirer où Properce invite Cynthie à pénétrer. Pontano préfère décrire une "scène de première vue" qui propose d'unir en couple le *puer* et la *nympha* se voyant pour la première fois, alors que Properce s'en tenait à la mise en présence des Muses et de Cynthie; c'est par la jeune femme que le *puer* peut être initié à la poésie érotique; c'est par la vision du *nemus* apollinien que Cynthie comprendra qu'elle inspire Properce. Le mouvement incoercible du désir entraîne vers l'élégie pour le poète néo-latin; il permet l'illusion de la confusion entre l'écrivain et l'individu. Properce avait ménagé la distance élaboratrice du texte qui ne suscite ni n'avive le désir, mais rend intense plutôt l'évocation des prédécesseurs illustres: Callimaque et Philétas, par la répétition des interrogatives (3.1.5–6) et la présence du vocabulaire sacré de l'inspiration (3.1.3–4). Le mythe littéraire du poète couronné (3.1.19–20) n'apparaît pas, dans ces conditions, comme la revendication d'une individualité, mais comme la légitimation de son appartenance à une culture grecque, hellénistique, qu'il latinise en se l'appropriant. L'Hélicon, la fontaine de Castalie, Apollon-Phébus à la lyre d'or sont les éléments d'un tableau dont Properce lui-même fait partie par le Songe, en 3.3. Là encore, l'impression dominante est celle d'une organisation attendue de l'espace symbolique des inspirations (épique/élégiaque) ayant pour figure centrale Apollon et non la scène d'une invite à l'amour; Properce, sous l'injonction du dieu, écrira pour la jeune femme esseulée, attendant celui qu'elle aime (v. 19–20); il n'a pas à parler seulement de lui-même pour lui-même; Properce évoque enfin les *orgia Musarum* et les *Veneris dominae uolucres* (v. 29, 31) pour susciter l'idée des mystères d'Erôs, alors que Pontano décrit le cortège dionysiaque, qui succède à l'apparition de la *nympha*, dans une atmosphère de fête profane (1.18.39–44): le poète regarde ce défilé où il reconnaît Pan (v. 45–48) et l'Arcadien, par son éloge de Bacchus, célèbre la *blanda uenus*, la *iucunda uoluptas*, les *lusus deliciaeque* (v. 55–56); le ton est ovidien, digne des *Fastes*, d'autant plus que tout se termine par la chute de la cruche de vin que porte Pan et les éclats de rire de Dionysos (v. 57–64). A l'apollinisme de Properce répond le dionysisme de Pontano. La fin du poème nous importe par sa poétique de la *consuetudo*: si la Muse de Pontano répugne encore à exprimer les accents de l'épopée homérique, c'est qu'elle s'est accoutumée au ton élégiaque; pour le moment, l'*ingenium* est façonné (v. 65–72). Le *furor poeticus* est ainsi rationalisé; Pontano, lecteur réfléchi des élégiaques, reste lui-même.

Dès lors, nous pensons être en mesure de pouvoir définir comment le poète néolatin concilie sa sensibilité personnelle avec l'utilisation de la mythologie qui est l'un des éléments d'héritage fondamentaux dans la République des Lettres. Le poème qui nous a semblé le plus intéressant à ce propos est l'élégie 1.17 à Stella, extraite de l'*Eridanus*. Il débute par une scène érotique:

> Nudasti, **mea uita**, sinus et sponte papillas
> admostique **meam** pectora ad ipsa **manum**
> **oraque** cum teneris iunxisti **nostra** labellis
> sedistique **meo** sarcina grata **genu**;
> ceruicem amplexa, leui mox uicta sopore
> concidis **in nostrum** languida facta **sinum**,
> longaque post fessos suspiria claudis ocellos,
> dum **tibi** sopitae serpit ad ossa quies.
> **Ipse tibi** tenuem procuro sedulus auram
> composita et moueo lenia flabra manu,
> **ipse tibi** somnos cantu leuo, cantus amores
> Sarnidis et Fauni dulcia furta refert . . .
> (*Eridanus*, 1.17.1–12).

La représentation *Ego / tu* domine, avant le récit de la légende; celui-ci, organisé selon le point de vue de Sarnis, amplifiera cette première représentation par l'emploi des mêmes déictiques jusqu'à produire des effets d'écho, aux vers 13–14 et 27–28:

> Faune, ueni, **tibi** Sarnis adest ad flumina nota;
> ad notas salices, candide Faune, ueni.
> (. . .)

> Faune, ueni, **te** Sarnis amat, suspirat et unum
> et parat in niueo gaudia multa sinu ...

Cette séquence achevée, Pontano reprend la mise en scène érotique du début:

> His **ego** mulcebam somnos. **Tibi** purpura mollis
> tingebat niueas flore decente genas,
> qualis ubi ad thalamos Hebe deducta mariti
> ad cupidi erubuit basia prima uiri. (31–34)

De nombreuses références mythiques s'ensuivent alors, afin de célébrer la beauté physique de Stella, tour à tour comparée à Hébé puis à Léda, à Hélène, à Laodamie, aux Grâces, à Thétis, à l'Aurore, à Dioné — cette liste n'est pas exhaustive. Le poète se remet ensuite à parler de Stella et de lui:

> At **tibi** perque genas roseisque infusa labellis
> ludit et in tenero gratia amica sinu,
> et quotiens blandos somno recludis ocellos,
> crediderim uel **te** posse mouere deos.
> Quosque moues; uerum custodia nostra tuetur,
> **teque meo** patior non abiisse **sinu**. (51–56)

L'énonciation de la subjectivité se fait par l'entrelacement d'un double registre: celui du couple poétique Pontano/Stella et celui de Sarnis/Faunus auxquels s'ajoutent les figures de couples mythiques; le poème nous apparaît structuré par ce chiasme du réel et du légendaire de la façon suivante:

> **Pontano/Stella** (v. 1–12)
> *Sarnis /Faunus* (v. 13–30)
> **Pontano/Stella** (v. 31–32)
> *Hébé /Hercule* (v. 33–34) + références légendaires
> **Pontano/Stella** (v. 51–fin du poème).

Mais de quel "réel" s'agit-il? La mythologie sert-elle de faire-valoir pour la représentation même du subjectif? Autrement dit, l'élégie 17 à Stella est-elle à lire comme autobiographique finalement, puisque le poète et son aimée apparaissent comme les seules figures réelles d'un poème saturé de fiction? Pour répondre à cette question, il convient de se souvenir de l'élégie 1.3 de Properce encore. C'est par les références aux mythes que ce texte commençait — Ariane, Andromède, la Bacchante —, retardant jusqu'au vers 7 l'énonciation de la première personne:

> talis uisa **mihi** mollem spirare quietem
> **Cynthia** non certis nixa caput manibus,
> ebria cum multo traherem uestigia Baccho

et quaterent sera nocte facem pueri.
(Properce, 1.3.7–10)

Or le texte n'établit pas une relation *Ego /tu*, mais une relation *Ego /haec*, indice ici d'une séparation annoncée (v. 11–12); lorsque Properce s'adresse à Cynthie, c'est en constatant que la nuit d'amour n'aura pas lieu (v. 21–26); il va jusqu'à imaginer des songes effrayants qui agitent le sommeil de sa maîtresse (v. 27–30); l'élégie s'achève sur le réveil et les récriminations de Cynthie (v. 35–46), *ego* et *tu* sont les mots de la confrontation et du déchirement. La rigidité de la scène est contenue dans la référence à Argus (Properce) surveillant Io (Cynthie). Plutôt que de penser que la subjectivité de Pontano donc réside dans l'évocation d'un "réel" qui se distinguerait du légendaire tout en se trouvant embelli par lui, il est préférable de considérer que cette subjectivité consiste avant tout en une écriture personnalisée du "topos". La réalité s'avère toute littéraire, tenant à ce que Pontano existe et fait exister Stella en s'opposant à la façon dont Properce lui-même existait en faisant exister Cynthie. Désormais nous sommes passés d'une écriture de la juxtaposition (l'élégie 1.18 de Pontano reprenant la hiérarchie des genres littéraires telle qu'elle apparaissait chez Properce) à une écriture de la différence, qui évite la superposition des motifs. Une réécriture.

Cependant, une situation semble originale dans la poésie élégiaque de Pontano: la déploration de la mort de l'épouse. Aucun des élégiaques classiques ne l'a dite; Properce avait évoqué le fantôme de Cynthie, mais celle-ci était sa *puella*. Or, dans les *Parthenopei siue Amorum libri*, 2.25, le poète s'adresse à son épouse défunte selon le rythme douloureux des première et seconde personnes:

> Quas **tibi ego** inferias, coniunx, quae munera soluam,
>   cum lacrimae et gemitus uerbaque destituant?
> (. . .)
>   **Mihi** mortua uiuis,
> uxor, et in nostro conderis ipsa sinu,
> (**uiua mihi** ante oculos **illa** obuersatur **imago**)
>   et **mecum** lusus deliciasque facis,
> **uiua** domum cultosque Lares remque ordine curas,
>   **uiua, Ariadna,** domi es, **uiua, Ariadna,** toro es,
> **mecum** perque hortos et culta uireta uagaris
>   et **mecum** noctes, **mecum** agis ipsa dies.
> Sic **mihi uiua** uales, sic est **mihi** grata senectus,
>   ut **tua mors** lasso uita sit ipsa seni.
> Haec ipse ad feretrum; at **tecum** mens ipsa moratur,
>   **tecum** post paucos laeta futura dies.
> (2.25.1–2, 7–18)

Assurément, nous pouvons reconnaître l'amour de Laodamie pour Protésilas, tel que Properce l'évoquait en 1.19; le poète s'y comparait, en effet, au héros fidèle qui ne pouvait oublier son épouse elle-même tout entière dans son désir pour lui:

>   Illic, quidquid ero, semper **tua** dicar **imago**:
>   traicit et fati litora magnus amor.
>   (Properce, 1.19.11–12)

L'expression *tua imago* possédait même une concision que n'a pas le vers 9 de Pontano. Nous pensons également au moineau de Lesbie, les vers 8 et 10 du poète néolatin rappelant les vers 1 et 2 du poème 2 composé par Catulle. Mais le ton de Pontano est autre: il ne reprend ni le thème propertien de l'amour fugace ni le badinage pathétique de l'amant de Lesbie. C'est que le poème est à lire comme une hypotypose: l'image de l'épouse est subjective, à la fois portrait, apparence qui donne l'illusion heureuse de la vie; représentation d'une réalité personnelle, Ariane continue d'exister par les mots du poème. Le signe le plus fort, donc, de cette énonciation de l'absence est la *uiua imago*, image vive de délicatesse dont le charme réside dans le paradoxe d'une mort féconde pour l'imaginaire. Ariane survit telle qu'en elle-même, ne ressemblant à aucune autre, comme son poète seul à écrire ce poème. Les lieux familiers, les jardins que hante la présence de l'épouse sont autant d'éléments pour un paysage intérieur, qui appartient aussi à un art poétique: Ariane évolue parmi les "topoi" d'une inspiration maîtrisée, le motif personnel d'un imaginaire amoureux qui est celui de Pontano, prend forme parmi des lieux communs. Le *tibi ego* du début, qui sépare encore, devient *tecum*, parce que le propre de l'écriture élégiaque est de réunir. Ariane ainsi nous apparaît comme une figure emblématique de l'inspiration pontanienne, dès lors que, grâce à elle, se retrouvent le passé et le présent, la vieillesse, la mort et l'amour de la vie; dans la République des Lettres aussi le passé n'est pas oublié, nourrissant la mémoire du poète qui sait en hériter. Déjà Catulle avait annoncé l'immortalité dionysiaque d'Ariane; Pontano écrit en termes humains cette apothéose.

M. Fuhrmann, il y a une trentaine d'années, considérait la littérature néo-latine avant tout comme une "littérature de réception", prolongement de la littérature latine de l'Antiquité classique et tardive. Cependant, plus récemment, H. Hofmann soulignait dans un article intitulé "Point de vue sur les méthodes et les perspectives des études néo-latines" paru dans *Les Cahiers de l'Humanisme*, t. I (2000), aux Belles-Lettres/Klincksieck (p. 12–13), que "la littérature néo-latine ne se limite pas à une tentative d'imitation ou d'émulation à l'égard de l'Antiquité classique en tant que modèle. Elle aspire plutôt à transposer celle-ci dans sa propre époque afin de la préserver en tant que telle (tout en soulignant sa continuité) et à lui attribuer une fonction dans le présent actuel." De fait, "dans les élégies, on fait la cour à la femme désirée comme Properce la faisait à Cynthie (...) bref, on a recours à l'ensemble des genres antiques pour mesurer le présent au passé et donner ainsi au présent une nouvelle signification et légitimité." Notre analyse de l'inspiration élégiaque chez Pontano s'inscrit dans cette double exigence de la réception du passé et de la présence vivante du présent. Nous avons vu comment l'*ingenium* du poète se fondait sur le *candor* des poètes élégiaques de la tradition classique et sur la *consuetudo*. En maintenant actuelle une énonciation ancienne de la subjectivité du sentiment amoureux, Pontano sait trouver, jusque dans les références à la mythologie, une originalité où peut transparaître le moi de l'individu. L'*Actius* insiste sur cette complémentarité de l'*ars ingenio coniuncta*, à propos de Cicéron, d'Ovide, même lorsque ceux-ci ne veulent pas montrer leur *ars*; c'est que la personnalité de l'écrivain se forme par l'assimilation des techniques d'écriture, ce qui n'exclut pas la personne en tant que présence éthique, caractère marquant de l'expression. Sans excès se manifeste l'existence du poète-individu. La thématique de la souffrance nous a semblé particulièrement représentative de cette poétique, puisque Pontano y trouve l'occasion d'être élégiaque, au sens pathétique du mot, c'est-à-dire d'être classiquement lui-même sans faire semblant d'être un autre.

Université de Nice

Ioannes Fabricius Montanus:
The Two Autobiographies

SIEGMAR DÖPP

The Alsatian Ioannes Fabricius Montanus, who lived from 1527 to 1566, worked for many years as a teacher and preacher in Switzerland, and is known for various works in Latin, both prose writings on scientific and religious subjects and poems. He was close to many humanists of his time and sought to support the Reformation in Switzerland.[1] In March 1565, at the age of thirty-eight, he published a brief autobiography in Latin prose; the book is dedicated to his cousin Wolfgang Haller. Fabricius tells us in his *Vita* that he wrote his autobiography during severe *turbae* and *procellae*, by which he means the confessional, political, and military conflicts of his time. Eight months later, on 5 November 1565, Fabricius finished a second autobiography in 109 elegiac couplets; its composition too was disturbed by conflicts, as Fabricius tells us in lines 211–214.[2] Both lives are structured chronologically, depicting the *curriculum vitae* of the author from his birth to the time of writing. In this paper I shall begin by surveying the content of both lives and then describe the picture which the author draws of himself. Lastly, I shall make a brief comparison with other Latin autobiographies from the Renaissance.

The prose life does not start with a proem, in which the author might have informed us about his reason for or intention in writing. Fabricius first mentions his birthplace: Bergheim in Alsace, from which he got his name Montanus. His uncle, Leo Jud, was born in the same place (§ 1). Fabricius identifies the year of his birth as

---

[1] For a more detailed account of Fabricius Montanus's life and works see Siegmar Döpp, *Ioannes Fabricius Montanus*, Abhandlungen der Akademie der Wissenschaften und der Literatur, Mainz (Stuttgart 1998), 5–9.

[2] I have had access only to a later edition, printed in *Miscellanea Tigurina*, vol. 3 (Zurich, 1724), 373–96 (prose); 396–402 (elegiacs). This text, with some corrections, is reprinted in Döpp, *Montanus*, 34–38 (prose [with division into paragraphs]); 39–45 (elegiacs). A German translation of both Lives may be found in Theodor Vulpinus, *Der lateinische Dichter Johannes Fabricius Montanus (aus Bergheim im Elsass) 1527–1566* (Strassburg, 1894).

that of the Sack of Rome. He also tells us that his mother had visited her brother Leo in Zurich six months before his birth. Both day and month of his birth are unknown to him, though he believes that it must have taken place in the autumn. Fabricius regards his mother's journey to Zurich as *fatale*, fateful for him: his mother thus brought him for the first time to the city which later would promote him in such a friendly fashion (§ 2). Fabricius gives no further information about his parents. His eldest brother, who was four years older than Fabricius, died before taking up his studies; the other brother, who was two years older, declined to go to university and became a stonecutter. Therefore, as Fabricius sees it, the way was paved for his own higher education, a fact which he refers to the grace of God (§ 3).

Next, the different phases of his education are described. He singles out three places: Zurich, where he arrived at the age of seven (§ 4); Basel, where he was supported by a relative and where he learned Greek; and Strasbourg, where he lived in the house of the humanist and Protestant Reformer Martin Bucer and read a comedy of Terence (§ 5). It was an illness that caused his parents to bring him back to his hometown, Bergheim. There they did not allow him to go to school for one year, since they feared that he might come into contact with the "papist" rite during the singing lessons. Instead he translated from the Latin Bible, under the supervision of his mother (§ 6). After his recovery he returned to Zurich, where he took up his studies again.

After the death of his uncle Leo Jud (1542) Fabricius worked for a while as a *lector* at a school (§ 7). Later a scholarship was awarded to him by the city of Zurich, and he continued his studies in Marburg (§ 7). This was during the Schmalkaldic War. From Marburg Fabricius travelled to Wittenberg, where he was expected by the the Neo-Latin poet Petrus Lotichius Secundus, whom he knew from Marburg (§ 8). In Wittenberg he also met Philipp Melanchthon, with whom he spoke at length (§ 9). He then travelled to Leipzig, where he attended lectures for a couple of days before he returned to Marburg (§ 10).

Here he interrupts his account for a *confessio*. When he had arrived at Marburg for the first time some years before, he had had no knowledge at all of Latin metre, and therefore was unable to distinguish a hexameter from a pentameter. The poet Lotichius became his mentor, and directed his attention to the composition of Latin verse and encouraged him to continue his poetic endeavours (§ 11).

Fabricius returned to Zurich in 1548 (§ 12). He became a *provisor* at the school of the local cathedral, but also worked as a preacher in a place close to Zurich. He sees his profession as guided by Providence: "quod non sine numine factum fuisse ... attestati sumus," he writes with a litotes, which is quite characteristic of his style (§ 12). Here again he interrupts his account of his professional career and tells us of the family he founded. He speaks about the early death of his first wife, his second marriage, and about their children, of whom only a few were still alive (§ 13). He then returns to his career. For six years (1551–1557) he was the head of the cathedral school for girls (Fraumünsterschule) at Zurich. Then he took over the diocese of Chur, where at the time of writing he had already lived for nine years, though initially he was intended for this post for three years only (§ 14). At the end of his prose autobiography Fabricius depicts his current mood. The troubled times prevent him from keeping on course with his studies (*studia*); he does not know to whom he might turn for help if not to God (§ 14).

Three features dominate the prose *Vita*: the education Fabricius received in school and at university; his meetings with important contemporaries, and his professional career. As far as his education is concerned, the individual stages are specified with great care, even if they were of short duration. In this context his journey to Wittenberg is described at great length. A number of his contemporaries he characterises as significant; I have not yet mentioned Heinrich Bullinger, Joachim Camerarius, and Erasmus, but there are many others, twenty-five in all. The greatest prominence is given to Melanchthon. Mentors and benefactors are mentioned with gratitude. Fabricius gives the important data of his professional career, but is reluctant to describe the confessional conflicts by which he was so much absorbed. Only the "papist" rite is mentioned, and that in the context of the singing lessons at school.

What he has to say about his education, his meetings with contemporaries, and his professional career has a common denominator: Fabricius's constant attempts to extend his knowledge, his unremitting efforts for acquiring learning — in a word, his *studia*. *Studia* is a central term of his prose autobiography. Fabricius is concerned with everything that to his great delight promotes his *studia*, with everything that to his great sorrow distracts him from his *studia*. He uses the term *studia* to signify all kinds of academic activity, including the prose writings which he does not specify. Similarly, he does not give the titles of any of his poems. Fabricius's description of his life is shaped by a way of looking at the world which contains another feature: God's care. In the important moments of his life Fabricius feels Providence at work. To sum up, in his prose autobiography Fabricius presents himself as a man who enthusiastically strives after learning, who feels greatly indebted to important contemporaries whom he has met, and who in times of distress trusts in the guidance of God.

I now come to Fabricius's poetic autobiography. It is written in the form of an elegiac letter. There are overlaps with the prose autobiography, but some aspects are omitted, others added.

The elegy opens with a proem of six lines. Fabricius addresses himself to a reader whose mind is open to poetry. Fabricius has this reader (in familiar formulaic fashion) enquire after the *patria* and the *parentes* of the poet, the way he has spent his life — in a phrase, the poet's *vitae condicio*. This reader represents, as we learn from line 6, future generations, the *veniens aetas*. The description starts with a praise of the poet's homeland, Alsace (7–14); the rivers Ill and Rhine are mentioned by name. A larger section (lines 15–26) is dedicated to his hometown, Bergheim. He particularly emphasises the important role Alsace has played in the humanistic movement. Again the Sack of Rome is mentioned to define the year of Fabricius's birth (27–30). Then he briefly speaks about his family. His father, about whom he had said nothing in his prose autobiography, was a poor man, but was held in esteem by his community. His two brothers were already dead (31–36).

When Fabricius reached the age of seven, his mother brought him to Leo Jud in Zurich. He had already touched upon this event in the prose autobiography, but now it is characterised as a particularly important turning point of his life. It was God's will, but also the wish of his parents and his uncle Leo, that he should be educated in the *ingenuae artes* and later go to university (37–44). He apostrophizes the Swiss people and the city of Zurich and expresses his attachment to both of them (45–52). He describes the moment when his mother was reunited with her brother Leo in Zurich (53–60) and when he had to take leave of his mother — a woeful scene, modelled on Ovid's farewell to his family in *Tristia* 1.3. In a second apostrophe Fabricius asks his host country, the *hospita tellus*, to indulge him in his tears (69–76). Along with God and his parents, he regards this country as the third decisive factor in his life. Leo Jud, Fabricius continues, introduced him to poetry for the first time. Jud's early death (1542) is mourned eloquently. With Leo, he says, the guide of his life, his light and teacher, has gone, and his own development as a poet has greatly suffered from this loss (v. 84; 89f). At that age he wasted much time in idleness, which he now regrets, but he excuses his teachers, since they repeatedly warned their pupil to get things right.

In the next section (103–134) Fabricius describes his first stay at the university of Marburg (from late 1545 onwards) and his first attempts at poetry; in this context he particularly mentions his meeting with the poet Lotichius. He repeats the confession already made in the prose autobiography: when he was a student, he knew nothing about dactyls and spondees; in the meantime, however, he had made substantial progress in Latin poetry — a success which was due to Lotichius, who most kindly helped him, but also to his own passion for poetry, which belonged to his very nature. As his models he mentions four Roman poets: Ovid, Tibullus, Horace, and Virgil. Admittedly, Fabricius concedes, he has not yet reached the top of Mount Parnassus, but for this shortcoming the civil war, with all its confusions inimical to the Muses, is made responsible. He then continues with the description of his journey to Wittenberg, which he undertook in order to speak with Melanchthon (135–168).

In lines 169f the poet announces that he now wishes to survey the rest of his life very briefly. First, he speaks about his work in Zurich (171–174). A longer section is devoted to his two marriages (175–200). Finally, there is a description of his activity in Chur (201–210). The poem ends with a reference to the disturbances of the present (211–214) and a glance at the future. God alone knows and determines what fate will be meted out to him (215–218).

Like the prose version, the poetic *Vita* addresses the working of God. Both lives close with the idea that the future is in the hands of God. But what about the other constituent parts of the autobiography? The poetic *Vita* also treats of Fabricius's meetings with contemporaries, though significantly fewer names are mentioned now (only eleven instead of twenty-five in the prose version). Already in his prose autobiography Fabricius had expressed his gratitude to the city of Zurich for its support. Much greater emphasis is laid upon this aspect in the poetic version. In his long apostrophe to the *urbs Tigurina* he shows his close attachment to the civil community and emphatically stresses the importance of the *hospita tellus*. On the other hand, the description of the various stages of his education is clearly reduced in the poetic version. The importance of his *studia*, which dominated the prose autobiography, is therefore diminished. This is not true, however, for all branches of the *studia*. Latin verse composition is a notable exception. Indeed, the development of his poetic work stands at the centre of the elegy.

In his prose autobiography Fabricius tended to style himself as a person who seeks to refine his knowledge and his learning; in the elegy he shifts the accent and portrays himself as a poet, who competes with the great poets of the ancient Romans and seeks to climb to the top of Mount Parnassus (127), with a large part of the way already behind him (115–118). It pains him greatly that contemporary confusions have prevented him from finishing his way to the top of the mountain of the Muses.

If we compare the two lives of Fabricius with other Latin autobiographies from the humanistic age,[3] the following points emerge: Fabricius seems to be the only person who wrote an autobiography both in prose and in verse. In some respects the prose autobiography is similar to the autobiographical sketch drawn by his friend Conrad Gessner (1516–1565) by 1545, a work where the *studia* also play a central part. By composing a life in verse, Fabricius joins a larger group of writers of the Renaissance.[4] Some of these follow the literary tradition founded by Ovid, who closed the fourth book of his *Tristia*, a collection of elegies, with a poem that can be called an *epistula posteritati*. It is this form of an elegiac *epistula posteritati* which Fabricius's poetic autobiography adopts. His humanistic predecessors here are Helius Eobanus Hessus (1488–1540)[5] and Clemens Ianicius (Klemens Janicki, 1517–1543).[6]

In each of his lives Fabricius treats topics which number among the traditional categories of Latin autobiographies: *genus, educatio,* and *res gestae*.[7] He does so without comparing himself to others and without saying anything about his physical appearance. His intellectual potential, his *ingenium*, is discussed only in the poetic *Vita*, and then only briefly (V. 84; 118). He does not get to speak of his habits and personal preferences. Nor does he give an explicit analysis, as Petrarch did in his prose letter to future generations, of his character. Fabricius's autobiographical interest focuses almost exclusively on the conditions and the development of his intellectual formation, of his learning. It is in this field that he allows the portrayal of deep emotions.

University of Göttingen

---

[3] See Georg Misch, *Geschichte der Autobiographie*, 4.2 (Frankfurt am Main, 1969), 657–738; Jozef IJsewijn, "Humanistic Autobiography," in *Studia humanitatis. Ernesto Grassi zum 70. Geburtstag*, ed. Eginhard Hora and Eckhard Kessler (Munich, 1973), 209–19.

[4] Presumably the longest one is that written by Antonio Astesano (1412–1468 [?]): *De ejus vita et fortunae varietate carmen*, ed. Armando Tallone, in L. A. Muratori, ed., *Rerum Italicarum scriptores*, vol. 14 (Città di Castello, 1912), 1005–1187.

[5] *Heroides* 3.9: *Eobanus Posteritati*, in Harry Vredeveld, ed., *Helius Eobanus Hessus, Dichtungen. Lateinisch und Deutsch*, vol. 3 (Bern, 1990), 476–83.

[6] *Tristia* 7, "De se ipso ad Posteritatem, cum in summo vitae discrimine versaretur, quod tamen evaserat," in Klemens Janicki, *Carmina*, ed. Jerzy Krókowski (Breslau, Warsaw, Cracow, 1966), 48–59 (with Polish translation); 351–353 (notes); text with French translation also in P. Laurens and C. Balavoine, eds., *Musae reduces. Anthologie de la poésie latine de l'Europe de la Renaissance*, vol. 2 (Leiden, 1975), 52–61.

[7] Compare Karl Enenkel, "Modelling the Humanist: Petrarch's *Letter to Posterity* and Boccaccio's Biography of the Poet Laureate," in *Modelling the Individual. Biography and Portrait in the Renaissance*, ed. idem, Betsy de Jong-Crane, and Peter Liebregts, Studies in Literature 23 (Amsterdam, 1998), 11–49.

The Renaissance Portrait of the Polish King Sigismund I in Bernard Wapowski's Chronica Polonorum

AGNIESZKA DZIUBA

The reign of Sigismund I (1506–1548) was undoubtedly the time of the flowering of Polish Renaissance culture. It was manifest not only in many new building projects but also in renovation works carried out on the initiative of the Jagiellonian monarch (the rebuilding of Wawel Castle — including Sigismund's famous chapel — in the spirit of the Renaissance is worth recalling here). Conceived on a wide scale, the patronage afforded by the Jagiellonian dynasty — later imitated by the Polish magnates — was particularly important for the intellectual development of Polish society. It not only created excellent conditions for literary activity and scientific research on the part of foreigners — Filippo Buonacorsi, Conrad Celtis, Peter Roizjusz, and others arriving in Poland in comparatively large numbers — but also did so for such talented people of poorer social origins as Klemens Janicki. Polish rulers, like those in Western Europe, placed their most gifted subjects in posts at court. Sigismund I had secretaries such as Jodok Ludwik Decjusz, Andrzej Krzycki, Jan Dantyszek, and, finally, Bernard Wapowski, almost all of them outstanding writers of this time. The fact of being close to the monarch and experiencing his constant care, which itself assured a secure existence, prompted in a number of such people the desire to repay him for his favours. That is why literature during Sigismund's reign abounds in eulogistic works, chiefly in poetic form. A general account of this heritage of eulogistic work, mostly written in Latin, has not, despite its quantity and quality, been undertaken so far.[1]

---

[1] Only minor observations have been devoted to this subject, as in the following: J. Nowak-Dłużewski, *Okolicznościowa poezja polityczna w Polsce*, Part 2: *Czasy Zygmuntowskie* (Warsaw, 1966); H. Dziechcińska, *Biografistyka staropolska w latach 1476–1627* (Wrocław, 1971); A. Budzisz, "Portret literacki Zygmunta Starego w epigramacie polsko-łacińskim XVI w.," in *Epigramat grecki i łaciński w kulturze Europy* (Poznań, 1997), 225–234.

As already indicated, Renaissance eulogistic literature in Poland includes works of prose as well as verse. Such works were not always entirely devoted to the glorification of the monarch; indeed, such *laudes personae* are more characteristic of the seventeenth century. The first half of the sixteenth century gave the reader works that had a precision of artistic point of view and where eulogistic comment was not of a kind to offend a humanist reader sensitive to the artistic principle of *decorum*. Respect for the monarch who was also the writer's patron was combined with respect for historical truth. This is to be seen in over sixty historical works that appeared in sixteenth-century Poland, and one of the authors of this kind of historiography is Bernard Wapowski.

Wapowski was born most probably in 1450 in Radochońce, near Cracow. In 1493 he and Nicholas Copernicus were pupils of Wojciech from Brudzew, an outstanding Polish mathematician. After finishing his studies at Cracow University, Wapowski left for Italy to study there, and in 1505 received his doctorate in canon law at Bologna. For the following ten years he stayed at the court of Popes Julius II and Leo X. In 1515 he returned to Poland and began his career at the court of Sigismund I, receiving the title of Historiographer Royal in 1522. He died in 1535.

If his career as a cleric developed in a traditional way, his work and its legacy were afflicted by ill fortune. He was the first Polish cartographer to gain high esteem in other countries. At Rome he worked with Marco de Beneveto on a critical study of Ptolemy's *Geographia*. However, the maps of Polish territories prepared by him — his *Tabula Sarmatiae* (1526–1528) and *Mappa in qua illustrantur ditiones Regni Poloniae ac Magni Ducatus Lithuaniae* (1526–1528) — have not been preserved. The fragments of them which had been discovered were destroyed by fire in the Warsaw insurrection. His chronicle covering the history of Poland from pre-Christian times down to 1535 suffered a similar fate. Because its author had been writing it until the moment of his death, he did not manage to correct it and improve it stylistically. Sigismund I appreciated the value of this piece of writing and made an attempt to find among his secretaries a person who would undertake the arduous task of preparing Wapowski's work for printing. There was nobody, however, who would complete the task, and so the *Chronica Polonorum* remained in manuscript form. One complete copy certainly remained in the possession of the most famous sixteenth-century historian of Polish and Lithuanian history, Martin Cromer. However, the manuscript which was presented by him to T. Płaza (the editor of Cromer's works) was already incomplete; that is, the part containing the beginning of the chronicle up to 1480 was missing. Of another manuscript copy only the folios covering the years between 1380 and 1535 remained. Until now, even the part of the *Chronica Polonorum* that has been preserved has not been the object of a critical edition. The remarks that follow in this paper are based on the text of *Chronicorum B. Vapovii pars posterior . . . Kroniki B. Wapowskiego z Radochoniec, kantora katedralnego krakowskiego, część ostatnia czasy podługoszowe obejmująca*, ed. J. Szujski (Cracow, 1874).

A precise analysis of all the surviving fragments of the work provides abundant proof that Wapowski was familiar with the principles of Renaissance historiography. In an extremely vivid, picturesque way he presents events on battlefields, and with the accuracy of a chronicler he quotes royal speeches and narrates events taking place at the royal court. The hero of the *Chronica Polonorum* is the Polish nation. It is its history in time of peace and war that Sigismund's royal historian describes. Nevertheless, alongside this collective hero — to some degree anonymous, though for the first time so realistically presented in Polish historiography — there appear outstanding individuals (kings, politicians, leaders, even influential townsmen) who are treated by the author as true creators of history — an aspect of the work that undoubtedly represents one of the features of the Renaissance chronicle. Therefore the style employed in descriptions of events is different in Wapowski's case from that found in his predecessors (Długosz, Miechowita, Decjusz), who frequently paid little attention to characters other than kings. Wapowski perceives not only the events that took place in Polish history but also the people who influenced them. In the course of reporting events he introduces brief accounts of the characteristics of the people appearing in his narrative.

It should also be noted that a given type of person tends to receive a certain pattern of commendation. The epithets that Wapowski uses to describe leaders most frequently remain the same and emphasise their military skills. Thus, while mentioning Mikołaj Kamienicki's death in 1515 (he was the first great crown hetman in Polish history), he describes him as *vir bellicis artibus praestantissimus* (137), and writes about one of the Polish squads during the war with the Turks: "Iacobus Sencignovius vir bellica laude praeclarus, mille equites Tartarorum post anceps cruentumque certamen fudit fugavitque" (147). Other descriptions of commanders and soldiers distinguished on the battlefield are, for example: *vir bellica laude famigeratissimus* (81), *vir fortis et disciplinae militariae peritus* (172), *vir rei bellicae experientissimus* (160), and *vir fortis et rei militaris peritus* (214).

However, Wapowski devotes most of his attention to his patron and employer, Sigismund I. From his very first reference to him, Wapowski sets out to write about this ruler only in complimentary terms, out of which he builds up a picture of him as an ideal ruler, wise politician, courageous commander, and ardent defender of the Christian faith. The king's characteristics are simultaneously presented in two ways: directly (brief remarks by the author about the king's virtues, in which epithets are mostly used in the superlative) and indirectly (by descriptions of the monarch's behaviour in particular situations and by quotations from speeches made by him).

The first remark about Sigismund that appears in Szujski's edition of *Kroniki B. Wapowskiego część ostatnia* (39–40) is concerned with how he took over the rule of the Głogów Duchy. Here Wapowski presents the prince as a providential saviour for this part of Silesia, a region ravaged by packs of brigands and complete lawlessness. The restoration of order in the Duchy, according to Wapowski, is attributable to Sigismund's fame and courage: "Pax inde ei provinciae et vicinis regionibus negociatoribus libere citro ultroque commeantibus facta est, non sine Sigismundi principis ingenti gloria, cuius nomen et virtus non sine omnium admiratione, iam inde amplificari ac ore omnium celebrari cepit" (40). Another instance of praise for this prince is found in the description of the ceremony of Aleksander I's election as king. Our writer reminds us here of the support that his younger brother received among the gentry gathered in Piotrków — support that could be prompted (according to Wapowski) only by the outstanding features of Sigismund's character: "Sigismundus quoque Casimiriades inter fratres iunior in senatu amicos et fautores habuit ob egregiam indolem, miramque prudentiae, mansuetudinis, iustitiae aliarumque heroicarum virtutum opinionem" (45). Numerous attributes with which Wapowski generously credits his monarch (e.g., *fortissimus rex* [81], *prudentissimus rex* [102], *excelsi atque invicti animi rex* [109], *vigilantissimus rex* [196], *optimus et clementissimus princeps* [206]) represent direct evaluations of Sigismund.

In addition to such direct praise there appear descriptions of situations in which the king is presented in the most positive fashion. Most frequently, each of these situations illustrates one of the virtues of the ideal monarch. Thus the account of the year 1508, during which the Poles were engaged in war with Moscow, concludes with words about the king's piety. Upon his return to Vilnius he immediately gave the order to celebrate thanksgiving services: "Sigismundus rex ad Divi Martini diem Vilnam ingressus, ob rem contra Moscovitas ac Tartaros eo anno bene gestam, indictis ad omnia templa et aras supplicationibus, Deo Optimo Maximo gratias egit, et laudes decantari multa omnium hilaritate mandavit" (83). Wapowski finds particularly convenient opportunities for praising Sigismund in the account he gives of the Congress of Vienna in 1515, lauding his erudition, political wisdom, dignity as a statesman, and majestic power as compared with that of other rulers gathered at the Congress. Beyond the description of the king's conduct during preparations for that gathering, the proceedings themselves or the ceremonies at their conclusion, our chronicler notes the conversations between the king and the Emperor Maximilian I, in which the Jagiellonian presents himself as a prudent and sagacious king of a Christian country: "Sigismundus Rex sententiam rogatus, ut est prudentia et animi magnitudine singulari, nunquam se in fide et virtute Maximiliani Caesaris haesitasse dixit. Se Regno suo egressum, ut tanti Principis conspectu et colloquio frueretur, iturum se, quo ille iuberet intrepide, ducturum se Vladislaum fratrem et eius liberos" [...] (133). Wapowski, quoting Sigismund's utterances, emphasises his fluency in Latin (e.g., "Ad haec Sigismundus Rex latino eloquio respondit [...]" [132]). Another of Sigismund's virtues described is the royal generosity which he displayed during the congress of monarchs at Vienna, when he is portrayed as the most munificent of the rulers: "Muneribus inde Reges inter se certarunt amplissimis, quibus etiam trium Regnorum Proceres sunt expleti, eorum Regum munificentia. In quo Sigismundi Poloniae Regis profusae liberalitatis maiestas supra omnes enituit" (134).

We should not be surprised at the strongly eulogistic character of Wapowski's portrayal of Sigismund, as he followed the route of other humanist chroniclers who depicted their protectors in the most favourable colours, or, in the case of a king, presented him as an ideal ruler, a providential statesman for a country on the verge of anarchy. It should at the same time, however, be emphasised that the kingly praise that comes from our historian's pen is fairly schematic in character, some epithets continuing to appear repeatedly in the description of his personality. It seems that Wapowski presented Zygmunt I Stary (Sigismund the Old) without overwhelming enthusiasm and as part of the business of only fulfilling his duty towards his ruler.

Although parts of his Chronicle devoted to the Polish monarch deserve to be seen as dictated by court fashion, their indisputable schematism allows us still to draw the conclusion that Wapowski makes an attempt in this way to diminish the importance of the descriptions devoted to the Jagiełłonian ruler and to give his chronicle the traits of a higher objectivity. For the beginning of the sixteenth century this attempt was extremely significant in the course of Polish historiography.

Lublin, Poland

What is a Hippopotamus?
A Problem in Renaissance
Taxonomy and Description

PETER FISHER

I should like to take as my starting-point a curious phrase which occurs in the natural history section of the *Historia de gentibus septentrionalibus (A Description of the Northern Peoples)* of Olaus Magnus, the sixteenth-century archbishop who wrote this account of his native Sweden and its surrounding countries. He is describing a strange sea-creature in the Baltic, whose habits he compares with those of the hippopotamus, which he categorizes as *piscis Nili fluminis*,[1] a fish in the River Nile. One's first amused reaction is to smile condescendingly and think that he has heard about the hippopotamus and its habitat, but has very little idea what it is.

Then, on reflection, you consider that he has ransacked the ancient classics for a great deal of his knowledge of animals, and that he must have read, almost certainly in Latin translation, Herodotus's account of this beast[2] and Aristotle's,[3] which repeats much the same details, and that of Pliny the Elder,[4] which is based on both. Here is Aristotle's description from the *Historia animalium,* in English translation.

> The Egyptian hippopotamus has a mane like a horse, is cloven-hoofed like an ox, and is snub-nosed. It has a haunch-bone like the cloven-footed animals, tusks which just show through, the tail of a pig, the neigh of a horse and the

---

[1] Olaus Magnus, *Historia de gentibus septentrionalibus* (Rome, 1555), facsimile ed. (Copenhagen, 1972), 21.38 (767); trans. P. Fisher and H. Higgens, 3 vols. (London, 1996–1998), 3:1123.

[2] Herodotus, *Historiae,* 2.71.

[3] Aristotle, *Historia animalium,* 502a, 589a. The following translation is based on that of A. L. Peck: *History of Animals,* trans. A. L. Peck and D. M. Balme, 3 vols. (Cambridge, MA, 1965–1991), 1:101–3.

[4] Pliny, *Naturalis historia,* 8.39.95.

size of an ass. It must have water to live in, but suffocates if it does not breathe air at intervals.

It is rather doubtful whether Aristotle had actually seen the animal, but he has enough information to allow him to class it among warm-blooded, viviparous quadrupeds.[5] In Rome the creature was shown publicly for the first time in 58 B.C., and Octavian exhibited one in the arena during the games of 29 B.C.[6] Nevertheless Pliny virtually repeats Aristotle's description, with the added detail of its impenetrable skin. Just over a century later Aelian classes it as an amphibian, along with otters and crocodiles.[7]

The ancient descriptions are passed down and inherited by the Middle Ages, but the image becomes vaguer and more distorted. Vincent of Beauvais in the thirteenth century follows Pliny, calling it *equus fluminis*, a *monstrum in oriente* of amazing shape and height. In the same period the English Franciscan friar, Bartholomaeus Anglicus, includes under the chapter heading *De piscibus* the information:

> Et talium piscium genera sunt antiphidia [i.e. amphibia], in Latina dubia, ab Isidoro dicta, "eo quod ambulandi in terris usum et natandi in aquis officium retinet" a natura, ut foce et cocodrilli, castores et hippopotami, id est fluvialis equi, et huiusmodi.[8]

In John Trevisa's rendering, completed about 1398, this becomes:

> And such a manere fisshe, as Ysider seith, is ycleped *antiphidia* and *dubia* in latyn, for he useth to go into the londe and swymme in the water, and holdeth the office of kynde as fisshes that ben yclepid *foce, cocodrilli, castores, ypotami* that ben water hors, and other suche.[9]

There is no doubt here that at the end of the fourteenth century seals, crocodiles, beavers, and hippopotamuses were still all lumped together under the heading of fish.

Like botany, Renaissance zoology started as a commentary on classical authors such as Aristotle, Pliny, and Aelian, and a good deal of effort was spent in trying to identify the plants and animals they had mentioned. Some pursued it as a literary interest, like the sixteenth-century Tuscan poet, Paulus Belmissurus of Bologna, who turned the first two books of Aristotle's *Historia animalium* into elegiac couplets in 1534.[10] But at the same time people began to collect specimens of plants and to

---

[5] Aristotle, *Hist. anim.*, 499b.

[6] Pliny, *Nat. hist.*, 8.40.96; Dio Cassius, *Historia Romana*, 51.22.5.

[7] Aelian, *Historia animalium*, 11.37.

[8] Bartholomaeus Anglicus, *De proprietatibus rerum* (Strasbourg, 1505), 13.26; the quotation is from Isidore *Etym.* 12.6.3.

[9] John Trevisa, *On the Properties of Things*, 3 vols. (Oxford, 1975–1998), 1:676.

[10] Cited in L. Thorndike, *A History of Magic and Experimental Science*, 8 vols. (New York, 1923–1958), 6: 257.

study fish, birds, and animals, especially of their own region, and to send examples to each other. Paulus Jovius writes on the fish to be found in Italian waters, and there are other accounts of fish to be found off Marseille and those to be seen in the Moselle.[11]

In the Middle Ages Albertus Magnus had recognized Aristotle's system of animal classification by body plan, i.e., vertebrates and invertebrates, and Aristotle had also led the way to linking structure with the function of creatures in their environment. Nevertheless in the Renaissance taxonomy has still a long way to go. In his *De piscibus marinis* some attempt is made by Guillaume Rondelet at a system of classification by appearance, way of life, habitat, and food, and he puts all his salt-water fish in one volume,[12] lumping all the rest into another volume of *aquatilia*, which includes crustaceans, shellfish, and amphibians, under the last of which are inserted frogs, beavers, and crocodiles.[13] Although he writes in his preface about the different kinds of fish, Pierre Belon calls his work of 1553 *De aquatilibus*, and again devotes a separate chapter to *amphibia quadrupedes vivipara*, which he says are *piscium magna ex parte consimiles*. Included in this section is the hippopotamus, with seals and beavers in the same category, and we soon come to the amphibious bipeds: tritons, nereids, naiads, and a monkfish that looks like a monk, all provided with engaging illustrations. He calls the hippopotamus a *monstrum aquaticum*, which takes its pleasure (*gaudere*) only in the River Nile, and is more like a pig or ox than a horse. His description is now on the right lines, for he has seen a living specimen in Constantinople, which he believes was given as a present to the Turkish sultan:

> Caput huic enorme fuit, et ad reliqui corporis collationem indecentissimum, quale vaccinum esse diceres, nullis praeditum cornibus, auribus ursinis, brevibus ac subrotundis, oris rictu usqueadeo vasto, ut leoninum superaret: certe humanum caput aequale potuisset. Patulas habebat nares, labra repanda atque resima, dentes prorsus equinos, obtusos tamen; oculos ac linguam praegrandes; collum, ut piscibus nullum, aut admodum breve: caudam, ut porci ac testudines, rotundam: reliquum obesissimi cuiusdam porci corpus esse diceres: pedes ita breves, ut quattuor a terra digitos vix attolleret; ungulae in porci formam diffissae: quae res nos inducebant, ut id animal non bene natare, sed fundum fluminis inhabitare ac passim in Nili profundo divagari crederemus.[14]

[Its head was huge and grotesquely out of proportion with the rest of its body, which you would have said was like an ox's; it had no tusks, but small, roundish ears, like those of a bear, and such vast, gaping jaws that they were larger

---

[11] Paulus Jovius, . . . *de Romanis piscibus libellus* (Rome, 1524); Petrus Gillius, *De Gallicis et Latinis nominibus piscium*, appended to trans. of Aelian (Lyons, 1533) (fish at Marseille); Carolus Figulus, *Ichthyologia seu dialogus de piscibus* (Cologne, 1540) (fish in the Moselle).

[12] Gulielmus Rondeletius, *De piscibus marinis* (Lyons, 1554), chap. 1–2 (1–34).

[13] G. Rondeletius, *Universae aquatilium historiae pars altera* (Lyons, 1555).

[14] Petrus Belonius, *De aquatilibus libri duo* (Paris, 1553), 1.4 (22).

than a lion's; they would certainly have accommodated a human head. It had wide nostrils, turned-up lips that bent back and teeth very like a horse's, but blunted; its eyes and tongue very large; its neck non-existent, like fishes', or at any rate quite short; its tail round, like that of a pig or tortoise; the remainder of its body you would have said was that of an extremely fat pig; its feet were so short that its four toes were only with difficulty lifted from the ground; its hooves cloven, like a pig's. All this leads me to believe that this animal does not swim well, but lives on the bottom of the river and wanders about in the deep waters of the Nile.]

He then provides a somewhat fantastic illustration on the opposite page of a hippo biting a crocodile's tail. Significantly, his description caused a good deal of dispute amongst scholars because it differed from those of Herodotus and Aristotle. Such was the tyranny of written authority.

Again in the following year Ippolito Salviani puts certain details about it in his work *De animalium aquatilium historia*. However, in his list he has returned to Aristotle, Pliny, Aelian and their copyists, calling it just as dangerous to man as the crocodile.[15]

Because there was some uncertainty about the classification of the seal, the Catholic Church in the Middle Ages and Renaissance was in two minds as to whether to allow its consumption on fast-days. According to *Grágás*, the corpus of Icelandic law dating back to the thirteenth century, seal and walrus flesh might only be eaten at the times when meat was allowed as part of the diet.[16] Even so, in some northern communities there may sometimes have been little else available, and in 1481 we find Pope Sixtus IV granting an application of Magnus Eyólfsson, bishop of Skálholt, to allow the Icelanders in his diocese to eat seal-meat in Lent and on other fast-days:

> temporibus quadragesime et aliis temporibus proprio possint sine scrupulo conscientie comedere quendam piscem marinum focam vulgariter nuncupatum qui universaliter dictis temporibus in aliis diocesibus comeditur.[17]

> [In Lent and at other times they may legitimately, without qualms of conscience, eat a certain sea-fish, popularly called seal, which is generally eaten at the said times in other dioceses.]

Our Catholic archbishop, Olaus Magnus, discusses this question in the mid-sixteenth century, and, with what was by now perhaps a familiar piece of logic-chopping, says that although the Church's leaders have constantly brought forward

---

[15] Hippolytus Salvianus, *Aquatilium animalium historiae liber primus* (Rome, 1554), List of contents s.v. Hippopotamus.

[16] *Grágás*, ed. G. Karlsson, K. Sveinsson, and M. Árnason (Reykjavík, 1992), 32.

[17] *Diplomatarium Islandicum* (*Íslenzkt fornbrévasafn*), 16 vols. to date (Reykjavík/Copenhagen, 1857–), 9 (1909–1913): 39–40.

reasons for and against its consumption on fast-days, he and other sensible authorities believe that if the seal has been caught on land it counts as meat, but if in the water it can be regarded as fish, and may therefore lawfully be eaten at such times.[18]

By the latter part of the century we reach the great encyclopaedic natural histories of Conrad Gesner, published between 1551 and 1558, and of Ulysse Aldrovandi, whose massive volumes on animals, birds, and fish begin to appear at the end of the century and continue well into the seventeenth. Both authors supply all that is known about each living thing up to their own day, with fabulous beasts like the unicorn or the sea-serpent thrown in. But there is little or no advance in taxonomy, and within each major category creatures are merely arranged in alphabetical order. Gesner still files the hippopotamus under *aquatilia*,[19] though in an edition of 1603, published well after his death, it is correctly removed to the class of [*bestiae*] *quadrupedes viviparae* (because its nature designed it to walk rather than swim); and Aldrovandi also includes it in his collection *De quadrupedibus digitatis*.[20]

It was left to the eminent Cambridge naturalist John Ray, at the end of the seventeenth century, to define fish properly, and to reject squids, crustaceans, molluscs, and, of course, water creatures like seals and turtles. So it was not until 1686, when this scholar produced the two volumes of *De historia piscium*, which he selflessly published under the name of Francis Willughby, his deceased friend who had collected many of the notes on which it was based, that a good working definition of fish is formulated. In his introduction Ray deplores the lax use of the term *piscis* in previous writers, and gives this first genuine definition. Fish are:

> ea tantum aquatilia, quae et sanguinea sunt et pinnis natant et pedibus carent, et in aquis perpetuo degunt, ibidem pariunt, nec umquam sponte in siccum exeunt, aut extra aquas diu vivere possunt.[21]

> [only those water creatures which contain blood, swim by means of fins, have no feet, spend all their time in water and produce their young there; they never come out on to dry land of their own accord and cannot live for very long out of water.]

He specifically excludes from this family the hippopotamus, crocodile, seals, manatees, and all other amphibians.

In antiquity there had been several lively and accurate representations of the hippo, including a frieze on the plinth of a statue preserved in the Vatican Museum, which depicts seven of these animals in the Nile threatening crocodiles and a number of pygmies in boats.[22] However, since ancient times, until the end of the sixteenth

---

[18] Olaus Magnus, *Historia*, 20.7; trans. Fisher and Higgens, 3:1038.

[19] Conradus Gesnerus, *Historia animalium*, 3 vols. (Zürich, 1551–1558), 3:495–501.

[20] Ulysses Aldrovandus, *De quadrupedibus digitatis viviparis* (Bologna, 1637), 181–94.

[21] F. Willughby, *De historia piscium*, 2 vols. (Oxford, 1686), 1.1.

[22] J. M. C. Toynbee, *Animals in Roman Life and Art* (London, 1973), 129.

century few Europeans had seen this creature, and no living specimen could be observed in western Europe before 1850, when one such animal was brought to the London Zoo.[23] It is perhaps not then surprising that Belon was taken to task because his account differed from those of Herodotus and Aristotle. In 1531 Vives had condemned the simple acceptance of Aristotle's writings and recommended a return to the observational practice which the Greek philosopher had himself advocated. Yet Gesner and Aldrovandi still gather a huge accumulation of authorities and in medieval fashion attribute moral qualities to animals. Everything is piled in: their use as food, as medicine, their capture, significance in heraldry, myths and symbolism, synonyms and etymology; and very little, if any, distinction is made between reliable and unreliable authors. For Aldrovandi the hippopotamus is a *belua amphibia, vorax et astuta* (an amphibious monster, voracious and cunning). Its size is emphasised (which is why it is called a horse), and in stature it is second only to the elephant. Nonetheless he does set down also the most recent, and most accurate description of this animal by Fabio Colonna, which I shall come to shortly.

Much of the older lore is repeated well into the seventeenth century, and we still find it in Robert Lovell's *Compleat History of Animals and Minerals* of 1661, or, as he prefers to call it, *Panzoologicomineralogia*, written now in English: wearing a hippopotamus tooth helps with haemorrhoids and eases toothache; the ashes of its skin applied with water dissolve spots; a piece of skin from its forehead tied to the groin is a great discourager of lechery, a remedy we probably have no reason to doubt; its skin also protects you from being struck by lightning.[24]

A turning-point however came when two preserved and stuffed hippopotamuses, caught at Damietta in Egypt, were exhibited in Rome in 1601 by the Neapolitan surgeon Federico Zerenghi, and described both by him in Italian and by Fabio Colonna in his *Ekfrasis de aquatilibus*, published in 1606. Colonna quotes the ancient portrayals and that of Belon only so that he can correct their mistakes from his own observation. He gives an accurate description, including measurements, with much detail about its teeth, and appends a realistic woodcut illustration, though he says that he wishes he could have seen it alive and then he could have drawn a better picture of it. Nevertheless he still persists in reproducing much of the old medicinal lore, like Dioscorides' statement that this creature's dried testicles are good for countering serpent bites.[25] However, now that a trustworthy description had been circulated, people were able to gain a true impression of this curious beast, and it was only left to Linnaeus to give a scientific description in 1758, and to classify it as zoologists know it today, *Hippopotamus amphibius*.[26] Someone who apparently did see the

---

[23] Bernhard Grzimek, ed., *Grzimek's Animal Life Encyclopedia*, 13 vols. to date (New York, 1972–), 13:116.

[24] R. Lovell, ΠΑΝΖΩΟΚΡΥΠΤΟΛΟΓΙΑ *sive Panzoologicomineralogia, or A Compleat History of Animals and Minerals* (Oxford, 1661), 108–9.

[25] Fabius Columna, *Minus cognitarum stirpium aliquot. . . . Item, De aquatilibus aliisque animalibus quibusdam paucis libellus* (Rome, 1616), *De aquatilibus*, Chap. 15 (xxviii–xxxv).

[26] Carolus Linnaeus, *Systema naturae*, facsimile of first volume of 10th ed. (1758) (London, 1939), 74.

Roman specimens in 1601 was Peter Paul Rubens, for in about 1617 he painted his *Hippopotamus and Crocodile Hunt*, with a very lifelike depiction of the hippopotamus seen from the front, a view which was not shown in any of the contemporary illustrations in the books of natural history.[27]

Anglia Polytechnic University

---

[27] See A. Balis, *Rubens' Hunting Scenes*, trans. P. S. Falla, Corpus Rubenianum Ludwig Burchard, 18.2 (London and Oxford, 1986), 72–74, 118–23.

Budé and the Republic of Letters

RICHARD I. FRANK

What was it that defined humanists? What did they share? In 1955 Paul Oskar Kristeller gave an answer: "Thus Renaissance humanism was not as such a philosophical tendency or system, but rather a cultural and educational program which emphasized and developed an important but limited area of studies. This area ... might be roughly described as literature ... Renaissance humanism must be understood as a characteristic phase in what may be called the rhetorical tradition in Western culture."[1] Humanists, then, were students of literature, but with a difference: "It was the novel contribution of the humanists to add the firm belief that in order to write and to speak well it was necessary to study and to imitate the ancients."[2]

Humanists, then, were part of an old rhetorical tradition, and if they stood for anything distinctive it was an emphasis on Greek and Latin. Educational reformers, in short; no more. Such was Kristeller's conclusion, and his authority has made it the dominant view today.

Humanists, however, would have disagreed. As witness the long letter written by Guillaume Budé to Erasmus in November of 1516. These two men were, with Juan Luis Vives and Thomas More, the recognized leaders of humanists all over Europe.[3] Budé's letter therefore deserves close attention.

Budé had sent Erasmus a copy of his new book, *De asse*, and asked him for a frank evaluation. Erasmus replied in a letter with some sharp criticisms. The letter we are considering in this paper gives Budé's response. He was troubled by Erasmus's criticisms, the more so perhaps because they were justified. In any case, in the course of his response he says a great deal about what he had in common with Erasmus and

---

[1] P. O. Kristeller, *Renaissance Thought and Its Sources*, ed. M. Mooney (New York, 1979), 22–24; first published in *The Classics and Renaissance Thought* (Cambridge, MA, 1955).

[2] Kristeller, *Renaissance Thought and Its Sources*, 24–25.

[3] Juan Luis Vives, *In Pseudodialecticos*, ed. Charles Fantazzi (Leiden, 1979), vii.

other humanists. Three themes emerge: (1) style, (2) aims, and (3) friendship. Let us consider each.

(1) Erasmus had raised the question of style, arguing that *De asse* was written in a Latin so difficult it could be understood only by readers who were erudite, had plenty of time for it, and were willing "to give as much effort to understanding the text as the author expended in writing it."[4] Furthermore, continues Erasmus, the book is full of digressions. They are learned and very interesting, but many a reader will say, "What does this have to do with the subject?" ("Quid ista ad Assem?")[5]

(2) Budé answers these criticisms directly, but links the question of style to that of aims, his second theme. Yes, he says, it is true that my book is written in a difficult style. In fact, it is "enigmatic," but that was done *on purpose*. "I realized at the time that it was to my advantage that I should be understood only by a few, and indeed in such a way that I could deny it" ("Sic referre mea id temporis existimabam, ut a paucis intelligerer").[6] The reason for this, continues Budé, was that I deplored the fact that the Church is involved in wars, and that priests seek ways to enrich themselves when instead they should be dedicating themselves to the things which bring us to Heaven.[7] In other words, he was saying things that could get him punished. But at this point he takes a new tack. The controversial ideas he has advanced are very similar, he says, to what Erasmus himself has published: "If someone should compare our writings, he might well conclude that I took my ideas from you, for I say almost exactly the same things about these matters as you do ('eadem de re eadem prope dicam'). When I read your essays 'On the Sileni' and 'War Is Sweet To Those Who Have Not Experienced It,' which you have given as a first installment on your promised book *Against War*, I find that we express the same ideas, although in different genres."[8]

Therefore, concludes Budé, the only difference between us is style: you say certain things in a controversial and light manner, whereas I say them — or, rather, I shout them — in the manner of an orator.[9] If my style is not to your taste, that is not important. For it is clear that our aims are the same: *Eodem certe tendimus*.[10]

(3) Next, after a few pleasantries about Dame Poverty, Budé abruptly turns to his third theme: friendship. François Deloynes, an eminent jurist, member of the Parlement de Paris, and patron of humanists, will soon write to Erasmus because, says Budé,

> I often show your letters to him, and to many others as well, so as to demonstrate to my friends that we are good friends, for it is by this means that I

---

[4] P. S. Allen, ed., *Opus epistolarum Des. Erasmi Roterodami* (Oxford, 1910), 2:369, #480, lines 236–239.

[5] Allen, *Opus epistolarum*, #480, line 259.

[6] Allen, *Opus epistolarum*, 2:394, #493, lines 124–128.

[7] Allen, *Opus epistolarum*, #493, lines 163–154.

[8] Allen, *Opus epistolarum*, #493, lines 158–160.

[9] Allen, *Opus epistolarum*, #493, lines 207–209.

[10] Allen, *Opus epistolarum*, #493, lines 239–240.

maintain my standing among those men who consider you the Varro of our age.[11]

Another friend is mentioned, Louis Ruzé, also a leading jurist and high official and patron of humanists, and then Budé concludes with a remarkable statement:

> Itaque iam tecum societatem amicorum coeo, si per te licet, praesertim cum me etiam ipsum, non meos tantum, tuum feceris; ut iam sit illud inter nos pactum non vulgaris amicitiae his verbis bona fide conceptum.[12]

[And so with your help we form a society of friends, the more so as you have made me as well as my friends your friends. And this is not an ordinary friendship but one based on this solemn agreement: whatever we acquire will be shared, and whatever friends we have will be held in common.]

In what follows it is clear that "whatever we acquire" refers to *knowledge*. So what we have is a group of scholars who treat each other as equals ("friends"), who feel bound to each other by direct or indirect ties ("friends in common"), and whose aim is to acquire and share knowledge. Here we meet the beginners of something new in European civilization, the emergence of which we celebrate in the theme of this Congress, the Republic of Letters.

The origins of the Republic are connected with the origins of Renaissance humanism, the rediscovery of classical texts. In 1417 Francesco Barbaro of Venice wrote to Poggio Bracciolini to praise him for bringing to light works of Lucretius and Manilius, as well as other classical texts: his achievements have brought "more assistance than ever and finer ornaments to this Republic of Letters."[13] At present that is the earliest known use of the term.[14] From the first it clearly referred to those who strove for "the revival of ancient learning," in other words, the humanists.[15] Its members honored "good letters"; its opponents were uneducated. In the volume of Erasmus's correspondence in which Budé's letter is printed there are numerous references to show that not only the term but also the group was well established. Thus Erasmus writes that he does not expect advancement in Prince Charles's court because "good letters are nowhere in less esteem than here, owing to the lack of education among the nobility."[16] Later he writes to Budé, who has asked him to evaluate his work: "On the merits of Budé a judgment has long since been pronounced by the leaders (*senatus*) of men of learning."[17] Thomas More writes to Erasmus about his

---

[11] Allen, *Opus epistolarum*, #493, lines 412–415.
[12] Allen, *Opus epistolarum*, #493, lines 432–436.
[13] P. Gordan, *Two Renaissance Book Hunters* (New York, 1974), 197, 199.
[14] So stated by Elizabeth Eisenstein, *The Printing Press As an Agent of Change* (Cambridge, 1979), 137, n. 287 (citing Gordan, *Two Renaissance Book Hunters*).
[15] Kristeller, *Renaissance Thought and Its Sources*, 31–32.
[16] Allen, *Opus epistolarum*, 2:255–256, #421, lines 136–138.
[17] Allen, *Opus epistolarum*, 2:368, #480, lines 216–217.

work soon to be published as *Utopia* that it may be approved by men of learning, even those in high places, "since whatever their power they have ignoramuses [*nebulones*] as equals and superiors."[18]

The association of *res publica litterarum* with classical texts — with humanism — was widespread. Thus a contemporary of Erasmus, and indeed his good friend, Juan Luis Vives, said that Macrobius, in preserving the *Dream of Scipio*, had "labored valiantly for the *litterariae reipublicae*."[19] By the early sixteenth century humanists formed the New Class of European society. They staffed the embassies, chanceries, and bureaucracies of the Renaissance state, and they trained men in the universities to play similar roles. Equally important is what they were not, the Old Class, the aristocrats trained for hunting and warfare, valuing birth rather than "good letters," valor rather than philosophy. Members of the Republic of Letters rejected the old values, warfare above all. So they were more than educational reformers.

One clear indication of what the humanists stood for comes later, from the career of Pierre Bayle. When he was forced to flee from France by the repressive policies of Louis XIV, he went to Rotterdam and, in 1684, founded a journal to voice opposition to the old regime of kings and aristocrats: and he called that journal *Nouvelles de la Republique des Lettres*. That publication marks the appearance of a new and important force in Europe: civil society. And in choosing the title he did, Bayle explicitly looked back to the humanists as his precursors.[20]

If the humanists were precursors of civil society, then the significance of that term deserves some attention. It was first used by Hegel in his *Philosophy of Right* (1821), in which he opposed it to the political society of the state. The state/civil society opposition was adopted by Marx and Marxists, and has recently been revived in political studies, in particular — ironically — in connection with the countries struggling to recover from communist regimes.[21]

Civil society is important because it encompasses the independent institutions strong enough to prevent the state from dominating and atomizing society.[22] It is a characteristic of modern, post-feudal societies. Under feudalism there was no civil society because the political realm was all-pervasive: "There is no talk of civil society as distinct from the state."[23]

What united humanists like Erasmus, Budé, and More was not only a passion for knowledge of Antiquity, but also a desire to use that knowledge to reform their own society. Erasmus's *Praise of Folly* denounces the cruelty and waste of war; even more significant, it violently attacks hunting, the favorite sport of aristocrats and their way of training for war: "Even the dung of dogs, I am sure, smells like cinnamon to

---

[18] Allen, *Opus epistolarum*, 2:372, #481, lines 64–70.

[19] Juan Luis Vives, *Opera Omnia*, ed. G. Mayans (Valencia, 1745; repr., London, 1964), 5:107.

[20] D. Goodman, *The Republic of Letters* (Ithaca, 1994), 12–14.

[21] Z. Pelczynski, *The State and Civil Society* (Cambridge, 1984), 1–13; E. Gellner, *Conditions of Liberty* (London, 1994), 1–9.

[22] Gellner, *Conditions of Liberty*, 5.

[23] Gellner, *Conditions of Liberty*, 55.

them." As for More, he declined to publish his correspondence with Budé because "what I have written is not sufficiently cautious and guarded to expose it to my enemies." His *Utopia*, like the *Praise of Folly*, sketches a society very different from the Europe of his day.[24]

So when the humanists created "a society of friends," standing together as equal participants in a cultural project, and standing apart from the dominant classes and institutions of their day, they were laying the foundations of a civil society. In this they fostered the transition in Europe from medieval to modern civilization. That takes us back to Jakob Burckhardt's view of the humanists as the class which led society from "the fantasies of the Middle Ages" and made the Italians "the first-born among the sons of modern Europe."[25] The great Swiss historian had the right idea, but we can understand it better now.

University of California–Irvine

---

[24] R. P. Adams, *The Better Part of Valor* (Seattle, 1962), 45–46 (Erasmus on hunting), 186–187, 141 (sharp contrast).

[25] W. Ferguson, *The Renaissance in Historical Thought* (Cambridge, MA, 1948), 189–192.

A Renaissance Treatise on Time: Lilio Gregorio Giraldi's De annis et mensibus

MAIA WELLINGTON GAHTAN

In his *Descrittione di tutta Italia*, Leandro Alberti characterized Lilio Gregorio Giraldi as an exceptionally erudite man with an exceptional memory: "Credo che pochi huomini hora (senza adulatione io dico) se ritrovano da egualiare a lui nella cognitione, tanto di lettere Grece come latine. Oltre di cio, e, di tanta tenacità di memoria (che penso) che quello havera letto una volta sempre gli sia presente" ("I believe that few men today (and I say this without adulation) can equal him in knowledge of Greek as well as Latin letters. In addition to this, he possesses such a tenacious memory that (I think) that if he has read something once, it is forever with him.")[1] Although Giraldi is mostly known today to historians of art for his discourse on ancient religion, *De deis gentium*, and is mostly admired by historians of literature for his dialogues discussing his contemporaries, his other scholarly works also merit attention for the originality of their subjects. *De annis et mensibus, caeterisque temporis partibus Dissertatio facilis et expedita, una cum calendario Romano et Graeco* (Basel, 1541) is a case in point, highly sought after in its own time but largely forgotten today. Andrea Alciati, for example, was so anxious to procure a copy of it that he wrote three letters asking a friend to send it to him. Francois Rabelais heavily annotated his copy.[2] Giraldi's book, a bewildering compendium of ancient philosophy, lore, and science, is not merely a discourse on calendars, as its title intimates. Rather, as a treatise on the ancient experience of time, it is unique in Renaissance scholarship.

Before *De annis et mensibus*, essentially three types of works took time as their

---

[1] Leandro Alberti, *Descrittione di tutta Italia* (Bologna, 1550), 313 v. Alberti's praise of Giraldi was cited in Giraldi's *Opera Omnia*.

[2] See Alciati's letters to Bonifacio Amerbach in Gian Luigi Barni, ed., *Le lettere di Andrea Alciato giureconsulto* (Florence, 1953), nos. 124, 127, 134. Rabelais' copy is discussed by Francesco Maiello, *Storia del calendario* (Turin, 1994), 81–82.

main subject. The longest tradition is that of the computus, a type of treatise developed in the early Middle Ages which explained how to reckon the calendar.[3] The computus provided not only astronomical formulas and mathematical principles, but also explanations of relevant units of time such as the year, month, day, and fractions of the day. The most important of these treatises, that by Bede, was probably not read by Giraldi, though he certainly knew the genre.[4] Most computuses were too late in date to be taken seriously by Giraldi, though he cites their sources, including Macrobius, Dionysius Exiguus, and Isidore of Seville.

Mainly in the thirteenth century, a philosophical literature developed around Aristotle's analysis of time in the fourth book of the *Physics*, read through the filters of Averroes and Avicenna. Thomas Aquinas contributed to this literature, as did Ockham, Duns Scotus, Bonaventure, and Roger Bacon. The scholastic philosophers addressed questions such as whether time exists, how it relates to movement, and which movements measure time.[5] They were intent upon refuting Augustine's analysis of time in his *Confessions*, and especially his contention that only present time exists. Giraldi's familiarity with such Aristotelian commentaries is evidenced by his introduction of these theoretical questions when discussing the meaning of *tempus*. Curiously, he neglects to include Augustine's point of view (which he surely knew), perhaps because he did not consider it representative of any ancient doctrine. He appears to have viewed these scholastic questions as pertinent to ancient Aristotelian philosophies of time.

A third type of time discourse which came of age in the Renaissance derived from antiquarian literature attempting to explain the Greek and Roman calendars. Notable among these efforts is Theodore Gaza's *De mensibus atticis*, published several times before Giraldi was writing. When discussing the Greek calendar, Giraldi cites Gaza repeatedly, agreeing with him on most points, though always supplying the ancient sources Gaza used.[6] No other modern treatise on ancient calendars is cited, though he refers to other antiquarian works such as Poliziano's *Miscellanea*, and occasionally to the works of modern poets such as Antonio Tebaldeo and Giovanni Pontano (in particular his *Urania*).

---

[3] On the computus, see Faith Wallis's introduction in *Bede. The Reckoning of Time*. (Liverpool, 1999); and the critical edition of the same text by Charles Jones, *Opera de Temporibus* (Cambridge, 1943), updated as *Bedae Venerabilis Opera 6, Opera Didascalia, 2: De Temporum Ratione*, ed. C. W. Jones, CCSL 123B (Turnhout, 1977). Wallis and Jones both cite most earlier bibliography.

[4] Although he cites Bede, he seems to have known only Bede's world chronicle (chapter 66 of Bede's computus which had been published separately in Venice in 1505) and his *De rerum natura*.

[5] On questions of time in scholastic philosophy, see Anneliese Maier, *Scienza e filosofia nel medioevo* (Milan, 1984), 155–267, and Helen S. Lang, *Aristotle's Physics and its Medieval Varieties* (Albany, 1992).

[6] On Theodore Gaza's activities in Ferrara, see John Monfasani, "L'insegnamento di Teodoro Gaza a Ferrara," in *Alla corte degli estensi*, ed. Marco Bertozzi (Ferrara, 1994), 5–17. In Giraldi's estimation, Gaza, "vir cum Graece tum Latine erudissimus elaboravit, ut eorum ordinem ostenderet." *De mensibus atticis* had been published several times before Giraldi began his treatise, most recently in Basel in 1536.

Giraldi drew from all of these sources for both content and organization. However, his treatise does not share a purpose with any of them. In organization, it is closest to the computus treatises which often include speculative definitions and etymologies. In approach, he is closest to the antiquarians, though his scope is much wider than a single text or a single calendar. In his overall grand sense of his task to define time and its parts, he may be closest to Aristotle and his commentators, though his method is historical and antiquarian rather than philosophical. The third-century author Censorinus, with his work *De die natali*, perhaps provides Giraldi's closest single model, but even he concentrates on calendrical units, and his book contains all kinds of other material.

Composed in 1539 and first published in 1541, Giraldi's antiquarian book on time was part of his effort to reintegrate himself into Ferrarese society. Having first sought his fortunes outside of his native city, Giraldi suffered several tragedies: first the death of his patron, Cardinal Ercole Rangone, during the Sack of Rome of 1527, and second, the murder of his dear friend Gianfrancesco Pico della Mirandola in 1533. At the time Giraldi had been living in Pico's house and barely escaped with his life. Having thus lost everything — including his books — a second time, Giraldi returned to Ferrara. Upon his return, his first serious publications were dedicated to Ercole II d'Este.[7] *De annis et mensibus* was dedicated to Ercole's heretical wife, Renée.

Giraldi's dedication stresses his book's general utility for all readers of the ancient authors. He notes that his appendix on ancient calendars could aid chronologers and calendar reformers like Johannes Stoeffler and Johannes Lucidus Samotheus. Giraldi's *De annis et mensibus* is his only book which could conceivably have been of direct relevance to the church, then in the throes of reforming the Julian calendar. The author remains distant, however, from the actual production of historical chronologies. He does not even offer the coherent synthesis of information promised by his title. Seeking to clarify the meaning of time in the ancient world through examples and citations, he offers many pieces of evidence, often contradictory, and usually without analysis. The reader is silently invited to pursue the problem further and to draw his or her own conclusions.[8]

Giraldi seems to have been less interested in the history of ideas than in presenting what he viewed as the simultaneous divergence of ideas which collectively illustrate the ancient experience of time. He begins with a long philosophical discourse on the concepts of *aevum*, eternity, and time. Noting that all other parts of time flow from these notions, Giraldi attempts to describe time's essential character. He may have gotten the idea of framing his discourse in these speculative philosophical terms from Censorinus, whose *De die natali* is the first text he cites. Giraldi quotes at length from

---

[7] Much of Giraldi's life story can be gleaned from his dedications. The only substantial biography is by Gian Andrea Barotti, *Memorie istoriche di letterati ferraresi* (Ferrara, 1777), who also cites all previous biographers. See also Girolamo Tiraboschi, *Storia della Letteratura Italiana* (Venice, 1824) 7:1133–1142 and 1853–1854 and Claudio Moreschini, "Per una storia dell'umanesimo latino a Ferrara," in *La rinascita del sapere*, ed. Patrizia Castelli (Ferrara, 1991), 168–188.

[8] A nice example of Giraldi's approach has been cited by Anthony Grafton, *Joseph Scaliger. A Study in the History of Classical Scholarship* (Oxford, 1993) 2:168–169.

Censorinus on the concept of *aevum*: its limitlessness, its mobility (it "steals" from the future to give to the past) and its incomprehensibility. Wearing his philological hat, he discusses sister terms such as *aeternitas*, though the extent of the evidence which he offers is well beyond ordinary philology.

Also beyond philology is his incorporation of ancient symbolism. In the case of *aevum*, he mentions several Egyptian figures — the snake biting its tail, a combined hieroglyph of the sun and moon, and the self-sufficient phoenix which feeds from its own flesh — and one Greek figure which he reproduces. This Greek figure, which Giraldi claims to have found in old Greek manuscripts, is a circle divided into four quadrants. Each quadrant is marked by a line protruding inward. As in the case of many of the passages he quotes, Giraldi does not offer an interpretation of these symbols.

His discussion of the relationship between eternity and time is equally delphic. Again, he includes widely diverging opinions but is reluctant to give any order whatsoever to this chaotic mass of philosophical commentary. He does not even distinguish between literary genres, treating poetry, philosophy, science, and visual symbols equally and in direct relation to one another. He cites Cicero, for whom time is "pars quaedam aeternitatis."[9] He cites Posidonius, for whom time was an incorporeal interval of the world's movement. He notes that the mythological figure of Saturn, child of Caelus, implies time's derivation from celestial (eternal) movement. After more fragmentary definitions, Giraldi launches into a long-argued scholastic problem taking Aristotle's *Physics* IV as its point of departure: would time still exist even if heavenly motion stopped? Narrative examples from the Bible and ancient history would argue that time cannot be defined as the motion of celestial bodies. Many more philosophical fragments follow, from Plato for whom time is eternity's moving image, to Jerome for whom time amends and preserves, to Lucretius's time as an accident: "tempus item per se non est."[10] Although they remain unordered, Giraldi's zeal and diligence in amassing these divergent opinions about time and eternity are also unparalleled. Many of these statements, while known to scholars of the classical tradition, had never before been brought together in a single treatise.

The existential sections are followed by discourses on segments or "spaces" of time, beginning with Varro's three epochs — the antediluvial, the mythical, and the historical — and moving on to other kinds of epochal divisions used by ancient and early medieval writers. He discusses various opinions about the world's age as well as the smaller divisions of time which can be identified with greater precision. These include the era, age, century, Jubilee, indiction, *lustrum*, year, the *tempus* or season, month, day (including *fasti* and *nefasti*), hour, moment, and other fractions of the hour. Treating each division as a separate problem, Giraldi proceeds by first defining the meaning of the term being discussed. The more complicated and muddled the concept, the more diverging quotations he gives. His often conflicting quotations point to problems in calculation and comprehension as well as to disjunctures in

---

[9] Giraldi, *De annis et mensibus*, 4 (from Cicero's *De inventione* 1.26).
[10] Giraldi, *De annis et mensibus*, 7 (from Lucretius, *De rerum natura* 1.459–60).

philosophy.[11] As we have seen in the case of *tempus*, he cites many authors. Only after he has satisfactorily explained the range of meaning of the concept does he offer etymological evidence. Many terms receive no etymology. Mostly, as in the case of *horae*, the etymological material serves to enrich the mystical texture of the word.

> Macrobius horas appellatas ait, quod horus sol dicatur, a quo horae. Marius vero Victorinus Trismegistus ait, cum esset in Aegypto sacrum quoddam animal Serapidi dicatum, & in toto die duodecies urinam fecisset, pari semper interposito tempore, per XII. horas diem dimensum esse, coniecisse, & exinde hunc horarum numerum emanasse, atque ideo horae dictae ab urina, hoc est, [*ouros*] ... Alii horas ita inventas tradunt. Coeli, ajunt, quadraturam in partes duodecim pro ratione musica dividi, & inde horarum manasse rationem, & aquam quae ex tenuissima caverna diffluebat, cum per totum diem excepissent, hanc in duodecim partes diviserunt, ex quibus horis nomen impositum, atque inde etiam vasis ipsis, quibus horas dimetiebantur, clepsydrae & hydrologia nuncupata.[12]

However, in some cases such as *aevum* (from "aetate omnium annorum" according to Varro), the etymology merely reinforces the meaning already discussed.

A unique slice of the ancient world and its terminology, Giraldi's topic also propels him back into his own times. When discussing epochs and the age of the world, for example, Giraldi inserts the canonical Christian view — that the world was created in 5200 B.C. — in between those of Varro, Plato, and Cicero. Since he is writing the book in 1539, this epoch had lasted 6739 years.[13] Similarly, when discussing the concept of Jubilee, he compares the Christian hundred-year version to the earlier Hebrew one of fifty years, noting that the Christians had rationalized theirs with the *secula* of pagan origin. He describes various changes in the length of the Christian Jubilee, ending with Paul II's final change to twenty-five years. The official rationale was that few men attain age fifty, but the ulterior motive was to increase revenues. Giraldi mentions the two Jubilees he himself celebrated, under Alexander VI in 1500 and under Clement VII in 1525, concluding this personal note with a mention of Charles V's sacking the city. Besides informing posterity about his own chronology, the insertion of these comments on contemporary practices reinforces the notion that time and time reckoning are human inventions with no great mystery or divine sanction behind them.

It is precisely because these ideas and definitions of time are human inventions that they risk being lost or misunderstood. By the time Giraldi was writing, for example, the fractional divisions of the hour were in the process of revision. The old

---

[11] Discussing the Romulan calendar which had only ten months, Giraldi argued that January was the first month, because Janus was around before Saturn. He uses the graphic evidence of Janus's two faces representing the old and new years as support.

[12] Giraldi, *De annis et mensibus*, 183–184.

[13] Giraldi, *De annis et mensibus*, 9–10. At two other points — when discussing the term *aera* (specifically the Christian era, 66) and *epacta* (129) — Giraldi also notes the date of the treatise's composition.

medieval divisions (probably created as analogies to other measuring systems) were gradually being replaced by the modern sixty-minute hour. Giraldi did not know how the ancients measured small units of time, and assumed that the medieval divisions in some way reflected earlier traditions. His discussion reflects a certain contentment in what he perceived as his culture's preservation of some parts of these ancient measuring systems.[14] It also reflects his suspicion that much information has not been preserved, and his awareness of the modern minute, the use of which was then still restricted to the astronomical sciences.

Giraldi begins his discussion of the fractions of the hour with Isidore of Seville's list: "Tempora momentis, horis, diebus, mensibus, annis, seculis aetatibusque dividuntur. Momentum est minimum atque angustissimum tempus a motu siderum dictum."[15] Two more lists of the hour's subdivisions follow, both of which ultimately derive from computus treatises: "Alii tempus distinguunt: seculum, aetas, annus, mensis, hebdomas, dies, quadrans, hora, punctum, momentum, uncia, atomus." The divisions were still in use, though probably not that common: "sunt ex nostris qui ita dirimunt."[16] He then explains the lengths of these units without citing ancient texts, adding the indiction (a fifteen-year segment used for tax purposes in late antique Rome) and the *lustrum* (a four-year or five-year segment deriving from the Greeks) to his list during the explanations, probably because the antiquity of these quantities is undisputed.

> In aetatem primum, quam mille annorum esse dicunt. Deinde in seculum, quod centum annorum. In indictionem, quam XV annorum statuunt. In lustrum, quae Graecis est olympias, quae perfectos quatuor annos continet. Tum in annum dividunt, quem in quatuor horas vel tempora distinguunt. Tempus in tres menses. Menses in hebdomadas quatuor. Hebdomadas in dies VII. Dies in quadrantes quatuor. Quadrans in sex horas dividitur. Porro hora in quatuor puncta. Punctum in decem momenta. Momentum, quod & momen apud antiquos vocitatum videmus, in uncias duodecim. Uncia in XLVII atomos. Atomos vero, ut vox ipsa indicat, dividi ac secari in partes non potest.[17]

---

[14] Paul Tannery, "Sur les subdivisions de l'heure durant l'Antiquité," in idem, *Mémoires scientifiques* 11 (Toulouse, 1912), 517–526, also believed that some of these medieval units had distant antique roots. Tannery also discusses the Greek circular symbol reproduced in Giraldi.

[15] Giraldi, *De annis et mensibus*, 11. Isidore's definition (*Etymologiae* 5.29) was partly lifted from Augustine, *De doctrina christiana* 2.22: 20–21: "neque enim ad rem pertinet, quod dicunt ipsum momentum minimum atque angustissimum temporis, quod geminorum partum disterminat, multum valere in rerum natura atque caelestium corporum rapidissima velocitate."

[16] Giraldi, *De annis et mensibus*, 11. After Giraldi, these units appear in a 1569 Venetian *Sacerdotale* and in Tomaso Garzoni's *Piazza Universale* of 1585. By 1795 they were no longer even comprehensible, as is attested in G. B. Gallicciolli, *Delle memorie venete antiche profane ed ecclesiastiche* (Venice, 1795), 357.

[17] Giraldi, *De annis et mensibus*, 11–12.

To further support the antiquity of these temporal divisions, Giraldi presents yet another list with a somewhat different array of small units which he claims to have found in an old book on weights and measures.[18]

As at other points in his treatise, the evidence does not all cohere. Trying to make sense of these tiny units of time that in his day had no practical or measurable value, Giraldi cites passages from earlier authors who use the words *momentum, punctum,* and *atom*. Good authorities like Lucretius, Terence, Cicero, and Jerome only provided support for Isidore's definition of the moment as simply a very brief length of time, though they confirm the shortness of the *punctum* and *atom*. According to Boethius, a minute is shorter than a *punctum*, but his text is late in comparison with Giraldi's classical sources.[19]

Realizing that the texts at his disposal would not yield more precise definitions, Giraldi moves on to the tiny divisions now used by astrologers: "Minutis nunc quidem LX astrologi dicunt horam constare," implying that not so long ago they used other systems. In this backhanded way, Giraldi was one of the first — and perhaps the first — to refer to the sixty-minute hour in a text aimed at a humanistic audience.[20] When Giraldi again brings up these tiny subdivisions in the context of explaining equinoctial or "clock" hours, he again contrasts the non-scientist's temporal divisions with those of the scientists: "naturalis diei pars est XXIIII quae in puncta IIII & XL momenta vel ut passim Astrologi loquuntur, in minutias vel minuta LX dividitur."[21] While Giraldi could not possibly have been aware how quickly and how total the change-over to the modern sixty-minute hour would be once clocks became accurate enough to record minutes, he clearly had some sense of the direction in which his culture was moving. In 1539, most were familiar with the *punctum*, and a few still used the *uncia* and *atom*, as today some scholars still use mechanical typewriters.

Giraldi was not opposed to innovations. He was fascinated by clocks and in fact ends his treatise with a description of a small portable clock in an eyeglass holder. This clock, owned by Leo X, accompanied the pope on his hunts and travels.[22]

---

[18] Giraldi, *De annis et mensibus*, 12: "Annum & mensum libram utrumque dici posse, quod ille ex XII mensibus, his ex XII horis constet; porro horam constare ex quinque punctis, X minutis, XV partibus, XL momentis, & LX ostentis: horamque diei secundum solis cursum quinque puncta habere, juxta vero lunam quatuor duntaxat."

[19] Giraldi, *De annis et mensibus*, 13. Boethius's minute was probably the medieval one which measured one-tenth of the hour. It is clear from Giraldi's discourse that he assumes Boethius's minute is the astronomical one, even though his "ancient treatises" give the medieval definition.

[20] Giraldi, *De annis et mensibus*, 13. He also mentions Ptolemaic degree minutes: dividing the twenty-four hours of the day into three hundred and sixty degree minutes, or each hour into fifteen parts.

[21] Giraldi, *De annis et mensibus*, 186. Although astronomers used minutes in the fifteenth century, they do not make their way into humanistic texts until the mid-sixteenth century in authors like Nicolo degli Agostini and Alessandro Citolini, *Tipocosmia* (Venice, 1561).

[22] Giraldi, *De annis et mensibus*, 196: "Ego in specilli oculari capulo Leonis X. Pont. horologium mirabiliter horas ostentans saepe conspexi, quo ille in venationibus itineribusque utebatur."

Naturally Leo X's clock is contextualized within a mini-history of timekeepers and their terminology including the first sundials, water clocks, gnomons, and automatic clocks. Giraldi was fascinated by all of these ingenious devices, but he was perhaps even more excited by the sense of wonder that each new type of clock aroused in its own time. For example, one wondrous mechanism was owned by Nicephorus Gregoras:

> Illa quoque Nicephori Gregorae instrumenta, quibus ratio cognoscendarum horarum noctis ex stellarum cursu traditur, miranda videri possunt.[23]

And more recently:

> Quo non illa miracula referendant: Quae hodie ex diverso metallo confecta, velut automata, sua sponte aguntur, haec donatus supra infraque rotulis, assidue circumactis ponderibus quibusdam libratis, ad stati motus temperamentum conficiuntur, in quibus non horas modo diurnas & nocturnas, sed & errantium caelestiumque signorum ortus & occasus conspiciuntur . . .[24]

As in many of his discourses, his analogies with the present serve to demonstrate both continuity and disunity with the past. Even if his contemporaries no longer marveled at nocturnal astrolabes, these objects had once had this awe-inspiring effect. Placed at the end of his book, Giraldi's mini-narrative of important and wondrous clocks shows that even familiar terms for these objects would have had different resonances in the ancient world than in his own.

While Giraldi might have written a treatise on time at any point in his troubled life, his decision to undertake the project several years after returning to Ferrara is probably not accidental. Since the Quattrocento, the university and the d'Este court had demonstrated a sustained interest in antiquarian and symbolic disquisitions on aspects of time, though no one had undertaken such a broad and ambitious project as Giraldi's.[25] Theodore Gaza's *De mensibus atticis*, so highly praised by Giraldi, was written while he was at the university in Ferrara. A few years later, Borso d'Este commissioned his celebrated and learned cycle of months for Palazzo Schifanoia, and Bernardo Lapini wrote his influential commentary on Petrarch's *Trionfi* in which each triumph was allegorized as a successive stage in man's existence. In the early sixteenth century, Ariosto allegorically described time, fate, and immortality in the famous lunar episodes of his *Orlando furioso*. In 1551, Vincenzo Cartari dedicated his Italian translation of Ovid's *Fasti* to Ercole II d'Este. During the 1540s and 1550s various

---

[23] Giraldi, *De annis et mensibus*, 195.

[24] Giraldi, *De annis et mensibus*, 196.

[25] Giraldi may originally have planned to dedicate his treatise on ancient time to Ercole. *De Herculis vita* (1539) and *De re nautica* (1540) had been dedicated to the duke. These books were being prepared for press just as Giraldi was composing his *De annis et mensibus*. Should they not achieve their desired effects, Giraldi would be in a position to direct his hopes towards a different patron.

artistic images of time were commissioned by Ercole II, including Dosso Dossi's *Night*, *Day*, and *Dawn*, Girolamo da Carpi's *Patience*, and Ercole II's medals which also represented Patience.[26] Finally, under Ercole II's son, Alfonso II (whose motto was "au lieu et temps"[27]), Bastianino and Camillo Filippi frescoed the ceiling of the master bedroom with Father Time, the Fates (or Hours), and the four times of day.

In many of these Ferrarese musings on time, as in the plays of Giambattista Giraldi Cinthio, humans are permitted only a passive role. Tending towards arcane antiquarian learning, these Ferrarese works emphasize time's general cyclicality and the role of fate in human affairs. Ercole's emblem of Patience is a case in point. It represents Patience chained to a stone next to a water clock. As time passes, water drains from the clock onto the chain, eroding the metal. Intently watching the clock, Patience is waiting until its water will set her free from her bonds. While Giraldi's learned work is not really comparable to this allegory, it shares a certain combination of curiosity and passivity. *De annis et mensibus* described and divided time in many ways, but nowhere does its author present the popular Ovidian monster, "tempus edax rerum" (*Metamorphoses* 15.234). Giraldi's time is not in competition with man; his "Ad lectorem" encapsulates this somewhat detached yet deterministic point of view:

> Dum nos secla, dies, menses metimur & annos,
> Obrepit tacito mors inopina gradu,
> Quae feret aethereamve diem, noctemve profundam.
> Acta tibi qualis, talis agenda dies.

Although not an original contribution to philosophy or science, *De annis et mensibus* is a highly original piece of Renaissance scholarship. Developed within a distinctly Ferrarese context, Giraldi's work goes beyond those of his Ferrarese contemporaries by considering time as a historical construct. Self-consciously writing in a period of intense research to reform the calendar and historical chronology, Giraldi may have been concerned that these advances or alterations to the present system would make earlier systems that much more remote. In the next century, Giraldi must have reasoned — correctly — that no one would still use the *momentum* or the *uncia*. Maybe these units would become like Romulus's ten-month year that still puzzles classicists. Giraldi expected his work to elucidate the ancient experience of time by clarifying terminology and by making ancient philosophical ideas available for modern consumption, but a second purpose in collecting this material on time may have been to preserve it in an age when not only the calendar but also the perception of even the tiniest fractions of time were changing for good. Although Giraldi did

---

[26] See Rudolf Wittkower, "Patience and Chance: The Story of a Political Emblem," *Journal of the Warburg and Courtauld Institutes* 1 (1937–1938): 171–177. Wittkower also discusses another related allegory of *Occasio* for which he believed Giraldi supplied iconographic advice.

[27] Ariosto provided the motto, "Loco et tempore." See Paolo Giovio, *Dialogo dell'imprese* (Rome, 1555), 51.

not succeed at this second task, he did produce the first general historical work on time. Through quotation, commentary, and juxtaposition with contemporary practice, Giraldi demonstrated that the ancient experience of time had its own distinct character, and thus, more generally, that the experience of time itself was culturally relative.

Baltimore, Maryland

Los reflejos plautinos en el latín de Descartes (Med. 1–3)

BENJAMÍN GARCÍA HERNÁNDEZ

El latín era la lengua por excelencia del humanismo literario, filosófico, y científico. Descartes lo había aprendido a fondo en el colegio de La Flecha, de manera que se expresaba en la lengua del Lacio con la naturalidad con que lo hacía en la materna. El latín era no sólo el vehículo ideal para la expresión de las grandes cuestiones filosóficas, sino una lengua de cultura capaz de moldear y dar forma a su pensamiento. Por ejemplo, Descartes se atiene rigurosamente a la importante oposición latina *mens/corpus* y rechaza las palabras *anima* y *spiritus* por su connotación de materialidad aérea; en su opinión, la única palabra que representa con propiedad la sustancia inmaterial del hombre es *mens*, sustantivo íntimamente unido desde el latín arcaico al verbo *cogitare*:[1]

> sum igitur praecise tantum *res cogitans*, id est, *mens*. (C. Adam et P. Tannery, eds., *Oeuvres de Descartes*, 11 vols. [Paris, 1996], 7:27.13)

Sin embargo, en la mayor parte de las traducciones de las *Meditaciones metafísicas* el concepto cartesiano de *mens* aparece falseado; la lengua francesa, en particular, no tiene una palabra que corresponda exactamente a la latina; y cuando se traduce *mens* por *esprit*, se traiciona el pensamiento del filósofo; otro tanto hacen quienes en español, pese a disponer de la palabra *mente*, siguen la pauta del francés traduciendo por *espíritu* o peor aún por *alma*. *Mens* encuentra también mejor correspondencia en el inglés *mind* que en *soul* y *spirit*.

---

[1] Cf. B. García Hernández, "La necesidad de volver al latín de los filósofos: el caso de *anima* y *mens* en las *Meditaciones* de Descartes," in *De Roma al siglo XX*, ed. A. M. Aldama, 2 vols. (Madrid, 1996), 2:710ss. Sobre el latín cf. de este mismo Congreso C. Vermeulen, "A Latin Translation of Descartes."

Del sistema filosófico de Descartes se han señalado numerosos precedentes, en lo que toca a su pensamiento y también a su expresión, y ninguno de ellos ha pasado tan desapercibido como el del comediógrafo latino Plauto. Sin embargo, no hay autor antiguo, medieval, o renacentista que haya ejercido una influencia mayor sobre el padre de la filosofía moderna. Esa influencia afecta a los conceptos fundamentales de su sistema, a su tono dramático, y, consiguientemente, se hace notar en su expresión.

Como hemos demostrado en nuestro libro *Descartes y Plauto*,[2] el filósofo francés construye su sistema filosófico sobre el argumento de la tragicomedia *Amphitruo* de Plauto. Sin embargo, mantuvo silencio absoluto sobre el origen de su inspiración. Cuando sus lectores y contradictores le señalaron ciertas analogías con san Agustín, no admitió que se hubiera inspirado en él; ésa fue una ocasión clara para haber revelado la fuente auténtica; pero no dio un paso que requería gran humildad científica y que habría supuesto ante sus contemporáneos desautorizar la base de su pensamiento. Cabe sospechar que, así como se sentía halagado por la relación con san Agustín, no tenía los mismos sentimientos respecto de la fuente plautina; y es que la autoridad literaria del gran cómico latino debía de distar mucho, a ojos de sus contemporáneos, del prestigio filosófico y teológico del padre de la Iglesia; así que Descartes se vio en la necesidad de guardar celosamente el secreto de su inspiración.

Ese secreto ha perdurado por más de tres siglos y medio. El nombre de Plauto ha estado siempre ausente de los estudios cartesianos; tan sólo hemos hallado dos referencias de la tragicomedia *Anfitrión*.[3] Una la vemos en el comentario de É. Gilson al *Discurso del Método*[4] y llega incluida en una cita de Justo Lipsio; en ella Alcmena concluye la loa de la victoria militar de su marido ponderando la excelencia de la *uirtus* como fuente de todos los bienes:

AL. — *Virtus omnia* in sese habet, *omnia* adsunt / *bona* quem penest uirtus (*Amph.* 652s.);

Descartes la glosa en la tercera parte del *Discurso*, donde dice cómo a la adquisición de las virtudes sigue la posesión de los demás bienes:

pour acquerir *toutes les vertus*, & ensemble *tous les autres biens*, qu'on puisse acquerir. (*Oeuvres*, 6:28.11–13)

La otra referencia plautina la dan los editores de Descartes a propósito del proverbio *noli irritare crabrones*, que éste usa en una carta del 31 de julio dirigida a Huygens (*Oeuvres*, 3:752.51), cuya formulación arranca de la expresión plautina *inritabis crabrones* (*Amph.* 707). Aunque es posible que el filósofo conociera el proverbio por al-

---

[2] B. García Hernández, *Descartes y Plauto: La concepción dramática del sistema cartesiano* (Madrid, 1997).

[3] Cf. García Hernández, *Descartes y Plauto*, 130s.

[4] Cf. É. Gilson, ed., *René Descartes, Discours de la Méthode: Texte et commentaire* (Paris, 1976), 261.

gún repertorio de la época, lo más seguro es que lo hubiera leído varias veces desde su juventud en la tragicomedia de Plauto.

Por otra parte, el filósofo italiano G. B. Vico señaló la sorprendente analogía entre el Genio maligno y el dios Mercurio y entre el *cogito* cartesiano y el que pronuncia Sosia en la primera escena de *Amphitruo*:

> Quare primum uerum aperit id esse Renatus: "Cogito: ergo sum." Et uero Plautinus Sosia non aliter, ac a genio fallaci Carthesii, aut a somnio diuinitus immisso Stoici, a Mercurio, qui ipsius imaginem sumpserat, in dubium de se ipso adductus, an sit, ad idem instar meditabundus huic primo uero acquiescit.
>
> Certe edepol, quom illum contemplo, et formam agnosco meam, quemadmodum ego saepe in speculum inspexi, nimis similis mei.
> . . . .
> Sed quom cogito, equidem certo sum ac semper fui.

(Giambattista Vico, *Le orazioni inaugurali, Il De Italorum sapientia e le Polemiche*, ed. G. Gentile e F. Nicolini [Bari, 1968], 139)

Pero Vico no llegó a sospechar que había una relación de dependencia entre Descartes y Plauto y luego su certera comparación ha sido menospreciada por la crítica cartesiana, mientras la crítica viquiana no ha sabido explotarla.[5]

1. Dependencia argumental y tono dramático

Descartes asume el papel del siervo Sosia enfrentado a su doble divino, el dios Mercurio, que lo despoja de su ser físico y de su experiencia psíquica y le hace dudar de su identidad, hasta que al final de la larga primera escena afirma su ser apoyándose en la realidad de su pensamiento:

> SO. — sed quom *cogito*, equidem certo idem *sum* qui semper fui.
> (*Amph.* 447)

Ésta es la fuente genuina del *cogito ergo sum*, la primera verdad en el orden del conocimiento; pero Descartes toma además directamente de *Amphitruo* sus tres figuras divinas. El Genio maligno es trasunto del dios Mercurio como doble de Sosia; el Dios falaz (*Deus fallax*) es asimismo el trasunto de Júpiter como doble de Anfitrión y responsable de la confusión que reina en la casa del general tebano. Incluso el Dios no falaz (*Deus non fallax*), garante de toda verdad y de todo conocimiento posterior a la formulación del *cogito*, tiene las trazas de ser un *deus ex machina*, como el Júpiter

---

[5] Cf. García Hernández, *Descartes y Plauto*, 191ss.; y, para mayor detalle, idem, "Vico acerca del *cogito* de Descartes y Plauto: Mucho más que una simple analogía," in *Pensar para el nuevo siglo: Giambattista Vico y la cultura europea*, ed. E. Hidalgo-Serna et al., 3 vols. (Napoli, 2001), 1:155–174.

plautino que en el desenlace de la tragicomedia revela la verdad de lo ocurrido a los miembros de la familia de Anfitrión.[6]

La caracterización del Genio maligno y la formulación del *cogito* serían pruebas suficientes para mostrar cómo Descartes se inspira en Plauto. He aquí la presentación de la figura del Genio maligno:

> Supponam igitur non optimum Deum, fontem ueritatis, sed *genium aliquem malignum*, eundemque summe potentem & *callidum*, omnem suam industriam in eo posuisse, ut *me falleret*. (*Oeuvres*, 7:22.23-26)

La maldad como cualidad más destacada, la astucia y la voluntad de engaño son las mismas características con las que se presenta el dios Mercurio como doble de Sosia:

> ME. — Quando imago est huius in me, certum est hominem eludere. / Et enim uero quoniam formam cepi huius in me[d] et statum, / decet et facta moresque huius habere me similis item. / Itaque me *malum* esse oportet, *callidum*, astutum admodum, / atque hunc telo suo sibi, *malitia*, a foribus pellere. (*Amph.* 265-269)

Estas cualidades no son exclusivas de Sosia, sino características de un personaje típico de la comedia plautina, el *seruus malus et callidus*, que se distingue por su función falaz. El Genio maligno une a ellas un sumo poder, que no es otro que el manifestado por el dios Mercurio, al arrogarse la persona y la experiencia de Sosia.

El famoso principio cartesiano ha sido extraído directamente del verso pronunciado por Sosia, citado anteriormente:

> SO. — sed quom *cogito*, equidem certo idem *sum* qui semper fui.
> (*Amph.* 447)

Ahora bien, la fórmula consabida *cogito ergo sum* no tiene lugar en las *Meditaciones*; en ellas se presenta de forma mucho más dramática. El filósofo trata de averiguar qué es él, una vez que se halla sometido a la acción impostora del Genio maligno; al igual que Sosia por obra de Mercurio, se ve despojado de su naturaleza corporal e incluso de su experiencia anímica; pero en ese momento se pregunta por su pensamiento:

> Cogitare? Hic inuenio: *cogitatio est*; haec sola a me diuelli nequit. *Ego sum, ego existo*; certum est. (*Oeuvres*, 7:27.7-9)

Como si respondiera a la violencia que ejerce el Genio maligno, concluye que sólo el pensamiento no le puede ser arrancado; por eso, en él consiste su esencia:

---

[6] Un avance con los elementos sustanciales de la inspiración plautina de Descartes lo dábamos ya en B. García Hernández, "La huella profunda e inexplorada de Plauto en el pensamiento cartesiano," in *Actas del I Congreso Andaluz de Estudios Clásicos* (Jaén, 1982), 208-214.

sum igitur praecise tantum *res cogitans*. (27.13)

Se ha dicho que el *cogito* es un entimema, al que le falta una premisa de carácter general (*qui cogitat est*); pero su formulación está condicionada por su origen; no surge de un razonamiento silogístico, sino de una reacción dramática; de ahí su expresión en primera persona. El tono dramático se percibe intensamente en numerosos párrafos de la segunda *Meditación*; el filósofo se enfrenta al Genio maligno como Sosia a su doble divino y, como éste, formula en primera persona no sólo su *cogito* y *sum*, sino todo el proceso de su duda:

Nunquid ergo saltem ego aliquid *sum*? Sed iam negaui me habere ullos sensus, & ullum corpus. *Haereo* tamen; ... (*Oeuvres*, 7:24.24–26)

Nonne ego ipse *sum* qui iam *dubito* fere de omnibus ... qui ... nolo decipi ...? (27.24ss)

Y la duda no está provocada por la posibilidad de caer en el error, sino por la de ser engañado y sometido al error por un impostor. Hay, pues, en las *Meditaciones* una clara actitud de enfrentamiento, desafío, y violencia entre el filósofo, que se expresa en primera persona, y sus antagonistas divinos, en particular el Genio maligno; ese tono dramático es reflejo del conflicto que viven los personajes plautinos, Sosia y Anfitrión, frente a sus dobles divinos, Mercurio y Júpiter.

Las tres primeras *Meditaciones* constituyen todo un drama.[7] En la primera el filósofo recorre la escala de la duda que afecta a la percepción de la realidad y a la identidad de su ser. En el duro combate que libra con las figuras divinas inductoras del engaño, esto es, con el Genio maligno y el Dios burlador, el filósofo logra afirmar su esencia mental, gracias a la conciencia de su pensamiento, esto es, gracias al *cogito*. Éste es el nudo dramático que se desarrolla en la segunda *Meditación*. En cambio, en la tercera cuenta con el auxilio del Dios no falaz que, como un *deus ex machina*, le garantiza la verdad de toda idea clara y distinta y le asegura el conocimiento del mundo extramental.

2. Dependencia expresiva

A la dependencia argumental se une la dependencia expresiva, de manera que el latín de las tres primeras *Meditaciones* es en muchos aspectos un calco del de Plauto; en particular las páginas 21–22 de la primera *Meditación*, 24–29 de la segunda, y 34–36 de la tercera, siempre de la edición de Adam y Tannery, contienen una fuerte relación intertextual, hasta el punto que el texto cartesiano es en ellas una especie de palimpsesto, en el sentido literario del título de G. Genette.[8] Muchas de las expresiones de origen plautino afectan a la concepción filosófica cartesiana y otras carecen de interés doctrinal; las primeras constituyen evocaciones directas del modelo de

---

[7] Cf. García Hernández, *Descartes y Plauto*, 152ss.
[8] G. Genette, *Palimpsestos: La literatura en segundo grado* (Madrid, 1989).

inspiración, y las segundas, que son reminiscencias quizás involuntarias, vienen a confirmar la deuda inspiradora del filósofo para con el cómico latino.[9]

P.-A. Cahné ha señalado que Descartes crea un tipo de frase compleja, correcta e indiferente a la armonía artística, en la que a veces se acumulan subordinadas, incisos y paréntesis.[10] Esto es algo que se confirma siguiendo su proceso creativo y comprobando cómo transforma la sintaxis plautina, en general más simple, o cómo la imita en ciertas estructuras complejas. He aquí una larga dubitación de Sosia, en la que predominan las oraciones simples introducidas por la anáfora de *nonne* o *non*:

> SO. — Quid, malum, *non sum ego* seruos Amphitruonis Sosia? / *nonne* hac noctu nostra nauis [huc] ex portu Persico / uenit, quae me aduexit? *nonne* me huc erus misit meus? / *nonne ego* nunc sto ante aedis nostras? *non* mihi est lanterna in manu? / *non* loquor? *non* uigilo? *nonne* hic homo modo me pugnis contudit? / fecit hercle: nam etiam [mi] misero nunc malae dolent. / Quid igitur ego *dubito*? (*Amph.* 403–409)

Y he aquí la réplica cartesiana, en la que la partícula *nonne* se reduce a su empleo inicial y se sustituye por la anáfora del pronombre *qui*, constituyendo un gran periodo de subordinadas de relativo:

> *nonne ego* ipse sum *qui* iam *dubito* fere de omnibus, *qui* nonnihil tamen intelligo, *qui* hoc unum uerum esse affirmo, nego caetera, cupio plura nosse, nolo decipi, multa uel inuitus imaginor, multa etiam tanquam a sensibus uenientia animaduerto? (*Oeuvres*, 7:28.24–29)

El gusto de Descartes por la oración de relativo se pone de manifiesto en la repetición de la fórmula de identidad que sigue al *cogito* de Sosia ("sed quom cogito, equidem certo idem sum qui semper fui"):

> *idem sum qui* imaginor (*Oeuvres*, 7:29.7s.);
> *idem ... sum qui* sentio (29.11);
> ille *idem qui* nunc *sum* (73.9);

en cambio, si los verbos aparecen en infinitivo, prefiere la estructura comparativa:

> si supponam me forte *semper fuisse ut* nunc *sum* (48.25s.);
> perfectiorem *futurum fuisse quam* nunc *sum*. (61.18s.)

---

[9] Para la distinción entre estos dos tipos de manifestaciones intertextuales, cf. A. Alvar Ezquerra, "Tipología de los procedimientos intertextuales en la poesía latina antigua," in *Actas del IX Congreso Español de Estudios Clásicos, V: Literatura latina*, ed. J. L. Vidal y A. Alvar (Madrid, 1998), 13s.

[10] P.-A. Cahné, *Un autre Descartes: Le philosophe et son langage* (Paris, 1980), 35, 245.

En la disputa que mantienen Mercurio y Sosia por poseer la persona de Sosia, Plauto emplea primero una oración completiva con *quin* y luego una consecutiva con la misma partícula:

>ME. — Tu me uiuos hodie *numquam facies quin sim* Sosia.
>SO. — Certe edepol tu me alienabis *numquam quin* noster *siem*.
>(*Amph.* 398s.)

Descartes, que manifiesta un tono desafiante similar frente al engaño del Genio maligno, las transforma en completivas con *ut*:

>& fallat quantum potest, *nunquam* tamen *efficiet, ut nihil sim* (*Oeuvres*, 7:25.8s.);
>fallat me quisquis potest, *nunquam* tamen *efficiet ut nihil sim*. (36.15s.)

El filósofo recurre a la disyuntiva *seu* para desgranar las diversas posibilidades del propio origen, en caso de negar la existencia de Dios:

>at *seu* fato, *seu* casu, *seu* continuata rerum serie, *seu* quouis alio modo me ad id quod sum peruenisse supponant. (*Oeuvres*, 7:21.20–22)

Este uso polisindético nos hace recordar la repetición de la partícula *siue* y de su variante *seu*, que Plauto pone en boca de Mercurio, para presentar una casuística similar dentro de la aplicación paródica al mundo teatral de una ley de soborno electoral:

>ME. — *siue* qui ambissent palmam histrionibus / *seu* quoiquam artifici –*seu* per scriptas litteras / *siue* [ipse] ambissit *seu* per internuntium–; / *siue* adeo aediles perfidiose quoi duint (*Amph.* 69–72);

o bien nos hace pensar en la detallada amenaza de Anfitrión, después de enfrentarse a su doble, esto es, a Júpiter:

>AM. — Certumst, intro rumpam in aedis: ubi quemque hominem aspexero, / *si*[*ue*] ancillam, *seu* seruom, *siue* uxorem, *siue* adulterum, / *seu* patrem, *siue* auom uidebo, optruncabo in aedibus. (1048–1050)

Hay una fórmula de prosecución (*pergam, perge*: "continuaré," "continúa") que usa Sosia, para manifestar que está dispuesto a llevar adelante las órdenes de su dueño, y Anfitrión, para expresar su voluntad de seguir la investigación de los hechos cerca de su mujer:

>SO. — Nunc *pergam* eri imperium exsequi et me domum capessere. / (*Amph.* 262)
>AM. — Nunc domum ibo atque ex uxore hanc rem *pergam* exquirere. / (1015)

AM. — *perge porro* dicere. (803)

Descartes recurre a ella para indicar la prosecución de su indagación de la verdad:

*perga*mque *porro* donec aliquid certi . . . cognoscam. (*Oeuvres*, 7:24.7ss.; 34.15)

En una pregunta de Mercurio y en la reflexión posterior de Sosia vemos una contraposición temporal, marcada por las partículas *nunc* y *antehac*:

ME. — Quid *nunc*? uincon argumentis, te non esse Sosiam? (*Amph*. 433)
SO. — Nam hicquidem omnem imaginem meam, quae *antehac* fuerat, possidet. / (458)

Esa misma contraposición se observa en las preguntas que se hace Descartes acerca de qué era antes de hallar el *cogito* y qué es ahora, sometido al poder del Genio maligno:

Quidnam igitur *antehac* me esse putaui? (*Oeuvres*, 7:25.25)
Quid autem *nunc*, ubi suppono deceptorem aliquem . . . me delusisse? (26.24ss.)

El uso recurrente de los indefinidos en la presentación de las figuras divinas es algo que ha llamado la atención de la crítica cartesiana.[11] Helos aquí:

Supponam . . . genium *aliquem* malignum. (*Oeuvres*, 7:22.23s.)
Suppono deceptorem *aliquem* potentissimum. (26.24s.)
Nunquid est *aliquis* Deus, uel quocumque nomine illum uocem. (24.21s.)
Veniebat in mentem forte *aliquem* Deum talem mihi naturam indere potuisse. (36.5ss.; 22; 24)
Sed est deceptor *nescio quis*, summe potens, summe callidus. (25.5ss.)
Fallat me *quisquis* potest. (36.15)

Pues bien, ese empleo refleja el que hace Plauto en relación con los dobles divinos, como personajes desconocidos e innominados, para sus doblados. Desde el principio Sosia manifiesta el temor de que los dioses le envíen a alguien para zurrarle la badana:

SO. — *Aliquem* hominem adlegent, qui mihi aduenienti os occillet probe. / (*Amph*. 183)

---

[11] J. L. Marion, *Sur la théologie blanche de Descartes* (Paris, 1981), 343s.; idem, *Sur le prisme métaphysique de Descartes* (Paris, 1986), 223ss.; idem, "The Essential Incoherence of Descartes' Definition of Divinity," in *Essays on Descartes' Meditations*, ed. A. O. Rorty (Berkeley, 1986), 297–338, 300s.

Mercurio, sabiendo que es Sosia quien se acerca, se refiere a él en aparte con el indefinido *nescioquis*:

> ME. — Certe enim hic *nescioquis* loquitur (331);

el mismo adjetivo aplica Anfitrión al embaucador de su mujer:

> AM. — *Nescioquis* praestigiator hanc frustratur mulierem. (830)

Y después de haberse encontrado con su doble, está dispuesto a hacerle frente, quienquiera que sea:

> Numquam edepol me inuitus istic ludificabit, *quisquis* est. (1041)

Descartes destaca sus dos certezas primordiales, la conciencia de su ser y la existencia de Dios, mediante el sentido exclusivo de *praeter* en frase negativa:

> & quamuis, ex quo de omnibus uolui dubitare, nihil adhuc *praeter me* & Deum existere certo cognoui.

Se trata de un uso común de esa preposición, probablemente inspirado en *Amphitruo*, donde Sosia se presenta ante Mercurio como siervo exclusivo de Anfitrión:

> Nec nobis *praeter me[d]* alius quisquam est seruos Sosia. (*Amph.* 400)

La contraposición entre placer y sufrimiento, característica del pensamiento epicúreo,[12] la hallamos en parecidos términos en la tragicomedia de Plauto y en las *Meditaciones*:

> AL. — Satin parua res est *uoluptatum* in uita atque in aetate agunda, / praequam quod *molestum* est? ita quoiqu' comparatum est in aetate hominum; / ita di[ui]s est placitum, *uoluptatem* ut *maeror* comes consequatur: / Quin *incommodi* plus *mali*que ilico adsit, boni si optigit quid. / (*Amph.* 633–636)

> sensique hoc corpus inter alia multa corpora uersari, a quibus uariis *commodis* uel *incommodis* affici potest, & *commoda* ista sensu quodam *uoluptatis*, & *incommoda* sensu *doloris* metiebar. (*Oeuvres*, 7:74.20–23)

---

[12] Cf. B. García Hernández, "Trasfondo filosófico y fondo precartesiano en *Amphitruo* de Plauto," in *La filología latina hoy: Actualización y perspectivas*, ed. A. M. Aldama et al. (Madrid, 1999), 2:995–1007, 1001s.

El verbo *depromere* indica la acción específica de sacar de la despensa. Sosia, mientras camina de noche, teme ir a parar al calabozo, de donde lo sacarán para trincharlo:

SO. — Ind' cras *quasi e promptaria cella depromar* ad flagrum. (*Amph.* 156)

Descartes lo aplica a la acción de extraer ideas de la mente, pero este uso abstracto no puede menos de hacernos recordar la descripción gráfica de Sosia:

Iam uero si ex eo solo, quod alicuius rei ideam possim *ex cogitatione* mea *depromere* (*Oeuvres*, 7:65.16s.);

sobre todo cuando el ablativo de origen va precedido de una partícula comparativa:

quoties tamen de ente primo & summo libet cogitare, atque eius ideam *tamquam ex* mentis meae *thesauro depromere*. [cf. Matt. 12:35, 13:52, Luc. 6:45] (67.21–23)

Aunque hay otras expresiones cartesianas que merecen ser cotejadas con sus paralelos plautinos, vamos a concluir aquí mencionando el uso de ciertos adverbios; entre ellos, el arcaísmo *noctu* (*Oeuvres*, 7:19.9) que Plauto emplea como variante de *nocte* en la larga dubitación de Sosia (*Amph.* 404), citada antes, y en tres ocasiones más (272, 412, 731); el doblete aliterante *satis superque* (*Oeuvres*, 7:25.10s.; *Amph.* 168); y el empleo restrictivo de *saltem* en frase interrogativa; así, bajo la presión del Genio maligno, Descartes se pregunta:

Nunquid ergo *saltem ego* aliquid *sum*? (*Oeuvres*, 7:24.24s.);

con el mismo tono con que Sosia inquiere a su doble divino, al verse desposeído de su persona:

SO. — Quis *ego sum saltem*, si non sum Sosia? (*Amph.* 438)

La influencia de *Amphitruo* no se limita a las tres primeras *Meditaciones*, pero en ellas resalta mucho más su marca dramática y su huella expresiva. Leyendo esas tres *Meditaciones* en latín, cualquiera que conozca a fondo la tragicomedia plautina, no tardará en sacar la impresión de que Descartes debía de conocerla casi de memoria o, al menos, debía haberla leído muchas veces desde su juventud. La clave que aclara este asiduo contacto con el texto plautino reside en el tercero de los famosos Sueños que el filósofo tuvo en 1619; en él habla de un *Corpus poetarum* que conocía muy bien. Se trata de la voluminosa obra editada por Pierre de Brosses (Petrus Brossaeus) en Lyon (1603) y en Ginebra (1611). No es casualidad que, después de unos fragmentos de Livio Andrónico y de Ennio, la primera pieza completa que contiene sea el *Amphitruo* de Plauto. Sin duda, éste era libro de cabecera del joven Descartes; debía de tenerlo desde la etapa escolar de La Flèche;[13] no en vano proceden de él otras muchas citas de poetas latinos diseminadas en las obras del filósofo. El episodio de los Sueños, relatado por su biógrafo A. Baillet,[14] recoge además el momento de inspiración entusiástica, en que se produce la concepción dramática de lo que un día sería el primer gran sistema filosófico de la época moderna.

Universidad Autónoma de Madrid

Bibliografía

Alvar Ezquerra, Antonio. "Tipología de los procedimientos intertextuales en la poesía latina antigua." In *Actas del IX Congreso Español de Estudios Clásicos*, V: *Literatura latina*, ed. J. L. Vidal y A. Alvar, 3–16. Madrid, 1998.

Adam, Charles, and Paul Tannery, eds. *Oeuvres de Descartes*. 11 vols. Paris, 1996.

Baillet, Adrien. *La vie de Monsieur Descartes*. 2 vols. Paris, 1691; repr. Hildesheim, 1972.

Brossaeus, Petrus. *Corpus omnium veterum poetarum latinorum secundum seriem temporum, et quinque libris distinctum*. 2 vols. Lugduni, 1603; Aureliae Allobrogum, 1611.

Cahné, Pierre-Alain. *Un autre Descartes: Le philosophe et son langage*. Paris, 1980.

García Hernández, Benjamín. "La huella profunda e inexplorada de Plauto en el pensamiento cartesiano." In *Actas del I Congreso Andaluz de Estudios Clásicos*, 208–214. Jaén, 1982.

———. "La necesidad de volver al latín de los filósofos: el caso de *anima* y *mens* en las *Meditaciones* de Descartes." In *De Roma al siglo XX*, ed. A. M. Aldama, 2 vols., 2:707–717. Madrid, 1996.

———. *Descartes y Plauto: La concepción dramática del sistema cartesiano*. Madrid, 1997.

———. "Trasfondo filosófico y fondo precartesiano en *Amphitruo* de Plauto." In *La filología latina hoy: Actualización y perspectivas*, ed. A. M. Aldama et al., 2 vols., 2:995–1007. Madrid, 1999.

———. "Vico acerca del *cogito* de Descartes y Plauto. Mucho más que una simple analogía." In *Pensar para el nuevo siglo. Giambattista Vico y la cultura europea*, ed. E. Hidalgo-Serna et al., 3 vols. 1:155–174. Napoli, 2001.

Genette, Gérard. *Palimpsestos: La literatura en segundo grado*. Madrid, 1989.

Gilson, Étienne. *René Descartes, Discours de la Méthode: Texte et commentaire*. Paris, 1976.

Marion, Jean-Luc. *Sur la théologie blanche de Descartes*. Paris, 1981.

———. *Sur le prisme métaphysique de Descartes*. Paris, 1986.

———. "The Essential Incoherence of Descartes' Definition of Divinity." In *Essays on Descartes' Meditations*, ed. A. O. Rorty, 297–338. Berkeley, 1986.

Plautus, T. Maccius. *Amphitruo*, ed. Ettore Paratore. Firenze, 1967.

Vico, Giambattista. *Le orazioni inaugurali, Il De Italorum sapientia e le Polemiche*, ed. G. Gentile e F. Nicolini. Bari, 1968.

---

[13] Cf. García-Hernández, *Descartes y Plauto*, 270ss.

[14] Cf. A. Baillet, *La vie de Monsieur Descartes*, 2 vols. (Paris, 1691; repr. Hildesheim, 1972), 1:81–86.

Petrarch's Poetics:
A Definition and Defense of Creativity
in the Familiares and Seniles

DONALD GILMAN

At the beginning of his epic *Africa* (1339–1343), Petrarch invokes the Muse to inspire within him the capacity to express in song the accomplishments of Scipio Africanus the Elder. Such a prayer, he recognizes, is a rhetorical trope, and he is consciously imitating the structure and style of Homer, Statius, and Lucan.[1] For Petrarch, though, convention and conviction converge; for, in calling upon the assistance of the Muse to sing of marvelous things, he acknowledges the need of a divine force to discover and convey the material of his verse. Poetry, then, combines the fact of experience and the fiction of expression. But Petrarch does not see himself solely as a rhetor-historian. In an invocation to Christ that follows his address to the Muse (1.15–25), he hopes to adapt historical event to a fictional form that, in turn, may relate to moral teaching. Thus the rhetorician is also a theologian who, combining the gifts of both Helicon and Parnassus, transmits a sacred vision through secular form.

As a historian, rhetorician, and moral philosopher, Petrarch is defining the role and responsibilities of the poet. Certainly, as Marjorie O'Rourke Boyle has argued, this view conflicts with the picture of the persona of the *Rime sparse* who details, in vernacular verse, the aspirations and anguish of a lustful sinner.[2] Rather, the writer

---

[1] Francesco Petrarca, *L'Africa*, ed. Nicola Festa, Edizione nazionale delle opere di Francesco Petrarca (Florence, 1926), 1: 69–72. All subsequent book and verse numbers correspond to this edition.

[2] Marjorie O'Rourke Boyle, *Petrarch's Genius: Pentimento and Prophecy* (Berkeley and Los Angeles, 1991), 1–10. According to Boyle, critics of the *Rime sparse* have stressed that Petrarch's obsession with Laura amounted to the sin of idolatry. See, for example, Thomas M. Greene, *The Light in Troy: Imitation and Discovery in Renaissance Poetry* (New Haven, 1982), 114–115; Robert M. Durling, "Petrarch's 'Giovene donna sotto un verde lauro'," *Modern Language Notes* 86 (1971):

of the *Africa* and the *Bucolicum carmen* is a poet-humanist who, according to Charles Trinkaus, practices both a *theologia poetica* and a *theologia rhetorica*.[3] Fictional forms and rhetorical techniques, then, represent the means to adapt historical fact or narrative fiction to the strictures of a truth allegorically expressed and interpreted. Besides Boyle and Trinkaus, Aldo Bernardo, Concetta Greenfield, Kenelm Foster, Pietro Paolo Gerosa, Craig Kallendorf, Nicholas Mann, and Carol Quillen have described this aspect of Petrarch's humanist poetics.[4] In spite of the accuracy of this research, though, three questions in the defining of poetic creativity require consideration: (1) the source of Petrarch's object of imitation; (2) the process whereby the poet converts abstract insight into concrete expression; and (3) the place of the poet and his craft in society. Furthermore, previous scholarship has taken into cursory account statements on the poetic process throughout his letters. However, such analyses have been indirect, with emphasis centered upon his poetry or his evolution as a humanist.[5] Both the *Familiares* and *Seniles* deserve separate attention; and, through an examination of Petrarch's thoughts on the poetic process recorded in these collections of letters, this study may perhaps explain more fully his theory on the process and purpose of poetic creativity.

The Material of Mimesis

In a letter written late in his life (*Seniles* 12.2), Petrarch proposes a concise but complete definition of poetic creativity:

> quid ergo officium eius est fingere, id est componere atque ornare, et veritatem rerum, vel mortalium, vel naturalium, vel quarumlibet aliarum artificiosis adumbrare coloribus, et velo amoenae fictionis obnubere.

1–20; John Freccero, "The Fig Tree and the Laurel: Petrarch's Poetics," *Diacritics* 5 (1975): 34–40; Giuseppe Mazzotta, "The *Canzoniere* and the Language of Self," *Studies in Philology* 75 (1978): 271–296. However, in studying Petrarch's rhetorical tradition, Boyle seeks to define his poetry not in moral but in humanist terms.

[3] Charles Trinkaus, *In Our Image and Likeness: Humanity and Divinity in Italian Humanist Thought*, 2 vols. (Chicago, 1970), chap. 15; idem, *The Poet as Philosopher: Petrarch and the Formation of Renaissance Consciousness* (New Haven, 1979), chap. 4. See also E. R. Curtius, *European Literature and the Latin Middle Ages*, trans. W. R. Trask (Princeton, 1967), 214–227.

[4] Aldo Bernardo, *Petrarch, Scipio, and the "Africa"* (Baltimore, 1962), especially chaps. 9 and 10; Pietro Paulo Gerosa, *Umanesimo cristiano del Petrarca* (Turin, 1966), chaps. 1 and 15; Concetta Greenfield, "Studies in Fourteenth and Fifteenth Century Poetics" (Ph.D. diss., University of North Carolina at Chapel Hill, 1971), 73–87; Kenelm Foster, *Petrarch: Poet and Humanist* (Edinburgh, 1984); Craig Kallendorf, *In Praise of Aeneas: Virgil and Epideictic Rhetoric in the Early Italian Renaissance* (Hanover, NH, 1989), chap. 2; Nicholas Mann, *Petrarch* (Oxford, 1984), esp. chaps. 2 and 6; Carol Quillen, *Petrarch, Augustine, and the Language of Humanism* (Ann Arbor, 1998).

[5] See, for example, Greenfield, "Studies," 81–82; Gerosa, *Umanesimo cristiano*, chap. 7, who discusses the themes and structure of the letters; Kallendorf, *In Praise of Aeneas*, 20, 28–30, 43–44, 46, 48–49; and numerous references scattered throughout the studies of Bernardo, Foster, Trinkaus, Mann, and Boyle.

[Their function is to invent, that is, to compose and adorn, and to sketch with artful colors the truth of things, whether mortal or natural or whatever else, and to cover it with a veil of neat fiction.][6]

For Petrarch, the process of invention involves a search for an object of imitation that, drawn from the poet's earthly surroundings, reflects the truth of reality. In several preceding sentences he affirms that poets do not misrepresent. Rather, fiction is a literary vehicle that conveys but covers truth. As a means to express a reality through literary ornamentation, poetry occupies a place in the arts distinct from grammar that stresses correctness of speech, and different from rhetoric that enables the orator to persuade. Although the poet employs the resources of the grammarian and the rhetorician, his task of perceiving and presenting "the truth of things" ("veritatem rerum") through a "veil of delightful fiction" ("velo amoenae fictionis") recalls the intermediary role of the ancient poet-seer who transmits to man divine insight in verse. Unlike Homer's unlettered bard, though, Petrarch's practicing poet, who invents, composes, and adorns a particular subject, is not an unconscious agent of the gods. Nevertheless, poetry, in spite of a fictional framework, enables the reader to discover truth. Thus, this seminal statement becomes a defense of an art that requires the use of allegory in its writing and interpretation.

According to Petrarch in *Familiares* 10.4, "poetry is not contrary to theology";[7] in fact, "theology is the poetry of God."[8] Truth, then, proceeds from God, thereby becoming the poet's object of imitation. In this frequently cited letter to his brother Gherardo, Petrarch demonstrates that the signified and the signifier sometimes diverge. For example, the single identity of Christ may emerge in discourse as a lion or lamb; and Christ employed narrative parables to describe the unfolding of divine purpose. According to Petrarch, Aristotle, too, sees the first theologians as poets who, as Varro, Suetonius, and Isidore affirm, praise the deities and describe the divine design. The *prisci theologi* are therefore poets who perceive and transmit the secrets of the heavens.[9] Conversely, Ambrose, Augustine, and Jerome are theologians who rely

---

[6] Francesco Petrarca, *Opera omnia*, 3 vols. (Basel: Henrichus Petrus, 1554), 1001. All page references to the *Seniles* correspond to this edition. The English translation is taken from Francis Petrarch, *Letters of Old Age*, trans. Aldo S. Bernardo, Saul Levin, and Reta A. Bernardo, 2 vols. (Baltimore, 1992), 2:455. Subsequent English translations from the *Seniles* will correspond to this edition.

[7] "theologie ... minime adversa poetica est": Francesco Petrarca, *Le Familiari*, ed. Vittorio Rossi, 4 vols., Edizione nazionale delle opere di Francesco Petrarca (Florence, 1933–1942), 2:301. All future volume and page references to the *Familiares* correspond to this edition. English translations from the *Familiares* correspond to those in *Letters on Familiar Matters*, trans. Aldo S. Bernardo, vol. 1 (Albany, 1975), vols. 2–3 (Baltimore, 1982 and 1985), here 2:455.

[8] "dicam theologiam poeticam esse de Deo," *Familiari*, 2:301; trans. Bernardo, 2:455.

[9] In his discussion of the *prisci theologi*, Petrarch was probably drawing upon two passages from Isidore of Seville, *Etymologiae*, ed. W. M. Lindsay, 2 vols. (Oxford, 1911), 1.39.11 and, especially, 8.7.1–3, where Isidore quotes from Suetonius's *De poetis*. See also Varro, who in his *De lingua latina*, ed. and trans. Roland G. Kent, 2 vols., Loeb Classical Library (Cambridge, MA, 1938), 7.36, briefly defines *vates*. See also Augustine, *De civitate Dei*, ed. and trans. Eva Matthews Sanford

upon the resources of language and rhythm to convey Christian doctrine. In both cases, the poet becomes a sort of seer who, as an intermediary between the spiritual and earthly, poeticizes a truth intelligible to man but often expressed by different modes of discourse.

Theological truth, then, becomes an appropriate topic of humanist verse. Through allusions to various ancient poet-seers (*Familiares* 24.12), and through analogies between Apollo and Christ (*Familiares* 10.4), Petrarch suggests the possibility of the poet's perception into the heavenly mysteries. Such visions are often divinely infused. In countering criticisms lodged against Nicola di Lorenzo, Petrarch refers, in *Familiares* 13.6, to Cicero's defense of the inspired poet Archias. Unfortunately, the truth revealed through inspired verse is often unappreciated, for Virgil was condemned for necromancy, and Petrarch himself recalls accusations of divination. The importance of divine inspiration, though, cannot be discounted. In *Seniles* 7.1 Petrarch does not specifically discuss poetic creativity. However, he does affirm man as an agent of God, for poets, like all human beings, respond to the call of their creator. In fact, as he stated in an earlier letter, Christian truth cannot be overlooked, and all literary works must conform to it (*Familiares* 6.2).

Poetic imitation may also derive from natural phenomena. In seeking an appropriate object of imitation, the poet may select images in his surroundings. However, such topics are frequently metaphors that conceal a truth and require interpretation. For example, on first reading, *Familiares* 9.4 appears to be a vituperation against lust. But the description of horses in heat reflects a higher meaning: the inconstancy of physical love. Sexual intercourse, Petrarch continues, may take the form of incest depicted in the relationship between Semiramis and her son. Again, a particular image conveys a more universal significance collected from earthly experiences. Vicissitudes exist in life, and images and legends become the material to depict suffering, delusion, and destruction. History also provides the material for the inventive process. In *Seniles* 2.1 Petrarch defends his portrayal of Mago in the *Africa* that, in turn, he borrowed from an incident included in Livy's account of the Second Punic War.[10] According to Petrarch, critics saw this account of the regrets of a dying man as an expression more Christian than pagan. Mago's recognition of his sins, though, is

---

and W. M. Green, 4 vols., Loeb Classical Library (Cambridge, MA, 1965), 18.14, and *De vera religione* 1.1–2, in PL 34. 121–123; Boccaccio, *Genealogie deorum gentilium libri*, ed. V. Romano (Bari, 1951), 14.8. For studies on the tradition, see especially D. P. Walker, *Spiritual and Demonic Magic: From Ficino to Campanella* (London, 1958), 18–24, and *The Ancient Theology* (London, 1972), chap. 1; Gerosa, *Umanesimo cristiano*, chap. 15; S. K. Heninger, Jr., *Touches of Sweet Harmony: Pythagorean Cosmology and Renaissance Poetics* (San Marino, CA, 1974), and idem, *Sidney and Spenser: The Poet as Maker* (University Park, PA, 1989), chaps. 2 and 3. Further, Petrarch alludes to these poets in his *Invectiva contra medicum*, in *Prose*, ed. G. Martellotti, P. G. Ricci, E. Carrara, and E. Bianchi (Milan, 1955), 674–677. However, in spite of their divine inspiration, their verse, according to Petrarch, lacks the validity of Christian poets'.

[10] *Africa* 6.885–918; Livy, *Ab urbe condita*, ed. and trans. B. O. Foster, F. G. Moore, E. T. Sage, and A. C. Schlesinger, 14 vols., Loeb Classical Library (Cambridge, MA, 1922–1959), 30.18.1–19.6. For a literary explication of this passage, see Gerosa, *Umanesimo cristiano*, 21–23.

hardly limited to a particular time, place, or creed. Historical fact is indeed an important touchstone; and the commonality of death, the awareness of human error, and the search for salvation are equally serious subjects for classical, biblical, and contemporary Christian writers. Both sensory perceptions and recorded happenings become therefore viable objects of poetic imitation that represent exemplary virtue (*Familiares* 6.4). Thus, as Petrarch deduces later in *Familiares* 9.4, poetry conforms to nature, thereby assuring that "nothing more natural can be imitated, nothing truer can be said" (*Familiares* 9.4).[11]

Mimesis also extends to literary texts. In an early letter, *Familiares* 1.8, Petrarch, like Horace and Seneca, sees invention as an eclectic process. Similar to bees that produce wax and honey from flowers, poets express in their own words the thoughts of earlier poets and philosophers.[12] Further, in a series of imaginary letters to past historians, rhetoricians, and poets (*Familiares* 24.2–12), he praises ancient learning and defends the reading of literature. By extension, the imitation of literary texts is valid, but it must also be limited in its application. His advice to Boccaccio in *Familiares* 23.19 seems especially pertinent. A poet, he notes, is not an ape. Rather, in appropriating another author's thoughts and language, the poet must refrain from slavish replication. In fact, originality appears to lie in a selection and an artistic mingling of effective images, genres, techniques, and tropes. The metaphor of the bees illustrates again the inventive process, for bees, like poets, do not gather flowers but construct honeycombs that reflect, through labor and blending, a single and better unity.

Invention, then, requires the identification of an appropriate object of imitation derived from natural phenomena, human experience, inspired vision, theological truth, or literary texts. Further, the poet serves as a seer who attains insight into the cosmic mysteries, but who conveys these visions to man in an intelligible, artistic form. A poetic process is therefore clearly implied, for the poet must discover and interpret the material of his proposed verse and, subsequently, accommodate his perceptions to the restrictions of accepted literary conventions. Nevertheless, any conversion of abstract thought to concrete expression raises questions that Petrarch anticipated but does not always fully answer in his letters.

A Poetic Process

As we have seen, Petrarch indicates that poetic practice is not a mindless replication of *sensibilia*. In fact, motivation prompts the poet to discover appropriate material. Like the unskilled bard who seems removed from social concerns, Petrarch's poet seeks in seclusion a contemplation that results in the finding of wisdom (*Familiares* 10.5). A disposition to create, moreover, extends to attitude. In lamenting the death of Tommaso Caloiro in *Familiares* 4.10, he notes the purgative powers of writ-

---

[11] "nichil fingi naturalius, nichil hoc verius dici posse": *Familiari*, 2:222; trans. Bernardo, 2:11.

[12] Horace, *Carmina*, ed. and trans. C. E. Bennett, Loeb Classical Library (Cambridge, MA, 1914), 4.2.27–32; Seneca, *Epistulae morales*, ed. and trans. Richard M. Gummere, 3 vols., Loeb Classical Library (Cambridge, MA, 1917), 84.3–10. See also Lucretius, *De rerum natura*, ed. and trans. Martin Ferguson Smith, Loeb Classical Library (Cambridge, MA, 1924), 3.9–11.

ing and, in *Familiares* 4.12, tells of the need to compose when sorrow and the regret of rejection oppress his mind. Petrarch does not directly relate the creative impuse to melancholy, thereby leaving it to later theorists to link creativity with a temperament previously described by Aristotle.[13] As he explains in *Familiares* 9.5, grief is alleviated by writing and, by extension, ends in an expression of eloquence. Writing is a labor but it stimulates and sustains a healthy mind, whereas pleasure characterizes a sick soul (*Seniles* 2.3).

Intentionality also affords the poet an opportunity to select a suitable subject. According to Petrarch, human intention motivates all human action (*Familiares* 19.12), and free will may end in pleasure or pain (*Familiares* 21.9). Certainly, his account of his ascent of Mont Ventoux (*Familiares* 4.1) attests metaphorically to the importance of the recognition of virtue and of the use of intention and effort to overcome earthly temptations to find eternal redemption. Petrarch returns to this theme throughout his letters (e.g., *Familiares* 7.17, 11.3, 12.16) and suggests its application to poetic creativity in *Familiares* 12.3. Adherence to grammatical rules, he observes, does not assure effective writing. As a human being, the poet confronts conflicts and must select one of two roads: earthly errors or spiritual satisfaction. Pythagoras and Virgil rejected the easier path of pleasure and, by respecting Nature as their guide, endured the narrow, thorny road that culminated in spiritual salvation (*Familiares* 12.3). In spite of Petrarch's numerous allusions to human errors and to the role of intention in the attainment of virtue and heavenly happiness, most of his thoughts on the relationship of human will and poetic creativity seem to be more directly recorded in his *De sui ipsius et multorum ignorantia liber*. As Trinkaus has demonstrated,[14] both Christian writers and rhetorical authors seek to identify and convey various aspects of wisdom. Writing, though, is not simply a description of virtue. Rather, the author, in striving to appreciate and actualize this ideal, assimilates its qualities and, through the use of words, incites the reader to love virtue and detest vice. As Petrarch views this thought in *Familiares* 3.1, redemption may not reside in poetry, but literature does become a means to attain salvation.

Thus poetic creativity is hardly an *ars mechanica*.[15] Although poetry results from the use of rhetorical resources, Petrarch advises aspiring poets, in the opening letter of the *Familiares*, to meditate on the subject to be conveyed. In spite of the significance of inspiration, Petrarch's practicing poet does not conform to the picture of

---

[13] Aristotle, *Problems I–XXXVIII*, ed. and trans. H. Rackham and W. S. Hett, 2 vols., Loeb Classical Library (Cambridge, MA, 1937), 954a20. For the origins and tradition of this idea, see Raymond Klibansky, Erwin Panofsky, and Fritz Saxl, *Saturn and Melancholy: Studies in the History of Natural Philosophy, Religion, and Art* (London, 1964).

[14] Trinkaus, *The Poet as Philosopher*, 107–112. See also Foster, *Petrarch: Poet and Humanist*, 149–150.

[15] Petrarch elaborates upon this idea in his *Invectiva contra medicum*. For an analysis of his view of the place of poetry within the sciences, see Greenfield, "Studies," 76–77. Foster, *Petrarch: Poet and Humanist*, 144–145, notes that Petrarch does not see himself as a passive agent of the gods, and that, although his poetry originates in the reading of Holy Scripture, it is not divinely inspired verse. Rather, it records a human wisdom consistent with divine truth.

Homer's blind poet or the Venerable Bede's account of the unskilled shepherd-bard Caedmon. A practicing poet may appear mad, but, in reality, he must consciously determine and select a moral quality to be expressed (*Seniles* 5.5). Thus he does not copy randomly collected sense-impressions; for, in his employment of reason that is required in the inventive process, the writer determines consciously and morally the subject to be interpreted and expressed.[16] Eloquence, though, complements wisdom (*Familiares* 21.10), and the poet must exercise a similar judgment in his use of appropriate forms. In *Seniles* 2.3, Petrarch alludes to Augustine's thoughts on art as "the memory of things experienced and enjoyed."[17] But the poet must also appreciate the significance of effective craftsmanship, for, "if experience really makes art, then practice begets, nourishes, and makes art perfect" (*Seniles* 2.3).[18]

The Place and Purpose of Poetry

Philosophy and eloquence are therefore interdependent (*Familiares* 1.9; *Seniles* 3.1); and, just as the poet may discover his object of imitation in literary texts, the writing of verse complies with the rhetorical process of talent, skill, and practice (*Familiares* 6.7). Petrarch does not seem to refer directly in his letters to the imitation of classical genres, but he does praise, in *Familiares* 24.4, Cicero and Virgil for their writing skills in prose and poetry respectively. Further, in two frequently cited letters, *Familiares* 10.4 and *Seniles* 4.5, he refers to his adoption of pastoral and epic forms in the writing of the *Bucolicum carmen* 1 and the *Africa*. Substance, though, seems to take precedence over style, and eloquence becomes the means to convey a moral message. Cicero and Virgil deserve admiration, but the psalmist David is the greatest poet for the beauty of his poetry's simplicity and the learning of its purity (*Familiares* 22.10).

In spite of the importance of substance, Petrarch affirms the essential role of form that provides a fiction to cover and convey a moral message.[19] Fables, such as Apollo's rape of Daphne, transmit truth (*Familiares* 11.6) that describes the violence and pain caused by passion. Similarly, he defines his *Bucolicum carmen* 1 as a didactic poem that contrasts the virtuous shepherd Monicus with his pleasure-seeking companion

---

[16] Grahame Castor, *Pléiade Poetics: A Study in Sixteenth Century Thought and Terminology* (Cambridge, 1964), chap. 12, describes a similar process employed by poets in sixteenth-century France.

[17] "artem rerum expertarum, placitarumque memoriam diffinivit": *Seniles*, 841; trans. Bernardo et al., 1:63.

[18] "Experientia siquidem artem facit, usus autem artem gignit, nutrit, ac perficit": *Seniles*, 841; trans. Bernardo et al., 1:62.

[19] Besides the letters, Petrarch emphasizes in his *Africa* the significance of allegory. The source of the poet's inspiration, he notes, lies in human experience, history, and nature (9.97–100), but the material is concealed by a veil of fiction (9.100–101). The reader, in turn, must make an effort to understand a message that will lead to his satisfaction (9.95–97). For a discussion of this passage, see Bernardo, *Petrarch, Scipio, and the "Africa,"* 264, as well as his analysis of Petrarch's use of allegorization throughout this study. Similarly, in the *Invectiva contra medicum*, ed. Martellotti et al., 669–670, Petrarch underscores the significance of literal and figurative interpretations, stressing the work of the poet as one of allegorizing fiction. See Greenfield, "Studies," 81. For Petrarch's use of allegory in his *Africa* and *Eclogues*, see Gerosa, *Umanesimo cristiano*, 318–319 and 321–323; Kallendorf, *In Praise of Aeneas*, 21–22; and Boyle, *Petrarch's Genius*, chaps. 2 and 3.

Silvius.[20] As he explains the narrative meanings of this poem in *Familiares* 10.4, the name Monicus evokes the image of a single eye that enables him to follow a path of moral rectitude. However, Silvius, as a denizen of the woods, wanders and enjoys his surroundings. The name and narrative, then, present a picture of the human situation that promises redemption for Monicus and condemnation for Silvius. Similarly, Petrarch describes, in *Seniles* 4.5, Virgil's *Aeneid* as a story that, through a series of allegories, depicts the journey of a perfect man. Through an analysis of two scenes, the burning of Troy and Dido's banquet, he sees the success of the hero's journey as a result of the use of reason over passion and a culmination of the triumph of virtue over vice.

As Petrarch remarks in the concluding book of his *Africa*, a sweet and varied structure (9.126–127) veils the foundation of truth. Poets, then, neither misrepresent nor mislead. In fact, at the beginning of *Seniles* 4.5, he defends Virgil's art, for the stories in the *Aeneid* are "gems wrapped in a napkin."[21] Military leaders may need neither philosophy nor poetry, but literature does inform and instruct (*Seniles* 4.4). And, if Mago in Livy's history and in Petrarch's *Africa* is pagan, his death shares characteristics of the repentant Christian *(Seniles* 2.1). Critics may attack (*Seniles* 2.1), but poetry advances knowledge and instills virtue (*Seniles* 1.5). Thus the reader, in removing the mantle of fiction, discovers a truth that becomes even more welcome after a difficult quest (*Seniles* 12.2).

In his creation of fiction, though, the poet is not a plagiarist. Through reading and study, he ruminates upon ideas, structures, and styles employed by ancient, biblical, and Christian authors. Tradition and originality coexist, for he must accommodate a particular perspective to established form. Virgil, then, was hardly a slavish imitator: in fact, he deserves a defense of his veneration for the past and of his individual voice that resonates in the present (*Familiares* 4.7). As Petrarch indicates in an early letter, *Familiares* 1.8, the poet's aim is to express in one's own thought and speech ideas borrowed and reworked from others. This shaping of present perspective to accepted form also implies the transcendent nature of poetry. In his final letter, *Seniles* 18.1, Petrarch reviews various stages of human development, and he sees the commingling of past and present perspectives as a fusion into a future vision to be appreciated by posterity. Likewise, creativity requires a knowledge of experience and poetic precedents that, adjusted to contemporary contexts, become through allegorization a reflection of eternal truth.

Conclusion

For Petrarch, then, the individual expression of poetry affords an insight into a universal wisdom that transcends time and place. Like the Lord's face depicted on Veronica's veil or on church walls (*Familiares* 9.13), poetic-philosophic themes culled

---

[20] For analyses of this poem, see Aldo S. Bernardo, "Petrarch's Attitude toward Dante," *Publications of the Modern Language Association* 70 (1955): 500–517; Gerosa, *Umanesimo cristiano*, 318–319; Kallendorf, *In Praise of Aeneas*, 19–22; and Boyle, *Petrarch's Genius*, 13–15 and 26.

[21] "gemmas lintheo obvolutas": *Seniles*, 868; trans. Bernardo et al., 1:139.

from scripture, theology, human experience, literary texts, or inspired vision provide the material to be selected and imitated in poetry. As an intermediary who fashions eternal truths to temporal forms, Petrarch's poet recalls characteristics of the poet-*vates*. However, he is not a passive agent of the gods, for, in serving as such a mediator, he recognizes the significance of study that enables him to convey a moral message intelligibly and eloquently. Unlike the physician attacked in the *Invectiva contra medicum*, though, the poet does not practice a scholastic science based upon syllogism and style; in expressing a wisdom in artistic form, he adheres to a rhetorical process that requires the successive steps of invention, disposition, and expression. Thus he reconciles the philosopher's search for truth and the rhetor's exercise of art, employing reason in his search for appropriate material, and expressing a wisdom beneficial to society. Although later theorists will borrow ideas of faculty psychology to elaborate on the use of judgment in the poetic process,[22] Petrarch affirms the role of study and thought in the creation of a text that illustrates and instructs a moral meaning. Allegorization becomes one of the means to attain this end. Thus his definition of the poet also suggests a defense of a craft that teaches a truth through a fiction created from the resources of talent and artifice. At the end of his *Familiares* (24.13), he describes his letters as trifles that weave together many things in a variety of styles.[23] In spite of the statements on poetic creativity scattered throughout the letters, Petrarch does depict and defend the poet-humanist as a seer and shaper of truth who, like Homer, conceals "with a splendid and transparent veil a very beautiful philosophy" (*Familiares* 24.12).[24]

Ball State University

---

[22] See, in particular, Murray Wright Bundy, *The Theory of Imagination in Classical and Mediaeval Thought*, University of Illinois Studies in Language and Literature 12 (Urbana, 1928), 179–198, 225, 230, 265; Castor, *Pléiade Poetics*, chap. 14.

[23] "librum e meis nugis multa rerum ac verborum imparitate contextum": *Familiari*, 4:264.

[24] Trans. Bernardo, 3:347, of the following passage: "pulcerrimam philosophiam ornatissimo ac tenuissimo velo," *Familiari*, 4:260.

Philosophy and Pedagogy in the Rhetoric of Giambattista Vico's De nostri temporis studiorum ratione *(1709)*

ROBERT GINSBERG

Giambattista Vico's service as Professor of Rhetoric at the University of Naples included an annual address composed in Latin at the opening of the academic year. The seventh such oration, *De nostri temporis studiorum ratione*, had the special conditions of being delivered, in 1708, in the presence of the Vice-Regent and the Cardinal, with the intention of being published by the university, which publication occurred the following year.[1] The oration is the first major statement of Vico's innovative and imaginative system of philosophy. It contains keys to most of the works of Vico to come. It is a world-class contribution to the philosophy of education; we may learn from it in our struggles with students and academic institutions. And it is a remarkable oratorical performance in the high spirit of humanism.

I propose to examine the educational core of Vico's vision and the highlights of his philosophical thought, especially as the oration fulfills his mission in teaching the students before him. Higher education and the pursuit of advanced scholarship are not matters of simply transmitting. They require participation. The heart of the art of teaching consists in its effective activation of the imagination and intellect of the learner. To awaken the scholar's full powers of mind and heart is to win over the person. To educate in this sense is to persuade. Not so much doctrinal as directional, the teaching draws the student onto the path of self-development. While much of our work as scholars takes the form of academic exercises, such as papers presented

---

[1] Giambattista Vico, "De nostri temporis studiorum ratione" (1709), in *Opere*, ed. Benedetto Croce, Giovanni Gentile, and Fausto Nicolini, 8 pts. (Bari: 1914–1941), pt. 1, *Le Orazione inaugurali*, ed. Giovanni Gentile and Fausto Nicolini. I will be citing the English translation, with page numbers identified parenthetically, by Elio Gianturco, *On the Study Methods of Our Time* (Ithaca, NY, 1990), with preface by Donald Phillip Verene.

at congresses and articles published in specialized journals and proceedings, our hope is that someday, somehow, our work will move the heart of someone.

Vico's discourse is built around the celebrated topic of the quarrel of the ancients and moderns. Every student at a European university heard about this, and every great figure of letters throughout the eighteenth century said something about it. In its present form, this recurrent theme is being debated by our universities in curricular terms of a return to the great books versus an expansion of contemporary interests. Vico greets the students at a formal occasion with an orientation to academic studies. Gianturco's rendition of the title as "On the Study Methods of Our Time" has been judiciously corrected by Donald Phillip Verene as "The Method of Studies." We can understand Vico as introducing students to "The Plan of Our Curriculum."

The comparative study of ancients and moderns as to their method of studies has direct practical value to the student in expanding knowledge. Learn more than the ancients, admonishes Vico, but recognize the limits of their — and our — ways of study (5). Vico has opened his consideration on the cautionary note that knowledge is limited because of human imperfection. A wise piece of instruction to the assembly of students at the beginning of their academic year! How we are to deal with the obstacles to learning draws the learners into the inquiry. Vico does not hold in suspension the resolution of the quarrel. He gives his answer at the outset (6): the moderns are more knowledgeable than the ancients. So he is not primarily engaged in debating the merits of ancients versus moderns; instead, he is using their differences as an organizational theme for his critique of modern education.

The problem is not only to recognize the merit of current pursuits of knowledge but to overcome their obstacles as well. We have to learn about learning. Vico is offering a learned approach to that task. Knowing how we may know helps us to know more and to know better. Vico is bringing to awareness self-consciousness about knowledge; thereby he shows the student's responsibility for higher education. The student is not a recipient of education but a seeker. How different this is from the vision of the student as an empty head, knowledge as a pile of subject matter, and the professor as a big shovel.

Vico draws the distinction (6) between new subject matters and new ways of study. His interest is how we are to study, involving three components: instruments, aids, and aims. Instruments are prerequisite disciplines, such as mathematics as presupposed by physics. These new methods of study have led to dazzling discoveries in modern times, ranging from physics and chemistry to pharmacology, medicine, and anatomy, and on to astronomy, geography, and even military science. In a couple of pages, Vico introduces the student to the exciting range of advances in knowledge, including those due to the microscope, telescope, and mariner's compass. A great part of the oration then consists of in-depth critical discussion of each of the fields of study. Something is bound to interest every student in one or another of the fields paraded, and the point of the presentation is not lost if, while some fields are discussed, the student should fall asleep. This is a model for lecturing which many of my colleagues have learned to follow.

Aids to learning include cultural conditions. Vico signals the invention of the printing press as the opening of "a multiple, diversified, almost boundless domain of culture" to scholars. Universities too are are institutions that aid modern learning: "the repositories of all our sciences and arts ... where the intellectual, spiritual, and linguistic abilities of men may be brought to perfection" (12). The door has been opened to the student by the university and by books to complete self-development as a human being. Vico's eloquent way of putting it inspires the student to relish the intimate connection between learning and becoming cultured. This is what you are here for, intimates the professor, and this is what we as a university exist for.

The explicit structure of the oration is a model of effective organization:

> Statement of the theme
> Its relevance to the audience
> Goal of the speaker
> Tripartite division of the approach
> Reminders (for the inattentive student) of the three prongs of the attack
> Examination of each field
> Summary
> Closing disclaimers
> Farewell.

This is the outer shell of convention. But we must look to the inner principles of persuasive organization.

In concentrating on methodology, Vico confronts the contributions of both Bacon and Descartes. The Lord Chancellor is mentioned from the first sentence, but strangely enough, Descartes's name is absent, although this is a powerful critique of Cartesianism. Vico takes a stand against Descartes's exclusion of probabilistic knowledge as lacking the sought-after certainty. Instead, "common sense arises from perceptions based on verisimilitude" (13). Whereas Descartes was seeking the perfect foundation upon which to construct all knowledge, Vico is attentive to the educational development of young people. We might say that Vico approves the pragmatic value of probability in the growth of individuals, whereas Descartes rejected it as a candidate for indubitable truth. Vico is considering the practice of pedagogy; Descartes was considering the foundations of epistemology. Descartes cooks up the hard-boiled ego; Vico prepares the ego omelette. In 1710, Vico was to tackle Descartes head-on in a critical monograph, "De Antiquissima Italorum Sapientia."

The rhetoric professor makes the case (13) that the practice of eloquence depends on common sense. He cautions against the "danger that instruction in advanced philosophical criticism may lead to an abnormal growth of abstract intellectualism, and render young people unfit for the practice of eloquence" (13). I have often seen a rigorous philosophical training, especially in symbolic logic and language analysis, for which Cambridge University must take much credit, lead to disaster for students as they turned to practical life where effective communication is required. Vico, in effect, is defending his students against the injudicious application of method. He praises the distinctive power of the young people's imagination. Imagination is to become the backbone of Vico's masterpiece, the *New Science*, first published in 1725.

Vico, the teacher, offers a nice mixture of caution and encouragement as the fuel of education. He has been establishing his character as sympathetic and learned. His persuasive presence creates that good rapport between teacher and student that facilitates the pleasure of learning. This is more than the authority of the orator. He explains, "in the art of oratory the relationship between speaker and listener is of the essence" (15). I imagine that at this point Vico is in eye-contact as well as ear-contact with his listeners. He has recognized the Aristotelian grounding of rhetoric in the audience.

Vico offers this educational plan: (1) First strengthen the common sense of the young. This will have good effect in character and speech. (2) Next strengthen their imagination and memory, which will give them access to the imaginative arts and law. The first two stages give credit for what students bring to the university; they will not lose these treasures which are to be fortified. (3) Then teach them philosophical criticism whereby they can be good judges of their own education. The critique comes in only when the student is ready for it. The educated person becomes responsible for the education of that person. Instead of dismantling access at the start of knowledge, the critical method comes into the life of the educated person as self-critical examination. The best of modern critique is conjoined to the best of ancient practice.

For students to hear that they are to become judges of their own education must be exciting, especially when Vico magnificently sums up their prospective accomplishments: "Were this done, young students . . . would become exact in science, clever in practical matters, fluent in eloquence, imaginative in understanding poetry or painting, and strong in memorizing what they have learned in their legal studies" (19). They will also get well-paying jobs, he might have added.

Vico's principal criticism of Cartesianism is its insistence on deductive method applied to fields, such as physics, where only probabilities arise (22–23). Vico introduces the image of a splendid house into which physics moves (21), though the foundations may be faulty (22). This may be an allusion to Descartes's image of demolition and construction from fresh foundations. But the habit of mind inculcated by deduction inhibits the development of "the student's specifically philosophic faculty": the power to detect analogies in what appear as disparate. This power expresses itself in metaphor, which is "the greatest and brightest ornament of forceful, distinguished speech" (24).

In my academic experience, I have observed that Vico's aesthetic critique of the deductive mind-set was borne out by the excessive training of the mind in symbolic logic that stifles the imagination. In the search for the deductive connections, the student, and the teacher, missed the big connections. Vico is correct that the narrow deductive training of the mind leads to weakness in expression. A lifeless, literal prosody still affects American philosophic writing to keep it from serving as a branch of letters. It is infected by a dry-rot of discourse.

Vico returns to his professorial specialty of eloquence (24–25). In the midst of a discussion of physics and geometry, he manages to defend eloquence in an eloquent passage with a flourish of several parallel tasks for the orator facing an uncultured audience. The diverse efforts are to be topped by concentration on a point to be taken home in the soul of the listener. Vico has been practicing what he preaches, though with an audience becoming cultured. He has made the students feel the point. This is just what he next says the orator must do (25). Participation in the thinking and its subsequent emotive development brings pleasure to the listener. The oration frequently turns the question of the best approach to studies into what is best for oratorical skill.

Even in the practice of medicine, Vico, joining Bacon, warns against the prevalence of deductive thinking. Medical judgment is probabilistic because it is centered on the changing particularity (32). "Nor am I," he asserts, "at the present moment, the same individual I was but a minute ago while talking of the sick: countless life-instants have already passed by" (32), one of the most startling things that any student might hear from a professor and one of the most troubling insights of modern thought. Vico at this point is talking about his talking: the temporality of discursive performance. But he is also talking about the existential identity that may change with each moment. This obliges the listener to reflect critically upon this speech-making and ponder how it reflects upon itself. If the speaker is confessedly self-conscious about the speech, then the listener may open the portal of self-consciousness about the listener's role in the speech-transaction. And the listener is thrown into doubt about the continuity of the listener's own identity. Who am I? is the unspoken question which Vico gets the student to raise—an unsettling experience, but it is cushioned about midway in the oration so that the student will calm down and sit through the rest.

In any case, Vico has spoken only of himself as changing each moment. He takes on the burden of this shocking condition for his listeners. They are both sharers in his predicament and separated from it, participants and observers. Vico has sown the seed of reflection whereby the student may ask, How am I different at this point in the lecture? How will be I different after it? What will I become during my education?

Vico is not making the commonplace observation that we change with time so that in senior years we are not quite who we were in youth. That would be an easily accepted observation by the young students listening to the forty-year-old professor. Instead, he claims that he is a different person from minute to minute. This is not the process of aging but the process of being. Between who I am as now writing and who I was a moment ago, innumerable moments have intervened at which I may have been different persons. At each moment of my life, I address my life anew. Not that I am becoming someone through stages, arriving at my true self. I become myself at every stage. Or better, each moment, rather than a becoming, is my being. I am who I am when I am each moment.

We have here the germ of a wonderful philosophy of the moment. The moment is not a mere momentary interval between stages of selfhood. The moment is the dwelling ground of my selfhood. I exist only in the moment. If I could realize the fullness of my moments of life that would be the momentous fulfillment of my life. But innumerable life-instants arise for me in which to renew my existence. Yet they are not endless, as Vico soberly remarks, for they all lead to death. I am a momentary being, passing away.

"But the great drawback of our educational methods," asserts Vico, "is that we pay an excessive amount of attention to the natural sciences and not enough to ethics" (33). This complaint echoed throughout the academic halls during the second half of the twentieth century. Because scientific knowledge of nature is more precise, we mistakenly rank it higher than efforts to understand human nature. The human phenomena, unlike natural phenomena, are subject to freedom of the will. The result is that human-centered subjects, especially politics, are neglected in the education of the young. This hinders their life in society, including speechmaking.

Notice how Vico in an orientation lecture to university studies is a vigorous critic of the shortcomings of education. Like all good faculty members, he offers this criticism with the aim of improving the curriculum. He is instructing the students — and his colleagues — that the university as cultural institution ought to change in order to advance knowledge. As a dispenser of knowledge, the university has an obligation to study the historical context of knowledge-seeking. It must be critical of present-day views of methodology as well as of old ones. It must seek out the weaknesses in education as well as its strengths. The university, as Vico is representing it, is a self-corrective culture of discovery. It advances its aims, and it conducts its revision, by means of discourse. The university, I would say, is not a given structure that tells us how we are to teach and learn, but a dialogue that we begin afresh as we arrive each day. The university is a self-discovering process.

In the course of illustrating how prudence may be garnered from judicious observation of cases taken from drama, Vico introduces the only humorous touch in the work, something sure to be appreciated by the young men who are his audience. He quotes a passage from Terence (37) about how the figures of virgin girls are shaped by their mothers (*Eunuchus* 313–314). The transition is between constriction of the mind that interfered with eloquence and constriction of the body, but the effect is a burst of humor following upon a burst of eloquence. The laugh, as usual in universities, is on the young women, though the passage is a striking description of the roots of anorexia nervosa.

Vico takes an unexpected turn to analyze the French language, which he finds more suitable for abstract reasoning than for "stately prose [or] for sublime verse" (40). He follows the view that the language we speak shapes how we think, not the reverse. What does this excursion into cultural linguistics have to do with the central theme? Because of the proclivities of their language, the French are credited, if not accused, of inventing the very method of philosophical criticism and deduction that has been opposed in this oration. In contrast, Italian is a dynamic language that evokes images and makes metaphorical connections (40–41). Vico stirs up his hearers' patriotic and linguistic pride by parading the names of Guicciardini, Boccaccio, Petrarch, Ariosto, and Tasso, who are compared favorably to both Greek and Roman writers. The passage calls for much expansion and substantiation by Vico, especially when he equates Tasso's verse to that of Virgil's.

But let us look at Vico's style in the passage. He lauds six modes of style in which five Italians are related to eight ancients. The passage culminates with a rhetorical question: "Shall we then not cultivate a language possessing such felicitous qualities?" You can hear with your reader's ear the sub rosa "sì!" expressed by the sea of Italian youth. We forget that this quintessential Italian experience is evoked by Vico's rhetorical skill *in Latin*. It is as if Vico has made his Latin speak Italian so that the listener to his Latin hears Italian, and later the reader of his Latin will hear Italian. Yet, for a long time, Vico did not practice what he preached. He continued to write in the academic language of Latin until he published the initial version of the *New Science*, his first work of substance in Italian, sixteen years later.

The worst part of the oration, from the point of the student-listener's ear, is an excessively long account of the history of law, given in section xi (47–58). Vico displays his broad knowledge of the cultural function of law in different epochs. This will be developed later in the cultural history of his *New Science* and the legal accounts of his *Universal Right*.[2] But on the present occasion, his listeners likely fell into a much-needed doze. In fairness to Vico, we must recognize that the printed version of the oration was likely padded with things that were not spoken. We all know that the publication of a paper is a different kind of academic exercise than its presentation. In the case of the former, we stuff it to the extent allowed by the page limit. I have been taking a risk in analyzing Vico's rhetorical performance as if the book were the speech.

As to the favored discipline of eloquence, Vico is showing its diminished role in the legal realm. Vico makes a great effort to wake up his hearers by a startling string of appositions that take the form, "In the past, law was . . . ; Today, law is . . ." (58–59). Twelve of these pithy comparisons are made. While the student may have lost interest in the ancient practices, interest is awakened by driving home the point about what is done today. Vico redeems his historical account by this pointed timeliness. A professional editor would have asked him to cut half the legal material from the printed version, or else build it up into a separate volume. The discussion is studded with technical terms, references to authors and schools of jurists, and fine points of social and political order. But Vico is sifting through all this rich substance to offer guidelines for pursuing present-day studies in law. A curricular tie in part justifies its inclusion, for at the university the study of eloquence is prerequisite to the study of law. Yet the disproportionateness and detail of the legal matter make us wonder if Vico is trying to convince parties other than the students of his expertise in law. He was later to throw himself into the competition for the chair of law at Naples, though with heartbreaking disappointment.

In the oddest turn in this academic welcoming speech, Vico arrives, a few pages before closing, at the failure of the university. He calls upon the professors to reform the curriculum with a unity in harmony with religion and the state.

Throughout the entirety of my academic career, I have heard calls for reforming a curriculum that offers only pieces for higher education while neglecting the education of the whole person. The method of studies in our universities is to fragment rather than integrate knowledge, to advance learning in disparate disciplines at the expense of developing the responsibility and wisdom of the student who is at the center of learning. While we are gifted with a multiplicity of methods exercised in many fields by scholars of considerable talent, the members of our faculties do not make sufficient effort to work together as teacher-scholars. They are not members of

---

[2] See Giambattista Vico, *Universal Right*, trans. Giorgio Pinton and Margaret Diehl (Amsterdam and Atlanta, 2000).

a Republic of Letters even within the walls of one university. Each of us is tyrant over a speciality. No one can presume to teach the teachers.

After this extensive introduction to the academic values offered by the university to its students, Vico throws such values in doubt by warning students that here their education may be "warped and perverted" (77). How can the students protect themselves against the very education they are on hand to receive? They must trust their professors. Yet therein lies the danger. This is the most sobering lesson taught by Vico in introducing all the fields of higher education to the student body: the university as the modern institution which makes such study possible is deficient. In its present organization of studies, it may harm students as much as benefit them. Revision of the institution is the professional responsibility of faculty members. Vico is taking this student-centered public occasion to exercise his responsibility as faculty member in making the case to his colleagues for change.

This right to criticize the university as an educational institution is integral to academic freedom. Such freedom has been too narrowly defined as the right of a faculty member to speak out on matters in that expert's field. But the university as a whole is every faculty member's field. In the interests of our student body, we may be obliged to speak against the structure, procedure, and spirit of our academic institution.

While Vico's colleagues might not have savored this critical turn, the students should have learned something about academic life of which Vico's performance is a taste. The paradox in which they are being encouraged to learn in an institution that nonetheless disserves their learning teaches them to open their minds. They have to learn about the shortcomings of their education. They thereby will take responsibility for their education. They will take away from this speech a critical openness to the many days of learning ahead.

Drawing to a conclusion, Vico calls the attention of listeners to his practice: "As you saw" (79). He praises "the intelligence of this assembly of listeners, every member of which knows how to reason with his own head and is fully conscious of his right to judge any author as he thinks best" (79). Such affirmation of the right and ability of the audience to judge is the fundamental principle of higher education.

Vico has pursued this inquiry into what we may learn by turning a critical eye on how we know. In the spirit befitting the academic occasion, he makes an eloquent case for the abundance of knowledge accessible to the human understanding. We may develop our natural faculties in order to seek further knowledge. A fine justification for university education! But we must also come to know the defects of our knowing, including the deficiency of the university.

Vico exercises the art of rhetoric in the act of discussing it. He exemplifies educational method and is engaged in educating in his discussion of education. In this Neo-Latin performance, he is winning over his listeners — and subsequently his readers — by what he is doing and by what he embodies, as well as by what he is arguing. This pedagogical, rhetorical, academic, stylistic, and philosophical tour de force is as winning at the beginning of the twenty-first century as it was at the beginning of the eighteenth.

The Pennsylvania State University

Orationes *concerning Letters at the University of Valencia in the Sixteenth Century*[1]

FERRAN GRAU CODINA

Let me introduce this paper with some words from the article "The Unity of Western Education" by J. W. Headlam, once Fellow of King's College Cambridge, published in 1915. This article is included in the book entitled *The Unity of Western Civilization*, edited by F. S. Marvin.[2]

> The School goes back to the very origin of our civilization; if we are to understand its nature, we must transfer ourselves in thought to those early days when the first missionaries planted in the Somerset valleys and on the stern Northumberland coast the Cross of Christ. (. . .) Wherever they came, among their first duties was to found schools in which to train men who would succeed them. (. . .) It was by the school that the boys were initiated into the common system of Western Christendom, and were made citizens of the greater world, the centre of which was in Rome.[3]

Headlam outlines the history — the unitary history — of western education, or as I would call it, instruction. Some pages later, Headlam says:

---

[1] This paper has been assisted by the research project "Estudios de textos latinos humanísticos de autores valencianos de los s. XVI al XVIII. Relevancia de los mismos en el contexto europeo" (PB 97–1389 Ministerio de Educación y Cultura). My thanks to David Martínez Matallín, Laura Ulzurrun de Asanza, and Paul Hamill for their revision of this text.
[2] J. W. Headlam, "The Unity of Western Education," in F. S. Marvin, ed., *The Unity of Western Civilization* (Oxford, 1915), 180–197.
[3] Headlam, "Unity of Western Education," 181–82.

That institution that was for so long the home of European unity has become the most useful agent for the perpetuation and exaggeration of national differences.... The national culture and national authors have at length forced their way into the schools, and the result has been that institutions which originally in reality, and for so long in appearance, were the vehicles for the expression of the common European civilization, have been almost entirely won over to the cause of the national expression.[4]

Finally, Headlam poses the question: "Is the older union of thought to be permanently lost?" The provisional answer is not an optimistic one, because he does not believe in "a spiritual and intellectual unity of the nations established on the basis of scientific education."[5] Why? Because "now in education it is the technical side of scientific progress which almost inevitably becomes most prominent, and the greater the advance in knowledge the more will this be true."[6] "None the less, a unity there is, but it is a deeper unity than this. It is the unity inherited from the past. Here we may find, not indeed a superficial uniformity, but a real unity of life and spirit."[7]

That article was published together with others on different aspects of unity, at a time, it must not be forgotten, of deep crisis in Europe early in the Great War.

In 1942, T. S. Eliot delivered a lecture as the Presidential Address at the meeting of the Classical Association at Cambridge on 15 April.[8] He argued that the study of Greek and Roman civilizations and languages was of a different nature for native Europeans from, for instance, that of Chinese antiquity or Egyptology. His point is that "a great literature is more than the sum of a number of great writers" and that "the continuity of a literature is essential to its greatness." European literature, even though made up of different national literatures, makes a related whole.[9] To understand a part, it is necessary to know the whole. The ideas of community and continuity are the basis of his argumentation. These ideas were also presented in the middle of an even deeper crisis in Europe, when his words seemed to be refuted by total war.

Against this background I would like to set in contrast our present-day world (different, of course, from that of Headlam and Eliot but still shaped by a national, that is, a partial education) and our own past.

Res publica litterarum implies unity of instruction in Europe. Different and diverse languages and nations were integrated in the past mainly by religion and education. So *Res publica litterarum* implies the function of school or university. But that expression, as well as *Res publica Christiana,* has a special connotation.

---

[4] Headlam, "The Unity of Western Education," 192.
[5] Headlam, "The Unity of Western Education," 193.
[6] Headlam, "The Unity of Western Education," 194.
[7] Headlam, "The Unity of Western Education," 197.
[8] T. S. Eliot, "The Classics and the Man of Letters," Presidential Address to the Classical Association on 15 April 1942, in *To Criticise the Critic and Other Writings* (London, 1965), 145–61.
[9] Eliot, "The Classics and the Man of Letters," 147, 150.

Res publica Christiana means the Church, but implies the community of Christians, who are citizens of such a spiritual republic. Res publica litterarum means a community of letters, that is, a community of disciplines (*universitas studiorum*) and a community of professors, students, and civil or ecclesiastical authorities who have to look after that community. The history of such expressions, although interesting, is not the subject of this paper, but is implied in the contents of orations delivered in the University of Valencia in the sixteenth century.

The orations in defence of letters in Spain have been studied by J. Fr. Alcina,[10] who has suggested that they owe a debt to both Erasmus of Rotterdam and the Italian philological humanism of the late *Quattrocento*, the latter represented mainly by Angelo Poliziano, and brought into Spain by Antonio de Nebrija, and implanted in Valencia by disciples of Nebrija such as Juan Andrés Estrany, Cosme Damián Savalls, or Miguel Jerónimo Ledesma, or other humanists like Francisco Decio, or physicians like Pedro Jaime Esteve.

All the orations share and make use of the commonplaces of humanism, but they also have peculiar features that throw light on the particular context of Valencia (or so I think); they also deal with recurrent topics through which we can catch a glimpse of the political and academic life of Valencia. The orations examined here are: (1) Cosme Damián Savalls' *Oratio paraenetica de optimo statu reipublicae literariae constituendo, Valentiae habita ad patres iuratos, senatumque Valentinum tum publicum, tum literarium mense octobri 1531* (St. Luke's Day being the course opening day); (2) Franciscus Decius's *De re literaria asserenda oratio ad Patres Iuratos Senatumque literarium Lucalibus ipsis publice habita Valentiae anno 1534* (published in 1535); (3) Franciscus Decius's *De scientiarum et academiae Valentinae laudibus, ad Patres Iuratos Senatumque literarium oratio, per Onofrium Clementem discipulum non poenitendum, publice habita. Anno 1547.* I shall also mention the dedicatory epistles written by Pedro Jaime Esteve and Miguel Jerónimo Ledesma.[11]

The three orations are exhortatory in character and have a similar structure and arrangement of subjects, and the same addressees: the *Iurati* of Valencia (city authorities), university professors, and students. Their exhortatory character lies in the fact that the orator reminds the addressees of their duties in so far as they are involved in the achievements of the University and are responsible for its members working at their best. Each part of the body depends on the others. Despite these similarities, the orations differ in tone, intensity, and the degree of bitterness and even virulence with which the audience is appealed to. Let us see now the main features of each oration.

The *Oratio paraenetica de optimo statu reipublicae literariae constituendo* has been studied by H. Rausell in her doctoral thesis in order to establish the Erasmianism of its author

---

[10] J. Fr. Alcina, "Poliziano y los elogios de las letras en España (1500–1540)," *Humanistica Lovaniensia* 25 (1976): 198–222.

[11] *Hippocratis Coi medicorum omnium principis Epidemiων liber secundus a Petro Iacobo Steve medico Latinitati donatus, et fusissimis commentariis illustratus, adiecta et singulis sententiis Graeca ueritate, quo facilius diligens lector quanta sit seruata fides intelligere possit* (Valentia, apud Ioannem Mey Flandrum, 1551) (B.N.M. /R. 26874); *GRAECARVM Institutionum compendium a Michaële Hieronymo Ledesma Valentino medico conscriptum* (Valentiae, excudebat Ioannes Mey, 1545) (B.N.M. /R.19072).

(Savalls).¹² So Rausell says that the sources of the *oratio* are a vernacular letter that Vives addressed to the *Iurati*, which Savalls states he has translated into Latin, and Erasmus's *De pueris statim ac liberaliter instituendis*. In the oration we find also highly favourable words relating to Erasmus, Vives, and other humanists such as G. Budé, Rudolf Agricola, Hermolao Barbaro, Poliziano, Pico della Mirandola, and, of course, Antonio de Nebrija, to whom he devotes great praise, and Andrés Estrany. Rausell is right, but we find the same kind of ideas in many other treatises, and as a matter of fact they furnish what we can call humanistic features. In this sense, what really distinguishes Savalls is that he mentions all these authors by name in a context where that practice is becoming unusual, if not dangerous, although he condemns Luther for dividing Christendom.

Moreover, there is an insistence on the importance of the university for the good health of society, so that *Iurati* must elect good professors because they are as important as the eyes to the body and the intellect to the soul. Places of learning are not dead buildings but a living community. The purpose of the professor is to sow virtue in the students, and in this sense it is better to have an intellectually mediocre professor than a competent but a morally irresponsible one. Students should love their professors, since they are their models to imitate.

In Decius's *De re literaria asserenda oratio,* there is a very similar approach, but the virulence with which Decius reprimands mainly the *Iurati* and professors stands out. In the dedicatory epistle his patron, Johannes Beruegalius, praises Decius's eloquence and makes a claim that will be found all over the forewords of other works, and also in amplified form in Decius's oration of 1547: Valencia is generous to foreigners, but mean and small-minded to its own citizens, its sons.[13]

In the *exordium* (there are marginal notes all through the text that indicate the parts of speech and figures — the *artificium* — in a very didactic way), Decius prepares his audience: although he is not saying anything new, nobody will hear what they are hoping for, because he is not so much praising letters as talking about the contempt for letters instead (so the *oratio* is more a *vituperatio* than a *laudatio*).

First of all, Decius questions the pride of the audience. He has seen with his very eyes the preeminence of the Germans and the Dutch, not because of their genius, but because of their hard work. So, by comparing Valencian people with North Europeans, he appeals to their pride and spirit of emulation. Professors are the first addressed, and accused of the harm suffered by the University. This harm is caused by two sorts of envy. The first divides students into factions. The second strives to secure audiences of students. Decius addresses himself to the *Iurati* in terms of very harsh invective, accusing them of corruption in the election of professors, and re-

---

[12] See Helena Rausell Guillot, "Una aproximación al erasmismo valenciano: Cosme Damián Çavall y Pedro Antonio Beuter, catedráticos, sacerdotes y erasmistas", Ph.D. diss., Universitat de València (1999).

[13] "Debet itaque Valentino Decio Valentia non minus; at quid minus dixi? imo multo magis pro tanto in patriam officio quam Romanus Populus Deciis illis Romanis multorum iam encomiis celebratissimis. Nisi plane filio suo aspera nouerca esse uult, quae ut alienis blanda parens esse solet Valentia" (p. 5).

minds them about their duties as *Iurati*. What really draws attention here is Decius's virulence in facing the *Iurati*. Decius also uses the same tone for students, whose laziness, carelessness, and somnolence contribute to their inferiority.

Past and future, forebears and posterity, are always present in his argumentation. We must be worthy of our forebears' legacy and transmit it to posterity. Thus the community moves on from generation to generation, including the *res publica litterarum*.

In the third oration, Decius's *De scientiarum et Academiae Valentinae laude* delivered twelve years later, in 1547, by a good disciple of his (Onofre Climent / Onofrius Clemens), the structure, subject, and circumstances of the oration are the same as in the previous speeches, but a praise of learning is added at the beginning: the liberal arts, that is, grammar, dialectic, rhetoric, and *mathematicae quatuor*, and medicine, law, and theology. Decius asks the *Iurati* for money and support and, of course, the appointment of the best professors. Nevertheless the University of Valencia can be compared now with the best universities: the humanities are taught, in part thanks to Mencía de Mendoza, Ledesma, and other professors; a man can be cultivated in Valencia. However, among his praises, Decius criticizes *Valentinorum mutabile semper ingenium*. And the bitterest complaint is that *excluditur filius, admittitur peregrinus*. Decius is not talking now about professors, but about preaching. Perhaps that has to do with a commonplace that describes Valencian people as hospitable and lovely (as A. Llull describes their ethos in his *De oratione libri septem* [Basel, 1558]), but not to their citizens. Valencian people are fond of novelty, and among novelties is the fashion for preaching by foreign preachers in a foreign language (I take this to be Castilian/Spanish). That makes people superficial. All of this is due both generally to human nature, and particularly to the Valencian ethos. In the second instance, envy of equals is attributed to the Valencian people. All the commonplaces about letters and the *Res publica litterarum* can be found in these exhortatory orations, but there is a particular feature: the protest against envy and jealousy among equals.

The same protest is found in other writings. In the dedicatory epistle of the translations of P. J. Esteve, he complains about the jealousy of his colleagues:

> Non dubito Bernarde magnifice, quin multi nos leuitatis ac petulantiae, nostramque hanc operam temeritatis, sint damnaturi, quos tamen partim liuore, partim uero maleuolentia idipsum facturos certo scio. (...) labentemque propemodum animum, ad firmam reuocasti spem, illud quidem egregie monens, bonorum hominum uirtutem imitatione, non inuidia dignam esse.

Similarly, Ledesma believes that for letters to flourish, *sophistae* must be eliminated from the University:

> Atque ut id certius sit, ac firmius Gymnasium celeberrimum in nostra hac urbe construere machinaris, in quo politiores litterae floreant, exulantibus scilicet nugis ac sophismatibus in hoc usque tempus cuncta tyrannide sua opprimentibus. Nam si scires quae hactenus scommata, quos cachinnos ac ronchos ex eo tempore, quo primum ex academia Complutensi in patriam remeaui tolerare

> solus a sophistis coactus sim, esset quod stupesceres, non parum illis occasionis praebente Stranei nostri uiri absolutissimi factione barbaris semper inuisa, cuius me esse unum intelligebant.

P. J. Núñez adopted a different style in his oration of 1553 (published in 1554), *De causis obscuritatis Aristoteleae et de illarum remediis*. But he left Valencia in 1556, complaining of incomprehension among academics in Valencia. He wrote a letter to Jerónimo Zurita which said:

> La aprobación que v. m. ha hecho de mis estudios me dá muy grande ánimo para passarlos adelante, porque si esso no fuesse, desesperaría no teniendo aquí persona con quien poder comunicar una buena corrección, o explicación, no porque no aya en esta Ciudad personas doctas, pero siguen muy diferentes estudios, y lo peor es desto, que querrían que nadie se aficionasse a estas letras humanas, por los peligros, como ellos pretenden, que en ellas ay, de como emienda el humanista un lugar de Cicerón, assí emendará uno de la escritura, y diziendo mal de comentadores de Aristóteles, que hará lo mismo de los doctores de la Iglesia; éstas, y otras semejantes necedades me tienen tan desatinado, que me quitan muchas veces las ganas de pasar adelante, las quales cobraré yo de cada día, viendo la aprobación que v. m. haze de mis estudios ...

A distance, I do not know if it is insurmountable, still separates our different nations and the education of their people. We all know that we belong to Europe, but what exactly is European culture? That is not so well established. For some, it may be the sum of different national cultures, but history offers us different exemples.

Headlam's and Eliot's words, with which I began, were like flowers in the middle of a vast battlefield. I do not know if envy was the cause of such a deep discord as we have seen, but a fearsome rivalry may be nourished by destructive envy (stronger among citizens and neighbours). We have the past, where a community of culture, religion and language was real, as an inspiration, and I think of a future for Europe (and for the world), which will be, as it were, a Europe of towns, and citizens, a Europe of humanity, not a Europe (or a world) of nations and states, in which a renewed *res publica litterarum* could be possible.

Universitat de València-Estudi General

George Herbert's Oration before King James, Cambridge 1623[1]

JOHN K. HALE

This paper seeks to answer three related questions about the oration delivered by George Herbert as University Orator to welcome the king and his heir in October 1623. How did Herbert please his audience by the Latin he performed? How far did the speech have a further purpose than pleasing, namely to advise his royal hearers about foreign policy? These two questions are "related" in a third: was the pleasing meant to assist the advice, as jam on a potentially unpalatable pill? To generate and judge answers we must first grasp several contexts of the 1623 event: biographical, political, ceremonial, and oratorical.

George Herbert, the eminent "Metaphysical" poet, was born in 1593 and rose swiftly up the career ladder he had chosen as a younger son from a noble family. After becoming a Fellow of his Cambridge college, Trinity, he was made Orator[2] in 1619. He became an MP as well in 1624 and 1625, but then advanced no further, his patrons having died.

Politically, 1623 was made a year of crisis by the actions of the Prince of Wales, the future King Charles I. When he set off for Spain to woo the King of Spain's daughter, this was in accordance with his father's peace policy. He set off in disguise, however, and since only a few knew of the plan, the kingdom seemed to lack its heir apparent — a security nightmare. In Spain, his courtship created equal uncertainty. The Spanish court and the British Resident were unclear about the extent of Charles's bargaining authority, there was the difference of religions to exacerbate negotiations, and besides, Charles acted in a whimsical way quite unsuited to Habsburg

---

[1] The paper was conceived as a tribute to my own university's Public Orator, Colin Gibson, and completed for the session on Cambridge Latin arranged by Craig Kallendorf for the IANLS. In addition to these two originators I must thank the Otago Classics Department Seminar, which heard a draft and helped improve it.

[2] This is the correct name of the office, as explained by another former Orator, James Diggle, *Cambridge Orations 1982–1993. A Selection* (Cambridge, 1994), x–xi.

formality.³ The King of Spain stalled, valuing harmony with the Papacy above humouring an eccentric young stranger. Months later, then, Charles came home, with nothing settled but feeling slighted. Through hurt pride he was now ready to put England behind the anti-Habsburg, anti-Catholic cause in Europe. There were good reasons, too, why he should: his sister the Queen of Bohemia might recover her kingdom, and many felt that Habsburg power needed curbing. And yet any such military action would flatly contradict his father's long-standing policy of peace.

Into this tension a cross-current intrudes. War with Spain would be very popular with Protestants at home, despite their normal dissatisfaction with the Anglican church settlement. They indeed turned out in jubilation to celebrate Charles's return. Charles found himself the hero of the hour and the saviour of his people, all achieved by failing! The sums of expenditure on the rituals of public joy — bonfires and bells, fireworks and street parties — broke all records.⁴

The ceremonial celebrations by Cambridge University took place on 8 October, only three days after Charles landed. Thus the gathering which heard Herbert's speech of congratulation ("Oratio Quâ auspicatissimum Serenissimi Principis Caroli Reditum ex Hispanijs celebrauit") was one of the earliest expressions of public feeling. Herbert addressed England's ears as well as Cambridge's. What would he present as the subjects' response, amidst the cross-currents created by Charles's startling exit and sudden return? Would he uphold the King's desire for peace with Spain, or the Prince's new desire for war, or something else? Would he diplomatically use well-chosen words to say nothing?

The final context needed is the oratorical. The Orator's role at Cambridge had always been to represent the University in good Latin, whether by letters or speeches. A number of such letters by Herbert survive, so diplomacy — if that were his key-note — would not surprise. But instead, his speech is by far the most ambitious of his surviving orations.⁵ He must have sought to say something out of the ordinary, to voice for his *alma mater* a hero's welcome. So now back to our first question: how did he welcome and entertain the nation's royalty at such a crisis? That he did rise to the occasion is clear from the speech's being specially printed by the University Press in the same year.⁶ To show by what sort and range and register of Latin he did it, by

---

³ For example, on a fancy he "startled the rigid propriety of the Spanish Court, by leaping into a garden in which the lady of his affections was walking. The poor girl shrieked and fled, and it was with some difficulty that the prince was persuaded, by the supplications of her guardian, to leave the place." See S. R. Gardiner, *History of England from the Accession of James I to the Outbreak of the Civil War, 1603–1642,* 10 vols. (London, 1883), 5: 52.

⁴ See David Cressy, *Bonfires and Bells. National Memory and the Protestant Calendar in Elizabethan and Stuart England* (London, 1989).

⁵ 12 pages, compared with 1, 2, and 1 in the edition used here, *The Works of George Herbert,* ed. F. E. Hutchinson (Oxford, 1941), 445–455, hereafter cited as "Hutchinson." Reference is to page and line of Hutchinson.

⁶ "Ex Officina CANTRELLI LEGGE, Almae *Matris* Cantabrigiae *Typographi.* 1623" (title-page reproduced facing Hutchinson, 444).

ORATIO

Quâ auspicatissimum Serenissimi

Principis
CAROLI,

Reditum ex Hispanijs celebrauit

Georgius Herbert

Academiæ   Cantabrigiensis

Orator.

Ex Officina Cantrelli Legge, Almæ
Matris Cantabrigiæ *Typographi.*
1623.

1623 title page of Herbert's speech of congratulation.

what tone and conceits and jokes, is my next task, in this pioneering account of the work's originality.

The opening is self-assured: "Veneranda Capita, / Viri grauissimi, / Pubes lectissima." The court, the teachers, and the pupils come in descending order, with pleasant phonetic patterning in the vs and rs of "Viri grauissimi," or the syntactical one which places the honorific adjectives before the "Capita" ("chief persons") but after the other groups listening. Such assurance might instill confidence but hardly rapture.

Another prominent feature, of the whole speech this time, is its multilingual interlarding. Greek words, phrases, lines, and passages (sometimes with variants) are frequent. But Herbert tosses in some German etymology and (of all things) a Spanish proverb. Whilst all this could be seen as a display of linguistic erudition normal to the University in its moments of display, comparable for instance with its verse anthologies replete with compositions in (say) Welsh or Persian, the amount of the Greek is unusual, the German is unexpected, and the Spanish (in the circumstances) audacious.

Audacity excused by joy fills much of the speech. For example, Herbert compares Charles to an elephant. Now the elephant is doubtless a noble and sagacious animal, but Herbert's conceit is more sprightly and preposterous as well as obvious and complimentary. When Charles went to Spain, why did he go alone, why oh why did he not take us all along with him: "siccine abijsti solus? cur non nos omnes tecum? cur non vt elephanti turres, ita tu patriam tecum portasti?" (451.7–8) The passage catches the fancy in several ways, from the engaging sound-pattern of the dentals through the quixotic image of Charles reversing the march of Hannibal to the emblem or cartoon of the prince carrying the nation on his back, like a howdah. A serious point and a compliment are being made too: the heir-apparent does carry the nation's well-being on his back, and does it with ease. In this image a rather special witty histrionics is on show.

Herbert follows up this flashy conceit with another one, less whimsical and more dramatic, in which he secretes a stronger public emotion: "Sic tunc omnes strepebant: huiusmodi lamentis & quiritationibus plena erant fora, nundinae, conciliabula, angiportus, Maeandri" ["Public places, marketplaces, places of assemblies, narrow lanes, winding ones"] (451.9–11). The asyndeton certainly exaggerates, again histrionically, but the imaging is a beautiful arching, aural as well as conceptual. Just as the Latin words progress from shorter to longer and from simpler to grander, then diminish and fade away (from two to three to six syllables, then four then three, and in rhythm from trochaic to dactylic then aside into molossus), so the progression of ideas has equal lucidity: from places where people congregate, sell and decide together, to their journeying home. This they do in small groups, then alone. Herbert is making vivid pictures of the nation discussing its absent prince and ends plangently on their dispersal homewards, still obsessed, perplexed, deprived of their beloved prince. The exaggeration, and the conscious artistry, enhance the emotional implication by cloaking the serious thrust. The thought "How we missed you!" is after all not likely to displease Charles, and anyway this was exactly the anxiety with which his absence had afflicted his ailing father.

A further sample bears out this claim that Herbert is deploying a disarming histrionics: the passage where he teases his colleagues en route to making a joke about

Charles's beard. He is rather careful about addressing Charles directly. In the "elephant" passage, for instance, he was talking to his colleagues *about* Charles, not to him (445.24–27). He seldom speaks to Charles: the clearest case is wholly compliment (451.27–34). In a further instance he is again addressing his fellow "Academici" (445.14 and 22), and again in teasing tones, but he is teasing *them*: he calls them "bookworms," "tineae estis helluones chartacei" (18–19). It is on the back of that wave that he compares the Prince's beard with that of a previous Charles, Charlemagne no less: "date mihi CAROLVM alterum, quamlibet *Magnum*, modò detis eum in flore, in vaginâ, in herbescenti viriditate; nondum ad spicam barbámque adultum" (19–21).[7] Charles cannot match Charlemagne for achievement, yet, nor for magnificence of beard,[8] but so much the better, because he has youth on his side. The fancy is an escapology, as Herbert escapes from a possibly damaging comparison through a clever (and truthful) compliment.

Nor has he finished with beards. After next insisting that he is not merely speech-making nor tinkling emptily ("Non rhetoricor, Academici, non tinnio," 445.21–22), and has indeed foresworn all such immaturity, he declares: "ego verō sentio, & quis sum ipse (barbam, hui, tam grauem) & apud quos dico, viros limatae auris atque tersae, quorum grauitate ac purpurâ non abutar." The parenthesis, I think, deprecates his own beard, which to judge by one portrait was indeed scrawny. He does this to placate his colleagues, who may not all have enjoyed being termed bookworms (even if it was done to please the Prince): he *is* serious, he is not rating his pitiful beard above their grave berobed wisdoms ("gravitate ac purpurâ," 445.27).

Still another tonal point emerges here. Whilst in general Herbert is displaying a huge Latin idiolect, as was and is expected of a University Orator (the *mot juste*, even if caviare to the general), locally he is letting off fireworks amidst prevailing erudition. "Hui!" is no dignified word, but an exclamation of astonishment, frequent in Roman comedy. Its use in context suggests spontaneity. Indeed, a clue to his whole stance may be present here, because the indicative mood in place of the usual subjunctive with indirect question ("sum," "dico") is another feature of comic Latin.[9] How much further, then, does this echoing of comedy go? Is Herbert posing as a Plautine clever slave?

Such speculation aside, Herbert does act silly, so silly that his listeners could either laugh or ignore (or doze). He denies juvenility yet is relying on it, to disarm criticism. Above all, he does this just *before* he talks about really dangerous topics, such as

---

[7] The typography of the printed version is reproduced here to show that it calls the attention of readers to the comparison, and so possibly suggests the emphases of the spoken oration hereabouts.

[8] A bushy one, "spicam Barbamque," where "spica" means a growth round an axis: Charlemagne's beard, trim and bushy, can be seen in such effigies as the reliquary from the Cathedral Treasury, Aachen.

[9] "There are many examples in early Latin (Plautus and Terence), and in the poets, where the indicative is retained in questions of fact which are clearly indirect": E. C. Woodcock, *A New Latin Syntax* (London, 1959), 134.

royal marriage-alliances and the question of war or peace. The fooling prepares for the serious plea, and so mitigates it.

In moving to our second question, whether Herbert had any purpose beyond pleasing, we must consider the context again and its rather complex probabilities. In so autocratic an age, and in the presence of two touchy royal personages, it may seem unlikely that he would offer advice, since foreign and ecclesiastical policy were involved together in any war against the Habsburgs, and both matters were in the king's domain. Nonetheless, when monarchs made a formal entry into a city or went on progress they would always be receiving speeches of welcome, which might include requests, and might verge onto advice too if expressed with sufficient generality. Even preachers might advise unpunished, as Peter McCullough's study shows.[10] It depended on what the advice was, and how conveyed, how timed, how strenuously pressed, and with what degree of particularity. Accordingly, we can approach Herbert's speech with an open mind, since examples of expression and suppression can both be found.[11]

Two of the very few published mentions of the speech will provide a starting-point. One historian said that "it was no secret that the prince had come back bent on war. . . . From Charles, rushing headlong into war, the lover of peace had no favour to expect."[12] And Herbert's editor, F. C. Hutchinson, declared that "Apart from the extravagant adulation of Charles, the most striking feature of Herbert's oration is the vehement indictment of war (447.26–449.11)."[13]

Hutchinson's statement, by giving such precise line-references, may suggest that Herbert moved suddenly into the vehement indictment and equally suddenly out of it. This is not so, however. The jam and the pill are nothing like so separate, and I shall argue that the transitions are more in keeping with the performance of the mixed persona that is being projected.

Here is how Herbert first mentions peace. He praises royal marriages in general, then Charles's wooing-journey in particular because he went to see for himself in such a vital dynastic matter. Short- and long-term interests alike are bound up in this marriage (447.21–26), "dum pacem, quâ tot iam annis impunè fruimur, hoc pacto fundatam cupit & perpetuam; quod quidem vbi gentium si non ab Hispano sperandum?" (28–31).[14] Reminding everyone why the wooing was undertaken, Herbert points to the absence of war throughout James's twenty-year reign. On that basis he

---

[10] Peter E. McCullough, *Sermons at Court. Politics and Religion in Elizabethan and Jacobean Preaching*, Cambridge Studies in Early Modern British History (Cambridge, 1998).

[11] In this connection it is worth remarking that the Stuarts relished progresses and entries less than Elizabeth had done, and also less as time went on. Contrast the magnificence of the constructions for James's first royal entry into London in 1604 with Charles's order in 1626 to put a stop to a London entry that had been planned (and paid for!). This struck witnesses as churlish. See David M. Bergeron, *English Civic Pageantry 1558–1642* (London, 1971), 4–5 and 107–108.

[12] Gardiner, *History of England*, 7:266–267.

[13] Hutchinson, 601.

[14] A perceptive a priori: if England wished for peace it was indeed Spain they had to treat with.

goes on to say the sweet Prince "desires" it to continue ("[Princeps] fundatam cupit & perpetuam"). Although the "Princeps" could be James, Charles could make the wish his own if he chose. Herbert is imputing, by a tactful ambiguity. And certainly if peace is wanted, it must be peace with *Spain*. Herbert is tacitly warning any warmongers listening that it is peace which royal policy favors.

Now ensue two pages in favor of peace (for the passage is longer than Hutchinson names). It comprises reasoning, in which he gives war its due, but then eulogy of peacetime in a heightened register contrasted with wartime; then reasoning again, and so back into a grateful praise of the prince who has so nobly sought peace at personal risk for his people. And *this* prince is Charles, just as if he were not the chief belligerent of the hour, but rather were being tacitly incorporated amongst the peace-lovers, since peace was the real meaning of his wooing-journey. If this bemused the young man, so much the better, rhetorically.

Selections will best demonstrate the rhetorical power which Herbert exerts in this crucial passage, and especially in his transitions. Here is where he warms to his theme: "certè fatendum est, anteferendam bello pacem, sine quâ omnis vita procella, & mundus solitudo" (448.7–8) War as *procella*, a "commotion" or "hurricane," comes from Cicero (*De Har. Resp.* 4) and Virgil (*Aeneid* 1. 594), the best of classical authors. Likewise, war as "solitudo" adapts from Tacitus the *mot* "ubi solitudinem faciunt, pacem appellant."[15] The emotional temperature rises higher: "Pace, filij sepeliunt patres; bello, patres filios: pace, aegre sanantur; bello, etiam sani intereunt" (8–15). The ordered antitheses may be standard topoi, but honed thus to dense expression they become plangent. They strike strongly if the aging James thought back to 1619 when he buried his eldest son, Prince Henry, or ahead to the time soon coming when Charles would bury him. Herbert gives another three such antitheses,[16] then caps the rising series of five with a couplet in Greek. It is so finely said that those who want only pleasure can enjoy the stylish expression, but those who are prepared to be persuaded, through their ears and in their hearts, will be.

Or again, at 448.32–449.16, after a cautious, thoughtful reminder not to underestimate peace (or take it for granted after twenty years of it), Herbert climbs higher still, to proclaim that war is a mutilation of God's own image: "Ecce lanienas omnimodas, truncata corpora, mutilatam imaginem Dei" [a rising threesome: "butchers' stalls, bodies, God's own image"]. The series plunges onward, into "pauxillum vitae ... vrbium incendia ... stupratas virgines ... infantulos plus lactis quàm cruoris emittentes" — heavily forensic, emotionally manipulative. He ends the paragraph with the exclamatory *gnome*, "Quàm cruenta gloria est, quae super ceruicibus hominum erigitur?" (449.9–10).

Next, lest he be thought a weak pacifist or blinkered ideologue he concedes that war is sometimes necessary (449.12): "Non nego bellum aliquando necessarium esse."

---

[15] *Agricola* 30, fin. Not the same point, but empowering Herbert's stronger, more disinterested one: "let us hang onto the real peace we do enjoy."

[16] "pace, securitas in agris est; bello, neque intra muros: pace, auium cantus expergefacit; bello, tubae ac tympana: pax nouum orbem aperuit; bellum destruit veterem" (448. 10–13).

Yet at once he qualifies the concession itself by adding "bellíque miserias gratas." But "gratas" to whom, seeing that war is all too close to us already, "praecipuè vbi velut ex continentibus tectis ad nos traiecturum est incendium"? The analogy of neighbors' house-fires must be a side-glance at the Thirty Years War.[17] Surely then, let us not *initiate* war, "Sed non est nostri bellum indicere." And now comes a clinching *sententia*: "prudentissimus Rex maturè prospiciet" and wages war only when he has to, and then terribly. "Rex" here is gnomic: this is the wisdom of *kings*. So perhaps *not* of a prince who is not yet a king?

That prince need not feel slighted, either, because the passage then modulates back by the end of the paragraph to Charles's own splendid wisdom and farsighted patriotism: "Illud autem, quod cuiuis clarissimè patet, etiam lusco, nunquam intueri satìs vel mirari possumus, nimirum infinitum Principis in suam gentem amorem, cui pacem quaesiuit suo capite, periculis suis" (449.34–37).

Even this may not be a direct adjuration to Charles; but when we turn the page and find that the next words are addressed explicitly to the Academici, it does seem in retrospect that the preceding words were aimed elsewhere, whether to the entire audience, or to James then Charles in especial. We cannot reconstruct exactly how Herbert performed his words, or where he was looking as he spoke, but this transition entails a gaze which had been traveling about, before settling safely on the Academici. There is a subtext of "who has ears to hear, let him hear" in the later stages of this appeal for peace. And its deliberately altering register, its moves between ratiocination or concession and emotional *hupsos*, look like an appeal not merely for applause (for the rhetorical pleasure which its figures and rhythms and revivified ancient exemplars would give), but an attempt to enlist the hearers' imaginations in the cause of peace.

Herbert is reminding Charles of why he had gone to Spain, and is seeking to make him feel good about the mission, not resentful about its failure: he has sought for peace, this valuable wonderful achievement of the all-wise James, at the risk of his own life. Elsewhere in the speech, Herbert urges on Charles the fact that by not having joined himself to the Infanta he can make a better alliance, perhaps across the Channel in France. This is not only putting a good face on the recent failure, but moving Charles in imagination forward into fresh opportunities for dynastic alliance. And whether embellishing the present or past or future, it is all construed into praise of the young Prince. His imagination is being levered away from hurt pride, back into self-respect.

Herbert's combined strategy can be seen at the close, where he joins elaborate praise to an alternative marriage alliance[18] and to the threat of war. And here, at last,

---

[17] There might be a pun on "continentibus" (adjacent houses) and "continens [terra]" (the mainland, the Continent of Europe).

[18] Charles is implored never to leave his land again ("precemur Deum immortalem, vt Princeps optimus nulla secunda itinera meditetur," 454.38–455.1). Or if he must, let him do it by the shortest route now he has discovered it ("Quod si necesse sit iterum exire patriâ, qui nunc inuenit viam, proximo itinere faciat," 455.7–8.) The meaning is obscure, perhaps deliberately: let him use this experience? or not go so far again? go to France not Spain? Could any or all of these

I find the conceits forced, as if the three things would not quite come together; yet the peroration exudes goodwill, and self-forgetful joy. Let my own reader judge.

I refer to the strained conceit, of the Infanta as Daphne and Charles as Apollo, in which Charles's love will now change into a laurel, one of triumph: "Apollo olim depositis radijs Daphnen deperijt, at illa mutata est in arborem triumphantem propriam: Noster etiam Princeps habuit Daphnen suam, cuius amor deinceps in triumphos & laurus mutabitur," 455.8–11. I call this strained because for one thing the "amor" was objective in the secondary discourse, Daphne being object of Apollo's desire, whereas when the primary discourse is reached the laurel becomes subjective and represents Charles's passion. Then, by another shift, Charles metamorphoses into a laurel tree, which will shelter his people till the cloud of war passes over, and for good measure will be the laurel awarded to composers of excellent words: "Nos vero, Auditores, diu iam peregrinati cum Principe, commodè peruenimus ad laurum hanc, vbi sub vmbrâ eius paulisper requiescamus: praesertim donec transeat nubes illa, quae vicinos adeò infestat: hìc enim securi sumus à pluuiâ, imò à fulmine: Obsecremus eum tantùm vt permittat nostram hanc *Inter victrices hederam sibi serpere Lauros*."

The final possible allusion I detect is to the sufferings of Germany in the Thirty Years War, already severe after only a few of those years. These are now being brought back into view by Herbert.[19] Against that black backdrop of war-clouds Herbert insinuates a pleasing, grateful image of a nation sheltering from war's rain and thunderbolts beneath its prince as a patron of the arts of peace.

The third question I raised in my introductory paragraph was about the relation between answers given to the first two. I suggested there first that the pleasure of the performance might be jam surrounding the pill of the advice against war. If the tone has hitherto been read aright, and if the reader agrees that its changes project a mixed, altering persona, we can characterize the speaker as follows. At times he is a harmlessly naive, but witty clown. These times tend to occur when he is approaching or broaching the contentious matter of peace. At other times he is the earnest advocate of peace. These times are fewer, being limited to the two pages we have examined and the peroration. During the rest of the oration, which has not been examined but which comprises a dispersed half of the whole, he is the mouthpiece of communal, even national joy. These adulations are spoken both as an academician and a loyalist. The triple persona and its fluctuations seek a triple, mixed response from the audience: pleasure, and the laughter of harmless delight for the wit and fooling; attention, with recall to fundamentals of royal policy and social truth, the thoughts about war and peace; and a glad complacency for the ample congratulations. The three come together in the peroration, that image of Charles as a laurel tree. The whimsy is shaky, but even that fact may disarm.

---

be hinted at by the vagueness? (One is of course influenced by hindsight; Charles married a princess of France just over a year later. However, presumably alternatives were now being discussed, and had already been.)

[19] 448.8–33, 448.34, 455.14; moving from generality or ancient instances towards contemporary ones.

Charles as Apollo blesses the arts, including oratory. And he finds himself linked, most flatteringly, with the laurels of peace.

The combined persona can be seen humanistically, as that of Horace, seeking "ridentem dicere verum."[20] (Compare "Many a true word is spoken in jest.") More exactly, the persona practises a series of deflections. His chameleon-like persona-shifts are not so much drawing attention to himself as deflecting any hostility from the message to the unimportant messenger. Similar deflections are being deployed when he talks to the Academici about the Prince, or when he implants the ideal of a "Princeps" who may be either the father or the son. He is seeking, obliquely, through self-dramatization and other skills, to persuade by pleasure. Pleasure is both end and means.

University of Otago

---

[20] Horace, *Satires*, 1.1. 24–25, "(Quamquam ridentem dicere verum / Quid vetat? ut pueris olim dant crustula blandi / Doctores, elementa velint ut discere prima.)" The cliché of jam-on-the-pill is given here in its Horatian expression.

Confession and Concession:
The Texts of Erasmus's Exomologesis

MICHAEL J. HEATH

Take a good look at the sort of people who will confound heaven and earth if anyone warns against the over-eager practice of confession; you will see men who are ravenous, covetous and devoted to their bellies. They make all this fuss because confession fuels their extravagance, their greed and their lust. Is it enough for the healing of souls to sport a cowl or a shaven head? Should this holy work be done by a bleary-eyed drunkard who's just stumbled out of an orgy? (156D)[1]

Surprisingly, this is not a passage from Erasmus's *Praise of Folly* or *Colloquies*; astonishingly, it is Erasmus trying to be magnanimous and conciliatory towards his critics. It is one of many passages added when in 1530 Erasmus revised his controversial book on confession, *Exomologesis sive Modus Confitendi*, first published in 1524.

At our Copenhagen congress, Erika Rummel presented evidence that Erasmus cared little about revising his own texts, usually complaining that he had no time to do so. She argued that Erasmus's natural eloquence and rhetorical skills amply compensated for this self-confessed reluctance to revise.[2] *Exomologesis* is a little-known exception. Its textual history is thus immediately interesting as a book that Erasmus conscientiously revised, largely in response to (or goaded by) contemporary critics. But it is also interesting as an example of Erasmus's accumulative method, in that he

---

[1] References to *Exomologesis* are to the Latin text in *Desiderii Erasmi Opera omnia*, ed. J. Le Clerc (Leiden, 1703–1706 [*LB*]), 5:145–170. The English versions are adapted from my translation in vol. 68 of the *Collected Works of Erasmus* (*CWE*) (Toronto, forthcoming).

[2] Erika Rummel, "With no Thought of Publication? Erasmus's *Manifesta Mendacia* as an Example of Spontaneous Writing," in *Acta Conventus Neo-Latini Hafniensis*, MRTS 120 (Binghamton, NY, 1994), 179–186.

added about fifty percent to his original text, but, like his admirer Montaigne, deleted almost nothing.

For Montaigne, of course, maintaining the original version enabled him to present a true if sometimes contradictory portrait of himself at different stages of his life. But what were Erasmus's motives for using an accumulative method? A possible affinity with Montaigne was their sceptical sense that on many topics one could never be sure that the last word had been said. Most often, however, Erasmus expanded his books for humanist and literary reasons. The *Adagia* were allowed to balloon almost out of control in the interests of scholarly completeness, of *copia*, and also because the genre of the book itself gradually changed, from a rhetorical handbook to a compendium of moral philosophy.

Elsewhere Erasmus enlarged earlier writings in order to clarify his position or to give fuller treatment to a complex subject; pertinent examples are his expansion of the relatively brief *Encomium matrimonii* into the massive and still controversial *Christiani matrimonii institutio*, or the little paragraphs on crusading in his pacific writings, which he worked up into the remarkably comprehensive *Consultatio de bello Turcis inferendo*.[3] In these cases, however, Erasmus rewrote himself in original books.

Another kind of accretion is evident in Erasmus's very numerous apologetic writings, his many *Responsiones* and *Apologiae*, where replies to critics are developed from the original passages at issue. But again these writings tend to take the form of separate and self-contained pamphlets or books. The same might have happened with the controversy over confession; the occasion of Erika Rummel's paper was her publication of a book called *Manifesta mendacia*, Erasmus's reply to critics of *Exomologesis* and *De esu carnium*. But *Manifesta mendacia* was not published, for reasons we can only guess at. In this case Erasmus chose the more discreet method of revising his original book; so discreet was he that the fact of the revision is not even mentioned on the 1530 title page. One minor artistic reason for the expansion may be that the 1524 book lacked a proper conclusion. Erasmus wrote it in Basel, perhaps with Froben breathing down his neck, demanding the next best-seller before it was properly finished; certainly in 1530 Erasmus supplied, at length, the rhetorically desirable summary and envoi.

But the enlargement of the original *Exomologesis* was above all polemical. The passage quoted at the beginning of this paper satirises critics of those (i.e., Erasmus) who suggest that the practice of confession requires reform. Erasmus declares that their motives are materialistic and self-serving. This was clearly a response to his own opponents, and in another satirical addition he came close to naming them. Ostensibly he is discussing the sort of commercial fiddles that require restitution to be made:

> These days, what wine-merchant will not pretend to the uninitiated that wine from Spain is actually from Beaune; or that Louvain wine is actually Rhenish? (165B)

---

[3] See my translations of the longer works: *The Institution of Christian Matrimony: Institutio christiani matrimonii*, trans. and annotated by Michael J. Heath, in *Collected Works of Erasmus*, 69 (Toronto-Buffalo-London, 1999), 203–438; and in *CWE* 64 (forthcoming).

Apart from showing that ill-informed wine-snobbery is nothing new, the fact that the bad wine comes from Spain and Louvain is an obvious gibe at specific opponents, the Spanish monks and the Louvain theologians who had attacked *Exomologesis* soon after its publication.[4]

The passages quoted so far do suggest that on confession Erasmus was himself unrepentant and unwilling to compromise. The more his previously neglected controversial writings are explored, the more clearly he emerges as a resolute and sometimes vituperative debater, rather than the fence-sitting master of compromise so often portrayed in the past.

However, it would be an over-simplification to say that in revising *Exomologesis* Erasmus simply stood his ground. In writing his pioneering work on Erasmus and the sacraments, John B. Payne was clearly (and understandably) unaware that the text had been revised, and thus accused Erasmus of hedging, of inconsistency, and of a lack of candour.[5] Eugénie Droz, also looking only at the final text, suggested that Erasmus had pursued a "tactique de la double vérité,"[6] doubtless the Franco-Scholastic equivalent of our British bureaucrat being "economical with the truth." For example, early in his revision Erasmus added a paragraph on the much-debated origin of confession which includes the sentence: "I am more inclined towards the party that believes that it was instituted by Christ" (147A). Payne rightly pointed out that this was at variance with Erasmus's view on the subject as expressed in his earlier polemic with Edward Lee and others. But it does represent a shift in emphasis which is observable elsewhere in the new *Exomologesis* and in Erasmus's *subsequent* replies to his critics. Similarly, an inserted passage on the beneficial effects of "certain external rites and ceremonies" (149D) hardly sounds like Erasmus at all; it certainly puzzled Payne, though, perceptively, he likened it to a passage in Erasmus's 1533 *De concordia*. Payne noted a number of these apparent inconsistencies, as well as an occasional softening of tone within the book, without of course being able to attribute them to Erasmus's confusing reluctance to sacrifice the text already published.

The divine origin of confession was one of the doctrinal issues on which Erasmus was prepared to retreat from the extreme position he had adopted in the *Annotations on the New Testament* in 1519 and in his reply to Edward Lee, where he had bluntly asserted that "we do not read that private confession was instituted by Christ."[7] Whereas in this polemic of 1520 he had exploited history to demonstrate the comparative modernity of auricular confession, in 1530, expanding the *Exomologesis*, he cited somewhat dubious historical parallels to suggest, on the contrary, a link with apostolic practices.

On issues such as these, it does appear that Erasmus made an effort to placate his Catholic critics. Indeed, on the *theory* of confession he arrived eventually at a

---

[4] Erasmus had already replied to his Spanish critics in 1528: see *LB* 9:1062–1064; *Manifesta mendacia* was a direct reply to four Louvain theologians.

[5] John B. Payne, *Erasmus: His Theology of the Sacraments* (Richmond, 1970), 181–213.

[6] Eugénie Droz, *Chemins de l'hérésie: textes et documents* (Geneva, 1970), 1:84.

[7] *LB* 9:255C.

relatively orthodox position, going so far as to describe his controversial earlier statements as "passing remarks."[8] An interesting way to demonstrate this is to construct another version of *Exomologesis* by excising the many passages recommended for deletion by the Tridentine Index; this produces a text consisting of perfectly harmless and orthodox pastoral advice, including an unblemished eulogy of confession. Erasmus had added passages, which clearly distanced him from the Reformers' stance on the question, on the necessity of confession (147A), on its sacramental status (145A),[9] and on the requirement to confess sinful thoughts as well as sinful deeds (148A), which, for example, Luther had denounced as an innovation introduced by "avaricious, inquisitive or tyrannical prelates."[10] Erasmus went so far as to accuse the Reformers themselves, perhaps teasingly, of inconsistency: "Even those who defend Luther's teachings admit that [confession] is salutary and not at all to be despised" (145B).

Teasing or not, the suggestion that common ground was to be found is borne out by other inserted passages which appear to echo some of Luther's views. A brief and decidedly sceptical parenthesis is added to a passage on the pope's power to define sin: "if in fact any mortal can make another guilty of sin" (158B).[11] Similarly, a pointed question is added to a passage on the necessity of confession: "Do you believe that God is false and will not fulfil his promises?" (161C), an argument frequently used by Luther to demonstrate the inutility of formal confession, or at least to question the need for a priest as mediator in penance.[12] Towards the end (167E) Erasmus inserted an attack on the logic of indulgences to which we shall return. Such characteristic eclecticism (or broad-mindedness) was unlikely to soothe Erasmus's Catholic critics.

Erasmus's irony was given full rein when it came to responding to the most nitpicking of the Louvain theologians' criticisms. They complained that he had enumerated only eight advantages of confession as against *nine* evils or disadvantages. In *Manifesta mendacia* Erasmus had been prepared to argue, rather lamely, that the confusion arose from his indiscriminate use of the terms *mala* and *incommoda*. But he was more than ready in 1530 to supply the all-important ninth "advantage" of confession, which he identified as readmission to the Christian fellowship, like a new baptism,

---

[8] In a letter to Lorenzo Campeggi a few months before the publication of *Exomologesis*: Ep. 1410 (*CWE* 10:157).

[9] As "part of a sacrament" [of Penance]; later in the treatise Erasmus consistently describes it as "sacramental penance."

[10] *Confitendi ratio* (1520), translated in *Luther's Works*, ed. J. Pelikan and H. T. Lehmann (St. Louis, 1955–1986), 39:32–33.

[11] The implication is that, like Luther (*Luther's Works*, ed. Pelikan and Lehmann, 39:31), Erasmus would define sin only as an offence against divine law, whereas in the early Church (and more recently, by implication), sin was regarded as an offence against the Church, with which the sinner must be reconciled.

[12] See for example *Sermon von dem Sacrament der Pusz*, translated in *Luther's Works*, ed. Pelikan and Lehmann, 35:12–14.

brought about by a confession properly made (153A).[13] The irony is that Erasmus was about to embark on a largely unorthodox exposition of the "proper" method of confessing. His mockery of his accusers' arithmetical pedantry was reinforced by a parting shot about the "principal advantages of confessing, which I know are in any case *innumerable*" (153C; my italics).

Predictably, it was Erasmus's views on the procedure prescribed for auricular confession that most enraged his Catholic critics and was to provoke the heaviest snipping of the censor's scissors. In exposing abuses arising from human failings and follies Erasmus was of course in his satirical element, and it is here that the sober theological and pastoral treatise turns into something of a tabloid exposé, with such colourful anecdotes as that of the scrupulous priest who refused to celebrate mass with a remnant of dinner lodged in his hollow tooth (158D), or that of the pastor who took an unhealthy interest in his flock's sex lives, where Erasmus's frank language also conveys the prurience to which the institution exposed its practitioners:

> It is right that a man who has seduced a woman should specify whether he has committed adultery with someone's wife, or committed incest with a nun, or whored with a prostitute, or fornicated with a single girl, or ravished a virgin, but he has no need to describe all the details of the act. (162C)

Was Erasmus himself too frank? It is interesting that his more prudish French translator actually bowdlerised some of the more graphic passages, perhaps on the grounds, noted by Erasmus himself elsewhere in the treatise, that to name some sins was akin to giving them wider currency.[14]

The Louvain theologians had bristled particularly at the following anecdote in the original work:

> Many people no doubt get complacent about their sins when they compare them with worse sins ... I heard a certain theologian, himself no stranger to ladies of easy virtue, say that he had heard that a certain spiritual director to a convent had confessed to debauching two hundred nuns. The man telling the tale was so pleased with himself that apparently it would never have crossed his mind to consider practising chastity. (154A)

Erasmus had already justified telling this story, in the unpublished *Manifesta mendacia*, on the grounds that he had named no names and, more cogently, that he had wished

---

[13] Thomas Tentler was impressed by the positive tone of this ninth advantage, without realising that it was an interpolation: "Forgiveness and Consolation in the Religious Thought of Erasmus," *Studies in the Renaissance* 12 (1965): 116. Payne, *Theology of the Sacraments*, 204–205 also noted its "traditionalism and concern for Church unity."

[14] In *La Maniere de se confesser* (1524), reprinted in Droz, *Chemins de l'hérésie*, 1:10–41, Claude Chansonnette (Claudius Cantiuncula) rendered *cum incubonibus aut cum brutis foedos congressus* (154A) as "compaignies des incubes et aultres non à nommer" (20), and omitted fornication from the list just quoted (34).

to prove that carnal sins need not engender despair.[15] In the additions to the *Exomologesis* itself Erasmus generally eschewed such abstract justifications, and indeed embellished the satire by adding ironic but fairly gratuitous passages aimed at a wider range of targets, including lustful courtiers, evil councillors (162D–E), and, most provocatively, "abbots", whom he inserted in a list of those in authority who sinfully waste their time whoring, drinking, and telling dirty stories (163A). Again, part of the new conclusion focusses on the dubious practices of restitution, with Erasmus raging not only against capitalists who enjoy their ill-gotten gains at small cost to their conscience and little more to their purse, but also against a Church which for a small fee will provide the necessary compositions and dispensations: "Even those who have robbed churches or monasteries can settle their conscience for a few coins" (165A).

It is thus no accident that the subtitle of Erasmus's book is *Modus confitendi*, suggesting that his principal concern was not the theory of penance, on which his position became more orthodox, but its practice. There was some irony here, too, as the subtitle recalled the most famous and popular of confessional manuals, Andrés de Escobar's *Modus confitendi*. One of the most frequently printed books of the fifteenth century, it often appeared in abridged form as a simple one-page "shopping list" of possible sins.[16] In 1530 Erasmus strengthened his attack on the "scrupulosity" encouraged by those unscrupulous confessors who caused their flock needless anxiety by insisting on completeness of confession and thus on the disclosure of the most trivial peccadilloes. The Louvain theologians had accused him of near-blasphemy in calling the modern form of confession more burdensome than the whole of Moses' law; rather than delete this hyperbole, Erasmus replied with an oblique scriptural defence, pointing out that in Acts 15 St. Peter lifted the burden of the Old Law from the Gentiles and even from the Jews (155B).

Erasmus did not spare the confessors in either version; having already described the most enthusiastic as "dirty, ignorant, frivolous, worthless, some of them not right in the head and many the worse for drink" (156B), he embellished this delightful portrait with the passage quoted at the beginning, where they reel away from drunken orgies to perform their holy task.

However, a notable feature of *Exomologesis* is that Erasmus, unlike the Reformers, was at least as severe on the behaviour of penitents as on that of confessors, and this sense of a conspiracy of malpractice is again reinforced in the additions. Having originally deplored some penitents' obsession with confessing trivia, observing sadly that "there is no shortage of priests who will pander to such people, or at least connive with them" (155E), he interpolated a passage to underline both the base motives of the priests "because they value the income that the recital brings more highly than the salvation of souls" and also the insouciance of the penitents: "Hence the joke you

---

[15] See the translation by Erika Rummel in *CWE* 71:119.

[16] See Thomas N. Tentler, *Sin and Confession on the Eve of the Renaissance* (Princeton, 1977), 40; Tentler's book is the essential study in this field.

hear many people make as they return from the priest: 'I've got rid of that load; I dumped the lot in a monk's cowl'" (155F).

However, in exposing the antics of wayward penitents, Erasmus was aiming at more than a mere reform of procedure; he was also making a plea for moral reform. In a remarkable catalogue of misdemeanours added in 1530 (164E–166B), he denounced such instantly recognisable figures as the shyster lawyer who will never admit incompetence, the trucker who will manage to "lose" some of the cargo en route, and the workman who will make a one-day job last four days, not to mention crooked city councillors and shady second-hand horse salesmen. All of them excuse their moral failings as mere "tricks of the trade" or "rules of the profession" which, they claim, everyone accepts. But all this rather obvious satire illustrates the need for conscience to play a role in public life and in business; for Erasmus, naturally, the most important element in true penitence was a humble and a contrite heart. In pursuit of this ideal, he also made a number of evangelical additions to his prescription for true confession, contrasting the benefits of Bible study, prayer, faith, and charity with those external works of satisfaction which too often lead only to complacency or hypocrisy.

The much expanded section on satisfaction is prefaced by an obvious allusion to Luther: "On this point I am not seeking a fight with those who say that satisfaction has no role to play in penance" (167E). Very true; what he did was to redefine works of satisfaction in line with his commitment to Christian charity, and in so doing to reject much ecclesiastical precedent. For example, he cast doubt on the scriptural or patristic basis of indulgences, and was outspoken on the pope's power to condone: "Where there is no charity, what use is a bull? Where charity is sufficient, the document is superfluous" (167E). He recommended spiritual and moral rehabilitation, drawing a parallel with the sort of community service practised (he claimed) by the more enlightened prison regimes in the secular world.

Erasmus's new conclusion is equally provocative. It is a recapitulation of the famous nine *incommoda*, condemned by the Louvain theologians and later excised by the papal censors. Erasmus proposed still more remedies for the perceived abuses of procedure, from the moral to the severely practical. But the tone here is modest, stripped of satirical exaggeration and earnestly intent on rectifying the notorious defects in procedure — many of which were also addressed, it has to be said, by the traditional manuals of confession. His overriding concern was to promote the essential pastoral and consolatory functions of the sacrament of penance and sacramental confession. In the additions as a whole, far from retreating into indecision and compromise, he pursued what can best be called an Erasmian line. On theoretical questions, he made concessions to the authority of the Church; but on procedural matters he made few concessions and, if anything, hardened his stance against contemporary abuses.

Here, some of his additional proposals demonstrate Erasmus's characteristic attention to detail. He recommended, for instance, that a sickroom be fumigated before the confessor enter to perform the last rites (169C). This refers back to the graphic portrayal, in the original text, of the health risks run by confessors, unable to avoid the stinking, disease-ridden breath of their penitents, or forced to enter the sickroom where a plague victim has just emptied his bowels or vomited (155A).

It has been suggested that such disturbing images derive from Erasmus's personal experience as a confessor.[17] Whether or not that is true, in 1530 Erasmus's personal involvement with his topic was made clear in another way. There comes a poignant moment when we realise that the ageing scholar's interest in confession is not merely academic. Already in the liminary epistle of 1524 Erasmus had hinted that his own ill health predisposed him to reflect upon the need for a clear conscience as his last day approached. In 1530 the personal note is still more apparent, and suggests that near the end Erasmus saw little harm and a great deal of benefit in confession as currently practised. In a tone which foreshadows the hopeful resignation of *De praeparatione ad mortem*, published four years later, Erasmus says:

> Those [*sc.* the Reformers] who teach that confession is not a necessity must decide for themselves whether they are well advised to do so. But if my mind were burdened with a mortal sin, I should not dare to approach the Lord's table, nor to await my last day, without being reconciled to God through a priest according to the long-accepted custom of the Church. (146A)

It may be that the ultimate explanation for Erasmus's unpublicised revision of his text was an all-too-human fear of eternal damnation.

King's College London

---

[17] Richard L. DeMolen, *The Spirituality of Erasmus of Rotterdam* (Nieuwkoop, 1978), 58. There is no documentary evidence for this.

Petrus Martyr de Angleria (Pietro Martire d'Anghiera): A Remarkable Italian Humanist and Historian of the New World

GERHARD HOLK

My first part, commenting on Petrus's career, has to include biographical facts like background, his studies, special circumstances, and turning points in his life. If we do not consider these, Petrus's humanistic efforts cannot be fully appreciated.

Petrus Martyr, born in 1457, was descended from a religious family of some wealth and cultural background at Arona on Lake Maggiore, Italy. He was named Petrus Martyr after an Inquisitor who was assassinated in 1252 and later canonized. Petrus was talented, ambitious, and of great learning capacity, and received his humanistic education at the school of the court of Milan, where the well-known humanist Franciscus Philelphus was active. Because of his excellent classical knowledge, he was encouraged to go to Rome, the very centre of humanism, but also an habitual place of resort for jealous or malicious soldiers of fortune. The centre of Christendom was at that time also a centre of worldly power, luxury, and above all nepotism. Petrus tried hard to get on there, but without the right connections there was no chance. Five years passed by and he had to content himself with an unpleasant teaching job outside Rome at Rieti. A year later he got the job of secretary to Francesco Negro, governor first of Perugia, then of Rome. Although this post did not correspond to his high level of learning, it helped him to make contacts with cultural circles at Rome and finally led to his admission into the circle of Pomponius Laetus, philologist, historian, archaeologist, and head of the Roman Academy. Pomponius Laetus's enthusiasm for various aspects of antiquity and his humanity made a lasting impression on Petrus. In particular he was led to the meticulous examination of historiographical evidence, to philological precision of textual criticism, and to securing reliable geographical and scientific information. He made friends with various humanists and influential personalities, but a career was not in the offing, although his interests and abilities were many-sided, extending to the political and diplomatic sphere. His current working conditions under the governor were bad, with slanderers and rivals omnipresent. His poetic talent helped him to counter-attack, and his sarcastic epigrams, of course written in Latin, did not prove ineffective. On top of that he cultivated the exchange of encomiastic and humorous epigrams appropriate for winning or strengthening friendships.

Because of his instinct for politics, he realized the precariousness of life in Italy. He saw how the current war between Pope Innocent VIII and King Ferdinand I of Naples was taking its toll on the population of Rome and threatened to provoke an intervention by the King of France. When, all of a sudden, the Spanish Count of Tendilla, Don Íñigo López de Mendoza, sent by the Catholic Kings, arrived in Italy and succeeded in persuading the Pope to come to terms with Naples (all this in pretty dramatic circumstances), Petrus reacted by writing a poem entitled "Inachus" in praise of the Spanish count and took care to have it conveyed to him.[1] Don Íñigo, an admirer of Italian culture, was pleased to be honoured by a well-known Italian humanist, and pleased to be presented as a hero of peace in a poem written in Latin. So he offered to take Petrus to Spain in order to present him to Queen Isabella of Castile and to King Ferdinand of Aragon, for the count was well aware that the Queen especially wanted to promote classical studies and culture at her court in order to keep pace with her European neighbours. Petrus accepted the invitation, although his friends urgently advised him not to leave Italy, pointing out that a distinguished Italian scholar would be out of place in a country of uneducated people where the nobility appreciated only wars and despised culture, where hardly anybody knew Latin, and where excessive pride would never acknowledge any merits in a foreigner. Petrus, however, had faith in the future and was looking forward to new prospects which he could not find in a country divided into a variety of more or less minor states, at times torn by wars and threatened by foreign intervention. Before leaving, in 1487, he promised to maintain his ties of friendship by writing letters from Spain and letting his friends know all about his experiences there. We should add that the "genus epistolare" especially was the form most congenial to him. It enabled him to maintain close ties with his friends and patrons and to write in his own way, that is, a way that was objective, functional, concise, speedy, and from a stylistic point of view independent of literary obligations. These characteristics were decisive for the form of his later major work, his *Decades de Orbe Novo*.

Petrus, Don Íñigo's guest at his Spanish residence, where the court was also staying, was introduced to the Catholic Kings. Watching the courtiers he realized that there was little interest in learning and antiquity, but he noticed a certain "magnitudo animi quasi Romana", that enabled them to go ahead with great enterprises and operations. Meanwhile, he succeeded in making friends with influential personalities, among others with Hernando de Talavera, bishop of Ávila and confessor to Queen Isabella, a learned man who had been a brilliant scholar at the University of Salamanca. However, the time of Petrus's arrival in Spain was not favourable. The war

---

[1] "Inachus" contains a comparison between the suffering of war and the lovely fruits of peace due to Don Íñigo's intervention.

against Moorish Granada had been dragging on for six years with ever-changing fortune. Petrus was fortunate to be admitted to the court and to get enrolled in the Queen's entourage. When asked what kind of service he wanted to render, he answered that he would like to participate in the fight against the Moors. His wish caught everybody by surprise, but was well thought out. His religious zeal, also shared by the Queen, was by no means his only motive. He felt that his position as a scholar amid the belligerent high nobility of the Court would be awkward, perhaps even absurd, particularly as the Court was going to move to Andalusia to be near the front line. In a way that corresponded to traditions of ancient Rome and was also obligatory upon courtiers in the Italian dynasties of his time, he wanted to demonstrate that a high level of learning and military service were not incompatible, but complemented each other. Queen Isabella granted his wish and had him assigned to the Royal Guards, where he had to endure great hardship and fatigue. His wartime experience broadened his mind and helped him to overcome some prejudices common to humanists, e.g., contempt of common people in general and intolerance of Moorish people. He felt sympathy with the suffering of the civil population during the long war. Whenever he could, he documented the events in letters to his friends, later included in his "Opus Epistolarum". The trustworthiness and accuracy of his presentation, and his consideration of various matters such as the nature of battlefields, and the state of mind among commanders and troops, are still esteemed today by contemporary historians.

As a combatant Petrus had risked his life and had received a war decoration, but as he had been a volunteer, he had to leave without achieving a military rank or receiving a title of nobility. Immediately after the war, we find him among the clergy of the metropolitan cathedral of Granada under its newly appointed archbishop, his friend Hernando de Talavera. This was the beginning of a career, of a "cursus honorum ecclesiasticus", which was to lead him on to dignities and benefices as time went on.

For Petrus his new spiritual life in conquered Granada was, however, intolerable. The subjected Moorish population tried to hold to their old beliefs. Considering the hostility of the crowds and the corresponding insecurity in town, the Christian clergy kept inside their locked cathedral (converted from the mosque). In this situation Petrus wrote to six influential Spanish friends to ask them to help him to obtain his immediate return to the Court which he had left during long intervals in the course of his four years of military service. The Queen consented. In order to make a lasting position at court possible, he was made canon of the cathedral of Granada, then chaplain of the Queen's chapel, and was granted the title "maestro en las artes liberales a los nobles". As an instructor of the young noblemen residing at the court, among them relatives of the sovereigns, and as the Queen's chaplain, he obtained a position of trust and witnessed all important events the Catholic Kings were involved in, among them the triumphant reception of Columbus returning from his first and sensational expedition. Petrus interviewed Columbus and his companions and sent letters communicating the news to his friends in Rome, Milan, and Granada. At the same time he began writing the first chapters of his *De Orbe Novo Decades*. He was fascinated and was looking forward to more news and information that could enlarge the knowledge of our world in many fields. Because of his manifold interests and the immediate notes he used to take, covering various aspects of the discoveries and of the New World, he became an expert on the Indies and was appointed Royal Chronicler.

Under the emperor Charles V a special Council for the Spanish colonies, called "Council for the Indies", was created. Petrus was appointed chronicler to this body, then full member and Imperial Senator, and he participated in drawing up laws and regulations for the American colonies. Approximately at the same time he reached the peak of his ecclesiastical career as Prior of Granada, Prior of Ocaña, and Abbot of Jamaica.

All the sovereigns under whom he served made use of his skill in negotiations, even sending him on precarious diplomatic missions[2] which partly were in the interest of popes: hence his appointment as Apostolic Protonotary. Throughout these activities for the Spanish Crown he remained responsible for the Latin version of the diplomatic correspondence sent to the courts of Europe.

Some Characteristics of His Major Work *De Orbe Novo Decades Octo*
First Personal Statements on the Purpose and Value of His Reports

In a letter written in 1494 (*Op. Epist.* 143) Petrus for the first time mentions that he has started to write books about the discoveries of the New World. His self-restraint is noteworthy. His aim is to provide scholars who intend to write major works with an enormous quantity of a new type of material. In Decade I of *De Orbe Novo*, chapter 10, Petrus defines his position as being that of a reporter of the New World. Thanks to Spain, he remarks, Europe has become acquainted with myriads of new peoples and scholars have been provided with ample material to write about. His own part is that of an intermediary and collector of information. He calls his reports "nuda collecta" and adds: "without elegance of style and literary embellishment." Although the alleged stylistic simplicity of his reports does him less than justice, he is basically right to refrain from any literary ambition in his *Decades*, because the content of his work is sensational enough and speaks for itself, particularly as his assignments in the service of the Crown leave him only little time. That is why he rejects the idea of writing a historical work, particularly as the discoveries and conquests are ongoing affairs, so that a historical description and evaluation would be out of the

---

[2] Under Queen Isabella of Castile Petrus Martyr was entrusted with a delicate and dangerous diplomatic mission to the Sultan of Egypt (1502). The Mohammedans in power resented the bad treatment of the defeated Moors in Spain and took reprisals against Christian pilgrims to the holy places in Palestine. Petrus Martyr succeeded in dissuading the Sultan from hostile actions against Christians. In 1504 Joanna, the declared successor to Queen Isabella, showed more and more signs of mental illness. Petrus Martyr had to support her, enduring her fits of madness and trying to induce her to deal at last with some governmental duties. When her husband, Philip of Burgundy, also declared successor to Queen Isabella, and his father-in-law, King Ferdinand of Aragon, who had been excluded from the succession, started arguing about supremacy, Petrus Martyr had to mediate (1505). When Charles V was taking over the reins in the different kingdoms of Spain, he did not want to appear in person in front of the "Cortes" of Valencia in order to take the oath of allegiance. But Valencia demanded his presence. So Petrus Martyr had to negotiate and mediate (1517).

question. The current reports, however, offer the opportunity of correcting doubtful information and of adding addenda whenever it seems appropriate. Finally he lets drop the remark that he wants to satisfy "per epistolas raptim scriptas" those whose wishes could not be ignored, this alluding to high-ranking recipients of his reports, mostly popes. For a clergyman it was appropriate to dedicate and send parts of his *Decades* to the pope in office, for the head of Christendom was directly concerned in Christianizing the natives of the New World. This kind of communication with the Holy See was of course equally in the interest of the Catholic Kings. Apart from these more formal reasons there are also personal ones. Petrus wants to get in touch and to keep in touch with Italian dignitaries at the highest level in order to find help and support if he should wish to, or should have to, leave Spain for whatever reason, or possibly also if he should get into trouble with the Spanish Inquisition, as Hernando de Talavera, his best friend and archbishop of Granada, had been. The popes who had received parts of his work were thrilled, passed on the news to their cardinals and diplomats, and asked him to continue to convey the latest news.

The eight *Decades de Orbe Novo* were written over a period of thirty-three years, from 1493 to his death in 1526, with two long breaks, lasting six and nine years respectively, mainly due to the prohibition of publication imposed by the Crown for reasons of secrecy.

In *Dec.* 5.1 (159), written in 1521, Petrus mentions the principles of his writing: "summa fides et integritas, brevitas et veritas", and calls his reports "commentarii", obviously following Caesar's "Bellum Gallicum". Petrus dedicated his first edition of *De Orbe Novo Decades Tres*, printed in 1516, to the emperor Charles V (38), dissociating himself from Spanish historians who meanwhile had started writing about the discoveries and the colonization of the Indies. He speaks "[de] historicis Hispanis, egregiis quippe viris, de generalibus tantum harum rerum inventis curam habentibus." We remember that Petrus has been trying to cover more than general facts, trying to grasp the special and unique traits in various areas. Due to his vivid sense of history, he feels obliged to take note of "miranda novaque, quae forte alias in voraces oblivionis fauces demersa latuissent."

Working Methods and Endeavours to Establish the Truth

Petrus had never seen the New World he was writing about. For this reason he was criticized by contemporary historians like Fernández de Oviedo, who stressed the importance of personal experience on the spot. Petrus anticipated reproaches like that (*Dec.* 7.7) and referred to authorities like Aristotle and Pliny the Elder who would never have been able to write their works if they had not relied on competent statements or reports of others.[3] A passage like *Dec.* 2.7 demonstrates his authority to collect information, his procedure, and his evaluation of all reports. Because of his special position at the Spanish Court, almost all famous explorers, among them Co-

---

[3] Petrus refers among other examples to Aristotle's *Historia animalium* in which Aristotle also adopted what had been observed by others who had been ordered by Alexander the Great to explore and investigate the animal world in remote parts of Asia.

lumbus, Núñez de Balboa, Magellán, Cortés, and Vespucci, had to give him a personal account of their discoveries, usually as guests at his hospitable home. After that, they had to give him a written version of their accounts. But he did not restrict himself to reports of explorers or of those in command. He listened also to selected representatives of Spanish colonists who came from remote areas of the New World in order to present their grievances to the authorities in Spain; he interviewed private travellers, ship-owners, and ordinary people returning from the West Indies. By interviewing people of various social classes, he took into consideration a variety of descriptions, opinions, and conflicts of interests.

The next procedure was sorting out irrelevant, contradictory, unlikely, or implausible statements. In order to clarify contradictions, eyewitnesses were called in. An important criterion for the adoption of reports was their contribution to cultural, historical, geographical, and scientific knowledge or understanding in various fields. There was also another category of documents at his disposal. The first maps of the New World drafted by discoverers like the brothers Columbus, Vespucci, and Morales, were helpful for his own orientation, but could not be publicly presented in detail, because they were classified as top secret. In addition Petrus seized every opportunity to examine objects and products brought by discoverers and presented to the Sovereigns, e.g., exotic plants, spices, fruit, rock samples, nuggets of precious metal, and commodities like tools, weapons, and also idols and treasures of various kinds.

Petrus's Objectivity

Petrus could not refrain from criticizing those who were responsible for noteworthy events if he thought it necessary. For all his admiration of the achievements of discoverers and conquerors, and for all his satisfaction at the extension of Christian belief in the Indies, he had reason enough for criticizing, for example, the rivalries and the laziness of Spanish noblemen, and the ruthless actions of the conquistadores and colonists against the Indians, especially the inhuman exploitation and even genocide which they practised.

The Scope of Petrus's Coverage

In line with his open-mindedness and manifold interests, Petrus does not confine himself to presenting specific events in detail. He also deals with reported botanic and zoological phenomena of the New World and their potential usefulness for human consumption and medical treatments. Moreover, he takes into consideration scientific and geographical phenomena like ocean currents, climate, the circumference of the earth, calculations of degrees of latitude, and measurements of distances. In the field of ethnology he treats the customs and religious ideas of the natives, their emotional life, and ethnic matters like craftsmanship, trade, and means of transport. This kind of universal coverage, characteristic of his extensive humanistic erudition, includes also philological and linguistic questions. He dealt for instance with the language of the inhabitants of the Antilles, compiled all the Indian words he could find out, and noted their stress and pronunciation. For experts in this field Petrus's notes are an important document of an idiom that died with the extermination of the original inhabitants about two decades after the arrival of Spanish colonists.

Petrus's References to the Ancient World and Their Purpose

Petrus's numerous references to classical mythology are nowadays sometimes completely misunderstood. In an article about *De Orbe Novo Decades Octo* in Kindler's *Neues Literaturlexikon* published in 1990 (11:277), B. Scharlau picks out a number of references to ancient myths indiscriminately and without considering the specific contexts, and says that the references are a projection of the Greek and Roman mythical world onto the newly discovered parts of the New World. That is why she declares that Petrus's work is a mixture of fantasy and empiricism, of exotic projection, mythical tradition and true story. Finally she seems to be at a loss over the fact that the *Decades* have enjoyed a long and continuing reception and many translations into numerous languages. As a humanist, Petrus is aware of the uniquely rich imagery and expressiveness of classical mythology. A suitable mythologem serves him as a code or a keyword that invokes a mythical archetype metaphorically transferrable to corresponding everyday situations. For instance, in *Decade* 7.4 (222), Petrus describes the royal decrees requiring just treatment of the native Indian population and the ensuing reality. He writes: "Spanish colonists, who came to the remote New World far away from their judges at home, were seized with greed for gold. Men who had left like gentle lambs changed after landing into rapacious wolves and forgot the royal decrees. A lot of them were reprimanded and punished." Petrus continues: "Quanto diligentius hydrae capita scinduntur, eo plura pullulare videntur." The ineffectiveness of laws and punishment cannot be expressed more clearly and more briefly than by the chosen mythologem.

For characterizing the uniqueness of the West Indian islands Petrus invokes (*Dec.* 3.7) the myth of the sea goddess Tethys and her daughters, the Nereids (or more exactly the Oceanides), who represent the islands he wants to describe. Tethys represents Haiti or Hispaniola as "domina atque genetrix", the Nereids the surrounding isles. He writes: "Habeat [sc. Hispaniola] mille atque iterum mille formosas, comptas ditesque Nereides nymphas quae ipsam, Fanquam Tethym alteram dominam & genetricem, circumsaepiant, comantique decentes." Then, describing the well-balanced mild climate, the remarkable fertility of some areas, the multiformity and beauty of landscapes, lakes, bays and inlets, describing too the botanical and zoological variety and novelties of the islands, he repeatedly refers to the mythical metaphor already quoted as a kind of leitmotiv in order to convey the magic and charm of this tropical paradise.

To sum up, it may be stressed that Petrus used his humanistic learning strictly for three purposes: first, of course, to enter upon a career that corresponded to his abilities and learning; second, to play his part as an esteemed and inspiring participant or correspondent in discussions with Italian and Spanish humanists, scholars, and his secular and ecclesiastical patrons; third, to explore new fields, thus becoming the first historian of the New World. He crowned his humanism with his humanity, his sense of justice, and his sympathy with those deprived of their rights or abandoned to their fates.

Hildesheim, Germany

Literature

Pietro Martire d'Anghiera (Petrus Martyr de Angleria). *Opera* (*Legatio Babylonica, De Orbe Novo Decades Octo, Opus Epistolarum*). Alcalá de Henares, 1530; facsimile repr. Graz 1966.

Lunardi, E. "Prospetto dei documenti relativi a Pietro Martire." In *Pietro Martire d'Anghiera nella storia e nella cultura. Atti del secondo convegno internazionale di studi americanistici, Genova, 1978*, 599–654. Genova, 1980.

De Bernardis, L. M. "Le dignità ecclesiastiche di Pietro Martire." In *Pietro Martire*, 75–80.

Bernecker, L., and Pietschmann, H. *Geschichte Spaniens*, 3rd ed. Stuttgart, Berlin, Köln, 2000.

Boscolo, A. "Pietro Martire Consigliere delle Indie e Abate di Giamaica." In *Pietro Martire*, 143–147.

Burckhardt, J. *Die Kultur der Renaissance in Italien*, 11th ed. Stuttgart, 1988.

Cantù, F. "Ideologia e storiografia in Pietro Martire." In *Pietro Martire*, 225–239.

Della Corte, F. I " 'Carmina' di Pietro Martire." In *Pietro Martire*, 187–194.

Ferro, G. "Interessi geografici nell' opera di Pietro Martire." In *Pietro Martire*, 485–493.

Lunardi, E. "Contributi alla biografia di Pietro Martire." In *Pietro Martire*, 3–62.

Lunardi, E., E. Magioncalda, and R. Mazzacane. *La Scoperta del Nuovo Mondo negli scritti di Pietro Martire*. Roma, 1988.

Klingelhöfer, H. *Peter Martyr von Anghiera, Acht Dekaden über die Neue Welt*. Darmstadt, 1972.

Lynch, J. *Spain 1516–1598: From Nation State to World Empire*. Oxford, 1991; repr. 1998.

Ponte, G. "Pietro Martire scrittore." In *Pietro Martire*, 151–174.

Repken, K., and R. Elze. *Studienbuch der Geschichte*, Bd. 2: *Frühe Neuzeit* 5th ed. Stuttgart, 1999; repr. 2000.

Wagner, H. R. *Peter Martyr and His Works*. New York, 1946.

On the Glory of Women: English and French Translations of Agrippa's Declamatio de nobilitate et praecellentia foeminei sexus *(1542–1726)*

BRENDA M. HOSINGTON

In 1509 Henricus Cornelius Agrippa von Nettesheim delivered a Latin *declamatio* on the nobility and preeminence of women at the University of Dôle, in Franche-Comté, where he had been appointed lecturer. His text served as a long introduction to a series of lectures on Johann Reuchlin's kabbalistic dialogue, *De verbo mirifico*, which were to incur the wrath of Jean Catilinet and end in Agrippa's removal from his post. As a result, Agrippa himself tells us, he held up the publication of the work for twenty years.

In his Letter to Maximilian Transsylvanus, Secretary to the Emperor Charles V, which prefaces the *De nobilitate et praecellentia foeminei sexus*, Agrippa explains how he had dedicated the Reuchlin lectures to Princess Margaret of Austria,[1] and delivered the *declamatio* on women in praise of her, "a unique example of women's excellence and nobility." The phrase that follows is revealing: "vt se praeside ac teste libellus ille non parum authoritatis caperet aduersus eos qui in foemineo sexu vituperando, nihil faciunt reliqui" (46). Agrippa, then, was aware that the *declamatio* presented views on women with which many, especially those "whose sole occupation is to criticize the female sex," would disagree. These views, in a nutshell, were as follows.

The *De nobilitate*, a strongly polemical work, argues forcefully that, while in terms of the soul women and men are equal, in name, order, place, created material, and station accorded by God, they are superior. Agrippa appeals to etymology, physiology, the Bible and the classics, history, the natural world, and contemporary writings that discuss the "woman question." When he borrows exempla of bad women from

---

[1] The Latin text quoted throughout is *De Nobilitate et praecellentia foeminei sexus. Edition critique d'après le texte d'Anvers 1529*, ed. R. Antonioli et al. (Geneva, 1990).

the many anti-feminist writings available, he subverts their traditional meaning to prove feminine virtue. Finally, he asserts that the oppression of women, supported by physicians, philosophers, the Bible, theologians, and lawyers, rests on custom, and all customs are arbitrary. Such oppression cannot be justified. Moreover, the supporting arguments, being flawed, can be used to demonstrate quite the opposite of what is intended: that women are in fact superior.

How serious was Agrippa in this defense of women, and how seriously did he take his *De nobilitate*? In his Letter to Maximilian, he asserts that he wants his work to be published with his other writings, "etiam si videam res haec quam sit exigua, et qua nulla elegantia dicendi reddita." He calls it a "libellum hunc quondam in pueritia mea conscriptum" and promises to present Margaret with more profound and serious works that will better represent his talents than "his pueritiae meae nugis" (46–47). This of course may simply be an example of the well-worn modesty topos. On the other hand, it may also be a means of defending himself against criticism. His preface to *De incertitudine et vanitate scientiarum* plays that very role, and its comments on *declamatio* also pertain to the *De nobilitate*. He defines the genre as one of mixed modes, shifting between playfulness and seriousness, between truth and fable: "non judicat, non dogmatizat, sed quae declamationis conditiones sunt, alia joco, alia serio, alia false, alia saeve dicit." *Declamatio*, he adds, expresses the opinions of both author and other commentators, yet sometimes offers arguments that are invalid.[2]

Agrippa's own mixed feelings towards his defense of women appear in his dedicatory letter to Margaret. He wavers between feeling audacious at being the first — or so he claims — to assert women's superiority over men and feeling shame at having taken such a position.[3] The word "pudor" occurs no fewer than three times in the first six lines of the letter, and Agrippa even goes so far as to say that to accord women pre-eminence over men is to denote "ingenii euirati," an "emasculated spirit." He wavers similarly between fearing to appear ungrateful for women's virtues should he remain silent and feeling shame at extolling them in print.

This ambiguity was not always understood by Agrippa's contemporaries or those who followed in his footsteps, nor is it always taken into consideration by modern critics. Some interpret his *De nobilitate* purely at face value, as an avant-garde feminist text. Others see it as an example of Renaissance paradox, an exercise in rhetoric, a flourish of epideixis, in which Agrippa's arguments run counter to popular anti-feminist conventions.[4] Most early commentators took him seriously and read the text

---

[2] "Henrici Cornelii Agrippae ... apologia adversus calumnias propter declamationem de Vanitate scientiarum, & excellentia verbi Dei, sibi per aliquos Lovanienses Theologistas intentatas," in *Opera*, 2 vols. (Lugduni per Beringos fratres: n.d.), 2.2:326–327.

[3] Agrippa was not actually the first to assert female superiority. Rodriguez del Padron da Camara did so in his 1430 *Triunfo das Donas*, translated into French by Fernand de Lucena in 1459 or 1460, and thought by Antonioli (*De Nobilitate*, 22) to be one probable source for the *De nobilitate*. Two other texts suggesting that women are superior in some aspects Agrippa probably did not know: Bartolomeo Gogio's *De laudibus mulierum*, composed in 1487 but never printed, and Maria Equicola's *De mulieribus*, possibly published in 1501, in which the author, like Agrippa, blames women's inequality on social customs.

[4] A range of opinions on this score is represented by, amongst others, Barbara Newman,

as a vigorous defense of women. It greatly influenced the *querelle des femmes* in France, while authors everywhere between 1400 and 1800 drew upon Agrippa's interpretation of Genesis and other biblical sources. In the sixteenth century alone it was translated into five languages, and many more translations would follow. The present study examines seven of these, four done into English and three into French, which cover the years 1542 to 1726. It discusses the liminary materials, various aspects of the text and translations, and their overall tone. In so doing, it attempts to ascertain how the translators, working in very different contexts and periods, interpret their original: as a serious feminist text, a witty and erudite example of rhetorical paradox, or a mixture of both.

The first English translation appeared in 1542 and was reissued in 1545. Entitled *A Treatise of the nobilitie and excellency of woman kynd*, it was the work of David Clapam, who in 1540 had already translated Agrippa's *De sacramento matrimonii declamatio*.[5] Clapam was a Cambridge graduate and well-connected proctor in the ecclesiastical courts. The second is in verse, *The Glory of Woman, or a Looking-glasse for Ladies*, published in 1652. It is by Hugh Crompton, known to Winstanley as a minor poet who dedicated one of his collections to Mary, Duchess of Richmond and Lennox.[6] The same year, Edward Fleetwood published a prose version, *The Glory of Women; or a Treatise declaring the excellency and preeminence of women above men*. I have discovered little about the translator, except that he was probably the brother of George Fleetwood who was one of the regicides condemned in 1660.[7] The fourth translation appeared eighteen years later, in 1670. It is by Henry Care and entitled *Female Pre-eminence or the Dignity and Excellency of that Sex above the Male*. Care is the best known of the four English translators, having been a political writer suspected of popish sympathies, a "petty fogger" who wrote against the Church of England, and who was also a translator of religious and medical works.[8]

"Renaissance Feminism and Esoteric Theology," *Viator* 24 (1993): 337–356; Marc van der Poel, *Cornelius Agrippa, the Humanist Theologian and his Declamations* (Leiden, 1997); Ian MacLean, *The Renaissance Notion of Woman* (Cambridge, 1980); and Constance Jordan, *Renaissance Feminism: Literary Texts and Political Models* (Ithaca, NY, 1990). For a definition of Renaissance paradox see Rosalie L. Colie, *Paradoxia epidemica. The Renaissance Tradition of Paradox* (Princeton, 1966), who points to Agrippa's exploitation of paradox in his *De incertitudine et vanitate scientiarum* and *Apologia adversus calumnias* although she does not mention his *De nobilitate* (400–401). Linda Woodbridge agrees that the *De nobilitate* is an example of Renaissance paradox, yet attributes a certain sincerity to Agrippa in his defense of women: *Women and the English Renaissance* (Urbana, IL, 1984), 34–44.

[5] *A Treatise of the nobilitie and excellencye of woman kynde, translated out of Latine into englysshe by David Clapam* (London, Thomas Berthelet, 1542). It is reissued by Berthelet in 1545 *along with a second edition of Clapam's The Commendation of Matrimony*, not as *The Commendation of Matrimony* as James Turner asserts in *One Flesh, Paradisal Marriage and Sexual Relations in the Age of Milton* (Oxford, 1987), 109.

[6] See William Winstanley, *Lives of the Most Famous English Poets* (London, 1687), 191. Crompton published *A Medley of Music and epigrammes* in 1657 and *Pierides or the Muses' Mount* possibly one year later.

[7] See the entry for Sir George Fleetwood in the *Dictionary of National Biography* 7:265–266.

[8] See the *Dictionary of National Biography* 3:954–955; and Anthony à Wood, *Athenae Oxonienses*

The three French translations under consideration span a shorter period. The first is anonymous: *Traité agréable & Curieux de la Noblesse & Excellence du Sexe de la femme par dessus celui de l'homme*, published in The Hague in 1686. It is followed by the 1713 *De la grandeur et de l'excellence des femmes audessus des hommes*, the work of Jean d'Arnaudin, the nephew of a famous theologian and himself the author of two religious works.[9] The last is Nicolas Gueudeville's *Sur la noblesse & excellence du sexe feminin*, published in Leiden in 1726 with, in the same volume, a translation of Agrippa's *De sacramento matrimonii* and *De incertitudine et vanitate scientiarum*. Gueudeville, a French Benedictine, forsook France and Catholicism for Holland and Calvinism. He translated a great number of books, including More's *Utopia* and Erasmus's *Praise of Folly* and *Colloquies*, and wrote several polemical works.[10]

The liminary materials in the *De nobilitate* comprise Agrippa's letter to Maximilian, his dedicatory epistle to Margaret, and a poem by a mysterious and unidentifiable L. Beliaquetus.[11] They appeared in all the editions available to our seven translators: Antwerp 1529, Cologne 1532 and 1598, two with no place of publication in 1567 and 1568, Grenoble, late sixteenth century, and the Lyon *Opera* of c. 1600 and its subsequent reprints. They are dealt with in various ways in the translations. Clapam ignores them and so, not surprisingly, does Crompton, since he says he has followed not the Latin text but an English prose translation, most certainly Clapam's. Fleetwood gives the Latin and English versions of the L. Beliaquatus poem and translates the letter to Maximilian very closely but omits the dedication to Margaret. Care simply alludes to the dedicatory epistle to Margaret in his own dedication to "no meaner princess, Katherine" [wife of Charles II]. The French translators demonstrate a similar independence. The 1686 anonymous translator gives a French version of the poem by L. Beliaquetus, which he places after the text of the *De nobilitate*. Arnaudin, like Clapam, ignores the liminary materials completely. Gueudeville, on the contrary, translates them all.

Perhaps of equal interest are the translator's own prefatory materials. While Clapam has none, Crompton, Fleetwood, and Care have dedications to various ladies. Crompton's dedicatee is his wife. He tells her he has chosen verse for his translation because, although he found the text "consonant in itselfe and reason", its tone was "dissonent" (A2). He has been encouraged by the fact that although poets seemed "lascivious" in praising women, they were well-intentioned. So much the more so, then, should he "paraphrase upon this so famous Tract, which is real and true." In his letter to the "Ingenious Reader" (A4), he declares himself ready to "illustrate women's glory" despite "the lash of many tongues," perhaps an echo of Agrippa's anxiety

---

2:469, as well as Macaulay, *History of England* (London, 1858), 2:218, n. 221.

[9] See the *Biographie universelle ancienne et moderne. Nouvelle édition publieé sous la direction de M. Michaud*. 45 vols. (Paris, 1843–[65]), 2:246.

[10] See the *Biographie universelle*, 18:69–70 and *La France littéraire ou Dictionnaire bibliographique*, éd. J.-M. Quérard. 11 vols. (Paris, 1827–1857), 1:94. The work against the Catholic church is *Dialogue de M. le baron de la Hontan et d'un sauvage d'Amérique* (Amsterdam, 1704).

[11] The French editors suggest that L. Beliaquetus might well be a pseudonym (45). The author could perhaps be Agrippa himself: both "L. Beliaquetus" and he call the *De nobilitate* a "libellus."

in his letter to Maximilian. He also confesses to omitting philosophers who do not support Agrippa's belief in women's superiority. Crompton's rather cavalier attitude towards his text is representative of the school of very free translation, represented by Denham and Cowley, and which inspired Dryden's disdain. It also demonstrates, however, how keen he was to put across Agrippa's defense of women and how seriously he took it.

Fleetwood dedicates his translation to "the Vertuous and Beautifull Female Sex of the Common-Wealth of England." We are told nothing of his translating methods, only that Agrippa is a "judicious learned Author" with whom he agrees completely "because when I behold your splendor and glittering beauty, I take it as a great confirmation of [Agrippa's] opinion" — a not wholly convincing reason (A3). Yet he, too, obviously takes Agrippa's treatise seriously.

Henry Care's translation is preceded by a friend's three poems, ostensibly in praise of women but in fact lauding Care and exhorting them to be grateful to him. There follows an "Epistle Dedicatory" to Queen Katherine in which Care reassures her that Agrippa's title will no longer scandalize and his work no longer be thought too lavish in praise of women because of her own preeminence and excellency (3) — an unconvincing and clichéd reason. In his "Preface to the Reader," however, he thanks Agrippa for revealing women's worth, although he gives the greater palm of victory to women themselves. He describes the *De nobilitate* as a "sally of the same Generosity" as the *De vanitate*, "that delights to engage on disadvantages, and bravely to assist the weaker party" (A2). Lastly, he praises Agrippa for his courage in defending women against men's calumnies. Again, the translator reads his source text as well intentioned and convincingly argued. This nevertheless does not prevent him from making some "Additions, and variation, to render it more smooth and gracefull to the present Age." In other words, he has taken the liberties that most translators of his age did in "improving" the original.

The French translators' own liminary materials demonstrate rather different attitudes towards Agrippa's defense. The "Avant Propos" to the 1686 anonymous French translation praises Agrippa for his erudition and courage in revealing to women how they can "égaler les hommes." Note the word "égaler," "to equal," and not "surpasser," "to surpass." The final sentence leaves us in no doubt as to the translator's opinion of Agrippa's encomium: it is likened to Apuleius's eloquent praise of an ass and Erasmus's brilliant praise of folly. In other words, this is a very clever piece of rhetoric but one not to be taken seriously (3a). Perhaps this is why he confesses he has not followed the original too closely, has removed some statements that did not agree with "saine religion," and has added some of his own (3b).

Arnaudin, in his very long "Preface," confesses his conversion to Agrippa's cause. His previous attitude towards women was based on grammar: as the masculine gender is superior to the feminine, so are men superior to women (a iii). He adds an argument to Agrippa's that he modestly calls "more convincing": men seek happiness in perfection and nobility; since they seek women's company, women must be perfect and noble (a vi). Arnaudin also tells us a little of his translating practices, which are typical of his age. He has taken some liberties with the text, removing tiresome and "unchaste" sentences here and there, making them more "polite," and changing the meaning in one place because "theologically unsound" and therefore damaging to the cause of women. He has also provided marginal notes to explain certain statements.

Our last translator, Nicolas Gueudeville, admits to no similar conversion to the cause of women. On the contrary, he offers a "Preface du traducteur" in which his criticism of Agrippa is biting. If, he says, Agrippa had argued with as much soundness as zeal, the text would have been humiliating for men; as it is, truth "is on our side." Agrippa is guilty of "pitiful sophistry" in arguing that female superiority resides in the fact that God created women last. Men and women are equally capable of doing good or evil (6). Finally, Gueudeville remains unconvinced by Agrippa's text and is faithful to his hallmark in translating: absolute freedom to rework the text and insert his own very firmly held political and religious views.

We have seen a variety of attitudes and reactions to the *De nobilitate* in the translators' liminary materials. It remains to be seen whether these are traceable in the translations themselves. Crompton, who called the work "real and true," and Fleetwood, who asserted that Agrippa's arguments are fully supported by Genesis, both translate with the freedom typical of their time, but their texts have a more subdued ring than Agrippa's. Neither achieves the playful tone of the original, probably because the translators did not understand it, thinking the *De nobilitate* an entirely serious work. Care, on the other hand, as James Turner has pointed out, "expresses much of the wit and social banter" and even adds "reassurances of playfulness."[12] Arnaudin, who confessed the text converted him to Agrippa's cause, adds footnotes suggesting that he has misunderstood Agrippa's teasing. For example, when Agrippa states that when women fall unexpectedly they nearly always do so on their backs ("ut si casu fortuitove cadendum sit, mulieres fere semper in tergum decidant"), a joke often found in medieval anti-feminist writings, Arnaudin criticizes the author for being "puérile et indigne du sérieux d'Agrippa" (37). Another footnote calls Agrippa's comments on females' ability to conceive without a man "faux et abusifs" (44), despite his accompanying statement that we cannot accept virgin births as true, except in the case of the Virgin Mary.

Three translators do appear to read the *De nobilitate* as a text containing elements of paradox. In rendering Agrippa's claim that the Scholastics can only prove the contrary of what he is saying by resorting to allegories, the 1686 French translator calls the work "ce paradoxe" (34). Henry Care mistranslates Agrippa's statement that his argument "ratum firmumque erit": "This may at first perhaps seem an odd Assertion, and extravagently Paradoxical" (17). At the end of the text, where Agrippa says simply "deinde a religione, a natura, ab humanis legibus, a uaria autoritate, ratione et exemplis promiscue demonstrauimus" (89), Gueudeville adds: "J'ai prouvé géométriquement, démonstrativement, invinciblement, mon paradoxe."

Of all the translators, it is indeed Gueudeville who takes the *De nobilitate* the least seriously. This is made evident in several ways: humorous statements added to the text, hyperbolic elaborations of some arguments, mostly those dealing with sexual matters, and sarcastic or mocking comments added about women where nothing in the original supports such an interpretation.

---

[12] Turner, *One Flesh*, 110.

Sometimes Agrippa himself is clearly tongue-in-cheek. For example, after praising the superiority of women in speech, he states as proof: "ut vix uspiam mulier muta reperiatur" (64). He is obviously responding ironically to one of the traditional criticisms of women found in misogynist texts, namely female garrulousness. This is accurately rendered by all the translators, but Gueudeville continues in mocking tone: "et la moindre harengère est plus forte sur ce chapitre-là que le plus habile avocat" [and the least fishwife is abler in that domain than the most skilful lawyer] (65). Care, too, adds to Agrippa's comment: "How sweet and insinuating are their compliments? How sudden their Answers? How ingenious their Retorts? How ready their Excuses? How neat their Evasions? How irresistible their Intreaties?" Thus he maintains the comic tone, even heightening it by hyperbole, yet without indulging in Gueudeville-like sarcasm.

This sarcastic tone is reserved in Agrippa's text for those who criticize women; it is never used when speaking of women themselves. In Gueudeville's translation, on the contrary, it is directed almost solely against them. For example, after Agrippa's list of cures associated with menstrual blood, Gueudeville adds acidly that even a woman's excrement can be a relic signaling a miracle (63). Throughout his text, woman is called "notre femelle," or "notre beau sexe." Neither term is used by Agrippa. Gueudeville's final sentence sums up his attitude to the text. Agrippa's sober "Ne ergo opus ipsum in nimis magnum uolumen exeat, hic illius finis esto" (89) is followed by a wish for "joie, et ce qui vaut mieux que tout le reste, une femme, si deja ne l'avez" [joy, and what's better than anything else, a woman — if you don't have one already].

Translations are a product of the context in which they are created, related to the cultural modes and social mores of their time as well as to ideological factors. This is amply proved by the translations under consideration. For example, Agrippa's text contains detailed references to subjects like menstruation, procreation without male assistance, and the genitals. Clapam translates some of these fairly accurately, although he often skips over the details. The later English and French translators, however, all either completely omit or severely curtail the references to menstruation and the genitalia. Arnaudin says clearly that he has changed, sweetened, or left out certain expressions "que la politesse de notre langue ne souffre pas, & que les oreilles chastes eussent entendues avec horreur" [which decorum in our language would not permit and which chaste ears would hear with horror] (e ii). Even the passage on Adam and Eve's nudity has been translated only partially "pour ne pas choquer les oreilles circonspectes, ou salir l'imagination" [in order not to shock circumspect ears or sully the imagination] (25). This is in keeping with eighteenth-century preoccupations with taste and correctness.

One ideological factor that influences the translation of Agrippa's *De nobilitate* is religion. Agrippa uses the Bible and Church Fathers for arguments and exempla. He also refers many times to the Catholic church and often praises the Blessed Virgin Mary as the "perfect and noblest example of the perfect and noble female sex."[13]

---

[13] Gueudeville also rejects this notion but not on theological grounds. He calls it simply "sophistry" (5b).

Arnaudin, nephew of a theologian, is troubled by Agrippa's assertion that Adam alone is responsible for original sin, a not, he says, very orthodox view that could be disproved by theologians. He even distances himself from the statement by pointing out he is only the translator, not the author (55).

Other shifts in the translations concern Catholicism and Protestantism. Clapam, working in the early 1540s, retains all references to the Catholic church and the Blessed Virgin Mary's immaculate conception and title as "mother of God", although he does omit Agrippa's assertion that she suffered no pains in childbirth because she was subject to no laws of nature. Despite the Schism a bare decade earlier, and the fact that he was highly thought of by both the ardent Protestant John Bale and William Cecil, Secretary of State to the equally ardent Protestant Edward VI,[14] Clapam feels no need to change Agrippa's text consistently, leaving references to "our Catholic church" and so on. The three later English translators, on the other hand, all do. "Ecclesia catholica" consistently becomes "Christian church" or simply "church." "Nostra ecclesia" becomes "the church." Mary is not once called the mother of God. Where reference is made to her being born without sin, Fleetwood and Crompton add, respectively, "(as some divines confirm)" and "(As some affirm)." There are too many examples of such changes for this to be accidental.

The mingling of judicious and at times facetious arguments in *De nobilitate* suggests that Agrippa was anxious to display his ability to create a work in the same vein as other humanist paradoxes. His espousing of the defense of women also suggests he was well aware of the *querelle des femmes* and changing humanist attitudes. But also in his mind was his desire to placate Margaret of Austria out of whose favor he had fallen in the years between 1509 and 1529. The resulting *declamatio* is one of endless ambiguities and subtleties that still tease the modern critic. Some of these Agrippa's translators render, others they omit or misinterpret. While Clapam, Crompton, Fleetwood, and Arnaudin seem to have interpreted the text as a serious defense of women and, indeed, in the case of Crompton and Arnaudin have even made changes to strengthen Agrippa's arguments, Care, the anonymous French translator, and Gueudeville perceived the text's playful tone. Yet even their response to this feature of the text varies. Care, although praising Agrippa for his courage in defending the superiority of women, calls it a "sally like the *De vanitate*." The anonymous French translator, in comparing the work to *The Golden Ass* and *The Praise of Folly*, clearly views it as satire, although he too praises Agrippa's courage and erudition. Of Gueudeville's interpretation there is no doubt. Agrippa has not convinced him of female superiority because his arguments are not sound. Despite these differences, all three, as we said earlier, perceive the paradoxical elements in the work. These seven translations, then, represent the same wide range of tone as Agrippa's text of 1529, and they pose the same tantalizing questions.

Université de Montréal

---

[14] See the *Dictionary of National Biography*, 4:371; and also John Bale, *Index Britanniae scriptorum quos ex variis bibliotheis non parro labore collegit Ionnes Baleus, cum aliis. John Bale's Index of British and Other Writers*, ed. Reginald Lane Poole with the help of Mary Bateson (Oxford, 1902), 60.

Neo-Latin Nonsense in Nabokov

AUGUST A. IMHOLTZ

To the question, what do Lewis Carroll and Vladimir Nabokov have in common, most people would probably answer something to the effect that the former wrote most famously, and the latter most infamously, about little girls. Humbert Humbert, the nymphet-obsessed narrator and anti-hero of Nabokov's novel *Lolita*,[1] was the cause of much moral outrage in America directed against its author some ninety years after the publication of Carroll's *Alice's Adventures in Wonderland*. But what Carroll and Nabokov really have in common is "logodaedaly" — playing games with words: and a few of those Latin and Neo-Latin word games we shall examine here.

At the end of chapter 8 of Part I of *Lolita*, Humbert Humbert says "Oh, my Lolita, I have only words to play with" (34). And play he does, often on several different levels. What Nabokov says in explicating a particularly difficult passage in his novel *Bend Sinister* for the Dutch translator Charles Timmer illustrates his technique. The phrase: "from the twinned night of the Keeweenawatin and the horrors of the Laurentian Revolution" means, according to Vladimir and Vera Nabokov's reply to Timmer:

> this is a hard passage. It develops simultaneously on several planes. The word "Keeweeanawatin" is a telescopic combination of two terms "Keewatin" (name of a schist of the Archaeozoic — the oldest — period) and "Keewanawan" (subdivision of the Protoerozoic). Laurentian belongs to the Archaeozoi, Permian to the Paleozoic . . . In other words, from the dimmest past into the present.[2]

---

[1] All citations from *Lolita* are to *The Annotated Lolita*, ed. with preface, introduction and notes by Alfred Appel, Jr. (New York, 1970). Page numbers of the Nabokov text are cited in parentheses following the quotation.

[2] Brian Boyd, *Vladimir Nabokov: The Russian Years* (Princeton, 1990), 316.

The Nabokov bibliography is quite a large one, with the paper chase for influence and echoes, to which I am not unwittingly about to add, encompassing a good deal of the world's literature. Critics have found in Nabokov's Lolita influences from the ancient Greek myth of Io to Melville's *Moby Dick* and from the Sumerian epic *Gilgamesh* to Mark Twain's *Huckleberry Finn*.[3] However many strata of texts and levels of experience might be buried in the novel, let us consider some of the verbal Roman fireworks Nabokov sets off.

A Neo-Latin Passage in Lolita

At a nearly climactic point in the novel, at least in the sexual sense, Humbert Humbert is overcome with passion as he holds Lolita on his lap. Word control is the first thing to go. "What's the katter with misses?" he mutters into her hair as he is about to moan and die (a clear sexual reference).

"If you must know," replies Lolita, "you do it the wrong way."
"Show wight ray," Humbert answers — another spoonerism.
"All in good time," responded the "spoonerette" — a manufactured word as though Lolita were the object of Humbert's spoonerisms.

Then comes the following macaronic Neo-Latin outburst:

Seva ascendes, pulsata, brulans, kitzelans, dementissima. Elevator clatterans, pausa, clatterans, populus in corridoro. Hanc nisi mors mihi adimet nemo! Juncea puellula, jo pensavo fondissime, nobserva nihil quidquam. (122)

To continue sketching the scene I should add that Humbert Humbert retires to the bathroom "where it takes him quite some time to shift back into normal gear" while he listens to Lolita's "oo's" and "gee's" of girlish delight as she looks at the garments and presents in the "treasure box" (i.e., the suitcase, but again a sexually charged phrase) that he has bought for her. Lolita's cries ironically echo those of Humbert Humbert's barely averted orgasm. This may be the most sexually explicit passage in the whole novel, but being in Latin and a macaronic mixture of other words from other languages it has been overlooked, not only by the morals police and censors in the United States but also by most of Nabokov's literary commentators. What we have here in Humbert Humbert's abruptly terminated stream of consciousness crescendo is a kind of Joycean verbal "coitus interruptus."

Here is the translation provided by Alfred Appel, Jr. in his commentary in *The Annotated Lolita*:

---

[3] S. E. Sweeney, "Io's Metamorphosis: Classical Subtext for Lolita," *Classical and Modern Literature* 10 (1990): 143–151; Laurie Clancy, *The Novels of Vladimir Nabokov* (London, 1984), 110; Charles Rowan Beye, "Gilgamesh, Lolita, and Huckleberry Finn," *Classical and Modern Literature* 9 (1989): 39–50.

The sap ascendeth, pulsates, burning, itching, most insane, elevator clattering, pausing, clattering, people in the corridor. No one but death would take this one away from me! Slender little girl, I thought most fondly, observing nothing at all.[4]

At best that is a poor literal crib and, in fact, is even a bit inaccurate. Nabokov deserves better. I cannot promise to reveal all the levels and interpret all of the possible allusions, but let us look at the passage more closely.

"Seva ascendes": "seva" comes from the French word "sève" meaning "sap" or "life force."[5] It derives from the Latin "sapa." In English it refers to the firmness and strength of flavor proper to any particular wine, a taste that lingers in the mouth. I suggest "seva" be taken in its sap sense as a figure for "semen." In Chapter 17 Humbert Humbert drinks his favorite concoction of gin and pineapple juice to fortify him for a sexual encounter with Charlotte, Lolita's mother, and as he waits he mows the lawn, deflowering the dandelions, and notes the reek of "sap mingled with pineapple."(75) "Ascendes" is best taken as a mistaken form of the Latin present participle "ascendens" or, if the "es" ending is retained, as direct address to the sap. "Sève ascendante" is also a botanical term as noted above.

"Pulsata": "having paused" may refer to the sap in Humbert's engorged member.

"Brulans": a Latinized present participle from the French verb "brûler" meaning to burn, which is often used figuratively in the sense of possessed by passion (e.g., "brûlant d'amour" and "brûlant du desir").[6]

"Kitzelans": we shall return to this interesting word in a moment.

"Dementissima": "most insane." Appel does not see that this, I believe, modifies "seva," the life's sap, which is not at all a reasonable entity. This is about Humbert's passion for his nymphets.

"Elevator": "the deliverer, one who rises up." (Note, as Humbert might have said in one of his frequent apostrophes, it is hard not to get carried away with this.) For this sense see 2 Kings 22:3 in the Vulgate. The reference is also probably to Humbert Humbert's member.

"Clatterans": another Latinized present participle, this time made from the English verb "clatter," which can have the sense, relevant here, of "the noise made by the collision of two sonorous bodies" (Lolita is on Humbert's lap).[7] Perhaps the indirect allusion here is that their bodies are not yet ringing.

"Pausa": halt or stop, and then "clatterans" again.

"Populus in corridoro": Appel is correct that this literally means "people in the corridor," but it is worth remembering that "populus" is related to the verb "popu-

---

[4] Appel, *The Annotated Lolita*, 375.

[5] "Seva ascendante" is a botanical technical term: Paul Imbs, *Trésor de la langue française. Dictionnaire de la langue du XIXe et du XXe Siècle, 1789–1960* (Paris, 1974), 1:431.

[6] Emile Littré, *Dictionnaire de la langue française* (Paris, 1964). 1:1290

[7] *Oxford English Dictionary*, 2nd ed. prepared by J. A. Simpson and E. S. C. Weiner (Oxford, 1989), 3:284. The earliest reference to "clatter" in this sense is from Lyte in 1578 and refers to aspen leaves which could scarcely be considered sonorous bodies.

lor" which means "to spread out, spoil, or despoil" while "corridor" of course is "the main passage" — another possible sexual reference.

"Hanc nisi mors mihi adimet nemo": This is in fact a quotation, a half-line, from Terence's *Andria*, a point not grasped by Appel.[8] Nor does he translate it correctly, for it should be a future indicative rather than a subjunctive: "only Death shall take her from me." Its use is ironic in that although death does claim Lolita, as the fictitious John Ray reveals in the novel's foreword, it is Clare Quilty (Humbert Humbert's double whose name to some critics indicates a play on the phrase "clearly guilty") who will take Lolita from Humbert Humbert, as will also Lolita's husband, Richard Schiller. Except for Nabokov's substitution of "mihi" for "mi," it is a direct quotation from Terence. The whole passage in the *Andria* (lines 694–697) has at least a little bearing on Humbert's own situation. Pamphilus is speaking to Mysis, maid of his beloved Glycerium:

> per omnis adiuro deos numquam eam me deserturum,
> non si capiundos mihi sciam esse inimicos omnis homines.
> hanc mi expetivi: contigit; conveniunt mores: valeant
> qui inter nos discidium volunt: hanc nisi mors mi adimet nemo.[9]

And in Betty Radice's translation for the Penguin Terence:

> By all the gods in heaven, I swear to you that I will never desert her, not if I knew that I would make the whole world my enemy. I sought her out and won her; we were made for each other. To hell with those who want to part us! Nothing shall take her from me except death.[10]

Has Humbert Humbert really won Lolita? Are their hearts one? He is about to find out that they are not. Humbert Humbert also does not realize that, like Pamphilus, he is an unhappy wretch — "miser" is the word the slave Davos uses. And Humbert Humbert knows that he must face the enmity of the whole world, or at least the outrage of 1950s middle America for his nympholepsy passion. The only critic who has noted the *Andria* quotation is David H. J. Larmour. He makes the same point as I do, which is so obvious that it must be the reason why Nabokov chose the line: "Humbert's situation is superficially similar to Pamphilus's: he is involved in a liaison which society finds unacceptable."[11] Unfortunately, he has nothing else to say about the "Seva" passage except to call it "a whole passage of linguistic confusion." It may be a little more than that at the hands of the master Vladimir Nabokov.

---

[8] Appel, *The Annotated Lolita*, 375.
[9] Sidney G. Ashmore, ed., *The Comedies of Terence* (New York, 1960), 35.
[10] Betty Radice, trans., *Terence: Phormio and Other Plays* (Baltimore, 1967), 55.
[11] David H. J. Larmour, "Nabokov *Philomelus*: The Classical Allusions in *Lolita*," *Classical and Modern Literature* 10 (1990): 145.

"Juncea puellula": a slender (bullrush-like) little girl. The words "juncea" and "puellula" occur in both Terence and Catullus.[12]

"Jo pensavo": Italian past tense, "I thought." This may be a tenuous reference to the passage in Canto XXIII of Dante's *Inferno* — a context not inappropriate to the situation in which Humbert finds himself. Here are Dante's lines in Singleton's translation: "I thought: they have been fooled because of us, and with such hurt and mockery as I believe must vex them greatly. If rage be added to their malice, they will come after us, fiercer than the dog to the leveret he snaps up."[13]

"Nobserva quidquam": Humbert Humbert may mean "nonobservans quidquam," as Appel suggests in his translation, "not observing anything." The point is that Lolita is not noticing what is happening sexually to Humbert.[14]

Now let us return to the key word: "kitzelans." According to the *Deutsches Wörterbuch*, the German word "kitzeln" primarily means "to tickle" or "to titillate." The Latin synonyms given by the *Wörterbuch* are "titillare" and "prurire." The word derives from the Althochdeutsch "chizilôn" and "chuzilôn," which in Mittelhochdeutsch becomes "kitzeln" with an "i" or "kützeln" with an umlauted "ü."[15] In addition to its ticklish sense, there are several meanings and usages of "kitzeln" that seem particularly relevant to Nabokov's depiction of Humbert's excited state.

Occasionally, for example, "kitzeln" is used as a euphemism for "coire," "to have sexual intercourse": "Leyrmatz wurde von einer jungfer, so einen hollandischen windbrommert im kützeln in die weite welt streichen liesze, befraget, warumb solcher blasianer so schrie?"[16] It also refers to the sensual side of joy and means "to arouse strongly," even "to excite oneself" — "mit fleischlicher liebe sich kutzelt."[17] Nouns reflecting these senses of the word include: "Kitzelfreude" — "love's sensual delight" — which is the equivalent of "liebesgenusz" and "Kitzeljagd" or "pursuit of love." The adjective "kitzelgierig" means "lusting, pruriently desiring."[18] The noun "Kitzler" is also derived from "kitzeln" and means "clitoris."[19] Nabokov uses the word with special effect later in the novel. Quilty, like Nabokov himself, is well versed in logomancy. When Humbert is examining hotel registers in his search for Quilty's pseudonyms, he says "[his] fiendish conundrum would ejaculate in my face." (252) The conundrum is one of Quilty's fictitious registered names, Dr. Kitzler, address: Eryx, Miss.; or, to translate: Dr. Clitoris, Venus, Miss, "Eryx" being, as Appel correctly notes, "a reference to the cult of Aphrodite with its practice of

---

[12] "Juncea" in Terence, *Eunuchus* 316. "Puellula" in Terence, *Phormio* 81; Catullus 55.9; 57.9; 59.57.

[13] Dante Alighieri, *The Divine Comedy: Inferno*, trans. with comm. Charles S. Singleton (Princeton, 1970), 235.

[14] Appel, *The Annotated Lolita*, 375.

[15] Jacob and Wilhelm Grimm, *Deutsches Wörterbuch* (hereafter *DW*) (Leipzig: 1873), 5:876.

[16] Grimm, *DW*, 5:878.

[17] Grimm, *DW*, 5:881.

[18] Grimm, *DW*, 5:875.

[19] Grimm, *DW*, 5:884.

religious prostitution, an Elymian settlement on a mountain above Drepana in western Sicily."[20]

The erotic German meanings of "kitzeln" are taken over wholesale in the Yiddish word "kitzln"[21] (pronounced "keets-lehn") and the Latinized present participle form with its "ans" ending could sound like a Yiddish form. But why a Yiddish exclamation at the height of Humbert Humbert's sexual reverie? It may be outrageous, but I would like to suggest that with this single Yiddish word uttered at the sexual climax of the book, for that as you see is what I think these macaronic lines constitute, Nabokov reveals what is only hinted at elsewhere throughout the novel: Humbert Humbert is Jewish. There are many allusions to such an identification, some of which were not seen even by Appel:

- Charlotte asks Humbert whether he had in his family "a certain strain," to which Humbert replies by asking whether she would want to marry him if his maternal grandfather had been, say, a Turk. She says it did not matter a bit; but that "if she ever found out I did not believe in *Our Christian God*, [italics added] she would commit suicide." (76–77) Racial identity for the Jews is conveyed through the female line.
- At the end of the same chapter, John Farlow, parent of one of Lolita's schoolgirl friends, says, "Far too many of the tradespeople here are Italians, but on the other hand we are at least spared — " "I wish," interrupted Jean [Farlow's wife who fears he is about to say "Jews"] with a laugh, "Dolly and Rosalie were spending the summer together." (81)
- Humbert Humbert is described as a "brand new American citizen of obscure European origin." (107)
- When Humbert and Lolita check in at the Enchanted Huntress Hotel, the desk clerk gives Humbert a Jewish-sounding name, Humberg, which he firmly, stridently, and overly nervously rejects. (120)
- Eva Rosen, another friend of Lolita's, and the only one who interests the perverted Humbert, is described as "a displaced little person from France." (192) ["Displaced persons" in the post-World War II period usually meant Jews.]
- Rita, a late replacement for Lolita, is described as a dark-haired, pale-skinned beauty who had "some Spanish or Babylonian blood." (260)
- "that silly cocker spaniel had perhaps been a baptized one." (263–264) Humbert wonders, Appel notes, whether in a hotel that advertised "near Churches" and "no dogs" "would accommodate only Christian dogs, because 'NEAR CHURCHES' was commonly used (circa 1940–1960) as a code sign, a discreet

---

[20] Appel, *The Annotated Lolita*, 379, 416.

[21] Personal communication from Mr. Zachary Baker, 7 July 2000. He quotes a Yiddish lyric of Aaron Lebedeff, "Khapt a kitsl in der shtil." See also German Galvin and Stan Tamarkin, *The Yiddish Dictionary Sourcebook: A Transliterated Guide to the Yiddish Language* (Hoboken, 1986), 207.

indication that only Gentiles were accepted."²² Why would Humbert worry either way unless he were not a Gentile?
- Again, Humbert Humbert describes himself with "French epithets, a Dorset yokel's knuckles, an Austrian tailor's flat fingers." (276) An Austrian tailor: does this mean an Austrian Jewish tailor?
- And finally, Quilty in his befuddled state says: "You are either Australian, or a German refugee. Must you talk to me, this is a Gentile's house you know." (299) Quilty surely means "Austrian" for "Australian" while the racial point is made quite clear in the next sentence.

If the supposition that "kitzln" is the Yiddish keyword unlocking the suggested but never openly stated racial origin of Humbert is correct, it is but one more example of Nabokov's gamesmanship. Nabokov himself, of course, was fiercely intolerant of any form of anti-Semitism both in his works and in his life. For example, he walked out of an American restaurant that served Gentiles only, threw out of his house a guest who had made an anti-Semitic remark, and, as Nabokov's biographer Brian Boyd says, speaking first of Nabokov's father:

> V. D. Nabokov eventually became the most outspoken defender of Jewish rights among all Russian gentiles trained in the law. His son [the author of Lolita] in turn would marry a Russian Jew, denounce anti-Semitism in his own works, and would escape Hitler with his wife and son only with the help of Russian Jewish émigrés still grateful for his father's sterling defense of their people.²³

Now to return to Classical Latin and Neo-Latin in *Lolita*, of which there is quite a lot. It can be divided into the following somewhat overlapping classes: direct quotations; puns; translations of American phrases into Latin; use of Latin words chosen to express additional levels of meaning; and Nabokov's wonderfully rich and often recondite Latinate English vocabulary.

In addition to the Terence quotation previously discussed, Nabokov's "O lente currite noctis equi" is both a pun [night mares and nightmares], which the author immediately glosses with "O softly run, nightmares," and a quotation. It occurs in Marlowe's *Tragedy of Doctor Faustus* (14.11.82) with an additional "lente," and Marlowe in turn is (as Proffer and Larmour note but Appel does not) echoing Ovid's *Amores* I.13.40.²⁴

Latin names and adjectives also play an important role in *Lolita*. Quilty's estate is called "Pavor Manor," a name which with its description parodies Poe's House of Usher. And "pavor" conveys not only fear but also sexual longing; likewise with

---

[22] Appel, *The Annotated Lolita*, 423.
[23] Boyd, *Vladimir Nabokov: The Russian Years*, 27. See also Appel, *The Annotated Lolita*, 424.
[24] Larmour, "Classical Allusions," 145. Also Karl Proffer, *Keys to Lolita* (Bloomington, 1968), 31.

"pavor nocturnus." Sometimes he glosses his arcane terms. In a potted history of sexual relations between old men and young girls Humbert Humbert says: "Here are some brides of ten compelled to seat themselves on the fascinum, the virile ivory in the temples of classical scholarship" (21). Humbert plays as well with Lolita's, Dolly's, Dolores's name: "Delectatio morosa. I spend my doleful days in dumps and dolors" (45). John Ray notes in the "Foreword" that "Haze" is not Lolita's real surname, but her first name "Dolores" is "too closely interwound with the inmost fiber of the book to allow one to alter it." Larmour points out that "dolores," the plural of "dolor," means "not only 'grief,' 'pain,' ... but also 'indignation,' 'resentment,' ... all of which Lolita displays towards Humbert."[25]

Nabokov's vocabulary throughout his English language works, by which I mean those written in English rather than translated from Russian into English, is full of Latin- and Greek-based words. Here is a small list from Lolita: fructuate, favonian, nictitating, ululations, pederosis, olisbos, lentigo, instar, lanugo, viatic, natorium, leporine, pavorine, matutinal, crepitating, tessellated, ancilla, and vibrissa. Appel believes Nabokov invented many of them, like "viatic," but such is not the case. "Viatic" and the others listed above are rare but legitimate English words.

Taxonomic Latin Nabokov learned well. Only in the past year has his "amateur" work as a lepidopterist, including many years of research in Harvard's Museum of Comparative Zoology, undergone a reevaluation which recognizes his skill and scientific acumen. In his poem "Discovery" Nabokov writes:

> I found it and I named it, being versed
> in taxonomic Latin; thus became
> godfather to an insect and its first
> describer — and I want no other fame.[26]

The butterfly is *Lycaeides sublivens* Nabokov, and toward the end of Nabokov's afterword, "On a Book Entitled *Lolita*," he says he thinks of Dolly Schiller, his Lolita, "dying in Gray Star (the capital town of the book), or the tinkling sounds of the valley town coming up the mountain trail on which I caught the first known female of *Lycaeides sublivens* Nabokov." (318)

Where did Nabokov learn his Latin? At his family's home in St. Petersburg and at their country estates of Vyra and Rozhdestveno, Nabokov was taught from a very early age by an English governess and a stream of private tutors. At the age of eleven his father enrolled him in the Tenishev School in St. Petersburg, one of the finest, most modern, and liberal schools in Russia. Since the Tenishev curriculum was directed to the sciences, classical languages were not studied. At least Nabokov says nothing in his autobiography *Speak, Memory* about Latin and Greek instruction. After he and his family in 1918 fled Russia for the Crimea, Nabokov hired in Yalta a tutor

---

[25] Larmour, "Classical Allusions," 146.
[26] Vladimir Nabokov, *Poems* (London, 1961), 15.

to teach him Latin.[27] Perhaps he was thinking of matriculating at Oxford, for which Latin would have been necessary. After he arrived in England, however, his friend Gleb Struve persuaded him to try Cambridge on the basis of his highly developed interest in lepidoptery. Here at Trinity College, where he was officially admitted on 1 October 1919, he read Russian and French after briefly experimenting with zoology — he seems to have preferred Pushkin to ichthyology. He finished with second class honors and left Cambridge for Berlin, where his family had settled, at the end of June of 1922.

Lolita, however, has only the most tenuous association with Cambridge. John Ray, Jr., the author of the "Foreword," may be a nominal echo of the brilliant seventeenth-century Cambridge biologist and father of natural history in Britain, John Ray, whom Nabokov greatly admired. Also, it may have been at Cambridge that Nabokov first began working on his brilliantly idiosyncratic Russian translation of *Alice's Adventures in Wonderland*, *Anya v Stranye Chudes*, which was published in Berlin in 1923. "A breeze from Wonderland" (133) is one of the many references in *Lolita* to Lewis Carroll's *Alice*; in fact, Carroll's influence on Nabokov and the evidence for it constitute a whole other topic unto itself. In any event, let us conclude, as we began, with reference to Lewis Carroll.

There is very little Latin per se in the *Alice* books, and, unlike Nabokov with his stylistic armorium of polysyllabic Latinate words, Carroll's style is almost entirely free of them.[28] Toward the end of his life, however, Carroll contributed a poem entitled "A Lesson in Latin" to *The Jabberwocky*, the newspaper of the Girls' Latin School in Boston, Massachusetts. In it he plays at some length upon the similarity between "amare," the infinitive of "amo," and the adjective "amarus" which means "bitter." The final lines of verses one and two are, respectively: "We've learned 'Amare' means to love!" and "'Amare! Bitter One' we cry." The third verse combines the two in its concluding lines:

> Our Latin lesson is complete:
> We've learned that Love is Bitter-Sweet!*[29]*

There is, I think, a little of Charles Lutwidge Dodgson himself in that sentiment and a lot of Humbert Humbert.

Beltsville, Maryland

---

[27] Boyd, *Vladimir Nabokov: The Russian Years*, 150.

[28] For discussion of Latin in Carroll, see the following: August A. Imholtz, Jr., "The Absent Ablative and the Search for Alice's Brother's Latin Grammar," *Classical Bulletin* 55 (1979): 46–47; idem, "Jam Sempiterne: A Note on Time in *Through the Looking-Glass*," *Jabberwocky: The Journal of the Lewis Carroll Society* 8 (1978–1979): 13–15; idem, "Latin and Greek Versions of 'Jabberwocky': Exercises in Laughing and Grief," *Rocky Mountain Review of Literature* 41 (1987): 21–28.

[29] Lewis Carroll, *The Complete Works of Lewis Carroll*, with an Introduction by Alexander Woollcott (London, 1939), 876–877.

Poetics and Ideology in Neo-Latin Poetry

HANS-ERIK JOHANNESSON

"Immature poets imitate, mature poets steal"
(T. S. Eliot)

With Italian Humanism the development of Latin language and literature was interrupted. The humanists returned to the sources of antiquity, *ad fontes*, and were inspired to create poetry in the language of Virgil and his contemporaries. The humanist poets were obsessed by the richness of Roman poetry: they recognized it as their ideal. But with Humanism there was also a new consciousness of historical distance, of a difference in time between the present and a great, proud past, a consciousness which has a parallel in the Hellenistic philologists and poets and *their* attitude to archaic and classical poetry. The ancient rhetorician Dionysius of Halicarnassus appreciated the "classics" of the fifth century B.C. more than the poets of his own time; in a similar way the Humanists valued the Roman poets higher than their medieval successors. This evaluation had consequences for literary *imitatio*.

The Humanist ideal had its origin in Roman *humanitas*, a concept coined by Cicero and by Quintilian made the basis of the rhetorical ideal. Rhetoric not only set up rules for speech; it was also the foundation of culture and education. Humanism transformed this into a cultural paradigm with a set of implications, literary, political, and religious. It saw its ideal realized in the age of Augustus, in the form in which Virgil had described it.

New studies of the literary practice of Roman poets have given us a deeper knowledge both of the intellectual play and of the ideological meaning of — not least — Virgil's *Aeneid* and *Georgics*. Virgil's works have been studied in relation to those of other Roman and Greek poets and have been shown to be veritable intertextual echo chambers. Virgil's transformation of the literary tradition by means of allusion ("arte allusiva")[1] has been recognized; the Italian critic Gian Biagio Conte has shown how Virgil makes use of "the epic code" and transforms the epic by means of intertextual references to different models in the epic tradition. It all results in what Conte calls a "polyphonic epic".[2] It is worth noticing that these interesting aspects have been little applied to the study of Renaissance, especially Neo-Latin poetry, which is so dependent on ancient, especially Virgilian, poetry.

I think scholars have often laid too much stress on the rhetorical aspect of Renaissance poetry and so neglected its specific literary aspects. Poetry was surely "rhetoricized" in certain ways, but not always in the reductive manner that has sometimes been claimed; I do not think you could say that Neo-Latin poetry was uniformly subordinated to the demands and rules of rhetoric. On the contrary, you could say that the distinctive features of poetry were emphasized in some poetics, for instance in those of the Italian humanist Hieronymus Vida. And Vida did so in an effort to imitate Virgil in a more complex way than has usually been understood.

Vida was famous all over Europe for his *Poeticorum libri tres*, which was first printed in 1517 (in Cremona), then in a revised edition in 1527; but his fame also rested on his epic *Christias*,[3] in which he emulated Virgil in the process of creating a Christian counterpart to the pagan *Aeneid*. The contemporary evaluation of Vida was mixed: some considered that he had written a poetics *ad usum mortuorum*, while others praised him, among these Julius Caesar Scaliger and Johannes Sturm; their own poetics were influenced by Vida's poetic programme. They considered Vida's *ars poetica* to be even better than those of both Aristotle and Horace (as a matter of fact Vida's poetics shows traces of an influence from Aristotle's poetics in his definition of the concept of *decorum*).

Vida wrote his poetics as an emulative *imitatio* of two models: Horace's *Ars poetica* and Virgil's *Georgics*. Like these, Vida's work is in hexameters; from the title one would expect that Horace was the most important model, but that is a superficial impression. Virgil is the main model both with reference to poetic technique (in particular the technique of allusion) and as a cultural paradigm or "ideology." With respect to the latter it exemplifies the educational/rhetorical programme of Quintilian. By "model" I mean a literary work or a corpus of texts by the same author that a poet takes as an object of *imitatio* (whether this is a servile imitation or creative transformation). I here agree with the view that ancient poetry was fashioned according to models, not genres. I also think that it can be more productive to interpret and explain Renaissance and Humanist poetry in this way. On Vida's part this means that there is a mixture of models, with the Virgilian model as the main one. Vida adopts and adapts Virgil's art of allusion to the literary tradition, in itself characterized by

---

[1] See Giorgio Pasquali, *Orazio lirico* (Florence, 1920).

[2] Gian Biagio Conte, *The Rhetoric of Imitation. Genre and Poetic Memory in Virgil and Other Latin Poets* (Ithaca, 1986).

[3] See *The De arte poetica of Marco Girolamo Vida*, trans. with comm. and with the text of c.1517 edited, by Ralph G. Williams (New York, 1976); Mario A. Di Cesare, *Vida's Christiad and Vergilian Epic* (New York and London, 1964).

multiple allusion, where often there is a hidden element. Thus you could also say that Vida's writing (with several models in mind) is part of his technique of allusion: the mixture of models forms a kind of "extended allusion." Another consequence is that, if you accept this theory of models, it will be more difficult to put Renaissance poems into a genre system. As a matter of fact we also see in the Renaissance the rise of many new poetic forms ("genera mixta").

The main model for Vida's "ars poetica" is not, as one might expect, and as is stubbornly still maintained by some scholars, Horace's *Ars poetica,* but rather another didactic poem, Virgil's *Georgics.*

> Saepe mihi placet antiquis alludere dictis,
> Atque aliud longe verbis proferre sub iisdem.
> Nec mea tam sapiens per sese prodita quisquam
> Furta redarguerit, quae mox manifesta probabunt
> Et nati natorum, et qui nascentur ab illis.
> (Vida, *De arte poetica* 3.257–261)

Vida's *Poetics* is the first Latin Renaissance poetics that in the form of didactic poetry takes Virgil as a model and at the same time accomplishes this with a literary technique that is meant to accord with, and even outdo ("out-Virgil") Virgil himself. Vida's poetry includes many references to Virgil (quotations and allusions). Sometimes he disguises an imitation of his work, for instance by changing a line-ending (e.g., 3.146f, a reference to the Fourth Eclogue). This disguised *imitatio* is close to literary theft, *furtum*, which is Vida's speciality. Vida has some recommendations for successful "theft": just go on stealing but be careful not to be detected, for instance by changing the word-order in the stolen lines. Critics who have been troubled by Vida's recommended *furtum* have not noticed his tongue-in-cheek approach here; they have not realized that Vida is so delighted with what we nowadays call the "intertextual" play with words.

I think it is hard *not* to see Vida's sort of *imitatio* as an equivalent to Virgil's art of allusion. I also think it is easy to agree with critics of that all too usual kind of comparative analysis which confines itself to detecting sources of a *locus* and gives up any attempt to decide the meaning of an allusion, quotation, or other reference. Ralph G. Williams (Vida's commentator) has some good remarks on that point:

> With authors of the subtlety of Vida, however, one's task is just begun when [one] has recognized the model: the writer assumes that his readers will have the ancient text as well in mind as he. The mark of excellence is how artfully the poet has used his source , and the meaning of the later passage or poem may be best — and sometimes may be only — understood in relation to the earlier one.[4]

---

[4] Williams, *De arte poetica,* 169.

The idea that the meaning of a (part of a) text is constituted by the tension between two (or more) texts is the vital point in Conte's understanding of Virgil's poetic technique, which he calls a "rhetoric of imitation" and where allusion has the character of metaphor. Williams has not himself seen the extent of this correspondence between Vida and Virgil, but once you have seen it, it stands out as both obvious and intended.

Vida's *imitatio* of Virgil does not concern poetical technique alone. Vida also transforms Virgil's cultural paradigm and puts forward a humanist programme, where the poet has a unique position:

> Just as for Quintilian the best type of citizen is he who is prepared to participate most fully in the civic and cultural life about him, that is, the orator, so for Vida the best and most exalted life open to youth is that of the humanist poet, one who can exercise all his powers in fulfilling Rome's function of teaching the nations, since her ability to rule the world has gone.[5]

The greatest task for a humanist poet according to Vida was to create a Christian epic poem. Vida saw such an epic as the third peak in the literary history of Europe, the first being Greek epic (Homer) and the second Roman epic (Virgil); finally, with the Medici in Florence, after a long period of European decline there were new conditions for cultural and literary greatness, corresponding to the ancient Roman ideal. In a letter to the *patres* of Cremona Vida expresses his opinion of Virgil as a model and his view that with the Roman poets *imitatio* was meant to be a transformation and improvement of Greek models:

> [the students] will realize, too, how much ornament and light Virgil conferred on this art through his preeminent genius; indeed, of all poets (and I am speaking not of our Latin authors only, but of the Greeks as well) I consider him easily the first. For, most noble Fathers, each time I read his divine poem I am struck by the idea that this preeminent poet was not simply writing history, but wished quite beyond this to give instructions on the poetic art itself, doing so to demonstrate how much the Greeks, from whom we received this study, were themselves wanting, and to show that whatever might be claimed for all other nations in this pursuit, our poets, for their part, always transformed and improved what they received from others.[6]

Like the *Georgics* Vida's poem is less a handbook than a panegyric to its subject; it contains a political design and artful digressions from the poetic subject to underline the political message. The prayer in the *Georgics* to Augustus for peace (1.466–514) has its counterpart in Vida's poem (2.588ff) with the statement that the leadership of Rome is gone and the wish that the city will at least maintain a leading position in

---

[5] Williams, *De arte poetica*, xxxvii.
[6] Williams, *De arte poetica*, 213.

the arts. The hope for political and religious power is directed to the Medici and Pope Leo X. There is a strong emphasis on the patriotic theme (*laus Italiae*) in this panegyric.

In 1577 Vida's *Poeticorum libri tres* was printed in Stockholm, probably to be used by students at the Collegium Regium which King John III had recently founded. I said before that it is remarkable that criticism of Northern European Neo-Latin poetry has paid almost no attention to the significance of Vida's work. One reason for the neglect might be the assumption that a poet and a poem with such a strong Catholic character could not have influenced Northern, Lutheran poets. Why then was Vida's poetics printed in Stockholm in 1577? I shall now discuss some aspects of the importance of Vida's work for some of this poetry.

The sixteenth century saw an increasing amount of Neo-Latin *epithalamia*. I will not now discuss the conditions and reasons for the frequent use of this kind of poem, but only state that there is a special *decorum*, a certain set of rules, regulating this poetry. The general aesthetics that the Swedish poet Ericus Jacobi Skinnerus followed when he composed his *Epithalamion* for the wedding of John III and Gunilla Bielke in 1585, or which Henricus Mollerus applied in a wedding poem for Gustav Vasa's daughter Katarina in 1559, seems to be the same for all those European poets addressing a panegyrical poem to a prince.

But there is also another side to this issue. The epithalamia for a Swedish royal or noble addressee have — beside the fact that they belong to the European cultural community — also a strong patriotic character (*laus Sueciae*). The Swedish poets mentioned above stress the fact that Gustav Vasa and John III are *Swedish* kings while Gunilla Bielke belongs to a *Swedish* noble family. The patriotism of these poems reflects and celebrates the increase of the Swedish state and the political and cultural ambition of the Swedish kings. We might observe the parallel in the patriotic and political themes in Virgil and Vida mentioned above. We also notice the strong didactic emphasis, which connects the poems with Vida's work. I prefer not to call the *epithalamia* a genre but rather a kind of poem characterized by certain themes and motifs connected with marriage. In many respects the *epithalamia* are quite different from one another. My point, briefly stated, is that some of these *epithalamia*, written in hexameters and with a noble or royal addressee, have characteristic features that connect them with Vida's poetics and didactic poetry. The *epithalamia* mentioned above show both a general resemblance and a specific similarity to Vida's Georgic poetics: the didactic form, cultural paradigm, patriotic theme transposed from the Medici to the Swedish royal court, the *laus Sueciae* motif, the multitude of allusions to models like Virgil, Lucretius, and Quintilian, and even specific references to Vida's *Christias*. The patriotism of Mollerus and Skinnerus, however, is different from that of Vida. In Mollerus's homage to Gustav Vasa there is no reference to Rome (as in Vida). Probably "Rome" had very strong implications of Catholicism, and as a matter of fact there is an element of anti-Catholicism in the poem (e.g., v. 866). In the *Romanitas* of Italian humanism the veneration of Virgilian poetry and of Catholicism was a stable combination; in Reformation Europe this cultural paradigm caused problems.

I will conclude with some reflections on Skinnerus's poem (1585) and the fact that Vida's poetics was actually there in Stockholm, printed in 1577. I will show in further detail in a forthcoming book that the type of poem I have discussed (Neo-Latin didactic panegyric) has a lot to do with Vida.

In the 1570s John III founded the Stockholm school (Collegium Regium) which for a couple of years was to be the centre of the Counter-Reformation in Sweden. Oskar Garstein in his *Rome and the Counter-Reformation in Scandinavia* (1992), and recently in a posthumous book, *Klosterlasse* (1998),[7] has vividly described the interesting figure, Laurentius Norvegus, who wanted to win Scandinavia back to Catholicism and in a short time gained the students' interest for this doctrine (some of them seem to have converted, secretly, of course). It was here, in this milieu, that Vida's treatise was introduced. We do not know much more about it beyond the fact of its being printed there, but we do know that Skinnerus (who in the 1580s — after "Klosterlasse" — had lost his influence and left Sweden) — was a professor at the Collegium, wrote a poem for the wedding of John III, demonstrating some of the characteristic features and political themes promoted by Vida, but at the same time with fierce attacks on the Pope and Catholicism. The irony of that is worth a mass.

Göteberg University

---

[7] Oskar Garstein, *Rome and the Counter-Reformation in Scandinavia. Jesuit Educational Strategy 1553–1622* (Leiden, 1992); idem, *Klosterlasse* (Oslo, 1998).

Exorcism and the Interstices of Language: Ruggle's Ignoramus and the Demonization of Renaissance English Neo-Latin[1]

HILAIRE KALLENDORF

Renaissance Neo-Latin is demonized in George Ruggle's 1615 play *Ignoramus*. Like other plays of the early seventeenth century which include episodes of exorcism, this play focuses on some of the symptoms of demonic possession. Demonic polyglossia, the devil's dark parody of the early Christian experience of speaking in tongues, was one of these symptoms. However, the fact that Neo-Latin is singled out for parody amidst other linguistic registers normally associated with demonic possession makes this play stand apart from other dramas about exorcism written during this period.

Its university setting — the play was performed before King James I at Cambridge in March 1615 — and its satire of the legal profession explain the play's focus on Latin instead of Greek, "Chaldean" or other "demonic" languages. But why did the playwright choose exorcism to satirize Latin instead of limiting the play's scope to mere ridicule of pedants and lawyers?

The answer is that exorcism, while itself a "hot topic" at this time in England, also provided a battleground for various competing languages and jargons. It was the perfect arena for the struggle over who understood Latin and who did not, and who possessed cultural power and who did not. Exorcism provided liminal spaces or interstices between languages at a time when a whole culture was in linguistic transition. As an extreme case of the linguistic anxiety felt in the culture as a whole, exorcism provided a forum for discussing issues of linguistic competence and authority.

---

[1] The author wishes to thank the Folger Institute for the opportunity to participate in its Symposium, "British Political Thought in Early Modern Europe: Mapping Networks and Practices of Political Exchange in the Sixteenth and Seventeenth Centuries," held at the Folger Shakespeare Library in Washington, DC, in May 2000. The Symposium provided a forum for testing the seeds of some of the ideas which were later incorporated into this paper.

The other characters in the play claim to hear the voice of the devil in Ignoramus, whose facility in Latin is presented as one of the signs of his demonic possession. In addition to physical symptoms, the state of demonic possession was characterized in the culture of Elizabethan and Jacobean England by either extraordinary speech or extraordinary absence of speech. These two possibilities are explained in Reginald Scot's *Discourse upon divels and spirits* as the different conditions resulting from inhabitation by two different kinds of demons:

> And if it be a subterrene diuell, it doth writh and bow the possessed, and speaketh by him, using the spirit of the patient as his instrument . . . when *Lucifugus* possesseth a man, he maketh him dumbe, and as it were dead: and these be they that are cast out . . . onelie by fasting and praier.[2]

The second condition, involving the extraordinary absence of speech, is not altogether unknown in the comic drama genre. Troilus speaks of "a still and dumb-discoursive devil / That tempts most cunningly" in Shakespeare's *Troilus and Cressida*.[3] Likewise, in *Gammer Gurton's Needle*, Gammer Gurton and Tib "sit as still as stones in the street, / As though they had been taken with fairies, or else with some ill sprite."[4]

More often, however, silence is not the problem in comic drama about demonic possession. Usually, in fact, the opposite affliction prevails: an abundance of speech, of extraordinary speech (as already mentioned, a parody of speaking in tongues), infuses the comic drama with hilarious vitality. Often this demonic proliferation of speech involves multiple foreign languages, to the point that the association of possession with polyglossia becomes a commonplace. We see this association, for example, in Marston's *The Malcontent* ("Phew! the devil: let him possess thee; he'll teach thee to speak all languages most readily and strangely")[5] as well as in Ben Jonson's *The Devil is an Ass*, where Fitzdottrel feigns demonic possession by speaking Greek, Spanish, and French.[6]

This association is developed further in *Ignoramus*. *Ignoramus* presents the story of the lovers Antonius, whose father is Theodorus, and Rosabella, whose custodian is Torcol (a pander). Theodorus sends Antonius from Bordeaux to London to bring back the rest of his family, whom he has not seen in nearly twenty years: his mother

---

[2] Reginald Scot, *The Discouerie of Witchcraft. With a Discourse upon divels and spirits, and first of philosophers opinions, also the maner of their reasoning hereupon; and the same confuted* (London: William Brome, 1584), 496.

[3] William Shakespeare, *The History of Troilus and Cressida*, in *The Riverside Shakespeare*, ed. G. Blakemore Evans (Boston, 1974), 4.4.90–91.

[4] *Gammer Gurton's Needle* (1575), in *Three Sixteenth-Century Comedies: Gammer Gurton's Needle by Mr. S., Roister Doister by Nicholas Udall, The Old Wife's Tale by George Peele* (New York, 1984), 1.2.25–26. "Mr. S." is thought to be William Stevenson.

[5] John Marston, *The Malcontent* (London, 1975), 1.3.30–31.

[6] Ben Jonson, *The Devil is an Ass*, ed. Gamini Salgado, in *Four Jacobean City Comedies* (New York, 1985), Act 5, Scene 3.

Dorothea, his twin brother Antoninus, and his stepsister Catherina (his remaining stepsister has been lost during childhood). Antonius, however, has other plans: with the help of his father's servant, Trico, he escapes from the ship bound for London. His purpose in doing this is to prevent the pander Torcol from giving his love Rosabella in marriage to Ignoramus, an English lawyer who speaks only in silly Neo-Latin legal jargon. Antonius and Trico enlist the help of Cupes and Friar Cola to trick the pander and Ignoramus. Following the idea of Polla, Cupes's wife, they convince other characters that Ignoramus is really possessed by a demon and in need of exorcism. During the exorcism ritual Ignoramus continues to pour forth jargon, so that each time he uses a legal phrase, the "exorcists" deliberately mistake it for the name of a familiar demon. Finally the "exorcists" remove him to a monastery where he will be tortured with fire — presumably a continuation of the exorcism ritual, the success of which remains undetermined. Antonius's long-lost family arrives from London, and they end up helping him to achieve his goal: they recognize that Rosabella is really his long-lost adopted sister, who had been promised to him in marriage so many years ago. The good servant Trico is rewarded, and Ignoramus is left in disgrace.

The main point of interest for us here is that the other characters are persuaded that Ignoramus is demon-possessed because of his Latin. They mistake his legal phrases for the names of demons who possess him. Some examples of his ridiculous language and its deliberate misapprehension are the following exchanges:

Ignoramus: Descedite vos, nebulones ut estis, cum vestra *Riota & Rowta*.
Cola: Duplex Daemon, *Riota & Rowta*. . . .

Ignoramus: Et praeter juncturam, si maritasset me, habuisset *Francum Bancum*.
Cola: Profuge sis *Francum Bancum*, separa te *Francum Bancum*. . . .

Ignoramus: Ignis ardeat vos: si dagarias capio, rumpam calvas coronas vestras.
Cola: Conjuro te, prodi dagarias.[7]

On one level, Ruggle's *Ignoramus* is simply another play involving exorcism which exploits the *topos* of polyglossia. Yet on another level, Ruggle's play is very different from the others. For one thing, it singles out Latin — as opposed to Greek, Aramaic, or "Chaldean" — to be an object of satire. Secondly — and this is of course the most obvious difference between it and most other plays written at this time about exorcism — it is written in Latin, not the vernacular, and thus utilizes the very language

---

[7] George Ruggle, *Ignoramus: comoedia coram rege Jacobo et Totius Angliae magnatibus per academicos Cantabrigienses habita: cum eorum supplemento quae, causidicorum municipalium reverentia, hactenus desiderabantur* (1615), 3rd ed. (London, 1658), 111, 112, 113 (Act 4, Scene 11). An English translation of the scene may be found in Robert Codrington, trans., *Ignoramus: a comedy as it was several times acted with extraordinary applause before the Majesty of King James: with a supplement which, out of respect to the students of the common law, was hitherto wanting* (London: For W. Gilbertson, 1662), sigs. P4v, Q1r, Q2r. Further references to both these books will be placed in the text.

it satirizes. What sort of complex linguistic game is going on here? In an attempt to answer this question, I shall explore both why Ruggle singled out Neo-Latin and what the religious and political ramifications of his choice are for our understanding of the linguistic battleground that was late Renaissance England.

Ruggle's choice of Neo-Latin in particular must be understood within at least two contexts: the university setting and the ongoing English satire against lawyers. To address these points, it is essential for understanding the *content* of this play to examine its *context* within the larger culture of the university and its academic drama. *Ignoramus* was based on Giambattista Della Porta's *La Trappolaria*.[8] Performed before the learned scholar/king James I at Cambridge on 8 March 1615 (1614 in the old style), this five-hour play drew an audience of two thousand to Trinity College. This performance is perhaps one of the best-documented to have occurred in Jacobean England; we even have the report of King James's reactions to the play from a contemporary witness: "his ma*ie*stie was much delighted with ye Playe and laughed exceedingly and offentymes with his handes and by wordes applauded it."[9] John Chamberlain reported in a letter that King James found it impossible to forget the play after this performance and, in fact, that he requested an encore at the nearby town of Royston on 6 May of the same year.[10] Evidently the play had been not merely a college production, but a political event designed to represent the whole university; students at Cambridge's major rival, Oxford, soon produced a torrent of satirical ballads about the play.[11]

What can this university context tell us about Ruggle's play in particular? At the minimum, we may assume that the play was written for a well-educated audience who could understand the language and appreciate the amount of effort that must have gone into writing such a long specimen of it. The use of Latin in this context makes a statement about who is educationally empowered and who is not, and it also valorizes the Latin language as the language of dramatic art as well as of humanistic learning.

---

[8] On the Neo-Latin university drama in England, see J. W. Binns, *Intellectual Culture in Elizabethan and Jacobean England: The Latin Writings of the Age* (Leeds, 1990), 120–140; and G. C. Moore Smith, *College Plays Performed in the University of Cambridge* (Cambridge, 1923). On *Ignoramus* and its relation to *La Trappolaria*, see Louise G. Clubb, *Giambattista Della Porta: Dramatist* (Princeton, 1965), 284; and Justin Loomis Van Gundy, *"Ignoramus": Comoedia Coram Regia Maiestate Jacobi Regis Angliae. An Examination of Its Sources and Literary Influence with Special Reference to Its Relation to Butler's "Hudibras"* (Lancaster, PA, 1906). *La Trappolaria*, in turn, was modeled on Plautus's *Pseudolus*.

[9] Alan H. Nelson, ed., *Records of Early English Drama: Cambridge* (Toronto, 1989), 542, quoted in Robert C. Evans, "Contemporary Contexts of Jonson's *The Devil is an Ass*," *Comparative Drama* 26 (1992): 140–176, here 166.

[10] *The Letters of John Chamberlain*, ed. Norman Egbert McClure (Philadelphia, 1939), 1:597–598, quoted in Evans, "Contemporary Contexts," 166.

[11] Two of the ballads were *Ignoramus, an excellent new song: to the tune of, Lay by your pleading, law lies a bleeding* (London: s.n., 1681), and *The Ignoramus ballad: to the tune of, Let Oliver now be forgotten* ([London?]: For N. T., 1681). Literary responses to *Ignoramus* are treated in Van Gundy, "*Ignoramus*," 65–98.

The second context we mentioned is the English tradition of legal satire. The literary tradition of demon-possessed lawyers would soon include such figures as Voltore in Jonson's *Volpone*[12] and Tangle in Middleton's *The Phoenix*.[13] John Chamberlain's contemporaneous epistolary account of King James's reactions to *Ignoramus* mentions the legal satire it contained and the responses it provoked:

> the King went again to Cambridge to see the play *Ignoramus* which hath so netled the Lawiers that they are almost out of all patience, and the Lord Chiefe Justice [Coke] both openly at the Kings Bench and divers other places hath galled and glaunced at schollers with much bitternes, and there be divers ynne of court men have made rimes and ballades against them, which they have aunswered sharply enough. ....[14]

The Master of Magdalene College, Barnabe Googe, likewise reported that the play had "woonderfully discontented the Lawyers," and he urged the Vice-Chancellor of Cambridge "to take som course for the staye of these bitter inuectives."[15]

What were all the lawyers, including Lord Chief Justice Coke, so upset about? And why the proliferation of ballads (clear adaptations of the play's subject, many of which have survived to this day) against the legal establishment? The play was written at least in part as a response to a local dispute in Cambridge (settled in 1612) in which a lawyer had offended the university. Edward Tucker has called *Ignoramus*

> the seminal work of literature in the molding of the *advocatus diaboli* convention. Greedy, lecherous, malicious yet easily duped, proud of his eloquence and his barbarous law jargon, educationally deficient, and frequently associated with the Devil, the lawyer's characterization follows a standard and predictable, though never tiresome, formula.[16]

The play clearly devalorized Latin as the language of the lawyers at the same time as it upheld the tradition of university plays written in Latin to demonstrate erudition and a connection to humanism.

---

[12] Ben Jonson, *Volpone* (1607), ed. Philip Brockbank (New York, 1969), Act 5, Scenes 10 and 12.

[13] Thomas Middleton, *The Phoenix* (1607), ed. John Bradbury Brooks (New York, 1980), Act 5, Scene 1.

[14] *The Letters of John Chamberlain*, 1:597–598, quoted in Evans, "Contemporary Contexts," 166.

[15] *Records of Early English Drama: Cambridge*, 552, quoted in Evans, "Contemporary Contexts," 166.

[16] Edward F. J. Tucker, "*Ignoramus* and Seventeenth-Century Satire of the Law," *Harvard Library Bulletin* 19.3 (1971): 329–330. Tucker has also prepared the facsimile edition of a manuscript of the play (Hildesheim, 1987). See also David Money's program essay for the performance of scenes from *Ignoramus* on 3 August 2000 in Peterhouse Theatre, Cambridge, at the Eleventh Congress of the International Association for Neo-Latin Studies.

These two contexts, the university setting and the anti-legal satirical tradition, help us to see both the positive and the negative valorizations of Neo-Latin within English culture at this time. But why does Ruggle demonize the language itself instead of merely those who use it, namely, scholarly pedants and lawyers? And why does he choose specifically the exorcism ritual as a vehicle for this satire?

Ruggle's self-deprecating posture of demonizing the same language he utilizes is intimately connected to the religious resonance of Latin in a Protestant country. For many Anglicans, Latin was still the language of the papacy and still the language of the Jesuit exorcists who had performed their rituals covertly at Denham in 1585 and 1586.[17] These exorcists were subjected to an exposé by Samuel Harsnett, who in 1603 published his *Declaration of Egregious Popish Impostures*.[18]

Writing only a little more than a decade after Harsnett's publication, Ruggle cannot escape the religious and political baggage that the choice of Neo-Latin brings with it in the England of 1615. He addresses the Catholic connotations directly and forcefully by staging an absurdly satirical exorcism in the middle of his own play. Officially Anglicans were not allowed to perform exorcisms at this time, but Ruggle fills Act 4, Scenes 10 and 11 with specific references which underscore the fact that Catholics are the precise targets of his satire. The hooded friars in the scene are obviously Catholic ("monachorum cucullis indutis," 107), and the exorcized demons in fact bear telling names that stress the anti-Catholic tone of the scene: "Gray-fryers," "Black-fryers," "Croched fryers" (113), then "porridge-bellied Fryers" (114). The exorcism is performed with props that only a Catholic priest would use: holy water, a chair and ropes, exorcized salt, and hallowed fire. An Anglican performing an unsanctioned exorcism would fast, pray, and ask God to cast out the demons, but the exorcizing priest in *Ignoramus* commands the demons to depart on his own authority. And finally, in a key phrase that shows how one early translator of the play understood these scenes, the Latin *mummatis & moppatis* (114) is expanded into "a mumming, and mopping, and such a moing" (trans. Codrington, sig. Q2r) with the last two gerunds echoing the "mopping and mowing" of Harsnett's account of the secret Jesuit exorcisms.[19]

The exorcism in this play is, of course, much more than simply a satire against the Jesuits. The exorcism ritual becomes an arena in which Latin and the vernacular engage in sophisticated linguistic battle. Supernatural knowledge of Latin was one of the surest signs that a person was possessed by the devil, particularly when that person

---

[17] See F. W. Brownlow, *Shakespeare, Harsnett, and the Devils of Denham* (London and Toronto, 1993).

[18] Samuel Harsnett, *A Declaration of Egregious Popish Impostures* (1603), in Brownlow, *Shakespeare, Harsnett*, 191–416.

[19] Brownlow, *Shakespeare, Harsnett*, 308. Harsnett describes how one of the demoniacs would "role [sic] her eyes, wrie her mouth, gnash her teeth, startle with her body, hold her armes and hands stiffe, make anticke faces, girne, mow, and mop like an Ape." Shakespeare also appropriated this phrase in one of Edgar's lines as Poor Tom: "Five fiends have been in poor Tom at once: of lust, as Obidicut; Hobbididence, prince of dumbness; Mahu, of stealing; Modo, of murder; Flibbertigibbet, of mopping and mowing, who since possesses chamber-maids and waiting-women" (*King Lear*, in *The Riverside Shakespeare*, ed. G. Blakemore Evans [Boston, 1974], 4.1.58–63).

was uneducated or illiterate. This is seen in an example from a 1638 treatise of a scholar who concluded that a common person was demon-possessed because he was able to recite a passage from Virgil.[20] A similar case was reported in Granada in 1650 when the Jesuit exorcist Diego Tello concluded that a man was possessed because he could speak Latin intelligibly.[21]

In essence, then, the "miracle" of polyglossia and the use of language as a litmus test for demonic possession were a painful reminder to high-culture humanists that knowledge of Latin was beginning to recede into the collective cultural past. Knowledge of Latin was not emphasized as much in medieval accounts of demonic possession and exorcism because it was assumed that Latin permeated even the language of daily life. It is a sign of just how much things had changed that most demoniacs were assumed to have no Latin unless it was by miraculous or diabolical means.

It is, of course, a sad statement about the educational state of affairs in Europe at this time to say that it was the Catholic exorcists who wielded this linguistic power and authority in one of the most highly-publicized ways. Sometimes these exorcists displayed their knowledge of Latin very publicly in order to build their *ethos* as capable demon-expellers. In one case in 1637–1642, the Spanish exorcist Luis de la Concepción recounts how at the church of Nuestra Señora de la Regla in San Lúcar he confronted a demon with Latin syllogisms after the manner of the scholastics. The demoniac proposed to the exorcist a syllogism that an "inexperienced" bystander approved as self-evident. The exorcist however argued to the contrary. The demoniac claimed in Latin that the exorcist did not know how to give a response; the exorcist responded that he knew nothing from his own knowledge and relied on the knowledge of God. The exorcist then proceeded to prove the demoniac's argument to be false by stating the major and minor premises in Latin "according to the manner of the schools." The demon was thus defeated and forced to leave the woman forever.[22] This case is a fascinating example of an exorcism presented as a rhetorical, scholastic, and linguistic battle.

Perhaps it would even be no exaggeration to say that England was mourning the loss of Catholic Latin learning at the same time as it was celebrating the Protestant new-found freedom of conscience. The Catholic Church and its writers such as St. Thomas Aquinas had been responsible for the medieval flowering of scholastic learning. Perhaps the English Protestants, especially in their Puritanical or Iconoclastic varieties, were somewhat chastened to discover that by rejecting Popery, they were also losing some Catholic Latin learning — as the modern proverb says, they were throwing out the baby with the bath water.

Linguistic anxiety finds expression in many forms within a culture in transition from one dominant mode of communication or instruction to another. Evidence of

---

[20] Meric Casaubon, *Of Credulity and Incredulity* (1668), intro. David G. Lougee (Delmar, NY, 1976), 149.

[21] Henry Charles Lea, *A History of the Inquisition of Spain* (New York, 1907), 4:350. He cites a manuscript in the Library of the University of Halle, Yc, 20, T. XVII.

[22] Fray Luis de la Concepción, *Práctica de conjurar* (1673), facs. ed. with preliminary note by Alexandre Venegas (Barcelona, 1983), 18–21.

this anxiety may be found, for example, in manuscript notes found in the margins of printed texts, where readers from this period translated (perhaps even with the aid of a dictionary) into English the Latin words and phrases interspersed through a primarily vernacular printed edition.[23]

The much-discussed Renaissance topos in Romance-language countries of the *questione della lingua* was an attempt by various vernaculars to take precedence over others by claiming a greater proximity to the original Latin. For example, in the first book of Baldassare Castiglione's *The Courtier*, translated into English by Sir Thomas Hoby in 1561, Lodovico (Lewis) proclaims to Federico (Fredericke) the primacy of Italian over other vernacular languages and, even more specifically, the primacy of Tuscan over other Italian dialects.[24] In England the question was not so much one of tracing a national linguistic heritage as it was one, particularly in the Renaissance, of appropriating the Latin classics and their medieval scholastic versions and adaptations. It was distressing to English humanists and university scholars such as Ruggle who were interested in keeping the Latin learning tradition alive that Catholics in some way "owned" Latin as their province of ritualistic dialogue. By writing a satire about Catholic exorcists in Latin, Ruggle was staking a claim to this linguistic territory. He was attempting to distance himself from the Catholic priests (some of whom, incidentally, were not very well educated and spoke a notoriously corrupt and macaronic Latin) while at the same time appropriating the language as a medium for English drama and university life.

Exorcisms functioned in the Renaissance as interstices between the natural and the supernatural worlds — as spaces in between where the divine could intrude into the human. In the linguistic realm, exorcisms also functioned as interstices between high and low culture, between education and illiteracy, between Neo-Latin and lack of Latin. The trajectory of Neo-Latin as a cultural commodity was far-ranging enough to earn it such contradictory descriptive adjectives as "miraculous" and "diabolical." The fact that Ruggle appropriated this commodity at this time and in this way need remain neither mysterious nor elusive. *In principio erat Verbum*, and Neo-Latin authors wanted many more *verba* to be *scripta* in Latin still. They did not want cultural baggage surrounding the use of Latin to stand in their way.

By writing his play in Latin and including in it a mock exorcism, Ruggle attempted to exorcize Neo-Latin of its Popish connotations. The exorcism was not successful, and Neo-Latin remained in some way demonized. The problem disappears when texts are written in the vernacular, and this, of course, is the solution that has prevailed in English literary history.

Princeton University

---

[23] In Folger Shakespeare Library 17854a, copy 2 of S. Michaelis, *The Admirable Historie of the Possession and Conversion of a Penitent Woman*, trans. W. B. (London, 1613), a very early reader (who signs the title page "Rbts Sctgr") translates all the Latin in the text and enters English into the margins; he also writes mottoes on the title page: "In omni sacrificio offeres Sal. Leu. 2." and "Accipe, Redde, Time."

[24] Baldassare Castiglione, *Il Cortegiano*, trans. as *The Book of the Courtier* by Thomas Hoby (1561), ed. Drayton Henderson (New York, 1928), 54.

Fray Alonso de la Veracruz's Views on the Legitimacy of the Spanish Conquest of America as Revealed in His De dominio infidelium et iusto bello *(1553–1554)*

ARNOLD L. KERSON

Fray Alonso de la Veracruz (1507–1584), born Alonso Gutiérrez in Caspueas (Guadalajara), Spain, studied at the Universities of Alcalá de Henares and Salamanca. There he was a disciple of the Dominican Francisco de Vitoria (1492/3–1526), the distinguished political and legal philosopher and theologian, considered by many as the founder of international law, and whose most influential works, or *relectiones*, that is, summaries or popularizations of ordinary lectures, were *De Indis recenter inventis relectio prior* (1532) and *De Indis, sive de iure belli hispaniorum in barbaris relectio posterior* (1532), both published for the first time in 1557. The former *relectio* discusses the legitimacy of the Spanish authority in the New World, while the latter completes the discussion by dealing with just and unjust wars, mainly in a theoretical sense.

Fray Alonso de la Veracruz took his theology degree at Salamanca, was ordained to the priesthood, and held a teaching position at the University of Salamanca when the Augustinian Fray Francisco de la Cruz persuaded him to go to Mexico. This he did with enthusiasm, and upon arriving at Veracruz, from which he assumed his new name, he entered the Augustinian Order.

Important for an understanding of Fray Alonso's character, as well as his key role in the cultural development of sixteenth-century Mexico, are the following facts. As soon as he became master of novices in his order, he began to wear coarse clothing, fasted more than the rule required, and slept on hard boards for only four or five hours each night in order not to waste time. Extremely serious, he urged his students not to waste it either, constantly repeating to them, "Habete rationem temporis," and objecting, for example, to chess-playing, saying that the time saved could be used to discuss St. Thomas's *Summa*. In his "free" time, he founded four libraries, and preached in Tarascan, the language of the people of Michoacán, in various Indian villages. His activist fame reached Charles V, who appointed him Bishop of León in Nicaragua. Fray Alonso is said to have exclaimed, paraphrasing both Psalm 22:22 ("Salva me ex ore leonis") and the Offertory of the Mass for the Dead ("liberas eas de ore leonis") and subtly punning "Ab ore leonis, libera me Domine," and flatly refusing this and any other administrative appointment.

Veracruz became the first Prime Professor of Philosophy at the Royal and Pontifical University of Mexico, inaugurated in 1553, and produced a number of works in Latin intended as basic texts for university students. Among them are: *Recognitio summularum* (1554), a resumé of the elementary principles of logic; *Dialectica resolutio* (1554), which, among other things, deals with Porphyry's Introduction to Aristotle's *Categories*, known as the *Isagoge*, a work which laid the foundations for all subsequent formal logic; and *Physica speculatio* (1557), an explanation of and commentary on Aristotle's *Physics*. However, his most significant work, the *De dominio infidelium et iusto bello*, which had been known to exist in manuscript form, did not come to light until the Jesuit Father Ernest J. Burrus discovered it in Mexico, and published a critical edition of the Latin text with an English translation in 1968, under the title *Defense of the Indians: Their Rights*.[1] Fray Alonso's *De dominio*, following the procedure of St. Thomas Aquinas in his *Summa Theologica,* is divided into eleven *dubia* and *quaestiones* (synonymous terms, in effect) which deal with various aspects of the relations between the Spaniards and the indigenous population of the New World. My study focuses on the ideas expressed in *quaestiones* 10 and 11 of the *De dominio,* which are concerned with the legitimacy of the conquest, and which bear a close similarity to ideas expressed in Vitoria's *De Indis*. The question arises as to what extent Veracruz derived his ideas from Vitoria, and the answer would require a thorough investigation. As his student in Salamanca, he was exposed to Vitoria's teachings and attended his *relectiones*. However, when Vitoria read his *De Indis* and *De iure belli*, in 1539, Fray Alonso was already in Mexico.

Veracruz's *De dominio* consists of 374 pages of printed text, which includes 945 paragraphs or sections. Because of space limitation, it is not possible to do justice to this document of great importance for the history of the Spanish conquest and colonization of America. My main purpose is to reveal the existence and the essence of the content of this Neo-Latin work, which must be considered a product of the sixteenth-century School of Salamanca, and which was totally unknown until Father Burrus published it in 1968. The School of Salamanca was headed by Vitoria, and consisted of such notables as the Dominican Domingo de Soto (1494–1560), Vitoria's star disciple, who was very active in the deliberations of the Council of Trent, and the great Jesuit theologians Luis de Molina (1535–1600) and Francisco Suárez (1584–1617).[2] What makes Veracruz unique is that he was the first philosopher-theologian

---

[1] *The Writings of Alonso de la Veracruz: II. Defense of the Indians: Their Rights. Latin Text and English Translation*. Sources and Studies for the History of the Americas (Rome: Jesuit Historical Institute, 1968). For the history of the discovery of the manuscript, see Prometeo Cerezo de Diego, *Alonso de la Veracruz y el Derecho de Gentes* (México, 1985), 45–48.

[2] The members of the School of Salamanca, whose main center of activities was the University

of the Salamanca group who was an eyewitness to the American reality, and this, of course, provided him with a perspective different from that of his co-religionists.

An important tradition at the University of Salamanca, strongly upheld by Vitoria, was the *relectio*, or "re-reading," sometimes known as the *repetitio*. This consisted of an unwritten lecture that each university professor was obligated to give at the completion of each academic year, before the entire university, on one of the more important themes dealt with in his course. One of the innovations implemented by Vitoria was that the *relectio* be written prior to its delivery so that none of the important passages could be lost by a memory lapse. The University of Mexico, whose entire system was a replica of that of Salamanca, immediately incorporated the practice of the *relectio*. Fray Alonso's *relectio*, which originally was untitled, and was read at the end of the 1553–1554 academic term, contained the basis of his *De dominio*. Since each speaker was allowed no more than two hours, the present text of the work we are considering is an obvious significant expansion of the original *relectio*, since it would take about ten hours to read it aloud. One may wonder why the *De dominio* never appeared in print during Fray Alonso's lifetime. The theory of scholars is that the nature of the content was too sensitive, given the heated polemics of the time, when, for example, the impassioned Fray Bartolomé de las Casas (1474–1566) condemned, with some exaggeration, the abuses committed by the Spaniards, while his opponent, Juan Ginés de Sepúlveda (1490?–1573), a distinguished humanist from Córdoba, in his *Democrates alter, sive de iustis belli causis apud indos*,[3] sought, by citing traditional arguments, to justify the conquest. It must also be noted that the Archbishop of Mexico from 1553 to 1572, Alonso de Montúfar, a Dominican, annoyed by a previous *relectio* by Veracruz, namely the *De decimis*, in which the Augustinian criticized the method of collecting tithes from the Indians as unjust, prohibited the publication of the *De dominio*.[4]

The first six "doubts" of the *De dominio* are of a practical nature, dealing with administrative matters.[5] "Doubts" 6 through 9 question whether the emperor is the master of the world, and whether the pope enjoys supreme authority, the conclusion being "no." The tenth and eleventh "doubts", or *quaestiones*, discuss the invalid, or unjustifiable, and valid, or justifiable, causes, respectively, for the waging of war against the natives of America.

The tenth *quaestio* consists of 140 paragraphs and eight *conclusiones*. It begins:

---

of Salamanca, had as their common goal a revitalization of traditional scholasticism, derived from St. Thomas.

[3] This work was first published, translated, and edited by Marcelino Menéndez y Pelayo, in *Boletín de la Academia de la Historia* 22 (1898): 257–369.

[4] The manuscript of the *Relectio de decimis habita in scholis publice in Universitate Mexicana a Magistro Alphonso edita anno 1555 relegenda sed non relecta* was found together with the manuscript of the *De dominio infidelium*. It was published, translated into English, and edited by Ernest J. Burrus, S.J., in *The Writings of Alonso de la Veracruz. Defense of the Indians* (Rome, 1976), 4.

[5] *The Writings*, 2:92–227.

[U]trum imperator vel rex Castellae potuit iustum bellum indicere istis barbaris. (606)[6]

Following scholastic procedure, Veracruz first points out opinions justifying war against the natives that are contrary to those that he will support. He refers to the concept of the universal sovereignty of the emperor over the entire world, the just deprivation of the *dominium* of the Indians and their possessions, their mental inferiority, and their practices of idolatry and human sacrifice as unjustifiable reasons to wage war. A number of Christian followers of such jurisconsults as Hostiensis, the cardinal of Ostia (ca. 1200–1271),[7] maintain with him:

Hodie non est iurisdictio, nec dominium, neque honor, neque potestas penes infideles; nam per adventum Christi, translata sunt in christianos; transfertur, enim, regnum de gente in gentem propter iniustitias suas, 23, quaestione paenultima, c. si de rebus. (624)

Veracruz totally rejects this concept, namely that only Christians have the right of dominion. Concluding that neither the emperor nor the pope is master of the world, he declares they have no right to deprive the natives of America of their dominion and jurisdiction. He bases himself on divine and natural law, and the law of nations, citing various church authorities (632–635). Had the unbelievers been subjects of the Roman Empire, as some falsely claim, the emperor could wage war against those who rebel; but the New World was never part of the Roman Empire: therefore war is not justified against the unbelievers of this territory (636). According to Veracruz, if missionaries had been first sent to preach to the Indians, and the latter had repulsed them, they might be justified in waging war. But such was not the case. Soldiers arrived first, and plundered and killed native peoples, for which reason war cannot be justified. Veracruz states that it was not enough for the soldiers to show the natives a Bible, and say that there was only one God and one supreme pontiff to whom they owed allegiance, and then attack the Indians if they resisted:

Necque sufficienter dicitur ad iustificationem quod ipsi milites armati ostenderent Bibliam, vel dicerent unum solum credendum Deum qui fecit caelum et terram, et quod unus esset pontifex summus, Dei vicarius in terris cui praestarent oboedientiam. (684–685)

This appears to be a veiled refutation of the *requerimiento*, literally "requirement", drawn up by the famous jurist Juan López de Palacios Rubios (1450?–1525), and which required each Spanish *conquistador* to have read by a notary, through an inter-

---

[6] The numbers in parentheses following the citations from the *De dominio* refer to the paragraphs in Burrus's edition, cited in note 1.

[7] Hostiensis (Henry of Segusio, Enrique Bartolomei), whose writings greatly influenced canon law in the thirteenth century.

preter, to the Indians. In a word, this document was a message from the king of Spain, indicating that they were now his subjects, and if they should resist this requirement, which began with the biblical creation of the world and was filled with legal technicalities, they would be enslaved, their wives taken away, and their goods confiscated. History has shown, however, that often the *requerimiento* was not translated, much to the detriment of the totally bewildered natives. If they listened peacefully to the preachers, and still refused to accept the Christian faith, they could not be forced "Patet: nullus debet ad fidem cogi" (689). This in fact was the shared opinion of the theologians of the School of Salamanca.

Regarding the sins of the Indians against natural law, such as idolatry, sexual promiscuity, adultery, polygamy, sodomy, and cannibalism, there were those who invoked the theocratic theory, derived from medieval thought, that these sins applied to all men, and therefore justified war. To the contrary, others, many of whom followed Thomistic scholasticism, maintained that pagans were not subject to these precepts of Christian law. Veracruz states:

> Ab hoc quod isti incolae huius Novi Orbis idola colerent et plures haberent deos, et in eis essent adulteria aut fornicationes simplices aut ebrietates, etiam si ista vitia frequentissima, non ea ratione iustum fuit bellum ad eos subiectandos et suo legitimo dominio exspoliandos. (693)

Veracruz, faithful to the School of Salamanca, gives a detailed number of "proofs," concluding that these sins do not justify war or the seizure of property. It is obvious that neither the emperor nor the sovereign pontiff may wage just war against Christians because of adultery, depriving them for that reason of their dominion; hence they may not do so against unbelievers. The deduction is logical, since adultery is a sin among Christians, and is more scandalous and detrimental to their common good than among unbelievers. Nowhere do we read that such a sin is a cause for war. As for theft, usury, and drunkenness, no action can be taken among the natives, since they were never subjects of the emperor either *de iure* or *de facto*, hence he has no jurisdiction over them (694–696).

As for the cultural and mental backwardness of the Indians adduced as a reason to deprive them of their dominion and subjugate them, Fray Alonso is the only member of the School of Salamanca who knew the Indians at first hand. Vitoria appears convinced of the mental backwardness of the Indians.[8] On the contrary, Fray Alonso has a high opinion of the Indians' rationality. He speaks of their orderly governments and laws before the arrival of the Spaniards. In effect,

---

[8] Vitoria writes: "Sed videtur quantum ad hoc eadem ratio de illis et de amentibus, quia nihil, aut paulo plus, valent ad gubernandum seipsos quam amentes": *De indis recenter inventis relectio prior*, in *Obras de Francisco de Vitoria. Relecciones Teológicas*, ed. Teófilo Urdanoz, O.P. (Madrid, 1960), 724.

> tales huius Orbis incolae non solum non sunt pueri aut amentes, sed suo modo
> praestantes et saltem ex ipsis aliqui qui suo modo praestantissimi sunt. (716)

The argument that the Indians are simple-minded, similar to children, and therefore may be subjugated, holds no validity, since St. Paul states in Galatians that children can enjoy true dominion, and have rights over property.⁹

The last title, or "doubt", *Quaestio* 10, denies that since God has abandoned the Indians, the Spaniards have a right to subjugate them. Veracruz alludes to a "vir gravis et religiosus" who defends this position, citing the Old Testament, wherein, in reference to the Canaanites and the Israelites,

> [Deus] . . . ob ipsorum peccata velit eos (i.e., Indos) destruere et Hispanorum manibus tradere et eo modo quo olim Chananaeos Deus Iudaeis dedit, sicut quidam alias vir gravis et religiosus ausus est probare. (720)

Ernest Burrus has no doubt that this "otherwise high-minded and conscientious person" is none other than Juan Ginés de Sepúlveda.¹⁰ Fray Alonso goes to great length, citing numerous church authorities and the Bible, to refute this concept.

> Quapropter ex illo non sumitur argumentum ad probandum quod sic licitum alios infideles debellare et suo dominio privare; in quo valde aberrant qui putant utrobique eandem causam. (745)

We now turn to *quaestio* 11, the valid causes for the subjection of the Indians by means of force. This part consists of 199 paragraphs and 15 *conclusiones*. The opening paragraph reads:

> Utrum detur aliqua causa iustificans bellum contra huius Novi Orbis incolas. (747)

In answer to this question, Veracruz begins by saying that the conquest could arguably be judged as unjustified. But since it is a *fait accompli*, there may be a justifying reason for sustaining it. He maintains that if the faith is proposed to the Indians seriously, with adequate proofs and reasons which they understand, then they are obligated to accept the faith. Cerezo de Diego faults Veracruz, who with excessive missionary zeal, confusing natural law with supernatural law, goes beyond the limits of the School of Salamanca by affirming that the Spanish monarch may force conversion on the Indians.¹¹

Says Veracruz,

---

[9] Gal. 4:1.
[10] *The Writings*, 2:513, n. 95.
[11] See Cerezo de Diego, *Veracruz*, 308.

Si istis barbaris insulanis sufficienter fuerit proposita fides ita ut ipsi credere teneantur, a suo superiore compelli possunt bello ad fidem suscipiendam de se, nec retrocessio timeatur. (759)

This contradicts St. Thomas, who writes that the act of faith depends on the free will of the individual (*ST* II–II q. 10, art. 8).[12] The pope, says Fray Alonso, could possibly deprive of their rights the Indian rulers who were an impediment to spreading the faith (809). Also, if an Indian king or ruler should exercise tyranny, this, which follows a long tradition in medieval political thought, would justify war (815). In addition, cannibalism and human sacrifice provide a legitimate cause for a just war. Says Fray Alonso:

Si barbari comedebant carnes humanas, sive innocentium, sive nocentium, quos sacrificabant, licite bello potuerunt subici et dominio suo legitimo alias privari si non desisterent. (824)

Veracruz also states that if one native nation is at war with another, Christians may ally themselves with the injured party, thus waging war against their adversary (847). According to him, if a native community is without a king or leader, the said community could elect to become subjects of the Spanish authorities. This is evident from natural law and from the law of nations (857). Also, if a commonwealth were ruled poorly by a legitimate but inept king, the Spaniards would have the right to replace that king by force (867). If some unbelievers should not allow Spaniards who meant no harm to move freely among them, war might be justified (901). Veracruz then maintains that the Spaniards have the right of travel, commerce, and the exploitation of precious minerals that are on unowned land. No one can impede the right of communication. Granted that the Indians of the New World were entitled to their rights as men of perfect republics, they then however become subject to the obligations of the international community. Veracruz sees the right to travel in a foreign territory as a natural right, or at least under the *ius gentium*, since man is a political animal, and travel is a natural consequence of the human condition (903). This derives from St. Augustine and St. Thomas, and is accepted by all those of the School of Salamanca. Should peacefully traveling Spaniards be attacked by Indians, they are justified in defending themselves (908). Cerezo de Diego sees Veracruz, regarding the right of communication, as proposing a new theory of free markets, which can be called "proto-liberalismo económico internacional," as opposed to the mercantile theories of the sixteenth to the eighteenth centuries.[13] The old system favors one's own country over another's, thus resulting in an unfavorable trade balance for the latter.

As Veracruz comes to the end of the rationale for the legitimate justification for the conquest, he goes from theory to reality, by saying that the conquest must be

---

[12] Cerezo de Diego, *Veracruz*, 315.
[13] Cerezo de Diego, *Veracruz*, 348.

accepted as a *fait accompli*, since the unstable situation of the Indians would make it difficult to carry on trade. He explains:

> cum rebus stantibus ut nunc sunt, et cognita conditione Indorum et eorum instabilitate, cum non posset Hispanorum natio manere pacifice, neque posset habere incolatum, neque alia exercere negotia honesta si dominarentur incolae, sequitur, inquam, quod iuste nunc dominium videtur esse apud imperatorem Catholicum, quidquid sit de iure et iustitia a principio; modo tamen non licet dubitare. (930)

However, he maintains that the legitimate native lords may not be deprived of their legitimate dominion, nor are private individuals to be despoiled of their personal property. In conclusion, unbelievers may not be warred against solely because they are unbelievers, nor may they be coerced to believe. And since the peoples of the New World must respect the basic tenets of the *ius gentium*, it follows that the rights of the conquered peoples must also be respected (945).

As Cerezo de Diego rightly concludes, if one compares the unjustifiable causes of Veracruz in the *De dominio* with the illegitimate titles of Vitoria in his *De Indis*, there is an evident parallel, although not a complete correspondence. Regarding the justifiable causes of Veracruz, although he shows a certain degree of independent thought, he coincides basically with the legitimate titles of Vitoria. This was logical, since the views of both men derived from principles shared with the scholastic-Thomist doctrine introduced by Vitoria and accepted by all his disciples.[14]

Vitoria's *De iure belli hispanorum in barbaros, relectio posterior*, the sequel or second part of *De Indis*, appears at first glance to be an abstract theory on what constitutes just cause for war, with no direct reference to the American Indian problem. However, there is the implication as to whether the conquest was justified. The conclusion consists of three *canones*, or rules, which obviously apply to the Indians as well as to wars between Christian princes. Vitoria begins by deploring war as "ultimae inmanitatis", that is, of the worst kind of savagery, to be avoided if possible. If not, due to just cause, then the aim of the victors should be peace and not the destruction of the enemy. Moderation and Christian humility must prevail.[15] These sentiments definitely coincide with those of Alonso de la Veracruz.

While Veracruz's *De dominio* lacks the concision, precision, and theological background of Vitoria's *De Indis*, it affords an eyewitness, direct study of the ethical norms of the colonial administration, something which the other members of the School of Salamanca could not provide. Finally, to quote the Mexican scholar Antonio Gómez Robledo, Veracruz was "el primer catedrático del Derecho de gentes" in the New World.[16] In effect, both Veracruz and Vitoria, judicial speculation aside, see the Conquest as an irreversible historical fact, to which there is a positive side. In view

---

[14] Cerezo de Diego, *Veracruz*, 362.
[15] See *Obras de Vitoria*, title 60, 857–858.
[16] "El problema de la Conquista en Alonso de la Veracruz," *Historia Mexicana* 23 (1974): 407.

of the instability of the Indians' situation, as well as the civilizing benefits that would accrue to them, no one could sensibly suggest that Spain abandon its dominion over the New World, even if a legal case could be made against it. What both men made very clear is that the Indians must be treated fairly and under Christian humanitarian principles.

The European enemies of Spain were responsible for the creation of the concept of the "Black Legend" ("La leyenda negra") which, among other things, accused her of destroying the great Indian civilizations. The respected historian Hubert Herring felt that the "Black Legend" required a "necessary rebuttal." He writes, in part:

> Spain did not topple the Indian peoples from an Elysian state of perfection to one of abysmal misery, despite the lyricists who dwell upon the communal happiness of the Incas and the democratic joys of the Aztecs. Spain did not destroy great Indian populations: there never were great populations.[17]

Spain, in effect, was the only colonial power that sustained the "Great Debate" ("El gran debate") concerning the legitimacy of the conquest. This debate produced such defenders of Indian rights as Las Casas, Vasco de Quiroga (1470–1565), Vitoria, and other members of the School of Salamanca, which included Fray Alonso de la Veracruz. Although not as well known as the distinguished men just cited, many scholars regard him as one of the truly eminent figures of sixteenth-century Spanish America.

Trinity College, Hartford

---

[17] Hubert Herring, *A History of Latin America* (New York, 1972), 152–153.

Bemerkungen zum Trophaeum Anglaricum von Leonardo Dati

THOMAS LINDNER

Der frühhumanistische italienische Dichter Leonardo Dati ist nach längerer Vergessenheit und literarhistorischer Mißachtung in letzter Zeit wieder etwas mehr in das Licht der Öffentlichkeit gerückt, insbesondere durch die erst jüngst erfolgte Neuausgabe seiner Tragödie *Hiensal*.[1]

Leben und Werk

Leonardo Dati (bzw. Leonardus/Lionardus Dathus) wurde in Florenz um 1408 (bzw. nach den Angaben seines Epitaphs im Herbst 1407) geboren.[2] Nach den üblichen Grammatik- und Rhetorikstudien wurde er zunächst Notar und nach 1435 "legum doctor." Durch Freundschaften und Kontakte zu den florentinischen Humanisten kam er auch in klerikale Kreise, wo er seine ersten literarischen Ambitionen pflegen konnte. In der Folge ließ Dati sich zum Priester weihen, ging nach Rom und wurde enger Vertrauter von Kardinal Giordano Orsini. Als die Kurie aber im Juni 1434 wegen der andauernden Kriege in Latium nach Florenz zog, kehrte auch Dati wieder in seine Heimatstadt zurück. Nach Orsinis Tod im Mai 1438 kam er in die Dienste von Kardinal Francesco Condulmer und war auch bei den Vorbereitungen des Konzils von Florenz im Jahr darauf beteiligt. 1441 nahm er am berühmten *certame coronario* teil, einem Dichterwettbewerb in *volgare,* der von Leon Battista Alberti organisiert wurde, und reüssierte mit seiner *scena De amicitia*. Doch er zerstritt sich offenkundig mit seinem Gönner Condulmer, was auch ein Zerwürfnis mit Papst Eugen IV. nach sich zog und ihn für etliche Jahre in Mißgunst von seiten der Kurie brachte. Doch Dati ließ sich nicht entmutigen und versuchte, sich auch weiterhin als

---

[1] *Hiensal* (auch: *Hiempsal, Hyempsal*) steht in der Tradition des Senecaschen Dramas und orientiert sich zudem an den humanistischen Vorbildern von Albertino Mussato und Gregorio Correr. Vgl. die durchaus kontroversiellen Editionen von J. R. Berrigan (*Humanistica Lovaniensia* 25 [1976]: 85–145) und A. Onorato (Messina, 2000).

[2] Vgl. Ristori, in *DBI* 33 (1987), 44f. (Vita); 51f. (Quellenangaben).

Dichter zu profilieren. Er schrieb zu Beginn der vierziger Jahre des 15. Jahrhunderts zwei vergilianisierende Eklogen (*Mirilta* und *Chirlo*) und vor allem das Gedicht, um das es in der Folge geht, *Trophaeum Anglaricum*. Durch dieses kam er seinem neuen Protektor Kardinal Ludovico Scarampi näher, söhnte sich mit der Kurie aus und wurde in den fünfziger Jahren päpstlicher Sekretär, sodann, unter Paul II., *primo segretario* und 1467 schließlich Bischof von Massa Marittima in der Kirchenprovinz Siena. Eine Ernennung zum Kardinal und Erzbischof von Florenz mißlang, was seine letzten Lebensjahre verbittern sollte; Leonardo Dati starb in den ersten Jännertagen 1472.[3]

Die Einschätzung und literarische Wertung Datis als Dichter ist durchaus ambivalent. Galt er seinen Zeitgenossen und den Späteren infolge des renommierten *certame coronario* als guter Poet, der vor allem durch seine Volgare-Gedichte ein breites Echo unter den Gebildeten hatte, wurde er von der deutschen Humanismusforschung des 19. Jahrhunderts diskreditiert und von Georg Voigt etwa als armseliger Dichterling bezeichnet.[4] Eine Neubewertung hat gegen Ende des 19. Jahrhunderts Francesco Flamini versucht, indem er die Inedita, eben die Handschriften, miteinbezogen hatte und somit in seinem eingangs erwähnten Artikel zu einer ausgewogenen Einschätzung kommen konnte: zu einer im großen und ganzen recht positiven Bewertung, indem er in Dati den größten lateinischen Dichter der Toskana im 15. Jahrhundert sieht: "Le sue poesie sono tutte, come dicono, *d'occasione;* spesso anzi dettate a penna corrente (ché Leonardo doveva essere facile verseggiatore) per gratificare a illustri personaggi e per accattare favori principeschi [. . .] Leonardo Dati non ha scritto, ch'io sappia, vasti poemi d'argomento mitologico o biblico o storico; non crea, non inventa, non favoleggia [. . .] Il Dati, in ogni modo, fu per la Toscana nella prima metà del secolo del Rinascimento quello che nella seconda il Poliziano: il migliore de' suoi poeti latini."[5] Dieses Urteil blieb allerdings eher isoliert, und noch 1976 kann man in der Literaturgeschichte des Quattrocento von Contini lesen, daß Datis Prosa und Poesie "atte a interessare unicamente gli eruditi" seien.[6]

Nichtsdestoweniger bestätigt sich die Einschätzung von Flamini bei einer detaillierten Lektüre und Analyse eines von Datis Hauptwerken, des *Trophaeum Anglaricum*. Es handelt sich hierbei um ein heroisches Kurzepos (Epyllion) von exakt 500 Hexametern, in welchem Dati die Schlacht bei Anghiari (Anglaricum) vom 29. Juni 1440 schildert, sie poetisch überhöht und dabei vor allem seinem Gönner Ludovico Scarampi, der als siegreicher Feldherr eine maßgebliche Rolle spielte, ein literarisches Denkmal setzte. Die viel nüchterneren geschichtlichen Ereignisse können anhand seines Epos sowie vor allem durch die Schilderungen in Machiavellis *Geschichte von Florenz* und Neri Capponis *Geschichte der Florentinischen Republik* im einzelnen rekon-

---

[3] Für eine ausführlichere Darstellung seines Leben und literarischen Gesamtwerks sei auf die alte Darstellung von Salvini in der Briefedition von Mehus (Florentiae, 1743) sowie vor allem auf die maßgebliche Studie von Flamini, "Leonardo di Piero Dati," und den umfänglichen Artikel von Ristori, "Dati, Leonardo," verwiesen.

[4] Zusammenfassend dazu Flamini, "Leonardo di Piero Dati," 81.

[5] Flamini, "Leonardo di Piero Dati," 81f.

[6] Contini, *Letteratura italiana*, 118.

struiert werden; es sei hier auf den historischen Beitrag von Mansetti-Bencini "La battaglia d' Anghiari" verwiesen. In dieser Auseinandersetzung ging es hauptsächlich um die Vorherrschaft von Florenz über die Toskana, die von Mailand aus von Filippo Maria Visconti und seinem General Niccolò Piccinino den Florentinern streitig gemacht werden sollte. Zu dieser Zeit hielt sich auch, wie bereits festgestellt, Papst Eugen IV. in Florenz auf, und gemeinsam mit den päpstlichen Milizen gelang es den Florentinern unter dem Oberbefehl von Kardinal Ludovico Scarampi, dem Patriarchen von Aquileia, in der entscheidenden Schlacht bei Anghiari in der Toskana nahe der umbrischen Grenze die Soldateska Piccininos verheerend zu schlagen, die Ansprüche der Visconti auf die Toskana zunichte zu machen und damit die Macht der Medici zu stärken.

Das *Trophaeum Anglaricum*

Dieses Kurzepos ist meines Wissen nur in einem einzigen Textzeugen überliefert, in einer Sammelhandschrift von Datis poetischen Werken, dem *Codex Riccardianus* 1207 aus dem 15. Jh., f. 47v–58r, der in einer zeittypischen italienischen Bastarda geschrieben wurde.[7]

Für die Erstpublikation 1994 habe ich einen Lesetext des *Trophaeum* erstellt und dort, wo der überlieferte Text für mich keinen Sinn ergab, eigenständig konjiziert; häufig sind das einfache Emendationen, wie z.B. V. 415 *tonaces* → *tenaces* "zäh, ausdauernd" (cj. *tonantes* Flamini), V. 485 *sepollit* → *sepellit* (immerhin mit -*ll*-!), V. 488 *valat* (was Flamini mit einem Fragezeichen im Text stehen ließ) → *volat* "eilt von dannen."

Die Interpunktion habe ich nach den Lesehilfen des Manuskripts eingerichtet, bin aber, wo syntaktisch oder stilistisch erforderlich, des öfteren davon abgewichen – Interpunktion ist ja immer schon ein Teil der Textinterpretation. Sodann habe ich die Orthographie nach dem Standard der klassischen Texte vereinheitlicht, d.h. im einzelnen wurden normalisiert: *e, e caudata, ae, oe; u, v;* hyperkorrektes -*ct*-; *xs, x; t, c;* hyperkorrektes *th; c, cc, c(c)h; tt, t* sowie hyperkorrektes *y : i.* Eine textkritische

---

[7] Manuskripttitel: *Tropheum anglaricum*. Eine Beschreibung dieser Handschrift findet sich in S. Morpurgo, *I manoscritti della reale biblioteca di Firenze* (Prato, 1900), *s.v.*; eine Nachprüfung in Kristellers *Iter italicum* brachte keine weiteren Manuskripte zum Vorschein. Etwa 185 Verse wurden von Flamini zur Illustration und Vertiefung seiner Einschätzung im genannten Artikel ediert; ich selbst habe 1994 eine vorläufige Edition mit deutscher Übersetzung erstellt und plane nunmehr gemeinsam mit Kurt Smolak eine umfassende kritische Edition und korrigierte Übersetzung mit Kommentar, was insofern schwierig ist, als die einzige bisher bekannte Handschrift, der zitierte Riccardianus, voller Fehler ist und manchmal ganz merkwürdige Korruptelen aufweist, die ich bisher nicht emendieren bzw. konjizieren konnte. Darüber verzweifelte auch Flamini, der ja nur einen kleinen Teil leider mit etlichen Lesefehlern publizierte, indem er in einer Fußnote klagt: "Ma in piú luoghi è scorretto [il manoscritto], e non arrivo a indovinarne la lezione genuina" (101). Ein weiterer wichtiger Punkt wird auch sein, einen Spezialisten für toskanische Landesgeschichte im 15. Jahrhundert zu konsultieren, der die lokalen Gegebenheiten aus eigener Forschung kennt; in der vorläufigen Übersetzung finden sich daher noch zahlreiche Lücken aufgrund mangelnder Detailkenntnisse der Ereignisse und Realien dieser Zeit und Gegend; dies gilt vornehmlich für noch nicht identifizierte Personen- und Ortsnamen.

Edition wird diese Standardisierungen entweder wieder rückgängig machen oder entsprechend kennzeichnen bzw. rechtfertigen.

Einzelprobleme

Im folgenden will ich mich ein paar sprachlichen und textuellen Schwierigkeiten zuwenden und einige Problemfälle diskutieren. Trivial sind Hyperkorrektismen wie etwa -*ct*- für genuines -*tt*-, z.B. *mictit* (V. 33) für *mittit*, *actonitum* (V. 62) für *attonitum* bzw. *actollere* (V. 129) für *attollere*, die sich in allen italienischen Handschriften der Zeit finden. Dies resultiert aus den bekannten italienischen Dubletten *fatto* ~ relatinisiertes *facto*. Ebenso sehr häufig ist hyperkorrektes *y*, etwa in *tryumphus*, *tryumphat*, *inclytus* sowie der Wechsel *tt : t*, etwa V. 455 *littora* neben einfachem *litora* etc.

In V. 22ff.

> Pars desperat opem, tamquam si nesciat usque,
> Quinam distineant hostem, pars **intus in orbe**
> Subtrepidat vitium, pars tunc in plebe cavendum
> Censet ieiuna (...)

findet sich das unscheinbare Syntagma *intus in orbe* als ein Beispiel für schwer verständliche Realien; das Ganze muß wohl heißen (es handelt sich um die Schilderung der Nöte der Florentiner, als sie von Piccinino bedrängt wurden): "Die einen geben die Hoffnung auf Hilfe auf, gleichsam ohne zu wissen, wie sie den Feind aufhalten könnten, die anderen — innen im Kreis — fürchten ein *vitium* (Fehler, Schande, Verrat), andere wiederum meinten, man müsse sich da hüten im (bzw. vor dem) hungrigen Volk." Was genau bedeutet *intus in orbe*? Ist das ein "Teil der inneren Führungsschicht," also des inneren Kreises, der einen Fehler, d.h. einen Verrat fürchtet? Man sollte aber wohl doch mit Flamini *intus in urbe* lesen (*o/u*-Wechsel sind aus paläographischer Sicht ja nichts Ungewöhnliches), was das Verständnis insofern erleichtern würde, als eben nunmehr ein Teil (*scil*. des Senats) inmitten der Stadt Florenz einen Aufstand fürchtet und somit im hungrigen Volk Vorsorge treffen muß.

In V. 32f.

> Sforsa comes proprias acies †**emutilat** ac se
> Deserit et Venetos mittitque accurrere Flori:

findet sich ein für mich noch nicht identifizierbares, deutlich so geschriebenes *emutilat*; vom Sinn her muß die Stelle lauten, daß Herzog Sforza die eigenen Scharen und sich "emutiliert," Venezien verläßt, wo er stationiert war, und sich anschickt, Truppen nach Florenz zum Entsatz zu entsenden.[8]

Ein ähnliches Problem findet sich in V. 163f.

---

[8] Wenn man hier *commutilat* liest, "er splittete die Truppen auf, " muß man eine metrische Dehnung in Kauf nehmen *(mutilare* klassisch mit kurzem *u*).

>   Mittere opem stringique arta obsidione Tifernum,
>   Ac regnum †experie iamiam se offerre Senensi.

Das Wort ist eindeutig lesbar, ergibt aber — für mich zumindest — keinen Sinn: Piccininos Kriegstaten werden geschildert, Furcht hätte sich in Florenz breitgemacht, die offene Schlacht wurde untersagt, nach Hilfe würde geschickt, Tifernum (das ist Città di Castello) werde durch einen dichten Belagerungsring zermürbt und er, also Piccinino, biete schon jetzt die Herrschaft der *experie Senensi*, den Sienesern also. Aber was ist *experie?* Ist hier vielleicht in *imperio* "der Obrigkeit" zu emendieren?

Manchmal kann man monströs anmutende Gebilde recht einfach entschärfen. Das gräzisierende *athicem* in V. 265f.

>   (...) Ille †athicem lustret nunc eminus hoste,
>   Et vincat nihilum (...)

ist wohl *aciem*. Piccinino feuert seine Mannen zur Schlacht an und gibt sich dabei als *detrectator Ludovici*: "Jener, d.h. Ludovicus, möge, wenn der Feind noch fern ist, seine Schlachtreihen mustern und wird nicht siegen." *Acies* kommt im Text freilich sehr oft vor; warum gerade an dieser Stelle pseudogräzisierendes *athicem* steht, bleibt immerhin merkwürdig.

In V. 463ff.

>   (...) fragor undique crescit
>   Armorum, saevit ferrum gaudetque cruore
>   Ignarum finis, cum †internictio summa,
>   Cumque hebetant vires fessis in caede lacertis.

wird das Kriegsgetümmel geschildert: "der Waffenlärm wächst immer noch auf allen Seiten, die Schwerter wüten und ergötzen sich am Blut, ohne an ein Aufhören zu denken, als (bis) die Kräfte den durch das Niedermetzeln müden Händen wichen." Vielleicht ist *internictio* (für *internecio/internicio*) mit dem metrisch auffälligen *cum* || *internictio-* Hiat eine Neuableitung auf *-tio*, um die Kürze von *-necio/-nicio* zu umgehen.

Im großen und ganzen ist der Text aber metrisch einwandfrei und nach den klassischen, d.h. vergilischen Mustern gebaut. Trotzdem taucht auch eine zäsurbedingte *productio* von auslautendem kurzen *e* des Infinitivs *capere* (V. 85) auf:

>   (...) De libertate caduca   83
>   Ille autem timuit, latebras atque oppida circum
>   Intentat caper**e**, neu sese in faucibus ipsis
>   Urgeat, ast habeat, quotiens remearit, asylum,

eine auffällige und für das *Trophaeum* ungewöhnliche, nichtsdestoweniger aus dem Mittellatein her durchaus übliche Lizenz. Es geht hier wieder um Piccinino, der um das unbeständige Kriegsglück fürchtet und sich anschickt, Schlupfwinkel und die

Städte ringsum einzunehmen, nicht um sich in den Engpässen aufzuhalten, sondern, wenn notwendig, ein Rückzugsgebiet zu haben.

Manchmal finden sich ganz merkwürdige Neuprägungen und *Hapax legomena:* In V. 328 etwa ein Verbum *andrivorat* 'Männer verschlingen', in V. 470 ein *laterones* für die Flanken des Heeres, und nicht selten ist die Syntax und Stilistik dunkel und verworren.

Aber *grosso modo* kann man doch der Kurzeinschätzung Rossis in *Il Quattrocento* zustimmen, Datis Werk sei "un carme eroico in cui descriveva con virgiliana eleganza di stile e di immagini la battaglia d'Anghiari" (245). Dies gilt umso mehr, wenn man sich das nachfolgende schöne Gleichnis zu Gemüte führt:

> Ac veluti pastor, si forte ululari et instet   73
> Pone lupus, caulas, ne iam sub nocte latenter
> Impetat, obducit trepidus fidusque tuetur
> Submissis canibus lucemque exspectat amicam;
> Ille fame et terrore simul stans haesitat anceps
> Atque avet atque timet; dum tandem postera lux est,
> Pastor opemque animumque capit furque exulat ultro,
> Sic exsanguis erat toto Florentia vultu,
> At sollers tamen, et spe pascebatur in horas.

Salzburg

Literatur (in Auswahl):

Vorläufige Gesamtedition: Th. Lindner, "Leonardo Dati, *Trophaeum Anglaricum* (neulat. Renaissance-Epos): Textkritische Revision der Handschrift Cod. Riccard. 1207, f. 47v–58r sowie deutsche Erstübersetzung," in F. Piel, *Leonardos Disegnio der Anghiarischlacht. Materialien und Dokumente zur Tavola Doria* (Falkenberg, 1994), 114–23.

J. R. Berrigan, "Leonardo Dati: *Hiensal Tragoedia*. A Critical Edition with Translation," *Humanistica Lovaniensia* 25 (1976): 85–145.

L. Bertolini, ed., *De vera amicitia. I testi del primo Certame coronario* (Ferrara, 1993).

G. (di Neri) Capponi, *Geschichte der Florentinischen Republik* (*Storia della repubblica di Firenze,* übers. H. Dütschke), 2 Bde. (Leipzig, 1876).

J.-F. Chevalier, "Dati, Leonardo (1408–1472)," in *Centuriae Latinae: Festschrift für Marie-Madeleine de la Garanderie* (Genf, 2001; im Druck).

G. Contini, *Letteratura italiana del Quattrocento* (Firenze, 1976).

F. Flamini, "Leonardo di Piero Dati poeta latino del secolo XV," *Giornale storico della letteratura italiana* 16 (1890): 1–107.

P. O. Kristeller, *Iter Italicum*, 6 Bde. (London/Leiden, 1963–1997).

N. Machiavelli, *Geschichte von Florenz* (*Istorie fiorentine / Historiae Florentinae,* übers. A. v. Reumont) (Wien, 1934).

I. Mansetti-Bencini, "La battaglia d'Anghiari," *Rivista delle biblioteche e degli archivi* 18 (1907): 106–27.

L. Mehus, ed., *L. Dathi Epistolae XXXIII* (Florentiae, 1743).

S. Morpurgo, *I manoscritti della reale biblioteca di Firenze* (Prato, 1900).
A. Onorato, ed., *Hyempsal,* Quaderni di filologia medievale e umanistica 4 (Messina, 2000).
R. Ristori, "Dati, Leonardo," in *Dizionario biografico degli italiani* 33 (Roma, 1987), 44–52.
V. Rossi, *Il Quattrocento,* 5. ed. (Milano, 1953).
G. Voigt, *Die Wiederbelebung des classischen Alterthums oder das erste Jahrhundert des Humanismus,* 2 Bde., 3. ed. (Berlin, 1893; Nd. 1960).

Un Soneto de Quevedo y
un Epigrama de Falcó

DANIEL LÓPEZ-CAÑETE QUILES

Hace diez años, en el I Simposio Internacional sobre Humanismo y Pervivencia del Mundo Clásico, celebrado en Alcañiz, provincia española de Teruel, presenté una comunicación titulada "Un epigrama de Falcó y un soneto de Quevedo."[1] La comparación de los dos poemas aludidos en el epígrafe quería demostrar la huella modeladora del primero respecto al segundo. Mi propósito era, así, ampliar la nómina de lecturas y fuentes quevedescas, y también ilustrar la influencia de la literatura neolatina del Renacimiento en la producción poética castellana de los Siglos de Oro. Esta relación entre ambas literaturas constituye hoy una realidad que no admite dudas,[2] pero que está lejos de ser conocida en toda su dimensión. La intercomunicación de los dos campos de estudio, el neolatino y el romance, es ciertamente cada vez mayor, pero el conocimiento de la literatura latina renacentista, al menos de la producida en España, es aún incompleto e interino: todavía hay muchos especímenes latinos del siglo XVI latentes en impresos antiguos que duermen, polvorientos, el sueño de los justos, y quién sabe cuántos de ellos pueden desmentir, si expuestos a la ciencia actual, la presunta originalidad de, supongamos, unos versos gongorinos. De ahí que los estudios de conjunto que abordan esta cuestión tienen por necesidad el carácter de balances provisionales y de estímulo urgente para la aportación de nuevos resultados. Y a tal fin quiere contribuir el trabajo que sigue, cuyo objeto y título son casi idénticos al presentado hace diez años; cambian, naturalmente, las composiciones estudiadas, y también el orden de análisis, que se ocupará en primer lugar del soneto de Quevedo.

Su texto dice así:

---

[1] In J. M. Maestre Maestre y J. Pascual Barea, eds., *Humanismo y Pervivencia del Mundo Clásico* (Cádiz, 1993), 1:557–564.

[2] Véase J. F. Alcina, "El latín humanístico y la cultura vernácula," in A. M. Aldama et al., eds., *La Filología Latina, hoy: Actualización y perspectivas* (Madrid, 1999), 2:729–746.

Inscripción de la estatua augusta
del César Carlos Quinto en Aranjuez

Las selvas hizo navegar, y el viento
Al cáñamo en sus velas respetaba,
Cuando, cortés, su anhélito tasaba
Con la necesidad del movimiento.

Dilató su victoria el vencimiento
Por las riberas que el Danubio lava;
Cayó África ardiente; gimió esclava
La falsa religión en fin sangriento.

Vio Roma en la desorden de su gente,
Si no piadosa, ardiente valentía,
Y de España el rumor sosegó ausente.

Retiró a Solimán, temor de Hungría,
Y, por ser retirada más valiente,
Se retiró a sí mismo el postrer día.[3]

La primera cuestión que se nos plantea tiene que ver con el título del poema, que le fue adjudicado por el editor póstumo de Quevedo, Jusepe González de Salas. Cuál es la "estatua augusta" de Carlos V a la que sirve de "inscripción" el presente soneto? A esta pregunta respondió uno de los máximos especialistas de Quevedo, James Crosby. Éstas fueron sus palabras textuales:

> El epígrafe que colocó González de Salas a este soneto nos dice que se trata de una estatua de Carlos V que estuvo en Aranjuez, y que se puede calificar de augusta. Del texto del poema se desprende que la estatua tendría un aspecto fuertemente militar, pero cortés, y que en ella estarían representados algunos de los enemigos vencidos por el Emperador. Estos datos sugieren que se trata de una famosa estatua que se titula "Carlos V dominando el Furor," lo que no es sino una traducción libre de la inscripción que se lee en el plinto: "Caesaris uirtute domitus furor." En las dos fotos que reproducimos, se observará no solamente las semejanzas ya mencionadas entre el soneto y la estatua, sino también que los versos siete y ocho cuadran muy bien con la representación plástica de la figura vencida, figura que en la primera mitad del siglo XVII fue llamada por Carducho "La Herejía," y también, en uno de los inventarios de Palacio, "El turco prisionero" (Eduardo Barrón, *Museo Nacional de Pintura y Escultura: Catálogo de la Escultura* [Madrid, 1908], 200, núm. 273). Por otra parte, sabemos que en el

---

[3] Francisco de Quevedo, *Obra Poética*, ed. José Manuel Blecua (Madrid, 1969), 1:418–419, nº 214.

mismo siglo XVII estuvo por algún tiempo en Aranjuez, entre otros lugares. La estatua es obra del escultor italiano Leone Leoni, a quien probablemente ayudó su hijo Pompeo, y fue terminada en el año 1564.[4]

José Manuel Blecua, autor de la edición canónica de la poesía quevedesca, cita la explicación de Crosby dándole su asentimiento,[5] también parecen mostrarse de acuerdo Ignacio Arellano y Lía Schwarz en su edición más reciente del mismo poema.[6] Yo, sin embargo, encuentro problemática la propuesta de la estatua de Leoni como modelo inspirador de los versos analizados. Éstos ensalzan la figura de Carlos V como conquistador y como caudillo militar, enumerando de manera más o menos explícita algunas de sus gestas bélicas. Quevedo se demora en el primer cuarteto celebrando, de manera tan pomposa como abstracta, las empresas navegadoras organizadas por Carlos V, tal vez las que tuvieron como destino y objeto la ampliación de los territorios conquistados en el Nuevo Mundo; éste había sido, al fin y al cabo, un argumento recurrente en la creación y la propaganda de la imagen heroica de Carlos V durante el siglo XVI, ya que permitía establecer una comparación, favorable para el emperador, entre sus navegaciones y las de Hércules: Carlos llegó más allá de las columnas del Alcida, y así, *plus ultra* fue lema recurrente en la iconografía y la panegírica imperial.[7] Desde el segundo cuarteto hasta el final se suceden, en llamativo contraste de extensión con la alabanza anterior de las glorias navegadoras, escuetas menciones de glorias bélicas específicas: las campañas en el Danubio y el Elba contra los protestantes, culminadas en la batalla de Mühlberg aparecen en los vv. 5–6; la expedición triunfante contra Túnez de 1535, en el v. 7; la represión de la revuelta de los moriscos de 1525–1526 en los vv. 7–8; los vv. 9–10 aluden al Saco de Roma y cautiverio del Papa Clemente VII en 1527, exhibición de "valentía ardiente, si no piadosa"; la sofocación del levantamiento de las comunidades es sugerida por el asordinado, casi eufemístico v. 11: "y de España el rumor sosegó ausente"; el 12 apunta a la retirada del sultán turco Solimán en Viena ante los ejércitos imperiales el año 1535; los dos últimos versos exaltan la abdicación de Carlos en favor de su hijo y su retirada a Yuste en 1556 como un acto de aún mayor valentía que, como tal, se alinea con las anteriores gestas y les sirve de culminación.[8]

Qué relación existe entre, por un lado, el contenido de este poema y la presentación de ese contenido, y por otro, el objeto referencial de la estatua de Leoni y la manera en que éste se plasma? El conjunto escultórico[9] tiene dos figuras: una es la del emperador, que aparece erguido y firme en atuendo guerrero, y la otra, la del

---

[4] James O. Crosby, *En torno a la poesía de Quevedo* (Madrid, 1967), 67–68.
[5] Quevedo, *Obra Poética*, ed. Blecua, 418–419.
[6] Francisco de Quevedo, *Un Heráclito Cristiano: Canta sola a Lisi y otros poemas*, ed. y estudio preliminar de Lía Schwarz e Ignacio Arellano (Madrid, 1998), 91–92, 715.
[7] Véase Fernando Checa Cremades, *Carlos V y la imagen del héroe en el Renacimiento* (Madrid, 1987), 196ss.
[8] La explicación de estos vv. está en Quevedo, *Un Heráclito Cristiano*, ed. Schwarz y Arellano, 91–92, 715.
[9] Una fotografía frontal y posterior puede verse en la obra y lugares citados de Crosby.

Furor, que yace en cadenas rendido a los pies de Carlos V. La obra de Leoni presenta, sí, una coincidencia con el poema de Quevedo: ambas exaltan el triunfo del emperador sobre el enemigo. A mi entender, sin embargo, las diferencias entre ambas obras son más llamativas que las semejanzas. Quevedo conmemora diversas victorias sobre enemigos particulares e históricos; Leoni nos presenta un solo enemigo, el Furor, y éste es abstracto: me cuesta concebir que esa mera figura alegórica le inspirase a Quevedo la enumeración de todos los triunfos específicos que encontramos en su soneto, el último de los cuales, no olvidemos, lo obtuvo Carlos V sobre sí mismo al retirarse y abdicar: es decir, el propio Carlos V sería — desde el punto de vista aquí cuestionado — uno de los enemigos representado por el Furor, pero eso me parece quizá poco decoroso y consonante con las intenciones encomiásticas del poeta. Es cierto que en el siglo XVII, como recuerda Crosby, existe una tradición que relaciona la escultura con la victoria en Túnez y que esa tradición "no duda en traducir la inscripción del plinto por 'Carlos V dominando el furor turco',"[10] y la victoria sobre el turco en Túnez es aludida por Quevedo; como también es verdad que en el mismo siglo XVII se interpretaba, diversamente, esa figura del Furor como una alegoría de la herejía protestante, y éste es otro enemigo cuya derrota celebra el soneto. Ahora bien, aun en el caso de que Quevedo conociese esas interpretaciones, la estatua reflejaría uno solo de los adversarios debelados por Carlos V, mientras que el soneto despliega a nueve de ellos. Por lo demás, si Quevedo se hubiera inspirado en la obra de Leoni, esperaríamos quizá en sus versos la mención del furor, que es central y evidente en el título de la escultura: esa palabra, sin embargo, brilla por su ausencia en todo el soneto.

Desde esta perspectiva, el título del poema parece inadecuado.[11] O si la obra de Leoni sirvió de fuente a Quevedo, hay que reconocer que Quevedo trató a su modelo con evidente libertad. Sin descartar esa filiación, creo, sin embargo, que el poeta tuvo ante sí otro modelo con el que presenta más semejanzas y que no es de índole escultórica sino literaria. Me refiero a unos versos del poeta valenciano Jaime Juan Falcó, nacido en 1522 y muerto en 1594, autor de un tratado sobre la cuadratura del círculo y, sobre todo, de una obra poética latina relativamente extensa y diversa. Su pluma fácil y venusta cultivó la lírica, la elegía, la égloga, y la sátira, así como el poema didáctico y la epopeya; pero ante todo, fue quizá su producción epigramática el fundamento principal de su reputación como escritor: recordemos que Baltasar

---

[10] Así Checa, *Carlos V*, 138ss.; véase 139, para más interpretaciones sobre el propósito de la estatua y su posible inspiración en Virgilio *Eneida* 1.291–296. Sobre la misma obra de arte y la historia de su producción, véase E. Plon, *Les maîtres italiens au service de la Maison d'Autriche: Léon Leoni sculpteur de Charles-Quint et Pompeo Leoni sculpteur de Philippe II* (Paris, 1887) (obra que conozco citada en el libro de Checa).

[11] Para otros casos de inadecuación en los títulos de González de Salas, cf. R. Álvarez Hernández, "Fuentes y originalidad de un soneto de Quevedo consagrado a Roma sepultada en sí misma," *Canente* 6 (1989): 15–27 (sobre el título del soneto "A Roma sepultada en sus ruinas"); Francisca Moya, "Salas, un humanista al trabajo," in J. M. Maestre Maestre, J. Pascual Barea, y L. Charlo Brea, eds., *Humanismo y pervivencia del mundo clásico II: Homenaje al Profesor Luis Gil* (Cádiz, 1997), 2:455–478, esp. 470 y n. 62.

Gracián lo celebrará en el siglo XVII otorgándole el honorable título de "el Marcial valenciano." Y entre sus epigramas precisamente está la composición que nos interesa:

VII
IN TVMVLVM CAROLI QVINTI IMPERATORIS

Parcite, mortales, nudos iam reddere montes,
    et Carolo tantas aedificare pyras.
Sit labor artificum solas ostendere palmas
    Caesaris, et tumulus Caesare dignus erit.
Prima triumphato stupefiat Gallia rege,
    procumbat supplex Caesaris ante pedes.
Ad dextrum stet Roma latus, Carthago sinistrum,
    altera capta tuis, altera capta tibi.
Sint alibi Turcae uertentes signa retrorsum,
    et iam iam pereant, ni ferat Ister opem.
Ante Deos iaceant exuti Saxones armis,
    Caedeque terribili decolor Albis eat.
Parte alia Alcidem sistat sua meta, tibique
    terra suos fines augeat, unda suos.
Vltima de seipso uictoria magna sequatur,
    sitque aliter magnus qui modo magnus erat.
His ita compositis, crescent miracula mundi:
    Octauum Caroli nobile funus erit.[12]

El epigrama, como vemos, tiene como tema central el mismo que el soneto: el encomio de una serie parecida de triunfos de Carlos V en la que se incardina, a modo de remate, la abdicación, puesta al mismo nivel, si no superior, que las victorias militares. Cierto: la presentación varía de un poeta a otro. En Falcó, la enumeración de las victorias es el contenido de sus instrucciones para un túmulo adecuado en honor del emperador: su poema es exhortativo. En el narrativo Quevedo, por el contrario, no existen semejantes recomendaciones funerarias. Ahora bien, éstas tampoco tienen sentido cuando el madrileño escribe, tal vez medio siglo después de muerto Carlos V: su omisión, pues, estaba justificada. Es cierto también que, en apariencia, los hechos celebrados pertenecen al acervo común de la historia, y que en la panegírica anterior de Carlos V hallamos, igualmente, ejemplos que consisten en el despliegue de los triunfos imperiales coronado por el elogio de la abdicación, considerada el triunfo supremo.[13] No he encontrado, sin embargo, ningún poema que concentre ese con-

---

[12] Jaime Juan Falcó, *Obras Completas, I: Obra Poética*, ed. crítica, trad., notas y estudio introductorio de Daniel López-Cañete Quiles (León, 1996), 1.7, p. 34. Véase la introducción para aquellas y otras noticias sobre la vida y obra de Falcó.
[13] Cf., e.g., el "Epigrama a la muerte del Emperador Carlos Quinto" de Hernando de Acuña, en *Varias Poesías*, ed. de L. F. Larios (Madrid, 1982), 355:

tenido en un número de versos parecido al de Quevedo, como sí ocurre en el caso de Falcó (obsérvese que éste desgrana las gestas del emperador en 12 versos [del 5 al 16], sólo dos menos que los 14 del soneto). Por otra parte, al margen del caso presente, existen indicios de que Quevedo leyó con provecho para su obra las poesías latinas de Falcó, un poeta admirado por otros grandes genios españoles de los Siglos de Oro.

En el trabajo mencionado al comienzo de esta comunicación traté de ilustrar esa hipótesis comparando otro epigrama de Falcó y otro soneto quevedesco, que pueden leerse allí; he aquí más textos convergentes de ambos autores cuyo parangón interesa. Un soneto al túmulo del Duque de Lerma se remata del modo siguiente:

>   No he de decirte el nombre de su dueño,
>   Que si lo sabes, parecerte ha poca
>   Toda aquesta grandeza a sus despojos.[14]

Por su parte, un breve epigrama de Falcó sobre el monasterio de San Lorenzo de El Escorial dice así:

DE TEMPLO DIVI LAVRENTII

>   O tu qui palles hac uisa mole, uiator,
>   ingredere ulterius, plusque stupebis opus.
>   Autorem taceo, nam si tibi dixero nomen,
>   illico rem tantam senseris esse nihil.[15]

>   Y al fin hubo otra vitoria
>   Que la más clara escurece
>   . . . .
>   Pues fue solo él vencedor
>   De su grandeza y valor,
>   Cuando del humano estado,
>   Despreciando el summo grado,
>   Ganó el Imperio mayor.

Compárense también estos versos de J. C. Calvete de Estrella, *El Túmulo Imperial, adornado de historias y letreros y epitaphios* (Valladolid, 1570), 14:

>   Hic ubi uix Atropos potuit perscindere filum,
>   Cum prius in Belgis, nato tot regna Philippo,
>   Se prorsus uincens, cum tot superauerit hostes,
>   Deponens etiam Imperium sponte ipse dedisset.

[14] Nº 219, ed. Blecua, 1:422–423.
[15] 1.16, ed. López-Cañete, 46.

Asimismo, en los *Sueños* de Quevedo leemos el siguiente pasaje:

> Y acogíme donde me señaló, y topé muchos demonios en el camino, con palos y lanzas, echando del infierno muchas mujeres hermosas, ... muchos malos confesores y muchos letrados. Pregunté que por qué los quería echar del infierno a aquellos solos, y dijo un demonio porque eran de grandísimo provecho para la población del infierno en el mundo: las damas, con sus caras y sus mentirosas hermosuras y buenos pareceres, los confesores con vendidas absoluciones y los letrados, con buenas caras y malos pareceres. Y que así los echaban porque trujiesen gente.[16]

Compárense estas líneas con el siguiente epigrama de Falcó contra Lutero:

DE LVTHERO

> Ad caeli portam fertur uenisse Lutherus,
>   sed Petrum hic cernens de fore uertit iter.
> Per loca purgandi noxas uestigia fecit;
>   non tamen agnouit, nam comes error erat.
> Venit ad infernas fauces, sed ianitor inquit:
>   "Aduena, siste pedem, non tibi porta patet.
> Plus nobis lucri uiuus quam mortuus affers.
>   Viue iterum ut ueniant millia multa uirum."[17]

El parecido entre los pasajes comparados es evidente y no necesita más comentario. No puedo afirmar con total certeza que los textos de Quevedo deriven de los de Falcó; pero incluso si no aceptamos este extremo, sí estaremos obligados a admitir la afinidad existente entre los ingenios de ambos autores. Esta afinidad, en fin, constituye un capítulo, si no voluminoso, sí ilustrativo de las conexiones y puntos de comunión entre literatura latina y literatura vernácula en el Renacimiento, un vasto campo a cuyo estudio las páginas anteriores esperan haber aportado alguna contribución y estímulo.

Universidad de Sevilla

---

[16] F. de Quevedo, *Los sueños*, ed. de Ignacio Arellano (Madrid, 1991), "Sueño del Infierno," 137–138.

[17] 1.85, ed. López-Cañete, 146.

Fuentes para los Comentarios de *Jodocus Badius Ascensius*

MARIANO MADRID CASTRO

Los comentarios de Badius (1462–1535) suponen un enorme volumen en el total de su obra. Constituyen la parte más importante después de sus trabajos gramaticales.[1] Tienen su origen en las explicaciones de clase, cuando enseñó latín en Valence y en Lyon (antes de 1492–1499).[2] Continuó escribiéndolos durante toda su vida.[3]

Sus trabajos sobre Baptista Mantuano

Entre la larga lista de obras que comenta Badius,[4] un capítulo importante es el dedicado a las de Baptista de Mantua (1447–1516). En 1513[5] editó en París una obra monográfica de los poemas de Spagnuoli. En ella se encuentra recogida gran parte de la obra poética del Mantuano, a la que acompañan comentarios suyos y de otros humanistas, como Murrho (1452–1494),[6] Brant (1458?–1521),[7] o Bruchterius (primera

---

[1] Ph. Renouard, *Bibliographie des impressions et des oeuvres de Josse Badius Ascensius, imprimeur et humaniste, 1462–1535* (Paris, 1908; repr. New York, 1965), 1:140.

[2] Renouard, *Bibliographie*, 1:10, 140. Existen algunos datos cronológicos seguros al respecto: en diciembre de 1488 y enero de 1489 se hallaba en Gante. Realizó un viaje a Italia, que hay que situar o bien antes de los meses indicados o después de ellos. En 1492 se encontraba en Lyon y, ya para esa época, había ejercido como profesor en Valence (Renouard, *Bibliographie*, 1:9).

[3] Hasta 1529, en que compone el último, a las *Filípicas* de Cicerón (Renouard, *Bibliographie*, 1:143, 156; 2:322–324). Siguió editando *Commentarii familiares* hasta 1532, si bien son revisiones de impresiones anteriores; la última, a Aulo Gelio (Renouard, *Bibliographie*, 1:156; 2:468).

[4] Las propias obras o sus autores se relacionan en Renouard, *Bibliographie*, 1:326: Terencio, Boecio, Juvenal y Persio, Cicerón, Horacio, Ovidio, Virgilio, *Expositiones* al uso de Salisbury, Pierre Bury o de Bur, Philippo Beroaldo, F. Ottavio, Salustio, *Navis Stultifera* (Sebastian Brant), Lucano, Valerio Máximo, Séneca, y Quintiliano.

[5] Número 232 del catálogo de E. Coccia, *Le edizioni delle opere del Mantovano* (Roma, 1960), 55.

[6] Mor, Murr o Morer. Cf. Hans G. Wackernagel, ed., *Die Matrikel der Universität Basel* (Basel, 1951), 1:54. Cf. Renouard, *Bibliographie*, 1: 147: Murr oder Mörer.

[7] La denominación vernácula del nombre, Brant, es la más usual. Incluso persiste cuando se

mitad del siglo XVI).⁸ De los ciento veintisiete títulos que Coccia atribuye⁹ al Mantuano, se incluyen en los tres volúmenes de esta monografía un total de ochenta y cuatro.

Según la investigación llevada a cabo, existen en España tres bibliotecas públicas en las que se conservan ejemplares de esta edición: Biblioteca Nacional de Madrid, Biblioteca Universitaria de Salamanca, y Biblioteca Universitaria de Valencia.¹⁰ En concreto, hemos trabajado con uno de los dos ejemplares disponibles en la Biblioteca Nacional y con el de Salamanca.

La lectura de los comentarios de Badius incluidos en esta edición nos revela multitud de fuentes explícitas. Respecto a ellas habría que diferenciar entre primarias y secundarias.¹¹ También se encuentra información dispersa que apunta a fuentes de más difícil determinación y que requieren un estudio específico.

El *corpus* analizado

Se ha limitado a los comentarios correspondientes a las siguientes obras del Mantuano: *Contra poetas impudice loquentes* y *De calamitatibus temporum*. El número total de fuentes que se cita en ellos se acerca al centenar.¹² Las más recurridas, nombradas por

---

latiniza su nombre de pila, e.g., *Collecta Sebastiani Brant in opus Baptistae Mantuani* (n. 14). *Stultifera navis* (traducción latina del original alemán *Das Narrenschiff*) es su obra más conocida, que le proporcionó fama internacional.

⁸ Jean Brouchier. Los datos biográficos de este autor son escasos. Precisamente, la referencia más importante para determinar los años en que vivió es la publicación del comentario a la obra del Mantuano *De fortuna Francisci Gonzagae*, editado por vez primera en París en 1512 (n° 210 del catálogo de Coccia, *Le edizioni*, 52). En los *Archives biographiques françaises* (ed. S. Bradley, London et al., s.a.), que recogen todas las obras biográficas francesas de los siglos XVII al XX, se establece como término *ante quem* la mencionada publicación. Las últimas obras de referencia son comentarios a Lucianus Scaphidius, Erasmo, y Simon de Colines en 1528. Esta información proviene de la obra de J. C. F. Hoefer, *Nouvelle biographie générale*, 46 vols. (Paris, 1855), 7:516.

⁹ Cf. Coccia, *Le edizioni*, 109–129.

¹⁰ Sólo uno de los tres volúmenes y mutilado.

¹¹ Entendiendo por ellas las que recibe a través un autor intermediario.

¹² En concreto, se han contabilizado un total de ochenta y ocho. El nombre empleado, así como el número de veces que aparecen se indica a continuación: Vergilius (209 veces), Ovidius (57), Servius (49), Vulgata (41), Plinius (33), Horatius (32), Iuvenalis (21), Homerus (20), Lucanus (14), Strabo (13), Iustinus (12), Statius (11), Augustinus (10), Cicero (10), Herodotus (9), Livius (9), Persius (9), Diodorus (8), Terentius (8), Tibullus (8), Seneca (7), Gellius (6), Hesiodus (6), Lucretius (6), Sallustius (6), Solinus (6), Valerius Maximus (6), Aristoteles (5), Plato (5), Donatus (4), Festus (4), Hieronymus (4), Macrobius (4), Tortellius (4), Valla (4), Baptista Mantuanus (3), Catullus (3), Curtius (3), Ennius (3), Lactantius (3), Medicus Tertius Ponticus (3), Nonius Marcellus (3), Plautus (3), Plutarchus (3), Propertius (3), Quintilianus (3), Apuleius (2), Iosephus (2), Martianus Capella (2), Martialis (2), Petrus Burrus (2), Q. Serenus (2), Silius Italicus (2), Varro (2), Afranius (1), Agathyrsides (1), Alexander (de Villedieu) (1), Antipatros Sidonius (1), Apollonius (1), Aristarchus (1), Ausonius (1), Avicenna (1), Badius Ascensius (1), Bergomensis chronographus (1), Boethius (1), Cato (1), Dionysius Thrax (1), Dioscorides (1), Ephorus (1), Euphorion (1), Eusebius (1), Fabius Pictor (1), Manlius Theodorus (1), Pacuvius (1), Philostephanus (1), Pindarus (1), Pius II (Aeneas Silvius Piccolomini) (1), Probus (1), Ps. Acron (1), Sappho (1), Simonides (1), Siponti-

orden de frecuencia son Virgilio (209 veces), Ovidio (57), Servio (49), la Vulgata (41), Plinio (33),[13] Horacio (32), Juvenal (21), Homero (20), Lucano (14), Estrabón (13), Justino (12), Estacio (11), Agustín (10), Cicerón (10), Heródoto (9), Livio (9), y Persio (9). A partir de este autor, la frecuencia con que aparecen los demás es algo menor. Entre los no nombrados aquí (véase n. 12) se encuentran autores coetáneos, como es el caso del propio Mantuano (en obras diferentes a la comentada, lógicamente), o de Valla.

Badius y otros comentaristas

La aludida edición de 1513 incluye piezas del Mantuano comentadas por más de un humanista, lo que nos brinda la posibilidad de cotejarlas. Para este fin, resulta especialmente útil el poema *Contra poetas impudice loquentes*, que dispone de dos comentarios, los de Badius y Murrho. Ello permite contrastar el uso de las fuentes en ambos. Respecto a *De calamitatibus temporum*, ha habido que recurrir a fragmentos con una extensión suficiente como para posibilitar la obtención de resultados satisfactorios. Algunos de los comentarios a esta última obra que Badius adjunta presentan el inconveniente de estar incompletos. Así ocurre con el de Murrho[14] a los libros 1 y 2[15] y el de Brant al libro 1. Han sido, pues, los comentarios de Badius y Brant al libro 2 *De calamitatibus* los elegidos para estudiar las relaciones entre ellos.

Fuentes citadas por Badius en el comentario al *Contra poetas*

Su número es muy superior al promedio que presenta en el otro comentario analizado. Hace referencia a cincuenta y un autores[16] entre los que ocupa un lugar pre-

---

nus (1), Suetonius (1), Theocritus (1), Theophrastus (1), Valerius Flaccus (1), Vegetius (1), Vitruvius (1), y Zoilus (1).

[13] Nos referimos a C. Plinio Segundo, el Viejo.

[14] Le sorprendió la muerte cuando no había concluido el comentario correspondiente al libro 1 *De calamitatibus*. Leemos (fol. 35v): "Coegit heu inexorabile fatum interpretationem hanc abrumpi imperfectamque relinqui. Nec potuit Sebastianus Murrho primae Parthenices et Secundae commentariolos revidere, recognoscere et castigare. Quod si, ut humanum est, in historiis, fabulis, geographia, astronomia abstrusi sensus interpretationem erratum miniusve [sic] absolutum aut tersum quiddam videbitur aut quod non aeque quadret, celeritati et indigesto labori vique dirae mortis absque Murrhonis infamia candidi lectores tribuere dignentur." En el fol. siguiente (36r) comienza propiamente el comentario sustitutivo de Brant con el siguiente encabezamiento: *Collecta Sebastiani Brant in opus Baptistae Mantuani quod Calamitatum inscribitur post commentarii Sebastiani Murrhonis defectum*. Antes de este encabezamiento, no obstante, ya se insertó el primer fragmento del trabajo de Brant (fol. 32v). Igualmente, quedan unas líneas de Murrho al final del libro 1 (fol. 42v) y en el libro 2 (fols. 48 y 52) compuestas, con toda seguridad, de forma anticipada al orden que iba siguiendo al redactar el comentario.

[15] Vid. n. 14. Presenta 7 líneas en el fol. 48, algo más de una página en el fol. 52. En este último pasaje no está indicado el nombre de Murrho, pero el fragmento presenta todas las trazas de pertenecer a este comentarista. En efecto, se repiten explicaciones que se han leído anteriormente en Badius. El comentario siguiente está encabezado por el nombre de su autor: Brant.

[16] Vergilius (44 veces), Ovidius (16), Servius (12), Horatius (11), Homerus (9), Plinius (6), Strabo (5), Terentius (5), Cicero (4), Iuvenalis (4), Tibullus (4), Augustinus (3), Lucretius (3),

eminente Virgilio, empleado cuarenta y cuatro veces. Es preciso recordar al respecto que la obra es de reducidas dimensiones.[17] Otros autores citados también en gran número son Ovidio (16 veces), Servio (12), Horacio (11), Homero (9), Plinio (6), Estrabón (5), y Terencio (5).

Fuentes citadas por Badius en el comentario al libro 2 *De calamitatibus*

Su número (29)[18] está en consonancia con el promedio habitual que presentan los comentarios del célebre impresor. Es cierto que en algunos pasajes aporta abundancia de fuentes, pero ello no ocurre con regularidad. Normalmente, da gran cantidad de información de carácter didáctico sin aludir a autores,[19] lo que explica la extensión de sus trabajos.

Los autores a los que acude con más frecuencia en el comentario al libro 2 son Virgilio (22 veces), Plinio (11), Vulgata (10), Juvenal (6), Horacio (5), Ovidio (5), Lucano (4), y Servio (4).

Fuentes citadas por Murrho en el comentario al *Contra poetas*

El panorama en este autor es bastante diferente. Ello se pone de manifiesto en el recuento, que arroja un resultado más bajo que en Badius respecto a la misma obra comentada (39 autores).[20] Además, las preferencias son otras. Para confirmar esto último, basta con hacer recuento de los autores más citados: Plinio (12 veces),

---

Nonius Marcellus (3), Persius (3), Plato (3), Valla (3), Aristoteles (2), Catullus (2), Diodorus (2), Ennius (2), Festus Pompeius (2), Hesiodus (2), Livius (2), Macrobius (2), Martialis (2), Propertius (2), Quintilianus (2), Seneca (2), Varro (2), Vulgata (2), Ps. Acron (1), Afranius (1), Gellius (1), Avicenna (1), Cato (1), Donatus (1), Herodotus (1), Josephus (1), Lactantius (1), Lucanus (1), Manlius Theodorus (1), Pacuvius (1), Plautus (1), Sallustius (1), Solinus (1), Statius (1), Suetonius (1), Theocritus (1), Theophrastus (1), y Valerius Maximus (1).

[17] Veinte hojas en tamaño octavo, incluyendo la presentación de la obra, el texto del Mantuano y el comentario de Badius.

[18] Vergilius (22 veces), Plinius (11), Vulgata (10), Iuvenalis (6), Horatius (5), Ovidius (5), Lucanus (4), Servius (4), Diodorus (3), Livius (3), Augustinus (2), Q. Curtius (2), Gellius (2), Iustinus (2), Persius (2), Solinus (2), Sallustius (2), Apuleius (1), Cicero (1), Fabius Pictor (1), Herodotus (1), Hieronymus (1), Petrus Burrus (1), Philostephanus (1), Seneca (1), Statius (1), Strabo (1), Terentius (1), y Tortellius (1).

[19] E.g., continua es su preocupación por mostrar el orden usual de los elementos de la oración, alterados tan frecuentemente por los poetas. La fórmula bajo la que se explica este aspecto particular del lenguaje poético es *ordo est* (que en ocasiones se señala en los escolios impresos de los comentarios). Vid. fols. 42v, 48r, 48v, 49r et passim. Este recurso es utilizado alguna vez por Murrho (en comentarios diferentes al que es objeto de comparación, e.g., en el del libro 1 *De calamitatibus*, fol. 9v). Nunca lo utiliza Brant, al menos en el comentario a los tres libros *De calamitatibus*.

[20] Plinius (12 veces), Strabo (11), Silius Italicus (9), Ovidius (7), Statius (7), Vergilius (7), Festus Pompeius (5), Martialis (5), Diodorus Siculus (4), Iuvenalis (4), Priscianus (3), Solinus (3), Catullus (2), Cicero (2), Gellius (2), Hieronymus (2), Horatius (2), Lactantius (2), Nonius Marcellus (2), Plautus (2), Propertius (2), Vulgata (2), Aristophanes (1), Diogenes Laertius (1), Hesiodus (1), Homerus (1), Hugucione da Pisa (1), Hyginus (1), Iohannes Ianuensis (1), Labeo (1), Macrobius (1), Nigidius (1), Persius (1), Plato (1), Plutarchus (1), Ptolemaeus (1), Scholia ad Apollonium Rhodium (1), Servius (1), y Varro (1).

Estrabón (11), Silio Itálico (9), Ovidio (7), Estacio (7), Virgilio (7), Festo Pompeyo (5), Marcial (5), Diodoro Sículo (4), y Juvenal (4).

Fuentes citadas por Brant en el comentario al libro 2 *De calamitatibus*

Son cincuenta y ocho en total.[21] El autor más citado es Virgilio, que aparece el doble de veces que el segundo en frecuencia, Ovidio. A ellos hay que añadir como fuentes más empleadas la Vulgata (31 veces), Servio (29), Plinio (21), Lucano (18), Estrabón (16), Justino (13), Solino (10), Diodoro (7), Livio (7), y Flavio Josefo (6).

Consideraciones en torno a los comentarios de Badius y Murrho al *Contra poetas impudice loquentes*

La nota más llamativa de Badius es la referencia continua a Virgilio: 44 veces, frente a 7 en Murrho. Ovidio, en cambio, el segundo autor más empleado por Badius, ocupa el cuarto lugar en frecuencia en el comentario de Murrho. Los dos siguientes autores en Badius son Servio (que aparece doce veces; citado sólo una en Murrho) y Horacio (11 veces; en Murrho 2 veces).

Badius aporta el testimonio de veinticuatro autores no empleados por Murrho.[22] Éste, por su parte, presenta quince que no aparecen en el comentario de Badius.[23]

Consideraciones en torno a los comentarios de Badius al *Contra poetas* y al libro 2 *De calamitatibus*

Si comparamos a Badius consigo mismo, esto es, las fuentes que emplea en sus comentarios — al *Contra poetas* y al *De calamitatibus temporum* 2 — llama la atención, sobre todo, la diferencia numérica en el uso de fuentes y testimonios en ambos trabajos. En el comentario al *Contra poetas* se encuentran un total de cincuenta y un autores citados, recogidos en algo más de 14 folios en formato de octavo.[24] Ello

---

[21] La relación completa de fuentes explícitas en el comentario de Brant al libro 2 *De calamitatibus* es la que sigue: Vergilius (64 veces), Ovidius (33), Vulgata (31), Servius (29), Plinius (21), Lucanus (18), Strabo (16), Iustinus (13), Solinus (10), Diodorus (7), Livius (7), Josephus (6), Festus (5), Herodotus (5), Horatius (4), Seneca (4), Cicero (3), Homerus (3), Iuvenalis (5), Lactantius (3), Pomponius (3), Appianus (2), Apuleius (2), Aristoteles (2), Boccaccio (2), Florus (2), Gellius (2), Plato (2), Statius (2), Valerius Maximus (2), Aeneas Silvius Piccolomini (1), Ambrosius (1), Aratus (1), Aristobulus (1), Athanasius (1), Augustinus (1), Baptista Mantuanus (1), Claudianus (1), Cornelius Celsus (1), Eusebius (1), Fabius Pictor (1), Hesiodus (1), Hyginus (1), Johannes de Ianua (1), Martialis (1), Persius (1), Philelphus (1), Philostephanus (1), Plautus (1), Priscianus (1), Prudentius (1), Quintilianus (1), Sallustius (1), Suetonius (1), Tacitus (1), Terentius (1), Thucydides (1), y Tibullus (1).

[22] Afranius, Aristoteles, Gellius, Avicenna, Cato, Donatus, Ennius, Herodotus, Josephus, Livius, Lucanus, Lucretius, Manlius Theodorus, Pacuvius, Quintilianus, Sallustius, Seneca, Suetonius, Terentius, Theocritus, Theophrastus, Tibullus, Valerius Maximus, y Valla.

[23] Aristophanes, Diogenes Laertius, Festus Pompeius, Gellius, Hieronymus, Hugucione da Pisa, Hyginus, Iohannes Ianuensis, Labeo, Nigidius, Plutarchus, Priscianus, Ptolemaeus, Scholia ad Apllonium Rhodium, y Silius Italicus.

[24] El texto poético comentado ocupa unos tres folios. El volumen total del opúsculo, que incluye dedicatoria, *index rerum et verborum*, texto y comentario es de 20 fols. del tamaño referido.

frente a los veintinueve correspondientes al comentario al libro 2 *De calamitatibus temporum*, escrito en 10 folios aproximadamente,[25] tamaño cuaternón, con lo que vienen a resultar casi el doble de extensos.

Sí hay coincidencia en relación a los autores más citados. En ambos comentarios son Virgilio (en *Contra poetas* 44 veces, en el libro analizado *De calamitatibus* 22); Ovidio, que ocupa el segundo lugar en *Contra poetas* (16 veces mencionado), desciende al sexto lugar en el *De calamitatibus*, libro 2. En este comentario es Plinio el Viejo el que ocupa el segundo lugar.

Consideraciones en torno a los comentarios de Badius y Brant al libro 2 *De calamitatibus*

No son de la misma extensión: Badius ocupa algo menos de 13 folios,[26] Brant algo más de 4. El primero recurre a un total de veintinueve autores, el segundo justamente al doble: cincuenta y nueve. Es, en cambio, curiosa la coincidencia de ambos en citar a Virgilio por delante de las demás fuentes. Badius lo emplea 22 veces, Brant 64. Ovidio y la Vulgata se encuentran también entre las primeras fuentes.[27] Del mismo modo, Servio, Lucano, y Plinio se encuentran entre los ocho primeros en ambos comentaristas.

Badius cita sólo cuatro autores[28] que no se encuentran entre los que aporta Brant. Éste, por su parte, hace referencia a treinta y tres que no aparecen en el trabajo de Badius.[29]

Conclusiones

Los datos que se ofrecen están, naturalmente, abiertos a multitud de interpretaciones. Por nuestra parte, hemos creído detectar algunos aspectos que se concretan en los puntos que siguen:

1) A lo largo del comentario, Badius aporta gran cantidad de información en distintos niveles: gramatical, histórico, literario, religioso, etc. La utilización que hace de las fuentes tiene la finalidad de enriquecer la explicación, aportando testimonios que orienten al lector. Al abordar el *Contra poetas* hace cincuenta y un alusiones a autores frente a treinta y nueve que hace Murrho; sin embargo, la extensión del comentario de Badius casi duplica a la de Murrho. La inquietud principal de Badius parece ser la

---

[25] En esta edición, unos 4 fols. contienen el comentario de Brant y algo más de tres el texto del Mantuano.

[26] Por ambas caras, se entiende.

[27] En Brant en segundo y tercero, con 33 y 31 veces respectivamente. En Badius en sexto y tercero, con 5 y 10 referencias respectivamente.

[28] Hieronymus, Petrus Burrus, Q. Curtius, y Tortellius.

[29] Aeneas Silvius Piccolomini, Valerius Maximus, Tibullus, Thucydides, Tacitus, Suetonius, Quintilianus, Prudentius, Priscianus, Pomponius, Plautus, Plato, Philelphus, Martialis, Lactantius, Josephus, Johannes de Ianua, Hyginus, Homerus, Hesiodus, Florus, Festus, Eusebius, Cornelius Celsus, Claudianus, Boccaccio, Baptista Mantuanus, Athanasius, Aristoteles, Aristobulus, Aratus, Appianus, y Ambrosius.

atención al lector, no dar muestras de erudición.[30] Este aspecto, por contra, sí puede achacársele a Brant, que en ocasiones cita autores desmesuradamente.[31]

2) La elección de fuentes para el comentario no está condicionada al tipo de texto que se explica. Al menos no solamente. En ello interviene de forma decisiva el criterio del comentarista, como parece desprenderse del uso diverso de fuentes que hacen Badius y Murrho cuando comentan la misma obra, el *Contra poetas*.

Los autores que preferentemente maneja Badius se repiten en los dos comentarios analizados. Vienen a ser Virgilio, Ovidio, Plinio el Viejo, Horacio, y Servio. Los dos primeros son muy empleados en los comentarios medievales por la interpretación alegórica de sus pasajes. A Cicerón y su obra los nombra en cinco ocasiones en los dos comentarios.[32] Con razón se podría decir que Badius no era propiamente un "ciceroniano". Este dato no parece baladí, sobre todo cuando se considera su situación en la controversia surgida entre Erasmo y Budé a raíz de la publicación en 1528 del *Ciceronianus, sive de optimo genere dicendi dialogus*.

3) La disparidad de las fuentes presentadas por Badius y Murrho apoya la tesis del desconocimiento que cada autor tuvo del comentario del otro al *Contra poetas*, cuestión ésta tratada en otro lugar.[33]

---

[30] Hay que suponer que los receptores de los comentarios de Badius no son tanto estudiantes universitarios como alumnos ya avanzados de lo que se conocía como "escuela latina" o *gymnasium* (vid. Comenius, *Didactica magna*, trad. S. López Peces [Madrid, 1986], 272 ss.), de edades comprendidas entre los 14 y 17 años. Hay en general, pues, menos fuentes citadas en los comentarios y, de ordinario, se refieren con menos detalle de lo que lo hacen Murrho y Brant. Este hecho debe de haber influido de manera notable en la creación del tópico respecto al latín de Badius, tildado de simple, a juzgar por las recriminaciones que se le dirigen una vez abierta la polémica entre Erasmo y Budé (vid. Renouard, *Bibliographie*, 1:26ss.). Germain Brice, amigo de Budé, escribe:

Scio Badium non esse prorsus ἄμουσον, verum qualis qualis est, talem se certe hominibus nostris hactenus probavit ut quoties de doctis sermo inter doctos incidit, de Badio plane οὐδεὶς λόγος.

Toussain, por su parte, le dedica este epigrama:

Desine mirari quare postponat Erasmus
    Budaeum Badio; plus favet ille pari.
        (En Renouard, *Bibliographie*, 1:27)

También los propios comentarios fueron denostados por sabios y eruditos contemporáneos y posteriores, aunque se plagiaron con fines didácticos en multitud de ocasiones (Renouard, *Bibliographie*, 1:140 ss.).

[31] E.g., en el fol. 53r de la edición manejada (París, 1513), se viene a citar una media de un autor por línea.

[32] Frente a las 66 en que remite a Virgilio o las 21 a Ovidio.

[33] M. Madrid Castro, "Badius' and Murrho's Commentaries on Baptista Mantuanus' *Contra poetas impudice loquentes*," in R. Schnur et al., eds., *Acta Conventus Neo-Latini Abulensis*, MRTS 207 (Tempe, AZ, 2000), 397–402.

4) Hay evidencias de que Brant utilizó y completó el comentario de Badius, como se desprende de que Brant repite prácticamente todos los autores que nombra Badius. No en vano, el trabajo de Badius se publicó siete años antes.[34]

UNED Motril

---

[34] Brant manifiesta en su comentario (fol. 48r): *Astra indicant annum Domini MCCCCCVI*. La primera edición del comentario de Badius hay que suponerla en 1499 (cf. Renouard, *Bibliographie*, 1:146). De hecho, en el comentario de Brant al libro 1 *De calamitatibus* aparece como fuente el comentario de Badius a este mismo libro 1 (fol. 40r).

Memory Training in Renaissance Education

JOHN R. C. MARTYN

In modern education, students seem to be almost incapable of memorizing anything, and Classics students now expect to be allowed to take in dictionaries and grammars for exams. By contrast, in Cicero's day there were no dictionaries, no grammars, and almost no encyclopaedias, and the papyrus rolls were extremely hard to read. Their capital letters were unseparated, and there was virtually no punctuation. Finding a particular passage in a roll of text must have been extremely time-consuming. Only a few scholars, and the better educated slaves, were able to read the rolls with any facility. According to Cicero, Simonides, one of the most brilliant of all the early Greeks, invented a system of mnemonics to remedy this problem, late in the sixth century B.C. At that time, the transmission of literature, history, science, and music depended almost entirely on oral skills, linked with well-trained memories. From then on, many similar works appeared on this topic, as generation after generation struggled with the problem of absorbing and remembering an ever-growing body of knowledge. Mind you, today most eight-year-olds can obtain almost all of their knowledge as they surf the net. But what one does with it all, and the CD racks full of encyclopaedias, is the modern problem.

In the fourth century B.C., Diogenes of Sinope was captured by pirates and sold to a Corinthian, Xeniades, as a tutor for his sons. Relying on his memory, the Cynic philosopher taught them many long passages of poetry and history, and aphorisms from his own works, and made them memorize these passages in order to train their own memories. Bear in mind that papyrus rolls containing the works of the Greek authors would have helped a scholar like him. By 167 B.C., the entire library of King Perseus of Macedonia had been brought over to Rome, after the King's capitulation to Aemilius Paullus at the battle of Pydna.

This influx of Greek texts had a dramatic effect on indigenous Roman culture, bringing in a new, Greek system of education and Greek models for philosophy, politics, religion, drama, and literature. Science and medicine were Greek imports also, and remained Greek thereafter. Only law was a Roman preserve. The so-called

"Scipionic Circle" had full access to this library of Paullus and his son, Scipio Aemilianus, a great patron of the arts. His friends included the inventor of Roman satire, Lucilius, the dramatist Terence, the Stoic Panaetius, and the historian Polybius. Other members of the circle, like Mucius Scaevola and Laelius, played a major part in codifying Roman law. This extraordinarily talented group was greatly admired by Cicero, who shared with them a passion for Greek culture.

In fact, one of Cicero's main services to posterity was his adaptation of Greek philosophy to his Latin works, for which he often had to coin new words, at times with the assistance of his publisher, Atticus, who was an expert in the Greek language. We know that Cicero could quote from almost all the Greek and Latin works available in his day, and he was extremely accurate, except for an odd connective or adjective. He quotes, for example, from the thirty books of *Satires* composed by Lucilius, written over a hundred years before, and although only forty verses appear, they cover most of the poems, and are used in eight of his works, including speeches and letters, and are almost word-perfect.[1] Aulus Gellius, in about A.D. 160, quoted from memory a six-line passage from book 8 of Ennius' *Annals,* with just one slip. Cicero knew over one hundred and fifty speeches of old Marcus Cato, delivered two centuries before his day. And Quintilian, the first professor of education in Rome, in about A.D. 100, expected his students to learn speeches and to memorize their own scripts. But he condemned other teachers who caned children when their memories let them down.[2]

Another writer who knew the *Satires* of Lucilius well was Lactantius, the "Christian Cicero", who quoted from memory a six-line passage attacking superstition. (One or two words differ from the version in Nonius.) The passage is quite striking and is still relevant, with the popular love today of horoscopes, and of witchcraft, Potter-style:[3]

> This man trembles at scarecrows and witches, established by our Fauns and Numa Pompiliuses, and he thinks that they are all-important. Just as baby boys believe that all bronze statues are alive and real men, so those fools think that false dreams are true, and believe that a heart beats in bronze statues. They are painters' galleries, nothing real, all fictitious.

Another test of memory was simultaneous dictation. The Elder Pliny tells us that Julius Caesar used to dictate four letters at the same time to four secretaries, and sometimes used as many as seven secretaries simultaneously. This feat reappeared in medieval and Renaissance times, as we shall see. Others from classical times with

---

[1] There are four in *De Oratore,* four in *De Finibus,* one each in the *Tusculan Disputations,* in *Brutus,* and in *De Natura Deorum,* and three in his *Letters to Atticus* (6.6.7, 13.21.3, 16.11.1).

[2] Aulus Gellius, *Noctes Atticae,* 20.10.1. Cicero, *Pro Murena* 14.30, starts with *proeliis promulgatis,* when the sword replaces wisdom and violence takes over rational debate.

[3] In Lactantius's great defense of Christianity, *Divinae Institutiones,* 1.22.13. Born in Africa, Lactantius was professor of rhetoric under Diocletian and became a Christian late in his life.

proverbial memories were Cyrus of Persia, who was believed to know the name of every soldier under him, Cineas, ambassador to Pyrrhus, and Marcus Cato himself, who wrote an encyclopaedia, treatises on medicine, jurisprudence, and military science, plus a major work on agriculture and seven books on Roman history.

All these works were stored in Cicero's memory-bank. In his old age, Cato exercised his mind by running over everything which he had said, heard, or done during the day; to him they were his "intellectual gymnastics," the "race-courses of his mind" — rather like Kim's game today. Any child at school in ancient Greece or Rome had a slate, and very little else. Long hours of rote learning was the only means of acquiring a wide knowledge. And most teachers used a cane to prod the memory, even though Quintilian recommended little cakes and incentives.[4]

In medieval times, little had changed. There were small collections of manuscripts in the scriptoria of monasteries, and a few well-stocked libraries, like the Pope's. But books were still very rare and costly, even when they replaced the papyrus rolls. In the third century A.D., with the growing demand for Bibles in particular, books (codices) began to appear, using folios of vellum, or sheets of papyrus, or thin boards of white acacia. But words were very slow to be separated, and Latin scribes used capitals until the fifth century, and uncials until the eighth. It was only when the lower-case Carolingian script appeared in the late eighth century that words were properly separated and punctuated, and book-production was encouraged by the emperor. This allowed the better-educated priests and lay people to read the holy texts.[5]

With the great shortage of texts, certainly until about A.D. 900, erudite monks had to memorize any works which were available to them personally, or on loan to their monastery. To achieve this, various mnemonic devices were developed, adapted from those of the Greco-Roman experts. Ironically, the increase in printed books led to an equal increase in works on memory training. This fact has been well documented by Mary Carruthers, in her important recent work on *Memory in Medieval Culture*. She rightly argues that no monastery had enough Bibles, or biblical commentaries or important classical texts, for ordinary monks or nuns to have more than a very small collection of their own. And so mnemonic techniques had to be used to help the monks memorize those many religious works which they were expected to know by heart.[6]

A well-known work in the field is the early eleventh-century treatise on memory by Hugh of Saint Victor, designed to train memories specifically to understand and

---

[4] For Cato's words, see Cicero, *De Senectute*, 11.38. For caning children, see Quintilian, *Institutio Oratoria*, 1.3.14–17, and 1.1.36: *maxime necessaria est oratori memoria*. His treatment of memory, based on Cicero's *De Oratore* and the *Rhetorica ad Herennium*, is in 11.2.1–51 (*omnis disciplina memoria constat*).

[5] Gregory the Great donated valuable manuscripts from his library to many newly-founded monasteries and nunneries, and to missionaries like Saint Augustine, as can be seen in his *Registrum Epistolarum*.

[6] Mary Carruthers, *The Book of Memory. A Study of Memory in Medieval Culture* (Cambridge, 1990), to which Elisabeth van Houts, *Memory and Gender in Medieval Europe 900–1200* (Toronto, 1999) is very much indebted.

interpret the Bible, without the aid of the text itself. John of Salisbury recalled with gratitude the daily memorizing exercises said to be given to him and his fellow pupils by their teacher, Bernard of Chartres. But for great feats of creative writing from memory alone, no one could surpass Thomas Aquinas, whose secretaries claimed that he too could dictate to three or four secretaries at once, just like Julius Caesar had done.[7]

The invention of printing certainly made self-education far easier, but one still needed to be wealthy to own a lot of books. A scholar might have half a dozen or so if he or she was lucky or rich. The early presses were extremely labor-intensive, and productions were very pricey. In fact, the first printed editions of Virgil's *Georgics* were almost as ornate in their lettering and illuminations as the finest and most expensive manuscripts. And yet no fewer than ten editions of the *Georgics* appeared in just five years, between 1467 and 1472.[8] This made it clear that there was a very strong thirst for new texts, but only libraries and the rich could afford them.

Despite this increased availability of religious and classical texts during the Renaissance, the vast majority of monks, priests, and scholars still relied on well-endowed monastic libraries, or on those of wealthy patrons, to establish and widen their theological and classical learning. A really retentive memory still remained a vital requirement in the training of any priest or scholar, or for that matter lawyer. When the eminent Scottish humanist George Buchanan was found guilty of deviations on articles of faith by the Inquisition in Lisbon, in July 1551, he was placed under house arrest in the monastery of São Bento. The prior claimed that his little monastery was totally unsuitable for a guest like Buchanan, a scholar and friend of the queen, but the Scot was forced to spend seven uncomfortable months there in isolation, until he was pardoned and left for France. While in his cell, Buchanan prepared his most successful literary work, his Latin paraphrases of the Psalms. In medieval times, all monks were expected to know all the Latin psalms by heart, and the same applied to Buchanan. Even when teaching in Coimbra, he owned only six or so books, among them Oecolampadius's *Excerpts from Greek Literature*, Stifelius's *Arithmetic*, and Cicero's *Defense of Milo*, the last two edited by Melanchthon, which could have proved dangerous. He also owned a few other speeches by Cicero. But he took none of these books with him to his monastic cell. And yet, while he was buried away there, his memory provided the framework and substance for his paraphrases. With some revisions, these were soon to astound the literary and religious circles in Paris with the beauty and elegance of their poetry. Over a hundred editions of these poems have been discovered, and their early publishers were none other than Henri Estienne and Plantin. Some of them were set to music. Through these poems, and friends in the Pléiade, Buchanan was introduced to the vivacious Mary, soon to be Queen of France and

---

[7] The year of John of Salisbury's birth is uncertain, but if 1115 is accepted, Bernard could not have taught him (he died in 1130).

[8] Andreas 1467, 1471; de Spira 1470, 1471; Mentelin 1470; Ahayes 1472; Bartol 1472; Fivizzano 1472; Gering 1472; and Girardanus 1472.

Scotland, and he followed her to the Highlands, to become her personal tutor. But that's another story.⁹

More interesting for mnemonics is an episode in the life of Prince Edward of Portugal, described by his teacher, André de Resende, in 1541. When the prince was still a teenager, he showed great originality and writing ability, and an amazing memory. The eminent Louvain scholar Nicolas Clenardo was attracted by a princely salary to the royal court to tutor young Edward. On his arrival, Clenardo addressed the boy in fluent Latin, and was surprised to be welcomed by him with an equally fluent Latin oration. King John was so impressed that he made Latin compulsory thereafter for all university classes. Later on, the prince was studying dialectics with his other tutor, Resende. They were reading the *principia* to the *Ars Rhetorica* of Johannes Caesarius, printed in Louvain in 1539, and they then turned to Aristotle, for light relief, presumably! His elder brother and a future king, Prince Henry, visited the two of them one day during their siesta, and Resende suggested that Edward should show his elder brother how well he was progressing. The young Prince closed his book, and gave his brother a resumé in Latin of Porphyry's *De Praedicabilibus,* Aristotle's *Categories,* and Plato's *Parmenides.* He did so with such fluency that Henry was astounded. Resende was also studying Cicero's *De Officiis* with the young prince, and they had just read chapter 7, *De Iustitia.* Edward recited this chapter from memory, word for word, and then recited all the critical notes. He then started at the last word of the chapter, and recited the text backwards, right to the very first word, without a pause. According to Resende, he often did this with other texts which they had been studying. Incidentally, Augustine admired his fellow-student, Simplicianus, who knew the works of Cicero and Virgil off by heart, and could use them most appositely, and could also recite books of Virgil's poems both forwards and backwards with great accuracy. Clenardo and Resende proved to be outstanding teachers, and Edward was their most brilliant student.¹⁰

Resende also saw the grown-up prince dictating to four secretaries simultaneously, just like Caesar and Aquinas. According to his tutor, Edward dictated one clause to one secretary, the next to another and so on, and then jumped back to the first, without a pause, and with every word in the right place. He maintained perfect continuity, as if dictating just one letter, without stopping. As well as his amazing memory and fluency in Latin, Edward showed a passionate devotion to God, wearing a rough hair shirt under his blouse and worshipping regularly in his private chapel. His elder brother, Alphonso, died early in the year, and Edward was very likely to

---

⁹ For a reliable biography of this great man, see I. D. McFarlane, *Buchanan* (1981). See also Philip J. Ford, *George Buchanan: Prince of Poets* (Aberdeen, 1982). For his psalms, besides the editions, there were many selections and translations, mostly into English. See McFarlane, *Buchanan,* 247, 263. They were published by Estienne and Plantin in 1556.

¹⁰ For the remarkable life and death of Prince Edward, see my edition and translation of the *Biographies of Prince Edward and Friar Pedro by André de Resende* (New York, 1997). Cyrus, Cineas, and Marcus Cato, mentioned above, were all picked out by Resende in his biography of Prince Edward. For a nearly contemporary expert on mnemonics, with an equally prodigious memory, see René Hoven, *Specimen artis memoriae . . . de Lambert-Thomas Schenckels* (1978): 121–126.

succeed John on the throne of Portugal, but he did not last long, dying of consumption, like Alphonso, just six months later, in October 1540, when barely twenty-five years old.

Memory training played a major part in the preservation of oral traditions, whether they were sagas built into the *Iliad* and *Odyssey* of Homer, tales of monks and ordinary families, women especially, vital for the social history of medieval and Renaissance times, or explanations of the world around them, sung by Aboriginal elders. The great oral poets and story-tellers could adapt and enrich a narrative with countless phrases and tales plucked from their memories. For the Aboriginals, these sagas were the basis of a boy's initiation, illustrated on trees or on the shifting sand, but kept alive in his memory. Few of them still survive, condemned as works of anti-Christ by the early English missionaries. Some have now been preserved on tape, as have just four or five of the six hundred or so Aboriginal languages once spoken throughout the country. In fact, when the whites first arrived, Aboriginal tribes living on one side of Sydney Harbor could not understand those on the other, like the belligerent tribes on opposite sides of the English Channel. Family stories are most important for medieval and Renaissance history, but they are even more important for the preservation of more ancient cultures, like that of the Aboriginals. The loss of most family histories, which explained their own myths as part of the world's creation, was one of the cruellest results of the 'stolen generation'. But that's another story also.[11]

University of Melbourne

---

[11] For living epics, see D. C. Rubin, *Memory in Oral Traditions* (Oxford, 1995).

Laughter and Humanism:
Unity and Diversity in
Thomas More's Epigrammata

ELIZABETH N. McCUTCHEON

Thomas More's *Epigrammata* is a particularly telling instance of the "Unity and Diversity" theme in the *Res publica litterarum* of Northern Renaissance humanism. The collection was twice printed in 1518, together with the third edition of the *Utopia* and a collection of epigrams by Erasmus, and printed in a separate volume two years later, in each instance by the press of Johann Froben.[1] The *Epigrammata* is otherwise a disparate and difficult work to describe. In some sense, indeed, it is a miscellany that delights and instructs (as the humanists would put it) because it is so varied. Fewer than a quarter of the poems included in the collection (two hundred and sixty in the 1518 editions, two hundred and sixty-nine in 1520, which omits two epigrams from 1518 and adds eleven new poems) are datable.[2] But they seem to have been written over a twenty-year or so period on all sorts of occasions — occasions that their titles often emphasize.[3] More's sources are also varied. He was the first to translate and publish many of the epigrams from the Planudean Anthology in Western Europe, and over one hundred poems are translations of or variations upon epigrams from the Greek text.[4] But he also adapts traditional jests and Aesopic fables, reworks material from any number of classical writers (including Plutarch, Seneca, Cicero, Diogenes Laertius, Plato, Aristotle, Lucian, Plautus, and Martial), weaves in biblical

---

[1] Thomas More, *Latin Poems*, vol. 3, pt. 2 of the *Complete Works of St. Thomas More*, ed. Clarence H. Miller, Leicester Bradner, Charles A. Lynch, and Revilo P. Oliver (New Haven, 1984), 3–9. All citations of More's Latin poems and English translations are from this edition.

[2] I am using the count supplied by More, *Latin Poems*, 9, 11. An additional ten poems are included at the end of this edition.

[3] More, *Latin Poems*, 10–11.

[4] More, *Latin Poems*, 61, 12. See also Alan Cameron, *The Greek Anthology from Meleager to Planudes* (Oxford, 1993), 182–185.

texts, and translates two near contemporaneous English love lyrics.⁵ Even so, this summary over-emphasizes what More borrowed and blurs the freshness and originality of the collection as a whole. More was a pioneer; the epigram did not become a popular form in Britain until after 1540.⁶

Formally and rhetorically, too, there is variety — the collection includes an ode, lyrics, and verse epistles, for instance, in addition to epigrams, and More delights in writing variations upon a theme or motif — as in his seven epigrams upon two beggars, one blind and one lame, who are each other's support. And there is a wide range of addressees, including King Henry VIII, potential patrons, humanist friends, More's children, the anonymous "Candidus," the French poet Brixius, a fat priest, a woman More loved long ago, unidentified readers (almost invariably male, learned, and sophisticated), and, in some instances, himself, along with dramatic dialogues and monologues. The topics are equally diverse — from foolish astrologers and cuckolds and a way to eliminate bad breath after eating leeks (by eating onions, and so on) to reflections upon kingship, government, and death. In mood, too, the epigrams and other poems vary. There are jokes, slapstick comedy, scatology, satiric jabs, expressions of friendship, encomia, ironic reflections, aphorisms, and epitaphs; a cluster or run of epigrams on a similar topic will be interrupted; and jests and gnomic treatments of mortality can follow one another in rapid succession. The epigrams are not nailed in place, either — indeed, historically, they proved easily detachable, and have made many subsequent appearances, which literary historians are still discovering.⁷

What, if anything, holds a miscellany like this together? One answer is what David Carlson calls the self-promotion or "magnification" of Thomas More.⁸ So he maintains that once "Each of these poems was ... deracinated from its original context of personal circulation and immediate occasion, and was reinscribed in the *Epigrammata* within an impersonal, strictly public monument to the poems' author," "the collection's ultimate subject matter is More and his mental and verbal dexterity."⁹ This is not a new claim: in 1959 H. A. Mason pointed out that the humanists "constituted a *vast mutual-admiration society*," and that "one of their principal activities was self-

---

⁵ J. B. Trapp, *Erasmus, Colet and More: The Early Tudor Humanists and Their Books* (London, 1991), 42, finds More's use of these two English songs startling.

⁶ Standard treatments of the Renaissance epigram include J. W. Binns, "Latin Translations from Greek in the English Renaissance," *Humanistica Lovaniensia* 27 (1978): 128–159; idem, *Intellectual Culture in Elizabethan and Jacobean England: The Latin Writings of the Age* (Leeds, 1990), chaps. 2–6; and Lawrence Ryan, "The Shorter Latin Poem in Tudor England," *Humanistica Lovaniensia* 26 (1977): 101–131. See too Ann Baynes Coiro, *Robert Herrick's "Hesperides" and the Epigram Book Tradition* (Baltimore, 1988), 45–77, which situates More's epigrams between classical models and later English epigrammatists.

⁷ In this connection see "Appendix D" by Charles Clay Doyle in More, *Latin Poems*, 695–744, and the many notes on sources and analogues that have appeared in *Moreana* and other journals.

⁸ David R. Carlson, *English Humanist Books: Writers and Patrons, Manuscript and Print, 1475–1525* (Toronto, 1993), 162.

⁹ David R. Carlson, "Reputation and Duplicity: The Texts and Contexts of Thomas More's Epigram on Bernard André," *English Literary History* 58 (1991): 261–281, here 265.

praise."[10] But Carlson's case is closely, if selectively, argued. Another critic has given a very different answer. Emphasizing the humanists' roles as advisors and teachers, Mary Thomas Crane argues that More and other humanist epigrammatists set out to "create a serious version of the epigram as a vehicle for humanist political and social aims."[11] What interests her, then, are the aphoristic and admonitory elements of a collection designed for authoritative moral instruction — primarily for More's superiors and inferiors.

The self-praise is undeniably there, and the epigrams were, in part, intended to instruct, although rarely as didactically as Crane posits. But either position overstates aspects of a much more nuanced and complex collection and seems to ignore the part that laughter or humor plays in a collection that is neither monumental, *pace* Carlson, nor the sober educational experience Crane describes. I see the *Epigrammata* rather as an open-ended, polyphonic collection that is often simultaneously serious and comic. What Carlson calls duplicity, then, is more often ambiguity, ambivalence, or equivocation — strategies that destabilize the epigrams, complicate attempts to derive a simple moral, and protect the author, while providing innumerable opportunities for joco-serious play and political and social commentary. In any case, their cleverness does not just demonstrate More's mental and verbal dexterity, but functions rather as a principle of coherence that serves many, albeit complex, social, political, and psychological purposes — the more so because the wit and humor that characterize so many of these epigrams are, to some extent, culturally determined: that is, they are expressions of the code by which More and his fellow humanists operated in pre-Reformation Europe.

Like other forms in this collection, the epigram is, itself, an inherently social form, one that almost invariably requires an addressee or audience, and More often emphasizes the addressee by using a direct address or a vocative.[12] Moreover, this collection was itself a cooperative venture: More, Erasmus, Beatus Rhenanus, and Froben were all participants in the production of a collection meant to appeal to and in some sense create an international community of humanists that could be defined, in part, by attitudes and values that evolved from and were sustained by their common participation in a reading experience that proved particularly appealing and effective, thanks to More's inimitable wit and humor. Unlike many of the forgettable collections of epigrams in the fifteenth century, then, or Erasmus's more sober, often devotional collection, More's are the product of someone who has rethought the na-

---

[10] Harold Andrew Mason, *Humanism and Poetry in the Early Tudor Period: An Essay* (London, 1959), 28.

[11] Mary Thomas Crane, *Framing Authority: Sayings, Self, and Society in Sixteenth-Century England* (Princeton, 1993), 146. Compare and contrast Coiro, *Robert Herrick's "Hesperides,"* which emphasizes the political aspects of More's epigrams by way of a far more nuanced reading.

[12] In *The Latin Epigrams of Thomas More*, ed. and trans. Leicester Bradner and Charles Arthur Lynch (Chicago, 1953), xxiv–xxv, Bradner and Lynch note that this is More's "most frequent deviation from his Greek originals": xxiv.

ture of the epigram and achieved something far more entertaining, aculeate, and memorable.[13]

Beatus Rhenanus makes comparable points in his prefatory letter to Willibald Pirckheimer, to whom the collection of More's epigrams was dedicated. He begins by introducing the two men, speaking about friendship, and stressing the many things that they shared as lawyers and writers who are learned, adept in Greek as well as Latin, heavily involved in public duties, honored by their respective sovereigns, well-to-do, generous, and able to appreciate the peculiar blend of wit, brevity, pleasure, learning, and point that constitutes a learned epigram.[14] These same attributes could characterize other readers of the epigrams as well, and indirectly define the nature of much of More's initial reading public, a humanist coterie. They also illustrate just how multiple and complex the allegiances of men like More and Pirckheimer were as they moved from law office to court and study.

Rhenanus gives even more attention to the epigrams themselves, emphasizing their humor and claiming that it would "be proper to say of More 'He is every inch pure jest,'"[15] a claim that is echoed by the decorated title page for the December 1518 edition of the epigrams, which includes figures of a fool and a satyr on pillars in the borders.[16] Interestingly, Rhenanus's remark is deleted in the 1520 edition, which also returns to the more serious title page that appeared in the first edition of the epigrams.[17] Both More's situation and Western Europe's had changed significantly between 1518 and 1520. In addition, Rhenanus's claim runs the risk of trivializing More's humor and the purposes it serves. It does a disservice, in other words, to More's blend of the jocular and the serious, and misrepresents the dynamic and delicate balance of a collection that is so frequently joco-serious. I prefer Erasmus's earlier description of More as one who played the role of Democritus, the laughing philosopher.[18]

Rhenanus is hyperbolic, in any case; while laughter takes many different forms in these epigrams — from coarse and homely jokes and satiric barbs to black comedy, urbane wit, various sorts of irony, and the gentlest of smiles — not every poem is humorous. But laughter, which a psychologist has recently called "a universal human signal,"[19] was recognized as a fundamental property of humankind by the humanists.[20] And it can be especially helpful in establishing a close relationship between an

---

[13] See, for instance, Ryan, "The Shorter Latin Poem," and Clarence H. Miller on "The Epigrams of More and Erasmus" in More, *Latin Poems,* 38–56.

[14] More, *Latin Poems,* 73–75.

[15] More, *Latin Poems,* 320 (note for Rhen. Pref. § 51).

[16] This title page is reproduced in *St. Thomas More: A Preliminary Bibliography of His Works and of Moreana to the Year 1750,* comp. R. W. Gibson (New Haven, 1961), 11.

[17] *St. Thomas More: A Preliminary Bibliography,* 8, 77.

[18] See Desiderius Erasmus, *The Praise of Folly,* trans. Clarence H. Miller (New Haven, 1979), 2.

[19] Robert R. Provine, "The Laughing Species," *Natural History* 109 (2000–2001): 72.

[20] M. A. Screech, *Laughter at the Foot of the Cross* (London, 1997), 1.

author and his or her readers.²¹ The group that laughs together stays together, as it were. More specifically, laughter can establish a bond of friendship — to appropriate Beatus Rhenanus's word — that is flexible enough to include both personal friendship and people allied in a common cause. This was crucial for the humanists. A trans-national European intellectual community, they rarely met in person, but — thanks to the printing press — they were able to create and sustain a group of like-minded scholars and administrators for whom solidarity was imperative as they engaged in battle (real or imagined) with those they thought of as barbarians, and sought to promote their own principles even as they struggled to balance loyalties (to God, king, profession, family, and self) that were not necessarily congruent. This means that laughter has programmatic, social, and psychological relevance, connecting More with the larger humanist community and vice versa, and reinforcing shared perceptions at the same time that (for better and worse) it excludes those with a different mind-set and opponents like Brixius, with whom More carried on a war of words. With this in mind, I should like to turn to More's collected epigrams and consider some instances of the kinds of laughter that were generated and the many different needs it met.

I shall start by mentioning a few of the epigrams that seem to be included largely to entertain, and thus serve a purpose similar to the kind of banter and table-talk that might occur at a dinner or in a garden or other setting where friends meet. Among these are four (116, 167, 235, and 245) that the Yale edition calls "sexually indelicate" and that the Louvain edition of 1565–1566, which was based on the 1518 edition, deleted, having a more pious audience and a different agenda in mind.²² The two that deal with rape unfortunately rely upon sexist notions, although one of them also exposes the chicanery of the lawyer, who can defend the rapist only by humiliating the young woman. But both passed muster with More and his friends, indicative of a kind of sixteenth-century bonding at work, which let a clearly male audience affirm their membership in a new (and elite) Republic of Letters.

In other instances, however, More's jokes and entertainments have a different and deeper resonance, and the humor is conjoined with something more serious. Consider "On a Fool" (106), a traditional joke that More translated from the Planudean Anthology. It is an example of a popular form (the "noodle") that reappears in a later humanist work, Robert Burton's *Anatomy of Melancholy,* although not attributed there to More.²³ The Yale translation renders More's version this way: "When the fleas bite Morio, he puts out his light and says, 'These fleas will not see me now,'" nicely preserving some part of More's word play, which connects the fleas that "mordent" with his own name.²⁴ But if More's version is self-promoting, it is also self-depre-

---

[21] See Audrey Bilger, *Subversive Comedy in Frances Burney, Maria Edgeworth, and Jane Austen* (Detroit, 1998), for an acute analysis of this function in a later group setting.

[22] More, *Latin Poems,* 9.

[23] Doyle, "Appendix D," in More, *Latin Poems,* 697–744; Elizabeth McCutcheon, "Robert Burton/Democritus Junior and Thomas More," *Moreana* 35, no. 135–136 (1998): 55–74, here 60.

[24] More, *Latin Poems,* 161, and the commentary to 106.3, 362.

catory and thus even more universalizing than Burton's more abstract, less dramatic version of "that stupid fellow [who] put out the Candle, because the biting fleas should not finde him."[25] Both versions, though, reflect major humanist preoccupations with folly and the nature of perception and self-deception that Democritus Junior's Preface to Burton's *Anatomy*, Erasmus's *Moria*, and More share.

Here, as elsewhere, More relies upon his mastery of narrative and dialogue. In this connection, consider another popular epigram (133), about the guest at a banquet who removed some flies from the wine-bowl before he drank and put them back afterwards, explaining, "I do not like flies; but then, I do not know — some of you may like them."[26] A joke, yes, which surprises by the incongruity between speech and act, but one that also plays ambiguously with questions of taste, decorum, and the nature of court life. For who, or what, is the butt of the joke: the speaker (seen as someone who is trying his best to be polite), or the situation, which the speaker is quasi-politely mocking? Where do we position ourselves when we laugh, in other words?

A number of More's epigrams, in particular those about kingship, are potentially even more subversive and often ambiguous, on account of More's choice of classical examples and his double-edged comments; as a result, the humor and the irony cut very deeply. More's version of the story about the peasant who sees the king (201) is a case in point. It seems that a rustic and very naïve peasant came to town, and watched as a huge crowd of people lined the street and shouted "The king is coming." But the poor peasant cannot see the king, even though one of the bystanders points to a man "resplendent with gold" on a tall horse. "I think you are making fun of me," he says; "To me he looks like a man in fancy dress."[27] According to a jest-book version of this joke, printed circa 1532, the joke is on the peasant, for not being "well nourished up and virtuously endoctrined."[28] So interpreted, the epigram reinforces the status quo. Yet a subversive reading that deflates the royal presence by insinuating that the king, too, is a man, however costumed, and/or that laughs at the populace for being taken in by the king's appearance, seems more likely, given attitudes expressed elsewhere in this collection.

Consider, for instance, the Aesop-like fable (180) about the smooth-tongued lion who offers to heal a sick fox by licking him, ingeniously explaining that: "You just do not know the power of my tongue." The fox politely demurs: " 'Your tongue,' said the fox, 'has healing powers; but the trouble is that such a good tongue has bad neighbors.' "[29] This is only one of at least three epigrams (compare 162 and 181) that involve lions. Traditionally considered the king of beasts, the lion had heraldic associations with the Tudor monarchy, and More made the link between King Henry

---

[25] Robert Burton, *The Anatomy of Melancholy*, ed. Thomas C. Faulkner, Nicolas K. Kiessling, and Rhonda L. Blair, 3 vols. (Oxford, 1989–1994), 1:56.

[26] More, *Latin Poems*, 175.

[27] More, *Latin Poems*, 233.

[28] Commentary in More, *Latin Poems*, 392. Compare David Rundle, "A New Golden Age? More, Skelton and the Accession Verses of 1509," *Journal of the Society for Renaissance Studies* 9 (1995): 58–76, here 58.

[29] More, *Latin Poems*, 215.

VIII and the lion explicit in a comment to Cromwell.[30] I think that all three are about the dangers of royal power, a point that becomes almost overt in 162, which addresses a courtier who boasts about the fun he has with the king, whom the epigrammatist compares to a "tamed" lion.[31] And More is even more aculeate in a very short epigram (115) that stings by exploiting a seemingly naïve pattern of question and answer. "What is a good king? He is a watchdog, guardian of the flock, who by barking keeps the wolves from the sheep. What is the bad king? He is the wolf."[32] Here More's analogy becomes a powerful indictment of tyranny — one of several political themes that he makes peculiarly his[33] — while the compression and the biblical echoes encourage a kind of black-comic humor (think of *Babe in the City* or a political cartoon) that makes the transformation from watch-dog to wolf particularly horrifying.

More wrote many other satires, like the epigram on the Frenchified courtier, Lalus (95), which both Rhenanus and a later humanist, Julius Caesar Scaliger, singled out for special praise.[34] Here More seems to have touched a particularly responsive chord, and the epigram anticipates similar satiric thrusts by Shakespeare, John Donne, and Ben Jonson. Relying on description and the much repeated jingle of Lallus, Gallicus, and Gallus, the speaker mocks a "friend" and fellow Englishman who affects everything French — even mistreating his servant, a Frenchman, as the French do — but can only speak French with an English accent. Once again More's epigram deflates, puncturing the affectation and pride that he elsewhere locates in characters like the fat priest; the astrologer who studies the stars but is blind to what is happening in his own house; and the greedy miser. From one point of view, these could be thought of as sophisticated versions of the man in a top hat who slips on a banana peel. In these instances, though, the humor, which is verbal, rather than dependent upon an actual fall, seems to extend beyond the individual case to adumbrate the absurdities or abuses of social systems that are typified by the feminized courtier, the cuckolded astrologer, or the ignorant or lazy priest.

A very different kind of laughter or wit is at least as important in More's collection — the wry smile of the ironist who claims, for example, that death and/or sleep is a leveler, so that the king is no better off than the beggar, Irus, and, in fact, may be worse off (40, 45, 46, 80, 107, 108, 110), although these epigrams (at least some of them) could be read in a rather different way — as evidence of frustration, if not

---

[30] I am grateful to Rhoda Schnur for reminding me of English heraldry. For More's remark, see William Roper, *The Life of Sir Thomas More*, in *Two Early Tudor Lives*, ed. Richard S. Sylvester and Davis P. Harding (New Haven, 1962), 228.

[31] More, *Latin Poems*, 205.

[32] More, *Latin Poems*, 165.

[33] Besides the introduction in Bradner and Lynch's edition and in *Latin Poems*, see Coiro, *Robert Herrick's "Hesperides,"* and Damian Grace, "Thomas More's *Epigrammata*: Political Theory in Poetic Idiom," *Parergon: Bulletin of the Australian and New Zealand Association for Medieval and Renaissance Studies* n.s. 3 (1985): 115–129.

[34] See the commentary in More, *Latin Poems*, 358, for 95.1–53.

rage, on the speaker's part. So they may function as a strategy for psychological survival or peace of mind in a world where, all too frequently, power rules. Consider, for instance, 80, "Death Unassisted Kills Tyrants" [Sola Mors Tyrannicida Est], which urges those "who have been cruelly persecuted at the hands of unjust men" to "take hope." Insisting that the tyrant too will be cast down from his high place, it concludes, grimly, that "The tables are turned: the man once so fearsome deserves only a laugh" [uicissim / Iam ridendus erit, qui metuendus erat].[35]

Related to these verses are those that ponder our attempts to control life or predict the future — attempts that are often evidence of misplaced pride, metaphoric blindness, or an exaggerated sense of self. A particularly well-known epigram, "What Is the Best Form of Government" (198), begins as if it were a dialogue about the advantages or disadvantages of a republic or a monarchy. The speaker makes a strong case for the former. But suddenly he interrupts himself: "Is there anywhere a people upon whom you yourself, by your own decision, can impose either a king or a senate?"[36] And this is just the first of several questions that transform what began as if it were a little treatise upon good government into something far more complex, unstable, and startling that alludes to More's *Utopia* by way of a pun ("Est ne usquam populus") at the same time that it deflates the speaker's pretensions and turns from theory to the ambiguities of political life.[37]

Similar epigrams hint of a world that resists our attempts to control it or of mysterious gaps between our intentions and the actual results. "On a Cat and a Mouse" (262), an epigram added to the collection in 1520, is a disarmingly "simple," and equivocal, instance, which plays with a favorite Morean metaphor, the trap, as it inverts and complicates an old proverb. Normally a cat first plays with a mouse and then eats it. In this case, though, the cat outwits itself, and the little mouse escapes the cat's outstretched paw and reaches a safe hiding place. But More further complicates this story; the speaker (a narrative "I") took the mouse from a trap to begin with and gave it to the cat. He concludes with a reverberating irony: the mouse would have "died in the trap if what ordinarily destroys it had not protected and saved it — a cat."[38] But this begs the question of the narrator's complicity and frustrated intentions. Embodied in even an apparently slight epigram, then, is a stance that generates some part of the wit and laughter that hover over or behind the collection. As Erasmus noted when he dedicated his *Moria* to More and compared him to Democritus, More is unusually sensitive and responsive to the multiple absurdities and ironies that characterize so much of life as we experience it, whether we be a mouse, a cat, a More, or whoever. For the story seems to have even deeper implications: it could well be a comment about both the equivocal nature of political life and the dangers of being too clever.

---

[35] More, *Latin Poems*, 145, 144.

[36] More, *Latin Poems*, 231.

[37] More, *Latin Poems*, 230. See the brilliant commentary by Clarence H. Miller, in *Latin Poems*, 50.

[38] More, *Latin Poems*, 275; compare commentary, 412.

More ended his 1518 collection with an unusually personal poem that celebrates his own marriage (or marriages), although it is not usually thought of as a marriage poem, since it is the epitaph he wrote for his first wife's tomb, which was supposed to be his second wife's and his own, as well. It is uniquely Morean and almost metaphysical in its comic wit, which disturbs readers who expect a more conventional epitaph. In fact, the Louvain edition of 1565–1566 deleted it — perhaps because it was seen as "sexually indelicate" (as the Yale edition posits) or because of its strange theology.[39] On the other hand, I read it as a love poem celebrating both the intimate and fruitful relationship that More and his first wife experienced — which made More the father of one son and three daughters — and the different, but no less happy relationship with his second wife and his four children. Indeed, More represents himself as unable to decide which wife was (or is) the "charior," the more beloved. "O, how happily we could have lived all three together," he concludes, "if fate and religion permitted. But the grave will unite us, and I pray that heaven will unite us too. Thus death will give what life could not" [At societ tumulus, societ nos obsecro coelum. / Sic mors, non potuit quod dare uita, dabit.][40] So More celebrates marriage, a bond that death normally severs, by imagining a *ménage à trois* that will endure beyond death, both here on earth and, he prays, in heaven.

Simultaneously personal and social, the epitaph touches several of the collection's most pervasive concerns — with life, with death, with human relationships and behavior — even noting how most stepmothers are very unlike More's second wife, Alice, who cared for his first wife's children so well. But tellingly, it also transforms them; for once, death is neither the terminus nor the leveler, but an unwitting agent for what More hopes will be an even more loving life together in heaven. Obviously this epigram is, and remains, occasional: it was written for the family tomb. But it is also an open-ended and witty ending for an otherwise disparate collection that daringly transforms a powerfully charged symbol — the marriage tie — to imagine life in heaven, a life that, in characteristically Morean terms, will be a societal one, where laughter will surely abound.[41]

University of Hawaii, Emerita

---

[39] More, *Latin Poems*, 9.

[40] More, *Latin Poems*, 271–273; 272.

[41] M. A. Screech's *Laughter at the Foot of the Cross* provides a useful context for this sort of laughter by way of its treatment of laughter in two other Renaissance humanists, Erasmus and Rabelais.

The Politics of Poetry:
A Quick Look at Robert Walpole, and
Two Thousand Other Cambridge Latin Poets

DAVID MONEY

This paper considers a few aspects of university commemorative poetry. The genre is quite widely known, but has rarely received very thorough attention from a literary, as opposed to a bibliographical, perspective.[1] Having written rather more about Oxford verses in the past, I here concentrate on Cambridge writers.[2] The two universities in fact follow a similar pattern, from the origins of the genre in the later sixteenth century until its demise, for whatever reason,[3] after 1763. The other universities in the British Isles participate only sporadically, and while continental institutions produced a vast mass of Neo-Latin, I am not aware of any comparable continuous tradition of commemorative anthologies, appearing in a regular format over a period of two centuries.[4] The numbers involved are considerable, representing a large proportion of active Neo-Latin writers; there were certainly more than the round figure of two thousand. Yet they are more than statistics: each single con-

---

[1] D. K. Money, *The English Horace: Anthony Alsop and the Tradition of British Latin Verse* (Oxford and London, 1998), esp. chap. 9; also, most recently, idem, "Free Flattery or Servile Tribute?" in J. Raven, ed., *Free Print and Non-Commercial Publishing since 1700* (Aldershot, 2000), 48–66. Both list further bibliography on the topic.

[2] Cf. D. K. Money, "'A Diffrent-sounding Lyre': Oxford Commemorative Verse in English," *Bodleian Library Record* 16 (1997): 42–92; for Cambridge volumes, see Money, *English Horace*, and especially H. Forster, "The Rise and Fall of the Cambridge Muses (1603–1763)," *Transactions of the Cambridge Bibliographical Society* 8 (1982): 141–172.

[3] A number of reasons may be suggested: e.g., gradual decline in the primacy of Latin, especially for original composition; a paucity of things worth celebrating, after 1763; changing political and academic fashions.

[4] I would be very interested to be proved wrong on this point, or to learn more of comparable traditions elsewhere; individual occasions throughout Europe, whether private or academic, regularly led to small collections. Oxford and Cambridge attempted something bigger.

tribution, however small or unoriginal, is evidence of another person's participation in Neo-Latin culture. We may illustrate this point by starting at the beginning of an alphabetical list.

Jonathan Acklom, of Clare Hall, wrote an accomplished Horatian ode, in fourteen alcaic stanzas, commencing "Veris sodales aequora temperant ...", to celebrate George II's successful return from the War of the Austrian Succession (1748), in which he was, as it turned out, the last British monarch to lead his troops into action. Acklom became a lawyer, was appointed Sheriff of Nottinghamshire in 1754, and died in 1806. The next poet, William Acton, made a smaller contribution, eight lines of elegiacs, to the volume on the death of William III and accession of Queen Anne (1702); he too attended Clare Hall, having been admitted a fellow-commoner in January 1700/1, a year before his short poem; he too was a person of some significance in public life, elected Member of Parliament for Orford, a town on the Suffolk coast, in 1722 and 1729, and High Sheriff of Suffolk in 1739. (Orford, as we will see, is itself a politically significant location.) The third in our alphabetical list is Thomas Adam of Trinity, who wrote forty lines of elegiacs for the first major verse collection, the manuscript presented to Queen Elizabeth I on her visit in 1564. Edward Adams subsequently offered sixty-two hexameters on the Peace of Utrecht (1713) as a newly graduated B.A. and fellow of King's; he died, insane, in college forty-two years later.

So too, no doubt, *lector benevole*, would you, if we continued with the full two thousand,[5] though even the dullest is a whole minute of our attention; and many are not dull at all. The four poets of the previous paragraph share one common feature: they only once ventured into print. Others were more adventurous. Two places further down, we meet John Adams (father of Edward); he wrote in 1683, as a young man (in exactly his son's later position), and then again alongside his son, though with a shorter piece, in 1713, by which time he was Provost of King's and Doctor of Divinity; as a Canon of Windsor, royal chaplain to William III and to Anne, and friend of Swift, he was another figure of substance among his contemporaries. His two poems come at times of personal significance: as a new graduate, and newly appointed head of his college. In each case, they may be gestures aimed at gaining attention and support in an unstable world, whether of academic life or public politics.

The purpose of these poems, like the authors' biographies, will undoubtedly have varied. Some probably stemmed from the pure pleasure of versifying, or genuine emotion at the event being celebrated. For most, however, I suspect that fame, or rather modest recognition of one's talents and future employability, was the spur. In this respect Neo-Latin verse is a useful accomplishment, cultivated for a practical purpose by practical men as well as learned amateurs. University verse is overwhelmingly a Neo-Latin genre, with English as a minority language (and a small place for Greek, Hebrew, and occasionally more learned, unreadable, tongues): the vernacular could

---

[5] Biographical details from J. and J. A. Venn, *Alumni Cantabrigienses* (Cambridge, 1922); listing from D. K. Money, *Database of British Latin Poets*: work in slow progress (with very much still to be done, though I have assembled a basic listing of Cambridge, and some Oxford, writers; a *Biographical Register* should appear, in print or electronic form, in due course).

usually be chosen, but was rejected by the majority of writers. We cannot, in general, assess the effectiveness of this form of collective literary self-advertisement; but its regular, frequent, and formal continuation suggests that it was felt to be of value, both by the university authorities and by the students (of all social classes) and college fellows who composed the poems.

What criteria are appropriate for studying the genre? We may consider the historical significance of individual authors, of particular collections, or of the genre as a whole. Or we may look for literary merit. Yet a poem that fails in aesthetic terms may have been a political success, helping to cement its author's career. Much Neo-Latin occasional poetry — in much the same way as similar vernacular writing — is open to the criticism of having little to say, and saying it in dull and conventional ways (sometimes with pointless reworking of classical forms, for a limited readership). Two thousand Cambridge poets would disagree. A sympathetic reassessment may well be appropriate, bearing in mind the poets' original aims, and the severe limitations of time and subject-matter within which they were forced to operate. Such a task was not easy, even for young men with rigorous training in composition on set themes; in the circumstances, it is their variety and elegance, rather than their formulaic qualities, that are surprising.

The topics of commemorative verse may seem unexciting to a modern critic. A public, united voice predominates over private emotion. Why should we read work that the authors themselves may not have cared much about? Their subjects, however, probably did matter rather more than we may think, especially in the seventeenth century. A royal marriage could spell life or death for a kingdom (as, for example, in the triumphant — but soon tragic — union of 1613 between James I's daughter Elizabeth and the Elector Palatine); princely births and deaths could blight or raise the political hopes of thousands; a new monarch's public policy would affect the religion of the nation, and thus the personal careers of virtually every academic poet, whether in the church or secular politics, both at a local level or, for the more ambitious, in a wider sphere. External war and peace, even the risk of civil war, hung on the events publicly commemorated by university Neo-Latin writers.

Minor or occasional writers provide both a readership and a context for major ones, whatever criteria we may use to confer privilege on a chosen canon. Without those surrounding lesser figures we have a distorted view of the centre. Few, if any, university poets show the quality, originality, and reasonably prolific production of "major" authors. Collectively, however, the university verses outweigh any "major" author for sheer quantity, and contain enough moments of skill to stand alongside the more modest productions of their famous colleagues, if not their greater works. While it is the firmly "minor" poet, contributing just once or twice, who is overwhelmingly typical, more serious commitment to the genre did regularly occur: take, for example, Joseph Beaumont, Master of Peterhouse, an active royalist, professor, and poet (in English and Neo-Latin). Beaumont contributed regularly from 1635 to 1695, appearing in fifteen volumes. He died in 1699, missing the chance for a final flourish in 1697. Was he too infirm at last, or sceptical of the cause? John Laughton of Trinity College, the most prolific composer, sent in over a thousand lines, to ten separate volumes. Another scholar's short epigram might still have made a difference to his life.

Many volumes could fruitfully be chosen for examination, to illustrate political attitudes or poetic responses to them. In the latter part of this paper, I will focus on the 1697 volume, for the Peace of Ryswyck that ended the Nine Years War, the first severe test of Britain's Revolution settlement. In 1697 we find a fully mature literary genre, established for over a century, and with two-thirds of a century still to run. For comparison, we may briefly consider some other years when peaceful events deserved commemoration. In 1623, it was Prince Charles's safe return, thankfully unwed, from Spain: an event also celebrated by George Herbert, as Cambridge's public orator.[6] Fifty-nine poets wrote for the official volume,[7] one sending nineteen poems. Unusually, the poets are identified only by initials and colleges.

Oliver Cromwell's victorious peace of 1654, after an external rather than a civil war, could fittingly be praised in Cambridge (as also in Oxford), the tensions of civil war having somewhat eased, and the traumatic ejections of many academics, like the last royalist volume, being well in the past. There is a nice punning title,[8] stressing Oliver's olive-branch of peace (Oxford made the same point in Greek). At least forty-eight poets contribute, many with several pieces, or one substantial offering. A number of well-known Cambridge names appear. Senior figures will have wanted to stress the loyalty of themselves and their colleges to the side that God currently favoured, whatever their private aspirations. Two pages of Latin hexameters are offered by James Duport (a major writer in Greek and Latin, especially of biblical paraphrase), and similarly long sets of hexameters by four others. Ralph Cudworth, then Master of Clare Hall, has a page of scazontes (limping iambics). William Dillingham of Emmanuel, later a significant Neo-Latin poet and anthologist,[9] sent a short alcaic ode, eight sapphic stanzas, and hexameters. Benjamin Whichcot (ejected from King's at the Restoration six years later) precedes Cudworth. Several poets were inspired to long alcaic poems, of twenty stanzas or more: William Bagge of Caius; Christopher Chalfont of King's; John Wray of Trinity (the longest, at twenty-seven stanzas, one hundred and eight lines); and W. Croone of Emmanuel. Jabez Brideoake of St John's managed ten alcaic stanzas. These, and other Horatian odes of the period (in a genuine Horatian form, rather than a pale vernacular imitation), may perhaps provide some context for Marvell's justly celebrated "Horatian Ode on Cromwel's Return from Ireland" of a few years previously.

And so to the Peace of 1697, coming like that of 1654 a few years after Revolution. Some poetic loyalties had been confused, with a pre-Revolutionary volume of 1688 cancelled out by the opposite sentiments of 1689.[10] Cambridge's title page emphasises William's achievement in restoring the peace of Europe: "GRATULATIO / Academiae Cantabrigiensis / De Reditu / *Serenissimi REGIS* / GULIELMI III. / post

---

[6] See the paper by J. K. Hale in this volume.

[7] *Gratulatio Academiae Cantabrigiensis de Serenissimi Principis Reditu ex Hispaniis exoptatissimo* ... (Cambridge, 1623).

[8] *Oliva Pacis ad illustrissimum celsissimum Oliverum ... De Pace cum foederatis Belgis feliciter sancita* ... (Cambridge, 1654).

[9] Money, *English Horace*, 39–42.

[10] Money, *English Horace*, 244–245.

/ *Pacem & Libertatem* / EUROPAE / Feliciter / Restitutam ./ Anno MDCXCVII. // Cantabrigiae: Typis Academicis."[11] There is much glee, as one might expect, at the foiling of Louis XIV's ambition. The prolific John Laughton fills four pages with a spirited, sarcastic, splenetic epode against Louis ("Lodoix"), entitled "Indignatio Libera". Some poets can give a distinctive twist to this theme. Gabriel Quadring, Master of Magdalene, has much the shortest offering from a head of house, a single epigram, entitled "*Sic Deum & Regem* GULIELMUM *affatur Ludovicus Magnus*":

> Qui soli possunt, obstant ingentibus ausis,
> Tu Deus Omnipotens, et Tu Rex Maxime Regum.

The title, and author's name and position, contain more words than the entire poem. Yet I am not sure that Quadring's is a weak or lazy effort. It is simple, with a striking conceit. The great Louis is forced to concede that only two greater powers can stand in his way: God, and the greatest of kings, William. The idea that Louis might actually say so is ludicrous; but Quadring's compliment to William is apt, recognising the magnitude of his achievement in stopping so great an adversary.

Like most of the volumes, that of 1697 has an impressive variety of literary forms. Robert Read of St John's eschews metre altogether, writing in the genre of the prose poem (or irregular inscription).[12] He begins by justifying this choice of form: joy must not be restrained by the bounds of metre: "Fuge *Musa, modis* refraenare / Laetitiam omnivagam, et quae / (Si quae unquam) nescia est *modi*." Correct formal appearance, however, clearly exercised the minds of the volume's editors. Unusually, they banish all the Greek poems to a separate section at the end, preceded by an interesting explanation: "Pauca quae sequuntur Carmina, commodiorem quidem locum cum superioribus alias habitura, ideo huc rejici placuit, Formis non aeque nitidis exprimenda; quod Typi novi Academici, iis excudendis destinati, nondum ad nos pervenerint." Owing to the delayed delivery of larger, suitably elegant Greek type to match the Latin, reasons of neatness override normal scholarly considerations. The book must be one of which the university can be proud in every respect, good-looking as well as learned. Despite the smaller type, and subordinate position, the seven Greek (and one Hebrew)[13] poets will have been proud of their substantial pieces. They are led by the hugely prolific, and equally eccentric, Professor Joshua Barnes, who could easily dash off a page of Homeric hexameters to *Basileus Ilermos* before

---

[11] In transcription, capitals used only for larger sizes of capital on original title page. Page references for poems discussed below: sig. C2r (Quadring), D1–2v (Laughton), K1v–2r (Bigot), M2v–N1r (Read), Q2r (Walpole), Aa2v–Bb1v (Wyllys), Hh2v–Kk2r (Greek).

[12] To be distinguished from the irregular variety of Pindaric ode, which retains (but mixes) traditional metre. For a vicious anti-Williamite prose poem, see Christ Church, Oxford, Wake MSS 18. 514 (quoted at Money, *English Horace*, 206).

[13] Hebrew by Thomas Bennett (orientalist; St John's; also wrote Hebrew on Queen Mary's death, 1694/5): D. K. Money and J. Olszowy, "Hebrew Commemorative Poetry," *Transactions of the Cambridge Bibliographical Society* 10 (1995): 549–576, here 572.

breakfast.¹⁴ Others, no doubt more laboriously, produced anacreontics, or more hexameters, including an extended pastoral dialogue from Samuel Cobb, a Theocritean idyll to match the Latin eclogues that regularly grace these volumes.

A typical example of a sapphic ode is provided by the splendidly named Isaac Bigot, of Clare Hall.¹⁵ He is, as it happens, one of the less bigoted contributors, preferring to dwell in charming Horatian fashion on the rural blessings of peace, as brought about by "ille Gallorum timor, ille magnae / Caesar Europae moderator." It is not a highly original piece of poetry; but it is well expressed, with attention to elegance of phrase, and appropriate modernising of classical terminology. A rather longer sapphic ode was written by Benjamin Wyllys, fellow of King's. It borrows shamelessly from Horace, starting "Est mihi Nonum superantis annum," and so on.¹⁶ After copying his first line and a half directly from his model, Wyllys allows some interesting variation, praising his variety of wines in more detail; naturally, the high table at King's College would surpass a Sabine farm. His first adonic, "Mitius uvis", different in sense, cleverly echoes the sound of "est hederae vis". Horace's original ode is fairly risqué, asking Phyllis (who unwisely lusts after young Telephus) to join him in celebrating Maecenas's birthday. It is not a political poem at all; but Wyllys can adapt it, more than doubling the length, and introducing much Augustan praise of William as "Caesar", victorious at the Boyne and Namur, or the "Auriacus Atlas", the Prince of Orange supporting the tottering kingdom. In his fourteenth stanza, Wyllys puts another direct Horatian borrowing to good effect:

> Mitte civiles super Urbe curas,
> Occidit fusum Mahumedis agmen,
> Ipse Sultanus fugit et Sabaudi
>   Signa Gradivi.

The defeat of the Dacians, in Horace,¹⁷ is transferred to a highly topical victory in the same general region. In that same year, 1697, Prince Eugene of Savoy had defeated the Turks at Zenta. Thus William's (and later Marlborough's) colleague had reduced a threat to the Empire, Britain's ally; it is flattering to William to compare his concern for the whole European situation to that of Augustus or Maecenas.¹⁸

There may also be a shocking personal element to Wyllys's poem, defensible only by reference to Horatian convention. He makes much reference to heavy drinking (a hundred toasts to William, even to Louis), to Bacchic orgies ("Orgiis adsis", "Sanius bacchor") made legitimate by William's victory. Most disgracefully, for a young col-

---

[14] Cf. Money, *English Horace*, 94–98; work on Barnes's Latin epic on the Black Prince, the *Franciad*, ed. D. K. Money and R. A. Kennedy, is in progress.

[15] Perhaps a Huguenot name? He is something of a mystery, not listed in Venn's *Alumni*.

[16] Horace, *Carmina* 4. 11. 1–2.

[17] Horace, *Carmina* 3. 8. 17–18.

[18] William had a leading role in building coalitions; the European angle is stressed in J. Scott, *England's Troubles* (Cambridge, 2000); cf. B. Cox, *King William's European Joint Venture* (Assen, 1995): detailed, but eccentric.

lege fellow and bachelor of arts (of course obliged by statute, like all holders of fellowships, to remain single), he has his own Phyllis, "Belinda, / Cara permultis, mihi praeter omnes / Cara Belinda." Dear to all, especially to me: she sounds like one of Cambridge's looser ladies, of whom Wyllys's Provost will scarcely have approved. Whether she existed, or he merely imagined her, he can have some daring fun, under the cloak of patriotic celebration and classical respectability. Wyllys himself had been at King's since 1690, as an Eton scholar, and fellow (1693); he was ordained in 1698/9, became an usher (junior schoolmaster) in Maidstone, Kent (1701), then was for many years a vicar in Northamptonshire, until his death in 1748. This lively piece of poetry seems the high point of an otherwise ordinary eighteenth-century career.

The most historically interesting of the hundred and twenty-nine contributors to the 1697 volume is Robert Walpole, who was for many years to dominate British politics and is often called the first "prime minister". Like Wyllys, though a few years younger, he came from Eton to King's, where he was a scholar from 1696 to 1698; thus the 1697 volume was his best chance to publish Neo-Latin, and he took it. In 1698, on the death on his older brother, Edward, Robert Walpole became heir to his father's estate, and withdrew unwillingly from college, "my father holding his resolution that I shall not any more reside here."[19] His father, who had a been something of a scholar, possessed a learned library, with Latin classics (and almost all Francis Bacon's works); the young Walpole was full of enthusiasm for study: nevertheless, learning about management and politics took precedence. A promising academic career was interrupted and a political career was launched. A memorable part of his years at Cambridge had probably been the sight of his verses in print, a full page (forty elegiac lines) in the university's presentation volume, with his name at its foot: "*Rob. Walpole, Coll. Regal. Alumn.*"

As far as I am aware, this early Neo-Latin work of Walpole's has not been studied (and is generally ignored) by historians and English scholars.[20] Of interest in itself, it also has implications for the discussion of Walpole's later career, particularly his turbulent relations with authors. During his long period of power, he was noted as a poor patron of letters in general, favouring those whose writing was politically useful.[21] Many prominent poets attacked him, whether as Tories (or crypto-Jacobites) or members of the so-called "patriot opposition".[22] On the other hand, his "consistent patronage of King's men and Etonians was a source of annoyance to many persons."[23] He clearly remembered his early associations; and the culture of Eton and

---

[19] Letter of resignation, 19 May 1698: J. H. Plumb, *Sir Robert Walpole: The Making of a Statesman* (London, 1956), 88. Library: Plumb, *Walpole*, 82. Cf. B. H. Hill, *Sir Robert Walpole: "Sole and Prime Minister"* (London, 1989), 18–24: "[a] seat in Parliament [was] now virtually his inheritance", at twenty-four.

[20] There is however a vast secondary literature on Walpole, which I have not attempted to digest for this paper (as well as numerous MSS, etc.); apologies if I have missed a discussion of the poem. Standard biographies noted above do not seem aware of it.

[21] B. A. Goldgar, *Walpole and the Wits* (Lincoln, NE, and London, 1976), 9–14.

[22] C. Gerrard, *The Patriot Opposition to Walpole* (Oxford, 1994).

[23] Quoted at *Dictionary of National Biography* 59 (London, 1899), 180.

King's was a Neo-Latin one, where such poetry as his own 1697 contribution was highly esteemed, and considered of practical value. He may even have felt, as a former Neo-Latin poet himself, some scorn for the vernacular bards clamouring for state handouts. Latin remained of real use to him: his son Horace wrote in 1742, "You know the Earl [by now he was ennobled, as Earl of Orford] don't speak a word of any language but English and Latin." As prime minister, he had no way of conversing with his employer, George I, "but very imperfectly in Latin."[24]

Walpole's poem begins by stressing Europe's fears at French preparations: their fraud, savagery, and famous pride (an effective tricolon, in the third line):

> Viderat instructos Europa in praelia Gallos,
>   Coeperat et tandem permetuisse sibi.
> Quo fraus, quo feritas, quo nota superbia tendat,
>   Cura, timor populis omnibus unus erat. (1–4)

Yet Britain herself had a treacherous leader (James II), who would not help to oppose Louis XIV; like the wicked pastors of Milton's "Lycidas", he aims to betray his flock:

> Horruit ante omnes Britannia moesta, tueri
>   Quod quae deberet dextra negaret opem.
> Intremuit, cum (quo non infelicior alter)
>   Ipse suas vellet prodere Pastor oves. (5–8)

Walpole then has a striking rhetorical flourish. Who can save us from present danger? The alliteration may seem heavy-handed (5 prominent "p"s in line 9; also "v" in 14, "g" in 15), but reflects the young poet's forceful enjoyment of the medium:

> Quisnam igitur praesens propiora pericula pellat?
>   Quem vocet Heroum, quem vocet illa Deum?
> Quem? nisi, qui potuit toties fulcire ruentem,
>   Victrici et toties reppulit arma manu,
> WILHELMUM. . . . (9–13)

Thus William saves Europe, and teaches Louis a lesson: a point made, in their different ways, by Quadring, and by Wyllys, from Walpole's own college. Walpole's sense of the urgency of the crisis; of Britain's catastrophic policy under James II, reversed by William's revolution; and of the nation's gratitude on the king's return, are all fitting for a future politician.

> Jam rediisti igitur, Princeps Optate; tuorum
>   Spes exples, praesens gaudia nostra foves.

---

[24] Mrs. P. Toynbee, ed., *Letters of Horace Walpole* (Oxford, 1903), 1:258.

> Semper grata Dies, nostris quae Te attulit oris,
> Quae cum pace ferat, gratior illa Dies. (23–26)

The classical language of a longed-for prince, ironically, echoes the terms regularly used by Jacobite Latin poets, hoping for their own restoration.[25] For both sides, political anniversaries were crucial; this day of peaceful return will rival that of Glorious Revolution. Walpole, soon to be in Parliament, anticipates the pleasure of voting annual subsidies:

> Quam laete vel Marte gravem Te excepimus olim,
> Annua testantur munera voce patrum. (27–28)

As in Cromwell's case (a connection not explicitly made, but possibly implicit), "Quam laete fulgebit Honos et frontis Oliva" (29). Let opponents, "vos infesti" (33) either cease complaints or abstain from the blessings of William's peace. The poem ends with a promise of enthusiastic loyalty:

> Ibimus, haud mora, confestim nos ibimus omnes,
> Quocunque ille vocat, quam jubet ille viam. (39–40)

It is no surprise, of course, to find loyalty in a loyal verse collection. Walpole's is a typical poem; he too is a typical Cambridge author, except in his later prominence. He writes powerfully and effectively, with an eye to the chief purpose of the genre: to attract favourable attention to the author. Soon after, as a young politician, he found a friend and patron in Edward Russell, Lord Orford, admiral at Britain's greatest naval victory in the Nine Years War, the battle of La Hogue (1692), when Jacobite hopes of an early reversal of the Revolution had been shattered.[26] (As Britain's leading statesman, it was this first patron's title he was to adopt.) Walpole's Cambridge verses — whether or not Russell read them — demonstrate exactly the qualities the admiral would have approved. Neo-Latin could be highly political, as Walpole's early acumen understood. It also required some learning and skill; one hesitates to imagine more recent politicians attempting to follow suit.[27] As I hope these few poems of 1697 suggest, there is much of value in these university poets, even if two thousand others from his university were not as influential as Walpole.

Wolfson College, Cambridge, and University of Sunderland

---

[25] E.g., Archibald Pitcairne: see Money, *English Horace*, and edn. by J. MacQueen (Bibliotheca Latinitatis Novae: forthcoming).

[26] Plumb, *Walpole*, 97; cf. P. Aubrey, *The Defeat of James Stuart's Armada, 1692* (Leicester, 1979).

[27] One gathers that Tony Blair, prime minister at the time of writing, was in a pop band at Oxford — perhaps the cultural, if not intellectual, equivalent.

Thomas More's De tristitia Christi as Theo-Drama

CLARE M. MURPHY

Thomas More's first printed English work was his *Life of John Picus, Earl of Mirandula*, which was also the first book to issue from the press of More's brother-in-law John Rastell, in 1510. It is not unusual that the greatest English humanist chose to publish a life of the Renaissance proto-humanist, especially since Giovanni Pico's nephew Gianfrancesco had some years earlier written the Latin *vita* which More now translated. That More may have to some extent identified with Pico I have shown elsewhere,[1] particularly as regards the similarities between what More wrote of Pico and what Erasmus was later to write of More in his letter of 23 July 1519 to Ulrich von Hutten (Allen, *Letters*, 999). And, the received wisdom tells us, More — having definitively decided to embrace not the priesthood but rather a wife — sought a lay model,[2] a role which the brilliant Florentine could perhaps fulfil, at least after his conversion. At the time of preparing this life, More was not far from the age Pico was when he died. Certain similarities between their lives and the possible discomfort he felt at Pico's sudden death at the age More was at the time of writing may help to explain why, when More comes to write of Pico's death, he lets the great humanist's attachment to Girolamo Savonarola carry the emotion of his narrative.

The Solution in *De tristitia*

The *Picus* was More's first published English work. What about his final work? *De tristitia tedio pavore et oratione Christi ante captionem eius* was written in the Tower of London by a man awaiting certain death. Now there was no other figure to carry the

---

[1] C. M. Murphy, "Humanist Values in Thomas More's Life of Giovanni Pico della Mirandola," in *Acta Conventus Neo-Latini Bariensis*, ed. J. F. Alcina et al., MRTS 184 (Tempe, AZ, 1998), 419–425.

[2] *The Life of SIR THOMAS MORE, Knight By His Great Grandson CRESACRE MORE, Esq.* (London, 1726); ed. and modernized by J. L. Kennedy (Athens, GA, 1941), 11.

emotion. More stands like Everyman in the medieval drama, who must go on the journey for which there is no travelling companion, at least no earthly one. Flannery O'Connor's short story "A Temple of the Holy Ghost" features a little girl, half brat and half serious thinker: "She thought she could never be a saint, but she could be a martyr if they killed her quick." Perhaps it was because of their former friendship that Henry VIII had More killed "quick," but More in the Tower knew that he might be awaiting partial hanging followed by drawing and quartering. Christ's "sadness", "weariness", and "fear" were More's own, as was Christ's "prayer", his Agony in the Garden.

More always had a sense of drama,[3] from his days as a page in Archbishop (of Canterbury) Morton's household when he climbed upon the stage with the players and took a part, until at the foot of the scaffold he asked for help going up, only because coming down he could shift for himself. In the Tower he turned to history's greatest drama, the Passion and Resurrection of Christ. In *My Dear Peter*, Elizabeth McCutcheon describes the three Mores who figure in *Utopia*.[4] The number of roles he plays in *De tristitia*, the number of masks he wears, is considerably larger, but all of us play at least one role in the Passion of Christ. By its nature, *De tristitia* is a highly theological work.

Hans Urs von Balthasar (1905–1988) singles out the hermeneutic nature of theology: "All theology is an interpretation of divine revelation. Thus, in its totality it can only be hermeneutics." This hermeneutics is played out in the Trinity and in the human being, for, in revealing himself in Christ, God interprets himself and thus gives "in broad outline and in detail, his plan for the world." The revelation of himself is the first hermeneutics. This first, however, is oriented and regulated by the second hermeneutics, his plan for the world — "for God does not play the world drama all on his own; he makes room for man to join in the acting," and it is through the Holy Spirit that God's language becomes intelligible to the human being. All this von Balthasar calls Theo-drama, theological dramatic theory. But Theo-drama is not played upon a stage for an audience to watch. As More did in Archbishop Morton's household, and as he does for the play-within-a-play in the Elizabethan drama *Sir Thomas More*, human beings must involve themselves in God's drama "if there is to be an integrated interplay."[5]

The Focus of *De tristitia*

The work opens at the conclusion of the Last Supper: "When Jesus had said these things, they recited the hymn and went out to the Mount of Olives," and ends with

---

[3] See for example Howard B. Norland, *Drama in Early Tudor Britain: 1485–1558* (Lincoln, NE, 1995), 111–127. Norland notes that More's father had served as Master of the Revels at Lincoln's Inn in 1488–1489 (112).

[4] E. McCutcheon, *My Dear Peter: The "Ars Poetica" and Hermeneutics for More's "Utopia"* (Angers, 1983), 17 ff.

[5] Hans Urs von Balthasar, *Theodramatik, Zweiter Band: Die Personen des Spiels, Teil 1, Der Mensch in Gott* (Einsiedeln, 1976); *Theo-Drama: Theological Dramatic Theory*, Volume II, *The Dramatis Personae: Man in God*, trans. Graham Harrison (San Francisco, 1990), 91.

"only then, after all these events, did they lay hands on Jesus, *tum demum primum manus iniectas in Iesum*."[6] There was joy as well as anguish at the Last Supper. It was, after all, a Passover meal among friends, at which Christ instituted the Eucharist, and in some views also the priesthood by the words "Do this in memory of me." Christ showed the necessity and beauty of service to others in the washing of the feet; Holy Thursday in Henry VIII's court still included the *Mandatum* or "Maundy", i.e., the washing of beggars' feet. For these reasons, Holy Thursday liturgies tend to be joyful, and are often followed by parties. Yet More avoids all this to focus on Christ's agony — and through it on his own.

More has a twofold imperative: to face the agony of fear of the possible torment his death could be, but most of all to find a reason for what he hoped to have the strength to do. Among the theological subjects treated in *De tristitia* are the Trinity, the Eucharist, free will, divine mercy, the quality of one's faith, and the necessity of prayer. But above all is the union of the two natures — divine and human — in the person of Christ. The crux of this hypostatic union may well be found in Christ's prayer during the Agony in the Garden: "Father, if it is possible, let this cup pass from me, yet not my will, but yours, be done" (Matthew 26:39; cf. Mark 14:36, Luke 22:42). Here Christ prays, More says, "not only in soul, but also in body" (CW 14: 145), since he is prostrate on the ground. (One is reminded of the ordinand, or the religious at final profession, prostrate during the Litany of the Saints, symbolically laying down their lives to rise and take up their crosses.) The Son of God could not have been ignorant of his Father's will, even though the Father as God could have spared him the cup of the Passion "if He had not imposed it on Him by an immutable decree." Christ also asked that his own will "might not be granted, if something else seemed better to His Father's will, which is absolutely best" (CW 14: 149). As God, Christ knows what will happen to him and for what cause. Why then does he pray that it not happen? His purpose, according to More, is instructive: to remind us that all Fatherhood proceeds from the first Person of the Trinity, both in heaven and on earth — that God the Father is so in a double sense: he is Father also by Creation, which is a sort of fatherhood (149).

The human father who begot us was in his turn created by God, explains More, but God creates from nothing. In calling twice on his Father, Christ acknowledges his natural father in heaven and signifies as well that he had no other father on earth — born of a virgin mother, but without male seed, therefore from nothing (CW 14: 151–153). "My father," says Christ, "if this cup cannot pass away without my drinking it, let your will be done" (CW 14: 177). More singles out the pronoun "my" (as in Matthew) for its twofold effect. It denotes affection, but it also makes clear that God is the father of Christ not only by creation, through which he is the father of all things, but also by nature. Christ taught us to pray "Our Father," but only he can pray to "my father" (CW 14: 179). As man, Christ can say "our"; as God, "my."

---

[6] The Yale Edition of the Complete Works of St. Thomas More, vol. 14, *De tristitia Christi*, ed. and trans. Clarence H. Miller (New Haven and London, 1976), 3, 625. All subsequent references to this work will be given in the body of the text as CW 14.

When Christ asks his Father to let the cup pass, he shows the "certain, immutable, unconstrained decision of His Father concerning His death" (CW 14: 179a). This is the only basis on which Christ calls something possible or impossible. If Christ saw himself as "ineluctably and necessarily destined to die," something determined by the stars or by fate, then it would have been "completely pointless" for him to add "let your will be done." The addition shows that he did not consider the Father's decision to be out of his control (CW 14: 179a–181). Two matters then for consideration: Christ "begged His Father to avert His death" and at the same time he "humbly submitted everything to the will of His Father." While we consider these two, writes More, "we must also constantly bear in mind that, though He was both God and man, [Christ] said all these things not as God, but insofar as He was man" (CW 14: 181). If the young More once identified himself with his literary subject Pico, the mature man waiting for death has found integrity of self and soul and pen in identification with the God who became man and let himself endure the sufferings human beings can face.

The analogy More uses to indicate the undivided nature of the hypostatic union is the favorite patristic one, that of soul and body in one human being. He points out that we sometimes speak of the one rather than the other: we say that martyrs go straight to heaven when they die, but we mean only their souls. We speak on the other hand of the proud, who are still only "dust and ashes" in their graves (CW 14: 183). Again the personal identification reveals itself. A prominent theme of *De tristitia* is that of willing and reluctant martyrdom, More fearing that his may be classed only in the latter group while he would wish it to be in the former. As for the proud man (eventually to be) turned to ashes in his grave, we need only to look to the son of Henry VII, in whose funeral sermon Bishop John Fisher evoked the familiar *fumus et umbra* theme in explaining why he refused to praise the late king's worldly glories.[7]

In the omnipotent person of Christ humanity and divinity were joined and made one no less closely than His immortal soul was united to a body which could die. Because he was divine Christ could say "I and the Father are one" [John 10:30] and "before Abraham came to be, I am" [John 8:58]. Because he was human he could say "The Father is greater than I" [John 14:28] and "A little while I am with you" [John 7:33, 13:33] (185).

The Drama of the Hypostatic Union

Why is hypostasis [= the Person] so important to More at this ultimate stage? This question is inseparable from a second: for what did More give his life? Clarence Miller ponders this question. For the "integrity of the self"? Yes. For "the irreducible freedom of the individual conscience"? Yes. For papal supremacy "as a sign of the supra-national unity of Western Christendom, past and present"? Yes. All these "are true as far as they go." "But in the last analysis," he continues, "More did not die for any principle, or idea, or tradition, or even doctrine, but for a person, for Christ"

---

[7] *The English Works of John Fisher*, coll. John E. B. Mayor, Part 1 (London, 1876; repr. 1935), 269–270.

(CW 14: 775). One might say that the God who is Christ made the death exigent; the man who is Christ made it bearable. This man, this person Christ, experienced the same sadness, weariness, and fear as More, prayed the same agonized prayer as More.

Von Balthasar writes of the hypostatic union: "When God says to a spiritual subject who that subject is for him, the eternally and abiding true God, when God says to it in the same breath why it exists — thus bestowing on it its divinely attested mission — at that point it can be said of a spiritual subject that it is a person." All this took place once, archetypally says the Swiss theologian, when Christ was given "definition" by his Father at his baptism by John: "This is my beloved son, in whom I am well pleased" (Matthew 3:17, Mark 1:11, cf. Luke 3:22). There is thus precise knowledge of who Christ is and of his mission, and the personhood of every Christian derives from that of Christ.[8] More, after sitting a while in his boat as they left their Chelsea home on 13 April 1534 — his final leave-taking of that home as it turned out — said to his daughter Margaret's husband, "Son Roper, I thank our Lord the field is won."[9] Perhaps this is More's strongest statement of personhood: "I know that I cannot sign the Oath of Succession. Whatever comes of that decision, I thank the Lord that I have been able to make that decision." In the Tower More must cling to that personhood, to that definition of self in a "divinely attested mission," sustained by his concentration on Christ's mission. In the very same paragraph Roper himself confides that he did not know what his father-in-law meant, but that he "conjectured afterwards, it was that the love he had to God wrought in him so effectually that it conquered all carnal affections [i.e., worldly feelings and emotions] utterly."

Where More's meditation concentrates on Christ's experience, von Balthasar describes the Agony in the Garden as the choice between two images of the Father, that of the all-powerful and good Father, who could let the cup pass from his son who is both God and man, and the image of the severe God of justice as seen through the heart and eyes of sinners, and is now appearing to the Son, who as a result of his sacrifice will be able to mediate with this Father in the defence of sinners. In his agony, says Balthasar, Jesus experiences "the terrible fear of not being able to perform what is demanded."[10] In *De tristitia* More's struggle with the will of the Father is perhaps best demonstrated in his anxious distinguishing between the willing and the reluctant martyr. He concludes finally that the martyr's witness of whichever nature is in itself a cause for our gratitude (CW 14: 239 and elsewhere).

Like More, von Balthasar discusses the singular phenomenon of Christ's sweating blood. "Only a conflict between God in heaven and God the representative of

---

[8] Von Balthasar, *Theodramatik* II/2, 190, 206–209, repr. in *In der Fülle des Glaubens: Hans Urs von Balthasar . . . Lesebuch* (Freiburg im Breisgau, 1980), and *The Von Balthasar Reader*, ed. Medard Kehl, S.J. and Werner Lösser, S.J., trans. Robert J. Daly, S.J. and Fred Lawrence (Edinburgh, 1982), 132.

[9] William Roper, *The Life of Sir Thomas More,* in *Two Early Tudor Lives,* ed. Richard S. Sylvester and Davis P. Harding (New Haven and London, 1962), 238.

[10] H. U. Von Balthasar, *Der dreifache Kranz: Das Heil der Welt im Mariengebet* (Einsiedeln, 1977), 45–47; *Reader,* 147.

sinners on earth" can explain it. The redemption, he writes, was accomplished because Christ as man freely chose to accept his Father's will that he be "God the representative of sinners on earth,"[11] and, as Eucharistic Prayer II of the Roman Catholic liturgy states, "he was given up to death, a death he freely accepted." This death is freely accepted when Jesus allows "them" "to lay hands on him."

And so More allows the same. Von Balthasar writes that, like Jesus, "the artist or scholar who is possessed by his or her mission knows himself or herself freely and totally only if he or she can pursue this most personal mission."[12] Clarence Miller, who personally handled the Valencia holograph and thus saw More's own revisions of his manuscript, shows how More's revisions indicate that he subsumed his own need to find relief from emotional distress into the production of a text that would sustain others in that and later times (CW 14: 748 ff.). More as artist could know himself "freely and totally" in pursuing "this most personal mission," identifying his own agony with Christ's, and expressing it by the *word*, as Christ himself is from the beginning the Word (John 1:1).

More loved not only the person Christ, but also Christ's church — however, cautions Miller, "only insofar as the church is made up of Christian persons in whom Christ is present and who constitute the mystical body of Christ" (CW 14: 775–776). The fledgling Church More contemplates in his long meditation on the Passion includes the betrayer Judas, toward whom his disdain is scathing (CW 14: 277). Yet around himself More also finds contemporary betrayers, for whom his disdain is also scathing: viciously sinful priests who administer the Eucharist unworthily, somnolent bishops who have betrayed Christ as surely as Judas did. Finally, in the fledgling Church are the apostles, sleeping away as Christ implores his Father and asks them to stay awake with him (Matthew 26:40, Mark 14:37–38, Luke 22:45–46).[13] More writes particularly of Peter, a warning against presumption, protesting that he will never deny Christ and then doing so three times in a row (CW 14: 217). Von Balthasar says that the apostles, whose "faith is not awake and prayerful enough, represent the Church in its average condition."[14] Yet More knew that the apostles would one day be martyrs all, as he probably would be. Whether willing or reluctant, they would no longer be average, supported into their complete witnessing by the grace of the same Christ who had called them into "definition" and personhood.

Moreanum
Université Catholique de l'Ouest

---

[11] Von Balthasar, *Der dreifache Kranz*, in *Reader*, 147. In his sermon on Psalm 129/130, the *De profundis*, John Fisher admonishes sinners to ". . . call unto Jesus Christ our advocate in heaven unto the father . . ." (*English Works*, 1:218).

[12] Von Balthasar, *Theodramatik*, in *Reader*, 133.

[13] For a study of both the sleeping apostles and the somnolent bishops, see Brenda Hosington, "'*Quid dormitis?*': More's Use of Sleep as a Motif in *De Tristitia*," in *Miscellanea Moreana: Essays for Germain Marc'hadour*, ed. Clare M. Murphy, Henri Gibaud, and Mario A. Di Cesare, MRTS 61 (Binghamton, NY, 1989), 55–69.

[14] Von Balthasar, *Der dreifache Kranz*, in *Reader*, 148.

The Metamorphoses of
De vita monachorum

STEPHEN MURPHY

To a considerable extent, what follows will develop the figure of *reticentia*.[1] I will not dwell on the definition of cento, a new text made from rearranged pieces of a previous one; nor on the long popularity of the Virgilian verse cento; nor on the first flourishing of cento in late antiquity, where Proba and Ausonius are the most important practioners; let alone the theoretical and formal discussions, which belong most prominently to Ausonius and Henri Estienne[2] (not to mention significant contributions from Giulio Roscio Hortino and Antonio Possevino).[3] *Non mihi si linguae centum, sint oraque centum.*

More important, I will probably end up begging the natural question: namely, so what? The traditional (modern critical) contempt for cento as an inevitably minor genre and a sure sign of decadent taste is not something to be attacked directly. But the following discussion of the most notorious text by the poet considered by his sixteenth-century contemporaries as the greatest modern centonist may give an idea of the interest of the poem, and of the form. If the interest of cento lies in its radicality, in the extremeness with which it pushes the intertextual relation to its limit, then my subject, Lelio Capilupi's *De vita monachorum* and its textual fortune, holds a privileged place.

First, a sketch of the editorial history of *De vita monachorum*. It may be best to proceed, not simply chronologically, but by the type of publication. In the *editio princeps*

---

[1] I have profited from suggestions by George Hugo Tucker and, especially, Hélène Cazes.

[2] Ausonius, preface to *Cento nuptialis*; H. Estienne, *Centonum veterum & parodiarum utriusque linguae exempla* (Geneva: H. Estienne, 1575).

[3] Antonio Possevino, dedicatory letter to Joachim Du Bellay, in both Lelio Capilupi, *Centones ex Virgilio* (Rome: Valerio Dorico, 1555), A 3–4, and *Capiluporum carmina* (Rome: Giovanni Gigliotti, 1590), 155–157; Possevino, *Bibliotheca selecta de ratione studiorum* [. . .] (Venice: Altobellus Salicatius, 1603), 2: ch. 24; "Camillo ac Prospero Capilupis clariss. adolescentibus Julius Roscius Hortinus S.P.D." (*Capiluporum carmina*, 389–394).

(Venice, 1543), *De vita monachorum* is paired with another cento by Capilupi, *Gallus*. The same texts reappear together in 1550.[4] Otherwise, *De vita monachorum* by itself is published only outside Italy, in Protestant territory: [Basel,] probably mid-1540s; [Zürich,] around the same date; Wittenberg, 1545; Edinburgh, 1565; and "Rome" (= Geneva), 1575.[5] Two collective editions of Capilupi's centos appear, both in Rome, in 1555 and 1590. The latter, entitled *Capiluporum carmina*, comprises not only Lelio's centos, but also his non-cento Latin verse, as well as the centos and verse of his nephew Giulio and the verse of his three brothers Ippolito, Alfonso, and Camillo. The last sort of publication in which *De vita monachorum* appears is anthologies or anthology-like works. The first of these that can be dated is the volume edited by Mathia Flacius Illyricus in Basel (1557), entitled *Varia doctorum piorumque virorum de corrupto ecclesiae statu poemata*, a title that gives an adequate idea of the ideological slant.[6] About the same time the cento appears in a similar polemical anthology *Sylva carminum in nostri temporis corruptelas* [...].[7] In 1575, Henri Estienne includes the entire text of *De vita monachorum* in his *Centonum veterum & parodiarum utriusque linguae exempla*.[8] In 1597 in Helmstadt, Heinrich Meibom prints Lelio's cento along with a number of others, including several by Giulio Capilupi.[9] Finally, a volume of *Virgilio-Centones* published in Köln in 1601 contains collected centos by Lelio, including a version of *De vita monachorum*.[10]

The other basic fact that must be mentioned explains the absence of Italian editions between 1555 and 1590. In late 1557, "Laelii Capilupi Cento ex Virgilio" is placed on the Roman index of forbidden books.[11] In order for *De vita monachorum* to appear again in Italy, it had to be revised. And, in fact, the editor of the 1590

---

[4] "Venetiis, 1550." However, Dennis Rhodes claims that this edition was printed in Lyons by Jean Pullon. See idem, "Lelio Capilupi and the 'Centones ex Virgilio'," *The Library*, ser. 6, 16 (1994): 208–218.

[5] For the identification of the Basel and Zurich editions, which are both n.p.n.p.n.d., see *Index Aureliensis* (Baden-Baden, 1965–), prima pars, tomus 6: 457. For the identification of Geneva rather than Rome for the 1575 edition, see Rhodes, "Lelio Capilupi," 214.

[6] 355–370: *De vita monachorum*.

[7] *Sylva carminum in nostri tempore corruptelas, praesertim religionis, sane quam falsa & festiva, ex diversis hinc inde autoribus collecta*, N.p.n.d., 112–127: *De vita monachorum*.

[8] 104–118.

[9] *Virgilio-Centones auctorum notae optimae antiquorum & recentium* [...] (Helmstadt: Jacobus Lucius, 1597).

[10] *P. Virgilii Maronis Opera* [...] *Quibus adiecti sunt Virgilio-Centones variorum Auctorum* (Köln: Bernardus Gualtherius, 1601). Second part: 67–76: *De aetate aurea & ferrea*. The important Neo-Latin anthology of Giovanni Matteo Toscano (*Carmina illustrium poetarum Italorum*, 2 vols. [Paris: A. Gorbinus, 1577]) includes the contents of the 1555 *Centones ex Virgilio* and more (2:308–340), minus *De vita monachorum*.

[11] See G. Hugo Tucker, "Mantua's 'Second Virgil': Du Bellay, Montaigne and the Curious Fortune of Lelio Capilupi's *Centones ex Virgilio* (Romae, 1555)," in *Ut granum sinapis: Essays on Neo-Latin Literature in Honour of Jozef IJsewijn*, ed. Gilbert Tournoy and Dirk Sacré (Leuven, 1997), 264–291, esp. 284–289.

Capiluporum carmina says explicitly that revision was undertaken by Giulio Capilupi, to accommodate his uncle's centos to the different climate.[12]

I would like to make three main points about the textual fortune of *De vita monachorum* (and, to varying degrees, about that of other centos by Lelio), although I make no pretense to an exhaustive treatment of any of them. First, the changes undergone by Lelio's cento include important paratextual elements. Second, the most important textual revisions of *De vita monachorum* are those made for the 1590 edition by Giulio Capilupi, but those are not the only revisions of interest. Third, to call Giulio's rewriting an expurgation is insufficient. He has created a different, though an obviously related poem, and one that intensifies the intertextual relationship posed by cento.

Among paratextual changes figures first the order of poems. The two notorious centos originally printed separately, *Gallus* and *De vita monachorum*, are the first two in the collected edition of 1555. In the section of the 1590 collected edition containing Lelio's centos, they become respectively the sixteenth and the eighteenth (out of nineteen).

There is also the matter of titles. Although *Gallus* and *De vita monachorum* come first in 1555, they are the only ones of the thirteen centos to lack titles, being headed only by a numeral. In 1590 both poems are again given titles, but *De vita monachorum* has become *De ætate aurea et ferrea*.

The next element is typographical rather than paratextual. The text of 1555 and that of 1590 are both in italics. However, both editions also use small roman capitals for certain words. In 1590, this occurs mainly with proper names the poet wants to emphasize or images to elucidate for panegyric purposes.[13] In the 1555 *De vita monachorum*, capitals are used more often as an aid to interpretation of common nouns. They alert the reader to the fact that a word is being used in a much different sense from that in Virgil: thus *fratres* and *sorores* mean friars and nuns, *claustra* means cloister.

This semantic use of typography is often clarified by marginal notes. One example occurs in *Gallus*, where a reader may be puzzled by the poet's use of the name Cacus, before understanding from a marginal note that Lelio derives the Italian *cazzo* from Cacus (naturally, only in the 1555 edition).[14] While marginalia are numerous in both collected editions, the two "Italian" editions of *Gallus* and *De vita monachorum* (Venice, 1543 and "Venice" [Lyons], 1550) lack any glosses. On the other hand, editions of *De vita monachorum* printed in Protestant cities share a tradition of polemical marginalia. Starting with the Basel edition, the marginal notes stress on the one hand the ordered structure of the poem (*Propositio, Invocatio, Narratio*, etc.), on the other the elements of monastic routine and ritual being mocked (*Matutini, Missae descriptio, Transubstantiatio, Confessio*, etc.), with an occasional cry of editorial indignation (*Misericordia, Proh pudor*).

---

[12] *Capiluporum carmina*, 154.
[13] For example, "Arduus insurgens & grandia LILIA quassans," glossed in the margin thus: "Insignes Regis Galliae, & familiae Estensis," 232.
[14] *Centones ex Virgilio*, 7.

A particular kind of marginalia present in several editions, as it is for centos at large, is the identification of Virgilian sources. Typically, to the left and right of each line (when each hemistich comes from a different place) is printed an abbreviation of the title (*Aeneid, Georgics, Eclogues*) and the number of the book (never the verse number). This is the case from the first edition of *Gallus* and *De vita monachorum*, in 1543, through Heinrich Meibom's inclusion of the latter poem in his anthology of 1597. The Virgilian *loci* do not appear with the text of *De vita monachorum* in Henri Estienne's *Centonum et parodiarum exempla* (1575), nor in the editions printed in Protestant countries. It may be that the identification of sources draws attention to the centonist's virtuosity and so distracts from the subversiveness of a cento such as *De vita monachorum*. In contrast, the Protestant stripping away of references would be a way of focusing attention on the satire in the text itself.

A final paratextual element is the title-page illustration. I will mention only two striking examples. On the title page of the Basel and Zürich editions of *De vita monachorum* a horned centaur wears a papal tiara and holds a sword in one hand and a flaming manuscript (maybe a papal bull) in the other as he tramples upon books. The reader will not be surprised by the anti-papal epigram on the verso or by the polemic marginalia.[15]

Upon opening the first collected edition, the 1555 Roman *Lælii Capilupi* [...] *Centones ex Virgilio*, one finds no information about the place, publisher, or date. One does find the image of an hourglass emerging from clouds and, more prominently, a bearlike or wolflike animal in the wilderness urinating and defecating. Since several centos refer to the Capilupi family as *genus luporum*, the figure may be an emblem of Lelio Capilupi. At the very least, it is an image of startling impertinence at the beginning of a collection that starts with Lelio's most controversial centos, *Gallus* and *De vita monachorum*. Surprisingly, in the 1590 *Capiluporum carmina*, with all its tidying-up of troublesome texts, the same image reappears. Here it is not on the title page of the whole volume, but on a separate page preceding the section with Lelio's centos.

My second point is that the revisions to *De vita monachorum* are not limited to the extensive changes that allowed it to be reprinted in 1590.[16] This is too vast a topic to be covered adequately here; the following example will have to serve. A line introduces a new character into the narrative of moral decline and strife which occupies the first part of *De vita monachorum*. He is given the name Asylas, a minor character in the *Aeneid* described as "hominum divumque interpres." In fact, the entire line from the *Aeneid* (10.175) is used here, starting in 1543: "Tertius ille hominum divumque interpres Asylas."

That is the reading of all editions until that of 1555, where we find substituted another Virgilian line, beginning "Ille quidem," which makes the whole line read:

---

[15] In both editions, the woodcut is accompanied by the same epigram, "In Pontificem vel Minotaurum." The Wittenberg edition reproduces the verses but not the woodcut.

[16] It would be more accurate to speak of different versions of the 1555 edition, since there appear to be at least five different printings of the collection. See Rhodes, "Lelio Capilupi," 215–217; Tucker, "Mantua's 'Second Virgil'," 278–284.

"Ille quidem ille hominum divumque interpres Asylas." What difference lies in that small change? The answer appears in the margin of the "Protestant" editions (Basel, Zürich, Edinburgh, "Rome" [1575]), where the original line is glossed thus: "Paulus tertius Papa." The same is true of Mathias Flacius Illyricus's 1557 anthology. Meibom's 1597 anthology has no marginal glosses, but he makes the same identification, with references, in an endnote. Lelio's use of the word *Tertius* has an internal logic in the poem's narrative (as we will see); Asylas is the third in a series of individualized figures. But the use of the number corresponding to the pope of the time (Paul III's long papacy lasted until 1549) must have seemed too good an opportunity to miss for the Protestant appropriators of Lelio's text.

As things stood in the mid-1550s, a change must have been felt necessary. Either Lelio, or the friends responsible for the first collective edition of his centos (Antonio Possevino and Fulvio Orsini), or the publisher Valerio Dorico made the accommodation. This comprises not only substitution of a vaguer *Ille quidem* for *Tertius*, but also of a new marginal gloss. Asylas is now identified as Bernardino Ochino. The figure of Asylas in Lelio's poem, at first presented favorably, then condemned as he flees and sows discord, could plausibly correspond to the great Sienese reformer. When this general of the Capuchin order and renowned preacher fled Italy in 1542 as accusations of heresy gathered about him, he caused a commotion in the Gonzaga circle that was Lelio's.[17] On the other hand, the flight of Asylas modulates somewhat murkily into a representation of "ille Paris cum semiviro comitatu," which fits easily with some of the contemporary condemnation of Paul III's nepotism.[18]

The 1590 *Capiluporum carmina* has the same reading and the same gloss for this line as the 1555 edition. However, even this officially approved insistence on Asylas as a condemnation of Bernardino Ochino was apparently not enough to settle the polysemy of the text. Protestants continued to refer to Paul III, and so when in 1601 an anthology of centos was published in Köln under Jesuit supervision it followed the 1590 version of Lelio's centos, but in *De vita monachorum* simply omitted the entire Asylas episode.

My third point concerns Giulio's rewriting of *De vita monachorum*. On the reading of the line introducing Asylas the editions of 1555 and 1590 agree, but there is little else on which they do so. Perhaps the best way to show the differences between these two versions, or these two poems, is to set out the structure of each. All earlier versions of *De vita monachorum* through 1555 proceed in the same way. The invocation declares the subject matter (*fratres*) and addresses Cardinal Ippolito d'Este. Then the first half of the poem follows a diachronic scheme. The narrative begins with primitive humanity, and traces the corruption that overtakes those who become monks. A series of three figures plays key roles in this process. The first is a pri-

---

[17] See Edmondo Solmi, "La fuga di Bernardino Ochino secondo i documenti dell' Archivio Gonzaga di Mantova," *Bullettino senese di storia patria* 15 (1908): 23–98.

[18] See the numerous epigrams on this subject in *Pasquinate romane del Cinquecento*, ed. Valerio Marucci et al., 2 vols. (Rome, 1983).

mordial lawgiver who organizes humanity into monastic orders and thus civilizes them. After the first corruptions of leisure have set in, the second figure to appear is *Vana superstitio*, an infernal plague that plunges all of Europe into strife. Third, as seen above, is Asylas. After bemoaning again the sad state of the contemporary world, and Italy in particular, the poet appeals to his protector Ercole Gonzaga, Duke of Mantua.

Another invocation at this point, this time to Calliope, marks the beginning of a new section. This part corresponds to a roughly synchronic scheme: no longer the history of monks, but their mores, what their daily life is like. Hence matins, mass with its crucial moments — offertory, elevation, Eucharist — then a sermon, then confession. Next, the monks' mealtime, presided over by their prior, followed by exercises and outdoor games. There follow begging, funeral ceremonies, then the evening meal, followed by sleep and sex. In a concluding apostrophe, the poet contrasts the monks' happy *otium* with the grimness of contemporary wars.

Now, if we assume that what Giulio had to do to make the poem acceptable for republication was eliminate the anti-monastic satire, it might seem that he faced an impossible task. In the double sense of its title — what monastic life has been, and what it is now — the poem seems full of its subject from beginning to end. And yet, in the same way that Lelio retains nothing of the plots of Virgil's poems while using Virgil's words, so Giulio is able to avoid adding much that is not already in Lelio's poem (and what he adds, of course, is Virgilian too), while coming up with something quite different.

Giulio retains the same invocation, and the same division into two parts, the first diachronic, the second synchronic. But in the initial declaration of subject matter, he changes the original "Fratres rerum dominos, gentemque togatam, [...] corda oblita laborum" to "totiusque ex ordine gentis / Mores et studia et populos, matresque virosque." In other words, the subject is generalized from monks to humanity. Rather than a narrative of the foundation and corruption of monastic orders, Giulio offers a story of human progress from barbarism to civilization to decadence. Naturally, the larger view was already latent in Lelio's account. By his anthropological turn, Giulio is able to maintain the three figures introduced in this section (the primordial lawgiver, *Vana superstitio*, and Asylas). But in doing so he empties them of their specificity. They become less allegorical, or veiled, referents and more mythical.

After paying the same attention to Italy's sad contemporary state, the second invocation sets in motion the synchronic section, as in Lelio's cento. But again Giulio displaces the subject, from *fortia facta Patrum* (where *Patres=Fratres*) to *Illustres animos* and, a little more concretely, *iuvenes*. In this way, Giulio preserves the narrative of worldly pastimes, transformed into the amusements of lively youth: mealtime, exercise, evening meal, sleep, sex. It is at this point that Giulio inserts the apostrophe "O fortunatae gentes," which is Lelio's final movement. Youth is enviable in its *quies* as war rages all around. But then comes the metamorphosis that enables Giulio to use much of the liturgical section from *De vita monachorum. Iuventus* goes to church, not to matins but morning mass. We find the same moments of the mass (although with an important revision of the elevation of the Eucharist), then the same sermon; confession leads finally to a prayer to Jesus Christ which ends the poem on a note both penitential and apocalyptic.

The different thrust of the new poem should be apparent in this substitution of youth and humanity for monks, and in its conclusion with liturgy rather than an ironic praise of *otium*. Although both poems share the same division between diachronic and synchronic sections, the sense of these perspectives is stood on its head. For Giulio, the temporal scheme is anthropological, not religious. In the synchronic section, the representation of mores, the difference between the two poems can be summed up simply as the presence and absence of irony. Those Lelio calls *Fortunatae gentes* he mocks, and as he sets such Virgilian phrases in a new context he makes them satirical. Giulio's context is also new, but he returns to the phrases' original serious and laudatory weight in Virgil. Ironically, we can see a sign of the absence of irony in Giulio's text through a declaration of its presence. Next to the speech preceding the description of gluttony at mealtime, a marginal note declares: "Ironice dictum." Naturally, no such note exists in the 1555 edition because Lelio's entire poem is ironic. This isolation, in the new version, of one limited and glaring case makes it clear how much irony has been emptied out.

If the youthful humanity Giulio represents can be praised finally without irony, it is because of the saving power of religious practice. This recuperation of Lelio's liturgical section is only one of the obvious signs of the Counter-Reformation orthodoxy of the 1590 edition. Even more than the panegyrics to the powerful that cram that edition, Giulio's *accommodatio* of his uncle's poem is instructive. It makes *De aetate aurea et ferrea* a poem also about the salvation of Lelio's cento, about the power of cento itself and the flexibility of writing from writing. I would like to avoid any pat opposition — between, for example, a playful High Renaissance textuality and a repressive post-Tridentine *rappel à l'ordre*; or casting Lelio as Ariosto to Giulio as Tasso. I have evoked questions not just of intertextuality and editorial ideology, but of the nature of censorship and literary compromise; questions that must be pursued elsewhere. *Non omnia possumus omnes.*

Wake Forest University

Hugo Grotius's Correspondence with His Brother Willem de Groot*

H. J. M. NELLEN

Over a period of many years Hugo Grotius (1583–1645) kept up a correspondence with his brother Willem de Groot (1597–1662). When Willem was born, Hugo was already thirteen years old and a third-year law student at the University of Leiden. It was not long before Hugo became a prominent scholar, who, after 1621 in particular, enjoyed great fame because of his Neo-Latin poetry as well as for his juridical studies and exegetical works. Willem de Groot, by contrast, was and remained a secondary figure.[1] He dabbled in the same disciplines as Hugo, and also wrote a couple of juridical studies, but he always realised that the status of his elder brother was beyond his reach. On 10 August 1611, when he was fourteen, Willem matriculated in the Faculty of Arts at Leiden University; later on, probably in September 1614, he began to study law. On 29 November 1616 he defended a "disputatio pro gradu" in Leiden and five days later, on 3 December 1616, he took his doctorate in law.[2] Willem also collaborated with Gerardus Joannes Vossius in order to publish a large selection of the Neo-Latin poetry written by Hugo in the *Poemata Collecta*.[3]

---

* I would like to express my gratitude to Steven Surdèl and Gerard Huijing for having a look at my text.

[1] M. Ahsmann, "Willem de Groot (1597–1662) en zijn studie te Leiden in het licht van brieven van zijn broer Hugo," *Tijdschrift voor Rechtsgeschiedenis* 50 (1982): 371–401; R. Huybrecht, "Willem de Groot," in *Biografisch Woordenboek van Nederland*, ed. J. Charité (Amsterdam, 1985) 2:198–199; H. J. M. Nellen, "Hoe Willem de Groot (1597–1662) een carrière in Delft misliep. Dagboeknotities van een pensionaris in spe," *Lias* 25 (1998): 231–256.

[2] Ahsmann, "Willem de Groot," 398–401.

[3] *Hugonis Grotii Poemata, collecta et magnam partem nunc primum edita a fratre Guilielmo Grotio* (Leiden, 1617) [= September 1616], with a dedication written by Willem de Groot, dated 1 September 1616. See J. ter Meulen and P. J. J. Diermanse, *Bibliographie des écrits imprimés de Hugo Grotius* (The Hague, 1950) (hereafter *BG*), no. 1; cf. MS. The Hague, Algemeen Rijksarchief (hereafter ARA), Eerste afd., Aanw. 1911 XXIII (Coll. H. de Groot), no. 32, W. de Groot to M. C.

In May 1619 Hugo Grotius was sentenced to life imprisonment for his involvement in the politics of Grand Pensionary Johan van Oldenbarnevelt. In March 1621, however, he managed to escape in a book-chest from the state prison at Loevestein Castle, and soon after settled in Paris. Here, from 1635, he served as the ambassador of the Swedish Crown, after enduring the bitter hardship of a long exile. Meanwhile, Willem tried to make a career for himself. He was sworn in as a lawyer in October 1618[4] and underwent further training in legal practice, and was soon able to earn his keep at The Hague.[5]

Hugo and Willem de Groot usually wrote to each other in Latin. They discussed a variety of subjects, such as Willem's law studies, the upbringing of Grotius's children, and many other problems he had to cope with during his exile, theological debates in the churches of Holland and France, the reception of Grotius's works, recent publications of his colleagues and other events in the world of learning, and, last but not least, contemporary political developments and the way in which these affected the private lives of the brothers. Their correspondence, a mixture of personal and general news, gradually grew in importance. In the loneliness of his exile in Paris, letter-writing offered Grotius a continuous stream of information on events at home.[6] What is more, from the middle of 1637 our scholar managed to carry out a full-scale plan for the publication of his works, including poetry, historical treatises, and commentaries on the Bible. This, however, had to be done in Holland, where he felt the political climate was more conducive to such an enterprise. Over a long period, therefore, Willem's main task was to advance the publication of Grotius's works. In that sense he may be considered his literary agent.[7]

The earliest letters date from the spring of 1614, the last few from August 1645, the month in which Hugo Grotius, the driving spirit behind the correspondence, died. So Hugo and Willem wrote to each other for more than thirty years. At first they wrote irregularly, whenever it suited them, but after Grotius went into exile in 1621 they exchanged letters more frequently, and from 1639–1640 onwards, when

---

Santenus, 28 September 1616. See also A. C. G. M. Eyffinger, *Grotius poeta. Aspecten van Grotius's dichterschap* (The Hague, 1981), 171–174.

[4] Ahsmann, "Willem de Groot," 374–375.

[5] See *Briefwisseling van Hugo Grotius*, ed. P. C. Molhuysen, B. L. Meulenbroek, P. P. Witkam, H. J. M. Nellen, and C. M. Ridderikhoff, 17 vols. (The Hague, 1928–2001) (hereafter *BW*), 17 (Supplement), no. 599A, from W. de Groot, 2 April 1620: "... iam Hagam addiscendae praxeos gratia commigravi. ..." Cf. MS. The Hague, ARA, Eerste afd., Aanw. 1911 XXIII, no. 32, Willem de Groot to his cousin De Bye, 14 April 1620. In this letter Willem reports that he has moved to The Hague: "... je vous fais sçavoir que j'ay entierement transporté depuis peu de jours mon domicile à La Haye. ..."

[6] This applies also to the weekly correspondence between Grotius and his brother-in-law Nicolaes van Reigersberch, although it was primarily focused on the exchange of political news.

[7] *BW* 8, no. 3135, to Willem de Groot, 26 June 1637, where a list of works due to be printed is concluded as follows: "Horum omnium te non tantum fratrem, sed et fautorem studiorum meorum esse nescium nolui, ut videas etiam, quae negotiis publicis superfluunt, tempora mihi non perire."

the preparation of Grotius's works for the press called for a continuous exchange of information, even once a week.[8]

Confidentiality is one of the most striking features of this correspondence. In the period from 1618 to 1621, when the incarcerated Grotius was receiving information on recent events from his family and friends, this was clearly necessary: the exchange of letters had to be organised in an atmosphere of strict secrecy. Nor did this change after Grotius escaped from Loevestein: although our learned ex-prisoner was now living at liberty, he could not freely communicate with his family and friends at home, as the controversial content of his letters was likely to threaten their safety. The publication in 1622 of the *Verantwoordingh*, the book in which Grotius defended the policy of Johan van Oldenbarnevelt,[9] put Willem de Groot in an awkward position. He was arrested when the judicial authorities in Holland managed to seize one of the letters in which Grotius informed his brother about the printing in Holland of this highly controversial work. Willem could not deny that he had been in the possession of the manuscript of Grotius's *Verantwoordingh*; this complicity in the publication of a "seditious libel" earned him some days of distress in a cell at the Gevangenpoort in The Hague.[10]

I will now dwell on one aspect of the services rendered by Willem de Groot. At his brother's request Willem kept a file which contained all recent Latin and Greek poetry. Every now and then Grotius sent poems he had composed on the occasion of events which had touched him. These poems were meant to be published in a volume entitled *Poemata Nova*.[11]

One fine example of such a poem, written in Greek, denounced the dismissal of Ludwig Camerarius, the Swedish ambassador in The Hague, from the diplomatic service.[12] Grotius very much regretted that, after a long dispute over areas of responsibility, his learned colleague Camerarius, scion of a famous family of humanists, had to cede his position to the upstart Petter Spiring Silvercrona, a rich entrepreneur and

---

[8] Even if they were short of matters to report, both correspondents acquitted themselves well of their task. Cf. *BW* 8, no. 3393, from Willem de Groot, 21 December 1637: "Etsi pauca iam scribenda occurrunt, officio tamen meo deesse nolui, ut vicissim a te saepiuscule litteras accipiam, quae me valde delectant."

[9] The *Verantwoordingh van de wettelijcke regieringh van Hollandt* . . . (Hoorn, 1622) appeared in November 1622. Some months before, in August 1622, Grotius had published a Latin translation, *Apologeticus eorum qui Hollandiae . . . praefuerunt* (Paris, 1622) (*BG* nos. 872 and 880).

[10] *BW* 17 (Supplement), nos. 775A and 827A, diary notes by W. de Groot, 2 August 1622 and 18–21 April 1623.

[11] *BW* 10, no. 4346, to W. de Groot, 22 October 1639. The original file containing Grotius's poetry is lost. Only the poems which Grotius happened to cite in the letters printed in the *Epistolae quotquot reperiri potuerunt* (Amsterdam, 1687; *BG* no. 1210) have been preserved. Cf. A. Eyffinger, *Inventory of the Poetry of Hugo Grotius* (Assen, 1982), xliii–li. A survey of the poetry to be published in the *Poemata Nova*: Eyffinger, *Inventory*, 54, 57–58; cf. 221–233.

[12] *BW* 12, nos. 5340 and 5375, to Willem de Groot, 31 August and [21] September 1641. On Ludwig Camerarius see O. Schutte, *Repertorium der buitenlandse vertegenwoordigers, residerende in Nederland 1584–1810* (The Hague, 1983), 488–489, and F. H. Schubert, *Ludwig Camerarius (1573–1651). Eine Biographie* (Kallmünz, 1955), esp. 387–409.

financier notorious for his arrogance and impetuousness, who took advantage of his wealth to get ahead:

> Κλαῖε Δαημοσύνη Καμεράριον εἰσορόωσα,
> Πλοῦτος ὅτι φρενοπληξ εἰο πλέον δύναται.

After a little while Willem confirmed receipt of the poem. He even translated it into Latin:

> Doctrina aspectu Camerarî percita plorat,
> Vis sua quod gazis est minor illicibus.

He realised that publication of the Greek epigram could not but harm the reputation of Spiring. Therefore he thought it wise to keep it to himself until further notice.[13] Whereupon Grotius told Willem that Spiring had no knowledge of Greek; neither would there be anyone to translate it for him. Nevertheless, he agreed to postpone the decision on publication until the *Poemata Nova* was ready for the press.[14]

Another poem sent to Willem was on Cardinal Jules Mazarin(i). It stressed the power and influence of the king's minister, who in a short period of time had managed to get France firmly in his grip and thus follow in the footsteps of his illustrious namesake:

> Ut Gallos domuit Romanus Julius armis,
> Romanus Gallos Julius arte domat.[15]

Honorific poems addressed to Grotius were also put in this file. At the end of a letter dated 12th June 1637, Grotius quoted a panegyric presented to him by a French gentleman, whose identity is unknown to us:

> (Galli nobilis epigramma:)
> Gallia, Scaligerum dederas male sana Batavis,
>   Grotiaden reddit terra Batava tibi.
> Ingratam expertus patriam venerandus uterque est,
>   Felix mutato erit uterque solo.

Like a second anonymous poem in the same vein, the lines quoted above are the poetic articulation of an idea first put into words by the French scholar Nicolas-Claude

---

[13] *BW* 12, no. 5394, from Willem de Groot, 30 September 1641.

[14] *BW* 12, no. 5412, to Willem de Groot, 12 October 1641: "Sensum epigrammatis abs te video bene perceptum. Ille, quem innuis, Graeca non intelligit et vix puto fore qui ei id interpretetur. Sed edine hoc epigramma an inter nos clausum teneri debeat, videbimus, ubi edentur poemata."

[15] *BW* 14, no. 6543, to Willem de Groot, 21 November 1643.

Fabri de Peiresc.[16] Grotius was very pleased with the subject of the poem. At that moment he was serving as the ambassador of the Swedish Crown in Paris and never tired of stressing that by entering Swedish service he had renounced his old native country.[17] Some years later he cited in a letter to Willem[18] the first lines of a eulogy by Lucius Cary, second Viscount Falkland, published in the English translation of the *Christus patiens*, a biblical drama that Grotius had first published in 1608:[19]

> Our Ages wonder, by thy birth the Fame
> Of Belgia, by thy banishment the Shame.

Grotius even elaborated on this theme in a funerary poem that he composed for himself in 1641. After his death it should be clear to everyone who passed his grave that he had long since broken off relations with Holland:

> Grotius hic Hugo est, Batavûm captivus et exul,
>   Legatus regni, Suedia magna, tui.[20]

Willem collected all Hugo's poems, but publication in a volume of *Poemata Nova* was never achieved. Compared with the other publishing projects, this Neo-Latin poetry was of minor importance. That is why an outsider like the famous Dutch poet

---

[16] *BW* 8, no. 3114, to Willem de Groot, 12 June 1637. Cf. Levesque de Burigny, *Vie de Grotius avec l'histoire de ses ouvrages* . . . (Amsterdam, 1754), 1:140–141, 2:203. Burigny gives another poem, written by A. Buchnerus, cited in *Vind[iciae] Grot[ianae]* (= *Hugonis Grotii, Belgarum Phoenicis, Manes ab iniquis obtrectationibus vindicati* . . . [Delft, 1727], 1:237) (with a reference to Augustus Buchnerus, *Poemata selectiora, nunc primum edita* . . . [Leipzig and Frankfurt, 1694; 2nd ed. 1720], 616):

> Gallia magnanimis dedit exorata Batavis
>   Dis geniti aeternum Scaligeri ingenium.
> Fallor an humanis male dura Batavia Gallis
>   Scaligerum magno reddidit in Grotio?

See also Pierre Gassendi, *Viri illustris Nicolai Claudii Fabricii de Peiresc, senatoris Aquisextiensis, vita*, in idem, *Opera Omnia* (Lyon, 1658; repr. Stuttgart-Bad Cannstatt, 1964), 5:289 (year 1621): ". . . tanti illum [Grotium] ducebat, ut in vicem Scaligeri affertum Galliae diceret. . . ."

[17] Cf. *BW* 8, nos. 2991 and 3148, to J. Witten, 12 March 1637 ("Suediae totum me dedi, Suedus sum adoptione animoque toto . . .") and 3 July 1637 ("Ego . . . regno Suedico me sine exceptione, sine ullo alio versum respectu tradidi . . .").

[18] *BW* 10, no. 4405, to Willem de Groot, 26 November 1639.

[19] Hugo Grotius, *Christs passion. A tragedie. With annotations* (London, 1640) (*BG* no. 43) [a5v]–[a7v]: "To the author." On Viscount Falkland (1610?–1643) see *Dictionary of National Biography* 9 (London, 1887), 246–251, and J. Tanner, *Lucius Cary, Viscount Falkland, Cavalier and Catalyst* (Ilford, Essex, 1974), esp. 5–6.

[20] *BW* 12, no. 5084, to Willem de Groot, 2 March 1641. Cf. Levesque de Burigny, *Vie de Grotius*, 2:77.

Constantijn Huygens will not have had any knowledge of Grotius's poem.[21] In 1644 Huygens presented Grotius with a copy of his own collection, entitled *Momenta desultoria*. At that time the relationship between the two poets was rather tense, as Huygens had twice attacked Grotius in anonymous poems. And then, suddenly, Grotius was praised as the best of Batavians, as can be seen from the following epigram:

> (Ad Grotium cum libro:)
> Grotiadae, summo Batavorum Belga Batavûm
> Infimus haec dono dat, dicat Hugenius.[22]

Grotius was not impressed by this eulogy. He reacted with an epigram in his own hand. We, the editors of his correspondence, had no knowledge of this poem when we were editing the letters dating from this period in his life. Willem de Groot, on the other hand, must have had a chance to see it, since he referred to it in one of his letters, saying that he could not understand why this poem of Grotius's contained such a sad farewell.[23]

As I discovered recently, the poem, unfortunately not complete, has been preserved by sheer coincidence. It will surprise no one that Willem plays an important part in the story of the circumstances under which the poem has come down to us.

Willem's readiness to help did not come to an end with Grotius's death in 1645. Unfortunately, it cannot be established how Willem coped with the death of his beloved brother. While still residing in The Hague, he managed to get by as far as it was possible for a close relative of one of the most controversial statesmen of the Republic.[24] In the meantime he was constantly reminded of Hugo Grotius, as the correspondence shows. At one point somewhere about 1616 one of his correspondents, Janus Casparius Gevartius,[25] had been given the opportunity to look at the manu-

---

[21] The court preacher André Rivet must, however, have been acquainted with the text, since he published his own version, alluding to Grotius's dismissal from Swedish service in 1645: A. Rivet, *Grotianae discussionis* ΔΙΑΛΥΣΙΣ. *Sive Vindiciae Apologetici sui, pro vera pace ecclesiae, contra subdolos mediatores* . . . (Rotterdam, 1646), 11:

> Grotius hic situs est, Batavûm captivus et exul,
> Regni exlegatus, Suedia magna, tui.

[22] Constantijn Huygens, *Momenta desultoria, poematum libri XI, edente Caspare Barlaeo* (Leiden, 1644); *BW* 15, no. 6977, from Willem de Groot, 25 July 1644; J. A. Worp, *De gedichten van Constantijn Huygens, naar zijn handschrift uitgegeven* (Groningen, 1892–1899), 3:299. Cf. H. J. M. Nellen, "Een Haags dichter over 'de Delftse Cicero'. Hugo Grotius in de brieven en gedichten van Constantijn Huygens," *De Zeventiende Eeuw* 3 (1987): 125–137.

[23] *BW* 15, no. 6984, dated 30 July 1644: "Tuum epigramma Hugeniano oppositum cur triste illud vale contineat nescio, et quid hoc responsi sit ignoro."

[24] Cf. Schutte, *Repertorium*, 551.

[25] From 27 September 1621 onwards Janus Casparius Gevartius (Jean-Gaspard Gevaerts) was registrar ("graphiarius," "griffier") of Antwerp; cf. *BW* 2, no. 711, from W. de Groot, 15 December 1621. He was the son of Jean Gevaerts, secretary ("secretaris") of Turnhout: see below, nn. 27, 29.

script of Grotius's *Annales et Historiae*.²⁶ Much later, in April 1656, that is, before the appearence of the first edition of this historical work, he sent a correction,²⁷ together with copies of letters by Grotius which were to be published in a posthumous collection like the *Epistolae ad Gallos*,²⁸ now to be called *Epistolae ad Belgas*.²⁹

What is quite remarkable is the fact that another correspondent, Dirck Graswinckel, who years before had assisted Grotius in editing his classic *De iure belli ac pacis*, approached Willem de Groot in 1661³⁰ with the request to explain a passage in a letter from 8 April 1637,³¹ which had been published meanwhile in the *Epistolae ad Gallos* (468).³² It was in this passage that Grotius had reminded Fabri de Peiresc of his "Vandalica et Gothica", a collection of texts by Procopius among others, which testified to the ancestry of the Swedish kingdom. This work, entitled *Historia Gotthorum*,³³ appeared in 1655 at the prompting of Isaac Vossius. It clearly served a political purpose: ancient roots of a state were an important criterion in determining its position in the diplomatic hierarchy of Europe. In his letter Grotius tells us that he was preparing this edition of historical sources "in honorem gentis, cui me in adoptionem dedi, a patria ter venundatus. Nosti legem XII tabularum." According to a rule in the Twelve Tables, a father should lose his paternal rights once he has offered his son for sale three times: "Si pater filium ter venum duuit [duit], filius a patre liber esto."³⁴

---

²⁶ Amsterdam 1657 (*BG* no. 741).

²⁷ The editors of the *Annales et Historiae* ignored the correction. Gevartius proposed to change the description "scriba Turnotanus" (*Annales et Historiae* [Amsterdam, 1657], 501), given to his father Jean Gevaerts, into "iurisconsultus." Jean Gevaerts was involved in the negotiations connected with the Twelve Years' Truce (1609–1621).

²⁸ Leiden 1648, second edition Leiden 1650 (*BG* nos. 1213–1214).

²⁹ MS. The Hague, ARA, Eerste afd., Aanw. 1911 XXIII, no. 33, Janus Casparius Gevartius to Willem de Groot, Antwerp, 24 April 1656: "Doleo equidem ob praefestinum ex hac urbe discessum tuum non licuisse mihi diutius frui optatissima consuetudine tua, in qua fraternam Hugonis Magni agnovi. Mitto eiusdem ad me epistolarum apographa. Si litterae eius ad Belgas quandoque prodibunt, perhonorificum mihi putabo et istas ibi legi. In Historia Belgica, — quam ante annos quadraginta Roterodami mihi exhibuit — , circa finem, ubi de primis Duodecennalium Induciarum fundamentis agit, et parentis mei ac D. Walravi Wittenhorstii mentionem facit, memini scriptum ibi esse 'Joannes Gevart[i]us, scriba Turnotanus.' Vellem obiter mutari et substitui: 'Joannes Gevartius, iurisconsultus'." Cf. MS. Leiden, University Library, BPL 214, fol. 9, Gevartius to [Pieter de Groot], 7 February 1650.

³⁰ MS. The Hague, ARA, Eerste afd., Aanw. 1911 XXIII, no. 33, from Dirck (Theodorus) Graswinckel, 26/27 August 1661. On Graswinckel (1600–1666) see D. P. M. Graswinckel, *Graswinckel. Geschiedenis van een Delfts brouwers- en regenten-geslacht* (The Hague, 1956), 90–117.

³¹ *BW* 8, no. 3016.

³² Graswinckel consulted the first edition of the *Epistolae ad Gallos* (Leiden, 1648; *BG* no. 1213).

³³ *Historia Gotthorum, Vandalorum et Langobardorum* (Amsterdam, 1655) (*BG* no. 735). Cf. F. F. Blok, *Isaac Vossius en zijn kring. Zijn leven tot zijn afscheid van koningin Christina van Zweden 1618–1655* (Groningen, 1999), 466–469.

³⁴ *Fontes iuris Romani antiqui*, 1: *Leges et negotia*, ed. C. G. Bruns et al., 7th ed. (Tübingen, 1909), 22, cited in Ulpian (*Fragmenta in Digestis aliisve collectionibus servata* 10.1) and Gaius (*Institutiones* 1.132).

Now, in 1661, Willem de Groot was asked by Graswinckel to explain this "ter venundatus". He himself could only think of the fact that Grotius had been condemned in 1619 to lifelong imprisonment and that he had been forced, after a short return from exile, to flee from Holland in 1632 because a price had been put on his head. A third case, however, was a puzzle to him. He only knew that Grotius had allied himself to Sweden. By way of proof he then cited a distich taken from a lost letter by Grotius to Joachim de Wicquefort.[35] Without any doubt this is the poem in which Grotius reacted to the donation of the *Momenta desultoria*, but unfortunately Graswinckel cited it only in part. Instead of the first syllables of the pentameter he placed only a few dots, perhaps because he had trouble deciphering Grotius's cramped handwriting:

> Grotius est Suecus, neque iam plus Belga, Batavis
> — — — — longum Huygenioque vale.[36]

We do not know what answer Willem de Groot gave to Graswinckel. Supposing that he did not fill in the dots himself, he must in any case have tried to explain the passage "ter venundatus" by mentioning that Grotius had been condemned three

---

[35] Joachim de Wicquefort (1596–1670), resident of Hessen-Kassel in the Dutch Republic, was involved in the distribution of Huygens's *Momenta desultoria*. Grotius received a copy from Wicquefort. Cf. *De briefwisseling van Constantijn Huygens (1608–1687)*, 4 (*1644–1649*), ed. J. A. Worp (The Hague, 1915), 33–34, H. Bruno to C. Huygens, 11 August 1644, and *De briefwisseling van Pieter Corneliszoon Hooft*, III (*1638–1647*), ed. H. W. van Tricht (Culemborg, 1979), 605, P. C. Hooft to C. Barlaeus, 12 August 1644; according to this last letter, Huygens had already received Grotius's poem in response: "T'onzer eerste bijeenkoomste verwacht ik ujt U.Eed. te hooren, oft de H. van Zuilichem zelf zijne gedichten aan den H. de Groot heeft gezonden, en wat U.Eed. gevoelen is van de twee veirskens daarop te rug gekoomen."

[36] The passage in Graswinckel's letter (above, n. 30) reads as follows: "Si vales, valeo; quod vel probent ipsae hae importunae nostrae, quibus molestiam tibi oggerit cum mea curiositas, tum et memoriae defectus. Ut autem ne cum Plautino servo [Plautus, *Epidicus* 2] odio hic ne nimium sim familiaris, in humanitate tua positum nosti. Curiositas mea versatur circa locum ex epistola beatissimae memoriae fratris tui, nostri cognati. Sic ille ad Nicolaum Peirescium — habetur in Epist. ad Gall. p. 468 — : 'Verti in Latinum sermonem Gothica et Vandalica, in honorem gentis cui me in adoptionem dedi ter venundatus. Nosti legem XII tabularum.' Bis venundatum et, cum — summa quidem cum iniuria — eam tulere sententiam quae nec illo nomine digna sit, scio, cumque item offerentem ab omni reipub[licae] administratione segregem vitam agere in patria non admisere, habitum pro reiectaneo, at tertio venum datus quod sit, nec factum scio, nec factum fuisse dici quo tempore potuerit aut possit, assequor. Scies tu id me — non dubito — melius; si placet, explica. Quod se Suecis adoptandum dederit, colligere potui ex illo quod sua manu ad Vicofortem scripsit:

> Grotius est Suecus, neque iam plus Belga, Batavis
> - - - - longum Huygenioque vale.

Non inaudivi tamen obtinuisse eo nomine diploma aliquod illius coronae aut reginae. Alterum est, quod nec teneam, cum ad manum hic non habeam [habeatur?] l[eges] XII tabularum, in quam legem verba ista intendantur. Sodes, et hoc me fasce leva."

times: apart from his conviction in 1619 and his expulsion in 1632, he was condemned a third time in a proclamation by the States-General of 24 November 1622 for publishing the *Verantwoordingh*.[37] Of course, I have looked for this poem in the estate of Constantijn Huygens, but I have not been able to find it. If this poem was indeed meant as a response, the full version might have been the following:

> Grotius est Suecus neque iam plus Belga, Batavis
>   [Nunc reddit] longum Huygenioque vale.[38]

I would be very much obliged to anyone who could offer me Grotius's authentic version.

Constantijn Huygens Instituut

---

[37] The text in C. Brandt and A. van Cattenburgh, *Historie van het leven des heeren Huig de Groot* (Dordrecht and Amsterdam, 1727), 1:302–303. Cf. *BG* no. 885 rem. 2.

[38] Professor Dirk Sacré (Leuven) helped me to fill in the missing words; he furthermore suggested the following alternatives: 'Iam mittit', 'Nunc dicit', 'Nunc mittit', and 'Exul ait'. Dr. Harm-Jan van Dam suggested: 'Dicit iam' and 'Dicit per', Dr. A. Eyffinger 'Dic igitur'.

Lusus *quidam* Westmonasterienses *ab oblivione nunc vindicandi: Appendix sive Contemporaneas res bina per saecula (1704–1905) orbe toto terrarum feliciter gestas quam lepide nonnulli poetae Londinienses Latinis versibus singulas usque depinxerint*

KARL AUGUST NEUHAUSEN

Neo-Latinam poesin, quam saeculis decimo sexto septimoque in cunctis Britanniae quoque regionibus reviruisse et deinde Cantabrigiae simul Oxoniique a duobus fere milibus poetarum esse constat excultam, ne vicesimo quidem ineunte vigere saeculo desiisse cum alii testantur auctores admodum multi, qui Musarum imbuti litteris Anglicanarum Victoriana floruerunt aetate, tum eo volumine carminum comprobatur, quod plus quam quadringentas et viginti paginas continens a. 1906 Londinii prodiit inscriptum *Lusus alteri Westmonasterienses sive Prologi et Epilogi ad fabulas in St. Petri Collegio actas collecti et iusta annorum serie ordinati. Quibus accedit Epigrammatum et Carminum delectus. Pars tertia* (1866–1905). Etenim copiosissima versuum haecce collectio claudit agmen illud uniforme collectaneorum trium, quibus duo per saecula deinceps inde ab a. 1704 usque poemata in collegio Westmonasteriensi celeberrima praeter Etonensem schola Britannorum publica Latino sermone condita comprehenduntur quorumque hodie paene prorsus oblitteratorum fundamenta iam Robertus Prior iecerat, cum a. 1730 primus *Lusus Westmonasterienses* divulgavit.

Est igitur hac mihi relatione propositum exemplis illustribus demonstrare selectis alterius *Lusuum Westmonasteriensium* editionis tertiam partem eandemque postremam — quod quidem opus collectaneis prioribus singulis (quorum unum a. 1863, altera quadriennio post erat emissum) ambitu praestat, vi momentoque vix cedit — contemporanea serie talium textuum Latinorum, quales in utraque universitate totius Angliae notissima compositi tum exstitisse traduntur, haud esse minoris putandam.

Quoniam haec eadem oratio die 4° m. Aug. a. 2000° inter eum habita conventum, quem undecimum Societas Internationalis Studiis Neolatinis Provehendis Cantabrigiae apud Britannos curaverat celebrandum, iam est publici facta iuris,[1] expedit profecto nunc — ut ibidem promisi — selectos textus eosdem, quos illo tempore nimis obtuli decurtatos, quam integerrimos huc afferre, quo facilius fusiusque retractentur, quam tum propter suppeditati mihi spatii penuriam licuit. Nam primum quidem, quaecumque Anglica voce carminibus florilegii Latinis aut inseri voluerunt editores aut addi notis seorsus adiectis, necesse me fuit praetermittere singula. Deinde trium in Plauti Terentiique fabulas epilogorum, quos e ducentis iisdemque excellentibus fere tunc eligendos decrevi, unum dumtaxat et id quidem anni 1872 exemplar paene totum potuit Latino saltem incolumi velut tenore praeberi, sed utriusque reliqui lusus exordium tantummodo typis rursus excusum est.

Itaque primi illius speciminis secundam partem, cuius medium obtinet locum Carolus Marx vir famosissimus, immutatum huc transferre constitui; ceteros autem duos lusus, quorum posterior est ultimus epilogorum totius anthologiae Westmonasteriensis, ita citabo, ut exhibeatur litterarum tanta congeries, quantam in conventu quidem illo Cantabrigiensi neglegere debui, sed in eiusdem Actis hisce permissam editoris H. Hofmann benignitate summa sum situs praesentare, ne parum niterent aut omnino denique evanescerent cum illa Latinae poeseos ipsius vigentis exemplaria tum eorundem commentarii perpetuis insignes adnotationibus vernaculo sermone confectis, quae documenta artis doctrinaeque litterariae tam splendida tot auctores Britannici colenda posteris tradidissent.

Exemplum I: Epilogus in Adelphos (1872)
Textus: *Lusus alteri Westmonasterienses*, pars 3 (1906), 38–43

Dramatis personae: Demea; Micio; Aeschinus; Ctesipho; Syrus; Sannio; Hegio; Sostrata (cum Anna); Canthara; Geta; Dromo; Parmeno

Secunda pars (41 s.) addito tertiae partis initio:

(*Enter three Internationals with Phrygian caps and paper and penny ink-pots.*)
                        DEM. Ohe!
      Isti sceptrigeri praedones terga dederunt!
          Nos vacuas sellas sumimus! Omen inest!
      Tempestive actum! nam nostrum est munus avitis
          De soliis reges trudere legitimos!
      Reges ac leges nos pellimus, ab-que-rogamus;
          Sunt pestes ambo. PAR. Tertia Religio est.
      Sartores tres en! convenimus! Internati-
          onales, necnon Κοσμοπολιτ-άθεοι

---

[1] Commentationem hanc ipsius praelectionis vice continent *Humanistica Lovaniensia* 50 (2001).

	Quantum inter nosmet nebulones distet et illos
	Non multis opus est dicere. SYR. Non opus est.
DEM.	Conventus noster toto hinc memorabilis orbe
	Dicetur; nos et posteri honore colent.
	Karl Mag. notus erat — Karl Marx,[2] mihi crede, futurus
	Notior in terris. PAR. (*aside*). Imperitare cupit?
DEM.	Nostra πολιτείας nova fundamenta tenetis.
SYR.	De paucis dubito. DEM. Clarius expediam.
	Audi jam — Imprimis omnis tibi simplice et uno
	Principio innixa est Res Socialis! PAR. Ita est.
DEM.	Si proprium, quid habes, fur rite es habendus et exlex;
SYR.	Vix capio — tiro sum — mea non mea sunt?
DEM.	Nil quicquam — Domina est Respublica. SYR. Quam pretio emi,
	Parva casa haud juris, quaeso, futura mei est?
DEM.	Non, inquam — rerum *nudus* permittitur usus:
	Possideas aliquid, fortiter id vetitum!
	Est modus in censu: sunt fines denique: acervus
	Crescit? at extemplo diminuendus erit.
	Cur dives quisquam existat me paupere? juris
	Hoc est communis; vox ea sacra valet.
	Omnino ex oculis hominum, descripta "meum" inter
	"Atque tuum" quondam, linea disperiit.
	Quippe agri, fundique, molae, fabricaeque, fodinae,
	Consolidatum aes, et quicquid ubique lucri est,
	Conflentur norma, quae vulgo dicitur Hotchpot;
	Divisum id cives convenienter alet.
PAR.	Audito hoc, ingens Gracchi laetabitur Umbra,
	Se vinci tandem fassa, dabitque manus.
DEM.	Immo — (*enter three Policemen*). PAR. Extra licitam sic an potabitis horam,[3]
	Audaces? moniti jam estis! abite cito!
	Vos propria excipiat "Cavum et Angulus",[4] ut vocitatur,
	Jam "caupona"! move te ocius!
	(*Exeunt, followed by Police. Enter three strong-minded females in masculine attire.*)

---

[2] Heinrich Karl Marx, one of the chief exponents of modern Socialism, born at Trèves in 1818, was the son of a Jew who was converted and had his family baptized as Christian Protestants. The first volume of his work on Capital — *Das Kapital, Kritik der politischen Ökonomie* — was published at Hamburg in 1867. He lived mainly in London during the latter part of his life and died in 1883.

[3] The Licensing Act which required public-houses to be closed at midnight was passed this year.

[4] The Hole and Corner.

SOS. Anna soror,
Salveto! ANN. et tu! SAX. et tu! SOS. Placet aula haec; prorsus amicas
Nos hic conventus, colloquiumque juvant.

Exemplum II: Epilogus in Phormionem (1902)
Textus: *Lusus alteri Westmonasterienses*, pars 3 (1906), 243–250

Scene: A University

Dramatis personae
Geta	A proctor
Phaedria	A scholarship
Davus	An official poet
Nausistrata	An American mother
Phormio	A millionaire
Demipho	A public orator
Chremes	A politician: Lord Rector
Hegio,	
Cratinus,	
Crito	Distinguished generals on tour
Dorio	A martial poet
Antipho	A School-Inspector
Sophrona	A gipsy

Post duas priores istius scaenae partes absolutas, simul ac Nausistrata nimis arroganter Americam ceteris rebus omnibus censuit anteponendam, eundem lusum poetae Westmonasterienses contexere hoc modo pergunt:

(*Exit NAUSISTRATA: Enter PHORMIO.*)
PHO.   Dic, hospes, cuius domus? GET. Haec collegia nostrae
          Sunt Academiae. PHO. (*aside*). Conicio, haec ego emam.
GET.   Aspicis, en, opus hoc Rhodii praegrande Colossi.[5]
PHO.   Magnificum est! (*aside*) et mox, conicio, meum erit.
       Dic, quanti est? GET. Quanti? quid vis, insane? quid audes?
          Hoc non venale est. PHO. Si quid habere volo,
            Illud emo: mea maxima per pontum organa vadunt
              Stellae Albae:[6] omnis merx nicotiana mea est,

---

[5] Mr. Cecil Rhodes by his will gave a large sum to his old college, Oriel, and established scholarships to be held at Oxford by Colonial and foreign students. He died 26 March 1902, aged forty-eight.

[6] At this time much alarm was caused by the fact that the White Star Line of Trans-Atlantic steamers had been purchased by an American Syndicate.

| | Et ferrum et carnes: ego cur, acquirere pauca |
| | Si possum, invideor? conicio, haec mea sunt. |

(*Exit PHORMIO.*)

GET. O fortunatos nimium, sua si loca norint,
 Americos! caelum mox, ut opinor, ement:
 Iam pridem in Tamesim Americus defluxit Ohio.
 O dolor! O hominum credula simplicitas!

(*Enter DEMIPHO and CHREMES with HEGIO, CRATINUS, and CRITO.*)

 Hei mihi, quos video? CHR. Sine me introducere claros
 Ductores.[7] Tu dic, Hegio. HEG. (*holding out his hat*). Mene rogas?

GET. Attat! quid quaeris? HEG. Quaerenda pecunia primum est.
 Nil das? Nonne luis vota? CHR. Age, fare, Crito.

CRA. De lare, de fundis manet anxia cura perustis.

CHR. Ultima nunc tecum verba, Cratine, manent.

CRA. De vetita nobis nunc libertate querendum est,
 O cives, cives. GET. Tu mihi civis? CRA. Ego.

HEG. Gallus apud Gallos. CRI. Germanus apud Germanos.

CRA. Inter vos igitur nonne Brittannus ero?

GET. Hem, quot sunt homines, tot gentes. HEG. Omnia fio
 Omnibus. DEM. At mos est, Hegio, cuique suus:
 Sunt qui dant nummos, sunt qui dant verba. Sed ite,
 Armaque pro patria sumite fida nova.

(*DEMIPHO bows the Advocates out.*)

 Nunc res nostra manet. CHR. (*climbing on to a fence*) De muro dicere
 malo.[8]
 Sum Libertatis verus amicus ego.

DEM. Tune? ubi sis nescis. GET. (*aside*) Hic iam locus est mihi nullus:
 Privata est haec lis (*exit*). CHR. Sit mihi cura meam
 Rem defendere. DEM. Abi, defensor! iungere ad utras
 Te partes mavis? CHR. (*aside*) Improbus ille abiit
 Deseruitque tabernaculum: quo denique vertar?
 Illuc me Imperium, huc Anglia parva vocat.
 (*to DEMIPHO*) Sed nostrum sub ovile, oro te, nonne redibis?

DEM. Numquam: tute phylacteria solus habe.
 A te sum definite disiunctus: at et mi
 Libertas cara est, sed simul Imperium.

(*Re-enter PHORMIO.*)

CHR. At saltem maneo dux hic. PHO. Mi ignosce, ego dux sum;
 Veni, vidi, emi; haec sunt mea, tuque meus.

(*CHREMES falls from fence at PHORMIO's feet.*)

---

[7] Three Boer leaders (Botha, De Wet, and Prinzloo) came to London this year on a mission.
[8] Sir Henry Campbell-Bannerman was described as "sitting on the fence."

DEM. Humptius in muro residebat Dumptius olim;
　　　　　　　Humptius at praeceps Dumptius hinc cecidit.
　　　　　Non dux sum, at maneo hic orator publicus. CHR. Id non
　　　　　　　Nescimus; surgis saepius atque ululas,
　　　　　Emergens subito veluti Ioannis ab arca.
DEM. 　　　Publica privatus iam loquor ex cathedra:
　　　　　Strenuitas[9] rebus sit in omnibus; omnia quisque
　　　　　　　Efficiat. PHO. Ventus, praetereaque nihil.
DEM. Purgatis tabulis demum efficientia fiet.
PHO. 　　　Non opus est mihi te. DEM. Non opus? ergo abeo,
　　　　　Quo possim solus solum mihi findere sulcum. (*Exit.*)
CHR. 　　　Ut doleo te non posse manere: vale.
(*Re-enter PHAEDRIA and GETA with DORIO.*)
PHO. Quid tibi vis? PHA. Academiam hanc intrare scholaris
　　　　　　　Quaero equidem; athletis aptus hic esse locus
　　　　　Dicitur. PHO. Egregiam laudem et spolia ampla reportes!
DOR. 　　　En Academiae gloria! PHO. At unde venis?
　　　　　Cuius et auspiciis? PHA. Me ad vos Australia misit.
DOR. 　　　Hic iuvenes nostros nobilis arte pilae
　　　　　Vicit delectos — et iam cupit esse scholaris.
PHA. 　　　Moralis virtus est mihi magna. PHO. Bene est.
DOR. Sunt quibus in satira videor nimis acer; at istis
　　　　　　　Non equidem athletis morigerare volo.
　　　　　Debemur Marti nos nostraque: tollite ludos:
　　　　　　　Sed laudo pedites et placet acer eques.
CHR. Tu moderaris equos qui non moderaberis irae?
PHA. 　　　Ni fallor, tibi erit ludere folle bonum.
DOR. Folle mihi! PHA. Sic. DOR. Lanigeri stulti! lutulenti[10]
　　　　　　　O fatui! PHO. Audire hunc non operae pretium est.
　　　　　Explorare velim quid noveris. GET. Heus, cape chartam.
PHA. 　　　Scribere non possum. DOR. Discipulus probus est!
PHO. Viva voce igitur tibi fac respondeat. GET. Esto:
　　　　　　　Scisne mathematicam? PHA. Plusve minusve. GET. Duo
　　　　　Et duo quot faciunt? responde. PHA. Quinque. DOR. Satisne
　　　　　　　Sanus es? GET. Euclides quis fuit? PHA. Id facile est:
　　　　　Repperit is lusum Pontis, quem ludimus omnes.[11]

---

[9] Lord Rosebery was at this time proclaiming the need of "efficiency" in the management of the state.

[10] "Flannelled fools" and "muddied oafs", contemptuous names applied to cricketers and footballers by Rudyard Kipling in a poem lately published.

[11] Now that Euclid has almost disappeared from English schools it is worth while to record that the difficult proposition Euclid 1.5 was called "pons asinorum". The reference shifts thus to the game of Bridge, then much in vogue.

DOR.	Tu, pol, non compos mentis. GER. Inepte puer!
PHA.	Nonne erat Euclidis famosus pons asinorum?
	Quattuor, ecce, sumus! ludere visne? PHO. Volo.
	(*to DORIO*) Divide tu chartas. DOR. Linquo. PHO. Placet esse triumphos
	Nullos. PHA. An ducam? GET. Scilicet. PHA. Interii!
	Quattuor en unae; reges quoque quattuor, et tres
	Reginae! GET. Lusum est: vincimur. PHA, O facinus!
	Omne tulit punctum qui chartas miscuit. Actum est:
	Sum fractus: quid agam nescio. GET. Novi equidem:
	(*indicating DORIO*) Educat hic pueros, ut mox educat in Afros.
DOR.	(*to PHAEDRIA*) Me sequere, atque armis fac cito des operam.
	Doctrina ut desit, tamen est laudanda voluntas.
(*Enter ANTIPHO.*)	
	Inspector vobis nempe cavendus erit.
(*Exeunt DORIO and PHAEDRIA.*)	
ANT.	Inspicienda mihi nunc est schola vestra; videndum est
	Num bene discipulos edoceatis. PHO. Eho,
	Unde tua id refert? ANT. Mihi lata rogatio nuper
	De doctrina.[12] PHO. Ast hic nil ditionis habes.
ANT.	An tu dissentis? CHR. Nobis mens conscia recti est;
	Nonconformistae nos sumus. PHO. Atque mihi
	Credita iam haec Academia est. ANT. Qui credita? PHO. Nescis
	Quanta sit in nummis vis posita Americis?
ANT.	Mercatura mihi non curae est; rebus in istis
	Infans sum:[13] sed non vestra probanda schola est.
PHO.	Arthure O princeps, seu Clara libentius audis,
	Infans es sane: nobile par eritis:
(*pointing to CHREMES*)	
	Scoticus hic infandus erit, tu Scoticus infans.
ANT.	Irritor: iuvenes colligam ut exagitem. (*Exit.*)
(*Re-enter DEMIPHO with SOPHRONA.*)	
DEM.	Non sum qualis eram. CHR. Quantum mutatus ab illo
	Oratore! PHO. Sed haec, quaeso, puella, quis est?
SOP.	Hunc monui palmam inspiciens quae fata manerent.
DEM.	Ah, nimium verum est. SOP. Fata redire iubent.
DEM.	Est depressa agri cultura, et gaudia desunt
	Quae solus sulcus praebuit; ergo iterum

---

[12] The Education Act of 1902.

[13] "I am a child in such matters," a famous saying of Mr. A. J. Balfour in a financial discussion. Mr. Balfour, then Prime Minister, was depicted in the Westminster Gazette as "Clara in Blunderland."

| | Orator fieri cupio. PHO. Me forte docebis |
| | Quae me sors maneat. Sed quis hic est strepitus? |

(*Re-enter HEGIO, CRATINUS, and CRITO with volunteers.*)

HEG. State! aciem duplicate! in frontem! lumina dextra!
   Lumina prae! placidi sistite! SOP. Macte, senex,
   Macte nova virtute armisque! HEG. Attendite! praesint
     Arma! inclinate arma! accelerate gradum!
   State! SOP. Ut vos metuent hostes, pavidisque cadet cor![14]
CHR.   Arripite hunc. CRI. (*trying to arrest PHO.*) Res est magna. PHO.
                        Goliath adest.
   (*to CHREMES*) An tu barbaricis rationibus uteris ipse,[15]
     Qui mala militibus dicere probra soles?
CHR.   Mene ea quae dico facere! at removere tyrannos
     Atque Academiam rursus habere volo.
PHO.   Sed mea dicatur fortuna. SOP. Age, porrige palmam.[16]
     Americus tu non amplius esse potes.
PHO.   Caelum, non patriam, mutant qui trans mare currunt.
GET.   Palmistarum artem lex vetat. SOP. Haud timeo.
   Sum dives; non lex eadem stat ditibus atque
     Pauperibus. (*To PHORMIO*) Quid tu? numquid inesse novi
   Mente tua sentis? PHO. Mirum est! iam me esse Brittannum
     Sentio, et exclamo "Surge, Brittannia," ego.
GET.   Ergo novum civem nos accipiamus, amici,
     Immemores veteris nunc inimicitiae.
OMNES (*singing*) Nam, quamvis fuerit temptatio magna, tenebat
     Natio non alia hunc ulla; Brittannus hic est.[17]
PHO.   (*advancing*) Sic maneam, maneatque Brittannia tota Brittannis,
     Et sumat partes haec schola nostra suas.
   Iam post tres annos renovamus ludicra; rursus
     Percurrunt nostri pulpita nota pedes.
   Interea subiere vices; bella, horrida bella
     Ceperunt finem; Pax sua regna novat:
   Iam schola nostra novi iurare in verba Magistri
     Est assueta; novus deinde Decanus adest:

---

[14] A cadet corps, attached to the Inns of Court R.V., was established at Westminster in 1902.

[15] Sir Henry Campbell-Bannerman had said that the British troops in South Africa were using "methods of barbarism."

[16] Palmistry was a good deal in fashion. There were amateurs at charity bazaars, and professionals sought for custom by advertisements. Various devices were tried to elude the law against fortune-telling.

[17] For in spite of all temptations
   To belong to other nations
   He remained an Englishman." (W. S. Gilbert's *H.M.S. Pinafore*)

Dicimus his "salvete": Domus sit cura fovere
    Antiquam famam, quam sine sorde gerat.
Iamque novum regem schola regia nostra salutat,
    Cui morti erepto "vivat" in Aede sonat:
Septimus Edwardus fama super aethere notus
    Vivat, et hic finis rite coronat opus:
Illi dum fidos cives producit alumnos,
    Floret, et aeternum floreat, alma Domus.

Exemplum III: Epilogus in Adelphos (1905)
Textus: *Lusus alteri Westmonasterienses*, pars 3 (1906), 273–279

Scene: The Westminster Golf Links. The last hole.
Flag marked XVIII "Domus".

Dramatis personae
Demea	A golfer
Micio	Another golfer
Geta	A caddie
Syrus	A Japanese Admiral
Dromo	A constable
Aeschinus	A motorist and Book Club Agent
Ctesipho	A Rugby football-player
Sostrata	A simple-liver, of the Hatless Brigade
Canthara	A lady swimmer
Sannio	An enthusiastic Frenchman
Hegio	The ghost of an English Admiral
Personae mutae	(A golf caddie and the ghost of an English Navy Captain)

Postquam Geta cum altero caducifero discessit, pilamalleatores eorundem domini Demea Micioque redeunt, ut ludere continuo pergant.

DEM.   (*wiping his lips*) Sic melius. Mihi certamen renovare videtur.
MIC.   Et mihi. Sed pueri quonam abiere duo?
    Et portare pares et — DEM. respondere parati.
MIC.   Arcades ambo. Heus, heus! GET. (*running up*). Adsumus. DEM. (*to MICIO*). Est tibi honor.
MIC. (*to GETA*). Da ferrum; armatus ferro tutissimus ibo.
GET.   Dirige nunc ictum: lumina fige pilae.
(*MICIO drives off*)
MIC.   A, nimium in dextram. Varium et mutabile semper
    Accipiter.[18] dubiumst quo sit itura pila

---

[18] The "Hawk" golf-ball.

         Illa. (*A shriek of pain is heard behind the stage: enter SYRUS in a fury.*)
                            SYR. Per imperium nostrum, Solisque Orientis
           Terram magnificam, perque meos proavos,
       Quis me sic tundit pilulis? in nomine Shinto
           Dic mihi. MIC. Peccavi: tu mihi da veniam:
       Factum improvisost. Sed quis tu? nonne Mikadi
           Nuntius es, nostri Nelsonis instar homo?
SYR.   Ille ego: quin veni huc, istum quod amicus amicum,
           Victorem victor, sic decorare volo.
(*Waves a laurel wreath.*)
       Sed quid tu ludis? MIC. Quod turbae "golfa" profanae
           Nomen habet, nobis nomine "goffa" placet.
DEM.   Nonne hoc novistis? numnamst tam barbara tellus?
SYR.   Immo non nobis ludere tempus erat,
       Dum minitabatur bellum: discrimine tali
           Cura est pro laribus pro patriaque mori.
       Sed nunc pax venit, nunc ludos discere multos,
           (Hocce tenes?) goffam et cetera, cura mihist.
(*A horn sounds from behind: enter AESCHINUS pursued by DROMO.*)
DRO. (*sternly*). Da numerum et nomen. AES. Quid feci? DRO. Sola per horam
           Quinque et triginta milia.[19] AES. (*indignantly*). Non potui.
       Sed ne me appelles in ius, aurum accipe densum.
DRO. (*effusively*) Accipio. AES. Currum fac tueare, precor.
(*Exit DROMO.*)
SYR.   Sed qualis tibi currus? AES. Habet duplicem ille cylindrum;
           Viginti validos viribus aequat equos:
       Nomen "Mors" dictumst vere; nam morte peremit
           Feles tres, pullos quattuor, octo canes:
       Quin et equos usque ad mortem perterruit acres,
           Et pavefecit anus decrepitosque senes.
DEM.   O monstrum! quid non motoria pectora cogis,
           Cursus sacra fames praecipitisque rotae?
SYR.   Sed quid fers? AES. Libros: libros non ulla legendi
           Nunc finis: libros *Tempora* suppeditant,[20]
       Quot quis cumque cupit gratis: mihi ferre laborist,
           Inque suburbanas distribuisse domos.
SYR. (*seeing CTESIPHO approach*). Sed quis adest? in veste filix argentea nigrast.[21]
           Quam sese ore ferens pectora quanta movet!
AES.   Credo equidem, nec vana fides, genus Antipodeum.

---

[19] The Motor Car Act, 1903, fixed the speed limit at 20 miles an hour.

[20] *The Times* had established a lending library.

[21] A team of New Zealand footballers had visited Great Britain with much success. Their jerseys were black, and were adorned with a silver fern.

Degeneres omnes arguet ille manus.
(*Enter CTESIPHO, running and passing a football from hand to hand.*)
CTE. Traicite, o comites, follem mihi passibus aequis.
Sic, sic, "tres partes"! Experientia adest.
Ast ubi, per Ditem, est "Octavae quinque"? ubi "Tergum"?
SYR. Dic qualis ludus sit tuus iste, precor.
CTE. Omnes per gentes hic ludus Ruga vocatur;
Nam leges illi Rugbia constituit.
Sed quis et unde venis, qui nescis talia! MIC. Mittit
Hunc tibi gens nobis associata fide.
CTE. Associata mihi non cordist formula: ludus
Hic semperque fuit semper eritque meus.[22]
Ludere sed voltis? OMN. Volumus. CTE. Bene. MIC. (*giving his Clubs to caddie*) Tu, puer, arma
Haec referes: nobis arbiter aequus eris.
CTE. Omnibus in partes abeundumst. Sic tibi follem
E medio pepuli: tu cape, deinde nota.
Hoc clama! o tardus nimium tu! sic data turbast!
Advenit in dextram! pellite calce pilam!
(*to AESCHINUS at half-back, who gets the ball from the scrum.*)
Traice nunc in tres partes, o traice follem,
"Dimidium tergum!" (*getting the ball*) iam mihi meta patet.
Ut capio, ut curro! (*He fumbles the ball and SYRUS gets it.*) Ut mi malus abstulit error
Follem! nunc tecum res mihi tota manet.
(*trying to collar SYRUS.*)
Ter sum conatus collo dare brachia circum,
Ter frustra refugis. Pone pilam! en habeo.
SYR. O fuscate puer, nimium ne crede colori.
(*throwing him*) En iacet en victus victor et omniniger!
MIC. Cambria, non sine dis infans animosa, corona[23]
Ipsa triumphali te decorare volet.
SYR. Arte mea hoc feci; quam si vos discere voltis,
Letalem amplexum cunctaque vos doceo.
CTE. Iupiter! ut iuvenes Iuiitsu[24] iure iuvantur!
(*getting up*) Hac arte instructus non metuam Americos:[25]
Namque agere et ruere et rapere et prosternere possim;
Frangam crura modis, brachia, colla bonis.

---

[22] This refers to the two sets of rules — the "Rugby" and the "Association" — under one or other of which football was commonly played.
[23] The only team that had beat the New Zealanders was the Welsh Fifteen.
[24] "Jiu-jitsu", a Japanese method of fighting without weapons; partly striking, partly wrestling.
[25] Football in America was a violent and dangerous game.

DEM.	Defessus sum currendo, follemque sequendo —
(*panting*)	Eminus. (*Enter SOSTRATA.*) At quaenam haec femina, nuda caput,
	Nuda pedes? SOS. Nocuumst operire caputque pedesque:[26]
	Mens sana in sano sit capite. GET. Et pedibus.
SOS.	Vivere naturae nos convenienter oportet:
	Maiorum in mores nempe redire decet.

(*She treads on a nail.*)

        Hem, perii! AES. Quidnamst? numnam punctura? SOS. Necessest
           Multa pati, si vis vivere simpliciter.
        Simplex vita mihi placuit. GET. Par illa Simoni,
           Cuius simplicitas vivit in ore virum:
        Simplex ille Simo cuidam fuit obvius imo
           Portanti ad festum crustula. DEM. Nonne taces?

SOS.	Surgere mane novo, *pontem* non ludere velle,[27]
	Rimarumque casam plenam habitare iuvat.
DEM.	Ista mihi quoque vita placebat rustica quondam.
(*sympathetically*)	
SOS.	Non nolo rursus nubere: sum vidua,
(*Engagingly*)	Sum sola. DEM. (*alarmed*). At non est tibi bissextilis hic annus.
	(*firmly*). Non est. Uni homini tristitia una sat est.

(*Enter CANTHARA.*)

        Ecce autem hoc aliud monstrum! num balnea quaeso,
           Liquisti nuper? cur tegis ipsa caput
        Manteli in tanto? dic, sodes. CAN. Nuper ab undis
           Absque freto Anglorum semianimis venio:[28]
        Nam per tres menses semper noctemque diemque
           Sustentata cibo, vi bovis et nucibus[29]
        Uvarum, dum saevit hiemps, dum marmora rident,
           In Gallos tendo — nec tamen advenio.

DEM.	Scilicet is generi labor est nunc curaque talis
(*shocked*)	Femineo. CTE. Grator. Macta puella tua

        Virtute, et tibi Fors fortunam det meliorem,
           Ut nando Burgen exsuperare queas.
GET. (*to CANTHARA*). Simplicitasne tibi vitae placet? CAN. I, tibi narra
           Haec ioca; certe habeo sat nimiumque salis.

(*Singing is heard behind the stage.*)

        "Eia age nunc, cives, bellandi tempus: ad arma!

---

[26] See *Punch* for some ridicule of the attempt to "live a simple life," going bareheaded and barefooted.

[27] The game of Bridge was very rife in society; cf. note 7 to Exemplum II.

[28] A Miss Kellerman, from Australia, had attempted to swim the Channel in rivalry of a man named Burgess.

[29] "Bovril" and "Grape Nuts" were much advertised foods.

	Sanguinolento nos ense tyrannus agit."[30]
	(Enter SANNIO.)
SAN.	Intenti corde, a, laeto sic imus ad Anglos,
(effusively)	Haec nostra ut iungat pectora fausta dies.[31]
	Vivat et Edvardus, Praetor quoque Londiniensis,
	Et Ludi vivant atque Fretense Cavum![32]
MIC.	Vos hominum generi quot quantaque dona dedistis,
	Vina mari sexu, femineoque modos:
	Redditis et scenae ioca vos et seria: Vernast
	Gallina[33] e vobis vestraque Sara dea.[34]
SAN.	At nos inter nos nunc amplectamur, amici.
	(SOSTRATA advances.)
	A, bene venisti.[35] SOS. Tu quoque, dulce caput.
SYR.	O si nunc Nelso vitales carperet auras,
	Heroi vestro gaudia quanta forent!
(HEGIO suddenly appears with one of his captains.)	
HEG.	Adsum. SAN. O nautarum dux invictissime, salve.
SYR.	O salve magni nominis umbra. HEG. Quis es?
MIC.	Aemulus hic laudisque tuae studiosus amator
	Hostilem classem mersit in ima maris:
	Ipse dedit signum par isti "Patria nostra
	Postulat ut faciat munera quisque sua:"
	Est socius noster. HEG. (to SYRUS). Sociis o digne Brittannis,
	Salve: nos inter sit diuturna fides.
SYR.	Mortuus es numquam: te, non moriture, saluto:
	Vivit adhuc nobis visque vigorque tuus.
HEG. (advancing).	Mirari nolite, mihi quod linquere visumst
	Elysias sedes; haec mihi causa viae:
(pointing to his companion.)	
	Hic, cui parebat navis Temeraria Pugnax,[36]
	Me voluit vestram nosse suamque Domum.
	O praeclaram illam lucem, cum duximus una
	Agmen in oppositas, acer uterque, rates;
	Primus ego; hic, parvo mihi proximus intervallo,
	Hostilem proram vinxit utrimque suae.

---

[30] "Aux armes, citoyens! Formez vos bataillons!" etc. Refrain of the "Marseillaise" by Rouget de L'Isle.

[31] L'Entente Cordiale, a friendly feeling that had grown up between France and England.

[32] The project of a tunnel under the Straits of Dover.

[33] The "Spring Chicken", a musical comedy adapted from the French.

[34] Sarah Bernhardt, the famous tragic actress, born in Paris, October, 1844.

[35] J. Benvenisti played Sostrata.

[36] Sir Eliab Harvey; referring to the ship named the "Fighting Temeraire."

Nunc agimus grates pro tot tantisque triumphis.
 Anglia, nunc vatis te meminisse decet,
Grandia qui cecinit resonanti carmine verba;
 "Haec ante hostiles Anglia nostra pedes
Non olim iacuit, numquam summissa iacebit,
 Ni prius intulerit volnus et ipsa sibi."[37]
Patria sic vigeat, sic vis virtusque noventur,
 Sic semper vobis floreat alma Domus!

Universität Bonn

---

[37] *King John,* Act V Sc. 7.

Gager's Meleager:
An Inventive Adaptation of Senecan Form

HOWARD B. NORLAND

First acted at Christ Church, Oxford, in February 1582, *Meleager* was William Gager's first dramatic success. It apparently was so well received that it was selected for a repeat performance three years later when the Earls of Pembroke and Leicester, accompanied by Sir Philip Sidney, visited the university. This revival, in January 1585, was marked by a new prologue and epilogue, in the latter of which the poet Sidney is identified with the tragic hero of the play; ironically Gager adds the wish that Sidney will escape the regrettable end of Meleager.[1] First printed in January 1593, the play was dedicated by Gager to the Earl of Essex, a rising star in Elizabeth's court, who like Sidney came to an early end. Whether one interprets this tragedy as a curse for its potential patrons or the author's bad luck in seeking patronage, it remains a memorable example of Latin neoclassical drama.

Gager in his dedicatory letter to Essex calls *Meleager* his "primogenitus," implying that it was his first completed dramatic composition. Closely following his Senecan model, Gager appropriates and adapts many scenes and lines from the tragedies ascribed to Seneca, especially *Medea* and *Hercules Oetaeus*, as Dana Sutton points out.[2] However, in transforming Ovid's 270-line narrative version of the Meleager myth from *Metamorphoses* (8:270–546) into some 1800 lines of drama, Gager made critical choices. His decision to follow the general outline of Ovid's story still allowed considerable latitude, and, while Gager incorporated many Ovidian motifs, he also introduced several new elements into the plot. It is in his inventive expansion of the Ovidian narrative to nearly twice the length of the typical Senecan tragedy that Gager demonstrates his creative skill.

---

[1] *William Gager: The Complete Works*, ed. Dana F. Sutton (New York, 1994), *Meleager*, Epilogue, 1920–1925. This foreboding epilogue is generally assumed to have been printed in its original form when the play was later published. (All further references to the text of the play and its translation are to this edition unless otherwise indicated.)

[2] See especially Sutton's notes to Acts I and II in his edition, 1.167–189.

By noting in his letter to the Academic Reader variants in different versions of the Meleager myth recounted by Homer, Ovid, and Antiphon, Gager justifies his adaptation of the classical tale. Following Seneca, Gager begins his play with an explanation of the provocation of the tragedy: the goddess Diana's anger at Oeneus for ignoring her in his sacrifices to the heavenly powers, an anger expressed by the Fury Megaera. As in the Senecan tragedies, *Agamemnon* and *Thyestes*, the motif of revenge is introduced by a supernatural figure who demands retribution for a perceived wrong; however, in this instance the irrationality of revenge is emphasized by the Fury.

Oeneus, the object of Diana's wrath in Ovid's version, is much more fully developed by Gager. Going beyond Ovid's explanation that in celebrating Ceres and Bacchus first Oeneus simply forgot Diana, Gager makes Oeneus an arrogant atheist who regards himself as equal if not superior to the gods. Perhaps the classical model for Oeneus was Oedipus, though as Boas points out, he more strikingly anticipates Tamburlaine,[3] who first appeared on the public stage in 1587, some five years after Gager's *Meleager*. Oeneus establishes his perspective in the opening lines of his first speech: "par diis superbis gradior, et caelo tenus, / inter tyrannos arduum caput effero" [I walk along, the equal of the prideful gods, and among other rulers I raise my lofty head to the sky] (2.472–473). This image of *hubris* is expanded in the dialogue that follows, as Oeneus stubbornly refuses to heed the traditional wisdom of the Senex and the prophetic vision of Althaea. His character remains static until he is informed of the death of Meleager, whereupon he blames himself for marrying a woman who has killed her son, though he never appears to grasp the fact that his impiety toward the gods led to the tragic outcome.

Atalanta's role is also much expanded in the play. Ovid describes her as an epicene warrior who evokes Meleager's desire, but in Gager's tragedy she is compared to the goddess Diana and to Jason's golden fleece. Her eagerness to prove her courage is expressed by her impatience to begin the hunt, but more definitive is her rejection of the womanly tasks of spinning and weaving for the masculine skills of the hunter. This preference links her, of course, to Diana, though her single-minded valor may also remind us of Virgil's female warrior Camilla who in the *Aeneid* outshines the men in battle.

Atalanta's repudiation of both beauty and marriage in her response to Meleager's and Philemon's attempts to persuade her to adopt the conventional female role demonstrates her independence of spirit. When reminded that beauty is transitory and must be exploited before it passes, Atalanta declares that she is ashamed of her physical charm and "nomine arridet magis / fortis vocari" [take[s] more pleasure in being called stout-hearted] (1.319–320). Being a "daughter" of Diana, Atalanta naturally prizes chastity, though in the dialogue between her and the besotted Meleager, drawn from Catullus's poetry, she characterizes virginity as a fragile rose which is valued only while it remains intact (1.355–364), and she represents marriage as a form of violation comparable to the pillaging of a city:

---

[3] Frederick S. Boas, *University Drama in the Tudor Age* (Oxford, 1914), 171.

> quae gravior illa nocte nox caelo exeat,
> castam puellam quae viro prodit truci,
> gremioque matris virginem teneram eripit,
> trepidam puellam matris amplexu eripit?
> quid peius hostes urbe iam capta patrant?
> quod ab hoste peius virgo patiatur nefas?

[What night can descend in the sky worse than that which gives over a chaste girl to a harsh man, tearing a gentle maiden from her mother's lap, tearing a frightened girl from her mother's embrace? What fouler deed can enemies commit during the sack of a city? What worse thing can a maiden undergo at the hands of a foeman?] (1.380–385)

Atalanta's view of men is extremely negative, to say the least, and her parting words to Meleager before leaving the stage appear to offer him no hope: "puella sapiens triste vitabit iugum. / vel sunt enim plerumque zelotypi viri, / vel dissoluti, vel nimis domini graves" [A wise girl avoids the sorry yoke. Men, for the most part, are jealous, dissolute, or harsh taskmasters] (1.405–407).

Identifying Queen Elizabeth with Atalanta in his Epilogue for Academics, Gager notes Elizabeth's harsh treatment of her suitors and praises her victory over a greater boar than the Calydonian, a possible allusion to the Catholic conspiracy in 1581 led by Campion and Parsons.[4] Gager describes the queen as a "stupenda virgo, bella seu tractet fera, / seu pacis artes" [a marvellous virgin whether waging harsh battles or plying the arts of peace] (Epil. 1903–1904), and concludes that all that is lacking is a poet to celebrate her deeds. This challenge appears to have been taken up by several poets in the two decades that followed, though clearly the most memorable identification of the queen carrying on Atalanta's role as a militant champion of chastity is Spenser's portrayal of Britomart in *The Faerie Queene*.

Giving the major players in the myth of the Calydonian boar more human dimensions, Gager represents Meleager as both persistent and impulsive. When he cannot win Atalanta with words, he threatens to take her by force. Burning with passion, he resembles the unrequited lover created by contemporary poets imitating Petrarch, including Sidney who, as we noted above, attended the second performance of the tragedy in 1585. Meleager is, however, also a brave and skilled hunter who outshines the heroes of ancient Greece in delivering the death blow to the ravaging boar. His offer of the victor's trophies, the head and hide of the boar, to Atalanta who had drawn the first blood, may at first glance appear to be a magnanimous act, but his motivation to buy her favor undercuts his generosity. His questionable honor is even more seriously jeopardized by his impulsive murder of his uncles when they challenge his action. Meleager may be essentially a victim of fate in Ovid's rendering, but in Gager's representation he is a victim of his passion for Atalanta and his own impulsive nature. In the wake of Atalanta's unremitting rejection of his suit, his attempt to win

---

[4] See Boas, *University Drama*, 177.

her hand by offering her the glory he has won in the hunt seems especially foolish.

In individualizing the major figures in the myth of the Calydonian boar, Gager often drew on classical precedents; nowhere is this more apparent than in his characterization of Althaea, who is only lightly sketched by Ovid. Faced with the divided loyalties of a mother and a sister after Meleager has killed her brothers, Gager's Althaea discusses her dilemma at length with the Nutrix who questions her decision to place a sister's revenge above a mother's love. Following the tenor of the Senecan Medea's internal debate over her love for her sons and her desire for revenge on Jason (*Medea*, 895–977), Althaea argues:

> mors est pianda morte, funus funere,
> furor furore, scelere pensandum est scelus.
> . . . .
> cruenta mater, at soror dicar pia,
> domusque nostra vindicis nomen feram.

[Death must be expiated by death, killing by killing, madness by madness, crime must be repaid by a crime. ... I shall be called a bloody mother, but a loyal sister, I shall bear the name of champion of this house] (4.1231–1232, 1236–1237).

Her placement of revenge over love does not, of course, resolve her dilemma but represents instead a further step in the progression of the tragedy. Rather than escaping retribution for her revenge like Seneca's Medea, Althaea in both Ovid and Gager goes mad after causing her son's death, and she takes final vengeance by killing herself with her son's sword that had killed her brothers. While modeling Althaea upon Medea, Gager does not allow the Senecan precedent to stultify his own creative spirit.

Gager's relationship to the Roman tragedian is further demonstrated by his adaptation of particular Senecan motifs in the dramatization of the myth. Forewarning of action to come is a common device in both Greek and Latin drama, but Seneca in reworking his Greek sources frequently emphasizes prophetic visions and supernatural signs that heighten or intensify the role of fate. In Gager's *Meleager* the Fury Megaera begins the action by expressing hatred for Oeneus, which she promises will reach fruition in "minae, caedes, furor" [menaces, murder, madness] (1.91). This establishes the tragic mood, but it also implies a supernatural direction of the action. In Act 2 as the conditions for tragedy are beginning to emerge, two further supernatural warnings are expressed. The first is the prophetic vision, which Althaea describes, of her mother's ghost entering her chamber and telling her of a dire catastrophe involving Althaea, her brothers, husband, and son. After the hubristic Oeneus dismisses this threat of portending fate as anxiety inspired by fear, the Soothsayer predicts the death of the rampaging boar but also alludes to an unnamed horror that causes his limbs to quake. As in Seneca, these direful anticipations intensify the atmosphere of gloom as they emphasize the inevitability of a tragic end.

Another classical dramatic device that Gager appears to have learned from Seneca is the addition of interlocutors to reveal the thoughts and motivations of the principal figures in the tragedy. In the first act Philemon appears in order to clarify Meleager's obsession with Atalanta; here Philemon's quiet reason contrasts with Meleager's impulsive nature. In addition, Philemon represents the conventional attitude toward woman's role in society; he argues that women should take up the distaff and loom and leave hunting and war to men. He serves a somewhat different function in Act 4 as Meleager begins to suffer when the fateful log is placed in the fire. Here Philemon's lack of understanding of what is happening to Meleager, and his lame advice on how to deal with the fateful malady, heighten the confusion and emphasize Meleager's victimization.

Similarly, Oeneus is accompanied by the Senex and Althaea by the Nutrix to elaborate the emotional and intellectual components of the issues that lead to tragedy. The Senex in Act 2 is a sounding board for Oeneus's *hubris*, but he also seems to personify reason in instructing his master about the implications and ramifications of his foolish arrogance. The interlocutor regularly serves a similar function in Seneca's tragedies, though in Gager's *Meleager* the Senex also reminds us of the good counselor in earlier educational and political moralities. Failing in his attempts to dissuade Oeneus from impiously threatening the gods, the Senex highlights Oeneus's atheism and arrogance which provoke divine vengeance. In the last act when Oeneus laments his change of fortune and the loss of his son, the Senex emphasizes the moral lesson to be learned by Oeneus's example. After offering the traditional consolation of an early death as an escape from the miseries of old age, the Senex goes on to decry the human ignorance and error that have made Fortune a god, and he directs the distraught Oeneus to fulfil his responsibilities as a father by giving Meleager a proper funeral. When Oeneus considers the punishment that awaits him after death, he succumbs to his delusions in a suicidal ending added by Gager. The Senex sums up the lesson to be learned from the mad Oeneus just before the two leave the stage for the last time: "en, ut superbos ultor insequitur deus, / et in furorem destinit nimius tumor!" [See how an avenging god pursues the arrogant, and how excessive pride ends in madness!] (5.1767–1768).

Althaea's Nutrix is added by Gager to flesh out the reasons the mother chose to kill her son. Although the Nutrix role here may superficially remind us of Phaedra's Nurse in Seneca's *Hippolytus*, in fact her function in Gager's tragedy is very different. Rather than abetting her mistress's immoral judgment as Phaedra's Nurse does, the Nutrix questions Althaea's priority of values; in a stichomythic dialogue reminding us of Seneca, the Nutrix registers the conventional view that a son is dearer than a brother, which emphasizes the unnaturalness of Althaea's insistence on placing her brothers' honor before her son's life. Another important aspect of the Nutrix role is as narrator. She prepares the audience for Althaea's entrance at the beginning of Act IV by describing the pain and anger that have brought her mistress to madness, and she returns in the last few minutes of the play to decry the costs of killing the boar by noting the deaths that followed, before providing the details of the suicides of Althaea and Oeneus. Like the other interlocutors modeled on Senecan precedents in Gager's play, the Nutrix serves a valuable function in interpreting and judging the principal characters' attitudes and actions.

Because much of the action in Senecan and neoclassical tragedy is narrated rather than represented, a witness's account of events is central to the tragic development. In *Meleager* the Nuntius provides a detailed account of the hunt for the Calydonian boar before the hunters appear on stage with the boar's head and hide. Elaborating upon Ovid's rendering in *Metamorphoses*, Gager's messenger alludes to the attempts of such famous warriors as Jason and Nestor but then focuses upon Atalanta's and Meleager's roles. Noting that Atalanta was the first to draw blood from the boar, the Nuntius indicates that her arrow only grazed the animal, while Meleager proved his prowess by single-handedly killing the boar with his spears. This description of the sequence of the action is important to the events that occur on stage when the hunters assemble. Meleager's determination to share with Atalanta the glory that he has clearly earned appears arbitrary in the context: it may win the maiden warrior's gratitude, but it elicits contempt from Meleager's uncles who interpret their nephew's gesture as prompted by love rather than honor. This report may not strike us as particularly Senecan, but its effectiveness in setting the stage for the crucial event from which the remaining tragic actions inevitably derive demonstrates Gager's dramatic skill.

More noticeably Senecan is Gager's employment of the chorus at the end of each act to comment on the preceding dialogue and to prepare the audience for what follows. Not interacting with the principal characters in the tragedy, the chorus is an extra-dramatic device designed to serve as a moral commentator, which may give more weight to the didactic nature of the tragedy than is found in Seneca, but in its role as a disembodied voice that directs audience response, it follows the Senecan model.

Although Gager modeled *Meleager* upon Senecan tragic form, he also introduced elements from contemporary stage practice, which resulted in a modification of neoclassical characteristics. Such an adaptation is perhaps most evident in Gager's representation of the tragic plot. While focusing the action of the play on a single crisis, the menace of the Calydonian boar and its consequences, in sound neoclassical fashion, Gager portrays the key events in the natural order in which they occur rather than in retrospective narratives of previous incidents. This progression of the action is structured in a cause-effect relationship that emphasizes individual responsibilities for crucial developments. The provocation of the tragic pattern, Oeneus's impiety in ignoring the goddess Diana, prompts her to send the Calydonian boar to ravage the kingdom. This leads to the hunt that brings Atalanta and Meleager together, which results in the quarrel between Meleager and his uncles, which in turn provokes him to kill them. This action causes Althaea to revenge their deaths by killing Meleager, and the death of Meleager provokes the suicides of both Althaea and Oeneus. While Gager maintains a unity of action observed in classical tragedy, his representation of the plot as a progressive chain of events follows popular stage practice.

Another contemporary innovation is Gager's staging of violence that in Seneca and classical tragedy was generally narrated. The Nuntius's account of the hunt is narrated in traditional neoclassical fashion, as noted above, but it also would have been very difficult to enact on stage. However, Meleager's stabbing of his uncles is represented, as well as his painful suffering induced by his mother. This revenge is particularly graphic in the simultaneous staging of Althaea's burning of the brand on one side of the stage, while on the other side the effects of the fire on Meleager are expressed by his physical sensations of burning.[5] The emotional moment is prolonged by Althaea's temporarily removing the brand from the fire and then thrusting it back in, but the audience is spared the final death throes of Meleager who, believing that he is pursued by the Fury Megaera, desperately runs off the stage. Gager returns to conventional neoclassical form in the final act by having the deaths of Althaea and Oeneus narrated.

Perhaps Gager's most significant departure from Senecan tragedy is his Christianizing of Senecan themes. Following the precedent of Senecan translators whose collected edition published in 1581 frequently added a Christian dimension to his tragedies,[6] Gager reinterprets Seneca's portrayal of fate and fortune. Rather than representing fate as a malevolent force imposed on helpless man and fortune as a capricious goddess who delights in man's crushed expectations, Gager emphasizes man's responsibility for the actions that lead to tragedy. Oeneus's impiety and arrogance, which cause him to scorn the forewarnings of tragedy, are compounded by Meleager's impulsiveness and Althaea's misplaced sense of duty to revenge her brothers' deaths. According to Gager, man may hubristically consider himself in control of his destiny or may foolishly blame fate or fortune for his own errors, but what he must realize is that divine Providence shapes our ends, as the Senex explains at the beginning of Act 5:

> humana fecit inscitia caelo deam
> fortunam, et error numen affinxit sacrum.
> non praevidentem si quid adversi opprimat,
> id omne sorti ascribitur, vanae deae.
> fortuna nulla est, alma nisi prudentia
> sit inane nomen. si sit, et curam gerat
> caeleste numen, nil temere nobis venit.
> quaecunque miseros fata mortales premunt,
> ea crede divum nutu et arbitrio regi.

[Human ignorance has made Fortune a goddess in heaven, and error has invented her as a divinity. If some reversal oppresses a man who has not foreseen it, this is all ascribed to the false goddess Fortune. There is no Fortune, unless fostering Providence is an empty word. If Providence exists, and [if the] heavenly divinity [has a care for us], nothing occurs to us at random. Whatever fates oppress us poor mortals, you must believe occur by divine will and judgment.] (5.1525–1533)

---

[5] Boas suggests that an inner stage was used for the dialogue between Althaea and the Nutrix (*University Drama*, 172–173), but this staging would unnecessarily complicate the production; simultaneous action on the two sides of the stage seems much more likely.

[6] See Howard B. Norland, "Adapting to the Times: Expansion and Interpolation in the Elizabethan Translations of Seneca," *Classical and Modern Literature* 16 (1996): 241–263.

This view of Fortune, which Gager also expressed in separate poems included in his notebook of miscellaneous works,[7] is, of course, not unique; in fact it expresses Gager's Christian faith in providence and divine judgment that underlies his moralistic interpretation of the characters' actions in the tragedy.

Gager was very conscious of the kind of tragic effect he meant to convey. In his letter addressed to the Academic Reader that prefaced his published edition of the play, he says that he introduced elements not found in Ovid — Atalanta's aversion to marriage and Oeneus's arrogance, impiety, and suicide — "ut tragoediae argumentum, maiore cum varietate, tum atrocitate pertexeretur" [so that the tragedy's plot might be embroidered with greater variety and horror]; but he goes on to explain that he excluded the metamorphoses of Meleager's sisters into birds lest this miraculous action detract from the tragic effect at the end of the play. Gager clearly seeks to enhance the tragic dimensions of the events in his adaptation of the Ovidian narrative, but he sidesteps the pessimism of his Senecan model in which Stoicism provides the only solace in the tragic end. Rather, Gager turns the play into a didactic lesson about the fruits of arrogance and impiety creating the tragic conclusion. The final choral ode includes the Stoical truism that the higher one's position in life the more vulnerable one is to danger, though it most emphatically declares that the impious are destroyed by divine vengeance. Therefore, "deos vereri discite" [Learn to fear the gods] (5.1868).

This didactic tone is registered throughout the play by the moralizing interlocutors as well as by the chorus. In the epilogue written for the performance given for Sidney and the Earls of Pembroke and Leicester the message may be directed particularly at Queen Elizabeth, but it also may be applied to men of authority and finally to us all:

> quicunque sceptro fretus ac solio tumens
> aureus avito spiritus altos gerit,
> nimiumque fidens, caelites temnit deos,
> te videat, Oeneu, videat eversam domum
> modo prepotentem, gentis Aetolae decus.
> hinc quemque par est facere documentum sibi,
> hoc quisque secum reputet exemplum domi.

[Whoever, relying on his scepter and, gilded, swells because of his ancestral throne, arrogant in spirit and overconfident, scorning the gods, let him see you, Oeneus, let him see your overthrown house, lately all-powerful, the glory of the Aetolian race. It is fair for every man to take this as an example for himself, let every one ponder this as a lesson for his own house.] (Epil. 1909–1915)

---

[7] See especially CVII, "De Fortuna", and CIII, "De Cupidine" in *Poems of William Gager*, British Library MS Add.22583 fols. 53–54.

Gager's didacticism at the end of the play may seem a bit overdone, but his moralizing should not distract us from his artistic accomplishment. His inventive application of Senecan form to Ovid's mythical tale established his reputation as the foremost academic playwright at Oxford and generated an interest in literary themes more fully explored by his artistic contemporaries.

University of Nebraska

In Gasparini Barzizzii De compositione *opusculum quaestiunculae*

JUAN Mᴬ NÚÑEZ GONZÁLEZ

Gasparino Barzizzio Bergomensi codicis M. Fabii Quintiliani *De Institutione Oratoria* integri fruendi facultas contigit non multo post illos libros retectos. Quorum lectione permotus opusculum (cui titulus *De compositione* exstat)[1] exarauit. Nam libros Quintiliani qui incuria temporum diutissime non exstiterant et in Transalpina Gallia ea tempestate reperti erant, diligenti cura et studio euoluit exhausitque, quibusdam Ciceronis[2] ac Cornificii Martianique Capellae additis, ea mente ut uetus Latine componendi ars renasceretur.

Cum omnis rhetorica Gasparini opusculi doctrina ex eis auctoribus sumpta uideretur, nonnulla tamen tractatus Medii Aeui de dictandi siue dictaminis arte cognominatos redolent. Quibus de locis igitur materiam disputandi dare inceptum est nobis hoc commentariolo.

In hac arte quidem componenda Gasparinum ex solis puris fontibus Ciceronis eiusque aequalium hausisse iure credideris, modo ut hanc exordii primam periodum perlegeris.[3]

> Cum omnis commodae, et perfectae elocutionis praeceptio in tres partes sit distributa, scilicet compositionem, elegantiam, et dignitatem; illud genus, quod ad

---

[1] Constat titulus idem qui in capite quarto libri noni codicis Ambrosiani Latini E 153 sup. apparet.

[2] Quamquam Gasparinus primus fuit etiam qui reppererit ac perlegerit integerrimos tres libros Ciceronis *De oratore, Brutum* et *Oratorem ad Brutum*; tamen dubium est si cogniti ei sint ante quam *De compositione* opus in lucem dederit. Cf. R. Sabbadini, *La scuola e gli studi di Guarino Guarini Veronese* (Catania, 1896), 7.

[3] Locos Gasparini laudauimus ex hac editione: *Gasparini Barzizzii Bergomatis et Guiniforti filii opera*, pars prima (Romae, MDCC XXIII).

compositionem attinet, tribus in rebus est positum, ordine, junctura, numero: quae nisi diligenter ab Oratore sint considerata, splendor pene omnis, uerborumque illa concinnitas tota intereat, necesse est. (*De compositione*, p. 1)

Cuius enim comprehensionis uerba sententiasque e tribus locis mutuatus uidetur esse: primum e *Rhetoricis* scriptis *ad Herennium*,[4] elocutionem diuisam in partes tres, scilicet dignitatem, elegantiam, compositionem; deinde ex *Institutionibus oratoriis* Fabii Quintiliani[5] compositionem in ordinem, iuncturam atque numerum distributam; postremum ex *Oratore ad Brutum*[6] Marci Ciceronis "concinnitatem" quo uocabulo unus Cicero ex ueterum rhetorum numero usus est. Nam nullo modo fieri potest ut "concinnitas" dictio in Cornificii aut Quintiliani operibus inueniatur.

Compositio enim non est in partes tres distributa a Cornificio (si quidem ab hoc auctore libri *Rhetorici ad Herennium* compositi sint) neque Cicero ordinem, iuncturam et numerum sub nomine compositionis complexus est. Enimuero Arpinas[7] uerborum collocationem (pro "compositione") in compositionem, concinnitatem atque numerum distributam docet. Porro illa dictio, "concinnitas", quasi concentus e figuris[8] quae Gorgias Leontinus primus inuenisse fertur ab uno Cicerone (ex antiquis rhetoribus) usurpata est.

Qua definitione constituta Barzizzius Quintilianum secutus de ordine uerborum ita disputat ut ipse inconsulte lapsus in turbidis riuulis (ex illis sane ueteribus profluentibus) esse uideatur:

"Ordo igitur est," inquit Barzizzius, "apta quaedam uerborum inter se naturalis uel artificialis dispositio." (*De compositione*, p. 1)

Quibus e uerbis uestigia doctrinarum quae ab infima antiquitate usque in recentiora tempora ueterem dicendi artem turbarunt nobis apparent. Etenim "dispositio" usurpata est hic pro illo quod "compositio" in ueteribus de elocutione libris nominatur. Hanc phrasin autem scilicet "uerborum dispositionem" in antiquis de arte oratoria scriptis reperire nullo modo possis usque in secundum nostri aeui saeculum, cum Iulius Victor, rhetor e latinorum minorum agmine (ut ita laudem qui post Quintilianum de dicendi arte disseruerunt) de compositione uerborum rettulisset haec uerba:

quod ad uerborum dispositionem pertinet satis plene docetur, cum de elocutione tractatur. De rerum uero dispositione per singula membra orationis, id est cum prooemio et narratione et ceteris traditum accepisti. (ed. Halm, 431.9)

---

[4] *Rhet. ad Her.* 4, 17.
[5] *Inst.* 9, 4, 22.
[6] *Orat.* 201.
[7] Cf. *Cicéron, L'Orateur*, ed. et trad. A. Yon (Paris, 1964), cxiii sqq.
[8] Haec sunt: similiter cadens, parison, contraria seu antitheta. Cf. Cic., *Orat.* 164 sq.

Cum dispositionem rebus argumentisue tantum, compositionem solis uerbis seu dictionibus collocandis adhibitam apud antiquos reperires, Iulius Victor tamen de uerborum rerumque dispositione aeque loquitur. Vt res ita se habeant, Cicero tamen semel "compositorem" dicit pro agendi nomine "dispositorem" declarante. "Compositor", inquam, et non "dispositor", ut coniici nobis liceat (sed nota ut "dispositor" in scriptis rhetoricis antiquis non appareat):

> "quem hoc uno excellere," inquit Cicero, "id est oratione, cetera in eo latere indicat nomen ipsum. non enim inuentor aut compositor aut actor ‹qui› haec complexus est omnia, sed et Graece ab eloquendo rhetor et Latine eloquens dictus est." (*Orat*. 61)

Haec Ciceronis uerba declarant agentia officiorum oratoris siue rhetoricae partium nomina, id est, inuentorem qui res inuenit, compositorem qui res inuentas disponit, actorem qui orationem dispositam agit, et cetera. Sed nunquam quidem inuenire nobis licuit compositionem pro dispositione seu dispositionem pro compositione in Ciceronis, Cornificii, Quintilianique scriptis de arte dicendi. Iulius Victor autem primus, ut supra diximus, hac phrase "uerborum dispositione" usus uidetur esse.

Alia uerba autem ex illa ordinis definitione quam supra memoraui, illum eruditissimum uirum, Gasparinum, in sermocinandi uel dictandi artibus Medii Aeui uersatum esse declarant. Nam illa sententia "naturalis seu artificialis dispositio" ex illo dicendi usu Aureae aetatis recedit et infimam antiquitatem redolet. Etenim Cicero naturalem dispositionem uocauit ipsam quae artificiosa ab auctore ad Herennium relata est. In libro secundo *De oratore* legimus ea uerba:

> cuius ratio est duplex; altera, quam adfert natura causarum, altera, quae oratorum iudicio et prudentia comparatur: nam ut aliquid ante rem dicamus, deinde ut rem exponamus, post ut eam probemus nostris praesidiis confirmandis, contrariis refutandis, deinde ut concludamus atque ita peroremus, hoc dicendi natura ipsa praescribit. (*De orat*. 2.307)

Eandem sententiam auctoris ad Herennium uerba declarant — ut mihi quidem uidetur — , sed Cornificius grammatico more illum tritum dispositionis ordinem, scilicet, principium seu exordium, narrationem, diuisionem, confirmationem, confutationem, et conclusionem seu perorationem ex institutione artis disponi asseuerat:

> Ex institutione artis disponemus, cum sequemur eam praeceptionem, quam in primo libro exposuimus, hoc est, ut utamur principio, narratione, diuisione, confirmatione, confutatione, conclusione. (*Rhet. ad Her*. 3.16)

In sequenti quidem capite aliam dispositionem esse, quae ab ordine artificioso recederit, nos certiores facit. Is ordo qui ab artis regulis recedit arbitrio oratoris fit si ab narratione necessitatis causa et non ab exordio incipiamus:

> Est autem alia dispositio, quae, cum ab ordine artificioso recedendum est, oratoris iudicio ad tempus adcommodatur; ut si ab narratione dicere incipiamus

aut ab aliqua firmissima argumentatione aut litterarum aliquarum recitatione; aut si secundum principium confirmatione utamur, deinde narratione aut si quam eiusmodi permutationem ordinis faciemus; quorum nihil, nisi causa postulat, fieri oportebit. (*Rhet. ad Her.* 3.17).

Et haec quidem uerba eandem uim habent atque illa ex secundo *De oratore* Ciceronis laudata: "altera quae oratorum iudicio et prudentia comparatur." Arpinas autem naturalem dispositionem uocat eandem quam artificiosam Cornificius docet. Sed nimirum recte uterque dixit. Quam prudenter enim intellexit germanam Ciceronis Cornificiique sententiam ille eruditissimus saeculi sexti et decimi uir, Benedictus Arias Montanus,[9] cum caneret:

Aemula naturae ratio, quam dicimus artem (vv. 3.67);
Partibus [sc. orationis] his etenim bis ter persoluerat omnem
dicendo effigiem quisquis iam rhetoris artem,
natura monstrante modum, didicit retulitque. (vv. 3.94–96)

Quidam[10] autem uiri docti nostri aeui existimarunt confusam atque discordem hanc doctrinam inter ueteres rhetores (sc. Ciceronem et Cornificium), sed, ut supra diximus, ordo orationis partium naturalis redigi in artem non repugnat. Atqui Sulpitius Victor,[11] Fortunatianus,[12] ac Martianus Capella eisdem Ciceronis Cornificiique paene uerbis usi, rebus tamen scholastico more mixtis, speciem dispositionis duplicem naturalem atque artificialem ita distinxerunt, ut ab illis infimae antiquitatis rhetoribus non recte intellecta doctrinae uis esse uideatur. Conferte exempli gratia hunc Martiani locum:

quae pars dispositio uocitatur, qua quid dicendum quoue loco, (. . .) prudenter inspicimus. Duplex igitur huius partis est ratio; aut enim naturalis est ordo aut oratoris artificio comparatur: naturalis, cum post principium narratio, partitio, propositio, argumentatio, conclusio epilogusque consequitur: artificio oratoris, cum per membra orationis quae dicenda sunt digerimus. Et hoc ex causae utili-

---

[9] In *Rhetoricorum libris quattuor* (Antuerpiae, MDLXIX), nuper critice instructis atque Hispane conuersis a Maria V. Pérez (Pace Augusta, 1984).

[10] Vt unum e pluribus laudem, cf. Maria V. Pérez, *Rhetoricorum libri quattuor*, 105, n. 4.

[11] "In dispositione plus artis est, quod tertium esse oratoris officium dixeramus: plurimi enim momenti est ea, quae inuenta sunt, aut utilitatem et uictoriae effectum digerere in ordinem atque disponere. In dispositione haec sunt: ordo cum ea, quae Graece appellatur οἰκονομία, dehinc elocutio, tum pronuntiatio. Ordo est, ut secundum textum naturalem singula persequamur, primum in partibus elocutionis, ut si scilicet primum exordium, tum narratio, tum partes argumentationis, peroratio demum extrema (. . .) Artificiosus ordo est, ut hunc ipsum ordinem, si ita causa poscit plerumque uertamus. Nam aliquando omittenda principia, aliquando subdiuidenda et interrumpenda narratio, ex parte ponenda et imperfecta argumentatione reddenda." (ed. Halm, 320)

[12] "Quot sunt generales modi dispositionis? duo. Qui? naturalis et artificialis, id est utilitatis." (ed. Halm, 120)

tate, non ex temporis serie coaptamus, ut pro Milone factum, cum quaestiones quasdam ante narrationem, ut praeiudicia refutaret, induxit, quod non ex ordine naturae, sed ex causae utilitate mutauit. (*Nupt.* 5.30)

His uerbis igitur Martianus Capella sententias Ciceronis Cornificiique scholastico more plane permiscuit. Cicero quidem ordinem orationis partium sicut omnia ad dicendi artem pertinentia esse naturae obsequentem passim uidetur dictitare. *Oratorem* enim ad Brutum scripsit Cicero eo consilio ut tanto uiro modulandae periodi obtrectatori oratorius numerus siue rhythmus e natura ductus aperte ostenderetur. Itaque narrat Tullius in tertio libro *De oratore* atque in *Oratore ad Brutum* theatra tota exclamare, si histrio unam syllabam aut breuiorem aut longiorem pronuntiauerit; et addidit multitudinem pedes non nouisse nec illud quod aut cur aut in quo offendat intellegere; longarum breuiumque syllabarum discrimen in auribus nostris collocauisse ipsam naturam.[13] Illud autem praeterea considerare oportebit ut Gasparinus in illo Martiani Capellae quinto libro (scilicet de rhetoricis) strenue uersaretur, praesertim ad oratorios numeros declarandos, ut ipse illic[14] memorauit.

Sed redeamus ad rem. Ordo quidem naturalis a Martiano Capella cognominatus idem est qui regulis artis non obsequens, sed propter utilitatem ab ordine artificioso, iudicio oratoris monstrante, recedere dicebatur, atque eo igitur artificiosus hic ordo non erat — si uero Ciceroni Cornificioque credimus — quod regulis bene dicendi artis a natura dictatis non obtemperaret. Illud igitur memorandum est, ut nunquam apud antiquos dispositionem, secundam rhetoricae partem, in naturalem atque artificialem speciem inuenire possis distinctam, sed passim apud recentiores laudatos. Ea de causa[15] forsitan, uir eruditus nostri aeui multisque in doctrinis uersatus, Henricus Lausberg, in artem cui titulus *Handbuch der literarischen Rhetorik. Eine Grundlegung der Literaturwissenschaft,*[16] quasi ueterem regulam, hanc duplicem speciem redigit, sed, ut supra uidimus, non recte.

Hac quidem uerborum rerumque permixtione moti, ut opinor, rhetores iuniores in nouam artis uocabulorum turbationem incesserunt, qui hac phrasi "uerborum dispositione" ordinem uerborum declarante usi sint.[17] Ad hanc calcem tamen non eos

---

[13] *De orat.* 3.195s: "quod ea sunt in communibus infixa sensibus nec earum rerum quemquam funditus natura esse uoluit expertem. Itaque non solum uerbis arte positis mouentur omnes, uerum etiam numeris ac uocibus. Quotus enim quisque est qui teneat artem numerorum ac modorum? At in eis si paulum modo offensum est, ut aut contractione breuius fieret aut productione longius, theatra tota reclamant." *Orat.* 173: "in uersu quidem theatra tota exclamant, si fuit una syllaba aut breuior aut longior; nec uero multitudo pedes nouit nec ullos numeros tenet nec illud quod offendit aut cur aut in quo offendat intellegit; et tamen omnium longitudinum et breuitatum in sonis sicut acutarum grauiumque uocum iudicium ipsa natura in auribus nostris collocauit."
[14] *De compositione,* 11: "Martianus uero quinto libro de nuptiis Philologiae & Mercurii, Ciceronis omissis, Quintilianique praeceptis, aliam rationem numerorum instituit; (...) cujus doctrina cum dilucidior sit, & ad intelligendum facilior, hoc loco a me primum commemorabitur."
[15] Intellige: quia rhetores Latini minores sic distinxerunt.
[16] München, 1960: §§ 446–452.
[17] Sic enim Iulius Victor, cuius haec uerba sunt: "quod ad uerborum dispositionem pertinet satis plene docetur, cum de elocutione tractatur. De rerum uero dispositione per singula membra

demorauit inuitus Quintilianus noster, qui in capitulo uigesimo tertio, capitis quarti, libri noni *Institutionis Oratoriae* de compositione in triplice specie distincta (sc. ordine, iunctura, numero) disputando, esse alium naturalem ordinem[18] dixisset[19] et paulo post ipsum ordinem rectum appellauisset. Cum Fabius de artificioso seu artificiali ordine uerborum non locutus esset, tantum de naturali, sed in rhetoricis tamen libris eae sententiae "ordo naturalis seu artificialis" ad dispositionem secundam rhetoricae partem pertinentes affuissent, uia igitur impedita non erat ut "dispositio" pro "compositione" et retrorsum usurparetur. Sed nota ut in antiquis scriptis de dispositione, secunda rhetoricae parte, "ordo" dispositionis collocationem orationis partium significet, in scriptis uero de compositione continuationem uerborum referat. Aldus quidem Scaglione, uir eruditissimus, doctrinam compositionis per medioaeuales dictaminis seu dictandi artes persecutus est,[20] attamen non solum eam uerborum tralationem — pro "uerborum compositione" scilicet "dispositionem" — non perspexerit, nisi fallor, uerum etiam a Iulio Victore ea uerba olim usurpata esse non animaduertit. Loci tamen auctorum quibus eam turbationem inspicere possis in Aldi Scaglione opere laudato non desunt. Sic "ordo artificialis" et "dispositio" fieri synonyma affirmare possis, ut in quadam *Summa dictaminis* arte saeculo decimo tertio ineunte ab ignoto uiro exarata, apparet. Quo in loco asseueratur artificialem ordinem uel dispositionem fieri ualde optatum si quando partes proprie transponantur et pulchrius ordinentur, ut "Petrum sincera dilectione prosequor et amplector."[21]. Exemplum quidem hoc est uerborum ordinis, sed huius artis auctor "dispositionem" quasi "artificialem ordinem" nuncupauit.

In alia autem *Summa dictaminis*, Guido Faua siue Faua Bononiensi (ca. 1200–ca. 1250) auctore, possis legere:

> In constructione duplex est ordo, scilicet naturalis et artificialis. Naturalis est ille qui pertinet ad expositionem, quando nominatiuus cum determinatione sua precedit et uerbum sequitur cum sua, ut EGO AMO TE. Artificialis ordo est illa compositio que pertinet ad dictationem, quando partes pulcrius disponuntur, qui sic a Tullio diffinitur: "Compositio artificialis est constructio dictaminis equabiliter perpolita."[22]

---

orationis, id est cum prooemio et narratione et ceteris traditum accepisti." (ed. Halm, 431.9)

[18] Haec eius uerba sunt: "est et alius naturalis ordo, ut 'uiros ac feminas, diem ac noctem, ortum et occasum' dicas potius quamquam et retrorsum." (*Inst.* 9.4.23)

[19] Quintilianus tamen de artificioso seu artificiali ordine non locutus est.

[20] In opere accuratissimo cui titulus *The Classical Theory of Composition from its Origins to the Present. A Historical Survey* (Chapel Hill, 1972).

[21] Apud Ch. Thurot, *Extraits de divers manuscrits latins pour servir à l'histoire des doctrines grammaticales au Moyen Age* (Paris, 1868; repr. Frankfurt am Main, 1964), 343s., loc. laud. ab A. Scaglione, *The Classical Theory of Composition*, 117.

[22] Apud A. Gaudenzi, *Il Propugnatore* 23 n.s. 3 (1890): 338. (loc. laud. ab A. Scaglione, in opere *The Classical Theory of Composition*, in adnotatione ad pedem paginae 117).

Nimirum enim perspicere possis ut compositionis definitio ex libris *Ad Herennium* deprompta eis dictionibus "artificiali" scilicet ac "dictamine" aucta sit. Haec enim sunt uerba Cornificii ad locum a medioaeuali dicendi magistro laudatum pertinentia:

> Compositio est uerborum constructio, quae facit omnes partes orationis aequabiliter perpolitas. (*Rhet. ad Her.*, 4.18)

"Dispositio" ergo, "compositio artificialis", atque "artificialis ordo" quasi synonyma in Mediae Aetatis artibus collocationem rite Latineque uerborum declarant. "Artificiale" igitur usi sunt quia ex dictandi arte hunc uerborum ordinem deprendissent. Etenim qua lege uerba in natiuis eorum linguis ordinentur, cum a natura dictata esse eis uiderentur, hanc grammatici iuniores naturalem uerborum collocationem decreuerunt.

Vt fit tamen uiris illis, qui totam uitam cura et studio ad litteras Latinas instaurandas egerunt atque tot tantosque aureae aetatis auctores diligenter perlegerunt, non licuit, quasi inuitis heredibus, eas barbaras foeditates (ut eorum uerbis utar) non mutuari.

Nam Barzizzius cum bonis atque antiquis Latine dicendi doctrinis operam studiose dedisset, Fortunaque audacem uirum iuuasset ut in primis codicem integrum Quintiliani *Institutionis Oratoriae* legeret, oculis tamen offusis deturpationem illam uitare nequiit. Vt uerborum sui linguae ordinem naturalem credidit Gasparinus, sic Latinae artificialem nuncupauit. Hoc accedit ut ipse ad uerborum ordinis uim declarandam hanc dictionem, scilicet "dispositionem", usurpet, sicut in huius disputationis exordio memoraui.

Hanc autem compositionis speciem duplicem, "naturalem", scilicet et "artificialem" quasi quoddam sigillum doctrinae Petri Rami Audomarique Talaei et qui eos[23] secuti sunt decernere possis. Nam Petrus Ramus discipulique naturalem esse compositionem deputarunt quae orationem modulans in uernaculis eorum linguis iudicibus auris superbissimis inueniretur; artificialem autem quae numeros uernaculis sermonibus ignotos et ea de causa a natura non praedictos rhythmos concinnaretur. Sed renascentes aures de correptione seu de productione syllabarum non iudicabant, ut de Afris infimae antiquitatis auribus Augustinus Hipponensis[24] rettulit. Namque Ciceroni ueteribusque oratoribus illis naturalis erat hic numerus siue rhythmus ideoque *Orator* populum in theatro reclamare histrionibus male numeros concinnantibus memorauit (cf. supra loc. laud.).

Alios autem locos laudare possim quibus inuito atque imprudente Barzizzio scholasticae grammaticae regulae exciderunt pessum dederuntque eius Latinitatem renas-

---

[23] Cf. K. Meerhoff, *Rhétorique et Poétique au XVIe siècle en France. Du Bellay, Ramus et les autres* (Leiden, 1986). Juan M. Núñez, "La doctrina de la *elocutio* en la retórica española del renacimiento," in *Actas del III Congreso Internacional de Humanismo y Pervivencia del Mundo Clásico* (Alcañiz, Hispania, in manibus impressoris).

[24] *Doct. christ.* 4.10.

centem. Cum Quintilianus enim dixisset Domitium Afrum soluisse in clausulas uerba traicere tantum asperandae compositionis gratia, exemplis duo propositis "gratias agam continuo" (ex oratione pro Cloatilla), et "eis utrisque apud te iudicem periclitatur Laelia" (ex oratione pro Laelia) addidissetque adeo refugisse teneram delicatamque modulandi uoluptatem ut currentibus per se numeris quod eos inhiberet obiceret,[25] intellexit tamen Gasparinus noluisse Domitium periodos cum finali uerbo concinnare eo consilio ut Quintiliani regulae[26] "uerbo cludere optimum esse" declarantis non pareret. At mihi quidem uidetur Fabius Quintilianus testari rhythmos, qui sine industria, sed tantum orationi ordinem rectum (sc. cum uerbo finali) seruanti accederent, Domitium turbauisse compositionis asperandae causa. Numeros igitur, non ordinem rectum, si recte intellexi, commouere uoluisse Domitium rettulit Quintilianus.

Iucundum est autem quo modo Gasparinus exemplum Cornificii ad hiperbata illustranda propositum interpretatus sit. Hic est locus auctoris *Ad Herennium*:

> ... et si uerborum transiectionem uitabimus, nisi quae erit concinna, qua de re posterius loquemur; quo in uitio est Caelius adsiduus, ut haec est: "In priore libro has res ad te scriptas, Luci, misimus, Aeli" (*Rhet. ad Her.*, 4.18).

Conferte hunc locum cum illo Barzizzii, ubi ipse, uersiculo illo *Annalium* Enni "saxo cere comminuit brum" memorato, ut opinor, interpretauit Coelium scripsisse ad Lucilium (nomen), non Lucium (praenomen) atque detraxisse ultimam nominis syllabam (scilicet "li") et primam verbi "emitto" (sc. "e"), unde "E" "li" pro hoc praenomine quod "Aeli" in uocandi casu est:

> Quo in vitio Caecilium quarto ad Herennium fuisse testatur Cicero cum inquit: "Has res ad te scriptas, Luci, misimus e li"; ubi "e" vocali ablata ex hoc verbo "misimus" et hac syllaba extrema "li" dempta ex hoc nomine Lucili, orationem quae ex se dilucida erat atque aperta confusam atque obscuram reddit. (*De compositione*, 10 sq.)

Illud etiam redolet Medii Aevi ludos scholasque quod Gasparinus Barzizzius (ut reliqui uiri docti sui aetatis) Ciceroni *Rhetoricos ad Herennium* libros auctori tribuit.

Universidad de Oviedo

---

[25] *Inst.* 9.4.31: "Solebat Afer Domitius traicere in clausulas uerba tantum asperandae compositionis gratia, et maxime in prohoemiis, ut pro Cloatilla: 'gratias agam continuo', et pro Laelia: 'eis utrisque apud te iudicem periclitatur Laelia.' Adeo refugit teneram delicatamque modulandi uoluptatem ut currentibus per se numeris quod eos inhiberet [et] obiceret."

[26] *Inst.* 9.4.26: "Verbo sensum cludere multo, si compositio patiatur, optimum est: in uerbis enim sermonis uis est."

La funzione e l'importanza dei nomi umanistici

KLÁRA PAJORIN

Una delle caratteristiche tipiche del movimento umanistico è che una gran parte degli autori aveva l'abitudine di scegliersi un nome umanistico, anticheggiante, per dimostrare anche col nome la propria appartenenza spirituale. Il precursore di tale usanza fu Francesco Petrarca, sebbene il suo nome non assomigliasse ai nomi umanistici dell'epoca successiva. Egli infatti, dal nome di suo padre, ser Petracco (una variante del nome Pietro) si creò un nome, che aveva un significato in latino: Petrarca = Petra + arca.[1] La creazione del nome di Petrarca rimase per lungo tempo senza seguaci, ma già all'inizio del '400 appaiono nomi che anticipano i nomi umanistici, come quelli di Antonio Beccadelli, di Leonardo Bruni, o di Antonio Averlino. Si sa che il Panormita creò il suo nome dal nome greco della sua città nativa, Palermo, mentre Leonardo Bruni formò il suo nome d'arte (*Aretinus*) dal nome latino di Arezzo; Averlino invece mutò radicalmente il suo nome in una parola (*Filarete*), che aveva un preciso significato in greco. Dalla metà del '400 nei nomi di due elementi compaiono sempre più spesso dei nomi noti nell'antichità; successivamente nell'accademia romana di Giulio Pomponio Leto nascono i nomi anticheggianti di tre elementi, ricalcati sul modello romano. Alla fine del '400 e all'inizio del '500 il nome anticheggiante era ormai una vera moda tra gli umanisti, e cominciava a diffondersi in tutti i ceti della società.[2]

La formazione dei nomi umanistici coincide col periodo iniziale della formazione dei nomi moderni di due elementi, costituiti da un nome di battesimo variabile e da un cognome, o nome di famiglia fisso. Gli umanisti, adeguandosi alle esigenze della società moderna, più che modificare il loro nome o ad adattarlo a modelli antichi, erano portati a ricrearlo; così, con la creazione dei loro nomi d'arte, contribuivano notevolmente alla diffusione dei nomi moderni di due o tre componenti. Come ben

---

[1] François Rigolot, *Poétique et onomastique. L'exemple de la Renaissance* (Genève, 1977), 107.
[2] Cf. Adolph Bach, *Deutsche Namenkunde*, 1.2. *Die deutschen Personennamen* (Heidelberg, 1953), 40–41.

sappiamo, l'uomo medievale aveva generalmente un nome fisso di un solo elemento, quello avuto nel battesimo, accompagnato da un epiteto attributivo. Quest'ultimo poteva cambiare volta per volta per la stessa persona, e non si ereditava. Come nome distintivo occasionale, si usava a volte il nome del padre (p. es. *Franciscus, filius Petri* oppure *Franciscus Petri*); a volte, per i magnati, il nome del feudo familiare, in altri casi, quello del luogo di nascita o di residenza, la professione, il titolo ecclesiastico o politico, il cosiddetto aggettivo d'onore, una vistosa caratteristica personale, ecc.[3] La nascita e l'uso del cognome fisso ed ereditario divenne indispensabile per lo sviluppo sociale dell' età moderna e per l'aumento del controllo e dell'attività amministrativa della Chiesa e dello stato.[4] Nella formazione dei nomi di due componenti l'Italia ebbe il primato. Il primo caso conosciuto risale al IX secolo a Venezia, il secondo al XII secolo a Firenze. Dall'Italia, l'uso di nomi di questo tipo giunse prima in Francia, dove attorno al 1300 i nomi di due elementi erano già frequenti tra i nobili,[5] e in seguito si diffuse anche in Germania e in Boemia. Nel XV secolo apparve anche in Ungheria,[6] ma per la sua diffusione generale ci volle molto tempo; si trattò di un processo lento, che si propagò per secoli in ogni regione europea. Per esempio, nella Germania dell'Ottocento c'erano ancora delle località, in cui le autorità furono costrette a introdurre i nomi di famiglia ereditari con la forza.[7] Nel XV secolo l'uso del cognome ereditario non era ancora generalmente diffuso neanche in Italia. Guarino Veronese p. es. aveva un solo nome (Guarino), e il suo nome distintivo gli venne dal luogo di nascita, mentre suo figlio Giovanni Battista portava come cognome il patronimico, nella forma del genitivo *Guarini*. Il nostro modo di concepire i nomi può portarci ad errori, nelle ricerche prosopografiche nel medioevo e nella prima età moderna. Padri e figli, con i loro relativi parenti, spesso figurano con cognomi diversi nei documenti scritti del XV secolo o di età anteriori, e questo è un fatto importante da considerare nelle ricerche. Ma troviamo esempi anche per il contrario. János Vitéz, arcivescovo di Strigonia, "padre dell'Umanesimo ungherese," p. es. si chiamava Ioannes de Zredna; il cognome da noi usato (Vitéz) è sconosciuto nelle fonti del XV secolo. Galeotto Marzio notò che uno dei suoi nipoti (il futuro *princeps* della *Sodalitas Litteraria Danubiana*; l'altro, come si sa, fu Janus Pannonius), si chiamava János Vitéz.[8] Sulla base di quest'unico dato, gli studiosi ungheresi cominciarono a chiamare János Vitéz anche lo zio, e così lo chiamano fino ad oggi.

---

[3] Cf. Paul Lehmann, "Mittelalterliche Beinamen und Ehrentitel," *Historisches Jahrbuch* 49 (1929): 215–239.

[4] Sándor Mikesy, "Miért alakultak ki vezetékneveink? [Perchè si sono prodotti i nostri cognomi?]" *Magyar Nyelv* 83 (1959): 5.

[5] Cf. Bach, *Deutsche Namenkunde*, 36, 80; Christiane Klapisch-Zuber, *Women, Family, and Ritual in Renaissance Italy* (Chicago–London, 1985), 283–284. Ringrazio Karl Schlebusch per aver richiamato la mia attenzione su questo libro.

[6] Béla Kálmán, *A nevek világa* [Il mondo dei nomi] (Budapest, 1973), 62–63.

[7] Bach, *Deutsche Namenkunde*, 76.

[8] Galeottus Martius Narniensis, *De egregie, sapienter, iocose dictis ac factis regis Mathiae*, ed. Ladislaus Juhász (Leipzig, 1934), 26.

Uno dei modi di creare un nome fu la traduzione del cognome in greco o in latino: ne abbiamo già visto alcuni esempi. Si creò così il nome Melanchthon da Schwarzerden, luogo di nascita dell'umanista. Desiderius Erasmus Roterodamus creò il proprio nome umanistico interpretando erroneamente il proprio nome originale (Geert Geerts) e traducendolo in latino e in greco. Il nome di Cuspinianus nacque dalla traduzione della prima metà del suo nome originario (Spiessheimer: *Spiess* = *cuspis*); un'analoga origine ebbe il nome del poeta Stephanus Taurinus d'Ungheria dal suo nome originale (Stieröchsel). Anche il nome Canisius si creò dalla traduzione del nome Hundt. Spesso il nome umanistico fu la traduzione di una parola che esprimeva una pecularietà (p. es. Curtius, Paulus, ecc.).[9] Si sarà formato così anche il nome di Georgios Gemisthos Plethon. Costituiscono un altro gruppo di nomi umanistici le varianti greche o latine di nomi beneauguranti; questo è il caso di Matthaeus Fortunatus, il filologo di origine ungherese, studioso del testo di Seneca, oppure di Georgius Polycarpus (Georgius de Kostolan, Kosztolányi György), umanista ungherese, genero di Giorgio Trebisonda. Com'è noto, nemmeno *Doctor Martinus*, grande riformatore della Chiesa, ebbe un nome di famiglia fisso; il suo cognome Luther deriva infatti dalla parola greca *eleutheros*.[10]

Molti nomi umanistici si formarono attraverso la *paronomasia* o l'*adnominatio*,[11] tecniche derivate dalla retorica antica. Ciò vuol dire che si usa un nome (o una parola), trasferendo il suo significato ad un'altra cosa o persona sulla base dell'identità o somiglianza del suono.[12] Anche il nome di Petrarca si formò con questo metodo. Questa figura retorica nel medioevo era conosciuta col nome di *figura etimologica*,[13] e forse era la figura più spesso adoperata. Del suo uso si potevano trovare numerosi esempi nelle *Etymologiae sive Origines* di Isidoro di Siviglia, uno dei manuali fondamentali, usati anche dagli umanisti. L'*adnominatio* o figura etimologica aveva un ruolo speciale nella *forma mentis* etimologica del medioevo, perché si pensava di trovare tramite essa il vero significato delle cose e dei fenomeni.[14] Possiamo trovare degli esempi del suo uso nella creazione dei nomi perfino nella seconda metà del XVI secolo. Ad esempio János Zsámboki (Ioannes Sambucus) si creò il cognome Sambucus (cioè sambuco) dal nome del suo luogo di nascita Samboc (Zsámbok).

Giovanni Pontano modificò il nome di battesimo con il metodo dell' *adnominatio* in Gioviano (*Iovianus*), ottenendo così un nome antico. Probabilmente con lo stesso

---

[9] Bach, *Deutsche Namenkunde*, 120–121.

[10] Bach, *Deutsche Namenkunde*, 82.

[11] *Ad Her.* 4.21.29.

[12] Cfr.: "ad idem verbum et nomen acceditur commutatione vocum aut litterarum, ut ad res dissimiles similia verba adcommodentur" (*Ad Her.* 4.21.29).

[13] Rigolot, *Poétique et onomastique*, 16.

[14] Sulla mentalità etimologica del medioevo cf. più dettagliatamente Ernst Robert Curtius, *Europäische Literatur und Lateinisches Mittelalter*, 2. Aufl. (Bern, 1954), 486–490; Friedrich Ohly, "Vom geistigen Sinn des Wortes," *Zeitschrift für deutsches Altertum und deutsche Literatur* 89 (1959): 1–23; Ilona Opelt, "Etymologie," in *Reallexikon für Antike und Christentum* (Stuttgart, 1966), 6:797–844; Roswitha Klinck, *Die lateinische Etymologie des Mittelalters* (München, 1970).

metodo si formò il soprannome *Corvinus* del re ungherese Mattia I. Suo padre Giovanni Hunyadi figura nei diplomi con il nome del podere della famiglia (Hunyad), oppure con il suo titolo supremo (*Ioannes gubernator*). Suo figlio maggiore Ladislao "vulgariter" si nomina Ladislaus Wajdafy (= il figlio del voivoda).[15] Péter Kulcsár ha dimostrato in modo convincente che Mattia ebbe il nome *Corvinus* dagli umanisti italiani, dal luogo d'origine di suo padre, Kovìn, in ungherese antico Keve (*Covinum*).[16] Questa scelta poteva esser influenzata anche dal corvo (*corvus*), presente nello stemma di famiglia, ma era importante anche che il nome *Corvinus* era ben noto nella storia antica, e così gli Italiani, facendo discendere Mattia dai Romani, potevano considerarlo come uno di loro. Il nome *Corvinus* figura per la prima volta in una lettera di Bartolomeo Fonzio del 1472. Il re stesso non lo usava, ma divenne il cognome del suo figlio naturale Giovanni, nato nel 1473.[17] L'origine romana poteva servire a legittimare l'ascesa di Mattia al trono del Sacro Impero Romano. Non è impossibile che fossero proprio gli umanisti italiani ad incoraggiare questa sua aspirazione. Ludovico Carbone già nel 1476 scrive apertamente di questa attesa: "Utinam dies illa cito adveniet, qua Romanorum regem, imperatoremque Matthiam videamus. /... /... quemadmodum super Matthiam apostolatus sortem cecidisse novimus, ita de altero Matthia nobis sperare conceditur fore aliquando, ut ei sors imperatoria contingat ..."[18] Possiamo presumere che anche il nome *Corvinus* potesse condizionare le aspirazioni e le azioni successive di Mattia.

I nomi umanistici finora citati sono legati in qualche modo al nome originale del loro portatore. All'accademia romana di Giulio Pomponio Leto — alla quale si fa risalire l'origine della moda dei nomi umanistici[19] — si sceglievano invece nomi di personaggi famosi dell'antichità. Secondo Bartolomeo Platina, Pomponio Leto "amore namque vetustatis, antiquorum praeclara nomina repetebat quasi quaedam calcharia quae nostram iuventutem aemulatione ad virtutem incitarent."[20] Pomponio Leto fu figlio naturale, non ebbe un cognome dal padre, e anche il suo nome *Iulius* fu un nome assunto.[21] Prese il suo nome umanistico probabilmente dal poeta antico *Pomponius*, che completò con l'aggettivo *Laetus*. *Philippus Callimachus Experiens* (Filippo Buonaccorsi) adottò il nome del poeta greco, e probabilmente volle esprimere il suo carattere personale con l'aggettivo *Experiens*. L'"Asclepiades" dell'accademia

---

[15] Gregorius Gyöngyösi, *Vitae fratrum eremitarum Ordinis Sancti Pauli Primi Eremitae,* ed. Franciscus L. Hervay (Budapest, 1988), 109.

[16] Péter Kulcsár, "A Corvinus-legenda [La leggenda di Corvinus]," in *Mátyás király* [Rex Mattia], ed. Gábor Bartha (Budapest, 1990), 17–35.

[17] Bartholomaeus Fontius, *Epistolarum libri III,* ed. Ladislaus Juhász (Budapest, 1931), l. 16. 26, p. 12.

[18] Lodovicus Carbo, *Dialogus de laudibus rebusque gestis r. Matthiae,* in *Analecta monumentorum Hungariae historicorum literariorum maximum inedita,* 1, ed. Franciscus Toldy (Pest, 1862; repr. ed. Geisa Érszegi, Budapest, 1987), 194.

[19] Francesco Saverio Quadrio, *Della storia e della ragione d'ogni poesia,* 1 (Bologna, 1739), 48; Michele Scherillo, *Le origini e lo svolgimento della letteratura italiana* (Milano, 1919), 96.

[20] Lo cita Vladimir Zabughin, *Giulio Pomponio Leto. Saggio critico,* 1 (Roma, 1909), 4.

[21] Zabughin, *Pomponio Leto,* 6.

portava il nome umanistico *Marcus Antonius Romanus*.[22] Presumibilmente era d'origine romana e trasse i primi due elementi del suo nome dal triumviro Marco Antonio. Niccolò Lelio Cosmico ebbe il secondo elemento del suo nome probabilmente da *Caius Laelius*, retore romano, conosciuto nell'opera intitolata *Laelius sive De amicitia* di Cicerone. Possiamo presumere che i membri dell'accademia si identificassero in qualche modo con i portatori originali dei loro nomi. Gli umanisti — come anche gli uomini antichi e medievali — credevano nell' *omen* e nel potere magico dei nomi. Questa credenza si indebolì — anche se solo in parte — con la formazione dei cognomi ereditari, i quali non indicavano più un carattere importante del loro portatore, ma sembravano in genere una serie di suoni senza alcun senso particolare.

Sembra che l'uso dei nomi umanistici diventasse frequente soprattutto nelle accademie, e nelle cerchie di scienziati, dopo la nascita dell'accademia romana di Pomponio Leto (verso la fine degli anni '60 del '400). Pomponio Leto ebbe una grande influenza sul celebre umanista tedesco, *Conradus Celtis Protucius* (Konrad Bickel, o Pickel), non solo nell'organizzazione delle accademie, ma anche per quanto riguarda i nomi umanistici. L'umanista tedesco formulò addirittura il principio che i poeti dovevano avere tre nomi.[23] Tra i letterati tedeschi infatti divenne frequente il nome umanistico di tre elementi. Ci basterà ricordare Helius Eobanus Hessus, Henricus Cornelius Agrippa (von Nettesheim), ecc.

Nella diffusione del nome umanistico ebbero un ruolo notevole la scuola ferrarese di Guarino Veronese e un suo famoso discepolo, Ioannes de Chesmicze, cioè *Ianus Pannonius*. Pare che tra gli umanisti fosse lui il primo a cambiare nome, scegliendo un vero nome antico. Descrisse quest'evento in un epigramma, in cui motivò il cambiamento del suo nome con il fatto che divenne poeta, dicendo indirettamente di aver cambiato il suo antico nome nobile in un nome ancor più illustre:

> Ioannes fueram, Ianum quem pagina dicit,
>   Admonitum ne te, lector amice, neges.
> Non ego per fastum sprevi tam nobile nomen,
>   Quo nullum totum clarius orbe sonat.
> Compulit invitum mutare vocabula cum me
>   Lavit in Aonio, flava Thalia, lacu.[24]

Dall' epigramma si capisce chiaramente che il nuovo nome di *Janus* si formò tramite l'*adnominatio*. A Ferrara i compagni di studio ungheresi dovevano pronunciare spesso il nome ungherese del poeta, János, che doveva ricordare a Guarino e ai suoi discepoli il nome del dio *Ianus*, essendo la forma fonica delle due parole quasi identica. Il cambiamento del nome dovette accadere prima del 1 ottobre del 1450, quando Tito

---

[22] Gioacchino Paparelli, *Callimaco Esperiente (Filippo Buonaccorsi)*, 2. ed. (Roma, 1977), 70 e passim.

[23] "Poetas esse trinomes." Lo cita Bach, *Deutsche Namenkunde*, 116.

[24] *Iani Pannonii . . . poemata omnia*, ed. József Teleki e Sándor Kovásznaj (Traiecti ad Rhenum, 1784), Ep. 1.130.

Vespasiano Strozzi finì i primi due volumi dell'*Erotica*,²⁵ perché già in quest'opera l'autore chiama il nostro poeta col nome *Ianus*. Il Nostro cambiò il primo elemento del suo nome, e usò il suo nome in questa forma anche nelle sue poesie. Il nome *Pannonius* lo ebbe a Ferrara come nome distintivo, ma egli stesso non lo usò mai. Si accontentò del suo nome unico, che fu più romano, più antico e più illustre del nome di tutti gli altri, e portato solo da lui: egli cambiò il nome cristiano di Giovanni col nome del dio più antico di Roma. Questo fu evidentissimo per i conoscitori dell'antichità, come per i poeti suoi compagni di Ferrara, i quali identificarono il nome del poeta con il nome del dio *Ianus*.²⁶

Il dio *Ianus*, con il suo nome ricco di significati, potrebbe anche essere il simbolo del movimento umanistico. Con questo nome il poeta pannonico trovò il suo vero nome come umanista, ma anche come persona e come poeta. Il nostro poeta sapeva tutto del dio di cui portava il nome, poiché conosceva tutte le fonti letterarie che lo riguardavano. I *Fasti* di Ovidio, il *De civitate Dei* di s. Agostino, i poeti e gli scrittori romani (Varrone, Virgilio, Servio, Orazio, Stazio, ecc.) costituivano una parte importante delle materie di studio della scuola di Guarino,²⁷ e Janus conosceva bene anche le due opere famose di Macrobio, fonti importantissime delle conoscenze sul dio Giano.²⁸ Nelle epistole poetiche scambiate con Giovan Battista Guarini, accetta in una forma semiseria l'attributo di bifronte (*Ianus Bifrons*) del dio Giano.²⁹ Il nome del dio era adatto ad esprimere anche l'orgoglio de Nostro di essere il primo poeta latino dell'antico *Barbaricum*, poiché egli sapeva di essere un valido emulatore dei poeti neolatini d'Italia. Giano, il dio del principio, aveva come epiteto fisso *Primus*, e anche nelle poesie del Nostro, accanto al nome del poeta figura quest'espressione. L'epiteto è sempre legato alla sua poesia. In un suo epigramma ferrarese il poeta esalta i suoi meriti:

> Quod legerent omnes, quondam dabat Itala tellus,
>   Nunc e Pannonia carmina missa legit.
> Magna quidem nobis haec gloria, sed tibi major,
>   Nobilis ingenio, patria facta, meo.³⁰

---

²⁵ *Die Borsias des Tito Strozzi. Ein lateinisches Epos der Renaissance,* hrsg. Walther Ludwig (München, 1977), 18, n. 33.

²⁶ Cf. l'epigramma di Roberto degli Orsi, in *Analecta ad historiam renascentium in Hungaria litterarum spectantia* . . . , ed. Jenö Ábel (Budapest, 1880), 106 e la poesia dello Strozzi in *Iani Pannonii . . . poemata omnia,* Ep. 2.5, ll. 25–26.

²⁷ Remigio Sabbadini, *La scuola e gli studi di Guarino Veronese* (Catania, 1896) 36, 52, 84, 105–108.

²⁸ Géza Vadász, "La pensée pythagorienne dans la poésie de Janus Pannonius," in *Mathias Corvinus and Humanism in Central Europe,* ed. Tibor Klaniczay and József Jankovics (Budapest, 1994), 235–240.

²⁹ Cf. *Analecta ad historiam,* ed. Ábel, 120. Cfr. l'epigramma di B. Guarini, 148.

³⁰ *Iani Pannonii . . . poemata omnia,* Ep. 1.61.

In un altro epigramma ferrarese, Janus chiama se stesso la prima gloria della Pannonia ("Ille ego Pannoniae, gloria prima, meae").[31]

Nel 1464 Janus seguì il re Mattia che stava per partire con il suo esercito in Bosnia per la seconda volta contro i Turchi. Il poeta si ammalò al campo, e descrisse in un'elegia quest'esperienza e il dolore di dover lasciare la vita. L'elegia imita i versi 1–56 dell'elegia tibulliana detta *di Corcyra*,[32] ma nonostante l'imitazione, è un capolavoro di tono personale. Come quella di Tibullo, anche l'elegia del poeta umanista finisce con un epitaffio, in cui Janus immortala il proprio nome, e usando l'epiteto *primus* per sè stesso, fissa come nome distintivo quest'unico "titolo" importante del suo nome:

> Hic situs est Ianus, patrium qui primus ad Histrum
> Duxit laurigeras, ex Helicone, Deas.[33]

La poesia citata è anche la testimonianza commovente del suo desiderio di pace. Janus già dalla prima gioventù si era impegnato per la pace. Ne è testimonianza la poesia intitolata *Pro pacanda Italia*, scritta in onore di Federico III, in occasione del ricevimento che diedero in suo onore a Ferrara (17 gennaio 1452),[34] dove l'imperatore si fermò durante il viaggio di ritorno dalla sua incoronazione a Roma. Alla poesia dovette aggiungere un significato particolare il fatto, che venne recitata proprio dal poeta che portava il nome del dio della pace. Non è impossibile che il pacifismo del poeta — attestato anche da altri due epigrammi contro la guerra (*Pro pace; Ad Martem, precatio pro pace*)[35] — fosse confermato anche da questa componente essenziale del significato del suo nome.

Il suono del suo nome induava che Janus apparteneva alla comunità degli umanisti, mentre il significato del nome lo aiutava a conoscere se stesso e ad autoidentificarsi. Quando il nome umanistico si diffuse dovunque come una moda, venne a mancare proprio quest'ultima sua funzione; diventò superflua anche la dimostrazione dell'appartenenza, perché la cultura umanistica era ormai accolta generalmente tra i letterati. Anche il nome *Ianus* diventò di uso comune (per esempio Ianus Vitalis, Aulus Ianus Parrhasius, Ianus Secundus, ecc.), usato da tutti quelli che si chiamavano Giovanni (Ioannes), non pensando più al suo significato originale. La moda del nome umanistico fu criticata da diversi autori, come per esempio da Ludovico Ariosto e

---

[31] *Iani Pannonii . . . poemata omnia*, Ep. 1.340.

[32] V. più ampiamente Klára Pajorin, "Janus Pannonius és Mars Hungaricus [J. P. e M. H.]," in *Klaniczay-emlékkönyv. Tanulmányok Klaniczay Tibor tiszteletére* [Memoria di Klaniczay. Saggi in memoria di Tibor Klaniczay], ed. József Jankovics (Budapest, 1994), 62.

[33] *Iani Pannonii . . . poemata omnia*, Ep. I. 9, ll. 117–118.

[34] *Iani Pannonii . . . poemata omnia*, *Silva panegyrica III*. Per la datazione e l'analisi della poesia v. József Huszti, *Janus Pannonius* (Pécs, 1931), 84–85.

[35] *Iani Pannonii . . . poemata omnia*, Ep. II. 8. e Ep. I. 7. Cf. più diffusamente Pajorin, "Janus Pannonius és Mars Hungaricus," 65–66.

Francesco Maturanzio.[36] Queste critiche basate su una considerazione moderna del nome (che abbiamo anche noi) contribuirono al processo, che portò alla scomparsa anche dell'ultimo requisito della mentalità medievale onomastica,[37] cioè dell'uso del nome umanistico.

MTA Irodalmi Intézet
(Institute for Literary Studies of Hungarian
Academy of Sciences)
Budapest, Hungary

---

[36] "Il nome che di apostolo ti denno / o d'alcun minor santo i padri, quando / cristiano d' aqua, e non d'altro ti fenno, / in Cosmico, in Pomponio vai mutando; / altri Pietro in Pierio, altri Giovanni / in Iano o in Iovian va riconciando; / quasi che 'l nome i buon giudici inganni / e che quel meglio t'abbia a far poeta / che non farà lo studio de molti anni" (L. Ariosto, *Sat.* VI, 53–66, citato da Scherillo, *Le origini e lo svolgimento*, 77). Per l'epigramma di Francesco Maturanzio, cf. Huszti, *Janus Pannonius*, 300.

[37] Sul cambiamento del nome nel Medioevo, cf. v. Gertrud Thoma, *Namensänderungen in Herrscherfamilien des mittelalterlichen Europa* (Kallmünz, 1985).

Coincidences and Differences between the Latin and the Spanish Poems, Treatises, and Epistles of Rudericus Carus (Rodrigo Caro)

JOAQUÍN PASCUAL BAREA

Rudericus Carus (Utrera, 1573–Seville, 1647) was an outstanding archaeologist and poet of the Spanish Golden Age, and he is well known for the historical treatises and the poems that he wrote in Latin and in the vernacular, particularly the *Song to the Ruins of Italica*.[1] He also used both languages in his letters and in his professional writings. Of course, this bilingual condition is not rare among other humanists.[2] But Carus adopted the legacy of Renaissance humanism more faithfully than any other writer of his time, particularly a sensibility and enthusiasm for antiquity. However, he is aware that the genuine principles of the Renaissance had already disappeared. This is quite clear from the following words written to the Aragonese scholar Andrés de Ustarroz on 23 May 1642:

> Lástima tenga vm. de los que vivimos en esta última Bética, que siendo madre en todas las edades de tan ilustres ingenios, se halla en este infelice tiempo tan prostrada, que en esta gran ciudad, lunbrera del mundo nuevo y viejo, no sé si se hallaran tres que traten estos estudios, y si alguno los trata, es o con vana

---

[1] This poem was translated into English by the American poet W. C. Bryant, and into Latin by T. Viñas and M. A. Caro. Cf. Tomás Viñas, *Versiones latinas de poesías hispanas* (Barcelona, 1927), xxix–xxx; Miguel Antonio Caro, *La Canción a las ruinas de Itálica. Introducción, versión latina y notas* (Bogotá, 1947).

[2] Cf. Joaquín Pascual, "Bilingual Cultures: The Learned Language and the Vernacular in Renaissance Seville and Ancient Rome," in *Latin and Vernacular in Renaissance Spain*, ed. Barry Taylor and Alejandro Coroleu, Cañada Blanch Monographs 3 (Manchester, 1999), 113–119.

ostentación y sin provecho público, o con ignorancia de los verdaderos principios, que es exercitarse en el glorioso polvo de la antigüedad.[3]

Humanistic Latin had already overcome the obsolete and useless controversies concerning Ciceronianism,[4] and a cultivated élite still tried to emulate in Latin the elegance of the classics, as much in the choice of words as in the variety of expression and the pleasant sonority of speech. Latin, besides being the basis of academic education, continued to be a language of literary prestige. In a *Memorial* written a few years before his death, Carus mentioned his poem *Baetis urbs* and a few other works in Latin, but he omitted his poetry and some books written in the vernacular, since they did not have such a high reputation. He also used Latin in some of his official submissions trying to institute new feasts in Seville, as well as in a few letters to Johannes Cintado, Franciscus de Bilches, and Josephus Fernández de Retes, among others who also wrote to him in the same language.[5] This use of Latin was not actually due to the need for communicating with learned scholars from other countries. It was rather the practice of a few people who sought to prolong the literary habits of humanism.

Carus's Latin prose is both natural and elegant. One of his correspondents praised the style of one of his Latin books by calling it "Flemish Latin". This is partly due to the influence exercised by authors such as Erasmus and Lipsius, as much in a direct way as through the teaching and works of García Matamorus, Arias Montanus, and other Spanish humanists. Carus knew that Latin would continue being the language of communication for academic and scientific purposes among European scholars, and he tried to use ancient words even to describe things that did not exist in antiquity. For instance, he suggested the name *thermopolium* for the chocolate shops that were already popular in Seville in the seventeenth century, since this word means, in Plautus's comedies, a place where hot and generally sweet drinks are sold.[6]

Carus wrote in Latin an interesting treatise on the ancient gods of Spain and Portugal, some annotations on the Spanish part of Nubiensis' *Geography*, and a commentary on his own edition of the *History* of pseudo-Dexter and other spurious texts. All these works deal with the whole Iberian Peninsula and have a European scope. His annotated edition of the *History* of pseudo-Dexter, which had been written in fact by a Jesuit from Toledo, might have been printed in France by Johannes Bellerus, in the new *Bibliotheca veterum patrum*, but Franciscus Vivarius did it first. In 1642 he sent his work *Veterum Hispanie Deorum Manes sive Reliquiae* to the Low Countries to be printed. But this manuscript got lost, and only the original MS version of 1628 has

---

[3] Biblioteca Nacional, Madrid, Ms. 8.389, f. 203; Ricardo del Arco y Garay, *La erudición española en el siglo XVII y el cronista de Aragón Andrés de Ustarroz* (Madrid, 1950), 336.

[4] Cf. Juan M. Núñez, *El ciceronianismo en España* (Valladolid, 1993).

[5] Carus wrote most of his letters in Spanish. The Biblioteca Capitular of Seville (BCS) contains the copy of many of them in MSS. 57–6–22 and 58–1–9, fols. 206, 236–252, 276–277, 290–292, etc.

[6] On 3 May 1641, his friend Hieronymus Pancorvus told him that he had written a panegyric to chocolate, since he was very fond of it (BCS, Ms. 58–1–9, fol. 189r).

been preserved in the Bodleian Library at Oxford, including his additions in the margins.[7] It was bound together with his Latin notes on several Spanish place names in Nubiensis' *Geography*, following a Latin translation from Arabic which had been printed in Paris. His mythological treatise does not follow the allegorical tradition; on the contrary, this literary and scientific work is based on the study of Latin inscriptions, coins, and other archaeological remains, as well as on the texts of the ancient authors. It also contains some interesting comments on comparative religion, etymology and folklore. This book was therefore a pioneer work among modern studies of the ancient gods of Europe.

When a book was expected to be read by more people if it was written in Spanish, Rudericus did not even need to explain why he did it that way.[8] This is the case with his treatises devoted to the antiquities of Utrera and the ancient *Conventus Hispalensis*, or to the illustrious figures of Seville and the ancient games, or dealing also with local and contemporary folklore. Since the ancient sources of these works were hardly understandable by most of his potential readers, he translated most of them into Spanish. These include Latin texts of more than forty authors from antiquity to the Renaissance. When the original was written in verse, he rendered it into Spanish verse too.[9] He also translated into Latin verse a vernacular proverb, "A quien Dios quiso bien, en Sevilla le dio de comer", following the practice of Ferdinandus Arceus, who had translated a collection of Castilian proverbs into Latin, and printed his book in Salamanca in 1533, and also of Joannes de Mal Lara.[10]

We know nearly fifty poems of Rudericus Carus. The number and range of his Latin and Spanish poems are similar, and they share the same literary theory, genres, and subjects. They also use the same rhetorical and poetic procedures to achieve the

---

[7] Five days before his death in August 1647, Carus bequeathed the manuscript of this work to the marquis of Estepa (†1658). Juan Lucas Cortés (†1701) owned it around 1676; after the auction of his books in 1702, it belonged to the Dutch philologist and poet Jacob Philip d'Orville (†1751), and his friend Pieter Burman was able to publish an epigram (now *Anth. Lat.* Riese 873) from this manuscript in his *Anthologia Veterum Latinorum Epigrammatum et Poematum*, 2 vols. (Amsterdam, 1773), 2:458, where he recommended Carus's treatise on the ancient gods of Spain to be printed. Cf. Joaquín Pascual Barea, "*Veterum Hispaniae deorum manes sive reliquiae*: noticias del tratado de Rodrigo Caro sobre la religión antigua en Hispania," paper at the III Congreso de la Sociedad de Estudios Latinos (Lugo and Santiago de Compostela, 2000), forthcoming.

[8] In 1540, Francus Leardus wrote an epigram for Petrus Mexía's *Silva de varia lección* to explain that the author preferred to write it in Spanish so that it could be read by more people. Cf. Joachim Pascual Barea, "Le Banquier génois Franco Leardo, un poète latin de Séville dans la première moitié du XVIème siècle," in *Acta Conventus Neo-Latini Bariensis*, ed. Rhoda Schnur et al., MRTS 184 (Tempe, AZ, 1998), 475–483 (here 483, poem VI). Mexía's book was eventually translated into Latin by Mambrini de Sabrino, and published at Lyon in 1556.

[9] Cf. Luis Gómez Canseco, *Rodrigo Caro, un humanista en la Sevilla del seiscientos* (Seville, 1986), 164–166.

[10] Cf. Antonio Serrano Cueto, *Los Adagiorum Quinquagenae quinque de Fernando de Arce*, Alcañiz, unpublished. We find that proverb among the *Refranes más famosíssimos de Mal Lara* (Seville, 1568), fols. 5v–7r. Cf. J. de Mal Lara, *Filosofía Vulgar*, ed. A. Vilanova, 4 vols. (Barcelona, 1958–1959), 1:157–161.

necessary elegance of poetry. We find therefore many similarities, connections, and mutual influences between them. Due to the older tradition of Latin literature, it is not surprising that the structure, procedures, images, topics, and even some phrases and words of the Spanish poems had been used first in the Neo-Latin literature. Carus's Latin poems, closer to ancient poetry in their language while contemporary in their subject-matter, frequently served as a bridge to adapt the classics to vernacular poetry. This is also true in the case of many other Renaissance poets, which illustrates the relationship between the poetry written in each language at that time.

Carus was aware of being a bilingual poet, and he collected some of his poems in a "quaderno [. . .] de sus versos en romance y en latín".[11] Marcelino Menéndez Pelayo was eager to see the publication of Carus's Latin and Spanish poetry, relating as it did to a great variety of genres of the humanistic tradition.[12] Some of his Latin and vernacular verses celebrated ancient ruins and other archaeological remains, which come to life in a very special way in the *naenia* of "*Cupido Pendulus*", in the "Song to the Ruins of Italica", and in the humorous poem about the ruined tower of "La Membrilla". The last-named poem is an autobiographical story, a Latin epistle in distichs from 1595, which was also addressed to his friend Joannes de Robles, a Latin poet and a Castilian writer and theorist. Carus wrote four religious poems in the vernacular and three in Latin: an ode and a hymn in imitation of Horace, and an epigram about a miracle by the Virgin; the ode is dedicated to the Virgin of Las Veredas of his native village, and the hymn to the skull of Euphrosyne, a relic of one of the eleven thousand martyrs of Cologne brought from the convent of the Beghards in Maastricht by the Spanish governor.

There are many coincidences in his Latin and Spanish poems belonging to the genre of the *laus urbis*. *Baetis urbs sive Vtricula* shares with the Spanish "silvas" devoted to Seville, Carmona, and Utrera, and even with the poem on the ruins of Italica, the same structure, literary resources, and contents, with slight variants depending on the particular features of each place. After the initial apostrophe, the five poems deal with the name and the foundation of each city, and all finish by mentioning their illustrious men and their martyrs and saints. While the ruins are the main topic in *Italica*, the situation of the three modern cities, the fertility of their lands and their other valuable products, are the central points in the other commendations of cities. Also lines 79–122 of the comic poem *Membrilla* include some of these elements: name and origin, natural wealth, patron saints and illustrious men, genius of the city, and so forth.

In *Baetis urbs*, the emulation of the classics is very carefully practised, even though a grammarian from the University of Salamanca, who had been the pupil of Sanctius, condemned the syntactic construction *fraudata colonos*. Through these three hundred

---

[11] BCS, MS. 58–1–9, fol. 72v. They might be those copied in 1645 from the autograph in MS. 57–3–24, fols. 45–57, under the title of *Carmina Cl. V. Ruderici Cari*.

[12] M. Menéndez Pelayo, "Programa de Literatura Española. Lección 82. Conservadores del buen gusto y de la tradición literaria del siglo XVI en la lírica. Escuela sevillana. Rodrigo Caro, sus poesías latinas y castellanas: la canción a las ruinas de Itálica, escrita en el siglo XVI, corregida en el XVII," in *Estudios y Discursos de Crítica Histórica y Literaria*, ed. E. Sánchez Reyes, 7 vols., in *Obras Completas* (Santander, 1941–1942), 1:60, 71.

and seven hexameters of classical elegance,[13] Rudericus tried to recover the past of his hometown. But the city of *Baetis* mentioned in the text of Strabo's *Geography* (3.2.1) might be indeed a misreading of *Italica* in the Greek transcription of these names. In that case, the author of the best Spanish poem on the ruins of Italica also used the language of Virgil to describe its natural wealth (*Baetis*, vv. 65–146), and to remember the exiling of the native Andalusian population and the new splendour brought by the Roman settlers according to Strabo (vv. 200–215):

>   [. . .] quam Caesar ademptam
>   priscis ruricolis Romano milite complet.
>   Huic diuisus ager ueteri migrante colono
>   diuisaeque domus alios uidere Penates.
>   Plebs, ciues, equites imitataque curia patres,
>   mores, iura, forum cedunt et sacra Quirino.
>   Totaque iam Baetim resonabat Roma per urbem
>   exiguam, nam magna decent te, Baetis, alumna
>   Aeneadum, aeterno quae iam praecellis honore
>   Romuleam priscumque audes ambire decorem
>   urbis patritiae dum Gaditana lacessis
>   moenia Balborum toties decorata trophaeis.
>   Hinc proceres uenere pii, hinc clara uirorum
>   militia atque toga praestantum fluxit origo,
>   quos non Cecropiae dedignarentur Athenae,
>   suspexit nam Roma suos [. . .]

Carus's laudatory poems in Latin belong to the genres of the Latin epicedium, epigram, and epitaph; they were also written for portraits and to recommend the books of some authors of his time. In his Castilian verses he used the sonnet, the *esparsa*, the quatrain, and the song to praise different people. Wit is one of the most common features in all these Latin and vernacular poems.[14] The following passage from Carus, who considered Góngora and Juan de Salinas the best authors of Spanish epigrams in his time, proves that literary theory concerning the Latin epigram was applied to the sonnet and other forms of vernacular verse:

---

[13] I have commented on some peculiarities of Carus's hexameters, pentameters, iambi, and Sapphics in "Algunas particularidades de prosodia y métrica latinas del Renacimiento," in *Estudios de Métrica Latina*, ed. Jesús Luque Moreno and Pedro Rafael Díaz y Díaz, 2 vols. (Granada, 1999), 2:747–766.

[14] Cf. Juan F. Alcina, "Entre latín y romance: modelos neolatinos en la creación poética castellana," in *Humanismo y pervivencia del Mundo Clásico*, 1, ed. José M. Maestre Maestre and Joaquín Pascual Barea, 2 vols. (Cádiz, 1993), 1:3–27 (here 5); Carmen Guzmán Arias and José I. Andújar Cantón, "El tratado de N. Mercerius sobre teoría epigramática," and Daniel López-Cañete, "Sobre el epigrama religioso en el Renacimiento," in *Humanismo y pervivencia del Mundo Clásico*, 2: *Homenaje al profesor Luis Gil*, ed. José M. Maestre Maestre, Joaquín Pascual Barea, and Luis Charlo Brea, 3 vols. (Cádiz, 1997), 2:865–870, 871–882 respectively.

En la poesía se inclinó [Salinas] a lo que comúnmente los españoles son inclinados, que es cifrar con viveza un conceto o muchos en pocos versos, ajustando de manera la propiedad de las voces que ninguna esté ociosa. Así lo pide el arte, y esta virtud resplendece en el príncipe de los poetas epigramatarios, Marco Valerio Marcial, también español de la Celtiberia, a quien admiró la Antigüedad romana y admirarán los siglos. Nuestra edad conoció a D. Luis de Góngora, hijo de aquella madre de eternos ingenios, Córdoba. Siguióles el Dr. Juan de Salinas con tanta propiedad y sales, que en este género no les es inferior, estrechando su Musa a aquellos preceptos que enseñó Quintiliano, también español, en el lib. 6, c. 3 de las *Institutiones oratorias*: 'dijo muchas gracias pero sin agravio de nadie' [. . .]. En lo que más resplendeció su agudeza fue en las alusiones y equívocos, en que no es inferior a los demás, antes superior en la pureza de la habla castellana [. . .].[15]

Some of Carus' own epigrams have these qualities, and Peter Burmann considered one of them very elegant and comparable to those written in the finest age of these things (*Anthologia Latina*, Riese 873). The painter Francisco Pacheco asked him to write the epigrams for the portraits of two of the chief poets of the Spanish Golden Age, Fernando de Herrera and Fray Luis de León.[16]

For a work of Francisco Tamayo now preserved at the Hispanic Society of America, Carus wrote a poem in Latin and another in the vernacular with the same contents. There are consequently many coincidences and points of dependence between them. The sonnet has the same structure as the Latin epigram, and they even share the final play of words. (Among others, Arias Montanus and Mal Lara had written such preliminary poems.) Again, the contents of a Latin distich and a Spanish quatrain by Carus praising Pancorvus are very similar, this being the result of a reciprocal and simultaneous poetic translation:

IN HIERONYMI PANCORVI LAVDEM DISTICHON

— Panem coruus habet rostro. Cur mel fluit inde?
— Ingenio panis redditur ore fauus.

---

[15] This praise for Salinas' poems, dated 16 May 1646, is quoted by Henry Bonneville, *Le poète sévillan Juan de Salinas (1562?–1643): vie et oeuvre* (Paris, 1969), 4.

[16] Francisco Pacheco, *Libro de descripción de verdaderos retratos de ilustres y memorables varones de Sevilla*, ed. Pedro Piñero Ramírez and Rogelio Reyes Cano (Seville, 1985) wrote about Fray Luis: "Para cumplimiento de su elogio y de mi deseo, no me contenté con menos, en honra de tan insigne varón, de que los versos latinos fuesen del licenciado Rodrigo Caro, y los castellanos de Lope de Vega en su *Laurel de Apolo*, con que se encarecen bastantemente" (69–71). In praise of Herrera, this father-in-law of Diego Velázquez wrote: "aunque muchos aventajados ingenios hicieron versos en su alabanza, me pareció poner aquí parte de un elogio de Pablo de Céspedes, por ser persona a quien estimó mucho Fernando de Herrera, después desta epigrama latina que el licenciado Rodrigo Caro ofreció a su retrato, digna de la erudición de su autor" (179). He praised Carus only as a Latin poet, since he certainly knew other good Spanish poets. Herrera and Fray Luis also wrote Latin poems.

REDONDILLA A JERÓNIMO PANCORVO

Cuervo es y pan celestial
trae en el pico, ¿cómo es miel?
Su ingenio es tal, que con él
lo que es pan, hace panal.

Many Latin poets wrote laudatory poems for Carus's own books too. Among them we can mention the professor of Antequera Joannes Aquilarius, Joannes Corderus Chamizo from Villamartín, Laurentius de Castillejos, Joannes Baptista Porcellus from Medina, Petrus Amador de Lazcano, the cosmographer Antonius Morenus, Joannes Ximenius, the Jesuit Bernardus Carus, and Ferdinandus Bajo Orihuela.

There were many other authors of Latin poems in Seville. But Castilian poetry had already reached a decisive maturity, and writing Latin was relegated to the members of religious orders and a few scholars. Latin hardly kept a place of privilege in the literary competitions organized in Seville from 1531 onwards. First as a Spanish poet, and later with a Latin inscription, Rudericus took part in the Sevillian competitions celebrating St. Ignatius's beatification in 1610 and the proclamation of Mary's Immaculate Conception in 1616. Many graduates, bachelors, as well as students and teachers of the English College, wrote poems for these competitions in both languages and in different genres. Among them we find the poet Thomas Barton and a few other British names, such as Richard Curtis, Henry Salkeld, Robert Smith, Edward Hopton, William Ashton (Aston), Nicholas Hannington, William Maurice, Andrew Barnes, and perhaps also Francis Guillaude, Thomas Piget, and Henry Valinger.[17] Their presence in Seville was due to the political exile imposed on Catholics by the religious persecution of the English Crown.

Rudericus Carus was a Latin humanist who lived at a time when Castilian already prevailed. This explains why he used both languages in his writings. In prose he preferred the vulgar tongue in his biographical and historical treatises about Utrera and Seville, or about the ancient games, thus interesting a public who for the most part did not understand Latin. He used Latin as an international language of culture in works of interest to other European scholars, such as his treatise on the ancient gods of Hispania, the *History* of pseudo-Dexter, and Nubiensis' *Geography*. As for his poems, he preferred Latin in the funeral compositions, but he used both languages in the commendations of cities and people, as well as in his poetry with a biographical, archaeological, or religious content. Carus also used Latin as the official language of the Catholic Church when he had to write a submission to the Vatican. Writing in Latin was also a humanistic entertainment in some of his poems and letters, particularly when this language better fitted the subject or the purpose in view. His case is

---

[17] Cf. Francisco de Luque Fajardo, *Relación de la fiesta que se hizo en Sevilla a la beatificación del glorioso San Ignacio* . . . (Seville, 1610); idem, *Relación de las fiestas de la cofradía de sacerdotes de San Pedro ad Vincula celebradas en su parroquial iglesia de Sevilla a la Purísima Concepción* (Seville, 1616).

certainly an interesting example of the situation of the *Respublica litterarum* in seventeenth-century Spain.

University of Cádiz

Rudericus Carus's Works Quoted

Antigüedades y principado de la ilustríssima ciudad de Sevilla y Chorographía de su convento jurídico o antigua chancillería (Seville, 1634), facs. Seville, 1982, 1998.

Días geniales o lúdicros, ed. Jean-Pierre Etienvre (Madrid, 1978).

Flavii Luci Dextri V. C. Omnimodae Historiae, quae extant Fragmenta, cum Chronico M. Maximi, et Helecae, ac S. Braulionis Caesaraugustanorum Episcoporum, Notis Ruderici Cari Baetici illustrata (Seville, 1627).

Memorial de Utrera, in *Obras de Rodrigo Caro*, 2 vols. (Seville, 1883), vol. 2.

Poesía castellana y latina e inscripciones originales. Estudio, edición crítica, traducción, notas e índices de Joaquín Pascual Barea (Seville, 2000).

Varones en letras naturales de la ilustrísima ciudad de Sevilla. Epistolario, ed. Santiago Montoto (Seville, 1915); *Varones insignes en letras* [...] *de Sevilla*, ed. Luis Gómez Canseco (Seville, 1992).

Veterum Hispaniae deorum manes sive reliquiae (1628) and *Excerpta ex libro geographiae Nubiensis, qui vocatur Relaxatio Animi curiosi, ab Nuba quodam Arabe composito.* Oxford, Bodleian Library, Ms. D'Orville 47.

Nuevos textos del teatro jesuítico en España, II: Las comedias Techmitius y Triunfo de la fe[1]

VICENTE PICON GARCIA

El objetivo de este trabajo, que se complementa con el del Profesor Á. Sierra aparecido en este mismo volumen, es presentar estas dos obras de teatro escolar jesuítico que permanecen aún inéditas y no han sido estudiadas ni figuran siquiera en ninguno de los catálogos existentes en España sobre este teatro. Se hallan también en un legajo de la Colección de Jesuitas de la Real Academia de la Historia de Madrid (R.A.H.) con la signatura 9/7262. Me limitaré a señalar los datos y aspectos fundamentales, que aparecerán completados y estudiados con más profundidad en la edición que de ellas estamos preparando.

La comedia *Techmitius* ocupa 28 folios (1r–28r) del manuscrito que la contiene, en el que figuran también composiciones en versos castellanos de algunos pasajes que en la comedia aparecen en prosa (33v–34v) y algunos borradores interesantes para la fijación del texto (35v–36v; 37r–38v).

En el manuscrito no figura el título de la pieza, pero, a juzgar por las formas en que aparece el nombre del protagonista en latín (e.g., el acusativo *Techmitium* con que se inicia el primer prólogo) debía ser *Techmitius*, con pronunciación asibilada *Techmisius*.

Tampoco figuran la fecha ni el lugar de representación. Sin embargo, la primera se puede deducir por un pasaje de la escena 2.4, donde Fraudencio, el antagonista de Techmisio, presenta la figura del Tiempo al personaje Donaire con esta alusión al Quijote de Cervantes: Frau.— "Ola ola Sor Donayre, encontrádose ha Sancho con su rocín, a fee de quien soy." Si la primera edición del Quijote apareció en el año 1604, como se sabe con certeza, se deduce que el término *post quem* para la fecha de composición de la obra y de su representación se puede situar en ese mismo año 1604 o después.

---

[1] El trabajo ha sido realizado en el marco de un proyecto de investigación (PB97–0053) financado por la DGICYT, titulado "El teatro escolar latino en España (1550–1650)."

El argumento básico es el siguiente: Techmisio, que se halla confundido por los males y los engaños que reinan en el mundo, quiere librarse de ellos y, para conseguirlo, pide consejo a sus compañeros Bellerfo y Discurso. Éste le elogia la astucia de Fraudencio, de ahí que, incitado por ello, Techmisio le encarga que vaya a consultarle el medio mejor para salir de su zozobra y librarse de los engaños; pero los consejos de Fraudencio les sumen en mayor confusión. Discurso entonces, por mediación de Donaire que se les une como compañero, acude a un historiador (Fileto) que le propone la historia como lección de vida y a un fisiólogo (Cosme Trapesunda) que le hace adivinaciones de alto vuelo, pero tampoco les sacan de sus dudas. Por eso se dirige finalmente al sabio Logiteo que le aconseja que Techmisio escuche el Consejo divino, por medio del cual alcanza la luz y vence a Fraudencio.

Los interlocutores son *Techmisius*, el protagonista confundido por los engaños y males del mundo; *Bellerfus* y *Discursus*, dos compañeros suyos; *Fraudentius*, el tramador de engaños; *Philetus*, historiador; *Philologus*, el astrólogo; Cosme Trapesunda, adivino; Donaire, un joven que colabora de *Discursus*; Domingo Ramos, un labrador, que intenta engañar astutamente a *Techmisius*; *Tempus*, figura alegórica que propone ver en su discurso lecciones de vida; *Democritus* y *Heraclitus*, filósofos con actitudes y consejos contrapuestos ante el acontecer: reírse o llorar; *Logiteus*, sabio consejero; y *Consilium diuinum*, descubridor de la luz y el camino para triunfar sobre el mal.

La comedia no sigue la ley clásica de los cinco actos como preferían los primeros autores del teatro escolar, sino que sólo contiene cuatro, con distinto número de escenas (1=5; 2=5; 3=3; 4=8), dos prólogos en latín y castellano respectivamente para explicar el argumento, otros tres en castellano para los actos 2, 3 y 4, y un epílogo también en castellano para la despedida.

Se trata de una comedia típica de colegio, de carácter moralizante, en la que se mezcla la prosa y el verso, el latín y el castellano. La presencia del latín en ella, para la fecha en que se compone, es destacada. Contiene en total 144 versos latinos y 200 líneas en prosa latina. Además, los diálogos en castellano se salpican con frecuencia de frases latinas, aforismos, sentencias, etc., que les confieren cierta gracia y sabor erudito. Los tipos de versos que se utilizan son senarios yámbicos (81), dímetros anapestos (20), hexámetros dactílicos (29), y dísticos elegíacos (7).

El autor distribuye estas partes compuestas en prosa o verso latino de un modo peculiar, de manera que la mayoría de las escenas que contienen latín las abre con versos latinos de buena factura, cuyo sentido parafrasea luego o lo amplía con versos castellanos, y las cierra con prosa latina, desarrollando en castellano el contenido de la escena que se extiende entre ambas partes. En las escenas que utiliza exclusivamente el castellano (1.2; 2.3; 2.4; 3.3; 4.6 y 7), destaca la 3.3 a la que confiere gran realismo reflejando el habla vulgar y el carácter astuto del labrador Domingo.

Para hacerse una idea de la calidad del latín de la pieza, véase la presentación de Fraudencio que el autor pone en sus propios labios:

(fol. 4v)   Act. 1 Sce 4
              Tech. Dis. Bell. Frau
Fraud.—   Fraudibus instructus regnat Fraudentius orbe
              atque regit regum celsa theatra dolis.

           Ipse per insidias nunc hos, nunc dej icit illos
                 ast alios technis sidera ad alta vehit.
           Montiuagus custos ouium me pectore gestat
                 ipse meis moderor legibus ampla fora
           Incultos habito saltus et compita et vrbes
                 et penetro latitans aulica tecta ducum
           Dulces blandicie risus fallacia verba
                 obsequiumque capit nescia corda mali
           Indicat haec vultus tegitur sed corde venenum
(fol. 5r) corde latent fraudes dulcia verba patent.
           Hinc fit vt immensum teneat Fraudentius orbem
           i[n]numere ac gentes numina nostra col{l}ant.

El *Triunfo de la Fe* ocupa 32 folios (1r–32r) del manuscrito que se completa a continuación con un coloquio sobre la vida solitaria. En él se da este título completo de la pieza en la rúbrica que la encabeza: "Triunfo de la fee div^a sobre la razon hum^a con la circuncision del entendim^o y de los cinco sentidos [y un coloquio de la vida solitaria]." Tampoco en este caso se recoge en dicha rúbrica el lugar y la fecha de representación, pero sabemos que se representó en Cádiz, el 1 de enero de 1573, porque así lo expresa explícitamente el autor en la información que nos da sobre la firma del cartel en que se anunciaba aquélla (fol. 1v: "[en el] "estudio de la compañia de Jesus de la jllse [ilustre] y antigua ciudad de cadiz") y la concesión de los premios (fol. 31r: "in hoc collegio societatis Iesu anno domini millesimo quingentesimo septuagessimo [sic] tertio Kalendis februarii").

El argumento de la obra es el siguiente: el Entendimiento o Razón representado por Philoteoro va en busca de los cinco sentidos y el sentido común representados por cinco pastores y su mayoral para que le den contentamiento, lo que logra al hacer caso a un rústico y otros compañeros que le encaminan con sus buenos consejos para encontrarse con aquéllos. La Fe, que busca fieles para la Iglesia, se encuentra con el Entendimiento y contienden ambos por determinar cuál de los dos es más importante, poniendo como jueces para dirimir la cuestión a las virtudes de la Prudencia y la Simplicidad. Mientras éstas se retiran a deliberar cuatro pastores y su mayoral realizan un entreacto para entretenimiento. Concluida la deliberación, las virtudes dan su veredicto, proclamando la superioridad de la Fe. Pero el Entendimiento, aunque acepta el cristianismo, no se somete del todo a la Fe, de ahí que salga a escena un Sacerdote a predicar a los sentidos la necesidad de circuncidarse. Realizada la circuncisión de éstos, se proclama el triunfo completo de la Fe.

La obra, de marcado carácter alegórico, está adobada con escenas realistas que buscan el entretenimiento. Los personajes principales, reales y alegóricos, son pocos (Fe, Entendimiento = Philoteoro, cinco sentidos y sentido común, Simplicidad, Prudencia, y Curiosidad, Sacerdos dei, el Licenciado Medinilla, y el Bachiller Aretino, cuatro pastores y su mayoral, y los pastores Glauco, Narciso, Audón); pero los actores que participan en ella son muy numerosos, para conferir así mayor suntuosidad a la acción y hacer intervenir en ella a más escolares. El manuscrito enumera hasta 67, detallando con precisión el papel asignado a cada uno y su indumentaria (5r–6r).

La pieza consta de cuatro actos y escenas, cinco argumentos, uno general y otro para cada acto, prólogo y epílogo, con esta peculiaridad: que el argumento del triunfo de la Fe se desarrolla propiamente en tres actos, pudiéndose suprimir el acto cuarto de la circuncisión, para adaptarse a otras fiestas. Además, esta acción básica de la obra se complementa con otros elementos dramáticos que le confieren gran variedad: un entremés como comienzo entre el Licenciado Medinilla y el Bachiller Aretino "para retardar la acçion tan esperada," según el autor; una égloga como interlocución primera tras el recitado del prólogo y del argumento antes de comenzar el acto 1; y otra segunda interlocución representada por cuatro pastores y su mayoral antes del 3 "para entretenimiento" del auditorio.

La pieza está compuesta en su mayor parte en castellano, pero es también significativa en varias partes de ella la presencia del latín:

— En el prólogo, que lo comienza a pronunciar un niño al que se le olvida y se equivoca, siendo rectificado por el maestro de retórica que lo comienza también en latín, pero acaba exponiéndolo en castellano (fol. 7v):

Puer.— Cyrus Xenophontius qui rerum gestarum gloriam cum disciplina et cognitione rerum vniuersarum coniunxit, humanissimi spectatores, Cirus, inquam, Xenophontius, cum —*aqui haze que se le oluida*— no, sino verum —no, sino cum... ¡o pobre de mi!, volauerunt, señores, las palabras que traya que dezir y se me a ydo ¡mal pecado! de la memoria el prologo y argumento de la acçion.

— En las letrillas, como la siguiente, que iba sembrando la Fe al aparecer en escena y que recoge el autor al final de la comedia (fols. 31v–32r):

fides sine operibus mortua est.	*non quecumq̧ vultis faciatis*
la fee sin obras es muerta	mas fuerte es aquel que vence
mas obrada da la vida	sus viciosas aficiones
con graçia y gloria cumplida	q̧ el que doma los leones

— En el acto 4, en las pláticas que el Sacerdote hace en latín y en castellano a cada uno de los sentidos, a las que responden éstos en parte también en latín.

— En uno de los tres epílogos, que hacen tres niños: el de en medio lo hace con una octava real, el de la derecha en latín, el de la izquierda en castellano (28v).

— En las palabras solemnes con que se sanciona la concesión de los premios a los mejores actores (31r).

— Y, sobre todo, en la égloga que precede inmediatamente a la acción central (9v–11v), cuyo género, forma, fin y modo de representarse el autor precisa así:

hazerse [ha] al prinçipio vna egloga pastoril y en lengua latina por exerçiçio y prouecho de los rrepresentantes della, que seran tres scholares en habito de zagales, en que trataran por su rrecreaçion, de cosas del campo conforme a su profeçion y entre estas jugaran vn poco a hecharse versos al modo que suelen los estudiantes en alabansas del niño jesus.

El pastor Glauco canta unas coplas en castellano. A continuación se acerca a saludarle Narciso y con él canta en hexámetros la alegría del campo y el descanso del ganado, con ecos virgilianos, sentados en un lugar bucólico. Audón se asoma desde dentro con el niño Jesús en brazos y recita dos estrofas sáficas para celebrar la circuncisión. Los pastorcillos sin hacerle caso celebran las estaciones del año en hexámetros, hasta que Audón, remedando el v. 55 de la *Égloga* 3 de Virgilio en la que Palemón invita a Menalcas y Damoetas a iniciar su amebeo, invita también a sus dos compañeros a dejar su certamen y a cantar sentados:

Audon. — *Mittite pastores alijs hec discutenda*
diçiteq unanimes quando conse[n]dimus omnes.
(cf. Verg. *Ecl.* 3.55: P. *Dicite: quandoquidem in molli consedimus herba*).

Glauco acepta, y el autor indica tras sus palabras el ceremonial con que deben realizar el certamen los tres pastorcillos.

Glauc. — *Eia age sed perdet qui nullum carmen habebit*
"tras cada distico de los sigt[es] el q acaba de dezir el suyo da al
que se sigue el niño Jesus con la letra final nombrandosela alto."

El propio Audón comienza la égloga con un dístico en el que saluda al niño, hijo de Dios hecho hombre:

Audon. — *Salue sancte puer patris generosa propago*
mundopifex nostro crimine factus homo.

Y a continuación la completan los tres cantando por turno en dísticos las loas al niño Jesús y expresándole sus peticiones y deseos.

Importancia excepcional posee el conjunto de noticias que nos ofrece el autor sobre la representación de la pieza antes y después de lo que constituye propiamente el texto del argumento dramático (7v–29r), y la multitud de acotaciones que también hace en este sentido a lo largo de ella.

Antes de dicho texto el autor indica que se debe poner en las puertas un cartel con características bien precisas para que sea conocido por todos, y tras exponer la finalidad pedagógica de la concesión de premios y el sentido de estas representaciones para fomentar la "emulación al exercicio de las letras" entre los autores y el "prouecho e consuelo del auditorio", explica con detalle las doce condiciones que deben figurar en el cartel para que sean observadas por los actores y los doce premios que les serán otorgados por orden riguroso, de acuerdo con la calidad de su respectiva actuación (2r–4v).

Acabada la pieza, tras el *valete* y *plaudite* de la despedida, el autor describe la solemne ceremonia de la distribución de los premios (29v–31r) exponiendo pormenorizadamente la forma como se debía engalanar el local en el que se distribuían, cómo debía ir vestida la personalidad que los otorgaba y su acompañamiento (música, instrumentos, etc.), lo que dicha personalidad debía decir (aludiendo de nuevo a la necesidad de insistir en la "emulacion" y el "provecho") y cómo debía decirlo en el discurso que pronunciara al efecto, señalando además las palabras que se debían repetir al dar los premios, con el fin de hacer una clara distinción entre los tres primeros galardonados y los siguientes. Las acotaciones que acompañan al texto se multiplican a lo largo de la obra indicando también con precisión la forma de representarla (vestido, voz, movimientos, etc.).

Constituye así esta pieza uno de los documentos más preciosos del teatro jesuítico, de la importancia que se daba en la Compañía de Jesús a esta actividad, del interés que en ella existía por suscitar la participación de los escolares en las obras para mejorar su formación y del cuidado exquisito que se observaba por ello para la preparación de las representaciones.

Éstos son a grandes rasgos los datos y características fundamentales de las dos obras señaladas.

Universidad Autónoma de Madrid

The Role of Latin in the Composition of Castiglione's Il libro del cortegiano

OLGA ZORZI PUGLIESE

Like many other early sixteenth-century Italian authors who were well versed in the Latin language, having had the benefit of a formal humanist training, Baldesar Castiglione opted, nevertheless, for the vernacular language as the vehicle for the majority of his writings. He adhered to Latin for a few of his secondary works, namely some poetry and letters, including the longer epistle on Guidubaldo da Montefeltro, duke of Urbino. Possibly following the example of Pietro Bembo in his *Gli asolani*, he chose Italian instead for his undisputed masterpiece, *Il libro del cortegiano*, the treatise in which he portrays life at court and delineates the concept of the ideal courtier. Castiglione was to devote at least fifteen years to revising and expanding the work before it went to press in 1528, and in the process he often focused on matters of style and language. In the final stages of composition he inserted a lengthy section of his dialogue on the issue of language in Book 1, debating mainly the question of which form of the vernacular was to be preferred, and presenting an eclectic theory that appears relatively open and comprehensive.

As far as the use of Latin in the text goes, any reader of the definitive printed version of the treatise will quickly realize that it is at best minimal.[1] Only a few phrases in Latin are to be found and these are mainly in Books 2 and 3. They are for the most part well-known sayings (e.g., "Si non caste, tamen caute", 3.20. 284), or witty remarks and puns, like that on the initials of pope Nicholas V, NPV, which are interpreted as "Nihil papa valet" (2.48. 192). An Italianate greeting that an unskilled speaker of Latin utters, "Deus det vobis bonum sero" (with the intended meaning of "evening", but actually meaning "late"), produces an ambiguous phrase which elicits from the interlocutor in the repartee a witty retort, in essence a curse: "Tibi malum cito" (2.63. 210).

---

[1] The edition cited here is the following: Baldassar Castiglione, *Il libro del cortegiano*, introd. Amedeo Quondam (Milan, 1981).

On the other hand, in his letters written in the vernacular,[2] Castiglione, like other contemporaries — Machiavelli, for example — used Latin for the opening and concluding formalities and also for single words, mainly prepositions and adverbs, such as *cum, continue,* and *tandem*. In certain cases these are merely chancery terms or graphic Latinisms, a kind of shorthand perhaps, that did not always reflect the actual pronunciation or enunciation, which was in all likelihood Italianized.

Leaving aside the minor writings, the bilingual or rather multilingual aspect that characterizes the text of *Il libro del cortegiano* is very limited. It becomes more consequential and substantial, though, when one traces the changes that the work underwent as Castiglione drafted and revised it before publishing it. I have been studying the early drafts of Castiglione's treatise, that is, the autograph fragments in the Mantuan manuscript still in the private archive of the Castiglioni family (MS. II 3 b), traditionally designated as A, and also some of the more complete versions of the first redaction housed in the Vatican, especially MSS. 8204 and 8205, conventionally referred to as B and C respectively. My collation of these manuscripts A, B, and C has produced interesting results. It has revealed significant variants, many of which had not been noted in published studies, at least not until Amedeo Quondam's recent volume on the drafts of *Il libro del cortegiano*.[3] The revisions that I have been examining pertain to the thematic content of the work (Castiglione's treatment of the topics of women, humour, and the court), and also to its formal structure, as *Il libro del cortegiano* evolved into an elaborate dialogue treatise. On the linguistic side, the variants relate to the peculiar use that Castiglione made of Spanish[4] and also to the utilization of Latin, which I focus on here.

In the early manuscripts of *Il libro del cortegiano* Castiglione resorts to Latin for different purposes, the first of which is editorial. In the documents consulted one finds the occasional autograph marginal or interlinear note that the author wrote to himself: *vacat* (B, fol. 72r) marks a section to be canceled; *alibi* and *hic ponatur* (A, fols. 21r–v, 93v) indicate a passage that is to be shifted from one point to another in the manuscript. In C a marginal annotation on fol. 228r bears the phrase "hic interponendus sermo Ottaviani" as a reminder concerning an insertion to be made.

Latin also found its way into the body of the text itself in the spoken phrases and

---

[2] I wish to thank Gae Pitman who prepared a list of the Latinisms used by Castiglione in the letters included in Baldassar Castiglione, *Le lettere*, ed. Guido La Rocca (Verona, 1978).

[3] Amedeo Quondam, *"Questo povero Cortegiano": Castiglione, il libro, la storia* (Rome, 2000).

[4] Since 1996 I have presented some of the results of my research in many venues and on various occasions in North America, Europe, and Africa. Two published essays are the following: "L'evoluzione della struttura dialogica del *Libro del cortegiano*," in *Il sapere delle parole: Studî sul dialogo latino e italiano del Rinascimento*, ed. Walter Geerts, Annick Paternoster, Franco Pignatti (Rome, 2001), 59–68; "Time and Space in the Composition of *Il libro del cortegiano*," *Studi d'italianistica nell'Africa australe/Italian Studies in Southern Africa*, vol. 14, no. 2 (2001). Special issue: "Time and Space in Italian Culture and Beyond," 17–32. A third essay is forthcoming: "The Development of Dialogue in *Il libro del cortegiano*: From the Manuscript Drafts to the Definitive Version," in *Printed Voices: The Renaissance Culture of Dialogue*, ed. Dorothea Heitsch and Jean-François Vallée, 93–108.

witticisms already alluded to; for example, the phrase "furiarum maxima iuxta me cubat", uttered by a "gentleman" to criticize his shrewish wife (2.61), is found in A, fol. 32v, and the words "oremus pro hereticis" (2.62) include bishops and other prelates, on fol. 33r; similarly, the puns on the titles of two popes are in B, fol. 151v. But all told, instances such as these are still few in number. Even when Castiglione later consulted more and more classical texts for the completion and elaboration of his treatise, as his letters and library inventories show,[5] he did not add further Latin phrases. On the contrary, he tended to eliminate them. Just as phrases in Spanish in the early drafts were eventually replaced by Italian equivalents, so too the Latin phrase referring to the "aurea . . . secula" in connection with the virtue of princes (A, fol. 90v) becomes "età d'oro" on fol. 91r of the same manuscript. It remains in the vernacular only in subsequent versions (e.g., C fol. 198r). Perhaps, in eliminating some of the few examples of Latin originally introduced, Castiglione was conforming to his theory of a courtly language, which would be refined and understood by all the educated nobility. The criterion of elegance and *sprezzatura*, so fundamental to his cultural program, may well have been the overriding one, even on the question of selecting an appropriate linguistic medium. Although he praises the study of other languages, Castiglione does warn against affectation, which might result from the use of foreign terms. He speaks in B, fols. 58v–59r, of the errors of many who, when speaking to persons they wish to impress, use affected language, "tirando le parole dal latino . . . di modo che per parere troppo savij si fanno tenere bestie" [lifting words from Latin, and thus wishing to appear too learned, they end up looking foolish].

Another document throws light on the topic under examination and illustrates the functional use that Castiglione made of the Latin language. Some of his autograph notes, namely the *taccuino* or notebook now located in the State Archives of Mantua, were examined and published by Guido La Rocca in 1980.[6] This critic claimed, quite accurately, that the notes, sketchy as they are, constituted the nuclei of the major treatise. Written in Latin and consisting mainly of lists of names and words, they touch upon topics relating to women, love, and language — topics that constitute important sections of the treatise. Among the notes studied by La Rocca there are several series of single statements and brief phrases. Some have already assumed dialogue form involving Cesare Gonzaga, Bernardo Bibbiena, and others as speakers. Other annotations consist of references to the narrative plot: "Custodiatur ut fugitivus" (La Rocca, "Un taccuino autografo," 370), for instance, is a note concerning the ending of the treatise. In the earlier redactions of the treatise (see C, fol. 321v), which this annotation must have preceded, it is told much more explicitly and clearly than in the ending of the vulgate text, that the misogynist Gaspar Pallavicino is "to be guarded like a fugitive" for fear, that is, that he might indeed flee before the discussion is completed.

---

[5] See Guido Rebecchini, "The Book Collection and Other Possessions of Baldassarre Castiglione," *Journal of the Warburg and Courtauld Institutes* 61 (1998): 17–52.

[6] Guido La Rocca, "Un taccuino autografo per il *Cortegiano*," *Italia medioevale e umanistica* 23 (1980): 341–373.

All together these fragments in the Archive notebook represent the preparatory phase of composition for Castiglione's masterwork. Some reflect what were to become fully worked out parts of the definitive version: e.g., the phrase "Disputatio de lingua etruscha" (La Rocca, "Un taccuino autografo," 370) announces the lengthy section on language inserted in the final stages of the revisions. Similarly, the notebook contains the following brief synopsis in Latin of the exemplary story of Camma: "Camma gallicana se et Sinorigem amantem, qui virum suum Sinatum interfecerat, simulatis nuptiis, ante simulachrum Diane veneno absumpsit" (363); it is eventually fleshed out to become a full chapter in the vulgate text (3.26). The Ficinian definition of "amor" as "desiderium fruendi pulchrum" (367) is the nucleus of the later fully worked-out section on Platonic love.[7] On the other hand, some Latin phrases listed in the notebook do not find corresponding passages in the treatise; clearly they remained undeveloped and were discarded. Similar lists of themes and concepts, some enunciated in Latin, are to be found at the beginning of B (fol. 3r). The phrase "de suis victoriis notis et aliis bonis condicionibus non loquatur" is developed into the discussion of the courtier's discreet praise of himself in 1.18 and 2.6–7.

What had been overlooked by the few readers of the early manuscript drafts in the private archive of the Castiglioni family in Mantua (that is, until Amedeo Quondam published it recently in his volume on the *Cortegiano* drafts, "*Questo povero Cortegiano*," 247–248), is a fragment which is perhaps of greater importance than those in the Archive studied by La Rocca. It is a brief passage in Latin, occupying a single side of a folio of A (fol. 84r).[8] The passage is acephalous, its first part missing; it is drafted in Latin, not in the vernacular; and it is expressed in expository prose that has not yet been completely transformed into dialogue, although the interlocutors Gaspar and Ottaviano (later to become Bembo and Ottaviano) are named. It is clear that the author eventually re-elaborated the passage, but he did not discard the original sheet, using the verso of it instead for a successive stage of composition and elaboration in the vernacular. Despite the brevity of the passage in question, it is clearly an outline of the core of Castiglione's theory of politics and incorporates concepts borrowed from Plutarch and Plato.[9] In this text Castiglione speaks of the *curialis* who uses the means at his disposal — those courtly arts probably specified in the missing introduction to the sketch — in order to gain the prince's ear. The purpose of the *curialis* is not the ruin of the prince and the people — something which might come about if he were to instil strange passions, and use adulation and all manner of evil. Rather, he is to teach the prince justice and other virtues ("ad docendum iustitiam et alias virtutes"). He who thus makes the prince good is most worthy, Castiglione states, just as he who does the opposite and poisons the public fountain is most evil.[10] Cas-

---

[7] Marsilio Ficino, *Commentarium in convivium Platonis, De amore*, I, 2: "Cum amorem dicimus pulchritudinis desiderium intelligite," ed. and trans. Raymond Marcel (Paris, 1956), 142.

[8] I wish to thank Professor Gian Carlo Alessio of the University of Venice for his help in transcribing the document.

[9] The documents published by Rebecchini, "Book Collection," show that Castiglione had copies of Plutarch and Plato in his library.

[10] Plutarch, in his treatise 53 on moral virtue dealing with the question why philosophers

tiglione adds that princes tend not to listen to reason since they do not wish to serve any superior. Therefore the courtier, under a veil — that is, using his art of courtiership — must teach him justice, prudence, and temperance. In this role he will be deemed most worthy. Referring to the fable of Jupiter who, through Mercury, sent the gifts of modesty and justice to humanity,[11] Gasparo objects that these are intrinsic virtues that no one feels the need to study and learn. To this observation Ottaviano, the principal interlocutor, replies that, although they are intrinsic, and no one admits to being evil, because it is contrary to nature, the virtues must be cultivated; otherwise one tends to go astray.[12]

This passage constitutes, as I have been able to determine, and as Quondam's analysis has confirmed ("*Questo povero Cortegiano*," 248), the heart of the discussion on politics, which eventually found its place in Book IV of the definitive version of the treatise. In it one finds the basic concepts that were then elaborated in the vernacular in the subsequent folios. For example, "nam nemo tam bene meretur de multis quam qui bonum facit principem, sicut etiam male qui malum" becomes in Italian the "corteggiano" who "meritarà molto maior laude e premio che per qual si voglia degna opera che far potesse al mundo, perché non è bene alchuno che così universalmente giovi come il bon principe, né male che così universalmente noccia come el mal principe" (fol. 85v). Many ideas still missing in the passage, some of them deriving from Aristotle, are added later: the reference to the classification of governments, the analogy of the father–son relation to describe the prince and his subjects, the concept of the prince as vicar of God, the discussion on war and peace and the contemplative and active lives, on the relation of the prince to his counselors, advice on the structure of government, and comments relating to the importance of religion and wealth.

Sketchy though it may be, the passage in the Mantua manuscript A, described here, represents the earliest phase that is extant and that can still be documented of his discussion on politics. Furthermore, it also reveals, I believe, the author's method of composition. It enables us to deduce that Castiglione gathered information and jotted down his ideas, in Latin, and then proceeded to reformulate and compose the section of his work in the vernacular. It certainly reflects La Rocca's conclusion about Castiglione's method of composition, which he described ("Un taccuino autografo," 359) as "un processo aperto di aggregazione tematica" (an open process of grouping together related topics). This procedure, interestingly enough, is at the opposite pole of a traditional treatise format, if it is assumed that treatises are built on basic principles through logical deduction. During the extended period of writing and revising, Castiglione appears to have elaborated and fused single units, a method which led to

---

should deal especially with the powerful (*Maxime cum principibus philosopho esse disserendum*), speaks of the great good achieved by one who makes good the person on whom so many depend. On the contrary, those adulators who corrupt kings and tyrants are punished as though they poured lethal poison into the public fountain from which all persons must draw water.

[11] Cf. Plato, *Protagoras*, chaps. 11–12.

[12] In chap. 13 Plato deals with acquired good.

certain discrepancies and to some unevenness that is still undeniably present in the definitive text. In the case of one set of the fragments that he examined, La Rocca does conclude correctly that they represent the preparatory work for the *Epistola* on Guidubaldo da Montefeltro, which was written in Latin. But for some of the others the critic does not seem to have grasped the full significance for the composition of *The Book of the Courtier*; at one point he hypothesizes that they were to be used at a later date by the author for other works to be written in Latin. He did not realize perhaps, as the passage on politics in the Mantua manuscript drafts of the *Cortegiano* also seems to indicate, that it may very well have been Castiglione's custom to begin composing his vernacular works — including *Il libro del cortegiano* — in Latin, probably collecting, listing, and jotting down materials which he then fitted into the structure or else completely discarded.

What the passage in the Mantua manuscript, together with the *taccuino* materials, show then is that the Latin language played an important role in the very first conception and formulation of works eventually written in the vernacular. This role is not limited to the insertion of Latin words and sayings interspersed in Italian prose, as the vulgate text might lead one to believe. Nor was it for Castiglione just a yardstick for measuring the validity of language and single words, as one critic put it.[13] The formulation of sections (perhaps of all sections) of the major work that Castiglione was writing in the vernacular probably began with phrases and then non-dialogic prose passages in Latin. Thus the drafts examined here, and especially the Latin passage on politics, enable us to observe at close hand the main role of Latin, perhaps an unsuspected one, as a compositional tool of fundamental significance adopted by one of the major Italian writers of the Renaissance.

University of Toronto

---

[13] Mario Pozzi, "Il pensiero linguistico di B. Castiglione," *Giornale storico della letteratura italiana* 156 (1979): 197n., refers to Latin as being for Castiglione, on linguistic matters, "il principale termine di controllo linguistico."

Milton and Cambridge

STELLA P. REVARD

John Milton entered Christ's College, Cambridge in the spring of 1625 at age sixteen and spent seven years of his life there. The Latin prose and poetry he composed while attending Cambridge University provides insight into Milton as a youthful undergraduate and also helps us trace his development as a writer of English prose and poetry. Already an accomplished Latinist at St. Paul's School in London, he perfected his Latin style in prose and poetry at the university, writing the Latin prose essays that were part of his university training and composing much of the Neo-Latin poetry that he was to print in 1645 in his collected *Poems*. It was as a Neo-Latin poet that he was received into the academic academies in Florence, Rome, and Naples when he journeyed to Italy in the late 1630s. Those skills that he honed at Cambridge as a writer of Latin prose won him even greater recognition in the European intellectual community in the 1650s. Engaged by Cromwell as Latin secretary, he conducted the correspondence with foreign governments and defended the newly formed English Commonwealth. As a polemicist he was known throughout Europe for the first and second defenses of the English people, composed in Latin prose. In the second defense, *Pro Populo Anglicano Defensio Secunda*, he includes an autobiographical section in which he looks back on his career at Cambridge, proclaiming his success at the University against an attack that he had been expelled from its walls.[1] Latin had served Milton well during his Cambridge years as a medium of personal and intellectual discourse, and it continued to serve him well years later.

---

[1] Milton writes: "after I had acquired a proficiency in various languages, and had made a considerable progress in philosophy, [my father] sent me to the University of Cambridge. Here I passed seven years in the usual course of instruction and study, with the approbation of the good and without any stain upon my character, till I took the degree of Master of Arts. After this I ... of my own accord retired to my father's house, whither I was accompanied by the regrets of most of the fellows of the college, who showed me no common marks of friendship and esteem" ("Second Defense of the English People," in *Complete Poems and Major Prose*, ed. Merritt Y. Hughes [New York, 1957], 828). All citations of Milton's work, unless otherwise noted, are to this edition.

During his seven years at Cambridge Milton must have been among its luminaries intellectually. However, the attitudes toward the university he expresses in both poetry and prose are at best ambiguous. Although he defends his university career in *Defensio Secunda*, he clearly experienced some difficulties at the beginning. In a Latin prose letter written in 1625 to his tutor Thomas Young he speaks of Cambridge as the "haunt of the Muses" where in peace and quiet, surrounded by his books, he devotes himself to study.[2] A year later, however, in a Latin elegy to Charles Diodati, he is less enthusiastic, having enjoyed a sojourn in his native London free to devote himself to his books, to the theater, and to girl-watching. He did not get along with his first tutor, William Chappell, and they were to part company soon afterwards, when Milton was assigned to a second tutor.[3] Elegy 1 glances sideways at this relationship, providing, as Milton characteristically does in his Latin elegies, a realistic, personal, and down-to-earth view. He refers in fact to his dislike of Cambridge and his reluctance to return.

> Iam nec arundiferum mihi cura revisere Camum,
>   Nec dudum vetiti me laris angit amor.
> Nuda nec arva placent, umbrasque negantia molles,
>   Quam male Phoebicolis convenit ille locus!
> Nec duri libet usque minas perferre magistri
>   Caeteraque ingenio non subeunda meo. (Elegia 1. 11–16)

[Now I have no concern to see the sedgy Cam again,
Nor does love of the forbidden quarters there constrain me.
The bare fields with no pleasant shade do not please me.
How badly that place suits the worshippers of Phoebus!
It is not fitting to endure the threats of a harsh tutor
And other indignities forced upon my spirit.]

However, he did return to Cambridge and, setting his stakes on being recognized for his proficiency in Latin poetry, embarked on an ambitious series of Latin poems. Four of these commemorate the deaths of older men who had or had had close connections with Cambridge University. I say commemorate rather than mourn, for though all these poems offer expressions of grief, they are basically poetic exercises in the art of the Neo-Latin funeral poem, which offer Milton the opportunity to demonstrate his command of mythological lore, his proficiency at Neo-Latin wit, as well as his mastery of Neo-Latin poetic forms: elegy, iambics, and ode.

---

[2] See Milton, *Private Correspondence and Academic Exercises*, trans. Phyllis B. Tillyard, intro. and comm. E. M. W. Tillyard (Cambridge, 1932).

[3] A letter to Alexander Gill Jr., dated 2 July 1628, also expresses dislike for Cambridge and a lack of congenial fellow students there. See *Private Correspondence and Academic Exercises*, ed. Tillyard and Tillyard, 7–80. Shawcross argues that this letter should be dated 2 July 1631: see John T. Shawcross, "The Dating of Certain Poems, Letters, and Prolusions Written by Milton," *English Language Notes* 2 (1965): 261–266.

Two of the poems commemorate the deaths of bishops (Lancelot Andrewes and Nicholas Felton), the two others the deaths of the Beadle of Cambridge University, Richard Ridding, and the Vice-Chancellor, John Gostlin. Although at the time of their deaths Andrewes and Felton were bishops of Winchester and Ely respectively, both men had important ties with Cambridge University. Close friends, they had been in turn undergraduates, fellows, and finally masters of Pembroke Hall. Although the verses to Andrewes and Felton make no mention of their university connection, Milton's audience would have been well aware that he was commemorating the deaths of two of its most distinguished alumni. In both poems he exploits neo-classical conventions, lamenting the cruelty of Death, excoriating Proserpina and the forces of a pagan underworld, and arriving finally at a semi-Christian, semi-classical resolution, wherein he depicts the bishops received into an Elysium-like heaven.

In the funeral poems to the Vice-Chancellor and Beadle, also written in the fall of 1626, Milton is no less classical in his references, but he also connects the men commemorated to their university positions. John Gostlin was a popular man, twice elected to the post of Vice-Chancellor, and was also noted as a physician.[4] Recalling how Gostlin had saved many from the plague that ravaged Cambridge in 1626, Milton praises his skills as one of Apollo's devotees. At the same time he remembers him as the leader who gave order to the "togaed society" at Cambridge — "Gentis togatae cui regimen datum" (30) — and wishes that he yet were present to lead the flock of Pallas. With a somewhat lighter touch, he also remembers Richard Ridding in his office as university beadle, a post which he had held for twenty years.[5] Beginning with a typical Neo-Latin witticism, Milton remarks that the super-beadle Death has gathered the university beadle to his company. He compares Ridding to the messenger Mercury and to the heralds sent by Agamemnon to Achilles. But he also pictures him carrying his glittering mace in the university processions and at the command of his "Apollo" (Gostlin) rousing the Cambridge assemblies, here also pictured in their "togas": "tu si iussus erat acies accire togatas" (11). Although his *funera* for Andrewes and Felton offer expressions of personal grief, Milton chooses in his poems for the Vice-Chancellor and Beadle to make himself the spokesman for the university. He calls upon the academic community to mourn for Ridding:

> Vestibus hunc igitur pullis, Academia, luge,
>   Et madeant lacrimis nigra feretra tuis.
> Fundat et ipsa modos querebunda Elegeia tristes,
>   Personet et totis naenia moesta scholis. (21–24)

> [Therefore, grieve, University, for this man, and wear mourning
>   vestments.

---

[4] John Gostlin was master of Gonville and Caius College and is buried in the college chapel. He was Regius Professor of Physics. He was popularly chosen over the appointee of James I to be master, and was twice Vice-Chancellor.

[5] Ridding took a degree from St. John's College, Cambridge, during the reign of Elizabeth.

May his black hearse be wet with your tears.
May plaintive Elegy herself pour forth sad laments,
and may all the schools resound with a lamenting song.][6]

Milton's skills as a Latinist did not go unnoted. In 1628 Milton was asked by a fellow of Christ's College to compose on his behalf a set of verses to be read at the July Commencement. He duly complied, producing a scholastic disquisition in Latin verse. We do not know whether the poem in question was "Naturam Non Pati Senium," a hexameter exercise that argues that nature is not subject to old age, or "De Idea Platonica," another debate in verse, one which attacks Plato's theory of ideal form.[7] Both these poems would fit the occasion and both are closely connected with the practice at Cambridge of writing scholastic debates in prose and verse.

Seven of Milton's prose debates, the *Prolusiones*, survive, published with his private Latin correspondence in 1674.[8] They give us another view of his relationship with his university. Milton had very definite views on the educational practices of his time, which he expressed both in the Latin prolusions written at Cambridge and in *Of Education*, a tract written in English that he published in 1644. In Prolusion 7, "Learning makes men happier than does Ignorance" [Beatiores reddit Homines Ars quam Ignorantia], he attacks scholasticism, maintaining that while the universities were in the grip of scholasticism nothing but ignorance prevailed (624). He also attacks scholasticism in *Of Education*, stating that "the usual method of teaching arts" to be "an old error of universities not yet recovered from the scholastic grossness of barbarous ages." Scholastic practices, he asserts, make acquisition of learning difficult (632). In Prolusion 3, "Against Scholastic Philosophy," he expresses the opinion that pursuit of inane arguments and of futile and barren controversies is vain and does nothing for the good of society and the honor of country. At Christ's College, however, he fulfilled the requirements of the university by composing and delivering orally the kind of exercise that was based on the old scholastic debate. Prolusions 4 and 5 demonstrate, as E. M. Tillyard has observed, Milton's ability to use the disputatious methods of his scholastic training.[9] Milton is quite emphatic, however, both in the prolusions and in *Of Education* about the university's faulty methods of teaching. In Prolusion 7 he points out the errors in teaching grammar, logic, metaphysics, law, and mathematics. In mathematics, for example, he notes that if the empty glory of demonstrations and other things which are of no value were eliminated, whole years

---

[6] As John Hale remarks, the poems for Ridding and Gostlin, as was the university custom, may have been pinned to the hearse cloth at the funeral. See John Milton, *Latin Writings, a Selection*, ed. and trans. John K. Hale, MRTS 191 (Tempe, AZ, 1998), 11.

[7] See John Carey in *Complete Shorter Poems* (Burnt Mill, 1971), 66. Carey believes that "De Idea Platonica" was the poem Milton described in a letter to Gill. Shawcross argues that both "Naturam" and "De Idea Platonica" were written in 1631. See Shawcross, "The Dating of Certain Poems," 261–266.

[8] Milton himself gave these undergraduate exercises to the printer to take the place of the official Latin correspondence for Cromwell that he was forbidden to print. Though he had clearly saved these university essays all his life, they might not have survived had they not been published before his death with his personal correspondence in this volume.

[9] See E. M. W. Tillyard, "Introduction," in *Private Correspondence and Academic Exercises*, xix.

would be gained in the process of learning (627). In *Of Education* he inveighs against the practice of "forcing the empty wits of children to compose themes, verses and orations, which are the acts of ripest judgment and the final work of a head filled by long reading and observing with elegant maxims and copious invention" (631). He deplores the fact that students are forced to memorize what they do not understand. He advocates that the best Latin texts be read, starting with reading the easy authors first, and saving logic and metaphysics until later when students had matured and could cope better with intellective abstractions. In that way students would not form the "ill habit which they get of wretched barbarizing against the Latin and Greek idiom with their untutored Anglicisms, odious to be read, yet not be avoided without a well-continued and judicious conversing among pure authors digested, which they scarce taste" (631). Suffice it to say, Milton avoided such barbarisms in his prose and poetry. In the 1640s when he himself was a schoolmaster, tutoring his nephews and other young men, Milton had the opportunity to put into practice the program of educational reforms that he first devised at Cambridge and which he advocated in *Of Education*.

The methods of argument that Milton mastered in his Latin prolusions lasted him throughout his long career as one of England's leading polemicists. The prolusions also tell us something about his relationship to his fellow undergraduates. Although we cannot date precisely or determine the order of composition of Milton's seven prolusions, it is probable, as Tillyard argues, that Prolusion 1, "Whether day or night is the more excellent," is the earliest, Prolusion 7 on "Learning and Ignorance" the last.[10] Prolusion 1 records an uneasy relationship of speaker to audience. Milton remarks on the hostility evident in many eyes, caused, he regrets, by the rivalry among proponents of different studies and different methods of study. However, by the time he delivers Prolusion 6, which dates from the summer of 1628, his relations with his fellow students seem to have ameliorated. Unwittingly revealing how much their disapprobation had stung him, he begins by remarking that he has lately perceived signs of favor, even from those previously most hostile to him. An academic oration he had given some months previously had received — to his surprise — warm applause. Therefore, he was strongly induced to undertake the present office by the newfound friendliness from members of his own college.[11] That he had been specifically chosen by his fellow students as principal speaker for the oration to be delivered at the time of the summer holidays proves, as Tillyard remarks, that by this time he was a popular or at least respected person. Not only members of his college, but also most of the young men of the university, as Milton writes in the headnote to the prolusion, were present.

The prolusion is divided into three parts. The first is an introduction in which he

---

[10] See Tillyard. Milton refers to his audience as *Auditores* (hearers) and as *Academici* (fellow students), formal terms he employs in all of the prolusions.

[11] Tillyard remarks: "That Milton was chosen to give it — before almost the entire university, as he tells us — proves that he was by this time a popular and respected person" ("Introduction," xxx).

defends with considerable earnestness the practice of these vacation exercises, arguing "That sportive exercises are occasionally not adverse to philosophic studies." The main body of the exercise is, as Tillyard describes it, "an elaborately comic entertainment" (xxx), complete with off-color jokes and the usual "ribbing" of college porters, tutors (conveniently absent for the occasion), and his fellow students. The final section concludes with an excursus into English verse and a promise to deliver such delights as are appropriate to English.

This part-Latin, part-English exercise presents a profile of Milton the undergraduate, who at the end of his third year at Cambridge was able to quit for a moment his earnest scholarly habits to share in a little fun. At first he seems, however, to take pains to defend his reputation as a serious student. He explains that he was just settling down to a course of extended literary and philosophical studies when he was called upon to devote himself instead to foolish trifles and inventions of new jests, as though, he exclaims, there were not fools enough already in the world! If he is to play the fool, he says, he will be a wise fool, for wise men such as Junius Brutus have before played the fool. And folly itself can have commendable uses, as its praise by Erasmus had demonstrated.

In praising folly, Milton is not simply endeavoring to win the good will of those fellow students who have called him to this exercise. True, he launches at this moment into hyperbolic praise of his audience as equal to those who flocked to hear Athenian orators such as Demosthenes and Aeschines. He even compares those partaking of his humble feast of jests to the gods who have sometimes deigned to share the banquets of mortals. But he also remarks seriously that sportive occasions are important occasions for cementing friendships. Friendship is one of the most important aspects of human life, argues the scrivener's son from London, who had earlier despaired of winning friends at Cambridge, but who now embraces this occasion as the sign of offered camaraderie from those who had previously shunned him.

We must examine carefully, however, Milton's disclaimer that he is unsuited to the task of praising mirth. Is this not the very poet who a few years later will neatly balance the opposing claims of Mirth and Melancholy in his twin poems, "L'Allegro" and "Il Penseroso"? Indeed, as he goes on to prove in this very prolusion, mirth is as necessary to human life as sober contemplation. The aspiring epic poet of *Paradise Lost* points out that even the divine Homer could divert his audience with comic subjects, as he demonstrated in his mock epic, *The Battle of the Frogs and Mice*, a piece included as authentic in most Renaissance editions of Homer. Jest and Jollity — the gifts of Milton's future goddess Mirth — are freely to be admitted into the academy, for to banish light-heartedness is also to banish serious study. The exercise of wit, Milton argues, sharpens the brain for other exercises, making it lively rather than dull. Conversely, no one can be the master of fine and clever wit who has not first learnt to behave seriously. There is evidence also that Milton practiced what he preached. Having composed serious Latin epitaphs on the deaths of bishops, a Vice-Chancellor, and a beadle in 1626, he penned two witty English epitaphs, "On the University Carrier," in 1631. These verses describe how Death has laid old Hobson in the dirt, and serve as comic counterparts of the elegies for great Winchester and noble Ely. Although Milton's talent for the comic has often been underestimated, he demonstrates in the sixth prolusion that he could play on the pipes of Pan as well as on Apollo's lyre. Commanding his audience, "Plaudite et ridete," he concludes the first section of the exercise, excusing whatever comic excesses he is about to commit on the grounds of the license due the occasion.

Little of what he has said so far prepares us for the scurrility and biting jests of the central section of the prolusion. Assuming the post of Dictator of the tottering Commonwealth of Fools, Milton immediately launches into a comic send-up at the expense of a now departed Sophister, who, he says, better deserves than he the post of Dictator of Fools. The Sophister mentioned had engaged in a recent student prank and led a band of students across Barnwell fields to destroy the town aqueduct. Milton next asks his audience to imagine that they are celebrating the feast of Hilaria, sacred to the Mother of the gods, or a festival dedicated to the god Laughter himself. In order to incite the appropriate laughter from his audience, he offers a series of off-color puns (the grossest of which is an Oedipal play on the words *sphinx* and *sphincter ani*). The porters who have attempted to restrain the coming-together of the comic assembly next become the victims of Milton's college humor. Imagining that the scene is a fiery furnace, he puns on the name of one such porter, Sparks, and the little sparks that he and his flaming brethren cause to fly about. He then lampoons the attending students by alluding to them as the dishes in the banquet that awaits them. Such occasional humor has a short life span. Although these tidbits provide little amusement for modern readers, they must have been the choicest of fare when offered up before a group of like-minded undergraduates attendant at the so-called feast of Hilaria.

The master of ceremonies on such occasions at Cambridge was called the Father of the Feast. Milton willingly takes on the title of Father, since it offers him the opportunity to requite those jesting classmates who had dubbed him the "Lady" or "Domina" of Christ's College. Good heavens, says Milton, in mock surprise, have I changed sex from woman to man, just like the fateful Tiresias or the mythic Caeneus? Exactly how much the epithet "Lady of Christ's" must have irked Milton is shown by the forcefulness with which he repudiates it and claims his rightful masculinity. Was I called a woman, he asks, because I lacked the aptitude for downing bumpers of drink like an athlete, or because my hand is uncallused by the plow, or because I have never shown my virility by visits to the brothel? I wish, he concludes, that those who named me woman could as easily leave off being asses as I quit the feminine.

After this personal aside, Milton proceeds with his task, taking up the role of Father and addressing his sons. True to the academic occasion and the scholasticism that fostered it, he describes the Father as the Aristotelian Ens (Being) and his sons as the Aristotelian categories or accidents of Ens: Substance, Quantity, Quality, Relation, Place, Time, Posture, Possession, Action, and Passion. But before he introduces his sons to the audience, he requests the license to move from Latin prose into English verse. Launching into English pentameter couplets, Milton greets his native language: "Hail native Languuage!" It is a significant moment. Up to this moment, Milton has made his claim of eminence at Cambridge by his expertise in Latin verse and prose. Now he openly courts favor in English verse — the language of Shakespeare, and yes, in the future, the language of Milton. But not yet in 1628. Apart from some psalm paraphrases and some occasional verses, Milton had composed few of the English poems that he would publish in 1645 with his Latin poetry. The Nativity ode, "L'Allegro" and "Il Penseroso," the mask *Comus*, and finally "Lycidas," the English monody that celebrates Cambridge life, had yet to be written. In contrast, many of the Latin poems had already been composed. So the "Lines at a Vacation Exercise" promise much. Milton longs to soar in thought "above the wheeling poles, and at Heav'n's door / Look in, and see each blissful Deity / How he before the thunderous throne doth lie, / Listening to what unshorn *Apollo* sings / To th' touch of golden wires, while *Hebe* brings / Immortal Nectar to her Kingly sire" (34–39) But not yet, he proclaims, can he play "wise *Demodocus*" at "King *Alcinous*' feast" (48–49): the achievements of the blind bard are forty years ahead in the future. Milton has only begun his apprenticeship as an English poet. So he resumes the role of Father and introduces his sons, who round out the entertainment with their speeches in English prose, the text of which has been lost.

Prolusion 6 shows Milton in his most expansive role at Cambridge, the spokesman for his college before the entire university. Nine years later Cambridge was to call upon him once more to contribute a poem to a volume intended to commemorate the death of Edward King, a fellow student whom Milton had known in his days at Christ's College. The animosities of old forgotten, Milton responds, producing the most idealized representation of Cambridge, once more employing his native language — and not Latin — as the medium for praise. He depicts the rustic charm of college life, describing himself and his friends as shepherds who daily drive afield their flocks (in pursuit of their studies) and who nightly enjoy the games and pastimes of university life, like fauns and satyrs dancing to the sound of rustic pipes and delighting their idealized tutor, a neo-classical Damoetas, who listens to their song. In this same monody, Milton, forgetting his previous slur on "reedy" or "sedgy Cam," portrays the river as a pastoral representation of the university, a reverend sire with mantle hairy and bonnet of sedge. Milton remembers the Cambridge of his youth with a warmth not often found in his Latin prose exercises or Latin poetry. But then by 1637 he was fast becoming one of Cambridge's most illustrious alumni. The Latin poetry and prose he produced while at the university give us insight into his poetic and personal development during a crucial period of his life.

Southern Illinois University, Edwardsville

Entertainment and Learning in the Neo-Latin Rebuses by the Seventeenth-Century Norwegian Nils Thomassøn

VIBEKE ROGGEN

Nils Thomassøn was born in 1605 or 1606 as the youngest son of the vicar of Oslo, Thomas Lagesøn. Like his brothers, Nils was well educated: he studied in Copenhagen, Rostock, Leiden, and Wittenberg, and took his Master's degree. At the age of twenty-five he was called home to take over as headmaster of the school of his home city, a city which had changed since his childhood. After a fire, the king, Christian IV, had taken the opportunity to move the town closer to the fortress of Akershus, and named the new town Christiania after himself. At that time Norway was not an independent state but under Danish rule; thus the king whose name the Norwegian capital bore for three hundred years was not Norwegian but Danish. Neither had Norway a university of its own; the few young men who were pursuing higher education had to start their studies in Copenhagen.

After a quarrel with one of the most powerful men of Christiania, Nils Thomassøn had to leave his position as headmaster in 1635. But the following year he was lucky enough to get a position as vicar of Toten, a rich parish in the countryside, some 120 km north of Christiania. His portrait is still preserved in the parish church there. Except for a short period of suspension because of a controversial leaflet he had written, Nils Thomassøn remained as vicar of Toten for the rest of his life. He died in 1662.

From the sources, we know that Nils Thomassøn wrote a number of books and leaflets, most of which, however, were not printed and are lost today. Even the leaflet which caused his suspension, and which in fact *was* printed, is lost. What we do have is a gratulatory poem, printed in the catechism of a contemporary, Christen Staphensøn Bang,[1] and one major work, *Cestus sapphicus*. The latter work is the subject of this study.[2]

---

[1] Christen Staphensøn Bang, *Postilla Catechetica,* 8 vols. (Christiania, 1650–1662), 2:48.
[2] See Vibeke Roggen, "Intellectual Play: Word and Picture. A Study of Nils Thomassøn's

Cestus sapphicus

Cestus sapphicus is a pretty little book with a varied content. It has a hundred and ten pages measuring 16.2 centimetres in height and was printed by Michael Thomassøn in Christiania in 1661.

The subject of *Cestus sapphicus* is marriage and married life, and the title may be translated "a love-belt in Sapphic stanzas". The word *cestus* or κεστός is taken from the *Iliad* 14.214ff., where Hera borrows Aphrodite's magic girdle in order to win back the love of her unfaithful husband Zeus. Nils Thomassøn writes in his introduction that the name of this book has been chosen for various reasons: because the girdle is a symbol of the connection between husband and wife in marriage, and also because the Greek word κεστός is connected with the verb κεντεῖν, to prick or sting (referring to embroidery). The most important element of *Cestus sapphicus* is thirty-one copperplate engravings giving graphic expression to a rebus poem. The artist who made the copperplates was the unemployed Norwegian priest Didrik Muus (1633–1706).

The Content of the Poem

The central part of *Cestus sapphicus* is a poem in thirty-one stanzas with marriage as its subject. Included in the book is a scheme in the form of a logical table, demonstrating how carefully the poem has been constructed.

The scheme has ten major parts. Part 1 is a definition, namely: what is marriage? In Part 4, the question is asked: who is the subject, that is, who wants to marry? The answer is: all persons of all nations and ages, and both sexes. Other parts contain a description of the advantages of marriage, the enemies of marriage, and rules for the married couple in order that their marriage should be happy.

As a whole, the scheme is a curious element of *Cestus sapphicus*, and a highly intellectual one. In that period, it was not uncommon to analyse poems and other kinds of works in the form of tables. For instance, the Danish professor Aders Krag analysed Horace's *Ars poetica* in this way.[3] Rosemond Tuve identifies elements derived from logic in English Renaissance poems, for example, definitions of love.[4] Tuve infers from her material that the poets used the logic they had learned at school for composing poetry; in *Cestus sapphicus* we have an example of a scheme which has been *published* along with the poem in question.

An Example: Stanza 23

What is regulated by the scheme is the content and structure of the poem. But the most striking element of this poem is its *form*, or, more precisely, the rebuses. The

---

Latin Rebus Book *Cestus sapphicus*. With Edition, Translation and a Corpus of Sources" (Ph.D. diss., Oslo University, forthcoming). In the following, I refer to my edition with page numbers and to the 1661 edition with folio numbers.

[3] Andreas Kragius, *Q. Horatii Flacci Ars Poetica, ad P. Rami dialecticam & rhetoricam resoluta* (Basle, 1583).

[4] Rosemond Tuve, *Elizabethan and Metaphysical Imagery: Renaissance Poetic and Twentieth-Century Critics* (Chicago and London, 1965), 301–302.

illustration shows one of the stanzas. For instance, the letters "sa" + the picture of Eve — *Eva* — give the word *saeva*, "wild". As we see, a word is presented partly through a picture, partly through letters.

In this stanza, stanza 23, we find different kinds of rebus figures. We have one plant, *scylla*, a squill, and a tree, *suber*, a cork-oak. There is also an ape; the solution involves, however, not the most usual name for ape, *simius* or *simia*, but *cluna*. Moreover, there are two female figures. Eve from the Old Testament is characterized by the tempting apple and the fig leaf. The other woman is an allegorical figure: Hope or, in Latin, *Spes*, traditionally depicted as a woman holding an anchor. Personifications of this type were common in Protestant churches in the form of paintings. The last three figures show an axle of a wagon, a mortar, and three horses harnessed together in front of a wagon.

Of these figures, some are concrete and easy to interpret, others are not. A necessary condition for a successful solving of the rebuses is the skill of combination: interpretation of the figure, knowledge of at least one Latin word for the object, and association with the surrounding text.

The reader of *Cestus sapphicus* meets with a challenge to solve more than two hundred rebuses in the form of pictures. Problems might arise: what if the reader could not manage to solve the rebuses? In that case, he might look at the rebus solutions, which are included in *Cestus sapphicus*. If there were still problems, these might be solved through the reading of the author's own commentaries.

The Rebus Genre

The rebus genre was popular in the Renaissance period, but mostly in vernacular literatures. Examples are found in French, e.g., "rébus de Picardie"; in Dutch, used by the Rederijkers; in Italian, artificial rebuses made by artists and members of literary societies; and in German, for instance, used on broadsheets, published as propaganda during the Thirty Years' War. An example of a Latin rebus is found in Denmark, over the entrance of the Round Tower in Copenhagen. But according to IJsewijn and Sacré in their *Companion to Neo-Latin Studies*, rebus poems in Latin are rare.[5] The only example they mention is, in fact, the *Cestus sapphicus*.

What is the Meaning of Such Rebuses?

In addition to word and picture, a rebus includes the elements of thinking and guessing, and also of game and entertainment. These two elements motivate the creator of the rebus as well as the reader. Both parties want to demonstrate their intelligence, wit, quick mind, and sharp thinking. Friedreich emphasizes in his description of riddles from 1860 the intellectual challenge connected with riddles:

Da das Aufgeben und Lösen von Räthseln einen bestimmten Grad von Wissen, von Verstand und Scharfsinn voraussetzt, so erscheint das Räthsel nicht allein

---

[5] J. IJsewijn and D. Sacré, *Companion to Neo-Latin Studies*, Part 2 (Supplementa Humanistica Lovaniensia 14) (Leuven, 1998), 130.

als ein Sinnbild der Weisheit selbst, und ist auch selbstbelehrend, sondern es kann auch dazu dienen, um die geistigen Fähigkeiten eines Andern zu prüfen.[6]

We get even closer to our rebuses through Dick Higgins's definition of "puzzle poem" in his *Pattern Poetry. Guide to an Unknown Literature* of 1987:

> By a puzzle poem, one usually means a piece in which the poet invites the reader to play a game, to solve the problem of what the poem means not by learned allusions or such-like, but by taking only the evidence given in the poem and working through it so as to give pleasure.[7]

Higgins's definition of the puzzle poem — including the rebus poem — emphasizes, as we see, words and expressions like "play a game", "solve the problem" and "pleasure". And both Higgins and Friedreich emphasize the game, to obtain pleasure by trying one's own wit as well as the wit of others.

Nils Thomassøn on *Cestus sapphicus* and Genre

From Nils Thomassøn's description of his poem, it is evident that he did not know the word *rebus* (first known from France in the sixteenth century). He uses the expression *picturatum carmen*, which may perhaps be translated "poem with figures".

Cestus sapphicus is dedicated to the hereditary prince of Denmark–Norway, Christian, later King Christian V. In connection with an address to the Prince, Nils Thomassøn modestly characterizes his work as *ludicrum exercitium*, which I translate as "playful literary work":

> Non ausus eram, *Serenissime Princeps,* hoc ludicrum exercitium *Vestræ Celsitudini* dedicare ni animo vim doctiores addidissent [. . .].[8]

In this connection, *ludicrum exercitium* expresses modesty: this poem is only a "playful literary work" (and not a weighty, serious one, befitting a prince). But Nils Thomassøn concludes otherwise: he explains that more learned men have given him courage, and as we understand, he does dedicate the book to the prince. He himself has argued in earlier parts of the introduction that such playful exercise, like other types of meaningful entertainment, is essential for human beings.

In his introduction, the author uses the word *lusus* of his work, and connects it with *ingenium*: "[. . .] figuræ potissimum sunt in hoc ingenii lusu [. . .]."[9] *Ingenii lusus,*

---

[6] J. B. Friedreich, *Geschichte des Räthsels* (Dresden, 1860), 84.

[7] Dick Higgins, *Pattern Poetry. Guide to an Unknown Literature* (Albany, 1987), 184.

[8] "I would not have dared, Most Serene Prince, to dedicate this playful literary work to Your Highness, if more learned men had not encouraged me [. . .]" (*Cestus sapphicus*, p. 7, fol. a4v).

[9] "The very best part of this intellectual game is the rebus figures" (*Cestus sapphicus*, p. 13, fol. Av).

STROPHA 23.

Scholion.

The twenty-third stanza of the rebus poem in *Cestus sapphicus*.

Transcribed Latin text, stanza 23:
    Vt maritus sa{eva} pericla {Scylla}e
    So{spes} evitet, Deus alme, f{axis},
    Atqve {cluna}clum, {Sagana}m s{triga}sqve
    Qvando {suber}rant!

English translation:
    Let the husband avoid Scylla's raging dangers
    unharmed, merciful God,
    and the sacrificial knife, Sagana, and other witches
    when they are wandering around.

"intellectual game", is a description which is rather close to Higgins's definition of puzzle poem.

In the commentary on the last stanza, the concept "genus" is used in the meaning of "genre". The author finds that it is about time to stop, quoting in this connection Isocrates, who says that "There is a point of satiety for everything".[10] Nils Thomassøn adds:

> [. . .] hæc litant veritati in *seriis,* qvidni in *ludicris,* qvale hoc fere carminis genus propter figuras.[11]

Here Nils Thomassøn characterizes the genre of his poem with the words *in ludicris,* which I translate as "in playful (matters)", and puts this in contrast to *in seriis,* in serious matters.

The Rebus Rules in *Cestus sapphicus*

The element of entertainment in *Cestus sapphicus* is connected with the rebuses, which quality is seen by the author as the core and the best part of the book. But the rebuses in *Cestus sapphicus* do not only entertain: they are also connected with learning. One learned element is the commentaries: to each of the thirty-one stanzas the author gives his own explanations, with suggestions for further reading. The rebus poem in itself is also highly intellectual in character, a fact which is proved primarily by the scheme in the form of a logical table. But essential for us here are the rebus rules: a list of ten "requisita" or formal rules for the rebuses, presented as a part of the introduction to the book. In what follows, we shall concentrate on these rebus rules.

Rule 1. The motif should belong to the category "concrete nouns" [Res quam figura notat debet esse in prædicamento substantiæ . . .].

> The meaning of this rule is that the motif should be apt for a picture. Almost all the pictures in *Cestus sapphicus* have concrete nouns as motifs. Exceptions in stanza 23 are the personified virtue Hope, and Eve from the Old Testament.

Rule 2. The motif cannot be a kind, but a species [Non potest esse genus . . . sed species . . .].

> The effect of this rule is to make it clear that in the case of, e.g., birds, the species is meant, not the general concept *avis,* bird. From Nils Thomassøn's practice we see that the same is true for trees and flowers. An example from stanza 23 is the cork-oak, *suber.*

---

[10] "πάντων εστι πλησμονή, Omnium rerum est satietas", *Cestus sapphicus,* p. 106, fol. M4r; Isoc. 1.20.

[11] "This is true where serious matters are concerned; why not then in playful (matters), such as this kind of near-poetry in representations" (*Cestus sapphicus,* p. 106, fol. M4r).

Rule 3. The noun that the figure depicts should be as remote as possible from the significance of the word into which it is placed [Nomen seu vocabulum quod notat figura oculis subjecta, debet quantum possibile distare . . . a significatione vocis in qua eadem ponitur].

This rule means that a figure word cannot have etymological connection with the word in the poem of which it forms a part. One example is the above-mentioned *suber* in our stanza; in the poem, this figure forms the prefix and the first part of the verb in *suberrant*, wander about.

This rule makes the task a lot more difficult for the rebus composer, since many possible rebuses cannot be used, and it makes the task more difficult for the reader too, since the obvious cannot be correct: the picture of, e.g., a heart (*cor* in Latin) does not mean a heart in the *text* — neither in a direct nor in a transferred meaning — but but rather stands for the string of letters "cor". This very figure is used in stanza 20, forming part of the adjective *cordo* (aftermath).

This rebus rule creates a need for commentaries, explanations, and references to learned works, in order to establish the etymology of word pairs. One example is *clepsydra* and *Clepsydra*: the figure of an hourglass is used to present the name of an actual fountain in Athens (stanza 14).

In stanza 19, the picture of a rake, *rastrum*, is used to form part of the word *serperastrum* (knee-splints). In the commentary, Nils Thomassøn states that *rastrum* is derived from *raritate dentium*. He refers to Martinius, who quotes an older authority:

> Papias: *Rastri ferramenta culturæ a raritate dentium dicti. hoc nomine & aratra dicuntur.* Idem melius: *Rastri a radendo terram.*[12]

We see that in this case Nils Thomassøn does not follow the etymology which Martinius finds best, but the less good one. It seems that his motive is to find an authority who says that "rastrum" is not derived from the same root as the last element of *serperastrum*; otherwise, he could not use the picture of a *rastrum* here.

Rule 4. Usually, one or more letters should accompany the picture [Litera una vel altera figuræ latine reddendæ directrix adsit . . .].

The meaning of this rule is, as it seems, to make it easier for the reader to interpret the picture: "in gratiam Lecturi". An example from the twenty-third stanza is that of the homonyms *scylla* and {*Scylla*}*e*. While the figure word has the meaning "squill", a plant, the word in the poem means the monster by the same name. And the letter "e" which is added gives the genitive case of the word in the poem.

---

[12] Quoted from Matthias Martinius, *Lexicon philologicum* (Bremen 1623), *s.v.* Rastrum.

Rule 5a. The same figure should not be repeated, but homonyms are allowed [Eadem figura non nisi semel pingatur; vox vero eadem sæpius poterit; modo vocabulum Homonymum ibidem repertum, plures figuras subministret].

An effect of this rule is to make it much more difficult to compose rebuses. The rule is broken once, in the case of *iris*, blue lily. This flower is used as a figure twice, in stanzas 2 and 21. We find also the homonym *iris* meaning rainbow (stanza 17). One possible explanation for the "illegal" repetition is that another object is meant, perhaps a hedgehog, called *iris* in Plautus's *Captivi*.[13]

From Nils Thomassøn's practice, as demonstrated in this rebus poem, it is clear that he not only allows homonyms, but uses as many as possible. Besides, he takes care to use the homonyms in such a way that they will be noted by the reader. *Ama*, for instance, has been used four times with different meanings in the poem. Of these four, two are in the same stanza, and both times included in forms of the verb *amare*.

Rule 5b. Every verse should contain at least one picture [Singuli versus unicam saltim contineant figuram . . .].

The meaning of this rule is, I think, to preserve the character of the rebus poem. This is a difficult rule for the author to obey: it must have been especially hard to invent one rebus or even two for the short versus *Adonicus*. But there is no verse without a picture in *Cestus sapphicus*.

From this rule, we see that the minimum number of figures allowed per stanza is four. In *Cestus sapphicus*, the lowest number found is five, while most stanzas have six or more figures. The highest number of figures in one stanza is twelve (stanza 22).

Rule 6. If the figure word has three syllables, the accent must be considered in both instances [Si vox figuræ est notata trisyllaba, accentus utrobique habenda est ratio . . .].

There are in *Cestus sapphicus* a number of figure words with three syllables. In such cases, the accent "in both instances" must be considered. ("In both instances" means in the figure word as well as in the word in the poem.) For example: one of the figure words in stanza 15 is *lucanus*, "beetle". When solved, the rebus forms part of the word *antelucanus*, an adjective with the meaning of "early in the morning". In both these words, the "a" is long, and consequently the syllable is stressed.

---

[13] v. 184. *Oxford Latin Dictionary* (Oxford, 1968), s.v. iris²: "N.B.: perh. better written *er*- (the form of the word extant in later Latin). A hedgehog."

Chil.1.   SCYLLA) vide Adag.Erasmi: nam evitata *Charybdi* in *Scyllam* incidi, hoc est
Cent.4. *dum vito gravius malum in alterum diversum incidi.*
       CLUNACULUM) est culter sanguinarius, qvod ad *clunes* dependeat, vel qvia *clunes*
hostiarum dividat. Fest.
       SAGAN) A nomen *Veneficæ qvæ Varum* puerum prætextatum suis *veneficiis* fasci-
navit, de qva Horat. 1. Serm. Sat. 8.
       STR.GAS) Mulieres *maleficas* antiqvi vocârunt Vid. Lex. Matth. Mart.   Sensus
st, hic ut *Sponsus & manifestas & clandestinas evitet machinas.*

FIGURÆ 23. Stroph.

SÆVA) Eva Evaallis voris Moder.
SCYLLÆ) Scylla Strand-Sÿg.
SOSPES) Spes Virgo anchoram tenens.
FAXIS) Axis Axel til en Vogn.
CLUNACLUM) Cluna Abe.
SAGANAM) Sagana Morter.
STRIGAS QFF) Triga Tre Hester for en Vogn.
SUBERRANI) Suber Korcke-Træ.

STRO.

The last part of the author's own commentaries to the twenty-third stanza and the rebus solutions to the stanza with translations into Norwegian.

Rule 7. The figure ought to be simple, not obscure [Figura sit facilis, non obscura ...].

It is not fair to use as motifs objects which can hardly be depicted, or hardly recognized, because this will make the reader's task too difficult and prolong it. The author gives some examples of words which are almost impossible to solve.

Rule 8. Two words may make one figure [Duo vocabula mutua ope possunt figuram constituere ...].

Each figure word must have the same spelling as the actual part of the word in the text. When space between words is concerned, however, rule 8 allows an exception: if one figure word "participates" in two words in the poem, the reader has to separate the words and add a space himself. One example is the figure *Atlas* in *sat lassus* (stanza 4).

Rule 9. Method.

The ninth rule describes the author's method for composing the rebus poem.

Rule 10. The figures should be of high quality.

Surely this rule has been obeyed by Nils Thomassøn: the figures are beautiful, demonstrating the motifs in an artistic way.

Conclusion

I have tried to demonstrate that our rebus book is a piece of entertainment literature in Latin. We have the author's word for this, and the element of entertainment is also what makes excuses necessary in his eyes. His excuses are, primarily, that all people have to relax sometimes. Moreover, there are meaningful kinds of entertainment, like his book, which points the way to European literature from Homer onwards. It does so through the rebuses themselves, as well as through the learned commentaries.

The rebus is seen historically as a playful genre. The entertainment lies in the task to be solved; it is entertaining to try one's brains, and try other persons' brains as well. To Nils Thomassøn, this was not enough: strict rebus rules represent more learning and more challenges — to his readers and, not least, to himself.

Oslo University

Illustris Blondelli Comparatio Pindari et Horatii: Les commentaires sur les œuvres de Pindare et d'Horace à la fin du XVIIe siècle

FRANÇOIS ROUGET

On sait quelle place les Anciens occupent dans le paysage culturel du Grand Siècle. Depuis l'ouvrage de référence que Jean Marmier a consacré à Horace,[1] on connaît son importance dans l'instruction délivrée au collège et dans le goût littéraire de l'époque.

Pourtant, une figure intéressante de la transmission de la tradition classique en France a été négligée jusqu'à présent: il s'agit de François Blondel (1617–1686), à qui l'on doit une *Comparaison de Pindare et d'Horace* publiée en français en 1673 (Paris, Cl. Barbin) et rééditée en 1686 (Amsterdam, W. Abraham), avant de connaître une diffusion européenne.[2]

Cet ouvrage mériterait un long examen. Blondel y résume la vie et l'œuvre des deux poètes lyriques. Il commente leurs textes et enrichit ses remarques par l'intermédiaire de Quintilien, Scaliger, Turnèbe et Heinsius, entre autres. Pourtant, s'il s'inspire de ces critiques et du modèle de la comparaison (comme J. C. Scaliger et R. Rapin), Blondel sait dépasser ses modèles et s'en écarter.

Dans les pages suivantes, nous aimerions rappeler le parcours bio-bibliographique de Blondel, puis indiquer les enjeux et les limites de son commentaire sur Pindare et Horace. Enfin, nous voudrions restituer sa *Comparaison* dans le contexte littéraire et le climat intellectuel de son temps et montrer son impact. Car au moment où Blondel édite son parallèle pour réhabiliter Pindare et promouvoir l'image d'Horace, Boileau, de son côté, fait paraître la traduction du *Traité du sublime* du pseudo-Longin, et l'*Art*

---

[1] *Horace en France au dix-septième siècle* (Paris, 1962).
[2] Éd. anglaise (Londres, Bennet, 1696); latine (*Illustris Blondelli comparatio Pindari et Horatii*), dans J. Le Paulmier, *Kritikon [. . .], sive Pro Lucano Apologia* (Lyon, 1704, 1707; Amsterdam, 1709).

poétique où il prend la défense des Anciens. Les deux écrivains fréquentent alors le même salon, partagent la même ferveur pour le lyrisme antique et leurs œuvres se recoupent, jusqu'à la disparition de Blondel peu avant que n'éclate publiquement la "Querelle des Anciens et des Modernes".

François Blondel: sa vie et son œuvre

Rappelons d'abord les grandes dates qui ont marqué l'existence et la carrière de François-Nicolas Blondel, cet humaniste versé dans les arts et les sciences. À ne pas confondre avec son homonyme, François Blondel, médecin, avec lequel il partage le goût de la science. Mais la comparaison s'arrête là. Le médecin (1609?–1682), professeur de botanique, est connu pour le rôle qu'il joua contre la réforme de l'aristotélisme à la Faculté et contre l'introduction du quinquina. Conservateur convaincu, il est l'auteur de commentaires et de traités de médecine en latin. Boileau se moque de lui dans l'*Arrest burlesque*.[3]

François-Nicolas Blondel, celui qui nous intéresse ici, est au contraire proche de Boileau. Né à Ribemont en 1618, F. Blondel, sieur des Croisettes, est le fils aîné d'un maître des requêtes de la reine mère, annobli en 1654. Versé dans les sciences et techniques, il fut reçu ingénieur de la marine, et chargé de lever le plan des principaux ports et places militaires en Espagne et au Portugal. Espion habile, à la solde de Mazarin, il semble avoir joué un rôle dans la révolte du Portugal contre la dépendance espagnole en 1640. Toujours impliqué dans les affaires extérieures de la France, il commanda la galère "La Cardinale" et se distingua lors de l'expédition de Sicile menée par le deuxième duc de Richelieu en 1647. À son retour, il fut chargé de dresser le plan des fortifications sur le littoral de Provence (1650–1651).

C'est à cette date que sa carrière prit un nouveau tournant. Il devint d'abord gouverneur de Louis-Henri de Brienne et entama avec celui-ci un grand tour européen pendant près de quatre ans. De retour en France, Henri de Loménie, secrétaire d'État, l'envoya en mission diplomatique à Berlin (1657), et à Constantinople (1658), où il s'accomplit fort bien de sa tâche.

Dès lors, sa réputation ira grandissant. De 1662 à 1668, le Roi en personne le chargea de renforcer les fortifications de Dunkerque, du Havre (1662), de restaurer le pont et la porte romaine de Saintes (1665), et de construire l'arsenal de Rochefort (1666). Cartographe, il leva les cartes marines des Antilles (1667–1669). Associé à l'Académie des Sciences (1669), puis nommé professeur de mathématiques au Collège royal (1671), il fut directeur de l'Académie d'architecture, chargé des ouvrages publics de la ville de Paris (1672–1674), maréchal de camp (1675), et enfin professeur de mathématiques du Dauphin (1683). Il mourut le 21 janvier 1686, l'année même où fut rééditée à Amsterdam la *Comparaison de Pindare et d'Horace*.

Voyageur infatigable, François Blondel se distingue aussi par son esprit d'inlassable curiosité. Éclectique, il commença par composer des vers (*La Solitude royale*, 1653), une *Relation de voyage de Berlin à Constantinople* (1658), des entretiens en latin sur la

---

[3] Paru anonymement en 1671. Voir Boileau, *Œuvres complètes*, éd. A. Adam et F. Escal (Paris, 1966), 325 et suiv. À noter que l'index de cette édition ne discrimine pas les deux hommes.

physique de Galilée, deux traités d'architecture qui firent autorité (*Résolution des quatre principaux problèmes d'architecture*, 1673, et *Cours d'architecture*, 1675–1683), une histoire du calendrier romain (1682), deux ouvrages de technique militaire (*L'Art de jetter les bombes*,[4] *Nouvelle manière de fortifier les places*, 1683) et le *Cours de mathématiques* (1683). Fin stratège et technicien compétent, F. Blondel fit partager son immense érudition en privé, en tant que précepteur, mais aussi en public, lors des séances qui réunissaient les beaux esprits du temps chez le Premier Président du Parlement de Paris, Guillaume de Lamoignon. C'est dans les discussions de ce cercle qu'il faut chercher l'origine de la *Comparaison de Pindare et d'Horace*, sur laquelle nous allons à présent nous pencher.

La *Comparaison de Pindare et d'Horace*

Dans sa préface, l'imprimeur rappelle au lecteur les circonstances de présentation, de rédaction, puis de publication du parallèle de Blondel. La fréquentation assidue de l'assemblée de savants, se réunissant une fois par semaine chez Lamoignon, puis le "commandement" ordonné par son président[5] de coucher par écrit la comparaison des deux grands lyriques, furent le point de départ de cet ouvrage. La comparaison, comme le précise Blondel, fut retouchée plusieurs fois aux fins de la publication. Reproduisant d'abord les citations de Pindare et d'Horace dans leur langue d'origine, l'auteur fut amené finalement à les accompagner de traduction en français afin d'atteindre un plus large lectorat. La vocation pédagogique apparaîtra plus nettement encore à la mort de Blondel puisque la *Comparaison* sera associée aux *Comparaisons* de René Rapin et reliée dans le même volume édité par Wolfgang Abraham. Rapin et Blondel appartenaient à l'entourage de Lamoignon et les deux hommes œuvraient à diffuser les Belles Lettres en France et en langue vernaculaire, depuis que les Jésuites s'étaient ralliés à l'enseignement en langue vulgaire.[6] Ceux-ci, d'ailleurs, selon le précepte de Quintilien, plaçaient dans l'étude des poètes anciens la base de l'éducation.

Mais quelle était la situation de Pindare et d'Horace au XVIIe siècle? Pour Pindare, si les éditions ne manquent pas jusqu'en 1623, on peut quand même préciser qu'il s'agit de rééditions. C'est à travers celles de F. Morel (1582, 1623), et de P. Estienne (1599), que Huet et Racine découvrent le poète thébain. Passé le premier quart du siècle, Pindare se fait plus discret dans la production éditoriale.

Pour Horace, il en va tout autrement, et Marmier a bien souligné le rôle qu'Horace joue dans l'enseignement, en particulier chez les Jésuites,[7] et la fortune de ses textes dans l'édition tout au long du XVIIe siècle. Virgile mis à part, Horace est le

---

[4] Publié à Paris (1683 et 1699), Amsterdam (1690), et La Haye (1685), le manuscrit en fut présenté au Roi dès 1675, de même que *L'Art de fortifier les places* en 1673. La publication en fut retardée afin de préserver le secret des techniques militaires françaises.

[5] Cf. *Comparaison de Pindare et d'Horace* (Amsterdam, 1686), fol A2 r, et p. 5. Toutes nos références renvoient à cette édition.

[6] Voir Marmier, *Horace en France*, 23.

[7] Voir aussi F. de Dainville, *L'Éducation des Jésuites (XVIe–XVIIIe siècles)*, textes réunis par M.-M. Compère (Paris, 1978), 168–170.

principal poète latin étudié, traduit, et commenté. Il figure dans toutes les bibliothèques, est inscrit à tous les programmes des collèges, et ses œuvres sont sans cesse rééditées. Jusqu'en 1670, les commentaires de Turnèbe et de Lambin dominent, et les éditions savantes de Muret, d'Estienne, ont encore la faveur des lettrés. Lorsque paraît la *Comparaison* de Blondel en 1673, on peut donc dire qu'elle répond à un intérêt constant pour le poète latin, à une ferveur générale. Mais elle se singularise surtout parce qu'elle remet à l'honneur l'œuvre de Pindare, généralement et largement éclipsée par celle d'Homère.

François Blondel sait alors fort bien que c'est là, sans doute, que réside l'un des attraits de son ouvrage. Mais avant d'en préciser le contenu, rappelons-en la composition. Après un court prologue (5), une dédicace à Lamoignon, Blondel rappelle la vie des deux lyriques (leurs origines, 5–7; leur pays, 7–9), et décrit leurs mœurs (leur foi, 9–12; leur éducation, 12–14; leurs qualités morales et leur tempérament, 14–29; leurs amours, 30–31). Blondel souligne aussi leur destin exceptionnel (31–35), éclaire leur époque (36–39), et détaille leurs œuvres (40–64 pour Pindare; 64–76 pour Horace). Et de conclure sur le génie respectif de chacun d'entre eux (76–78).

Cette brève analyse comparée du lyrisme antique se signale par la précision de son érudition et la passion dont fait preuve le commentateur. Blondel procède par comparaison et tente de souligner les mérites et les défauts de chacun d'entre eux.

Ses idées sur Pindare sont nourries de ses lectures nombreuses. Blondel s'appuie sur Quintilien, Pausanias, Elien, sur Horace même qui avoue sa dette à l'égard du Thébain (*Odes*, 4.2). Le portrait qu'il trace du poète est nuancé, mesuré, en ce qui concerne sa personne et ses mœurs. Fils d'un joueur de flûte, originaire de Béotie "dont les peuples ont toujours passé pour grossiers" (7), Pindare fut pourtant pieux et ses œuvres illustrent sa vertu et sa dévotion aux dieux. Ce qui est déjà très bien pour un païen! Blondel croit même percevoir dans son œuvre des réminiscences de l'Ancien Testament (15). Ainsi christianisé, ce poète est rendu plus proche de nous, plus acceptable aussi. Face à l'adversité, Pindare adopte en outre une attitude toute chrétienne de compréhension et de pardon (22), et il n'a "jamais mal parlé de personne" (22). Bref, un portrait élogieux que seul le goût démesuré de l'argent semble nuancer (26). Car Pindare était cupide et il a vendu sa poésie au plus offrant. Autre excès, son penchant pour l'amour, en particulier "l'amour des Garçons" (Théoxène, 31), que Blondel tente de comprendre d'après les mœurs de l'Antiquité. Heureusement, il se rachète par son œuvre (malgré ses détracteurs) et sa gloire posthume.

Blondel est fasciné par les témoignages de louanges qui sont parvenus jusqu'à lui et par l'étendue de son génie. L'examen de ses œuvres n'occupe pas moins de 25 pages d'un parallèle qui en compte à peine 73. Blondel s'efforce de mettre en valeur la beauté des vers, leur musicalité, leur variété, la grandeur de leur élévation. Il en profite aussi pour donner un bref aperçu de ce qu'était le lyrisme officiel en Grèce, de son caractère national. Les quinze dernières pages de cet examen visent à souligner les plus beaux passages et les réussites lyriques de Pindare. Blondel se sent ému (51), séduit par la douceur de ses vers, ébloui par la richesse des vocables (52). Il juge que la description qu'il fait de l'Etna dans la 1ère *Pythique* "a quelque chose de divin" (53). Il renvoie à "mille autres beaux endroits" (55), savoure "l'austérité de sa diction, de ses sentences, de ses figures [. . .]" (56). Quand Blondel note certains défauts, il ne fait alors que reprendre des critiques générales comme s'il n'osait se dissocier totalement du jugement commun. D'autant qu'il prend sa défense en avançant l'argument qu'il nous faut toujours essayer de comprendre Pindare d'après son époque et non pas en fonction du goût de la nôtre.[8] À chaque reproche avancé, celui-ci rétorque et le réduit à néant.[9] Bref, le jugement ici tourne à l'éloge à peine camouflé. Et Blondel se range dans le sillage du pseudo-Longin pour faire valoir que les rares défauts relevés chez Pindare (de "petites taches", des "negligences", 62–63) ne font que rehausser la valeur de ses réussites.

L'examen d'Horace suit le même cheminement. Mais soit parce qu'il est mieux connu du public, soit que son génie procède en partie de l'œuvre de Pindare, Blondel lui accorde moins de place (12 pages). D'origine modeste, Horace est pourtant différent de mœurs et de caractère: impie, libertin, mais loyal et fidèle à l'autorité du père. Horace comme Pindare furent "de treshonnestes gens eu égard aux mœurs et à la manière d'agir des temps où ils ont vécu" (14), mais ils furent amoureux et vaniteux. Pourtant, Horace se singularise par sa liberté d'esprit, son indépendance à l'égard de ses protecteurs. Il a certes des défauts mais il en a conscience et tente de se corriger, et il prône dans ses vers une conduite morale irréprochable (20). Son désintéressement est admirable, sa générosité éclate partout (26–27). Comme Pindare, il était animé de pensées lascives, voluptueuses, détestables; comme lui aussi, il eut des détracteurs, mais sa gloire eut raison de leurs médisances.

Passons à l'examen de ses œuvres (64–76). Blondel note la supériorité d'Horace sur Pindare en ce qu'il "a eu la liberté de choisir les sujets les plus propres à son génie et à l'humeur où il se trouvoit" (65). Suivant l'autorité de Quintilien, il reprend son jugement qui fait d'Horace un poète moins sublime mais plus égal (*Instit. orat.* 10.1. 94–96). Son "style médiocre" (moyen) "a des charmes inimitables", ses odes adoptent tous les tons, du plus élevé au plus mélancolique. Ses épîtres, au contraire, charment par leur humilité, et ses satires touchent Blondel plus que celles de Juvénal, contre l'avis de Scaliger. Sur ce point, Blondel va défendre Horace pour s'opposer et se démarquer de l'auteur de la *Poétique* (69–70). Blondel n'a pas assez de mots pour louer ses satires et l'épître aux Pisons, et il lui vient en aide pour expliquer contre ses prédécesseurs les raisons qui ont pu le pousser à décrier Plaute (73–75). À nouveau, c'est au nom de l'histoire que Blondel veut pardonner à Horace: "Il faut bien plustot attribuer ce jugement d'Horace au goust de son siecle, qui estoit ennemy des mauvaises bouffonneries" (75). Même s'il nie vouloir "deffendre la réputation d'Horace" (75), Blondel attaque avec virulence les jugements des "sçavants critiques d'aujourd'huy" (76).

Au total, Blondel tente de sauvegarder le prestige de chacun des deux poètes lyriques, bien qu'il rétablisse l'équilibre en faveur de Pindare qui "a quelque chose de plus surprenant qu'Horace, et tend pour ainsi dire, au divin" (76). Mais Horace, lui,

---

[8] Cf. "De vouloir neanmoins tout condamner sur ce principe, ce seroit, ce me semble, aller trop viste, et faire comme ceux qui n'estant jamais sortis de leur Ville, ne sçauroient souffrir sans rire aucun habillement étranger" (58); voir aussi 59.

[9] Voir 61–62, entre autres.

"a bien plus d'etendue, de sçavoir et de connoissance que Pindare, plus d'egalité, plus de douceur et d'enjoüement et beaucoup moins de deffauts". On voit alors Blondel rejoindre le jugement commun qui préfère le poète latin au grec, mais au terme d'un examen des œuvres qui réhabilite Pindare et la notion de sublime, si importante dans les débats de l'esthétique classique vers 1670.

Blondel montre aussi qu'il connaît son histoire littéraire gréco-latine et que son jugement prétend à l'indépendance. À partir des commentaires et des éditions antérieurs, il bâtit un examen solide et personnel. Son originalité consiste à reprendre un exercice rhétorique classique pour le marquer de son empreinte. À l'instar de Plutarque, du pseudo-Longin (que Boileau traduit en 1673), de Scaliger, mais aussi de ses contemporains (G. de Balzac, R. Rapin, puis Ch. Perrault),[10] Blondel emploie le parallèle pour analyser, juger, et prendre position. Mais, pour la première fois, il rédige une comparaison en forme des deux grands lyriques antiques, ce qui manquait chez ses prédécesseurs. Blondel concrétise donc un projet latent. Il rédige aussi, et il ne pouvait l'ignorer, un ouvrage dont le sujet figure parmi ceux qui étaient proposés aux collégiens par les manuels de Jésuites, tel la *Ratio* de 1586: "Qua in re Homerum Virgilio, Pindarum Horatio posthaberes ex Scaligeri Critico et Hypercritico?"[11] La présence insistante de Quintilien et de Scaliger dans la *Comparaison* de 1673, sa réédition en 1686 à la suite des *Comparaisons* de Rapin, semblent conforter l'hypothèse que ce livre correspondait à un exercice pédagogique, oratoire, dicté par le goût mondain.

S'il doit beaucoup au pseudo-Longin[12] (par l'intermédiaire de Boileau?), il révèle pourtant une certaine liberté de pensée qui l'amène parfois à s'écarter de la tradition, à contredire Scaliger (69, 72–75), à le dépasser (35, 53, 55)[13], et même à l'ignorer (65). On voit ainsi que la *Comparaison*, loin d'être un simple exercice rhétorique, contribue à réévaluer la place du lyrisme antique, cela pour tenter de définir l'esthétique classique contemporaine.

---

[10] Voir respectivement les *Parallèles ou Vies des hommes illustres*, trad. J. Amyot, qui définit ainsi le parallèle d'après Plutarque: "... il se meit à escrire ceste œuvre excellente des Vies, qu'il appella Parallelon, comme qui diroit d'accouplement ou assortissement pource qu'il accouple un Grec avec un Romain, mettant leurs vies l'une devant l'autre, et les conferant ensemble, selon qu'ilz se sont trouvez avoir entre eux conformité de nature, de mœurs et d'adventures, en examinant ce que l'un a eu de meilleur ou de pire, de plus grand ou de plus petit, que l'autre ..." L'abbé Tallemant fit paraître une nouvelle traduction en 1663–1665, ainsi que La Serre en 1681 et Dacier en 1694. Voir J. C. Scaliger, *Poetices libri septem*, 1561, livre 5; R. Rapin, *Comparaisons* (1664–1671); *Réflexions sur la poétique d'Aristote et sur les ouvrages des poètes anciens et modernes* (1674); G. de Balzac, *Les Entretiens* (1657), 31 (Malherbe et Ronsard); Ch. Perrault, *Parallèle des Anciens et des Modernes ...*, 1688–1694.

[11] Cité par de Dainville, *L'Éducation des Jésuites*, 177.

[12] Voir le chap. 27 dans la traduction de Boileau, "Si l'on doit preferer le mediocre parfait au sublime qui a quelques defauts", dont le titre résume bien l'enjeu esthétique qui sépare Pindare d'Horace. Pourtant, finalement, Blondel s'écarte du pseudo-Longin pour préférer le "mediocre" au sublime.

[13] Voir *Poetices libri septem*, 5.7, "Horatii et Graecorum comparatio".

Blondel et l'esthétique classique

François Blondel était bien introduit à la Cour et dans les salons et académies parisiens. On le retrouve ainsi dans l'académie de Guillaume de Lamoignon. Dès 1667, on note la présence de Boileau, de Rapin, de Gui Patin (père de celui-ci), de l'abbé Fleury, parmi les dix-huit membres qui se réunissent tous les lundis de 5 à 7.[14] À chaque séance, un sujet savant est choisi et l'un des membres présente une dissertation. À quelle date Blondel a t-il rejoint le cercle de Lamoignon ? Il est difficile de le dire, mais on peut supposer que Blondel dût profiter de ses courts séjours à Paris, interrompus par ses missions en province et à l'étranger, pour y participer.

Toujours est-il qu'au début de la décennie 1660–1670, on remarque la prédominance des questions de poétique au programme de cette académie. Au moment où Blondel fait paraître sa *Comparaison*, R. Rapin a entamé la publication de ses *Comparaisons* (*Démosthène et Cicéron*, 1670 ; *Homère et Virgile*, 1664 ; *Platon et Aristote*, 1671).[15] Mais surtout, en 1674, on voit paraître l'*Art poétique* (le texte en avait été révélé partiellement dès 1673) et le *Traité du sublime* par Boileau, et les *Réflexions sur la poétique d'Aristote* de Rapin. Les questions du sublime, du génie et de l'art, du naturel et des règles, parcourent l'ensemble de ces textes tout comme la *Comparaison* de Blondel.[16] Il s'agit à chaque fois de définir qui l'emporte entre Aristote et Platon, Homère et Virgile, Pindare et Horace. Malgré quelques divergences d'opinion, une communauté d'esprit semble réunir ces savants. Tous sont convaincus du principe de l'imitation, du génie naturel de l'artiste, et de la supériorité des Anciens sur les Modernes.

À cet égard, le corpus des textes publiés par ces lettrés s'oppose aux revendications de leurs contemporains. Même s'il faut attendre la lecture du *Siècle de Louis Le Grand* par Perrault à l'Académie en 1687, puis la parution de son *Parallèle* (1688, 1690, 1692, 1694) pour voir éclater la "Querelle des Anciens et des Modernes",[17] en vérité les débats entre les partisans des deux clans étaient apparus dès 1669. Des Marests de Saint-Sorlin en 1670 avait publié sa *Comparaison de la langue et de la poésie française avec la grecque et la latine*, qu'il réédita en 1673 avec un *Traité pour juger des poètes grecs, latins et français*. Ce fut le début des hostilités. Comme ceux de ses émules, l'ouvrage de Blondel a pour but de prôner la grandeur et la force dans l'inspiration et l'écriture poétique. C'est pourquoi il réhabilite Pindare et son sens du sublime. De leur côté, Rapin compose son traité *Du grand ou du sublime dans les mœurs* et Boileau traduit le pseudo-Longin.

À lire la *Comparaison* de Blondel, on perçoit quelques allusions ou insinuations à ces débats houleux. Il persifle certains "Grammairiens" (64), s'en prend à certains commentateurs comme Scaliger (69), Juste Lipse (69, 73), Turnèbe même (73). Mais il ne polémique pas, à l'inverse de Boileau. Ce n'est donc pas sur ce terrain que les

---

[14] Cf. A. Adam, *Histoire de la littérature française du XVIIe siècle* (Paris, 1962), 3:15 et suiv., et Marmier, *Horace en France*, chap. 5.

[15] La première publication en volume date de 1684 (Paris), et sera reprise en 1686 (Amsterdam).

[16] Cf. Marmier, *Horace en France*, 88.

[17] Cf. Adam, *Histoire*, 3:143–50.

deux érudits se rejoignent, mais sur le plan des idées et de l'admiration pour les Anciens, en particulier pour Pindare, Horace et le genre de l'ode. Antoine Adam a bien montré que l'*Art poétique* de Boileau devait beaucoup à la fréquentation de ses contemporains, à Claude Fleury et à l'abbé Cotin. Il doit sans doute aussi à la lecture de la *Comparaison* de Blondel. Celui-ci, par exemple, liste la variété des sujets traités dans les odes pindariques ("les Jeux, les Ris, les Graces et l'Amour") qui trouvent un écho au chant II lorsque Boileau décrit les sujets de l'ode: "Elle peint les festins, les danses et les ris" (v. 67). Ailleurs, c'est la traduction que Boileau fit du pseudo-Longin qui semble avoir influencé Blondel. Celui-ci cite le *Traité du sublime* à plusieurs reprises (50–52), et ses remarques sur Pindare sont sans doute nourries des commentaires du rhéteur grec sur Pindare au chapitre 27 ("Si l'on doit preferer le mediocre parfait au sublime qui a ses defauts").[18] Mais la comparaison ne s'arrête pas là. Dans son parallèle (61–62), Blondel reprend les critiques faites par certains de ses contemporains à la première *Olympique* de Pindare: "Je voy des personnes sçavantes qui trouvent à redire au commencement de la premiere Ode de Pindare. C'est une chose excellente que l'eau. Et qui n'approuvent pas qu'ayant à faire une comparaison fort relevée, il se soit servy de celle de l'eau, qui est trop vile et trop basse pour produire aucune idée de grandeur dans nostre esprit. [. . .]". Et d'expliquer au lecteur que le recours à l'image de l'eau est voulu de Pindare qui s'adresse "à un Tyran de Syracuse, où l'on suivoit la doctrine d'Empedocle [. . .]" qui considérait "cet Element comme le principe qui leur [aux Siciliens] avoit donné l'Estre".

Ce débat semble donc remonter au début des années 1670 au moins. On constate avec curiosité que cette querelle sera reprise par Perrault au livre I de son *Parallèle* (1688)[19] et par Boileau retorquant à Perrault dans ses *Réflexions critiques sur quelques passages du rheteur Longin* (1694). Perrault reproche à Pindare son "galimatias" et ridiculise par avance toute tentative pour expliquer le début audacieux de la première *Olympique*.[20] Et Boileau lui réplique en l'accusant de ne comprendre ni l'esprit du poète thébain, ni de ne le traduire convenablement (*Réflexion VIII*). Sa défense de la comparaison pindarique s'inspire directement de la justification de Blondel, quinze ans plus tôt: "On sera donc assez surpris icy de voir que cette bassesse et ce galimatias appartiennent entierement à Monsieur P. qui en traduisant Pindare, n'a entendu ni le Grec, ni le Latin, ni le François. C'est ce qu'il est aisé de prouver. Mais pour cela, il faut sçavoir, que Pindare vivoit peu de temps aprés Pythagore, Thalés, et Anaxagore, fameux Philosophes Naturalistes [. . .]. L'opinion de Thalés, qui mettoit l'eau pour le principe des choses, estoit surtout celebre. Empedocle Sicilien [. . .] avoit encore poussé la chose plus loin qu'eux [. . .]".[21]

---

[18] Voir la *Comparaison*, 62–63.
[19] On se souvient que dans ce dialogue Perrault met en scène les personnages du cercle de Lamoignon, où le Président tente de convaincre son épouse des charmes de la poésie pindarique.
[20] Voir le *Parallèle*, livre I (Paris, 1688), 27–30.
[21] Voir *Œuvres complètes*, 528.

Mais c'est toute la *Réflexion VIII* qu'il faudrait citer tellement elle semble le décalque des remarques de Blondel. Malgré la publication tardive des textes polémiques de Perrault et Boileau concernant Pindare, il n'est pas interdit de supposer que leurs ouvrages n'aient rendu publique une querelle qui était notoire dès 1670.[22]

Bref, on le voit, l'apport littéraire de François Blondel n'est pas négligeable. S'il a contribué à mieux faire connaître Pindare à ses contemporains (dont Boileau), il a aussi joué un rôle dans la "Querelle des Anciens et des Modernes", un rôle surtout posthume puisque celle-ci n'éclate publiquement à l'Académie que l'année suivant la disparition de Blondel (1686).

Ce savant, versé dans les humanités, les sciences, et les techniques, impliqué dans les débats de son temps, a cherché à imprimer sa marque dans tout ce qu'il entreprenait. Sa *Comparaison* permet d'éclairer l'histoire des idées poétiques et théoriques, et joue un rôle sous-estimé par la critique, à l'image de son rédacteur.

La postérité garde pourtant le souvenir de sa réputation européenne puisque sa comparaison fut traduite en plusieurs langues au début du XVIIIe siècle. Esprit vraiment curieux que ce François Blondel, à la fois sensible à la musicalité des rythmes antiques et passionné par la trajectoire des obus!

Queen's University, Canada

---

[22] Perrault, d'ailleurs, continuera cette querelle jusqu'en 1692 (*Parallèle*, 3ᵉ partie, 160 et suiv.), où les mérites d'Horace et de Pindare sont comparés. De son côté, Boileau fait paraître ses *Réflexions* en 1694 mais les neuf premières avaient été rédigées entre 1692 et 1694.

Personajes femeninos en el De viris illustribus Urbis Romae a Romulo ad Augustum *(1779) de Charles François Lhomond*

JOSÉ MANUEL RUIZ VILA

Antes de abordar el estudio de los personajes femeninos en una obra titulada *De viris illustribus*, expondremos brevemente cuál es su contenido.[1] Se trata de un compendio de historia romana escrito para facilitar el aprendizaje del latín; no debemos olvidar que Lhomond dedicó la mayor parte de su vida a la enseñanza. Pero no sólo éste era su fin, sino también lograr una correcta educación tomando como modelo las virtudes de los grandes hombres de Roma. Esto no nos tiene que llevar a pensar que en esta obra sólo aparezcan los más notables personajes romanos como Rómulo o Régulo; al contrario, figuras históricas como la de Tarquinio el Soberbio, último rey de Roma, sirven igualmente como modelo de comportamiento a evitar. En cuanto al modo de narrar todos los acontecimientos de la historia de Roma, Lhomond en cierta medida se disculpa por su estilo quizás no muy elevado. Él mismo llega a justificarse argumentando que sólo trata de conseguir que los alumnos, aparte de conocer la historia romana, adquieran un mínimo de soltura con el latín, ya tendrán tiempo después para pulir el estilo.

¿Qué fuentes utiliza? El propio Lhomond menciona, en el prólogo al *De viris*, tres autores: Tito Livio, Valerio Máximo, y Floro. No obstante, en su catálogo de hombres ilustres podemos rastrear testimonios de otras dos obras más no mencionadas: un

---

[1] Hacemos aquí un resumen de lo ya expuesto en J. M. Ruiz Vila, "Fuentes historiográficas latinas del *De viris illustribus Urbis Romae a Romulo ad Augustum* (1779) de Charles François Lhomond," *Cuadernos de Filología Clásica: Estudios Latinos* n.s. 16 (1999): 423–448. A él remitimos para un estudio en mayor profundidad sobre el *De viris*, su contenido, su estructura y sus fuentes.

Liber de viris illustribus Urbis Romae atribuido falsamente a Aurelio Víctor[2] y el *Breviarium historiae Romanae* de Eutropio. De estos cinco autores van a ser Tito Livio y Pseudo Aurelio Víctor sus fuentes principales, remitiéndose sólo al *Epitome* de Floro, a los *Facta et dicta memorabilia* de Valerio Máximo, y al *Breviarium* de Eutropio en ocasiones muy puntuales. Todas estas fuentes las hemos señalado en el aparato de fuentes con el que acompañamos los textos latinos con la idea de ver cómo se sirve de sus modelos, qué datos omite y cuáles destaca en función de sus intenciones didácticas. Hemos marcado en negrita aquellos pasajes que Lhomond tomó al pie de la letra, resaltando por su parte en *cursiva* aquellas partes que han sido motivo de adaptación o simplificación con fines escolares.

Personajes femeninos en el *De viris*

Abordamos en el presente trabajo el estudio de diez personajes femeninos, de la historia mítica de Roma en su mayor parte. Todos ellos aparecen en el *Ab Urbe condita* de Livio, pero no así en todos los compendios sucesivos que se realizaron como el *De viris* anónimo, el *Breviarium* de Eutropio, o el *Epitome* de Floro. La mayoría sí aparece, sin embargo, en los *Facta* de Valerio Máximo. Curiosamente, todos los personajes que Lhomond selecciona tienen cabida también en el *De viris* anónimo, principal fuente de su obra junto con Livio.[3]

Vamos a ver qué tratamiento da Lhomond a las mujeres en un libro que, como su título indica, está dedicado por entero a los varones. Hay que tener también muy en cuenta el público al que estaba dedicada la obra: los alumnos del colegio parisino en el que enseñaba latín. La mayor parte de los personajes femeninos aparecen citados porque no le quedaba más remedio, dada su importancia en la historia de Roma. Otros, por el contrario, van a tener entidad propia, como es el caso de *Cloelia virgo*.

Uno de los aspectos más destacados del estilo de Lhomond, y que se ve muy bien reflejado en los retratos femeninos, es la falta de opiniones personales (cada vez que aparecen en Livio, él las suprime), así como la ausencia de dramatismo, como por ejemplo en el caso de la violación de Lucrecia. Todo elemento sangriento y cruel ha sido retirado o, por lo menos, mitigado, pensando siempre en sus jóvenes lectores.

Textos

La primera mujer a la que Livio hace mención, Lavinia, está ausente del relato de Lhomond, dado que no forma parte propiamente de la historia de Roma. Asimismo tampoco aparece la figura de Eneas. El relato comienza en Rómulo y Remo siguiendo la pauta del *De viris illustribus* anónimo.

---

[2] Sobre la autoría de esta obra, cf. el prólogo a la edición de Fr. Pichmayr (Leipzig, 1966) en la Bibliotheca Teubneriana.

[3] A propósito de estudios sobre la mujer en las fuentes utilizadas por Lhomond, podemos destacar varios artículos; sobre Tito Livio, cf. C. Gallardo y Á. Sierra, "Tópicos sobre la mujer en la historia romana de Tito Livio," in *La mujer en el mundo antiguo* (Madrid, 1986), 299–306; R. Delicado Méndez, "La mujer en Tito Livio," *Estudios Clásicos* 113 (1998): 37–46; por lo que respecta a Aurelio Víctor, cf. H. W. Bird, "Aurelius Victor on Women and Sexual Morality," *Classical Journal* 78 (1982): 44–48.

Rhea Silvia

La primera mujer que aparece en el *De viris* es Rea Silvia, la madre de Rómulo y Remo. Su aparición en el relato es fugaz, y encontramos una omisión con respecto a todas las fuentes: la violación que sufrió por parte del dios Marte. En este fragmento la fuente principal es Pseudo Aurelio Víctor del que toma el pasaje literal pero omite sutilmente *a Marte compressa* (1.1). No parecía un buen dato a tener en cuenta por parte de sus alumnos. En el mismo episodio de Rea Silvia aparece también Acca Laurencia, esposa de Fáustulo, pastor del ganado real, que se encarga de cuidar a los gemelos. Lhomond omite deliberadamente el rumor que ofrece Livio (y ninguna fuente antigua más hasta Petrarca[4] en su *De viris illustribus*) de que esta Laurencia fuera llamada *lupa* por vender su cuerpo (*volgato corpore* dice Livio [1.4.7]) y no una *lupa* en sentido real.

Como vemos, pues, dos omisiones relacionadas directamente con la moral. Si estamos ante una obra que debe servir de *exemplum*, no parece lógico que hechos como una violación y acusaciones de prostitución, tengan cabida.

> **Proca, rex Albanorum**, duos **filios, Numitorem et Amulium habuit.** / **Numitori, qui** natu maior erat, regnum reliquit; sed **Amulius, pulso fratre,** *regnavit,* / **et ut eum sobole privaret, Rheam Sylviam eius filiam Vestae sacerdotem** *fecit,* **quae** /
> 5 tamen **Romulum et Remum uno partu edidit.** / Quo cognito, **Amulius ipsam in vincula** *coniecit,* **parvulos** alveo impositos **abiecit in Tiberim,** / qui tunc **forte super ripas** erat **effusus;** sed, relabente flumine, eos **aqua in sicco** reliquit. **Vastae tum in iis locis solitudines erant.** (1.24)[5]

1–2	Vir. ill. 1.1		**5**	Eutr. 1.1
2–3	Liv. 1.30.10		**5–7**	Vir. ill. 1.1
3–4	Vir. ill. 1.1		**7–9**	Liv. 1.4.4–6.

Tarpeia

La segunda mujer que aparece en el *De viris* de Lhomond es la misma que en el de Aurelio Víctor. Ambos autores suprimen la figura de Hersilia, esposa de Rómulo, que ante las súplicas de las sabinas pide a Rómulo que perdone a sus padres y permita así la concordia del Estado (1.11.2). Abordamos ahora el personaje de Tarpeya, una mujer que aparece marcada ya desde Livio bajo el signo de la traición y el engaño. En su

---

[4] Cf. la *Vita de Romulo primo Romanorum rege* en su *De viris illustribus* 1.3–5. Citamos por la siguiente edición: F. Petrarca, *De viris illustribus*, ed. Guido Martellotti (Florencia, 1964).

[5] La numeración corresponde al capítulo y a la página, de acuerdo a la última edición del texto latino: Abbé Lhomond, *De viris: Les grands hommes de Rome*, ed. et trad. Jacques Gaillard (París, 1995). El text de Lhomond también en: http://www/thelatinlibrary.com/lhomond.viris.html. Cf. nuestra reseña en *Boletín Informativo de Madrid* 31 (1999): 67–70.

intento por engañar a los sabinos pidiendo lo que llevaban en el brazo izquierdo (las armas) a cambio de entrar en la ciudad, cayó en su propia trampa y fue asesinada por traidora. En este caso, Lhomond, intentando convertir esta leyenda en un *exemplum* para sus alumnos, termina el episodio de forma sentenciosa con la frase: "sic impia proditio celeri poena vindicata est," frase de su propia cosecha.

> **Sabini ob** virgines **raptas bellum adversus Romanos sumpserunt, et cum Romae appropinquarent, Tarpeiam virginem nacti** sunt, **quae aquae causa sacrorum hauriendae descenderat.** Huius pater Romanae praeerat arci. **Titus Tatius** Sabinorum
> 5 dux Tarpeiae **optionem muneris dedit, si exercitum suum** *in Capitolium* **perduxisset. Illa petiit quod Sabini in sinistris manibus gerebant, videlicet annulos et armillas. Quibus dolose promissis, Tarpeia Sabinos in arcem perduxit, ubi Tatius eam scutis obrui praecepit. Nam** et scuta in laevis habue-
> 10 rant. Sic impia proditio celeri poena vindicata est. (2.30)

1–10 Vir. ill. 2.4–14

Horatia

La tercera mujer que aparece en el *De viris* se encuentra dentro del capítulo dedicado a Tulo Hostilio, tercer rey de Roma. Vamos a referirnos aquí al famoso episodio de la lucha entre Horacios y Curiacios. La lucha entre unos y otros la resume Lhomond muy brevemente, siendo en este pasaje Livio su fuente principal. En el episodio siguiente de esta historia, el asesinato de la hermana, las similitudes son, si cabe, todavía mayores, a pesar de lo cual queremos comentar ciertos aspectos. Comprobamos cómo Lhomond, al igual que Aurelio Víctor, despoja a la hermana del Horacio de su condición de *virgo* (o al menos la omite). Una característica fundamental de la adaptación de Lhomond es el respeto, en la medida de lo posible, por diálogos que Livio atribuye a los personajes históricos. Suelen aparecer en el *De viris* de Lhomond sin adaptar o, al menos, con escasos cambios. La intención parecía clara: acercar poco a poco a los alumnos al estilo de Livio. En este caso concreto, del texto del *Ab urbe condita* omite *mortuorum vivique* conservando sólo *patriae* quizás en un intento de suavizar las duras palabras que profiere a su hermana el Horacio. Livio lo califica de crimen atroz, aunque más tarde lo justifica en función de la *virtus* exigible a todo ciudadano romano. Vemos aquí, por tanto, un ejemplo práctico de lo que mencionábamos más arriba: intento a toda costa de Lhomond de suavizar el dramatismo de algunas escenas de la historia mítica de Roma.

> **Princeps ibat Horatius,** *trium fratrum* **spolia prae se gerens. Cui obvia fuit soror, quae desponsa fuerat uni ex Curiatiis,** *viso*que **super humeros fratris paludamento sponsi, quod ipsa confecerat,** flere et **crines** *solvere coepit.* **Movit feroci iuveni**
> 5 **animum comploratio sororis in tanto gaudio publico: stric-**

to itaque gladio transfigit puellam, simul eam **verbis increpans: "Abi hinc cum immaturo amore ad sponsum; oblita fratrum, oblita patriae. Sic eat quaecumque Romana lugebit hostem."** (4.40)

1–9 Liv. 1.26.2–5

Tanaquil

Abordamos ahora varios personajes que en Livio aparecen marcados como símbolos de ambición, capaces de hacer caer al más honrado de los varones. Lhomond las incluye en su relato, pero mitiga esos aspectos tan negativos que les imprime Livio. La primera que vemos es Tanaquil, esposa de Tarquinio Prisco, de la que Lhomond sólo se atreve a decir que era *auguriorum perita*, pero sin mencionar esa ambición que dice Livio, aunque la caracterización del personaje no es muy positiva dejando entrever en varias ocasiones su carácter ambicioso y manipulador, como en la ocasión en la que oculta la muerte de su esposo para propiciar el ascenso al reino de Servio, niño al que habían adoptado.

Additur haec fabula: scilicet ei **advenienti aquila pilleum sustulit,** et super carpentum, ubi Tarquinius sedebat, cum magno clangore volitans, rursus capiti apte reposuit; inde sublimis abiit. **Tanaquil coniux auguriorum perita regnum ei portendi in-**
5 **tellexit:** / itaque virum complexa iussit eum alta sperare. **Has spes cogitationesque secum portantes, urbem ingressi sunt /** ... **Servius Tullius** matre nobili, sed *captiva*, natus est. **Cum in domo Tarquinii Prisci educaretur,** ferunt prodigium visu eventuque mirabile accidisse. **Flammae species** *pueri dormientis*
10 **caput amplexa est. Hoc viso Tanaquil summam ei dignitatem portendi intellexit; coniugi suasit ut eum non secus ac liberos suos educaret.** Is *postquam* **adolevit, a Tarquinio gener assumptus est; et cum** Tarquinius **occisus esset, Tanaquil,** celata eius morte, **populum** *ex superiori parte aedium* **allocuta, ait** re-
15 gem, **gravi quidem, sed non letali vulnere accepto, petere, ut, interim dum convalescit, Servio Tullio dicto audientes essent. Servius Tullius quasi precario regnare coepit, sed recte imperium administravit.** (6.48–7.52)

1–5 Vir. ill. 6.3–4
5–6 Liv. 1.34.10
7–18 Vir. ill. 7.1–5

Tullia

De acuerdo con la tradición las hijas de Servio Tulio se casaron con los hijos de Tarquinio Prisco. Se trataba de dos hermanas de carácter bien distinto. Aurelio Víctor califica a una de *ferox* y a la otra como *mitis*. Los hijos de Tarquinio parecían estar dotados del mismo carácter opuesto de las hijas de Servio. De ahí que, como dice Aurelio Víctor: "ut omnium mentes morum diversitate leniret, ferocem miti, mitem feroci in matrimonium dedit" (7.15). Sin embargo, ¿casualmente quizás?, los cónyuges que habían sido calificados como *mites* mueren de forma un tanto extraña. Livio asegura que se trata de un crimen y da esta opinión tan misógina que, por supuesto, Lhomond omite: "malum malo aptissimum; sed initium turbandi omnia a femina ortum est" (1.46.7). Por su parte, el *De viris* de Pseudo Aurelio se muestra más comedido y dice que murieron "seu forte, seu fraude" (7.16) dejando al lector la elección. Lhomond toma estas palabras al pie de la letra sin añadir nada, pero omitiendo, eso sí, las opiniones misóginas de Livio, que atribuye claramente la autoría a la *ferox Tullia*. En este pasaje, tomado del capítulo dedicado a Servio Tulio, sexto rey de los romanos, no aparece Livio por ninguna parte, y es que este pasaje está marcado por connotaciones peyorativas hacia la mujer, como por ejemplo las palabras que Livio atribuye a la *ferox Tullia*: "si tu is es cui nuptam esse me arbitror, et virum et regem appello; sin minus, eo nunc peius mutata res est quod istic cum ignavia est scelus. Quin accingeris?" (1.47.3–4).

Servius Tullius filiam alteram ferocem mitem alteram *habebat*. Duo quoque Tarquinii Prisci filii longe dispares moribus erant: Tullia ferox Tarquinio miti nupserat; Tullia vero mitis Tarquinio feroci; sed **mites, seu forte, seu fraude, perierunt: feroces**
5   **morum similitudo coniunxit. Statim Tarquinius superbus a Tullia incitatus, advocato senatu, regnum** *paternum* **repetere coepit: qua re audita, Servius dum ad curiam contendit, iussu Tarquinii gradibus deiectus, et domum refugiens interfectus est. Tullia** carpento vecta **in forum properavit,** virum
10   e curia evocavit, **et prima regem salutavit: a quo iussa a turba decedere, cum domum rediret, viso patris corpore, mulionem evitantem super ipsum corpus carpentum agere praecepit. Unde vicus ille Sceleratus dictus est.** (7.54–56)

1–13   Vir. ill. 7.15–19

Lucretia

Estamos, sin duda, ante uno de los episodios de mayor crueldad y dramatismo de la historia mítica de Roma: la violación de Lucrecia por parte de Tarquinio el Soberbio, hecho que puso fin a la monarquía en Roma. En este punto dos van a ser las fuentes principales de Lhomond: el *Ab urbe condita* y el *De viris illustribus*. El texto de Lhomond resulta mucho menos violento que el de Livio; no es de extrañar dada la finalidad educativa de la obra. Por ejemplo, la escena tan sanguinaria que ofrece Livio al escribir *eum in corde defigit* (1.58.11) se ve mitigada en *se occidit*, tomado a su vez de Pseudo Aurelio (9.4). Es curiosa aquí, sin embargo, la ausencia de los diálogos livianos, tan habituales en otros capítulos. El famoso pasaje que comienza con las no menos conocidas " 'tace, Lucretia,' inquit; 'Sex. Tarquinius sum; ferrum in manu est; moriere, si emiseris vocem'" (1.58.2) queda reducido a *Lucretiae vim attulit*.

> **Incidit de uxoribus mentio:** / cum unusquisque suam laudaret, placuit experiri. Itaque equis Romam petunt. Regias nurus in convivio et luxu deprehendant. / Pergunt inde Collatiam. / **Lucretiam** Collatini **uxorem inter ancillas in**
> 5 **lanificio** inveniunt. Ea *ergo caeteris praestare* **iudicatur**. / **Paucis interiectis diebus, Sextus Collatiam** *rediit*, / **et Lucretiae vim attulit. Illa postero die, advocatis patre et coniuge, rem exposuit, et se cultro, quem sub veste texerat, occidit.** / *Conclamant* **vir paterque,** / **et in exitium regum** *coniurant*. (8.58)

1	Liv. 1.57.6	5–6	Liv. 1.58.1
1–3	Vir. ill. 9.1	6–8	Vir. ill. 9.4
3–4	Liv. 1.58.8	8–9	Liv. 1.58.12
4–5	Vir. ill. 9.2	9	Vir. ill. 9.5

Cloelia Virgo

El personaje que viene a continuación destaca por encima de todos los demás en la obra de Lhomond por ser la única mujer a la que se le dedica un capítulo independiente. Todas las demás aparecen siempre subordinadas a las acciones de los hombres. A diferencia de Livio, en cuya obra, a partir de este momento, la aparición de la mujer se convierte en accidental, en Lhomond encontramos todo un capítulo dedicado a una mujer en una obra titulada *De viris*. Entremezcla en este capítulo Lhomond las fuentes de forma hábil para producir un relato muy breve pero narrando todo lo necesario de la historia de esta mujer, destacando al final del relato, a diferencia de la mayoría de las fuentes, el gran honor que le hizo el pueblo romano de realizarle una estatua ecuestre en la vía Sacra, aunque todo apunta a que se trataba de una estatua dedicada a una diosa, de donde pudo arrancar la leyenda. Podría parecer en principio un contrasentido dedicarle un capítulo, pero el valor de esta doncella bien lo merecía como *exemplum*.

> **Porsenna Claeliam virginem nobilem inter obsides accepit.** / **Cum** *eius* **castra haud procul ripa Tiberis locata essent,** / **Claelia deceptis custodibus noctu egressa, ecum, quem sors dederat, arripuit, et Tiberim traiecit.** / **Quod ubi regi nun-**
> 5 **tiatum est, primo** ille **incensus ira Romam legatos misit ad Claeliam obsidem reposcendam. Romani** eam excedere **restituerunt.** / Tum *rex virginis* **virtutem admiratus,** / *eam laudavit,* **ac parte obsidum donare se dixit, permisitque ut ipsa quos vellet, legeret. Productis** *obsidibus,* / **Claelia virgines pueros-**
> 10 **que elegit quorum aetatem iniuriae obnoxiam sciebat,** et cum iis in patriam rediit. / **Romani novam in femina virtutem**

> novo genere honoris, statua equestri, donavere. In summa
> via sacra, fuit posita virgo insidens equo. (12.70)

1	Vir. ill. 13.1	7	Vir. ill. 13.3
2	Liv. 2.13.6	7–9	Liv. 2.13.9
3–4	Vir. ill. 13.1	9–11	Vir. ill. 13.3
4–7	Liv. 2.13.7–9	4–13	Liv. 2.13.11

Veturia et Volumnia

Siguiendo en la línea de las mujeres ilustres de la historia de Roma nos encontramos con Veturia y Volumnia, madre y esposa de Coriolano respectivamente. Ambas, con sus ruegos y súplicas, consiguen que Coriolano desista de asediar Roma, su patria, cual traidor. El relato en Lhomond es extremadamente breve y se omite todo elogio hacia estas mujeres, a diferencia de Livio, que dice de ellas: "quoniam armis viri defendere urbem non possent, mulieres precibus lacrimisque defenderent" (2.40.3).

> 5 Tum **Veturia** *Coriolani mater,* et **Volumnia** uxor **duos parvos filios secum** *trahens,* **castra hostium** *petierunt.* Ubi matrem aspexit Coriolanus: "O patria," inquit, "vicisti iram meam admotis matris meae precibus, cui tuam in me iniuriam condono." **Complexus inde suos castra** *movit,* et exercitum **ex agro Romano** *abduxit.* Coriolanus postea a Volscis, **ut proditor, occisus** dicitur. (17.86)

1	Liv. 2.40.4
3	Liv. 2.40.10
4	Vir. ill. 19.4

Virginia

En el capítulo dedicado a Lucio Virginio Centurio, Lhomond se dedica fundamentalmente a narrar otro vergonzoso episodio de la historia de Roma, que culminó con la caída de los decenviros. Nos referimos a Virginia, plebeya hija de Lucio Virginio que acepta ser sacrificada antes de caer bajo la lascivia del decenviro Apio Claudio. En este episodio de nuevo se mezclan las fuentes, aunque cabe destacar que la mayor parte del texto es propio de Lhomond. Éste omite la introducción que hace Livio del relato, equiparando el hecho y las consecuencias a la violación de Lucrecia: "sequitur aliud in urbe nefas, ab libidine ortum, haud minus foedo eventu quam quod per stuprum caedemque Lucretiae urbe regnoque Tarquinios expulerat, ut non finis solum idem decemviris qui regibus sed causa etiam eadem imperii amittendi esset" (3.44). Lhomond vuelve a presentar a la mujer como víctima, pero no se compadece de ella en ningún momento, se limita a suavizar la crueldad que se aplica hacia ella.

> Anno trecentesimo ab urbe condita, pro duobus consulibus decemviri creati sunt, qui allatas e Graecia leges populo proponerent.

> **Unus ex iis Appius Claudius** *virginem plebeiam* **adamavit, quam cum** Appius **non posset / pretio ac spe pellicere, clienti suo negotium dedit,** / ut eam *in servitutem* **deposceret: facile victurus cum ipse esset et accusator et iudex.** / Lucius Virginius puellae pater tunc aberat militiae causa. Cliens igitur **virgini venienti in forum iniecit manum,** *affirmans suam esse servam: eam sequi se iubet;* / ni faciat, minatur se cunctantem vi abstracturum. **Pavida puella stupente,** ad clamorem nutricis **fit concursus.** / Cum ille puellam non posset abducere eam, vocat in ius ipso Appio iudice. Interea missi nuntii ad Virginium properant. **Is prima luce Romam advenit, cum iam civitas in foro expectatione erecta staret.** Virginius statim in forum lacrimabundus et civium opem implorans filiam **suam deducit.** / Appius obstinatum gerens animum in tribunal ascendit, et Virginiam clienti suo addixit. **Tum pater, ubi nihil usquam auxilii vidit; "Quaeso,"** inquit, **"Appi, ignosce patrio dolori,** sine me filiam ultimo alloqui." **Data venia, pater filiam in secretum abducit. Ab lanio** *cultrum arripit,* **et pectus puellae transfigit.** / Tum ferro sibi viam facit, et respersus cruore **ad exercitum profugit.** (19.86–90)

3–4 Vir. ill. 21.2		**10**	Liv. 3.44.7
4–5 Liv. 3.44.4–5		**12–15**	Liv. 3.47.1
5–6 Vir. ill. 21.2		**17–20**	Liv. 3.48.4–5
7–9 Liv. 3.44.6		**21**	Vir. ill. 21.3

Hemos visto en este breve estudio el tratamiento que Lhomond da a las mujeres de la historia mítica de Roma. En la mayoría de los casos, salvo la virgen Clelia, los personajes femeninos aparecen tratados rápidamente sin detenerse en sus virtudes o sus defectos. Lhomond los cita porque se hacen imprescindibles para el curso de la historia, pero no porque deban figurar por méritos propios. Caso aparte es la *virgo Clelia* que, con un capítulo para ella sola, ve cómo, por su valor y valentía, está a la altura de figurar en un catálogo exclusivamente masculino. Pero de la misma manera que decimos que las describe con trazo rápido, sin entrar en mayor detalle, también hay que dejar muy claro que, en la mayoría de los casos, omite cualquier tipo de connotación peyorativa o misógina.

Universidad Complutense de Madrid

La versione latina dell'Iliade di Giuseppe Pasquali Marinelli

CARLO SANTINI

Sulla biografia del poeta neo-latino Giuseppe Pasquali Marinelli (PM), nato a Camerano in provincia di Ancona nel 1793 e ivi morto nel 1875, la documentazione più aggiornata è rappresentata dal saggio recente di Massimo Morroni;[1] l'opera di PM resta comunque tuttora del tutto sconosciuta, né a renderla più nota ha contribuito un congresso tenutosi a Camerano nel 1993, perché gli atti dei lavori non sono stati pubblicati. L'opera in versi di PM è assolutamente monumentale: segnaliamo qui, accanto alla versione latina dei due poemi omerici, l'esposizione in versi delle *Institutiones juris civilis*, la versione di buona parte del *Vecchio Testamento*, della *Divina Commedia*, dei *Sepolcri* del Foscolo e della *Messiade* di Klopstock, nonché tre poemi epici sulla battaglia di Castelfidardo (*De pugna ad Castrumficardum*), di Mentana (*De pugna ad Nomentum*) e sulla presa di Roma (*Romae expugnatio*), dove PM esprime il suo lealismo nei confronti dello Stato Pontificio e quindi la sua avversione per il processo di unificazione nello stato italiano unitario. Buona parte di detta produzione di alcune decine di migliaia di esametri è edita, ma resta una parte rilevante di inediti presso la biblioteca comunale di Camerano.

Dopo un periodo di gestazione di venti anni la versione latina dell'*Iliade* vede la luce ad Ancona nel 1869 presso la tipografia degli eredi Baluffi; un anno dopo gli tiene dietro quella dell'*Odissea*. Le due versioni sono segnalate con il primo premio all'Esposizione Provinciale di Ancona del 1872 con la seguente motivazione: "perché dettate in elegante latinità, concorrono a mantener vive la tradizione e la coltura della Lingua latina."[2]

Lo stesso PM parla in un componimento tuttora inedito (il n. CXVII dell'autografo presso la Biblioteca Comunale di Camerano) della genesi della traduzione; qui immagina di aver avuto una visione in cui "umbra est Maeonidae sic mihi visa loqui"

---

[1] M. Morroni, *Le età di un poeta. Biographia literaria* (Ancona, 1993).
[2] Cf. il catalogo dell'Esposizione Provinciale di Ancona 1872 preparatoria all'esposizione mondiale di Vienna del 1873. Relazione dell'Ufficio di Presidenza dei Giurati (Ancona: 1873), 82.

invitando proprio lui, cultore del latino "inimica aetate," all'opera del tradurre i due poemi epici "Eja age, carminibus latiis jam vertere nostram / suscipe Odysseam, suscipe et Iliaden"; il racconto, pur aneddotico, implica tuttavia un certo coefficiente di autenticità, perché quello di PM è stato, credo, l'ultimo tentativo di una versione poetica in latino già in piena età della filologia positivista. Parlare delle traduzioni latine di Omero significa aprire un capitolo non solo di storia dell'Umanesimo, ma anche della storia del tradurre. A prescindere dagli esempi del mondo classico, l'età delle versioni latine dei poemi omerici inizia nel nome di Leonzio Pilato, che traduce sia l'*Iliade* sia l'*Odissea* (1358–62 circa) dietro richiesta di Boccaccio, e si conclude nel XIX secolo con la *editio Didotiana* sul testo di Dindorf attraverso un catalogo ricco di quasi cinquanta lemmi.[3] Quella del Pilato fu versione letterale con vari fraintendimenti ed errori, dovuti alla scarsa perizia della lingua latina, ma a questa prima prova tennero poi seguito le versioni parziali di alcuni grandi umanisti (Valla, Poliziano); a partire dalla metà del XVI secolo, e precisamente dopo la versione poetica dell'*Iliade* di Eoban Hesse (Basilea 1540), comincia tuttavia a venir meno il proposito della traduzione in versi latini con l'eccezione di quella del gesuita messicano Francisco Javier Alegre e del gesuita raguseo Raimondo Cunich[4] (Roma 1776).

Ogni discorso sul modo migliore di tradurre Omero implica nel XVIII secolo un accenno al nome di Melchiorre Cesarotti. Cesarotti ha ben presente quanto sia spinoso nel caso specifico il dilemma tra traduzione letterale e traduzione poetica, ragion per cui inizia nel 1786 la pubblicazione di una versione letterale in prosa italiana dell'*Iliade*, terminata nel 1794 alla quale affianca un rifacimento in versi sciolti che intitola *L'Iliade o La morte di Ettore*. Cesarotti, da buon filologo, come dimostra la sua versione letterale che rappresenta una vera e propria enciclopedia omerica con molte ricche annotazioni al testo ("la Critica filologica abbraccia tutto ciò che si riferisce all'Erudizione antica, che può ridursi a sei capi, vale a dire la Mitologia, la Geografia, le arti, le opinioni, i costumi, le usanze,")[5] si rende perfettamente conto dell'impossibilità di dar vita ad una traduzione d'arte, che rispetti rigorosamente l'originale; in questa prospettiva "risolsi" — scrive — "di dar a' miei lettori due Traduzioni in cambio di una: la prima in verso e Poetica, la seconda in prosa ed accuratissima, quella libera, disinvolta, e per quanto mi fu possibile originale, questa schiava della lettera fino allo scrupolo, e tale che quanto al senso e al valor preciso dei termini potrà servire di Testo a chi non intende la lingua."[6]

Sempre nell'ambito delle versioni in italiano due casi opposti agli inizi del XIX secolo sono quelli rappresentati dalla versione di Vincenzo Monti (1810–1811) e dagli *Esperimenti di traduzione dell'Iliade* attuati da Ugo Foscolo nel corso di tre lustri dal 1807 fino alle minute degli ultimi anni (1822–1826). Il primo, "portato ad ammirare

---

[3] A. Pertusi, *Leonzio Pilato tra Petrarca e Boccaccio* (Venezia–Roma, 1964), 521–529.

[4] Sulla figura del Cunich (1719–1794) cf. M. Vigilante, "Cunich, Raimondo," in *Dizionario biografico degli Italiani*, vol. 31 (Roma, 1985), 378–380.

[5] Cfr. *L'Iliade o la Morte di Ettore. Poema omerico ridotto in verso italiano dall'abate M. Cesarotti*, tomo IV [= *Ragionamento storico-critico*] (Venezia, 1795), 321.

[6] *L'Iliade*, 210.

la grande favola iliaca al punto da perderne di vista il testo in quanto tale e i problemi che vi erano connessi,"⁷ trascorre veloce sul testo greco basandosi sostanzialmente sulle versioni latine, tra le quali in particolare quella di Cunich, ed italiane, mentre il secondo sente quanto siano ardui i problemi del tradurre, soprattutto per quanto riguarda la resa del patrimonio formulare.

Nel caso di PM, che con grande determinazione ha scritto solo in versi latini, il progetto di una traduzione poetica è una scelta obbligata. Non è quindi casuale che il nome di Cunich — unito a quello di Bernardo Zamagna, anche lui gesuita e raguseo nonché discepolo del primo e traduttore latino, a sua volta, dell'*Odissea* in versi (Venezia e Siena 1777) — compaia dopo la dedica in distici elegiaci al cardinale Lorenzo Barili nella *prolusio* in esametri, là dove PM espone il suo pensiero per quanto concerne la *ratio vertendi*. La versione di Cunich era stata infatti valutata dai critici dei suoi tempi con particolare favore, tanto da assurgere al rango di modello, che avrebbe reso inutili ulteriori altri lavori in questa direzione, come quello di PM (vv. 1–3: "Maeonidae Iliaden latiis mandare Camoenis / aggrederis? nonne haec eadem vulgata Latinis / Cunichii est numeris, plausuque excepta secundo?"). La critica di PM nei riguardi del Cunich muove da una considerazione generale che colloca la tecnica del tradurre in una dimensione letteraria sua propria, ben diversa quindi dalla semplice padronanza linguistica⁸ (vv. 20–23: "qui callet utrasque / linguas, ex qua vertit, et in quam vertit oportet, / aiunt, egregie vertat. — non hercule: multum / nam distant, linguam callere et vertere recte"). Cunich dà prova di notevole competenza nella lingua greca, circostanza questa che, come vedremo, non si può dire per PM, ma la sua dottrina non garantisce a priori il successo, che dipende invece dalla capacità di entrare in sintonia con il modello (vv. 24–26: "ut vertas, potius quam docta scientia linguae, / indolis efficiet paritas qua scriptor uterque / conveniant"). Se è dunque vero — scrive PM — che al traduttore deve essere riconosciuto lo stesso ruolo dell'autore (v. 39: "haud tamen interpres, verum ipse videbitur auctor") per essere riuscito a riservarsi una sorta di autonomia nella sua sfera linguistica, Cunich invece, da un lato, rivela palesemente il peso del modello (*gravem se ferre catenam*) e dall'altro diluisce, proprio per tale soggezione, il *Maeonidae generosum ac nobile vinum*, oltrepassando di tremila versi il testo greco, con la conseguenza che l'originale ha perso vigore (v. 60: *sine nervis*, v. 67: *elumbem*) e lo stile è divenuto prolisso (v. 60: *carmine praeduro prolixoque*; v.66 s.: *pleraque laxe diceret*; v. 67: *fluxam poesim*).

È tuttavia abbastanza singolare che anche Cunich aveva dichiarato propositi analoghi nell'ampia *Operis ratio eidem Cl. V. ab interprete reddita*, che precede la sua versione dell'*Iliade*. Qui ammette infatti che i modi di tradurre sono sostanzialmente due, il primo dei quali è quello di quanti "verbum e verbo convertunt, singulas voces

---

⁷ M. Mari, "Introduzione," in Vincenzo Monti, *Iliade di Omero*, vol. 1 (Milano, 1990), 29.

⁸ Il pensiero di PM in merito al concetto di traduzione dipende a sua volta, come risulta anche da una sua nota alla *prolusio*, da Tommaso Ceva, gesuita e letterato milanese (1648–1737) che in una delle *Sylvae* (Mediolani, 1718) dedicata alla traduzione in latino della *Gerusalemme liberata* portata a compimento dal fratello Cristoforo [Christophoro Cevae e societate Jesu *De eiusdem versione Latina Torquati Tassi*, 54 ss.] ne celebra la perfetta corrispondenza contestuale con il modello.

religiose, atque adeo superstitiose adnumerant, nihil eo, quo positum est loco, mutare audent" (xx), ma questo genere di traduzione, se risulta idoneo per opere il cui precipuo scopo consiste nel fornire al lettore notizie ed informazioni, appare invece inadatto e spiacevole (*injucundum, ineptum*) per la versione d'arte ("si quis transferat ad oratores, aut ad poetas, qui non magis rerum pondere, quam verborum splendore commendantur"). Cunich sembra quindi perseguire il miraggio di una traduzione che riesca a conservare il livello formale del modello, vale a dire ne riproduca il contesto stilistico.

Come si vede entrambi propongono come finalità una sorta di "calco" nell'intento di far rivivere in modo autonomo nella traduzione il mondo poetico dell'originale; scrive appunto PM in una lettera del 19 giugno 1872 che "primo e sostanziale pregio di una versione si è che produca nell'animo del lettore quel medesimo effetto che vi produce l'originale, con non minor forza, eleganza e fluidità di verso. Ciò si ottiene quando la versione non sembra versione, quantunque renda l'originale."[9] Gli esiti rischiano tuttavia di apparire controversi soprattutto quando si è dinnanzi ad uno dei maggiori problemi per il traduttore della *Kunstsprache* omerica, vale a dire la formularità, che è sempre stata per altro un parametro di classificazione per quanti hanno lavorato sul *Fortleben* di Omero, sicché come osserva L. E. Rossi: "sarebbe interessante vedere come i singoli *traduttori* si sono comportati di fronte alla formularità."[10] Rispetto a questo modulo fondamentale PM, differentemente da quanto ha fatto Cunich, sceglie la strada della sostanziale omissione, così come è stato ben illustrato da Flammini nel caso della *Odissea*[11] conseguendo lo scopo di rispettare le proporzioni del modello ("neve sit uberior copia neu brevior") e addirittura di ridurlo in scala minore. Si tratta infatti di 14917 versi rispetto ai 15692 del testo greco, cioè in termini statistici il 5.57% in meno rispetto al 19.74% in più di Cunich (18790 versi).

La scelta di PM può essere considerata in certa qual misura anticipatrice di una presa d'atto alla quale la critica si accingerà con il saggio di Milman Parry solo sessanta anni dopo. Il sistema formulare quale appare in Omero, proprio in virtù dei principi di economia (esiste una sola formula per ogni idea essenziale in una determinata condizione metrica) e di esaustività (esiste una formula per ogni idea essenziale ed ogni condizione metrica) che lo governano, risulta essere nel momento ottimale del processo di trasmissione orale dell'epica greca. La definizione di formula come "une expression qui est régulièrement employée, dans les mêmes conditions métriques, pour exprimer une certaine idée essentielle"[12] implica infatti che proprio perché funzionali al codice formale (stilistico, linguistico, e metrico) del testo le formule risultino quindi virtualmente intraducibili per l'impossibilità di familiarizzare il lettore al rapporto nome-epiteto.[13]

---

[9] Morroni, *Le età di un poeta*, 79.

[10] L. E. Rossi, "I poemi omerici come testimonianza di poesia orale," vol. 1 di *Storia e civiltà dei Greci* (Milano, 1989), 136.

[11] G. Flammini, "Giuseppe Pasquali Marinelli traduttore dell'Odissea," in S. Baldonicini, ed., *Studi in memoria di A. Valentini* (Pisa–Roma, 2000), 131–165.

[12] M. Parry, *L'épithète traditionelle dans Homère* (Paris, 1928), 16.

[13] Parry, *L'épithète traditionelle*, 215.

A queste considerazioni si aggiunge anche l'accertata scarsa conoscenza della lingua greca[14] di PM, che lo induce a ricorrere di volta in volta a don Marino Marinelli[15] per consiglio, per la revisione degli elaborati, e anche per indagini e verifiche presso la biblioteca del seminario di Osimo, dove era disponibile il testo greco con la versione letterale latina di J. H. Lederlin e S. Bergler[16] assai diffusa in quei tempi. Tale condizione di minorità linguistica non ha tuttavia distolto dall'impresa il PM, che invece porta avanti questo lavoro secondo alcune precise scelte di metodo. La prima di queste è rappresentata dalla sostanziale equivalenza di dimensioni con il modello, circostanza che lo induce ad attenersi agli stessi due criteri già evidenziati per la versione dell'*Odissea*, che consistono sia nell'omissione ovvero nella "resa misurata"[17] degli epiteti fissi, sia nella "fusione in un solo verso di due esametri dell'originale" laddove, in contesto dialogico, il primo dipenda da qualche espressione formulare.[18] Se quindi gli epiteti sono sovente tralasciati (e al riguardo è evidente il contrasto con la traduzione letterale della *editio Didotiana*), non è detto che essi debbano sempre sparire e ovunque come dimostra la presenza costante di espressioni come *rex hominumque Deumque* oppure di *galea insignis* (κορυθαίολος).

Accanto a questo criterio è per altro evidente, come vedremo con qualche esempio, l'intenzione di creare, tramite modificazioni e aggiunte non irrilevanti al testo greco, un sistema di ponderazione e di *colores*, che rappresenti un costante riferimento ai codici del genere epico, quali sono stati fissati nel contesto della lingua latina[19] — inutile aggiungere a questo punto che tali modificazioni e accrescimenti dipendono in larga misura dal dettato epico dell'*Eneide*.

Il primo assaggio relativo alla tecnica della traduzione in PM corrisponde ai sette versi incipitari della *propositio* dell'*Iliade*, proprio per la loro riconosciuta e collaudata citabilità mnemonica come anche per il carattere esemplare ed esemplificativo rispetto all'intera opera; PM li porta ad otto:

> *Iram*, quam Peleo natus concepit Achilles,
> *diva, cane*; exitialem iram, quae plurima Grajis
> damna tulit, multasque virum provolvit ad Orcum
> ante diem fortes animas, ipsosque reliquit
> alitibus diris canibusque voracibus escam.
> Sic Superum Patri visum, cum, lite coorta,
> indociles flecti, discordia discidit ardens
> Æaciden divumque regumque Agamemnona regem

---

[14] Morroni, *Le età di un poeta*, 48.

[15] Sulla figura di Marino Marinelli (Ancona, 1820–1884), presenza costante nell'epistolario di PM, cf. Morroni, *Le età di un poeta*, 25 e n. 235.

[16] Homeri *Opera* quae extant omnia Grece et Latine [. . .], curante Stephano Berglero, Transilvano (Patavii, 1791).

[17] Flammini, "Giuseppe Pasquali Marinelli traduttore dell'Odissea," 141.

[18] Flammini, "Giuseppe Pasquali Marinelli traduttore dell'Odissea," 138.

[19] Cf. quanto scrivo su Virgilio e la definizione della lingua epica classica in P. Poccetti, C. Santini, D. Poli, *Una storia della lingua latina* (Roma, 1999), 279–282.

conservando la posizione incipitaria di quella che è "la prima parola del Poema, come ne è l'elemento," come chiosa Foscolo, ma rinunciando a mantenere nel primo verso gli altri due segni determinanti θεά e ἄειδε, come avrebbe meritato invece, sempre per Foscolo, "la venerazione di tutti i secoli per questo verso."[20] Cunich al contrario, così come rimprovera[21] al predecessore cinquecentesco Eoban Hesse di avere modificato arbitrariamente tali segni con dei sinonimi ("*Dic* mihi magnanimi Pelidae *Musa furorem*"), li colloca tutti nel primo verso ("*Iram, diva,* trucem Pelidae *concine* Achillei").

PM ha notato anche la marcatura per enjambement di οὐλομένην che conserva in qualche misura nella ripresa in epanalessi ("Iram . . . exitialem iram"). Alcune aggiunte corrispondono invece a sue scelte individuali: la forma *ante diem* accentua il motivo della morte prematura dei giovani guerrieri (προΐαψεν), ma il sintagma è stato senza dubbio recepito dal modello virgiliano, cf. *Aen.* 1.374: "*ante diem* clauso componet Vesper Olympo," nella stessa posizione metrica, e 4.697 "sed misera *ante diem* subitoque accensa furore" (che qui si riferisce alla morte prematura di Didone), oltre che dalla versione italiana del Monti, cf. 1, vv. 3–4: "molte *anzi tempo* all'Orco / generose travolse alme d'eroi." Un'accentuazione di *colores* è rappresentata dalla coppia *alites diri* e *canes voraces* con l'aggettivo per ogni nome in virtù dell'equivalenza ponderale, come anche dalla scelta di personificare *discordia*, che diviene soggetto nel testo latino al posto dei due contendenti — ed al riguardo va ancora una volta riconosciuta l'influenza esercitata dal testo di Monti, cf. 1.8: "primamente disgiunse aspra contesa." Viene anche rovesciato l'ordine dei nomi propri che stanno agli estremi della struttura ad anello del verso greco: Ἀτρεΐδης . . . Ἀχιλλεύς. Alla sfera delle ripetizioni verbali tipica dell'epica latina appartengono la coppia allitterante <u>discordia discidit</u> e gli altri riscontri fonici come l'omoteleuto *divum regumque* e il poliptoto *regum regem* che realizza con il genitivo enfatico l'epiteto ἄναξ ἀνδρῶν di Agamennone.

Per la definizione della specifica qualità della traduzione di PM può qui valere un assaggio di indagine che analizza alcune divaricazioni dal testo greco, che risultano essere tanto più significative quanto più paiono configurarsi come il frutto di una scelta di gusto.

L'incontro di Ettore con Paride e Elena a Z 312–368 offre lo spettro delle possibilità di trasformazioni interpretative realizzate da PM. Ai vv. 307 sg. del testo latino la marcatura moralistica nei confronti di Paride "invenit hic fratrem, *studio fulgentia vano* / versantem arma manu" è esplicitata dalle notazioni sia del brillare delle armi, sia della vanità del personaggio, notazioni che risultano entrambe aggiunta e specificazione rispetto alla tenuta impassibile nell'esposto omerico, cf. Z 321 τὸν δ'εὗρ' ἐν θαλάμῳ περικαλλέα τεύχε' ἔποντα. Il v. 310 della redazione latina "juxta *Argiva* aderat, *famulabus* pensa ministrans" trasforma l'etnico in un richiamo allusivo rispetto a Ἀργείη δ' Ἑλένη di Z 323, proponendo altresì l'intenzionale romanizzazione della scena con l'iperarcaico dativo rispetto a μετ' ἄρα δμωῇσι γυναιξὶν / ἧστο, καὶ ἀμφιπόλοισι περικλυτὰ ἔργα κέλευν. Infine a v. 330 la redazione latina con le

---

[20] *Esperimenti di traduzione dell'Iliade* di Ugo Foscolo, ed. G. Barbarisi (Firenze, 1961/1967), 13.
[21] Cf. XXIX.

parole di Elena "Levir care *mihi, quae* tot sum causa malorum" rappresenta un'edulcorazione rispetto alla forma esplicitamente intensa del greco δᾶερ ἐμεῖο κυνὸς κακομηχάνου ὀκρυοέσσης (Z 344).

L'aderenza di PM ai fenomeni linguistici e stilistici del testo greco appare talvolta elevata, nonostante la sua imperfetta conoscenza della lingua, come ad esempio nel caso di ὀλλύντας τ' ὀλλυμένους τε di Λ 83 tradotto "*cedentes* atque *cadentes*" (11.83) oppure μειλιχίοις ἐπέεσσιν. ἀμείλικτον δ' ὅπ' ἄκουσαν di Λ 137, che viene reso "verbis sic *mollibus* illi / orabant flentes: non *mollia* rettulit heros" (11.136–137); in altri casi PM preferisce utilizzare per una voce specialistica del greco un'altra di categoria analoga, come a Λ 147 ὅλμον, "a round smooth stone," che diviene "ut buxum versatile," oppure una voce del tutto generica, come a Λ 183 Ἴδης ἐν κορυφῇσι καθέζετο πιδηέσσης, dove l'attributo πιδήεις "rich in springs" della montagna diviene l'anodino "praecelsae Idae," che solo per acrofonia potrebbe essergli accostato.

Ho già osservato che i connotati virgiliani della versione di PM risultano ben riconoscibili. La glossa di Servio segnala le varie occasioni in cui Virgilio utilizza in modo ragionato e cauto i moduli espressivi del testo omerico. Non sappiamo se PM abbia mai avuto accesso a Servio, ma la sua conoscenza di Virgilio gli consente di ricostruire per la sua versione dell'*Iliade* alcune delle riprese virgiliane. Cito al riguardo vari casi come PM 1.510 s. "per tempora divae / *nutavere* comae : *trem*uit concussus *Olympu*s" (A 528: Ἢ καὶ κυανέῃσιν ἐπ' ὀφρύσι νεῦσε Κρονίων, 530 μέγαν δ' ἐλέλιξεν Ὄλυμπον) da correlare a *Aen.* 9.105, "adnuit et totum *nutu trem*efecit *Olympu*m," oppure PM 5.119 s. "praeterea, quae *mortales* tibi densa tegebat / mox oculos, *nubem eripui*" (E 127: ἀχλὺν δ' αὖ τοι ἀπ' ὀφθαλμῶν ἕλον, ἣ πρὶν ἐπῆεν) che corrisponde ad *Aen.* 2.604 ss. "namque omnem, quae nunc obducta tuenti / *mortalis* hebetat visus tibi, et umida circum / caligat, *nubem eripiam*" e ancora PM 6.291 "*frange manu telum* Diomedis, *et ipsum* / *sterne solo* ad Scaeas" (Z 306–307: ἆξον δὴ ἔγχος Διομήδεος, ἠδὲ καὶ αὐτὸν / πρηνέα δὸς πεσέειν Σκαιῶν προπάροιθε πυλάων) da confrontare con *Aen.* 11.484 "*frange manu telum* Phrygii praedonis *et ipsum* / pronum *sterne solo*," e ancora PM 8.275 s. "*purpureum veluti florente papavera* in horto / *demittit*, foetu ac verno *caput* imbre gravatum" (Q 306–307) da confrontare con *Aen.* 9.435 ss.: "*purpureus veluti* cum *flos* succisus aratro / languescit moriens lassove *papavera* collo / *demisere caput*" e infine PM 22.87, "*mala gramina pastus*" (Χ 94 βεβρωκὼς κακὰ φάρμακα) identico a *Aen.* 2.471, "*mala gramina pastus*."

Ma, a prescindere da queste riprese che potremmo definire come riprese di secondo livello, quello che appare in ogni modo abbastanza evidente è il travestimento virgiliano di episodi omerici che pure non dipendono direttamente dallo stesso contesto diegetico e figurale dal quale sono desunti, ma che ad esso in qualche misura alludono. Anche qui basterà produrre alcuni esempi: Ettore si rivolge a Paride invitandolo a combattere, 6.316: "quid stas? *rumpe moras*: te te prius *eripe tectis* / quam succensa super procumbant moenia Troiae" (Z 331: ἀλλ' ἄνα, μὴ τάχα ἄστυ πυρὸς δηΐοιο θέρηται) con parole analoghe a quelle con le quali Virgilio fa svegliare Enea dal fantasma di Ettore nell'ultima notte di Troia, cf. 2.289: "heu fuge, nate dea, *teque his* ait *eripe tectis*;" l'ombra di Patroclo invita Achille a seppellirlo con la formula "eja age *rumpe moras*, me conde sepulcro" a 23.73 (Ψ 71: θάπτε με ὅττι τάχιστα) che troviamo anche in *Aen.* 4.569 "heia age *rumpe moras*," dove la situazione parenetica dei due contesti è analoga (Patroclo appare in sogno di Achille ~ Mercurio appare in sogno ad Enea) e si ricordi anche *Aen.* 9.13, "*rumpe moras* omnis" (Iri appare a Turno).

Un'ulteriore testimonianza su come PM lavora sul testo omerico modificandolo alla luce sia degli stilemi e del gusto formale dell'epica latina sia per i suggerimenti del testo virgliano appare anche in un passo propriamente descrittivo, quale è la descrizione del θώραξ offerto in dono da Cinira a Agamennone e descritto a Λ 25–28 al momento che l'eroe lo sta indossando. Qui (11.24–29) PM preferisce al numerale la forma composta dell'avverbio numerale con distributivo, che è della lingua epica latina anche perché suggerita dalla *ratio* metrica e varia scambiando abilmente i colori dei metalli (τοῦ δ᾽ ἤτοι δέκα οἶμοι ἔσαν μέλανος κυάνοιο, / δώδεκα δὲ χρυσοῖο καὶ εἴκοσι κασσιτέροιο ~ "hanc cyani *denae, bis senae divitis* auri, *bisque decem* stanni, variabant undique zonae"), inserisce inoltre a v. 27 una nota, *squalentia tergora picti* dei κυάνεοι δράκοντες, che ha per presupposto la citazione virgiliana di *Georg.* 4.13, "absint et *picti squalentia terga* lacerti," tanto più pertinente visto che le lucertole sono anche esse rettili e presentano il dorso screziato e squamoso come i serpenti della corazza ageminata.

Un ultimo angolo prospettico alla luce del quale valutare la versione di PM resta infine il confronto con la versione d'arte del Cunich, che il grande successo aveva canonizzato e dalla quale, nonostante le critiche mossele, PM in varia misura dipende. Soltanto l'approntamento di un *index verborum*, attualmente non disponibile, potrebbe evidenziare in dettaglio il grado di dipendenza di PM da Cunich, che segue a sua volta i modelli di Virgilio e Ovidio; tuttavia anche questa modesta campionatura può servire da esempio, come 24.210–211 Cunich: "*Dardanide, confide animo*, gelidumque pavorem / mitte: malae haud venio tibi namque huc *nuncia sortis*" ~ PM 168–169: "*Dardanide, confide animo*, moestumque timorem / abjice: non adsum crudelis *nuntia sortis*," e ancora 24.585–587 Cunich: "quem *fortasse premunt infenso* pectore *circum* / *finitimi nec adest qui* cladem ac *triste repellat* / exitium" ~ PM 465–467: "illum *forte premunt* nunc *infesto* agmine *circum* / *finitimi nec adest qui* vim *triste*mque *repellat* / perniciem."

In conclusione l'interrogativo sulla qualità del progetto letterario che presiede a questa traduzione e sul tipo di lettore al quale PM pensava di rivolgersi sembra evidenziare un ambito culturale, presumibilmente non vasto, né sofisticato, ma determinato a mantenersi tenace custode di quella produzione neo-latina che è frutto dell'istruzione seminariale e gesuitica. I grandi modelli, Cunich e Monti,[22] non soddisfano PM, anzi la straordinaria inventiva di Monti, che ricerca la magniloquenza declamatoria anche a costo di alterare il testo omerico purché l'opera divenga "la più

---

[22] Cunich e Monti, che dal primo era stato largamente influenzato, sono congiunti per altro anche nella pubblicistica del tempo, come sta a illustrare la *Collezione delle similitudini contenute nella Iliade di Omero estratte fedelmente dalle due più celebri versioni, l'una latina del p. Raimondo Cunich* [...] *l'altra italiana del Cav. Vincenzo Monti* (Roma, 1830).

completa espressione della civiltà napoleonica"[23] gli è sostanzialmente estranea, nonostante le riprese che abbiamo visto. La critica di PM nei confronti del Monti viene alla luce in un punto specifico, quando scrive che "molto errò il Monti, quando tradusse *Mi restava Ettorre, l'unico Ettorre*" ad Ω 499–501, perché, così come aveva già notato Chateaubriand, in questo modo il traduttore italiano faceva proferire a Priamo in prima battuta un nome che Achille sicuramente aborriva.[24]

In definitiva proporrei al riguardo per questa traduzione dell'*Iliade* la formula di officina artigianale dove la traduzione è realizzata con grande impegno, pari consapevolezza e anche quella dose di gusto letterario che guarda a soluzioni plurime[25] per evitare ogni trasposizione meccanica nel rapporto tra due lingue.

Università di Perugia

---

[23] Mari, "Introduzione," 5.

[24] Cf. le *Osservazioni sopra alcuni passi della versione dell'Iliade fatta dal Monti* che stanno in allegato all'edizione della versione latina dell'*Iliade* di PM, 464.

[25] Si vedano in proposito anche le conclusioni alle quali giunge anche F. Stok, "G. Pasquali Marinelli e le sue parafrasi bibliche in esametri latini," in *Scritti in onore di I. Gallo*, ed. Luigi Torraca (Napoli, 2002), 497–523.

Erasmus von Rotterdam,
"Ratio seu methodus verae theologiae"

PAUL GERHARD SCHMIDT

Fidel Rädle zum 65. Geburtstag

Sie kennen alle die unfreundliche Bemerkung über bestimmte Lehrer, denen man nachsagt, sie hätten ihren Beruf nur deshalb gewählt, weil sie zu allem anderen unfähig seien. Dieses Verdikt lautet: "Those who can, do, those who cannot, teach." Oder, auf Philologen bezogen: "Wer von der Sache nichts versteht, spricht über Methode." Wer sich mit Texten beschäftigt, kann in der Tat solche Methodiker benennen, die vor der mühsamen kleinteiligen Textarbeit in das Reich der hohen Theorie flüchten, wo man unbekümmert um die störende Realität erstaunliche Einsichten und Zusammenhänge konstruiert, die in immer kürzer werdenden Zeitabständen durch immer erstaunlichere Betrachtungsweisen abgelöst werden, die sich in einer rasch veraltenden Terminologie präsentieren.

Gehört Erasmus, als Herausgeber des griechischen Neuen Testaments ein textnaher Philologe, in diese Kategorie der Thesenritter? Gemeinsam mit der Edition des *Novum Testamentum graece* erschien 1516 seine "Methodus", drei Jahre später bei der zweiten Auflage des NT die "Ratio seu Methodus". Die "Methodus" von 1516 und die "Ratio seu Methodus" von 1519 stimmen in ihren Grundgedanken und auch in manchen Formulierungen überein. Der auch in der Titelform erkennbare Unterschied zwischen beiden Texten besteht in ihrem Umfang. Die "Methodus" ist eine unter dem Diktat der Ungeduld entstandene kleine Schrift von ca. 20 Druckseiten, die "Ratio seu Methodus" ist fast zehnmal so umfangreich. Erasmus hat das Verhältnis der beiden Texte, über die ich im folgenden sprechen werde, mit einem Vergleich aus der Küche verdeutlicht. So wie sparsame Wirte das übriggebliebene Essen vom Vortag unter die neu zubereiteten Speisen mischen, sie sozusagen strecken und durch Würzen eine Einheit herstellen, so habe er den älteren Aufsatz in den neuen eingehen lassen. Wir kennen alle diese Praxis, greifen selbst vielleicht manchmal zu diesem Rezept, gestehen es aber selten so souverän ein wie Erasmus, der sich beim Herstellen seines Textes bereitwillig über die Schultern schauen läßt.

Erasmus kannte als guter Rhetor die Regeln für eine gute Darlegung, wonach man zunächst dem Hörer und Leser unbedingt das ihm Bekannte in Erinnerung rufen muß, ehe man ihn mit neuen Gedanken konfrontiert. Es ist eine subtile Form der *Captatio benevolentiae*: der Adressat wird nicht direkt angesprochen und auch nicht mehr oder minder unverhohlen als kompetent bezeichnet; man erinnert ihn vielmehr sehr diskret an gemeinsame Kenntnisse und Denkformen. Auf diesem Weg stellt sich ein Einvernehmen zwischen dem Autor und seinem Publikum ein; der Leser wird an unstrittige Fakten und Einsichten erinnert und sieht keinen Anlaß zum Widerspruch. Ist diese Harmonie stabilisiert, kann der Autor die ihm wichtigen neuen Wege einschlagen und Gedanken äußern, die ein unvorbereitetes Publikum *a limine* zurückweisen würde. Bei der Suche nach Konsens läßt sich das Institut der Tradition vorzüglich instrumentalisieren. Leser und Autor haben zwar nicht dieselben Pläne für die Zukunft, aber ein gemeinsames geistiges Erbe. In der "Methodus", vor allem aber in der "Ratio" greift Erasmus deshalb zur Harmoniestiftung auf die Kirchenväter und auf das lateinische Mittelalter zurück.

Es fehlt leider immer noch eine umfassende Studie über sein Verhältnis zum Mittelalter. Soweit ich bisher sehe, hat Erasmus — anders als viele seiner Zeitgenossen — Schultexte und Schriften des Mittelalters nicht pauschal verurteilt. Er hat ja selbst Alcher von Lüttich ediert und war bereit, mittellateinischen Texten unvoreingenommen zu begegnen. Kritisch stand er vielen Formen der Hagiographie gegenüber. Lobreden auf Heilige ästimierte er nicht, Hymnen gehörten nicht zu den literarischen Texten, die ihn erbauten, und geradezu verhaßt war ihm eine Sonderform der mittelalterlichen Hymnik, die Sequenz. Er bezeichnete sie als ärgerlich und lächerlich zugleich und hätte den Konzilsvätern von Trient begeistert seine Zustimmung signalisiert, als sie wenige Jahre nach seinem Tod von den fast 5000 Sequenzen des Mittelalters nur noch eine Handvoll akzeptierten, die dann in das *Missale Romanum* unter Papst Pius V. aufgenommen wurden. So reizbar Erasmus auf Auswüchse des Heiligenkultes und auf das Reliquienunwesen reagierte, so positiv stand er mittellateinischen Texten gegenüber, die lexikalische und grammatische Fragen behandeln. Je mehr antikes Sprachgut sie boten, desto lieber waren sie ihm. So zog er Isidor dem Johannes de Garlandia vor, und er verschmähte nicht den Gräcismus. Der hermeneutische Zugang des lateinischen Mittelalters zur Bibel, besonders die allegorische Schriftauslegung, stieß auf seine Zustimmung. Er sah das Mittelalter und sich selbst in der Nachfolge von Augustins *De doctrina christiana*, wie er an vielen Stellen von "Methodus" und "Ratio" bekundet. Selbst den Hauptvertreter der scholastischen Methode, Thomas von Aquin, führt er in seiner Methodenlehre so an, daß er bei keinem seiner zeitgenössischen Leser Anstoß erregte.

Als moderner Leser, der die Entwicklung des Schriftverständnisses und der Schriftauslegung nach Erasmus kennt, wird man bei seinen einführenden und um Einverständnis werbenden Textpartien immer stärker von der Spannung und Neugier gepackt, wie es Erasmus gelingen wird, seine eigenen Gedanken den Lesern so zu vermitteln, daß sie folgen können. Warum ist es denn notwendig, fragt Erasmus sie, neben dem lateinischen Text des Neuen Testaments auch den griechischen zu kennen? Schließlich existiert doch die Vulgata. Warum denn Griechisch und sogar Hebräisch lernen? Ohne Hieronymus direkt zu kritisieren, setzt Erasmus einem fingierten Gesprächspartner auseinander, daß es idiomatische Redewendungen gibt, die sich nicht literaliter von einer Sprache in die andere übertragen lassen. Dem Einwand, daß die Erlernung der heiligen drei Sprachen zeitaufwendig und schwierig sei, hält er die Fortschritte der Didaktik entgegen, die es ermöglichten, in relativ kurzer Zeit zu einem ausreichenden Kenntnisstand zu gelangen. Der Theologe solle diese Sprachen ja nicht in allen ihren Feinheiten beherrschen; es genüge, wenn er in der Lage sei, die Texte in ihrem fremden Charakter zu erfassen und zu verstehen. Selbst im höheren Lebensalter sei man in der Lage, noch Griechisch zu erlernen; der alte Cato und Augustin hätten erst nach der Lebensmitte Griechisch gelernt, Rudolf Agricola sich mit 40 Jahren dem Hebräischen zugewendet. Wer aber diese leichte Mühe scheue, die für einen Theologen notwendig sei, laufe Gefahr, mit falsch übersetzten Lehrsätzen in die Irre zu geraten und Irrtümer zu verbreiten. Bei allem Respekt vor Thomas von Aquin seien derartige Irrtümer auch diesem *vir diligentissimus* unterlaufen. Durch unachtsame, nachlässige und ungebildete Abschreiber und Übersetzer würden Texte depraviert, selbst die Bibel sei von diesem Verfallsprozeß nicht ausgenommen. Um sich nicht als Neuerer darzustellen, erinnert Erasmus seine Leser daran, daß diese Erkenntnis der mittelalterlichen Kirche nicht fremd war. Er hätte die Bibelkorrektorien, die im 13. Jahrhundert von französischen Dominikanern revidierte sogenannte Pariser Bibel nennen können; er verweist dagegen auf einen Konzilsbeschluß, der seinen Intentionen noch besser entspricht. Es handelt sich um den Sprachenkanon des Konzils von Vienne aus dem Jahr 1312. Der Beschluß forderte die Einrichtung von Lehrstühlen für Arabisch und Hebräisch an den Universitäten Paris, Oxford, Bologna und Salamanca und an der Kurie: eine Forderung, die aus Mangel an geeigneten Lehrern nicht verwirklicht werden konnte. Der Konzilsbeschluß hatte im übrigen andere Motive, als Erasmus sie unterstellt. Die Kenntnis der Sprachen sollte die christliche Mission befördern, nicht den biblischen Text revidieren helfen. Man nimmt derartige eigenmächtige Deutungen des Erasmus mit leichtem Schmunzeln zur Kenntnis; die Tradition der mittelalterlichen Kirche bietet ihm Material, das er sich in seinem Sinn aneignete. Es ist die Wachsnase der *Auctoritas*, die ein jeder umformen kann.

Obwohl Augustin mit der griechischen Sprache nur oberflächliche Bekanntschaft hatte und die hebräische nicht verstand, hat er dennoch in *De doctrina christiana* die Kenntnis dieser Sprachen zum Verständnis und zur Wiederherstellung der *sacri codices* für unentbehrlich gehalten — mit anderen Worten, was Augustin zwar forderte, aber selbst nicht einzulösen vermochte, bietet ein anderer, ich nenne ihn "einen zweitern Augustin". Dieser zweite Augustin ist dank seiner Kenntnis der Sprachen in der Lage, das zu verstehen, was er liest. Der wahre Theologe wird nicht nur durch Sprachkenntnisse definiert: Er ist zugleich durch sein Studium zum besseren Menschen geworden. Erasmus zitiert in diesem Zusammenhang den Jakobusbrief (3:17): Wer die Weisheit erlangt hat, soll sie freundlich und sanftmütig verkünden, nicht besserwisserisch und hartnäckig disputieren, nicht streitlustig und rechthaberisch sein; die Weisheit, die von Gott stammt — Erasmus macht daraus: die Weisheit der Theologen — ist bescheiden, friedfertig, umgänglich, voll Erbarmen, sie zeitigt gute Früchte, sie verstellt sich nicht und sie verurteilt nicht. Es gibt daneben auch eine irdische, ja sogar eine teuflische Weisheit, die auch im Jakobusbrief erwähnt wird, aber Erasmus verzichtet darauf, aus dieser Bibelstelle einen polemischen Seitenhieb gegen seine theologischen Gegner abzuleiten. Es liegt ihm bei "Methodus" und "Ratio" ja daran, sich dem Leser nicht als gefährlichen Neuerer, sondern als friedfertigen Theologen bzw. Philologen darzustellen, der den Beschlüssen der Kirche und den Worten der Heiligen Schrift folgt.

Denn Erasmus verlangt dem Leser seiner Bibelhermeneutik viel ab. Wer zum wahren Schriftsinn vordringen will, muß nicht nur den Text, sondern vor allem den Kontext beachten.[1] Er muß sich vergegenwärtigen, wer spricht, für wen etwas gesagt wird, in welcher Zeit und bei welcher Gelegenheit, was vorher gesagt wurde und was anschließend folgt. Manche Worte richtete Jesus an seine Jünger, andere an das Volk. Er antwortete anders den Pharisäern, die ihm eine Falle stellen wollten, anders denen, die in aller Schlichtheit eine Frage an ihn richteten. Der Theologe muß die vielen Tropen und Figuren des Neuen Testaments bedenken, wenn er den Sinn einer Aussage erfassen will. Er muß sich fragen, ob Christus einen Satz als Mensch oder in seiner göttlichen Natur ausspricht oder beim Gespräch mit der Kananäerin aus der Denkweise eines Juden heraus spricht; d.h. der Theologe muß die Rolle der Sprecher beachten, es geht um die *observata ratio personarum*.[2]

Ebenso muß der Theologe die Zeit berücksichtigen. Analog zur *observata ratio personarum* steht hier die *observata varietas temporum*. Was zur Zeit des Alten und Neuen Testaments über die Juden ausgesagt wurde, ist nicht automatisch auf die Christen zu übertragen, sondern kann nur allegorisch gedeutet werden. Als Beispiel nennt Erasmus u.a. die Polygamie. Über den in diesem Zusammenhang zentralen Begriff der *accommodatio* hat mein Freiburger Kollege Peter Walter in seiner Habilitationsschrift das Nötige gesagt;[3] es handelt sich um das paulinische *omnia omnibus factus*, die Verwandlungsfähigkeit des pfiffigen Paulus, wie Erasmus sagt, der proteusartig oder wie ein Chamäleon die notwendige Anpassungsfähigkeit an seine Umwelt aufweist.

Erasmus, so habe ich bisher gezeigt, will in erster Linie die philologische Interpretation der Bibel als genuin theologische Aufgabe darstellen, sich als Fortsetzer der patristischen und scholastischen Traditionen ausgeben und von der Tatsache ablenken, daß er die Bibel wie jeden anderen weltlichen Text interpretiert. Die Zeitgebundenheit der Bibelsprache spielt in seinen Ausführungen eine große Rolle; der Text präsentiert sich in seiner Auslegung nicht als das zeitlose Wort Gottes, sondern als die kontextuell gebundene Äußerung von Menschen, die sich menschlich verhielten.

Erasmus selbst erliegt in mehreren Teilen der "Ratio" solchen Zeitströmungen. Er vergleicht die von Christus selbst unterwiesenen Jünger und ihr Hirtenamt nach Christi Tod mit der Ausbildung der Priester seiner Zeit. Aus der Gegenüberstellung von Bibelstellen über Reichtum und Armut, etwa über den reichen Mann und den armen Lazarus, leitet er Folgerungen über das sittliche Verhalten der Geistlichen seiner Zeit ab. Erasmus wäre nicht Erasmus, wenn er bei dieser Gelegenheit darauf verzichtet hätte, in aller Vorsicht die Lebensweise der Prälaten seiner Zeit zu kriti-

---

[1] Erasmus von Rotterdam, *Ausgewählte Schriften*, hrsg. Werner Welzig. 3. Band: *In Novum Testamentum Praefationes. Vorreden zum Neuen Testament. Ratio. Theologische Methodenlehre*, übers., eingeleitet und mit Anmerkungen versehen von Gerhard B. Winkler (Darmstadt, 1967), 178–179.

[2] Erasmus, *Ratio*, 184–185.

[3] Peter Walter, *Theologie aus dem Geist der Rhetorik. Zur Schriftauslegung des Erasmus von Rotterdam* (Mainz, 1991), 46–47.

sieren.⁴ Nach Lastern geordnet werden Berichte aus dem Neuen Testament aufgeführt — z.B. die *gloria inanis*, die sich darin äußert, daß die Mutter der Söhne des Zebedäus Christus darum bittet, daß ihre Söhne im Himmel zu seiner Rechten und zu seiner Linken sitzen dürfen (Matt. 20: 25ff). Christus gibt eine Antwort, die zunächst auf den Geltungsdrang dieser beiden Jünger bezogen ist, die aber auch, wie Erasmus sagt, schon im Blick auf die Prälaten der christlichen Kirche gegeben ist. Denn sie leiden besonders unter der Geltungssucht und dem Ehrgeiz, dem *studium honoris* und dem *morbus* der *ambitio*. Im Blick auf die Prälaten der späteren Zeiten habe Christus zu seinen Jüngern gesagt, der Menschensohn ist nicht gekommen, um sich dienen zu lassen, sondern um zu dienen, ja sein Leben hinzugeben für viele ... "ut animam suam det pro multis. Papae, quantum haec oratio discrepat ab ambitionis affectu!" Die Interjektion "papae" wird von unseren Lexika gern mit "Potztausend" übersetzt; der Satz des Erasmus ließe sich auf deutsch etwa mit den Worten wiedergeben: "Potztausend, wie wenig hat dieser Satz Christi mit dem Streben nach Ruhm zu tun" oder "Welten liegen zwischen diesem Satz und dem Streben nach Ruhm." In der Übertragung von Gerhard B. Winkler wird der Passus "Papae, quantum haec oratio discrepat ab ambitionis affectu" etwas anders wiedergegeben, nämlich so: "Wie ganz anders als die Äußerung des Geltungsdranges müssen diese Worte dem Papst in den Ohren klingen."⁵ Winklers *lapsus*, die Verwechslung von *papaé* und *pápae*, bietet ein schönes Beispiel dafür, daß eine theologische Vorerwartung zu philologischem Schiffbruch führt.

Erasmus mag sicher an dieser Stelle den Papst im Auge gehabt haben, aber er argumentierte nicht so direkt. Der Leser wird stets aufgefordert, eine von Erasmus herangezogene Stelle des Neuen Testaments selbständig auf seine Zeit zu übertragen. Unter Verzicht auf die reiche kommentierende Literatur geht Erasmus jeweils *ad fontem*; er fordert den Leser auf: "Blättere das ganze Neue Testament durch, nirgends wirst du eine Vorschrift finden, die sich auf die Zeremonien bezieht. Wo gibt es ein Wort über Speisen oder Kleidung, wo irgendeine Erwähnung des Fastens? Christus nennt allein die Liebe als sein Gebot. Durch die Zeremonien kommt es zu Spaltungen, durch Liebe zum Frieden."⁶

Was als Apologie und Werbeschrift begann, wird allmählich zu einer wohldosierten Anklage. Erasmus wußte nur zu gut, daß nur eine methodologische Schrift nicht zu einer grundlegend neuen hermeneutischen Methode würde führen können. So greift er häufig auf vertraute Vorstellungen zurück. Er stellt sie aber jeweils auf subtile Weise zur Disposition; z.B. referiert er die mittelalterliche Dreiteilung der menschlichen Gesellschaft in die Stände der *laboratores*, *bellatores* und *oratores*.⁷ Zwei Stände nimmt er wortlos als gegebene Fakten hin, während er beim Priesterstand die Frage stellt, ob denn die Privilegien dieser Gruppe sich wirklich so eindeutig aus der Bibel ableiten lassen, wie es die Tradition der Kirche bis zu seiner Zeit unaufhörlich tat. Er greift keineswegs den Text der Bibel als vielmehr die *ratio* ihrer Ausleger an, und er

---

⁴ Erasmus, *Ratio*, 268–269.
⁵ Erasmus, *Ratio*, 272–273.
⁶ Erasmus, *Ratio*, 302–303.
⁷ Erasmus, *Ratio*, 194–195.

zeigt auf, daß diese Hermeneuten ihrerseits neue Ausleger und Interpreten gefunden hatten, die jeweils auf andere Theologen einwirkten. In bis zu zehnfacher Brechung werden die Worte Christi gedeutet; der Grundtext geht verloren, die Kommentatoren kommentieren nur noch ihre Vorgänger. Über die Beschäftigung mit der Sekundärliteratur und über den fehlenden Bezug auf den Originaltext äußert sich Erasmus mehr als verbittert. Er nimmt einzig die Theologen in Cambridge und die in Löwen von seiner Kritik aus; sie verhalten sich moderat, während man in Paris verantwortungslos interpretiert.[8] Um das zu demonstrieren, berichtet er von der Predigtreihe eines Theologen in Paris. Bisher ist diese Anekdote nicht verifiziert worden. Es könnte sein, daß Erasmus sie erfunden hat, um die von ihm nicht geliebte Sorbonne der Lächerlichkeit preiszugeben.

Ein Theologe, der über das Gleichnis vom Verlorenen Sohn predigte, habe dieses Thema an 40 aufeinanderfolgenden Tagen behandelt, um die gesamte Fastenzeit von 40 Tagen damit zu füllen. Natürlich reicht eine so kurze Bibelstelle nicht für 40 lange Predigten. Der geistliche Herr sei daher auf den Gedanken verfallen, den verlorenen Sohn auf seiner Reise in die Fremde zu begleiten. An jedem Tag habe er einen Tag der Reisestation des jungen Verschwenders beschrieben: die Wirtshäuser, in denen er abgestiegen, was er dort gegessen, welchen Lastern er sich hingegeben, wie er an einer Wassermühle vorbeigekommen usw., jeweils mit Bibelstellen garniert, die aus anderen Kontexten stammten oder frei erfunden waren. Mit der Bibel habe diese Predigtserie nichts mehr zu tun gehabt.[9]

Was hier als Auswuchs einer ausufernden Methode bibelfreier Theologie gebrandmarkt wurde, wird die Zustimmung von Erasmus' Hörern gefunden haben, die dadurch dann auch auf seine Forderung eingestimmt wurden, daß einzig die Quellen zu befragen seien.

"Methodus" und "Ratio" sind zunächst als Apologie und Werbeschrift konzipiert, verwandeln sich aber zunehmend in Kampfansagen und bereiten den Bruch mit einer Jahrhunderte hindurch bestehenden Tradition einer Bibelinterpretation vor, die den Text auf die Funktion eines Stichwortgebers reduzierte. Indem Erasmus die Auswüchse kritisiert, stellte er die patristische und mittelalterliche Bibelexegese grundsätzlich in Frage; stets zwar mit der beschwichtigenden Formel "docere est animus, non irritare,"[10] aber doch mit dem Hinweis auf die eigene Zeit, die auch ihre Pharisäer aufweise: "Habent enim et nostra tempora suos Phariseos ac rabbinos. Ab illis omne malum oritur"[11] — eine für Erasmus eindeutige und kühne Aussage. Ambiguität und Ängstlichkeit wird man Erasmus nach der Lektüre der "Ratio" nicht vorwerfen können, seinen persuasiven Diskurs wird man bewundern.

Seminar für Lateinische Philologie des Mittelalters
der Universität Freiburg

---

[8] Erasmus, *Ratio*, 488–489.
[9] Erasmus, *Ratio*, 422–425.
[10] Erasmus, *Ratio*, 214–215.
[11] Erasmus, *Ratio*, S. 338–339.

Nuevos textos del teatro jesuítico en España, I: Parenesia y Demophilus

ANGEL SIERRA DE COZAR

El objeto de este trabajo, juntamente con el presentado por el profesor V. Picón en este mismo volumen, es dar a conocer cuatro nuevos manuscritos de otras tantas piezas del teatro de colegio de los jesuitas en España, que se conservan en la Real Academia de la Historia (RAH), de Madrid.[1] Se trata de dos testimonios nuevos de obras ya conocidas, *Parenesia* y *Demophilus,* y otros dos de obras de las que hasta ahora no se tenía noticia, tituladas *Techmisio* y *El triunfo de la Fe.*

Las cuatro piezas forman parte del legajo 9/7262 (signatura antigua 11-11-2/42) de la sección de Jesuitas de la Biblioteca de la RAH. De su existencia informaba el P. Lecina en su catálogo al anotar escuetamente "varios dramas" en su reseña del contenido del legajo. En las páginas que siguen me ocuparé, sucintamente, de las dos primeras.[2]

En principio, la información sobre nuevos testimonios de un texto ya conocido debería partir de su comparación con los antiguos. Por suerte o por desgracia, el cierre temporal de la sección de manuscritos de la Biblioteca Nacional (BN) ha hecho imposible la realización de este trabajo. No obstante, es tan sucinto lo publicado sobre los textos conocidos, que estos de ahora, supuestamente repetidos, podemos conside-

---

[1] Este trabajo se integra en el PB97-0053, "Teatro escolar latino en España (1550-1650)", financiado por la DGICYT.

[2] Cf. Mariano Lecina, S.J., *Catálogo de los 116 legajos existentes en la sección titulada jesuitas de la Biblioteca de la Real Academia de la Historia* (Madrid, 1895). La rareza de este catálogo explica que la indicación de su autor haya pasado hasta ahora inadvertida. Por otra parte, el carácter unitario, y el aspecto descuidado y desordenado de los textos explica que el recopilador de la conocida Colección de Cortes, que agrupa a la mayor parte del teatro de colegio conservado, no los tuviera en cuenta.

rarlos como nuevos — y en parte realmente lo son, como veremos, aun sin conocer en detalle los que posiblemente fueron sus modelos.

Los textos "antiguos" de estas dos comedias fueron dados a conocer por M. Molina hace no muchos años, al describir el contenido de un manuscrito de la BN, procedente del Colegio de jesuitas de Córdoba (BN, MS. 15.404), añadiéndolo a un recuento general del teatro neolatino en España.[3] Sobre los nuevos textos, y en especial sobre las dos piezas que nos ocupan, es particularmente breve, limitándose "a las notas más significativas y los nuevos datos ... dejando para un estudio posterior el examen detallado de las obras." "Por lo demás" — añade a modo de resumen — "las obras presentan los rasgos característicos de este teatro de colegio ...: en ellas hallamos coros ..., mezcla de prosa y verso, latín y castellano, entreactos y pasatiempos — con el típico sabor popular que tanta fortuna tendría — prólogos explicativos en latín y en castellano, multitud de personajes, a menudo alegóricos ... y una temática alegorizante cuyo núcleo es la efímera y falsa felicidad que proporcionan los bienes terrenales frente al goce de una paz eterna celestial. Son obras, pues, que se insertan plenamente en el tipo de teatro alegórico-simbólico con fines didácticos que iniciara a mediados del XVI el Padre Acevedo."[4] Por último, destaca un dato común a ambas comedias: el uso de un segundo prólogo dialogado para defender el uso del latín junto al castellano y la elección de un tema edificante, en razón de la doble finalidad de aquel teatro de "instruir a los alumnos y educar al vulgo."

No me consta que el autor de ese primer acercamiento a estas comedias haya llevado a cabo el examen detallado que las circunstancias le obligaban a aplazar. Veamos, pues, si el examen de los nuevos textos permite añadir algo a lo ya conocido.

Con respecto a "nuestra" *Parenesia*, nada tendríamos que decir aquí, ya que se trata de una obra escrita totalmente en castellano. Sin embargo, el análisis puramente externo de su desarrollo da pie a algunas observaciones de interés en relación precisamente con el uso del latín y de la lengua vernácula en el teatro de colegio. El desarrollo dramático de la obra podría sintetizarse en el siguiente esquema:

PARENESIA

6v			
Acto Prim°	scena 1ª		Amartano (verso)
7r	scena 2ª		Dificultad Amartano (verso y prosa)
8r	scena 3 2ª		Dilaçion oluido Difficultad Amarta. (prosa)
9v	sçena 3ª		Cupedio Aleator DeTractor Dilacion Letheo (p.)

---

[3] M. Molina Sánchez, "El teatro de los jesuitas en la provincia de Andalucía: nuevos datos para su estudio," in J. M. Maestre et al., eds., *Humanismo y pervivencia del mundo clásico*, 2 vols. (Cádiz, 1993), 2:643–654. Aparte de la *Parenesia* (fols. 1r–42v) y el *Demophilus*, éste bajo el título de *Demophilea, de vera et ementita fœlicitate* (fols. 82r–127v), el MS contiene otras cuatro piezas teatrales: *Acolastus, Dialogus . . . de praestantissima scientiarum eligenda, Zenonia,* y *Gadirus herculanus.*

[4] Molina, "El teatro de los jesuitas," 650, 653.

10v			
Actus 2us.		Sçena 1ª	[paranesius stimul. amart. dificultad] (añadidos)
			Paranesius (verso) [stimulus] (diálogo, prosa)
	12r	~~Scena 2ª~~	~~Paranesio Estimulo Amartano Diffi.~~
	13v	Scena ~~3~~ 2ª	Dilacion Letheo Pharanesio estimulo (p.)
	15r	Scena 3ª	Dilatio Aleatorius detractor cupedius
16v			
	en lugar de entreacto		stimulo letheo Pensamiento y cinco sentidos (p.)
18r			
Acto 3º		scena 1ª	stimulo Temor. (Diálogo, prosa; Temor solo, verso)
	19v	scena 2ª	Temor stimulo Imfortunio breuedad fragilidad
	20r	(espacio en blanco; luego aparecen Letheo Paranesio Dilacion) (p.)	
	20v	scena 3ª	Timor imfort Br. fra, stimu (v.)
21r		finis actus tertij	
Acto 4ª		scena 1ª	Dilacion y oluido Paranesio y Amartano (p.)
	21v	scena 2 ª	Aleator deTrastor Cupedio
			Dilatio Letheo Paranesio Amarthano (v. y p.)
	23v	scena 3ª	Pensamiento y los 5 sentidos Temor y estimulo (p.)
25r			
Acto 5º		scena Primª	Paranesio (p. y v.)
			Dilacion letheo dificultad Amartano estimulo (p.)
	27r	scena 2ª	Paranesio Amar. Dila. Let. Diffi.
			Temor Infort. Fragili. breuedad stimulo (p.)
	29r	~~scena 4ª~~	~~Pareneçio Fragilidad breuedad infortunio temor stimulo~~ (v.)
	30r	scena 3 ª	Pax alegria Pareneçio Temor breuedad fragilidad imfortunio estimulo amarthano Letheo [cum]? Parasitibus (p.)

De un rápido examen de los datos puestos de relieve en este cuadro se deduce que la nueva *Parenesia* deriva de una versión anterior castellano-latina, de la que se ha eliminado el latín. Así lo indican el proceso de fusión de escenas, que en mayor o menor medida afecta a todos los actos, y la variación en el nombre de los personajes.

Los indicios de reducción del número de escenas, significativos en sí mismos, lo son aún más comparados con los procedimientos habituales de la comedia *Demophilus*: comienzo de escena en verso latino seguido de glosa en verso castellano, alternancia latín/castellano dentro de una misma escena y existencia de escenas exclusivamente en latín o en castellano para determinados contenidos. En cuanto a los nombres de los personajes basta comparar, e.g., el nombre de los tres truhanes en la relación de personajes (Glotón, Jugador, Murmurador), con el que tienen en los encabezamientos de escena, u oscilaciones como Dilatio/Dilación o Stimulus/Estímulo.

Por si esto fuera poco, dos diferencias en relación con la *Parenesia* del manuscrito de la BN llevan indefectiblemente a la misma conclusión: frente a las 84 páginas de allí, aquí tenemos 50, y en el prólogo dialogado de la nueva no se plantea si será en castellano o en latín.

En el manuscrito de la BN ambas obras están fechadas: la fecha del *Demophilus* (Granada, 1584), que coincide con datos presentes también en el texto nuevo, no hace al caso; la *Parenesia* se representó en Córdoba en 1580. El manuscrito de la RAH contendría por tanto una versión posterior, reflejando tal vez el abandono del latín que se generalizaba a comienzos del XVII.

En cuanto al contenido de las dos comedias, sus semejanzas y diferencias podrían plasmarse en los dos esquemas siguientes:

Parenesia

            Amartano   (Eubulo)
Cupedius
Aleator
Detractor
                        Parenesius
            Difficultas
                            Stimulus

            Dilatio   Timor Dei
            Letheo   Pensamiento   Infortunium
                       5 sentidos   Breuitas vitæ
                                         Fragilitas corporis
                          Pax
                          Alegria

Demophilvs

            (falsa)   pax   (vera
            Fœlicitas   spes   Fœlicitas)
                             relligio
Honor
Opulentius   Inspiratio
Delicius   *Demophilus*

                        Philautus   Infamia
                       Desiderium   Egestas
                  Discursus   Aegritudo

Ambitianus   Veritas — Verbum divinum
Cressicus
                        Honor
           Timon   Dives
                      Experientia

En uno y otro caso, las figuras que dan nombre a la comedia constituyen el centro de una constelación de personajes que se distribuyen a izquierda y derecha en torno a ellas, según su pertenencia al bando del bien o del mal. Las dos comedias consisten en el enfrentamiento de estos dos contingentes por la posesión de la figura central. En cuanto al desarrollo argumental, estos conflictos recuerdan el viejo "Nissens'ches Schema" de las batallas en Livio: entablado el combate se mantiene por un tiempo *aequis viribus*, luego el frente romano (las fuerzas del bien) comienza a ceder, y cuando ya se encuentra a punto de ser derrotado, reacciona, se recupera y termina aniquilando al enemigo. Sólo que aquí el papel activo corresponde a la "presa" en interacción con sus enemigos o con su salvador.

Poco más se puede añadir a partir de la comparación de uno y otro esquema, salvo señalar la mayor complejidad, variedad, y cohesión del *Demophilus*, y ejemplificar con determinados grupos de personajes lo apuntado antes del empleo exclusivo del latín o del castellano para determinados contenidos o escenas: el núcleo formado por Timon–Ambitianus–Cressicus se expresa en latín sobre un tema académico: la filosofía sobre la felicidad; en cambio Honor–Dives–Experientia forman un tribunal ante el que comparece la felicidad para ser juzgada, un tribunal que se recrea en un juego de metáforas en clave jurídica, intraducible al latín, destinado a dibujar sonrisas complacidas en el auditorio, acomodados burgueses entendidos en leyes padres de alumnos.

Echemos finalmente una ojeada a la literariedad/latinidad del texto de *Demófilo*. Tenía mucha razón M. Molina en subrayar la importancia de los prólogos y la viveza de los entreactos y pasatiempos. En *Demófilo* hay tres entreactos señalados como tales — 1°, 2° y último — , y en mi opinión, por su contenido, un entreacto 3°, presentado en el manuscrito como última escena del acto, seguramente por estar parcialmente en latín. En él intervienen Demófilo con los suyos (= los criados de Fœlicitas) y el parásito Tristán en lo que puede valer para nosotros como un documento pedagógico:

ACTVS 3 SCENA VLTIMA

HON. —Pero ¿es posible que no tenéis otro entretenimj^{to} sino ese? Auíanme dicho q. despues q. salistes de casa de aquel bachiller de grammática soys grande poeta latino.

TRIST. —¡Bueno es eßo! Nacieronme los dientes êla fuente cabalina, y estoy harto de andar entre los laureles del Helicón o del Parnaso ¿y viéneme agora con eso?.

HON. —Aora pues, dezidnos algo de lo q. auéis compuesto estos dias.

TRIST. —Vna epigrama le dire en verso elegíaco q. hize lamentando la pérdida de mi capote y quexándome de la fortuna. Escuche, y despauil[e el en]tendim[iento]

Est fallax fortuna mihi, temer[ar]ia ceca
preceps inconstans lubrica fluxa vaga

Aprenda: exordium sumptum ab antiqua pictura.

Vestis versicolor contexit serica corpus
heu pictam clamidem cartula picta tulit.

Narración descriptiua: *pictam* y *picta* †. . .† paululum inmutata atque deflexa in or(a-ti)one ponuntur ¡que también tiene la persona sus puntillos de rethorico!

> *Aurea commiβi prætiosa nomismata ludo*
> *sed mansit nûmis nuda crumena meis.*

Periphrasis: illustris tropus cum id quod [uno] verbo dici poterat pluribus dicitur. ¡q. galano modo de hablar! Para dezir jugué y perdí dixe: *aurea* etc.

> *Reieci ex humeris ~~lusurus~~ pulchrû lusurus amictû*
> *atq. itidem fuerunt inuida fata mei.*

Conclusión. *Fuerunt* cô la penult[a] breue; figura sistole frequens apud claros poetas, Sylio ytalico: *terruerunt pauidos accensa ceraunia nautas*, n(uest)rô lyrico: *dij tibi diuitias dederunt artêq. fruendi* y finalm[te] el poeta latino: *Obstipuit steteruntque. comæ et uox faucibus hæsit.* Nóteme esos sp(irit)ûs poéticos ...

¿Qué les parece? Abobados los he dexado. ¡Oh, pues si me oyera en mis tiempos, cuando yo era muchacho: con qué agudeza hablaba y escriuía! Decíame el bachiller mi amo — Dios haya su alma —: "Tú me succederás en la cátedra, hijo." Dado he quenta de mi pérdida, señor Demófilo, y si no remedia el daño, sin duda hara Tristán un Ovidio de Tristibus, y si esto no bastara haremos un Juvenal en sátiras contra su auaritia y laçería.

La *vis comica* del fragmento residía, sin duda, en su valor de reflejo burlesco de modos de enseñanza o textos escolares al uso, herederos en parte de la impostación retórica del comentario transmitida a través de los *commenta ad Terentium*. Aquí en un breve epigrama de ocho versos se enfoca bajo la óptica de un discurso: *exordium*, narración, conclusión.

Tonos mucho menos amables presenta la figura del gramático en el entreacto 2º, expuesta a la ironía y el desprecio del personaje Discurso, interpretado, según se deduce del propio texto, por un muchacho de 14 años. El Gramático es un necio que se queja, en un lenguaje ridículo, del desprecio en que yace su ciencia: "están las letras el dia de oi supeditadas, digo oppresas y aspernadas, *et ut uno uerbo dicam, assis, teruncii, flocci, pili non faciunt*"; que está orgulloso de tener su ejemplar de los *Adagia* ilegible a fuerza de subrayados, notas, ilustraciones, escolios, glosématas, y apéndices; que apela a la autoridad de nueve gramáticos — de Varrón a Nebrija — , pero que preguntado por Discurso sobre dónde encontrar la felicidad, no se le ocurre otra cosa que mandarlo al diccionario: ¿Felicidad? En el Calepino, letra F con diptongo œ, añadiendo en un alarde de erudición superflua la distinción establecida por Valla entre *prosper* y *felix*. Sintomáticamente el muchacho (Discurso) manifiesta su desprecio mediante refranes castellanos que ponen al mismo nivel de locura al gramático y al astrólogo de los entreactos anteriores: "¡otro que bien bayla! ¡Topado se ha Sancho con su rocín!"..., etc. Filosofía vulgar frente y por encima de los adagios de la tradición recogida por Erasmo.

El latín del *Demófilo* — excepción hecha de algunos versos logrados[5] — es en general un latín bastante pobre, reiterativo y esquemático, a veces casi se diría que escrito para que los actores tengan algo que decir. Únicamente en un par de escenas

---

[5] Entre los méritos de la comedia hay que colocar el esfuerzo del autor por ofrecer ejemplos de versificación latina en distintos ritmos y medidas, sobre el modelo de Séneca.

del acto cuarto la semejanza de las situaciones le lleva a recuperar algo de la tradición de la comedia romana con ecos directos de Terencio, pero no sin que el léxico terenciano (cf. nota 6) se incruste en una frase que tiene un aire algo así como biblico o eclesiástico.

En 4.4 el idilio entre Demophilus y Fœlicitas se rompe; y acaba como los idilios rotos: con lágrimas, indignación y reproches:

ACTUS 4 SCÆN. 4ª

DISC. — Hem fallacem Fœlicitatem, ementitam inanem!
PHIL. — Proh, nugacem fœminam!
DESID. — Fa[s]cinatricem maleficam!
DEMO. — Præceps hic famulorum interuentus noui cuiuspiam mali index est, ... quid inclamatis, ~~pueri~~.?

. . . .

DISC — Satis me dolose in fraudem induxit Fœlicitas; sed ego me in pedes.
DEMO. — Vobiscum etiam actum est fraudulenter?
DESID. — Promißa fides illam ab impia cogitatione non reflexit neque a scelere represßit vlla infamiæ suspicio.[6]

. . . .

DEMO. — Alieno ergo animo a nobis est Fœlicitas.
DESID — Res ipsa indicat.[7]

Esto se ponía sobre los escenarios de los colegios en 1584. Veinte años antes Acevedo había estrenado su *Occasio*, una obra tejida con las "intertextualidades" más diversas, un verdadero centón literario, capaz de inspirar a Cervantes por sus innovaciones escénicas.[8] La edición crítica traducida y anotada de las obras dramáticas de Acevedo a cargo de un equipo de latinistas de la Universidad Autónoma de Madrid, entre los que me cuento y a cuyo frente se encuentra V. Picón, deberá hacer revisar ese prejuicio heredado sobre la nula entidad de este teatro, moralista y simbólico desde sus comienzos, es cierto, pero también en sus comienzos más próximo y abierto a la recepción e interacción con los clásicos y al ideal educativo de un humanismo cristiano, mucho más de lo que muestran ejemplos como estos de la segunda generación de maestros de latinidad entre los jesuitas, cuando, aparte de las naturales diferencias de capacidad y estudios entre autores, el lema *virtus versus litteras* se había hecho más combativo.[9]

Universidad Autónoma de Madrid

---

[6] Cf. Ter. *Ad.* 306–307: "quem neque fides neque iusiurandum . . . / repressit neque reflexit."
[7] Ter. *Ad.* 338: "Iam primum illum alieno animo a nobis esse res ipsa indicat."
[8] Cf. Á. Sierra de Cózar, "El posible modelo de Cervantes en las comedias del P. Pedro Pablo de Acevedo," *Cuadernos de Filología Clásica: Estudios Latinos*, n.s. 15 (1998): 561–571.
[9] V. Picón, et al., *Teatro escolar latino del s. XVI: La obra de Pedro Pablo de Acevedo, S.I., I: Lucifer furens, Occasio, Philautus, Charopus* (Madrid, 1997).

Zamość: Das letzte Bollwerk der Renaissance in Polen

JERZY STARNAWSKI

Jan Zamoyski (1542–1605), der als Oberfeldherr und Großkanzler des Königreichs Polen sein Leben beendete, war in seiner Jugend Student der Universität Padova, wo er ein Jahr lang die Würde des Rektors bekleidet hatte und wo er die Dissertation *De senatu Romano* (Venetiis 1563) fertigstellte.

Er war mit dem größten Dichter der polnischen Renaissance, Jan Kochanowski (1530–1564), befreundet. Als Zamoyski seine zweite Frau, Krystyna Radziwiłłówna, heiratete, dichtete Kochanowski für diese Hochzeit ein bedeutendes Drama, *Die Abfertigung der griechischen Gesandten*. Die Vorstellung fand während des Hochzeitsfestes am 12. Januar 1578 in Jazdow bei Warschau statt. Der Spielleiter Wojciech Oczko (1537–1599) hat seine Aufgabe in erstaunlicher Schnelligkeit erledigt, denn er hatte den Text des Schauspiels erst am 23. oder 24. Dezember erhalten.

Nach der Inszenierung der *Abfertigung der griechischen Gesandten,* einer Tragödie, die das Thema der *Ilias* entlehnte, wurde ein lateinisches Poem von Kochanowski, *Orpheus Sarmaticus,* zur Leier gesungen, das die Idee der letzten Worte des Schauspiels weiterführte, nämlich die Warnung vor dem Kriege.

Die Abfertigung der griechischen Gesandten wurde noch im Jahre 1578 in Warschau veröffentlicht. In diesem Jahr jagte der König Stefan Batory in Zamech, dem Landgut von Zamoyski. Aus diesem Anlaß verfaßte Kochanowski zwei lateinische Gedichte: *Dryas Zamchana,* zu dem auch eine polnische Übersetzung erschien, und *Pan Zamchanus.* Beide wurden am 8. Mai 1578 in Anwesenheit des Königs vorgetragen. Die Wälder in der Gegend von Zamech hat der Dichter in seiner Einbildungskraft mit Faunen und Satyrn bevölkert und die Jagdgöttin Diana gepriesen. Pan Zamchanus war ein Waldgott, der in Zamech wohnte. Das Gedicht ist ein Monolog, eine Apostrophe an den König, eine Glorifikation des Monarchen.

Die zweite Frau von Zamoyski ist am 28. Februar 1580 gestorben. Der Kanzler heiratete am 13. Juni 1583 Gryzelda Batory, die Tochter des Fürsten von Siebenbürgen, eine Nichte des Königs. Zu der Hochzeit, die im Königsschloß Wawel gefeiert wurde, schrieb Kochanowski zwei lateinische Gedichte, die beide 1583 in Krakau herausgegeben wurden: *In nuptiis Illustrium Joan/nis/ de Zamoscio /.../ ac Griseldis Bathorreae /.../ Epithalamion* und *Ad Stephanum Bathorreum, Regem Poloniae inclytum, Mischo debellato et Livonia recuperata Epinicion.* Das zweite Gedicht ist nicht das einzige, in dem Kochanowski den König als Sieger des Krieges 1579–1580 verherrlicht hat. Im Feldzug gegen Moskau hat Zamoyski teilgenommen und drei Städte erobert. Der 52. *Duodenarius* in dem *Epinicion* hat ihren Sieg gepriesen.

Der Chronist der Hochzeit war Reinhold Heidenstein (1553–1620), *historiographus regius,* Verfasser der *De nuptiis illustrium Joannis de Zamoscio /.../ ac Griseldis Bathorreae /.../ epistola* (Cracoviae, 1583). Es war auch das Thema der lateinischen und polnischen Dichtungen.

Im Jahre 1560 hat Jan Zamoyski die Stadt Zamość gegründet. Als Hauptbaumeister hat er aus Italien Bernardo Morando geholt. In den Plänen des Kanzlers sollte sie eine "ideale Renaissance-Stadt" werden. Die Stadt hat während der Bauzeit der Dichter Sebastian Fabian Klonovic (um 1545–1602) besichtigt, der seine lateinischen Werke unter dem Namen Acernus veröffentlichte. In dem Gedicht *Roxolania* (Cracoviae, 1584, wahrscheinlich 1581 entstanden) wandte sich Acernus in der Invokation an die Musen mit den Worten:

>   Dicite, quod surgit coelo arridente Zamoscum,
>   Dicite, nam vobis nascitur illa domus. (V. 13–14)

Der neuen Stadt hat der Dichter 20 Verse gewidmet (V. 1281–1300). Er schrieb u. a.:

>   Moenia bellator Gradivus ahenea iecit
>   Hostibus adversis et metuenda dedit.
>   "Hic mihi cara quies — dixit — mea cura Zamoscum,
>   Parcite iam vestro, Martia bella, deo.
> 1295 Urbis adhuc fuerant quondam incunabula nostrae,
>   Qua nunc has moles surgere forte vides."[1]

Einige Jahre später war Klonovic-Acernus in Zamość Schulleiter (1589–1592), später wohnte er in Lublin als Bürgermeister.

Die Stadt Zamość entwickelte sich zu einem polnischen Padova mit dem schönen Ringplatz, dem Renaissance-Rathaus und einigen Kirchen und Gebäuden im Renaissance-Stil. Georg Braun (Georgius Braunius Agrippinus, gest. 1616) hat in seinem Hauptwerk *Theatri praecipuarum totius mundi orbium libri* (1512 ff.) im 6. Buch *Novum Zamoscium* geschildert und begann seine Beschreibung mit folgenden Worten:

> Ioannes de Zamoscio, Magnus Polonici Regni Cancellarius et Generalis exercituum Dux, illustri genere sed virtute et rebus gestis multo illustrior, ut de patria

---

[1] Vgl. Sebastian Acernus, *Roxolania,* hrsg. Mieczysław Mejor (Warszawa, 1996), 22–96; hrsg. Elzbieta Kolbus, *Humanistica Lovaniensia* 47 (1998): 175–211.

bene mereretur, in omnes partes animum versans, magno sed laudabili ausu eam nova civitate augere constituit [. . .] arcem suam Zamoscium unde gentile ipsi nomen, egregie munire novisque substructionibus exornari curavit.[2]

Georgius Dousa, der 1597 durch Polen nach Konstantinopel reiste, schrieb in seinem lateinischen Werk *De itinere suo Constantinopolitano epistola* über die guten Eigenschaften Zamoyskis, indem er mit solchen Worten der Stadt Zamość gedachte:

> Nihil autem magis innatum eius erga patrios lares amorem declarare possit quam haec ipsa civitas, quam propriis sum(p)tibus a fundamentis extruxit, moenibus et propugnaculis adversus hostium impetum validissimis munivit, et a suo nomine Zamoscium appellavit.[3]

Die erste literarische Gesellschaft in Polen entstand am Ende des 15. Jh., als Konrad Celtis nach Krakau kam und die *Sodalitas litteraria Vistulana* begründete. Wir haben keinen Beweis, daß Jan Zamoyski etwas Ähnliches ins Leben zu rufen versuchte, jedoch ist bezeugt, daß es in seiner Umgebung viele hochbegabte Männer, Schriftsteller und Gelehrte gab. Rutger zur Horst schrieb in seinem parenthetischen Werk *Cancellarius* (1628), daß David Hilchen, Reinhold Heidenstein, Simonides und Rutger Lewel dem Kanzler Zamoyski nahestanden:

> [. . .] isti quattuor Zamoscio erant familiarissimi, his in mensa aliquid proponere solebat, tandem post longas pro et contra disputationes et discursus summa cum gravitate concludebant.[4]

David Hilchen kam zu Zamoyski um das Jahr 1588 als Botschafter von Riga und ist in Zamość geblieben. Dort hat er manche Werke veröffentlicht, u. a. *Clypeus innocentiae et veritatis* (1604) und ein Beileidsgedicht *Paregoria* (1605) für Jan Lipski aus Goraj, einem nicht weit von Zamość entfernten Städtchen.

Der schon genannte Reinhold Heidenstein schrieb über Zamoyski in einigen seiner historischen Werke; nach dem Tode des Großkanzlers war er dessen erster Biograph und verfaßte die Schrift *De vita Ioannis Zamoscii* (1606), die unter Benutzung einer Handschrift des 18. Jahrhunderts erstmals im Jahre 1861 veröffentlicht wurde.

Den größten Dichter der neuen Stadt Zamość, Szymon Szymonowic (1558–1629), der sich Simonides nannte, hat Zamoyski um 1586 kennengelernt und ihn im Jahre 1588 nach Zamość eingeladen; doch kam er erst 1598 nach Zamość. Er wohnte früher in Lemberg und stand mit Zamoyski in Korrespondenz. Er hatte schon mehrere lateinische Dichtungen publiziert, zu denen sich ab 1588 einige über Zamoyski ge-

---

[2] Vgl. Georgius Braunius, *Theatri praecipuarum totius mundi urbium libri VI* (Coloniae Agrippinae, 1618), K. 53r–v.

[3] Vgl. *Thesaurus Graecarum antiquitatum, contextus et designatus ab Jacobo Gronovio*, Bd. 6 (Venetiis, 1725), 3364.

[4] Vgl. Leon Szyperski, *De Simonis Simonidae vita, ingenio, poesi* (Vratislaviae, 1875), 15.

sellten, z.B. *Flagellum livoris* (Cracoviae, 1558), ein Zyklus von 19 Oden zur Verherrlichung Zamoyskis nach seinem Sieg bei Byczyna, und *Aelinopean* (Leopoli, 1589), ein Zyklus von 16 kleinen Gedichten, auch zur Verherrlichung des Kanzlers nach dessen Sieg in den südöstlichen Gegenden des Königreiches.

Zamoyski hat Simonides als Nachfolger Kochanowskis betrachtet. Er wandte sich an ihn, da er die Dichtungen der Dichter Andrzej Zbylitowski, Joachim Bielski und des schon genannten Acernus schätzte. So entstand in Zamość eine "docta sodalitas", die jedoch nicht streng organisiert war. Dafür entstand eine Akademie, die in der Bulla des Papstes Klemens VIII. vom 29. Oktober 1594 genehmigt wurde. Sie wurde erstmals im Jahre 1595 von dem Kanzler einberufen, jedoch erst am 23. September 1601 von König Sigismund III. bestätigt.

Die *Academia Samoscensis* wurde als eine Ergänzung der *Academia Cracoviensis* angesehen. Die weltlichen Unterrichtsgegenstände wurden hier ausführlicher behandelt als in Krakau, und es wurde hier eine andere Konzeption realisiert: die jungen Knaben, die in Zamość ihre Ausbildung begonnen hatten, konnten sie an der Akademie fortsetzen, d.h. die ganze Ausbildung bis zum Universitätsstudium konnte man in derselben Schule durchlaufen. Die Unterrichtsanstalt wurde in erster Linie für die adelige Jugend aus dem Ritterstand begründet; die Knaben wurden auch im Reiten unterrichtet, daher wurde sie auch *Hippeum* genannt.

Bei der Besetzung der Lehrstühle stützte sich Zamoyski auf die Vorschläge des Simonides, der als Erzieher des Sohnes des Kanzlers, Tomasz Zamoyski (1594–1635), an den Hof in Zamość kam, doch selbst keinen Lehrstuhl erhielt. Die vornehmsten Gelehrten der *Academia Samoscensis* waren Laurentius Starnigel (ab 1595, gest. 1639), Joannes Ursinus (ab 1595, gest. 1613), Melchior Stephanides (ab 1595, gest. 1638) und Adam Bursius (ab 1596, gest. 1611). Der Großkanzler ließ den Professoren reichlich Versorgung zuteil werden, was Szymon Starowolski in seinem Werk *Scriptorum Polonicorum Hekatontas* (1625, 2. ed. 1627) bescheinigt; er schrieb über Joannes Ursinus: "[. . .] magnum auctoritatis et gratiae locum apud Ducem Zamoscium obtinuit, a quo stipendiis non contemnendis invitatus [. . .]."[5] Jeder Professor erhielt ein Haus auf dem Ringplatz. Auf dem Plan der Stadt Zamość, der sich im dortigen Museum befindet, können wir noch heute sehen, welches Haus Adam Bursius gehörte.

Bei der Inauguration der Akademie hat Zamoyski einen Aufruf unter dem Titel *Ad Cives Polonos de Academia Zamoscensis Prophasis* (1594) veröffentlicht. Aus dem Betrieb der *Academia Samosciensis* entstand das Lehrbuch *Grammaticae methodicae libri IV* von Joannes Ursinus, das 1619 gedruckt, aber schon früher in den Vorlesungen verwendet wurde. Bedeutende Leistungen wurden im Kreis von Zamość in der Philologie erbracht. In der Epoche, in der die ersten gedruckten Ausgaben (*editiones principes*) der griechischen und römischen Schriftsteller erschienen, war der Anteil polnischer Humanisten an diesen Unternehmungen nicht groß; denn erstens haben die Römer niemals die Karpaten überschritten und daher in unserem Lande keine Handschriften hinterlassen, und zweitens konnten in unseren Breiten keine Papyri so viele

---

[5] Vgl. Simonis Starovolsci, *Tractatus tres* (Vratislaviae, 1733); *Scriptorum Polonicorum Hekatontas*, 88.

Jahrhunderte überdauern. Doch zwei Namen der polnischen Philologen aus der Zeit der Renaissance sind in der ganzen Welt berühmt: Andrzej Patrycy Nidecki (1522–1587), der Ciceros Fragmente herausgegeben hat (1561 ff.) und mit Zamoyski in Korrespondenz stand, und Adam Bursius, der Verfasser der *Dialectica Ciceronis* (Samosci, 1604). Das Werk von Bursius war nicht das einzige aus dem Gebiet der Philologie, das in der *Academia Samosciensis* vorbereitet wurde. Szymon Birkowski (Professor ab 1607, gest. 1616) hatte, bevor er den Lehrstuhl übernahm, die Schrift *De collocatione verborum* von Dionysios von Halikarnassos (1602) herausgegeben. Simonides versuchte sich ebenfalls an editorischen Tätigkeiten (Pseudo-Herennius, der heilige Epiphanius), jedoch hat er die Ausgaben nicht zu Ende geführt.

Simonides hat während seines Aufenthalts in Zamość (oder in Czerniźcin, wo er von Zamoyski ein Landgut erhalten hatte) dem Großkanzler manche Dichtungen gewidmet, nämlich *Repotia Zamosciana* (Leopoli, 1592), ein Gedicht aus Anlaß der Heirat des Oberfeldherrn mit der vierten Frau, Barbara Tarnowska, und *Imagines dietae Zamoscianae,* ebenfalls 1592 entstanden, jedoch erst zehn Jahre später (1602) gedruckt. Im ersten Gedicht wurde das Lob Zamoyskis mit den Worten des Flusses Wieprz ausgedrückt, wobei sich die Nymphen, Vepriades genannt, aus der Tiefe des Stroms erheben. Die zweite Dichtung ist ein Zyklus emblematischer Verse für die Porträts im Schloßsaal. Die berühmtesten Dichtungen von Simonides, die in Zamość entstanden, sind: *Hercules Prodiceus* (1602), über Herkules, der den Weg der Tugend, nicht des Lasters gewählt hat; *Pentesilea* (1618), ein Drama über die verderblichen Folgen der weiblichen Leidenschaft, und vor allem die polnischen *Idyllen* (1614), die schönsten in unserer Literatur, in denen er zum polnischen Theokrit und polnischen Vergil (als Verfasser von *Bucolica*) wurde.

Zamoyskis Freude über das Hippeum dauerte nur zehn Jahre. Der schon genannte Georg Braun schrieb über ihn:

> Quocirca huiusmodi laudum praecones prae Myrone illo statuario, Phidia et Apelle pictoribus, et Praxitele sculptore, admiratione digni videntur. Caeterum quum tot huius imperatoris erga Regnum Poloniae extent merita, cum quonam potius eum conferam? Cum Cyrone Persarum illo laudatissimo? An cum Atheniensium Duce Themistocle? Cum Philippo Macedone an Pericle? Sed cum nullo melius eum conferri posse, quam cum Magno Constantino arbitror.[6]

Man kann diesen Worten ein Fragment aus der Biographie Zamoyskis in Starowolskis *Scriptorum Polonicorum Hekatontas* zur Seite stellen:

> In tantum deinde profecerat, ut philosophiae tam plane gnarus esset, quam Plato; geometer quasi Boethius; in numeris Macrobio similis; in dicendo alter Demosthenes; agriculturam quam Vergilius novit; in politicis vero ipsi Stagyraeo par visus; in bellis gerendis Iulio Caesari.[7]

---

[6] Braunius, *Theatri . . . urbium.*
[7] Starovolsci, *Hekatontas,* 37.

Beide Zitate sind freilich Banalitäten der Renaissance.

Der große französische Geschichtsschreiber Jacques-Auguste De Thou (lateinisch Thuanus, gest. 1617) hat in seinem Riesenwerk *Historiarum sui temporis libri CXXVIII* im 5. Band nach dem Tode des Großkanzlers und Oberfeldherrn eine kurze Notiz über ihn eingefügt, in der er mit ein paar Worten auch au das Hippeum erinnerte:

> [...] insignem Academiam in urbe cognomine a se condita in Belsensi praefectura VIII a Leontopoli Russiae Poloniae metropoli miliarib[us] instituit et anno MDXCIV Id[ibus] Maiis ludum aperuit, professorib[us] eximio stipendio ad eam Cracovia invitatis [...].[8]

Der genannte Bursius hat während der ersten jährlichen Gedächtnisfeier in Zamość eine Rede gehalten, die er unter dem Titel *Oratio funebris in anniversario depositionis Illustrissimi [...] Joannis Zamoscii* (1606) veröffentlicht hat. Über das Hippeum sagte er darin folgendes:

> [...] sapientissimus Zamoscius instituit in eadem urbe sua Academiam, cultissimum seminarium omnium bonorum, artium optimarum, scientiarum, virtutum, seminarium Ecclesiae Dei sacerdotum, seminarium Reipub[licae] bonorum civium, seminarium omnis generis hominum, omni ordini, conditionique huius imperii utilium, lucem sapientiae quae non solum huic Roxolaniae parti sed ubique gentium dux sit honestae vitae, magistra morum, officium virtutum.[9]

Simonides sorgte nach dem Tode des Großkanzlers für die Besetzung der Lehrstühle in der Academia. Szymon Birkowski wurde schon genannt; außer ihm kamen folgende Gelehrte: Tomasz Drezner (ab 1610, gest. 1617), Wojciech Nowopolski (ab 1610, gest. 1644), und Kaspar Solski (ab 1616, gest. 1653). Simonides widmete den Kollegen und Freunden Gedichte, darunter Ursinus, Ciekliński und Hilchen. Piotr Ciekliński (1558–1604) war der zweite begabte polnische Dichter im Zamość-Kreis am Ende des 16. und Anfang des 17. Jahrhunderts. Er hat eine polnische Bearbeitung der Komödie *Trinummus* von Plautus veröffentlicht (1597). Die Handlung wurde in Polen, genauer in Lemberg, lokalisiert. Das Schauspiel wurde wahrscheinlich am Hofe des Jan Ostroróg in Busk, nicht weit von Zamość entfernt, aufgeführt. In Zamość entstand auch die Übersetzung einer Komödie des Aristophanes, entweder von Simonides oder von Ciekliński.

Auf Veranlassung des schon genannten David Hilchen, der seit 1591 noch als Syndikus in Riga mit Zamoyski mehrere Begegnungen hatte und der 1603 nach dem Streit mit seiner Stadt in Zamość Schutz gefunden hatte, schrieb Daniel Hermann (gest. 1601) ein Gedicht *De Marte cum Musis in nova Academia Samosciana coniuncto*

---

[8] Vgl. Jacobus Augustus Thuanus, *Historiarum sui temporis*, Bd. 5 (Coloniae Allobrogum, 1630), 1179–1780.

[9] Vgl. Adam Tytus Działyński, ed., *Collectanea vitam resque gestas Ioannis Zamoscii [...] illustrantia* [...] (Posnaniae, 1861), 207.

Carmen (1594). Die Einleitung dazu hatte Hilchen geschrieben. Der Verfasser forderte darin, daß die Jugend von Livland und Preußen nach Zamość gehen soll, um dort zu studieren ("si qui ingenium praeclaris quibusque artibus excolere volunt, et linguam simul Polonam et Latinam discere cupiunt, Samosciam Urbem petant"). Hermanns Gedicht wurde von Hilchen, dem Verfasser der Vorrede, als "copiosus, varius" und "eruditus" gerühmt. In seiner Vorrede bewunderte er auch den Großkanzler und Oberfeldherrn als Begründer der Akademie und schickte ihm Wünsche für erfolgreiche Unternehmungen.

Daniel Hermann, der Verfasser des Gedichts, hat das Hippeum mit den antiken Unterrichtsanstalten, aber auch mit den französischen und italienischen Hochschulen verglichen, er schätzte jedoch die *Academia Samosciensis* höher; denn dort würden die gelehrten Musen mit Mars vereinigt.

Unter dem Mäzenatentum des Großkanzlers ist die Übersetzung von Ovids *Metamorphosen* von Jakub Zebrowski entstanden, die zum ersten Mal nach dem Tode von Zamoyski, 1636, veröffentlicht wurde. Szymon Starowolski, ein Polyhistor und Verfasser vieler Bücher, war in seiner Jugend Hofmann des Großkanzlers und Oberfeldherrn.

Die Akademie in Zamość existierte bis 1784, jedoch ihre Blütezeit lag in den letzten Jahren des 16. und den ersten Jahrzehnten des 17. Jahrhunderts und dauerte letztlich nur bis zum Tode von Simonides, der die Pläne des Begründers treu ausgeführt hatte. Unter Simonides' Leitung entwickelten sich die anderen Dichter, die einen wirklichen Kreis bildeten. Der größte von ihnen wurde im Jahrhundert von Angelo Maria Durini *Pindar Latinus* genannt. Stanisław Grochowski, der Herausgeber des Gedichts *Divus Stanislaus* (1604), schrieb an Bernard Maciejewski über den Verfasser: "magni ingenii et excellentis doctrinae vir." Stanisław Reszka schrieb direkt an Simonides: "Josepho tuo nihil vidi castius, Divo Stanislao nil maturius, Aelinopeane nil vehementius."[10] Der berühmte Justus Lipsius spendete Simonides folgendes Lob: "Macte, spondeo tibi, paucos in Europa esse (et est ingens poëtarum copia, ut apum), paucos, inquam, qui meo quidem sensu sic scribant."[11] Scaliger, vielleicht nicht weniger berühmt, pries den Großkanzler als Dichter, der "écrit fort bien,"[12] und der schon genannte Dousa ehrte Simonides mit den Worten, daß er "quanto orchestrae plausu Parnassi collem institerit."[13] Zamość war also zur Zeit des Großkanzlers und Oberfeldherrn Zamoyski und zur Zeit des lateinischen Dichters Simonides wirklich das letzte Bollwerk der polnischen Renaissance.[14]

Universität Łódz

---

[10] Vgl. Simonis Simonidae *Opera omnia* procurante Angelo Maria Durini (Varsoviae, 1772), 252, 332–333. Simonides hat in seiner Jugend das Drama *Castus Ioseph* herausgegeben (1587). *Divus Stanislaus* und *Aelinopean* wurden schon genannt.

[11] Vgl. Simonidae *Opera*, 41.

[12] Vgl. Józef Kallenbach, *Les humanistes polonais* (Fribourg, 1891), 35.

[13] Kallenbach, *Les humanistes polonais,* 37.

[14] So hat der große polnische Gelehrte Stanisław Łempicki Zamość genannt.

L'Umanesimo scandinavo di Olaus Magnus

FABIO STOK

Olaus Magnus (Olåf Mansson) è una delle figure più rilevanti dell'Umanesimo svedese. Nato nel 1490 a Linköping (Östergötland), dopo aver ultimato gli studi in Germania (a Rostock e in altri centri) collaborò con Sten Sture il Giovane e, per qualche anno, con Gustavo Vasa. Dopo l'adesione di quest'ultimo alla Riforma luterana (1527) seguì in esilio il fratello Johannes (Jöns Månsson, 1488–1544), arcivescovo di Uppsala (titolo ricoperto, dopo la morte del fratello, anche da Olaus), rimasto fedele alla Chiesa romana. Nel 1539 Olaus pubblicò a Venezia la *Carta marina*,[1] la prima importante rappresentazione cartografica della Scandinavia. Partecipò in seguito al Concilio di Trento e trascorse gli ultimi anni di vita a Roma, dove dette alle stampe l'*Historia de gentibus septentrionalibus* (1555), un monumentale trattato sulla geografia e sulle popolazioni dell'Europa settentrionale.[2] Morì nel 1557.

L'opera ebbe un grande successo editoriale e costituì per un paio di secoli la principale fonte di conoscenza della Scandinavia nella cultura europea:[3] fino verso la metà del sec. XVII ne vennero pubblicate oltre venti edizioni, oltre a diverse traduzioni in italiano, francese, neerlandese, tedesco ed inglese.

---

[1] Cf. E. R. Knauer, *Die "Carta Marina" des Olaus Magnus von 1539* (Göttingen, 1981).

[2] Cf. J. Ijsewijn, *Companion to Neo-Latin Studies*, vol. 2 (Leuven, 1998), 353.

[3] Sulla diffusione delle opere dei fratelli Magnus, cf. il sondaggio di A. Maranini, "Edizioni postillate di Giovanni e Olaus Magnus in alcune biblioteche emiliane," *Classiconorroena* 2 (1993): 5–6. Sull'utilizzazione letteraria dell'*Historia*, cf. J. E. Hankins, "Milton and Olaus Magnus," in *Studies . . . T. W. Baldwin* (Urbana, 1958), 305–310; A. Perelli, "Olaus Magnus' *History* and Torquato Tasso's *Torrismondo*," in *Tra Testo e Contesto. Studi di scandinavistica medievale*, ed. C. Santini (Roma, 1994), 13–20. Cf. inoltre — in Olaus Magnus, *A Description of the Northern Peoples, 1555*, ed. P. G. Foote, 3 vols. (London, 1989) — P. Cherchi, "Antonio de Torquemada e Olao Magno," 21–32; A. Perelli, "Olao Magno a Ferrara: l'*Alfeo* di Orazio Ariosti," 209–244; e C. Vecce, "Olao Magno e Jorge Luis Borges," 411–423.

In epoca recente l'*editio princeps* dell'*Historia* venne riproposta in edizione anastatica da John Granlund,[4] che aveva pubblicato già un ampio commento dell'opera, in lingua svedese.[5] Negli ultimi anni sono state pubblicate una parziale traduzione in spagnolo[6] e una traduzione annotata in inglese.[7] Le opere di Olaus (e del fratello Johannes) sono state il tema di un convegno internazionale svoltosi a Roma nel 1996.[8]

Nella prefazione dell'*Historia* Olaus colloca la propria opera nella tradizione dei grandi geografi ed esploratori dell'Antichità ed accenna ad una propria personale esperienza di esplorazione, in riferimento probabilmente alla missione da lui effettuata in Norvegia e nella Svezia settentrionale nel 1518–1520. Un esame anche superficiale dell'opera rivela però che essa non è affatto una cronaca o il resoconto delle esplorazioni dell'autore, ma un complesso trattato in 22 libri nel quale sono citati numerosissimi autori antichi e medievali, per lo piú non attinenti a quel mondo del Settentrione che è l'oggetto del libro. L'*Historia* contiene, va precisato, anche notizie di carattere documentario (ne vedremo oltre un esempio), derivate cioè dalla conoscenza e dall'esperienza diretta dell'autore; ma la parte nettamente preponderante dell'opera è fatta di citazioni e di parafrasi di fonti libresche, spesso raccolte in forma di centoni.[9] Anche per le notizie relative ai *mirabilia*, alle quali l'*Historia* deve molta della sua fortuna letteraria, più che di tradizioni locali Olaus risente del modello classico costituito, per questo aspetto, soprattutto dalla *Naturalis historia* di Plinio il Vecchio.[10]

L'insistente accostamento fra fonti classiche e mondo del Settentrione che Olaus propone nella sua *Historia* risponde ad un progetto culturale che non è stato ancora analizzato con precisione, e che è connesso all'atteggiamento di Olaus nei confronti dell'Umanesimo europeo e quindi di quella *Res publica litterarum* di cui ci stiamo occupando.

Converrà partire, nella nostra esplorazione, da Johannes Magnus, il fratello di Olaus. La sua *Historia de omnibus Gothorum Sueonumque regibus*, pubblicata da Olaus nel 1554, ebbe un'influenza considerevole nella storiografia svedese successiva, per l'affermazione di quell'ideologia "goticistica" che sarà in auge soprattutto negli anni dell'espansionismo svedese di Gustavo Adolfo.[11] Nella costruzione storiografica di Jo-

---

[4] Cf. Olaus Magnus, *Historia de gentibus Septentrionalibus, Romae 1555*, intro. J. Granlund (Copenhagen, 1972).

[5] Cf. Olaus Magnus, *Historia om de Nordiska Folken i Svensk översättning*, utg. av Michaelisgillet, 1909–1925; Kommentar: J. Grandlund, 4 vol. (Uppsala, 1951; rist. Östersåla, 1976).

[6] Olao Magno, *Historia de las gentes septentrionales*, ed. J. D. Terán Fierro (Madrid, 1989).

[7] Olaus Magnus, *A Description of the Northern Peoples*, ed. Foote.

[8] *I fratelli Giovanni e Olao Magno. Opere e cultura fra due mondi. Atti del Convegno internazionale: Roma-Farfa*, ed. C. Santini (Roma, 1999).

[9] Per i primi capitoli del libro 1, cf. F. Stok, "Olao Magno e la scoperta del Nord," in *Columbeis*, vol. 6, ed. S. Pittaluga (Genova, 1997), 105–124.

[10] Cf. R. Scarcia, "La tradition de la paradoxographie classique dans l'oeuvre d'Olaus Magnus," in *Tra Testo e Contesto*, 55–66; L. De Anna, "Mostri e alterità in Olao Magno," in *I fratelli*, 101–115.

[11] Cf. J. Svennung, *Zur Geschichte des Göticismus* (Stockholm, 1967); K. Johannesson, *The Renaissance of the Goths in Sixteenth-Century Sweden*, trad. J. Larson (Berkeley, 1991); idem, "The Goths as Vision and Propaganda in Swedish History," in *I fratelli*, 157–166.

hannes, gli Svedesi sono i discendenti dei Goti, la popolazione germanica stanziatasi, dopo la caduta dell'Impero Romano, nei Balcani, in Italia e nella penisola iberica. Questa operazione consentiva a Johannes da una parte la rivalutazione dei "barbari" Goti (analoga a quella effettuata nella stessa epoca, sulla scorta di Tacito, per i Germani), descritti quale popolazione eroica e moralmente integra chiamata a salvare il Cristianesimo dopo la caduta dell'impero; dall'altra la nobilitazione degli Svedesi, funzionale alla politica nazionale ed antidanese di Gustavo Vasa. L'operazione promossa da Johannes si configura, nel complesso, quale versione moderna di un genere che aveva avuto notevole fortuna nella tarda Antichità e nel Medioevo, quello dell'*origo gentis*:[12] Johannes, del resto, si riallacciava dichiaratamente a Cassiodoro e a Jordanes, che avevano proposto un'operazione di questo tipo per i Goti.

L'adesione di Olaus al progetto storiografico del fratello è rilevabile già nella prefazione della sua *Historia*, dove egli delinea un canone storiografico "gotico" che comprende Saxo Grammaticus, Cassiodoro, Iordanes, Paolo Diacono, Procopio, i contemporanei Albert Krantz e Francesco Irenico e lo stesso Johannes Magnus. Già nella definizione di questo canone Olaus evidenzia però una certa autonomia rispetto alle posizioni del fratello: mi riferisco alla presenza in esso, in posizione di rilievo, del danese Saxo Grammaticus, autore dal quale Johannes, nella sua *Historia*, prende frequentemente le distanze, per l'orientamento anti-danese che caratterizza il suo Goticismo. I *Gesta Danorum* di Saxo, pubblicati a Parigi nel 1514, erano stati del resto utilizzati, negli anni successivi, a favore delle rivendicazioni danesi sulla Svezia.[13] Analoghe riserve sono rilevabili, nell'opera di Johannes, anche nei confronti di un altro degli autori citati da Olaus, Albert Krantz, autore di una *Cronica regnorum aquilonarium* pubblicata dopo la morte di Johannes, ma della quale quest'ultimo possedeva, fin dal 1525, un esemplare manoscritto.[14]

L'atteggiamento nazionalistico non è ovviamente estraneo ad Olaus: esso è rilevabile, come è stato osservato, già nella *Carta marina*, nella collocazione decentrata assegnata allo Iutland rispetto alla penisola scandinava.[15] Nella più tarda *Historia*, però, Olaus assume una prospettiva più meditata, che lo porta a trattare non del solo regno di Svezia, su cui verteva l'opera del fratello, ma più in generale delle *gentes septentrionales*, e ad adottare una prospettiva che pone l'accento, più che sulla particolarità e sull'esclusività, sulla comune appartenenza delle popolazioni settentrionali non solo alla stirpe gotica, ma anche a quella germanica e (come vedremo), più in generale, al mondo antico.

Nell'elaborazione di questo progetto Olaus tenne certamente conto della già citata *Germaniae exegesis*, pubblicata nel 1518 da Francesco Irenico (Franz Friedlieb, 1495–1549) e largamente utilizzata nell'*Historia*. Irenico aveva effettuato un'operazione nei confronti delle fonti antiche per diversi aspetti analoga a quella di Johannes, volta a

---

[12] Cf. — anche per la bibliografia precedente — H. Wolfram, "Le genre de l'Origo gentis," *Revue belge de philologie et d'histoire* 68 (1990): 789–801.
[13] Cf. Johannesson, *The Renaissance of the Goths*, 103–105.
[14] M. E. Ruggerini, "Gli idoli del tempio di Uppsala," in *I fratelli*, 281 n.
[15] Cf. Johannesson, *The Renaissance of the Goths*, 180.

nobilitare l'antichità germanica emersa, nei decenni precedenti, soprattutto in seguito alla riscoperta della *Germania* di Tacito.[16] Di notevole interesse è il fatto che Irenico comprendesse nella propria rivalutazione anche la tradizione "gotica", includendola nella più generale cultura germanica.

Olaus, con la sua *Historia*, estende ulteriormente la riscoperta della tradizione "gotica" e delinea una civiltà "antica" che comprende non solo i popoli del Settentrione, Goti e Germani, ma gli stessi Romani, accomunati da analoghi valori civili e morali. Questa operazione, di cui mostrerò alcuni esempi, è connessa ovviamente agli obiettivi che Olaus si proponeva con la sua opera. Johannesson ha insistito sul ruolo di *Fürstenspiegel* che l'*Historia* avrebbe dovuto avere, per le classi dirigenti svedesi (lo stesso accumulo di citazioni classiche terrebbe conto della scarsità di libri in circolazione nella Svezia dell'epoca).[17] È difficile, tuttavia, ricostruire con sicurezza l'idea che Olaus poteva avere, negli anni '50, della diffusione svedese della propria opera; almeno in parte la sua *Historia* presuppone un pubblico internazionale (quello che effettivamente ebbe). L'*Historia* esprime, però, l'idea che Olaus aveva dell'Umanesimo svedese: un'idea nella quale l'antica solidarietà fra i Goti e il mondo classico costituisce il fondamento di un Umanesimo europeo fortemente integrato, unificato dalla cultura classica (oltre che, nella visione dei fratelli Magnus, dalla centralità della Chiesa cattolica).

In questa prospettiva l'*Historia* si configura quale una *summa* culturale di carattere enciclopedico,[18] come si evince già dall'*inscriptio* dell'*editio princeps*, che vale la pena trascrivere integralmente, in quanto evidenzia anche l'attenzione con cui Olaus curò la stampa della propria opera:[19]

> Historia de gentibus septentrionalibus, earumque diversis statibus, conditionibus, moribus, ritibus, superstitionibus, disciplinis, exercitiis, regimine, victu, bellis, structuris, instrumentis, ac mineriis metallicis, & rebus mirabilibus, necnon universis pene animalibus in septentrione degentibus, eorumque natura. Opus ut varium, plurimarumque rerum cognitione refertum, atque cum exemplis externis, tum expressis rerum internarum picturis illustratum, ita delectatione iucunditateque plenum, maxima lectoris animum voluptate facile perfundens. Avctore Olao Magno Gotho archiepiscopo Upsalensi Suetiae & Gothiae primate. Cum indice locupletissimo. Cautum est privilegio Iulii III Pont. Max. ne quis ad decennium imprimat.

Alla cura tipografica del testo e delle annesse xilografie corrisponde l'elaborata struttura formale dell'*Historia*, che rinvia da una parte al modello pliniano, dall'altra

---

[16] Cf. G. Cordes, *Die Quellen der Exegesis Germaniae des Franciscus Irenicus* (Tübingen, 1966).

[17] Cf. Johannesson, *The Renaissance of the Goths*, 163–168.

[18] Cf. F. Stok, "Enciclopedia della comunicazione nella *Historia* di Olao Magno," in *I fratelli*, 387–410.

[19] Cf. C. Santini, "Strategie della comunicazione nella *Historia* di Olao Magno," in *I fratelli*, 309–331.

all'*Hexaemeron* di Ambrogio e al *De civitate Dei* di Agostino, del quale replica il numero dei libri, 22.[20] Anche la simmetrica suddivisione in due parti (di 11 libri ciascuna) obbedisce all'esigenza di integrare i diversi aspetti dell'antichità nordica, evitando di assegnare un ruolo eccessivamente marcato all'evangelizzazione della Scandinavia. Ispirandosi probabilmente all'analoga operazione proposta per i Danesi dal citato Saxo Grammaticus, Olaus propone una visione fortemente integrata della storia dei popoli settentrionali, parallela e contigua a quella del mondo antico in epoca precedente alla diffusione del Cristianesimo.

Cercherò di avvalorare questa lettura dell'opera di Olaus con l'esame di alcuni capitoli dell'*Historia*, tratti tutti dal libro 14 ("De variis conditionibus Aquilonarium populorum"), che è dedicato a quella che oggi chiameremmo l'antropologia delle popolazioni settentrionali: Olaus esamina in particolare l'abbigliamento (capp. 1–2), la famiglia e il matrimonio (capp. 3–16), la giustizia (capp. 17–25), e l'educazione (capp. 26–28).

Nella *praefatio* Olaus anticipa quella che è la tesi principale dell'intero libro, cioè l'originaria moralità delle popolazioni scandinave. In apertura egli cita le più importanti testimonianze di autori antichi e tardoantichi sulla Scandinavia:

> Mirari quispiam non debet, in amplissimis Septentrionalium terris, praesertim peninsulae Scandianae (quam Plinius ob incompertam magnitudinem alterum orbem & Iordanes ac Paulus Diaconus vaginam sive officinam gentium appellant), diversitatem fore habituum ac vestimentorum pariter & morum ac conditionum, circa incolarum convictum & cohabitationem adventantium alienigenarum ac iudicia utriusque, & quam syncera tranquillitate veteribus institutis olim adhaerentes singuli concorditer vivere dicebantur.

La definizione che Olaus attribuisce a Plinio il Vecchio è in realtà attribuita da quest'ultimo alla popolazione degli Hilleviones, *quae alterum orbem terrarum eam appellat*; da parte sua Plinio ritiene la Scandinavia un'isola *inconpertae magnitudinis* (*Nat. Hist.* 4.96). La definizione di *vagina gentium* è del solo Iordanes (*Get.* 4.25), mentre Paolo Diacono si limita ad indicara la Scandinavia quale luogo d'origine di numerose popolazioni emigrate (*Hist. Lang.* 1.1). Il brano citato, e gli altri che propongo oltre, evidenziano anche il non sempre facile latino di Olaus, il cui stile nervoso e concitato, come ha osservato Johannesson, si differenzia notevolmente da quello pacatamente "ciceroniano" del fratello Johannes.[21] Isacson, sulla base di un sondaggio effettuato sul libro 15, ha definito il suo latino "clumsy and unidiomatic."[22]

All'originaria moralità delle popolazioni scandinave Olaus contrappone, nella *praefatio*, la corruzione introdotta recentemente dai Luterani:

---

[20] Cf. Johannesson, *The Renaissance of the Goths*, 205–206.
[21] Cf. Johannesson, *The Renaissance of the Goths*, 163.
[22] Cf. K. Isacson, "A Study of Non-Classical Features in Book XV of Olaus Magnus' *Historia de gentibus septentrionalibus* 1555," *Humanistica Lovaniensia* 38 (1989): 189.

ubi nunc crescente discordia paucissimi sua orte contenti videntur. In quo rursus mirandum non est, dum eo processit astuta hominum pernicies, ut quisque suae destructionis factus sit artifex ingeniosus, foris scilicet habitu discissus & intus in mente corruptus, foris legibus parere simulans & ubique disseminans dolos. Quorum tandem effectu & exitu ad ultimum infamiae plenus & omnibus odiosus e vita discedet.

La polemica antiluterana affiora correntemente nell'*Historia*, e riflette l'orientamento che Olaus recepì, negli anni dell'esilio, dal Concilio di Trento. Particolarmente significativo, per questo aspetto, è il passo in cui Olaus, dopo aver lodato la naturale *verecundia* delle popolazioni settentrionali, rimprovera agli *haeretici Lutherani* l'introduzione di raffigurazioni pittoriche di *nudae mulieres*, che comunque "numquam tamen naturalem candorem in gente castis moribus instituta extinguere valuerunt" (13.50).

Affrontando nel cap. 3 il tema dei matrimoni nobiliari ("De nuptiis Illustrium ac Nobilium personarum"), Olaus fornisce alcune notizie ricavate dalle *Variae* di Cassiodoro (una delle citate *auctoritates* "gotiche"), relative al matrimonio di re Theidahadus (cf. 10.3 del 534). Sulla base di queste notizie, relative ovviamente agli Ostrogoti del sec. VI, egli formula un giudizio sulla "moralità" che caratterizzerebbe, in ambito matrimoniale, le popolazioni della Scandinavia:

> Vera autem ornamenta matronarum non vestes sed pudicitia (Pythagora teste) aestimantur. Nec visum est umquam in Septentrionalibus regnis ut mulieres pendentibus margaritis in auribus ornarentur, quia ibi turpe in foemina, turpe in milite & turpissimum in Principe reputaretur.

Il rinvio a Pitagora ed il relativo contesto derivano da Giustino, che a 20.4.12 scrive che *vera ornamenta matronarum pudicitiam, non vestes esse*. È peraltro probabile che non leggesse Giustino direttamente, ma tramite il *De institutione* di Francesco Patrizi (cf. 4.5), una delle fonti più utilizzate dell'*Historia*. Il passo evidenzia la tecnica utilizzata correntemente da Olaus, per la quale alla realtà scandinava sono attribuiti contesti che nelle fonti (nel nostro caso Cassiodoro e Giustino/Patrizi) sono relativi a tutt'altre tematiche. Questa operazione è fondata su quello che costituisce il postulato fondamentale dell'opera di Olaus, la solidarietà che legherebbe l'antichità nordica e quella classica.

Questo postulato è evidenziato, nel passo in esame, dall'opposizione che Olaus propone fra le antiche popolazioni scandinave, rispettose di una moralità testimoniata nel mondo classico da Pitagora, e le popolazioni "selvagge" del Nuovo Mondo:

> Insuper & fatuus diceretur & esset qui labiis gemmas aut margaritas pro ornatu alligaret, prout Petrus Martyr in descriptione novi orbis meminit, videlicet quod Reges & magnates Indorum in populo talem ornatum certatim gestant in labiis suis.

Per la notizia relativa alle Americhe Olaus dovrebbe essersi basato sul *De novo orbe* di Pietro Martire d'Anghiera (1530), dove però non si parla di gioielli ma solamente di perle. A prescindere da questa imprecisione, l'operazione di Olaus è di un certo interesse quale testimonianza dell'atteggiamento della cultura dell'epoca nei confronti del Nuovo Mondo. Nel contesto dell'*Historia* l'opposizione Scandinavia/Americhe è chiaramente finalizzata ad avvalorare quell'accostamento fra antichità scandinava ed antichità classica che Olaus persegue nella sua opera.

Un altro buon esempio della tecnica compilatoria di Olaus è offerto dal cap. 4, relativo alle doti ("De rigore pudicitiae & armorum interpretatione"). Dopo aver fornito alcune notizie ricavate dalle *Gesta Danorum* di Saxo Grammaticus, Olaus si sofferma sul particolare per cui la dote nuziale è costituita, nella tradizione nordica, da armi:

> Dos quidem a marito offertur, sed non ad muliebres delicias aut novae nuptae comptum vel fastum, ut significatione intervenientium armorum in nuptiis declararetur quod (sicuti in hasta, quae signat prima veterum connubia olim fuisse violenta ex raptu) etiam uxores fortibus & bellicosis coniunctae severum & minime effoeminatum sed virilem cultum magna operando probarent. Nam & hastam Iunoni consecratam esse veteres Romani existimabant & eius statuae ut plurimum hastae innixae cernuntur. Hasta enim significat nuptias olim ferro diremptas: framea vero & scutum ut feminae meminisse debeant ex illustri seu nobili stirpe (ut eam communiter cum marito defendant) prodiisse. Hisque consummatis cum pactione dotis hasta solemni ritu eiicitur extra fenestram palatii nuptialis, in signum mutui foederis & perpetuae cohabitationis.

Dell'antica pratica del rapimento a scopo nuziale Olaus tratta più dettagliatamente nel cap. 9, dove essa è attribuita però alle popolazioni baltiche e slave. Anche in questo contesto, va osservato, la valutazione che Olaus propone del fenomeno è tutt'altro che negativa, come rivela già il parallelo che egli propone, in quell'occasione, con il ratto delle Sabine ad opera di Romolo.

Nel capitolo in esame, la notizia relativa alla lancia dedicata dai Romani a Giunone è ricavata da un'altra delle fonti correnti dell'*Historia*, il *Cornu copiae* di Niccolò Perotti (1489).[23] L'accostamento che Olaus propone fra realtà classica e realtà scandinava è ben evidenziato dal "nam" che introduce questa notizia, che è volta evidentemente a confermare l'appartenenza delle due realtà ad una stessa dimensione etica. La notazione successiva, sul significato che avrebbero le diverse armi assegnate in dote, sembra dello stesso Olaus. La successiva notizia sull'uso di gettare la lancia *extra fenestram palatii nuptialis* è invece documentata da fonti seicentesche, e costituisce quindi la più antica testimonianza su questa consuetudine. È questo un esempio significativo del modo in cui Olaus tende a sovrapporre notizie disparate, ricavate in parte da fonti in parte da testimonianze dirette, in termini non sempre ricostruibili con precisione.

I capp. 15 e 16 sono dedicati all'adulterio ("De adulteris ac poena eorum") e ve-

---

[23] Cf. N. Perotti, *Cornu copiae*, 1.123, ed. J.-L. Charlet e altri (Sassoferrato, 1989). Cf. anche F. Stok, "Perotti e Olao Magno," *Studi Umanistici Piceni* 16 (1996): 123–136.

dono anch'essi giustapposte notizie sulla realtà contemporanea e notizie tratte da fonti classiche. Significativa, in questo senso, appare già l'apertura del cap. 15, con il suo richiamo ai grandi poeti latini e alle loro città di origine:

> Quemadmodum praeclarae urbes Italiae ob excellentissima hominum ingenia vel facinora pro eorum perpetuanda memoria ingentes statuas posuere, ut Verona suis [sic] Plinii, Mantua Virgilii, Roma Herculi, ita & Germanicae ac Gothicae civitates ob heroica gesta statuas virorum excellentium in locis publicis apponere non dubitarunt, ut Brema sui Rolandi & Scheningia vetustissima urbs Ostrogothorum sui Thuronis longi, qui duobus concatenatis saxis rationabili causa ad clavam in humeris descendentibus pingitur, quia honestum & iustum illi visum est lege multare vel caede corripere qui matrimonialem pudicitiam spurca oppressione defoedare praesumebant.

Ho riprodotto il passo dell'*editio princeps*, curata dallo stesso Olaus, che contiene però forse qualche errore di stampa (non sono chiari, nella costruzione sintattica del brano, il plurale "suis", che potrebbe essere riferito ai due Plinii, e l'isolato dativo "Herculi"). La diffusione delle statue di "Rolando" nella Germania settentrionale è ben documentata: una prima statua di "Rolando" era stata eretta a Brema attorno al 1181; quella esistente all'epoca di Olaus risaliva al 1404. Funzione analoga, legata all'amministrazione della giustizia, aveva anche la statua di "Ture Lång" esistente a Skänninge, raffigurata nella xilografia che accompagna il capitolo dell'*Historia* nell'*editio princeps*.

Seguono un ennesimo riferimento polemico alla riforma luterana, alla quale è attribuita anche qui in questo caso la responsabilità di aver introdotto costumi immorali (con un significativo inciso sulla frequenza comunque bassa degli adulteri nella città di Skänninge) e, con il consueto salto temporale con cui Olaus accosta correntemente fonti antiche e testimonianze moderne, il rinvio ad un autore che abbiamo già incontrato fra le fonti dell'*Historia*, il "gotico" Cassiodoro, ancora per un passo delle *Variae* (9.18.9, del 533–534), relativo questa volta ad una legge di Athalaricus:

> Sed tractu temporis Lutheranorum impunita libidine haec statua deleta est, ne vel signo vel terrore vel poene metu a scelerato opere vel proposito eius aspectu revocarentur impuri. Nullibi tamen in toto Septentrione severius puniri solent diversorum generum malefactores, maxime adulteri (rarissime licet reperti), quam in hac urbe. Quia, ut Cassiodorus lib. IX in edicto Alarici Regis Gothorum asserit, impium est iudices illis esse remissos, quos coelestis pietas non patitur impunitos.

Analoga commistione antico/moderno è rilevabile, sempre a proposito della repressione dell'adulterio, nel cap. 16, dove Olaus cita di seguito una legge municipale del re Magnus Erikson (sec. XIV) ed un brano di Plutarco:

> Mulier adulterans testimonio sex virorum deprehensa perdit dotem & quicquid secum tulit in cohabitationem viri qui ea suscipiet, immo vitae utriusque potes-

tatem habet & haereditatis eorundem vigore municipalium legum patriae Gothorum & Sueonum [...]. Ne autem hoc solum in gentibus his praticari videatur, simile apud Plutarchum Problemate centesimo quintodecimo de Cumaeis, quomodo Onobotim mulierem sic appellatam in adulterium repertam in forum deductam & saxo impositam, omnibus spectandam proponebant, inde super asinum collocatam & circa urbem pervectam in eundem locum restitui oportebat, unde infamis reddita est, & ab eodem tempore lapis tamquam impurus & delectabilis vitabatur.

Con il titolo *Problemata* Olaus si riferisce a due dei *Moralia* plutarchei, le *Quaestiones Romanae* e le *Quaestiones Graecae*, pubblicate con questo titolo e numerazione continua, nella traduzione latina, di Giampietro di Lucca (1477).[24] L'episodio citato da Olaus è a *Mor.* 291F: la *mulier* "Onobotis" di cui egli parla, va precisato, è frutto di un'erronea interpretazione che eredita dall'edizione a stampa, dove il gr. ἡ ὀνοβάτις, "che cavalca l'asino", è diventato un nome proprio. Olaus segnala, in questo caso, la somiglianza fra le due notizie, tratte dalla storia svedese recente e da quella romana antica. Ad esse egli ne aggiunge una terza, relativa ai Germani del I sec. d. C. descritti da Tacito:

Praetera legislatore Tuiscone prioribus seculis inter alias scelestorum poenas una fuit levior, ut adulterae uxori maritus abscisis crinibus nudae verbera iniiceret, ut refert Cornel. Tacitus.

Nella *Germania* (cf. cap. 19) Tacito non attribuisce però a Tuisto la consuetudine che egli descrive (e che è attestata peraltro anche da fonti longobarde): Tuisto è citato da Tacito, ma al cap. 2, genericamente come legislatore dei Germani. La sovrapposizione si spiega con il fatto che Olaus non ha utilizzato direttamente la *Germania* di Tacito, ma le riprese che ne aveva fatto Francesco Irenico nella sua *Germaniae exegesis*: da quest'ultima opera egli riprende il rinvio a Tacito che propone nell'*Historia*.

Gli esempi proposti sono sufficienti, direi, ad evidenziare la tendenza di Olaus ad assimilare consuetudini, usi e valori comuni alle popolazioni settentrionali (Goti e Germani) a quelle dell'Antichità classica, ricorrendo spesso ad attribuzioni e a sovrapposizioni che possono anche suscitare qualche perplessità. Esse rivelano una tecnica di compilazione, mediante la quale Olaus utilizza per il mondo settentrionale fonti che con esso non presentavano alcuna attinenza, ma insieme anche il progetto culturale dell'Umanesimo di Olaus.

Università di Roma Tor Vergata

---

[24] Cf. F. Stok, "Olao Magno e Plutarco," *Classiconorroena* 6 (1995): 12–14.

L'epopea di Elia Berger sulla Santa Croce e la storia ungherese

LÁSZLÓ SZÖRÉNYI

Elia (in ungherese, Illés) Berger (1562–1645) è una delle figure più significative della letteratura neolatina ungherese, e nello stesso tempo una delle meno conosciute. Ciò non dipende solo dal minore interesse degli studiosi per l'età rodolfina, rispetto all'umanesimo ungherese del s. XV, o alla produzione poetica e storiografica dei Gesuiti e degli Scolopi in Ungheria, ma anche dalla convinzione generale che la sua principale opera storica, *Tria volumina Historiarum, videlicet Chronologia cum sua Isagoge* (tra i tanti titoli, che si leggono nella redazione manoscritta, questo è, secondo il Kulcsár, il più fondato) fosse rimasta incompleta e che fosse comunque definitivamente perduta. In effetti, nel 1603 il Berger aveva chiesto all'imperatore Rodolfo II — re d'Ungheria col nome di Rodolfo I — di nominarlo (sull'esempio di altri illustri predecessori come Antonio Bonfini, Johannes Sambucus, e Gian Michele Bruto) storiografo reale della corte ungherese.[1] La sua richiesta, grazie all'appoggio dell'arciduca Mattia, fu accolta dal sovrano nel 1604; Berger mantenne questa carica sia sotto Rodolfo, sia sotto il suo successore Mattia II; il titolo di storiografo reale gli fu confermato anche da Ferdinando II e nel 1637 da Ferdinando III. Il Berger, in cambio di un modesto stipendio, doveva consegnare a scadenze regolari determinate parti della sua opera storiografica; all'inizio del 1641 ormai tre grossi volumi erano pronti per essere stampati e furono consegnati ai Gesuiti per essere sottoposti al controllo della censura. Non sappiamo i motivi che impedirono di fatto la pubblicazione dell'opera, mentre anche il testo manoscritto rimaneva sepolto e ignorato da tutti nella Biblioteca Universitaria di Budapest, là dove fu ritrovato, solo cinque anni fa, da Péter Kulcsár.[2] Ci auguriamo che alla riscoperta segua in tempi brevi la pubblica-

---

[1] Cf. Eleonore Novotny, *Johannes Sambucus (1531–1584), Leben und Werk* (Wien, 1975); D. Caccamo, "Gian Michele Bruto," 1517–1592," in *Dizionario biografico degli Italiani*, 14 (Roma, 1972), 730–734.

[2] Péter Kulcsár, "Berger Illés történeti művei" (con estratto francese, "Les oeuvres historiques d'Illés Berger"), *Magyar Könyvszemle* 110 (1994): 245–259.

zione di un'opera, che finora è stata citata come una leggenda della storia della storiografia e che merita di essere finalmente conosciuta e studiata.

La perdita della sua opera principale — della cui stessa esistenza si era giunti persino a dubitare — ha messo in ombra anche tutta l'altra vasta e varia produzione del Berger, sia in versi che in prosa. Prima del Kulcsár solo Vilmos Fraknói (1843–1924), che è uno dei più attenti studiosi della storia culturale ungherese, dedicò un saggio al Berger.[3] In esso tuttavia il Fraknói si limitava ad una ricerca sulla genesi dell'opera storica perduta, trattando delle altre sue opere con grande superficialità. Alla base di tale atteggiamento, vi era senza dubbio una condanna globale di tutta la produzione dell'età rodolfina, giudicata nel suo insieme manieristica o pre-barocca. In seguito, pur essendosi progressivamente modificato questo giudizio così tendenzioso, nessuno si è finora occupato della produzione del Berger.

La lettura delle sue opere "minori" mi ha indotto invece a considerare il Berger come un autore particolarmente interessante, che — a parte il titolo di storiografo di corte — aveva meritato anche quello di *poeta laureatus* o *poeta Caesareus*. L'intera raccolta della sua produzione in latino meriterebbe di essere letta ed analizzata; ma per far questo bisognerebbe cominciare col ristamparla, visto che delle edizioni seicentesche delle sue opere non sono rimasti che pochi esemplari, che si conservano solo in alcune fra le maggiori biblioteche europee. Un primo passo in questa direzione mi sembra possa essere l'analisi della prima opera pubblicata dal Berger. Si tratta di un poema epico in 3000 esametri, diviso in tre libri, che fu stampato ad Olomouc, da Giorgio Handelius, nel 1600.

Il poema — seguendo il costume dell'epoca — ha un titolo lunghissimo: *Rapsodiae de Cruce, insigniis Regni Hungarici sanctissimis, et de gestis pro Cruce Christi inclutorum Hungariae Regum faelicissimis: secundum fidem historicam pro Immortalitate Gloriae Hungariae, pro nomine Christi tot seculis Pugnantis* ("Rapsodie sulla Croce, emblema santissimo del regno di Ungheria, e sulle gesta gloriosissime degli incliti sovrani ungheresi fatte per la Croce di Cristo, narrate sulla base della verità storica, per la gloria immortale dell'Ungheria, che per tanti secoli ha combattuto a difesa del nome di Cristo"). Il ruolo di sottotitolo è svolto da una citazione dalla lettera di San Paolo ai Galati (6:14): "Nobis absit gloriari, nisi in Cruce Domini Nostri Jesu Christi" ("Sia lontano da me il vantarmi in nome di ogni altra cosa, all'infuori della Croce del Nostro Signore Gesù Cristo"). Il contenuto, fortemente ideologico, del poema è sintetizzato emblematicamente nell'incisione del frontespizio interno, che nel cerchio simboleggiante il cosmo pone cinque cerchi minori: nel cerchio centrale il crocifisso con citazioni di brani evangelici collocate al posto delle piaghe di Cristo, a sinistra di questa figura un globo imperiale simboleggiante gli imperi, a destra una croce con le estremità allargate in una corona d'alloro, simboleggiante la sovranità; in alto il monogramma greco di Cristo, una croce di Sant'Andrea, e un'ancora, che, insieme ai segni dell'Alfa e dell'Omega, costituiscono il simbolo della gloria; infine la duplice croce dell'emblema nazionale ungherese, che simboleggia la vittoria. Alla base si colloca il

---

[3] Vilmos Franki (Fraknói), "Berger Illés magyar királyi historiographus" ("Elia Berger, storiografo reale ungherese"), *Századok* 6 (1873): 373–390.

motto collegato all'illustrazione emblematica, che — decifrata come rebus e come logogrifo combinati tra di loro — può essere ricostruita come segue: *Christus Alpha et Omega, vincit in imperiis, Crux Christi regnat triumphatque* ["Cristo, che è l'alfa e l'omega, vince sugli imperi, la croce di Cristo impera e trionfa"].

L'opera, nelle sue 161 pagine non numerate, comprende una prefazione in prosa e circa tremila esametri. Il destinatario della dedica è l'arcivescovo di Strigonio (Esztergom) Giovanni Kutassi (1545–1601), cancelliere di Rodolfo II, luogotenente dell'Ungheria, noto mecenate.[4] La prefazione è in sostanza un'analisi araldica, in cui Berger elenca e mette a confronto gli emblemi dei popoli antichi con quelli delle nazioni moderne. Egli passa in rassegna il Marte dei Traci, l'aquila dei Romani, la freccia dei Persiani, il fulmine degli Schipetari, l'ariete degli Armeni e, per converso — con riferimento all'epoca più recente — l'aquila polacca, i leoni azzurri degli Spagnoli, la fascia argentea in campo rosso dell'Austria, e il leone ceco. La conclusione è prevedibile: nessuna nazione possiede un'insegna più nobile dell'Ungheria: questa è la stessa Santa Croce, assegnata dal papa al primo re santo — che ha guidato gli Ungheresi sulla via della conversione cristiana — come simbolo profetico della successiva consacrazione degli Ungheresi a cavalieri, destinati a combattere i nemici della Santa Croce. Per questo nella sua epopea, suddivisa in rapsodie, il poeta intende descrivere gli antecedenti e la storia di questa lotta durata per secoli. Ispirandosi alle opere di Antonio Bonfini[5] e dei suoi continuatori, sua fonte principale per la storia ungherese, egli vuol dimostrare come il filo conduttore della storia della nazione ungherese sia stata sempre la lotta contro i nemici della Croce, lotta che ha avuto persino due re martiri: Wladislao I, caduto nella battaglia di Varna (1444), e Luigi II, morto nella battaglia di Mohács (1526). Contro i Turchi, inorgogliti dall'insegna della mezza luna, la lotta continua ancora, e l'arcivescovo dedicatario dell'opera è uno dei promotori di questa guerra santa.

Non v'è dubbio che l'opera abbia tratto ispirazione da quella guerra antiturca promossa da Rodolfo II, detta "guerra dei tredici o dei quindici anni" e dall'ideologia dominante in quegli anni (1591–1606). L'idea dominante alla corte absburgica era che quella avrebbe dovuto essere l'ultima guerra; di fatto i successi iniziali ottenuti da Rodolfo e dai suoi alleati, avevano diffuso la speranza che l'impero ottomano potesse essere sconfitto definitivamente.[6] Quest'ideologia poteva tuttavia essere formulata in diversi modi. Berger ha deciso di non porre in primo piano il punto di vista imperiale della dinastia Absburgica, ma di considerare gli ultimi eredi di quella dinastia — e in particolare Rodolfo — come gli esecutori testamentari di una missione salvifica dell'intera umanità, la cui storia risale addirittura alla prima origine della specie umana.

Il libro 1 (1–43) si divide in quattro rapsodie. La prima rapsodia celebra le lodi

---

[4] Cf. *Memorabilia Basilicae Strigoniensis* (Budapest, 1856), 88.

[5] G. Rill, "Bonfini, Antonio, 1427/1437–1502/1505," in *Dizionario biografico degli Italiani*, 12 (Roma, 1970): 28–30; cf. István Dávid Lázár, *Antonio Bonfini storico umanista ascolano* (Ascoli Piceno, 1993).

[6] Alexander Randa, *Pro republica christiana. Die Walachei im "Langen" Türkenkrieg der Katholischen Universalmächte 1593–1609* (München, 1964).

della Santa Croce, in parte con riferimento alla simbolica araldica della prefazione. Secondo la finzione del poema la nascita mistica della croce si riconduce naturalmente all'Eden, dove l'albero sacro — come un microcosmo — avrebbe unificato in sé i quattro elementi originari. Questo albero va identificato con quello del paradiso terrestre, di cui i nostri progenitori — seguendo il consiglio infernale del serpente — mangiarono il frutto proibito. Immediatamente dopo il peccato originale, per la volontà di Dio l'albero si trasforma in croce per simboleggiare il trionfo finale su Satana. Segue — in corrispondenza ai cànoni dell'epica — la riunione nell'Averno, in cui Satana incita i propri diavoli contro la Santa Croce. Prima vuol far annientare i Cristiani dalle aquile romane, ed è lui che ispira le persecuzioni contro i Cristiani. Però, fin dal momento della morte di Cristo, la Croce ha praticamente trionfato sull'imperatore Tiberio; in seguito Roma si è convertita alla fede cristiana e più tardi persino l'imperatore Giuliano l'apostata muore confessando la sua sconfitta. La seconda rapsodia — arretrando nella cronologia — ritorna a Costantino il Grande, narrando il sogno antecedente alla battaglia di ponte Milvio e il modo in cui la croce fu scelta come insegna imperiale al posto delle aquile. La terza rapsodia invece narra come il re persiano Cosroe avrebbe rubato la reliquia della Santa Croce; segue la visione dell'imperatore Eraclio, grazie alla quale egli riesce a sconfiggere i Persiani, riportando trionfante la reliquia nella propria capitale. Questo evento della leggenda della Santa Croce viene interpretato dall'autore come auspicio della successiva lotta contro l'Islam; perciò egli narra a questo punto la genesi della *setta* di Maometto. Nella quarta e ultima rapsodia del primo libro, Berger canta l'unno Attila, il re pagano ritenuto l'antenato dei Magiari che vuole occupare Roma, ma di fronte all'intervento del papa e soprattutto atterrito dall'apparizione miracolosa della Croce, si allontana dalle mura della città sacra. La sua morte è orribile, come i peccati da lui commessi nella prima notte di nozze, e la sua anima sprofonda nel mondo infernale.[7] I Magiari pagani, discendenti di Attila, sparsero il terrore in Italia, per vendicare la sua morte; ma Carlo Magno riuscì a domare la loro violenza. Seguendo l'imprecisa cronologia di Bonfini, Berger identifica infatti con i Magiari/Unni gli Avari, annientati da Carlo Magno.[8]

Il secondo libro — diviso anch'esso in quattro rapsodie (43–61) — ha per titolo *Conversio Hungarorum ad Crucem* ("La conversione degli Ungheresi alla Croce"). In questo libro il poeta introduce dei cambiamenti interessanti nella tradizione relativa alla figura di santo Stefano (967 o 977), il primo re che ha convertito gli Ungheresi. In primo luogo, egli trasforma il motivo del "sogno", così come è tramandato dalla leggenda di Hartvicus (Cartuizio).[9] Nella versione originale, è la madre di santo Stefano, Sarolt, a vedere in sogno il protomartire Stefano che le predice la nascita, la grandezza, e la santità futura del figlio; proprio per questo il bambino, che aveva in

---

[7] Cf. *Attila e gli Unni*, ed. Silvia Blason Scarel (Roma, 1995).

[8] Cf. Péter Kulcsár, *Bonfini magyar történetének forrásai és keletkezése* (con estratto italiano, "Fonti e genesi della storia ungherese di Bonfini") (Budapest, 1973).

[9] "Legenda S. Stephani regis maior et minor, atque legenda ab Hartvico episcopo conscripta," ed. Emma Bartoniek, in *Scriptores Rerum Hungaricarum*, ed. Emericus Szentpétery (Budapest, 1938), 2:361–440; sulle vite dei re ungheresi v. László Makkai, "The History of Hungary until 1849," in *Information Hungary*, ed. Ferenc Erdei (Budapest, 1968), 175–250.

origine il nome pagano Vajk, fu battezzato Stefano. Nella versione di Berger, invece, è il futuro padre, Géza, che sogna la Santa Croce, come annunzio della nascita del figlio. In tal modo Stefano nasce come vero e proprio portatore di croce (*cruciger*). Inoltre Berger pretende di identificare la Santa Corona — mandata secondo la tradizione dal papa Silvestro II a Stefano — con l'emblema della croce in essa raffigurato. E' proprio questo che simboleggia l'apparizione della Croce: essa vuole "fidanzare" (cioè impegnare) gli Ungheresi — a partire dal loro primo re cristiano — come soldati consacrati della Croce. Perciò anche al papa Silvestro II appare in sogno la Croce per comunicargli la vocazione di Stefano, re degli Ungheresi; per questo il papa gli manda la doppia croce apostolica, da cui deriverà lo stemma della nazione ungherese! Dopo questa duplice visione il poeta fa pronunziare al re Stefano un discorso: d'ora in poi saranno proprio gli Ungheresi ad assumersi la missione, che anticamente era stata degli imperatori Costantino il Grande ed Eraclio. Essi lotteranno nel segno della Croce contro gli infedeli e, se sarà necessario, adotteranno come insegna quel simbolo sacro. In seguito a ciò gli Ungheresi giurano sulla Croce.

Il terzo libro non a caso è il più esteso (61–161), data la vastità dell'argomento, che si deduce dal sottotitolo: *Gesta Crucigerorum regum Hungariae* ("Imprese dei re ungheresi portatori della croce"). In esso si narra in ordine cronologico la storia dei re ungheresi da Stefano I (o santo Stefano) a Rodolfo I. Ovviamente l'estensione dei diversi capitoli varia a seconda delle fonti a disposizione, ma anche del diverso rilievo della personalità di ciascun sovrano. Così la narrazione delle imprese di santo Stefano diventa una vera e propria apoteosi; in particolare il poeta interpreta la vittoria del re sull'imperatore Enrico come un patto di alleanza. Dopo aver rapidamente passato in rassegna i successori diretti, coinvolti in conflitti dinastici, un grande rilievo è attribuito al settimo sovrano dopo santo Stefano, Ladislao I o san Ladislao (1040–1095), che — secondo una tradizione — sarebbe stato eletto condottiere nella prima Crociata, e solo la morte prematura gli avrebbe impedito di partecipare all'impresa. La grandezza di Ladislao è accentuata dall'interpretazione assolutamente negativa della personalità del suo successore, re Colomanno (1085–1116). Un ruolo di primo piano è assegnato ad Andrea II (1176/77–1235), che partecipò davvero ad una crociata, occupando trionfalmente Damietta e portando con sè diverse reliquie dalla Terra Santa in Ungheria; per queste imprese egli è paragonato all'imperatore Eraclio. A proposito di Andrea II, va sottolineato un episodio, che non ha alcun rapporto con la Santa Croce, ma si collega invece alla concezione tradizionale dell'aristocrazia ungherese. Secondo Berger, Andrea II avrebbe emanato il decreto chiamato "Bolla d'Oro," in base al quale (secondo un'interpretazione tendenziosa) la nobiltà ungherese avrebbe il diritto di opporsi legittimamente agli atti illegittimi del re, da essa liberamente eletto. Questa clausola fu cancellata alla fine del secolo XVII dalla Dieta di Sopron, sotto l'imperatore e re Leopoldo I; durante il Seicento, anzi, persino all'inizio del Settecento è stata questa la base di riferimento di tutte le insurrezioni e guerre d'indipendenza antiabsburgiche.[10] Particolare rilievo assumono in questa parte del poema le imprese del re

---

[10] *De Bulla Aurea II regis Hungariae MCCXXII Andreae*, ed. Lajos Besenyei, Géza Érszegi e Maurizio Pedrazza, Gorleo (Verona, 1999).

Béla IV (1206–1270) che ha ricostruito il paese devastato dai Mongoli nel 1241. L'estesa lamentazione posta in bocca al re riassume tutti quei ricordi funesti delle devastazione di Tartari, Mongoli e Turchi, che dall'umanesimo ungherese in poi sono diventati un vero motivo topico della letteratura ungherese. Interessante notare che il fiume Danubio è definito qui per la prima volta (a quanto ci è dato conoscere) come la lacrima della patria: tale immagine poetica rimarrà viva fino alla letteratura ungherese del Novecento.[11]

In seguito all'estinzione del ramo maschile dei re della casa degli Árpád (1301) viene qui messa in particolare risalto — in relazione al motivo della Croce — la figura di Carlo Roberto d'Angiò e ancor più quella di suo figlio, Luigi il Grande. A proposito di quest'ultimo, viene attribuito alla sua fedeltà nei confronti del re e alla sua devozione per la Croce persino il fatto di aver espulso dal suo paese quegli ebrei che non avevano voluto convertirsi. Il Berger esalta anche la figura del re, poi imperatore, Sigismondo di Lussemburgo, benché egli fosse stato sconfitto a Nicopoli dai Turchi infedeli. Egli considera suo titolo di merito la lotta condotta contro gli eretici Ussiti, che in senso lato egli interpreta come lotta a difesa della Santa Croce. Wladislao I Jagellone (1424–1444), re di Ungheria e di Polonia, caduto a Varna, è interpretato naturalmente come uno dei maggiori eroi: il poeta utilizza qui per la prima volta dei paragoni omerici. Tuttavia egli condanna il re per aver violato i giuramenti di pace conclusi con i Turchi a Szeged; giustamente il sultano Murad (*Amurathes*) ringrazia Dio per aver punito quei cristiani che — seguendo il consiglio del cardinale Giuliano Cesarini — avevano infranto il loro giuramento sulla Croce. Berger segue qui fedelmente l'interpretazione della sconfitta di Varna, che si legge in un celebre epigramma composto da Giano Pannonio, o a lui attribuito, epigramma che fu molto popolare nel periodo della Riforma, che identificava la fallacia papale con i perfidi consigli del cardinale.[12] Berger giudica invece del tutto negativamente Ladislao V (1440–1457) di Absburgo, che — violando il proprio giuramento — ha giustiziato Ladislao, figlio maggiore di Giovanni Hunyadi, mentre con la stessa intensità esalta la dinastia dei Corvini. In primo luogo egli inserisce tra i re ungheresi lo stesso Giovanni Hunyadi — che in realtá era solo governatore — e aggiunge che il papa avrebbe inserito nel calendario la festa della "Transfiguratio Christi" per far ricordare eternamente dalla Chiesa la vittoria di Hunyadi contro i Turchi a Belgrado (1456).

Il capitolo dedicato a Mattia Hunyadi (o Corvino) (1443–1490) è l'apoteosi di tutta l'opera. Tutte le imprese di Mattia, non solo le campagne trionfali contro i Turchi, ma anche quella contro gli Ussiti e perfino la riconquista di Vienna sottratta agli Absburgo, nell'impostazione del poeta dimostrano che Mattia ha servito nel modo più illustre la Santa Croce (impostazione sorprendente da parte di un poeta che poneva tutte le sue speranze di carriera in un imperatore absburgico). Il Danubio trasformato

---

[11] Cf. *Amore e libertà. Antologia di poeti ungheresi*, ed. Marta Dal Zuffo e Péter Sárközy (Roma, 1997).

[12] Cf. Robert C. Jenkins, *The Last Crusader, or the Life and Times of Cardinal Jullian, of the House of Cesarini* (London, 1861).

in lacrime nel periodo dell'invasione tartara ora viene ritrasformato nel Dio *Danubius* che innalza la testa dalle schiume e decora la testa con la corona della gloria per gli Ungheresi. Da santo Stefano in poi Mattia è il primo che viene di nuovo paragonato dal poeta a Costantino il Grande e ad Eraclio. Nell'esaltazione di Mattia arriva persino ad esclamare:

> Maior eras mundo, MATHIA, nec tuus orbis
> Te capit, EVROPE Regum tu maximus ille es (130)

["Eri più grande del mondo, Mattia, il mondo che è tuo non ti racchiude: tu sei il più grande fra i sovrani di Europa"][13]

Dopo la morte di Mattia, il poeta tratta di Wladislao II Jagellone (1456–1516), sotto il regno del quale scoppiò la rivolta dei contadini di Dózsa, che adottarono la croce come emblema. Berger considera questo come un'offesa nei confronti della Santa Croce, comparabile solo alla rottura della pace, confermata col giuramento sulla croce, nel periodo di Wladislao I, e considera che ambedue gli atti avevano giustamente provocato la vendetta divina. La grandezza del re Mattia — ponendo la sua figura accanto a quella dei due Wladislao — viene così ancor di più accentuata. Il poeta esprime i propri lamenti nei confronti di Luigi II, caduto nella battaglia di Mohács contro Solimano il Grande, ed esalta sua moglie — appartenente alla casa degli Absburgo — come annunciatrice degli eventi futuri. Nella lamentazione soggettiva inserita in seguito alla morte di Luigi, il poeta riassume l'enorme sacrificio di sangue versato dagli Ungheresi in difesa della Croce. Berger tratta piuttosto rapidamente di re Giovanni (1487–1540) di Szapolya o di Scepusio, incoronato dopo la battaglia dal partito nazionale; infatti in definitiva egli è diventato alleato dei Turchi. In questo contesto non manca neanche uno sfogo anticlericale, con forti connotazioni protestanti, contro il governatore Giorgio Martinuzzi (1482–1551) che originariamente era stato un frate paolino, divenuto poi cardinale e che — secondo il poeta — ha consegnato la capitale del paese in mano ai Turchi, grazie alla menzogna di un frate cappuccino (1482–1551). È importante notare che Elia Berger era nato protestante e solo dopo i suoi studi effettuati ad Heidelberg si era convertito alla fede cattolica.

Particolarmente significativa è l'esaltazione della figura di Ferdinando I, dato che proprio questo re rese permanente il dominio della casa degli Absburgo sul trono ungherese. Con un colpo di scena audace, il poeta attribuisce a Ferdinando il merito di aver concluso il "matrimonio" della Croce con le aquile, come emblemi araldici, cacciati da Vienna poco prima da Mattia. Grazie a queste nozze simboliche, gli Absburgo, diventando re dell'Ungheria, allo stesso tempo diventano pure autentici portatori della croce. In altre parole, la loro vocazione al governo universale del mondo cristiano non deriverebbe dagli imperatori romani, ma dai santi sovrani ungheresi. Con questo spirito sono descritte le gesta degli imperatori Ferdinando e Massimiliano;

---

[13] Cf. Tibor Klaniczay, *Mattia Corvino e l'umanesimo italiano* (Roma, 1974).

poiché il poeta si concentra solo sulle *imprese compiute dai sovrani*, egli senza nemmeno un accenno alla morte eroica di Niccolò Zrínyi attribuisce a Massimiliano il merito di aver ucciso sotto le mura di Szigetvár il diavolo incarnato (come Lutero per i cattolici, così il sultano è qui considerato come il frutto di nozze diaboliche),[14] arrestando in questo modo l'irresistibile avanzata dei Turchi. Ora tutti, anche i potenziali lettori del poema di Berger, conoscevano in Europa l'impresa eroica di Zrínyi;[15] e tuttavia essi dovevano comprendere il valore allegorico di questa interpretazione e non considerarla come un'esaltazione adulatoria degli Absburgo, visto che gli Absburgo — secondo il poeta — erano gli eredi diretti della missione storica assegnata ai sovrani ungheresi dalla stessa Croce. Questa interpretazione della morte del sultano è significativa; morto il maggiore alleato del demonio, a Rodolfo non rimaneva che portare a compimento quella vittoria, ricevendo in premio la corona della gloria. In questo modo, la conclusione del poema si ricollega alla sua parte iniziale, dove — dopo un prologo in Cielo — avevamo trovato l'assemblea infernale dei demoni e la loro decisione di condurre un'eterna lotta contro la Santa Croce. Se, come è prevedibile, Rodolfo riuscirà a sconfiggere definitivamente i Turchi, egli sconfiggerà anche il potere di Satana, fondando il dominio della Croce e riportando in tal modo di fatto il Paradiso in terra.

La brevità del mio saggio mi impedisce di procedere oltre in quest'analisi. Mi sembra tuttavia di poter affermare che il poema di Berger rappresenta una vera svolta nell'ambito della letteratura neolatina ungherese. Infatti, a partire dagli *Annales* — il poema epico perduto che il Sambuco attribuiva a Giano Pannonio — l'aspirazione costante degli umanisti ungheresi è stata quella di creare un'epopea nazionale.[16] Berger è stato il primo a realizzare questo ideale, unendo tra loro elementi apparentemente contrastanti, come la tradizione ungaro/magiara e quella della dinastia absburgica. Egli ha *magiarizzato* non solo l'intera storia ungherese, ma addirittura tutta la storia dell'umanità, interpretata in senso cristiano. In lingua ungherese la grande epopea barocca sarà fondata da un pronipote dell'eroe di Szigetvár, Miklós (Niccolò) Zrínyi. Le sue fonti epiche sono in parte identiche a quelle di Berger: Omero, Virgilio, Lucano, Claudiano, Girolamo Vida, ecc. Li accomuna il tentativo dell'impostazione universalistica della lotta contro i Turchi in modo da farle assumere una rilevanza cosmica e da farla diventare parte della lotta eterna tra Dio e Satana.[17] Ma assolutamente peculiare è l'illusione di Berger di poter integrare e fondere, in una linea di continuità, le gloriose tradizioni magiare con le glorie della dinastia imperiale

---

[14] Cf. Aby Warburg, *Heidnisch-antik Weissagung im Wort und Bild zu Luthers Zeiten* (Heidelberg, 1920).

[15] Sulla popolarità del tema della morte eroica di Zrínyi nell'epoca, v. la collana poetica *De Sigetho Hungariae propugnaculo a Turca Anno Christi M.D.LXVII obsesso et expugnato* [...] (Witebergae, Excudebat Matthaeus Vvelach, M.D.LXXVII; ristampa anastatica Budapest, 1987).

[16] Cf. László Szörényi, *Arcades ambo. Relazioni letterarie italo-ungheresi e cultura neo-latina* (Catanzaro, 1999), 79–99.

[17] Cf. Amedeo Di Francesco, "Concezione etica e modelli epici italiani nell'*Assedio di Sziget* di Miklós Zrínyi," in *Venezia e Ungheria nel contesto del Barocco europeo*, ed. V. Branca (Firenze, 1970), 351–370.

absburgica. Questa illusione ebbe una durata brevissima. Già nel 1604 — poco dopo la stesura del poema — l'aristocrazia ungherese si ribellò contro il dominio di Rodolfo. Da allora in poi, la tradizione storica ungherese, da Attila a Mattia Corvino, diventa patrimonio nazionale e non può essere associata alle imprese di una dinastia straniera.[18]

Per concludere vorrei aggiungere che sarà solo alla fine dell'Ottocento, nell'utopia di Maurizio Jókai (1825–1904) — il maggior romanziere romantico ungherese — ossia nell'epopea in prosa *Romanzo del secolo futuro* (*A jövõ szàzad regénye*) che la tradizione dei re santi si ricongiunge con quella degli Absburgo, naturalmente proiettandosi nel "secolo futuro" e cioè nel XX secolo. In quel secolo in cui il contrasto tra nazione e dinastia diventa ormai superato, perché il diavolo è chiamato *russo* e *comunista*. . . .[19]

MTA Irodalmi Intézet
(*Institute for Literary Studies of Hungarian Academy of Sciences*)
Budapest, Hungary

---

[18] Cf. *Attila, the Man and his Image,* ed. Franz Bäuml e Marianna D. Birnbaum (Budapest, 1993).

[19] Cf. *Anthologie de la Prose Hongroise,* ed. Jean Hankiss e Léopold Molnos (Paris, 1938), 87–92.

Die Aeneis-Allegorese in *Cristoforo Landinos* Disputationes Camaldulenses

NIKOLAUS THURN

Cristoforo Landinos *Disputationes Camaldulenses* sind in der Forschung gern und häufig bearbeitet worden,[1] handelt es sich doch bei ihnen um ein philosophisch und sozialgeschichtlich bedeutsames Werk, das in einer Zeit des angeblichen Übergangs von jenseits-gewandtem Mittelalter und diesseitsbezogener Neuzeit die Frage nach dem Primat von *vita activa* und *vita contemplativa* aufgreift. Im folgenden soll jedoch nicht der, bereits hinlänglich untersuchte, neuplatonische Hintergrund Landinos beobachtet werden, noch soll das Werk aufgrund der historischen Um-

---

[1] Vgl. u.a. E. Grassi, *Humanismus und Marxismus. Zur Kritik der Verselbständigung von Wissenschaft* (Hamburg, 1973), 120–129; P. Laurens, "Pius Aeneas, héros de la vie contemplative dans les *Disputationes Camaldulenses*," in *Les loisirs et l'héritage de la culture classique. Actes du XIIIe Congrès de l'Association Budé*, ed. J. M. André, J. Angel et P. Demont, Collection Latomus 230 (Brüssel, 1996), 441–451; M. Lentzen, "Zur Problematik von *vita activa* und *vita contemplativa* in den *Disputationes Camaldulenses* von Cristoforo Landino*," in *Acta Conventus Neo-Latini Torontonensis, Proceedings of the Seventh International Congress of Neo-Latin Studies*, ed. Alexander Dalzell, Charles Fantazzi, and Richard J. Schoeck, MRTS 86 (Binghamton, 1991), 429–437; E. Müller-Bochat, *Leon Battista Alberti und die Vergil-Deutung der Disputationes Camaldulenses. Zur allegorischen Dichtererklärung bei Cristoforo Landino*, Schriften und Vorträge des Petrarca-Instituts 21 (Köln, 1968); U. Rombach, *Vita Activa und Vita Contemplativa bei Cristoforo Landino* (Stuttgart, 1991); Th. H. Stahel, "Cristoforo Landino's Allegorization of the *Aeneid*: Books III and IV of the *Camaldolese Disputations*" (Ph.D. diss., Johns Hopkins University, 1968); A. Vallone, "La linea esegetica: Benvenuto, Landino, Vellutello," in *Ricerche dantesche* (Lecce, 1967); J. B. Wadsworth, "Landino's *Disputationes Camaldulenses*, Ficino's *De Felicitate* and *L'Altercazione* of Lorenzo de' Medici," *Modern Philology* 50 (1952): 23–31; R. Weiss, *Cristoforo Landino. Das Metaphorische in den Disputationes Camaldulenses* (München, 1981); E. Wolf, "Die allegorische Vergilerklärung des Cristoforo Landino," *Neue Jahrbücher für das klassische Altertum* (1919): 453–479; C. Zintzen, *Index zu Cristoforo Landino* (Köln, 1998), XV–XIX; idem, "Zur *Aeneis*-Interpretation des Cristoforo Landino," *Mittellateinisches Jahrbuch* 20 (1985): 193–215.

stände, aus denen es erwachsen ist, erklärt werden. Mein Blickwinkel wird ein vorwiegend formaler sein: die Eckpfeiler von Landinos Dante-Allegorese sollen auf die gesamte *Aeneis* übertragen werden, um damit herauszuarbeiten, wie eine Interpretation der *Aeneis* als Ganzes angelegt ist. Dabei möchte ich dem formalen Vorgehen der allegorischen Entwicklung folgen und ein Prinzip aufdecken, das meines Wissens für Landinos Vergildeutung noch nicht beachtet wurde. In einem zweiten Schritt werde ich versuchen, ebenfalls formal die zweite Hälfte der *Disputationes Camaldulenses* mit den ersten beiden Büchern zu verbinden.

Jener zweite Teil der *Disputationes* ist immer aufs neue untersucht worden, in dem Landino durch sein Sprachrohr Leon Battista Alberti eine allegorische *Aeneis*-Interpretation vorträgt, die, in deutlicher Tradition von Fulgentius und Bernardus Silvestris stehend, dennoch ein Maß an Geschlossenheit und ansprechender Form aufweist, daß in ihr die humanistische, allegorische Interpretationsweise zur Blüte gekommen zu sein scheint. Der Schluß lag auf der Hand, daß die Vergil-Allegorie im 3. und 4. Buch die exemplarische Durchführung des im 1. Buch besprochenen Problems vom Verhältnis zwischen *vita activa* und *vita contemplativa* darstellt, und daß damit ein richtiges Verständnis der Allegorese das richtige und aus dem ersten Teil der *Disputationes* nicht eindeutig erschließbare Verständnis der Position Landinos in dieser Frage klären könnte.

Die *Disputationes Camaldulenses* wurden wohl 1472 fertiggestellt, gedruckt aber erst um 1480. Im ersten Buch findet sich ein Disput zwischen Leon Battista Alberti, der die *vita contemplativa*, und Lorenzo de' Medici, der die *vita activa* vertritt. Abschließend finden wir in den Worten Albertis so etwas wie eine Versöhnung der beiden Lebensprinzipien: sie bedingen einander. Im zweiten Buch wird das *summum bonum* nach einer Repetition der antiken philosophischen Antworten christlich in der Annäherung an Gott definiert. Die Vergil-Allegorese der beiden folgenden Bücher teilt sich in das Buch 3, wo die ersten vier Bücher der *Aeneis*, und das Buch 4, wo die Bücher fünf und sechs gedeutet werden.

Die Renaissance hat die *Aeneis* vornehmlich als ein panegyrisch ausgerichtetes Werk gelesen.[2] Gelobt wird jedoch kein sterblicher Mensch, sondern im jeweiligen Protagonisten werden stellvertretend die Tugenden an sich gelobt und die Laster kontrastierend getadelt. Auch der Aeneas Landinos ist solch ein Protagonist. Aeneas ist in Landinos Augen der Mensch, der sich zuerst von den Verlockungen der Sünden freimacht, dann in Karthago der Verlockung der *vita civilis* nicht erliegt und so schließlich nach Italien gelangt, wo er das *summum bonum* findet. Einzelne Orte, Stationen und Personen der Irrfahrten des Aeneas werden als Symbole für Sünden und Tugenden verstanden: so ist Troia das körperhafte und Karthago das aktive Leben.

Die bisherigen Interpretationen haben diese Deutung recht gut herausgearbeitet. Als Eckpfeiler der Allegorie werden im großen und ganzen einhellig folgende grobe Schritte anerkannt: Aeneas entsagt der *vita voluptuosa* mit seiner Flucht aus Troia, er läßt die *vita activa* in Karthago hinter sich und gelangt im sechsten Buch durch seine

---

[2] Vgl. C. Kallendorf, *In Praise of Aeneas. Virgil and Epideictic Rhetoric in the Early Italian Renaissance* (London, 1989).

Unterweltsreise zur *vita speculativa* und dem *summum bonum*. Diese Deutung ist aber keine selbstverständliche: Landinos Interpretation hört zwar mit dem sechsten Buch auf, die *Aeneis* aber geht weiter. Was, soll man sich nun vorstellen, bliebe Aeneas da noch zu tun, wenn er doch den Ort der Kontemplation bereits erreicht hat?[3] Wozu muß er da noch die Kämpfe in Latium durchstehen? Landino selbst hat diese Frage im vierten Buch der *Disputationes* (*Cam.* 4.209–211) anhand der Prophezeiung der Sibylle in *Aen.* 6.83–84 genau so formuliert, und er gibt darauf als Antwort eine Kurzinterpretation seiner Allegorie der Kämpfe in Italien. Zwar verheißt die Sibylle Aeneas mit den Worten *sed terris graviora manent* noch größere Kämpfe in Italien, bei diesen handelt es sich aber nicht — wenn man sie allegorisch auslegt — um externe Kämpfe im praktischen Leben, sondern um interne des Geistes:[4] "Cum enim a communi vita ac hominum coetu te in solitudinem vindicaveris, tunc acriores quasdam veluti faces earum rerum, quas reliquisti, memoria admovet et illarum desiderio acerrimo insurgunt morsus." Das heißt, Aeneas kämpft in Italien — allegorisch gedeutet — nicht einen wirklichen Kampf im praktischen Leben, sondern einen des Geistes, um die Erinnerung an das Leben und die Möglichkeit der Begierde zu vergessen: er ist wie ein Einsiedler, der, in der *vita contemplativa* befindlich, noch von den Phantasien des Lebens geplagt wird.[5]

Aeneas wird also im sechsten Buch zwar das *summum bonum* insofern erreicht haben, als er dies im Elysium zu sehen bekommt; aber er hat damit nicht das höchste, dem Menschen mögliche Sein erreicht. An die von mir eben zitierte Passage schließt Landino eine kurze Skizze an, wie denn die Bücher 7–12 zu verstehen seien. Sie seien ein zweiter Kampf um Troia, wiederum um eine Frau und wiederum mit einem Achilles; aber während Troia das körperhafte Leben bedeutet habe, bedeute Italien das Leben in der *speculatio*; und so würde Aeneas hier nicht unterliegen und fliehen müssen, sondern — ich zitiere — als *victor triumphansque parto regno redeat*.

Für Landino sind also die ersten sechs Bücher nicht eine abgeschlossene Einheit,

---

[3] Rombach, *Vita Activa und Vita Contemplativa*, 149; S. 159 sieht im zweiten Teil der *Aeneis* das praktische Leben verwirklicht: "Als er aber dieses höchste Ziel des Menschen erreicht, verheißt ihm die Sibylle noch härtere Proben als die bisherigen. Sie deutet voraus auf die Kämpfe in Latium und damit über den höchsten Akt der Erkenntnis hinaus und zurück in die Praxis."

[4] *Cam.* 4.209: "Quae omnia gravia ac periculis plena cum perpessus fuerit, quonam modo in Italia duriora passurus est? Non tamen procul a vero aberrat Sibylla. Cum enim a communi vita ac hominum coetu te in solitudinem vindicaveris, tunc acriores quasdam veluti faces earum rerum, quas reliquisti, memoria admovet et illarum desiderio acerrimo insurgunt morsus. ... Venit in Italiam Aeneas, verum eo virtutum genere, quae purgatoriae appellantur, a quibus antea quam penitus expiata sit mens necesse est, ut acerrimum bellum, quem admodum nostri aiunt, spiritus adversus carnem gerat. ... In Italia vero, cum nondum cupiditatem rerum humanarum deponere valeat animus, bella excitantur, aspera illa quidem, sed non in quibus veluti apud Troiam succumbat, sed unde victor triumphansque parto regno redeat."

[5] Vgl. *Cam.* 4.210: "Humanam enim societatem cum deserimus, aut in ferinam vitam per insaniam et atram bilem degeneramus aut heroico robore supra hominem erigimur."

die man allegorisch deuten kann, während die folgenden Bücher lose und ohne Sinn darauf folgen; er präsentiert ein Gesamtkonzept von der *Aeneis*.

Landino behauptet bekanntlich, Homer, Vergil und Dante hätten in derselben Weise ihre Werke aufgebaut und zum selben Ende geführt: Homers Werk sei nichts als ein Lob der Tugend;[6] Vergil habe dieses gewußt und mit Aeneas den Menschen schildern wollen, der sich von den Lastern entsühnt, mit Tugenden ausstattet und schließlich zum höchsten Gut gelangt.[7] In diesem wiederum sei ihm Dante gefolgt.[8]

Um auf ein Gesamtverständnis der *Aeneis*-Interpretation zu kommen, muß man die Worte Landinos ernst nehmen, daß seiner Meinung nach Dante Vergil minutiös gefolgt sei: in diesem Sinne muß die Interpretation der *Divina Commedia* durch Landino mit der Interpretation der *Aeneis* in ihrem Gesamtkonzept und nicht nur hinsichtlich deren erster Hälfte oder allein des sechsten Buches deckungsgleich sein. Der Kommentar der *Divina Commedia* gibt damit den Schlüssel zu einem Verständnis der Allegorie in der *Aeneis*.

Landino hat in seinem Dantekommentar nun die gesamte *Divina Commedia* behandelt. Dabei hat er den Gedanken der drei bzw. vier Tugendstufen, wie ihn Macrobius im Kommentar zum *Somnium Scipionis* (1.8.4ff.) verbreitete, auf den Weg Dantes durch Hölle, Fegefeuer und Himmel angewendet.[9] Mit Hilfe der *virtutes civiles* gelangt Dante unversehrt durch die Hölle, mit Hilfe der *virtutes purgatoriae* reinigt er sich im Aufstieg über den Läuterungsberg, und mit Hilfe der *virtutes animi iam purgati* vermag er sich zum Himmel aufzuschwingen.[10]

Diese Konstruktion können wir auch für Landinos Deutung des sechsten Buches der *Aeneis* wiederfinden, auch wenn Aeneas eigentlich mit Karthago die *virtutes civiles* hinter sich gelassen hat. Landino erklärt im 4. Buch der *Disputationes* (*Cam.* 4.212ff.) die Notwendigkeit der Unterweltschau für die Perfektion von Aeneas: damit der Mensch in der *vita contemplativa* dazu bereit wird, die Laster völlig zu besiegen, muß er sich auf der Schwelle zu ihr (*in limine contemplandarum rerum positus*) die Laster und

---

[6] *Cam.* 3.118: "[sc. opinor] totam Homeri poesim laudem virtutis continere."

[7] *Cam.* 3.119: "ut idem in suo Aenea efficere voluerit, quod ille antea in Ulixe finxerat. Quapropter pulcherrimis poeticisque figmentis eum nobis virum informavit, qui plurimis ac maximis vitiis paulatim expiatus ac deinceps miris virtutibus illustratus id, quod summum homini bonum est quodque nisi sapiens nullus assequi potest, tandem assequeretur."

[8] *Cam.* 4.190: " ... Dantem ... habemus, qui eius itineris, quo mundum omnem ab imis Tartaris ad supremum usque caelum peragrat, in eo sibi illum ducem fingit, in quo summum hominis bonum perquirens miro quodam ingenio unicam Aeneida imitandam proponit, ut, cum pauca omnino inde excerpere videatur, nunquam tamen, si diligentius inspiciemus, ab ea discedat ..."

[9] M. Lentzen, "Cristoforo Landinos Dantekommentar," in *Der Kommentar in der Renaissance* (Boppart, 1975), 167ff.

[10] Vgl. Lentzen, "Landinos Dantekommentar," 174.

die kommenden Gefahren im Geiste vergegenwärtigen.[11] Er befindet sich zwar bereits in der *contemplatio*, nicht aber im völligen Besitz der zweiten Tugendstufe, sondern erst auf dem Weg dazu. Nachdem Aeneas die Laster auf seinem Weg mit der Sibylle kontemplativ kennengelernt hat, reinigt er sich von ihnen theoretisch und mit Hilfe der Erkenntnis. Landino faßt Aeneas' Gang im vierten Buch der *Disputationes* (*Cam.* 4.253.19ff.) zusammen: "Hac igitur ratione impulsus Maro, cum ad summum bonum perducere hominem velit, ita Aeneam instituendum curat, ut primo vitia omnia edoceat, deinde illis eum expiatum ad campos Elysios perducat." Der Weg zum Elysium beginnt mit einer Waschung, d. h. mit der *expiatio* vom Schmutz der Sünden, und ist gestaltet — ganz wie in Dantes Purgatorium — als der pythagoreische Buchstabe, das Y, Symbol für die Entscheidung zwischen Tugend und Laster. Der Weg wird damit zur *purgatio*, zur Reinigung von den Sünden. Lorenzo de' Medici setzt nun im Gespräch die *Aeneis* auf Dantes *Divina Commedia* um: "Nunc enim demum perspicio, quid sibi velit Danthes, qui primum ad inferos descendat atque inde emergens nullam aliam viam nisi per purgatoria loca ad caelum inveniat." An den Seelen im Elysium kann Aeneas nun exemplarisch den Weg und das Ziel des Menschen erkennen: nun erst ist er ganz im Besitz der *virtutes purgatoriae*; er tritt so in die Ebene der nächsten Tugendstufe ein. Dies ist zwar das *summum bonum*, aber nun gilt es, dieses mit den *virtutes animi iam purgati* zu bewahren, und damit muß Aeneas ihrer erst einmal überhaupt völlig inne werden.[12]

In Landinos Interpretation findet sich die *Divina Commedia* aber nicht nur auf das sechste Buch, sondern auch auf die *Aeneis* als Ganzes angewendet. Aeneas' Weg in den Büchern 1–4 ist der Weg von der Sünde bis zur Erreichung der *virtutes civiles*. Auch im Erwerb der zivilen Tugenden kann man erkennen, daß Landino eine Dreigliederung vor Augen hatte: zuerst befindet sich Aeneas in Troia (allegorisch die *vita voluptuosa*), das untergeht. Hier, wie nicht anders im sechsten Buch, erwähnt Landino den pythagoreischen Buchstaben, diesmal um zu zeigen, daß sich Aeneas für die seelische, Paris für die fleischliche Venus entschieden habe. Auf seinem Weg nach Karthago besiegt Aeneas die Laster. In Karthago endlich lernt er die *vita civilis* in ihrer positiven Verwirklichung kennen. Auch hier kann man also ein Kennenlernen der Laster, ein Sich-Reinigen und Gereinigt-Sein beobachten, das damit endet, daß Aeneas von den Tugenden erfüllt ist und sich auf die nächst höhere Stufe begibt, mit

---

[11] 219.7: "Quod cum petit, ostendit mentem praemonstrante ipsa doctrina in sensualitatem descendere. Vult enim vitia, quae ab ea sunt, penitus cognoscere."

[12] So ist auch Landinos Bemerkung zu verstehen, daß Dante den ersten sechs Büchern der *Aeneis* gefolgt sei (vgl. M. Lentzen, *Studien zur Dante-Exegese Cristoforo Landinos* [Köln–Wien, 1971], 154, der Landinos Dante-Kommentar zitiert: "Ma tutta questa è fictione d'Homero, el quale niente altro per quella dimostra, se non chome L'huomo trascorrendo per molti vitii e dipoi purgandosene arriva al sommo bene. Il che imitò Virgilio ne' primi sei libri de' Eneide, et Danthe in queste tre cantiche sequitò Vergilio." Man sollte hier nicht hineinlesen, daß Landino lediglich die ersten sechs Bücher für in dieser Weise interpretierbar hielt: Er schreibt, Vergil habe die ersten sechs Bücher als eine Nachahmung der *Odyssee* verfaßt und Dante sei wiederum Vergil gefolgt. Dies schließt nicht aus, daß Vergil der gesamten *Aeneis* eine einheitliche Allegorie zugrundegelegt habe.

der er nach Italien gelangt. Die Spiele, die Aeneas im fünften Buch abhält, werden von Landino dabei selbst als unwichtig und lediglich zur *delectatio* des Lesers gehörend ausgeklammert (*Cam.* 4.199); seine Überfahrt wird aber bereits durch die *virtutes purgatoriae* ermöglicht.

Die Erinnerung an das Fleischliche ist in Landinos Interpretation des Orakels der Sibylle der Gegenstand der Kämpfe in Italien: dies entspricht seiner Definition der dritten Tugendstufe, die ja die Erinnerung an die Laster gänzlich löschen soll.[13] Landino hat sich entschieden, nicht aufzuzeigen, auf welche Weise man sich vorstellen sollte, daß sich die erste Stufe beim Erwerb der *virtutes animi iam purgati*, das Kennenlernen dessen, von dem man sich zu befreien wünscht, vollziehen könnte. Vielleicht hätte er die Völkerkataloge in *Aen.* 8–9 als ein solches Kennenlernen gedeutet. Die Kämpfe in Italien wären dann die Reinigung in dieser Tugendstufe, der Tod von Turnus der endgültige Sieg, dem — außerhalb der *Aeneis* gelegen, aber von Landino mit den Worten *triumphans parto regno* gleich anfangs angelegt — die Errichtung eines Königreiches der Troianer und Latiner folgen müßte.

Man sieht, wie zumindest auf den ersten Teil der *Aeneis* einerseits eine Gliederung in die *virtutes civiles* 1–4 und die *virtutes purgatoriae* in Buch 6 erfolgt ist, und wie gleichzeitig jede einzelne Tugendstufe dreigeteilt ist in die für ihren Erwerb notwendigen drei *actus*: *cognitio vitiorum*, *purgatio* und *illustratio*.[14] Sie wiederum korrespondieren auffällig mit den drei Tugendstufen.

In seiner Konstruktion in Makro- und Mikro-Ordnung, also den porphyrischen Tugendstufen und den zu ihrem Erwerb jeweils neu ablaufenden, stets gleichen Vorgängen, scheint mir dies Konzept verwandt mit der Schrift *De coelesti hierarchia* des Dionysius Areopagita, deren Inhalt längst allgemeines Kulturgut geworden war.[15] Hier gibt es neun Arten von Engeln, die in drei Ordnungen untergebracht sind. Aufsteigend sind die drei Ordnungen jeweils vornehmlich für eine andere Tätigkeit zuständig: zuerst "reinigen" die einen (*purgatio*), dann "erleuchten" die nächsten (*illustratio*), und die dritten bringen schließlich zur Vollendung (*perfectio*). In jeder einzelnen Stufe aber findet sich dasselbe Schema wieder: von den Engeln der unteren Ordnung sind die *Angeli* die den Menschen "reinigenden", die *Archangeli* die den Menschen "erleuchtenden", die *Principatus* aber die zur Perfektion bringenden Kräfte. Ähnliches bewirken die Engel der zweiten Stufe für die mittleren, und so fort.

Noch ein weiterer Punkt ist beim Erwerb der Tugendstufen zu beachten: sie laufen chronologisch aufeinanderfolgend ab. Das ergibt sich natürlich einmal aus der Tatsache, daß man die nächst höhere nicht erreichen kann, ohne im Besitz der vor-

---

[13] *Cam.* 3.154f.: "Verum audi iam tertium illud eorum genus, quorum animi ab omni vitiorum labe procul absint. Hi igitur in eo prudentiam exercent, non ut delectu quodam habito divina terrenis praeferant, sed ut illa sola noscant solaque, veluti nihil aliud sit, intueantur. Adhibent autem temperantiam, non ut cupiditates coerceant, sed illas penitus ignorent. Eadem ratio erit fortitudinis. Illa enim perturbationes non vincit, sed ignorat. Quin optabit dura atque horrenda sibi offerri, non ut victoriam assequatur, sed ut in eorum oblivione perpetua firmitate perduret."

[14] Diese drei Stufen finden sich sogar im — für die Großinterpretation weniger wichtigen — Betrachten der Bilder vor dem Gang zur Sibylle: vgl. *Cam.* 4.206.

[15] Vgl. etwa Thomas v. Aquin, *Summa Theologiae*, 1.1.quaest. 108; Dante par. 28.

ausgegangenen zu sein. Es ist aber zu bemerken, daß diese zeitliche Abfolge es Landino leicht macht, neben einer allegorischen Deutung der *Aeneis* als eines Werkes, das den Erwerb dieser Tugendstufen aufzeigt, auch gleichzeitig die Deutung des Fulgentius einzubeziehen, in der *Aeneis* würden die einzelnen Lebensalter des Menschen dargestellt.[16] Insofern handelt es sich nicht um die Darlegung eines philosophischen Wertekanons, sondern, bedingt durch die Koppelung an einen zeitgebundenen Vorgang, um einen auf den einzelnen Menschen Aeneas zugeschnittenen Lebenslauf.

Eine richtig verstandene Deutung der Allegorese Landinos würde also lauten: Aeneas durchläuft die drei Tugendstufen der *virtutes civiles* (Buch 1–4), *virtutes purgatoriae* (Buch 6) und *virtutes animi iam purgati* (Buch 7–12). Buch 5 ist vor allem der Erquickung des Lesers gewidmet. Dabei lernt Aeneas in der jeweiligen Tugendstufe erst die Laster kennen, reinigt sich dann von ihnen und kommt am Ende in den vollen Besitz der Tugenden. In Buch 12 der *Aeneis* hat er sich — aber das ist pure Vermutung — wohl gerade mit dem Töten von Turnus von den Lastern in der letzten Tugendstufe gereinigt; der Triumph, das Erringen des Königreiches werden aber von Vergil nicht mehr explizit erzählt. Gleichzeitig altert Aeneas im Erwerb der Tugendstufen ebenso, wie es Fulgentius dargelegt hatte. Seine endliche Heimkehr im Triumph bedeutet deshalb letztlich seinen Tod; oder, wie es Ovid in *Met.* 14.581–608 beschrieben hatte, seine Vergöttlichung. Aeneas' Vergöttlichung wiederum fände so ihre Entsprechung in Landinos Deutung von Herkules auf dem Berg Oeta, die er in Nachfolge von Coluccio Salutati in *De vera nobilitate* darlegt.

Ganz frei von Widersprüchen ist Landinos Interpretation aber nicht: folgt man seiner stillschweigenden Gleichung der *virtutes civiles* als *vita activa*, finden die *virtutes purgatoriae* in der *vita contemplativa* statt. Ist dem aber so, müßte ihr Erwerb ausschließlich an das 6. Buch der *Aeneis* gekoppelt sein. Doch bereits Aeneas' Überfahrt von Karthago nach Italien wird von Landino mit den *virtutes purgatoriae* in Zusammenhang gebracht.[17] Noch größere Schwierigkeiten wären mit einer Erklärung der zweiten Hälfte der *Aeneis* verbunden gewesen.

Landino endete mit dem sechsten Buch der *Aeneis* wohl deshalb, weil mehr zum Thema der *vita activa* und *contemplativa* nicht zu sagen war. Einer minutiösen Deutung der zweiten Hälfte der *Aeneis* hätten sich grundsätzliche Probleme in den Weg gestellt: Erstens hätte Landino eine so große Fülle an Details — ähnlich wie im 5. Buch die Spiele — beiseite schieben müssen, daß die Gültigkeit der Allegorie an sich fragwürdig geworden wäre. Zweitens hätte er immer wieder darauf hinweisen müssen, daß es sich hier um eine pagane Konstruktion handele, die ein Christ nicht in

---

[16] Vgl. *Cam.* 3.120: "Troiae igitur oritur Aeneas, per quam urbem recte, ut puto, primam hominis aetatem intelligimus, in qua, cum ratio adhuc omnis consopita sit, solus sensus regnat."
[17] *Cam.* 4.203: "Nam adventus in Italiam ostendit habitum virtutum iam contractum ita, ut a proposita vita non sit discessurus Aeneas, non tamen earum virtutum, quae sunt animi iam purgati — nam nihil sibi difficile iam proponeretur — , sed earum, quas dicunt purgatorias."

allen Details gelten lassen könne.[18] Und drittens bezieht sich die höchste Tugendstufe auf eine Kategorie Mensch, die keine der am Dialog beteiligten Persönlichkeiten weder verkörperte noch verkörpern wollte, ja die so singulär ist, daß man sie wohl als Ideal, kaum aber als aus eigener Kraft erreichbar annehmen konnte. Ein ähnlicher Schluß brachte auch Petrarca in *De Vita Solitaria* dazu, als er im ersten Buch (1.4) die Tugendstufen erwähnt, in Bezug auf jene dritte Tugendstufe desillusioniert zu schreiben: "Hec perfectorum sunt, qui ubi sint nescio; sed et qui fuerunt, solitudinem amarunt, et si quis unquam superest, quamvis hoc virtutum gubernaculo tutus in alto naviget, puto tamen solitudinis portum amet." Grundsätzlich läßt sich natürlich damit schon bei Petrarca das Schwinden des Interesses am Leben der Heiligen, am Einsiedler- und Mönchswesen bemerken, aber man sollte nicht vergessen, an welchen Ort Landino die *Disputationes* verlegt hat und welche Tradition gerade das Kloster Camaldoli verkörpert.[19]

Sind nun Landinos Bücher 3–4 lediglich eine Veranschaulichung des ersten Buches? Auf diese Frage, die die verschiedensten Lösungen erhalten hat, kann man eine Antwort geben, die aus dem formalen Aufbau des Werkes abgeleitet ist: Buch 1 widmete sich der *vita activa* und *contemplativa* als zweier Pole und endete mit der Versöhnung beider als einander bedingenden Kräfte bei der Ausführung jeder Lebensart. Buch 2 zeigte auf, was man zu erstreben hat: das *summum bonum* ist eine Annäherung an Gott. Buch 3–4 dagegen zeigen an einem Beispiel, wie es erstrebt werden kann.

Insofern teilen sich die *Disputationes Camaldulenses* in drei Arbeitsschritte: eine Gliederung der Lebensarten im ersten Buch, ein Aufzeigen der Zweckbezogenheit des Lebens im zweiten Buch, und ein Beweis der Möglichkeit, ein solches Leben zu leben, in dem Beispiel von Aeneas:[20] ähnlich findet man sie im 5. Buch von Ciceros *Tuskulanen*, denen doch Landino "ad unguem"[21] gefolgt sein soll: Cicero zählt in *Tusc.* 5.68–72 die drei *partes* auf, denen sich der Philosoph, der ja allein die *vita beata*

---

[18] Ähnliche Bemerkungen finden sich in Landinos Kommentar der *Divina Commedia* einerseits auf Homers *Odyssee* und andererseits, um zu erklären, warum Virgilio Dante nur bis zum Purgatorium begleitet. Vgl. Lentzen, *Studien*, 129f.

[19] Während bisher stets darauf hingewiesen wurde, daß die Widmung sich an einen in beiden Lebensarten sich auszeichnenden Fürsten richtete oder daß das Werk ja mit Lorenzo de' Medici einen Protagonisten und in seinem Bruder Piero einen zu Erziehenden besaß, von denen man kaum ein Bekenntnis zur reinen *vita contemplativa* erwarten konnte, ist meines Wissens bisher noch nicht hinreichend darauf aufmerksam gemacht worden, daß Landino das Gespräch in einem Kloster spielen läßt und es nach ihm benennt, das Zentrum eines Einsiedlerordens war.

[20] In diesem Zusammenhang muß bemerkt werden, daß die Person Aeneas die einzige mythologische ist, die in der Exemplasammlung von Valerius Maximus als Exemplum auftaucht: Val. Max. 1.8.7. Gewiß handelt es sich bei der *Aeneis* um Dichtung, und Landino betont dies ja auch mehrfach. Aber nichtsdestoweniger wird in Aeneas ja den Menschen ein Vorbild vorgeführt.

[21] So Marsilio Ficino in einem Brief an Bartolomeo Scala (zitiert auch von Lentzen, *Studien*, 153, Anm. 48), op. 1.667: "Ciceronis dialogos imitatur ad unguem, felicem virum fabricat felicissime."

kennt, widme: der Physik, Ethik und Logik.[22] In 5.83–88 nennt er dann die *fines*, welche die verschiedenen philosophischen Schulen der *vita* zugesprochen haben, damit sie *beata* zu nennen sei.[23] In 5.88 beginnt dann der letzte Teil, wo Cicero anhand vieler historischer Beispiele aufzeigt, daß die angeblichen Übel wie Armut und Verbannung einem Weisen nicht schaden können. Ist auch Ciceros Darstellung verschlungen, und mag eine heutige Interpretation diese Gliederung nicht im selben Maße gelten lassen, für einen Leser des 15. Jahrhunderts sind im 5. Buch der *Tuskulanen* deutlich diese drei Schritte auf eine *Quaestio* über die *vita beata* angewendet: *partes*, *fines* und *exempla*.

Inhalt der *Disputationes* ist damit nicht vornehmlich die Frage nach dem Primat von *vita activa* und *contemplativa*, sondern eine Untersuchung über das tugendhafte Leben schlechthin, dessen Teile, Ziele sowie ein Beispiel, wie man es erreichen konnte, aufgezeigt werden. So wie bei Cicero Logik, Physik und Ethik Teile der philosophischen Betrachtung sind, so ist natürlich auch die *vita activa* Teil des tugendhaften Lebens. Die Frage einer *vita composita* oder *mixta* stellt sich damit nicht — jedenfalls insofern man sie als Zugeständnis an die Interessen etwa eines Lorenzo de' Medici oder Federigo da Montefeltro versteht — , da die Lebensarten, wenn es um ihre höchste Stufe geht, überwunden werden durch das Leben des Vollendeten, der als Einsiedler oder — in allerhöchster Vollendung — als wahrer Heiliger in die Stadt wie das Schaf "mitten unter die Wölfe" (Matt. 10:16) geschickt, sich dieser Polarität entzieht. Doch dies bleibt ein fernes Ideal, das Landino selbst in der Allegorese nur mit kurzen Worten skizziert hat.[24]

Universität Rostock

---

[22] Cic. *Tusc.* 5.68: "ex quo triplex ille animi fetus existet, unus in cognitione rerum positus et in explicatione naturae, alter in descriptione expetendarum fugiendarumque rerum ‹et in ratio›ne vivendi, tertius in iudicando quid cuique rei sit consequens, quid repugnans, in quo inest omnis cum subtilitas disserendi tum veritas iudicandi."

[23] Cic. *Tusc.* 5.84: "Sunt autem haec de finibus, ut opinor, retentae defensaeque sententiae: . . ."

[24] Beeinflußt von Cristoforo Landinos Allegorie hat sein Schüler Ugolino Verino sein Epos *Carlias* konzipiert. Vgl. meinen soeben erschienen Kommentar: N. Thurn, *Kommentar zur 'Carlias' des Ugolino Verino*, Humanistische Bibliothek, Reihe II: Texte, Bande 33 (München, 2002). Hier wird der Weg des Helden wirklich allegorisch bis hin zum Status eines Heiligen verfolgt. Weitere "Verwirklichungen" des hier skizzierten allegorischen Konzepts sind mir nicht bekannt; es ist aber bemerkenswert, daß sich in Marginalien und Kommentaren des *Orlando Furioso* die Behauptung findet, Ariost habe in den Protagonisten den Weg zur Vollendung über die drei Tugendstufen darstellen wollen: vgl. M. Behr, *Romanzi di Cavalleria* (Rom, 1987), 12.

Joannes Dantiscus and Italian Neo-Latin Poetry

PIOTR URBAŃSKI

Joannes Dantiscus lived between 1485 and 1548, and was an eminent Polish Renaissance poet, diplomat, and bishop. In his literary output he used almost all the genres which were popular in the Renaissance: elegy, epigram, epithalamion, threnody, epinicion, itinerary, satire, letter, and liturgical hymnody. In his poetry there are many borrowings from Virgil, Ovid, Statius, Claudian, Tibullus, Horace, Propertius, Martial, Ausonius, and Prudentius. He employed eleven kinds of classical metres. His Latin was pure and clear, quite similar to rhythmical prose.[1]

The classical background of Dantiscus's poetry was described by Stanisław Skimina in 1948 and fully shown in his 1950 edition.[2] He carried out his work, however, in the manner of traditional philology, that is to say by investigating verbal similarities and lexical borrowings from Roman authors as well as by analyzing prosody. This method does not suffice for contemporary Neo-Latin studies, as there are three important but completely overlooked questions: (1) the way of using the classical

---

[1] I would like to thank the Andrew W. Mellon Foundation for a grant in support of my research, and the Harvard University Center for Italian Renaissance Studies, Villa I Tatti, Florence for its hospitality in 1999. I am deeply grateful to all the members of the I Tatti community, especially the Director, Professor Walter Kaiser, Dr. Nelda Ferace, the Librarian, Dr. Michael Rocke, and Professor Salvatore I. Camporeale, for creating an excellent intellectual atmosphere and for their help.

The best introduction to Dantiscus is Zbigniew Nowak, *Jan Dantyszek — portret renesansowego humanisty* [*Joannes Dantiscus — Portrait of a Renaissance Humanist*] (Wrocław, 1982). In English, see Harold B. Segel, *Renaissance Culture in Poland: The Rise of Humanism, 1470–1543* (Ithaca and London, 1989), chap. 7: "At the Courts of Kings and Emperors: Dantiscus as Diplomat and Poet." See also Jozef IJsewijn and W. Bracke, eds., *Joannes Dantiscus (1485–1548): Polish Ambassador and Humanist* (Brussels, 1996); this includes a nineteenth- and twentieth-century bibliography.

[2] Stanisław Skimina, *Twórczość poetycka Jana Dantyszka* [*The Poetry of Joannes Dantiscus*] (Kraków, 1948). Also, *Ioannis Dantisci Poetae Laureati Carmina*. Edidit, praefatione instruxit, annotationibus illustravit Stanislaus Skimina (Cracoviae, 1950). All quotations are taken from this edition.

tradition; (2) the cultural context of poetry; (3) the relationship between Dantiscus's output and earlier and contemporary Neo-Latin poetry, considered by using what is now called the concept of intertextuality.

Generally, we may say that the questions posed above are the main problems of Neo-Latinists who have been educated primarily as classicists and come from such a background; it is often very difficult to perceive Neo-Latin literature as an autonomous collection of texts which indeed imitate classical authors but are independent as far as their cultural context is concerned. In the field of Polish Neo-Latin studies there are two main opinions concerning (1) the position and function of Neo-Latin literature, and (2) reasons why we should be interested in it. Some scholars say that Neo-Latin is an international, cross-border literature; it exists just as French, English, and Polish literatures do. This view may be called the "Curtius view" and is very important if we want to see Early Modern Europe as a cultural unity, as a "*concordia discors*". The second set of scholars argues that it is necessary to consider Neo-Latin literature as a part of national literature. We could not understand Polish literature without carefully reading both Polish and Latin works written in Poland. Of course, it is true if we remember that about fifty percent of Polish literature of the sixteenth and seventeenth centuries was written in Latin.

Undoubtedly in the case of Dantiscus only the first task needs to be undertaken, mainly owing to the lack of high literary Polish in the time of the poet's activity. His poetry and literary activity should be examined as a part of the European humanistic movement. My case study is therefore carried out against the background of Italian Neo-Latin poetry. Paradoxically, this is difficult for various reasons.

(1) On account of Dantiscus's German origins the poet was deeply rooted in German culture. At the age of fourteen he decided to join Polish political life and was sent by his father to the school in Grudziądz to improve his Polish. Next he began to study in the University of Greifswald in Pomerania (1499) and thereafter came into close contact with German and other north European (especially Netherlandish) humanists. Furthermore, Erasmus was his main master. Dantiscus joined Erasmian circles both in Cracow and in Spain. Moreover, we must remember that the inspiration of Erasmus was felt by the poet more keenly than by many other of his Polish followers. Dantiscus not only perceived the literary-philological values of Erasmian *bonae litterae* but also noticed and understood all their deep moral tendencies and implications.[3]

(2) It is quite easy to describe Dantiscus's knowledge of the classics. We can at least say that it was typical for his period. Moreover, the research done by Skimina demonstrated the poet's classical background; at our disposal we also have a list of the classical books that were in Dantiscus's possession. Yet, on the other hand, we can say almost nothing about his knowledge of Neo-Latin poetry. We can ask whether he knew, for example, the main fourteenth- and fifteenth-century authors, or rather

---

[3] See Maria Cytowska, "Erazmianizm w literaturze polskiej XVI wieku" ["Erasmianism in sixteenth-century Polish Literature"], in *Studia porównawcze o literaturze staropolskiej* [*Comparative Studies in Old-Polish Literature*], ed. Teresa Michałowska and Jan Ślaski (Warsaw, 1980), 19.

whether he was familiar with poets contemporary with him. What Neo-Latin poets did he read and own in his library?

(3) Even if we were sure that Dantiscus knew, for example, poetry by Poliziano or Pontano, we might ask whether they were the poet's literary masters. The cases of Poliziano and Pontano are real ones because Jan Harhala and Stanisław Skimina have argued that Dantiscus borrowed two genres from them: the silva (*Silvula de victoria Sigismundi, De profectione Sigismundi, De nostrorum temporum calamitatibus silva*)[4] and the hendecasyllabion (*Hendecasyllabi ad Georgium Sabinum*). But is it really enough to claim Dantiscus as Poliziano's and Pontano's follower? I do not think so. Perhaps he borrowed inspiration directly from classical sources (i.e., Statius and Catullus). Besides, we are not sure if it was possible for Dantiscus to have read Poliziano, Pontano, or other Neo-Latin poets. He studied at the university for such a short time and then was engaged in so many political affairs that it is impossible to establish his reading list.[5]

(4) The problem of the imitation of Neo-Latin authors is very complicated. We can thus formulate the next question. Is it possible to settle upon true verbal similarities and borrowings as in the case of classical texts? Again, I do not think so. Some time ago I started to work on the imitation and emulation of Sarbievius's poetry in England. It was very satisfying as far as poems in English were concerned, different from what was the case with the Latin ones. While reading poems by Anthony Alsop I was quite sure that I was looking at lines borrowed from Sarbievius. Also, the mood of some of the verses was quite familiar to me. But I asked myself: Sarbievius or Horace? Did Alsop imitate Horace in this poem directly or through Sarbievius's poem? When later I consulted the excellent book and edition by David Money,[6] I did not find there any suggestions of possible connections between Alsop and Sarbievius. Therefore I am afraid it is completely useless to search for lexical or phraseological similarities between Neo-Latin authors. So if we are going to establish the "Neo-Latin tradition" in Dantiscus's poetry, we should achieve it not as the philologists used to do — by reference to the classical tradition — but in a modern, intertextual way — that is, by an indication not only of real sources but also of all possible similarities and analogies that could have been in the consciousness of a contemporary literary audience.

Moreover, as some scholars argue, Dantiscus was very independent as a poet, with the exception of his very early poems, such as the *Epithalamium Sigismundi et Barbarae*

---

[4] According to Harhala, Poliziano's *Silvae* are the direct source of the first poem, not Statius. See Jan Dantyszek [Joannes Dantiscus], *Utwory poetyckie* [*Poems*], trans. Jan Harhala, with a life of Dantiscus by Ryszard Ganszyniec (Lwów, 1937), 20 (commentary).

[5] On the knowledge of Italian authors in Cracow see (in English) Jacqueline Glomski, "Italian Influences on Early Humanist Educational Theory at Cracow (1495–1530)," in *Acta Conventus Neo-Latini Bariensis*, MRTS 184 (Tempe, AZ, 1998), 285–292; eadem, "The Italian Grammarians and Early Humanism at Cracow," *Studi Umanistici Piceni* 19 (1999): 47–53.

[6] David K. Money, *The English Horace: Anthony Alsop and the Tradition of British Latin Verse* (Oxford, 1998). See also the review by Colin Burrow, "A Pickwick among Poets, Exiled in the Fatherland of Pickled Fish," *London Review of Books* (19 August 1999): 21–22.

(1512), where he followed Paulus Crosnensis. It is also possible to show a turning point when he abandoned the imitation of classical sources.[7]

So what can we do if we are interested in describing the relationship between Dantiscus and the Italian Neo-Latin poets and their poetry? I would like to signal the following questions:

(1) Are there any Neo-Latin poets mentioned by Dantiscus himself?
(2) What could we say about his personal knowledge of contemporary Italian poets and humanists? Was this knowledge on a literary level as well?
(3) In which poems might we suspect that Dantiscus joined the contemporary discussion on poetry (that is, the problem of literary relationships at the level of literary genre)?
(4) Are there any poets whose literary method as well as choice of cultural attitude were similar and/or analogical to those of Dantiscus?

These questions constitute a starting point for the next part of this paper, which will be only a preview of a research project necessary for preparing a modern edition of Dantiscus's poetry, which will include intertextual and intercultural relationships.

Are there any Neo-Latin poets mentioned by Dantiscus himself?

The first place where we could hope to find some names of contemporary poets is the poem *De Virtutis et Fortunae differentia somnium* (1510). Here there is a description of Virtus's retinue where we find mentioned many names of politicians, rulers, and philosophers. As regards poets, we read:

> Pascua qui cecinit, qui rura et grandia bella,
>   Subsequitur, primus laurea serta gerit.
> Hunc sacri longo comitantur in ordine vates,
>   Quos noscis; frustra nota referre velim. (427–430)

So, poets whom you know; it is vain to mention their names. Of course these names could be very interesting for us: perhaps among them there were not only classical authors.

In fact, there is only one well known Neo-Latin poet directly mentioned by Dantiscus himself as his source. Let us quote:

> Quodsi forte licentia Catulli
> Interdum vel et utimur Marulli,

---

[7] See Jan Harhala, "Przedmowa tłumacza" ["Translator's introduction"], in Dantyszek [Dantiscus], *Utwory poetyckie* [*Poems*], xii–xiv. Harhala argues that Dantiscus's imitation is rather external, in that he imitated only themes and literary form; but through a close reading of his poems it is possible to define their themes and stylistic unity. Cf. Skimina, *Twórczo ę poetycka* [*Poetry*], 140–141.

> Fit, cum copia largior negatur
> Intento gravibus subinde rebus.
> (Hendecasyllabi ad Georgium Sabinum [1539], 2.59–62)

Dantiscus mentions Michael Marullus (c. 1453–1500) for only one reason (besides the marvellous rhyme). Marullus, like Catullus in antiquity, used to employ the hendecasyllable and that is why his poems could be a kind of useful pattern, especially when Dantiscus as a bishop was involved in affairs more important than poetic *inventio*.

Also in the *Hendecasyllabi*, Pietro Bembo (1470–1547) is mentioned, as a friend of both Sabinus and Dantiscus. Obviously they knew each other personally:

> Quod porro quereris, gemis dolesque
> Mortem coniugis optimique Bembi,
> Tecum condolui, piis utrisque,
> Orans, Manibus ut quies beata
> Detur cum superis [. . .] (3.31–36)

In Dantiscus's poetry the relationship with Riccardo Bartolini is the best substantiated one.[8] It has been recently described by Barbara Milewska-Waźbińska,[9] so it will be enough to summarize. In the course of the Congress of Vienna (1515) Dantiscus wrote three poems which involved Bartolini: *De profectione Sigismundi, Ricardo Bartholino*, and *Ad lectorem Hodoeporici*. The first is a kind of a poetic competition, a response to Bartolini's *Hodoeporicon*, published together with it in Vienna. The second contains an explanation of some current moral and political problems discussed by both humanists. And the third is a eulogy of Riccardo's poem. The Italian poet is praised for his very realistic and detailed description of contemporary events. All these poems are unique examples of the intimate humanistic dialogue which, here, is a reflection on Dantiscus's and Bartolini's opinions about the aim of poetry. It is a real dialogue of texts and ideas.

What we could say about Dantiscus's personal knowledge of contemporary Italian poets and humanists?
Was this knowledge on a literary level as well?

I think Petrus de Ravenna, a professor of law at the University of Greifswald, was the first Italian Neo-Latin poet whom Dantiscus met in person. However, Dantiscus was a student in Greifswald for only a few months, so we do not know whether he had the chance to read Petrus's poems or to become familiar with his literary tastes.

---

[8] See his biography in *Dizionario bibliografico degli italiani*, 6 (Rome, 1964), 626–627, s.v. "Bartolini, Riccardo."

[9] B. Milewska-Waźbińska, "The Poetry of Joannes Dantiscus in the Diplomatic Service," in *Joannes Dantiscus (1485–1548): Polish Ambassador and Humanist*, 109–114. See also Skimina, *Twórczość poetycka [Poetry]*, 33–37.

(Unfortunately an edition of Petrus's *Carmina*, Lübeck 1499, has been unavailable to me up to now.) At any rate, as Paulus Crosnensis — whom Dantiscus probably also met in Greifswald, but surely did in Cracow — was Dantiscus's master as a poet (this has been proven by Skimina), it would be interesting to attempt to confirm the same role in the case of Petrus also.

In 1505, at the age of twenty, Dantiscus was in Italy for the first time. However, although he arrived there to study at the university and to refine his humanistic culture, he stayed in Italy only for a very short time (at Venice) and then went on a pilgrimage to the Holy Land. So it very unlikely that he had any opportunity to become familiar with the Italian Neo-Latin poets then. Of course, later he visited Italy several times. On the return journey from the Holy Land he stayed in Sicily, Naples, and Rome. In 1524 he visited Venice and Bari, and five years later Genoa, Mantua, and Bologna. We certainly know that he became familiar with Vittoria Colonna and her cultural circle, as well as with Lasarius Bonamico and Francesco Berni. But perhaps only when he came to Spain did Dantiscus have the best opportunity to read Italian Neo-Latin poetry. The fact overlooked is that, while staying in Spain and performing the functions of an ambassador of the Polish King (1524–1530), Dantiscus met two Italian Latin poets, Baldassare Castiglione and Andrea Navagero, who were performing similar duties. We can be quite sure that they were Dantiscus's colleagues and, perhaps, literary masters. I believe it is necessary to try to analyze possible analogies between the secular poetry written by Dantiscus and Castiglione, as well as that by Navagero.

At this point, brief mention should be made of some points proposed by previous students of Dantiscus. In his first piece of poetry, the *De Virtutis et Fortunae differentia somnium*, there are some similarities to Dante's *Divina Commedia* and Petrarch's *De remediis utriusque fortunae*. Unfortunately, these similarities have not been sufficiently described. Otherwise, this poem has a prefatory verse by the Italian professor of Greek Johannes Silvus Amatus who had taught in Cracow since 1504. Amatus praises Dantiscus as a Tibullan poet,[10] but the text has nothing to do with Tibullus.

Next, in the description of Voluptas's Palace in the *Carmen paraeneticum ad Constantem Alliopagum* (1539), some similarities to Palingenius's *Zodiacus vitae* have been observed. (This is the first alleged example of Polish familiarity with Palingenius.) Unfortunately, this has not been explained in detail, but has only been given as a very general observation that does not offer any proof.

Much information about Dantiscus's relations with Italian humanists and poets could be found in the huge collection of his letters kept in the Centre for Studies on the Classical Tradition in Poland and East-Central Europe, at the University of Warsaw; however, it is not certain that one could find there records concerned with all of Dantiscus's colleagues. To give an example, one could mention the archbishop Philippo Archinto. Though their correspondence has not survived up to the present day, we can be sure that they both were in close contact. There is no doubt that Archinto's *Christiana de Fide et Sacramentis explanatio* was published by Dantiscus and

---

[10] The text is available in Skimina's edition of Dantiscus, *Carmina*, 306.

recommended in his pastoral letter as a catechism for the diocese of Warmia (Ermland). This book emerged from the trend of the Catholic Counter-Reformation, which led to the Council of Trent. Moreover, in the spirit of the programme of ministry being developed in Italy at that time, and, even more significant, on the basis of cultural and literary programmes prompted by the reformist trend, Dantiscus composed his *Hymni aliquot ecclesiastici* (printed in 1548).[11]

In which poems might we suspect that Dantiscus joined the contemporary discussion on poetry (that is to say, the problem of literary relationship at the level of literary genre)?

I think that *Hymni*, the book mentioned above, could be the answer. A proposition suggested by Ann Moss should be the starting point for future investigation:

> This negation [of mythological hymnody expressed in the beginning of the *Hymni*] separates the hymns of Dantiscus from the classicising language of a whole universe of Christian humanist poetry, elaborated with particular enthusiasm by the Italians (G. F. Pico, Sannazaro, Mantuan, and their like). Dantiscus parodies the language of the Latin humanists in order to refuse their verbal style and, implicitly, their compromising vision of a Christianity accommodated to pagan taste. He also rejects, again in stylistic parody recognisable to the "literary" reader, the cruder style of contemporary vernacular hymn-writers.[12]

So it is important to compare *Hymni* to some central example of Italian Latin humanist hymnography. I think that a comparison of *Hymni* with *Meditatio in hebdomada olivarum* by Lancino Corti and other poets *minorum gentium*, would be entirely fruitful [13] Zaccaria Ferreri (1479–1524), who was a nuncio in Poland (1520–1521) and the author of the *Hymni novi ecclesiastici iuxta veram metri et Latinitatis normam*,[14] seems to be an especially interesting *comparandus*,[15] all the more so as replacing the old Breviary hymns was his aim (his book was inspired by Pope Leo X and approved by Clement VII).

---

[11] See Piotr Urbański, *Natura i łaska w poezji polskiego baroku (okres potrydencki): Studia o tekstach* [*Nature and Grace in the Poetry of the Polish Baroque (Post-Trent Period): Analysis of Literary Texts*] (Kielce, 1996), chap. 1: *"Hymny Jana Dantyszka — próba interpretacji"* [*"Hymni* by Joannes Dantiscus — an Attempt at Interpretation"].

[12] Ann Moss, "Johannes Dantiscus, Hymn-Writer," in *Munera Philologica Georgio Starnawski ab amicis collegis discipulis oblata*, ed. Krzysztof A. Kuczyński, Zbigniew J. Nowak, and Hanna Tadeusiewicz (Łódź, 1992), 158.

[13] Studies by Ann Moss: "The Counter-Reformation Latin Hymn," in *Acta Conventus Neo-Latini Sanctandreani*, ed. Ian D. McFarlane, MRTS 38 (Binghamton, 1986), 371–378; "Latin Liturgical Hymns and their Early Printing History, 1470–1520," *Humanistica Lovaniensia* 36 (1987): 112–137; and "Latin Liturgical Hymns of the Reformation Crisis (1520–1568)," *Humanistica Lovaniensia* 40 (1991): 73–111.

[14] Published: In aedibus L. Vincentius et A. Perusia, Romae, 1525, 1549.

[15] See *Dizionario biografico degli italiani*, 46 (Rome, 1996), 809–811, s.v. "Ferreri, Zaccaria."

Marcantonio Flaminio is another important author. Although his *Carminum sacrorum libellus* was published a little later than Dantiscus's *Hymni*, it is possible that Dantiscus became acquainted with it before it was printed.

Are there any poets whose literary method as well as choice of cultural attitude were similar and/or analogical to those of Dantiscus?

This is the most complicated problem, so I would like to give some suggestions and names only:

Iacobo Sadoleto and his programme of Christian humanism and participation in the preparation for the Council of Trent.
Celio Calcagnini, who was very close to Erasmus, especially in the consideration of the concept of human freedom.
A relationship between Dantiscus's concept of Christian culture and the circle of Italian poets and humanists that produced the *Coryciana* (Giano Vitale, Francesco Franchini, and others).
Marcantonio Flaminio and Dantiscus: the similarity of their biographies and their understanding of poetry. Both Flaminio's and Dantiscus's literary lives may be divided into two periods, secular and religious (hymnography). On the other hand, these poets were completely different as far as Ciceronianism was concerned.
Baptista Spagnoli called Mantuanus (1447–1516): his *De calamitatibus temporum* compared with Dantiscus's *De nostrorum temporum calamitatibus silva*. It is important to note that Mantuanus was praised by Dantiscus's master Erasmus and called the *Christianus Maro*. In the sixteenth century Mantuanus's poems were reprinted many times all over Europe. His presentation of a humanistic reformist type of Christianity made him especially popular North of the Alps. It is possible that Dantiscus did know Mantuanus's poems. In addition, Mantuanus belongs to a small group of Neo-Latin poets well known for a long time after their death. For instance, in seventeenth-century England he was still widely read in grammar schools (as Sarbievius and sometimes Castiglione were).

This paper has been concerned with possible relationships as well as influences. In ending, I should like to quote two passages from one of Dantiscus's best poems, the *De nostrorum temporum calamitatibus silva*, printed in Bologna (1529–1530). The following statement from the very beginning of this poem (*Ad lectorem*) is evidence and expression of Dantiscus's consciousness about changes on the cultural map in his time. It was really something new that a poet from Sarmatia (read "Poland") should publish his poem in Italy and perhaps find an audience there:

> Cum nova delectent, nova, lector, Sarmata vates
> Edidit in Latio carmina; nonne placent?
> Si re non alia, placeant novitate, quod ante
> In Latio vates Sarmata rarus erat. (1–4)

Later we read:

> Hos modo praecipites numeros ne sperne, quod atrum
>   Squalorem vultus temporis huius habent,
> Sarmata vel Latios quod perstrepit inter olores
>   Sub gelido natus, qua riget Ursa, polo,
> Hic ubi Sarmaticum vagus Istula fertur in aequor
>   Et tuta portum cum statione beat. (509–514)

University of Szczecin

Paolo Paladino: militare e umanista alla corte di Federico d'Aragona

SEBASTIANO VALERIO

La figura e l'opera di Paolo Paladino, militare e letterato di origine dalmata, rappresentano un capitolo poco noto della storia civile e letteraria del mezzogiorno aragonese. Si è a lungo creduto che il Paladino fosse pugliese, originario della Lesina garganica, mentre egli proveniva dall'isola di Lesina (poi detta Pharos), allora sotto il dominio di Venezia.[1] A generare l'equivoco fu colui che per primo segnalò la figura di questo autore, De Marinis, che nella descrizione dell'unico codice manoscritto che conserva l'opera del Paladino ipotizzò questa provenienza,[2] lamentando comunque una grande difficoltà di reperire notizie certe e affidabili sul suo conto. Tutto quanto conosceva, De Marinis lo apprendeva dal codice 60 della Biblioteca Universitaria di Valencia, un bell'esemplare, integro anche nella rilegatura, proveniente dalla Biblioteca Aragonese di Napoli, di cui aveva seguito la dispersione.[3] Risulta composto di due sezioni omogenee: la prima conserva un'orazione pronunciata dal Paladino e dedicata a Federico, su cui mi soffermerò, mentre la seconda una raccolta di liriche in cui si alternano distici elegiaci e sonetti volgari, sempre dedicata all'Aragonese.

Sulla base del titolo attribuito a Federico d'Aragona, luogotenente generale del regno, è stato facile datare il codice ad un periodo ragionevolmente compreso tra il gennaio e i primi di ottobre del 1496, lasso di tempo in cui Federico assunse questa

---

[1] È questa la notizia riportata da N. De Blasi e A. Varvaro, "Napoli e l'Italia meridionale," in *Letteratura Italiana. Storia e Geografia:* 2. *L'età moderna*, ed. A. Asor Rosa (Torino, 1993), 1:285: "Allo stesso ambiente cortigiano prossimo a Federico va ricondotta anche l'opera del rimatore Paolo Paladino da Lesina, che raccolse per il 'suo illustrissimo principe' una serie di componimenti latini e volgari (questi ultimi una quindicina)."

[2] Cfr. T. De Marinis, *La biblioteca Napoletana dei re d'Aragona* (Milano, 1952), 2:120–121.

[3] M. Gutiérrez del Caño, *Catálogo de los manuscriptos existentes en la Biblioteca universitaria de Valenza* (Valencia, 1930), 2:4–5 (§ 1720–1721).

carica, prima di diventare re alla morte del nipote Ferrandino, sopraggiunta, come è noto, il 7 ottobre di quell'anno.

Le fonti erudite, che pur non numerose si occupano del Paladino, fanno emergere la figura di un giovane, colto e sensibile condottiero, distintosi in particolar modo come marinaio e morto prematuramente. Poco è noto invece della sua attività di letterato, mentre Agostino Fortunio ricorda il padre di Paolo, Nicolò Paladino, autore di un "omnis gestae rei commentariolum," rimasto inedito.[4] Presso la Biblioteca Universitaria di Spalato si conserva nella carte finali del codice M 10, risalente al sec. XVIII, un'opera dal titolo *De Nicolai Palladini Pharii equitis aurati Paulique eius filii militiaeque memorabilibus gestis Historiola*.[5] Non so dire con estrema certezza se questa "historiola" possa corrispondere al "commentariolum" di cui scriveva Fortunio, ma l'opera possiede tutti i caratteri del commentario e in tal senso anche la narrazione in terza persona da parte dell'autore rientrerebbe nella topica del genere. L'opera è interamente dedicata alle figure dei due Paladino, Nicolò e Paolo, e riporta spesso con toni enfatici episodi di battaglie navali con i Turchi avvenute nell'Adriatico, a partire dal 1474 fino al 1499. Di Paolo si legge che fu *corporis praepotens* e *facundia excellens*; la carriera militare del giovane Paladino è seguita dal 1494 in poi, dall'anno in cui le truppe venete guidate da Antonio Grimani scendono nel mezzogiorno a dar manforte agli Aragonesi. A Paolo viene riconosciuta anzitutto la dote dell'*humanitas*, che coniugata al coraggio e all'intelligenza bellica ne faceva un esempio da lodare e seguire. L'*historiola* infatti si sofferma con compiaciuta attenzione sul comportamento da lui tenuto in occasione della conquista di Monopoli (1496). L'impresa fu di particolare importanza per le sorti della guerra; aveva fatto impressione con quanta forza e determinazione i Veneti si fossero impossessati del porto pugliese, saccheggiando pesantemente la città; Paolo Paladino, secondo l'*historiola*, preferì rendere ai Monopolitani la sua parte del bottino, conquistandosi così enorme riconoscenza.

In sostanza Paolo sembra avere vissuto, accanto al padre, le vicende salienti della guerra condotta per mare dai Veneziani contro gli invasori francesi, non mancando di difendere le coste dal pericolo turco. Egli fu a seguito della flotta del Grimani

---

[4] Cfr. A. Fortunio, *Historiarum Camaldulensium libri tres. Ubi aliarum quoque religionum, militiarumque vera inserta est suis locis origo. In fine vero Ambrosii generalis, & interpretis Graeci eximij habetur vita* (Camaldoli, 1575).

[5] Cfr. P. O. Kristeller, *Iter Italicum* 5 (Leiden, 1990), 446. Ringrazio il prof. D. Novakovic che mi ha gentilmente fornito la riproduzione fotografica del manoscritto. Il codice contiene una raccolta di scritti vari sulla cultura dalmata: *Oratio Fratris Vincentii Priboevii O.P. de origine successibusque Slavorum*, Venetiis MDXXXII (fol. 1); *Encomium Thomae Nigro alias episcopi Scradonensis et Traguriensis in vigilias Magistri Vincentii Priboevii O.P.* (fols. 1v–2). Priboevius, orazione *ad Petrum Vitaleum* MDXXV (fol. 2v); Leonardus Ales, epigramma; Nicolai Dominei Arbensis *carmen*, Venetiis per Joannem Antonium et fratres de Salis MDXXXII; *Dell'origine et successi de gli Slavi* oratione di M. Vincenzo Pribevo da Lesena già recitata da lui nella medesima città et hora tradotta dalla lingua latina nell' italiana da Bellisario Malaspalli da Spalato, datata Spalato MDXCV (è il testo, già edito da Manuzio nel 1545, da cui sono tratte le notizie biografiche sul Paladino riportate da Gliubich); Priboevio, orazione a Pietro Vidali; *De Nicolai Palladini Pharii . . . Paulique eius filii militia ac memorabilibus gestis historiola per Joannem Perlotum edita*.

anche in uno dei passaggi più delicati e complessi di quella spedizione, vuoi dal punto di vista militare, vuoi dal punto di vista diplomatico, l'assedio di Taranto, che si protrasse per tutto il 1496. L'*historiola*, che a lungo si sofferma sull'avvenimento, ricorda che questa circostanza dimostrò la lealtà nei confronti degli Aragonesi dei Veneti, che si rifiutavano di occupare Taranto, disposta a cedere a loro piuttosto che alle truppe di Federico. Fu dunque nel corso di questo assedio che Paolo Paladino pronunciò l'orazione conservata nel codice valenziano. La fama e l'importanza del giovane Paladino nel frattempo crescevano, tanto che a partire proprio dal 1496 si affollano le note sul suo conto nei *Diari* del Sanudo. Grazie a questa fonte sappiamo che Paolo Paladino nella seconda metà di quell'anno si allontanò da Taranto assediata, come confermato anche da altre fonti, tra le quali l'*Historiola*: qui si dice che fu particolarmente apprezzato per le sue doti politiche e per la sua saggezza, tanto che divenne, sempre in quel tempo, un fidato consigliere di Bartolomeo Giorgio, proconsole della flotta veneta, che si avvalse del suo consiglio proprio in occasione dell'assedio di Taranto quando il Paladino entrò nel merito di questioni relative *ad rempublicam bene gerendam*, che poi altro non è che il tema dell'orazione.

L'*incipit* è dominato da un primo e immediato paragone tra il principe Federico e il re persiano Artaserse, citato nei *Regum et imperatorum apophthgmata*: il principe avrebbe dovuto seguire l'esempio che Plutarco aveva già portato a Traiano e accettare di buon grado anche quel modestissimo dono che ora Paolo Paladino gli offriva.

Si tratta di un vero e proprio panegirico, in cui l'opera di Federico viene esaltata da molti punti di vista, a cominciare proprio dai numerosi paragoni con grandi re dell'antichità proposti in apertura. Un massiccio dispiegamento di elementi eruditi caratterizza questo esordio tutto sommato breve, eccedendo la stessa topica della "falsa modestia", e creando, volutamente, un contrasto stridente tra l'affermazione della modestia del dono offerto e il ricorso tanto ostentato a testi classici spesso rari e preziosi. Accanto a questo un altro *topos* caratterizza l'*exordium*: la contrapposizione tra lettere e armi, anche qui con una preziosa variante. Non compare una discussione sulla superiorità delle lettere o delle armi oppure una rivendicazione da parte dell'autore di averle con successo praticate entrambe, ma piuttosto si denuncia un'aperta alterità che non significa comunque una classificazione di merito. La guerra sembra però avere interrotto un impegno letterario che altrimenti sarebbe stato più continuo e maggiormente gratificante anche dal punto di vista dei risultati poetici. Paolo Paladino quindi enuncia apertamente l'oggetto attorno a cui verterà la sua trattazione: "Et nobis in illo circa tuum non mansisse et circa tuum domi mansisse et sic circa duo haec tantummodo succinte tamen versandum est."

Che cosa intenda Paolo Paladino per *domi mansisse* è presto detto: un principe non nasce né per sé né per i propri cari; la sua vita appartiene allo stato e alla dinastia e a difendere e mantenere il dominio della propria dinastia sullo stato deve essere spesa. Citando indirettamente Genesi 1:26 e trovando conferma di quanto in esso affermato nel mito pagano di Prometeo, Paolo Paladino accostava finemente il mito delle origini elaborato in ambito cristiano e quello elaborato nella mitologia pagana, e proseguendo su questa strada di conciliazione tra classicità e cristianesimo, riconosceva come nell'animo umano spirasse un afflato divino, riportando la dottrina neoplatonica dell'anima che poteva leggere in Agostino, *De civitate Dei* 10.2. Anche Cicerone

(*Paradoxa* 1.14.6) è chiamato in causa in questa discussione sulla natura dell'anima il cui fine è distinguere tra principi che si fanno guidare dagli istinti animali e principi che lasciano che le loro azioni siano mosse da quanto di più nobile risiede nell'anima umana: naturalmente Federico appartiene a questa seconda schiera.[6] La capacità "politica" di Federico, secondo l'oratore dalmata, si evincerebbe proprio dalla volontà che ha mostrato in passato di viaggiare, di conoscere, di farsi apprezzare per il mondo, novello Ulisse, "qui mores hominum vidit et urbes,"[7] rifiutando le mollezze della vita di corte e rinunciando a restare "ut coeteri regum pueri in aulis et auleis degens." Qui però la lode fin troppo manierata lascia spazio ad una considerazione di estremo interesse, perché il *non mansisse* ha consentito al principe aragonese non tanto di accumulare una generica esperienza di vita, quanto piuttosto di conoscere e confrontare diversi modelli di stato, democrazie, oligarchie, aristocrazie e addirittura di avere avuto a che fare con tiranni, riuscendo ovunque a farsi apprezzare per le straordinarie doti di umanità. Si apre qui una lunga digressione nella quale pare di sentire tutti i *topoi* degli *specula principum*, a cominciare da una breve ma importante discussione sullo stato ideale, che qui sembra più che altro rispondere, in conclusione, ad una monarchia illuminata, retta da un re "filosofo."

Paolo Paladino rifiutava senza mezzi termini la tirannide, e così gli *exempla* negativi di principato proposti erano Giulio Cesare, che riteneva che *regnandi causa* fosse lecito violare ogni regola, e Nerone a cui veniva attribuito il detto, riportato in Svetonio, "sit unus imperator, sit unus rex."[8] Proprio Seneca è chiamato a rendere piena testimonianza di come un principe debba essere e non è certo casuale che egli, vittima del potere dispotico di Nerone, sia chiamato a svolgere questo ruolo. Il sacrificio del "re iniquo" gradito a Giove, con l'esplicito richiamo all'*Hercules furens*, l'affermazione tratta dal *Thyestes*, 388 ("rex est qui metuit nihil...") servono a ricordare che Federico avrebbe potuto essere re ma non lo ha voluto e se era già cosa divina il regnare, il potere regnare e rifiutarlo lo era a maggior ragione, perché se avere l'opportunità di governare un regno era in potere della sorte, rinunciarvi era un atto di libero arbitrio. Quindi Paladino, riprendendo le fila del discorso, pare finalmente convergere verso il vero cuore del "panegirico", la guerra in atto, in cui proprio la capacità di mediazione di Federico e i rapporti politici da lui fondati con il suo attivismo avevano dato i frutti più concreti. Pian piano, emerge la realtà storica, fino a questo punto paludata dietro la coltre dell'erudizione: la presenza delle truppe venete è il frutto di quanto il principe aragonese aveva seminato in gioventù e qui coglie l'occasione di ricordare che della flotta veneta faceva parte anche la nave proveniente

---

[6] Non manca ancora il ricorso ad una fittissima erudizione anche in questo passo: "Inde et ita in *Paradoxis* Tullius: 'tu cum tibi sive Deus, sive natura (ut ita dicam) mater omnium rerum dederit animum praestabilius nihil est aut divinius' et deinde continuat: 'sic te abiicies atque prosternes tamquam inter hominem et quadrupedem interesse nihil putes?', veluti serenissime Princeps, vulgarioris animi Reges et Monarchae plurimi non putaverunt de quibus ad differentiam generositatis tuae in libris *Cosmographiae* suae Strabo et in historiis Polybius, hic diffusius de aliquo, ille circumcisius de plaerisque uterque tamen latissime dissertantur": fol. 5rv.

[7] fol. 6v.

[8] Omero, *Iliade*, 2.204–205.

"ex pharia insula (quae nunc Lexina dicitur),"[9] al cui comando era ancora Nicolò Paladino, coadiuvato dal giovane figlio.

Sembra che così si voglia sottolineare l'importanza del ruolo svolto "in obsidione ista tarentinorum"[10] dalle truppe venete che non solo in questa circostanza, ricorda Paladino, hanno coadiuvato l'azione di Federico, il cui merito maggiore è proprio quello di avere coinvolto le truppe della Serenissima in questa guerra, azione compiuta proprio grazie alle sue *peregrinationes*, novello Bacco, Perseo, Ercole o Ulisse, eroi o dei che conquistarono la fama proprio visitando terre e popoli diversi, ma con un certo gusto per l'iperbole, Paolo Paladino riconosce la superiorità di Federico perché costoro talvolta *efferarunt*, mentre il principe aragonese agì sempre con umanità. L'esercizio di queste virtù, l'esercizio di quella mitezza, di quell'*humanitas*, di cui si è già detto, hanno nei fatti salvato il regno e la dinastia. L'umanista dalmata sa di poter parlare dell'invasione di Carlo VIII come di una vicenda di cui ormai si stavano liquidando gli ultimi fastidiosi strascichi; perché se Federico, viaggiando ha assicurato quel reticolo di relazioni internazionali che hanno permesso di congregare una forte armata per liberare il regno, bisogna rimarcare — sostiene Paladino — che proprio la capacità di rinunciare agli "strata mollia" e alle "domesticae deliciae" ha guadagnato all'aragonese anche la stima dei *provinciales* e dunque con una sola azione aveva conquistato la stima degli stranieri e quella dei sudditi, vincendo così, anzitutto con la raccolta di consenso, la battaglia contro gli invasori e la battaglia, per certi versi più difficile, contro i nemici interni della monarchia, quei baroni che da sempre avevano osteggiato il potere regio. Cosicché, per tornare alla questione posta in capo all'orazione, Federico ha servito la patria tanto viaggiando, quanto soggiornando in essa. Un'affermazione di questo genere deve ancora indurre alla riflessione perché essa veniva portata al cospetto di una città, Taranto, asserragliata non per respingere i Veneziani, ma per non cedere agli Aragonesi.

Nei fatti la retorica celebrativa del panegirico cela una situazione di estrema delicatezza politica di cui il giovane Paladino sembra preoccupato, come molti del resto a quell'epoca. E si coglie altresì tutto l'imbarazzo del militare "veneziano" in Puglia, un po' soldato dell'esercito di Ferrandino impegnato contro l'invasore francese e un po' egli stesso invasore, come dimostravano i fatti di Monopoli. La celebrazione delle doti di Federico non ripercorre semplicemente una diffusa topica comportamentale, ma si tratta, piuttosto che di una pura "celebrazione", di un invito a prediligere determinati modi di agire e di governare: combattere la guerra più che con le armi, con la *modestia* e i *boni mores* era quanto di maggiormente auspicabile si potesse immaginare nella situazione di fatto, nell'assedio di Taranto.

Per mesi infatti la città aveva resistito ad un durissimo assedio, costellato di numerosissimi e sanguinosissimi scontri.[11] Quando i Tarantini compresero di non poter

---

[9] fols. 9v–10r.
[10] fol. 10r.
[11] Cf. G. C. Speziale, *Storia militare di Taranto* (Bari, 1930), 45–54. Si narra ad esempio che il primo comandante delle truppe veneziane, Marco Cizeno (ma Speziale erroneamente scrive Zeno), fu duramente sconfitto dopo un maldestro tentativo di sbarco e che a seguito della sconfitta

più contare sull'apporto dei francesi, ormai in rotta, cercarono di evitare in ogni modo la vendetta degli Aragonesi. Nella seconda metà di quell'anno (1496) particolarmente intensi si fecero i rapporti diplomatici tra Taranto, Venezia e gli Aragonesi, per trattare una resa indolore. Sappiamo che a partire da settembre i Tarantini chiesero con insistenza di potere cedere le armi ai Veneziani ed essere da loro amministrati, come già altri porti pugliesi e che se la Serenissima non avesse accettato, avrebbero preferito darsi ai Turchi.[12] Nelle note inviate da Venezia in Puglia si coglie tutto l'imbarazzo dei Veneziani di fronte ad una proposta allettante ma che di certo avrebbe reso ancora più tesi i rapporti con gli Aragonesi. La risoluzione che fu presa da Venezia fu quella di rifiutare la richiesta di Taranto ma di impegnarsi diplomaticamente sui due fronti per "indure quel populo a la devution dil re Federico"[13] e d'altro canto "imporre" a Federico di rispettare Taranto, concedendo alla città ribelle "immunità et exemptione."[14]

L'esaltazione dell'*humanitas* di Federico così più che ad un atto di dovuta lode risponde ad un consiglio estremamente pratico, quello di risparmiare Taranto, come già aveva fatto in altre circostanze con altre città ribelli:

> Sic advolutae civitates ante pedes tuos tanquam divina quadam maiestate coram constitutae veniam postulaverunt, utque ignosceres utque expectatus eas occupatas reciperes, rogaverunt. Recepisti, ignovisti, pepercisti atque omnes umbra tua invictissima protexisti.

Se l'orazione fu pronunciata al cospetto di un Federico che non si fregiava ancora del titolo di re, dunque prima dell'ottobre 1496, quando ancora non vi erano stati pronunciamenti ufficiali riguardo alle richieste dei tarantini a Venezia, è pur vero che, per chi assediava ormai da tempo la città, quella situazione doveva essere ben nota ancora prima che fosse ufficialmente posta. D'altro canto la proposta che Paladino faceva, senza mai citare Taranto, su come regolare i rapporti con i *provinciales*, coincide in maniera non generica con quella che poi Venezia avrebbe fatto ufficialmente a Federico divenuto re, per il tramite di Andrea Zancan, nel dicembre dello stesso anno. E la cosa in effetti fu poi messa in pratica quando, nel febbraio del 1497, Taranto cadde ma fu risparmiata dal saccheggio. Ad ogni modo l'orazione dovrebbe essere datata ad un periodo precedente all'agosto 1496, perché in quella data, come concordemente riportato da più fonti, il Paladino prese direttamente il comando della nave paterna, a seguito di una malattia che costrinse Nicolò a rientrare a Lesina, mentre nell'orazione Paolo fa intendere di essere ancora in compagnia del padre. Dopo questa

---

fu costretto a rientrare in patria. Cfr. anche G. Giovane, *De antiquitate, et varia Tarentinorum fortuna, libri octo* (Napoli, 1589), 8.3: 128–133.

[12] Cf. Marin Sanuto, *I Diarii*, ed. F. Stefani (Venezia, 1879), 1:704. Nell'ottobre del 1496 i comandanti delle truppe veneziane in Taranto, Melchiorre Trevisan e Antonio Grimani, sono direttamente coinvolti nelle trattative. Quindi, verso la fine dell'anno fu inviato Antonio Zancan a dirimere la questione.

[13] *Diarii*, 1:378.

[14] *Diarii*, 1:380.

vicenda, nell'aprile 1499, i *Diarii* di Sanudo ricordano Paolo accanto al padre, ormai ottantenne e malato e quindi tacciono altre notizie al suo riguardo,[15] come fa anche l'*Historiola* che si conclude con la narrazione di vicende avvenute nel 1499. Ciò potrebbe rafforzare l'ipotesi che si tratti proprio del commentario scritto da Nicolò Paladino. Non è dato di conoscere le circostanze in cui trovò la morte il Paladino, ma è probabile che sia rimasto coinvolto nella rotta della flotta veneziana agli ordini di Antonio Grimani, avvenuta il 12 agosto 1499 per mano dei Turchi presso le isole Sporadi nel mar Egeo.[16]

Università di Bari

---

[15] *Diarii*, 2: 621 (§ 246): "*Item* fo aldito la diferentia di do liesignani, zoè di Polo Paladin, venuto per nome di suo padre miser Nicolò, el cavalier, stato 7 volte soracomito, et per la gratia è exente et ha privilegio fato per pregradi che ogni volta volesse andar soracomito per Liesna potesse andare, tamen è vechio: per questo suo fiol diceva voler andar; a l'incontro Jacomo Barbichii over de Barbis electo al presente soracomito, per il consejo, diceva voler andar lui; et mandati fuora fo ditto Michiel Nicolò Paladin haver anni 80, è sordo et non vol andar; et fo terminato per la signoria in favor de l'altro."

[16] Cfr. S. Romanin, *Storia documentata di Venezia* (Venezia, 1856), 5:138.

Juan Ginés de Sepúlveda, Epistolarum libri Septem, *Salamanca, 1557: Testamento Literario de un Humanista*

JUAN JESÚS VALVERDE ABRIL

La práctica epistolar de Francesco Petrarca, condicionada, aunque no exclusivamente, por el descubrimiento en 1345 de las cartas de Cicerón a Ático, a Quinto, y a Bruto, dio una orientación nueva a un género literario, el epistolar, que estaba llamado a ser, en tanto que instrumento propagandístico de las corrientes ideológicas y espirituales y receptáculo de los avances científicos y de las novedades literarias, un elemento activo fundamental en el abandono de formas de pensamiento típicamente medievales y en la conformación de una ideología moderna.[1]

En efecto, el papel fundamental que jugó la epístola en los siglos XV y XVI resulta evidente con el solo hecho de considerar la producción librera relacionada con este género literario. Pensemos, por ejemplo, en las numerosas ediciones aparecidas en las tres últimas décadas del siglo XV, no sólo del epistolario de Cicerón, sino también de otros autores latinos como Plinio el Joven o Séneca, e incluso de algunos autores griegos.[2] Pensemos también en los tratados de preceptiva teórica, que intentaban orientar dentro de los márgenes éticos y estéticos del movimiento cultural imperante la práctica epistolar, entre otros: las *Elegantiolae* de Agostino Dati (Colonia, 1470), los

---

[1] Cf. C. H. Clough, "The Cult of Antiquity: Letters and Letter Collections," in idem, ed., *Cultural Aspects of the Italian Renaissance* (Manchester, 1976), 33–67; V. R. Giustiniani, "La communication érudite: les lettres des humanistes et l'article moderne de revue," in *La correspondance d'Érasme et l'épistolographie humaniste*, Travaux de l'Institut Interuniversitaire pour l'étude de la Renaissance et de l'Humanisme 8 (Bruxelles, 1985), 109–133.

[2] Cf. Clough, "The Cult of Antiquity," 43–44.

Rudimenta grammatices de Nicolò Perotti (1473),[3] el *Ars epistolandi* de Francesco Negri (Venecia, 1488), el *Tractatus de condendis epistolis* de Konrad Celtis (Ingolstadt, 1492),[4] los *Commentaria epistolarum conficiendarum* de Heinrich Bebel (Tübingen, 1500), las distintas redacciones del tratado de Erasmo sobre la composición de epístolas, como la *Breuissima maximeque compendiaria conficiendarum epistolarum formula* (Erfurt, 1520, edición ésta no reconocida por el autor),[5] el *Libellus de conscribendis epistolis* (Cambridge, 1521, aparecido también en una edición pirata), y finalmente la versión autorizada con el título de *Opus de conscribendis epistolis* (Basilea, 1522; luego revisada y corregida en 1534),[6] o para finalizar el *De conscribendis epistolis* de Luis Vives (Amberes, 1534).[7] Y pensemos, por último, en las colecciones de cartas y misceláneas, realizadas por los propios autores o por sus allegados y discípulos, que fueron apareciendo por toda la geografía europea, como las de Petrarca, Leonardo Bruni, Francesco Filelfo, Eneas Silvio Piccolomini, Marsilio Ficino, Angelo Poliziano, entre los italianos;[8] o, sin ir más lejos, las colecciones del propio Erasmo.[9]

En el caso que aquí nos ocupa, el de Juan Ginés de Sepúlveda, un humanista de formación eminentemente italiana, nos encontramos con una colección de cartas que

---

[3] Cf. C. G. Alessio, "Il *De componendis epistolis* di N. Perotti e l'epistolografia umanistica," *Res Publica Litterarum* 11 (1988): 9–18.

[4] Cf. F. J. Worstbrock, "Die Brieflehre des Konrad Celtis: Textgeschichte und Autorschaft," in *Philologie als Kulturwissenschaft: Festschrift für Karl Stackmann zum 65. Geburtstag*, ed. L. Grenzmann et al. (Göttingen, 1987), 242–269.

[5] Cf. A. Jolidon, "Histoire d'un opuscule d'Érasme: La *Brevissima maximeque compendiaria conficiendarum epistolarum formula*," in I. D. McFarlane, ed., *Acta Conventus Neo-Latini Sanctandreani*, MRTS 38 (Binghamton, 1986), 229–243.

[6] Cf. Erasmus, *De conscribendis epistolis*, ed. J.-C. Margolin, in *Des. Erasmi Roterodami Opera Omnia* (Amsterdam, 1971), 1.2:581–709; A. Gerlo, "The *Opus de conscribendis epistolis* of Erasmus and the Tradition of the *ars epistolica*," in R. R. Bolgar, ed., *Classical Influences on European Culture, A.D. 500–1500* (Cambridge, 1971), 103–114; J. R. Henderson, "Erasmus on the Art of Letter-Writing," in J. J. Murphy, ed., *Renaissance Eloquence: Studies in the Theory and Practice of Renaissance Rhetoric* (Berkeley, 1981), 331–355; H. Funke, "Epistolographie und Rhetorik: Beobachtungen zu Erasmus' *De conscribendis epistolis*," *Res Publica Litterarum* 10 (1987): 93–99; J. R. Henderson, "The Composition of Erasmus' *Opus de conscribendis epistolis*: Evidence for the Growth of a Mind," in A. Dalzell, C. Fantazzi, R. J. Schoeck, eds., *Acta Conventus Neo-Latini Torontonensis*, MRTS 86 (Binghamton, 1991), 147–154; H. Vredeveld, "Towards a Critical Edition of Erasmus's *De conscribendis epistolis*," *Humanistica Lovaniensia* 48 (1999): 8–69.

[7] Cf. J. L. Vives, *De conscribendis epistolis*, ed. C. Fantazzi (Leiden, 1989); J. R. Henderson, "Defining the Genre of the Letter: Juan Luis Vives' *De conscribendis epistolis*," *Renaissance and Reformation* 19 (1983): 89–105.

[8] Cf. Clough, "The Cult of Antiquity," 36–43. A propósito de la epístola en suelo peninsular, cf. D. W. Bleznick, "Epistolography in Golden Age Spain," in S. Bowman et al., eds., *Studies in Honor of Gerald E. Wade* (Madrid, 1979), 11–21; J. N. H. Lawrance, "Nuevos lectores y nuevos géneros literarios: apuntes y observaciones sobre la epistolografía en el primer Renacimiento español," in V. García de la Concha, ed., *Literatura en la época del Emperador*, Acta Salmanticensia: Academia literaria renacentista 5 (Salamanca, 1988), 81–99.

[9] Cf. Des. Erasmi Roterodami *Opus epistolarum*, ed. P. S. Allen, H. M. Allen, y H. W. Garrod, 12 vols. (Oxford, 1906–1958), 1:593–602.

él mismo seleccionó de entre las que formaban su correspondencia y que con la ayuda de su amigo Diego de Neila entregó a la imprenta.

La colección, compuesta por ciento tres documentos epistolares (ochenta y nueve de Sepúlveda, y los catorce restantes remitidos a él por sus corresponsales), ha llegado hasta nosotros en tres ediciones distintas que enumeramos a continuación:[10]

1. Ioannis Genesii Sepuluedae Cordubensis, artium et sacrae theologiae doctoris, historici Caesarei *Epistolarum libri septem*, in quibus cum alia multa quae legantur dignissima traduntur, tum uarii loci grauiorum doctrinarum eruditissime et elegantissime tractantur (Salmanticae: apud Ioannem Mariam da Terranova et Iacobum Archarium, 1557).

2. Ioannis Genesii Sepuluedae Cordubensis, sacrosanctae theologiae doctoris, Caroli V imperatoris historici *Opera quae reperiri potuerunt omnia*, nunc primum singulari studio in Hispania, Italia et Gallia ad publicam utilitatem conquisita et iam simul in lucem edita (Coloniae Agrippinae: in officina Birckmannica, sumptibus Arnoldi Mylij, 1602), 119–289.

3. Ioannis Genesii Sepuluedae Cordubensis *Opera omnia cum edita tum inedita*, accurante Regia Historiae Academia, 4 vols. (Matriti: ex typographia regia de la Gazeta, 1780), 3:72–389.

Claro que además de estas ediciones algunas epístolas se han transmitido de forma aislada, unas veces en manuscritos originales o copias,[11] otras veces en colecciones impresas.[12] Pero para entender esa decisión de Sepúlveda de publicar parte de su epistolario, creemos que es oportuno recordar, aunque sea someramente, las circunstancias vitales que precedieron y que, al margen de cualquier moda, creemos que determinaron la publicación de los *Epistolarum libri septem*.

Cuando se encontraba en la cima de su carrera como traductor de Aristóteles, cuando por su trabajo como exegeta se había ganado la admiración de los personajes más influyentes de la corte pontificia, Sepúlveda acudió a la llamada de Carlos V, que demandaba sus servicios como historiador imperial, y volvió a la patria allá por el año de 1536. Recién llegado de Italia gozó del favor y del respeto de los nobles y príncipes españoles, con los que convivía allá donde la corte estuviera asentada. Pero Sepúlveda no llegó a adaptarse por completo a la vida de la corte española. Eso se

---

[10] Cf. Á. Losada, *Juan Ginés de Sepúlveda a través de su «Epistolario» y nuevos documentos* (Madrid, 1949; repr. Madrid, 1973), 336–341, 371–374. Citaremos las cartas según la numeración con que aparecen en nuestro trabajo: J. J. Valverde Abril, "Io. Genesii Sepuluedae *Epistolarum libri septem*, Introducción, edición, traducción, notas e índices" (Tesis doctoral, Universidad de Granada, 2001).

[11] El original de la carta enviada a Erasmo con fecha de 23 de mayo de 1534 (1.6) se encuentra en la Biblioteka Uniwersytecka Wrocław, MS. R 254.69, fols. 65r–66v; el de la carta 3.6 se halla en la Biblioteca Apostolica Vaticana, MS. 3904, fol. 310r–v (hay copia en la Biblioteca de El Escorial, MS. J–II–22, fols. 176v–178r).

[12] Las *Epistolae clarorum uirorum . . . a Ioanne Michaele Bruto comprehensae atque nunc primum in lucem editae* (Lugduni: haeredes Seb. Gryphi, 1561) recogen nueve cartas de las que aparecen en los *Epistolarum libri septem* (1.9; 1.12; 2.12; 2.13; 2.14; 3.17; 3.18; 3.19; y 3.20). Otra recopilación de cartas, las *Epistolae Clarorum uirorum selectae de quamplurimis optimae* (Coloniae Agrippinae: Ioannem Gymnicum, 1586), recoge las cartas 1.12; 2.13; y 2.14.

desprende del hecho de que prefiriese abandonarla por temporadas, que con el paso del tiempo se van haciendo cada vez más largas, y llevar una vida aislada en su finca del Gallo, en Sierra Morena,[13] y en su Pozoblanco natal.

La situación fue a peor a partir de 1545, cuando intentó publicar su *Democrates secundus* y se encontró con la oposición de algunos círculos de poder y de intelectuales, encabezados por fray Bartolomé de las Casas. Desde entonces su vida se vio salpicada de polémicas, unas más agrias que otras, como ésta en torno a su *Democrates secundus* o sobre la compensación de los pecados, o sobre la interpretación de algunos pasajes del Nuevo Testamento. Sus enemigos se valieron en dichas polémicas de todos los recursos de que dispusieron y no dudaron en levantar contra él el rumor de que la Inquisición estaba estudiando sus escritos para acusarlo de hereje.[14] A la vista de estas circunstancias no es de extrañar, por tanto, que se decidiese a publicar parte de su correspondencia, su obra literaria más personal; y así, dar a conocer al gran público su verdadera personalidad y atajar las calumnias que sus enemigos habían lanzado contra él.

Así pues, Sepúlveda solicitó permiso de impresión a las autoridades y lo obtuvo con fecha de 30 de agosto de 1553.[15] Ello indica que entonces ya debía existir un *liber epistolarum*; y es de suponer, en atención a la cronología de las cartas incluidas en la colección, que ese *liber* constaba únicamente de cinco libros, los cinco primeros de los siete que luego aparecieron en prensa. En efecto, en ellos no hay ninguna epístola que se pueda datar con posterioridad a esa fecha.[16] Pero el retraso en la aparición definitiva del volumen, cuatro años hasta 1557, debió permitir a Sepúlveda incluir otros dos libros al plan original de la obra, el 6 y el 7, con cartas enviadas o recibidas durante esos años.

Una vez concluida esta breve descripción de las circunstancias que rodearon la publicación de los *Epistolarum libri septem* de Sepúlveda, se impone un estudio intrínseco de los mismos. Con tal fin y dentro de los múltiples detalles de un epistolario que merecen la atención del lector, nos limitaremos a dos aspectos que nos parecen fundamentales para entender esta colección de cartas como lo que es, una obra de creación literaria: primero, los criterios de selección aplicados en la constitución de la obra y tipología epistolar; y segundo, el estilo epistolar de Sepúlveda.

I

En lo que respecta a los criterios que Sepúlveda siguió en la selección de las cartas que incluyó en la colección, y, en definitiva, a la finalidad que presidió la publicación de la obra (la de ofrecer a la comunidad un retrato fidedigno de sí mismo como

---

[13] Cf., e.g., las epístolas 4.10; 6.6.
[14] Cf. las epístolas 6.11; 7.2.
[15] La cédula de impresión aparece en la primera edición de los *Epistolarum libri septem*, fols. 2r–3v.
[16] A propósito de la cronología de las epístolas que conforman la colección, cf. Valverde Abril, "Sepulvedae *Epistolarum libri*," LXX–LXXXVI.

individuo de sabiduría e integridad moral contrastadas — *vir bonus dicendi peritus* —), éstos deben ser los mismos que venían operando en la formación de antologías y colecciones de epístolas formadas desde la Antigüedad hasta el Renacimiento.[17] En ese sentido no es de extrañar que sean las cartas más brillantes desde el punto de vista del estilo o las más notables por su contenido histórico, moral, o doctrinal las que se incluyan en una colección de este tipo. A estas razones debe añadirse otra: la emulación del modelo ciceroniano con toda la diversidad de cartas que éste ofrece.

En principio están ausentes de la colección de Sepúlveda todos los prefacios de sus obras publicadas hasta la fecha, que, pese a la forma epistolar que adoptaron, eran auténticos prólogos con todos los elementos constitutivos de los mismos.[18] Asimismo faltan las cartas que envió a Melchor Cano,[19] que Sepúlveda consideraba como otra más de las apologías que escribió con motivo de la defensa de su *Democrates secundus*.[20]

Entre las cartas que sí tuvieron cabida en sus *Epistolarum libri* caben destacar las de tono privado que envió a sus amigos y colegas a propósito de las vicisitudes (unas veces positivas, y otras bastante negativas) que le tocaron vivir. En este sentido algunas cartas son meramente informativas, como la epístola 1.10, que escribe a Gian Matteo Giberti informándole de que ha sido nombrado historiador imperial; o como aquella otra (5.5) que relata los acontecimientos de la Junta de Valladolid en la que se debatió la pertinencia de la publicación de su *Democrates secundus*.

Siguiendo el ejemplo de Cicerón, se incluyen también cartas de recomendación, como la dirigida a Miquel Mai en favor de Juan Sora (3.3); cartas de felicitación y agradecimiento, como la enviada a Rodolfo Pío (3.4); cartas de exhortación a jóvenes para que se apliquen a sus estudios, como la que envió a Sebastián de León (3.11), o la dirigida a Alfonso Guzmán (3.14). También da cabida en esta colección a cartas que nos informan de las actividades literarias de nuestro autor, como la que envió a Mencía de Mendoza (3.1) a propósito de su trabajo como historiador imperial; o las que remitió a los impresores parisinos Simon de Colines (3.10) y Michel de Vascosan (5.13; 5.14) acerca de la publicación de su traducción de la *Política* de Aristóteles. En este breve recuento que estamos realizando no deberíamos olvidar aquellas epístolas escritas a amigos por el mero placer de escribir, como la epístola enviada a Íñigo de Mendoza (2.3), en la que relata unos escabrosos acontecimientos ocurridos en Roma en ausencia del pontífice Clemente; o como la epístola remitida a Leopoldo de Austria (6.6), en la que pondera las excelencias de su finca de Sierra Morena.

Pero, sin duda, las que forman el grupo más numeroso son las que cabe denominar *epistolae disputatoriae*. Como ejemplos podemos citar algunas de las dirigidas a Erasmo

---

[17] Cf. G. Constable, *Letters and Letter-Collections* (Turnhout, 1976), 60.

[18] Cf. A. Porqueras Mayo, *El prólogo en el Renacimiento español* (Madrid, 1965); T. Janson, *Latin Prose Prefaces: Studies in Literary Conventions* (Stockholm, 1964), 116; M. Pade, "The Dedicatory Letter as a Genre: The Prefaces of Guarino Veronese's Translation of Plutarch," in *Acta Conventus Neo-Latini Torontonensis*, 559–568.

[19] Las cartas se conservan en la Biblioteca Nacional de Madrid (MS. 5785, fols. 291–308). Aparecen editadas en Io. Genesii Sepulvedae *Opera Omnia*, 3:1–71.

[20] Cf. epístola 5.9.

(aquellas en las que se debate la interpretación de algunos pasajes bíblicos, 1.4 a 1.8); las epístolas a Contarini acerca de la reforma del calendario (2.13 a 2.15); o las remitidas a Hernán Núñez, el Pinciano, en las que se discuten algunos problemas de crítica textual concernientes a la obra de Plinio el Viejo, y otros asuntos relativos a la filosofía natural (3.15 a 3.19). También es digna de mención la epístola 5.2, dirigida a Martín Oliván, en la que defiende el estudio de las letras griegas de la acusación que algunos le imputaban de ser el origen de la herejía luterana.[21] O como la epístola 7.1, en la que afronta el problema doctrinal de la salvación de los paganos a través del cumplimiento del derecho natural, y aplica esta teoría al caso particular de Aristóteles, cuya ética es a juicio de Sepúlveda perfectamente compatible con la ideología cristiana y católica.

Pero Sepúlveda era consciente de que este tipo de cartas contravenía en cierto modo la preceptiva teórica epistolar, que no consideraba propiamente cartas aquellas que el autor había concebido como libros.[22] De ello se excusa Sepúlveda en el prólogo a la edición, siguiendo el ejemplo de las cartas de san Jerónimo:

> Si quis autem longiores de rebus literatis commentationes epistolas inepte nominari contendat, is poterit equidem per me eosdem libros epistolares, ut a quibusdam Hieronymi epistolae inscribuntur, appellare. (*Praef.* 21)

II

Así pues, si desde el punto de vista de la tipología epistolar el "ciceronianismo" de Sepúlveda se ve atenuado por la inclusión en los *Epistolarum libri* de cierto tipo de cartas derivado de la práctica epistolográfica cristiana, ese "ciceronianismo" se hace patente si consideramos la fraseología y el estilo empleado por Sepúlveda en sus epístolas.

Si por algo se caracteriza el discurso literario epistolar es por la aparición dentro del mismo de ciertos *topica* epistolares que pueden ser tanto de ideas como de lengua y que lo diferencian de otros discursos literarios que en el devenir histórico resultaron tan cercanos a él como el de la oratoria.[23] Ésa es la razón de que en los estudios más recientes sobre epistolografía se preste mayor atención a estos detalles.[24] Comencemos por los *topica* de ideas.

El primero y más importante, porque delata uno de los fundamentos en los que se basa la concepción teórica de la epístola, es el de considerarla como un diálogo entre amigos ausentes. Sepúlveda se dirige a Gasparo Contarini en los siguientes términos:

---

[21] Cf. L. Gil Fernández, *Panorama social del Humanismo español, 1500–1800*, 2ª ed. (Madrid, 1997), 210–211.

[22] Demetr. *Eloc.* 231; cf. Henderson, "Erasmus on the Art of Letter-Writing," 344; Clough, "The Cult of Antiquity," 49.

[23] Cf. P. Cugusi, *Evoluzione e forme dell'epistolografia latina* (Roma, 1983), 73–104.

[24] Cf., e.g., K. Thraede, *Grundzüge griechisch-römischer Brieftopik* (München, 1970); C. D. Lanham, *Salutatio Formulas in Latin Letters to 1200: Syntax, Style, and Theory*, Münchener Beiträge zur Mediävistik und Renaissance-Forschung 22 (München, 1975).

Mihi enim suauissimum est tecum ... per literas, quando coram negatur huiusmodi conferre sermones. (2.12.11)

Y a Mencía de Mendoza dice:

Ex literis quas ... misisti intellexi tibi, quando coram negatur, non ingratum fore ut per literas colloqueremur. (3.1.2)

En numerosas ocasiones se hace alusión a la pretendida brevedad de la carta, tan repetida en las preceptivas teóricas como poco respetada en la práctica. En efecto, Sepúlveda se siente en la obligación de excusarse cuando entiende que la extensión de la epístola que ha escrito supera ciertos límites. Ejemplos paradigmáticos de lo que decimos son sendas cartas, dirigidas a Martín de Oliván y a Guillermo van Mâle, en las que escribe:

> Haec ad te pluribus uerbis scripsi. (5.5.22)
> Haec apud te pluribus fortasse quam oportuit commemoraui. (7.9.12)

En otros tantos lugares pide nuestro autor excusas por el retraso con el que responde a sus interlocutores. Dice al mismo van Mâle:

Nolim ... ulla mea uel obliuione tui, uel negligentia factum fuisse putes ut ad te tam sero scriberem deque meis rebus certiorem facerem. (7.9.1)

A Gian Matteo Giberti dirige estas palabras:

Quod tam longo interuallo ad te scribam noli mea uel obliuione uel negligentia commissum existimare, sed quod diu mihi ad scribendum nullum satis idoneum argumentum in mentem uenit. (1.11.1)

Y a Francesco Florido Sabino:

Accepi literas tuas ... ad quas quominus ante rescripserim non obliuio tui ..., sed partim multae meae occupationes fuerunt in causa, partim quod cui literas ad te darem nemo erat. (2.9.1)

Por lo que respecta a los *topica* de lengua, esa misma preceptiva teórica impone la utilización de un *sermo cotidianus*, con las implicaciones léxicas y sintácticas que eso supone, como la de evitar períodos excesivamente largos o la de cultivar un estilo descuidado y desprovisto de *ornatus*.[25] Así se debe entender el empleo de formas del

---

[25] Demetr. *Eloc.* 229; Cic. *epist.* 9.21.1; *Rhet. min.* p. 589 (Halm); Vives *Conscr.* 71. Para un juicio sobre el estilo epistolar de Sepúlveda, cf. M. Menéndez Pelayo, "Apuntes sobre el ciceronianismo en España y sobre la influencia de Cicerón en la prosa latina de los humanistas españoles,"

imperativo como *scito* (1.1.5; 1.4.3; 1.10.3; 3.1.3; etc.); la aparición de la expresión *crede mihi* (1.3.4; 1.15.4; 3.4.1; 3.17.8; 3.19.1); o el uso de construcciones propias de la lengua hablada como la de *habeo* + participio: *exploratum habemus* (1.4.1). En ese mismo sentido debemos interpretar el recurso a imprecaciones y expedientes humorísticos, de los que la epístola dirigida a Francisco de Toledo (2.11) ofrece un buen ejemplo. Éste personaje se había burlado de que Sepúlveda no hubiese querido emprender un viaje en barco por temor a un posible naufragio y le había recordado el caso de Trebacio, del que Cicerón se burlaba por parecidas circunstancias. A eso repone Sepúlveda:

> Quem tu mihi Trebatium narras? ... Illud igitur haud dubie (nec me fallis) significare uoluisti, homo uafer, me nihilo magis in Ligustico mari nuper natare uoluisse quam illum olim in oceano Britannico. ... Sed heus tu, dum talia ludis, memento etiam in iocis retinere aliquam aequitatem. (2.11.3–4)

Sin embargo, la tratadística admite y aconseja igualmente que el nivel lingüístico empleado en las cartas, según el principio del *decorum*, debe adaptarse al tema y al destinatario de la carta.[26] Por eso no es de extrañar que los *Epistolarum libri* ofrezcan un espectro estilístico tan variopinto como distintos son los destinatarios de las cartas y diversa la temática en ellas tratada.

Pero, desde luego, lo más definitorio desde el punto de vista formal y lo exclusivo de la epístola es que se trata de un discurso literario abierto por unas fórmulas estereotipadas de saludo (*inscriptio*) y cerrado por otras de despedida (*subscriptio*). No es éste un aspecto carente de importancia, pues los cambios producidos en esas fórmulas marcan en cierta medida la historia del género epistolar.

Por lo que respecta a Sepúlveda, los complicados y farragosos saludos de las cartas medievales ceden paso a otros más sencillos y escuetos de inspiración ciceroniana. Lo normal en el caso de Sepúlveda es que al nombre del remitente en nominativo siga el del destinatario en dativo, más la frase en tercera persona: S[alutem] P[lurimam] D[icit]. A dicho nombre pueden acompañar el posesivo *suus* en señal de afecto o el *titulus honoris* como muestra de respeto. Y en esto no hay trato de preferencia para las grandes personalidades. Nuestro autor saluda al príncipe Felipe (3.6) con unas palabras (*Io. Genesius Sepulueda Philippo, Hispaniarum principi, S.P.D.*) que difieren muy poco de las que dedica a Sebastián de León (3.11), uno de sus secretarios (*Io. Genesius Sepulueda Sebastiano Leoni S.P.D.*).

En cuanto a la despedida Sepúlveda sigue igualmente el procedimiento clásico en sus dos variantes, la breve: *Vale* (passim); o la ampliada: *Vale et me, quod mutuo facis, ama* (3.12.3). Eso sí, cuando facilita la fecha de la carta, suele recurrir a giros pro-

---

in *Bibliografía Hispanolatina clásica*, ed. E. Sánchez Reyes, 10 vols. (Santander, 1950–1953), 3:262.

[26] Cic. *epist*. 15.21.4; Iul. Vict. *rhet*. p. 105 (Giomini-Celentano); Erasmus *Conscr*. pp. 36–38 (Smolak).

piamente cristianos como: *anno Christi nati* (1.3.6; 1.4.19; etc.), *anno a Christo nato* (1.6.19), o sencillamente *anno Christi* (1.9.11; 1.11.10; etc.).

No obstante y en contra de lo que pudiera parecer, podemos afirmar que dichas fórmulas no resultan en absoluto acartonadas, sino que cobran nueva vida a manos de nuestro autor, que se vale de ellas, y de variantes de las mismas, como otro expediente más para expresar valores filofronéticos característicos de la carta, como la amistad y el respeto. Del príncipe Felipe se despide como sigue:

Vale, princeps humanissime, cui omnia laeta feliciaque precor. (3.6.17)

Y de su amigo Juan de Toledo lo hace del siguiente modo:

Vale et primo quoque tempore uolente deo profecturis bene precaberis. (2.10.8)

Otro rasgo destacado de las cartas de Sepúlveda, igual que de las ciceronianas, es la utilización del griego,[27] que se puede entender como un rasgo más de la lengua hablada de la clase alta romana del siglo I a.C. En los autores posteriores perdió, no obstante, ese carácter y se utilizó como otro procedimiento estilístico más de imitación del modelo. Tal es el caso de Erasmo;[28] y también de nuestro autor, que unas veces lo emplea para nombrar con su denominación técnica conceptos filosóficos o fenómenos naturales: πωγωνίας (2.7.6); παρήλιος (2.7.9); εὐετηρία (4.7.16); αὐτάρκεια (4.7.17); y en otras otras ocasiones lo utiliza para dotar a la expresión de mayor brillantez: κἀμοῦ συνεργοῦντος (3.9.1); ὡς κομικός θησί (3.19.2). Del mismo modo son relativamente frecuentes las citas de poetas griegos, principalmente Homero y Hesíodo; dichas citas son unas veces literales: κεραμεὺς κεραμεῖ κοτέει, καὶ τέκτονι τέκτων (5.10.12; cf. Hes. *Op.* 25); otras reelaboradas *ad artem*: La frase Ἀλλὰ τί σε σπεύδοντα καὶ αὐτὸν ὀτρύνω (3.17.3) está inspirada en unos versos de la *Ilíada* (8.293–294).

Retomando, en fin, las ideas que hemos venido esbozando a lo largo de nuestro estudio, podemos decir que Sepúlveda siguió una costumbre ampliamente extendida entre sus coetáneos cuando publicó parte de sus epístolas. Éstas, por razones propias a su naturaleza, se mostraban como el medio más fehaciente de mostrarse ante la comunidad como un individuo sabio y probo. Que Sepúlveda supo utilizar este procedimiento para defenderse de las calumnias que sus contrincantes (Fray Bartolomé de las Casas, Melchor Cano, entre otros) habían lanzado contra él, es algo que no escapa a nadie. Desde el punto de vista formal se muestra como un ciceroniano, pero en la

---

[27] Cf. R. B. Steele, "The Greek in Cicero's Epistles," *American Journal of Philology* 21 (1900): 387–410; Cugusi, *Evoluzione e forme*, 83–91; B. Baldwin, "Greek in Cicero's Letters," *Acta Classica* 35 (1992): 1–17; G. O. Hutchinson, *Cicero's Correspondence: A Literary Study* (Oxford, 1998), 13–15.

[28] Cf. E. Rummel, "The Use of Greek in Erasmus' Letters," *Humanistica Lovaniensia* 30 (1981): 57–92.

concepción de la carta sigue postulados propiamente cristianos, puesto que la considera un instrumento privilegiado para la comunicación científica y doctrinal. En todo ello podemos ver otro reflejo más del eclecticismo de Sepúlveda, fruto de la asimilación que nuestro autor obró de todas las corrientes estéticas y filósoficas que conoció en su singladura vital.

Universidad de Granada

The Religious Beliefs of Hadrianus Junius (1511–1575)

DIRK VAN MIERT

Historical research into the effects of the Reformation schism on members of the Republic of Letters has in the past focused on the conflicts which differences in religious beliefs produced among humanists in the sixteenth and seventeenth centuries. This is not surprising if one looks at their position. Religious matters were closely interwoven with political interests, and humanists were frequently dependent on the influential and powerful figures of their time in order to make a living. Therefore humanists often became spokesmen for the men they served, and thus their positions were polarised.

However, today we tend to focus less on the differences than on the similarities between the humanists.[1] It is sometimes fairly difficult actually to map the personal religious beliefs of some of them unless they made their position clear in treatises on the subject of religion. On the eve of the Dutch Revolt a number of humanists of different beliefs were aware that they had a great deal in common with their fellow humanists, even though they refrained from stressing that in public. Here I will present the case of the Dutch humanist Hadrianus Junius as an example of the fact that, in reality, things were not as black-and-white and in opposition to each other as they might seem. As regards sources, I will limit myself mainly to his correspondence. I shall discuss his position as a Catholic during his first stay in England and analyse his defence against the allegation of his being a Protestant, taking into account the complicating circumstances of the historical context. This discussion will show that it is difficult to conclude anything about Junius's religious beliefs. Nevertheless, in the second half of this paper, I shall try to do so.

---

[1] A recent example is Judith Pollman, *Religious Choice in the Dutch Republic. The Reformation of Arnoldus Buchelius (1565–1641)* (Manchester, 1999).

Junius in England: 1543–1550[2]

Junius had come to England at the invitation of the conservative Catholic Edmund Bonner, Bishop of London, whom he had met in Paris in the early 1540s. When Junius had crossed the Channel, it turned out that Bonner was unable to act as his patron. Instead, therefore, Junius began to serve Henry Howard, Earl of Surrey, poet and son of the Duke of Norfolk, England's premier nobleman, in the role of tutor to his children. Norfolk was part of the Catholic group who had brought about the execution of Thomas Cromwell in 1540 for having arranged a marriage between Henry VIII and the Protestant daughter of the German Duke of Cleves, a marriage which turned out to be unhappy as well as politically useless. Norfolk, together with Bishop Stephen Gardiner, counteracted the Protestant forces at Henry's court. Gardiner himself had been tutor to Henry Howard, so during this period in England Junius was in the midst of a powerful conservative Catholic group. What, then, did Junius think about the Protestantising of the Anglican Church, carried through under the young Edward VI, who succeeded his father in February 1547?

At the request of his correspondents, Junius reported on some of those changes in letters of that period.

> They banish the images of the saints and votive tablets from the churches; altars and walls speak the word of God. Only God knows the hearts of mortal men. Oh, if only they would speak in their conduct and in reality what their tongues utter! Sermons addressed to the people take place almost daily. The holy liturgy, cast out for a time, has recovered its former place, though as a rule care is taken to see that, when Mass is offered, there should be someone to receive communion. The service is sung in the vernacular. Holy Communion is received very reverently, though in both kinds by everyone, and frequently, though in this matter those who remain attached to the old order of things and those from abroad are allowed to do as they wish. The same goes for confession, whether public or private. Processions are done away with, as are ceremonies and Masses for the dead. The use of lamps, torches, and lights has ceased, except for two candles on the main altar. Priests are free to marry if they wish. However things stand, everyone is allowed to have his own opinion.[3]

---

[2] For a detailed account of Junius's whereabouts in England, and of his contacts, see the excellent chapter on him in M. Aston, *The King's Bedpost. Reformation and Iconography in a Tudor Group Portrait* (Oxford, 1993), 176–199.

[3] "Templis exulant Divorum imagines et tabulae votivae: arae et parietes verbum Dei loquuntur: corda mortalium solus novit Deus; o si moribus et re ipsa loquerentur, quod linguae sonant. Conciones tantum non quotidianae ad populum fiunt. Res divine semel explosa nunc pristinum locum recepit, id tamen fere cavetur, ut cum sacrificio sit qui communionem participet: Eadem vernaculo sermone cantatur. Sacra Synaxis pie admodum, sed tamen duplici specie ab universis percipitur, idque frequenter, at relicto tamen antiquum tenentibus exterisque libero hac in re arbitrio. Idem observatur et in confessione vel publica vel auriculari. Pompae abrogatae, Ceremoniae et Sacra pro defunctis antiquata. Lychnorum, facum et lucernarum in templis usus extinctus, praeter binas in princip[ali] ara: sacerdotibus patent connubia volentibus. Utcunque res se ha-

The measures referred to here clearly reflect the Edwardian Injunctions of 1548, so this undated letter may well date from that year. The letter from which the following passage is taken may well belong to the same year, as Junius uses almost exactly the same words:

> On the whole I would have you think that the school of Martin [Luther] is restored here. Statues are banned from churches, all their walls speak the word of God, as does nearly everyone, so far as talking is concerned. Would that their lives did not differ from their tongues! Their services are conducted in the vernacular. In recent weeks these were rather more severely controlled than is now the case as regards not saying Mass unless there was someone to receive communion with the priest. Similarly, it was stipulated that the Host should not be elevated higher than the head of the celebrant, but that has been set aside and the old usage restored, since the Emperor's settlement with Germany [sc. the Augsburg Interim of 1548] became known. There are sermons almost daily. Priests are free to marry and little honour is paid to them unless they hold ecclesiastical office. Almost all church rites have fallen out of use. The vicars and pastors of the Church are obliged to possess the Bible and Erasmus's *Paraphrases*, together with the homilies appointed for feast days (they call them "Postils"), all rendered into English. There is one Holy Communion for all, received under both kinds (as they say); but every foreign "nation" is free to maintain its religion intact. Everyone freely enjoys the right to make confession either privately or publicly.[4]

The following fragment may well be from the same period, as the rite of the "res divina" is spoken of as having been restored to its former place:

> The liturgy, whose authority on the whole was weak, has been restored almost to its former respect by the bishops, save that they have done away with the

---

beat, sua cuique libera manet sententia" (Junius to Nicolaus Poelenburgius, in Hadrianus Junius, *Epistolae, quibus accedit ejusdem vita et Oratio de artium liberalium dignitate: numquam antea edita. Cum indice* [Dordrecht, 1652], 19–20).

[4] "In universum Martinianam scholam revocatam huc velim existimes. Imagines templis exulant, parietes omnes verbum Dei loquuntur, atque ore tenus plaerique omnes, ac utinam a lingua non dissentiret vita. Sacra vernaculo sermone obeuntur: fuitque in iis paulo severior disciplina superioribus hebdomadis, quam nunc est, non sacrificare, nisi esset qui cum sacerdo[te] simul communicaret, non allevare supra caput panem sacratum fas erat: id nunc obliteratum, in pristinum ritum abiit, posteaquam cum Germania concors Caesaris rescriptum innotuit. Conciones sunt prope quotidianae. Sacerdotibus conjugia patent; iisque nisi Ecclesiasticis nullus est honos. Ritus templorum exolevere pene omnes. Ecclesiae vicarii & pastores Biblia, & Erasmi *Paraphrases* cum concionibus in Dies Festos (Postillas nominant) omnia Anglico sermone reddita habere coguntur. Sacra Synaxis cunctis mortalibus una est sub duplici (ut vocant) percepta specie: sua tamen cuilibet nationi exterae manet integra religio. Confessionis sive auricularis sive publicae liberum jus omnibus" (Junius to Rogerus Beverovicius) (*Epistolae* [1652], 23–24).

Elevation [of the Host], giving more weight instead to the Holy Communion. Furthermore, the sacraments and rites of Baptism, Matrimony, Confirmation, Churching of Women, Holy Unction, Burial, etc., have all been restored to their former position, except that they are to be performed in English. As regards the heresies of the Anabaptists and Libertines, enquiry is being made, since, it is said, the desire is to root them right out: however, much is done but little completed; many words, little action.[5]

I conclude these citations with a small phrase from another letter: "I also send you [...] the new face of the British Church, or rather the changed form of worship that is taking root here, this hastily translated out of the vernacular" (Junius to Cornelius Joannes, 19 September [1548]).[6]

Attack and Defence

It is therefore surprising that Junius, in 1548, dedicated his Greek-Latin Dictionary to the young King Edward, addressing himself to him in the terms: "Serenissimo Eduardo Angliae regi, fidei defensori, & supremo Anglicanae Ecclesiae a Christo capiti". This dedication caused Junius considerable trouble in later life.

In the 1564 Tridentine *Index librorum prohibitorum*, Junius's name is mentioned among the "authors of the First Class", whose works were condemned in their entirety.[7] He was so listed in the reissue of this *Index* brought out at Antwerp by Plantin in 1570. However, in the Appendix to this *Index*, drawn up at the instigation of the Duke of Alba in 1569 and published together with it, Junius is listed among the writers of the "Second Class", and now only the heading of his Dictionary's dedication to Edward VI is condemned: "Hadriani Iunii nempe medici titulus Praefationi praefixus in nonnullis exemplaribus lexici Graecolatini: eo titulo excepto, caetera eius

---

[5] "Rei divinae, cujus tenuis admodum erat authoritas, pristinus fere honos assertus est per Episcopos, nisi quod elevationem abrogarint, communionem vero sacrosanctam magis sanxerint, propterea sacra ritusque Baptismi, Matrimonii, Confirmationis, Lustrationis a puerperio, Sacrae Unctionis, Sepulturae, etc., in gradus restituta sunt omnia, nisi quod Anglicana lingua obiri illa placuit. In haereses Anabaptistarum et Libertinorum, qui hic suppullulascere incipiebant, anquiritur, quod eas radicitus sublatas velint, πολλὰ μὲν ποιοῦντες, ὀλίγα δὲ διατελοῦντες, ῥημάτων ἅλις, ἔργων δὲ σπανίως" (Junius to Martinus Petreius, in Hadrianus Junius, *Epistolae selectae, nunc primum editae*, ed. P. Scheltema [Amsterdam, 1839], 13).

[6] "Mitto itidem meam Echo de Germaniae rebus mense Majo biduo absolutam. Et τὸν νεωτερισμὸν τῆς ἐκκλησιάς Βρεττανικῆς ἢ τὴν μετάλλαξιν καὶ μᾶλλον ῥίζωσιν τῆς αὐτόθι θρησκείας tumultuario studio obiter conversum e lingua vernacula" (Junius, *Epistolae* [1652, 45]).

[7] Probably because the *Appendix Bibliothecae Gesneri* (Zürich, 1555) already mentions that his Greek-Latin dictionary was dedicated to Edward VI. See F. H. Reusch, *Der Index der Verbotener Bücher. Ein Beitrag zur Kirchen- und Literaturgeschichte*, Bd. 1 (Bonn, 1883; repr. Darmstadt, 1976), 366.

opera legi possunt, quod nihil contra sanam doctrinam habeant, et auctorem ipsum constet Catholicam fidem profiteri."[8]

What action had Junius undertaken to get his name cleared and the original condemnation reduced so drastically?

The first thing he did was to ask Benito Arias Montano for advice. The Spanish biblical scholar had come to Antwerp in the spring of 1568 to advise on the Antwerp Polyglot Bible project. A year later, the compilation of a new *Index of Forbidden Books* (the Appendix already mentioned) was entrusted to Montano, who had to form a team that included theologians from the University of Louvain. It was published in February 1570, and in a letter to Montano the following May Junius expresses his surprise at finding so many publishers in it. The problem for him was that even the books issued by those publishers were condemned, yet he needed some of these because he was busy writing a historical work. He could judge for himself which books were good and which were not: did he not have a doctorate in philosophy and medicine?[9] Strangely enough, in this letter nothing is said about Junius's own name appearing in this *Index*. It is therefore not completely clear what the positive comment regarding Junius made by Cardinal Granvelle writing to Arias Montano on 20 July 1570 refers to: whether to Junius's name being cleared or to his having been given permission to consult forbidden books;[10] yet, in a letter of 10 November — written in 1573, according to Rekers — Junius thanks Montano for his help in achieving "the removal of false suspicion [...]. Trusting to your advice, I have written to the people you told me to write to."[11]

---

[8] See *Index librorum prohibitorum* [...] *auctoritate Santiss. D.N. Pij IIII. Pont. Max. comprobatur cum Appendice in Belgio, ex mandato Regiae Cathol. Maiestatis confecta* (Antwerp: Plantin, 1570), 28, 63. See also Reusch, *Index der Verbotener Bücher*, 1:366, who mistakenly dates Junius's defence to before 1564.

[9] "Perlectus est a me prohibitorum librorum Index operosus, in quo mirifice me torquet, quod primi nominis impressores, e quorum officinis, optimos utriusque linguae authores prodiisse constat, damnatos legam, cum quibus pariter et authorum ipsorum abolitio sanciri videtur: deinde sollicitum me facti tanta vis omnigenum scriptorum, qui (ut de Fuchsio alii[s]que medicis, quibus insuevimus, taceam) historiam scribenti mihi materiam suppeditare possent [...]. Neque vero ita cerebri cavum me, aut a judicio inopem existimem, ut nequeam capitis atque inguinis discrimina nosse: neque ita sum puer, ut gladius mihi (juxta paroemiam) committi non debeat. Quin jam degustatus mihi est arboris scientiae boni malique succus. Quorsum haec omnia, nimirum ut si ratione ulla fieri queat, ut quum anno abhinc tricesimo Bononiae Doctoratus titulos cum in philosophia, tum in medicina acceperim, data legendi quidvis et profitendi authorite, nunc tua ope beneficioque concedatur usus lectioque librorum mediae classis" (Junius to Arias Montano, 1 May 1570) (Junius, *Epistolae*, ed. Scheltema, 45).

[10] "El negocio del Sr Adriano Iunio tracté de muy buena gana con Su Santidad por la afición que le tengo por las mismas causas que v.m. apunta, y aún más especialmente por ver la cuenta que v.m. dél tiene y el juicio que dél hace" (cited in B. Rekers, *Benito Arias Montano (1527–1598)* [London–Leiden, 1972], 150 [no. 67]).

[11] "Postquam singulari tua benignitate et incomparabili candore uti frui mihi licuit in instituenda justa mei purgatione [...]. Itaque tui consilio fretus scripsi ad quos jusseras" (Junius to Arias Montano, [10 November 1572]) (Junius, *Epistolae* [1652], 252–253).

This remark must refer to the defence Junius wrote to the congregation of cardinals.[12] Here Junius calls the condemnation of his books in the *Index* of Pope Paul IV (Junius mistakenly writes "Paulus Tertius") a false accusation ("falsum crimen"). He had always been innocent of any scandalous deed ("flagitii purum"). Junius was especially affected by the fact that *all his books* were forbidden; and this only because he had addressed Edward VI in the terms cited here earlier. Junius first disowns responsibility on his own part: he had had doubts about the right title to employ in addressing the king but had acted on the advice of his friends. Thus Charles V's ambassador, Franciscus Dilfus or François van der Dilft, warned him more than once that he should use the the king's official title. England was a bad place to be at that time, Junius adds, but the king was still very young and uncorrupted. In fact, Junius had acted on the advice of influential men of unquestioned loyalty. Besides, he continued, the Council of States in the Low Countries itself did not refrain from using this title in letters to the King of England. To stress further that he had no personal responsibility in the matter, Junius added that not to use the proper title would have been considered a capital offence.

After this *refutatio*, he starts his attack. The Pope had been misled by slanderers and miserable backbiters. If he, Junius, were a Protestant, would he not have known that he risked persecution and exile by Mother Church on returning to his own country? In fact the reason why he had left England in 1550 was precisely the religious turmoil in which that country found itself.

Junius could have added another powerful argument. After the untimely death of

---

[12] "Etsi nihil ambigam P.C. non defuturos in sanctissimo isto conventu, qui absentis rationem aut omnino non habendam, aut certe pensi nullius ducendam existimaturi sint, in spem tamen certam erigit me vestra cum aequitas, tum prudentia, ut arbitrer vos non passuros tantae labis vel solam suspicionem in vobis residere, ut caussa incognita cadat, qui se pro criminis exorte gerit: quae certe ignorata, ut nemo rite condemnari potest, ita cognita non dubium quin ab aequissimis omnibus innocentia nostra in tuto statuatur. Cui enim tanta vecordia innata fuerit, qui non salutarem judiciorum literam, quam lugubrem illam malit? Quod si tantum mihi esset ingenii flumen, tanta dicendi vis, tantaque copia, ut pro loci consessusque dignitate verba facere, expectationique aurium satisfacere me posse considerem, facilis explicandi mei foret ratio: nunc tanto me commoveri animo magis par est, quod nec usu satis, nec ingenio valeam, ut in hac luce delectissimorum virorum, reique publicae columinum digne caussam meam tuear: illud tamen unum me recreat, quod sit quaedam ita perspicua veritas, quae nulla re infirmari queat. Velut ignis aquae immersus, e vestigio restinguitur, ita et falsum crimen, in opinionis integrum flagitiique purum collatum, mox aboletur atque corruit. Quod quale sit, succincta oratione explicabo, sed ita, ut non tam brevitate oratiunculae meae, quam rei veritate crimen intentatum ponderetis, siquidem (quod a veteribus sapienter dictum est) veritas simplex est, et ambagium fugitans sermo. Vos interim obstestatos velim, P.C. ut tribus verbis, quicquid est rei, explicaturo mihi auribus favere tantisper dignemini, dum seriem rei pariter et vitae rationem obiter delibem. Districtum est a Sacrorum Rege, sive Pontifice Max. Paulo Tertio fulmen in meum nomen, quo librorum meorum, qui varii in lucem exierunt, lectione interdicitur, non alia de causa, uti reor (neque enim sinistrae alicujus opinionis ac diversae a communi Orthodoxorum persuasione mihi sum conscius) quam quod Angliae Regi Edovardo, quos praeferebat titulos, in epistola quadam nuncupatoria Lexici Graeci, a me evulgati, attribuerim, quae res ad hunc modum habet." (*Epistolae* [1652], 390–392)

Edward in 1553, his successor, Mary Tudor, married Philip of Spain. Junius went to considerable pains to write an epic poem in praise of the Catholic couple which was to be presented on the occasion of their wedding. Perhaps he did not refer to this now because of the painful memory of having incurred twice as much expense in the composition of the poem and travelling to England to present it as the whole project brought him: he complains on different occasions about the low reward he received from the Spanish king.[13] This anecdote indicates the most important reason why, I think, Junius had dedicated his earlier work to Edward: his desperate search for a patron. His maecenas, Henry Howard, had been executed in January 1547, only days before Henry VIII died. When Howard was arrested a few weeks earlier, his library had been pillaged and Junius's own had suffered serious loss.[14]

Close Contact with Non-Catholics

At first sight, there was no reason for the scrupulous compilers of the 1569 Appendix not to believe Junius. But had they taken a closer look, things could have turned out more difficult for our humanist. In the first place, there is the dedication itself. Junius praises not only the great talents of Edward but also those of his royal father, Henry VIII, whose virtues, he declares, Edward has inherited, and includes a two-page eulogy of the boy-king's uncle and "governor", Protector Somerset, celebrating his successful campaign of 1547 against the Scots. By the time Junius's Dictionary appeared, Somerset was becoming the driving force behind the Protestantising of the Church of England.

Furthermore, during his stay in England, Junius maintained a friendly correspondence with men who were outspokenly supportive of the new religion. There is a letter to Walter Haddon, distinguished academic lawyer, man of letters, Neo-Latin poet, and friend of the influential Protestant reformer, Martin Bucer, explicitly asking him to greet on his behalf Thomas Smith, another academic lawyer at Cambridge and Protestant scholar, just as Haddon was.[15] There is also a letter to John Cheke, who was to take refuge abroad during the reign of Mary. There is yet another letter — to Nicholas Wotton, Secretary of State — in which Junius defends the Dutch shopkeeper Walter Lynne, who had published several theological translations and had, as Junius puts it, put much effort into "promoting evangelical truth": that is to say,

---

[13] See C. L. Heesakkers, "The Ambassador of the Republic of Letters at the Wedding of Prince Philip of Spain and Queen Mary of England: Hadrianus Junius and his *Philippeis*," in *Acta Conventus Neo-Latini Abulensis. Proceedings of the Tenth International Congress of Neo-Latin Studies, Ávila 4–9 August 1997*, ed. R. Schnur et al., MRTS 207 (Tempe, AZ, 2000), 325–332.

[14] "Absente me procul in Nordfolkia, dum capitis arcessitur Maecenas tum meus, Comes Surrianus, pars bona bibliothecae meae, quae in Musaeo istius adservabatur, direpta fuit" (Junius to an unknown addressee; date unknown, presumably 1548) (Junius, *Epistolae*, ed. Scheltema, 4). See also: "Direpta mihi praeter locuples stipendium etiam biblioteca haud contemnanda" (Junius to Vulcanius; date unknown) (Junius, *Epistolae* [1652], 179).

[15] See C. L. Lees, *The Poetry of Walter Haddon* (The Hague, 1967), 22–23.

Protestantism.[16] Finally, in a letter to his life long friend Martinus Aedituus [Martin Coster], he says he has greeted on his behalf John à Lasko, Bernardino Ochino, Petrus Alexandrius and Walter Delenius (Delen), people who are known to have been Protestant reformers who found shelter in London during the reign of Edward VI.[17]

Of course, writing letters to Protestants does not in itself mean that Junius himself was a Protestant; but the fact that he wrote in defence of Walter Lynne does indicate that Junius, at the personal level, was not hostile to every Protestant, even though he was not particularly fond of Protestantism in general, as is clear from the letters of his quoted above. Lack of party zeal made it all the easier for him to dedicate his work to Edward VI. The makers of the 1569 Appendix perhaps did not mention Junius's dedication of his *De anno et mensibus commentarius* to Edward — a dedication where he highly praises the King's tutor, John Cheke — because our humanist reworked the dedication (and parts of the treatise) in 1556 so as to make it suitable to be dedicated to Queen Mary Tudor.

Though the cardinals eventually accepted that Junius had always been a good Catholic, they had more reason to distrust him at the time he wrote in his own defence than during his English period in the 1540s.

The 1560s and 1570s were an extremely important time for the emancipation of the Northern Low Countries. One of the major features of those years is the change undergone as regards religion. During the 1570s one city after another turned Protestant. At this time Junius lived in Haarlem, where he had contacts with people like the painter Maarten van Heemskerk and the poet-philosopher Dirck Volckertsz Coornhert. The latter was accused of being a libertarian, a free-thinker, by his contemporaries, though today he is regarded, in religious terms, as a "perfectist".[18] He

---

[16] "Illustrissimae tuae Celsitudinis genibus supplex advolvitur Gualterus Lynne opis omnis indigus, quam Serenissima Regia Majestas tuaque Illustrissima Celsitudo ceu ex uberrimis fontibus affluenter prestare possunt: qui cum ad exemplum illorum (si magnis pusilla componere fas est) ita se comparaverit hactenus, ut studium, diligentiam, curam, omnemque operam in promovendo Evangelicae veritatis profectu, quantam vires paterentur, poriendam sibi duceret [. . .]" (Junius in the *Libellus Supplex*, attached to his letter of 8 March 1550 to Wotton, who was Secretary of State from 15 October 1549 to 5 September 1550) (see *Epistolae* [1652], 34–36 [p. 34]). Junius had already met Wotton in 1543, when he handed over to him the dedication of Petrus Nannius's *Oratio de obsidione Lovaniensi*. Together with this work, Junius carried with him Nannius's *Orationes duae gratulatoriae de felici Caesaris [. . .] adventu*, with a dedication to Bishop Bonner. This is probably how Junius came into contact with this bishop of London. (Both dedications are given in A. Polet, *Une Gloire de l'humanisme belge. Petrus Nannius 1500–1557* [Louvain, 1936], 279–281.) Walter Lynne had settled in England before 1540 and published theological books in the period 1547–1550. He was mainly a translator into English and did not print any books by himself. He had a shop in St. Paul's Churchyard. Possibly, Junius knew him from this shop. See E. G. Duff, *A Century of the English Book Trade* (London, 1905), 95–96.

[17] See Junius to Aedituus, 21 January [1548] (*Epistolae* [1652], 152). Cranmer was instructed by Protector Somerset to invite learned refugees to his palace at Lambeth, where Norfolk also kept a household.

[18] According to "Perfectism", it is possible for a Christian, after great effort and by the grace

had much criticism of the Catholic Church but also loathed the doctrines of Calvinism. He was first and foremost the champion of religious freedom. Other important contacts of Junius were with Plantin and Arias Montano, both of whom are known to have been members of the Family of Love or at least to have co-operated with the Familists.[19] From 1565 onwards, all Junius's works were published by the Antwerp printer. The correspondence between Junius and Plantin consists of a large number of relatively short but intimate letters, where Junius brings in the name of Arias Montano more than once. The latter, as a servant of the Spanish king, detested the iconoclasm of the 1560s in the Low Countries, but when he came to Antwerp he was introduced to the circle of Plantin, which included people of a Familist stamp. Brought face to face with Rome's opposition to the publication of the Antwerp Polyglot Bible in 1572, on the one hand, and with the harsh way in which the Spanish troops tried to suppress Protestantism in the Low Countries, on the other, he began to doubt the merits of Mother Church.[20]

In 1565 Junius became acquainted with the young and talented Dutch humanist Janus Dousa, to whom he dedicated his edition of Martial in 1568. Junius wrote a letter of recommendation to introduce the young Dousa to Elizabeth I of England when he was engaged in a minor embassy.[21] The exact status of this "legatiuncula" is not known, but in a poem to the Queen Dousa warned her of the approaching end of 'religious liberty' (not 'Protestantism').[22]

In 1568 Junius dedicated one of his own works to the Queen: his translation of Eunapius's *Lives of the Philosophers*. Though this time he did not employ any sort of title referring to her as "Defender of the Faith" or "supreme Head of the Church in England", he could have chosen another, less suspect, sovereign as patron for the work. Catholics in England were exposed to persecution in 1568. Furthermore, Junius wrote a friendly letter to Philip Howard — son of Thomas Howard, fourth

---

of God, to be able to obey, in spite of original sin, all the commandments given by God in the Old and New Testaments. See, for example, Dirck Volckertsz Coornhert, *Op zoek naar het hoogste goed*, Uitgegeven, ingeleid en van aantekeningen voorzien door H. Bonger (Baarn, 1987), 17. For the contacts between Junius and Coornhert, see B. Becker, *Bronnen tot de kennis van D.V. Coornhert* (The Hague, 1928), 14. Junius wanted Coornhert to be the translator of his *Emblemata* (Antwerp, 1565): see Junius, *Epistolae*, ed. Scheltema, 63. As for the contacts between Junius and Heemskerck, Junius produced a number of inscriptions for engravings by Maarten van Heemskerck and his copiers Harmen Muller and Philippus Galle. See I.M. Veldman, "Maarten van Heemskerck and Hadrianus Junius: The Relationship between a Painter and a Humanist," in *Simiolus. Netherlands Quarterly for the History of Art* 17 (1974): 35–54.

[19] See Rekers, *Arias Montano*, 71, 77. For further examination of the issue of whether Plantin was a member of the Family of Love, see P. Valkema Blouw, "Was Plantin a Member of the Family of Love? Notes on His Dealings with Hendrik Niclaes," *Quaerendo. A Quarterly Journal from the Low Countries devoted to Manuscripts and Printed Books* 23 (1993): 3–23.

[20] See Rekers, *Arias Montano*, 38.

[21] See C. L. Heesakkers and W. M. S. Reinders, *Genoeglijk bovenal zijn mij de muzen. De Leidse Neolatijnse dichter Janus Dousa (1545–1604)* (Leiden, 1993), 31.

[22] The phrase is that of J. A. van Dorsten, *Poets, Patrons and Professors. Sir Philip Sidney, Daniel Rogers and the Leiden Humanists* (Leiden–London, 1962), 28.

Duke of Norfolk — who was unstable in his religious allegiance but seems to have been more of a Protestant than a Catholic.[23] In view of all these facts, it is not surprising that Junius has by some scholars been categorised as a non-Catholic.[24] What then are we to think about Junius's opinions on religion?

Junius as Philologist and Scholar

Junius never engaged much in religious affairs. He wrote to Rome defending his position as a Catholic, but in the years of Edward VI he kept on corresponding with scholars from the University of Cambridge, which was inclined towards Protestantism in the 1540s, sending them very polite, not to say begging, letters. It may be that Junius did have personal objections on religious grounds against those correspondents, but what could he do? He was desperate for a patron and sought someone influential — a scholar — with whom he could identify himself. His correspondents are mainly scholars: Junius was a well-known and greatly respected member of the "Respublica literaria". In order to keep things this way, he tried not to get involved in too many political or religious matters. We see a focus on scholarly affairs: he would touch upon religious issues only at the request of his correspondents, and even then would hide his personal feelings if it was better for him to do so. There is a striking parallel here with what one finds in his most important work: the *Batavia*, a piece of cultural history which he wrote in discharge of his office as historiographer to the States of Holland and which was to form the first part of a trilogy on the history of Holland. Though it gave every opportunity for references to politics or religion, in the *Batavia* Junius avoids touching upon political or religious current affairs and focuses solely on scholarly subjects.[25]

He had always had more interest in philological subjects. His numerous editions and translations of ancient writers; his philological annotations in his *Animadversorum libri sex* (Basel, 1556); his Greek-Latin dictionary; his famous dictionary in eight languages (the *Nomenclator omnium rerum propria nomina . . . indicans* [Antwerp, 1567]);[26] his *Adagiorum Centuriae VIII cum dimidia* (Basel, 1558), a supplement to Erasmus's *Adagia*; his edition of Ravisius Textor's *Epitheta*; and his plan to prepare an edition of Suidas's *Lexicon*: all these things show that Junius was far more interested in scholarly subjects than in religion.

He is explicit about religion in only two cases. Ari Wesseling published in 1991 a sarcastic satire by Junius against the Anabaptist David Joris: we have already cited the passage in a letter from which it is clear that he had little sympathy for this sect.

---

[23] M. F. S. Hervey, *The Life, Correspondence and Collections of Thomas Howard, Earl of Arundel* (Cambridge, 1921), 4.

[24] For example, P. Noordeloos, *Cornelius Musius [Mr. Cornelis Muys], Pater van Sint Agatha te Delft, Humanist / Priester / Martelaar* (Utrecht–Antwerp, 1955), 261.

[25] See D. van Miert, "Adriano Junio y su *Batavia*," in *Actas del III Simposio sobre humanismo y pervivencia del Mundo Clásico, Alcáñiz*, ed. J. M. Maestre Maestre and J. P. Barea (Cádiz, forthcoming).

[26] See G. de Smet, "De *Nomenclator* van Hadrianus Junius," *Handelingen van de Zuidnederlandse Maatschappij voor Taal- en Letterkunde* 8 (1954): 61–73.

Second, in his supplement to Erasmus's *Adagia*, he attacks the Flagellants.[27] His other — very few — references to controversial matters in his *Adagia* are summed up by Wesseling, who comments: "Whether it was fear of getting into trouble with secular and ecclesiastical authorities, or rather a conciliatory attitude that held him back from voicing his opinion on political and religious matters, we will probably never know."[28] Though I cannot prove anything, I wish to make a suggestion here. If it was fear, the fact remains that Junius's need for money and a patron led him to dedicate a dictionary to a Protestant king. But was it just the need for money that made Junius an opportunist? I do not think so. In 1568 his need for money was less than it had been. He was an official historiographer now, and though we do not know of any document testifying to his earnings at Haarlem, where he acted as physician to the city, it may be assumed that he was financially better off than during his English period. Besides, Junius states in 1559 that his second wife had brought him a good dowry. In 1568 he apparently had the resources to cross the Channel to present his translation of Eunapius to Elizabeth I, in contrast to his deplorable financial situation in 1553. It was not a case of Junius's being deterred by fear of getting into trouble. Moreover, his close contacts with enemies of the Spanish King indicate merely that he supported the Dutch Revolt like a number of other Catholics. Therefore I think that there is reason to assume that Junius had "a conciliatory attitude", as Wesseling puts it.

A Tolerant Catholic

In my view, Junius belonged to the kind of enlightened people who, like Coornhert, were in favour of religious tolerance. He did not have this attitude from the start of his life; he learned it by experience. Sickened at the end of his life by the Spanish armies, which sacked his hometown of Haarlem and destroyed his library, he may have got to the point of repudiating zealous Catholicism, just like many other Catholics in the Low Countries.[29] There is no indication whatsoever that he had been a member of the Family of Love. His fierce attack on the Anabaptist David Joris makes such a suggestion very unlikely. I prefer to conclude that he did not really care so much about taking sides. He must have spoken about the subject of religion with people like Coornhert and was bound to share their conclusions on religious freedom (let us not forget that Junius did not actually publish his attack on David Joris). Only such a tolerant attitude can explain the seemingly contradictory pattern of his dedications and his unwillingness to address controversial matters. However, when con-

---

[27] "Junius is apparently thinking of Italian Flagellant rituals, which he may have watched during his stay in that country": Ari Wesseling, "David Joris, 'Son of God'. An Unpublished Satire by the Dutch Humanist Hadrianus Junius," *Nederlands Archief voor Kerkgeschiedenis* 71 (1991): 53.

[28] Wesseling, "David Joris," 57.

[29] "Doleo certe ejus [Pulmanni] vicem et doctis hominibus suam spem tolli Iberia aut barbara potius ista tempestate deploro, quae ut ingemiscenda, ita rursus ferenda est" (Junius to Plantin [1569]) (*Epistolae*, ed. Scheltema, 37).

fronted with the limits imposed on him by religious or political authorities, he had no hesitation in putting forward his case and defending himself.

We see here a gap between the everyday reality of the world of power and politics, in which humanists were forced to choose a side in a polarised political and religious situation, and, on the other hand, the enlightened attitude of some members of the Republic of Letters. There was diversity and conflict at the official level, and unity at the personal level. I hope I have shown that Junius focused on the latter.

Universiteit van Amsterdam

The Cranevelt Letters and Rome

MICHIEL VERWEIJ

At the heart of Leuven University Library is preserved a collection of letters that is considered one of its main treasures. This collection consists of private letters sent to Franciscus Craneveldius or Van Cranevelt (1485–1564), Doctor of Laws, pensionary of Bruges, and from 1522 member of the Mechlin Parliament.[1] Apart from his busy legal activities, he devoted himself to the study of *bonae litterae* as well as to a correspondence with many leading humanists. Among these rank first and foremost Erasmus, Thomas More, and especially Juan Luis Vives. They are paralleled by a pleiad of humanists from the Leuven circle, such as Adrianus Barlandus, Gerard Geldenhouwer, Johannes Borsalus, and Petrus Curtius, as well as from the Bruges circle, such as Cranevelt's best friend Johannes Fevynus or his protégé Leonardus Clodius. The letters date from the 1520s and were discovered in the twentieth century in two

---

[1] Cf. H. de Vocht, *Literae virorum eruditorum ad Franciscum Craneveldium 1522–1528. A Collection of Original Letters Edited from the Manuscripts and Illustrated with Notes and Commentaries*, Humanistica Lovaniensia 1 (Louvain, 1928) (=*Litt.Cran.*); J. Ijsewijn, D. Sacré, G. Tournoy, and M. Verweij, "Litterae ad Craneveldium Balduinianae. A Preliminary Edition," *Humanistica Lovaniensia* 41 (1992): 1–85; 42 (1993): 2–51; 43 (1994): 15–68; 44 (1995): 1–78 (=*Litt.Bald.*). A definitive edition of *Litt.Bald.* is being prepared. The newly found letters from Thomas More have also been edited separately by H. Schulte Herbrüggen, *Morus ad Craneveldium litterae Balduinianae novae / More to Cranevelt: New Baudouin letters*, Supplementa Humanistica Lovaniensia 11 (Leuven, 1997). Schulte Herbrüggen gives on pp. 40–44 a general evaluation of Cranevelt as a collector of his correspondence. On Cranevelt see P. G. Bietenholz and T. B. Deutscher, *Contemporaries of Erasmus. A Biographical Register of the Renaissance and Reformation*, 3 vols. (Toronto–Buffalo–London, 1985–87) (hereafter *CE*), 1:354–355; an extensive biography can be found in de Vocht, *Litt.Cran.*, xxxiii–lxxxvii (overlooked in *CE*); a shorter survey is also provided by Schulte Herbrüggen, *Morus ad Craneveldium*, 30–33. A detailed study of the relation between Cranevelt and Erasmus is being prepared by the present author (this study will also discuss the relations between Erasmus and some other correspondents of Cranevelt mentioned below, such as Fevynus, Borsalus, Barlandus, Geldenhouwer, and Hezius).

parts. Two bundles of letters from 1522 to 1528 were rescued from the 1914 sack of Leuven and edited by Henry de Vocht in 1928, while a new bundle was discovered at a London auction by Hubert Schulte Herbrüggen, subsequently bought by the Belgian King Baudouin Foundation, and published by the late Josef IJsewijn and his team. The subjects discussed in this correspondence are of great variety: apart from strictly private matters, literary and scholarly questions are raised and politics are debated. While the great age of discoveries did not leave many traces, the Lutheran Reformation did: this in fact is one of the main topics. Apart from this, the activities of much admired persons such as Erasmus fill many lines, as we will have some occasion to see.

The present paper intends to focus attention on one specific aspect of this important source for the study of early sixteenth-century Humanism in the Low Countries, namely, relations with, and the significance of, the city of Rome.

As far as we know, Cranevelt never visited Rome himself. However, one of his most faithful correspondents, Johannes Fevynus, did, although we do not gather much information about his journey.[2] The interest of the present subject lies elsewhere.

It is surmised that one of Cranevelt's professors in Leuven was Adrian Floris Boeiens of Utrecht, who later was to be elected pope, taking the name of Adrian VI (reg. 1522–1523).[3] Another possibility is that Cranevelt, who must have remained in Leuven until 1515, met the future pope in a more exalted official position at Leuven University: it is well known that Adrian was a very important person there before he became counsellor to Charles V and regent of Spain. However that may be, it is a fact that Cranevelt reacted enthusiastically to Adrian's election. A poem probably composed by himself has survived among the collection of letters mentioned earlier and celebrates the beginning of a new era, which, however, was not to last long and would achieve little.[4] This poem may have been written shortly after news of the

---

[2] On Fevynus see *CE*, 2:26; De Vocht, *Litt.Cran.*, general introduction, xci–xcix; the newly found *Litt.Bald.* furnish some new details about his life and personality which could not have been used earlier. Fevynus went to study in Italy and visited Bologna, Pavia, and Rome. He returned a *iuris utriusque doctor*, but it is not known at which university he obtained his degree. His Roman visit is mentioned only once, when he refers to a Nicolaus Petri as his companion in *Litt.Cran.* 64. In *Litt.Bald.*, 30, he wonders why Cranevelt did not consult him on a question about Italian topography, as he had been there himself.

[3] See on Adrian *CE* 1:5–9; J. Coppens and M.E. Houtzager, *Paus Adrianus VI. Herdenkingstentoonstelling: Gedenkboek, Catalogus* (Utrecht–Leuven, 1959); L. Altringer, "Hadrian VI. (1522–1523)," in *Hochrenaissance im Vatikan. Kunst und Kultur im Rom der Päpste, I. 1503–1534* (Bonn, 1999), 48–54 ; P. Nissen, *Adrianus VI. Een biografie* (Amsterdam, 2000). Adrian was buried in the church of S. Maria dell'Anima: his tomb may be the most concrete object a reader of this article and possible visitor to Rome can still find with regard to this subject; cf. M. Verweij, "Een suggestie voor de Romereis: de Santa Maria dell'Anima. Het Rome van de 'Leuvense' paus Adrianus VI," *Kleio. Tijdschrift voor oude talen en antieke cultuur* 29 (1999–2000): 16–27.

[4] This poem was published as *Litt. Bald.* 100. The text is dated ca. 15 March 1522 and is in Cranevelt's own handwriting. The fact that three versions are given may suggest that the final choice had not yet been made, and so, that Cranevelt was indeed the author of the poem himself.

election reached Bruges. Furthermore, it may be that writing this poem was equally part of an attempt to attract attention from Charles V himself, whose triumphs are celebrated as well, at a moment when Cranevelt appears to have been looking for a new position.[5] At any rate, notwithstanding the possibility of an additional purpose, it is clear that Adrian's election was greeted warmly. Another poem which summarises the events of 1522 mentions Adrian's election as well and refers to him explicitly, and maybe even with some pride, as "one of our country" (*nostras*).[6] Indeed, and this is vital for our understanding in this matter, Adrian was considered as "one of us" and he enjoyed a sympathetic and keen interest on the part of the Cranevelt circle.

That appears also from a curious reference made by Fevynus to a chair Adrian used to use in Leuven, which is referred to informally and humorously as "a pontifical chair": Cranevelt should not torment himself about visiting Peter's chair at some point as he can see this one at home.[7] It seems to have been quite a handy chair capable of moving on wheels from one desk to another and spinning round on an axis, as is shown by a sketch in the letter. The casual and to a certain extent almost joking tone shows that Fevynus and Cranevelt considered Adrian really as someone known to themselves, as a valued acquaintance.

Possibly the most interesting evidence of this attitude towards Adrian VI and in a certain way the culmination of Cranevelt's Roman contacts is a draft letter written by Cranevelt to the pope himself.[8] It is a somewhat belated letter of congratulation on Adrian's election. As Cranevelt also mentions his own activities over the past few years, it seems justified to assume that they really had been acquainted personally in Leuven. However, they seem not to have been regular correspondents or really close friends. The tone of the letter is respectful, but certainly not servile.

From Fevynus's letter about the chair it may be deduced that Cranevelt might even once have wanted to go to Rome himself. However, in this case it seems unlikely that he would have thought of seeking a new job in Rome at that particular moment, as so many of his countrymen tried to do in Adrian's reign. Cranevelt had been appointed to a higher position himself a few months before he wrote his letter to Adrian, but one of the characteristics of Adrian's pontificate is the high percentage

---

[5] Cf. *Litt.Bald.* 103 (6 March 1522), which is the reply by a high Guelders official to a lost letter by Cranevelt exploring his chances with the duke of Guelders.

[6] Cf. *Litt.Cran.* 11.9: "Nostratem Ianus Pontificemque dedit." The poem is attributed to Geldenhouwer or Clodius, in whose hand the surviving document is written.

[7] Cf. *Litt.Cran.* 21 (by Fevynus, early November 1522?): "[nempe ut mihi effingas] sedem, sed ferream, sed pontificiam; n[ec est] quur te maceres ob aliquando visendam Petri sedem, cum h[anc domi] videris." The text is rather mutilated at some points, but the reference to Adrian's chair is clear enough. Of course, *domi* is a suggestion by the editor, and it may stand either for Cranevelt's own house or for Adrian's former residence. Cf. T. Padmos and G. Vanpaemel, eds., *De geleerde wereld van keizer Karel. Catalogus tentoonstelling Wereldwijs. Wetenschappers rond keizer Karel* (Leuven, 2000), 62–63, n. 26.

[8] Viz. *Litt. Cran.* 25 (12 November 1522).

of officials appointed from the Low Countries,⁹ and some of Cranevelt's correspondents belonged to this class.

One of these is Conrad Vecerius of Luxembourg, who originally belonged to the Court of Maximilian and Charles V and who left for Rome early in 1523.¹⁰ He delivered Adrian's funeral oration. Later he was admitted to Clement VII's *familia* and delivered the sermon in the Sistine Chapel on Ash Wednesday 1525. He published both orations as well as an account of Adrian's journey to Rome. He died in Rome in 1526 or 1527. Vecerius was Cranevelt's most important personal contact in Rome during Adrian's pontificate and immediately afterwards: three letters written by Vecerius in Rome survive,¹¹ and Vecerius refers to letters by Cranevelt himself which have been lost. He also provided some news of the events just before Adrian's departure from Spain.¹² Vecerius was in Spain himself at the time, so naturally this topic of news presented itself, but in view of what we have already seen, it may have been even more gratifying for Cranevelt than Vecerius thought it.

However, Vecerius was not the only or even the most important source of information for the Cranevelt circle as such. Fevynus, a member of the Chapter of St. Donatian in Bruges and well acquainted with Marcus Laurinus, Erasmus's trusted friend, also received news from sources which most of the time cannot be identified. Often he transmitted it to Cranevelt. Since the autumn of 1522 Cranevelt had lived in Mechlin, while Fevynus remained in Bruges, and thus their correspondence lost some of its daily informality, but it became a more suitable instrument for the exchange of important news features. In this way Fevynus announces an expected meeting between the emperor and the pope in November 1522, though it in fact never took place.¹³ The question of Luther was to have been its subject, a topic that always interested the Cranevelt circle. Later Fevynus repeats a false rumour that Adrian had fled to Viterbo during a plague.¹⁴ It may be that one of Fevynus's sources was the same Vecerius: Fevynus refers to some documents he would receive, and it is

---

⁹ Cf. W. A. J. Munier, "Nederlandse curialen en hofbeambten onder het pontificaat van Adriaan VI," *Mededelingen van het Nederlands Historisch Instituut te Rome*, 3. reeks, 10 (1959): 199–226.

¹⁰ See on Vecerius *Litt. Cran.* 12 intr., which has to be supplemented by the new information from *Litt. Bald.*: cf. *Litt. Bald.* 10 intr.

¹¹ Viz. *Litt. Cran.* 68 (5 August 1523), 73 (18 September 1523), and 77 (15 October 1523).

¹² Cf. *Litt. Cran.* 12 (7 August 1522): "Quum etiamnum in portu ageremus, scripsit ad Caesarem Hadrianus pontifex, sese iampridem accinctum navigationi Italicae; gratum habiturum si priusquam solvat, convenire in certum locum deque communibus rebus coram colloqui statuereque possit"; 17 (30 September 1522). The last letter is heavily damaged and the allusion to Adrian is partially a conjecture by de Vocht.

¹³ Cf. *Litt. Cran.* 22, tentatively dated to the first days of November 1522: "Qui hec secum nova attulit, profectus est in [aulam] apud Principem Margaretam; post audiemus congre[ssum] Pontificis et Imperatoris si modo quid possint in L[utherum]."

¹⁴ Cf. *Litt. Cran.* 29 (4 December 1522): "Hic nihil est novi, nisi quod quidam adfirmabant venisse liter[as] ex Venetiis Turcam obiisse mortem. Pontifex, Urbe relict[a] diei itinere, agit Viterbii." Possibly both pieces of news were transmitted in the same letter from Venice, but the news immediately following about a Leuven vacancy makes it impossible to obtain any certainty about this matter.

suggested that this may be the report on Adrian's journey written by Vecerius.[15] That he had his own contacts is clear from a reference in a letter from April, where he repeats news he has just received from the Eternal City.[16]

From the material discussed so far it is evident that personal interest in Adrian VI and acquaintance with men like Vecerius were the most important stimuli and characteristics of Cranevelt's contact with Rome. Besides, it is clear that there must have been some regular exchange of news, the exact amount of which, however, remains hidden in darkness to us.

Adrian's pontificate did not last long. After a short illness, he died on 14 September 1523, not much regretted by the Roman people. As could be expected, news of this illness and rumours of its fatal result soon reached Bruges and Mechlin. In fact Fevynus seems to mention a rumour of Adrian's illness the day before the pope died.[17] Four days after Adrian's death Vecerius wrote about it in *Litt.Cran.* 73. Cranevelt made some notes on this letter, among which is part of the first epitaph on the pope.[18] Cranevelt passed a copy of Vecerius's letter to Fevynus, as appears from a note he made on the back of Fevynus's next letter.[19] It is assumed that Cranevelt passed Vecerius's letter also to other friends, as was his custom, and that in this way it could have been an important source for the chapter on Adrian in the *De rebus gestis ducum Brabantiae* by the Leuven professor and Erasmian humanist Adrianus Barlandus. This circulation of letters is an essential element in the spread of information in this period.

As a very important piece of information, Adrian's death was also mentioned in other letters dating from these weeks.[20] We are also kept informed, mostly by Fe-

---

[15] Cf. *Litt. Cran.* 33 (6 January 1523): "cum accepero Apostolicas tunc rescribam latius." Nothing certain can be said about this matter, except for the obvious fact that news from Rome was considered worthwhile to report and that Fevynus had his own contacts.

[16] Cf. *Litt. Cran.* 53 (17 April 1523): "Ex Urbe intelligo Urbini ducem profectum Pontificis nomine cum Colunnensi Cardinali in Pannoniam." This fact was connected with the danger from the Ottoman Empire, news about which was eagerly collected. This danger was one of Adrian's constant worries.

[17] Cf. *Litt. Cran.* 72 (13 September 1523): "[De morbo Romani Pontificis] ac [isthic] admiramur rumorem sparsum, sed nunc vanum de extrema valetudine." Again the reference to Adrian rests on a conjecture by de Vocht.

[18] On the fourth page, preceded by a pointing hand: "Hic nihil sibi infelicius duxit esse in vita quam quod impera[ret]." De Vocht suggests that Cranevelt received this epitaph from Fevynus, but there is no evidence for this: in fact, this text cannot be found in any letter by Fevynus actually preserved. As Cranevelt meticulously collected his correspondence, the absence of any positive indication in one of Fevynus's letters might be considered an *argumentum ex silentio* to the effect that the text of the epitaph did *not* reach Cranevelt by Fevynus.

[19] Viz. *Litt. Cran.* 75 (2 October 1523). Cranevelt's note, "Rescripsi XXa Octobris et misi epistolam Ludii Vegerii ad me ex Urbe Rhoma." *Ludii* is an allusion to the contents of Vecerius's letter, where the word *theatrum* repeatedly occurs.

[20] Viz. by Martinus Dorpius in *Litt. Cran.* 74 (30 September 1523) and by Fevynus in *Litt. Cran.* 75 (2 October 1523) and 76 (4 October 1523), this last letter being a reply to a letter by Cranevelt and a supplement to Fevynus's letter of two days earlier.

vynus, of such events as the conclave for the election of Adrian's successor[21] and the flight of Nicolaas van der Poorten, executor of Adrian's will, who was unjustly suspected by the Roman populace of having stolen all the money he could get.[22] In this last letter Fevynus apparently paraphrases news direct from Rome.

A special item in the Cranevelt letters consists of two letters from Adrian VI and Clement VII respectively, both concerning Erasmus, the *princeps* of the humanists, much admired by both Cranevelt and Fevynus. After the beginning of the Lutheran Reformation Erasmus had to cope with critics from both sides. Erasmus himself remained loyal to the Church of Rome, but had to seek protection from the reigning pope in order to silence fervent Catholic critics.[23] In fact this was the most important value that the papal briefs had for Erasmus, but they had only moderate success. Erasmus had been anxious after Adrian's election about possible condemnation without a chance of being heard, but in fact received two letters of protection from him (Allen 1324 and 1338, answering Allen 1304/1310 and 1329 respectively). The exact appraisal of the relation between Adrian and Erasmus is not relevant here: suffice it to say that there was a certain difference of interest between them, as Adrian thought Erasmus to be a prime candidate for undertaking the Catholic defence and tried to secure his co-operation, while Erasmus mainly needed Adrian's confirmation of support.[24] On the other hand, the question of Erasmus's position was followed with a keen interest by the Cranevelt circle.

Cranevelt had been used on previous occasions as an essential agent in Erasmus's defence in the Low Countries, as Erasmus had sent him some letters which Cranevelt could distribute among his fellow humanists or use against his opponents.[25] In the same way Erasmus now sent to Cranevelt a copy of Adrian's first letter to himself.[26] Apart from this copy, another one survived which was made by Gerard Geldenhouwer, a close friend of Cranevelt and secretary to the bishop of Utrecht, and remained

---

[21] Cf. *Litt. Cran.* 78 (by Fevynus; 31 October 1523): "De statu Romano, accepimus Cardinales 36 Conclave (quod vocant) intrasse; Gallos item illius collegii treis equis desultorii[s] et insperato supervenisse; nihildum tamen certi quisnam pontifex futurus: faxit Deus ut is aut melior sanctiorque Hadr[iano] sit, aut certe neutri partium favens, quisquis is fuerit."

[22] Cf. *Litt. Cran.* 81 (again by Fevynus; 30 November 1523). See, on Van der Poorten, dean of Eindhoven, *Litt. Cran.* 81 intr.

[23] See on Erasmus's position in general E. Rummel, *Erasmus and his Catholic Critics*, 2 vols., Bibliotheca Humanistica et Reformatorica 45 (Nieuwkoop, 1989). See on Erasmus and Rome in general also J. IJsewijn, "I rapporti tra Erasmo, l'umanesimo Italiano, Roma e Giulio II," in *Humanisme i literatura neollatina. Escrits seleccionats*, ed. col·lecció J. L. Barona, Col·lecció honoris causa 12 (Valencia, 1996), 87–103; J. B. Trapp, "Erasmus und Rom," in *Hochrenaissance im Vatikan*, 407–411.

[24] Cf. Verweij, "Een suggestie voor de Romereis, 2," 66–76.

[25] One bundle of such a collection has survived (*Litt. Cran.* 3–9, 14–36), though there must have been more (cf. *Litt. Bald.* 80 and 82 or *Litt. Cran.* 139).

[26] Viz. *Litt. Cran.* 28.

among his collection of notes on contemporary events.²⁷ Although it will never be established with absolute certainty, it seems highly probable that Geldenhouwer made his copy of this letter from the one Cranevelt had received. In any case, it again illustrates how certain documents circulated and how information was transmitted at a time with far fewer possibilities of communication than we are used to now.

After Adrian's death attempts to slander Erasmus started again and rumours of this situation, which was positively threatening for Erasmus, reached Bruges. In this case it appears that Fevynus's superior, the Bruges dean Marcus Laurinus, received a letter of a highly confidential nature written by Erasmus himself. Generally, Fevynus was allowed to read Erasmus's letters, but in this case things were different and he was told only in general terms about the Roman intrigue. Fevynus was very worried and wrote twice to Cranevelt about this matter.²⁸ In the end, however, all was well and Erasmus obtained papal protection once again. As in the case of the letter from Adrian, he sent a copy of this one from Clement VII to Cranevelt, which is the only copy of the letter to survive in the form as it was received by Erasmus.²⁹ In this way Cranevelt was being informed about this aspect of Roman politics, and he was used as well as a possible defender of Erasmus's interests in the Low Countries. In the story of Cranevelt's Roman relations these copies of letters from Adrian VI and Clement VII to Erasmus form a category of their own, as the focus of attention here is Erasmus rather than the pope or Rome.

With Adrian's death the amount of news from Rome and interest in it lessened, but it did not disappear. Another former official of Adrian introduced himself, namely Albertus Pigge from the Overijssel town of Kampen.³⁰ He also was a Leuven theologian and had been invited to Rome by Adrian. He may have been known to Cranevelt from his Leuven period. However that may be, Pigge and Cranevelt kept up a correspondence from 1524 to 1527, when, subsequently upon the Sack of Rome, Pigge must have returned to the Low Countries. In this period Pigge was Cranevelt's main contact in Rome and ensured a continuation of news from there. In Rome Pigge must have met Nicolas Herco Florenas, a former acquaintance of

---

²⁷ See on Geldenhouwer *CE* 2:82–84; I. Bejczy, S. Stegeman, and M. Verweij, *Gerard Geldenhouwer van Nijmegen (1482–1542). Historische werken* (Hilversum, 1998). The collection of notes is commonly known as the *Collectanea* and was edited by J. Prinsen in 1901 (*Collectanea van Gerardus Geldenhauer Noviomagus*; the letter can be found on pp. 133–137). See on this letter also M. Verweij, "Erasmus in the *Collectanea*, 1520–1530, of Gerard Geldenhouwer (1482–1542)," *Lias* 25 (1998): 31–41, here 38.

²⁸ Cf. *Litt. Cran.* 89 (24 January 1524) and 91 (2 February 1524). On these letters see M. Verweij, "Fevynus and Some Dark Rumours on Erasmus, Bruges Jan.–Feb. 1524," *Wolfenbütteler Renaissance Mitteilungen* 22 (1998): 5–9.

²⁹ Viz. Allen 1438 = *Litt. Cran.* 101 (30 April 1524). Allen dates this letter according to the Vatican minutes to 3 April. See on this question M. Verweij, "Remarks on Some So-called Erasmian Correspondence," *Humanistica Lovaniensia* 46 (1997): 114–126, here 121–122.

³⁰ On Pigge see *CE* 3:84–85; *Litt. Cran.* 97 intr. The letters written by Pigge from Rome are *Litt. Cran.* 97 (9 April 1524), 108 (15 June 1524), 114 (10 July 1524), 192 (2 June 1526), 197 (7 July 1526), 208 (9 November 1526), and 220 (5 January 1527). One letter written by Cranevelt to Pigge (but apparently never sent) has come down to us as *Litt. Cran.* 196 (27 June 1526).

Cranevelt, who visited Rome in 1526 and also wrote one letter to Cranevelt from the Eternal City: he was a humanist on a Grand Tour.[31]

It thus appears that epistolary contacts between Rome and Bruges or Mechlin were more frequent than might be expected at first sight, especially if one takes into account the fact that Rome is the only city outside the Low Countries figuring in this way in the Cranevelt letters. Cranevelt, however, apparently did not know any Italian humanists: his contacts were with men from Leuven University circles whom he would have met in Leuven and who followed Adrian after his election as pope. In fact, Adrian is the central theme of this correspondence. The most interesting document in this perspective, perhaps, is Cranevelt's own letter to the pope.

Apart from furnishing some information on a few Netherlanders in Rome in this period, the Cranevelt letters show how news was transmitted from a considerable distance and equally how this news was valued and circulated. The most important fact, however, is that they illustrate an aspect, neglected until now, of the Netherlandish presence in Rome during and immediately following the pontificate of Adrian. This presence is generally considered a leading characteristic of his pontificate, and in this light it may be interesting to note that in the Cranevelt letters interest was focused on this group almost entirely. It was perhaps the only period when the Low Countries had any real influence on Roman matters, and the Leuven presence in it was conspicuous. Interest in personal acquaintances who had made their way in Rome, together with sympathy for Pope Adrian and the expectations of his reign, lay at the bottom of Cranevelt's Roman connection.

Seminarium Philologiae Humanisticae
KULeuven

---

[31] On Herco Florenas see *Litt. Cran.* 154 intr. His letter from Rome is *Litt. Cran.* 181 (21 March 1526).

The Central Position of the Authors of Late Antiquity in Humanist Thought: The Case of Aeneas Silvius Piccolomini[1]

ZWEDER VON MARTELS

Or do you think it right that the learned should allow the Roman tongue [...] to which so many excellent branches of learning — to which the Christian religion itself — have been entrusted, [...] to die out in order not to give offence to the ignorant conceit of these individuals? Surely you do not judge it to be right that you should be the cause that great writers — I shall not mention Cicero, Quintilian, and others of this sort, but rather Cyprian, Jerome and Augustine — should perish, and that in in their place the *Catholicon*, Holcot, Bricot and Gorra should be read?[2]

This quotation from Erasmus is illustrative of the central importance humanists were wont to attribute to the Christian authors of Late Antiquity, the long period of cultural efflorescence following the political turmoil and the wars of the

---

[1] I am grateful to Professor Alasdair MacDonald who corrected the English of this article and made valuable suggestions.

[2] *Opera omnia Desiderii Erasmi Roterodami*, 1.2: *De conscribendis epistolis*, ed. J.-C. Margolin (Amsterdam, 1971), 219–220: "An aequum censes, vt docti romanam linguam, cui tot egregiae disciplinae, cui christiana religio concredita est, sinant intermori, ne quid offendant istorum indoctam arrogantiam? Num par esse iudicas committere vt intereant, non dicam Cicero, Quintilianus, et huius generis caeteri sed Cyprianus, Hieronymus, Augustinus, vt pro his legatur Catholicon, Holcot, Bricot et Gorra." In my translation I follow only in part that of Charles Fantazzi, which as a result of his changes of word order and a too free rendering no longer reflects Erasmus's meaning. See *Collected Works of Erasmus* (Toronto, 1985), 25:17, esp.: "Surely you do not think it fair that Cyprian, Jerome and Augustine — not to mention Cicero, Quintilian, and others like them — should be condemned to oblivion so that in their place the *Catholicon*, Holcot, Bricot, and Gorra may be read?"

middle of the third century A.D., and lasting until the Middle Ages set in. What I hope to show in this article — taking as my main example Aeneas Silvius Piccolomini — is that Christian and other authors of Late Antiquity are not to be regarded as a *quantité négligeable*, and that we do wrong to overlook Renaissance references to authors of that earlier period. However, I suspect that this is precisely what many of us are inclined to do when we encounter, next to the great names of Virgil, Cicero, Seneca, and Tacitus, other less familiar names such as Solinus, Isidore of Seville, and a plethora of Church Fathers. The undervaluing of such writers is the result of a long-lasting process, which, as far as the Christian authors are concerned, started with the Reformation, when the former organic coherence of the western cultural tradition began to disintegrate. The age of Classicism and its ensuing influence was, in general, unsuitable for the encouragement of any interests other than classical ones.[3] In my opinion, the relation between Late Antiquity and the Renaissance has not been studied adequately, although, of course, the references to pagan and Christian authors of Late Antiquity by Neo-Latin authors — beginning with Petrarch — have in many cases not escaped notice. But a full understanding of the importance of Late Antiquity for the Renaissance is lacking, and much work still has to be done before this can be attained. However, it may be that a turning point has now been reached, thanks to a new broadening of interests precipitated by various circumstances in the last forty years or so. The study of Neo-Latin, but also the study of Late Antiquity, has immensely benefited from this change. As a consequence, it is now inevitable that students of Late Antiquity and those of the Renaissance will meet each other sooner or later.

In outline, the following subjects will be treated in this paper. First, I briefly explain why, in my view, the integration of Late Antiquity into the whole of Latin studies is essential for the future development of (Neo-)Latin studies. Thereafter, I turn to Aeneas Silvius, first calling to mind some of the decisive moments of his life in connection with the theme of this paper. I then give an impression of the specific texts and authors which he recommended to young students, and of his vision of the development of the Latin literary tradition. The final part of the paper consists of a brief treatment of two examples showing influences from Christian authors of Late Antiquity. Before I begin with these points, I should like to enter a caveat: it will be difficult to stay within the boundaries of each consecutive historical period. Our rigorous modern division into epochs such as Classical Antiquity, Late Antiquity, the Middle Ages and so on is a relatively late invention, and is now becoming more and more problematic, since students are less inclined to keep within such traditionally prescribed areas. For Aeneas Silvius, at any rate, the separating lines between historical periods were always rather vague.

---

[3] On this subject, see Z. Von Martels, "Begrafenis en wederopstanding: een studie naar het wee en wel van het Neolatijn in de negentiende en twintigste eeuw," in *Limae labor et mora: opstellen voor Fokke Akkerman ter gelegenheid van zijn zeventigste verjaardag,* ed. idem, P. Steenbakkers, and A. Vanderjagt (Leende, 2000), 220–232.

Still, one often finds the Italian Renaissance designated by the circumscribing formulation of *Die Wiederbelebung des classischen Altertums*, as the title of Georg Voigt's famous book once defined it. With that, in essence, the great authors of pagan Antiquity spring to mind: names such as Virgil, Cicero, Ovid, Seneca, and Tacitus. These are still the authors taught at our schools today, and this fact may seem to imply that there is a convenient and pleasant similarity among (a) these modern times of ours, (b) the Renaissance, and (c) pagan antiquity. Unfortunately, there is only a shadow of truth in this supposition. As compared with ourselves, the humanists read and used the authors of the past in a quite different way, and for quite other purposes. In fact, they did this not so much for the sake of intellectual studies within small circles, but rather in order to make a way for themselves outside the walls of the university and into public life. Furthermore, the canon of authors studied by the humanists was not constricted by the normative and aesthetic ideas of the nineteenth century, but was one which had grown out of the Middle Ages. In general terms we may say that the present is to a great extent determined by its immediate past: we ourselves are involved first and foremost in an ongoing debate with the views of our parents and our not too distant forebears; at a generous reckoning, this dialectic goes back a mere two or three centuries. If this rule is conceded, much of what the Italian humanists were doing, therefore, was bound to be in reaction to the culture and tradition of the late Middle Ages. This means that they lived in a Christian world,[4] and one which had an intellectual basis in Late Antiquity. Moreover, the Italian humanists were wont often to read about the esteemed authors of the classical age through the eyes of the writers of Late Antiquity, while the latter, in their turn, had helped to shape the Middle Ages. Hence the frequent citations from Solinus, Isidore of Seville, Macrobius, Boethius, and from commentators such as Donatus and so on. Unfortunately, we tend most readily to perceive that which we have been taught, and we are often blind to elements that are unknown or strange to us. With these thoughts in mind, I shall attempt to bring a few corrections to the traditional perception of Aeneas Silvius Piccolomini, and, in so doing, try to direct attention back to Late Antiquity.

Aeneas Silvius Piccolomini was born in 1405, in Corsignano, which was later renamed by him as Pienza. For some time Piccolomini studied under Filelfo, but like Petrarch, Salutati, Bruni, Valla, Rudolf Agricola, and many other early humanists, he had also studied law for a couple of years. This fact should not be underestimated, even though, like many other humanists, he does not speak with enthusiasm about his law studies. Nonetheless, it was the study of law which brought them into contact with texts of the *Corpus Juris Civilis* of Justinian, and also with canon law based on both Roman law and Christian doctrine. Both kinds of law had some of their main roots in Late Antiquity. It should also be noted that humanists could benefit from this combination of studies, as they sought careers for themselves as secretaries, ambassadors, or those performing other public functions. Some insight into the juridical and theological complications of the dealings of society was required in such professions,

---

[4] See, in fact, Paul Oskar Kristeller, "Paganism and Christianity," in idem, *Renaissance Thought and its Sources*, ed. Michael Mooney (New York, 1979), 66–81.

and this proved to be no less useful than proficiency in Latin and skill in writing elegant letters and orations. Thanks to their study of literature, humanists had sharpened their historical perspective and their ability to relativise and with ease to adapt themselves to new situations. An interesting example of Piccolomini's intimate knowledge of law is to be found in his famous letter to his father concerning the illegitimate son which he had begotten by an English woman. After Piccolomini had sent the baby to his impecunious and aged parents, his father had written him letters of complaint. In appeasing his father, Piccolomini used some delightful arguments, derived from Boccaccio's *Decameron*, and also some more serious ones, from the Bible, classical authors, and natural law, as found in the glosses of Johannes Teutonicus. The letter in which these arguments appear is, therefore, an excellent example of the skilful way in which Piccolomini used tradition in order to convince a reader of what he thought was prudent and right.[5]

A sensational event in Piccolomini's life was his decision in 1444 to renounce the world and be ordained priest. Fourteen years later, he was elected pope, taking the name Pius II. A characteristic feature of his character was the unbending determination with which he pursued his goal. Already before the fall of Constantinople, in 1453, he had decided that a crusade against the Turks ought to be organized, but, after the refusal of all kings and princes to take up the cause, he, as pope, decided that he would have to lead the crusade himself. Fulfilling this duty, he died on board his crusader ship in 1464, still waiting in Ancona for departure.

What more did Piccolomini read? One recalls his deep love of Virgil, to whom he keeps referring. In a letter of 5 December 1443 to Sigismund, king of Austria, Piccolomini gives us an idea of the other authors he valued. He states that "nothing should be learned so that one has to unlearn it. But we must always assume the best things for imitation." He then recommends classical authors such as Quintilian, Cicero, Livy, Caesar, Virgil, and Pliny. As well as post-classical ones such as Vegetius, Macrobius, and Solinus, he also mentions Christian ones such as Isidore, Augustine, Ambrose, Gregory, and Lactantius, and he adds suggestions for specific disciplines such as geography and agriculture. Greek writers are absent, except for Aristotle's political works and Plutarch's educational writings, both in Latin translation. The list contains no medieval authors: according to Piccolomini, Thomas Aquinas, Peter of Blois, and others should not be imitated, for they cannot teach. However, he regards the culture of his own time as a continuation of Classical and Late Antiquity. This becomes clear

---

[5] See G. Kisch, *Enea Silvio Piccolomini und die Jurisprudenz* (Basel, 1967), 103–108. For more literature on the relation between law and humanism, see R. G. Witt, *In the Footsteps of the Ancients: The Origins of Humanism from Lovato to Bruni,* Studies in Medieval and Reformation Thought 74 (Leiden, 2000), 92. For Piccolomini's letter to his father of September 20, 1443, see R. Wolkan, *Der Briefwechsel des Eneas Silvius Piccolomini*, Fontes Rerum Austriacarum 61 (Vienna, 1909), 188–191, esp. 189; for Johannes Teutonicus, see Gratian, *Decretum emendatum et notationibus illustratum, una cum glossis* (Turin, 1620), col. 4, s.v. "Quid sit ius naturale." Piccolomini's letter will be discussed in a separate article by the present author.

when he recommends Francesco Barbaro's book on marriage, and — in Piccolomini's letter on education to King Ladislaus — other contemporary authors.[6]

Piccolomini praised these ancient authors for the fact that they had laid the foundations for various disciplines; as such, they are the best teachers. For Piccolomini, Antiquity forms a continuum, coming to an end only after the transformations affecting Latin had left things past recovery. This picture is corroborated by his sketch of the development of the Latin language. Piccolomini, in his life of Bruni in the *De viris illustribus*, notes that Latin has undergone continuous changes. The embellishment of, and interest in, literature had increased until Cicero's time. At that point it had attained its greatest fulness, and was unable to grow any further; this situation, moreover, lasted until the time of Jerome and Gregory, though not without some diminishment; after that, however, it perished completely.[7] As a result, Ciceronian Latin was a much looser and more relative concept for Piccolomini than for us today. Under the influence of later developments, we are accustomed to take the term "Ciceronian Latin" literally, and not as a designation for a more general tradition.

The canon of authors mentioned by Piccolomini was meant for students and their teachers. He himself, however, followed another course. Twice he quotes Pliny the Elder's view that even the most foolish book contains something of value.[8] We should therefore not be surprised to find in Piccolomini's works many (often hidden) borrowings from writings of contemporaries, and a considerable number of medieval authors as well. He often used these authors as a source of inspiration!

There was a continuous debate in the Renaissance about the important question of whether Christians should be allowed to read pagan authors. After he had become a bishop, Piccolomini did not avoid this issue in his letters and orations. His historical approach to life, his belief in the changing nature of material things, and, at the same time, in the permanent value of particular virtues, had armed him against what one might call ideological philosophers and theologians. Rather, he followed eclectic thinkers like Cicero and Pliny the Elder, and in so doing he sought advice from the Christian defenders of these Romans, for example, the Church Fathers such as Sts. Jerome, Ambrose, and Basil. These great men had allowed pagan texts to be read, if only with a discerning mind. The reason for this permission was that pagan literature could also help one to distinguish between vice and virtue.[9] Such passages show that

---

[6] Letter of Aeneas Silvius to Duke Sigismund of Austria, of 5 December 1443, in Wolkan, *Briefwechsel*, 222–236, esp. 228–231. For a more extensive educational programme, see Aeneas Silvius's letter to King Ladislaus entitled *De liberorum educatione*, of February 1450, in Wolkan, *Briefwechsel*, pt. 2, 103–158.

[7] E. S. Piccolomini, *De viris illustribus*, ed. A. van Heck, Studi e testi 341 (Città del Vaticano, 1991), 34.

[8] For Pliny the Elder's attitude, see Pliny the Younger, *Epistulae*, 3.5.10. For Piccolomini's quotation, see *Aeneae Syluii Pii II Pontificis Maximi in historiam rerum ubique gestarum locorumque descriptionem praefacio* in *Opera omnia* (Basel, 1571; repr. Frankfurt, 1967), "nec liber tam ineptus, qui non afferat aliquid emolumenti." In his letter to King Ladislaus of February 1450, Piccolomini adds that Pliny's words do not apply to children (see Wolkan, *Briefwechsel*, 103–158, esp. 144).

[9] See Aeneas Silvius's letter to Zbigniew Olésnicki of 27 October 1453 in Wolkan, *Brief-*

Piccolomini, after his ordination, had become more selective in what was to be singled out from tradition. Moral reasons, as much as practical ones, became the decisive arguments in the defence of pagan literature.

The Bible, Church Fathers, and ecclesiastical literature had an ever greater effect upon Piccolomini's mind as he grew older and wiser; the *Commentarii*, composed during his papacy, are proof of this. Philological studies have been made of passages such as that mentioning the boat race at the Lago di Bolsena after the model of Virgil's Fifth Book of the *Aeneid*,[10] but the numerous passages inspired by Christian authors have hardly drawn any attention. What strikes us time and again is that Pius, without distancing himself from his Christian conviction, tries, as much as possible, to *integrate* elements from the pagan and Christian traditions. Two examples may suffice. First, Piccolomini was fascinated with the idea of personal glory, which had preoccupied Cicero and Sallust, but after them many ambitious men as well. Long before his election as pope, Piccolomini was aware that, according to the Church Fathers, the classical form of the idea of earthly fame was incompatible with the Christian belief that one's soul lives on after death, either suffering a wretched lot or joining the company of blessed spirits, as a consequence of which we, in our actions, should be preoccupied with the future of our soul and not with temporary fame on earth. But in the preface to his *Commentaries*,[11] Pius, with a sense of realism, combines the best of both ways of thinking. He confirms the Christian belief that after death souls do not benefit from the reputation they may have enjoyed on earth. On the other hand, he adds that it cannot be denied that while men live they take pleasure in the glory of the present, which they hope will continue after death. So glory becomes — as it seems, in the footsteps of Augustine[12] — a psychological incentive for brilliant intellects, and, as Pius emphatically adds, an even greater incentive than the hope of heavenly life. The thought of glory makes it easier for such spirits to endure criticism. This is especially true, Pius continues, for the Pope of Rome, whom almost all men abuse while he lives among them, but praise when he is dead.

---

wechsel, pt. 3, 315–347, esp. 342 ff.; J. D. Mansi, ed., *Pii II. P.M. olim Aeneae Piccolominei Senensis Orationes politicae et ecclesiasticae*, 3 vols. (Lucca, 1755–1759), 1:38–54, esp. 48 ff. (*Oratio II Habita Basileae in Divi Ambrosii celebritate*). For the importance of Basil's defence of the reading of the pagan poets, see, Kristeller, "Paganism and Christianity," esp. 73, 272 (n. 25).

[10] Norbert Seeber, *Enea Vergilianus: Vergilisches in den "Kommentaren" des Enea Silvio Piccolomini (Pius II.)*, Commentationes Aenipontanae 30 (Innsbruck, 1997).

[11] *Pii II commentarii rerum memorabilium que temporibus suis contigerunt ad codicum fidem nunc primum editi*, ed. A. van Heck, 2 vols., Studi e testi 312–313 (Città del Vaticano, 1984), 1: *Praefatio*. For the translation, see *The Commentaries of Pius II: Books I–XIII*, trans. F. A. Gragg, intro. L. C. Gabel (Northampton, 1937–1957), 9.

[12] For Augustine, who regarded glory as a reward and a compensation for the burdens connected with public responsibility, see A. J. Vermeulen, *The Semantic Development of Gloria in Early-Christian Latin*, Latinitas christianorum primaeva 12 (Nijmegen, 1956), 49. For the classical concept of *gloria* see A. D. Leeman, "Gloria: Cicero's waardering van de roem en haar achtergrond in de wijsbegeerte en de Romeinse samenleving" (Ph.D. diss., University of Leiden, 1949).

In this example, then, we witness the happy reconciliation of two formerly contradictory views.

My second example of the influence of Christian ideas on Piccolomini's thought concerns the responsibility and duty of princes. An early formulation of his views on this issue is to be found in the oration which he gave before Pope Nicholas V on 5 June 1452. There, on behalf of the German emperor, he asked the pope for permission to organize a crusade against the Turks. Combining three short passages of Cicero's *De officiis*, the orator stated:

> Princes, says the [Prophet], should think things worthy of princes. It was for the sake of enjoying the benefits of justice that the kings of the Medes heretofore, as we are told by Herodotus, and the kings of all peoples, as Cicero believes, were created, as the men who ward off injuries, and who, if they are willing to listen to the right precepts of the great Plato and other philosophers, will try to direct the management of the state not to their own interest but to that of those who are entrusted to them.[13]

In other words, the king is chosen by the people to protect the latter from injustice; and second, the king is not chosen to benefit from the state, but the state should benefit from the actions of the king.

From his later actions, it is clear that Piccolomini was here thinking as much of the duties of the emperor as of his own responsibilities, first as bishop, later as cardinal and pope. He chose as his main task the defence of Christemdom against the Turks. His *De Asia* describes how the Christian world had constantly been threatened since the rise of Islam and had finally been pushed back within the boundaries of Europe. Only a crusade could redress this situation. The orations which Piccolomini gave at Frankfurt and Mantua, and on various other occasions, show the evolution of his thinking, which eventually led to his bold decision around 1462 that he himself would head the Christian army against the Turks, since otherwise no prince would be prepared to fight for this holy goal. Interestingly, in his last great oration to his cardinals, in November 1463, Pius still clung to his old conviction that the leader is responsible for his people; the leader should stand up for justice. This time, as he spoke to his cardinals, he could not use Cicero's words, but he found assurance and

---

[13] A. F. Kollarius, *Analecta monumentorum omnis aevi Vindobonensia*, 2 vols. (Vienna, 1762), 1:76: *Aeneae Silvii Episcopi Senensis, qui postea Pius Papa II fuit, Historia rerum Friderici III Imperatoris*; see esp. 308: "Principes, inquit Sapiens, quae sunt digna Principe cogitabunt. 'Reges apud Medos,' ut Herodotus inquit, apud omnes, ut Cicero sensit, 'justitiae fruendae causa' sunt creati, 'injuriarum propulsatores,' qui si Platoni magno voluerint auscultare, caeterisque Philosophis recta monentibus obedire, 'procurationem Rei Publicae non ad suam, sed ad eorum, qui sibi commissi sunt, utilitatem' convertere conabuntur." Words derived from Cicero's *De officiis*, 2.41, 3.74 and 1.85 are in single quotation marks. A slightly different (but probably incorrect) version of this text is to be found in Mansi, ed., *Orationes politicae*, 1:164 (*Oratio X. Ad Nicolaum V. PP. ut Caesarem Fridericum in Turcos passagium parantem modis omnibus adjuvare velit*). The introductory words here are taken from Isaiah 32:8 [Vg.].

support in the traditional language of the church. He mentions his papal duty to defend his Church from bad influences, which he saw creeping in from all sides; he spoke of the need to follow the martyrs of the Church, and of his desire to imitate Christ, who had given his life for the people in order to preserve what was right and just.[14] The step from the pagan world of Cicero to the world of the Church Fathers was not such a great one for a man who was wont to extract the best elements from the European tradition as a whole.

What has been said about the influence of the Christian authors of Late Antiquity on Piccolomini can easily be extended to non-Christian writers of that era. Solinus, for instance, a writer today almost unanimously reviled on account of his style and subject matter, was cited at least thirteen times in Pius's *De Asia*; indeed he praised him elsewhere as a "not unreliable author" ("Solinus ... non futilis auctor").[15] I am confident that with some effort we shall easily find many more such examples. What is required, however, is the will to move away from the traditional approach taken to Latin literature during the last two centuries, where, generally speaking, the great classical authors have been regarded as the exclusive standard, to the detriment of all later periods. As far as Piccolomini is concerned, one should perhaps constantly keep in mind how Jacob Burckhardt described this humanist — whom, in one of his letters, he had called his "Liebling"![16] — as someone who "dem Normalmenschen der Frührenaissance wie wenige andere nahe kommt."[17] In these words Burckhardt expressed his deep admiration for the harmonious and natural way in which Piccolomini had used his talents in accordance with the intellectual culture of his time.[18] This culture was grounded upon the many layers of the long Latin tradition, and — as I have tried to demonstrate — Piccolomini, with great common sense, left none of these layers unused.

---

[14] *Pii II commentarii rerum*, 2:764–775; *The Commentaries of Pius II*, trans. Gragg, pp. 817–827. About his role, see R. Vaughan, *Philip the Good: The Apogee of Burgundy. A History of Valois Burgundy* (London, 1970). For a discussion of this period of Pius's life, from a different angle, see A. G. Jongkees, "Pie II et Philippe le Bon, deux protagonistes de l'union chrétienne," in *Burgundica et varia: Keuze uit de verspreide opstellen van prof. dr. A. G. Jongkees hem aangeboden ter gelegenheid van zijn tachtigste verjaardag*, ed. E. O. van der Werff, C. A. A. Linssen, and B. Ebels-Hoving (Hilversum, 1990), 172–190.

[15] Josephus Cugnoni, *Aeneae Silvii Piccolomini Senensis . . . opera inedita descripsit ex codicibus chisianis vulgavit notisque illustravit* (Rome, 1883), 280.

[16] Ludwig von Pastor, *Tagebücher, Briefe, Erinnerungen*, ed. W. Wühr (Heidelberg, 1950), 273.

[17] J. Burckhardt, *Die Kultur der Renaissance in Italien*, Gesamtausgabe 5 (Basel, 1930), 215.

[18] For an evaluation of Burckhardt's utterances, see B. Widmer, *Enea Silvio Piccolomini in der sittlichen und politischen Entscheidung*, Basler Beiträge zur Geschichtswissenschaft 88 (Basel-Stuttgart, 1963), 1–3.

Index

Adrian VI, pope, 84, 596–602 *passim*
Aelian, 194, 196, 476
Aeneas Sylvius Piccolomini (Pope Pius II), 15, 116n., 126, 338n., 341n., 342n., 574, 604–10 *passim*
Aesop, 116n., 351, 356
Agricola, Rudolf, 164–66, 168–70, 250, 505, 605
Agrippa, Heinrich Cornelius, von Nettesheim, 279–86 *passim*, 431
Alberti, Leon Battista, 321, 545n., 546
Albertus Magnus, 195
alchemy, 105, 144
Aldrovandi, Ulisse, 197, 198
Aldus Manutius, 14–15, 17, 65, 66, 68, 566n.
Alexander VI, pope, 211
allegory, 24, 26–27, 29–32, 34–41 *passim*, 115, 117, 118–19, 231, 284, 332, 343, 382, 445, 504, 506, 510, 542, 545–53 *passim*
Ambrose of Milan, 231, 341n., 342n., 529, 606, 607
America, *see* Columbus, Christopher; Mexico; New World, discovery and conquest of
Anjou, house of, 115–20, 540
Anne, queen of England, 362
Antipater of Sidon, 338n.
Antiphon, 410
Apollonius Rhodius, 338n., 340n., 341n.
Appian, 341n., 342n.
Apuleius, 23–41, 283, 286, 338n., 340n., 341n.

Aquinas, Thomas, 208, 309, 311, 312, 317, 318, 348, 349, 504, 505, 550n., 606
Aratus, 50, 341n., 342n.
Arias Montano, Benito, 422, 436, 440, 587, 591
Ariosto, *Orlando furioso*, 214, 244, 383, 433, 553n.
Aristophanes, 161, 340n., 341n., 522
Aristotle, 96, 98, 99, 163n., 193–94, 196, 209, 231, 234, 242, 252, 275, 338n., 340n., 341n., 342n., 351, 575
   Categories, 312, 349, 461
   Ethics, 165, 578
   Historia animalium, 193–95, 198, 275n.
   Physics, 208, 210, 312
   Poetics, 153, 298, 478n., 479
   Politics, 453, 577, 606
Athanasius of Alexandria, 341n., 342n.
Athenaeus, *Deipnosophistae*, 155–62 *passim*
Augustine of Canterbury, 347n.
Augustine of Hippo, 218, 231, 235, 317, 338n., 339, 340n., 341n., 349, 425, 505, 603, 606, 608
   City of God, 231–32n., 432, 529, 567
   Confessions, 208
   De doctrina christiana, 212n., 425, 504, 505
Aulus Gellius, 337n., 338n., 340n., 341n., 346

Aurelius Victor (ps.-) (historian), 484–88
Ausonius, 377, 555
   Mosella, 55, 338n.
autobiography, 161–62, 181–85 *passim*
Averroes (Ibn Rushd), 208
Avicenna (Ibn Sina), 208, 338n., 340n., 341n.

Bacon, Francis, 241, 243, 367
Bacon, Roger, 208
Badius Ascensius, Jodocus, 337–44 *passim*
Baptista Mantuanus, 337–44 *passim*, 561, 562
Barbaro, Ermolao, 12, 13, 17, 18, 250
Barbaro, Francesco, 2
Baronius, Cardinal, 158
Bartholomaeus Anglicus, 194
Bartolini, Riccardo, 559
Barzizzio, Gasparino, 419–26 *passim*
Basil of Caesarea, 165, 607
Bayle, Pierre, 1, 204
Beatus Rhenanus, 18–19, 353, 354–55, 357
Bede, 208, 235
Bembo, Pietro, 49, 449, 559
Berger, Elias, 535–43 *passim*
Bernardus Silvestris, 546
Beroaldo, Filippo, 12, 13, 16, 17, 337n.
   commentary on Apuleius, 23, 24, 34, 36, 37–41 *passim*
Bessarion, Cardinal, 9, 10
Bible, 27, 122, 182, 210, 235, 279–80, 285, 316, 338n., 339, 340, 341, 342, 351–52, 493, 501n., 503–8, 536, 576, 578, 587, 591, 606, 608; *see also* Genesis
Blondel, François-Nicolas, 474–81 *passim*
Boccaccio, Giovanni, 21, 23, 24, 29–33 *passim*, 40, 115–16, 119, 233, 244, 341n., 342n., 494
   Decameron, 606

Boethius, 153, 213, 337n., 338n., 605
   De musica, 160
Boiardo, Matteo Maria, 115
Boileau, Nicolas, 474, 478, 479, 480, 481
Bonaventure, 208
Brant, Sebastian, 337, 339, 341, 342–44
Bruni, Leonardo, 126, 427, 574, 605
Buchanan, George, 151–53, 348
Budé, Guillaume, 201–5, 250, 343
Bussi, Giovanni Andrea, 8–12, 36–37
Byzantine literature, 161, 351, 429, 592

Caesar, Julius, 128, 275, 346, 348, 349, 388, 568, 606
Callimachus, 171, 175
Calvin, John, 128, 591
Capilupi, Lelio, 377–83 *passim*
Caro, Rodrigo, 435–42 *passim*
Carroll, Lewis, 287, 295
de las Casas, Bartolomé, 313, 319, 576, 581
Casaubon, Isaac, 155–62 *passim*
Cassiodorus, 527, 530, 532
Castiglione, Baldassare, 560, 562
   Il cortegiano, 310, 449–54 *passim*
Cato the Elder, 340n., 341n., 346, 347, 505
Catullus, 67–68, 158n., 168, 171, 179, 291, 338n., 340n., 410, 557
Celtis, Conrad, 187, 431, 519, 574
Censorinus, 209–10
Cervantes, Miguel de, *Don Quixote*, 443, 515
Charles I, king of England, 253–54, 256–62, 364
Charles II, king of England, 282
Charles V, emperor, 17, 83–101, 211, 274, 275, 279, 312, 330–34, 575, 588, 596, 597, 598
Christian V, king of Norway, 466
Christianization, literary, 11, 26–27, 31–33, 36, 38, 165, 229, 231–32,

236, 415–16, 447, 457, 476, 546, 551–52, 561, 567, 578, 582, 605, 607–8, 610
Cicero, 100, 122, 123, 165, 180, 211, 213, 232, 235, 252, 259, 297, 338n., 339, 340n., 341n., 343, 345–46, 351, 521, 567–68, 603, 604, 605, 606, 607, 608, 610
 Ad Herennium (ascr.), 420–22, 425–26, 521
 De Amicitia, 165, 431
 De Officiis, 349, 609
 De Inventione, 210
 Letters (*Epistulae*), 10, 122, 168, 346n., 573, 577, 578, 579n., 580
 Oratorical works, 419–26 *passim*
 Philippics, 337n.
 Pro Milone, 348, 423
 Tusculan Disputations, 552–53
Cinthias, poem, 115–20 *passim*
Clairambault, Louis, 57
classicism, literary, 24–25, 43–60 *passim*, 62, 145–53 *passim*, 175, 177, 179, 277, 366, 367, 436, 438, 457, 479–80, 515, 526, 527, 530, 532–33, 561, 567, 569, 604
Claudian, 153, 341n., 342n., 542, 555
Clement VI, pope, 118
Clement VII, pope, 96, 211, 331, 561, 577, 598, 600, 601
Clement VIII, pope, 520
Colonna, Fabio, 198
Coluccio Salutati, 2, 551, 605
Columbus, Christopher, 49, 54, 273, 275–76
Constantine, emperor, legend of, 538, 539, 541
Copernicus, Nicholas, 188
van Cranevelt, Franciscus, 595–602 *passim*
Cromwell, Oliver, 364, 369
Cyprian of Carthage, 603

Dante Alighieri, 115, 291, 493, 548–49, 550n., 552n., 560

Dantiscus (Dantiszek), Jan, 187, 555–63 *passim*
Dati, Leonardo, 145, 147, 150–51, 321–26 *passim*
Della Porta, Giambattista, 306
Descartes, René, 217–27 *passim*, 241, 242
didactic poetry, 43–60 *passim*, 235, 299, 301, 302, 332
Diodorus Siculus, 338n., 340n., 341
Diogenes Laertius, 164, 340n., 341n., 351
Dionysius the Areopagite (ps.-), 550
Dionysius Exiguus, 208
Dionysius of Halicarnassus, 297, 521
Dionysius Thrax, 338n.
Dioscorides, 157, 198, 338n.
Doissin, Louis, 59
Donatus (grammarian), 338n., 340n., 341n., 605
Donne, John, 357
Dousa, Janus, 591
drama, 145–53 *passim*, 303–10 *passim*, 371–76 *passim*, 395–408 *passim*, 409–17 *passim*, 443–48 *passim*, 509–15 *passim*, 517, 521
Duns Scotus, 208

Edward VI, king of England, 286, 584–85, 586, 588, 589, 590, 592
elegiac poetry, 171–80 *passim*, 184, 194, 332, 555, 565
Elizabeth I, queen of England, 362, 409, 411, 416, 591, 593
England, Latin in, 253–62 *passim*, 303–10 *passim*, 361–69 *passim*, 395–408 *passim*, 409–17 *passim*; *see also individual authors*
Ennius, 338n., 340n., 341n., 346, 426
Eobanus Hessus, Helius, 185, 431, 494, 498
epic poetry, 229, 298, 300, 322–26 *passim*, 332, 366n., 460, 493–501 *passim*, 537–43 *passim*, 558
Epicureanism, 163, 170, 225

epigram, 66, 332–34, 351–59 *passim*, 361–69 *passim*, 388, 438, 439–41, 513, 555
Epiphanius of Salamis, 521
epistolography, 272, 274–75, 352, 385–93 *passim*, 555, 573–82 *passim*, 595–602 *passim*
epithalamium, 301, 302, 517–18, 521, 555, 557–58, 589
Erasmus of Rotterdam, 94, 96–97, 100–1, 152, 156–57, 166, 169, 183, 201–5, 249–50, 263–70 *passim*, 343, 351, 353, 429, 436, 556, 562, 577, 585, 596, 598, 600, 603
  Adagia, 514, 592, 593
  Antibarbari, 2
  Colloquies, 282
  epigrams, 351, 353
  Exomologesis, 263–70 *passim*
  Letters, 17, 201–4, 371, 574, 580n., 581, 595, 600–1
  Ratio . . . verae theologiae, 503–8 *passim*
  Praise of Folly, 282, 283, 286, 356, 358, 460
ethnography, 525–33 *passim*
Eton College, 367, 395
Eugenius IV, pope, 321, 323
Eunapius (sophist), 591, 593
Euripides, 134, 150, 152, 153, 161
Eutropius (historian), 484
Eusebius of Caesarea, 338n., 341n., 342n.

Fabricius Montanus, Ioannes, 181–85 *passim*
Falcó, Jaime Juan, 329, 332–35 *passim*
Fellon, Thomas, 55–56
Ferdinand and Isabella, monarchs of Aragon and Castile, 272–73, 274n., 275
Ferrara, court of, 208–15, 431–33, 525n.
Ferrara-Florence, Council of, 321

Festus Pompeius (historian), 338n., 340n., 341, 342n.
Ficino, Marsilio, 164–65, 166–67, 452, 545n., 552n., 574
Filelfo, Francesco, 9, 12, 271, 341n., 342n., 574, 605
Florence, scholarship in, 23, 33–34, 166–68, 321, 323
Florus (historian), 483, 484
football, in Latin, 400, 404–5
Fracastoro, Girolamo, *Syphilis*, 44, 48–50, 53, 55n., 57
Frederick III, emperor, 433
Frederick of Aragon, 565–71 *passim*
Fulgentius, 23, 24–27, 30, 34–35, 38, 40, 41, 546, 551

Gager, William, 409–17 *passim*
Galileo, 59
Gambara, Lorenzo, 58
Gaza, Theodore, 8, 10, 208, 214
Genesis, book of, as model, 26, 27, 35, 58, 281, 284, 285, 538, 567
Geoponica, 157
George II, king of England, 362
George of Trebizond, 429
Gesner, Conrad, 197, 198
Giannettasio, Nicolò Parthenio, 54, 57, 58
Gilbert and Sullivan, in Latin, 402
Giovio, Paolo (Paulus Jovius), 195, 215n.
Giraldi, Lilio Gregorio, 207–16 *passim*
golf, in Latin, 403–4
Greek Anthology, 351, 355
Greek language, as cultural factor, 304, 345–46, 351, 354, 362, 365, 388, 427, 429, 504–5, 578, 581
Gregory I (the Great), pope, 347n., 606, 607
Gregory Naziazen, 158
Grotius, Hugo, 385–93 *passim*
Guarini, Battista, 126
Guarini, Guarino, 7, 419n., 428, 431, 432, 577n.

Gustav Vasa, king of Sweden, 301, 525, 527

Heinsius, Daniel, 473
Henry VIII, king of England, 352, 356–57, 372, 373, 584, 589
Herbert, George, 253–62 passim, 364
Herodotus, 193, 196, 198, 338n., 339, 340n., 341, 609
Hesiod, 50, 338n., 340n., 341n., 342n., 581
historiography, 123–24, 126–27, 128–29, 188–91, 271, 535–36, 575, 577, 592, 593
Homer, 157, 176, 229, 234, 338n., 339, 340, 341n., 342n., 365, 410, 460, 542, 548, 581
　Iliad, 172, 350, 464, 517, 568n., 581
　　in Latin, 493–501 passim
　Odyssey, 49, 53, 350, 548n., 549n., 552n., 568
　　in Latin, 493, 496, 497
Horace, 165, 184, 233, 338n., 339, 340, 341, 343, 366, 432, 438, 473–81, 555, 557
　Ars poetica, 298, 299, 464, 477
humanism, 2, 11, 12, 13, 69, 72–73, 124, 126, 128, 165–70, 183, 185, 201–5, 232, 239–46, 249–52, 271, 277, 297, 300, 301, 307, 310, 321, 351, 352, 353–55, 356, 427–34, 435–36, 494, 515, 525–33, 556–62, 583, 594, 595–96, 603–6; see also individual localities
Hungary, scholarship in, 428–31, 433, 535–43
Huygens, Constantijn, 390
hymnography, 555, 561–62

Iamblichus, 164
Innocent VIII, pope, 272
Inquisition, 94–95, 121–22, 127, 275, 309, 348, 576
Isidore of Seville, 194, 208, 212, 231, 429, 504, 604, 605, 606

Isocrates, 468

James I, king of England, 258–60, 303, 306, 307, 363
James II, king of England, 368
Janus Pannonius, 428, 431–33, 540, 542
Jerome, 15, 165, 210, 213, 231, 338n., 340n., 341n., 342n., 504–5, 578, 603, 607
Jesuits, 54, 55, 56, 57, 59, 443–48, 475, 478, 495n., 509–15, 535
John, king of Portugal, 349–50
John III, king of Sweden, 301
John Chrysostom, 157, 158
Jonson, Ben, 304, 307, 357
Jordanes, 527, 529
Josephus, 338n., 340n., 341, 342n.
　Antiquitates Judaicae, 127
Julius II, pope, 70n., 76, 188
Julius III, pope, 92, 528
Justin (historian), 338n., 339, 340n., 341, 530
Juvenal, 11, 12, 337n., 338n., 339, 340, 341, 477

Kaempfer, Engelbert, 131–38 passim

Lactantius, 338n., 340n., 341n., 342n., 346, 606
Landino, Cristoforo, 15, 545–53 passim
Latin language, as cultural factor, 14, 303–10, 329, 335, 354, 361–69, 435–38, 441, 444, 446, 449–54, 510–13, 606, 607
law, study of, 605–6
Le Febvre, François-Antoine, 57
Leo X, pope, 85, 86, 87, 95, 188, 213–14, 301, 561
Leto, Pomponio (Pomponius Laetus), Giulio, 13, 271, 341n., 342n., 427, 430, 431
Lhomond, Charles François, 483–91 passim
Lipsius, Justus, 436, 479, 523

"Longinus", *On the Sublime*, 152, 473, 477, 478, 479, 480
Lotichius Secundus, Petrus, 182, 184
Louis XIV, king of France, 53, 59, 204, 365, 368
Livy, 232, 236, 338n., 339, 340n., 341, 483, 484–91 *passim*, 513, 606
Lucan, *De Bello Civile*, 149n., 153, 229, 337n., 338n., 339, 340, 341, 342, 542
Lucas, Jean, 59
Lucian, 36, 351
Lucilius, 346
Lucretius, 45, 50, 65, 203, 210, 213, 233n., 338n., 339n., 341n.
Luther, Martin, 83–101, 128, 250, 266, 269, 335, 429, 598

Machiavelli, Nicolo, 126, 127, 322, 450
Macrobius, *Commentary on the Dream of Scipio*, 15, 54, 204, 208, 211, 338n., 340n., 432, 548, 605, 606
Magnus, Olaus, 193–99 *passim*, 525–33 *passim*
Manilius, 48, 160, 203
Marius Victorinus, 211
Marmion, Shakerly, 35
Martial, 11, 12, 13, 68, 333, 338n., 340n., 341, 342n., 351, 440, 555, 591
Martianus Capella, 24, 30, 34, 338n., 419, 422–23
Marullus, Michael, 62–68 *passim*, 74, 77, 558–59
Mary I, queen of England, 589, 590
Mary Queen of Scots, 348–49
Mary, Virgin, veneration of, 285–86, 438, 441
de'Medici, Cosimo, 166–68
de'Medici, Lorenzo, 546, 553
Melanchthon, Philipp, 121–29 *passim*, 182, 183, 184, 348, 429
Merula, Giorgio, 9–10, 12, 13

Mexico, scholarship in, 121–29 *passim*, 311–19 *passim*, 494
Middleton, Thomas, 307
Milton, John, 368, 455–62 *passim*
More, Thomas, 201, 203–4, 205, 595
  De tristitia Christi, 371–76 *passim*
  Epigrammata, 351–59 *passim*
  Letters, 595n.
  Utopia, 282, 351, 358, 372
Muret, M.-A., 152–53
Muslims, war against, 272–73, 274n., 330, 331, 332, 333, 366, 433, 537, 538, 540, 541, 542, 566, 571, 599n., 606, 609

Nabokov, Vladimir, 287–95 *passim*
Nebrija, Antonio de, 249, 250, 514
Netherlands (Low Countries), scholarship in the, 385–93 *passim*, 583–94 *passim*, 595–602 *passim*
New World, discovery and conquest of, 45, 49, 54, 273–77, 311–19, 331, 530–31; *see also* Columbus, Christopher
Nicander, 56
Nicholas V, pope, 449, 609
Noceti, Charles, 57
Norway, scholarship in, 193–99 *passim*, 463–72 *passim*

Ockham, William of, 208
onomastics, 427–34 *passim*
Ovid, 50, 171–72, 180, 184, 337n., 338n., 339, 340, 341, 342, 343, 410, 411, 412, 416, 500, 555, 605
  Amores, 293
  Ars Amatoria, 172
  Fasti, 176, 214, 432
  Metamorphoses, 47–48, 49, 51n., 52, 54n., 56, 58, 60, 147, 149, 153, 213, 409, 414, 416, 417, 523, 551
  Tristia, 106, 107, 143, 184, 185, 514

Paladino, Paolo, 565–71 *passim*
Pasquali Marinelli, Giuseppe, 493–501 *passim*
pastoral, 115–20, 173, 175–76, 235–36, 462, 521, 558
patristics, *see individual authors*
Patrizi, Francesco, 10, 530
Paul II, pope, 8, 211, 322
Paul III, pope, 90, 91, 92, 381
Paul IV, pope, 588
Paul the Deacon, 527, 529
Pausanias, 476
Persius, 337n., 338n., 339, 340n., 341n.
Peter Martyr d'Anghiera, 83–84, 85, 86–88, 271–78 *passim*, 530–31
Petrarch (Petrarca), Francesco, 2, 7, 15, 28, 52, 115, 182, 214, 229–37 *passim*, 244, 411, 427, 429, 560, 573, 574, 604, 605
  De viris illustribus, 485
  De vita solitaria, 552
philology, *see* humanism; textual criticism
Pico della Mirandola, Gianfrancesco, 561
Pico della Mirandola, Giovanni, 13, 250, 371, 374
Pindar, 338n., 473–81 *passim*
Pirckheimer, Willibald, 354
Pius V, pope, 504
Platina, Bartolommeo, 430
Plato, 163–70 *passim*, 210, 211, 338n., 340n., 341n., 342n., 351, 452, 458, 609
  Parmenides, 349
  Protagoras, 453n.
Plautus, 217–27 *passim*, 306n., 338n., 340n., 341n., 342n., 351, 436, 470, 477, 522
Plethon, George Gemistus, 429
Pliny the Elder, *Historia naturalis*, 7–21 *passim*, 56, 157, 193–94, 196, 275, 338n., 339, 340, 341, 342, 343, 346, 526, 528, 529, 578, 606, 607

Pliny the Younger, *Letters*, 573, 607n.
Plutarch, 127, 338n., 340n., 341n., 351, 452, 478, 532–33, 567, 577n., 606
Poggio Bracciolini, 2, 36, 203
Poland, scholarship in, 187–91 *passim*, 517–23 *passim*, 555–63 *passim*
Politian (Angelo Poliziano), 12, 13, 15, 16, 18, 72, 73, 172, 208, 249, 250, 322, 494, 557, 574
Polybius, 162, 346, 568n.
Pontano, Giovanni, 47–48, 50, 52, 53, 68, 71, 116, 171–80 *passim*, 208, 429, 557
  "sodalitas" of, 61–82 *passim*
Porphyry, *De Praedicabilibus*, 349
  Isagoge, 312
printing, impact of, 7–8, 11, 94, 240–41, 347, 348, 355
Priscian, 74, 340n., 341n., 342n.
Procopius, 391, 527
Propertius, 171, 172, 173–79 *passim*, 338n., 340n., 555
Protestantism, 83–101 *passim*, 121–29 *passim*, 143, 144, 158–59, 181–82, 250, 254, 266, 282, 286, 301, 302, 308, 309, 310, 331, 332, 378, 379, 380, 381, 525, 529–30, 532, 541, 578, 583–94 *passim*, 596, 600; *see also* Luther, Martin
Prudentius, 152, 341n., 342n., 555
Ptolemy, *Geographia*, 188, 340n., 341n.

Quevedo, Francisco de, 329–33, 334, 335
Quintilian, *Institutiones oratoricae*, 2, 73, 297, 298, 300, 301, 337n., 338n., 340n., 341n., 342n., 346, 347, 419–21, 424, 425, 426, 440, 473, 475, 476, 477, 478, 603, 606
Quintus Curtius, 338n., 340n., 342n.

Ramus, Petrus (Pierre de la Ramée), 425

Rapin, René, 52–54, 57, 473, 475, 478, 479
Reformation, *see* Luther, Martin; Protestantism
Reuchlin, Johann, 279
rhetoric, 44, 124–26, 201, 241, 242–43, 249, 251, 253–62, 297, 298, 300, 349, 419–26, 429, 478, 504, 513–14
Rome, 7, 8, 13, 596, 597–602 *passim*
Rudolf II, emperor, 105, 109, 139, 140, 142, 143, 535–36, 537, 542–43

Sallust, 121–29 *passim*, 337n., 338n., 340n., 341n., 608
Sannazaro, Jacopo, 61–82 *passim*, 115, 173, 561
Sanudo, Marino, 567, 570n., 571
Sappho, 107, 108, 110–11, 112, 338n.
satire, 303–10, 332, 352, 356–57, 380–83, 513–14, 555
Saxo Grammaticus, 527, 529, 531
Scaevola (Scévole), 58–59
Scaliger, Joseph Justus, 160
Scaliger, Julius Caesar, 298, 357, 473, 477, 478, 479, 523
science, 45, 193–99, 271, 276, 578
Seneca, 145, 146, 149–51, 152–53, 233, 337n., 338n., 340n., 341n., 351, 409–17 *passim*, 514n., 568, 604, 605
  Letters, 171, 573
Sepúlveda, Juan Ginés de, 83, 89–101 *passim*, 313, 316, 573–82 *passim*
Servius, 74, 338n., 339, 340, 341, 342, 343, 432, 499
Shakespeare, William, 308n., 357, 461
  in Latin, 408
  Troilus and Cressida, 304
Sigismund I, king of Poland, 187–91 *passim*, 557–58
Sigismund III, king of Poland, 520
Silius Italicus, 338n., 340n., 341, 514
Simonides, 338n., 345

Sixtus I, pope, 196
Sixtus IV, pope, 11
Solinus, 338n., 340n., 341, 604, 605, 606, 610
Spain, scholarship in, 247–52 *passim*, 435–42 *passim*, 443–48 *passim*, 509–15 *passim*, 556, 560, 573–82 *passim*
Statius, 153, 229, 338n., 339, 340n., 341, 432, 555, 557
Stephen I, king of Hungary, 537, 538–39, 541
Stoicism, 99, 163, 170, 346, 416
Strabo, 338n., 339, 340, 341, 439, 568n.
Strozzi, Filippo, 17, 18
Strozzi, Tito Vespasiano, 431–32
Suda, the, 161, 592
Suetonius, 15, 231, 339n., 340n., 341n., 342n., 568
Sweden, scholarship in, 193–99 *passim*, 301–2, 525–33 *passim*

Tacitus, 259, 341n., 342n., 527, 528, 533, 604, 605
Tarillon, François, 56
Tasso, Torquato, 244, 383, 495n., 525n.
Terence, 182, 213, 244, 290, 291, 337n., 338n., 339n., 340, 341n., 346, 515
  Andria, 290
  parodies of, 396–408 *passim*, 515
textual criticism, 7–21, 128, 156–62, 271, 494, 503–8, 520–21, 578, 592
Theocritus, 339n., 340n., 341n., 366, 521
Theophrastus, 339n., 340n., 341n.
Thomas, Loup, 59
Thucydides, 341n., 342n.
Tibullus, 171, 172, 184, 338n., 339n., 341n., 342n., 433, 555, 560
tragedy, 145–53 *passim*, 409–17 *passim*
Trent, Council of, 91, 92, 121, 504, 525, 530, 561, 562, 586

Urban VI, pope, 117, 119

Valerius Flaccus, 339n.
Valerius Maximus, 337n., 338n., 340n., 341n., 342n., 483, 484, 552n.
Valla, Giorgio, 13
Valla, Lorenzo, 15, 73, 116n., 124, 126, 339, 340n., 341n., 494, 514, 605
Vanière, Jacques, 54–55
Varro, 210, 211, 231, 338n., 340n., 432, 514
Vegetius, 339n., 606
Venice, printing at, 7–8, 13
Veracruz, Fray Alonso de la, 311–19
Vergil (Virgil), 50, 184, 234, 235, 244, 297, 309, 326, 337n., 338n., 339, 340, 341, 342, 343, 349, 377, 379, 382, 383, 432, 439, 542, 555, 604, 605, 606
   Aeneid, 48, 49, 149n., 153, 168n., 236, 259, 297, 298, 332n., 380, 410, 497, 498, 499–500, 545–53 *passim*, 608
   Eclogues, 115, 117, 172, 299, 322, 380, 447, 521
   Georgics, 43, 45–47 *passim*, 48, 49, 51, 52, 53, 56, 60, 297, 298, 299, 300, 348, 380, 500
   legend of, 232, 532
Veschambez, Guillaume, 59

Vico, Giambattista, 219, 239–46 *passim*
Vida, Marco Girolamo, *Christias*, 298, 300, 301, 542
   On the Art of Poetry/De Arte Poetica, 298–301
   On Chess, 44, 57
   On Silkworm Raising, 50–52, 57
   Rhetorica, 44
Vincent of Beauvais, 194
visual art, 33–34, 197, 199, 214–25, 236, 330–32, 465, 521, 536–37
Vitoria, Francisco de, 311, 312–13, 315n., 318, 319
Vitruvius, 339n.
Vives, Juan Luis, 198, 201, 204, 250, 574, 579n., 595

Walpole, Robert, 367–69
Wapowski, Bernard, 187–91 *passim*
Weston, Elizabeth Jane (Westonia), 105–13 *passim*, 139–44 *passim*
Westminster School, 395–408 *passim*
William III, king of England, 362, 364–65, 366, 368
women writers, 105–13, 140–41

Xenophon, 116n.

Zamoyski, Jan, 517–23 *passim*
Zoilus, 339n.
Zwingli, Ulrich, 90